MANAGEMENT AND COST ACCOUNTING

Sixth Edition

MANAGEMENT AND COST ACCOUNTING

Alnoor Bhimani
London School of Economics and Political Science

Charles T. Horngren
Stanford University

Srikant M. Datar
Harvard University

Madhav V. Rajan
Stanford University

PEARSON

Harlow, England • London • New York • Boston • San Francisco • Toronto • Sydney • Auckland • Singapore • Hong Kong
Tokyo • Seoul • Taipei • New Delhi • Cape Town • São Paulo • Mexico City • Madrid • Amsterdam • Munich • Paris • Milan

PEARSON EDUCATION LIMITED
Edinburgh Gate
Harlow CM20 2JE
United Kingdom
Tel: +44 (0)1279 623623
Web: www.pearson.com/uk

Original edition, entitled *Cost Accounting* published by Prentice-Hall Inc., Upper Saddle River, New Jersey, USA
© 1999 by Prentice-Hall, Inc.

First edition published in Great Britain under the Prentice Hall Europe imprint in 1999 (print)
Second edition published in 2002 (print)
Third edition published 2005 (print)
Fourth edition published 2008 (print)
Fifth edition published in 2012 (print and electronic)
Sixth edition published in 2015 (print and electronic)

The rights of Alnoor Bhimani, Charles T. Horngren, Srikant M. Datar and Madhav V. Rajan to be
identified as authors of this work have been asserted by them in accordance with the Copyright,
Designs and Patents Act 1988.

Pearson Education is not responsible for the content of third-party Internet sites.

ISBN: 978-1-292-06346-1 (print)
      978-1-292-06353-9 (PDF)
      978-1-292-06348-5 (eText)

British Library Cataloguing-in-Publication Data
A catalogue record for the print edition is available from the British Library

Library of Congress Cataloging-in-Publication Data
A catalog record for the print edition is available from the Library of Congress

10 9 8 7 6 5 4 3 2 1
18 17 16 15 14

Front cover image: Getty Images

Print edition typeset in 10/12pt Sabon MT Pro Regular by 35
Print edition printed in Slovakia by Neografia

NOTE THAT ANY PAGE CROSS REFERENCES REFER TO THE PRINT EDITION

In memory of Charles T. Horngren 1926–2011

Chuck Horngren revolutionised cost and management accounting. He loved new ideas and introduced many new concepts. He had the unique gift of explaining these concepts in simple and creative ways. He epitomised excellence and never tired of details, whether it was finding exactly the right word or working and reworking assignment materials.

He combined his great intellect with genuine humility and warmth and a human touch that inspired others to do their best. He taught us many lessons about life through his amazing discipline, his ability to make everyone feel welcome, and his love of family.

It was a great privilege, pleasure, and honour to have known Chuck Horngren. Few individuals will have the enormous influence that Chuck had on the accounting profession. Fewer still will be able to do it with the class and style that was his hallmark. He was unique, special and amazing in many, many ways and, at once, a role model, teacher, mentor and friend.

He is deeply missed.

Alnoor Bhimani
London School of Economics and Political Science

Srikant M. Datar
Harvard University

Madhav V. Rajan
Stanford University

AB: For all children whose lives were lost in meaningless violent circumstances in 2014

SD: Swati, Radhika, Gayatri, Sidharth

MVR: Gayathri, Sanjana, Anupama

BRIEF CONTENTS

PART I — Management and cost accounting fundamentals

PART II — Accounting information for decision making

PART III — Planning and budgetary control systems

CONTENTS

PART I

Management and cost accounting fundamentals

CHAPTER 1
The accountant's role in the organisation

CHAPTER 2
An introduction to cost terms and purposes

CHAPTER 3
Job-costing systems

CHAPTER 4
Process-costing systems

PART II

**Accounting information for
decision making**

PART III

Planning and budgetary control systems

CHAPTER 14
Motivation, budgets and responsibility accounting   424

CHAPTER 15
Flexible budgets, variances and management control: I   462

CHAPTER 16
Flexible budgets, variances and management control: II   492

CHAPTER 17
Measuring yield, mix and quantity effects   526

PART IV

Management control systems and performance issues

PART V

Quality, time and the strategic management of costs

GUIDE TO THE CASE STUDIES

Case number	Case details	Short/long	Manufacturing/service	Budgeting	Pricing	Ethical issues	Environmental issues	Activity-based costing	Behaviour/organisation factors	Cash flow	Costing system	Profit/loss measurement	ROI	Transfer pricing system	Management control system	Balanced scorecard	Performance measurement	Variance	Market assessment/competitor analysis	Tableau de bord	Strategic issues	Profitability	Country/area of origin
PART 1																							
101	**The European Savings Bank:** Legal and ethical issues involved in software piracy.	short	SS			●			●														Europe
102	**The ethical dilemma at Northlake:** How far does the notion of 'different costs for different purposes' extend?	mid	M			●	●														●		USA
103	**Electronic Boards plc:** Design of costing systems for a firm operating in a high-tech environment. Simplistic vs complex costing.	short	M	●				●	●		●						●				●		N/A
PART 2																							
201	**Permaclean Products plc:** Analysis of costs and price-demand information using past sales data to make decisions on product pricing.	mid	M		●						●	●										●	UK
202	**Tankmaster Manufacturing Company:** ABC in an altered production environment. Behavioural, organisational and cultural issues are explored.	mid	M					●	●		●										●		UK
203	**Siemens Electric Motor Works:** Considers how a cost system can align with a new corporate strategy.	long	M		●				●	●						●	●	●		●	●		Germany
204	**Colombo Frozen Yogurt:** Explores adapting to competitive markets and development of strategies according to market.	short/mid						●	●		●	●					●		●				USA
PART 3																							
301	**Zeros plc:** Use of ROI to measure divisional performance. Use of costing systems to produce meaningful profit statements.	mid	M	●	●			●			●	●	●				●					●	UK
302	**Instrumental Ltd:** Analysis of budgeted vs actual performance for different organisational functions. Considers strategic vs operational issues.	mid	M	●	●			●	●		●	●					●	●			●		UK

Case number	Case details	Short/long	Manufacturing/service	Budgeting	Pricing	Ethical issues	Environmental issues	Activity-based costing	Behaviour/organisation factors	Cash flow	Costing system	Profit/loss measurement	ROI	Transfer pricing system	Management control system	Balanced scorecard	Performance measurement	Variance	Market assessment/competitor analysis	Tableau de bord	Strategic issues	Profitability	Country/area of origin
303	**Hereford Steak Houses:** Use of variance analysis in the restaurant industry. Variance calculations using both standard and flexible budgets.	short	SS	•	•					•		•			•		•	•					UK
	PART 4																						
401	**BBR plc:** Transfer-pricing problem where divisional interests are pitted against total corporate profitability.	mid	M	•	•	•			•	•	•			•			•	•					UK
402	**Cresta Plating Company Ltd:** Considers issues of decentralisation and responsibility.	long	M	•	•	•			•	•	•	•	•	•			•					•	UK
403	**Clayton Industries, Inc.:** Discusses centralisation, sourcing and strategy issues.		SS						•			•			•				•		•		Germany
	PART 5																						
501	**High-Tech Ltd:** Importance of strategy and cost allocation within the IT manufacturing industry. Considers just-in-time inventory systems.	long	M & SS		•			•	•		•	•				•	•			•	•	•		N/A
502	**Empire Glass Company:** Considers control and responsibility alignment issues.																						
503	**Osram:** Analysis of potential savings made by newer, more efficient consumables as opposed to traditionally used ones.	mid/long	M	•	•						•	•							•			•	Germany
504	**Coors:** Demonstrates importance of supply chain management and compares strategies through the use of EVA.	long	M						•		•	•			•	•	•				•		USA

PREFACE

Accounting shapes our lives. It changes organisations and alters our social, economic and physical environment. Whether or not we engage in producing and/or reading accounting information, it influences what we can and cannot do and, therefore, affects our well-being. Corporate decisions regarding new product developments, pricing strategy, staff recruitment and salary levels are generally influenced by accounting information. The way in which a manager acts is often associated with how he or she reacts to accounting data. At times, accounting motivates certain types of behaviour and discourages others. In most organisations, decisions, actions and human behaviour find direct links with the nature, use and focus of accounting information. This text is about understanding the preparation and use of management and cost accounting information in this light.

Whereas management accounting is concerned with the measurement and reporting of financial and other types of information to managers in their pursuit of organisational and other goals, cost accounting is more concerned with information on the acquisition and consumption of resources. Cost accounting tends to provide a useful input into management accounting. Our concern is to encompass both management and cost accounting, stressing particularly the design, use and role of accounting information in the management of organisational activities. The intent is to balance technical detail and organisational insight so as to discuss issues of primary interest to the discharge of management activities. The focus is thus on technical and organisational concepts, analyses and practice vis-à-vis management decision making.

Management and cost accounting is a dynamic discipline which interacts with many facets of the organisational environment in which it exists across nations, industrial settings and management functions. It entails the application both of long-established techniques and of newly emerging concepts. Consequently, the book covers conventional topic areas such as job costing and process costing, cost–volume–profit relationships, capital investment decisions and budgetary control systems in the light of changes in modern-day operational circumstances. In addition, we have addressed innovative approaches in management accounting which relate to, for example, quality concerns, throughput concepts, non-financial performance issues and strategic analysis. Throughout the book's chapters we point to emerging themes within the field of management accounting which are regarded as important for organisations seeking to evolve their management accounting systems. Additionally, we discuss the possible implications for management accounting practices of management and organisational concerns which are recent but fast evolving. We point, therefore, to the relevance of many issues, including sustainability, digitisation, knowledge management and intellectual capital, enterprise governance, Big Data and inter-organisational cost management, which hold significance for potential management accounting practice changes.

We have also explicitly incorporated discussions of the management accounting implications of the use of flexible organisational technologies in the production and delivery of physical goods and services. Further, some of the potential influences of e-business innovations, the 'digitisation' of the economy and Internet technologies on management accounting practices are considered. The rise of Web applications and social networking present important lessons of interest to management accountants. The convergence of telecommunications and digital technologies embedded within the Internet has given rise to the restructuring of business activities while also bringing to the fore questions concerning the continued relevance of established management accounting principles within highly web-enabled enterprises. We are now in a more mature and advanced phase of the growing impact of the Internet on society and the economy.

Although no established body of research exists in this domain, our intent is to highlight some of the management accounting implications brought about by the Internet.

Throughout the text an emphasis is placed on developing a context-based understanding of management and cost accounting practices. By this, we mean that, although generalisations need to be made to introduce topics and issues, it is essential to recognise that these practices are highly dependent upon the situational and organisational factors within which such application takes place. We therefore discuss global themes and concepts in management and cost accounting while stressing the need to understand the context in which it is practised. This focus extends to addressing issues of social and ethical concern. Enterprise governance as an issue of increasing corporate concern is discussed at some length. Likewise, the deployment of social media platforms by enterprises and deriving insights from 'Big Data' analysis are regarded as being of very significant concern to management accounting developments. Rather than accord a separate chapter to consider organisational and social aspects of management accounting, we integrate this perspective throughout the text to lend it a greater degree of realism.

This text pays particular attention to concerns and issues within an international setting. Our endeavour to cover fundamental concepts and techniques of management and cost accounting, while also highlighting the diversity of approaches and practices which management and cost accounting are viewed to encompass in different countries, has made the writing of this text a unique and interesting challenge. We draw comfort from the realisation that other management accounting texts have begun to attempt to present a similar mix of practical examples, case studies and coverage of research findings while also sharing our preference for the format and structure adopted here. In this edition we provide new illustrative examples, survey findings and case studies relating to many global enerprises, and have drawn on a wide range of business writings. This is regarded as an important feature of this book, especially with the growing number of economies which are shaped by and affect globalisation forces. Moreover, we consider management accounting changes under the 'new normal' conditions facing economies as they recover from the global economic crisis which started in 2008.

Deciding on the sequence of chapters in a management and cost accounting textbook which spans introductory through to relatively detailed analysis of material is a challenge. Every lecturer has a favourite way of organising his or her course. The five-part structure of this text and the sequencing of chapters have been designed to facilitate fexibility and diversity in the teaching of different topic areas and the use of the text for a range of courses and levels. An outline of the coverage and component chapters of each part is given in the part openers.

Assessment material

This book includes a high quantity and broad range of assessment material to further facilitate the use of the text on a diverse range of courses:

- **Review questions** These short questions encourage students to review and/or critically discuss their understanding of the main topics and issues covered in each chapter, either individually or in a group.

- **Exercises** These comprehensive questions are graded and grouped by their level of difficulty: basic, intermediate and advanced. Each question is preceded by a note of its topic coverage and an indication of the time it should take to complete. Where appropriate, the exercises include questions taken from recent examinations of several professional accountancy bodies. There is an average of fourteen exercises per chapter. Fully worked solutions to a selection of exercises in each chapter (identified by an asterisk) are provided in Appendix A.

Case study problems

At the end of each of the five parts are problem-based illustrative cases. Each is more substantive and typically more demanding than the end-of-chapter exercises, integrating topics from several chapters in each of the core parts of the text, allowing you to apply your understanding of accounting concepts, issues and techniques within a broader organisational context, and to develop your critical thinking and analytical skills. The questions which follow the case material include some aspects suitable for group discussion/assignment.

Appendix B: Compound and interest rate tables

Students will need to use these tables in studying Chapter 13 of the text and undertaking the end-of-chapter exercises. For ease of reference, we recommend students make a photocopy of these pages.

Glossary

This comprises an alphabetical listing of all the key terms, including a concise definition, so allowing revision of all the key concepts and techniques in the text.

Academic supplements

Lecturers who adopt this text are provided with a range of additional materials to assist in the preparation and delivery of courses. These include:

- complete, downloadable Instructor's Manual with teaching ideas and solutions to end-of-chapter exercises not given in the text;
- suggested solutions to all case study problems;
- editable PowerPoint slides and overhead projector masters, organised by chapter, allowing you to provide a lecture or seminar presentation (and/or to print handouts). These incorporate colourful graphics, outlines of chapter material, text exhibits, additional examples and graphical explanations of difficult topics;
- solutions to additional questions and spreadsheet problems.

Alnoor Bhimani
Srikant Datar
Madhav Rajan
January 2015

AUTHORS'
ACKNOWLEDGEMENTS

We are indebted to many individuals for their ideas and assistance. Our primary thanks go to the many academics and practitioners who have advanced our knowledge of management and cost accounting. Aside from the many individuals in North America who have contributed in one way or another, we would like to thank the following who have provided material for inclusion in the text, or who have painstakingly commented on chapters in draft form, or have otherwise helped the review process:

David Adnum, Wrexham Business School
Farah Ahamed, Farahahamed.com
Thomas Ahrens, University of United Arab Emirates
John Ahwere-Bafo, Royal Holloway, University of London
Jasim Al-Ali, Manchester Metropolitan University
Mohammed Al-Omiri, Umm Al-Qurag University
Michael Anderson, Copenhagen Business School
Denise Ashworth, Manchester Metropolitan University
Richard Barker, Said Business School, University of Oxford
Ronnie Barnes, London Business School
Elisabetta Barone, Henley Business School
Ken Bates, Victoria University of Wellington
Niels Boberg Bøgh, Syddansk Universitet
Jane Broadbent, Royal Holloway, University of London
Mick Broadbent, University of Hertfordshire
Michael Bromwich, London School of Economics
Werner Brugemann, University of Ghent
Ariela Caglio, Bocconi University
Salvador Carmona, IE University
Christopher Chapman, Imperial College London
Peter Clarke, University College Dublin
Ciaran Collolly, Queen's University Belfast
John Currie, National University of Ireland
Jay Dahya, Baruch College
Claire Dambrin, ESCP Europe
Shanta Davie, Newcastle University Business School
Zsuzsa Deli-Gray, ESSCA
Jeremy Dent, London Business School
Angelo Ditillo, Bocconi University
Robert Dixon, University of Durham
John Duran, University College Cork
Pam Edwards, Manchester School of Management
Roy Edwards, University of Southampton
Jeremy Fernando, Imperial College London
Ian Fisher, Liverpool John Moores University
Victor Franco, ISCTE, Portugal
Florian Gebreiter, Aston University
Miles Gietzman, Bocconi University

Pauline Gleadle, University of East Anglia
Robert Greenhalgh, Nottingham University
Tom Groot, University of Amsterdam
Frank Hartmann, Erasmus University
Mostafa Hassan, Shaqra University
Tord Haversjo, Royal Technical University
Joachim Hebrendt, Luneburg University, Germany
Jos Hexspoor, Tilbury University, the Netherlands
John Innes, University of Dundee
Evelyn Kapteyn, Haagse Hogeschool
Vicky Kiosse, Exeter University
Claes-Goran Larsson, Umea Universitet
Michel Lebas, Hautes Etudes Commerciales
Alan Lowe, Aston University
Kari Lukka, Turku School of Economics
Maria Major, ISCTE, Portugal
Carolyn Malinowski, University of East London
Teemu Malmi, Aalto University
Alyson McLintock, University of Nottingham
Anette Mikes, HEC Lausanne
Peter Miller, London School of Economics
Tony Miller, Durham University
Yuval Millo, University of Leicester
Falconer Mitchell, Edinburgh University
Jodie Moll, University of Manchester
Jan Mouritsen, Copenhagen Business School
Bill Neale, Bradford University
Alexander Niess, ESC Rennes
Bill Nixon, University of Dundee
Deryl Northcott, AUT University
Vincent O'Connell, University of Amsterdam
Hiroshi Okano, Osaka City University
David Otley, Lancaster University
Jatin Pancholi, Middlesex University
Sepideh Parsa, Middlesex University
Mike Partridge, University of Brighton
Mark Pilkington, University of Westminster
Mike Pogue, University of Ulster
Iver Poulsen, Syddansk Universitet
David Preen, University of Brighton
Paolo Quattrone, Edinburgh University
Flemming Rasmusses, Technical University of Denmark
Leonardo Rinaldi, Royal Holloway, University of London
Hanno Roberts, Norwegian School of Management
Keith Robson, HEC Paris
Carsten Rohde, Copenhagen Business School
Robin Roslender, University of Dundee
Ken Shackleton, Glasgow University
Hanna Silvola, Allto University
Prabhu Sivabalan, UTS
Peter Smidt, Vrije University, the Netherlands
Kazbi Soonawalla, University of Oxford
Heather Stewart, Southampton Institute of Higher Education

Rennie Tjerkstra, University of Kent
Mathew Tsamenyi, Birmingham University
Chin Bun Tse, University of Salford
Juhani Vaivio, Aalto University
Herman van der Meulen, Nijenrode University, the Netherlands
Gerrit Vjige, Twente University, the Netherlands
Fred Vlotman, Tilburg University, the Netherlands
Hassan Yazdifar, University of Salford
Luca Zan, Università degli Studi di Bologna, Italy

At Pearson Education Limited:

Rebecca Pedley, Acquisitions Editor
Carole Drummond, Project Editor

Finally, we would like to thank the following professional accountancy bodies for their assistance and permission to reproduce copyright material:

The Association of Chartered Certified Accountants
The Institute of Chartered Accountants in England and Wales
The Institute of Chartered Accountants of Scotland
The Chartered Institute of Management Accountants
The Institute of Chartered Accountants in Ireland

PUBLISHER'S ACKNOWLEDGEMENTS

We are grateful to the following for permission to reproduce copyright material:

Figures

Figure 1.3 from *Strategic Finance: Achieving High Corporate Performance*, Strategy Press (Bhimani, A., 2013), reproduced with permission; Figure 1.7 from CIMA Code of Ethics for Professional Accountants, CIMA 2010, reproduced with permission; Figure 14.2 from *Accounting and Human Behaviour*, Haymarket (A. Hopwood, 1974), reproduced with permission from Haymarket; Figure 22.3 adapted from 'Tableau de bord and French reaction on the balanced scorecard, paper presented at the EAA Conference, Athens 18–20 April, p. 30 (Bourguignon, A., Malleret, V. and Norreklit, H. 2001), http://www.hec.edu/var/fre/storage/original/application/b238ea034d08e3b258e080d334376553.pdf; Figure 22.5 from 'Environmental Management Accounting' in A. Bhimani (ed.), *Contemporary Issues in Management Accounting*, Oxford University Press (Soonawalla, K., 2006) pp. 381–6, by permission of Oxford University Press; Figure 22.6 adapted from Environmental Management Accounting in A. Bhimani (ed.), *Contemporary Issues in Management Accounting*, Oxford University Press (Roberts, H., 2006) pp. 308–28, by permission of Oxford University Press.

Text

Case Study 1.01 from 'Software piracy – who does it impact?', *Issues in Accounting Education*, 9(1), Spring (Christiansen, A. and Eining, M.M., 1994). Reproduced with permission from the American Accounting Association. Permission conveyed through Copyright Clearance Center, Inc.; Case study 1.02 from 'The ethical dilemma at Northlake', *CMA Magazine*, March (Grant, R., 1993), reproduced with permission from Centre for Accounting Ethics; Case study 1.03 from 'Electronic boards plc. in D. Otley, D. Brown and C. Wilkinson, eds, *Case Studies in Management Accounting*, Philip Allan Publishers (Innes, J. and Mitchell, F., 1988), reproduced with permission; Case study 2.02 based on a case written by Ken Bates, Warwick University; Case study 2.03 from Professors Robin Cooper and Karen Hopper Wruck, 1990, © 1990 by the President and Fellows of Harvard College. To order copies or request permission to reproduce materials, call 1-617-783-7831, write to Harvard Business School Publishing, Watertown, MA 02472, or go to http://www.hbsp.harvard.edu. No part of this publication may be reproduced, stored in a retrieval system, used in a spreadsheet or transmitted in any form or by any means – electronic, mechanical, photocopying, recording or otherwise – without the permission of Harvard Business School; Case study 2.04 adapted from Colombo frozen yogurt: activity-based costing applied to marketing costs, *Cases from Management Accounting Practice*, 15 (Saly, J. and Guy, T., 2000), reproduced with permission; Case study 3.01 from Zeroes plc in D. Otley, D. Brown and C. Wilkinson, eds, *Case Studies in Management Accounting*, Philip Allan Publishers (Mitchell, F., 1988), reproduced with permission; Case Study 3.02 from 'Profit variance analysis: a strategic focus', *Issues in Accounting Education*, Fall, pp. 396–410 (Govindarajan, V. and Shank, J., 1989). Reproduced with permission from the American Accounting Association. Permission conveyed through Copyright Clearance Center, Inc.; Case study 3.03 from Thomas Ahrens, United Arab Emirates University and Christopher Chapman, Imperial College London; Case study 4.01 from

BBR plc in D. Otley, D. Brown and C. Wilkinson, eds, *Case Studies in Management Accounting*, Philip Allan Publishers (Emmanuel, C. R. 1988) reproduced with permission; Case study 4.03 from Clayton Industries, Peter Arnell, Country Manager for Italy, Harvard Business School Cases (Bartlett, C. A., and Barlow, B. H.), reproduced with permission; Case study 5.01 adapted from High-tech Limited, *Cases from Management Accounting Practice*, vol. 16 (Prather-Kinsey, J., 2001), reproduced with permission; Case study 5.02 from Professor David F. Hawkins, © 1964 President and Fellows of Harvard College. To order copies or request permission to reproduce materials, call 1-800-545-7685, write to Harvard Business School Publishing, Boston, MA, 02163, or go to http://www.hbsp.harvard.edu. No part of this publication may be reproduced, stored in a retrieval system, used in a spreadsheet, or transmitted in any form or by any means – electronic, mechanical, photocopying, recording or otherwise – without the permission of Harvard Business School; Case study 5.03 adapted from Osram in *IMA Cases from Management Accounting Practice*, vol. 17, Institute of Management Accounting Practice (Shank, J. and Carr, L., 2002) reproduced with permission; Case study 5.04 adapted from Coors: balanced scorecard in *IMA Cases from Management Accounting Practice*, vol. 15, Institute of Management Accounting Practice (Grove, H., Cook, T. and Richter, K., 2000) reproduced with permission; Extract on page 5 from 'Changing times: management accounting, research and practice from a UK perspective' in A. Bhimani (ed.), *Contemporary Issues in Management Accounting*, Oxford University Press (Scapens, R.W., 2006) pp. 329–54, by permission of Oxford University Press; Extract on page 16 is an extract from *Competent and Versatile: How Professional Accountants in Business Drive Sustainable Success of The Professional Accountants in Business (PAIB)*, published by The International Federation of Accountants (IFAC) in August 2011, and is used with permission of IFAC; Exercises 4.15 and 10.17 from ACCA Financial Information for Management, Part 1, June 2004. We are grateful to the Association of Chartered Certified Accountants (ACCA) for permission to reproduce past examination questions. The suggested solutions in the exam answer bank have been prepared by us, unless otherwise stated; Exercises 6.16, 6.17 and 6.23 adapted from CMA, Institute of Certified Management Accountants (ICMA); Exercise 6.18 from ACCA Financial Information for Management, Part 1, June 2007; Exercises 7.13 and 17.14 from ACCA Financial Information for Management, Part 1, June 2006; Exercises 7.14, 12.16, 16.15 and 21.25 from ACCA Financial Information for Management, Part 1, June 2005; Exercises 7.15, 16.16 and 16.17 from ACCA Financial Information for Management, Part 1, June 2004. We are grateful to the Association of Chartered Certified Accountants (ACCA) for permission to reproduce past examination questions. The suggested solutions in the exam answer bank have been prepared by us, unless otherwise stated; Exercises 7.16 and 7.21 from CIMA Management Accounting Pillar Managerial Level 1 Paper, November 2006, reproduced with permission; Exercise 8.28 from CIMA Management Accounting Pillar Managerial Level Paper, May 2006, reproduced with permission; Exercises 9.16, 14.16, 14.18, 16.23, 17.11, 18.17, 18.18, 19.15, 19.16, 19.20, 21.17 and 22.17 adapted from CMA; Box on page 332 adapted from www.lloydstsb.com (July 2014). Please note that Lloyds TSB regularly review their accounts and the rates are subject to change; Exercise 11.15 from CIMA Management Accounting Pillar Managerial Level Paper, 21 November 2006, reproduced with permission; Exercises 11.19 and 13.14 from Association of Chartered Certified Accountants, Pilot Paper 2.4, Financial Management and Control. We are grateful to the Association of Chartered Certified Accountants (ACCA) for permission to reproduce past examination questions. The suggested solutions in the exam answer bank have been prepared by us, unless otherwise stated; Exercise 13.19 adapted from NAA Research Report, no. 35, pp. 83–5, reproduced with permission; Exercise 13.22 from CIMA 2010 Chartered Institute of Management Accountants, Specimen Examination Paper 1, reproduced with permission; Exercises 14.21 and 14.23 from CIMA Management Accounting Pillar Managerial Level Paper, May 2001, reproduced with permission; Exercises 16.18, 17.15 and 18.20 from CIMA Management Accounting Pillar Managerial Level Paper, November 2006, reproduced with permission; Exercise 18.21 from CIMA Management Accounting Pillar Managerial Level Paper, reproduced with permission; Exercise 18.23 from Chartered Institute of Management Accountants, Intermediate Level, Management Accounting Decision Making, November 2003, reproduced with permission; Exercise 22.18 from Chartered Institute of Management Accountants, Intermediate Level, Management Accounting – Performance Management, November 2003, reproduced with permission.

Photographs

Alamy Images: 648, Lenscap 575; Corbis: David Atlas/Retna Ltd 225, Pascal Della Zuana/Sygma 384, Brent Smith/Reuters 441, Wolfgang Kaehler 474, Dave Caulkin/Pool 645, Alexandra Walker/ Reuters 698; Digital Vision Ltd: 162, 333; Getty Images: 707, Bloomberg 99, AFP 594; Pearson Education Ltd/Naki Kouyioumtzis 106; Stockbyte: 332.

All other images © Pearson Education

In some instances we have been unable to trace the owners of copyright material, and we would appreciate any information that would enable us to do so.

Photographs

PART I

Management and cost accounting fundamentals

The first part of the book is intended to provide an introduction to fundamental concepts and ideas in management and cost accounting. Chapter 1 considers the role of accounting and accountants in organisations. Chapters 2–7 discuss relevant technical and broader organisational issues in the design and functioning of cost systems. Specifically, Chapter 2 provides an introduction to costing terminology and its aims. Chapters 3 and 4 discuss what might be considered ends of a continuum in costing systems: job order costing and process costing. Chapter 5 addresses fundamental cost allocation issues while Chapter 6 deals with joint-costing situations. The final chapter in this part discusses absorption costing and variable costing as two distinct approaches to stock costing.

CHAPTER 1

The accountant's role in the organisation

Former accountants have headed many large companies across the world, including Coca-Cola, P&O, Gulf Oil, Bass, Royal Bank of Scotland, Asda and Nike. Finance leaders' roles in organisations change continuously. About 30% of Fortune 500 (the 500 largest US industrial corporations by revenue) Chief Executive Officers spend the first four years of their careers developing a strong foundation in finance (Sanders 2011). In the UK, half of FTSE 100 (a share index of the 100 companies listed on the London Stock Exchange with the highest market capitalisation) CEOs have a background in accounting or financial management (Savage 2014). What is clear is that from back office accountant to front-line executive, the rapid rise of the chief financial officer is unrivalled by any other corporate role (Karaian 2014). Certainly, since the global financial crisis of 2008, accountants are far more involved in risk management, business strategy and communications than ever before (CFO/ACCA 2009). The evidence points to a growing managerial engagement by accountants in modern enterprises. In many organisations, the accountant's duties are intertwined with management planning, control and decision making. Accounting in such organisations is considered to provide a very good training field for senior management positions.

The study of management and cost accounting yields insights into the changing roles and relationships between managerial activities and accounting intelligence. What types of decisions do managers make? How can accounting help managers make these decisions? Are managerial needs proactively being met by management and cost accounting solutions? This book addresses these questions. In this chapter we look at some dimensions of the role of management accounting in modern enterprises, why management accounting is subject to continual change and where the accountant fits into the organisation. A consideration of these issues will give us a framework for studying the succeeding chapters.

Learning objectives

After studying this chapter, you should be able to:

- Differentiate management accounting from financial accounting and cost management

- Recognise the growing role of strategy in management accounting processes

- Identify five broad purposes of accounting systems

- Understand how accounting can influence planning, control and decision making

- Distinguish between the scorekeeping, attention-directing and problem-solving functions of management accounting

- Recognise that economic benefits and costs are to be considered alongside contextual and organisational process issues in the design, implementation and use of accounting systems

- Describe evolving themes that are shaping management accounting systems

- Discuss forces of change in management accounting, including enterprise structure, digitisation, intellectual capital and knowledge management

Accounting, costing and strategy

Management accounting, financial accounting and cost accounting

A distinction is often made in practice between management accounting and financial accounting. **Management accounting** measures and reports financial information as well as other types of information that are intended primarily to assist managers in fulfilling the goals of the organisation. Additionally, a management accounting system is an important facet of overall organisational control, as is discussed later in this book. The Chartered Institute of Management Accountants (CIMA) – the largest association of management accountants in the UK – considers management accounting to be an integral part of management. It considers management accounting as combining accounting, finance and management with the leading-edge techniques needed to drive successful businesses. Professional management accountants apply the principles of accounting and financial management to create, protect, preserve and increase value for the shareholder of for-profit and not-for-profit enterprises in the public and private sectors. They might engage in the identification, generation, presentation, interpretation and use of relevant information relevant to:

- inform strategic decisions and formulate business strategy;
- plan long-, medium- and short-term operations;
- determine capital structure and fund that structure;
- design reward strategies for executives and shareholders;
- inform operational decisions;
- control operations and ensure the efficient use of resources;
- measure and report financial and non-financial performance to management and other stakeholders;
- implement corporate governance procedures, risk management and internal controls;
- explore the potential for managerial and organisational value creation.

Financial accounting focuses on external reporting that is directed by authoritative guidelines. Organisations are required to follow these guidelines in their financial reports to outside parties. **Cost accounting** measures and reports financial and non-financial information related to the organisation's acquisition or consumption of resources. It provides information for both management accounting and financial accounting.

Financial accounting is guided by prescribed accounting principles. These principles define the set of revenue and cost measurement rules and the types of item that are classified as assets, liabilities or owners' equity in balance sheets. Sources of authority for accounting regulation differ across countries. In Spain, for instance, the Instituto de Contabilidad y Auditoria de Cuentas (ICAC) has been appointed by the government for this purpose. In the UK, the Financial Reporting Council has the authority to issue accounting standards. The FRC's regulator philosophy is underpinned by its belief that promoting confidence in corporate reporting and governance can make the creation of wealth more likely. In France, the Autorité des Normes Comptable (ANC), a public body, oversees accounting legislation, whereas in Denmark, the Føreningen af Statsautoriserede Revisører (FSR), a professional accounting body, oversees the setting of accounting standards. Other bodies which are concerned with accounting standards include: in Australia, the Australian Accounting Standards Board (AASB); in China, the China Accounting Standards Committee (CASC); and in South Africa, the South Africa Accounting Standards Board. In contrast, management accounting is not restricted by those accounting principles acceptable for financial reporting. For example, a car manufacturer may present a particular estimated 'value' of a brand name (say, the Volvo brand name) in its *internal* financial reports for marketing managers, although doing so is not in accordance with the legal framework within which externally oriented financial reports can be prepared in Sweden.

In some countries, close links exist between accounting information produced internally for managers and that intended for the compilation of external financial accounts. For instance, the French Plan Comptable Général (PCG) provides a model for integrating the needs of corporate management with the requirements of statute and fiscal authorities. In Portuguese enterprises, the Chart of Accounts is used both as a detailed coding matrix and as a management tool and a way of involving personnel in the operations of their individual organisations (see Alexander et al. 2011).

While the work of management accountants and financial accountants tends to be organisation-specific, some broad differences generally exist. They may be categorised as follows:

- *Regulations*. Management accounting reports are generally prepared for internal use and no external regulations govern their preparation. Conversely, financial accounting reports are generally required to be prepared according to accounting regulations and guidelines imposed by law and the accounting profession.

- *Range and detail of information*. Management accounting reports may encompass financial, non-financial and qualitative information which may be very detailed or highly aggregated. Financial accounting is usually broad-based, lacking detail and intended to provide an overview of the position and performance of an organisation over a time period. It tends to focus on financial information.

- *Reporting interval*. Management accounting reports may be produced frequently – on an hourly, daily or weekly basis, possibly to span several years. The interval covered by management accounting information will be dictated by the decision-making and control needs of the information users. Conversely, financial accounting reports are produced annually. Some large companies also produce semi-annual and quarterly reports.

- *Time period*. Management accounting reports may include historical and current information but also often provide information on expected future performance and activities. Financial accounting reports provide information on the performance and position of an organisation for the past period. They tend to be backward-looking.

Cost management and accounting systems

A central task of managers is cost management. We use the term **cost management** to describe the actions managers undertake in the short-run and long-run planning and control of costs that increase value for customers and lower the costs of products and services.

An important component of cost management is the recognition that prior management decisions often commit the organisation to the subsequent incurrence of costs. Consider the costs of handling materials in a production plant. Decisions about plant layout and the extent of physical movement of materials required for production are usually made before production begins. These decisions greatly influence the level of day-to-day materials handling costs once production begins. For this reason, cost management has a broad focus. It typically includes the continuous reduction of costs and encompasses the whole life cycle of the product from product conception to deletion. Cost management is often carried out as a key part of general management strategies and their implementation. Examples include enhanced customer satisfaction programmes, quality initiatives and more efficient supplier relationships management via the Internet.

Managers around the globe are becoming increasingly aware of the importance of the quality and timeliness of products and services sold to their external customers. In turn, accountants are particularly sensitive to the quality and timeliness of accounting information required by managers. For example, a management accounting group at Johnson & Johnson (a manufacturer of many consumer products) has a vision statement that includes the phrases 'delight our customers' and 'be the best'. The success of management accounting depends on whether managers perceive their decisions as being improved by the accounting information provided to them. This does not necessarily imply that management accountants should shed past techniques and practices, but that they will undergo change in line with how they and other managers believe they can be most effective. There is evidence that, in many organisations, accountants are regarded as 'hybrid accountants' who combine the skills of business managers with those of accountants. Scapens notes that:

> **The accountants' analytical skills, supplemented by extensive knowledge of the business, can put the management accountant in a position to recognise the more strategic impacts and value creation potential of decisions taken in the individual areas of the business. Such a role for the management accountant is crucial for the organisation as it helps to integrate the various activities and functions of the business.** (2006, p. 339)

Management accounting's primary purpose is to enhance value creation within both private and public sector organisations. The management accountant must make use of a sound body of knowledge as well as abide by ethical guidelines (discussed in the appendix of this chapter). Of particular relevance is the growing contribution which management accountants make to strategic financial management information production and analysis and to strategic management action itself.

Strategic decisions and management accounting

Many organisations seek to be more expansionist, entrepreneurial, risk taking and innovative as a conscious move away from inwardly focused management techniques. Entirely new markets are emerging for products and services and avant-garde innovative firms are reaping significant benefits. Consider, for instance, the Oculus Rift, a virtual reality headset produced by the company Ocular VR. Facebook's CEO Mark Zuckerberg paid $2 billion for the company in 2014 to help Facebook's mission to 'make the world more open and connected' (Zuckerberg 2014) by tying in to Oculus VR's mission 'to experience the impossible'. Zuckerberg says of the headset 'When you put it on, you enter a completely immersive computer generated environment, like a game, or a movie scene or a place far away. The incredible thing about the technology is that you feel like you're actually present in another place with other people.' Peter Berkman (www.peterberkman. tumblr.com/post/80827337212) identifies Facebook's value creation possibilities from the Oculus VR acquisition:

> **Between head and iris tracking, in-game data, and Facebook's incredible systems – there will be a plethora of information to mine . . . Facebook will know where you're looking, what you're doing, and how long you do it. . . . When they cross-reference that with all the other information they already have on a billion people . . . the data is actively . . . used as a way to make Facebook more revenue.**

Big Data analysis is altering the value creation possibilities that are increasingly open to companies and, as a consequence, the opportunities for management accounting practitioners to process different forms of data in diverse ways for managerial use. Consider also the service of M-PESA, which is operated by Safaricom – Kenya's largest mobile operator. M-PESA is used by more than a quarter of the country's population to 'zap' money via mobile telephones from one location to another. Customers can convert real money into 'e-float', which is credited to a person's mobile-money account. E-float can be used to make purchases or it can be converted into cash by M-PESA agents. The system has altered significantly the economics of trading. Such forays into new markets via technological innovations have many financial implications which management accounting tools can help assess.

Research reveals that companies that emphasise creating long-term value for shareholders are likely to outperform those that focus on preserving shareholder value in the short term. Companies whose primary focus is on internal control and value preservation do not increase their stock market valuations as effectively as those that look outside for opportunities to create value. Outperformers in business are those with the strategic and external awareness to evolve and change when need arises. Studies have also revealed that performance-based pay focusing on highly tangible near-term measurable variables damages the creation of longer-term shareholder value. At the heart of such findings are the emerging roles that management accounting is starting to play in enterprises. Management accounting information is called upon not only to help managers make balanced decisions in the face of organisational changes and the opportunities their environments offer but increasingly also to monitor and evaluate strategic progress.

The trend for professional institutes of management accounting is to reorient the field towards strategic management information preparation and analysis and the actual participation of management accountants in such activities. Operational accounting techniques and issues continue to be relevant but their roles are being recast in the context of their contributions and relationships with organisation-wide financial management and strategic concerns.

The shift towards managerial and strategic engagement rather than just acting as providers of largely financial information about enterprises allows management accountants to align their work to the changing business and organisational landscape. The beginning of the millennium has seen a radical shift in the economic context in which companies operate. Early in the twentieth century, the Ford Motor Company demonstrated the ability of mass production to lower the price of a product by 60% or more. This enables consumption to move its focus away from elite consumers to the masses. Today, another transformation is taking place away from mass consumption to a focus on individuals. New societal and enterprise forms are being created to serve individual end-users. Consumers, in many sectors, are building platforms, tools and relationships which enable a high degree of personalisation. Companies such as Amazon.com, eBay, Apple, YouTube and Facebook fall into this new category. Interactive technologies allow consumers greater self-determination. The owner of a tablet computer, for instance, is allowed a new experience where consumption is self-defined at a fraction of the old cost. Assets, information, relationships and management are now 'distributed' because of the availability of the Internet, mobile computing, wireless broadband and new software applications. As a result, individualised goods and services can now be experienced at very low costs. Organisations are strategically seeking to engage in a form of 'distributed capitalism' (Zuboff 2010). Management accountants are now called upon to understand, control and manage such new cost structures. Even though many management accounting concepts used in traditional industrial and service sectors continue to find application, new circumstances are also reshaping management accounting activities.

Accounting systems and management controls

What are the objectives of accounting systems? Is Tata's management control system more effective than Audi's? Is Nestlé's more effective at planning than Cadbury's? This section provides an overview of the broad purposes of accounting and management control systems, illustrating the role of accounting information.

The major purposes of accounting systems

The accounting system is among the most significant quantitative information systems in almost every organisation. This system aims to provide information for five broad purposes:

- *Purpose 1: Formulating overall strategies and long-range plans.* This includes new product development and investment in both tangible (equipment) and intangible (brands, patents or people) assets, and frequently involves special-purpose reports. Increasingly, many organisations seek market-, supplier- and customer-based information for determining longer-term strategic action.

- *Purpose 2: Resource allocation decisions such as product and customer emphasis and pricing.* This frequently involves reports on the profitability of products or services, brand categories, customers, distribution channels, and so on.

- *Purpose 3: Cost planning and cost control of operations and activities.* This involves reports on revenues, costs, assets, and the liabilities of divisions, plants and other areas of responsibility.

- *Purpose 4: Performance measurement and evaluation of people.* This includes comparisons of actual results with planned results. It can be based on financial or non-financial measures.

- *Purpose 5: Meeting external regulatory and legal reporting requirements where they exist.* Regulations and statutes often prescribe the accounting methods to be followed. Financial reports are provided by some organisations to shareholders who are making decisions to buy, hold or sell company shares. These reports ordinarily attempt to adhere to authoritatively determined guidelines and procedures which exist in many European countries.

Each of the purposes stated here may require a different presentation or reporting method. Accountants combine or adjust the method and data to answer the questions from particular internal or external users.

The nature of management-oriented accounting information alters in line with changes in the business environment. Over the past decade, many enterprises have experienced a shift from a traditional monitoring and control perspective to a more business- and support-oriented focus. This requires a broad-based understanding of the business, with management accountants working alongside managers in cross-functional teams rather than in a separate accounting function. Some present-day key influences on changes in accounting information include:

- an increased pace of change in the business world
- shorter product life cycles and competitive advantages
- a requirement for more strategic action by management
- the emergence of new companies, new industries and new business models
- the outsourcing of non-value-added but necessary services
- increased uncertainty and the explicit recognition of risk
- novel forms of reward structures
- increased regulatory activity and altered financial reporting requirements
- more complex business transactions
- increased focus on customer satisfaction
- new ethics of enterprise governance
- the need to recognise intellectual capital
- enhancing knowledge management processes.

In this book we consider the accounting information implications of many of these developments.

Planning and control

There are many definitions of planning and control. Study the left side of Exhibit 1.1, which uses planning and control at *The Sporting News* (SN) as an illustration. We define **planning** (the top box) as choosing goals, predicting results under various ways of achieving those goals, and then deciding how to attain the desired goals. For example, one goal of SN may be to increase operating profit. Three main alternatives are considered to achieve this goal:

1 Change the price per newspaper.
2 Change the rate per page charged to advertisers.
3 Reduce labour costs by having fewer workers at SN's printing facility.

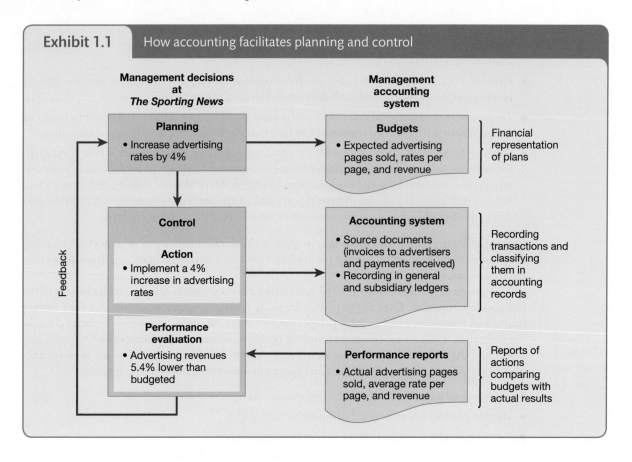

Exhibit 1.1 How accounting facilitates planning and control

Assume that the editor, Bérangère Saunier, increases advertising rates by 4% to €5200 per page for March 2015. She budgets advertising revenue to be €4 160 000 (€5200 × 800 pages predicted to be sold in March 2015). A **budget** is the quantitative expression of a plan of action and an aid to the coordination and implementation of the plan.

Control (the bottom box in Exhibit 1.1) covers both the action that implements the planning decision and deciding on performance evaluation and the related feedback that will help future decision making. With our SN example, the action would include communicating the new advertising-rate schedule to SN's marketing sales representatives and advertisers. The performance evaluation provides feedback on the actual results.

During March 2015, SN sells advertising, sends out invoices and receives payments. These invoices and receipts are recorded in the accounting system. Exhibit 1.2 shows the March 2015

Exhibit 1.2 Advertising revenue performance report at *The Sporting News* for March 2015

	Actual results	Budgeted amounts	Variance
Advertising pages sold	760	800	40 unfavourable
Average rate per page	€5 080	€5 200	€120 unfavourable
Advertising revenue	€3 860 800	€4 160 000	€299 200 unfavourable

advertising revenue performance report for SN. This report indicates that 760 pages of advertising (40 pages less than the budgeted 800 pages) were sold in March 2015. The average rate per page was €5080 compared with the budgeted €5200 rate, yielding actual advertising revenue in March 2015 of €3 860 800. The actual advertising revenue in March 2015 is €299 200 less than the budgeted €4 160 000. Understanding the reasons for any difference between actual results and budgeted results is an important part of **management by exception**, which is the practice of concentrating on areas not operating as expected (such as a cost overrun on a project) and placing less attention on areas operating as expected. The term **variance** in Exhibit 1.2 refers to the difference between the actual results and the budgeted amounts.

The performance report in Exhibit 1.2 could spur investigation. For example, did other newspapers experience a comparable decline in advertising revenue? Did the marketing department make sufficient efforts to convince advertisers that, even with the new rate of €5200 per page, advertising in the SN was a good buy? Why was the actual average rate per page €5080 instead of the budgeted rate of €5200? Did some sales representatives offer discounted rates? Did a major advertiser threaten to transfer its advertising to another newspaper unless it was given a large rate-per-page reduction? Answers to these questions could prompt Saunier to take subsequent actions, including, for example, pushing marketing personnel to renew efforts to promote advertising by existing and potential advertisers.

A well-conceived plan includes enough flexibility so that managers can seize opportunities unforeseen at the time the plan is formulated. In no case should control mean that managers cling to a pre-existing plan when unfolding events indicate that actions not encompassed by the original plan would offer the best results to the company.

Planning and control are so strongly intertwined that managers do not spend time drawing artificially rigid distinctions between them. Unless otherwise stated, we use control in its broadest sense to denote the entire management process of both planning and control. For example, instead of referring to a management planning and control system, we will refer to a management control system. Similarly, we will often refer to the control purpose of accounting instead of the awkward planning and control purpose of accounting.

Do not underestimate the role of individuals and groups in management control systems. Both accountants and managers should always remember that management control systems are not confined to technical matters such as the type of computer system used and the frequency with which reports are prepared. Management control is primarily a human activity that tends to focus on how to help individuals do their jobs better. For example, it is often better for managers to discuss personally with underperforming workers how to improve performance rather than just sending those workers a report highlighting their underperformance.

Moreover, do not view accounting's intended roles as being shared by all organisations. Accounting practice tends to be informed by technical considerations but is always indicative of many organisational, social and political processes which are specific to the enterprise context. Thus, two equally profitable companies of the same size within the same industry and having comparable accounting systems at their disposition may exhibit very different uses and purposes served by these accounting systems. This is because, although accounting systems may be designed with similar aims in mind, users of accounting information will perceive different possibilities and priorities as to the roles accounting can play within their organisations. Do not be surprised to see accounting systems in practice being used in ways which reflect the preferences and idiosyncrasies of their users rather than the predefined functions identified by accounting information system designers.

Feedback: a major key

Exhibit 1.1 shows a feedback loop from control back to planning. Feedback involves managers examining past performance and systematically exploring alternative ways to improve future performance. It can lead to a variety of responses, including the following:

Use of feedback	Example
• Tracking growth	• Unilever monitors the attainment of its 'Path to Growth' sales and operating margin targets.
• Searching for alternative means of operating	• Mbarara University Hospital compares internal processing versus third-party managing (outsourcing) of its accounts receivable operations.
• Changing methods for making decisions	• Lombard Odier & Cie, a Swiss private banking institution whose success is built on customised confidential client service, provides tailor-made financial information to customers after assessing client preferences in terms of communication mode and format.
• Making predictions	• Siemens adopts a team-based new product development process with input from both manufacturing and marketing following an analysis of information flows.
• Changing operations	• Land Rover reduces scrap, obsolescence and lost material and improves stock turns after establishing innovative supplier relationships.
• Changing the reward system	• Convent, Germany's leading producer of crisps and salted snacks, has established data-recording links with customers to minimise use of its shelf space while maximising return for both retailers and Convent alike.

Scorekeeping, attention-directing and problem-solving functions

Management accountants can be considered to perform three important functions: scorekeeping, attention directing and problem solving. **Scorekeeping** refers to the accumulation of data and the reporting of reliable results to all levels of management. Examples are the recording of sales, purchases of materials, and payroll payments. **Attention directing** attempts to make visible both opportunities and problems on which managers need to focus. Examples are highlighting rapidly growing markets where the company may be underfunding its investment and highlighting products with higher-than-expected rework rates or customer-return rates. Attention directing should focus on all opportunities to add value to an organisation and not just on cost-reduction opportunities. **Problem solving** refers to the comparative analysis undertaken to identify the best alternatives in relation to the organisation's goals. An example is comparing the financial advantages of leasing a fleet of vehicles rather than owning those vehicles.

Accountants serving the scorekeeping function accumulate data and report the results to all levels of management. Accountants serving this function are responsible for the reliability of the reported information. The scorekeeping function in many organisations requires processing numerous data items (millions of items in some cases). Computerised information systems are used by these organisations to automate scorekeeping tasks so that they are executed as flawlessly as possible.

Many organisations which automate scorekeeping have management accountants concentrating solely on the attention-directing or problem-solving function. The titles of these individuals differ. Positions may exist for 'cost systems and financial reporting', 'planning and analysis', 'forecasting' and 'manufacturing analysis and support'. Yoplait, the French yogurt-making company, has staff positions for 'operations analysis', 'budget analysis and reporting' and 'marketing and sales analysis'.

Costs, benefits and context

This book regards management accounting as encompassing the assessment of costs, benefits and context. That is, one criterion for choosing among alternative accounting systems is how well they are perceived to help achieve organisational goals in relation to the costs of those systems and the context within which they are to operate. Many studies indicate that the functioning of management accounting systems is affected as much by behavioural and social factors as by technical ones. This book identifies many changes in the field. However, it is clear that in many instances, resistance to management accounting change is caused by behavioural attitudes rather than technical flaws in the accounting innovations. At times, resistance to management accounting change can be associated with incompatibilities between the new system and the norms or taken-for-granted ways of thinking within the organisation.

As customers, managers buy a more elaborate management accounting system when its perceived expected benefits exceed its perceived expected costs and only after due consideration of contextual factors is undertaken. Although the benefits may take many forms, managers take decisions that seek to help better attain goals (both personal and organisational).

Consider the installation of a company's first budgeting system. Previously, the company had probably been using some historical record keeping and little formal planning. A major benefit of installing the budgeting system is that it compels managers to plan more formally. They may make a different, more profitable set of decisions than would have been done by using only a historical system. Thus, in this instance, the expected benefits exceed the expected costs of the new budgeting system. These costs include investments in computer hardware and software, in training people, and in ongoing operating costs of the system. Naturally, the enhanced formality of the new system must be compatible with the values and inclinations of its intended users.

The measurement of costs and benefits and developing an understanding of context are seldom easy. This is because we cannot assume rational-economic behaviour on the part of managers and accountants. In other words, accounting systems cannot just be chosen after their benefits and costs have been assessed and compared (at least conceptually). There are differences across organisations in the patterns and processes of adoption and routinisation of accounting systems as well as in how extensively accounting information is used by managers. Sometimes, an understanding of these differences can be obtained by studying the context in which accounting information is used and the process whereby the accounting systems influence and are affected by their context. Some organisations such as Amazon, Capital One, Barclays Bank and Yahoo are regarded as a new breed of company 'competing on analytics'. These analytical firms consider both qualitiative and quantitative information. For example, eBay undertakes 'extensive and varied analyses by performing randomized tests of Web page variations before making any changes to the Web site or the business model' (Davenport et al. 2010, p. 22). Clearly, organisational context is important to consider, but so too is country context in the design of management accounting systems and in understanding differences in the ways in which their information output is used. For instance, the number of qualified accountants varies significantly from one European country to another (see Exhibit 1.3). A better understanding of context can help you

Exhibit 1.3	Qualified accountants in Europe
Country	**Accountants per 10 000**
UK	23.0
Germany	8.0
Italy	7.5
Sweden	5.1
Denmark	5.0
France	4.0
Finland	3.5
The Netherlands	3.0
Belgium	2.5
Spain	1.0
Greece	0.8

Source: Bhimani, A. (2015) *Strategic Finance: Achieving High Corporate Performance* (London: Strategy Press). Reproduced with permission.

decide whether these differences are indicative of, say, more use being made of accounting information by managers in Germany as opposed to the Netherlands, or whether there are more legal requirements for producing accounting information in the UK than in France, or perhaps whether accounting information users in Italy desire more detailed accounts than those in Spain.

As Harrison and McKinnon (2007, p. 114) observe: 'Individuals crossing national and cultural borders to work require an understanding of the differences in management control practices they are likely to encounter, and sensitivity to the cultural underpinnings of those practices'.

Consider also the fact that some organisations will face important barriers in implementing new accounting systems whereas others will not. Perhaps this is due to differences in enthusiasm by senior managers towards altering accounting systems. Managers differ in their perception of the usefulness of accounting information. Insights into the context within which and the process by which accounting information is used can tell us much about differences in the choice and use of accounting systems in organisations. In this book, you will be encouraged to think about the economic aspects of management accounting while also being encouraged to consider factors relating to the organisational and social context of accounting systems. The cost–benefit–context approach provides a solid point for analysing accounting issues. Assessing context and process issues can be useful in choosing and designing accounting information systems and in considering how they will be used.

Themes in the design of management accounting systems

The design of a management accounting system should be guided by the challenges facing managers. Exhibit 1.4 presents four key themes that are important to managers seeking to make effective planning and control decisions. Management accounting can play a key role in helping managers focus on these four themes.

1 *Customer focus.* Customers are pivotal to the success of an organisation. The number of organisations aiming to be 'customer-driven' is large and increasing. For example, consider Uchumi, one of the largest commercial retailing companies in Kenya. The company is highly customer-centric:

> **Our success is based on listening and responding to customers. Our steering wheel has six segments – the top one being customer service. We have put systems in place to listen to our customers. We are well aware that if we stop listening and do not respond to our customers' needs they will choose to shop elsewhere.**   (www.uchumi.com)

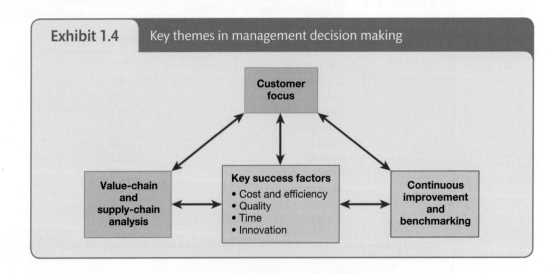

Exhibit 1.4   Key themes in management decision making

The challenge facing managers is to continue investing sufficient (but not excessive) resources in customer satisfaction such that profitable customers are attracted and retained. We discuss this theme in Chapter 12 where we address customer performance measures and customer-profitability analysis.

2 *Value-chain and supply-chain analysis.*

The **value chain** is the sequence of business functions in which utility (usefulness) is added to the products or services of an organisation. These functions are as follows:

- **Research and development (R&D)** – the generation of, and experimentation with, ideas related to new products, services or processes.
- **Design of products, services or processes** – the detailed planning and engineering of products, services or processes.
- **Production** – the coordination and assembly of resources to produce a product or deliver a service.
- **Marketing** – the manner by which individuals or groups (a) learn about and value the attributes of products or services, and (b) purchase those products or services.
- **Distribution** – the mechanism by which products or services are delivered to the customer.
- **Customer service** – the support activities provided to customers.

Do not interpret Exhibit 1.5 as implying that managers should proceed sequentially through the value chain. There are important gains to be realised (in terms of, say, cost, quality, and the speed with which new products are developed) from having the individual parts of the value chain work concurrently.

Senior managers (including those from individual parts of the value chain) are responsible for deciding the organisation's overall strategy, how resources are to be obtained and used, and how rewards are to be given. This task covers the entire value chain. IKEA, the Swedish home furnishings retailer, focuses on analysing its value-added chain in order to reduce its costs while enhancing perceived value by the customer: unassembled furniture is profitably sold direct from the warehouse to customers who prize easy assembly instructions and family-oriented showrooms. Such efforts have helped IKEA attain the stature of a number 1 brand in Europe and Africa according to Brand Channel rankings.

Accounting is a major means of helping managers to administer each of the business functions presented in Exhibit 1.5 and to coordinate their activities within the framework of the organisation as a whole. This book focuses on how accounting aims to assist managers in these tasks.

The term **supply chain** describes the flow of goods, services, and information from cradle to grave, regardless of whether those activities occur in the same organisation or other organisations. Consider the beverage products of Coca-Cola or Pepsi-Cola. Many companies

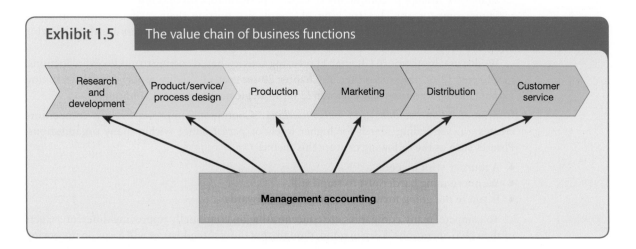

Exhibit 1.5   The value chain of business functions

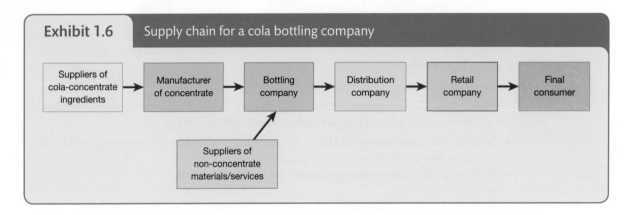

Exhibit 1.6   Supply chain for a cola bottling company

play a role in bringing these products to the final consumers. Exhibit 1.6 presents an overview of the supply chain. Cost management emphasises integrating and coordinating activities across all companies in the supply chain as well as across each business function in an individual company's value chain. To illustrate, both Coca-Cola and Pepsi-Cola bottling companies work with their suppliers (such as glass and can companies and sugar manufacturers) to reduce their materials-handling costs.

We discuss this theme in Chapter 15 on variance analysis, Chapter 12 on target costing and Chapter 21 on just-in-time (JIT) and supply-chain analysis.

3 **Key success factors.** These operational factors directly affect the economic viability of the organisation. Customers are demanding ever-improving levels of performance regarding several (or even all) of the following:

- *Cost*. Organisations are under continuous pressure to reduce the cost of their products or the services they sell to customers.
- *Quality*. Customers expect higher levels of quality and are less tolerant of low quality than in the past.
- *Time*. Time has many components, including the time taken to develop and bring new products to market, the speed at which an organisation responds to customer requests, and the reliability with which promised delivery dates are met. Organisations are under pressure to complete activities faster and to meet promised delivery dates more reliably than in the past in order to increase customer satisfaction.
- *Innovation*. There is now a heightened perception that a continuing flow of innovative products or services is a prerequisite for the ongoing success of most organisations.

Managers attempt to continually track their performance on the chosen key success factors *vis-à-vis* competitors. This tracking of companies outside their own organisation alerts managers to changes in the external environment that their own customers are also observing and evaluating.

We discuss this theme in Chapter 11 on using activity-based costing to guide cost reductions; in Chapter 12 on target costing; in Chapter 20 on cost of quality reports, bottlenecks and manufacturing lead time and Chapter 22 on strategic management accounting.

4 *Continuous improvement and benchmarking.* Continuous improvement by competitors creates a never-ending search for higher levels of performance within many organisations. Phrases such as the following capture this theme:

- A journey with no end.
- We are running harder just to stand still.
- If you're not going forward, you're going backwards.

To compete, many companies are concentrating on continually improving different aspects of their own operations. Keep in mind, though, that different industries will focus on improving different operational factors. For example, airlines seek to improve the percentage of their flights that arrive on time. Internet companies seek to improve the percentage of each 24-hour period that customers can access their online systems without delay. Sumitomo Electric Industries, the Japanese manufacturer of electric wire and cable, has daily meetings so that all employees maintain a continuous focus on cost reduction. Continuous improvement targets are often set by benchmarking or measuring the quality of products, services and activities of the company against the best known levels of performance found in competing companies. Many companies within industry groups exchange information for the purpose of performance benchmarking.

We discuss this theme in the sections in Chapter 14 on kaizen budgeting, Chapter 15 on continuous improvement and standard costs, and Chapter 9 on learning curves.

These four themes frequently overlap. For example, customer focus (theme 1) is now a key ingredient in new product development at many companies (theme 2). Product designers are encouraged to search for cost-reduction opportunities at all stages in the value chain and supply chain (theme 3) and to cross-compare operational performance with competitor products (theme 4). The Concepts in Action box below describes how some companies choose their e-business strategies to integrate the four themes.

While these four themes are of relevance to many managers in modern enterprises, the design of management accounting systems must also take into account the peculiarities and contextual characteristics of organisations. Although the form of one management accounting system within a particular organisation may appear to be similar to that of another, management accounting systems designers must attempt to learn about the organisational context in which the system is to operate. The relevance of understanding organisational specificity and the potential of accounting systems is discussed further in Chapter 22.

Concepts in action   Management accounting beyond the numbers

When you hear the job title 'accountant', what comes to mind? The accountant who does your tax return each year? Individuals who prepare budgets at Dell or Sony? To people outside the profession, it may seem like accountants are just 'numbers people'. It is true that most accountants are adept financial managers, yet their skills do not stop there. To be successful, management accountants must possess certain values and behaviours that reach well beyond basic analytical abilities, working in cross-functional teams and as business partners of managers. It is not enough that management accountants are technically competent in their area of study. They also need to be able to work in teams, to learn about business issues, to understand the motivations of different individuals, to respect the views of their colleagues, and to show empathy and trust.

Promoting fact-based analysis and making tough-minded, critical judgements without being adversarial

Management accountants must raise tough questions for managers to consider, especially when preparing budgets. They must do so thoughtfully and with the intent of improving plans and decisions. Consider Northern Rock, a UK-based building society formed in 1965 but nationalised in February 2008 following credit problems. Management accountants at Northern Rock should have raised questions about whether the company's risky mortgage lending and its strategy of securitisation would be profitable if housing prices declined.

Leading and motivating people to change and be innovative

Implementing new ideas, however good they may be, is seldom easy. When Unilever, the Anglo-Dutch multinational consumer goods company, sought to install an enterprise resource planning system and outsource part of its accounting activities, Christian Kaufmann, the company's European Managing Director of Finance Business Services, knew this would make 'a very big organisation much slicker and more agile. And that, of course, has an impact on culture'. He made sure that the vision for change was well understood throughout the company. Operational excellence measures which focused on a few key metrics were developed.

Concepts in action   continued

Source: Corbis/HBSS

Communicating clearly, openly, and candidly

Communicating information is a large part of a management accountant's job. A few years ago, Pitney Bowes Inc. (PBI), a $4 billion global provider of integrated mail and document management solutions, implemented a reporting initiative to give managers feedback in key areas. The initiative succeeded because it was clearly designed and openly communicated by PBI's team of management accountants.

Having a strong sense of integrity

Management accountants must never succumb to pressure from managers to manipulate financial information. They must always remember that their primary commitment is to the organisation and its shareholders. At WorldCom, under pressure from senior managers, members of the accounting staff concealed billions of dollars in expenses. Because the accounting staff lacked the integrity and courage to stand up to and report corrupt senior managers, WorldCom landed in bankruptcy. Some members of the accounting staff and the senior executive team served prison terms for their actions.

Sources: Dash, E. and Sorkin, A.R. (2008) 'Government seizes WaMu and sells some assets', *New York Times*, 25 September, http: www.nytimes.com/2008/09/26/business/26wamu.com; Garling, W. (2007) 'Winning the transformation battle at the Defense Finance and Accounting Service', *Balanced Scorecard Report*, May–June, http://cb.hbsp.harvard.edu/cb/web/product_detail.seam?R=B0705C-PDF-ENG; Gollakota, K. and Gupta, V. (2009) 'WorldCom Inc.: what went wrong?', Richard Ivey School of Business, Case No. 905M43. London, ON: University of Western Ontario, http://cb/hbsp.harvard.edu/cb/web/product_detail.seam?R=905M43-PDF-ENG; Green, M., Garrity, J., Gumbus, A. and Lyons, B. (2002) 'Pitney Bowes calls for new metrics', *Strategic Finance*, May, http://www.allbusiness.com/accounting-reporting/reports-statements-profit/189988-1.html; the-financedirector.com/features/feature84724, 'Unilever's simplified structure' (11 May 2010).

Forces of change in management accounting

Over time, the emphasis placed on the four themes in Exhibit 1.4 may change and new themes may emerge. If management accountants are to remain useful to the organisations within which they work, they need to keep current with changes in management practices. The International Federation of Accountants has established a Professional Accountants in Business Committee (PAIB) with responsibility to provide guidance on management accounting issues to IFAC member bodies and the more than one million professional accountants worldwide working in commerce, industry, the public sector, education and the not-for-profit sector (see www.ifac.org).

The PAIB in its report *Competent and Versatile: How Professional Accountants in Business Drive Sustainable Organisational Success* (August 2011) noted that professional accountants in business support and further the strategic, financial and operational aims of the organisations in which they work. They play a role:

- as *creators of value*, by taking leadership roles in the design and implementation of strategies, policies, plans, structures, and governance measures that set the course for delivering sustainable value creation;

- as *enablers of value*, by informing and guiding managerial and operational decision making and implementation of strategy for achieving sustainable value creation, and the planning, monitoring and improvement of supporting processes;

- as *preservers of value*, by ensuring the protection of a sustainable value creation strategy against strategic, operational and financial risks, and ensuring compliance with regulations, standards and good practices;

- as *reporters of value*, by enabling the transparent communication of the delivery of sustainable value to stakeholders.

The report stresses that the work of professional accountants, ultimately, contributes to developing sustainable organisations and financial markets and strong international economies.

Clearly, the role of accountants pervades many aspects of both management and information provision. In the context of the consequences of the global economic crisis which began in 2008, the role of finance specialists is of specific significance to governments, regulators, financial markets and to public and private organisations. The PAIB report identifies some specific challenges relating to the movement towards models of sustainable economies and corporate responsibility; balancing compliance requirements with the need to drive organisational performance and remaining globally competitive; and in some contexts, the need for government expenditure and debt to be reduced, while enhancing accountability and transparency.

Changes across economies which have taken place over the recent past point to aspects of management accounting change of concern to many practising management accountants around the globe. In this book we attempt to identify many of these emerging trends while also highlighting management accounting approaches which have had a longer past but which continue to be relevant for many enterprises.

Are there other pressures for management accounting to change? It is possible that management accounting systems designed for organisations operating in more stable markets are not ideal in contexts where market opportunities have become very short-lived (see Bhimani 2015). Organisations that traditionally were centralised and which are no longer capable of providing the type of information required by managers today may be shaping alterations in management accounting output. This view holds not only for profit-seeking enterprises but also for not-for-profit and (public sector) organisations (Allen 2000; Lapsley 2000; Smith 2000). There are many instances of accounting systems and processes being assigned a more prominent role in the management of public services. This is the case for both short-term operational and longer-term capital investment decision making (Moll and Humphrey 2007). The traditional functional specialisation of some organisations may have produced systems of performance measures and reward incentives which are fragmented and no longer adequate for modern integrated operations that emphasise cross-functional processes. Emerging flexible organisational technologies which have made possible the shift from selling mass-market, generic products and services to servicing potentially more profitable niche market and special-purpose products in much smaller volumes, have, in some instances, also given rise to the perceived need for altered cost management practices.

Many management accounting thinkers have commented on the desirability for more management accounting information which stresses non-financial metrics and performance measures that supports total quality management and value-chain concepts as well as activity accounting, benchmarking and target costing (see Hopper et al. 2007; Mitchell et al. 2012; Wickramasinghe and Alawattage 2007). In some organisational contexts, management accounting information reports now elaborate on pricing strategies and costing issues to recognise that a majority of resources are focused on the design, development and marketing stages of the products' life cycles. A constantly altering valuation of the product's characteristics by the customer is perceived to be enhancing the prospect for 'attribute costing' (Roslender and Hart 2003). In some organisations, capturing real-time market and external information is as significant as understanding cost incursions involved in carrying out internal operational activities. Management accounting is regarded by some scholars as increasingly playing a valuable role in different organisational forms of consumerism (Jeacle 2007). Understanding the customer and the competition is viewed as essential for corporate survival which has led to management accounting processes becoming more externally oriented (Bhimani and Bromwich 2010).

Whereas traditional management accounting techniques have been internally orientated, the e-business environment within which modern enterprises increasingly operate forces a higher level of interactive relationships with suppliers, alliances and customers. The scope for outsourcing as opposed to producing in-house is on the increase for most organisations. E-business management principles in the face of opportunities offered by Internet technologies make it potentially desirable for organisations to consider new distribution and communication channels within supplier–assembler–customer networks. Likewise, auxiliary administrative and support functions such as personnel management, accounting processes and computer hardware and software can be more readily outsourced via application service providers and web-based service operators. The high level of interactivity between what were traditionally seen as external and internal segments has removed the precision of such differentiation. It is now less clear what is internal to the company and what is external. Traditional control frameworks, now have to address altered demands placed on accounting information systems and the communication process, taking account of knowledge management priorities (Bhimani 2006; Busco et al. 2007; Hartmann and Vaassen 2003; Kraus and Lind 2007). This will no doubt continue to challenge highly defined and focused management accounting systems. Strategic management accounting (discussed in Chapter 22) considers ways of balancing management accounting information which is internally as well as externally oriented so as to seamlessly integrate aspects of the two to engender effective decision making and performance evaluation.

Many organisations are today increasingly 'virtual' in that they perform a largely coordinating and resource allocation function across market entities with very little investments in traditional physical-assets bases. One principal asset base of the virtual organisation is its intellectual capital. One can think of intellectual capital as the combined knowledge resources of an enterprise (Roberts 2006; 2007). Whenever a firm produces and sells a new product or service, it adds to its knowledge base by accumulating experience (see Chapter 9) and gaining insights from the design, production and marketing processes. Intellectual capital can include know-how, work-related knowledge, entrepreneurial élan, customer loyalty, brands, trademark, corporate culture and cost management systems among other dimensions of capital. Building intellectual capital is dependent on organisational process tracking, measurement and reporting. For some enterprises, these represent new priorities for management accounting. Nevertheless it is important for companies to develop appropriate ways of assessing and measuring intellectual capital to provide overall evaluation and long-term assessment of an organisation's competitiveness. A related issue concerns management accounting's objectives within organisations to abet knowledge creation. Accounting has always been concerned with information production, processing and reporting, and management accounting specifically with providing managers with information-based intelligence. As many organisations are increasingly harnessing wealth creation through intangible intellectual resources, knowledge creation and management grow in importance. Differentiating between data which management accountants interpret into meaningful information for managers and knowledge which is information that is made actionable, becomes particularly relevant. The relevance of management accounting activities which seek to generate confidence in information which enables knowledge creation and which addresses the non-physical characteristics of production processes is continuing to grow.

The virtual organisation is characterised by coordination in the absence of centralisation of ownership, facilities, resources or operations. The production capability of the virtual organisation stems from the electronic integration of resources and expertise which is widely distributed among an alliance of participants. Ultimately, it might be expected that as organisational structures, priorities and modes of operations change, so pressures will mount for management accounting systems to alter their information focus. Factors like external outlook, speed of reporting, capture of operational complexity, customer responsiveness, total life-cycle concerns, strategic integration and emerging e-business issues are likely to continue to impinge on demands made of management accounting. No doubt the management accountant's role in organisations will continue to be seen as potentially very significant in the years to come. It is intended that this book will help you think about technical, organisational and wider global issues of concern to management accountants.

Summary

The following points are linked to the chapter's learning objectives.

1 Cost accounting measures and reports financial and other information related to an organisation's acquisition or consumption of resources. It is an important component of both management accounting and financial accounting.

2 Cost management and strategy are increasingly relevant aspects of management accounting processes.

3 Accounting systems are intended to provide information for five broad purposes: (a) formulating overall strategies and long-range plans, (b) resource allocation decisions such as product and customer emphasis, (c) cost planning and cost control, (d) performance measurement, and (e) meeting external regulatory and legal reporting obligations.

4 Accounting influences planning, control and decision making through budgets and other financial benchmarks, its systematic recording of actual results and its role in performance evaluation.

5 In most organisations, management accountants perform scorekeeping, attention-directing and problem-solving functions. The first function emphasises the importance of the integrity of information, while the other two emphasise the helper role of the accountant.

6 Economic benefits and costs in the design, implementation and use of accounting systems need to be assessed in the light of organisational context and process issues. Assessing costs, benefits and context is important to understanding the functioning of management accounting in enterprises.

7 A variety of management forces and trends is shaping the design and uses of management accounting systems.

8 Economic and global factors are affecting management accounting thinking and practices, including organisational structure changes, digitisation, the growing significance of intellectual capital and knowledge management, sustainability issues, the rise of 'Big Data', and national and international measures to deal with governance, risk and economic growth issues.

Appendix

Professional ethics

Ethical guidelines

Professional accounting organisations representing management accountants exist in many countries. For example, CIMA in the UK provides a programme leading to membership of the institute. Membership signals that the holder has passed the admission criteria and demonstrated the competence of technical knowledge required by the CIMA to become a chartered management accountant.

To become a CIMA member, students complete operational, management and strategic levels of professional qualifications and a test of professional competence in management accounting. Ten examinations are required. Three years' relevant practical experience is also required to qualify (see www.cimaglobal.com for more information).

Management accounting topics are also covered by several other professional bodies. The syllabus for the examinations of the Association of Chartered Certified Accountants (ACCA) has 14 papers. Three years of practical experience and the completion of a Professional Ethics module are also requirements (see www.accaglobal.com). Other accounting bodies include the

Institute of Chartered Accountants in England and Wales (ICAEW) (see http://www.icaew.co.uk) and the Institute for Chartered Accountants of Scotland (ICAS) (see http://www.icas.org.uk). These institutes have requirements that cover proficiency in general management topics as well as professional accounting and ethics topics.

Professional accounting organisations play an important role in promoting a high standard of ethics. The CIMA has issued a code of ethical guidelines for its members, just as the Institute of Management Accountants (IMA) in the US has issued ethical principles in its IMA Statement of Ethical Professional Practice (2005). Exhibit 1.7 presents a summary of CIMA's 'fundamental principles'.

Exhibit 1.7	Summary of CIMA's ethical guidelines

Fundamental principles – to achieve the objectives of the profession, accountants have to observe the following fundamental principles:

1 *Integrity* – A professional accountant should be straightforward and honest in all professional and business relationships. Integrity also implies fair dealing and truthfulness.

2 *Objectivity* – A professional accountant should not compromise their professional or business judgement because of bias, conflict of interest or the undue influence of others.

3 *Professional competence and due care* – A professional accountant should maintain professional knowledge and skill at the level required to ensure that clients or employers receive a competent professional service. A professional accountant should act diligently in accordance with applicable technical and professional standards when providing professional services.

4 *Confidentiality* – A professional accountant should refrain from disclosing outside the firm or employing organisation confidential information acquired as a result of professional and business relationships without proper and specific authority unless there is a legal or professional right or duty to disclose. Confidential information acquired as a result of professional and business relationships should not be used for personal advantage of the professional accountant or the advantage of third parties.

5 *Professional behaviour* – A professional accountant should comply with relevant laws and regulations and should avoid any actions that the professional accountant knows or should know may discredit the profession.

Source: Chartered Institute of Management Accountants (CIMA) (2010) *CIMA Code of Ethics for Professional Accountants* (London: CIMA). Reproduced with permission.

Typical ethical challenges

Ethical issues can confront management accountants in many ways. The following examples are illustrative.

- **Case A.** A management accountant, knowing that reporting a loss for a software division will result in yet another 'rightsizing initiative' (a euphemism for lay-offs), has concerns about the commercial viability of software for which R&D costs are currently being capitalised. The divisional manager argues vehemently that the new product will be a 'winner' but has no credible evidence to support the opinion. The last two products from this division have not been successful in the market. The management accountant has many friends in the division and wants to avoid a personal confrontation with the division manager. Should the management accountant require the R&D to be expensed immediately owing to the lack of evidence regarding its commercial viability?

● **Case B.** A packaging supplier, bidding for a new contract, offers the management accountant of its customer an all-expenses-paid weekend to Disneyland Paris for her and her family. The supplier does not mention the new contract when making the invitation. The accountant is not a personal friend of the supplier. She knows operating cost issues are critical in approving the new contract and is concerned that the supplier will ask details about bids by competing packaging companies.

In each case the management accountant is faced with an ethical challenge. Case A involves competence, objectivity and integrity, whereas case B involves confidentiality and integrity. Ethical issues are not always black or white. For example, the supplier in case B may have no intention of raising issues associated with the bid. However, the appearance of a conflict of interest in case B is sufficient for many companies to prohibit employees from accepting free 'gifts' from suppliers.

Key terms

management accounting (3)	**problem solving** (10)
financial accounting (3)	**value chain** (13)
cost accounting (3)	**research and development (R&D)** (13)
cost management (4)	**design of products, services or processes** (13)
planning (7)	**production** (13)
budget (8)	**marketing** (13)
control (8)	**distribution** (13)
management by exception (9)	**customer service** (13)
variance (9)	**supply chain** (13)
scorekeeping (10)	**key success factors** (14)
attention directing (10)	

References and further reading

Alexander, D., Britton, A. and Jorissen, A. (2011) *International Financial Reporting and Analysis* (Hampshire, UK: Cengage).

Allen, D. (2000) 'Management accountancy in the public sector', *Management Accounting* (February), pp. 44–5.

Bhimani, A. (2006) 'Management accounting and digitisation', in A. Bhimani (ed.) *Contemporary Issues in Management Accounting* (Oxford: Oxford University Press), pp. 69–91.

Bhimani, A. (2015) *Strategic Finance: Achieving High Corporate Performance* (London: Strategy Press).

Bhimani, A. and Bromwich, M. (2010) *Management Accounting: Retrospect and Prospect* (Oxford: CIMA/ Elsevier).

Busco, C., Giovannoni, E. and Riccaboni, A. (2007) 'Globalisation and the international convergence of management accounting', in T. Hopper, D. Northcott and R. Scapens (eds) *Issues in Management Accounting* (Harlow: FT Prentice Hall).

CFO/ACCA (2009) *The CFO's New Environment* (London: CFO/ACCA).

Davenport, T. (2006) 'Competing on analytics', *Harvard Business Review*, January.

Davenport, T., Harris, J. and Morison, R. (2010) *Analytics at Work: Smarter Decisions, Better Results* (Boston, Mass.: Harvard Business Press).

Harrison, G. and McKinnon, J. (2007) 'National culture and management control', in T. Hopper, D. Northcott and R. Scapens (eds) *Issues in Management Accounting* (Harlow: FT Prentice Hall).

Hartmann, F. and Vaassen, E.H. (2003) 'The changing role of management accounting and control systems', in A. Bhimani (ed.) *Management Accounting in the Digital Economy* (Oxford: Oxford University Press), pp. 112–31.

Hopper, T., Northcott, D. and Scapens, R. (eds) (2007) *Issues in Management Accounting* (Harlow: FT Prentice Hall).

Jeacle, I. (2007) 'Management accounting for consumerism', in T. Hopper, D. Northcott and R. Scapens (eds) *Issues in Management Accounting* (Harlow: FT Prentice Hall).

Karaian, J. (2014) *The Chief Financial Officer: What CFOs Do, the Influence They Have, and Why It Matters* (London: Economist Books).

Kraus, K. and Lind, J. (2007) 'Management control in international relationships', in T. Hopper, D. Northcott and R. Scapens (eds) *Issues in Management Accounting* (Harlow: FT Prentice Hall).

Lapsley, I. (2000) 'Management accounting and the state: making sense of complexity', *Management Accounting Research*, pp. 169–73.

Mitchell, F., Norreklit, H. and Jakobsen, M. (2012) *The Routledge Companion to Cost Management* (London: Routledge).

Moll, J. and Humphrey, C. (2007) 'Management accounting and accountants in the public sector: the challenges presented by public-private partnerships', in T. Hopper, D. Northcott and R. Scapens (eds) *Issues in Management Accounting* (Harlow: FT Prentice Hall).

Roberts, H. (2006) 'Making management accounting intelligible', in A. Bhimani (ed.) *Contemporary Issues in Management Accounting* (Oxford: Oxford University Press).

Roberts, H. (2007) 'Knowledge resources and management accounting', in T. Hopper, D. Northcott and R. Scapens (eds) *Issues in Management Accounting* (Harlow: FT Prentice Hall).

Roslender, R. and Hart, S. (2003) 'In search of strategic management accounting: theoretical and field study perspectives', *Management Accounting Research*, pp. 255–81.

Sanders, J. (2011) 'The path to becoming a Fortune 500 CEO', www.forbes.com/sites/2011/12/05.

Savage, R. (2014) 'Who knew? The average FTSE 100 CEO is a 54-year-old male accountant', www.managementtoday.co.uk/news/1292054, 29 April.

Scapens, R.W. (2006) 'Changing times: management accounting, research and practice from a UK perspective', in A. Bhimani (ed.) *Contemporary Issues in Management Accounting* (Oxford: Oxford University Press), pp. 425–54.

Smith, M. (2000) 'Strategic management accountancy in the public sector', *Management Accounting* (January), pp. 40–3.

Wickramasinghe, D. and Alawattage, C. (2007) *Management Accounting Change: Approaches and Perspectives* (London: Routledge).

Zuboff, S. (2010) 'Creating value in the age of distributed capitalism', *McKinsey Quarterly* (4), pp. 45–55.

Zuckerberg, M. (2014) www.facebook.com/zuck/posts/10101319050523971, 25 January 2014.

CHAPTER 1

Assessment material

Review questions

1.1 The accounting system should provide information for five broad purposes. Describe them.

1.2 Distinguish between *management accounting* and *financial accounting*.

1.3 Describe the business functions in the value chain.

1.4 Explain the meaning of *cost management*.

1.5 'Knowledge of technical issues such as computer technology is necessary but not sufficient to becoming a successful accountant.' Do you agree? Why?

1.6 Peter Drucker, a noted business observer, made the following comment in an address to management accountants: 'I am not saying that you do not need a "cop on the beat", you do . . . But your great challenge is to get across to your associates your ability to identify the opportunities – to identify the wealth-producing characteristics.' Do you agree? Explain.

1.7 As a new accountant, reply to this comment by a plant manager: 'As I see it, our accountants may be needed to keep records for shareholders and for the tax authorities – but I don't want them sticking their noses in my day-to-day operations. I do the best I know how. No pen-pushing bean-counter knows enough about my responsibilities to be of any use to me.'

1.8 When explaining a motor vehicle market-share turnaround, Citroën stated: 'We listened to what our customers wanted and acted on what they said. Good things happen when you pay attention to the boss.' How might management accountants at Citroën apply this same perspective to their own tasks?

1.9 A leading management observer stated that the most successful companies are those which have an obsession for their customers. Is this statement pertinent to management accountants? Explain.

1.10 Changes in the way managers operate require rethinking the design and operation of management accounting systems. Describe five themes that are affecting both the way managers operate and developments in management accounting.

Exercises

Basic level

*1.11 **Financial and management accounting** (15–20 minutes)

Anne-Jorun Sørensen, an able electrical engineer, was informed that she was going to be promoted to assistant plant manager. Anne-Jorun was elated but uneasy. In particular, her knowledge of accounting was sparse. She had taken one course in financial accounting but had not been exposed to the management accounting that her superiors found helpful.

---

* Fully worked solutions to exercises thus marked are provided in Appendix A.

Sørensen planned to enrol in a management accounting course as soon as possible. Meanwhile, she asked Siri Aspelund, an assistant controller, to state two or three of the principal distinctions between financial and management accounting using some concrete examples.

As the assistant controller, prepare a written response to Sørensen.

*1.12   Purposes of accounting systems (10 minutes)

The European Sports Management Group (ESMG) manages and promotes sporting events and sporting personalities. Its managers are currently examining the following reports and accounting statements:

a Five-year projections for expanding into managing sports television networks for satellite television.

b Income statement to be included in a six-month interim report to be sent to investors.

c Profitability comparison of cricket tournaments directed by different managers, each of whom receives a percentage of that tournament's profits.

d Monthly reports of office costs for each of the 14 ESMG offices throughout Europe.

e Statement showing the revenues ESMG earns from different types of sporting event (for example, squash, triathlon and cricket).

Required

Classify the reports in parts a–e into one of the five major purposes of accounting systems.

1.13   Value chain and classification of costs, computer company (15 minutes)

Compaq Computer incurs the following costs:

a Electricity costs for the plant assembling the Presario computer line of products.

b Transportation costs for shipping Presario software to a retail chain.

c Payment to David Kelley Designs for design of the Armada Notebook.

d Salary of a computer scientist working on the next generation of minicomputers.

e Cost of Compaq employees' visit to a major customer to illustrate Compaq's ability to interconnect with other computers.

f Purchase of competitors' products for testing against potential future Compaq products.

g Payment to a television station for running Compaq advertisements.

h Cost of cables purchased from an outside supplier to be used with the Compaq printer.

Required

Classify each of the cost items in parts a–h into a component of the value chain shown in Exhibit 1.5.

1.14   Value chain and classification of costs, pharmaceutical company (15 minutes)

Boots the Chemist incurs the following costs:

a Cost of redesigning blister packs to make drug containers more tamperproof.

b Cost of videos sent to doctors to promote sales of a new drug.

c Cost of website's 'frequently asked questions' for customer enquiries about usage, side-effects of drugs, and so on.

d Equipment purchased by a scientist to conduct experiments on drugs yet to be approved by the government.

e Payment to actors on a feature to be shown on television promoting new hair-growing product for balding men.

f Labour costs of workers in the packaging area of a production facility.

g Bonus paid to a salesperson for exceeding the monthly sales quota.

h Cost of the courier service to deliver drugs to hospitals.

Required

Classify each of the cost items in parts a–h into a component of the value chain shown in Exhibit 1.5.

1.15 **Uses of feedback** (10 minutes)

Six uses of feedback are described in the chapter:

a Changing goals.

b Searching for alternative means of operating.

c Changing methods for making decisions.

d Making predictions.

e Changing the operating process.

f Changing the reward system.

Required

Match the appropriate letters from the preceding list to each of the following items.

1 The Potters Bar University system explores subcontracting its gardening operations to a private company instead of hiring its own gardeners.

2 Sales commissions are to be based on total operating profit instead of total revenue.

3 Fiat adjusts its elaborate way of forecasting demand for its cars by including the effects of expected changes in the price of crude oil.

4 The hiring of new sales personnel will include an additional step: an interview and evaluation by the company psychologist.

5 Quality inspectors at Volvo are now being used in the middle of the production process as well as at the end of the process.

6 Virgin enters the telecommunications industry.

7 Worker assignments on an assembly line are made by teams instead of directed by a foreman.

1.16 **Scorekeeping, attention directing and problem solving** (15 minutes)

For each of the following activities, identify the major function (scorekeeping, attention directing or problem solving) the accountant is performing.

a Preparing a monthly statement of Spanish sales for the BMW marketing vice-president.

b Interpreting differences between actual results and budgeted amounts on a performance report for the customer warranty department of Tefal.

c Preparing a schedule of depreciation for forklift trucks in the receiving department of a Hewlett-Packard plant in Scotland.

d Analysing, for a Toshiba international manufacturing manager, the desirability of buying some semiconductors made in Ireland.

e Interpreting why a Birmingham distribution centre did not adhere to its delivery costs budget.

f Explaining a Niceday shipping department's performance report.

g Preparing, for the manager of production control of a German steel plant, a cost comparison of two computerised manufacturing control systems.

h Preparing a scrap report for the finishing department of a Volvo parts plant.

   i Preparing the budget for the maintenance department of Mont-Blanc Hospital.

   j Analysing, for a Volkswagen product designer, the impact on product costs of some new headlight lamps.

1.17 Scorekeeping, attention directing and problem solving (15 minutes)

For each of the following activities, identify the major function the accountant is performing – scorekeeping, attention directing or problem solving.

   a Interpreting differences between actual results and budgeted amounts on a shipping manager's performance report at a Lada distribution centre.

   b Preparing a report showing the benefits of leasing motor vehicles versus owning them.

   c Preparing adjusting journal entries for depreciation on the personnel manager's office equipment at Crédit Suisse.

   d Preparing a customer's monthly statement for an Argos store.

   e Processing the weekly payroll for the University College Dublin maintenance department.

   f Explaining the product-design manager's performance report at an Audi division.

   g Analysing the costs of several different ways to blend materials in the foundry of a Krupp plant.

   h Tallying sales, by branches, for the sales vice-president of Unilever.

   i Analysing, for a senior manager of British Telecom, the impact of a contemplated new product on net income.

   j Interpreting why a Moulinex sales district did not meet its sales quota.

1.18 Changes in management and changes in management accounting (15 minutes)

A survey on ways organisations are changing their management accounting systems reported the following:

   a Company A now reports a value-chain income statement for each of the brands it sells.

   b Company B now presents in a single report all costs related to achieving high quality levels of its products.

   c Company C now presents estimates of the manufacturing costs of its two most important competitors in its performance reports, in addition to its own internal manufacturing costs.

   d Company D reduces by 1% each month the budgeted labour-assembly cost of a product when evaluating the performance of a plant manager.

   e Company E now reports profitability and satisfaction measures (as assessed by a third party) on a customer-by-customer basis.

Required

Link each of the above changes to one of the key themes in the new management approach outlined in Exhibit 1.4.

1.19 Planning and control, feedback (15–20 minutes)

In April 2014, Bérangère Saunier, editor of *The Sporting News* (SN), decides to reduce the price per newspaper from €0.70 in April 2014 to €0.50 starting 1 May 2014. Actual paid circulation in April is 7.5 million (250 000 per day × 30 days). Saunier estimates that the €0.20 price reduction would increase paid circulation in May to 12.4 million (400 000 × 31 days). The actual May circulation turns out to be 13 640 000 (440 000 × 31 days). Assume that one goal of SN is to increase operating profit. The budgeted increase in circulation would enable SN to charge higher advertising rates in later months of 2014 if those budgeted gains actually occur. The actual price paid in May 2014 was the budgeted €0.50 per newspaper.

Required

1 Distinguish between planning and control at SN, giving an example of each.

2 Prepare a newspaper revenue performance report for SN for May 2014 showing the actual results, budgeted amounts and the variance.

3 Give two types of action Saunier might take based on feedback on the May 2014 circulation revenue.

1.20   Professional ethics and reporting divisional performance (10–15 minutes)

Marguerite Devallois is division controller and Jacques Clément is division manager of the Royaume de la Chaussure SARL, a shoe company. Devallois has line responsibility to Clément, but she also has staff responsibility to the company controller.

Clément is under severe pressure to achieve budgeted division income for the year. He has asked Devallois to book €200 000 of sales on 31 December. The customers' orders are firm, but the shoes are still in the production process. They will be shipped on or about 4 January. Clément said to Devallois, 'The key event is getting the sales order, not shipping of the shoes. You should support me, not obstruct my reaching division goals.'

Required

1 Describe Devallois's ethical responsibilities.

2 What should Devallois do if Clément gives her a direct order to book the sales?

Intermediate level

1.21   Responsibility for analysis of performance (20–30 minutes)

Kari-Anna Nedregotten is the new corporate controller of a multinational company that has just overhauled its organisational structure. The company is now decentralised. Each division is under an operating vice-president who, within wide limits, has responsibilities and authority to run the division like a separate company.

Nedregotten has a number of bright staff members. One of them, Signy Henriksen, is in charge of a newly created performance-analysis system. Henriksen and staff members prepare monthly division performance reports for the company president. These reports are division income statements, showing budgeted performance and actual results, and they are accompanied by detailed written explanations and appraisals of variances. In the past, each of Henriksen's staff members was responsible for analysing one division; each consulted with division line and staff executives and became generally acquainted with the division's operations.

After a few months, Øyvind Hedby, vice-president in charge of Division C, stormed into the controller's office. The gist of his complaint follows:

'Your staff are trying to take over part of my responsibility. They come in, snoop around, ask hundreds of questions, and take up plenty of our time. It's up to me, not you and your detectives, to analyse and explain my division's performance to central headquarters. If you don't stop trying to grab my responsibility, I'll raise the whole issue with the president.'

Required

1 What events or relationships may have led to Hedby's outburst?

2 As Nedregotten, how would you answer Hedby's contentions?

3 What alternative actions can Nedregotten take to improve future relationships?

*1.22   Software procurement decision, ethics (30 minutes)

Walter von Stolzing is the Innsbrück-based controller of Beckmesser GmbH, a rapidly growing manufacturer and marketer of Austrian food products. Stolzing is currently considering the purchase of a new cost management package for use by each of its six manufacturing plants and its many marketing personnel. There are four major competing products being considered by Stolzing.

Pogner 1-2-3 is an aggressive software developer. It views Beckmesser as a target of opportunity. Every six months Pogner has a three-day users' conference on the Costa del Sol. Each conference has substantial time left aside for 'rest and recreation'. Pogner offers Stolzing an all-expenses-paid visit to the coming conference. Stolzing accepts the offer believing that it will be very useful to talk to other users of Pogner software. He is especially looking forward to the visit as he has close relatives living near Marbella.

Prior to leaving, Stolzing received a visit from the president of Beckmesser. She shows him an anonymous letter sent to her. It argues that Pogner is receiving unfair favourable treatment in the Beckmesser software decision-making process. The letter specifically mentions Stolzing's coming 'all-expenses-paid trip to Marbella during the depths of Innsbrück's winter'. Stolzing is deeply offended. He says he has made no decision and believes he is very capable of making a software choice on the merits of each product. Beckmesser currently does not have a formal written code of ethics.

Required

1 Do you think Stolzing faces an ethical problem as regards his forthcoming visit to the Pogner's users' group meeting? Refer to Exhibit 1.4. Explain.

2 Should Beckmesser allow executives to attend users' meetings while negotiating with other vendors about a purchase decision? Explain. If yes, what conditions on attending should apply?

3 Would you recommend Beckmesser develop its own code of ethics to handle situations such as this one? What are the pros and cons of having such a written code?

1.23 Planning and control decisions: Internet company (30 minutes)

WebNews.co.uk is an Internet company. It offers subscribers multiple online services ranging from an annotated TV guide to local-area information on restaurants and cinemas. It has two main revenue sources:

- Monthly fees from subscribers. Recent data are:

Month/Year	Actual number of subscribers	Actual monthly fee per subscriber
June 2013	28 642	£14.95
December 2013	54 813	£19.95
June 2014	58 178	£19.95
December 2014	86 437	£19.95
June 2015	146 581	£19.95

- Banner advertising fees from companies advertising on WebNews.co.uk page sites. Recent data are:

Month/Year	Advertising revenues
June 2013	£400 988
December 2013	£833 158
June 2014	£861 034
December 2014	£1 478 072
June 2015	£2 916 962

The following decisions were made in the June to October 2015 period:

a June 2015. Decision to raise the monthly subscription fee from £19.95 per month in June 2015 to £24.95 per month in July 2015. The £19.95 fee first applied in December 2013.

b June 2015. Decision to inform existing subscribers that the July 2015 subscription fee would be £24.95.

c July 2015. Decision to upgrade the content of its online services and to offer better Internet mail services.

d October 2015. Demotion of manager of marketing after significant slowing of subscriber growth in accounts and revenues. Results include:

Month/Year	Actual number of subscribers	Actual monthly fee per subscriber
July 2015	128 933	£24.95
August 2015	139 419	£24.95
September 2015	143 131	£24.95

Budgeted amounts (set in June 2015) for the number of subscribers were 140 000 for July 2015, 150 000 for August 2015, and 160 000 for September 2015.

e October 2015. Decision to reduce the monthly subscription fee from £24.95 per month in September 2015 to £21.95 in October 2015.

Required

1 Distinguish between planning decisions and control decisions at WebNews.co.uk.

2 Classify each of the decisions a–e as a planning or a control decision.

1.24 **Problem solving, scorekeeping and attention directing: Internet company** (continuation of Exercise 1.23) (30 minutes)

Management accountants at WebNews.co.uk can play three key roles in each of the five decisions described in Exercise 1.23: problem solving, scorekeeping and attention directing.

Required

1 Distinguish between the problem-solving, scorekeeping and attention-directing roles of a management accountant at WebNews.co.uk.

2 For each of the five decisions outlined in Exercise 1.23, describe a problem-solving, scorekeeping or attention-directing role. Where possible, provide your own example of an information item that a management accountant could provide for each decision.

CHAPTER 2

An introduction to cost terms and purposes

This chapter explains several widely recognised cost concepts and terms. They will help us demonstrate the multiple purposes of cost accounting systems, which we will stress throughout the book.

Various cost concepts and terms are useful in many contexts, including decision making in all areas of the value chain. They help managers decide such issues as: How much should we spend on research and development? What is the effect of product design changes on manufacturing costs? Should we replace some production assembly workers with a robot? Should we spend more of the marketing budget on sales promotion coupons and less on advertising? Should we outsource some engineering and production activities? Should we provide a freephone number for customer enquiries regarding our products? Such questions require an understanding of costs.

Understanding costs is useful for determining ways of containing costs. Many accountants and financial managers within companies expand efforts to achieve this.

A recent survey of 301 senior executives from a range of industries and from around the world indicated the importance of understanding costs before considering which to cut. The executives reported that significant cuts had to be made after the onset of the global economic downturn from September 2008. The main object of cost reduction was to swiftly lower variable costs in response to lower demand. More than half the executives took a highly targeted approach focusing on a particular geography or function. The reason for knowing costs was to cut them! In the longer run, cost cutting focused on fixed-cost structures, such as those involved in designing and delivering products or services. Cost consciousness underlies cost-containment strategies (see Dolan et al. 2010). Generally, when times are good, companies focus on selling as much as they can. Costs gain less attention. When times are difficult, companies shift their emphasis from selling to cutting costs.

An understanding of how costs behave is highly relevant to most business decisions. Consider BMW's decision to lower annual costs by 'several hundred million euros a year' (Taylor 2014). The company's decision was made to offset higher expenses to meet emission standards and to develop new electric and hybrid cars in Australia in 2017. The company cited high labour costs and the need to reduce expenses by A$3800 per vehicle (Shankar 2014).

Learning objectives

After studying this chapter, you should be able to:

- Define and illustrate a cost object
- Distinguish between direct costs and indirect costs
- Explain cost drivers, variable costs and fixed costs
- Understand why unit costs must be interpreted with caution
- Distinguish between service-sector, merchandising-sector and manufacturing-sector companies
- Differentiate between capitalised costs and revenue costs
- Describe the three categories of stock commonly found in many manufacturing-sector companies
- Explain how different ways of computing product costs are appropriate for different purposes

Costs in general

Cost objects

Accountants usually define **cost** as a resource sacrificed or forgone to achieve a specific objective. Most people consider costs as monetary amounts (such as shillings, euros, pounds or yen) that must be paid to acquire goods and services. For now, we can think of costs in this conventional way.

To guide their decisions, managers often want to know how much a certain thing (such as a new product, a machine, a service or a process) costs. We call this 'thing' a **cost object**, which is anything for which a separate measurement of costs is desired. Exhibit 2.1 provides examples of several different types of cost object.

Exhibit 2.1	Examples of cost objects
Cost object	**Illustration**
● Product	An eighteen-speed bicycle
● Service	An airline flight from Paris to Dubai
● Project	An aeroplane assembled by Airbus for BA
● Customer	All products purchased by Rolls-Royce (the customer) from Lucas
● Brand category	All soft drinks sold by a PepsiCo bottling company with 'Pepsi' in their name
● Activity	A test to determine the quality level of a television set
● Department	A department within a government environmental agency that studies air emissions standards
● Programme	An entrepreneurship showcase programme of a university

Cost accumulation and cost assignment

A costing system typically accounts for costs in two basic stages:

1 It *accumulates* costs by some 'natural' (often self-descriptive) classification such as materials, labour, fuel, advertising or shipping.

2 It *assigns* these costs to cost objects.

Cost accumulation is the collection of cost data in some organised way through an accounting system. **Cost assignment** is a general term that encompasses both (1) tracing accumulated costs to a cost object, and (2) allocating accumulated costs to a cost object. Costs that are *traced* to a cost object are direct costs, and costs that are *allocated* to a cost object are indirect costs. Many accounting systems accumulate **actual costs**, which are the costs incurred (historical costs), as distinguished from budgeted or forecasted costs.

In some organisations, stage 1 (cost accumulation) and stage 2 (cost assignment) occur simultaneously. Consider the purchase by Airbus of 100 business-class seats to be installed in an A330-200 aeroplane to be sold to BA. This transaction could be coded to a general ledger account such as materials (the cost accumulation stage) and simultaneously coded to three separate cost objects (the cost assignment stage):

● a department (assembly)

● a product (A330-200 product line)

● a customer (BA).

Alternatively, stage 1 (cost accumulation) could occur first, followed by stage 2 (cost assignment). For example, the 100-seat purchase by Airbus could first be coded to the materials account, then subsequently assigned to a department, then reassigned to a product, and finally reassigned to a customer. Advances in information-gathering technology (such as barcoding) are facilitating the simultaneous assignment of costs to more than one cost object at the time costs are incurred.

Remember, managers assign costs to designated cost objects to help decision making. For example, costs may be assigned to a department to facilitate decisions about departmental efficiency. Costs may also be assigned to a product or a customer to facilitate product or customer profitability analysis.

Direct costs and indirect costs

Cost tracing and cost allocation

A major question concerning costs is whether they have a direct or an indirect relationship to a particular cost object.

- **Direct costs of a cost object** are costs that are related to the particular cost object and that can be traced to it in an economically feasible (cost-effective) way.
- **Indirect costs of a cost object** are costs that are related to the particular cost object but cannot be traced to it in an economically feasible (cost-effective) way. Indirect costs are allocated to the cost object using a cost-allocation method.

Take a tennis racket as a cost object. The cost of the carbon fibre used to make that racket is a direct cost. Why? Because the amount of material used in making the racket can easily be traced to the racket. The cost of lighting in the factory where the racket was made is an indirect cost of the racket. Why? Because although lighting helped in the making of the racket (the workers needed to see), it is not cost effective to try to determine exactly how much lighting cost was used for a specific racket.

Managers prefer to make decisions on the basis of direct costs rather than indirect costs. Why? Because they know that direct costs are more accurate than indirect costs. The relationship between these terms is summarised in Exhibit 2.2.

Cost tracing is the assigning of direct costs to the chosen cost object. **Cost allocation** is the assigning of indirect costs to the chosen cost object. *Cost assignment* encompasses both cost tracing and cost allocation.

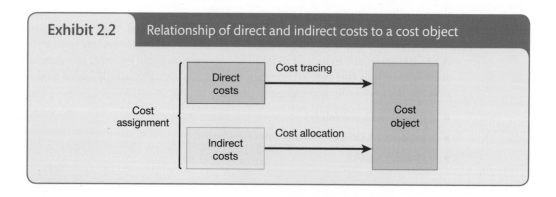

Exhibit 2.2   Relationship of direct and indirect costs to a cost object

Factors affecting direct/indirect cost classifications

Several factors will affect the classification of a cost as direct or indirect:

1 *The materiality of the cost in question.* The higher the cost in question, the more likely the economic feasibility of tracing that cost to a particular cost object. Consider a mail-order catalogue company. It would probably be economically feasible to trace the courier charges for delivering a package directly to each customer. In contrast, the cost of the invoice paper included in the package sent to the customer is likely to be classified as an indirect cost because it is not economically feasible to trace the cost of this paper to each customer. The benefits of knowing the exact number of (say) £0.05 worth of paper included in each package typically do not justify the costs of money and time in tracing the costs to each package.

2 *Available information-gathering technology.* Improvements in this area are enabling an increasing percentage of costs to be classified as direct. Barcodes, for example, allow many manufacturing plants to treat certain materials previously classified as indirect costs as direct costs of products. Barcodes can be read into a manufacturing cost file by waving a 'wand' in the same quick and efficient way that supermarkets now enter the cost of many items purchased by their customers.

3 *Design of operations.* Facility design can impact on cost classification. For example, classifying a cost as direct is helped if an organisation's facility (or part thereof) is used exclusively for a specific product or specific cost object, such as a particular customer.

This book examines different ways to assign costs to cost objects. For now, be aware that one particular cost may be both direct and indirect. How? *The direct/indirect classification depends on the choice of the cost object.* For example, the salary of an assembly-department supervisor may be a direct cost of the assembly department at Fiat but an indirect cost of a product such as the Fiat 500 Pop.

Cost drivers and cost management

The continuous cost reduction efforts of competitors create a never-ending need for organisations to reduce its own costs. Cost reduction efforts frequently identify two key areas:

1 Focusing on **value-added activities**, that is, those activities that customers perceive as adding value to the products or services they purchase.

2 Efficiently managing the use of the cost drivers in those value-added activities.

A **cost driver** (also called a *cost generator* or *cost determinant*) is any factor that affects total costs. That is, a change in the level of the cost driver will cause a change in the level of the total cost of a related cost object. Costs that do not vary in the short run and have no identifiable cost driver in the short run may in fact have a cost driver in the long run.

Exhibit 2.3 presents examples of cost drivers in each of the business functions of the value chain. Some cost drivers are financial measures found in accounting systems (such as direct manufacturing labour costs and sales), while others are non-financial variables (such as the number of parts per product and the number of service calls). We now discuss the role of cost drivers in describing cost behaviour.

Cost management is the set of actions that managers take to satisfy customers while continuously reducing and controlling costs. A caveat on the role of cost drivers in cost management is appropriate. Changes in a particular cost driver do not automatically lead to changes in overall costs. Consider the number of items distributed as a driver of distribution labour costs. Suppose that management reduces the number of items distributed by 25%. This reduction does not

Exhibit 2.3	Examples of cost drivers of business functions in the value chain

Business function	Cost driver
• Research and development	• Number of research projects • Labour hours on a project • Technical complexity of projects
• Design of products, services and processes	• Number of products in design • Number of parts per product • Number of engineering hours
• Production	• Number of units produced • Direct manufacturing labour costs • Number of set-ups • Number of engineering change orders
• Marketing	• Number of advertisements run • Number of sales personnel • Sales
• Distribution	• Number of items distributed • Number of customers • Weight of items distributed
• Customer service	• Number of service calls • Number of products serviced • Hours spent servicing products

automatically translate to a reduction in distribution labour costs. Managers must take steps to reduce distribution labour costs, perhaps by shifting workers out of distribution into other business functions needing additional labour or by laying off some distribution employees.

Two types of cost behaviour pattern: variable costs and fixed costs

Management accounting systems record the cost of resources acquired and track their subsequent use. Tracing these costs allows managers to understand how these costs behave. Let us now consider two basic types of cost behaviour pattern found in many of these systems: variable costs and fixed costs. A **variable cost** is a cost that changes in total in proportion to changes in the related level of total activity or volume. A **fixed cost** is a cost that does not change in total despite changes in the related level of total activity or volume. Costs are defined as variable or fixed with respect to a specific cost object and for a given time period. Consider costs at the Bursa-based plant of the Oyak–Renault alliance in Turkey. The company produces to a capacity of 300 000 vehicles with sales exceeding €3.3 billion in 2013. The Renault Symbol III went on sale in the Turkish, Algerian and Tunisian market in 2013.

- *Variable costs.* If Oyak–Renault buys a steering wheel at €600 for each of its Symbol cars, then the total cost of steering wheels should be €600 times the number of cars assembled. This is an example of a variable cost, a cost that changes in total in proportion to changes in the cost driver (number of cars). The variable cost per car does change with the number of cars assembled. Exhibit 2.4 (Panel A) illustrates this variable cost. A second example of a variable

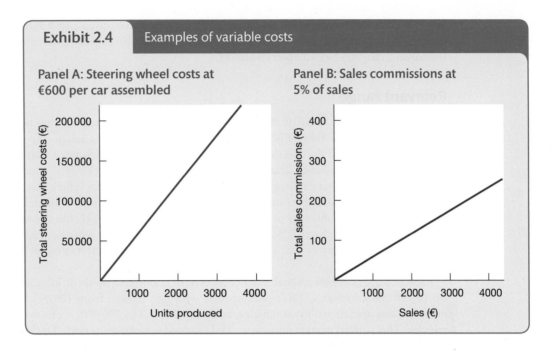

Exhibit 2.4   Examples of variable costs

Panel A: Steering wheel costs at €600 per car assembled

Panel B: Sales commissions at 5% of sales

cost is a sales commission of 5% of each sales euro. Exhibit 2.4 (Panel B) shows this variable-cost example.

- *Fixed costs.* Oyak–Renault may incur €20 million in a given year for the leasing and insurance of its Symbol plant. Both are examples of fixed costs: costs that are unchanged in total over a designated range of the cost driver during a given time span. Fixed costs become progressively smaller on a per-unit basis as the cost driver increases. For example, if Oyak–Renault assembles 10 000 Symbol vehicles at this plant in a year, the fixed cost for leasing and insurance per vehicle is €2000 (€20 million ÷ 10 000). In contrast, if 50 000 vehicles are assembled, the fixed cost per vehicle becomes €400.

Do not assume that individual cost items are inherently variable or fixed. Consider labour costs. An example of purely variable labour costs is the case where workers are paid on a piece-work basis. Some textile workers are paid on a per-shirt-sewn basis. Often, labour costs are appropriately classified as fixed where employment conditions restrict an organisation's flexibility to assign workers to any area that has extra labour requirements.

Major assumptions

The definitions of variable costs and fixed costs have important underlying assumptions:

1 Costs are defined as variable or fixed with respect to a specific cost object.

2 The time span must be specified. Consider the €20 million rent and insurance that Oyak–Renault pays for its Symbol plant. This amount may be fixed for one year. Beyond that time, the rent and insurance may be renegotiated to be, say, €22 million for a subsequent year.

3 Total costs are linear. That is, when plotted on ordinary graph paper, a total-variable-cost or a total-fixed-cost relationship to the cost driver will appear as an unbroken straight line.

4 There is only one cost driver. The influences of other possible cost drivers on total costs are held constant or deemed to be insignificant.

5 Variations in the level of the cost driver are within a relevant range (which we discuss in the next section).

Variable costs and fixed costs are the two most frequently recognised cost behaviour patterns in existing management accounting systems. Additional cost behaviour patterns are discussed in subsequent chapters (see Chapters 9 and 11).

Relevant range

A **relevant range** is the range of the cost driver in which a specific relationship between cost and the level of activity or volume is valid. A fixed cost is fixed only in relation to a given relevant range (usually wide) of the cost driver and a given time span (usually a particular budget period). Consider the Swedish-based Trans-Europe Transport Company (TETC), which operates two refrigerated vehicles that carry agricultural produce to market. Each vehicle has an annual fixed cost of €400 000 (including an annual insurance cost of €150 000 and an annual registration fee of €80 000) and a variable cost of €12 per kilometre of hauling. TETC has chosen kilometres of hauling to be the cost driver. The maximum annual usage of each vehicle is 120 000 kilometres. Suppose that in the current year (2016) the predicted combined total hauling of the two vehicles is 170 000 kilometres.

Exhibit 2.5 shows how annual fixed costs behave at different levels of kilometres of hauling. Up to 120 000 kilometres, TETC can operate with one vehicle; from 120 001 to 240 000 kilometres, it can operate with two vehicles; and from 240 001 to 360 000, it can operate with three vehicles. This pattern would continue as TETC added vehicles to its fleet. The bracketed section from 120 001 to 240 000 is the range at which TETC expects the €80 000 fixed costs to be valid given the predicted 170 000-kilometre usage for the year.

Fixed costs may change from one year to the next. For example, if the annual registration fee for refrigerated vehicles is increased in 2017, the total level of fixed costs will increase (unless offset by a reduction in other fixed items).

Relationships of types of costs

We have introduced two major classifications of costs: direct/indirect and variable/fixed. Costs may simultaneously be:

- direct and variable
- direct and fixed
- indirect and variable
- indirect and fixed.

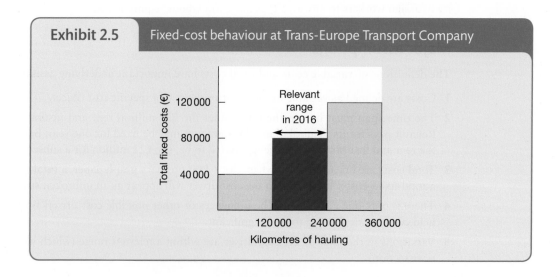

| **Exhibit 2.5** | Fixed-cost behaviour at Trans-Europe Transport Company |

Exhibit 2.6	Examples of simultaneous direct/indirect and variable/fixed-cost classifications

		Assignment of costs to cost object	
		Direct cost	**Indirect cost**
Cost behaviour pattern	**Variable cost**	*Cost object*: Assembled car *Example*: Tyres used in assembly of car	*Cost object*: Assembled car *Example*: Power costs where power usage is metered only to the plant
	Fixed cost	*Cost object*: Assembled car *Example*: Salary of supervisor on Renault Symbol assembly	*Cost object*: Assembled car *Example*: Annual lease cost at Symbol plant line

Exhibit 2.6 presents examples of simultaneous cost classifications with each of the four cost types.

Total costs and unit costs

Meaning of unit costs

Accounting systems typically report both total-cost and unit-cost numbers. A **unit cost** (also called an **average cost**) is calculated by dividing some amount of total cost by the related number of units. The units might be expressed in various ways. Examples are hours worked, packages delivered or cars assembled. Suppose that €980 000 of manufacturing costs were incurred to produce 10 000 units of a finished good. Then the unit cost would be €98:

$$\frac{\text{Total manufacturing costs}}{\text{Number of units manufactured}} = \frac{€980\ 000}{10\ 000} = €98 \text{ per unit}$$

If 8000 units are sold and 2000 units remain in ending stock, the unit-cost concept helps in the assignment of total costs for the income statement and balance sheet:

Cost of goods sold in the income statement, 8000 units × €98	€784 000
Closing stock of finished goods in the balance sheet, 2000 units × €98	196 000
Total manufacturing costs of 10 000 units	€980 000

Unit costs are found in all areas of the value chain – for example, there are unit costs for product design, sales calls and customer-service calls.

Use unit costs cautiously

Unit costs are averages. As we shall see, they must be interpreted with caution. For decision making, it is best to think in terms of total costs rather than unit costs. Nevertheless, unit-cost numbers are frequently used in many situations. For example, assume that the president of the Jazz Society at the University of Antwerp is deciding whether to hire a music group for a forthcoming party. The group charges a fixed fee of €1000. The president may intuitively calculate a unit cost for the group when thinking about an admission price. Given the fixed fee of €1000, the unit cost is €10 if 100 people attend, €2 if 500 attend, and €1 if 1000 attend. Note, however, that with a fixed fee of €1000 the *total cost* is unaffected by the attendance level, while the *unit cost* is a function of the attendance level. In this example, each attendee is considered to be one unit.

Concepts in action   How Zipcar helps reduce Twitter's transport costs

Soaring gas prices, high insurance costs and hefty parking fees have forced many businesses to re-examine whether owning corporate cars is economical. In some cities, Zipcar has emerged as an attractive alternative. Zipcar provides an 'on demand' option for urban individuals and businesses to rent a car by the week, the day or even the hour. Zipcar members make a reservation by phone or Internet, go to the car park where the car is located (usually by walking or public transport), use an electronic card or iPhone application that unlocks the car door via a wireless sensor, and then simply climb in and drive away. Rental fees begin around $8 per hour and $75 per day, and include petrol, insurance and some mileage (usually around 180 miles per day).

Currently, business customers account for a growing proportion of Zipcar's revenues. In the UK, the business segment is growing at 20% per year. Let's think about what Zipcar means for companies. Many small businesses own a company car or two for getting to meetings, making deliveries, and running errands. Similarly, many large companies own a fleet of cars to shuttle visiting executives and clients back and forth from appointments, business lunches, and the airport. Traditionally, owning these cars has involved very high fixed costs, including buying the asset (car), costs of the maintenance department and insurance for multiple drivers. Unfortunately, businesses had no other options. Now, however, companies like Twitter can use Zipcar for on-demand mobility while reducing their transport and overhead costs. Based in downtown San Francisco, Twitter managers use Zipcar's fleet of Mini Coopers and Toyota Priuses to meet venture capitalists and partners in Silicon Valley. 'We would get in a Zipcar to drive down to San Jose to pitch investors or go across the city', says Jack Dorsey, the micro-blogging service's co-founder. 'Taxis are hard to find and unreliable here'. Twitter also uses Zipcar when travelling far away from its headquarters, like when visiting advertisers in New York and technology vendors in Boston, forgoing the traditional black sedans and long taxi rides from the airport. From a business perspective, Zipcar allows companies to convert the fixed costs of owning a company car to variable costs. If business slows, or a car isn't required to visit a client, Zipcar customers are not saddled with the fixed costs of car ownership. Of course, if companies use Zipcar too frequently, they can end up paying more overall than they would have paid if they purchased and maintained the car themselves. Along with cutting corporate spending, car-sharing services like Zipcar reduce congestion on the road and promote environmental sustainability.

Users report reducing their vehicle miles travelled by 44%, and surveys show CO_2 emissions are being cut by up to 50% per user. Beyond that, each shared car takes up to 20 cars off the road as members sell their cars or decide not to buy new ones – challenging the whole principle of owning a car. 'The future of transportation will be a blend of things like Zipcar, public transportation, and private car ownership', says Bill Ford, Ford's executive chairman. But the automaker isn't worried. 'Not only do I not fear that, but I think it's a great opportunity for us to participate in the changing nature of car ownership'. Avis Budget acquired Zipcar in 2013 for $1500m based on the group's prediction that people will increasingly want to buy ways of getting around (referred to as mobility solutions) rather than buying cars.

Sources: Keegan, P. (2009) 'Zipcar – the best new idea in business', *Fortune*, 27 August, http://money.cnn.com/2009/08/26/news/companies/zipcar_car_rentals.fortune/; Olsen, E. (2009) 'Car sharing reinvents the company wheels', *New York Times*, 7 May, http://www.nytimes.com/2009/05/07/business/businessspecial/07CAR.html; Zipcar, Inc. (n.d.) 'Zipcar for business case studies', http://www.zipcar.com/business/is-it/case-studies (accessed 8 October 2009); Murray, J. (2013) 'Zipcar looks to move business service into the fast lane', www.businessgreen.com, 24 July.

Costs are often neither inherently fixed nor variable. Much depends on the specific context. Consider the €1000 fixed fee that we assumed was to be paid to the music group. This is just one way the music group could be paid. Possible payment schedules that might be considered include:

- Schedule 1: €1000 fixed fee
- Schedule 2: €1 per person attending + €500 fixed fee
- Schedule 3: €2 per person attending.

Under schedules 2 and 3, the euro amount of the payment to the music group is not known until after the event.

The effects of these three payment schedules on unit costs and total costs for five attendance levels are shown in Exhibit 2.7.

Exhibit 2.7	The effects of the three payment levels on unit costs and total costs for five attendance levels					
	Schedule 1: €1000 fixed		Schedule 2: €1 per person + €500 fixed		Schedule 3: €2 per person	
Number of persons attending	Total cost	Unit cost	Total cost	Unit cost	Total cost	Unit cost
50	€1000	€20	€550	€11	€100	€2
100	1000	10	600	6	200	2
250	1000	4	750	3	500	2
500	1000	2	1000	2	1000	2
1000	1000	1	1500	1.5	2000	2

The unit cost under schedule 1 is calculated by dividing the fixed cost of €1000 by the attendance level. For schedule 2, the unit cost is calculated by first determining the total cost for each attendance level and then dividing that amount by that attendance level. Thus, for 250 people, schedule 2 has a total cost of €750 (€500 + 250 × €1), which gives a unit cost of €3 per person. Schedule 3 has a unit cost of €2 per person for any attendance level because the music group is to be paid €2 per person with no fixed payment.

All three payment schedules would yield the same unit cost of €2 per person only if 500 people attend. The unit cost is not €2 per person under schedule 1 or schedule 2 for any attendance level except 500 people. Thus, it would be incorrect to use the €2 per person amount in schedule 1 or 2 to predict what the total costs would be for 1000 people. Consider what occurs if 250 people attend and the group is paid a fixed fee of €1000. The unit cost is then €4 per person. *While unit costs are often useful, they must be interpreted with extreme caution if they include fixed costs per unit.* When estimating total cost, think of variable costs as an amount per unit and fixed costs as a lump-sum total amount.

The key relationships between total costs and unit costs are summarised in Panel A of Exhibit 2.8. Panel B illustrates these relationships for schedule 3 where the university social club pays the music group on a variable basis (cost of €2 per person). Panel C illustrates schedule 1 where the music group is paid a fixed amount (cost of €1000).

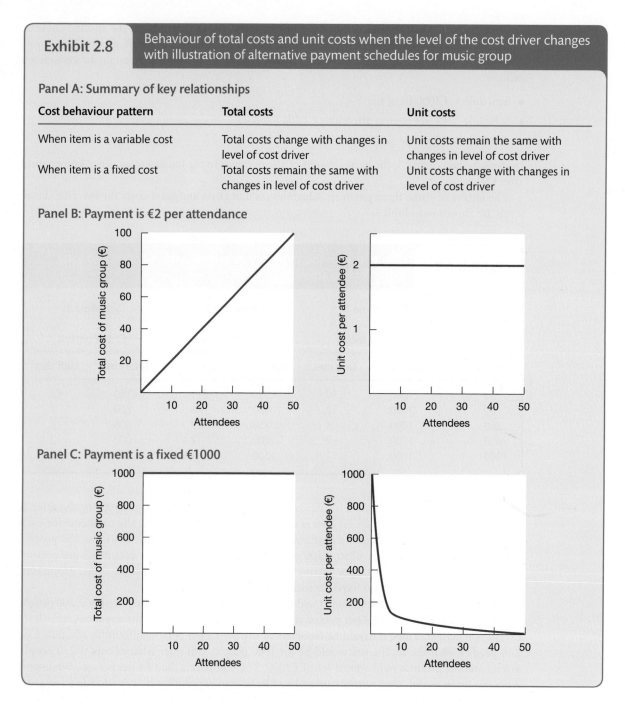

| Exhibit 2.8 | Behaviour of total costs and unit costs when the level of the cost driver changes with illustration of alternative payment schedules for music group |

Panel A: Summary of key relationships

Cost behaviour pattern	Total costs	Unit costs
When item is a variable cost	Total costs change with changes in level of cost driver	Unit costs remain the same with changes in level of cost driver
When item is a fixed cost	Total costs remain the same with changes in level of cost driver	Unit costs change with changes in level of cost driver

Panel B: Payment is €2 per attendance

Panel C: Payment is a fixed €1000

Financial statements and cost terminology

We now consider costs included in the income statements or balance sheets of service-, merchandising- and manufacturing-sector companies. One key distinction of costs is their classification as capitalised or expensed when they are incurred:

● **Capitalised costs** are first recorded as an asset (capital) when they are incurred. These costs are presumed to provide future benefits to the company. Examples are costs to acquire computer equipment and motor vehicles. These costs are written off to those periods assumed to benefit from their incurrence. For example, the cost of acquiring motor vehicles is written off as a depreciation expense that occurs each year of the expected useful life of the vehicle.

- **Revenue costs** are recorded as expenses of the accounting period when they are incurred. Examples are salaries paid to marketing personnel and monthly rent paid for administrative offices.

These two categories of costs apply to companies in all three sectors of the economy.

Service-sector companies

Service-sector companies provide services or intangible products to their customers – for example, legal advice or an audit. These companies do not have any stock of tangible product at the end of an accounting period. Examples include law firms, accounting firms, advertising agencies and television stations. Labour costs are typically the most significant cost category, often being as high as 70% of total costs.

Exhibit 2.9 presents an income statement for Ahamed & Partners, a law firm specialising in libel lawsuits. The customers (clients) of this law firm receive legal advice and representation on their behalf in court and in negotiations. Salaries and wages constitute 67.3% of total operating costs (€970 000 ÷ €1 442 000).

The operating-cost line items for service companies will include costs from all areas of the value chain (production of services, marketing, and so on). There is not a line item for cost of goods sold in the income statement of Ahamed & Partners. Why? Because the business sells only services or intangible products to its customers.

Exhibit 2.9	Service-sector income statement

Ahamed & Partners income statement for the year ended 31 December 2015

Revenues		€1 600 000
Costs		
Salaries and wages	€970 000	
Rent	180 000	
Depreciation	105 000	
Other costs	187 000	1 442 000
Operating profit		€158 000

Merchandising- and manufacturing-sector companies

Merchandising-sector companies provide tangible products they have previously purchased in the same basic form from suppliers. Merchandise purchased from suppliers but not sold at the end of an accounting period is held as stock. The merchandising sector includes companies engaged in retailing (such as book stores or department stores), distributing or wholesaling. **Manufacturing-sector companies** provide tangible products that have been converted to a different form from that of the products purchased from suppliers. At the end of an accounting period, a manufacturer has stock that can include direct materials, work in progress or finished goods. Examples are computer, food processing and textile companies.

Merchandising and manufacturing companies differ from service companies in their holding of stocks. **Stock-related costs** (also called **inventoriable costs**) are those costs associated with the purchase of goods for resale (in the case of merchandise stock) or costs associated with the acquisition and conversion of materials and all other manufacturing inputs into goods for sale (in the case of manufacturing stocks). Inventoriable costs become part of cost of goods sold in the period in which the stock item is sold. **Operating costs** are all costs associated with generating revenues, other than cost of goods sold. (The term *operating costs* is sometimes used to include cost of goods sold. In this book, we do not include costs of books sold in operating costs.) We now consider the financial statements for Cellular Products, a manufacturer of telephone systems for large enterprises.

Manufacturing-sector example

The manufacturing sector differs from the merchandising sector in that the products sold to customers are converted to a different form from that of the products purchased from suppliers. This distinction results in the manufacturers having one or more of the following types of stock:

1 **Direct materials stock.** Direct materials in stock and awaiting use in the manufacturing process.

2 **Work-in-progress stock.** Goods partially worked on but not yet fully completed. Also called **work in process.**

3 **Finished goods stock.** Goods fully completed but not yet sold.

In this chapter we assume that all manufacturing costs are inventoriable. The term *absorption costing* is used to describe the method in which all manufacturing costs are inventoriable. Chapter 6 further discusses this method and *variable costing*, in which only variable manufacturing costs are inventoriable. Fixed manufacturing costs under variable costing are treated as *period costs*, that is, they are treated as expenses in the period in which they are incurred rather than being inventoried.

The language of management accounting has specific terms for manufacturing costs. Three terms in widespread use are direct material costs, direct manufacturing labour costs and indirect manufacturing costs.

1 **Direct material costs** are the acquisition costs of all materials that eventually become part of the cost object (say, units finished or in process), and that can be traced to the cost object in an economically feasible way. Acquisition costs of direct materials include goods-in (inward delivery) charges, sales taxes and customs duties.

2 **Direct manufacturing labour costs** include the compensation of all manufacturing labour that is specifically identified with the cost object (say, units finished or in process), and that can be traced to the cost object in an economically feasible way. Examples include wages and fringe benefits paid to machine operators and assembly-line workers.

3 **Indirect manufacturing costs** are all manufacturing costs considered to be part of the cost object (say, units finished or in process), but that cannot be individually traced to that cost object in an economically feasible way. Examples include power, supplies, indirect materials, indirect manufacturing labour, plant rent, plant insurance, property taxes on plants, plant depreciation and the salaries of plant managers. Other terms for this cost category include **manufacturing overhead costs** and **factory overhead costs.** We use *indirect manufacturing costs* and *manufacturing overhead costs* interchangeably in this book.

Two terms used in manufacturing-cost systems are prime costs and conversion costs. **Prime costs** are all direct manufacturing costs. As information-gathering technology improves, companies may add other direct-cost categories. For example, power costs might be metered in specific areas of a plant that are dedicated to the assembly of separate products. In this case, prime costs would include direct materials, direct manufacturing labour and direct metered power. Computer software companies often have a 'purchased technology' direct manufacturing-cost item. This item, which covers payments to third parties who develop software programs included in a product, would also be included in prime costs. **Conversion costs** are all manufacturing costs other than direct materials costs. These costs are for transforming direct materials into finished goods.

The income statement of a manufacturer, Cellular Products, is shown in Exhibit 2.10 (Panel A). Cost of goods sold in a manufacturing company is calculated as follows:

$$\begin{array}{c}\text{Opening finished} \\ \text{goods stock}\end{array} + \begin{array}{c}\text{Cost of goods} \\ \text{manufactured}\end{array} - \begin{array}{c}\text{Closing finished} \\ \text{goods stock}\end{array} = \text{Cost of goods sold}$$

Exhibit 2.10	Income statement and schedule of cost of goods manufactured or manufacturing-sector company

Panel A: Cellular Products income statement for the year ended 31 December 2015 (€000)

Revenues		€210 000
Cost of goods sold		
Opening finished goods, 1 January 2015	€22 000	
Cost of goods manufactured (see Panel B)	104 000	
Cost of goods available for sale	126 000	
Closing finished goods, 31 December 2015	18 000	108 000
Gross margin (or gross profit)		102 000
Operating costs		70 000
Operating profit		€32 000

Panel B: Cellular Products schedule of cost of goods manufactured* for the year ended 31 December 2015 (€000)

Direct materials		
Opening stock, 1 January 2015	€11 000	
Purchases of direct materials	73 000	
Cost of direct materials available for use	84 000	
Closing stock, 31 December 2015	8 000	
Direct materials used		€76 000
Direct manufacturing labour		17 750
Indirect manufacturing costs		
Indirect manufacturing labour	4 000	
Supplies	1 000	
Heat, light and power	1 750	
Depreciation – plant building	1 500	
Depreciation – plant equipment	2 500	
Miscellaneous	500	11 250
Manufacturing costs incurred during 2015		105 000
Add opening work-in-progress stock, 1 January 2015		6 000
Total manufacturing costs to account for		111 000
Deduct closing work-in-progress stock, 31 December 2015		7 000
Cost of goods manufactured (to income statement)		€104 000

* Note that the term *cost of goods manufactured* refers to the cost of goods brought to completion (finished) during the year, whether they were started before or during the current year. Some of the manufacturing costs incurred during the year are held back as costs of the closing work-in-progress stock; similarly, the costs of the opening work-in-progress stock become part of the cost of goods manufactured for the year. Note too that this schedule can become a schedule of cost of goods manufactured and sold simply by including the opening and closing finished goods stock figures in the supporting schedule rather than directly in the body of the income statement as in Panel A.

For Cellular Products in 2015, the corresponding amounts (in thousands, Panel A) are

$$€22\ 000 + €104\ 000 - €18\ 000 = €108\ 000$$

Cost of goods manufactured refers to the cost of goods brought to completion, whether they were started before or during the current accounting period. In 2015, these costs amount to €104 000 for Cellular Products (see the schedule of cost of goods manufactured in Panel B of Exhibit 2.10). The manufacturing costs incurred during 2015 (€105 000) is a line item in Panel B. This item refers to the 'new' direct manufacturing costs and the 'new' manufacturing overhead costs that were incurred during 2015 for all goods worked on during 2015, regardless of whether all those goods were fully completed during this year.

The manufacturing costs of the finished goods include direct materials, other direct manufacturing costs, and indirect manufacturing costs. All these are inventoriable costs; they are assigned to work-in-progress stock or finished goods stock until the goods are sold. Inventoriable costs include the costs of assets that facilitate the manufacturing process and (typically) become part of indirect manufacturing costs. For example, the costs of the blast furnace of a steel company are first capitalised at the time of construction. These costs subsequently become part of steel stock costs as depreciation on the blast furnace is included in indirect manufacturing costs over the useful life of the blast furnace.

Newcomers to management accounting frequently assume that indirect costs such as rent, telephone and depreciation are always costs of the period in which they are incurred and are unconnected with stocks. However, if these costs are related to manufacturing *per se*, they are indirect manufacturing costs and are inventoriable. Operating-cost items in the income statement in Panel A of Exhibit 2.10 include: (1) the expensing of capitalised costs (such as depreciation on a fleet of delivery vehicles or depreciation on computers purchased for marketing personnel), and (2) the cost of items recorded as an expense as incurred (such as the salaries of customer-service representatives).

Differences exist across companies in the way accounting terms are defined. Consider a direct labourer, such as a lathe operator or an assembly-line worker, who earns gross wages calculated on the basis of a regular wage rate of €20 per hour. This person receives fringe benefits (employer contributions to the employee's National Insurance, life insurance, and so on) totalling, say, €8 per hour. Some companies classify the €20 as direct manufacturing labour cost and the €8 as manufacturing overhead cost. Other companies classify the entire €28 as direct manufacturing labour cost. The latter approach is conceptually preferable because these payroll fringe benefit costs are a fundamental part of acquiring manufacturing labour services. The magnitude of fringe benefits makes this issue important. Countries where fringe benefit costs are over 30% of wage rates include Italy (105%), France (90%), Germany (86%), the UK (43%) and the USA (38%).

The many meanings of product costs

An important theme of this book is 'different costs for different purposes'. This theme can be illustrated with respect to product costing. A **product cost** is the sum of the costs assigned to a product for a specific purpose. Exhibit 2.11 illustrates three different purposes:

1 *Product pricing and product emphasis.* For this purpose, the costs of all those areas of the value chain required to bring a product to a customer should be included.

2 *Contracting with government agencies.* Government agencies frequently provide detailed guidelines on the allowable and non-allowable items in a product-cost amount. For example, some government agencies explicitly exclude marketing costs from reimbursement to contractors and may reimburse only a part of R&D costs. Hence, the bracket in Exhibit 2.11 shows that a specific contract may provide for recovering all design and production costs and part of R&D costs.

3 *Financial statements.* The focus here is on inventoriable costs. In most countries, generally accepted accounting principles in manufacturing companies allow only manufacturing costs to be assigned to products reported in the financial statements.

Exhibit 2.11 illustrates how a product-cost amount may include only inventoriable costs in the financial statements, a broader set of costs for reimbursement under a government contract, and a still broader set of costs for pricing and product emphasis.

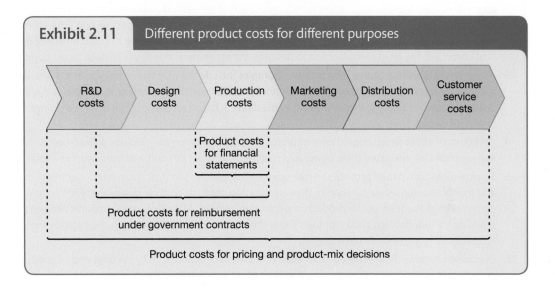

Exhibit 2.11   Different product costs for different purposes

Classification of costs

This chapter has provided many examples of cost classifications that have various purposes. Classifications can be made on the basis of:

1 Business function

    a Research and development
    b Design of products, services and processes
    c Production
    d Marketing
    e Distribution
    f Customer service

2 Assignment to a cost object

    a Direct costs
    b Indirect costs

3 Behaviour pattern in relation to changes in the level of a cost driver

    a Variable costs
    b Fixed costs

4 Aggregate or average

    a Total costs
    b Unit costs

5 Assets or expenses

    a Inventoriable (product) costs
    b Period costs.

Summary

The following points are linked to the chapter's learning objectives.

1 A cost object is anything for which a separate measurement of costs is desired. Examples include a product, service, project, customer, brand category, activity, department and program.

2 A direct cost of a cost object is any cost that is related to the cost object and can be traced to that cost object in an economically feasible way. Indirect costs are costs that are related to the cost object but cannot be traced to that cost object in an economically feasible way. A cost may be direct regarding one cost object and indirect regarding other cost objects. This book uses the term *cost tracing* to describe the assignment of direct costs to a cost object and the term *cost allocation* to describe the assignment of indirect costs to a cost object.

3 A cost driver is any factor that affects costs. Examples include the number of set-ups and direct-labour hours in manufacturing and the number of sales personnel and sales euros in marketing. A variable cost is a cost that does change in total in proportion to changes in a cost driver. A fixed cost is a cost that does not change in total despite changes in a cost driver.

4 Unit costs of a cost object should be interpreted with caution when they include a fixed-cost component. When making total cost estimates, think of variable costs as an amount per unit and fixed costs as a total amount.

5 Service-sector companies provide services or intangible products to their customers. In contrast, merchandising- and manufacturing-sector companies provide tangible products to their customers. Merchandising companies do not change the form of the products they acquire and sell. Manufacturing companies convert materials and other inputs into finished goods for sale. These differences are reflected in both the balance sheets and income statements of companies in these sectors.

6 Capitalised costs are first recorded as an asset when they are incurred. They become cost of goods sold when the product is sold. Period costs are expensed in the period in which they are incurred.

7 The three categories of stock found in many manufacturing-sector companies depict stages in the conversion process: direct materials, work in progress and finished goods.

8 Managers may assign different costs to the same cost object depending on its purpose. For example, for financial reporting purposes, the (inventoriable) costs of a product include only manufacturing costs. In contrast, costs from all areas of the value chain can be assigned to a product for decisions on pricing and product emphasis.

Key terms

cost (31)
cost object (31)
cost accumulation (31)
cost assignment (31)
actual costs (31)
direct costs of a cost object (32)
indirect costs of a cost object (32)
cost tracing (32)
cost allocation (32)
value-added activities (33)
cost driver (33)
variable cost (34)
fixed cost (34)
relevant range (36)
unit cost (37)
average cost (37)
capitalised costs (40)
revenue costs (41)

service-sector companies (41)
merchandising-sector companies (41)
manufacturing-sector companies (41)
stock-related costs (42)
inventoriable costs (42)
operating costs (42)
direct materials stock (42)
work-in-progress stock (42)
work in process (42)
finished goods stock (42)
direct material costs (42)
direct manufacturing labour costs (42)
indirect manufacturing costs (42)
manufacturing overhead costs (42)
factory overhead costs (42)
prime costs (42)
conversion costs (43)
product cost (44)

References

Dolan, K., Murray, M. and Duffin, K. (2010) 'What worked in cost cutting – and what's next', www.McKinseyQuarterly.com, January.

Shankar, Sneha (2014) 'Toyota announces exit from Australia', *International Business Times*, 29 September, http://www.ibtimes.com/toyota-announces-exit-australia-2017-cutting-2500-jobs-follows-ford-gm-holden-after-65-years-1554290.

Taylor, E. (2014) 'BMW plans multi-million euro annual cost cuts', reuters.com, 18 June.

CHAPTER 2

Assessment material

Review questions

2.1 Define *cost object* and give three examples.

2.2 Which costs are considered direct? Indirect? Give an example of each.

2.3 Describe how a given cost item can be both a direct cost and an indirect cost.

2.4 Give three factors that will affect the classification of a cost as direct or indirect.

2.5 What is a *cost driver*? Give one example for each area in the value chain.

2.6 What is the *relevant range*? What role does the relevant range concept play in explaining how costs behave?

2.7 Explain why *unit costs* must often be interpreted with caution.

2.8 Describe how service-, merchandising- and manufacturing-sector companies differ from each other.

2.9 What are the three major categories of the inventoriable costs of a manufactured product?

2.10 Define the following: direct materials costs, direct manufacturing labour costs, indirect manufacturing costs, prime costs and conversion costs.

Exercises

Basic level

2.11 Total costs and unit costs (10 minutes)

A student association has hired a music group for a graduation party. The cost will be a fixed amount of €40 000.

Required

1 Suppose 500 people attend the party. What will be the total cost of the music group? The unit cost per person?

2 Suppose 2000 people attend. What will be the total cost of the music group? The unit cost per person?

3 For prediction of total costs, should the manager of the party use the unit cost in requirement 1? The unit cost in requirement 2? What is the major lesson of this problem?

*2.12   Total costs and unit costs (15 minutes)

George Mathenge is a well-known motivational speaker. The Europe Speaker's Bureau (ESB) wants Mathenge to be the sole speaker at an all-day seminar. Mathenge's agent offers ESB the choice of three possible fee arrangements:

- Schedule 1:   €8000 fee
- Schedule 2:   €20 per person + €2000 fixed fee
- Schedule 3:   €50 per person.

Each attendee will be charged a €200 fee for the all-day seminar.

Required

1 What is ESB's fixed cost and variable cost for hiring Mathenge under each alternative schedule?

2 For each schedule, calculate the total cost and unit cost per seminar attendee if (a) 50 attend, (b) 200 attend, and (c) 500 attend. Comment on the results.

2.13   Total costs and unit costs (10 minutes)

Weltferien AG markets vacation packages to Tenerife from Dresden. The package includes a round-trip flight on Saxon-Air. Weltferien pays Saxon-Air €60 000 for each round-trip flight. The maximum load on a flight is 300 passengers.

Required

1 What is the unit cost to Weltferien of each passenger on a Saxon-Air round-trip flight if there are (a) 200, (b) 250, or (c) 300 passengers?

2 What role can the unit-cost figures per passenger calculated in requirement 1 play when Weltferien is predicting the total air-flight costs to be paid next month for Saxon-Air carrying 4000 passengers on 15 scheduled round-trip flights?

2.14   Classification of costs, service sector (15–20 minutes)

Presta-Serviços SA is a marketing research firm that organises focus groups for consumer product companies. Each focus group has eight individuals who are paid €9000 per session to provide comments on new products. These focus groups meet in hotels and are led by a trained independent marketing specialist hired by Presta-Serviços. Each specialist is paid a fixed retainer to conduct a minimum number of sessions and a per-session fee of €360 000. A Presta-Serviços staff member attends each session to ensure that all the logistical aspects run smoothly.

Required

Classify each of the following cost items as:

a Direct or indirect (D or I) costs with respect to each individual focus group.

b Variable or fixed (V or F) costs with respect to how the total costs of Presta-Serviços change as the number of focus groups changes. (If in doubt, select the cost type on the basis of whether the total costs will change substantially if a large number of groups are conducted.)

You will have two answers (D or I; V or F) for each of the following items:

Cost item	D or I	V or F
A Payment to individuals in each focus group to provide comments on new products		
B Annual subscription of Presta-Serviços to *Consumer Reports* magazine		
C Phone calls made by Presta-Serviços staff member to confirm individuals will attend a focus group session. (Records of individual calls are not kept)		

Cost item	D or I	V or F

D Retainer paid to focus group leader to conduct 20 focus groups per year on new medical products

E Hotel meals provided to participants in each focus group

F Lease payment by Presta-Serviços for corporate office

G Cost of tapes used to record comments made by individuals in a focus group session. (These tapes are sent to the company whose products are being tested)

H Petrol costs of Presta-Serviços staff for company-owned vehicles. (Staff members submit monthly bills with no mileage breakdowns)

2.15 **Classification of costs, merchandising sector** (15–20 minutes)

Crescendo Srl operates a large store in Milan. The store has both a film (video/DVDs) section and a musical (compact discs and tapes) section. Crescendo reports revenues for the film section separately from the musical section.

Required

Classify each of the following cost items as:

a Direct or indirect (D or I) costs with respect to the film section.

b Variable or fixed (V or F) costs with respect to how the total costs of the film section change as the number of films sold changes. (If in doubt, select the cost type on the basis of whether the total costs will change substantially if a large number of films are sold.)

You will have two answers (D or I; V or F) for each of the following items:

Cost item	D or I	V or F

A Annual retainer paid to a film distributor

B Electricity costs of Crescendo store (single bill covers entire store)

C Costs of films purchased for sale to customers

D Subscription to *Video-Novo* magazine

E Leasing of computer software used for financial budgeting at Crescendo store

F Cost of popcorn provided free to all customers of Crescendo

G Earthquake insurance policy for Crescendo store

H Freight-in costs of films purchased by Crescendo

Intermediate level

2.16 **Cost drivers and the value chain** (15 minutes)

A Toyota analyst is preparing a presentation on cost drivers. Unfortunately, both the list of its business function areas and the accompanying list of representative cost drivers are accidentally randomised. The two lists now on the computer screen are as follows:

Business function area	Representative cost driver
A Design of Products/Processes	**1** Number of cars recalled for defective parts
B Customer Service	**2** Number of machine assembly hours
C Marketing	**3** Number of research scientists
D Research and Development	**4** Hours of computer-aided design (CAD) work
E Distribution	**5** Number of sales personnel
F Production	**6** Weight of cars shipped

Required

1 Match each business function area with its representative cost driver.

2 Give a second example of a cost driver for each of the business function areas of Toyota.

2.17 **Computing cost of goods manufactured and cost of goods sold** (20–25 minutes)

Calculate cost of goods manufactured and cost of goods sold from the following account balances relating to 2015 (in € millions):

Property tax on plant building	0.45
Marketing, distribution and customer-service costs	5.55
Finished goods stock, 1 January 2015	4.05
Plant utilities	2.55
Work-in-progress stock, 31 December 2015	3.90
Depreciation of plant building	1.35
General and administrative costs (non-plant)	6.45
Direct materials used	13.05
Finished goods stock, 31 December 2015	5.10
Depreciation of plant equipment	1.65
Plant repairs and maintenance	2.40
Work-in-progress stock, 1 January 2015	3.00
Direct manufacturing labour	5.10
Indirect manufacturing labour	3.45
Indirect materials used	1.65
Miscellaneous plant overhead	0.60

2.18 **Income statement and schedule of cost of goods manufactured** (25–30 minutes)

Howell Ltd has the following account balances (in millions):

For specific date		For year 2015	
Direct materials, 1 January 2015	£15	Purchases of direct materials	£325
Work in progress, 1 January 2015	10	Direct manufacturing labour	100
Finished goods, 1 January 2015	70	Depreciation – plant building	
Direct materials, 31 December 2015	20	and equipment	80
Work in progress, 31 December 2015	5	Plant supervisory salaries	5
Finished goods, 31 December 2015	55	Miscellaneous plant overhead	35
		Revenues	950
		Marketing, distribution and	
		customer-service costs	240
		Plant supplies used	10
		Plant utilities	30
		Indirect manufacturing labour	60

Required

Prepare an income statement and a supporting schedule of cost of goods manufactured for the year ended 31 December 2015. (For additional questions regarding these facts, see the next problem.)

2.19 **Interpretation of statements** (continuation of Exercise 2.18) (20–25 minutes)

Refer to the preceding problem.

Required

1 How would the answer to the preceding problem be modified if you were asked for a schedule of cost of goods manufactured and sold instead of a schedule of cost of goods manufactured? Be specific.

2 Would the sales manager's salary (included in marketing, distribution and customer-service costs) be accounted for differently if Howell Ltd were a merchandising company instead of a manufacturing company?

3 Plant supervisory salaries are usually regarded as indirect manufacturing costs. Under what conditions might some of these costs be regarded as direct manufacturing costs? Give an example.

4 Suppose that both the direct materials used and the plant depreciation were related to the manufacture of 1 million units of product. What is the unit cost for the direct materials assigned to those units? What is the unit cost for plant building and equipment depreciation? Assume that yearly plant depreciation is calculated on a straight-line basis.

5 Assume that the implied cost behaviour patterns in requirement 4 persist. That is, direct materials costs behave as a variable cost and depreciation behaves as a fixed cost. Repeat the computations in requirement 4, assuming that the costs are being predicted for the manufacture of 1.2 million units of product. How would the total costs be affected?

6 As a management accountant, explain concisely to the CEO why the unit costs differed in requirements 4 and 5.

2.20 **Finding unknown balances** (20–25 minutes)

An auditor for the Inland Revenue is trying to reconstruct some partially destroyed records of two taxpayers. For each of the cases in the accompanying list, find the unknowns designated by letters A to D (figures are assumed to be in £000).

	Case 1	Case 2
Debtors, 31 December 2015	£6 000	£2 100
Cost of goods sold	A	20 000
Creditors, 1 January 2015	3 000	1 700
Creditors, 31 December 2015	1 800	1 500
Finished goods stocks, 31 December 2015	B	5 300
Gross margin	11 300	C
Work in progress, 1 January 2015	0	800
Work in progress, 31 December 2015	0	3 000
Finished goods stocks, 1 January 2015	4 000	4 000
Direct material used	8 000	12 000
Direct manufacturing labour	3 000	5 000
Indirect manufacturing costs	7 000	D
Purchases of direct material	9 000	7 000
Revenues	32 000	31 800
Debtors, 1 January 2015	2 000	1 400

2.21 **Fire loss, computing stock costs** (30–40 minutes)

A distraught employee, Guy Pirault-Manne, put a torch to a manufacturing plant on a blustery day, 26 February 2015. The resulting blaze completely destroyed the plant and its contents. Fortunately, certain accounting records were kept in another building. They revealed the following for the period from 1 January 2015 to 26 February 2015:

Direct materials purchased	€3.2 million
Work in progress, 1 January 2015	€680 000
Direct materials, 1 January 2015	€320 000
Finished goods, 1 January 2015	€600 000
Indirect manufacturing costs	40% of conversion costs
Revenues	€10 million
Direct manufacturing labour	€3.6 million
Prime costs	€5.88 million
Gross margin percentage based on sales	20%
Cost of goods available for sale	€9 million

The loss was fully covered by insurance. The insurance company wants to know the historical cost of the stocks as one factor considered when negotiating a settlement.

Required

Calculate the cost of:

1 Finished goods stock, 26 February 2015.

2 Work-in-progress stock, 26 February 2015.

3 Direct materials stock, 26 February 2015.

2.22 **Comprehensive problem on unit costs, product costs** (30 minutes)

Overtoom International Nederland BV manufactures and sells metal shelving. It began operations on 1 January 2015. Costs incurred for 2015 (V stands for variable; F stands for fixed) are as follows:

Direct materials used costs	€280 000 V
Direct manufacturing labour costs	60 000 V
Plant energy costs	10 000 V
Indirect manufacturing labour costs	20 000 V
Indirect manufacturing labour costs	32 000 F
Other indirect manufacturing costs	16 000 V
Other indirect manufacturing costs	48 000 F
Marketing, distribution and customer-service costs	245 700 V
Marketing, distribution and customer-service costs	80 000 F
Administrative costs	100 000 F

Variable manufacturing costs are variable with respect to units produced. Variable marketing, distribution, and customer-service costs are variable with respect to units sold. Stock data are as follows:

	Opening 1 January 2015	Closing 31 December 2015
Direct materials	0 kg	2000 kg
Work in progress	0 units	0 units
Finished goods	0 units	? units

Production in 2015 was 100 000 units. Two kilograms of direct materials are used to make one unit of finished product.

Revenues in 2015 were €873 600. The selling price per unit and the purchase price per kilogram of direct materials were stable throughout the year. The company's ending stock of finished goods is carried at the average unit manufacturing costs for 2015. Finished goods stock, at 31 December 2015, was €41 940.

Required

1 Direct materials stock, total cost, 31 December 2015.

2 Finished goods stock, total units, 31 December 2015.

3 Selling price per unit 2015.

4 Operating profit 2015. Show your computations.

*2.23 Budgeted income statement (continuation of Exercise 2.22) (30 minutes)

Assume management predicts that the selling price per unit and variable cost per unit will be the same in 2016 as in 2015. Fixed manufacturing costs and marketing, distribution and customer-service costs in 2016 are also predicted to be the same as in 2015. Sales in 2016 are forecast to be 122 000 units. The desired closing stock of finished goods, 31 December 2016, is 12 000 units. Assume zero closing stock of both direct materials and work in progress. The company's closing stock of finished goods is carried at the average unit manufacturing costs for 2016. The company uses the first-in, first-out stock method. Management has asked that you prepare a budgeted income statement for 2016.

Required

1 Units of finished goods produced in 2016.

2 Budgeted income statement for 2016.

Advanced level

*2.24 Variable costs and fixed costs (5–20 minutes)

Lutukka Oy owns the rights to extract minerals from beach sands in Enare Lappmark. Lutukka has costs in three areas:

a Payment to a mining subcontractor who charges €80 per tonne of beach sand mined and returned to the beach (after being processed on the mainland to extract three minerals: ilmenite, rutile and zircon).

b Payment of a government mining and environmental tax of 50 per tonne of beach sand mined.

c Payment to a barge operator. This operator charges €150 000 per month to transport each batch of beach sand – up to 100 tonnes per batch per day – to the mainland and then return to Enare Lappmark (that is, 0–100 tonnes per day = €150 000 per month; 101–200 tonnes = €300 000 per month, and so on). Each barge operates 25 days per month. The €150 000 monthly charge must be paid even if less than 100 tonnes is transported on any day and even if Lutukka requires fewer than 25 days of barge transportation in that month.

Lutukka is currently mining 180 tonnes of beach minerals per day for 25 days per month.

Required

1 What is the variable cost per tonne of beach sand mined? What is the fixed cost to Lutukka per month?

2 Plot one graph of the variable costs and another graph of the fixed costs of Lutukka. Your plots should be similar to Exhibits 2.4 and 2.5. Is the concept of relevant range applicable to your plots?

3 What is the unit cost per tonne of beach sand mined (a) if 180 tonnes are mined each day, or (b) if 220 tonnes are mined each day? Explain the difference in the unit-cost figures.

2.25 Revenue and cost recording and classifications, ethics (25–30 minutes)

Aran Sweaters Ltd designs and markets wool jumpers to many retailers and distributors around Europe. Its corporate headquarters are situated in Dublin, Ireland. Manufacturing is done by a subcontractor (O'Neil's Clothing Ltd) on Achill Island. The local council in Achill Island grants locally-owned companies a 20% income tax rebate if the ratio of their domestic labour costs to total costs exceeds 25%. Domestic labour costs are defined as the employment costs of all employees who are Achill residents. Siobhan Sheridan, the newly appointed controller of Aran Sweaters, has recently been examining payments made to O'Neil's. She observes that O'Neil's purchased wool from Aran Sweaters (€3 million in 2015). Aran Sweaters paid O'Neil's €12 million for the jumpers manufactured on Achill in 2015. Based on her industry experience, the €12 million amount is very low. She was told it was 'a great deal' for Aran Sweaters. There is also a sizable payment by Aran Sweaters to the Swiss subsidiary of O'Neil's (€4.8 million in 2015). Sheridan is told by the O'Neil's CEO that this payment is for fabric design work that O'Neil does with Aran Sweaters. Aran Sweaters has included the €4.8 million payments in its own product design cost. The director of product design at Aran Sweaters told Sheridan it is an 'off-statement' item that historically he has neither responsibility for nor any say about. To his knowledge, O'Neil's uses only Aran Sweaters designs with either zero or minimal changes.

O'Neil's domestic labour costs in 2015 were €3.6 million while its total costs were €10 million. Included in this €3.6 million was €1.3 million for labour fringe benefits (for health insurance, etc.). A component of this €1.3 million is €600 000 for life insurance for O'Neil's executives. Aran Sweaters helped arrange this life insurance policy. It negotiated with the insurance company managing its own executive life insurance plans to include the O'Neil's executives at rates much more favourable than those available in Achill.

Required

1 What concerns should Sheridan have about the revenue and cost numbers in Aran Sweaters' financial reports?

2 Which (if any) of the concerns in requirement 1 raise ethical issues for Sheridan? Explain.

3 What steps should Sheridan take to address the ethical issues you identify in requirement 2?

CHAPTER 3

Job-costing systems

How much does it cost Ernst & Young to audit Yamaha? How much does it cost Kraft to promote its new pre-sliced, cracker-sized cheese? How much does it cost Peugeot to manufacture and sell an iOn all-electric car to a customer? How much does it cost Apple to incorporate wi-fi and Bluetooth within an iPad? Managers ask these questions for many reasons, including formulating overall strategies, determining product and service emphasis and pricing, engaging in cost control and meeting external reporting obligations. This chapter presents concepts and techniques that guide the responses to such questions. Chapter 11 will refine some ideas presented here.

Costing systems aim to report cost numbers that indicate the manner in which particular cost objects – such as products, services and customers – use the resources of an organisation. Before we explore the details of costing systems, three points are worth noting:

1 The cost–benefit–context approach we discussed in Chapter 1 is of relevance in designing and choosing costing systems. The costs of elaborate systems, including the costs of educating managers and other personnel, can be quite high. Managers may choose to install a more sophisticated system if they believe that its benefits will outweigh its costs. In practice, experienced managers tend to act on intuition rather than a fully quantified cost–benefit analysis. Behavioural, political and institutional factors generally influence accounting information systems choice and design.

2 Systems tend to be tailored to the underlying operations and not vice versa. Any significant change in underlying operations is likely to justify a corresponding change in the accompanying costing systems. Systems fail when operating managers perceive them as misleading, useless or incompatible with their management style.

3 Costing systems are only one source of information for managers. Generally, managers combine cost information with non-financial metrics and qualitative information when making decisions.

Learning objectives

After studying this chapter, you should be able to:

- Describe the building block concept of costing systems
- Distinguish between job costing and process costing
- Outline a six-step approach to job costing
- Distinguish actual costing from normal costing
- Understand job costing in service and manufacturing contexts
- Describe key source documents used in job-costing systems
- Understand how the steps in the production process are tracked in a job-costing system
- Describe alternative methods of dealing with period-end under- or overallocated indirect costs

The building block concept of costing systems

Let us briefly review some terms introduced in Chapter 2 that we will use in discussing costing systems:

- *Cost object* – anything for which a separate measurement of costs is desired.
- *Direct costs of a cost object* – costs that are related to the particular cost object and can be traced to it in an economically feasible (cost-effective) way.
- *Indirect costs of a cost object* – costs that are related to the particular cost object but cannot be traced to it in an economically feasible (cost-effective) way. Indirect costs are allocated to the cost object using a cost-allocation method.

The relationship among these three concepts is shown in Exhibit 3.1.

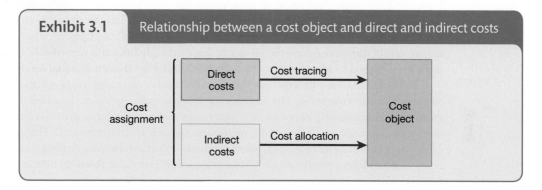

Exhibit 3.1 Relationship between a cost object and direct and indirect costs

Two concepts not previously defined are also important when discussing costing systems:

- **Cost pool** – a grouping of individual cost items. Cost pools can range from the very broad (such as a company-wide total-cost pool for telephones and fax machines) to the very narrow (such as the costs of operating a car used by a travelling salesperson).
- **Cost-allocation base** – a factor that is the common denominator for systematically linking an indirect cost or group of indirect costs to a cost object. A cost-allocation base can be financial (such as direct labour costs) or non-financial (such as the number of car kilometres travelled). Companies often seek to use the cost driver of the indirect costs as the cost-allocation base. For example, the number of kilometres travelled may be used as the base for allocating motor vehicle operating costs among different sales districts.

These five terms constitute the building blocks that are considered relevant in the design of costing systems.

Job-costing and process-costing systems

Companies frequently adopt one of two basic types of costing system to assign costs to products or services:

- **Job-costing system.** In this system, costs are assigned to a distinct unit, batch or lot of a product or service. A job is a task for which resources are expended in bringing a distinct product or service to market. The product or service is often custom-made, such as an audit by an accounting firm or a gearbox system for a particular car system.
- **Process-costing system.** In this system, the cost object is masses of identical or similar units. The cost of a product or service is obtained by using broad averages to assign costs to masses of identical or similar units. The customers all receive the same product (such as teddy bears or soda ash).

These two types of costing system are best viewed as ends of a continuum:

Most companies have costing systems that are neither pure job costing nor pure process costing. Rather, they combine elements of both job costing and process costing. For now, we introduce these two systems by focusing on their pure versions. Exhibit 3.2 presents examples of job and process costing in the service, merchandising and manufacturing sectors.

The products or services accounted for with job costing can differ greatly. Accounting firms typically define individual audits as jobs, which can differ markedly in complexity among clients. An aircraft assembly company may define an individual aircraft for a specific customer as a job. Customers usually differ in their specifications about electronic equipment, size of toilet cubicles and so on. In these examples, the service or product is distinct and identifiable. Job-costing systems are designed to accommodate the cost accounting for these individual services or products.

Companies that use process costing provide similar (in many cases identical) products or services to their customers. For example, a bank usually provides the same service to all its customers in processing deposits. A magazine publishing company provides the same product (say, a weekly issue of *Le Point* or *The Times*) to each of its customers. The customers of an oil-refining company all receive the same product – crude oil. Process-costing systems average the costs of providing a similar product or service to different customers to obtain a per unit cost. Chapter 4 discusses process costing in more detail.

Exhibit 3.2	Examples of job costing and process costing in the service, merchandising and manufacturing sectors		
	Service sector	**Merchandising sector**	**Manufacturing sector**
Job costing used	• Accounting firm audits • Advertising agency campaigns	• Sending a catalogue to a mailing list • Special promotion of a new store product	• Aircraft assembly • House construction
Process costing	• Deposit processing • Postal delivery (standard items)	• Grain dealing • Processing new magazine subscriptions	• Oil refining • Beverages production

Job costing in service organisations using actual costing

Service-sector companies provide their customers with services or intangible products. Within the service sector, jobs often differ considerably in terms of their length, complexity and resources used. Examples include a service call to repair a television, an audit engagement, the making of a musical and a university research project for a government agency.

Job costing of an audit engagement

Lindsay & Associates is a public accounting firm. Each audit engagement is viewed as an individual job. Lindsay bids a fixed fee for each audit in advance of doing the work. A key issue for Lindsay is the cost of an audit engagement. A record of costs on previous jobs enables it to make informed estimates of the costs of potential future jobs. The more knowledgeable Lindsay is about its own costs, the more likely it is to price jobs so that it makes a profit on those accepted.

First, consider the actual costing system Lindsay uses to determine the cost of individual jobs. Actual costing is a costing method that traces direct costs to a cost object by using the actual direct-cost rate(s) times the actual quantity of the direct-cost input(s) and allocates indirect costs based on the actual indirect-cost rate(s) times the actual quantity of the cost-allocation base. The Tracy Transport audit illustrates **actual costing**. In November 2014, Lindsay was awarded the 2015 Tracy Transport audit job for a fee of €86 000. The 2015 audit job was done in the January to March 2015 period and covers Tracy Transport's 2014 financial year.

General approach to job costing

The six steps taken in assigning costs to individual jobs are presented here. They apply equally to job costing in the service, merchandising or manufacturing sectors.

Step 1: Identify the job that is the chosen cost object In this example, the job is the annual audit of the financial statements of Tracy Transport.

Step 2: Identify the direct costs for the job Lindsay identifies only one category of direct costs when costing individual audit jobs – professional labour. Each auditor keeps a daily time record for tracing professional labour-hours to individual audit jobs. These records show that the Tracy Transport job used 800 professional labour-hours. The actual direct-labour cost rate is €51 per hour. The actual direct-labour cost rate is the average rate at which professional labour is paid (actual total professional compensation divided by actual total direct labour-hours worked) during the period in which the Tracy Transport audit was done. Lindsay traces the actual direct-labour costs for the Tracy Transport job as €40 800 (€51 × 800).

Step 3: Identify the indirect-cost pools associated with the job Lindsay groups all its individual indirect costs into a single cost pool called audit support. This cost pool represents all costs in Lindsay's Audit Support Department. The indirect cost pool consists of a variety of individual costs, such as general audit and secretarial support, that are less predictable and less traceable to jobs than direct labour. Hence, the actual indirect cost rate can often only be calculated on an actual basis at the end of the year. In 2015, indirect costs totalled €12 690 000 (€4 990 000 for 'other-labour-related costs' plus €7 700 000 for 'non-labour-related costs').

Step 4: Select the cost-allocation base to use in allocating each indirect-cost pool to the job The allocation base selected for the audit support indirect-cost pool is professional labour-hours. Total professional labour-hours worked in 2015 were 270 000.

Step 5: Develop the rate per unit of the cost-allocation base used to allocate indirect costs to the job The actual indirect-cost rate for Lindsay in 2015 is €47 per professional labour-hour:

$$\text{Actual indirect-cost rate} = \frac{\text{Actual total costs in indirect-cost pool}}{\text{Actual total quantity of cost-allocation base}}$$

$$= \frac{€4\ 990\ 000 + €7\ 700\ 000}{270\ 000}$$

$$= \frac{€12\ 690\ 000}{270\ 000}$$

$$= €47 \text{ per professional labour-hour}$$

The actual indirect costs allocated to the Lindsay audit job are €37 600 (€47 × 800).

Step 6: Assign the costs to the cost object by adding all direct costs and all indirect costs The information from steps 1 to 5 can now be used to calculate the 2015 actual cost of the Lindsay audit:

Direct job costs traced	
Professional labour, €51 × 800	€40 800
Indirect job costs allocated	
Audit support, €47 × 800	37 600
	€78 400

Recall that Lindsay was paid €86 000 for the 2015 Tracy Transport audit. Thus, the actual costing system shows a €7600 operating profit (€86 000 − €78 400) on this audit job.

Exhibit 3.3 presents an overview of the Lindsay job-costing system. This exhibit includes the five building blocks of this chapter: cost object, cost pool, direct costs of a cost object, indirect costs of a cost object and cost-allocation base. Costing-system overviews like Exhibit 3.3 are important learning tools. We urge you to sketch one when you need to understand a costing system. (The symbols in Exhibit 3.3 are used consistently in the costing-system overviews presented in this book. For example, a triangle always identifies a direct cost.)

Source documents

Managers and accountants gather the information that goes into their cost systems through **source documents**, which are the original records that support journal entries in an accounting system. Time records are Lindsay's main source documents. All professional staff members record how they spend each half-hour of the day. At the end of each week, the number of total professional labour-hours spent on each job (both for the most recent week and the cumulative total since the start of the job) is tabulated. The accuracy of information on how employees

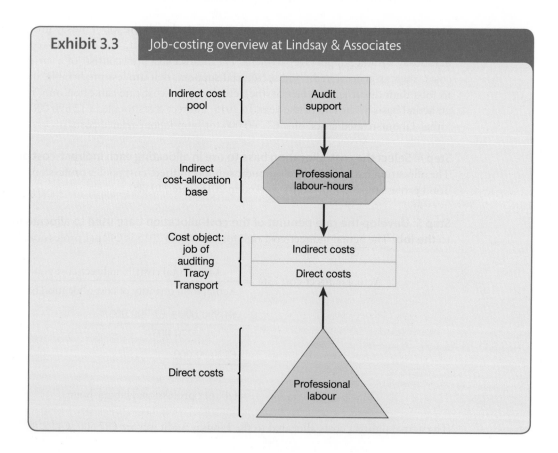

Exhibit 3.3   Job-costing overview at Lindsay & Associates

spend their time is important, especially in service organisations, where labour costs often make up over half of total costs. Accounting and law firms often impose penalties on personnel who do not submit accurate time records when required. Computers simplify the recording and preparation of job-cost information.

Normal costing

The difficulty of calculating actual indirect-labour costs for each job means that Lindsay & Associates has to wait until the end of 2015 to calculate the actual costs on individual jobs done in 2015. Managers often want more timely information about 'actual' job costs. This demand for more timely information has prompted the use of alternatives to the actual costing method described earlier in this chapter. The alternatives are practical responses to the desire for a timely approximation of average actual costs of various jobs. Now we discuss normal costing, whereby budgeted rather than actual amounts are used to calculate indirect-cost rates. The following 2015 budgeted data pertain to the total operations of Lindsay & Associates:

	Budget
Total professional labour-hours worked	288 000
Direct costs	
Total professional labour costs	€14 400 000
Indirect costs	
Total other labour-related costs	5 328 000
Total non-labour-related costs	7 632 000
	€12 960 000

Exhibit 3.4 provides details underlying these amounts.

Exhibit 3.4	Income statement for Lindsay & Associates: 2015 budget and 2015 actual results			

	2015 Budget		2015 Actual	
Revenues		€33 120		€29 700
Costs				
Professional labour costs		14 400		13 770
Other labour-related costs				
Office staff	€2 030		€1 840	
Information specialists	1 008		1 230	
Administrative	1 252		1 100	
Other	1 038	5 328	820	4 990
Non-labour-related costs				
Professional liability insurance	2 160		2 069	
Professional development	880		540	
Occupancy	2 000		1 913	
Telephone/fax/copying	1 430		1 530	
Travel	770		718	
Other	392	7 632	930	7 700
Total costs		27 360		26 460
Operating profit		€5 760		€3 240

A **normal costing** method traces direct costs to a cost object by using the actual direct-cost rate(s) times the actual quantity of the direct-cost input and allocates indirect costs based on the budgeted indirect-cost rate(s) times the actual quantity of the cost-allocation base(s). Both actual costing and normal costing trace direct costs to jobs in the same way. For the Lindsay & Associates 2015 audit of Tracy Transport, the actual direct costs traced equal €40 800 – the actual direct-cost rate of €51 per professional labour-hour times the actual quantity of 800 hours.

The difference between the actual costing and normal costing methods is that actual costing uses an actual indirect-cost rate while normal costing uses a budgeted indirect-cost rate to cost jobs. Recall that Lindsay & Associates groups all its individual indirect costs into a single cost pool called audit support. The budgeted amount for audit support in 2015 is €12 960 000. The allocation base for the audit support indirect-cost pool is professional labour-hours. In 2015, the budgeted quantity is 288 000 hours. The budgeted indirect-cost rate for 2015 is €45 per professional labour-hour:

$$\text{Budgeted indirect-cost rate} = \frac{\text{Budgeted total costs in indirect-cost pool}}{\text{Budgeted total quantity of cost-allocation base}}$$

$$= \frac{\text{€5 328 000} + \text{€7 632 000}}{288\ 000\ \text{hours}}$$

$$= \frac{\text{€12 690 000}}{288\ 000\ \text{hours}}$$

$$= \text{€45 per professional labour-hour}$$

Under normal costing, each hour of professional labour on jobs in 2015 is assigned the actual direct-cost rate of €51 and the budgeted indirect-cost rate of €45. The 2015 cost of the Tracy Transport audit using normal costing is €76 800:

Direct job costs traced	
Professional labour, €51 × 800	€40 800
Indirect job costs allocated	
Audit support, €45 × 800	36 000
	€76 800

Normal costing uses actual direct costs because these costs are known and can be quickly traced to a job. Indirect costs, by definition, cannot be traced to jobs. Moreover, actual indirect costs are less predictable and not known until the end of the year. Normal costing uses budgeted rates for indirect costs to estimate or approximate the actual indirect costs of a job soon after the job is completed.

The building industry illustrates the use of normal costing. Here, materials are purchased at a price known at the purchase date and labour is paid on an hourly rate basis that is set at the time workers are hired. Actual cost information on both major direct-cost categories can thus be calculated as construction takes place. Indirect costs are allocated using a budgeted rate.

Note that normal costing uses a predetermined (budgeted) rate for allocating indirect costs, €45 here. In contrast, actual costing used a €47 rate. Chapter 11 discusses alternative approaches to accounting for these differences when reporting individual job costs and when preparing income statements and balance sheets.

Job costing in manufacturing

We now discuss job costing in manufacturing. This includes a transaction-by-transaction summary of how a costing system tracks the purchase of manufacturing inputs, their conversion into work in progress and then into finished goods and finally their sale. The six-step approach to job costing illustrated above is also applicable to the manufacturing sector. We illustrate this approach using the Wallace Company, which manufactures specialised machinery for the papermaking industry at its Glasgow plant. Wallace uses a normal costing method – that is, actual costs for direct-cost items and budgeted costs for indirect-cost items.

Step 1: Identify the job that is the chosen cost object The job in this case is a pulp machine manufactured for the Merseyside Paper Company in 2015.

Step 2: Identify the direct costs for the job Wallace identifies two direct manufacturing cost categories: direct materials and direct manufacturing labour.

Step 3: Identify the indirect-cost pools associated with the job For product-costing purposes, Wallace uses a single indirect manufacturing cost pool termed manufacturing overhead. This pool represents the indirect costs of the Glasgow Manufacturing Department. It includes items such as depreciation on equipment, energy costs, indirect materials and indirect manufacturing labour and salaries.

Step 4: Select the cost-allocation base to use in allocating each indirect-cost pool to the job Wallace uses machine-hours as the allocation base for manufacturing overhead.

Step 5: Develop the rate per unit of each cost-allocation base used to allocate indirect costs to the job Wallace budgets 2015 manufacturing overhead costs to be €1 280 000 and the 2015 quantity of machine-hours as 16 000. Hence, the 2015 budgeted indirect-cost rate for manufacturing overhead is €80 per machine-hour (€1 280 000 ÷ 16 000 hours).

Step 6: Assign the costs to the cost object by adding all direct costs and all indirect costs The cost of the machine job for Merseyside Paper is €10 135.

Direct manufacturing costs		
Direct materials	€4 606	
Direct manufacturing labour	1 329	€5 935
Indirect manufacturing costs		
Manufacturing overhead		
(€80 × 52.5 machine-hours)		4 200
Total manufacturing costs of job		€10 135

Exhibit 3.5 presents an overview of the job-costing system for the manufacturing costs of the Wallace Company.

Wallace uses its job-costing system to help manage the costs in its Glasgow Manufacturing Department as well as to determine the cost of individual jobs such as the Merseyside Paper machine. The Manufacturing Department is an important cost object, as is each job manufactured. The relationship between these two important goals of a job-costing system is shown in Exhibit 3.6.

Source documents

Source documents are the original records that support journal entries in an accounting system. The key source document in a job-costing system is a **job cost record** (also called a **job cost sheet**). This document records and accumulates all the costs assigned to a specific job. Exhibit 3.7, Panel A, shows a typical job cost record at the Wallace Company. Source documents also exist for individual items in a job cost record. Consider direct materials. The basic source document is a **materials requisition record**, which is a form used to charge departments and job cost records for the cost of the materials used on a specific job. Panel B shows a materials requisition record for the Wallace Company. The basic source document for direct manufacturing labour is

Exhibit 3.5   Job-costing overview for manufacturing costs at the Wallace Company

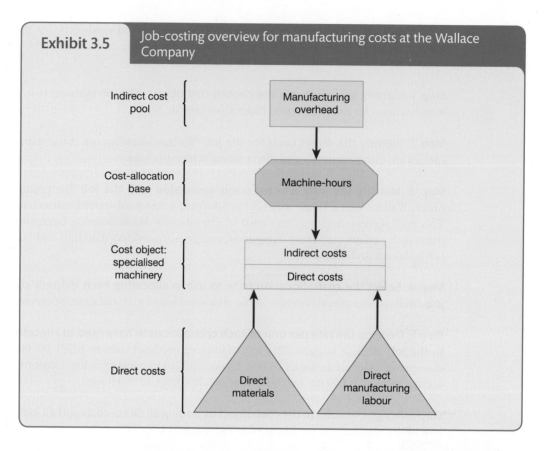

Exhibit 3.6   Department and job costing at the Wallace Company

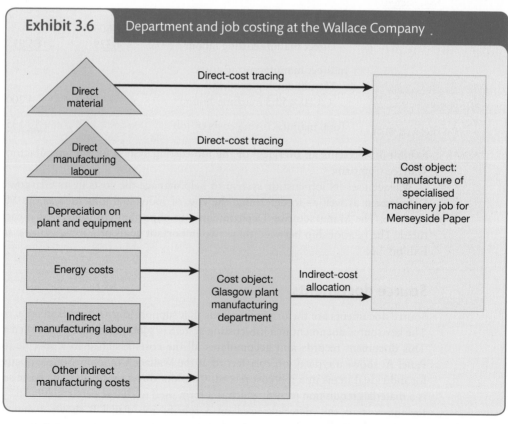

Exhibit 3.7 Source documents at the Wallace Company: job cost record, materials requisition record and labour time record

Panel A

JOB COST RECORD

JOB NO: WPP298   CUSTOMER: Merseyside Paper
Date started: 7 Feb. 2015   Date completed: 3 April 2015

DIRECT MATERIALS

Materials requisition no.	Part no.	Date received	Quantity used	Unit cost	Billing amount
③ 2015:198	MB 468-A	9 Feb. 2015	8	€14	€112
2015:268	TB 267-F	11 Feb. 2015	12	€63	756
					•
					•
					•
Total					€4606

DIRECT MANUFACTURING LABOUR

Labour time record no.	Employee no.	Period covered	Hours used	Hourly rate	Billing amount
③ LT 232	551-87-3076	16–22 Feb. 2015	25	€18	€450
LT 247	287-31-4671	16–22 Feb. 2015	16	18	288
					•
					•
					•
Total					€1329

MANUFACTURING OVERHEAD

Cost pool category	Allocation base	Allocation base units used	Allocation base rate	Billing amount
Manufacturing	Machine-hours	52.50	€80	€4200
				•
				•
				•
Total				€4200
TOTAL BILLABLE JOB COST				€10135

Panel B

MATERIALS REQUISITION RECORD

Materials requisition record no: 2015:198
Job No: WPP 298   Date: 9 Feb. 2015

Part no.	Part description	Quantity	Unit cost	Total cost
MB468-A	Metal brackets	8	€14	€112

Issued by: B. Clyde   Date: 9 Feb. 2015
Received by: L Daley   Date: 9 Feb. 2015

Panel C

LABOUR TIME RECORD

Labour time record no: LT 232

Employee name: G.L. Cook   Employee no: 551-87-3076

Employee classification code: Grade 3 Machinist

Week start: 16 Feb. 2015   Week end: 22 Feb. 2015

Job. no.	M	T	W	Th	F	S	Su	Total
WPP298	4	8	3	6	4	0	0	25

Supervisor: R. Stuart   Date: 23 Feb. 2015

a **labour time record**, which is used to charge departments and job cost records for labour time used on a specific job. Panel C in Exhibit 3.7 shows a typical labour time record for the Wallace Company. The reliability of job cost records depends on the reliability of the inputs. Problems occurring in this area include materials recorded on one job being 'borrowed' and used on other jobs and erroneous job numbers being assigned to material or labour inputs.

In many costing systems, the source documents exist only in the form of computer records. With barcoding and other forms of online information recording, the materials and time used on jobs are increasingly being recorded without human intervention.

An illustration of a job-costing system in manufacturing

We will use the Wallace Company to illustrate in some detail how a job-costing system operates in manufacturing. Recall that its job-costing system has two direct-cost categories (direct materials and direct manufacturing labour) and one indirect-cost pool (manufacturing overhead). See Exhibit 3.7. The following example considers events that took place in September 2015.

General ledger and subsidiary ledgers

As we have noted, a job-costing system has a separate job cost record for each job. This record is typically found in a subsidiary ledger. The general ledger combines these separate job cost records in the Work-in-Progress Control account, which pertains to all jobs undertaken.

Exhibit 3.8 shows T-account relationships for the Wallace Company's general ledger and illustrative records in the subsidiary ledgers. Panel A shows the general ledger section that gives a 'bird's-eye view' of the costing system; the amounts are based on the illustration that follows. Panel B shows the subsidiary ledgers and the basic source documents that contain the underlying details – the 'worm's-eye view'. General ledger accounts with the word *control* in their titles (such as Materials Control and Creditors Control) are supported by underlying subsidiary ledgers.

Software programs guide the processing of transactions in most accounting systems. Some programs make general ledger entries simultaneously with entries in the subsidiary ledger accounts. Other software programs make general ledger entries at, say, weekly or monthly intervals, with entries made in the subsidiary ledger accounts on a more frequent basis. The Wallace Company makes entries in its subsidiary ledger when transactions occur and then makes entries in its general ledger on a monthly basis.

A general ledger should be viewed as only one of many tools that assist management in planning and control. To control operations, managers not only use the source documents in the subsidiary ledgers, they also study non-financial variables such as the percentage of jobs requiring rework.

Explanations of transactions

The following transaction-by-transaction summary analysis explains how a job-costing system serves the twin goals of (1) department responsibility and control, and (2) product costing. These transactions track stages (a) to (d):

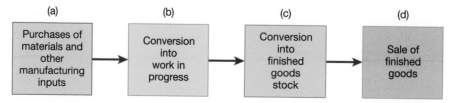

It is the existence of stages (b) and (c) that makes the costing of manufactured products more detailed than the costing of services and merchandise described earlier.

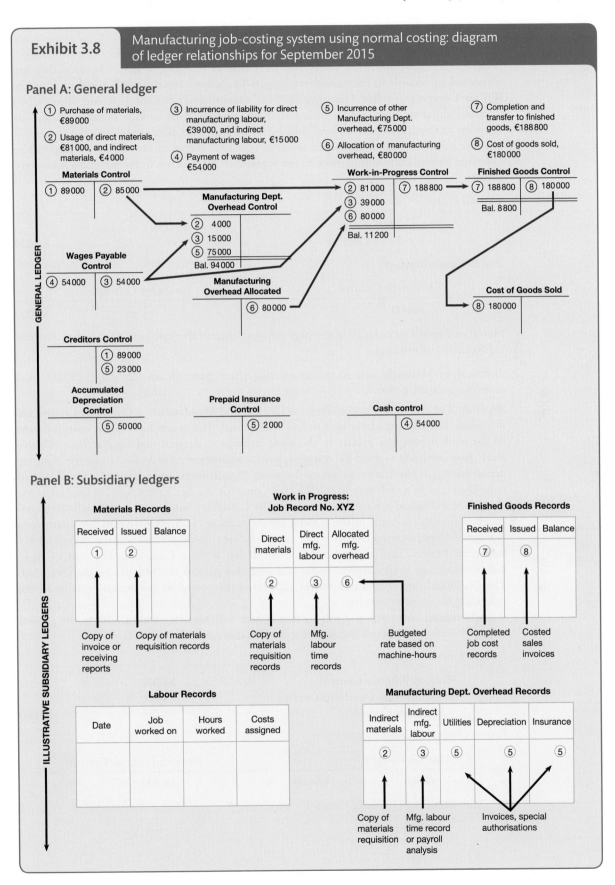

Exhibit 3.8 Manufacturing job-costing system using normal costing: diagram of ledger relationships for September 2015

1 *Transaction*: Purchases of materials (direct and indirect), €89 000 on account.

Analysis: The asset Materials Control is increased. The liability Creditors Control is increased. Both accounts have the word *control* in their title in the general ledger because they are supported by records in the subsidiary ledger. The subsidiary records for materials at the Wallace Company – called *Materials Records* – maintain a continuous record of additions to, and reductions from, stock. At a minimum, these records would contain columns for quantity received, issuance to jobs and balance (see Panel B of Exhibit 3.8). There is a separate subsidiary materials record for each type of material in the subsidiary ledger. The following journal entry summarises all the September 2015 entries in the materials subsidiary ledgers:

Journal Entry:

Materials Control	89 000	
Creditors Control		89 000

Post to General Ledger:

Materials Control		Creditors Control		
a 89 000			a	89 000

Materials Control includes all material purchases, whether the items are classified as direct or indirect costs of products.

2 *Transaction*: Materials sent to manufacturing plant floor: direct materials, €81 000 and indirect materials, €4000.

Analysis: The accounts Work-in-Progress Control and Manufacturing Overhead Control are increased. The account Materials Control is decreased. The assumption is that costs incurred on the work in progress 'attach' to the work in progress, thereby making it a more valuable asset. Responsibility is fixed by using *materials requisition records* as a basis for charging departments for the materials issued to them. Requisitions are accumulated and posted monthly to the general ledger at the Wallace Company. As direct materials are used, they are charged to individual job records, which are the subsidiary ledger accounts for the Work-in-Progress Control account in the general ledger account. Indirect materials are charged to individual Manufacturing Departments' overhead cost records, which comprise the subsidiary ledger for Manufacturing Overhead Control at the Wallace Company. The cost of these indirect materials is allocated to individual jobs as a part of the Manufacturing Overhead. The Manufacturing Overhead Control account is the record of the *actual costs* in all the individual overhead categories.

Each indirect-cost pool in a job-costing system will have its own account in the general ledger. Wallace has only one indirect-cost pool: manufacturing overhead.

Journal Entry:

Work-in-Progress Control	81 000	
Manufacturing Overhead Control	4 000	
Materials Control		85 000

Post to General Ledger:

Materials Control			Work-in-Progress Control	
a 89 000	b 85 000	b	81 000	

Manufacturing Overhead Control	
b 4 000	

3 *Transaction*: Manufacturing labour wages liability incurred, direct (€39 000) and indirect (€15 000).

Analysis: The accounts Work-in-Progress Control and Manufacturing Department Overhead Control are increased. Wages Payable Control is also increased. Labour time records are used to trace direct manufacturing labour to Work-in-Progress Control (see Panel B of Exhibit 3.8) and to accumulate the indirect manufacturing labour in Manufacturing Department Overhead Control. The indirect manufacturing labour is, by definition, not being traced to the individual job. Department managers are responsible for making efficient use of available labour.

Journal Entry:

Work-in-Progress Control	39 000	
Manufacturing Overhead Control	15 000	
Wages Payable Control		54 000

Post to General Ledger:

Wages Payable Control			Work-in-Progress Control	
	c	54 000	b	81 000
			c	39 000

Manufacturing	Overhead Control	
b	4 000	
c	15 000	

4 *Transaction*: Payment of total manufacturing payroll for the month, €54 000. (For simplicity, payroll withholdings from employees are ignored in this example.)

Analysis: The liability Wages Payable Control is decreased. The asset Cash Control is decreased.

Journal Entry:

Wages Payable	54 000	
Cash Control		54 000

Post to General Ledger:

Wages Payable Control			Cash Control	
d	54 000	c	54 000	
			d	54 000

For convenience here, wages payable for the month is assumed to be completely paid at month-end.

5 *Transaction*: Additional manufacturing overhead costs incurred during the month, €75 000. These costs consist of utilities and repairs, €23 000; insurance expired, €2000; and depreciation on equipment, €50 000.

Analysis: The indirect-cost account of Manufacturing Overhead Control is increased. The liability Creditors Control is increased, the asset Prepaid Insurance Control is decreased and the asset Equipment is decreased by means of a related contra asset account Accumulated Depreciation Control. The detail of these costs is entered in the appropriate columns of the individual manufacturing overhead cost records that make up the subsidiary ledger for Manufacturing Overhead Control. The source documents for these distributions include invoices (for example, an electricity bill) and special schedules (for example, a depreciation schedule) from the accounting officer responsible.

Journal Entry:

Manufacturing Overhead Control	75 000	
Creditors Control		23 000
Accumulated Depreciation Control		50 000
Prepaid Insurance Control		2 000

Post to General Ledger:

Creditors Control			Manufacturing Overhead Control		
	a	89 000	b	4 000	
	e	23 000	c	15 000	
			e	75 000	

Accumulated Depreciation Control			Prepaid Insurance Control		
	e	50 000		e	2 000

6 *Transaction*: Allocation of manufacturing overhead to products, €80 000.

Analysis: The asset Work-in-Progress Control is increased. The indirect-cost account of Manufacturing Overhead Control is, in effect, decreased by means of its contra account, called **Manufacturing Overhead Allocated**. This is the record of manufacturing overhead allocated to individual jobs on the basis of the budgeted rate multiplied by actual units used of the allocation base. It comprises all manufacturing costs that are assigned to a product (or service) using a cost-allocation base because they cannot be traced to it in an economically feasible way. The 2015 budgeted overhead rate used by Wallace is €80 per machine-hour. The overhead cost allocated to each job depends on the machine-hours used on that job. The job record for each individual job in the subsidiary ledger will include a debit item for manufacturing overhead allocated. It is assumed that 1000 machine-hours were used for all jobs, resulting in a total manufacturing overhead allocation of $1000 \times €80 = €80\ 000$.

Note that a subsidiary entry is made for Manufacturing Overhead Allocated when machine-hours are used on a job. These entries are made to the individual job records in the subsidiary ledger. In contrast, subsidiary entries are made for Manufacturing Overhead Control when actual transactions occur during the period.

Journal Entry:

Work-in-Progress Control	80 000	
Manufacturing Overhead Allocated		80 000

Post to General Ledger:

Manufacturing Overhead Allocated			Work-in-Progress Control		
	f	80 000	b	81 000	
			c	39 000	
			f	80 000	

7 *Transaction*: Completion and transfer to finished goods of eight individual jobs, €188 800.

Analysis: The asset Finished Goods Control is increased. The asset Work-in-Progress Control is decreased. The total costs of each job are calculated in the subsidiary ledger as each job is completed. Given Wallace's use of a normal costing method, this total will consist of *actual* direct materials, *actual* direct manufacturing labour and budgeted manufacturing overhead that is allocated to each job.

Journal Entry:

Finished Goods Control	188 800	
Work-in-Progress Control		188 800

Post to General Ledger:

Work-in-Progress Control				Finished Goods Control	
b	81 000	g	188 800	g	188 800
c	39 000				
f	80 000				

8 *Transaction*: Cost of Goods Sold, €180 000.

Analysis: The €180 000 amount represents the cost of goods sold in sales transactions with customers during September 2015. The account Cost of Goods Sold is increased. The asset Finished Goods Control is decreased.

Journal Entry:

Cost of Goods Sold	180 000	
Finished Goods Control		180 000

Post to General Ledger:

Finished Goods Control				Cost of Goods Sold	
g	188 800	h	180 000	h	180 000

At this point, please pause and review all eight entries in the illustration. Be sure to trace each journal entry, step by step, to the general-ledger accounts in the general ledger section in Panel A of Exhibit 3.8.

Budgeted indirect costs and end-of-period adjustments

Budgeted indirect-cost rates have the advantage of being more timely than actual indirect-cost rates. With budgeted rates, indirect costs can be assigned to individual jobs on an ongoing basis rather than waiting until the end of the accounting period when actual costs will be known. However, the disadvantage of budgeted rates is that they will probably be inaccurate, having been made up to 12 months before actual costs are incurred. We now consider adjustments made when the indirect costs allocated differ from the actual indirect costs incurred.

Underallocated indirect costs occur when the allocated amount of indirect costs in an accounting period is less than the actual (incurred) amount in that period. **Overallocated indirect costs** occur when the allocated amount of indirect costs in an accounting period exceeds the actual (incurred) amount in that period.

Under- or overallocated indirect costs = Indirect costs incurred − Indirect costs allocated

Equivalent terms are **underapplied (or overapplied) indirect costs** and **underabsorbed (or overabsorbed) indirect costs.**

The Wallace Company has a single indirect-cost pool (Manufacturing Overhead) in its job-costing system. There are two indirect-cost accounts in its general ledger that pertain to manufacturing overhead:

- Manufacturing Overhead Control, which is the record of the actual costs in all the individual overhead categories (such as indirect materials, indirect manufacturing labour, power and rent).

- Manufacturing Overhead Allocated, which is the record of the manufacturing overhead allocated to individual jobs on the basis of the budgeted rate multiplied by actual machine-hours.

Assume the following annual data for the Wallace Company:

Manufacturing Overhead Control	Manufacturing Overhead Allocated
Bal. 31 Dec. 2015 1 200 000	Bal. 31 Dec. 2015 1 000 000

The €80 budgeted indirect-cost rate is calculated by dividing budgeted manufacturing overhead of €1 280 000 (the numerator) by the 16 000 budgeted quantity of machine-hours (the denominator). The €1 200 000 debit balance in Manufacturing Overhead Control is the sum of all the actual costs incurred for manufacturing overhead in 2015. The €1 000 000 credit balance in Manufacturing Overhead Allocated results from 12 500 actual machine-hours worked on all the jobs in 2015 times the budgeted rate of €80 per hour.

The €200 000 difference (a net debit) is an underallocated amount because actual manufacturing overhead costs exceed the allocated amount. This €200 000 difference in 2015 arises from two reasons related to the computation of the €80 budgeted hourly rate:

1 *Numerator reason (budgeted indirect costs)*. Actual manufacturing overhead cost of €1 200 000 is less than the budgeted amount of €1 280 000.

2 *Denominator reason (budgeted quantity of allocation base)*. Actual machine-hours of 12 500 are less than the budgeted amount of 16 000 hours.

There are two main approaches to disposing of this €200 000 underallocation of manufacturing overhead in Wallace's costing system: (1) the adjusted allocation rate approach and (2) the proration approach.

Adjusted allocation rate approach

The adjusted allocation rate approach, in effect, restates all entries in the general ledger by using actual cost rates rather than budgeted cost rates. First, the actual indirect-cost rate is calculated at the end of each period. Then, every job to which indirect costs were allocated during the period has its amount recalculated using the actual indirect-cost rate (rather than the budgeted indirect-cost rate). Finally, end-of-period closing entries are made. The result is that every single job cost record – as well as the closing stock and cost of goods sold accounts – accurately represents actual indirect costs incurred.

The widespread adoption of computerised accounting systems has greatly reduced the cost of using the adjusted allocated rate approach. Consider the Wallace Company example. The actual manufacturing overhead (€1 200 000) exceeds the manufacturing overhead allocated (€1 000 000) by 20%. The actual 2015 manufacturing overhead rate was €96 per machine-hour (€1 200 000 ÷ 12 500 machine-hours) rather than the budgeted €80 per machine-hour. At year-end, Wallace could increase the 2015 manufacturing overhead allocated to each job in that year by 20% using a single software directive. The directive would apply to the subsidiary ledger as well as to the general ledger. This approach increases the accuracy of each individual product cost amount and the accuracy of the end-of-year account balances for stocks and cost of goods sold. This increase in accuracy is an important benefit. After-the-fact analysis of individual product profitability can provide managers with useful insights for future decisions about product pricing and about which products to emphasise. Such decisions are improved by having more accurate product-profitability numbers on prior jobs.

Proration approach

Proration is the term we use to refer to spreading of under- or overallocated overhead among closing stocks and cost of goods sold. Consider the Wallace Company where manufacturing overhead is allocated on the basis of machine-hours. Materials are not allocated any overhead costs. It is not until materials are put into work in progress that machining of them commences.

Only the closing work-in-progress and finished goods stocks will have an allocated manufacturing overhead component. Hence, in our Wallace example, it is only these two Closing Stock accounts (and Cost of Goods Sold) for which end-of-period proration is an issue. Assume the following actual results for the Wallace Company in 2015:

	End-of-year balances (before proration)	Manufacturing Overhead Allocated component of year-end balances (before proration)
Work in Progress	€50 000	€13 000
Finished Goods	75 000	25 000
Cost of Goods Sold	2 375 000	962 000
	€2 500 000	€1 000 000

There are three methods for prorating the underallocated €200 000 manufacturing overhead at the end of 2015.

Method 1

Proration is based on the total amount of indirect costs allocated (before proration) in the closing balances of Work in Progress, Finished Goods and Cost of Goods Sold. In our Wallace Company example, the €200 000 underallocated overhead is prorated over the three pertinent accounts in proportion to their total amount of indirect costs allocated (before proration) in column 3 in the following table, resulting in the closing balances (after proration) in column 5.

(1)	Account balance (before proration) (2)	Indirect costs allocated component in the balance in column (2) (3)		Proration of €200 000 Manufacturing Overhead Underallocated (4)		Account balance (after proration) (5) = (2) + (4)
Work in Progress	€50 000	€13 000	(1.3%)	0.013 × €200 000 =	€2 600	€52 600
Finished Goods	75 000	25 000	(2.5%)	0.025 × 200 000 =	5 000	80 000
Cost of Goods Sold	2 375 000	962 000	(96.2%)	0.962 × 200 000 =	192 400	2 567 400
	€2 500 000	€1 000 000	(100.0%)	1.000 ×	€200 000	€2 700 000

The journal entry for this proration would be:

Work-in-Progress Control	2 600	
Finished Goods Control	5 000	
Cost of Goods Sold	192 400	
Manufacturing Overhead Allocated	1 000 000	
Manufacturing Overhead Control		1 200 000

This journal entry results in the 2015 closing balances for Work in Progress, Finished Goods and Cost of Goods Sold being restated to what they would have been had actual cost rates rather than budgeted cost rates been used. Method 1 reports the same 2015 closing balances as does the adjusted allocation rate approach.

Method 2

Proration is based on total closing balances (before proration) in Work in Progress, Finished Goods and Cost of Goods Sold. In our Wallace Company example, the €200 000 underallocated overhead is prorated over the three pertinent accounts in proportion to their total closing balances (before proration) in column 2 in the following table, resulting in the closing balances (after proration) in column 4:

(1)	Account balance (before proration) (2)		Proration of €200 000 Manufacturing Overhead Underallocated (3)		Account balance (after proration) (4) = (2) + (3)
Work in Progress	€50 000	(2%)	0.02 × €200 000 =	€4 000	€54 000
Finished Goods	75 000	(3%)	0.03 × 200 000 =	6 000	81 000
Cost of Goods Sold	2 375 000	(95%)	0.95 × 200 000 =	190 000	2 565 000
	€2 500 000	100%	1.00	€200 000	€2 700 000

For example, work in progress is 2% of the €2 500 000 total, so we allocate 2% of the underallocated amount (0.02 × €200 000 = €4000) to work in progress.

The journal entry for this proration would be:

Work-in-Progress Control	4 000	
Finished Goods Control	6 000	
Cost of Goods Sold	190 000	
Manufacturing Overhead Allocated	1 000 000	
Manufacturing Overhead Control		1 200 000

Note that if manufacturing overhead had been overallocated, the Work in Progress, Finished Goods and Cost of Goods Sold accounts would be decreased (credited) instead of increased (debited).

Method 3

Proration is based on year-end write-off to Cost of Goods Sold. Here the total under- or overallocated overhead is included in this year's Cost of Goods Sold. In our Wallace Company example, the journal entry would be:

Cost of Goods Sold	200 000	
Manufacturing Overhead Allocated	1 000 000	
Manufacturing Overhead Control		1 200 000

Wallace's two Manufacturing Overhead accounts are closed out with all the difference between them now included in Cost of Goods Sold. The Cost of Goods Sold after proration is €2 375 000 before proration + €200 000 underallocated overhead amount = €2 575 000.

Choice among approaches

Choice among the approaches should be guided by how the resultant information is to be used. The reported account balances under the approaches are

		Proration approach		
	Proration based Adjusted allocation rate approach	Method 1: Proration on indirect costs allocated component of ending balances	Method 2: based on total ending balances	Method 3: Write-off to Cost of Goods Sold
Work in Progress	€52 600	€52 600	€54 000	€50 000
Finished Goods	80 000	80 000	81 000	75 000
Cost of Goods Sold	2 567 400	2 567 400	2 565 000	2 575 000
	€2 700 000	€2 700 000	€2 700 000	€2 700 000

If managers wish to develop the most accurate record of individual job costs for profitability analysis purposes, the adjusted allocation rate approach is preferred. The proration approaches do not make any adjustment to individual job cost records.

If the purpose is confined to reporting the most accurate stock and cost of goods sold figures, either the adjusted allocation rate or the method 1 proration should be used. Both give the same ending balances of Work in Progress, Finished Goods and Cost of Goods Sold that would have been reported had an actual indirect-cost rate been used. Method 2 is frequently justified as being a lower-cost way of approximating the results from method 1. The implicit assumption in method 2 is that the ratio of manufacturing overhead costs allocated to total manufacturing costs is similar in Work in Progress, Finished Goods and Cost of Goods Sold. Where this assumption is not appropriate, method 2 can yield numbers quite different from those of method 1. Many companies use method 3 for several reasons. First, it is the simplest. Second, the three methods often result in similar amounts for ending Work in Progress, Finished Goods and Cost of Goods Sold.

This section has examined end-of-period adjustments for under- or over-allocated indirect costs. The same issues also arise when budgeted direct-cost rates are used and end-of-period adjustments must be made.

Summary

The following points are linked to the chapter's learning objectives.

1 The building blocks of a costing system are cost object, direct costs, indirect costs, cost pool and cost-allocation base. Costing-system overview diagrams present these concepts in a systematic way. Costing systems aim to report cost numbers that reflect the way that chosen cost objects (such as products, services or customers) use the resources of an organisation.

2 Job-costing systems assign costs to a distinct unit of a product or service. In contrast, process-costing systems assign costs to masses of similar units and calculate unit costs on an average basis. These two costing systems are best viewed as opposite ends of a continuum. The costing systems of many companies combine some elements of both job costing and process costing.

3 A general approach to job costing involves identifying (a) the job, (b) the direct-cost categories, (c) the indirect-cost categories, (d) the cost-allocation bases, (e) the cost-allocation rates, and (f) adding all direct and indirect costs.

4 Actual costing and normal costing differ in their use of actual or budgeted indirect-cost rates.

	Actual costing	Normal costing
Direct-cost rates	Actual rates	Actual rates
Indirect-cost rates	Actual rates	Budgeted rates

Both methods use actual quantities of direct-cost inputs and actual quantities of the allocation bases for allocating indirect costs.

5 Costing systems aim to report cost numbers that reflect the way chosen cost objects use the resources of an organisation. This is the case for service, merchandising and manufacturing environments.

6 Three key source documents in a job-costing system are a job cost record, a materials requisition record and a labour time record.

7 The transactions in a job-costing system in manufacturing track (a) the acquisition of materials and other manufacturing inputs, (b) their conversion into work in progress, (c) their eventual conversion into finished goods, and (d) the sale of finished goods. Each of the stages (a) to (d) in the manufacture/sale cycle can be represented by journal entries in the costing system.

8 The theoretically correct alternative to disposing of under- or overallocated indirect costs is to prorate that amount on the basis of the total amount of the allocated indirect cost in the ending balances of stocks and cost of goods sold. For simplicity, many organisations write off any such amount to Cost of Goods Sold.

Key terms

cost pool (57)
cost-allocation base (57)
job-costing system (57)
process-costing system (57)
actual costing (59)
source documents (60)
normal costing (62)
job cost record (63)
job cost sheet (63)

materials requisition record (63)
labour time record (66)
manufacturing overhead allocated (70)
underabsorbed/underallocated/
    underapplied indirect costs (71)
overabsorbed/overallocated/overapplied
    indirect costs (71)
proration (72)

CHAPTER 3

Assessment material

Review questions

3.1 Define cost pool, cost tracing, cost allocation and cost allocation base.

3.2 'In the production of services, direct materials are usually the major cost.' Is this quote accurate? Explain.

3.3 How does a job-costing system differ from a process-costing system?

3.4 Why might an advertising agency use job costing for an advertising campaign for Pepsi while a bank uses process costing for the cost of current account withdrawals?

3.5 Distinguish between actual costing and normal costing.

3.6 What are two major goals of a job-costing system?

3.7 Describe the role of a manufacturing overhead allocation base in job costing.

3.8 Give two reasons for under- or overallocation of indirect costs at the end of an accounting period.

3.9 Describe alternative ways to prorate end-of-period adjustments for under- or overallocated indirect costs.

3.10 Why might a company prefer the adjusted allocation rate approach over a proration approach to under- or overallocated indirect costs?

Exercises

Basic level

*3.11 Computing indirect-cost rates, job costing (20–30 minutes)

Michel Scaramouche, the president of Tax-Assistance SA, is examining alternative ways to calculate indirect-cost rates. He collects the following information from the budget for the year:

- Budgeted variable indirect costs: €10 per hour of professional labour time
- Budgeted fixed indirect costs: €50 000 per quarter.

The budgeted billable professional labour-hours per quarter are:

January–March	20 000 hours
April–June	10 000 hours
July–September	4 000 hours
October–December	6 000 hours

Scaramouche pays all tax professionals employed by Tax-Assistance on an hourly basis (€30 per hour, including all fringe benefits).

Tax-Assistance's job-costing system has a single direct-cost category (professional labour at €30 per hour) and a single indirect-cost pool (office support that is allocated using professional labour-hours).

Tax-Assistance charges clients €65 per professional labour-hour.

Required

1 Calculate budgeted indirect-cost rates per professional labour-hour using:

   a Quarterly budgeted billable hours as the denominator
   b Annual budgeted billable hours as the denominator.

2 Calculate the operating profit for the following four customers using:

   a Quarterly-based indirect-cost rates
   b An annual indirect-cost rate:

   • Jean-Baptiste Roquelin: 10 hours in February
   • Violette Leduc: 6 hours in March and 4 hours in April
   • Alphonse Dudet: 4 hours in June and 6 hours in August
   • Francine Leclerc: 5 hours in January, 2 hours in September and 3 hours in November.

3 Comment on your results in requirement 2.

3.12   Computing direct-cost rates, consulting firm (15–20 minutes)

Zimmermann GmbH is an international consulting firm. Its annual budget includes the following for each category of professional labour:

Category	Average salary	Average fringe benefits	Billable time for clients (hours)	Vacation and sick leave (hours)	Professional development (hours)	Unbilled time due to lack of demand
Director	€140 000	€60 000	1 600	160	240	0
Partner	105 000	45 000	1 600	160	240	0
Associate	60 000	20 000	1 600	160	240	0
Assistant	38 000	12 000	1 600	160	240	0

Required

1 Calculate the budgeted direct-cost rate for professional labour (salary and fringe benefits) per hour for (a) directors, (b) partners, (c) associates, and (d) assistants. Use budgeted billable time for clients as the denominator in these computations.

2 Repeat requirement 1. Use the sum of budgeted billable time, vacation and sick leave time and professional development time as the denominator in these calculations.

3 Why are the rates different between requirements 1 and 2? How might these differences affect job costing by Zimmermann GmbH?

3.13   Accounting for manufacturing overhead (15 minutes)

Consider the following selected cost data for Schwarzmetal GmbH for 2015.

Budgeted manufacturing overhead	€7 000 000
Budgeted machine-hours	200 000
Actual manufacturing overhead	€6 800 000
Actual machine-hours	195 000

Schwarzmetal's job-costing system has a single manufacturing overhead cost pool (allocated using a budgeted rate based on actual machine-hours). Any amount of under- or overallocation is immediately written off to Cost of Goods Sold.

Required

1 Calculate the budgeted manufacturing overhead rate.

2 Journalise the allocation of manufacturing overhead.

3 Calculate the amount of under- or overallocation of manufacturing overhead. Is the amount significant? Journalise the disposition of this amount on the basis of the closing balances in the relevant accounts.

3.14 Proration of overhead (Z. Iqbal, adapted) (20 minutes)

Ti-Enne Srl uses a normal costing system with a single manufacturing overhead cost pool and machine-hours as the allocation base. The following data are for 2015:

Budgeted manufacturing overhead	€4 800 000
Overhead allocation base	Machine-hours
Budgeted machine-hours	80 000
Manufacturing overhead incurred	€4 900 000
Actual machine-hours	75 000

Machine-hours data and the closing balances (before proration of underallocated or overallocated overhead) are as follows:

	Actual machine-hours	2015 end-of-year balance
Cost of Goods Sold	60 000	€8 000 000
Finished Goods	11 000	€1 250 000
Work in Progress	4 000	€750 000

Required

1 Calculate the budgeted manufacturing overhead rate for 2015.

2 Calculate the under- or overallocated manufacturing overhead of Ti-Enne in 2015. Prorate this under- or overallocated amount using:

   a Immediate write-off to Cost of Goods Sold

   b Proration based on closing balances (before proration) in Work in Progress, Finished Goods and Cost of Goods Sold

   c Proration based on the allocated overhead amount (before proration) in the closing balances of Work in Progress, Finished Goods and Cost of Goods Sold.

3 Which proration method do you prefer in requirement 2? Explain.

3.15 Job costing with single direct-cost category, single indirect-cost pool, law firm (15–20 minutes)

Tricheur et Associés is a recently formed law partnership. Jean Racine, the managing partner of Tricheur et Associés, has just finished a tense telephone call with Blaise Rascal, president of Morges-Guyère, Sarl. Rascal complained about the price Tricheur charged for some conveyancing legal work done for Morges-Guyère. He requested a breakdown of the charges. He also indicated to Racine that a competing law firm, Andrault & Maque, was seeking more business with Morges-Guyère and that he was going to ask them to bid for a conveyancing job next month. Rascal ended the telephone call by saying that if Tricheur bid a price similar to the one charged last month, Tricheur would not be hired for next month's job.

Racine is dismayed by the telephone call. He is also puzzled because he believes that conveyancing is an area where Tricheur et Associés has much expertise and is highly efficient. The Morges-Guyère telephone call is the bad news of the week. The good news is that yesterday Racine received a call from its only other client (Verrerie de Lausanne) saying it was very pleased with both the quality of the work (primarily litigation) and the price charged on its most recent case.

Racine decides to collect data on the Morges-Guyère and Verrerie de Lausanne cases. Tricheur et Associés uses a cost-based approach to pricing (billing) each legal case. Currently, it uses a single direct-cost category (for professional labour time) and a single indirect cost pool (general support). Indirect costs are allocated to cases on the basis of professional labour-hours per case. The case files show the following:

	Morges-Guyère	Verrerie de Lausanne
Professional labour time	104 hours	96 hours

Professional labour costs at Tricheur et Associés are €70 an hour. Indirect costs are allocated to cases at €105 an hour. Total indirect costs in the most recent period were €21 000.

Required

1 Why is it important for Tricheur et Associés to understand the costs associated with individual cases?

2 Present an overview diagram of the existing job-costing system.

3 Calculate the costs of the Morges-Guyère and Verrerie de Lausanne cases.

3.16 Job costing: fill in the blanks (20–30 minutes)

Eldorado SA is a management consulting firm. Its job-costing system has a single direct-cost category (consulting labour) and a single indirect cost pool (consulting support). Consulting support is allocated to individual jobs using actual consulting labour-hours worked on a job. It is currently examining the actual and normal costs of a strategy review job for Pablo Café that required 70 actual hours of consulting labour. The internal cost expert decides to test your understanding of cost concepts.

Required

1 Fill in the blanks for the Pablo Café job:

	Actual costing		Normal costing	
Direct job costs	€ ?	(€55 × ?)	€ ?	(€ ? × ?)
Indirect job costs	2 660	(€ ? × ?)	2 800	(€ ? × 70)
Total job costs	€ ?		€ ?	

2 Fill in the blanks for Eldorado:

	Budgeted amounts for 2015	Actual amounts for 2015
Consulting labour compensation	?	?
Consulting labour-hours	18 000 hours	?
Consulting support costs	?	€798 000

*3.17 Job costing, normal and actual costing (20 minutes)

Idergard AB assembles residential homes. It uses a job-costing system with two direct-cost categories (direct materials and direct labour) and one indirect cost pool (assembly support). Direct labour-hours is the allocation base for assembly support costs. In December 2014, Peterson budgets 2015 assembly support costs to be SKr 8 000 000 and 2015 direct labour-hours to be 160 000.

At the end of 2015, Idergard is comparing the costs of several jobs that were started and completed in 2015.

Construction period	Mora model February–June 2015	Solna model May–October 2015
Direct materials	SKr 106 450	SKr 127 604
Direct labour	SKr 36 276	SKr 41 410
Direct labour-hours	900	1 010

Direct materials and direct labour are paid for on a contract basis. The costs of each are known when direct materials are used or direct labour-hours are worked. The 2015 actual assembly support costs were SKr 6 888 000 while the actual direct labour-hours were 164 000.

Required

1 Calculate the (a) budgeted and (b) actual indirect-cost rates. Why do they differ?

2 What is the job cost of the Mora model and the Solna model using (a) normal costing and (b) actual costing?

3 Why might Idergard Construction prefer normal costing over actual costing?

3.18 Job costing, journal entries (30 minutes)

The Editions Sorbonne is wholly owned by the university. It performs the bulk of its work for other university departments, which pay as though the Editions Sorbonne were an outside business enterprise. The Editions Sorbonne also publishes and maintains a stock of books for general sale. A job-costing system is used to cost each job. There are two direct-cost categories (direct materials and direct manufacturing labour) and one indirect cost pool (manufacturing overhead, allocated on the basis of direct-labour costs).

The following data (in €000) pertain to 2015:

Direct materials and supplies purchased on account	€800
Direct materials used	710
Indirect materials issued to various production departments	100
Direct manufacturing labour	1300
Indirect manufacturing labour incurred by various departments	900
Depreciation on building and manufacturing equipment	400
Miscellaneous manufacturing overhead* incurred by various departments	550
(ordinarily would be detailed as repairs, photocopying, utilities, etc.)	
Manufacturing overhead allocated at 160% of direct manufacturing labour costs	?
Cost of goods manufactured	4120
Revenues	8000
Cost of goods sold	4020
Stock, 31 December 2014:	
Materials control	100
Work-in-progress control	60
Finished goods control	500

* The term 'manufacturing overhead' is not used uniformly. Other terms that are often encountered in printing companies include 'job overhead' and 'shop overhead'.

Required

1 Present an overview diagram of the job-costing system at the Editions Sorbonne.

2 Prepare general journal entries to summarise 2015 transactions. As your final entry, dispose of the year-end over- or underallocated manufacturing overhead as a direct write-off to Cost of Goods Sold. Number your entries. Explanations for each entry may be omitted.

3 Show posted T-accounts for all stocks, Cost of Goods Sold, Manufacturing Overhead Control and Manufacturing Overhead Allocated.

For more details concerning these data, see Exercise 3.19.

3.19   Job costing, journal entries and source documents (continuation of Exercise 3.18)
(20 minutes)

For each journal entry in your answer to Exercise 3.18, (a) indicate the source document that would most probably authorise the entry and (b) give a description of the entry into the subsidiary ledgers, if any entry needs to be made there.

*3.20   Job costing, engineering consulting firm (20–35 minutes)

Solucions SA, an engineering consulting firm, specialises in analysing the structural causes of major building catastrophes. Its job-costing system in 2015 had a single direct-cost category (professional labour) and a single indirect-cost pool (general support). The allocation base for indirect costs is professional labour-costs. Actual costs for 2015 were:

Direct costs	
Professional labour	€100 million
Indirect costs	
General support	190 million
Total costs	€290 million

The following costs were included in the general support indirect cost pool:

Technical specialists' costs	€8 million
Telephone/fax machine	6 million
Computer time	37 million
Photocopying	4 million
Total costs	€55 million

The firm's data-processing capabilities now make it feasible to trace these costs to individual jobs. The managing partner is considering whether more costs than just professional labour should be traced to each job as a direct cost. In this way, the firm would be better able to justify billings to clients.

In late 2015, arrangements were made to expand the number of direct-cost categories and to trace them to seven client engagements. Two of the case records showed the following:

	Client case 304	Client case 308
Professional labour	€200 000	€200 000
Technical specialists' costs	20 000	60 000
Telephone/fax machine	10 000	20 000
Computer time	20 000	40 000
Photocopying	10 000	20 000
Total direct costs	€260 000	€340 000

Required

1 Present an overview diagram of the 2015 job-costing system. What was the actual indirect cost rate per professional labour-euro?

2 Assume that the €55 million of costs included in the 2015 general-support indirect cost pool were reclassified as direct costs. The result is a system with five direct-cost categories. Calculate the revised indirect-cost rate as a percentage of:

a Professional labour-costs.
b Total direct costs.

3 Calculate the total costs of jobs 304 and 308 using:

a The 2015 costing system with a single direct-cost category and a single indirect cost pool (professional labour-costs as the allocation base)

b A costing system with five direct-cost categories and a single indirect cost pool (professional labour-costs as the allocation base)

c A costing system with five direct-cost categories and a single indirect cost pool (total direct costs as the allocation base).

4 Assume that clients are billed at 120% of total job costs (that is, a mark-up on cost of 20%). Calculate the billings in requirement 3 for jobs 304 and 308 for the (a), (b) and (c) costing systems.

5 Which method of job costing in requirement 3 do you favour? Explain.

3.21 Job costing, accounting for manufacturing overhead, budgeted rates (25–30 minutes)

Giannacopoulos SA uses a job-costing system at its Korinthos plant. The plant has a Machining Department and an Assembly Department. Its job-costing system has two direct-cost categories (direct materials and direct manufacturing labour) and two manufacturing overhead cost pools (the Machining Department, allocated using actual machine-hours, and the Assembly Department, allocated using actual labour cost). The 2015 budget for the plant is as follows:

	Machining Department	Assembly Department
Manufacturing overhead	€1 800 000	€3 600 000
Direct manufacturing labour cost	€1 400 000	€2 000 000
Direct manufacturing labour-hours	€100 000	€200 000
Machine-hours	50 000	200 000

Required

1 Present an overview diagram of Giannacopoulos's job-costing system. What is the budgeted overhead rate that should be used in the Machining Department? In the Assembly Department?

2 During the month of February, the cost record for Job 494 shows the following:

	Machining Department	Assembly Department
Direct material used	€45 000	€70 000
Direct manufacturing labour cost	€14 000	€15 000
Direct manufacturing labour-hours	1 000	1 500
Machine-hours	2 000	1 000

What is the total manufacturing overhead allocated to Job 494?

3 Balances at the end of 2015 are as follows:

	Machining Department	Assembly Department
Manufacturing overhead incurred	€2 100 000	€3 700 000
Direct manufacturing labour cost	–	€2 200 000
Machine-hours	55 000	–

Calculate the under- or overallocated manufacturing overhead for each department.

3.22   Overview of general-ledger relationships (30–40 minutes)

Budenmayer BV is a small machine shop that uses highly skilled labour and a job-costing system (using normal costing). The total debits and credits in certain accounts just before year-end are as follows:

	30 December 2015	
	Total debits	**Total credits**
Materials Control	€100 000	€70 000
Work-in-Progress Control	320 000	305 000
Manufacturing Department Overhead Control	85 000	–
Finished Goods Control	325 000	300 000
Cost of Goods Sold	300 000	–
Manufacturing Overhead Allocated	–	90 000

All materials purchased are for direct materials. Note that 'total debits' in the stock accounts would include beginning stock balances, if any.

The preceding accounts do not include the following:

a The manufacturing labour costs recapitulation for the 31 December working day: direct manufacturing labour, €5000 and indirect manufacturing labour, €1000.

b Miscellaneous manufacturing overhead incurred on 30 December and 31 December: €1000.

Additional information

- Manufacturing overhead has been allocated as a percentage of direct manufacturing labour costs through 30 December.
- Direct materials purchased during 2015 were €85 000.
- There were no returns to suppliers.
- Direct manufacturing labour costs during 2015 totalled €150 000, not including the 31 December working day described previously.

Required

1 Calculate the stock (31 December 2014) of Materials Control, Work-in-Progress Control and Finished Goods Control. Show T-accounts.

2 Prepare all adjusting and closing journal entries for the preceding accounts. Assume that all under- or overallocated manufacturing overhead is closed directly to Cost of Goods Sold.

3 Calculate the ending stock (31 December 2015), after adjustments and closing, of Materials Control, Work-in-Progress Control and Finished Goods Control.

CHAPTER 4

Process-costing systems

A process-costing system is a costing system in which the cost of a product or service is obtained by assigning costs to masses of like or similar units. Unit costs are then calculated on an average basis. Process-costing systems are used in industries that cost like or similar units of products, which are often mass produced. In these industries, relatively homogeneous products are processed in a very similar manner. Industries using process costing in their manufacturing area include chemical processing, oil refining, pharmaceuticals, plastics, brick and tile manufacturing, semiconductor chips, and breakfast cereals.

The principal difference between process costing and job costing is the extent of averaging used to calculate unit costs of products or services. The cost object in a job-costing system is a job that constitutes a distinctly identifiable product or service. Individual jobs use different quantities of manufacturing resources, so it would be incorrect to cost each job at the same average manufacturing cost. In contrast, when like or similar units are mass produced and not processed as individual jobs, process costing averages manufacturing costs over all units produced.

Knowing what products cost is important information for stock valuation, pricing decisions and product profitability analysis. Companies also use product costs to measure how well they are doing in managing and reducing costs. For example, SABMiller, one of the world's leading brewing and beverage companies with more than 200 beer brands and over 70 000 employees across 75 countries, makes extensive use of process costing. It compiles information from brewing and packaging operations and tracks beer movement and quality measures. Process-costing information allows SABMiller to prepare and monitor beer loss reports.

Organisations which produce similar products can be very complex. Consider, for instance, the view of the former CEO of the world's seventh largest oil company, Peter Voser, of Royal Dutch Shell. He complained in a company-wide memo that costs were too high, the organisation was too complex and its culture too 'consensus-oriented'. He called for a 'strong performance ethic' by which he meant:

> I like to keep things simple and clear in the way I run the company. For me, execution needs to be competitive. It's about absolute clarity on strategy and what you want on operational performance. Everyone needs to know what is expected of them.
>
> (Peter Voser, cited in Gumbel 2009, p. 79)

We consider strategy issues in later chapters.

As we examine process costing in this chapter, we will be concerned only incidentally with controlling and managing costs and evaluating performance. Our primary focus is on determining the cost of products or services and on stock and cost of goods sold valuation. Operation costing as applied to batches of similar products is discussed in the appendix to this chapter.

Learning objectives

After studying this chapter, you should be able to:

- Recognise when process-costing systems are appropriate
- Describe key steps in process costing
- Calculate and use equivalent units
- Prepare journal entries for process-costing systems
- Demonstrate the weighted-average method of process costing
- Use the first-in, first-out (FIFO) method of process costing
- Show how standard costs simplify process costing
- Apply process-costing methods to cases with transferred-in costs

Illustrating process costing

In a **process-costing system**, the unit cost of a product or service is obtained by assigning total costs to many identical or similar units. In a manufacturing process-costing setting, each unit is assumed to receive the same amount of direct materials costs, direct manufacturing labour costs and indirect manufacturing costs. Unit costs are then calculated by dividing total costs by the number of units.

The principal difference between process costing and job costing is the *extent of averaging* used to calculate unit costs of products or services. In a job-costing system, individual jobs use different quantities of production resources. Thus, it would be incorrect to cost each job at the same average production cost. In contrast, when identical or similar units of products or services are mass produced, and not processed as individual jobs, process costing averages production costs over all units produced.

The easiest way to learn process costing is by example. Consider the following illustration.

Example 4.1

Euro-Défense SA manufactures thousands of components for missiles and military equipment. These components are assembled in the Assembly Department. Upon completion, the units are immediately transferred to the Testing Department. We will focus on the Assembly Department process for one of these components, DG-19. Every effort is made to ensure that all DG-19 units are identical and meet a set of demanding performance specifications. The process-costing system for DG-19 in the Assembly Department has a single direct-cost category (direct materials) and a single indirect-cost category (conversion costs). **Conversion costs** are all manufacturing costs other than direct material costs. These include manufacturing labour, indirect materials, energy, plant depreciation, and so on. Direct materials are added at the beginning of the process in Assembly. Conversion costs are added evenly during Assembly. These facts are summarised in Exhibit 4.1.

Process-costing systems separate costs into cost categories according to the timing of when costs are introduced into the process. Often, as in our Euro-Défense example, only two cost classifications, direct materials and conversion costs, are necessary to assign costs to products. Why? Because *all* direct materials are added to the process at one time and *all* conversion costs are generally added to the process uniformly through time. If, however, two different direct materials are added to the process at different times, two different direct material categories would be needed to assign these costs to products. Similarly, if manufacturing labour is added to the process at a

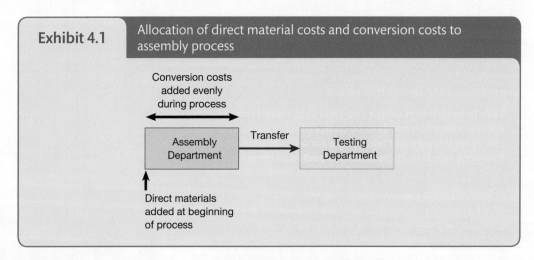

Exhibit 4.1   Allocation of direct material costs and conversion costs to assembly process

time that is different from other conversion costs, an additional cost category (direct manufacturing labour costs) would be needed to separately assign these costs to products.

We will use the production of the DG-19 component in the Assembly Department to illustrate process costing in three cases:

1 Process costing with zero opening and zero closing work-in-progress stock of DG-19, that is, all units are started and fully completed by the end of the accounting period. *This case presents the most basic concepts of process costing and illustrates the key feature of averaging of costs.*

2 Process costing with zero opening work-in-progress stock but some closing work-in-progress stock of DG-19, that is, some units of DG-19 started during the accounting period are incomplete at the end of the period. *This case builds on the basics and introduces the concept of equivalent units.*

3 Process costing with both some opening and some closing work-in-progress stock of DG-19. *This case adds more detail and describes the effect of weighted-average and first-in, first-out (FIFO) cost flow assumptions on cost of units completed and cost of work-in-progress stock.*

We start with the simple case and work towards the more detailed and more complex cases.

Case 1: Process costing with no opening or closing work-in-progress stock

On 1 January 2015, there was no opening stock of DG-19 units in the Assembly Department. During January 2015, Euro-Défense started, completed assembly of, and transferred out to the Testing Department, 400 DG-19 units.

Data for the Assembly Department for January 2015 are:

Physical units for January 2015	
Work in progress, opening stock (1 January)	0 units
Started during January	400 units
Completed and transferred out during January	400 units
Work in progress, closing stock (31 January)	0 units
Total costs for January 2015	
Direct material costs added during January	€32 000
Conversion costs added during January	24 000
Total Assembly Department costs added during January	€56 000

Euro-Défense records direct material and conversion costs in the Assembly Department as these costs are incurred. By averaging, the assembly costs per unit of DG-19 are €56 000 ÷ 400 units = €140, itemised as follows:

Direct material costs per unit (€32 000 ÷ 400)	€80
Conversion costs per unit (€24 000 ÷ 400)	60
Assembly Department costs per unit	€140

This case shows that in a process-costing system, unit costs can be averaged by dividing total costs in a given accounting period by total units produced in that period. Because each unit is identical, we assume all units receive the same amount of direct materials and conversion costs. This approach can be used by any company that produces a homogeneous product or service but has no incomplete units when each accounting period ends. This situation frequently occurs in service-sector organisations. For example, a bank can adopt this process-costing approach to calculate the unit cost of processing 100 000 similar customer deposits made in a month.

Case 2: Process costing with no opening but a closing work-in-progress stock

In February 2015, Euro-Défense places another 400 units of DG-19 into production. Because all units placed into production in January 2015 were completely assembled, there is no opening stock of partially completed units in the Assembly Department on 1 February 2015. Customer delays in placing orders for DG-19 prevent the complete assembly of all units started in February. Only 175 units are completed and transferred out to the Testing Department.

Data for the Assembly Department for February 2015 are:

Physical units for February 2015

Work in progress, opening stock (1 February)	0 units
Started during February	400 units
Completed and transferred out	175 units
Work in progress, closing stock (28 February)	225 units

The 225 partially assembled units as of 28 February 2015 are fully processed with respect to direct materials. Why? Because all direct materials in the Assembly Department are added at the beginning of the assembly process. Conversion costs, however, are added evenly during the assembly process. Based on the work completed relative to the total work required to complete the DG-19 units still in the process, an Assembly Department supervisor estimates that the partially assembled units are, on average, 60% complete as to conversion costs.

Total costs for February 2015

Direct material costs added during February	€32 000
Conversion costs added during February	18 600
Total Assembly Department costs added during February	€50 600

The accuracy of the completion percentages depends on the care and skill of the estimator and the nature of the process. Estimating the degree of completion is usually easier for direct materials than it is for conversion costs because the quantity of direct materials needed for a completed unit and the quantity of direct materials for a partially completed unit can be measured more easily. In contrast, the conversion sequence usually consists of a number of basic operations for a specified number of hours, days or weeks, for various steps in assembly, testing, and so forth. Thus, the degree of completion for conversion costs depends on what proportion of the total effort needed to complete one unit or one batch of production has been devoted to units still in progress. This estimate is more difficult to make accurately. Because of the difficulties in estimating conversion cost completion percentages, department supervisors and line managers – individuals most familiar with the process – often make these estimates. Still, in some industries no exact estimate is possible or, as in the textile industry, vast quantities in progress prohibit the making of costly physical estimates. In these cases, all work in progress in every department is assumed to be complete to some reasonable degree (for example, one-third, one-half or two-thirds complete).

The key point to note in Case 2 is that a partially assembled unit is not the same as a fully assembled unit. Faced with some fully assembled and some partially assembled units, how should Euro-Défense calculate (1) the cost of fully assembled units in February 2015, and (2) the cost of the partially assembled units still in progress at the end of February 2015?

Euro-Défense calculates these costs by using the following five steps:

- Step 1: Summarise the flow of physical units of output.
- Step 2: Compute output in terms of equivalent units.
- Step 3: Compute equivalent unit costs.
- Step 4: Summarise total costs to account for.
- Step 5: Assign total costs to units completed and to units in closing work in progress.

Physical units and equivalent units (steps 1 and 2)

Step 1 tracks the physical units of output. Where did the units come from? Where did the units go? The physical units column of Exhibit 4.2 tracks where the physical units came from – 400 units started, and where they went – 175 units completed and transferred out, and 225 units in closing stock.

Step 2 focuses on how the output for February should be measured. The output is 175 fully assembled units plus 225 partially assembled units. Since all 400 physical units are not uniformly completed, output in step 2 is computed in *equivalent units*, not in physical units.

Equivalent units is a derived amount of output units that takes the quantity of each input (factor of production) in units completed or in work in progress, and converts it into the amount of completed output units that could be made with that quantity of input. For example, if 50 physical units of a product in closing work-in-progress stock are 70% complete with respect to conversion costs, there are 35 (70% × 50) equivalent units of output for conversion costs. That is, if all the conversion cost input in the 50 units in stock were used to make completed output units, the company would be able to make 35 completed units of output. Equivalent units are calculated separately for each input (cost category). Examples of equivalent-unit concepts are also found in non-manufacturing settings. For instance, universities often convert their part-time student enrolments into full-time student equivalents.

Exhibit 4.2	Steps 1 and 2: Summarise output in physical units and calculate equivalent units, Assembly Department of Euro-Défense SA, for February 2015		
	(Step 1)	**(Step 2) Equivalent units**	
Flow of production	**Physical units**	**Direct materials**	**Conversion costs**
Work in progress, opening	0		
Started during current period	400		
To account for	400		
Completed and transferred out during current period	175	175	175
Work in progress, closing*	225		
225 × 100%; 225 × 60%		225	135
Accounted for	400		
Work done in current period only		400	310

* Degree of completion in this department: direct materials, 100%; conversion costs, 60%.

When calculating equivalent units in step 2, focus on quantities. Disregard euro-amounts until after equivalent units are computed. In the Euro-Défense example, all 400 physical units – the 175 fully assembled ones and the 225 partially assembled ones – are complete in terms of equivalent units of direct materials. Why? Because all direct materials are added in the Assembly Department at the initial stage of the process. Exhibit 4.2 shows output as 400 *equivalent* units for direct materials because all 400 units are fully complete with respect to direct materials.

The 175 fully assembled units are completely processed with respect to conversion costs. The partially assembled units in closing work in progress are 60% complete (on average). Therefore, the conversion costs in the 225 partially assembled units are *equivalent* to conversion costs in 135 (60% of 225) fully assembled units. Hence, Exhibit 4.2 shows output as 310 *equivalent* units with respect to conversion costs – 175 equivalent units assembled and transferred out and 135 equivalent units in closing work-in-progress stock.

Calculation of product costs (steps 3, 4 and 5)

Exhibit 4.3 shows steps 3, 4 and 5. Together, they are called the *production cost worksheet*. Step 3 calculates equivalent-unit costs by dividing direct materials and conversion costs added during February by the related quantity of equivalent units of work done in February (as calculated in Exhibit 4.2).

We can see the importance of using equivalent units in unit-cost calculations by comparing conversion costs for the months of January and February 2015. Observe that the total conversion costs of €18 600 for the 400 units worked on during February are less than the conversion costs of €24 000 for the 400 units worked on in January. However, the conversion costs to fully assemble a unit are €60 in both January and February. Total conversion costs are lower in February because fewer equivalent units of conversion costs work were completed in February (310) than were in January (400). If, however, we had used *physical* units instead of *equivalent* units in the per-unit calculation, we would have erroneously concluded that conversion costs per unit declined from €60 in January to €46.50 (€18 600 ÷ 400) in February. This incorrect costing might have prompted Euro-Défense, for example, to lower the price of DG-19 inappropriately.

Exhibit 4.3	Steps 3, 4 and 5: Calculate equivalent-unit costs, summarise total costs to account for, and assign costs to units completed and to units in closing work in progress, Assembly Department of Euro-Défense SA, for February 2015		
		Total production costs	**Direct materials**	**Conversion costs**

		Total production costs	Direct materials	Conversion costs
(Step 3)	Costs added during February	€50 600	€32 000	€18 600
	Divide by equivalent units of work done in current period (Exhibit 4.2)		÷ 400	÷ 310
	Cost per equivalent unit		€80	€60
(Step 4)	Total costs to account for	€50 600		
(Step 5)	Assignment of costs:			
	Completed and transferred out (175 units)	€24 500	(175* × €80) + (175* × €60)	
	Work in progress, closing (225 units):			
	Direct materials	18 000	225† × €80	
	Conversion costs	8 100		135† × €60
	Total work in progress	26 100		
	Total costs accounted for	€50 600		

* Equivalent units completed and transferred out from Exhibit 4.1, step 2.
† Equivalent units in closing work in progress from Exhibit 4.1, step 2.

Step 4 in Exhibit 4.3 summarises total costs to account for. Because the opening balance of the work in progress is zero, total costs to account for (that is, the total charges or debits to Work in Progress – Assembly) consist of the costs added during February – direct materials of €32 000, and conversion costs of €18 600, for a total of €50 600.

Step 5 in Exhibit 4.3 assigns these costs to units completed and transferred out and to units still in process at the end of February 2015. *The key idea is to attach euro amounts to the equivalent output units for direct materials and conversion costs in (a) units completed, and (b) closing work in progress calculated in Exhibit 4.2, step 2. To do so, the equivalent output units for each input are multiplied by the cost per equivalent unit calculated in step 3 of Exhibit 4.3.* For example, the 225 physical units in closing work in progress are completely processed with respect to direct materials. Therefore, direct materials costs are 225 equivalent units (Exhibit 4.2, step 2) × €80 (cost per equivalent of direct materials calculated in step 3), which equals €18 000. In contrast, the 225 physical units are 60% complete with respect to conversion costs. Therefore, the conversion costs are 135 equivalent units (60% of 225 physical units, Exhibit 4.2, step 2) × €60 (cost per equivalent unit of conversion costs calculated in step 3), which equals €8100. The total cost of ending work in progress equals €26 100 (€18 000 + €8100).

Journal entries

Journal entries in process-costing systems are basically like those made in job-costing systems with respect to direct materials and conversion costs. The main difference is that, in process costing, there is often more than one Work-in-Progress account, one for each process – in our example, Work in Progress – Assembly and Work in Progress – Testing. Euro-Défense purchases direct materials as needed. These materials are delivered directly to the Assembly Department. Using euro amounts from Exhibit 4.3, summary journal entries for the month of February at Euro-Défense are:

1 Work in Progress – Assembly   32 000
    Creditors Control   32 000

    To record direct materials purchased and used in production
    during February

2 Work in Progress – Assembly   18 600
    Various accounts   18 600

    To record Assembly Department conversion costs for February;
    examples include energy, manufacturing supplies, all
    manufacturing labour and plant depreciation

3 Work in Progress – Testing   24 500
    Work in Progress – Assembly   24 500

    To record cost of goods completed and transferred from Assembly to
    Testing during February

Exhibit 4.4 shows a general framework for the flow of costs through the T-accounts. Notice how entry 3 for €24 500 follows the physical transfer of goods from the Assembly to the Testing Department. The key T-account, Work in Progress – Assembly, shows a closing balance of €26 100, which is the opening balance of Work in Progress – Assembly in March 2015.

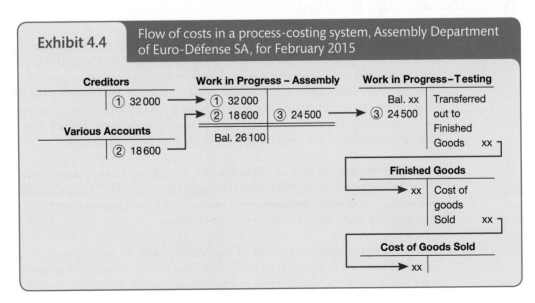

Exhibit 4.4 Flow of costs in a process-costing system, Assembly Department of Euro-Défense SA, for February 2015

Case 3: Process costing with both some opening and some closing work-in-progress stock

At the beginning of March 2015, Euro-Défense had 225 partially assembled DG-19 units in the Assembly Department. During March 2015, Euro-Défense placed another 275 units into production. Data for the Assembly Department for March 2015 are:

Physical units for March 2015	
Work in progress, opening stock (1 March)	225 units
Direct materials (100% complete)	
Conversion costs (60% complete)	
Started during March	275 units
Completed and transferred out during March	400 units
Work in progress, closing stock (31 March)	100 units
Direct materials (100% complete)	
Conversion costs (50% complete)	

Total costs for March 2015		
Work in progress, opening stock		
Direct materials (225 equivalent units × €80 per unit)	€18 000	
Conversion costs (135 equivalent units × €60 per unit)	8 100	€26 100
Direct material costs added during March		19 800
Conversion costs added during March		16 380
Total costs to account for		€62 280

We now have incomplete units in both opening and closing work-in-progress stock to account for. Our goal is to use the five steps we described earlier to calculate (1) the cost of units completed and transferred out, and (2) the cost of closing work in progress. To assign costs to each of these categories, however, we need to choose a stock cost-flow method. We next describe the five-step approach to process costing using two alternative stock cost-flow methods – the weighted-average method and the first-in, first-out method. The different assumptions will produce different numbers for cost of units completed and for closing work in progress.

Weighted-average method

The **weighted-average process-costing method** calculates the equivalent-unit cost of the *work done to date* (regardless of the period in which it was done) and assigns this cost to equivalent units completed and transferred out of the process and to equivalent units in closing work-in-progress stock. The weighted-average cost is the total of all costs entering the Work in Progress account (regardless of whether it is from opening work in progress or from work started during the period) divided by total equivalent units of work done to date. We now describe the five-step procedure introduced in Case 2 using the weighted-average method.

Step 1: Summarise the flow of physical units The physical units column of Exhibit 4.5 shows where the units came from – 225 units from opening stock and 275 units started during the current period – and where they went – 400 units completed and transferred out and 100 units in closing stock. These data for March were given above.

Step 2: Compute output in terms of equivalent units As we saw in Case 2, even partially assembled units are complete in terms of direct materials because direct materials are introduced at the beginning of the process. For conversion costs, the fully assembled physical units transferred

	(Step 1)	(Step 2) Equivalent units	
Flow of production	**Physical units (given p. 000)**	**Direct materials**	**Conversion costs**
Work in progress, opening	225		
Started during current period	275		
To account for	500		
Completed and transferred out during current period	400	400	400
Work in progress, closing*	100		
100 × 100%; 100 × 50%		100	50
Accounted for	500		
Work done to date		500	450

Exhibit 4.5 — Steps 1 and 2: Summarise output in physical units and calculate equivalent units, weighted-average method of process costing, Assembly Department of Euro-Défense SA, for March 2015

* Degree of completion in this department: direct materials, 100%; conversion costs, 50%.

out are, of course, fully completed. The Assembly Department supervisor estimates the partially assembled physical units in March 31 work in progress to be 50% complete (on average).

The equivalent-units columns in Exhibit 4.5 show the equivalent units of work done to date – equivalent units completed and transferred out and equivalent units in closing work in progress (500 equivalent units of direct materials and 450 equivalent units of conversion costs). Notice that the equivalent units of work done to date also equal the sum of the equivalent units in opening stock (work done in the previous period) and the equivalent units of work done in the current period, because:

$$\begin{array}{c}\text{Equivalent units} \\ \text{in opening} \\ \text{work in progress}\end{array} + \begin{array}{c}\text{Equivalent units} \\ \text{of work done in} \\ \text{current period}\end{array} = \begin{array}{c}\text{Equivalent units} \\ \text{completed and} \\ \text{transferred out} \\ \text{in current period}\end{array} + \begin{array}{c}\text{Equivalent units} \\ \text{in closing} \\ \text{work in progress}\end{array}$$

The equivalent-unit calculation in the weighted-average method is concerned only with total equivalent units of *work done to date* regardless of (1) whether the work was done during the previous period and is part of opening work in progress, or (2) whether it was done during the current period. That is, the weighted-average method *merges* equivalent units in opening stock (work done before March) with equivalent units of work done in the current period. Thus, the stage of completion of the current-period opening work in progress *per se* is *irrelevant* and *not* used in the calculation.

Step 3: Compute equivalent-unit costs Exhibit 4.6, step 3, shows the calculation of equivalent-unit costs separately for direct materials and conversion costs. The weighted-average cost per equivalent unit is obtained by dividing the sum of costs for opening work in progress and costs for work done in the current period by total equivalent units of work done to date. When calculating the weighted-average conversion cost per equivalent unit in Exhibit 4.6, for example, we divide total conversion costs, €24 480 (opening work in progress, €8100, plus work done in current period, €16 380) by total equivalent units, 450 (equivalent units of conversion costs in opening work in progress and in work done in current period), to get a weighted-average cost per equivalent unit of €54.40.

Exhibit 4.6	Steps 3, 4 and 5: Calculate equivalent-unit costs, summarise total costs to account for, and assign costs to units completed and to units in closing work in progress, weighted-average method of process costing, Assembly Department of Euro-Défense SA, for March 2015

		Total production costs	Direct materials	Conversion costs
(Step 3)	Work in progress, opening (given p. 92)	€26 100	€18 000	€8 100
	Cost added in current period (given p. 92)	36 180	19 800	16 380
	Cost incurred to date		€37 800	€24 480
	Divide by equivalent units of work done to date (Exhibit 4.5)		÷ 500	÷ 450
	Cost per equivalent unit of work done to date		€75.60	€54.40
(Step 4)	Total costs to account for	€62 280		
(Step 5)	Assignment of costs:			
	Completed and transferred out (400 units)	52 000	(400* × €75.60) + (400* × €54.40)	
	Work in progress, closing (100 units):			
	Direct materials	7 560	100† × €75.60	
	Conversion costs	2 720		50† × €54.40
	Total work in progress	10 280		
	Total costs accounted for	€62 280		

* Equivalent units completed and transferred out from Exhibit 4.5, step 2.
† Equivalent units in closing work in progress from Exhibit 4.5, step 2.

Step 4: Summarise total costs to account for The total costs to account for in March 2015 are described in the example data on page 92 – opening work in progress, €26 100 (direct materials, €18 000 and conversion costs, €8100) plus €36 180 (direct material costs added during March, €19 800, and conversion costs, €16 380). The total of these costs is €62 280.

Step 5: Assign these costs to units completed and to units in closing work in progress The key point in this step is to cost all work done to date: (1) the cost of units completed and transferred out of the process, and (2) the cost of closing work in progress. Step 5 in Exhibit 4.6 takes the equivalent units completed and transferred out and equivalent units in closing work in progress calculated in Exhibit 4.5 step 2, and attaches euro amounts to them. These euro amounts are the weighted-average costs per equivalent unit for direct materials and conversion costs calculated in step 3. For example, note that the total cost of the 100 physical units in closing work in progress consists of:

Direct materials:
  100 equivalent units × Weighted-average cost per equivalent unit of €75.60   €7 560
Conversion costs:
  50 equivalent units × Weighted-average cost per equivalent unit of €54.40   2 720
Total costs of closing work in progress   €10 280

The following table summarises the total costs to account for and the €62 280 accounted for in Exhibit 4.6. The arrows indicate that costs of units completed and transferred out and in closing work in progress are calculated using average total costs obtained after merging costs of opening work in progress and costs added in the current period.

Costs to account for		Costs accounted for calculated at weighted-average cost	
Opening work in progress	€ 26 100	Completed and transferred out	€ 52 000
Costs added in current period	36 180	Closing work in progress	10 280
Total costs to account for	€ 62 280	Total costs accounted for	€ 62 280

Before proceeding, please pause and review Exhibits 4.5 and 4.6 carefully to check your understanding of the weighted-average method. Note that Exhibit 4.5 deals only with physical and equivalent units but no costs. Exhibit 4.6 shows the cost amounts.

Using euro amounts from Exhibit 4.6, summary journal entries under the weighted-average method for the month of March at Euro-Défense SA are:

1 Work in Progress – Assembly   19 800
      Creditors Control   19 800

   To record direct materials purchased and used in production
   during March

2 Work in Progress – Assembly   16 380
      Various accounts   16 380

   To record Assembly Department conversion costs for March; examples
   include energy, manufacturing supplies, all manufacturing labour, and
   plant depreciation

3 Work in Progress – Testing   52 000
      Work in Progress – Assembly   52 000

   To record cost of goods completed and transferred from
   Assembly to Testing during March

The key T-account, Work in Progress – Assembly, under the weighted-average method would show the following:

Work in Progress – Assembly

Opening stock, 1 March	26 100	③ Completed and transferred out to Work in Progress – Testing	52 000
① Direct materials	19 800		
② Conversion costs	16 380		
Closing stock, 31 March	10 280		

First-in, first-out method

In contrast to the weighted-average method, the **first-in, first-out (FIFO) process-costing method** assigns the cost of the previous period's equivalent units in opening work-in-progress stock to the first units completed and transferred out of the process, and assigns the cost of equivalent units worked on during the current period first to complete beginning stock, then to start and complete new units, and finally to units in closing work-in-progress stock. This method assumes that the earliest equivalent units in the Work in Progress – Assembly account are completed first.

A distinctive feature of the FIFO process-costing method is that work done on opening stock before the current period is kept separate from work done in the current period. Costs incurred in the current period and units produced in the current period are used to calculate costs per equivalent unit of work done in the current period. In contrast, equivalent-unit and cost-per-equivalent-unit calculations in the weighted-average method merge the units and costs in opening stock with units and costs of work done in the current period.

We now describe the five-step procedure introduced in Case 2 using the FIFO method.

Step 1: Summarise the flow of physical units Exhibit 4.7, step 1, traces the flow of physical units of production. The following observations help explain the physical units calculations.

	Exhibit 4.7	Steps 1 and 2: Summarise output in physical units and calculate equivalent units, FIFO method of process costing, Assembly Department of Euro-Défense SA, for March 2015

	(Step 1)	(Step 2) Equivalent units	
Flow of production	**Physical units**	**Direct materials**	**Conversion costs**
Work in progress, opening (given p. 93)	225	(work done before current period)	
Started during current period (given p. 93)	275		
To account for	500		
Completed and transferred out during current period:			
From opening work in progress*	225		
225 × (100% – 100%); 225 × (100% – 60%)		0	90
Started and completed	175†		
175 × 100%, 175 × 100%		175	175
Work in progress, closing‡ (given p. 93)	100		
100 × 100%; 100 × 50%		100	50
Accounted for	500		
Work done in current period only		275	315

* Degree of completion in this department: direct materials, 100%; conversion costs, 60%.

† 400 physical units completed and transferred out minus 225 physical units completed and transferred out from opening work-in-progress stock.

‡ Degree of completion in this department: direct materials, 100%; conversion costs, 50%.

- The first physical units assumed to be completed and transferred out during the period are the 225 units from the opening work-in-progress stock.

- Of the 275 physical units started, 175 are assumed to be completed. Recall from the March data given on page 93 that 400 physical units were completed during March. The FIFO method assumes that the first 225 of these units were from opening stock; thus 175 (400 – 225) physical units must have been started and completed during March.

- Closing work-in-progress stock consists of 100 physical units – the 275 physical units started minus the 175 of these physical units completed.

- Note that the physical units 'to account for' equal the physical units 'accounted for' (500 units).

Step 2: Calculate output in terms of equivalent units Exhibit 4.7 also presents the computations for step 2 under the FIFO method. *The equivalent-unit calculations for each cost category focus on the equivalent units of work done in the current period (March) only.*

Under the FIFO method, the work done in the current period is assumed to first complete the 225 units in opening work in progress. The equivalent units of work done in March on the opening work-in-progress stock are calculated by multiplying the 225 physical units *by the percentage of work remaining to be done to complete these units*: 0% for direct materials, because the opening work in progress is 100% complete with respect to direct materials, and 40% for conversion costs, because the opening work in progress is 60% complete with respect to conversion costs. The results are 0 (0% × 225) equivalent units of work for direct materials and 90 (40% × 225) equivalent units of work for conversion costs.

Next, the work done in the current period is assumed to start and complete the next 175 units. The equivalent units of work done on the 175 physical units started and completed are calculated by multiplying 175 units by 100% for both direct materials and conversion costs, because all work on these units is done in the current period.

Finally, the work done in the current period is assumed to start but leave incomplete the final 100 units as closing work in progress. The equivalent units of work done on the 100 units of closing work in progress are calculated by multiplying 100 physical units by 100% for direct materials (because all direct materials have been added for these units in the current period) and 50% for conversion costs (because 50% of conversion costs work has been done on these units in the current period).

Step 3: Calculate equivalent-unit costs Exhibit 4.8 shows the step 3 calculation of equivalent-unit costs *for work done in the current period only* for direct materials and conversion costs. For example, we divide current-period conversion costs of €16 380 by current-period equivalent units for conversion costs of 315 to obtain cost per equivalent unit of €52.

Step 4: Summarise total costs to account for The total production costs column in Exhibit 4.8 presents step 4 and summarises the total costs to account for in March 2015 (opening work in progress and costs added in the current period) of €62 280, as described in the example data (p. 92).

Exhibit 4.8	Steps 3, 4 and 5: Calculate equivalent-unit costs, summarise total costs to account for, and assign costs to units completed and to units in closing work in progress, FIFO method of process costing, Assembly Department of Euro-Défense SA, for March 2015

		Total production costs	Direct materials	Conversion costs
	Work in progress, opening	€26 100	(costs of work done before current period)	
(Step 3)	Costs added in current period (given p. 92)	36 180	€19 800	€16 380
	Divide by equivalent units of work done in current period (Exhibit 4.7)		÷ 275	÷ 315
	Cost per equivalent unit of work done in current period		€72	€52
(Step 4)	Total costs to account for	€62 280		
(Step 5)	Assignment of costs:			
	Completed and transferred out (400 units):			
	Work in progress, opening (225 units)	€26 100		
	Direct materials added in current period	0	0* × €72	
	Conversion costs added in current period	4 680		90* × €52
	Total from opening stock	30 780		
	Started and completed (175 units)	21 700	(175† × €72) + (175† × €52)	
	Total costs of units completed and transferred out	52 480		
	Work in progress, closing (100 units):			
	Direct materials	7 200	100‡ × €72	
	Conversion costs	2 600		50‡ × €52
	Total work in progress, closing	9 800		
	Total costs accounted for	€62 280		

* Equivalent units used to complete opening work in progress from Exhibit 4.7, step 2.
† Equivalent units started and completed from Exhibit 4.7, step 2.
‡ Equivalent units in closing work in progress from Exhibit 4.7, step 2.

Step 5: Assign costs to units completed and to units in closing work in progress Finally, Exhibit 4.8 shows the step 5 assignment of costs under the FIFO method. The costs of work done in the current period are first assigned to the additional work done to complete the opening work in progress, then to the work done on units started and completed during the current period, and finally to the closing work in progress. *The easiest way to follow step 5 is to take each of the equivalent units calculated in Exhibit 4.7, step 2, and attach euro amounts to them (using the cost-per-equivalent-unit calculations in step 3).* The goal is to determine the total cost of all units completed from opening stock and from work started and completed in the current period, and the costs of closing work in progress done in the current period.

Notice that the 400 completed units are of two types: 225 units come from opening stock, and 175 units are started and completed during March. The FIFO method starts by assigning the costs of the opening work-in-progress stock of €26 100 to the first units completed and transferred out. This €26 100 is the cost of the 225 equivalent units of direct materials and 135 equivalent units of conversion costs that comprise opening stock. The work that generated these costs was done in February, so these units are costed (see data on page 92) at the February prices of €80 for direct materials and €60 for conversion costs [(225 × €80) + (135 × €60) = €26 100]. As we saw in step 2, an additional 90 equivalent units of conversion costs are needed to complete these units in the current period. The current-period conversion costs per equivalent unit is €52, so €4680 (90 × €52) of additional costs are needed to complete the opening stock. The total production costs for the units in opening stock are €26 100 + €4680 = €30 780. The 175 units started and completed in the current period consist of 175 equivalent units of direct materials and 175 equivalent units of conversion costs. These units are costed at the cost per equivalent unit in the current period (direct materials, €72 and conversion costs, €52) for a total production cost of €21 700.

Under FIFO, the closing work-in-progress stock comes from units that were started but not fully completed during the current period. The total cost of the 100 partially assembled physical units in closing work in progress consists of:

Direct materials:	
100 equivalent units × cost per equivalent unit in March of €72	€7 200
Conversion costs:	
50 equivalent units × cost per equivalent unit in March of €52	2 600
Total costs of work in progress on 31 March	€9 800

The following table summarises the total costs to account for and the costs accounted for of €62 280 in Exhibit 4.8. Notice how under the FIFO method, the layers of opening work in progress and costs added in the current period are kept separate. The arrows indicate where the costs in each layer go (that is, to units completed and transferred out or to closing work in progress). Be sure to include the costs of opening work in progress (€26 100) when calculating the costs of units completed from opening stock.

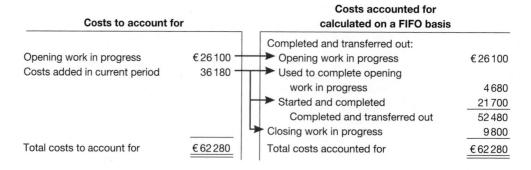

Costs to account for		Costs accounted for calculated on a FIFO basis	
		Completed and transferred out:	
Opening work in progress	€ 26 100	Opening work in progress	€ 26 100
Costs added in current period	36 180	Used to complete opening work in progress	4 680
		Started and completed	21 700
		Completed and transferred out	52 480
		Closing work in progress	9 800
Total costs to account for	€ 62 280	Total costs accounted for	€ 62 280

Before proceeding, you are advised to pause and review Exhibits 4.7 and 4.8 carefully to check your understanding of the FIFO method. Note that Exhibit 4.7 deals only with physical and equivalent units but no costs. Exhibit 4.8 shows the cost amounts.

The journal entries under the FIFO method parallel the journal entries under the weighted-average method. The only difference is that the entry to record the cost of goods completed and transferred out would be for €52 480 under the FIFO method instead of for €52 000 under the weighted-average method.

Only rarely is an application of pure FIFO ever encountered in process costing. As a result, it should really be called a *modified* or *departmental* FIFO method. Why? Because FIFO is applied within a department to compile the cost of units transferred *out*, but the units transferred *in* during a given period usually are carried at a single average unit cost as a matter of convenience. For example, the average cost of units transferred out of the Assembly Department is €52 480 ÷ 400 units = €131.20 per DG-19 unit. The Assembly Department uses FIFO to distinguish between monthly batches of production. The succeeding department, Testing, however, costs these units (that consist of costs incurred in February and March) at one average unit cost (€131.20 in this illustration). If this averaging were not done, the attempt to track costs on a pure FIFO basis throughout a series of processes would be unduly cumbersome.

Concepts in action   ExxonMobil and accounting differences in the oil patch

Source: Getty Images/Bloomberg

In 2012, ExxonMobil was number two on the Fortune 500 annual ranking of the largest US companies. The company had $420 billion dollars in revenue and more than $40 billion in profits. Believe it or not, however, by one measure ExxonMobil's profits are understated. ExxonMobil, like most US energy companies, uses last-in, first-out (LIFO) accounting. Under this treatment, ExxonMobil records its cost of inventory at the latest price paid for crude oil in the open market, even though it is often selling oil produced at a much lower cost. This increases the company's cost of goods sold, which in turn reduces profit. The benefit of using LIFO accounting for financial reporting is that ExxonMobil is then permitted to use LIFO for tax purposes as well, thereby lowering its payments to the tax authorities.

In contrast, International Financial Reporting Standards (IFRS) do not permit the use of LIFO accounting. European oil companies, such as Royal Dutch Shell and British Petroleum, use the first-in, first-out (FIFO) methodology instead when accounting for inventory. Under FIFO, oil companies use the cost of the oldest crude in their inventory to calculate the cost of barrels of oil sold. This reduces costs on the income statement, therefore increasing gross margins.

Assigning costs to inventory is a critical part of process costing, and a company's choice of method can result in substantially different profits. For instance, ExxonMobil's 2012 net income would have been $4.3 billion lower under FIFO. If US firms used IFRS they would be forced to adopt FIFO for financial and tax reporting, and they would have to pay additional taxes on the cumulative savings to date from showing a higher cost of goods sold in LIFO. Companies such as ExxonMobil, Coca-Cola and Novartis produce many identical or similar units of a product using mass-production techniques.

The focus of these companies on individual production processes gives rise to process costing. This chapter describes how companies use process costing methods to determine the costs of products or services and to value inventory and cost of goods sold (using methods like FIFO).

Source: Exxon Mobil Corporation *2012 Annual Report* (Irving, TX: Exxon Mobil Corporation); Kaminska, I. (2010) 'Shell, BP and the increasing cost of inventory', *Financial Times*, 'FT Alphaville' blog, 29 April; Reilly, D. (2006) 'Big oil's accounting methods fuel criticism', *Wall Street Journal*, 8 August.

Comparison of weighted-average and FIFO methods

The following table summarises the costs assigned to units completed and to units still in process under the weighted-average and FIFO process-costing methods for our example:

	Weighted average (from Exhibit 4.6)	FIFO (from Exhibit 4.8)	Difference
Cost of units completed and transferred out	€52 000	€52 480	+€480
Work in progress, closing	10 280	9 800	−€480
Total cost accounted for	€62 280	€62 280	

The weighted-average closing stock is higher than the FIFO closing stock by €480, or 4.9% (€480 ÷ €9800). This is a significant difference when aggregated over the many thousands of products that Euro-Défense makes. The weighted-average method in our example also results in lower cost of goods sold and hence higher operating income and higher income taxes than does the FIFO method. Differences in equivalent-unit costs of opening stock and work done during the current period account for the differences in weighted-average and FIFO costs. Recall from the data on page 92 that direct materials costs per equivalent unit in opening work-in-progress stock is €80, and conversion costs per equivalent unit in opening work-in-progress stock is €60. These costs are greater than the €72 direct materials and €52 conversion costs per equivalent unit of work done during the current period. This reduction could be due to a decline in the prices of direct materials and conversion cost inputs or could be a result of Euro-Défense becoming more efficient.

For the Assembly Department, FIFO assumes that all the higher-cost units from the previous period in opening work in progress are the first to be completed and transferred out of the process, and closing work in progress consists of only the lower-cost current-period units. The weighted-average method, however, smooths out cost per equivalent unit by assuming that more of the lower-cost units are completed and transferred out, and some of the higher-cost units are placed in closing work in progress. Hence, in this example, the weighted-average method results in a lower cost of units completed and transferred out and a higher closing work-in-progress stock relative to FIFO.

Cost of units completed and, hence, operating income can differ materially between the weighted-average and FIFO methods when (1) the direct materials or conversion costs per unit vary significantly from period to period, and (2) the physical stock levels of work in progress are large in relation to the total number of units transferred out of the process. Thus, as companies move towards long-term procurement contracts that reduce differences in unit costs from period to period, and reduce stock levels, the difference in cost of units completed under the weighted-average and FIFO methods will decrease.[1]

Managers need information from process-costing systems to aid them in pricing and product-mix decisions and to provide them with feedback about their performance. The major advantage of FIFO is that it provides managers with information about changes in the costs per unit from one period to the next. Managers can use this information to evaluate their performance in the current period compared with a benchmark or compared with their performance in the previous period. By focusing on work done and the costs of work done during the current period,

---

[1] For example, suppose opening work-in-progress stock for March is 125 physical units (instead of 225) and suppose cost per equivalent unit of work done in the current period (March) is direct materials, €75, and conversion costs, €55. Assume all other data for March are the same as in our example. In this case, the cost of units completed and transferred out would be €52 833 under the weighted-average method and €53 000 under the FIFO method, and the work-in-progress closing stock would be €10 417 under the weighted-average method and €10 250 under the FIFO method (calculations not shown). These differences are much smaller than in the chapter example. The weighted-average closing stock is higher than the FIFO closing stock by only €167 or 1.63% (€167 ÷ €10 250) compared with 4.9% higher in the chapter example.

the FIFO method provides useful information for these planning and control purposes. The weighted-average method merges unit costs from different periods and so obscures period-to-period comparisons. The major advantages of the weighted-average method, however, are its computational simplicity and its reporting of a more representative average unit cost when input prices fluctuate markedly from month to month.

Note that unlike in job-costing systems, activity-based costing (see Chapter 11) has less applicability in process-costing environments. Why? Because products are homogeneous and hence use resources in a similar way. Furthermore, each process – assembly, testing, and so on – corresponds to the different (production) activities. Managers reduce the costs of activities by controlling the costs of individual processes.

Standard-costing method of process costing

As we have mentioned, companies that use process-costing systems produce masses of identical or similar units of output. Setting standards for quantities of inputs needed to produce output is often relatively straightforward in such companies. Standard costs per input unit may then be assigned to these physical standards to develop standard costs per output unit.

The weighted-average and FIFO methods become very complicated when used in process industries that produce a wide variety of similar products. For example, a steel-rolling mill uses various steel alloys and produces sheets of various sizes and of various finishes. Both the items of direct materials and the operations performed are relatively few. But used in various combinations, they yield such a *wide variety* of products that inaccurate costs for each product result if the *broad* averaging procedure of actual process costing is used. Similarly, complex conditions are frequently found, for example, in plants that manufacture rubber products, textiles, ceramics, paints, and packaged food products. The standard-costing method of process costing is especially useful in these situations.

Under the standard-costing method, teams of design and process engineers, operations personnel, and management accountants determine *separate* standard or equivalent-unit costs on the basis of the different technical processing specifications for each product. Identifying standard costs for each product overcomes the disadvantage of costing all products at a single average amount, as under actual costing.

Computations under standard costing

We again use the Assembly Department of Euro-Défense SA as an example, except this time we assign standard costs to the process. The same standard costs apply in February and March of 2015:

Direct materials	€74 per unit
Conversion costs	54 per unit
Total standard manufacturing costs	€128 per unit

Data for the Assembly Department are:

Physical units for March 2015

Work in progress, opening stock (1 March)	225 units
Direct materials (100% complete)	
Conversion costs (60% complete)	
Started during March	275 units
Completed and transferred out during March	400 units
Work in progress, closing stock (31 March)	100 units
Direct materials (100% complete)	
Conversion costs (50% complete)	

Total costs for March 2015

Work in progress, opening stock as standard costs		
Direct materials: 225 equivalent units × €74 per unit	€16 650	
Conversion costs: 135 equivalent units × €54 per unit	7 290	€23 940
Actual direct materials costs added during March		19 800
Actual conversion costs added during March		16 380

Exhibit 4.9	Steps 1 and 2: Summarise output in physical units and calculate equivalent units, use of standard costs in process costing, Assembly Department of Euro-Défense SA, for March 2015

	(Step 1)	(Step 2) Equivalent units	
Flow of production	Physical units	Direct materials	Conversion costs
Work in progress, opening (given p. 101)	225		
Started during current period (given p. 101)	275		
To account for	500		
Completed and transferred out during current period:			
From beginning work in progress*			
225 × (100% – 100%); 225 × (100% – 60%)	225	0	90
Started and completed	175†		
175 × 100%, 175 × 100%		175	175
Work in progress, closing‡ (given p. 101)	100		
100 × 100%; 100 × 50%		100	50
Accounted for	500		
Work done in current period only		275	315

* Degree of completion in this department: direct materials, 100%; conversion costs, 60%.

† 400 physical units completed and transferred out minus 225 physical units completed and transferred out from opening work-in-progress stock.

‡ Degree of completion in this department: direct materials, 100%; conversion costs, 50%.

We illustrate the standard-costing method of process costing using the five-step procedure introduced earlier in the chapter. Exhibit 4.9 presents steps 1 and 2. These steps are identical to the steps described for the FIFO method in Exhibit 4.7. Work done in the current period equals direct materials (275 equivalent units) and conversion costs (315 equivalent units).

Exhibit 4.10 shows the step 3 calculation of equivalent-unit costs. Step 3 is easier under the standard-costing method than it is under the weighted-average and FIFO methods. Why? Because the cost per equivalent unit does not have to be calculated, as was done for the weighted-average and FIFO methods. Instead, the costs per equivalent unit *are* the standard costs: direct materials, €74, and conversion costs, €54. Using standard costs also simplifies the computations for assigning the total costs to account for to units completed and transferred out and to units in closing work-in-progress stock.

The total costs to account for in Exhibit 4.10, step 4, that is, the total debits to Work in Progress – Assembly, differ from the total debits to Work in Progress – Assembly under the actual cost-based weighted-average and FIFO methods explained earlier in the chapter. Why? Because, *as in all standard-costing systems*, the debits to the Work-in-Progress account are at standard costs rather than actual costs. These standard costs total €61 300.

Exhibit 4.10, step 5, assigns total costs to units completed and transferred out and to units in closing work-in-progress stock, as in the FIFO method. Step 5 attaches euro amounts, using standard costs, to the equivalent units calculated in Exhibit 4.9. These costs are assigned first to complete opening work-in-progress stock, then to start and complete new units, and finally to start new units that are in closing work-in-progress stock. Note how the total costs accounted for in step 5 of Exhibit 4.10 (€61 300) equal the total costs to account for.

	Total production costs	Direct materials	Conversion costs
(Step 3) Standard cost per equivalent unit (given p. 101)		€74	€54
Work in progress, opening (given p. 101)			
Direct materials, 225 × €74; Conversion costs, 135 × €54	€23 940		
Costs added in current period at standard costs			
Direct materials, 275 × €74; Conversion costs, 315 × €54	37 360	20 350	17 010
(Step 4) Costs to account for	€61 300		
(Step 5) Assignment of costs at standard costs:			
Completed and transferred out (400 units):			
Work in progress, opening (225 units)	€23 940		
Direct materials added in current period	0	0* × €74	
Conversion costs added in current period	4 860		90* × €54
Total from opening stock	28 800		
Started and completed (175 units)	22 400	(175† × €74) + (175† × €54)	
Total costs of units transferred out	51 200		
Work in progress, closing (100 units):			
Direct materials	7 400	100‡ × €74	
Conversion costs	2 700		50‡ × €54
Total work in progress, closing	10 100		
Total costs accounted for	€61 300		
Summary of variances for current performance			
Costs added in current period at standard prices (see step 3 above)		€20 350	€17 010
Actual costs incurred (given p. 102)		19 800	16 380
Variance		€550F	€630F

Exhibit 4.10   Steps 3, 4 and 5: Calculate equivalent-unit costs, summarise total costs to account for, and assign costs to units completed and to units in closing work in progress, use of standard costs in process costing, Assembly Department of Euro-Défense SA, for March 2015

* Equivalent units to complete opening work in progress from Exhibit 4.9, step 2.
† Equivalent units started and completed from Exhibit 4.9, step 2.
‡ Equivalent units in closing work in progress from Exhibit 4.9, step 2.

Accounting for variances

Process-costing systems using standard costs usually accumulate actual costs incurred separately from the stock accounts. The following is an example. The actual costs are recorded in the first two entries. Recall that Euro-Défense purchases direct materials as needed and that these materials are delivered directly to the Assembly Department. The total variances are recorded in the next two entries. The final entry transfers out the completed goods at standard costs.

1   Assembly Department Direct Materials Control (at actual)   19 800
        Creditors Control   19 800

To record direct materials purchased and used in production during March. This cost control account is debited with actual costs and immediately credited with standard costs assigned to the units worked on (entry 3 below)

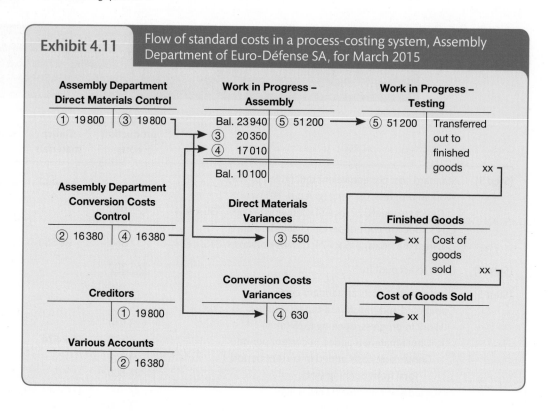

Exhibit 4.11 Flow of standard costs in a process-costing system, Assembly Department of Euro-Défense SA, for March 2015

2 Assembly Department Conversion Costs Control (at actual)   16 380
       Various accounts   16 380

   To record Assembly Department conversion costs for March

Entries 3, 4 and 5 use standard cost euro amounts from Exhibit 4.10.

3 Work in Progress – Assembly (at standard costs)   20 350
       Direct Materials Variances   550
       Assembly Department Direct Materials Control   19 800

   To record actual direct materials used and total direct
   materials variances

4 Work in Progress – Assembly (at standard costs)   17 010
       Conversion Costs Variances   630
       Assembly Department Conversion Costs Control   16 380

   To record actual conversion costs and total
   conversion costs variances

5 Work in Progress – Testing (at standard costs)   51 200
       Work in Progress – Assembly (at standard costs)   51 200

   To record costs of units completed and transferred
   out at standard cost from Assembly to Testing

Variances arise under the standard-costing method, as in entries 3 and 4 above. Why? Because the standard costs assigned to products on the basis of work done in the current period do not equal the actual costs incurred in the current period. Variances can be measured and analysed in little or great detail for planning and control purposes, as described in Chapters 15 and 16. Exhibit 4.11 shows how the standard costs flow through the accounts.

Transferred-in costs in process costing

Many process-costing systems have two or more departments or processes in the production cycle. As units move from department to department, the related costs are also transferred by monthly journal entries. If standard costs are used, the accounting for such transfers is relatively simple. However, if the weighted-average or FIFO method is used, the accounting can become more complex. We now extend our Euro-Défense SA example to the Testing Department. As the assembly process is completed, the Assembly Department of Euro-Défense immediately transfers DG-19 units to its Testing Department. Here the units receive additional direct materials, such as crating and other packing materials to prepare the units for shipment, at the *end* of the process. Conversion costs are added evenly during the Testing Department's process. As units are completed in Testing, they are immediately transferred to Finished Goods. Exhibit 4.12 summarises these facts.

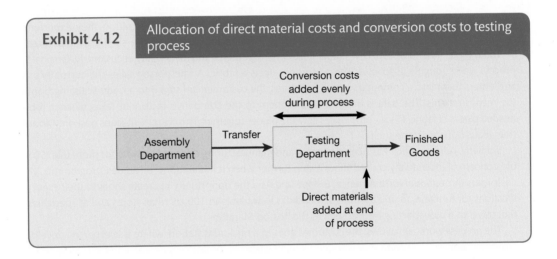

Exhibit 4.12   Allocation of direct material costs and conversion costs to testing process

Data for the Testing Department for the month of March 2015 are:

Physical units for March 2015

Work in progress, opening stock (March 1)	240 units
Transferred-in costs (100% complete)	
Direct materials (0% complete)	
Conversion costs (5/8 or 62.5% complete)	
Transferred in during March	400 units
Completed during March	440 units
Work in progress, closing stock (March 31)	200 units
Transferred-in costs (100% complete)	
Direct materials (0% complete)	
Conversion costs (80% complete)	

Concepts in action   Hybrid costing for customised products at Levi Strauss and at Adidas

Source: Pearson Education Ltd/Naki Kouyioumtzis

Levi Strauss, the company that invented blue jeans more than a century ago, is now able to produce individually customised jeans by means of computer-controlled technology. A computer graphic designer in Boston, Sung Park, came to Levi Strauss with the idea. He realised that a pattern for a piece of clothing is just a big computer graphic, except that the lines of the graphic image are cut instead of drawn. He also realised that, whereas the sizing of men's jeans is fairly straightforward – based on simple waist and inside leg dimensions – the sizing of women's jeans is much more complicated – a function not only of waist size and inside leg, but also hip size and the variance in the difference between waist and hip sizes. His female friends complained about the frustration they experienced from not being able to find off-the-shelf jeans that fitted them well.

Today there are a number of Levi Strauss stores where women – and men – can get custom-fit 'Original Spin' jeans. The process works roughly as follows. The customer selects a fabric. A salesperson takes the customer's measurements and enters them into a computer; or, in a few stores, the customer can step into a body-scanning booth that records the measurements. The data is then sent via modem to the company's factory in Texas, where a robot cuts out the needed pieces of fabric. Finally, employees sew the pieces together. The custom-fit jeans cost only about US$10 more than jeans bought off the shelf.

Similarly, Adidas, which has been designing and manufacturing athletic footwear for more than 90 years, took the old concept of individually crafted shoes a step further when it initiated the 'mi adidas' programme. Mi adidas allows customers throughout North America, Europe and Asia the opportunity to create shoes to their exact personal specifications for function, fit and aesthetics. Mi adidas is available in 100 US retail stores and at specialised mobile units that travel to major sporting events, such as the Boston Marathon.

The process works as follows: the customer goes to a mi adidas station, where a salesperson develops an in-depth customer profile, a 3-D computer scanner develops a scan of the customer's feet, and the customer selects from over 200 different styles and colours for his/her modularly designed shoe. The resulting data are transferred to an Adidas plant, where small, multiskilled teams produce the customised shoe.

Historically, costs associated with individually customised products have generally fallen into the domain of job costing. Levi Strauss and Adidas, however, use hybrid-costing systems – job costing for the material and customisable components that customers choose, and process costing to account for the conversion costs of production. The cost of making each pair of jeans or shoes is calculated by accumulating all production costs and dividing by the number of pairs made. Even though each pair is different, the cost of making each pair is the same.

This combination of customisation with certain features of mass production is called *mass customisation*. It is the consequence of being able to digitise information that individual customers indicate is important to them. Various products that companies are now able to customise within a mass-production setting (e.g. personal computers, windows, bicycles) still require a lot of human intervention and job costing of materials. But as manufacturing systems become flexible, process costing is used to account for the standardised conversion costs.

Sources: Copley News Service, 14 February 2000; Montgomery, R. (1995) 'The genie of jeans Newton entrepreneur enlists computer for customized Levi's', *Boston Globe*, 4 January; Levi Strauss annual reports; Lee, L. (2006) 'Sewing up the iPod market', *Business Week*, 12 January; Seifert, R. (2002) 'The "mi adidas" mass customization initiative', IMD Case Studies (IMD-6-0249) (Cranfield: ECCH); Tait, N. (2004) 'How "mi adidas" provides personalized style, fit', *Apparel*, 1 January; 'adidas America to introduce running customization shoe at 2002 LaSalle Bank Chicago Marathon', *Chicago Athlete*, 2 October 2002.

Costs of testing department for March 2015

Work in progress, opening stock[2]

Transferred-in costs (240 equivalent units × €140 per equivalent unit)	€33 600	
Direct materials	0	
Conversion costs (150 equivalent units × €120 per equivalent unit)	18 000	€51 600
Transferred-in costs during March		
Weighted-average (from Exhibit 4.6)		52 000
FIFO (from Exhibit 4.8)		52 480
Direct material costs added during March		13 200
Conversion costs added during March		48 600

Transferred-in costs (also called **previous department costs**) are the costs incurred in a previous department that are carried forward as the product's cost when it moves to a subsequent process in the production cycle. That is, as the units move from one department to the next, their costs are transferred with them. Thus, calculations of Testing Department costs consist of transferred-in costs as well as the direct materials and conversion costs added in Testing.

Transferred-in costs are treated as if they are a separate type of direct material added at the opening of the process. In other words, when successive departments are involved, transferred units from one department become all or a part of the direct materials of the next department; however, they are called transferred-in costs, not direct material costs.

Transferred-in costs and the weighted-average method

To examine the weighted-average process-costing method with transferred-in costs, we use the five-step procedure described earlier (page 88) to assign costs of the Testing Department to units completed and transferred out and to units in closing work in progress. Exhibit 4.13 shows

Exhibit 4.13	Steps 1 and 2: Summarise output in physical units and calculate equivalent units, weighted-average method of process costing, Testing Department of Euro-Défense SA, for March 2015

Flow of production	(Step 1) Physical units (given p. 000)	(Step 2) Equivalent units		
		Transferred-in costs	Direct materials	Conversion costs
Work in progress, opening	240			
Transferred in during current period	400			
To account for	640			
Completed and transferred out during current period	440	440	440	440
Work in progress, closing*	200			
200 × 100%; 200 × 0%; 200 × 80%		200	0	160
Accounted for	640			
Work done to date		640	440	600

* Degree of completion in this department: transferred-in costs, 100%; direct materials, 0%; conversion costs, 80%.

---

[2] The opening work-in-progress stock is the same under both the weighted-average and FIFO stock methods because we assume costs per equivalent unit to be the same in both January and February. If the cost per equivalent unit had been different in the two months, the work-in-progress stock at the end of February (beginning of March) would be costed differently under the weighted-average and FIFO methods. If this were the case, the basic approach to process costing with transferred-in costs would still be the same as described in this section, only the opening balances of work in progress would be different.

		Total production costs	Transferred-in costs	Direct materials	Conversion costs
(Step 3)	Work in progress, opening (given p. 105)	€51 600	€33 600	€0	€18 000
	Costs added in current period (given p. 105)	113 800	52 000	13 200	48 600
	Costs incurred to date		€85 600	€13 200	€66 600
	Divide by equivalent units of work done to date (Exhibit 4.13)		÷ 640	÷ 440	÷ 600
	Equipment-unit costs of work done to date		€133.75	€30	€111
(Step 4)	Total costs to account for	€165 400			
(Step 5)	Assignment of costs:				
	Completed and transferred out (440 units)	€120 890	(440* × €133.75) + (440* × €30) + (440* × €111)		
	Work in progress, closing (200 units):				
	Transferred-in costs	26 750	200† × €133.75		
	Direct materials	0		0† × €30	
	Conversion costs	17 760			160† × €111
	Total work in progress, closing	44 510			
	Total costs accounted for	€165 400			

Exhibit 4.14 — Steps 3, 4 and 5: Calculate equivalent-unit costs, summarise total costs to account for, and assign costs to units completed and to units in closing work in progress, weighted-average method of process costing, Testing Department of Euro-Défense SA, for March 2015

* Equivalent units completed and transferred out from Exhibit 4.13, step 2.
† Equivalent units in closing work in progress from Exhibit 4.13, step 2.

steps 1 and 2. The computations are basically the same as the calculations of equivalent units under the weighted-average method for the Assembly Department in Exhibit 4.5, except for the addition of transferred-in costs. The units are fully completed as to transferred-in costs because these costs are simply carried forward from the previous process. Note, however, that direct materials costs have a zero degree of completion in both the opening and closing work-in-progress stocks because, in Testing, direct materials are introduced at the end of the process.

Exhibit 4.14 describes steps 3, 4 and 5 for the weighted-average method. Note that opening work in progress and work done in the current period are combined for purposes of computing equivalent-unit costs for transferred-in costs, direct materials, and conversion costs.

Using the euro amount from Exhibit 4.14, the journal entry for the transfer out from Testing to finished goods stock is:

Finished goods Control   120 890
    Work in Progress – Testing   120 890
To record cost of goods completed and transferred from Testing to finished goods

Entries to the key T-account, Work in Progress – Testing, follow (from Exhibit 4.14).

Work in Progress – Testing			
Opening stock, 1 March	51 600	Transferred out	120 890
Transfered-in costs	52 000		
Direct materials	13 200		
Conversion costs	48 600		
Closing stock, 31 March	45 510		

Transferred-in costs and the FIFO method

To examine the FIFO process-costing method with transferred-in costs, we again use the five-step procedure. Exhibit 4.15 shows steps 1 and 2. Other than considering transferred-in costs, the computations of equivalent units are basically the same as those under the FIFO method for the Assembly Department shown in Exhibit 4.7.

Exhibit 4.16 describes steps 3, 4 and 5. Note that the costs per equivalent unit for the current period in step 3 are only calculated on the basis of costs transferred in and work done in the current period. In steps 4 and 5, the total costs to account for and accounted for of €165 880 under the FIFO method differ from the corresponding amounts under the weighted-average method of €165 400. Why? Because of the different costs of completed units transferred-in from the Assembly Department under the two methods (€52 480 under FIFO and €52 000 under weighted average).

Using the euro amount from Exhibit 4.16, the journal entry for the transfer of completed units to finished goods stock is:

Finished goods Control	122 360	
Work in Progress – Testing		122 360

To record cost of goods completed and transferred from Testing to finished goods

---

Exhibit 4.15   Steps 1 and 2: Summarise output in physical units and calculate equivalent units, FIFO method of process costing, Testing Department of Euro-Défense SA, for March 2015

	(Step 1)	(Step 2) Equivalent units		
Flow of production	Physical units	Transferred-in costs	Direct materials	Conversion costs
Work in progress, opening (given p. 107)	240	(work done before current period)		
Transferred-in during current period (given p. 107)	400			
To account for	640			
Completed and transferred out during current period:				
From opening work in progress*	240			
240 × (100% – 100%); 240 × (100% – 0%);				
240 × (100% – 62.5%)		0	240	90
Started and completed	200†			
200 × 100%; 200 × 100%; 200 × 100%		200	200	200
Work in progress, closing‡ (given p. 107)	200			
200 × 100%; 200 × 0%; 200 × 80%		200	0	160
Accounted for	640			
Work done in current period only		400	440	450

* Degree of completion in this department: Transferred-in costs, 100%; direct materials, 0%; conversion costs, 62.5%.
† 440 physical units completed and transferred out minus 240 physical units completed and transferred out from opening work-in-progress stock.
‡ Degree of completion in this department: transferred-in costs, 100%; direct materials, 0%; conversion costs, 80%.

		Total production costs	Transferred-in costs	Direct materials	Conversion costs
	Exhibit 4.16 Steps 3, 4 and 5: Calculate equivalent-unit costs, summarise total costs to account for, and assign costs to units completed and to units in closing work in progress, FIFO method of process costing, Testing Department of Euro-Défense SA, for March 2015				
	Work in progress, opening (given p. 000)	€51 600	(costs of work done before current period)		
(Step 3)	Costs added in current period (given p. 000)	114 280	€52 480	€13 200	€48 600
	Divide by equivalent units of work done in current period (Exhibit 4.15)		÷ 400	÷ 440	÷ 450
	Cost per equivalent unit of work done in current period		€131.20	€30	€108
(Step 4)	Total costs to account for	€165 880			
(Step 5)	Assignment of costs:				
	Completed and transferred out (440 units):				
	Work in progress, opening (240 units)	€51 600			
	Transferred-in costs added in current period	0	0* × €131.20		
	Direct materials added in current period	7 200		240* × €30	
	Conversion costs added in current period	9 720			90* × €108
	Total from opening stock	68 520			
	Started and completed (200 units)	53 840	(200† × €131.20) + (200† × €30) + (200† × €108)		
	Total costs of units completed and transferred out	122 360			
	Work in progress, ending (200 units):				
	Transferred-in costs	26 240	200‡ × €131.20		
	Direct materials	0		0‡ × €30	
	Conversion costs	17 280			160‡ × €108
	Total work in progress, closing	43 520			
	Total costs accounted for	€165 880			

* Equivalent units used to complete opening work in progress from Exhibit 4.15, step 2.
† Equivalent units started and completed from Exhibit 4.15, step 2.
‡ Equivalent units in closing work in progress from Exhibit 4.15, step 2.

Entries to the key T-account, Work in Progress – Testing, follow using information from Exhibit 4.16.

Work in Progress – Testing

Opening stock, 1 March	51 600	Transferred out	122 360
Transferred-in costs	52 480		
Direct materials	13 200		
Conversion costs	48 600		
Closing stock, 31 March	43 520		

Remember that in a series of interdepartmental transfers, each department is regarded as being separate and distinct for accounting purposes. All costs transferred in during a given accounting period are carried at one unit-cost figure, as described when discussing modified FIFO, regardless of whether previous departments used the weighted-average method or the FIFO method.

Points to remember about transferred-in costs

Here are some points to remember when accounting for transferred-in costs:

- Remember to include transferred-in costs from previous departments in your calculations.

- In calculating costs to be transferred on a FIFO basis, do not overlook the costs assigned at the opening of the period to units that were in process but are now included in the units transferred. For example, do not overlook the €51 600 in Exhibit 4.16.

- Unit costs may fluctuate between periods. Therefore, transferred units may contain batches accumulated at different unit costs. For example, the 400 units transferred in at €52 480 in Exhibit 4.16 using the FIFO method consist of units that have different unit costs of direct materials and conversion costs when these units were worked on in the Assembly Department (see Exhibit 4.8). Remember, however, that when these units are transferred to the Testing Department, they are costed at *one* average unit cost of €131.20 (€52 480 ÷ 400) as in Exhibit 4.14.

- Units may be measured in different terms in different departments. Consider each department separately. For example, unit costs could be based on kilograms in the first department and litres in the second department. Accordingly, as units are received in the second department, their measurements must be converted to litres.

Hybrid-costing systems

Product-costing systems do not always fall neatly into the categories of job costing or process costing. A **hybrid-costing system** blends characteristics from both job-costing systems and process-costing systems. Job-costing and process-costing systems are best viewed as the ends of a continuum (Exhibit 4.17).

Product-costing systems must often be designed to fit the particular characteristics of different production systems. Many production systems are a hybrid – they have some features of custom-order manufacturing and other features of mass-production manufacturing. Manufacturers of a relatively wide variety of closely related standardised products tend to use a hybrid-costing system. Consider Renault, the car manufacturer. Cars may be manufactured in a continuous flow, but individual units may be customised with a special combination of engine size, gears, in-car stereo

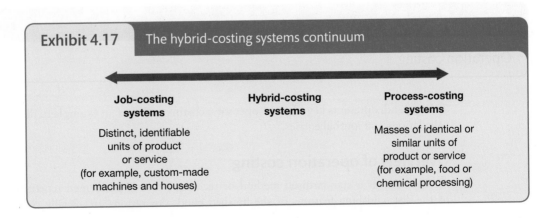

Exhibit 4.17   The hybrid-costing systems continuum

Job-costing systems

Distinct, identifiable units of product or service (for example, custom-made machines and houses)

Hybrid-costing systems

Process-costing systems

Masses of identical or similar units of product or service (for example, food or chemical processing)

system, and so on. Companies develop hybrid-costing systems in such situations. The Concepts in Action in this chapter describes a hybrid-costing system at Levi Strauss and at Adidas. The appendix to this chapter explains *operation costing*, a common type of hybrid-costing system.

Summary

The following points are linked to the chapter's learning objectives.

1　A process-costing system is used to determine the cost of a product or service when masses of identical or similar units are produced. Unit costs are computed by first assigning costs to these similar units and then dividing by the number of these units. Industries using process-costing systems include food, textiles and oil refining.

2　The five key steps in a process-costing system using equivalent units are (a) summarise the flow of physical units of output, (b) compute output in terms of equivalent units, (c) compute equivalent-unit costs, (d) summarise total costs to account for, and (e) assign total costs to units completed and to units in closing work in progress.

3　Equivalent units is a derived amount of output units that takes the quantity of each input in units completed or in work in progress, and converts it into the amount of completed output units that could be made with that quantity of input. Equivalent-unit calculations are necessary when all physical units of output are not uniformly completed during an accounting period.

4　Journal entries in a process-costing system are similar to entries in a job-costing system. The main difference is that in a process-costing system, there is a separate Work-in-Progress account for each department.

5　The weighted-average method of process costing computes unit costs by focusing on the total costs and the total equivalent units completed to date and assigns this average cost to units completed and to units in closing work-in-progress stock.

6　The first-in, first-out (FIFO) method of process costing assigns the costs of the opening work-in-progress stock to the first units completed, and assigns the costs of the equivalent units worked on during the current period first to complete beginning stock, then to start and complete new units, and finally to units in closing work-in-progress stock.

7　The standard-costing method simplifies process costing because standard costs serve as the costs per equivalent unit when assigning costs to units completed and to units in closing work-in-progress stock.

8　The weighted-average process-costing method computes transferred-in costs per unit by focusing on total transferred-in costs and total equivalent transferred-in units completed to date, and assigns this average cost to units completed and to units in closing work-in-progress stock. The FIFO process-costing method assigns transferred-in costs in opening work in progress to units completed, and the costs transferred in during the current period first to complete opening work-in-progress units, then to start and complete new units, and finally to units in closing work-in-progress stock.

Appendix

Operation costing

This appendix presents key ideas of operation costing and uses an example to illustrate relevant calculations and journal entries.

Overview of operation costing

An **operation** is a standardised method or technique that is performed repetitively regardless of the distinguishing features of the finished good. Operations are usually conducted within departments. For instance, a suit maker may have a cutting operation and a hemming operation within a single department. The term *operation*, however, is often used loosely. It may be a synonym for a department or a process; for example, some companies may call their finishing department a finishing process or a finishing operation.

Operation costing is a hybrid-costing system applied to batches of similar products. Each batch of products is often a variation of a single design and proceeds through a sequence of selected (though not necessarily the same) activities or operations. Within each operation, all product units are treated exactly alike, using identical amounts of the operation's resources. Batches are also termed production runs.

Consider a business that makes suits. Management may select a single basic design for every suit that the company manufactures. Depending on specifications, batches of suits vary from each other. One batch may use wool; another batch, cotton. One batch may require special hand stitching; another batch, machine stitching. Other products that are often manufactured in batches are semiconductors, textiles and shoes.

An operation-costing system uses work orders that specify the needed direct materials and step-by-step operations. Product costs are compiled for each work order. Direct materials that are unique to different work orders are specifically identified with the appropriate work order as in job-costing systems. The conversion cost for each unit passing through a given operation is the same regardless of the work order. Why? Because each unit passing through an operation uses identical amounts of that operation's resources. A single average conversion cost per unit is calculated as in process costing. For each operation, this amount is calculated by aggregating conversion costs and dividing by all units passing through that operation. Our examples assume only two cost categories, direct materials and conversion costs. Of course, operation costing can have more than two cost categories. The costs in each category are identified with work orders using job-costing or process-costing methods as appropriate.

Managers often find operation costing useful in cost management because operation costing focuses on the physical processes, or operations, of a given production system. For example, in the manufacturing of clothing, managers are concerned with fabric waste, the number of fabric layers that can be cut at one time, and so on. Operation costing captures the financial impact of the control of physical processes. Feedback from an operation-costing system can therefore provide essential insight into the control of physical processes and the management of operational costs.

An illustration of operation costing

Consider Aran Sweaters Ltd, a clothing manufacturer that produces two lines of blazers for department stores. Wool blazers use better-quality materials and undergo more operations than do polyester blazers. Let us look at the following operations in 2015:

	Work order 423	Work order 424
Direct materials	Wool	Polyester
	Satin full lining	Rayon partial lining
	Bone buttons	Plastic buttons
Operations		
1 Cutting cloth	Use	Use
2 Checking edges	Use	Do not use
3 Sewing body	Use	Use
4 Checking seams	Use	Do not use
5 Machine sewing of collars and lapels	Do not use	Use
6 Hand sewing of collars and lapels	Use	Do not use

Suppose work order 423 is for 50 wool blazers and work order 424 is for 100 polyester blazers. The following costs are assumed for these two work orders, which were started and completed in March 2015:

	Work order 423	Work order 424
Number of blazers	50	100
Direct material costs	€6 000	€3 000
Conversion costs allocated:		
Operation 1	580	1 160
Operation 2	400	–
Operation 3	1 900	3 800
Operation 4	500	–
Operation 5	–	875
Operation 6	700	–
Total manufacturing costs	€10 080	€8 835

As in process costing, all product units in any work order are assumed to consume identical amounts of conversion costs of a particular operation. Aran Sweaters' operation-costing system uses a budgeted rate to calculate the conversion costs of each operation. For example, the costs of operation 1 might be budgeted as follows (amounts assumed):

$$\begin{array}{l} \text{Operation 1 budgeted} \\ \text{conversion cost} \\ \text{rate in 2015} \end{array} = \frac{\text{Operation 1 budgeted conversion costs in 2015}}{\text{Operation 1 budgeted product units in 2015}}$$

$$= \frac{€232\ 000}{20\ 000\ \text{units}}$$

$$= €11.60\ \text{per unit}$$

The budgeted conversion costs of operation 1 include labour, power, repairs, supplies, depreciation and other overheads of this operation. If some units have not been completed so that all units in operation 1 have not received the same amounts of conversion costs, the conversion cost rate is calculated by dividing budgeted conversion costs by the *equivalent units* of conversion costs.

As goods are manufactured, conversion costs are allocated to the work orders processed in operation 1 by multiplying the €11.60 conversion costs per unit by the number of product units processed. The conversion costs of operation 1 for 50 wool blazers (work order 423) are €11.60 × 50 = €580, and for 100 polyester blazers (work order 424) are €11.60 × 100 = €1160. If work order 424 contained 75 units, its total costs in operation 1 would be €870 (€11.60 × 75), 150% rather than 200% of the cost of work order 423. If equivalent units have been used to calculate the conversion cost rate, costs are allocated to work orders by multiplying the conversion cost per equivalent unit by the number of equivalent units in the work order. Direct material costs of €6000 for the 50 wool blazers (work order 423) and €3000 for the 100 polyester blazers (work order 424) are specifically identified with each order as in a job-costing system. Note that operational unit costs are assumed to be the same regardless of the work order, but direct material costs vary across orders as the materials themselves vary.

Journal entries

Actual conversion costs for operation 1 in March 2015 (assumed to be €24 400) are entered into a Conversion Costs account:

1 Conversion Costs	24 400	
Various accounts (such as Wages Payable and Provision for Depreciation)		24 400

Summary journal entries for assigning costs to the polyester blazers (work order 424) follow. Entries for the wool blazers would be similar.

Of the €3000 of direct materials for work order 424, €2975 are used in operation 1. The journal entry for the use of direct materials, which are traced directly to particular batches, for the 100 polyester blazers is:

2	Work in Progress, Operation 1	2975	
	Materials Stock Control		2975

The allocation of conversion costs to products in operation costing uses the budgeted rate €11.60 times the 100 units processed, or €1160.

3	Work in Progress, Operation 1	1160	
	Conversion Costs Allocated		1160

The transfer of the polyester blazers from operation 1 to operation 3 (recall that the polyester blazers do not go through operation 2) would be entered in the journal as follows:

4	Work in Progress, Operation 3	4135	
	Work in Progress, Operation 1		4135

After posting, Work in Progress, Operation 1 account appears as follows:

Work in Progress, operation 1

2	Direct materials	2975	**4**	Transferred to Operation	34 135
3	Conversion costs allocated	1160			

The costs of the blazers are transferred through the pertinent operations and then to finished goods in the usual manner. Costs are added throughout the year in the Conversion Costs and Conversion Costs Allocated accounts. Any over- or underallocation of conversion costs is disposed of in the same way as over- or underallocated manufacturing overhead in a job-costing system.

Key terms

process-costing system (86)
conversion costs (86)
equivalent units (89)
weighted-average process-costing method (92)
first-in, first-out (FIFO) process-costing method (95)

transferred-in costs (107)
previous department costs (107)
hybrid-costing system (111)
operation (112)
operation costing (113)

Reference

Gumbel, P. (2009) 'Meet Shell's new CEO', *Fortune*, 20 July, p. 79.

CHAPTER 4

Assessment material

Review questions

4.1 Give three examples of industries that often use process-costing systems.

4.2 In process costing, why are costs often divided into two main classifications?

4.3 What problems might arise in estimating the degree of completion of an aircraft blade in a machining shop?

4.4 Describe the distinctive characteristic of weighted-average computations in assigning costs to units completed and closing work in progress.

4.5 Describe the distinctive characteristic of FIFO computations in assigning costs to units completed and closing work in progress.

4.6 Identify a major advantage of the FIFO method for purposes of planning and control.

4.7 Identify the main difference between journal entries in process costing and those in job costing.

4.8 Why should the accountant distinguish between transferred-in costs and additional direct material costs for a particular department?

4.9 'Previous department costs are those incurred in the preceding accounting period.' Do you agree? Explain.

4.10 'There's no reason for me to get excited about the choice between the weighted-average and FIFO methods in my process-costing system. I have long-term contracts with my materials suppliers at fixed prices.' State the conditions under which you would (a) agree and (b) disagree with this statement, made by an accountant. Explain.

Exercises

Intermediate level

4.11 **No opening stock** (25 minutes)

Europe Electronics SNC manufactures microchips in large quantities. Each microchip undergoes assembly and testing. The total assembly costs during January 2015 were:

Direct materials used	€720 000
Conversion costs	760 000
Total manufacturing costs	€1 480 000

Required

1 Assume there was no opening stock on 1 January 2015. During January, 10 000 microchips were placed into production and all 10 000 microchips were fully completed at the end of January. What is the unit cost of an assembled microchip in January 2015?

2 Assume that during February 10 000 microchips were placed into production. Further assume the same total assembly costs for January are also incurred in February, but only 9000 microchips are fully completed at the end of February. All direct materials had been added to the remaining 1000 microchips. However, on average, these remaining 1000 microchips were only 50% complete as to conversion costs. (a) What are the equivalent units for direct materials and conversion costs and their respective equivalent unit costs for February? (b) What is the unit cost of an assembled microchip in February?

3 Explain the difference in your answers to requirements 1 and 2.

*4.12 Journal entries (continuation of Exercise 4.11) (20 minutes)

Refer to requirement 2 of Exercise 4.11.

Required

Prepare summary journal entries for the use of direct materials and conversion costs. Also prepare a journal entry to transfer out the cost of goods completed. Show the postings to the Work in Progress account.

4.13 Equivalent units and equivalent unit costs (25 minutes)

Consider the following data for the satellite assembly division of Aéro-France:

	Physical units (satellites)	Direct materials	Conversion costs
Opening work in progress (1 May)*	8	€4 968 000	€928 000
Started in May	50		
Completed during May	46		
Closing work in progress (31 May)†	12		
Costs added during May		€32 200 000	€13 920 000

* Degree of completion: direct materials, 90%; conversion costs, 40%.
† Degree of completion: direct materials, 60%; conversion costs, 30%.

Required

1 Calculate equivalent units of work done in the current period for direct materials and conversion costs. Show physical units in the first column.

2 Calculate cost per equivalent unit of opening work in progress and of work done in the current period for direct materials and conversion costs.

*4.14 Equivalent unit computations, benchmarking, ethics (20–25 minutes)

Radhika Khrishna is the corporate accountant of Manchester Suits plc. Manchester Suits has 20 plants worldwide that manufacture basic suits for retail stores. Each plant uses a process-costing system. At the end of each month, each plant manager submits a production report and a production-cost report. The production report includes the plant manager's estimate of the percentage of completion of the closing work in progress as to direct materials and conversion costs. Khrishna uses these estimates to calculate the equivalent units of work done in each plant and the cost per equivalent unit of work done for both direct materials and conversion costs in each month. Plants are ranked from 1 to 20 in terms of (a) cost per equivalent unit of direct materials and (b) cost per equivalent unit of conversion costs. Each month Khrishna publishes a report that she calls 'Benchmarking for Efficiency Gains at Manchester Suits'. The top three ranked plants on each category receive a bonus and are written up as the best in their class in the company newsletter.

Khrishna has been pleased with the success of her benchmarking programme. However, she has heard some disturbing news. She has received some unsigned letters stating that two plant managers have been manipulating their monthly estimates of percentage of completion in an attempt to become best in class.

Required

1 How and why might plant managers 'manipulate' their monthly estimates of percentage of completion?

2 Khrishna's first reaction is to contact each plant accountant and discuss the problem raised by the unsigned letters. Is that a good idea?

3 Assume that the plant accountant's primary reporting responsibility is to the plant manager and that each plant accountant receives the telephone call from Khrishna mentioned in requirement 2. What is the ethical responsibility of each plant accountant (a) to Radhika Khrishna and (b) to Manchester Suits in relation to the equivalent unit information each plant provides for the 'Benchmarking for Efficiency' report?

4 How might Khrishna gain some insight into whether the equivalent unit figures provided by particular plants are being manipulated?

4.15   Process Costing (From ACCA Financial Information for Management, Part 1, June 2004)
(40 minutes)

Duddon Ltd makes a product that has to pass through two manufacturing processes, I and II. All the material is input at the start of process I. No losses occur in process I but there is a normal loss in process II equal to 7% of the input into that process. Losses have no realisable value.

Process I is operated only in the first part of every month followed by process II in the second part of the month. All completed production from process I is transferred into process II in the same month. There is no work in progress in process II.

Information for last month for each process is as follows:

Process I

Opening work in progress	200 units (40% complete for conversion costs) valued in total at £16 500
Input into the process	1900 units with a material cost of £133 000
Conversion costs incurred	£93 500
Closing work in progress	50% complete for conversion costs

Process II

Transfer from process I	1800 units
Conversion costs incurred	£78 450

1650 completed units were transferred to the finished goods warehouse.

Required

1 Calculate for process I:
   a the value of the closing work in progress; and
   b the total value of the units transferred to process II.

2 Prepare the process II account for last month.

3 Identify TWO main differences between process costing and job costing.

Advanced level

*4.16   Transferred-in costs, equivalent unit costs, working backwards (30 minutes)

Le Roi du Plastique Sarl has two processes – extrusion and thermo-assembly. Consider the June 2015 data for physical units in the thermo-assembly process of Le Roi du Plastique: opening work in progress, 15 000 units; transferred in from the Extruding Department during September, 9000; closing work in progress, 5000. Direct materials are added when the process in the Thermo-assembly Department is 80% complete. Conversion costs are added evenly during the process. Le Roi du Plastique uses the weighted-average process-costing method. The following information is available.

	Transferred-in costs	Direct materials	Conversion costs
Opening work in progress at cost	€90 000	–	€45 000
Cost per equivalent unit of opening work in progress	€6	–	€5
Costs added in current period	€58 500	€57 000	€57 200
Cost per equivalent unit of work done in current period	€6.50	€3	€5.20

Required

1 For each cost element, calculate equivalent units of (a) opening work in progress and (b) work done in the current period.

2 For each cost element, calculate the equivalent units in closing work in progress.

3 (a) For each cost element, calculate the percentage of completion of opening work-in-progress stock and (b) for each cost element, calculate the percentage of completion of closing work-in-progress stock.

4.17   Transferred-in costs, weighted-average method (35–40 minutes)

Telemark-Kjemi AS manufactures an industrial solvent in two departments – mixing and cooking. This question focuses on the Cooking Department. During June 2015, 90 tonnes of solvent were completed and transferred out from the Cooking Department. Direct materials are added at one point in time during the process. Conversion costs are added uniformly during the process. Telemark-Kjemi uses the weighted-average process-costing method. The following information about the actual costs for June 2015 is available.

	Transferred-in costs		Direct materials		Conversion costs	
	Equivalent tonnes	Total costs	Equivalent tonnes	Total costs	Equivalent tonnes	Total costs
Work in progress, 1 June	40	NOK 40 000	0	NOK 0	30	NOK 18 000
Work done in June	80	NOK 87 200	90	NOK 36 000	75	NOK 49 725
Completed in June	?	?	?	?	?	?
Work in progress, 30 June	?	?	?	?	?	?

Required

1 Calculate the equivalent tonnes of solvent completed and transferred out and in closing work in progress for each cost element.

2 Calculate cost per equivalent unit for opening work in progress and work done in current period.

3 Summarise total costs to account for and assign these costs to units completed (and transferred out) and to units in closing work in progress using the weighted-average method.

4.18   Transferred-in costs, FIFO method (35–40 minutes)

Refer to the information in Exercise 4.17. Suppose that Telemark-Kjemi uses the FIFO method instead of the weighted-average method in all its departments. The only changes under the FIFO method are that the total transferred-in cost of opening work in progress is NOK 39 200 and that the cost of work done in the current period is NOK 85 600.

Required

Do Exercise 4.17 using the FIFO method.

4.19   Transferred-in costs, standard costing method (35–40 minutes)

Refer to the information in Exercise 4.17. Suppose Telemark-Kjemi determines standard costs of NKr 1050 per (equivalent) tonne of transferred-in costs, NOK 390 per (equivalent) tonne of direct materials and NOK 640 per (equivalent) tonne of conversion costs for both opening work in progress and work done in the current period.

Required

Do Exercise 4.17 using the standard costing method.

4.20   Weighted-average method (25 minutes)

Euro-Défense is a manufacturer of military equipment. Its Tourcoing plant manufactures the Déca-Pite missile under contract to the French government and friendly countries. All Déca-Pites go through an identical manufacturing process. Every effort is made to ensure that all Déca-Pites are identical and meet many demanding performance specifications. The product-costing system at the Tourcoing plant has a single direct-cost category (direct materials) and a single indirect-cost category (conversion costs). Each Déca-Pite passes through two departments – the Assembly Department and the Testing Department. Direct materials are added at the opening of the process in Assembly. Conversion costs are added evenly throughout the two departments. When the Assembly Department finishes work on each Déca-Pite, it is immediately transferred to Testing.

Euro-Défense uses the weighted-average method of process costing. Data for the Assembly Department for October 2015 are:

	Physical units (missiles)	Direct materials	Conversion costs
Work in progress, 1 October*	20	€460 000	€120 000
Started during October	80		
Completed during October	90		
Work in progress, 31 October†	10		
Costs added during October		€2 000 000	€935 000

* Degree of completion: direct materials, ?%; conversion costs, 60%.
† Degree of completion: direct materials, ?%; conversion costs, 70%.

Required

1 For each cost element, calculate equivalent units of work done in October 2015 in the Assembly Department. Show physical units in the first column.

2 For each cost element, calculate cost per equivalent unit of opening work in progress and of work done in October 2015.

3 Summarise the total Assembly Department costs for October 2015 and assign these costs to units completed (and transferred out) and to units in closing work in progress using the weighted-average method.

4 Prepare a set of summarised journal entries for all October 2015 transactions affecting Work in Progress – Assembly. Set up a T-account for Work in Progress – Assembly and post the entries to it.

4.21   FIFO method (continuation of Exercise 4.20) (20 minutes)

Required

Do Exercise 4.20 using the FIFO method of process costing. Explain any difference between the cost of work completed and transferred out and cost of closing work in progress in the Assembly Department under the weighted-average method and the FIFO method.

4.22   Weighted-average method (25 minutes)

Sligo Toys Ltd manufactures one type of wooden toy figure. It buys wood as its direct material for the Forming Department of its Ballinode plant. The toys are transferred to the Finishing Department, where they are hand-shaped and metal is added to them.

Sligo Toys uses the weighted-average method of process costing. Consider the following data for the Forming Department in April 2015:

	Physical units (missiles)	Direct materials	Conversion costs
Work in progress, 1 April*	300	€7 500	€2 125
Started during April	2 200		
Completed during April	2 000		
Work in progress, 30 April†	500		
Costs added during April		€70 000	€42 500

* Degree of completion: direct materials, 100%; conversion costs, 40%.
† Degree of completion: direct materials, 100%; conversion costs, 25%.

Required

1 Summarise the total Forming Department costs for April 2015, and assign these costs to units completed (and transferred out) and to units in closing work in progress using the weighted-average method.

2 Prepare a set of summarised journal entries for all April transactions affecting Work in Progress – Forming. Set up a T-account for Work in Progress – Forming and post the entries to it.

4.23   FIFO computations (continuation of Exercise 4.22) (20 minutes)

Required

Do Exercise 4.22 (1) using FIFO and four decimal places for unit costs. Explain any difference between the cost of work completed and transferred out and cost of closing work in progress in the Forming Department under the weighted-average method and the FIFO method.

4.24   Transferred-in costs, weighted-average (related to Exercises 4.22 and 4.23) (30 minutes)

Sligo Toys Ltd manufactures wooden toy figures at its Ballinode plant. It has two departments – the Forming Department and the Finishing Department. (Exercises 4.22 and 4.23 focused on the Forming Department.) Consider now the Finishing Department, which processes the formed toys through hand-shaping and the addition of metal. For simplicity here, suppose all additional direct materials are added at the end of the process. Conversion costs are added evenly during Finishing operations.

Sligo Toys uses the weighted-average method of process costing. The following is a summary of the April 2015 operations in the Finishing Department:

	Physical units (toys)	Transferred-in costs	Direct materials	Conversion costs
Work in progress, 1 April*	500	€17 750	€0	€7 250
Transferred-in during April	2 000			
Completed during April	2 100			
Work in progress, 30 April†	400			
Costs added during April		€104 000	€23 100	€38 400

* Degree of completion: transferred-in costs, 100%; direct materials, 0%; conversion costs, 60%.
† Degree of completion: transferred-in costs, 100%; direct materials, 0%; conversion costs, 30%.

Required

1 Summarise the total Finishing Department costs for April 2015, and assign these costs to units completed (and transferred out) and to units in closing work in progress using the weighted-average method.

2 Prepare journal entries for April transfers from the Forming Department to the Finishing Department and from the Finishing Department to Finished Goods.

4.25   **Transferred-in costs, FIFO costing** (continuation of Exercise 4.24) (30 minutes)

Required

1 Using the FIFO process-costing method, do the requirements of Exercise 4.24. The transferred-in costs from the Forming Department for the April opening work in progress are €17 520. During April, the costs transferred in are €103 566. All other data are unchanged.

2 Explain any difference between the cost of work completed and transferred out and cost of closing work in progress in the Finishing Department under the weighted-average method and the FIFO method.

CHAPTER 5
Cost allocation

Cost allocation is an inescapable problem in nearly every organisation. How should the airline costs of a trip to attend job interviews from London to Dubai to Tunis and then return to London be allocated among the prospective employers in Dubai and Tunis? How should university costs be allocated among undergraduate programmes, graduate programmes and research? How should the costs of expensive medical equipment, facilities and staff be allocated in a medical centre? How should manufacturing overhead be allocated to individual products in a multiple-product company such as Heinz?

Finding answers to cost-allocation questions is difficult. The answers are seldom entirely right or clearly wrong. Nevertheless, in this chapter, we will try to obtain some insight into cost allocation and to understand the dimensions of the questions, even if the answers seem elusive. Regardless of your profession, you will undoubtedly be faced with many cost-allocation questions in your career. We first concentrate on the allocation of costs to departments and subsequently emphasise the allocation of costs to individual products, services, customers or jobs. Chapter 6 considers costing issues which arise when two or more products are simultaneously produced with each other and where joint costs are allocated to products and services.

Learning objectives

After studying this chapter, you should be able to:

- Describe how a costing system can have multiple cost objects
- Outline four purposes for allocating costs to cost objects
- Discuss key decisions faced when collecting costs in indirect cost pools
- Describe how the single-rate cost-allocation method differs from the dual-rate method
- Explain how the choice of budgeted versus actual allocation rates changes the risks that managers face
- Distinguish between direct allocation, step-down and reciprocal methods of allocating support department costs
- Distinguish between the incremental and stand-alone cost-allocation methods
- Outline the consequences of the inappropriate use of an allocation base
- Describe why managers may find cost hierarchy-based reports useful in their decisions

Purposes of cost allocation

Indirect costs of a particular cost object are costs that are related to that cost object but cannot be traced to it in an economically feasible or cost-effective way.

Indirect costs often comprise a sizable percentage of the costs assigned to cost objects such as products, distribution channels and customers. Exhibit 5.1 illustrates four purposes for allocating indirect costs to such cost objects:

1 to provide information for economic decisions

2 to motivate managers and employees

3 to justify costs or calculate reimbursement

4 to measure income and assets for reporting to external parties.

The allocation of one particular cost need not satisfy all purposes simultaneously. Consider the salary of an aerospace scientist in a central research department of Aérospatiale. This salary cost may be allocated as part of central research costs to satisfy purpose 1 (economic decisions); it may or may not be allocated to satisfy purpose 2 (motivation); it may or may not be allocated to a government contract to justify a cost to be reimbursed to satisfy purpose 3 (cost reimbursement); and it must not be allocated (under generally accepted accounting principles) to stock to satisfy purpose 4 (income and asset measurement).

Exhibit 5.1	Purposes of cost allocation
Purpose	**Illustrations**
1 To provide information for economic decisions	• To decide whether to add a new airline flight • To decide whether to make a component part of a television set or to purchase it from another manufacturer • To decide on the selling price for a customised product or service
2 To motivate managers and employees	• To encourage the design of products that are simpler to manufacture or less costly to service • To encourage sales representatives to push high-margin products or services
3 To justify costs or calculate reimbursement	• To cost products at a 'fair' price, often done with government defence contracts • To compute reimbursement for a consulting firm that is paid a percentage of the cost savings resulting from the implementation of its recommendations
4 To measure income and assets for meeting external regulatory and legal reporting obligations	• To cost shares for financial reporting to shareholders, bondholders and so on. (Under generally accepted accounting principles, inventoriable costs include manufacturing costs but exclude R&D, marketing, distribution and customer-service costs.)

Different costs are appropriate for different purposes. Consider product costs of the following business functions in the value chain:

Research and Development > Design > Production > Marketing > Distribution > Customer service

The same combination of costs in these six business functions typically will not satisfy each of the four purposes in Exhibit 5.1. For the economic-decision purpose (for example, product pricing), the costs in all six functions should be included. For the motivation purpose, costs from more than one function are often included to emphasise to managers how costs in different functions are related to each other. For example, many Japanese and German companies require product designers to incorporate costs further down the chain than design (such as distribution and customer service, as well as manufacturing) into their product-cost estimates. The aim is to focus attention on how different product-design options affect the total costs of the organisation. For the cost-reimbursement purpose, the particular contract will often stipulate whether all six of the business functions or only a subset of them are to be reimbursed. For instance, for the purpose of income and asset measurement for reporting to external parties, inventoriable costs under generally accepted accounting principles usually include only manufacturing costs (and product-design costs in some cases). In most European countries, R&D costs can be capitalised (over up to five years) although there are countries (such as Germany and the UK) where research costs must be written off in the accounting period in which they are incurred.

Cost allocation and costing systems

We will use Fontaine Informatique to illustrate how costs incurred in different parts of an organisation can be assigned and then reassigned when costing products, services, customers or contracts. Fontaine Informatique has two manufacturing divisions. The Microcomputer Division manufactures its Roseau, Roseau Portable and Super Roseau products. The Roseau and Roseau Portable are assembled at its Antwerp, Mataró and Longvic plants. The Super Roseau is assembled at its Tourcoing plant. The Peripheral Equipment Division manufactures printers, cables and other items used with its computer products. It has plants in Antwerp and Rotterdam.

Exhibit 5.2 presents an overview of the costing system at the Antwerp assembly plant of the Microcomputer Division. This plant assembles the Roseau line and the Roseau Portable line. The area within the box in Exhibit 5.2 shows a costing system overview for the Model A version of the Roseau. Fontaine Informatique has manufacturing plants located in France, Belgium, the Netherlands and Spain. It has marketing operations in more than 20 countries. Every month it consolidates accounting information from each of its operations to use in its planning and control decisions. A detailed costing overview of this company-wide system would be sizably more complex than that in Exhibit 5.2.

The costing system for the Antwerp plant portrayed in Exhibit 5.2 highlights two important points. First, it highlights how there are multiple cost objects in most costing systems. Examples at the Antwerp plant include the Plant Maintenance Department, the Roseau Assembly Department, the Roseau Portable Assembly Department and the separate products in the Roseau Assembly Department – for example, Roseau Models A, B and C. Note, however, that Exhibit 5.2 presents only a small subset of the separate cost objects at the Antwerp plant. Other examples include the Procurement Department, the Energy Department and the various Roseau Portable products.

Exhibit 5.2 also highlights how an individual cost item can be simultaneously a direct cost of one cost object and an indirect cost of another cost object. Consider the salary of the Plant Maintenance Department manager. This salary is a direct cost traced to the Plant Maintenance Department. Fontaine Informatique then allocates the costs of this department to the two Assembly Departments at the Antwerp plant using units produced as the allocation base. In turn, the costs of the two Assembly Departments are allocated to individual products, such as the Roseau Model A, using assembly machine-hours as the allocation base. Thus, the salary of the Plant Maintenance Department manager is both an indirect cost of each computer assembled at the plant and a direct cost of the Plant Maintenance Department.

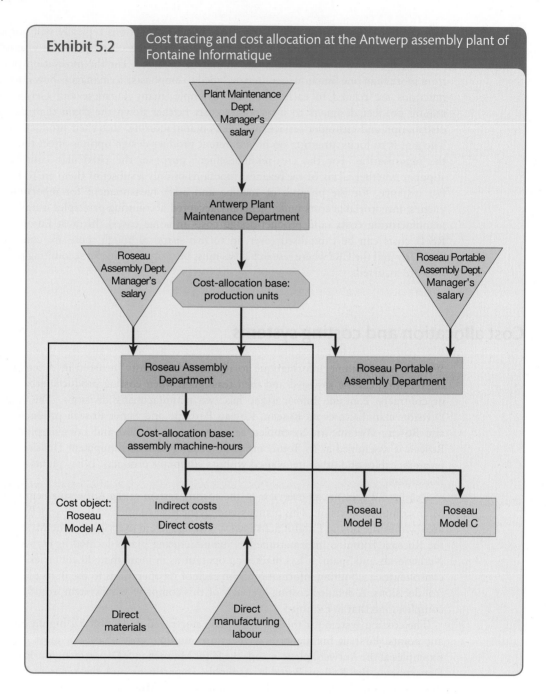

Exhibit 5.2 Cost tracing and cost allocation at the Antwerp assembly plant of Fontaine Informatique

Indirect cost pools and cost allocation

The indirect costs of products assembled at the manufacturing plants of Fontaine Informatique include (1) costs incurred at corporate headquarters and (2) costs incurred at the manufacturing plants. Exhibit 5.3 illustrates cost pools at both levels (1) and (2).

Choices related to indirect costs

Fontaine Informatique has several key choices to make when accumulating and subsequently allocating the indirect costs to products of the Microcomputer Division:

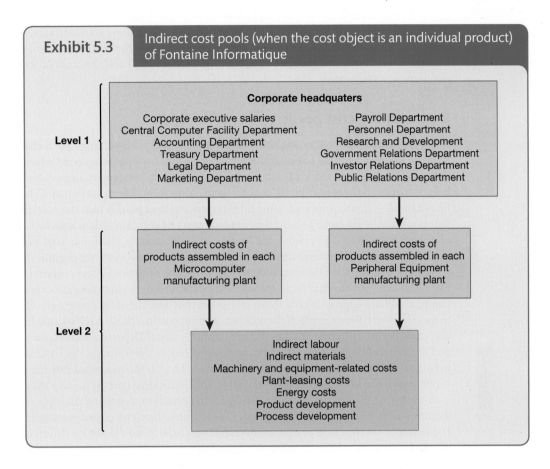

Exhibit 5.3   Indirect cost pools (when the cost object is an individual product) of Fontaine Informatique

- Which cost categories from corporate headquarters and the other divisions should be included in the indirect costs of the Microcomputer Division? Should all of the corporate headquarters cost pools in Exhibit 5.3 be allocated, or should only a subset of them be allocated? For example, some companies exclude corporate public relations from any corporate cost allocations to the divisions; division managers have little say in corporate public relations decisions and would object to allocations as 'taxation without representation'.

- How many cost pools should be used when allocating corporate costs to the Microcomputer Division? A *cost pool* is a grouping of individual cost items. One extreme is to aggregate all corporate costs into a single cost pool. The other extreme is to have numerous individual corporate cost pools. The concept of homogeneity (described in the following section) is important in making this decision.

- Which allocation base should be used for each of the corporate cost pools when allocating corporate costs to the Microcomputer Division? Examples include the following:

Cost pool	Possible allocation bases
Corporate executive salaries	Sales; assets employed; operating profit
Treasury Department	Sales; assets employed; estimated time or usage
Legal Department	Estimated time or usage; sales; assets employed
Marketing Department	Sales; number of sales personnel
Payroll Department	Number of employees; payroll euros
Personnel Department	Number of employees; payroll euros; number of new employees

- Which allocation base should be used when allocating the indirect-cost pools at each manufacturing plant to the products assembled in those plants? Examples include number of parts assembled in each product, direct manufacturing labour-hours, machining-hours and testing-hours.

These allocation bases for both corporate and plant indirect costs are illustrative only. Managers' choices of allocation bases depend on the purpose served by the cost allocation (see Exhibit 5.1), the criteria used to guide the cost allocation (see Exhibit 5.2) and the costs of implementing the different allocation bases.

Determining cost pools

A **homogeneous cost pool** is one in which all the activities whose costs are included in the pool have the same or a similar cause-and-effect relationship or benefits-received relationship between the cost allocator and the costs of the activity. Why is homogeneity important? Because using homogeneous indirect-cost pools enables more accurate product, service and customer costs to be obtained. A consequence of using a homogeneous cost pool is that the cost allocations using that pool will be the same as would be made if costs of each individual activity in that pool were allocated separately. The greater the degree of homogeneity, the fewer cost pools required to explain accurately the differences in how products use resources of the organisation.

Assume that Fontaine Informatique wishes to use the cause-and-effect criterion (that is, identify the variable or variables that cause resources to be consumed) to guide cost-allocation decisions. The company should aggregate only those cost pools that have the same cause-and-effect relationship to the cost object. For example, if the number of employees in a division is the cause for incurring both corporate Payroll Department costs and corporate Personnel Department costs, the payroll cost pool and the personnel cost pool could be aggregated before determining the combined payroll and personnel cost rate per unit of the allocation base. That is, the combined rate per unit of the allocation base is the same as the sum of the rates if the individual cost pools were allocated separately.

A variety of factors may prompt managers to consider recognising multiple cost pools where a single cost pool is currently being used. One factor is the views of line managers and personnel. For example, do they believe important differences exist in how costs are driven or how products use the facilities not currently being recognised using a single cost pool? A second factor is changes made in plant layout, general operations and so on, such that all products do not use the facility in an equivalent way. A third factor is changes in the diversity of products (or services) produced or in the way those products use the resources in the cost pool. Improvements in information and communication technology continuously expand the ability to develop multiple cost pools.

Allocating costs from one department to another

In many cases, the costs of a department will include costs allocated from other departments. Three key issues that arise when allocating costs from one department to another are (1) whether to use a single-rate method or a dual-rate method, (2) whether to use budgeted rates or actual rates, and (3) whether to use budgeted quantities or actual quantities.

Single-rate and dual-rate methods

A **single-rate cost-allocation method** pools all costs in one cost pool and allocates them to cost objects using the same rate per unit of the single allocation base. There is no distinction between costs in the cost pool in terms of cost variability (such as fixed costs versus variable costs). A **dual-rate cost-allocation method** first classifies costs in one cost pool into two subpools (typically into a variable-cost subpool and a fixed-cost subpool). Each subpool has a different allocation rate or a different allocation base.

Consider the Central Computer Department at the corporate headquarters of Fontaine Informatique (shown in Exhibit 5.3). For simplicity, assume that the only users of this facility are the Microcomputer Division and the Peripheral Equipment Division. The following data apply to the coming budget year:

Fixed costs of operating the facility	€300 000	per year
Total capacity available	1 500	hours
Budgeted long-term usage (quantity) in hours		
Microcomputer Division	800	
Peripheral Equipment Division	400	
Total	1 200	
Budgeted variable costs per hour in the		
1000–1500-hour relevant range	€200	per hour used

Under the single-rate method, the costs of the Central Computer Department (assuming budgeted usage is the allocation base and budgeted rates are used) would be allocated as follows:

Total cost pool: €300 000 + (1200 budgeted hours × €200)	€540 000	per year
Budgeted usage	1 200	hours
Budgeted total rate per hour rate: €540 000 ÷ 1200 hours	€450	per hour used
Allocation rate for Microcomputer Division	€450	per hour used
Allocation rate for Peripheral Equipment Division	€450	per hour used

The rate of €450 per hour differs sizably from the €200 budgeted variable cost per hour. The €450 rate includes an allocated amount of €250 per hour (€300 000 ÷ 1200 hours) for the fixed costs of operating the facility. These fixed costs will be incurred whether the computer runs its 1500-hour capacity, its 1200-hour budgeted usage, or even, say, only 600 hours' usage.

Using the €450 per hour single-rate method (combined with the budgeted usage allocation base) transforms what is a fixed cost to the Central Computer Department (and to Fontaine Informatique) into a variable cost to users of that facility. This approach could lead internal users to purchase computer time outside the company. Consider an external supplier that charges less than €450 per hour but more than €200 per hour. A division of Fontaine Informatique that uses this supplier rather than the Central Computer Department may decrease its own division costs, but the overall costs to Fontaine Informatique are increased. For example, suppose the Microcomputer Division uses an external supplier that charges €360 per hour when the Central Computer Department has excess capacity. In the short run, Fontaine Informatique incurs an extra €160 per hour because this external supplier is used (€360 external purchase price per hour minus the €200 internal variable costs per hour) instead of its own Central Computer Department.

When the dual-rate method is used, allocation bases for each different subcost pool must be chosen. Assume that the budgeted rates are used. The allocation quantities chosen are budgeted usage for fixed costs and actual usage for variable costs. The total budgeted usage of 1200 hours comprises 800 hours for the Microcomputer Division and 400 hours for the Peripheral Equipment Division. The costs allocated to the Microcomputer Division would be as follows:

Fixed-cost function:		
(800 hours ÷ 1200 hours) × €300 000	€200 000	per year
Variable-cost function	€200	per hour used

The costs allocated to the Peripheral Equipment Division would be:

Fixed-cost function:		
(400 hours ÷ 1200 hours) × €300 000	€100 000	per year
Variable-cost function	€200	per hour used

Assume now that during the coming year the Microcomputer Division actually uses 900 hours but the Peripheral Equipment Division uses only 300 hours. The costs allocated to these two divisions would be computed as follows:

Under the single-rate method

Microcomputer Division	$900 \times €450 = €405\ 000$
Peripheral Equipment Division	$300 \times €450 = €135\ 000$

Under the dual-rate method

Microcomputer Division	$€200\ 000 + (900 \times €200) = €380\ 000$
Peripheral Equipment Division	$€100\ 000 + (300 \times €200) = €160\ 000$

One obvious benefit of using the single-rate method is the low cost of implementation. It avoids the often expensive analysis necessary to classify the individual cost items of a department into fixed and variable categories. However, a single-rate method may lead divisions to take actions that appear to be in their own best interest but are not in the best interest of the organisation as a whole.

An important benefit of the dual-rate method is that it signals to division managers how variable costs and fixed costs behave differently. This important information could steer division managers into making decisions that benefit the corporation as well as each division. For example, it would signal that using a third-party computer supplier who charges more than €200 per hour could result in Fontaine Informatique's being worse off than if it had used its own Central Computer Department, which has a variable cost of €200 per hour.

Budgeted versus actual rates

The decision whether to use budgeted cost rates or actual cost rates affects the level of uncertainty that user departments face. Budgeted rates let the user departments know the cost rates they will be charged in advance. Users are then better equipped to determine the amount of the service to request and, if the option exists, whether to use the internal department source or an external supplier. In contrast, when actual rates are used, the user department will not know the rates charged until the end of the period.

Budgeted rates also help motivate the manager of the support department (for example, the Central Computer Department) to improve efficiency. During the budget period, the support department, not the user departments, bears the risk of any unfavourable cost variances. Why? Because the user department does not pay for any costs that exceed the budgeted rates. The manager of the support department would probably view this as a disadvantage of using budgeted rates, especially when unfavourable cost variances occur because of price increases outside the department's control.

Some organisations recognise that it may not always be best to impose all the risks of variances from budgeted amounts completely on the support department (as when costs are allocated using budgeted rates) or completely on the user departments (as when costs are allocated using actual rates). For example, the two departments may agree to share the risk (through an explicit formula) of a large, uncontrollable increase in the price of materials used by the support department.

Budgeted versus actual usage allocation bases

The choice between actual usage and budgeted usage for allocating department fixed costs can also affect a manager's behaviour. Consider the budget of €300 000 fixed costs at the Central Computer Department of Fontaine Informatique. Assume that actual and budgeted fixed costs are equal. Assume also that the actual usage by the Microcomputer Division is always equal to the budgeted usage. We now look at the effect on allocating the €300 000 in total fixed costs when actual usage by the Peripheral Equipment Division equals (case 1), is greater than (case 2) and is less than (case 3) the budgeted usage. Recall that the budgeted usage is 800 hours for the Microcomputer Division and 400 hours for the Peripheral Equipment Division. Exhibit 5.4 presents the allocation of total fixed costs of €300 000 to each division for these three cases.

In case 1, the fixed-cost allocation equals the expected amount. In case 2, the fixed-cost allocation is €40 000 less to the Microcomputer Division than expected (€160 000 vs €200 000). In case 3, the fixed-cost allocation is €40 000 more than expected (€240 000 vs €200 000). Consider case 3. Why is there an increase of €40 000 even though the Microcomputer Division's actual and budgeted usage are exactly equal? Because the fixed costs are spread over fewer hours of usage. Variations in usage in another division will affect the fixed costs allocated to the Microcomputer Division when fixed costs are allocated on the basis of actual usage. When actual usage is the allocation base, user divisions will not know how much cost is allocated to them until the end of the budget period.

When budgeted usage is the allocation base, user divisions will know their allocated costs in advance. This information helps the user divisions with both short-run and long-run planning. The main justification given for the use of budgeted usage to allocate fixed costs relates to long-range planning. Organisations commit to infrastructure costs (such as the fixed costs of a support department) on the basis of a long-range planning horizon; the use of budgeted usage to allocate these fixed costs is consistent with this long-range horizon.

| Exhibit 5.4 | Effect of variations in actual usage on departmental cost allocations |

	Actual usage		Budgeted usage as allocation base		Actual usage as allocation base	
Case	Microcomputer Division	Peripheral Equipment Division	Microcomputer Division	Peripheral Equipment Division	Microcomputer Division	Peripheral Equipment Division
1	800 hours	400 hours	€200 000*	€100 000†	€200 000*	€100 000†
2	800 hours	700 hours	€200 000*	€100 000†	€160 000‡	€140 000‖
3	800 hours	200 hours	€200 000*	€100 000†	€240 000§	€60 000#

$$* \quad \frac{800}{(800+400)} \times €300\,000 \qquad † \quad \frac{400}{(800+400)} \times €300\,000 \qquad ‡ \quad \frac{800}{(800+700)} \times €300\,000$$

$$§ \quad \frac{800}{(800+200)} \times €300\,000 \qquad ‖ \quad \frac{700}{(800+700)} \times €300\,000 \qquad # \quad \frac{200}{(800+200)} \times €300\,000$$

If fixed costs are allocated on the basis of estimated long-run use, some managers may be tempted to underestimate their planned usage. In this way, they will bear a lower fraction of the total costs (assuming all other managers do not similarly underestimate). Some organisations offer rewards in the form of salary increases and promotions to managers who make accurate forecasts of long-range usage. (This is the carrot approach.) Alternatively, some organisations impose cost penalties for underpredicting long-range usage. For instance, a higher cost rate may be charged after a division exceeds its budgeted usage. (This is the stick approach.) It is often the case that a business unit within a large enterprise establishes a final budget for the following year which looks a lot like the one its managers proposed at the beginning of the budget-setting process and which is not much different from the actual performance for the previous year. The reason for this is that managers often get 'anchored'. Lovallo and Sibony (2014) explain that 'anchoring' is a well-known psychological bias whereby one piece of information sticks in one's mind and influences interpretation of subsequent information, even if one is unaware of it. They state that 'In the case of budgeting, getting stuck in the same numbers from year to year is almost unavoidable.'

Allocating costs of support departments

Operating departments and support departments

Many organisations distinguish between operating departments and support departments. An **operating department** (also called a **production department** in manufacturing companies) adds value to a product or service that is observable by a customer. A **support department** (also called a **service department**) provides the services that maintain other internal departments (operating departments and other support departments) in the organisation. Support departments at Fontaine Informatique include the Legal Department and the Personnel Department at corporate headquarters.

Support departments create special accounting problems when they provide reciprocal support to each other as well as support to operating departments. An example of reciprocal support at Fontaine Informatique would be the Legal Department's providing services to the Personnel Department (such as advice on compliance with employment law) and the Personnel Department's providing support to the Legal Department (such as advice about the hiring of solicitors and secretaries). To obtain accurate product, service and customer costs at Fontaine Informatique requires inclusion of support department costs as well as operating department costs. More accurate support department cost allocations results in more accurate product, service and customer costs.

Be cautious here for several reasons. First, organisations differ in the departments located at the corporate and division levels. Some departments located at corporate headquarters of Fontaine Informatique (for example, R&D) are located at the division level in other organisations. Second, organisations differ in their definitions of *operating department* and *support department*. Always try to ascertain the precise meaning of these terms when analysing data that include allocations of operating department costs and support department costs. Third, organisations differ in the percentage of total support costs allocated using the methods described in this section. Some companies allocate all support department costs using one of the methods outlined below. Other companies only allocate *indirect* support department costs using these methods, with all *direct* support costs traced to the appropriate operating department.

Support department cost-allocation methods

We now examine three methods of allocating the costs of support departments: *direct*, *step-down* and *reciprocal*. To focus on concepts, we use the single-rate method to allocate the costs of each support department.

Consider Honnigsvåg, AS, which manufactures engines used in electric power generating plants. Honnigsvåg has two support departments (Plant Maintenance and Information Systems) and two operating departments (Machining and Assembly) in its manufacturing facility. Costs are accumulated in each department for planning and control purposes. For stock costing, however, the support department costs of Honnigsvåg must be allocated to the operating departments. The data for our example are listed in Exhibit 5.5. The percentages in this table can be illustrated by reference to the Plant Maintenance Department. This support department provides a total of 8000 hours of support work: 20% (1600 ÷ 8000) goes to the Information Systems support department; 30% (2400 ÷ 8000) to the Machining Department; and 50% (4000 ÷ 8000) to the Assembly Department.

Direct allocation method

The **direct allocation method** (often called the **direct method**) is the most widely used method of allocating support department costs. This method allocates each support department's costs directly to the operating departments. Exhibit 5.6 illustrates this method using the data in Exhibit 5.5.

Exhibit 5.5   Data for allocating support department costs at Honnigsvåg for 2015

| | Support departments | | Operating departments | | |
	Plant Maintenance	Information Systems	Machining	Assembly	Total
Budgeted manufacturing overhead costs before any interdepartment cost allocations	€600 000	€116 000	€400 000	€200 000	€1 316 000
Support work furnished					
By Plant Maintenance					
Budgeted labour-hours	–	1 600	2 400	4 000	8 000
Percentage	–	20%	30%	50%	100%
By Information Systems					
Budgeted computer time	200	–	1 600	200	2 000
Percentage	10%	–	80%	10%	100%

Exhibit 5.6   Direct method of allocating support department costs at Honnigsvåg for 2015

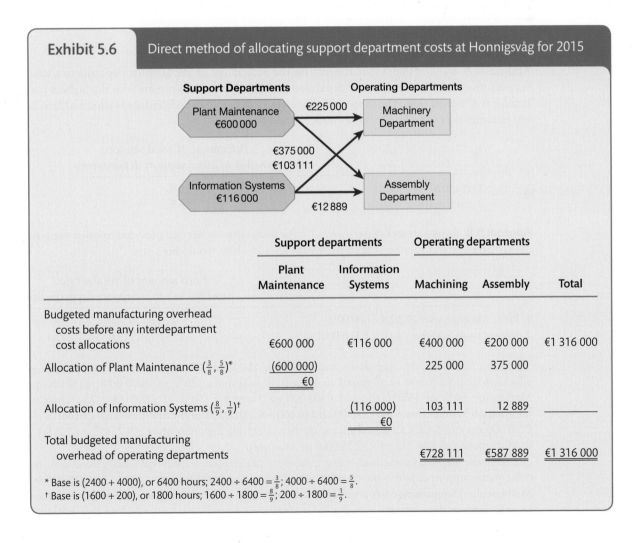

| | Support departments | | Operating departments | | |
	Plant Maintenance	Information Systems	Machining	Assembly	Total
Budgeted manufacturing overhead costs before any interdepartment cost allocations	€600 000	€116 000	€400 000	€200 000	€1 316 000
Allocation of Plant Maintenance $(\frac{3}{8}, \frac{5}{8})^*$	(600 000)		225 000	375 000	
	€0				
Allocation of Information Systems $(\frac{8}{9}, \frac{1}{9})^\dagger$		(116 000)	103 111	12 889	
		€0			
Total budgeted manufacturing overhead of operating departments			€728 111	€587 889	€1 316 000

* Base is (2400 + 4000), or 6400 hours; $2400 \div 6400 = \frac{3}{8}$; $4000 \div 6400 = \frac{5}{8}$.
† Base is (1600 + 200), or 1800 hours; $1600 \div 1800 = \frac{8}{9}$; $200 \div 1800 = \frac{1}{9}$.

Note how this method ignores both the 1600 hours of support time rendered by the Plant Maintenance Department to the Information Systems Department and the 200 hours of support time rendered by Information Systems to Plant Maintenance. The base used to allocate Plant Maintenance is the budgeted total maintenance labour-hours worked in the operating departments: 2400 + 4000 = 6400 hours. This amount excludes the 1600 hours of support time provided by Plant Maintenance to Information Systems. Similarly, the base used for allocation of Information Systems costs is 1600 + 200 = 1800 hours of computer time, which excludes the 200 hours of support time provided by Information Systems to Plant Maintenance.

The benefit of the direct method is its simplicity. There is no need to predict the usage of support department resources by other support departments.

Step-down allocation method

Some organisations use the **step-down allocation method** (sometimes called the **step allocation method** or **sequential allocation method**), which allows for *partial* recognition of the services rendered by support departments to other support departments. This method requires the support departments to be ranked (sequenced) in the order in which the step-down allocation is to proceed. The costs in the first-ranked support department are allocated to the other support departments and to the operating departments. The costs in the second-ranked department are allocated to those support departments not yet allocated and to the operating departments. This procedure is followed until the costs in the last-ranked support department have been allocated to the operating departments. Two ways to determine the sequence to allocate support department costs are as follows:

Approach A Rank support departments on the percentage of the support department's total support provided to other support departments. The support department with the highest percentage is allocated first. The support department with the lowest percentage is allocated last. In our Honnigsvåg example, the chosen order would be:

	Percentage of total service provided to other support departments
1 Plant Maintenance	20%
2 Information Systems	10%

Approach B Rank support departments on the total euros of service provided to other support departments. In our Honnigsvåg example, the chosen order would be:

	Euro amount of total service provided to other support departments
1 Plant Maintenance (0.20 × €600 000)	€120 000
2 Information Systems (0.10 × €116 000)	€11 600

Exhibit 5.7 shows the step-down method where the Plant Maintenance cost of €600 000 is allocated first; €120 000 is allocated to Information Systems (20% of €600 000); €180 000 to Machining (30% of €600 000); and €300 000 to Assembly (50% of €600 000). The costs in Information Systems now total €236 000 (€116 000 + €120 000 from the first-round allocation). This €236 000 amount is then allocated among the two operating departments: €209 778 ($\frac{8}{9}$ × €236 000) to Machining and €26 222 ($\frac{1}{9}$ × €236 000) to Assembly.

Under the step-down method, once a support department's costs have been allocated, no subsequent support department costs are allocated or circulated back to it. Thus, once the Plant Maintenance Department costs are allocated, they receive no further allocation from other (lower-ranked) support departments.

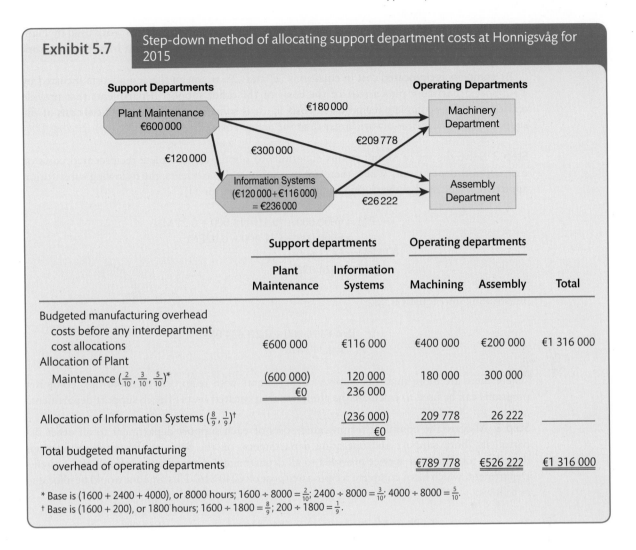

Exhibit 5.7   Step-down method of allocating support department costs at Honnigsvåg for 2015

	Support departments		Operating departments		
	Plant Maintenance	Information Systems	Machining	Assembly	Total
Budgeted manufacturing overhead costs before any interdepartment cost allocations	€600 000	€116 000	€400 000	€200 000	€1 316 000
Allocation of Plant Maintenance $(\frac{2}{10}, \frac{3}{10}, \frac{5}{10})^*$	(600 000) €0	120 000 236 000	180 000	300 000	
Allocation of Information Systems $(\frac{8}{9}, \frac{1}{9})^†$		(236 000) €0	209 778	26 222	
Total budgeted manufacturing overhead of operating departments			€789 778	€526 222	€1 316 000

* Base is (1600 + 2400 + 4000), or 8000 hours; 1600 ÷ 8000 = $\frac{2}{10}$; 2400 ÷ 8000 = $\frac{3}{10}$; 4000 ÷ 8000 = $\frac{5}{10}$.
† Base is (1600 + 200), or 1800 hours; 1600 ÷ 1800 = $\frac{8}{9}$; 200 ÷ 1800 = $\frac{1}{9}$.

Reciprocal allocation method

The **reciprocal allocation method** allocates costs by explicitly including the mutual services provided among all support departments. Theoretically, the direct method and the step-down method are less accurate when support departments provide services to one another reciprocally. For example, the Plant Maintenance Department maintains all the computer equipment in the Information Systems Department. Similarly, Information Systems provides database support for Plant Maintenance. The reciprocal allocation method enables us to incorporate interdepartmental relationships *fully* into the support department cost allocations. That is, Plant Maintenance is allocated to Information Systems and Information Systems is allocated to Plant Maintenance; each is allocated to the operating departments as well. Implementing the reciprocal allocation method requires three steps.

Step 1 Express support department costs and reciprocal relationships in linear equation form. Let PM be the *complete reciprocated costs* of Plant Maintenance and let IS be the complete reciprocated costs of Information Systems. We then express the data in Exhibit 5.5 as follows:

$$PM = €600\ 000 + 0.1IS \qquad (1)$$
$$IS = €116\ 000 + 0.2PM \qquad (2)$$

The 0.1IS term in equation (1) is the percentage of the Information Systems work used by Plant Maintenance. The 0.2PM term in equation (2) is the percentage of the Plant Maintenance work used by Information Systems.

By **complete reciprocated cost** in equations (1) and (2), we mean the actual costs incurred by a support department plus a part of the costs of the other support departments that provide service to it. This complete reciprocated costs figure is sometimes called the **artificial costs** of the support department; it is always larger than the actual costs.

Step 2 Solve the set of simultaneous equations to obtain the complete reciprocated costs of each support department. Where there are two support departments, the following substitution approach can be used. Substituting equation (2) into equation (1),

$$PM = €600\ 000 + [0.1(€116\ 000 + 0.2PM)]$$
$$= €600\ 000 + €11\ 600 + 0.02PM$$
$$0.98PM = €611\ 600$$
$$\therefore PM = €624\ 082$$

Substituting into equation (2),

$$IS = €116\ 000 + 0.2(€624\ 082)$$
$$= €240\ 816$$

Where there are more than two support departments with reciprocal relationships, computer programs can be used to calculate the complete reciprocated costs of each support department.

Step 3 Allocate the complete reciprocated costs of each support department to all other departments (both support and operating departments) on the basis of the usage proportions (based on total units of service provided to all departments). Consider the Information Systems Department, which has a complete reciprocated cost of €240 816. This amount would be allocated as follows:

To Plant Maintenance ($\frac{1}{10} \times$ €240 816)	€24 082
To Machining ($\frac{8}{10} \times$ €240 816)	192 653
To Assembly ($\frac{1}{10} \times$ €240 816)	24 082
Total	€240 817

Exhibit 5.8 presents summary data pertaining to the reciprocal method.

One source of confusion to some managers using the reciprocal cost-allocation method is why the complete reciprocated costs of the support departments, €864 898 (€624 082 and €240 816 in Exhibit 5.8), exceed their budgeted amount of €716 000 (€600 000 and €116 000 in Exhibit 5.5). The excess of €148 898 (€24 082 for Plant Maintenance and €124 816 for Information Systems) is the total costs that are allocated among support departments. The total costs allocated to the operating departments under the reciprocal allocation method are still only €716 000.

Overview of methods

Assume that the total budgeted overhead costs of each operating department in the example in Exhibits 5.6 to 5.8 are allocated to individual products on the basis of budgeted machine-hours for the Machining Department (4000 hours) and budgeted direct labour-hours for the Assembly Department (3000 hours). The budgeted overhead allocation rates associated with each support department allocation method (rounded to the nearest euro) are set out in Exhibit 5.9.

These differences in budgeted overhead rates with alternative support department cost-allocation methods can be important to managers. For example, consider a cost-reimbursement

Exhibit 5.8	Reciprocal method of allocating support department costs at Honnigsvåg for 2015

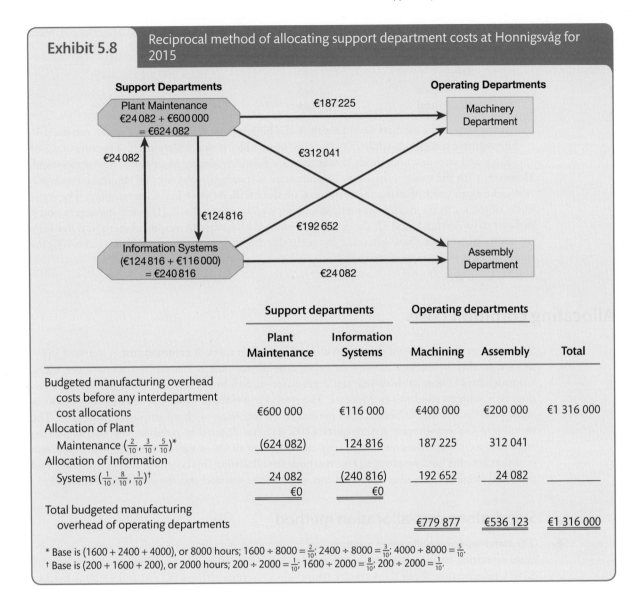

	Support departments		Operating departments		
	Plant Maintenance	Information Systems	Machining	Assembly	Total
Budgeted manufacturing overhead costs before any interdepartment cost allocations	€600 000	€116 000	€400 000	€200 000	€1 316 000
Allocation of Plant Maintenance $(\frac{2}{10}, \frac{3}{10}, \frac{5}{10})$*	(624 082)	124 816	187 225	312 041	
Allocation of Information Systems $(\frac{1}{10}, \frac{8}{10}, \frac{1}{10})$†	24 082 €0	(240 816) €0	192 652	24 082	
Total budgeted manufacturing overhead of operating departments			€779 877	€536 123	€1 316 000

* Base is (1600 + 2400 + 4000), or 8000 hours; 1600 ÷ 8000 = $\frac{2}{10}$; 2400 ÷ 8000 = $\frac{3}{10}$; 4000 ÷ 8000 = $\frac{5}{10}$.
† Base is (200 + 1600 + 200), or 2000 hours; 200 ÷ 2000 = $\frac{1}{10}$; 1600 ÷ 2000 = $\frac{8}{10}$; 200 ÷ 2000 = $\frac{1}{10}$.

Exhibit 5.9	The budgeted overhead allocation rates associated with each support department allocation method

Support department cost-allocation method	Total budgeted overhead costs after allocation of all support department costs		Budgeted overhead rate per hour for product-costing purposes	
	Machining	Assembly	Machining (4000 machine-hours)	Assembly (3000 labour-hours)
Direct	€728 111	€587 889	€182	€196
Step-down	789 778	526 222	197	175
Reciprocal	779 877	536 123	195	179

contract that uses 100 machine-hours and 15 assembly labour-hours. The support department costs allocated to this contract would be:

Direct	€21 140	(€182 × 100 + €196 × 15)
Step-down	22 325	(€197 × 100 + €175 × 15)
Reciprocal	22 185	(€195 × 100 + €179 × 15)

Use of the step-down method would result in the highest cost reimbursement to the contractor.

The reciprocal method, while conceptually preferable, is not widely used. The advantage of the direct and step-down methods is that they are relatively simple to calculate and understand. However, with the ready availability of computer software to solve sets of simultaneous equations, the extra costs of using the reciprocal method will, in most cases, be minimal. The more likely obstacles to the reciprocal method's being widely adopted are: (1) many managers find it difficult to understand, and (2) the numbers obtained by using the reciprocal method differ little (in some cases) from those obtained by using the direct or step-down method. In the UK, the direct method is the most widespread.

Allocating common costs

We next consider two methods used to allocate common costs. A **common cost** is a cost of operating a facility, operation, activity or other cost object that is shared by two or more users. Consider Paul O'Shea, a third-year undergraduate student in Galway who has been invited to an interview with an employer in Moscow. The round-trip Galway–Moscow airfare costs €1200. A week prior to leaving, O'Shea is also invited to an interview with an employer in Prague. The round-trip Galway–Prague airfare costs €800. O'Shea decides to combine the two recruiting steps into a Galway–Moscow–Prague trip that will cost €1500 in airfare. The €1500 is a common cost that benefits both employers. Two methods for allocating this common cost between the two potential employers are now discussed: the stand-alone method and the incremental method.

Stand-alone cost-allocation method

The **stand-alone cost-allocation method** uses information pertaining to each cost object as a separate operating entity to determine the cost-allocation weights. For the airfare common cost of €1500, information about the separate (stand-alone) return airfares (€1200 and €800) is used to determine the allocation weights:

$$\text{Moscow employer:} \quad \frac{€1200}{€1200 + €800} \times €1500 = 0.60 \times €1500 = €900$$

$$\text{Prague employer:} \quad \frac{€800}{€800 + €1200} \times €1500 = 0.40 \times €1500 = €600$$

Advocates of this method often emphasise an equity or fairness rationale. That is, fairness occurs because each employer bears a proportionate share of total costs in relation to their individual stand-alone costs.

Incremental cost-allocation method

The **incremental cost-allocation method** ranks the individual cost objects and then uses this ranking to allocate costs among those cost objects. The first-ranked cost object is termed the *primary party* and is allocated costs up to its cost as a stand-alone entity. The second-ranked cost object is termed the *incremental party* and is allocated the additional cost that arises from there being two users instead of only the primary user. If there are more than two parties, the non-primary parties will need to be ranked.

Consider Paul O'Shea and his €1500 airfare cost. Assume that the Moscow employer is viewed as the primary party. O'Shea's rationale was that he had already committed to go to Moscow. The cost allocations would then be:

Party	Costs allocated	Costs remaining to be allocated to other parties
Moscow (primary)	€1200	€300 (€1500 − €1200)
Prague (incremental)	300	0

The Moscow employer is allocated the full Galway–Moscow airfare. The non-allocated part of the total airfare is allocated to the Prague employer. Had the Prague employer been chosen as the primary party, the cost allocations would have been Prague, €800 (the stand-alone Galway–Prague return airfare) and Moscow, €700 (€1500 − €800). Where there are more than two parties, this method requires them to be ranked and the common costs allocated to those parties in the ranked sequence.

Under the incremental method, the primary party typically receives the highest allocation of the common costs. Not surprisingly, most users in common cost situations propose themselves as the incremental party. In some cases, the incremental party is a newly formed 'organisation' such as a new product line or a new sales territory. Chances for its short-term survival may be enhanced if it bears a relatively low allocation of common costs.

A caution is appropriate here as regards O'Shea's cost-allocation options. His chosen method must be acceptable to each prospective employer. Indeed, some prospective employers may have guidelines that recruiting candidates must follow. For example, the Moscow employer may have a policy that the maximum reimbursable airfare is a seven-day advance booking price in economy class. If this amount is less than the amount that O'Shea would receive under (say) the stand-alone method, then the employer's upper limit guideline would govern how much could be allocated to that interviewer. O'Shea should obtain approval before he purchases his ticket as to which cost-allocation method(s) each potential employer views as acceptable.

Cost-allocation bases and cost hierarchies

Companies make changes in their costing systems at varying degrees of regularity. The prompts to these changes vary. In some cases, it is a change in the operations (for example, an increase in automation or a change in the products manufactured). It can also be a change in information-gathering technology. Another prompt is a change in the products or services offered by competitors (for example, a competitor separately selling as individual products items that were previously sold as a bundle for a single price).

As companies change from labour-paced to machine-paced operations, they increase their use of machine-hours-related allocation bases. In **labour-paced operations,** worker dexterity and productivity determine the speed of production. Machines function as tools that aid production workers. Direct manufacturing labour costs or direct manufacturing labour-hours may still capture cause-and-effect relationships here, even if operations are highly automated. In contrast, in **machine-paced operations,** machines conduct most (or all) phases of production, such as movement of materials to the production line, assembly and other activities on the production line and shipment of finished goods to the delivery bay areas. Machine operators in such environments may simultaneously operate more than one machine. Workers focus their efforts on supervising the production line and general troubleshooting rather than on operating the machines. Computer specialists and industrial engineers guide the speed of production. In machine-paced operations, machine-hours will probably better capture cause-and-effect relationships than the direct labour-hours allocation base.

Consequences of an inappropriate allocation base

Cost figures play a key role in many important decisions. If these figures result from allocation bases that fail to capture cause-and-effect relationships, managers may make decisions that conflict with maximising long-run company net income. Consider the use of direct manufacturing labour costs as an allocation base in machine-paced manufacturing settings. In this environment, indirect-cost rates of 500% of direct manufacturing labour costs (or more) may be encountered. Thus, every €1 of indirect manufacturing labour costs has a €6 impact (€1 in direct costs + 500% per €1 in indirect costs) on reported product costs. Possible negative consequences include the following points:

1 Product managers may make excessive use of external suppliers for parts that have a high direct manufacturing labour content.

2 Manufacturing managers may pay excessive attention to controlling direct manufacturing labour-hours relative to the attention paid to controlling the more costly categories of materials and machining. By eliminating €1 of direct manufacturing labour costs when the indirect-cost rate is 500% of these costs, €6 of reported product cost can be eliminated. When the indirect-cost rate is 500% of these costs, managers can control much of the accounting amounts allocated to products by controlling direct labour use. However, this action does not control the larger materials and machining costs actually incurred.

3 Managers may attempt to classify shop-floor personnel as indirect labour rather than as direct labour. As a result, part of these labour costs will be allocated (inappropriately) to other products.

4 Products may be under- or overcosted. The danger then arises that a company will push to gain market share on products that it believes are profitable when in fact they are unprofitable. Similarly, the company may neglect products that are profitable because it believes they are unprofitable.

Cost drivers and allocation bases

When a cause-and-effect criterion is used, the chosen allocation bases are cost drivers. Because a change in the level of a cost driver causes a change in the total cost of a related cost object, the use of cost drivers as allocation bases increases the accuracy of reported product costs. However, not all chosen cost-allocation bases are cost drivers. Consider the following reasons for using bases that are not cost drivers.

1 Improving the accuracy of individual product costs may be less important to a company than other goals. Think about the goal of restraining the growth in headcount (the number of employees on a company's payroll). Several Japanese companies use direct manufacturing labour-hours as the cost-allocation base, while acknowledging that such labour-hours are not the most important driver of their manufacturing overhead costs. The purpose of this choice is to send a clear signal to all managers that reduction in headcount is a key goal.

   Managers may also prefer direct manufacturing labour-hours as an allocation base so as to promote increased levels of automation. Using this allocation base, product designers are motivated to decrease the direct manufacturing labour content of the products they design. Management may view increased automation as a strategic necessity to remain competitive in the long run.

2 Information about cost-driver variables may not be reliably measured on an ongoing basis. For example, managers often view the number of machine set-ups as a driver of indirect manufacturing costs, but some companies do not systematically record this information.

3 Accounting systems with many indirect-cost pools and allocation bases are more expensive to use than systems with few cost pools and allocation bases. The investment required to develop and implement a system with many indirect cost pools – and to educate users about it – can be sizable. Unfortunately, some firms place a low priority on investments in their internal accounting systems, given that the benefits from such investments are frequently difficult to quantify.

Cost assignment and cost hierarchies

One extreme approach to cost assignment is to fully assign every cost to each individual unit of a product or service. There is growing interest in cost hierarchy systems that stop short of this full assignment of costs. A *cost hierarchy* is a categorisation of costs into different cost pools on the basis of either different classes of cost drivers or different degrees of difficulty in determining cause-and-effect relationships. Not all costs in a cost hierarchy are driven by unit-level product or unit-level service-related variables. Four levels of costs in the product-based cost hierarchy are: (1) output unit-level costs, (2) batch-level costs, (3) product-sustaining costs, and (4) facility-sustaining costs. Activity-based costing systems (see Chapter 11) often differentiate these four levels.

Is the product-costing system broken?

A viewer knows when a television set no longer works. A driver knows when a motor vehicle no longer starts. The breakdown of many products is easy to detect. The breakdown of a product-costing system is not. Nonetheless, guidelines for assessing whether a product-costing system is broken have long existed (Cooper 1987). Although no one individual guideline is conclusive, collectively they can flag the need for a detailed review of an existing product-costing system. The following four questions focus on these guidelines:

1 Can managers easily explain changes in profit margins from one period to the next? (If they cannot, one explanation is that the existing system is broken.)

2 Can managers easily explain why their bids for business are successful or unsuccessful? (If they cannot, one explanation is that the costing system is broken.)

3 Does the costing system have a small number of cost pools, and are the items in each cost pool heterogeneous? (Reducing heterogeneity will require an increase in the number of cost pools.)

4 Are competitors pricing their high-volume products comparable to ours at prices substantially lower than our cost figure? (One explanation is that we are overcosting these products.)

Answering no to questions 1 and 2 and yes to questions 3 and 4 are red-flag responses to the overall question of whether a product-costing system is broken. An individual company that gives a red-flag response to all four of these questions should quickly examine whether its existing costing system should be significantly changed.

Summary

The following points are linked to the chapter's learning objectives.

1 A *cost object* is anything for which a separate measurement of costs is desired. Costing systems in organisations have multiple cost objects (departments, products, services and customers), meaning many individual costs are allocated and reallocated several times before becoming an indirect cost of a specific cost object.

2 The four purposes of cost allocation are to provide information for economic decisions, to motivate managers and employees, to justify costs or calculate reimbursement and to measure income and assets for meeting external regulatory and legal reporting obligations. Different cost allocations may be appropriate depending on the specific purpose.

3 A cost pool is a grouping of individual cost items. Two key decisions related to indirect cost pools are the number of indirect-cost pools and the allowability of individual cost items to be included in those cost pools.

4 A single-rate cost-allocation method pools all costs in one cost pool and allocates them to cost objects using the same rate per unit of the single allocation base. In the dual-rate method, costs are grouped in two separate cost pools, each of which has a different allocation rate and which may have a different allocation base.

5 When cost allocations are made using budgeted rates, managers of divisions to which costs are allocated face no uncertainty about the rates to be used in that period. In contrast, when actual rates are used for cost allocation, managers do not know the rates to be used until the end of the accounting period.

6 The three main methods of allocating support department costs to operating departments are the direct, step-down and reciprocal. The direct method ignores any reciprocal support among support departments. The step-down method allows for partial recognition while the reciprocal method provides full recognition of support among support departments.

7 Common costs are the costs of operating a facility, operation or activity area that are shared by two or more users. The stand-alone cost-allocation method uses information pertaining to each operating entity to determine how to allocate the common costs. The incremental cost-allocation method ranks cost objects and allocates common costs first to the primary cost object and then to the other remaining (incremental) cost objects.

8 The use of an inappropriate cost allocation base can cause products to be manufactured less efficiently, management to be misfocused and products to be mispriced in the marketplace.

9 There is growing interest in cost hierarchies, which are categorisations of costs into different cost pools based on either different classes of cost drivers or different degrees of difficulty in determining cause-and-effect relationships.

Key terms

homogeneous cost pool (128)
single-rate cost-allocation method (128)
dual-rate cost-allocation method (128)
operating department (132)
production department (132)
support department (132)
service department (132)
direct allocation method (132)
direct method (132)
step-down allocation method (134)

step allocation method (134)
sequential allocation method (134)
reciprocal allocation method (135)
complete reciprocated cost (136)
artificial costs (136)
common cost (138)
stand-alone cost-allocation method (138)
incremental cost-allocation method (138)
labour-paced operations (139)
machine-paced operations (139)

References and further reading

Bhimani, A. (1996) *Management Accounting: European Perspectives* (Oxford: Oxford University Press).

Bromwich, M. (1997) *Accounting for Overheads: Critique and Reforms* (Sweden: Uppsala University Press).

Clarke, P.J. (1997) 'Management accounting practices in large Irish manufacturing firms', *Irish Business and Administrative Research*, pp. 136–52.

Cooper, R. (1987) 'Does your company need a new cost system?', *Journal of Cost Management*, Spring.

Harrison, G. and McKinnon, J. (2007) 'National culture and management control', in T. Hopper, D. Northcott and R. Scapens (eds) *Issues in Management Accounting* (Harlow: FT Prentice Hall).

Lovallo, D. and Sibony, O. (2014) 'Is your budget process stuck on last year's numbers?', McKinsey and Co., www.mckinsey.com/insights/corporate_finance.

CHAPTER 5
Assessment material

Review questions

5.1 Why might the classification of a cost as a direct cost or an indirect cost of a cost object change over time?

5.2 How can an individual cost item, such as the salary of a plant security guard, be both a direct cost and an indirect cost at the same time?

5.3 A given cost may be allocated for one or more purposes. List four purposes.

5.4 How do cost–benefit considerations affect choices by a company about the allocation of indirect costs to products, services or customers?

5.5 Distinguish among the three methods of allocating the costs of service departments to production departments.

5.6 Distinguish between two methods of allocating common costs.

5.7 Different costs for different purposes means that a cost allocated for one purpose is not allocated for another purpose. Do you agree?

5.8 Why is the distinction between labour-paced and machine-paced operations important when selecting indirect-cost allocation bases?

5.9 Describe two consequences of using direct manufacturing labour-hours as an allocation base in a machine-paced work environment.

Exercises

Basic level

5.10 **Alternative allocation bases for a professional services firm** (15 minutes)

Germinal et Associés provides tax advice to multinational firms. Germinal charges clients for (a) direct professional time (at an hourly rate) and (b) support services (at 30% of the direct professional costs billed). The three professionals in Germinal and their rates per hour are:

Professional	Billing rate per hour
Thérèse Raquin	€500
Jeanne Rozerot	120
Claude Bernard	80

Germinal has just prepared the May 2015 bills for two clients. The hours spent on each client are as follows:

	Hours per client	
Professional	Fortune Plassans	Au Bonheur des Dames
Raquin	15	2
Rozerot	3	8
Bernard	22	30
Total	40	40

Required

1 What amounts did Germinal bill to Fortune Plassans and Au Bonheur des Dames for May 2015?

2 Suppose support services were billed at €50 per labour-hour (instead of 30% of labour costs). How would this change affect the amounts Germinal billed to the two clients for May 2015? Comment on the differences between the amounts billed in requirements 1 and 2.

3 How would you determine whether labour costs or labour-hours is the more appropriate allocation base for Germinal's support services?

*5.11 Cost allocation, use of a separate machining cost pool category (10 minutes)

Azu-Cena Ltda is a manufacturer of motorcycles. Production and cost data for 2015 are as follows:

	500 cc model	1000 cc model
Units produced	10 000	20 000
Direct manufacturing labour-hours per unit	2	4
Machine-hours per unit	8	8

A single cost pool is used for manufacturing overhead. For 2015, manufacturing overhead was €6.4 million. Azu-Cena allocates manufacturing overhead costs to products on the basis of direct manufacturing labour-hours per unit.

Azu-Cena's accountant now proposes that two separate pools be used for manufacturing overhead costs:

- Machining cost pool (€3.6 million in 2015)
- General plant overhead cost pool (€2.8 million in 2015).

Machining costs are to be allocated using machine-hours per unit. General plant overhead costs are to be allocated using direct manufacturing labour-hours per unit.

Required

1 Calculate the overhead costs allocated per unit to each model of motorcycle in 2015 using the current single-cost-pool approach of Azu-Cena.

2 Calculate the machining costs and general plant overhead costs allocated per unit to each model of motorcycle assuming that the accountant's proposal for two separate cost pools is used in 2015.

3 What benefits might arise from the accountant's proposal for separate pools for machining costs and general plant costs?

5.12 Cost allocation with a non-financial variable, retailing (15–20 minutes)

Jyvaskyla Oy is a retail chain of supermarkets. For many years, it has used gross margin (selling price minus cost of goods sold) to guide it in deciding on which products to emphasise or de-emphasise. And, for many years, it has not allocated any costs to products. It changed its internal reporting system recently and goods handling costs are now allocated to individual products on the basis of cubic volume. (Most products are delivered to the shelves in cartons. A detailed study showed that cubic volume was the major driver of Jyvaskyla's goods handling costs. These costs make up over 30% of non-cost-of-goods-sold costs of Jyvaskyla.) The following data focus on four products in April 2015:

Product	Revenue per carton	Cost of goods purchased per carton	Volume (cubic metres)
Breakfast cereal	€82	€56	24
Dairy product	64	52	12
Paper towels	36	26	24
Toothpaste	100	74	12

Each supermarket has a weekly report on product contribution:

	€	
Revenue		R
Cost of goods sold		C
Gross margin (GM)		R – C
Goods handling costs		D
Product contribution (PC)	€	GM – D

The April 2015 goods-handling cost allocation rate is €0.50 per cubic metre.

Required

1 Calculate the gross margin for each of the four products. Rank these four products using their gross margin percentage.

2 Calculate the product contribution for each of the four products. Rank these four products using the product contribution to revenue percentage.

3 Compare your ranking in requirement 2 with that in requirement 1. How is the requirement 2 analysis useful to Jyvaskyla management?

Intermediate level

5.13 Cost allocation in centres, alternative allocation criteria (15–20 minutes)

Brian McGarrigle went to Les Arcs for his annual winter vacation. Unfortunately, he suffered a broken ankle while skiing and had to spend two days at the Hôpital de Grasse. McGarrigle's insurance company received a €4800 bill for his two-day stay. One item that caught McGarrigle's eye was an €11.52 charge for a roll of cotton wool. McGarrigle was a salesman for Boots and knew that the cost to the centre of the roll of cotton wool would be in the €2.20 to €3.00 range. He asked for a breakdown of how the €11.52 charge was derived. The accounting office of the centre sent him the following information:

a	Invoiced cost of cotton wool roll	€2.40
b	Processing of paperwork for purchase	0.60
c	Supplies room management fee	0.70
d	Operating-room and patient-room handling charge	1.60
e	Administrative centre costs	1.10
f	University teaching-related recoupment	0.60
g	Malpractice insurance costs	1.20
h	Cost of treating uninsured patients	2.72
i	Profit component	0.60
	Total	€11.52

McGarrigle believes the overhead charge is excessive. He comments, 'There was nothing I could do about it. When they come in and dab your stitches, it's not as if you can say, "Keep your cotton wool. I've brought my own."'

Required

1 Calculate the overhead rate Hôpital de Grasse charged on the cotton wool.

2 What criteria might Hôpital de Grasse use to justify allocation of each of the overhead items **b** to **i** in the preceding list? Examine each item separately and use the allocation criteria listed in Exhibit 5.2 in your answer.

3 What should McGarrigle do about the €11.52 charge for the cotton wool?

*5.14   Single-rate versus dual-rate cost-allocation methods (15–20 minutes)

Alxenor SA has a power plant designed and built to serve its three factories. Data for 2015 are as follows:

Factory	Usage in kilowatt-hours	
	Budget	Actual
Kifisia	100 000	80 000
Iraklion	60 000	120 000
Chalandri	40 000	40 000

Actual fixed costs of the power plant were €1 million in 2015; actual variable costs, €2 million.

Required

1 Calculate the amount of power costs that would be allocated to Iraklion using a single-rate method.

2 Calculate the amount of power costs that would be allocated to Iraklion using a dual-rate method.

5.15   Single-rate versus dual-rate allocation methods, support department (20 minutes)

The Fredensborg power plant that services all manufacturing departments of Fabri-Danmark AS has a budget for the coming year. This budget has been expressed in the following terms on a monthly basis:

Manufacturing departments	Needed at practical capacity production level* (kilowatt-hours)	Average expected monthly usage (kilowatt-hours)
Roskilde	10 000	8 000
Køge	20 000	9 000
Nysted	12 000	7 000
Ålborg	8 000	6 000
Totals	50 000	30 000

* This factor was the most influential in planning the size of the power plant.

The expected monthly costs for operating the department during the budget year are DKr 15 000: DKr 6000 variable and DKr 9000 fixed.

Required

1 Assume that a single cost pool is used for the power plant costs. What Danish krone amounts will be allocated to each manufacturing department? Use (a) practical capacity and (b) average expected monthly usage as the allocation bases.

2 Assume a dual-rate method; separate cost pools for the variable and fixed costs are used. Variable costs are allocated on the basis of expected monthly usage. Fixed costs are allocated on the basis of practical capacity. What Danish krone amounts will be allocated to each manufacturing department? Why might you prefer the dual-rate method?

5.16   Allocation of common costs (20–30 minutes)

Rolf, Ilse and Ulrich are members of the Frankfurt Fire Brigade. They share an apartment that has a lounge with the latest wide-screen TV. Ulrich owns the apartment, its furniture and the wide-screen TV. He can subscribe to a cable television company that has the following packages available:

Package	Rate per month
A Basic news	€32
B Premium movies	25
C Premium sport	30
D Basic news and premium movies	50
E Basic news and premium sport	54
F Premium movies and premium sport	48
G Basic news, premium movies and premium sport	70

Rolf is a TV news addict, has average interest in movies and no interest in sport ('they are overpaid dummies'). Ilse is a movie buff, likes sport and avoids the news ('it's all depressing anyway'). Ulrich is a sports fan, has average interest in news and no interest in movies ('I always fall asleep before the end'). They all agree that the purchase of the €70 total package is a 'win-win-win' situation.

Each works on a different eight-hour shift at the fire station, so conflicts in viewing are minimal.

Required

1 What criteria might be used to guide the choice about how to allocate the €70 monthly cable fee among Rolf, Ilse and Ulrich?

2 Outline two methods of allocating the €70 among Rolf, Ilse and Ulrich.

5.17   Allocation of travel costs (20 minutes)

Catherine MacDougall, a third-year undergraduate student at a university near Edinburgh, received an invitation to visit a prospective employer in Nice. A few days later, she received an invitation from a prospective employer in Copenhagen. She decided to combine her visits, travelling from Edinburgh to Nice, Nice to Copenhagen and Copenhagen to Edinburgh.

MacDougall received job offers from both companies. Upon her return, she decided to accept the offer in Copenhagen. She was puzzled about how to allocate her travel costs between the two employers. She gathered the following data:

Regular round-trip fares with no stopovers	
Edinburgh to Nice	£1400
Edinburgh to Copenhagen	£1100

MacDougall paid £1800 for her three-leg flight (Edinburgh to Nice, Nice to Copenhagen, Copenhagen to Edinburgh). In addition, she paid £30 for a taxi from her home to Edinburgh Airport and another £30 for a taxi from Edinburgh Airport to her home when she returned.

Required

1 How should MacDougall allocate the £1800 airfare between the employers in Nice and Copenhagen? Show the actual amounts you would allocate and give reasons for your allocations.

2 Repeat requirement 1 for the £60 taxi fares at the Edinburgh end of her travels.

5.18   Support department cost allocation; direct and step-down methods (30 minutes)

Olympiakos SA provides outsourcing services and advice to both government and corporate clients. For costing purposes, Olympiakos classifies its departments into two support departments (Administrative/Human Resources and Information Systems) and two operating departments

(Government Consulting and Corporate Consulting). For the first quarter of 2015, Olympiakos incurs the following costs in its four departments:

Administrative/Human Resources (A/HR)	€600 000
Information Systems (IS)	€2 400 000
Government Consulting (GOVT)	€8 756 000
Corporate Consulting (CORP)	€12 452 000

The actual level of support relationships among the four departments for the first quarter of 2015 was:

			Used by		
		A/HR	IS	GOVT	CORP
Supplied	A/HR	–	25%	40%	35%
by	IS	10%	–	30%	60%

The Administrative/Human Resource support percentages are based on headcount. The Information Systems support percentages are based on actual hours of computer time used.

Required

1 Allocate the two support department costs to the two operating departments using the following methods:

   a Direct method
   b Step-down method (allocate Administrative/Human Resources first)
   c Step-down method (allocate Information Systems first).

2 Compare and explain differences in the support department costs allocated to each operating department.

3 What criteria could determine the sequence for allocating support departments using the step-down method? What criterion should Olympiakos use if government consulting jobs require the step-down method?

5.19   **Manufacturing cost allocation, use of a conversion cost pool category, automation**
(20–30 minutes)

Euro-Medi Plc manufactures a wide range of medical instruments. Two testing instruments (101 and 201) are produced at its highly automated Limerick plant. Data for December 2015 are as follows:

	Instrument 101	Instrument 201
Direct materials	€100 000	€300 000
Direct manufacturing labour	€20 000	€10 000
Units produced	5 000	20 000
Actual direct labour-hours	1 000	500

Manufacturing overhead is allocated to each instrument product on the basis of actual direct manufacturing labour-hours per unit for that month. Manufacturing overhead cost for December 2015 is €270 000. The production line at the Limerick plant is a machine-paced one. Direct manufacturing labour is made up of costs paid to workers minimising machine problems rather than actually operating the machines. The machines in this plant are operated by computer specialists and industrial engineers.

Required

1 Calculate the cost per unit in December 2015 for instrument 101 and instrument 201 under the existing cost accounting system.

2 The accountant at Euro-Medi proposes combining direct manufacturing labour costs and manufacturing overhead costs into a single conversion costs pool. These conversion costs would be allocated to each unit of product on the basis of direct materials costs. Calculate the cost per unit in December 2015 for instrument 101 and instrument 201 under the accountant's proposal.

3 What are the benefits of combining direct manufacturing labour costs and manufacturing overhead costs into a single conversion costs pool?

5.20   Segment reporting and cost hierarchies (20 minutes)

Koala Ltd has only two divisions: A and B. The following data apply to Division A.

Fixed costs controllable outside division	€100 000
Net revenues	1 500 000
Variable marketing and administrative expenses	200 000
Total traceable costs	1 000 000
Total variable costs	600 000

Required

1 Prepare a segment report for Division A that differentiates between the performance of the manager and the performance of the division.

2 Division B's net revenue is €3 million and its contribution margin is €1.2 million. The segment margin (contribution by division of Division B) is €700 000.

   a Determine fixed costs traceable to Division B.
   b Determine variable costs of Division B.

3 Koala's corporate costs unallocated to divisions are €400 000. Determine Koala's income.

5.21   Departmental cost allocation, university computer-service centre (20–30 minutes)

A computer-service centre of Madrid University serves two major users, the department of Engineering and the department of Humanities and Sciences (H&S).

Required

1 When the computer equipment was initially installed, the procedure for cost allocation was straightforward. The actual monthly costs were compiled and divided between the two departments on the basis of the computer time used by each. In October, the costs were €100 000. H&S used 100 hours and Engineering used 100 hours. How much cost should be allocated to each department? Suppose costs were €110 000 because of various inefficiencies in the operation of the computer centre. How much cost would then be allocated? Does such an allocation seem justified? If not, what improvement would you suggest?

2 Use the same approach as in requirement 1. The actual cost-behaviour pattern of the computer centre was €80 000 fixed cost per month plus €100 variable cost per hour used. In November, H&S used 50 hours and Engineering used 100 hours. How much cost would be allocated to each department? Use a single-rate method.

3 As the computer-service centre developed, a committee was formed that included representatives of H&S and Engineering. This committee determined the size and composition of the centre's equipment. The committee based its planning on the long-run average utilisation of 180 monthly hours for H&S and 120 monthly hours for Engineering. Suppose the €80 000 fixed costs are allocated through a budgeted monthly lump sum based on long-run average utilisation. Variable costs are allocated through a budgeted unit rate of €100 per hour. How much cost should be allocated to each department? What are the advantages of this dual-rate allocation method over other methods?

4 What are the likely behavioural effects of lump-sum allocations of fixed costs? For example, if you were the representative of H&S on the facility planning committee, what would your biases be in predicting long-run usage? How would top management counteract the bias?

Advanced level

*5.22 Cost allocation for all cost categories in the value chain, different costs for different purposes (30–40 minutes)

Laser Tecnologia Srl develops, assembles and sells two product lines:

- Product Line A (laser scanning systems)
- Product Line B (laser cutting tools).

Product Line A is sold exclusively to the Italian Department of Defence under a cost-plus reimbursement contract. Product Line B is sold to commercial organisations.

Laser Tecnologia classifies costs in each of its six value-chain business functions into two cost pools: direct product-line costs (separately traced to Product Line A or B) and indirect product-line costs. The indirect product-line costs are grouped into a single cost pool for each of the six functions of the value-chain cost structure:

Value-chain indirect product-line cost function	Base for allocating indirect costs to each product line
1 R&D	Hours of R&D time identifiable with each product line
2 Product design	Number of new products
3 Production	Hours of machine assembly time
4 Marketing	Number of salespeople
5 Distribution	Number of shipments
6 Customer service	Number of customer visits

Summary data in 2015 are:

	Product Line A: direct costs (millions)	Product Line B: direct costs (millions)	Total indirect costs (millions)	Product allocation base for indirect costs	Product Line A units of allocation base	Product Line B units of allocation base
R&D	€10.0	€5.0	€20.0	R&D time	6 000 hours	2 000 hours
Product design	2.0	3.0	6.0	New products	8 new products	4 new products
Production	15.0	13.0	24.0	Machine-hours	70 000 machine-hours	50 000 machine-hours
Marketing	6.0	5.0	7.0	Salespeople	25 people	45 people
Distribution	2.0	3.0	2.0	Shipments	600 shipments	1400 shipments
Customer service	5.0	3.0	1.0	Customer visits	1000 visits	4000 visits

Required

1 For product pricing on its Product Line B, Laser Tecnologia sets a preliminary selling price of 140% of full cost (made up of both direct costs and the allocated indirect costs for all six of the value-chain cost categories). What is the average full cost per unit of the 2000 units of Product Line B produced in 2015?

2 For motivating managers, Laser Tecnologia separately classifies costs into three groups:

- upstream (R&D and product design)
- manufacturing
- downstream (marketing, distribution and customer service).

Calculate the costs (direct and indirect) in each of these three groups for Product Lines A and B.

3 For the purpose of income and asset measurement for reporting to external parties, inventoriable costs under generally accepted accounting principles for Laser Tecnologia include manufacturing costs and product design costs (both direct and indirect costs of each category). At the end of 2015, what is the average inventoriable cost for the 300 units of Product Line B on hand? (Assume zero opening stock.)

4 The Department of Defence purchases all Product Line A units assembled by Laser Tecnologia. Laser is reimbursed 120% of allowable costs. Allowable cost is defined to include all direct and indirect costs in the R&D, product design, manufacturing, distribution and customer-service functions. Laser Tecnologia employs a marketing staff that makes many visits to government officials, but the Department of Defence will not reimburse Laser for any marketing costs. What is the 2015 allowable cost for Product Line A?

5 'Differences in the costs appropriated for different decisions, such as pricing and cost reimbursement, are so great that firms should have multiple accounting systems rather than a single accounting system.' Do you agree?

CHAPTER 6

Cost allocation: joint-cost situations

Rather than emphasise costing either for single-product companies or for companies in which individual products are separately produced, we now consider costing for the more complex case where two or more products are simultaneously produced with each other. Costs incurred in this more complex case are termed joint costs. A joint cost is the cost of a single process that yields multiple products simultaneously. Although joint costs sometimes pose problems of allocation, it may be possible to trace resources consumption to ultimate cost objects such as individual products or organisational units. This can be useful in making certain types of managerial decision. This chapter examines methods for allocating joint costs to products and services.

Learning objectives

After studying this chapter, you should be able to:

- Identify the split-off point(s) in a joint-cost situation

- Distinguish between joint products and by-products

- Provide several reasons for allocating joint costs to individual products

- Explain alternative methods of allocating joint costs

- Identify the criterion used to support market-based joint-cost allocation methods

- Describe the irrelevance of joint costs in deciding to sell or further process

- Distinguish alternative methods of accounting for by-products

Meaning of joint products and by-products terms

Consider a single process that yields two or more products (or services) simultaneously. The distillation of coal, for example, gives us coke, gas and other products. The cost of this distillation process would be called a **joint cost**. Joint costs are thus the costs of a production process that yields multiple products simultaneously. The juncture in the process when one or more products in a joint-cost setting become separately identifiable is called the **split-off point**. An example is the point where coal becomes coke, gas and other products. **Separable costs** are costs incurred beyond the split-off point that are assignable to one or more individual products. At or beyond the split-off point, decisions relating to sale or further processing of individual products can be made independently of decisions about other products.

Various terms have arisen in conjunction with production processes. A **product** is any output that has a positive sales value (or an output that enables an organisation to avoid incurring costs). **Joint products** all have relatively high sales value but are not separately identifiable as individual products until the split-off point. When a single process yielding two or more products yields only one product with a relatively high sales value, that product is termed a **main product**. A **by-product** has a low sales value compared with the sales value of the main or joint product(s). **Scrap** has a minimal sales value. The classification of products as main, joint, by-product or scrap can change over time, especially for products (such as tin) whose market price can increase or decrease by, say, 30% or more in any one year.

Exhibit 6.1 shows the relationship between the terms defined in the preceding paragraph. Be careful. These distinctions are not firm in practice. The variety of terminology and accounting practice is bewildering. Always gain an understanding of the terms used by the particular organisation with which you are dealing.

Industries abound in which single processes simultaneously yield two or more products. Exhibit 6.2 presents examples of joint-cost situations in diverse industries. In each example in Exhibit 6.2, no individual product can be produced without the accompanying products appearing, although sometimes the proportions can be varied. A poultry farm cannot kill a turkey wing; it has to kill a whole turkey, which yields breast, drumsticks, giblets, feather meal and poultry meal in addition to wings. In this example, the focus is on building up costs of individual products as disassembly occurs. This focus contrasts with prior chapters that emphasise building up costs of individual products as assembly occurs.

In some joint-cost settings, the number of outputs produced exceeds the number of products. This situation can occur where an output, produced as an inherent part of the joint production

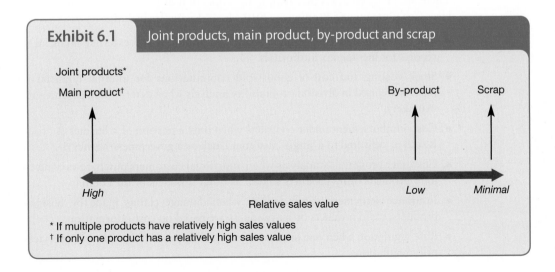

Exhibit 6.1   Joint products, main product, by-product and scrap

Joint products*

Main product†

By-product   Scrap

High   Low   Minimal

Relative sales value

* If multiple products have relatively high sales values
† If only one product has a relatively high sales value

process, is recycled without any value being added by its production. For example, the offshore processing of hydrocarbons to yield oil and gas also yields water as an output, which is recycled back into the sea. Similarly, the processing of mineral ore to yield gold and silver also yields dirt as an output, which is recycled back into the ground. The water and dirt in these examples typically are not classified as products, but they are outputs. No entries are made in the accounting system to record their processing. The physical quantity of these outputs can be large relative to the physical quantity of outputs that are recorded in the accounting system as products. It is only those outputs that have a positive sales value that are typically labelled products.

Exhibit 6.2	Examples of joint-cost situations
Industry	**Separable products at the split-off point**
Agriculture	
Lamb	Lamb cuts, offal, hides, bones, fat
Raw milk	Cream, liquid skim
Turkeys	Breast, wings, drumsticks, giblets, feather meal, poultry meal
Mining industries	
Coal	Coke, gas, benzol, tar, ammonia
Copper ore	Copper, silver, lead, zinc
Petroleum	Crude oil, gas, raw liquefied petroleum gas
Salt	Hydrogen, chlorine, caustic soda
Chemical industries	
Raw liquefied petroleum gas	Butane, ethane, propane
Semiconductor industry	
Fabrication of silicon-wafer chips	Memory chips of different quality (as to capacity), speed, life expectancy and temperature tolerance

Why allocate joint costs?

There are many contexts that require the allocation of joint costs to individual products or services (see Bhimani and Bromwich, 2010, ch. 2). Examples include:

- Stock costing and cost-of-goods-sold computations for external financial statements and reports for income tax authorities.
- Stock costing and cost-of-goods-sold computations for internal financial reporting. Such reports are used in division profitability analysis when determining compensation for division managers.
- Cost reimbursement under contracts when only a portion of a business's products or services is sold or delivered to a single customer (such as a government agency).
- Customer profitability analysis where individual customers purchase varying combinations of joint products or by-products as well as other products of the company.
- Insurance settlement computations when damage claims made by businesses with joint products, main products or by-products are based on cost information.
- Rate regulation when one or more of the jointly produced products or services are subject to price regulation.

Approaches to allocating joint costs

There are two basic approaches to allocating joint costs:

1 Allocate costs using market-based data (for example, revenues). Three methods that can be used in applying this approach are:

   a the sales value at split-off method
   b the estimated net realisable value (NRV) method
   c the constant gross-margin percentage NRV method.

2 Allocate costs using physical measure-based data such as weight or volume.

We have previously emphasised both the cause-and-effect and benefits-received criteria for guiding cost-allocation decisions. In joint-cost settings, it is not feasible to use the cause-and-effect criterion to guide individual product-cost allocations. Joint costs, by definition, cannot be the subject of cause-and-effect analysis at the individual product level. The cause-and-effect relationship exists only at the joint process level. The benefits-received criterion leads to a preference for methods under approach 1. Revenues, in general, are a better indicator of benefits received than are physical measures such as weight or volume.

In the simplest situation, the joint products are sold at the split-off point without further processing. We use this case first (Example 6.1) to illustrate the sales value at split-off method and the physical measures method using volume as the metric. Then we consider situations involving further processing beyond the split-off point (Example 6.2) to illustrate the estimated NRV method and the constant gross-margin percentage NRV method.

To highlight each joint-cost example, we make extensive use of exhibits in this chapter. We use the following notation:

Joint product or main product   By-product or scrap

To enable comparisons across the methods, we report for each method individual gross-margin percentages for individual products.

Example 6.1

Farmers' Dairy purchases raw milk from individual farms and processes it up to the split-off point, where two products (cream and liquid skim) are obtained. These two products are sold to an independent company, which markets and distributes them to supermarkets and other retail outlets.

Exhibit 6.3 presents an overview of the basic relationships in this example. Summary data for May 2015 are as follows:

- Raw milk processed: 440 litres (440 litres of raw milk yield 400 litres of good product with a 40-litre shrinkage):

	Production	Sales
Cream	100 litres	80 litres at €2 per litre
Liquid skim	300 litres	120 litres at €1 per litre

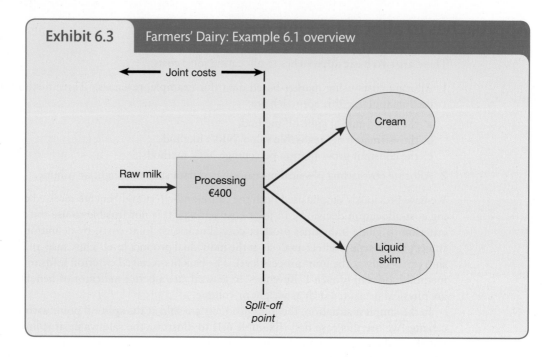

Exhibit 6.3   Farmers' Dairy: Example 6.1 overview

- Stocks:

	Opening stock	Closing stock
Raw milk	0 litre	0 litre
Cream	0 litre	20 litres
Liquid skim	0 litre	180 litres

- Cost of purchasing 440 litres of raw milk and processing it up to the split-off point to yield 100 litres of cream and 300 litres of liquid skim: €400.

How much of the joint costs of €400 should be allocated to the closing stock of 20 litres of cream and 180 litres of liquid skim? The joint production costs of €400 cannot be uniquely identified with or traced to either product. Why? Because the products themselves were not separated before the split-off point. The joint-cost-allocation methods we now discuss can be used for costing the stock of cream and liquid skim as well as determining cost of goods sold.

Sales value at split-off method

The **sales value at split-off method** allocates joint costs on the basis of the relative sales value at the split-off point of the total production in the accounting period of each product. In Exhibit 6.1, the sales value at split-off of the May 2015 production is €200 for cream and €300 for liquid skim. We then assign a weighting to each product, which is a percentage of total sales value. Using this weighting, we allocate the joint costs to the individual products, as shown in Exhibit 6.4.

Note that this method uses the sales value of the *entire production* of the accounting period. The joint costs were incurred on all units produced and not just those sold. Exhibit 6.5 presents the product-line income statement, using the sales value at split-off method of joint-cost allocation. Use of this method has enabled us to obtain individual product costs and gross margins. Both cream and liquid skim have gross-margin percentages of 20%. The equality of the gross-margin percentages for the two products is a mechanical result reached with the sales value at split-off method when there are no beginning stocks and all products are sold at the split-off point.

Exhibit 6.4	Allocation of joint costs using the sales value at split-off method		
	Cream	Liquid skim	Total
1 Sales value at split-off point (cream, 100 litres × €2; liquid skim, 300 litres × €1)	€200	€300	€500
2 Weighting (€200 ÷ €500; €300 ÷ €500)	0.40	0.60	
3 Joint costs allocated (cream, 0.40 × €400; liquid skim, 0.60 × €400)	€160	€240	€400
4 Joint production costs per litre (cream, €160 ÷ 100 litres; liquid skim, €240 ÷ 300 litres)	€1.60	€0.80	

Exhibit 6.5	Farmers' Dairy product-line income statement for May 2015: joint costs allocated using sales value at split-off method		
	Cream	Liquid skim	Total
Sales (cream, 80 litres × €2; liquid skim, 120 litres × €1)	€160	€120	€280
Joint costs			
Production costs (cream, 0.4 × €400; liquid skim, 0.6 × €400)	160	240	400
Deduct ending stock (cream, 20 litres × €1.60; liquid skim, 180 litres × €0.80)	32	144	176
Cost of goods sold	128	96	224
Gross margin	€32	€24	€56
Gross-margin percentage	20%	20%	20%

The sales value at split-off point method exemplifies the benefits-received criterion of cost allocation. Costs are allocated to products in proportion to their ability to contribute revenue. This method is both straightforward and intuitive. The cost-allocation base (sales value at split-off) is expressed in terms of a common denominator (euros) that is systematically recorded in the accounting system and well understood by all parties.

Physical measure method

The **physical measure method** allocates joint costs on the basis of their relative proportions at the split-off point, using a common physical measure such as weight or volume of the total production of each product. In Example 6.1, the €400 joint costs produced 100 litres of cream and 300 litres of liquid skim. Joint costs using these quantities are allocated as shown in Exhibit 6.6.

Exhibit 6.7 presents the product-line income statement using this method of joint-cost allocation. The gross-margin percentages are 50% for cream and 0% for liquid skim.

The physical weights used for allocating joint costs may have no relationship to the revenue-producing power of the individual products. Using the benefits-received criterion, the physical measure method is less preferred than the sales value at split-off method. Consider a mine that extracts ore containing gold, silver and lead. Use of a common physical measure (tonnes) would result in almost all the costs being allocated to the product that weighs the most – lead, which has the lowest revenue-producing power. As a second example, if the joint cost of a pig were assigned to its various products on the basis of weight, loin pork chops would have the same cost per

Exhibit 6.6	Allocation of joint costs using the physical measure method		
	Cream	**Liquid skim**	**Total**
1 Physical measure of production (litres)	25	75	100
2 Weighting (100 litres ÷ 400 litres; 300 litres ÷ 400 litres)	0.25	0.75	
3 Joint costs allocated (cream, 0.25 × €400; liquid skim, 0.75 × €400)	€100	€300	€400
4 Joint production costs per litre (cream, €100 ÷ 100 litres; liquid skim, €300 ÷ 300 litres)	€1	€1	

Exhibit 6.7	Farmers' Dairy product-line income statement for May 2015: joint costs allocated using the physical measure method		
	Cream	**Liquid skim**	**Total**
Sales (cream, 80 litres × €2; liquid skim, 120 litres × €1)	€160	€120	€280
Joint costs			
Production costs (cream, 0.25 × €400; liquid skim, 0.75 × €400)	100	300	400
Deduct closing stock (cream, 20 litres × €1; liquid skim, 180 litres × €1)	20	180	200
Cost of goods sold	80	120	200
Gross margin	€80	€0	€80
Gross-margin percentage	50%	0%	28.6%

kilogram as pigs' trotters, lard, bacon, bones and so forth. In a product-line income statement, the pork products that have a high sales value per kilogram (for example, loin pork chops) would show a fabulous 'profit', and products that have a low sales value per kilogram (for example, bones) would show consistent losses.

Obtaining comparable physical measures for all products is not always straightforward. Consider oil and gas joint-cost settings, where oil is a liquid and gas is a vapour. Use of a physical measure, such as barrels, will require technical assistance from chemical engineers on how to convert the vapour into a measure additive with barrels of oil. Technical personnel outside accounting may be required when using some physical measures in joint-cost-allocation situations.

Example 6.2

Assume the same situation as in Example 6.1 except that both cream and liquid skim can be processed further:

- Cream → Butter cream: 100 litres of cream are further processed to yield 80 litres of butter cream at additional processing (separable) costs of €280. Butter cream is sold for €6.25 per litre.

- Liquid skim → Condensed milk: 300 litres of liquid skim are further processed to yield 200 litres of condensed milk at additional processing costs of €520. Condensed milk is sold for €5.5 per litre.

Sales during the accounting period were 48 litres of butter cream and 180 litres of condensed milk. Exhibit 6.8 presents an overview of the basic relationships. Stock information is as follows:

	Opening stock	Closing stock
Raw milk	0 litres	0 litres
Cream	0 litres	0 litres
Liquid skim	0 litres	0 litres
Butter cream	0 litres	32 litres
Condensed milk	0 litres	20 litres

Example 6.2 will be used to illustrate the estimated net realisable value (NRV) method and the constant gross-margin percentage NRV method.

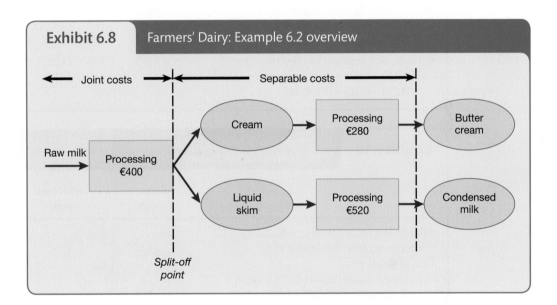

Exhibit 6.8   Farmers' Dairy: Example 6.2 overview

Estimated net realisable value method

The **estimated net realisable value (NRV) method** allocates joint costs on the basis of the relative *estimated net realisable value* (expected final sales value in the ordinary course of business minus the expected separable costs of production and marketing of the total production of the period). Joint costs would be allocated as shown in Exhibit 6.9.

Exhibit 6.10 presents the product-line income statement using the estimated NRV method. The gross-margin percentages are 22.0% for butter cream and 26.4% for condensed milk.

Estimating the net realisable value of each product at the split-off point requires information about the subsequent processing steps to be taken (and their expected separable costs). (The estimated NRV method is clear-cut when there is only one split-off point. When there are multiple split-off points, however, additional allocations may be required if processes subsequent to the initial split-off point remerge with each other to create a second joint-cost situation.) In some plants, such as in petrochemicals, there may be many possible subsequent steps. Companies may frequently change further processing to exploit fluctuations in the separable costs of each processing stage or in the selling prices of individual products. Under the estimated NRV method, each such change would affect the joint-cost-allocation percentages. (In practice, a set of standard subsequent steps is assumed at the start of the accounting period when using the estimated NRV method.)

Exhibit 6.9	Allocation of joint costs using the estimated NRV method		
	Butter cream	Condensed milk	Total
1 Expected final sales value of production (butter cream, 80 litres × €6.25; condensed milk, 200 litres × €5.5)	€500	€1100	€1600
2 Deduct expected separable costs to complete and sell	280	520	800
3 Estimated NRV at split-off point	€220	€580	€800
4 Weighting (€220 ÷ €800; €580 ÷ €800)	0.275	0.725	
5 Joint costs allocated (butter cream, 0.275 × €400; condensed milk, 0.725 × €400)	€110	€290	€400
6 Production costs per litre [butter cream (€110 + €280) ÷ 80 litres; condensed milk (€290 + €520) ÷ 200 litres]	€4.875	€4.05	

Exhibit 6.10	Farmers' Dairy product-line income statement for May 2015: joint costs allocated using the estimated NRV method		
	Butter cream	Condensed milk	Total
Sales (butter cream, 48 litres × €6.25; condensed milk, 180 litres × €5.5)	€300	€990	€1290
Cost of goods sold			
Joint costs (butter cream, 0.275 × €400; condensed milk, 0.725 × €400)	110	290	400
Separable processing costs	280	520	800
Cost of goods available for sale	390	810	1200
Deduct closing stock (butter cream, 32 litres × €4.875; condensed milk, 20 litres × €4.05)	156	81	237
Cost of goods sold	234	729	963
Gross margin	€66	€261	€327
Gross-margin percentage	22.0%	26.4%	25.3%

The sales value at split-off method is less complex than the estimated NRV method as it does not require knowledge of the subsequent steps in processing. However, it is not always feasible to use the sales value at split-off method. Why? Because there may not be any market prices at the split-off point for one or more individual products. Market prices may not first appear until after processing beyond the split-off point has occurred.

Constant gross-margin percentage NRV method

The **constant gross-margin percentage NRV method** allocates joint costs in such a way that the overall gross-margin percentage is identical for all the individual products. This method entails three steps:

Exhibit 6.11	Farmers' Dairy for May 2015: joint costs allocated using constant gross-margin percentage NRV method		
	Butter cream	**Condensed milk**	**Total**
Step 1			
Expected final sales value of production:			
(80 litres × €6.25) + (200 litres × €5.5)		€1600	
Deduct joint and separable costs (€400 + €280 + €520)		1200	
Gross margin		€400	
Gross-margin percentage (€400 ÷ €1600)		25%	
Step 2			
Expected final sales value of production			
(butter cream, 80 litres × €6.25;			
condensed milk, 200 litres × €5.5)	€500	€1100	€1600
Deduct gross margin, using overall gross-margin			
percentage (25%)	125	275	400
Cost of goods sold	375	825	1200
Step 3			
Deduct separable costs to complete and sell	280	520	800
Joint costs allocated	€95	€305	€400

1 Calculate the overall gross-margin percentage.

2 Use the overall gross-margin percentage and deduct the gross margin from the final sales values to obtain the total costs that each product should bear.

3 Deduct the expected separable costs from the total costs to obtain the joint-cost allocation.

Exhibit 6.11 presents these three steps for allocating the €400 joint costs between butter cream and condensed milk. To determine the joint-cost allocation, Exhibit 6.11 uses the expected final sales value of the *total production* of the period (€1600) and *not* the actual sales of the period. The joint costs allocated to each product need not always be positive under this method. Some products may receive negative allocations of joint costs to bring their gross-margin percentages up to the overall company average. The overall gross-margin percentage is 25%. A product-line income statement for the constant gross-margin percentage NRV method is presented in Exhibit 6.12.

The tenuous assumption underlying the constant gross-margin percentage NRV method is that all the products have the same ratio of cost to sales value. A constant ratio of cost to sales value across products is rarely seen in companies that produce multiple products but have no joint costs. The main advantage of this method, however, is that it is easy to implement.

Comparison of methods

Which method of allocating joint costs should be chosen? Because the costs are joint in nature, managers cannot use the cause-and-effect criterion in making this choice. Managers cannot be sure what causes what cost when examining joint costs. The benefits-received criterion leads to a preference for the sales value at split-off point method (or other related revenue or market-based methods). Additional benefits of this method include:

1 No anticipation of subsequent management decisions. The sales value at split-off method does not presuppose an exact number of subsequent steps undertaken for further processing.

2 Availability of a meaningful common denominator to calculate the weighing factors. The denominator of the sales value at split-off method (euros) is a meaningful one. In contrast, the

Exhibit 6.12	Farmers' Dairy product-line income statement for May 2015: joint costs allocated using constant gross-margin percentage NRV method		
	Butter cream	**Condensed milk**	**Total**
Sales (butter cream, 48 litres × €6.25; condensed milk, 180 litres × €5.5)	€300.0	€990.0	€1290.0
Cost of goods sold			
Joint costs (from Exhibit 6.11)	95.0	305.0	400.0
Separable costs to complete and sell	280.0	520.0	800.0
Cost of goods available for sale	375.0	825.0	1200.0
Deduct closing stock (butter cream, 32 litres × €4.6875*; condensed milk, 20 litres × €4.125†)	150.0	82.5	232.5
Cost of goods sold	225.0	742.5	967.5
Gross margin	€75.0	€247.5	€322.5
Gross-margin percentage	25%	25%	25%

* 375 ÷ 80 litres = €4.6875.
† 825 ÷ 200 litres = €4.125.

physical measure method may lack a meaningful common denominator for all the separable products (for example, when some products are liquids and other products are solids).

3 Simplicity. The sales value at split-off method is simple. In contrast, the estimated NRV method can be very complex in operations with multiple products and multiple split-off points. The total sales value at split-off is unaffected by any change in the production process after the split-off point.

The purpose of the joint-cost allocation is important. Consider rate regulation. Market-based measures are difficult to use in this context. It is circular to use selling prices as a basis for setting prices (rates) and at the same time use selling prices to allocate the costs on which prices (rates) are based. Physical measures represent one joint-cost-allocation approach available in rate regulation.

Concepts in action   Chicken processing: costing on the disassembly line

Source: Digital Vision Ltd

Chicken processing operations provide many examples where joint and by-product costing issues can arise. Each chicken is killed and then 'disassembled' into many products. Every effort is made to obtain revenue from each disassembled item.

White breast meat, the highest revenue-generating product, is obtained from the front end of the bird. Dark meat is obtained from the back end. Other edible products include chicken wings, giblets and kidneys. There are many non-edible products, including feathers and blood, the head, feet and intestines. The non-edible products have a diverse set of uses. Examples include poultry feathers (used in bedding and sporting goods); poultry leftover parts such as bones, beaks and feet (ground into livestock pellets and fertiliser); and poultry fat (used in animal feed and pet food).

Poultry companies use individual product cost information for several purposes. One purpose is in customer profitability analysis. Customers (such as supermarkets and fast-food restaurants) differ greatly in the mix of products purchased. Individual product cost data enable companies to determine differences in individual customer profitability. A subset of products is placed into frozen storage, which creates a demand for individual product cost information for stock valuation.

Companies differ in how they cost individual products. Some companies classify white breast meat as the single main product in their costing system. All other products are then classified as by-products. Market selling prices of the many by-products are used to reduce the chicken processing costs that are allocated to the main product. The white breast meat is often further processed into many individual products (such as trimmed chicken and marinated chicken). The separable cost of this further processing is added to the cost per kilogram of deboned white breast meat to obtain the cost of further processed products.

Other companies might classify any product sold to a retail outlet as a joint product. Such products include breast fillets, half breasts, drumsticks, thighs and whole legs. All other products are classified as by-products. Revenue from by-products is offset against the chicken processing cost and is allocated among the joint products. The average selling prices of products sold to retail outlets are used to allocate the net chicken processing cost among the individual joint products. The distribution costs of transporting the chicken products from the processing plants to retail outlets are not taken into account when determining the joint-cost-allocation weights.

No allocation of joint costs

All of the preceding methods of allocating joint costs to individual products are subject to criticism. As a result, some companies refrain from joint-cost allocation entirely. Instead, they carry all stocks at estimated NRV. Income on each product is recognised when production is completed. Industries that use variations of this approach include meat packing, canning and mining.

Accountants ordinarily criticise carrying stocks at estimated NRV. Why? Because income is recognised *before* sales are made. Partly in response to this criticism, some companies using this no-allocation approach carry their stocks at estimated NRV minus a normal profit margin.

Exhibit 6.13 presents the product-line income statement with no allocation of joint costs for Example 6.2. The separable costs are assigned first, which highlights for managers the cause-and-effect relationship between individual products and the costs incurred on them. The joint costs are not allocated to butter cream and condensed milk as individual products.

Exhibit 6.13	Farmers' Dairy product-line income statement for May 2015: no allocation of joint costs		
	Butter cream	**Condensed milk**	**Total**
Produced and sold (butter cream, 48 litres × €6.25; condensed milk, 180 litres × €5.5)	€300	€990	€1290
Produced but not sold (butter cream, 32 litres × €6.25; condensed milk, 20 litres × €5.5)	200	110	310
Total sales value of production	500	€1100	1600
Separable costs	280	520	800
Contribution to joint costs and operating profit	€220	€580	800
Joint costs			400
Gross margin			€400
Gross-margin percentage			25%

Irrelevance of joint costs for decision making

No technique for allocating joint-product costs should guide management decisions regarding whether a product should be sold at the split-off point or processed beyond split-off. When a product is an inevitable result of a joint process, the decision to process further should not be influenced either by the size of the total joint costs or by the portion of the joint costs allocated to particular products. Ultimately, all joint-cost allocations to products are, to a degree, arbitrary.

Sell or process further

The decision to incur additional costs beyond split-off should be based on the incremental operating profit attainable beyond the split-off point. Example 6.2 assumed that it was profitable for both cream and liquid skim to be further processed into butter cream and condensed milk, respectively. The incremental analysis for these decisions to process further is as follows:

Further processing cream into butter cream

Incremental revenue (€500 – €200)	€300
Incremental processing costs	280
Incremental operating profit	€20

Further processing liquid skim into condensed milk

Incremental revenue (€1100 – €300)	€800
Incremental processing costs	520
Incremental operating profit	€280

Example 6.3

Atilla-Parfums jointly processes a speciality chemical that yields two perfumes: 50 ml of Chimène and 150 ml of Nicomède. The sales values per millilitre at split-off are €6 for Chimène and €4 for Nicomède. The joint costs incurred up to the split-off point are €880. The manager has the option of further processing 150 ml of Nicomède to yield 100 ml of Psyché. The total additional costs of converting Nicomède into Psyché would be €160 and the selling price per millilitre of Psyché would be €8. Exhibit 6.14 summarises the relationships in this example.

Exhibit 6.14   Atilla-Parfums: Example 6.3 overview

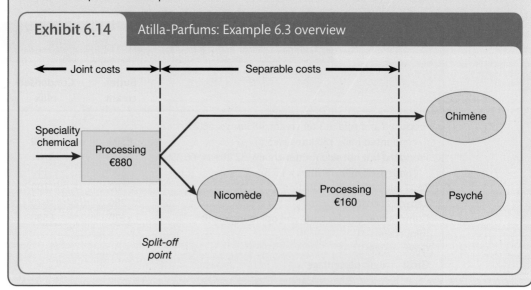

The amount of joint costs incurred up to split-off (€400) – and how it is allocated – is irrelevant in deciding whether to process further cream or liquid skim. Why? Because the joint costs of €400 are the same whether or not further processing is done.

Many manufacturing companies constantly face the decision of whether to process further a joint product. Meat products may be sold as cut or may be smoked, cured, frozen, canned and so forth. Petroleum refiners are perpetually trying to adjust to the most profitable product mix. The refining process necessitates separating all products from crude oil, even though only two or three may have high revenue potential. The refiner must decide what combination of processes to use to get the most profitable mix of crude oil, gas, butane, ethane, propane and the like.

In designing reports for managers' decisions of this nature, the accountant must concentrate on incremental costs rather than on how historical joint costs are to be allocated among various products. The only relevant items are incremental revenue and incremental costs. This next example illustrates the importance of the incremental cost viewpoint.

The correct approach in deciding whether to further process Nicomède into Psyché is to compare the incremental revenue with the incremental costs, if all other factors such as invested capital and the time period are held constant:

Incremental revenue of Psyché $(100 \times €8) - (150 \times €4)$	€200
Incremental costs of Psyché, further processing	160
Incremental operating profit from converting Nicomède into Psyché	€40

The following is a total income computation of each alternative. The revenues reported for each product are Chimène (50 ml at €6 per ml = €300), Nicomède (150 ml at €4 per ml = €600) and Psyché (100 ml at €8 per ml = €800).

	Alternative 1: Sell Chimène and Nicomède	Alternative 2: Sell Chimène and Psyché	Difference
Total revenues	(€300 + €600) €900	(€300 + €800) €1100	€200
Total processing costs	880	(€880 + €160) 1040	160
Operating profit	€20	€60	€40

As we can see from our example, it is profitable to extend processing and to incur additional costs on a joint product as long as the incremental revenue exceeds incremental costs.

Conventional methods of joint-cost allocation may mislead managers who rely on unit-cost data to guide their sell-or-further-process decisions. For example, the physical measure method (millilitres in our example) would allocate the €880 joint costs as follows:

Product	Millilitres produced	Weighting	Allocation of joint costs
Chimène	50	50 ÷ 200 = 0.25	0.25 × €880 = €220
Nicomède	150	150 ÷ 200 = 0.75	0.75 × €880 = 660
	200		€880

The resulting product-line income statement for the alternative of selling Chimène and Psyché would erroneously imply that the company would suffer a loss by selling Psyché:

	Chimène	Psyché
Revenues	€300	€800
Costs		
Joint costs allocated	220	660
Separable costs	–	160
Cost of goods sold	220	820
Operating profit	€80	€(20)

Accounting for by-products

Processes that yield joint products often also yield what are frequently referred to as by-products – products that have relatively low sales value compared with the sales value of the main or joint product(s). We now discuss accounting for by-products. To simplify the discussion, consider a two-product example consisting of a main product and a by-product.

Example 6.4

Deen's Grossierderij BV processes meat from slaughterhouses. One of its departments cuts lamb shoulders and generates two products:

- shoulder meat (the main product) – sold for €60 per pack
- hock meat (the by-product) – sold for €4 per pack.

Both products are sold at the split-off point without further processing, as Exhibit 6.15 shows. Data (number of packs) for this department in July 2015 are as follows:

	Production	Sales	Opening stock	Closing stock
Shoulder meat	500	400	0	100
Hock meat	100	30	0	70

Total manufacturing costs of these products were €25 000.

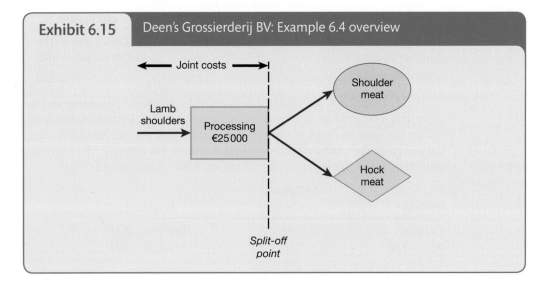

Exhibit 6.15   Deen's Grossierderij BV: Example 6.4 overview

Accounting methods for by-products address two major questions:

1 When are by-products first recognised in the general ledger? The two basic choices are (a) at the time of production, or (b) at the time of sale.

2 Where do by-product revenues appear in the income statement? The two basic choices are (a) as a cost reduction of the main or joint product(s), or (b) as a separate item of revenue or other income.

Combining these two questions and choices gives four possible ways of accounting for by-products (Exhibit 6.16).

Exhibit 6.16   Four ways to account for by-products

By-product accounting method	When by-products are recognised in in general ledger	Where by-product revenues appear in income statement	Where by-product stocks appear on balance sheet
A	Production	Reduction of cost	By-product stock
B	Production	Revenue or other income item	reported at (unrealised) selling prices
C	Sale	Reduction of cost	By-product stock
D	Sale	Revenue or other income item	not recognised

Exhibit 6.17 presents the income statement figures and stock figures that Deen's Grossierderij would report under each method. Methods A and B recognise the by-product stock at the time of production. Note, however, that by-product stocks are reported on the balance sheet at selling prices rather than at a cost amount. One variation of methods A and B is to report by-product

---

Exhibit 6.17   Deen's Grossierderij BV income statement for July 2015

	By-product accounting method			
	A	**B**	**C**	**D**
When by-products are recognised in general ledger	At production	At production	At sale	At sale
Where by-product revenues appear in income statements	Reduction of cost	Revenue item	Reduction of cost	Revenue item
Revenues				
Main product: shoulder meat (400 × €60)	€24 000	€24 000	€24 000	€24 000
By-product: hock meat (30 × €4)	–	120	–	120
Total revenue	24 000	24 120	24 000	24 120
Cost of goods sold				
Total manufacturing costs	25 000	25 000	25 000	25 000
Deduct by-product net revenue (30 × €4)	120	–	120	–
Net manufacturing costs	24 880	25 000	24 880	25 000
Deduct main product stock*	4 976	5 000	4 976	5 000
Deduct by-product stock (70 × €4)	280	280		
Total cost of goods sold	19 624	19 720	19 904	20 000
Gross margin	€4 376	€4 400	€4 096	€4 120
Gross-margin percentage	18.23%	18.24%	17.07%	17.08%
Inventoriable costs (end of period)				
Main product: shoulder meat	€4 976	€5 000	€4 976	€5 000
By-product: hock meat†	280	280	0	0

* (100 ÷ 500) × net manufacturing costs.
† Shown at selling prices.

stocks at selling price minus a 'normal profit margin'. This variation avoids including unrealised gains as an offset to cost of goods sold in the period of production. One version of method A deducts the estimated NRV of the by-product(s) from the joint costs before the remainder is allocated to individual joint products. Another version of method A deducts the estimated NRV of the by-product(s) from the total production costs (joint costs plus separable costs).

Methods C and D are rationalised in practice primarily on grounds of the relative insignificance of by-products. By-products are sometimes viewed as incidental. Methods C and D permit managers to 'manage' reported earnings by timing when they sell by-products. Managers may stockpile by-products so that they have flexibility to give revenue a 'boost' when most propitious for them.

Deen's Grossierderij uses method B in its accounting system. This method highlights how each saleable product contributes to its total revenues. Over time, the revenues contributed by individual products can vary. Method B enables managers to track these changing contributions easily.

Summary

The following points are linked to the chapter's learning objectives.

1 A joint cost is the cost of a single process that yields multiple products. The split-off point is the juncture in the process when the products become separately identifiable.

2 Joint products have relatively high sales value and are not separately identifiable as individual products until the split-off point. A by-product has a low sales value compared with the sales value of a joint product. Individual products can change from being a by-product or a joint product when their market prices move sizably in one direction.

3 The purposes for allocating joint costs to products include stock costing for external financial reporting, internal financial reporting, cost reimbursement under contracts, customer profitability analysis, insurance settlements and rate regulation.

4 The accounting methods available for allocating joint costs include using market selling price (either sales value at split-off or estimated net realisable value) or using a physical measure. Choosing not to allocate is also an option.

5 The benefits-received criterion leads to a preference for revenue or market-based methods such as the sales value at split-off point method. Additional pros of this method include not anticipating subsequent management decisions on further processing, using a meaningful common denominator and being simple.

6 The incremental-cost analysis emphasised elsewhere in this book applies equally to joint-cost situations. No techniques for allocating joint-product costs should guide decisions about whether a product should be sold at the split-off point or processed beyond split-off because joint costs are irrelevant.

7 By-product accounting is an area where there is much inconsistency in practice and where some methods used are justified on the basis of expediency rather than theoretical soundness. By-products can be recognised at production or at the point of sale. By-product revenues can appear as a separate revenue item or an offset to other costs.

Key terms

joint cost (153)
split-off point (153)
separable costs (153)
product (153)
joint products (153)
main product (153)
by-product (153)

scrap (153)
sales value at split-off method (156)
physical measure method (157)
estimated net realisable value (NRV)
   method (159)
constant gross-margin percentage NRV
   method (160)

References and further reading

Bhimani, A. and Bromwich, M. (2010) *Management Accounting: Retrospect and Prospect* (Oxford: CIMA/Elsevier).

Labro, E. (2006) 'Analytics of costing system design', in A. Bhimani (ed) *Contemporary Issues in Management Accounting* (Oxford: Oxford University Press), pp. 217–42.

CHAPTER 6

Assessment material

Review questions

6.1   What is a joint cost?

6.2   Define separable costs.

6.3   Give two examples of industries in which joint costs are found. For each example, what are the individual products at or beyond the split-off point?

6.4   Why might the number of products in a joint-cost setting differ from the number of outputs? Give an example.

6.5   Provide three reasons for allocating joint costs to individual products or services.

6.6   Give two limitations of the physical measure method of joint-cost allocation.

6.7   Which joint-cost-allocation method is supported by the cause-and-effect criterion for choosing among allocation methods?

6.8   'Managers must decide whether a product should be sold at split-off or processed further. The sales value at split-off method of joint-cost allocation is the best method for generating the information managers need.' Do you agree? Why?

6.9   'Managers should consider only additional revenues and separable costs when making decisions about selling now or processing further.' Do you agree? Why?

6.10 Describe an accounting method that would eliminate some key inconsistencies that often arise in by-product reporting.

Exercises

Basic level

6.11   **Matching terms with definitions** (10 minutes)

Terms

a Split-off point

b Joint cost

c Separable cost

d By-product

e Joint product

f Product

Definitions

1 Product with low sales value compared with the sales value of the main or joint product(s).

2 Any output that has a positive sales value.

3 Junction in the process when one or more products in a joint-cost setting become separately identifiable.

4 Cost of a single process that yields multiple products simultaneously.

5 Cost incurred beyond the split-off point that are assignable to one or more individual products.

6 Product that is one of two or more products with relatively high sales value but not separately identifiable until the split-off point.

Required

Match each term with its appropriate definition.

6.12 Estimated net realisable value method (10 minutes)

Miljø-Såpe AS produces two joint products, cooking oil and soap oil, from a single vegetable oil refining process. In July 2015, the joint costs of this process were NOK 24 000 000. Separable processing costs beyond the split-off point were cooking oil, NOK 30 000 000; and soap oil, NOK 7 500 000. Cooking oil sells for NOK 50 per drum. Soap oil sells for NOK 25 per drum. Miljø-Såpe produced and sold 1 000 000 drums of cooking oil and 500 000 drums of soap oil. There are no beginning or ending stocks of cooking oil or soap oil.

Required

Allocate the NOK 24 000 000 joint costs using the estimated NRV method.

Intermediate level

*6.13 Joint-cost allocation, insurance settlement (20–30 minutes)

Galinha-Esquina SA grows and processes chickens. Each chicken is disassembled into five main parts. Information pertaining to production in July 2015 is as follows:

Parts	Kilograms of product	Wholesale selling price per kilogram at end of production line
Breast	100	€1.10
Wings	20	0.40
Thighs	40	0.70
Bones	80	0.20
Feathers	10	0.10

Joint costs of production in July 2015 were €100.

A special shipment of 20 kg of breasts and 10 kg of wings has been destroyed in a fire. Galinha-Esquina's insurance policy provides for reimbursement for the cost of the items destroyed. The insurance company permits Galinha-Esquina to use a joint-cost-allocation method. The split-off point is assumed to be at the end of the production line.

Required

1 Calculate the cost of the special shipment destroyed using (a) the sales value at split-off point method, and (b) the physical measure method using kilograms of finished product.

2 Which joint-cost-allocation method would you recommend that Galinha-Esquina use?

*6.14 Accounting for a main product and a by-product (30 minutes)

Claude Deux-Bussy is the owner and operator of Boissons Barbe-Bleue Sarl, a bulk soft-drink producer. A single production process yields two bulk soft drinks, Pelléas (the main product) and Mélisande (the by-product). Both products are fully processed at the split-off point and there are no separable costs.

Summary data for September 2015 are as follows:

- Cost of soft-drink operations = €120 000
- Production and sales data

	Production (litres)	Sales (litres)	Selling price per litre
Main product (Pelléas)	40 000	32 000	€20.00
By-product (Mélisande)	8 000	5 600	2.00

There were no opening stocks on 1 September 2015. The following is an overview of operations:

Required

1 What is the gross margin for Boissons Barbe-Bleue under methods A, B, C and D of by-product accounting described on p. 167?

2 What are the stock amounts reported in the balance sheet on 30 September 2015 for Pelléas and Mélisande under each of the four methods of by-product accounting cited in requirement 1?

3 Which method would you recommend Boissons Barbe-Bleue to use? Explain.

6.15   Joint costs and by-products (W. Crum, adapted) (35–45 minutes)

Pohjanmaan Oy processes an ore in Department 1, out of which come three products, L, W and X. Product L is processed further through Department 2. Product W is sold without further processing. Product X is considered a by-product and is processed further through Department 3. Costs in Department 1 are €800 000 in total; Department 2 costs are €100 000; and Department 3 costs are €50 000. Processing 600 000 kg in Department 1 results in 50 000 kg of product L, 300 000 kg of product W and 100 000 kg of product X.

Product L sells for €10 per kg. Product W sells for €2 per kg. Product X sells for €3 per kg. The company wants to make a gross margin of 10% of sales on product X and also allow 25% for marketing costs on product X.

Required

1 Calculate unit costs per kilogram for products L, W and X, treating X as a by-product. Use the estimated NRV method for allocating joint costs. Deduct the estimated NRV of the by-product produced from the joint cost of products L and W.

2 Calculate unit costs per kilogram for products L, W and X, treating all three as joint products and allocating costs by the estimated NRV method.

6.16   Estimated net realisable value method, by-products (CMA, adapted) (30 minutes)

Flori-Dante Srl grows, processes, packages and sells three joint apple products: (a) sliced apples that are used in frozen pies, (b) apple sauce, and (c) apple juice. The apple peel, processed as animal feed, is treated as a by-product. Flori-Dante uses the estimated NRV method to allocate costs of the joint process to its joint products. The by-product is inventoried at its selling price when produced; the net realisable value of the by-product is used to reduce the joint production costs before the split-off point. Details of Flori-Dante production process are presented here:

- The apples are washed and the peel is removed in the Cutting Department. The apples are then cored and trimmed for slicing. The three joint products and the by-product are recognisable after processing in the Cutting Department. Each product is then transferred to a separate department for final processing.

- The trimmed apples are forwarded to the Slicing Department, where they are sliced and frozen. Any juice generated during the slicing operation is frozen with the apple slices.

- The pieces of apple trimmed from the fruit are processed into apple sauce in the Crushing Department. The juice generated during this operation is used in the apple sauce.

- The core and any surplus apple pieces generated from the Cutting Department are pulverised into a liquid in the Juicing Department. There is a loss equal to 8% of the weight of the good output produced in this department.
- The peel is chopped into animal feed and packaged in the Feed Department. It can be kept in cold storage until needed.

A total of 270 000 kg of apples were entered into the Cutting Department during November. The following schedule shows the costs incurred in each department, the proportion by weight transferred to the four final processing departments and the selling price of each end-product.

Processing data and costs November 2015

Department	Costs incurred	Proportion of product by weight transferred to departments	Selling price per kilogram of final product
Cutting	€60 000		
Slicing	11 280	33%	€0.80
Crushing	8 550	30	0.55
Juicing	3 000	27	0.40
Feed	700	10	0.10
Total	€83 530	100%	

Required

1 Flori-Dante uses the estimated NRV method to determine stock cost of its joint products; by-products are reported on the balance sheet at their selling price when produced. For the month of November 2015, calculate the following:

   a The output for apple slices, apple sauce, apple juice and animal feed, in kilograms.
   b The estimated NRV at the split-off point for each of the three joint products.
   c The amount of the cost of the Cutting Department assigned to each of the three joint products and the amount assigned to the by-product in accordance with corporate policy.
   d The gross margins in euros for each of the three joint products.

2 Comment on the significance to management of the gross-margin monetary information by joint product for planning and control purposes, as opposed to stock-costing purposes.

6.17 **Joint product/by-product distinctions, ethics** (continuation of Exercise 6.16) (20–30 minutes)

Flori-Dante classifies animal feed as a by-product. The by-product is inventoried at its selling price when produced; the net realisable value of the product is used to reduce the joint production costs before the split-off point. Prior to 2015, Flori-Dante classified both apple juice and animal feed as by-products. These by-products were not recognised in the accounting system until sold. Revenues from their sale were treated as a revenue item at the time of sale.

Flori-Dante uses a 'management by objectives' basis to compensate its managers. Every six months, managers are given 'stretch' operating-income to revenue ratio targets. They receive no bonus if the target is not met and a fixed amount if the target is met or exceeded.

Required

1 Assume that Flori-Dante managers aim to maximise their bonuses over time. What by-product method (the pre-2015 method or the 2015 method) would the manager prefer?

2 How might an accountant gain insight into whether the manager of the Apple Products division is 'abusing' the accounting system in an effort to maximise his bonus?

3 Describe an accounting system for Flori-Dante that would reduce 'gaming' behaviour by managers with respect to accounting rules for by-products.

6.18   Processing cost issues (From ACCA Financial Information for Management, Part 1, June 2007) (25 minutes)

A company simultaneously produces three products (X, Y and Z) from a single process. X and Y are processed further before they can be sold; Z is a by-product that is sold immediately for $6 per unit without incurring any further costs. The sales prices of X and Y after further processing are $50 per unit and $60 per unit respectively. Data for October are as follows:

	$
Joint production costs that produced 2500 units of X, 3500 units of Y and 3000 units of Z	140 000
Further processing costs for 2500 units of X	24 000
Further processing costs for 3500 units of Y	46 000

Joint costs are apportioned using the final sales value method.

Required

Calculate the total cost of the production of X for October.

Advanced level

*6.19   Net realisable value cost-allocation method, further process decision (20–30 minutes)

Langholmen-Sverige AB crushes and refines mineral ore into three products in a joint-cost operation. Costs and production for 2015 were as follows:

- · Department 1, at initial joint costs of SKr 420 000, produces 20 000 kg of Vadstena, 60 000 kg of Vättervik and 100 000 kg of Birgitta.
- Department 2 processes Vadstena further at a cost of SKr 100 000.
- Department 3 processes Vättervik further at a cost of SKr 200 000.

Results for 2015 are:

- Vadstena: 20 000 kg completed; 19 000 kg sold for SKr 20 per kg; closing stock, 1000 kg.
- Vättervik: 60 000 kg completed; 59 000 kg sold for SKr 6 per kg; closing stock, 1000 kg.
- Birgitta: 100 000 kg completed; 99 000 kg sold for SKr 1 per kg; closing stock, 1000 kg; Birgitta required no further processing.

Required

1   Use the estimated NRV method to allocate the joint costs of the three products. Calculate the total costs and unit costs of closing stock.

2   Calculate the individual gross-margin percentages of the three products.

3   Suppose Langholmen-Sverige receives an offer to sell all of its Vättervik product for a price of SKr 2 per kg at the split-off point before going through Department 3, just as it comes off the production line in Department 1. Using last year's figures, would Langholmen-Sverige be better off by selling Vättervik that way or processing it through Department 3 and selling it? Show computations to support your answer. Disregard all other factors not mentioned in the problem.

6.20   Alternative joint-cost-allocation methods, further process decision (40 minutes)

Jerónimos Ltda produces two products, turpentine and methanol (wood alcohol), by a joint process. Joint costs amount to €120 000 per batch of output. Each batch totals 40 000 litres: 25% methanol and 75% turpentine. Both products are processed further without gain or loss in volume. Separable processing costs include: methanol, €0.75 per litre, and turpentine, €0.5 per litre. Methanol sells for €5.25 per litre; turpentine sells for €3.5 per litre.

Required

1 What joint costs per batch should be allocated to the turpentine and methanol, assuming that joint costs are allocated on a physical measure (number of litres at split-off point) basis?

2 If joint costs are to be assigned on an estimated NRV basis, what amounts of joint cost should be assigned to the turpentine and to the methanol?

3 Prepare product-line income statements per batch for requirements 1 and 2. Assume no opening or closing stocks.

4 The company has discovered an additional process by which the methanol can be made into a pleasant tasting alcoholic beverage. The new selling price would be €15 per litre. Additional processing would increase separable costs by €2.25 per litre (in addition to the €0.75 separable cost required to yield methanol). The company would have to pay excise taxes of 20% on the new selling price. Assuming no other changes in cost, what is the joint cost applicable to the methanol (using the estimated NRV method)? Should the company use the new process?

6.21   Alternative methods of joint-cost allocation, product-mix decisions (40 minutes)

Schmidsendl GmbH buys crude vegetable oil. Refining this oil results in four products at the split-off point: A, B, C and D. Product C is fully processed at the split-off point. Products A, B and D can be individually further refined into Super A, Super B and Super D. In the most recent month (December), the output at the split-off point was:

Product A	300 000 litres
Product B	100 000 litres
Product C	50 000 litres
Product D	50 000 litres

The joint costs of purchasing the crude vegetable oil and processing it were €100 000.

Schmidsendl had no beginning or ending stocks. Sales of product C in December were €50 000. Total output of products A, B and D was further refined and then sold. Data related to December are as follows:

	Separable processing costs to make super products	Sales
Super A	€200 000	€300 000
Super B	80 000	100 000
Super D	90 000	120 000

Schmidsendl had the option of selling products A, B and D at the split-off point. This alternative would have yielded the following sales for the December production:

Product A	€50 000
Product B	30 000
Product D	70 000

Required

1 What is the gross-margin percentage for each product sold in December, using the following methods for allocating the €100 000 joint costs: (a) sales value at split-off, (b) physical measure, and (c) estimated NRV?

2 Could Schmidsendl have increased its December operating profit by making different decisions about the further refining of products A, B or D? Show the effect on operating profit of any changes you recommend.

6.22   **Joint and by-products, estimated net realisable value method** (CPA, adapted) (30 minutes)

Protomastoras SA produces three products: Alpha, Beta and Gamma. Alpha and Gamma are joint products and Beta is a by-product of Alpha. No joint costs are to be allocated to the by-product. The production processes for a given year are as follows:

a   In Department 1, 110 000 kg of direct material Rho are processed at a total cost of €120 000. After processing in Department 1, 60% of the units are transferred to Department 2 and 40% of the units (now Gamma) are transferred to Department 3.

b   In Department 2, the material is further processed at a total additional cost of €38 000. Seventy per cent of the units (now Alpha) are transferred to Department 4 and 30% emerge as Beta, the by-product, to be sold at €1.20 per kg. Separable marketing costs for Beta are €8100.

c   In Department 4, Alpha is processed at a total additional cost of €23 660. After this processing, Alpha is ready for sale at €5 per kg.

d   In Department 3, Gamma is processed at a total additional cost of €165 000. In this department, a normal loss of units of Gamma occurs, which equals 10% of the good output of Gamma. The remaining good output of Gamma is then sold for €12 per kg.

Required

1   Prepare a schedule showing the allocation of the €120 000 joint costs between Alpha and Gamma using the estimated NRV method. The estimated NRV of Beta should be treated as an addition to the sales value of Alpha.

2   Independent of your answer to requirement 1, assume that €102 000 of total joint costs were appropriately allocated to Alpha. Assume also that there were 48 000 kg of Alpha and 20 000 kg of Beta available to sell. Prepare an income statement through gross margin for Alpha using the following facts:

a   During the year, sales of Alpha were 80% of the kilograms available for sale. There was no opening stock.

b   The estimated NRV of Beta available for sale is to be deducted from the cost of producing Alpha. The closing stock of Alpha is to be based on the net costs of production.

c   All other cost and selling price data are listed in a–d.

Collaborative learning exercise

6.23   **Joint-cost allocation, process further or sell by-products** (CMA, adapted) (75 minutes)

Nor-Pharma AS manufactures three joint products from a joint process: Altox, Lorex and Hycol. Data regarding these products for the fiscal year ended 31 May 2015 are as follows:

	Altox	Lorex	Hycol
Units produced	170 000	500 000	330 000
Selling price per unit at split-off	€3.50	–	€2.00
Separable costs	–	€1 400 000	–
Final selling price per unit	–	€5.00	–

The joint production cost up to the split-off point where Altox, Lorex and Hycol become separable products is €1 800 000 (which includes the €17 500 disposal costs for Dorzine as described below).

The president of Nor-Pharma, Gro Seljord, is reviewing an opportunity to change the way in which these three products are processed and sold. Proposed changes for each product are as follows:

- Altox is currently sold at the split-off point to a manufacturer of vitamins. Altox can also be refined for use as a medication to treat high blood pressure; however, this additional processing would cause a loss of 20 000 units of Altox. The separable costs to further process Altox are estimated to be €250 000 annually. The final product would sell for €5.50 per unit.

- Lorex is currently processed further after the split-off point and sold by Nor-Pharma as a cold remedy. The company has received an offer from another pharmaceutical company to purchase Lorex at the split-off point for €2.25 per unit.

- Hycol is an oil produced from the joint process and is currently sold at the split-off point to a cosmetics manufacturer. Nor-Pharma's Research Department has suggested that the company process this product further and sell it as an ointment to relieve muscle pain. The additional processing would cost €75 000 annually and would result in 25% more units of product. The final product would be sold for €1.80 per unit.

The joint process currently used by Nor-Pharma also produces 50 000 units of Dorzine, a hazardous chemical waste product. The company pays €0.35 per unit to dispose of the Dorzine properly. Nor-Chem, AS, is interested in using the Dorzine as a solvent; however, Nor-Pharma would have to refine the Dorzine at an annual cost of €43 000. Nor-Chem would purchase all the refined Dorzine produced by Nor-Pharma and is willing to pay €0.75 for each unit.

Instructions

Form groups of two or more students to complete the following requirements.

Required

1 Allocate the €1 800 000 joint production cost to Altox, Lorex and Hycol using the estimated NRV method.

2 Identify which of the three joint products Nor-Pharma should sell at the split-off point in the future and which of the three main products the company should process further in order to maximise profits. Support your decisions with appropriate calculations.

3 Assume that Nor-Pharma has decided to refine the waste product Dorzine for sale to Nor-Chem and will treat Dorzine as a by-product of the joint process in the future.

  a Evaluate whether Nor-Pharma made the correct decision regarding Dorzine. Support your answer with appropriate calculations.

  b Explain whether the decision to treat Dorzine as a by-product will affect the decisions reached in requirement 2.

CHAPTER 7

Income effects of alternative stock-costing methods

Profit figures capture the attention of managers in a way few other numbers do. Consider three examples:

- Planning decisions typically include an analysis of how the considered options affect future reported profit.
- Increases in reported profit are the object of many decisions related to cost reduction.
- Reported profit is a key number in the performance evaluation of managers.

The reported profit number of manufacturing companies is affected by cost accounting choices related to stock. In this chapter we examine two such choices:

1 Stock-costing choices – the choices here relate to which costs are to be recorded as stock when they are incurred. We discuss two alternatives: variable costing and absorption costing.

2 Denominator-level choices – the choices here relate to the pre-selected level of the cost-allocation base used to set budgeted fixed manufacturing cost rates. We discuss four alternatives: theoretical capacity, practical capacity, normal utilisation and master-budget utilisation.

Learning objectives

After studying this chapter, you should be able to:

- Identify what distinguishes variable costing from absorption costing

- Construct income statements using absorption costing and variable costing

- Explain differences in profit under absorption costing and variable costing

- Understand how absorption costing influences performance evaluation decisions

- Describe the various denominator-level concepts that can be used in absorption costing

- Explain how the choice of denominator level affects reported operating profit and stock costs

PART ONE: Stock-costing methods

The two most commonly encountered methods of costing stock are variable costing and absorption costing. Absorption costing is the required method under generally accepted accounting principles for external reporting in most countries. Management accountants most frequently use variable costing for decision making and performance evaluation purposes.

Variable costing and absorption costing

These two methods differ in only one conceptual respect: whether fixed manufacturing costs (both direct and indirect) are 'inventoriable' costs. In other words, fixed manufacturing costs are allocated to product rather than expenses on a period basis. If the former treatment is adopted, then a proportion of fixed manufacturing costs will be carried forward to future periods in closing stocks. Recall from Chapter 2 that *inventoriable costs* for a manufacturing company are costs associated with the acquisition and conversion of materials and all other manufacturing inputs into goods for sale; these costs are first recorded as part of stock and then subsequently become an expense when the goods are sold.

Variable costing is a method of stock costing in which all variable manufacturing costs are included as inventoriable costs. All fixed manufacturing costs are excluded from inventoriable costs; they are costs of the period in which they are incurred. **Absorption costing** is a method of stock costing in which all variable manufacturing costs and all fixed manufacturing costs are included as inventoriable costs. That is, stock 'absorbs' all manufacturing costs. Throughout this chapter, to emphasise underlying concepts, we assume that the chosen denominator level for computing the variable and fixed manufacturing overhead allocation rates is a production-output-related variable. Examples include direct labour-hours, direct machine-hours and units of production output.

We will use Centurion, which manufactures speciality clothing belts, to illustrate the difference between variable costing and absorption costing. (The variable- versus absorption-costing choice is but one of several pertaining to stock costing. For example, decisions related to cost flows – FIFO, LIFO, weighted average, and so on – must also be made.) Centurion uses a normal costing system. That is, its direct costs are traced to products using actual prices and the actual inputs used and its indirect (overhead) costs are allocated using budgeted indirect cost rate(s) times actual inputs used. The allocation base for all indirect manufacturing costs is units produced. The allocation base for all variable indirect marketing costs is units sold. (Only manufacturing costs are included in inventoriable costs.)

To keep our focus on variable- versus absorption-costing issues, we assume the following for 2015:

- The budgeted number and actual number of units produced are equal (1 100 000 units).
- The budgeted number and actual number of units sold are equal (1 000 000 units).
- The budgeted and actual fixed costs are equal.
- Work in progress is minimal.
- No opening stock on 1 January 2015.
- All variable costs are driven by an output-unit-related variable. (We assume, for example, that batch-level and product-sustaining costs are zero.)

With 2015 production of 1 100 000 units and sales of 1 000 000 units, the closing stock on 31 December 2015 is 100 000 units.

The per unit and total actual costs for 2015 are shown in Exhibit 7.1.

Exhibit 7.1	Centurion's per unit and total costs for 2015	
	Per unit	**Total costs**
Variable costs		
Direct materials	€3.50	€3 850 000
Direct manufacturing labour	1.60	1 760 000
Indirect manufacturing costs	0.90	990 000
Manufacturing costs	6.00	6 600 000
Direct marketing costs	0.80	800 000
Indirect marketing costs	1.60	1 600 000
Marketing costs	2.40	2 400 000
Total variable costs	€8.40	€9 000 000
Fixed costs		
Direct manufacturing costs	€0.30	€330 000
Indirect manufacturing costs	1.70	1 870 000
Manufacturing costs	2.00	2 200 000
Direct marketing costs	2.10	2 100 000
Indirect marketing costs	3.40	3 400 000
Marketing costs	5.50	5 500 000
Total fixed costs	€7.50	€7 700 000

The heart of the difference between variable and absorption costing for financial reporting is accounting for fixed manufacturing costs:

		Direct	Indirect
Same under both methods {	**Variable**	Direct manufacturing cost	Indirect manufacturing
Differs under both methods {	**Fixed**	Direct manufacturing cost	Indirect manufacturing

For stock valuation under both methods, all variable manufacturing costs (both direct and indirect) are costs which remain unexpired until the stock is sold. That is, they are first recorded as an asset when they are incurred. Under variable costing, fixed manufacturing costs (both direct and indirect) are deducted as a period cost in the period in which they are incurred. Examples of variable direct manufacturing costs are direct materials and direct manufacturing labour. An example of a fixed direct manufacturing cost is the annual lease cost of a machine dedicated to the assembly of a single product. The annual lease cost of a building in which multiple products are assembled illustrates a fixed indirect manufacturing cost. Under absorption costing, fixed manufacturing costs are initially treated as stock-based costs. They then become expenses in the form of cost of goods sold when sales occur. The unit inventoriable costs for Centurion under the two methods are set out in Exhibit 7.2.

Exhibit 7.3 presents the variable-costing and absorption-costing income statements for Centurion in 2015. The variable-costing income statement differentiates between fixed and variable costs. It entails the determination of a 'contribution margin' which represents sales less variable costs. We refer to this type of income statement as the 'contribution' format. The absorption-costing income statement calculates a 'gross margin' which represents sales less cost of goods sold. Why these differences in format? The distinction between variable and fixed costs is central to variable costing; the contribution format highlights this distinction. The distinction between manufacturing and non-manufacturing costs is central to absorption costing;

Exhibit 7.2	Centurion's unit inventoriable costs under variable and absorption costing			
	Variable costing		**Absorption costing**	
Variable manufacturing costs				
Direct materials	€3.50		€3.50	
Direct manufacturing labour	1.60		1.60	
Indirect manufacturing costs	0.90	6.00	0.90	6.00
Fixed manufacturing costs				
Direct manufacturing costs			0.30	
Indirect manufacturing costs			1.70	2.00
Total inventoriable costs		€6.00		€8.00

the gross-margin format highlights this distinction. Many companies using absorption costing do not make any distinction between variable and fixed costs in their accounting system.

See how the fixed manufacturing costs of €2 200 000 are accounted for in Exhibit 7.3. The income statement under variable costing deducts the €2 200 000 lump sum as a period cost in 2015. In contrast, the income statement under absorption costing regards each finished unit as absorbing €2 of fixed manufacturing costs. Under absorption costing the €2 200 000 is initially treated as a product cost in 2015. Given the preceding data for Centurion, €2 000 000 subsequently becomes an expense in 2015 and €200 000 remains part of closing finished goods stock, 100 000 units × €2, at 31 December 2015. The variable manufacturing costs are accounted for in the same way in both income statements in Exhibit 7.3.

Never overlook the heart of the matter. The difference between variable costing and absorption costing centres on accounting for fixed manufacturing costs. If stock levels change, operating profit will differ between the two methods because of the difference in accounting for fixed manufacturing overhead. Compare sales of 900 000, 1 000 000 and 1 100 000 units by Centurion in 2015. Fixed manufacturing costs would be included in the 2015 expense as follows:

	Fixed manufacturing costs treated as an expense in 2015
Variable costing, whether	
● sales are 900 000, 1 000 000 or 1 100 000 units	€2 200 000
Absorption costing, where	
● sales are 900 000 units, €400 000 (200 000 × €2) held back in stock	€1 800 000
● sales are 1 000 000 units, €200 000 (100 000 × €2) held back in stock	€2 000 000
● sales are 1 100 000 units, €0 held back in stock	€2 200 000

Some companies use the term **direct costing** to describe the stock-costing method we call *variable costing*. Direct costing is an unfortunate choice of terms for two reasons.

(1) Variable costing does not include all direct costs as inventoriable costs. Only direct variable manufacturing costs are included. Any direct fixed manufacturing costs and any direct non-manufacturing costs (such as marketing) are excluded from inventoriable costs. (2) Variable costing includes as inventoriable costs not only direct manufacturing costs but also some indirect costs (variable indirect manufacturing costs).

Exhibit 7.3	Comparison of variable-costing and absorption-costing income statements for the year ended 31 December 2015 for Centurion (in €000)	

Panel A: Variable costing

Revenues: €17.00 × 1 000 000 units		€17 000
Variable costs		
Opening stock	€0	
Variable cost of goods manufactured:		
€6.00 × 1 100 000	6 600	
Cost of goods available for sale	6 600	
Closing stock: €6.00 × 100 000	600	
Variable manufacturing cost of goods sold	6 000	
Variable marketing costs	2 400	
Adjustment for variable cost variances	0	
Total variable costs		8 400
Contribution margin		8 600
Fixed costs		
Fixed manufacturing costs	2 200	
Fixed marketing costs	5 500	
Adjustment for fixed cost variances	0	
Total fixed costs		7 700
Operating profit		€900

Panel B: Absorption costing

Revenues: €17.00 × 1 000 000 units		€17 000
Cost of goods sold		
Opening stock	€0	
Variable manufacturing costs:		
€6.00 × 1 100 000	6 600	
Fixed manufacturing costs:		
€2.00 × 1 100 000	2 200	
Cost of goods available for sale	8 800	
Closing stock: €8.00 × 100 000	800	
Adjustment for manufacturing variances	0	
Cost of goods sold		8 000
Gross margin		9 000
Marketing costs		
Variable marketing costs	2 400	
Fixed marketing costs	5 500	
Adjustment for marketing variances	0	
Total marketing costs		7 900
Operating profit		€1 100

Comparison of variable costing and absorption costing

Our next example explores the implications of accounting for fixed manufacturing costs in more detail. Daxenberger manufactures and markets telescopes. It uses a standard costing system for both its manufacturing and marketing costs. (For ease of exposition, we assume that Daxenberger uses a standard costing system for all its operating costs, that is, it uses standards (or budgeted estimates) for both variable and fixed costs in both its manufacturing and marketing. Standard costing systems are further discussed in Chapters 14 and 15. It began business on 1 January 2015 and it is now March 2015. The chairman asks you to prepare comparative income statements for January 2015 and February 2015. The simplified unit data that are available are set out in Exhibit 7.4.

The standard variable manufacturing costs per unit of €20 include €11 for direct materials. For simplicity, we assume all fixed manufacturing costs are indirect product costs.

We assume work in progress is minimal. There were no opening or closing stocks of materials. On 1 January 2015, there was no opening stock of finished goods. In order to highlight the effect of the 'production-volume variance', we assume that actual costs and actual volumes were equal to budgeted costs and budgeted volumes during January and February of 2015; in other words, there were no other variances (variances are discussed in Chapters 15 and 16). The standard fixed manufacturing cost per unit is €16 (€12 800 ÷ 800). Thus the key standard cost data per unit are

Variable costs

Standard variable manufacturing costs	€20
Standard variable marketing costs	19
Total variable costs	€39

Manufacturing costs

Standard variable manufacturing costs	€20
Standard fixed manufacturing costs	16
Total manufacturing costs	€36

Assume that managers at Daxenberger receive a bonus based on reported monthly income. The following points illustrate how the choice between variable and absorption costing will affect Daxenberger's reported monthly income and hence the bonuses their managers will receive.

Exhibit 7.4	Unit data available for Daxenberger at March 2015	
Unit data	**January 2015**	**February 2015**
Opening stock	0	200
Production	600	650
Sales	400	750
Closing stock	200	100
Other data		
Selling price		€99
Standard variable manufacturing costs per unit		€20
Standard variable marketing costs per unit		€19
Standard fixed manufacturing costs per month		€12 800
Standard fixed marketing costs per month		€10 400
Budgeted denominator level of production per month		800 output units

Comparative income statements

Exhibit 7.5 contains the comparative income statements under variable costing (Panel A) and absorption costing (Panel B) for Daxenberger in January 2015 and February 2015. The operating profit numbers are

	January 2015	February 2015
1 Absorption costing	€4 000	€20 200
2 Variable costing	800	21 800
3 Difference (1) − (2)	€3 200	€(1 600)

In Panel A, variable costing, all variable-cost line items are at standard cost except the last line item, 'Adjustment for variances'. This line item would include any variance related to variable-cost items (which are zero in our Daxenberger example). In Panel B, absorption costing, all cost of goods sold line items are at standard cost except the last line item, 'Adjustment for variances'. This line item would include all manufacturing cost variances. Only the production-volume variance is relevant in our Daxenberger example.

Keep the following points in mind about absorption costing as you study Panel B of Exhibit 7.5:

1 The inventoriable costs are €36 per unit, not €20, because fixed manufacturing costs (€16) as well as variable manufacturing costs (€20) are assigned to each unit of product.

2 The €16 fixed manufacturing costs rate was based on a denominator level of 800 units per month (€12 800 ÷ 800 = €16). Whenever *production* (not sales) deviates from the denominator level, a production-volume variance arises. The amount of the variance is €16 multiplied by the difference between the actual level of production and the denominator level.

3 The production-volume variance, which relates to fixed manufacturing overhead, exists only under absorption costing and not under variable costing. (All other variances, discussed in Chapters 15 and 16, exist under both absorption costing and variable costing.)

4 The absorption-costing income statement classifies costs primarily by *business function*, such as manufacturing and marketing. In contrast, the variable-costing income statement features *cost behaviour* (variable or fixed) as the basis of classification. Absorption-costing income statements need not differentiate between the variable and fixed costs. Exhibit 7.5 does make this differentiation for Daxenberger in order to highlight how individual line items are classified differently under variable- and absorption-costing formats.

Explaining differences in operating profit

If the stock level increases during an accounting period, variable costing will generally report less operating profit than absorption costing; when the stock level decreases, variable costing will generally report more operating profit than absorption costing. These differences in operating profit are due solely to moving fixed manufacturing costs into stock as stock increase and out of stock as they decrease.

The difference between operating profit under absorption costing and variable costing can be calculated by formula 1 below, which is illustrated with Exhibit 7.5 data. This formula assumes that the amounts used for opening and closing stock are after proration of manufacturing overhead variances (see Chapter 3).

Exhibit 7.5	Daxenberger: Comparison of variable costing and absorption costing income statements for January 2015 and February 2015

Panel A: Variable costing

	January 2015	February 2015
Revenue*	€39 600	€74 250
Variable costs		
Opening stock	0	4 000
Variable cost of goods manufactured[†]	12 000	13 000
Cost of goods available for sale	12 000	17 000
Closing stock[‡]	4 000	2 000
Variable manufacturing cost of goods sold	8 000	15 000
Variable marketing costs[§]	7 600	14 250
Total variable costs (at standard)	15 600	29 250
Contribution margin (at standard)	24 000	45 000
Adjustment for variable-cost variances	0	0
Contribution margin	24 000	45 000
Fixed costs		
Fixed manufacturing costs	12 800	12 800
Fixed marketing costs	10 400	10 400
Total fixed costs (at standard)	23 200	23 200
Adjustment for fixed cost variances	0	0
Total fixed costs	23 200	23 200
Operating profit	€800	€21 800

* $400 \times €99 = €39\ 600;\ 750 \times €99 = €74\ 250.$
[†] $600 \times €20 = €12\ 000;\ 650 \times €20 = €13\ 000.$
[‡] $200 \times €20 = €4000;\ 100 \times €20 = €2000.$
[§] $400 \times €19 = €7600;\ 750 \times €19 = €14\ 250.$

Panel B: Absorption costing

	January 2015	February 2015
Revenue*	€39 600	€74 250
Cost of goods sold		
Opening stock	0	7 200
Variable manufacturing costs[†]	12 000	13 000
Fixed manufacturing costs[‡]	9 600	10 400
Cost of goods available for sale	21 600	30 600
Closing stock[§]	7 200	3 600
Total cost of goods sold (at standard)	14 400	27 000
Gross margin (at standard costs)	25 200	47 250
Adjustment for manufacturing variances	3 200 U	2 400 U
Gross margin	22 000	44 850
Marketing costs		
Variable marketing costs[#]	7 600	14 250
Fixed marketing costs	10 400	10 400
Total marketing (at standard)	18 000	24 650
Adjustment for marketing variances[‖]	0	0
Total marketing	18 000	24 650
Operating profit	€4 000	€20 200

* $400 \times €99 = €39\ 600;\ 750 \times €99 = €74\ 250.$
[†] $600 \times €20 = €12\ 000;\ 650 \times €20 = €13\ 000.$
[‡] $600 \times €16 = €9600;\ 650 \times €16 = €10\ 400.$
[§] $200 \times (€20 + €16) = €7200;\ 100 \times (€20 + €16) = €3600.$
[‖] January 2015 has €3200 unfavourable (U) production-volume variance $(600 - 800) \times €16 = €3200$ unfavourable.
  February 2015 has €2400 unfavourable production-volume variance $(650 - 800) \times €16.00 = €2400$ unfavourable.
[#] $400 \times €19 = €7600;\ 750 \times €19 = €14\ 250.$

Formula 1

$$\begin{pmatrix} \text{Absorption-costing} \\ \text{operation} \\ \text{profit} \end{pmatrix} - \begin{pmatrix} \text{Variable-costing} \\ \text{operation} \\ \text{profit} \end{pmatrix} = \begin{pmatrix} \text{Fixed} \\ \text{manufacturing} \\ \text{costs in} \\ \text{closing stock} \end{pmatrix} - \begin{pmatrix} \text{Fixed} \\ \text{manufacturing} \\ \text{costs in} \\ \text{opening stock} \end{pmatrix}$$

January 2015: $\qquad$ €4000 − €800 = (200 × €16) − (0 × €16)
$$€3200 = €3200$$
February 2015: $\qquad$ €20 200 − €21 800 = (100 × €16) − (200 × €16)
$$-€1600 = -€1600$$

Fixed manufacturing costs in closing stock are a current-period expense under variable costing that absorption costing defers to future period.

Two alternative formulae can be used if we assume that all manufacturing variances are written off as period costs, that no change occurs in work-in-progress stock and that no change occurs in the budgeted fixed manufacturing overhead rate between accounting periods:

Formula 2

$$\begin{pmatrix} \text{Absorption-costing} \\ \text{operation} \\ \text{income} \end{pmatrix} - \begin{pmatrix} \text{Variable-costing} \\ \text{operation} \\ \text{income} \end{pmatrix} = \begin{pmatrix} \text{Units} \\ \text{produced} - \text{Units} \\ \text{sold} \end{pmatrix} \times \begin{pmatrix} \text{Budget fixed} \\ \text{manufacturing} \\ \text{costs rate} \end{pmatrix}$$

January 2015: $\qquad$ €4000 − €800 = (600 − 400) × €16
$$€3200 = €3200$$
February 2015: $\qquad$ €20 200 − €21 800 = (650 − 750) × €16
$$-€1600 = -€1600$$

Formula 3

$$\begin{pmatrix} \text{Absorption-costing} \\ \text{operation} \\ \text{income} \end{pmatrix} - \begin{pmatrix} \text{Variable-costing} \\ \text{operation} \\ \text{income} \end{pmatrix} = \begin{pmatrix} \text{Closing} \\ \text{stock in} - \text{Opening} \\ \text{stock in} \\ \text{units} \quad \text{units} \end{pmatrix} \times \begin{pmatrix} \text{Budget fixed} \\ \text{manufacturing} \\ \text{costs rate} \end{pmatrix}$$

January 2015: $\qquad$ €4000 − €800 = (200 − 0) × €16
$$€3200 = €3200$$
February 2015: $\qquad$ €20 200 − €21 800 = (100 − 200) × €16
$$-€1600 = -€1600$$

Effect of sales and production on operating profit

The period-to-period change in operating profit under variable costing is driven solely by changes in the unit level of sales, given a constant contribution margin per unit (that is, unit sales less unit variable costs). Consider for Daxenberger the variable-costing operating profit in February 2015 versus that in January 2015:

$$\begin{pmatrix} \text{Change in} \\ \text{operating profit} \end{pmatrix} - \begin{pmatrix} \text{Contribution} \\ \text{margin} \end{pmatrix} = \begin{pmatrix} \text{Change in unit} \\ \text{sales level} \end{pmatrix}$$

$$€21\ 800 − €800 = (€99 − €39) × (750 − 400)$$
$$€21\ 000 = €60 × 350$$
$$€21\ 000 = €21\ 000$$

Exhibit 7.6	Daxenberger: Effect on absorption-costing operating profit of different production levels holding the unit sales level constant, data for February 2015 with sales of 750 units

	February 2015 production level				
	550	**650**	**700**	**800**	**850**
Unit data					
Opening stock	200	200	200	200	200
Production	550	650	700	800	850
Goods available for sale	750	850	900	1 000	1 050
Sales	750	750	750	750	750
Closing stock	0	100	150	250	300
Income statement					
Revenues	€74 250	€74 250	€74 250	€74 250	€74 250
Opening stock	7 200	7 200	7 200	7 200	7 200
Variable manufacturing costs*	11 000	13 000	14 000	16 000	17 000
Fixed manufacturing costs†	8 800	10 400	11 200	12 800	13 600
Cost of goods available for sale	27 000	30 600	32 400	36 000	37 800
Closing stock‡	0	3 600	5 400	9 000	10 800
Cost of goods sold (at standard cost)	27 000	27 000	27 000	27 000	27 000
Adjustment for manufacturing variances§	4 000 U	2 400 U	1 600 U	0	800 F
Total cost of goods sold	31 000	29 400	28 600	27 000	26 200
Gross margin	43 250	44 850	45 650	47 250	48 050
Total marketing and administrative costs	24 650	24 650	24 650	24 650	24 650
Operating profit	€18 600	€20 200	€21 000	€22 600	€23 400

* €20 per unit.
† Assigned at €16 per unit.
‡ €36 per unit.
§ (Production in units – 800) × €16. All written off to cost of goods sold at end of the accounting period.

Note that under variable costing, Daxenberger managers cannot increase operating profit (and hence their bonuses) by producing for stock.

Under absorption costing, however, period-to-period change in operating profit is driven by variations in *both* the unit level of sales and the unit level of production. Exhibit 7.6 illustrates this point. The exhibit shows how absorption-costing operating profit for February 2015 changes as the production level in February 2015 changes. This exhibit assumes that all variances (including the production-volume variance) are written off to cost of goods sold at the end of each accounting period. The opening stock in February 2015 of 200 units and the February sales of 750 units are unchanged. Exhibit 7.6 shows that production of only 550 units meets February 2015 sales of 750. Operating profit at this production level is €18 600. By producing more than 550 units in February 2015, Daxenberger increases absorption-costing operating profit. Each unit in February 2015 closing stock will increase February operating profit by €16. For example, if 800 units are produced, closing stock will be 250 units and operating profit will be €22 600. This amount is €4000 more than the operating profit with zero closing stock (250 units × €16 = €4000) on 28 February 2015. Recall that Daxenberger's managers receive a bonus based on monthly operating profit. Absorption costing enables them to increase operating profit (and hence their bonuses) by producing for stock.

Exhibit 7.7 compares the key differences between variable and absorption costing.

Exhibit 7.7	Comparative income effects of variable costing and absorption costing			

Question	Variable costing	Absorption costing	Comment
Are fixed manufacturing costs inventoried?	No	Yes	Basic theoretical question when these costs should be expensed as period costs
Is there a production volume variance?	No	Yes	Choice of denominator level affects measurement of operating profit under absorption costing only
How are the other variances treated?	Same	Same	Highlights that the basic difference is the accounting for fixed manufacturing costs, not the accounting for any variable manufacturing costs
Are classifications between variable and fixed costs routinely made?	Yes	Not always	Absorption costing can be easily modified to obtain sub-classifications for variable and fixed costs, if desired (for example, see Exhibit 7.3, Panel B)
How do changes in unit stock levels affect operating profit?			Differences are attributable to the timing of when fixed manufacturing costs become period costs
Production = sales	Equal	Equal	
Production > sales	Lower*	Higher†	
Production < sales	Higher	Lower	
What are the effects on cost–volume–profit relationships?	Driven by unit sales	Driven by unit sales level and unit production level	Management control benefit: effects of changes in production level on operating profit are easier to understand under variable costing

* That is, lower operating income than under absorption costing.
† That is, higher operating income than under variable costing.

Capsule comparison of stock-costing methods

Variable costing or absorption costing may be combined with actual, normal or standard costing (discussed in Chapters 15 and 16). Exhibit 7.8 presents a capsule comparison of a job-costing record under six alternative stock-costing systems:

Variable costing	Absorption costing
1 Actual costing	4 Actual costing
2 Normal costing	5 Normal costing
3 Standard costing	6 Standard costing

The data in Exhibit 7.8 represent the debits to job-costing account (that is, the amounts assigned to product) under alternative stock-costing systems.

Variable costing has been a controversial subject among accountants – not so much because there is disagreement about the need for delineating between variable and fixed costs for management

Exhibit 7.8	Capsule comparison of alternative stock-costing systems		
	Actual costing	**Normal costing**	**Standard costing**
Absorption costing / **Variable costing** — Variable direct conversion costs*	Actual prices × Actual inputs used	Actual prices × Actual inputs used	Standard prices × Standard inputs allowed for actual output achieved
Variable indirect manufacturing costs	Actual variable indirect rates × Actual inputs used	Budgeted variable indirect rates × Actual inputs used	Standard variable indirect rates × Standard inputs allowed for actual output achieved
Fixed direct manufacturing costs	Actual prices × Actual inputs used	Actual prices × Actual inputs used	Standard prices × Standard inputs allowed for actual output achieved
Fixed indirect manufacturing costs	Actual fixed indirect rates × Actual inputs used	Budgeted fixed indirect rates × Actual inputs used	Standard fixed indirect rates × Standard inputs allowed for actual output achieved

* Conversion costs are all manufacturing costs minus direct materials costs.

planning and control, but because there is a question about using variable costing for *external* reporting. Those favouring variable costing for external reporting maintain that the fixed portion of manufacturing costs is more closely related to the capacity to produce than to the production of specific units. Supporters of absorption costing maintain that stock should carry a fixed manufacturing cost component. Why? Because both variable and fixed manufacturing costs are necessary to produce goods, both types of cost should be inventoriable, regardless of their having different behaviour patterns.

Absorption costing (or variants close to it) is the method most commonly used for the external regulatory purpose of accounting systems. For external reporting to shareholders, most companies around the globe tend to follow the generally accepted accounting principle that all manufacturing overhead is inventoriable.

Performance measures and absorption costing

Undesirable stockbuilding

Absorption costing enables managers to increase operating profit in the short run by increasing the production schedule independent of customer demand for products. Exhibit 7.6 shows how a Daxenberger manager could increase February 2015 operating profit from €18 600 to €22 600 by producing an additional 250 units for stock. Such an increase in the production schedule can increase the costs of doing business without any attendant increase in sales. For example, a manager whose performance is evaluated on the basis of absorption-costing income may increase production at the end of a review period solely to increase reported income. Each additional unit produced absorbs fixed manufacturing costs that would otherwise have been written off as a cost of the period.

The undesirable effects of such an increase in production may be sizable and they can arise in several ways as the following examples show.

1   A plant manager may switch production to those orders that absorb the highest amount of fixed manufacturing costs, irrespective of the customer demand for these products (called 'cherry picking' the production line). Some difficult-to-manufacture items may be delayed, resulting in failure to meet promised customer delivery dates.

2   A plant manager may accept a particular order to increase production even though another plant in the same company is better suited to handle that order.

3   To meet increased production, a manager may defer maintenance beyond the current accounting period. Although operating profit may increase now, future operating profit will probably decrease because of increased repairs and less efficient equipment.

Current criticisms of absorption costing have increasingly emphasised its potentially undesirable incentives for managers. Indeed, one critic labels absorption costing as 'one of the black holes of cost accounting', in part because it may induce managers to make decisions 'against the long-run interests' of the company.

Proposals for revising performance evaluation

Critics of absorption costing have made a variety of proposals for revising how managers are evaluated. Their proposals include the following:

1   Changing the accounting system. As discussed previously in this chapter, variable costing reduces the incentives of managers to stockbuild. An alternative approach is to incorporate into the accounting system a charge for managers who tie up funds in stock. The higher the amount of stock held, the higher the stock holding charge.

2   Changing the time period used to evaluate performance. Critics of absorption costing give examples where managers take actions that maximise quarterly or annual income at the potential expense of long-run income. By evaluating performance over a three- to five-year period, the incentive to take short-run actions that reduce long-term income is lessened.

3   Careful budgeting and stock planning to reduce management's freedom to build excess stock. For instance, the budgeted monthly balance sheets have estimates of the value of stock. If the actual stock values exceed these estimated amounts, top management is alerted to investigate the stock build-ups.

4   Including non-financial as well as financial variables in the measures used to evaluate performance. Companies are currently using non-financial variables, such as the following, to monitor managers' performance in key areas:

a $\dfrac{\text{Closing stock in units this period}}{\text{Closing stock in units last period}}$

b $\dfrac{\text{Sales in units this period}}{\text{Closing stock in units this period}}$

Any build-up of stock at the end of the year would be signalled by tracking the month-to-month behaviour of these two non-financial stock measures (where a company manufactures or sells several products, the two measures could be reported on a product-by-product basis).

Concepts in action | Absorption costing and the bankruptcy of US automakers

In the years leading up to the 2008 recession, General Motors, Ford and Chrysler were producing new vehicles in excess of market demand. This led to large inventories on car dealers' lots across the United States. At the same time, profits were rising and executives at these three companies were achieving their short-term incentive targets. How is this possible? Absorption costing may hold the answer.

In 2009, General Motors and Chrysler filed for bankruptcy and appealed for government aid. Yet these automakers had abundant excess capacity. They also had enormous fixed costs, from factories and machinery to workers whose contracts protected them from layoffs when demand was low. To 'absorb' these costs, the automakers produced more cars while using absorption costing. The more vehicles they made, the lower the cost per vehicle, and the higher the profits on their income statements. In effect, the automakers shifted costs from their income statements to their balance sheets.

Ultimately, this practice hurt the automakers by driving up advertising and inventory costs. 'When the dealers couldn't sell the cars, they would sit on the lots,' said Dr Karen Sedatole, a Michigan State professor who co-authored a study on the topic. 'They'd have to go in and replace the tyres, and there were costs associated with that.' The companies also had to pay to advertise their cars, often at discounted prices using rebates, employee pricing and 0% financing promotions. General Motors and Chrysler ran out of cash for operations and making loans available for car buyers. In January 2009, the US government used $24.9 billion in bailout funds to rescue General Motors and Chrysler.

Sources: Segarra, M. (2012) 'Lots of trouble', *CFO Magazine*, March; Bruggen, A., Krishnan, R. and Sedatole, K.L. (2011) 'Drivers and consequences of short-term production decisions: evidence from the auto industry', *Contemporary Accounting Research*, 28(1), pp. 83–123.

PART TWO: Denominator-level concepts and absorption costing

Now we examine how alternative denominator-level concepts affect fixed manufacturing overhead rates and operating profit under absorption costing. Reported cost numbers can be sizably affected by the choice of a denominator level. This can be important in many contexts, such as pricing and contracting based on reported cost numbers.

Alternative denominator-level concepts

We use a coconut juice bottling plant to illustrate several alternative denominator-level concepts. Cocobot is a specialist Sri Lankan company with a new process. It produces 500 ml bottles of coconut juice. The variable manufacturing costs of each bottle are €0.35. The fixed monthly manufacturing costs of the bottling plant are €50 000. Cocobot uses absorption costing for its monthly internal reporting system and for financial reporting to shareholders. Cocobot could use any one of at least four different denominator-level concepts for computing the fixed manufacturing overhead rate – theoretical capacity, practical capacity, normal utilisation and master-budget utilisation. Whichever the denominator-level concept, Cocobot defines its denominator in output units (500 ml bottles of coconut juice).

Theoretical capacity and practical capacity

The term *capacity* means constraint, an upper limit. **Theoretical capacity** is the denominator-level concept that is based on the production of output at full efficiency for all of the time. Cocobot can produce 2400 bottles an hour when the bottling lines are operating at full speed. There is a maximum of two 8-hour shifts per day following a trade union agreement. Thus, the theoretical monthly capacity would be:

$$2400 \text{ per hour} \times 16 \text{ hours} \times 30 \text{ days} = 1\,152\,000 \text{ bottles}$$

Theoretical capacity is theoretical in the sense that it does not allow for any plant maintenance, any interruptions because of bottle breakages on the filling lines, or a host of other factors. While it is a rare plant that is able to operate at theoretical capacity, it can represent a goal or target level of usage.

Practical capacity is the denominator-level concept that reduces theoretical capacity for unavoidable operating interruptions such as scheduled maintenance time, shutdowns for holidays, and so on. Assume that the practical hourly production rate is 2000 bottles an hour and that the plant can operate 25 days a month. The practical monthly capacity is thus:

$$2000 \text{ per hour} \times 16 \text{ hours} \times 25 \text{ days} = 800\,000 \text{ bottles}$$

Engineering, economic and human factors are important to consider when estimating theoretical or practical capacity. Engineers at Cocobot's plant can provide input on the technical capabilities of machines for filling bottles. In some cases, however, an increase in capacity may be technically possible but not economically sound. For example, the trade union may actually permit a third shift per day but only at unusually high wage rates that clearly do not make financial sense in the coconut juice market. Human-safety factors, such as increased injury risk when the line operates at faster speeds, are also important to consider.

Normal utilisation and master-budget utilisation

Both theoretical capacity and practical capacity measure the denominator level in terms of what a plant can supply. In contrast, normal utilisation and master-budget utilisation (discussed further in Chapters 14 and 15) measure the denominator level in terms of demand for the output of the plant. In many cases, budgeted demand is well below the supply available (productive capacity).

Normal utilisation is the denominator-level concept based on the level of capacity utilisation that satisfies average customer demand over a period (say, of two to three years) that includes seasonal, cyclical or other trend factors. **Master-budget utilisation** is the denominator-level concept based on the anticipated level of capacity utilisation for the next budget period. These two denominator levels can differ – for example, when an industry has cyclical periods of high and low demand or when management believes that the budgeted production for the coming period is unrepresentative of 'long-term' demand.

Consider our Cocobot example of coconut juice production. The master budget for 2015 is based on production of 400 000 bottles per month. Hence the master-budget denominator level is 400 000 bottles. However, Cocobot senior management believes that over the next one to three years the normal monthly production level will be 500 000 bottles. They consider the 2015 budgeted production level of 400 000 bottles to be 'abnormally' low. Why? A major competitor has been sharply reducing its coconut juice prices and has also been spending enormous amounts on advertising. Cocobot expects that the lower prices and advertising blitz will be a short-run phenomenon and that in 2015 the market share it has lost to this competitor will be regained.

A major reason for choosing master-budget utilisation over normal utilisation is the difficulty of forecasting normal utilisation in many industries with long-run cyclical patterns. A similar problem occurs when estimating 'normal' demand. Some marketing managers are prone to overestimating their ability to regain lost market share. Their estimate of 'normal' demand for their product may be based on an overly optimistic outlook (a case of counting chickens before they have hatched).

Effect on financial statements

Cocobot has budgeted fixed manufacturing costs equivalent to €50 000 per month. Assume that actual costs are also €50 000. To keep this example simple, we assume all fixed manufacturing costs are indirect. The budgeted fixed manufacturing overhead rates in May 2015 for the four alternative denominator-level concepts discussed are:

Denominator-level concept (1)	Budgeted fixed manufacturing overhead per month (2)	Budgeted denominator level (in bottles) (3)	Budgeted fixed manufacturing overhead cost rate (4) = (2) ÷ (3)
Theoretical capacity	€50 000	1 152 000	€0.0434
Practical capacity	50 000	800 000	0.0625
Normal utilisation	50 000	500 000	0.1000
Master-budget utilisation	50 000	400 000	0.1250

The budgeted fixed manufacturing overhead rate based on master-budget utilisation (€0.1250) is more than 180% above the rate based on theoretical capacity (€0.0434).

Assume now that Cocobot's actual production in May 2015 is 460 000 bottles of coconut juice. Actual sales are 420 000 bottles. Also assume no opening stock on 1 May 2015 and no variances in manufacturing for May 2015. The manufacturing plant sells bottles of coconut juice to another division for €0.50 per bottle. Its only costs are variable manufacturing costs of €0.35 per bottle and €50 000 per month for fixed manufacturing overhead. Cocobot writes off all variances to cost of goods sold on a monthly basis.

The budgeted manufacturing costs per bottle of coconut juice for each denominator-level concept is the sum of €0.35 in variable manufacturing costs and the budgeted fixed manufacturing overhead costs (shown from the preceding table).

Denominator-level concept (1)	Variable manufacturing costs (2)	Budgeted fixed manufacturing overhead cost rate (3)	Total manufacturing costs (4) = (2) + (3)
Theoretical capacity	€0.35	€0.0434	€0.3934
Practical capacity	0.35	0.0625	0.4125
Normal utilisation	0.35	0.1000	0.4500
Master-budget utilisation	0.35	0.1250	0.4750

Each denominator-level concept will result in a different production-volume variance.

$$\text{Production-volume variance} = \left(\begin{array}{c} \text{Denominator} \\ \text{level in} \\ \text{output units} \end{array} - \begin{array}{c} \text{Actual} \\ \text{output} \\ \text{units} \end{array} \right) \times \begin{array}{c} \text{Budget fixed} \\ \text{manufacturing overhead} \\ \text{rate per output unit} \end{array}$$

Theoretical capacity	= (1 152 000 − 460 000) × €0.0434
	= €30 033 U (rounded up)
Practical capacity	= (800 000 − 460 000) × €0.0625
	= €21 250 U
Normal utilisation	= (500 000 − 460 000) × €0.1000
	= €4000 U
Master-budget utilisation	= (400 000 − 460 000) × €0.1250
	= €7500 F

Exhibit 7.9 shows how the choice of a denominator affects Cocobot's operating profit for May 2015. Using the master-budget denominator results in assigning the highest amount of fixed manufacturing overhead costs per bottle to the 40 000 bottles in closing stock. Accordingly, operating profit is highest using the master-budget utilisation denominator. Recall that Cocobot had no opening stock on 1 May 2015, production in May of 460 000 bottles and sales in May of 420 000 bottles. Hence, the closing stock on 31 May is 40 000 bottles. The differences among the operating profit for the four denominator-level concepts in Exhibit 7.9 are due to different amounts of fixed manufacturing overhead being inventoried:

Denominator-level concept	Fixed manufacturing overhead in 31 May 2015 stock
Theoretical capacity	40 000 × €0.0434 = €1736
Practical capacity	40 000 × 0.0625 = 2500
Normal utilisation	40 000 × 0.1000 = 4000
Master-budget utilisation	40 000 × 0.1250 = 5000

Thus, in Exhibit 7.9 the difference in operating profit between the master-budget utilisation concept and the normal utilisation concept of €1000 (€8000 − €7000) is due to the difference in fixed manufacturing overhead inventoried (€5000 − €4000).

Exhibit 7.9	Cocobot: Income statement effects of alternative denominator-level concepts for May 2015			
	Theoretical capacity	**Practical capacity**	**Normal utilisation**	**Master-budget utilisation**
Sales, €0.50 × 420 000	€210 000	€210 000	€210 000	€210 000
Cost of goods sold (COGS)				
Opening stock	0	0	0	0
Variable manufacturing costs*	161 000	161 000	161 000	161 000
Fixed manufacturing overhead costs[†]	19 964	28 750	46 000	57 500
Cost of goods available for sale	180 964	189 750	207 000	218 500
Closing stock[‡]	15 736	16 500	18 000	19 000
Total COGS (at standard costs)	165 228	173 250	189 000	199 500
Adjustment for manufacturing variances[§]	30 033 U	21 250 U	4 000 U	7 500 F
Total COGS	195 261	194 500	193 000	192 000
Gross margin	14 739	15 500	17 000	18 000
Marketing costs	10 000	10 000	10 000	10 000
Operating profit	€4 739	€5 500	€7 000	€8 000

* €0.35 × 460 000 = €161 000

[†] Fixed manufacturing overhead costs:
€0.0434 × 460 000 = €19 964
€0.0625 × 460 000 = €28 750
€0.1000 × 460 000 = €46 000
€0.1250 × 460 000 = €57 500

[‡] Closing stock costs
(0.35 + 0.0434) × (460 000 − 420 000) = €15 736
(0.35 + 0.0625) × (460 000 − 420 000) = €16 500
(0.35 + 0.1000) × (460 000 − 420 000) = €18 000
(0.35 + 0.1250) × (460 000 − 420 000) = €19 000

[§] The only variance for Cocobot in May 2015 is the production-volume variance. See text for the computations.

Summary

The following points are linked to the chapter's learning objectives.

1 Variable costing and absorption costing differ in only one respect: how to account for fixed manufacturing overhead costs. Under variable costing, fixed manufacturing overhead costs are excluded from inventoriable costs and are a cost of the period in which they are incurred. Under absorption costs, these costs are inventoriable and become expenses only when a sale occurs.

2 The variable-costing income statement is based on the contribution margin format. The absorption-costing income statement is based on the gross-margin format.

3 Under variable costing, reported operating profit is driven by variations in unit sales levels. Under absorption costing, reported operating profit is driven by variations in unit production levels as well as by variations in unit sales levels.

4 Managers can increase operating profit when absorption costing is used by producing for stock even when there is no immediate demand for the extra production. Critics of absorption costing label this as the major negative consequence of treating fixed manufacturing overhead as an inventoriable cost. Such negative consequences can be highlighted by using non-financial as well as financial variables for performance evaluation.

5 The denominator level chosen for fixed manufacturing overhead can greatly affect reported stock and operating profit amounts. In some cases it can also affect pricing and contract reimbursement. Denominator levels focusing on the capacity of a plant to supply product are theoretical capacity and practical capacity. Denominator levels focusing on the demand for the products a plant can manufacture are normal utilisation and master-budget utilisation.

6 The smaller the denominator level chosen, the higher the fixed manufacturing overhead cost per output unit that is inventoriable.

Appendix

Breakeven points in variable and absorption costing

This appendix considers breakeven point calculations (discussed further in Chapter 8) under variable and absorption costing. If variable costing is used, the breakeven point (where reported operating profit is zero) is unique: there is only one breakeven point. It is a function of (1) fixed costs, (2) unit contribution margin and (3) sales level in units. Holding (1) and (2) constant, operating profit rises as the sales level in units rises and vice versa. As the level of sales in units rises, operating profit rises and vice versa. In our Daxenberger illustration for February 2015, the following holds:

$$\text{Breakeven number of units} = \frac{\text{Total fixed costs}}{\text{Unit contribution margin}}$$

$$\text{Let } Q = \text{Number of units sold to break even}$$

$$Q = \frac{\text{€12\,800} + \text{€10\,400}}{\text{€99} - (\text{€20} + \text{€19})}$$

$$= \frac{\text{€23\,200}}{\text{€60}}$$

$$= 387 \text{ units (rounded)}$$

Proof of breakeven point:

Revenues: €99 × 387	€38 313
Costs: €39 × 387	15 093
Contribution margin	23 220
Fixed costs	23 200
Operating profit (rounding error)	€20

If absorption costing is used, the breakeven point (reported operating profit of zero) is not unique. The following formula, which can be used to calculate the breakeven point under absorption costing, highlights several factors that will affect the breakeven point:

$$\begin{array}{c} \text{Breakeven} \\ \text{number} \\ \text{of units} \end{array} = \cfrac{\text{Total fixed costs} + \left[\begin{array}{c}\text{Fixed} \\ \text{manufacturing} \\ \text{cost rate}\end{array} \times \left(\begin{array}{c}\text{Breakeven} \\ \text{sales in} \\ \text{units}\end{array} \times \begin{array}{c}\text{Units} \\ \text{produced}\end{array}\right)\right]}{\text{Unit contribution margin}}$$

Consider Daxenberger in February 2015:

$$Q = \frac{€12\,800 + €10\,400 + [€16(Q - 650)]}{€99 - (€20 + €19)}$$

$$= \frac{€23\,200 + €16Q - €10\,400}{€60}$$

$$€60Q = €12\,800 + €16Q$$

$$€44Q = €12\,800$$

$$Q = 291 \text{ units (rounded)}$$

Proof of breakeven point:

Revenues: €99 × 291		€28 809
Cost of goods sold		
Cost of goods sold (standard):	€10 476	
€36 × 291		
Production-volume variance:	2 400	12 876
(800 − 650) × €16		
Gross margin		15 933
Marketing costs		
Variable marketing: €19 × 291	5 529	
Fixed marketing	10 400	15 929
Operating profit (rounding error)		€4

The breakeven point under absorption costing depends on (1) fixed costs, (2) unit contribution margin, (3) sales level in units, (4) production level in units and (5) the denominator level chosen to set the fixed manufacturing costs rate. For Daxenberger in February 2015, a combination of fixed costs of €23 200, unit contribution margin of €60, units sold of 291 (rounded), 650 units produced and an 800-unit denominator level would result in an operating profit of zero. Note, however, there are many combinations of these five factors that would give an operating profit of zero.

We see that variable costing accords with cost–volume–profit analysis. Managers using variable costing can easily calculate the breakeven point or any effects that changes in the sales level in units may have on operating profit. In contrast, managers using absorption costing must also consider the unit production level and the denominator level before making such computations.

Suppose in our illustration that actual production in February 2015 was equal to the denominator level, 800 units. Also suppose that there were no sales and no fixed marketing costs. All the production would be placed in stock and so all the fixed manufacturing overhead would be included in stock. There would be no production-volume variance. Thus, the company could break even with no sales whatsoever. In contrast, under variable costing the operating loss would be equal to the fixed costs of €12 800.

Key terms

variable costing (179)

absorption costing (179)

direct costing (181)

theoretical capacity (191)

practical capacity (192)

normal utilisation (192)

master-budget utilisation (192)

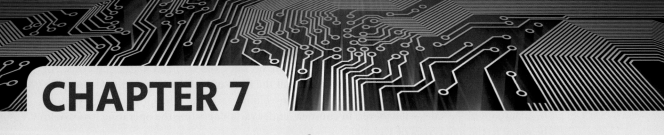

CHAPTER 7

Assessment material

Review questions

7.1 Differences in operating profit between variable and absorption costing are due solely to accounting for fixed costs. Do you agree? Explain.

7.2 The term variable costing could be improved by calling it variable manufacturing costing. Do you agree? Why?

7.3 Explain the main conceptual issue under variable and absorption costing regarding the proper timing for the release of fixed manufacturing overhead as expense.

7.4 'Companies that make no variable-cost/fixed-cost distinctions must use absorption costing and those that do make variable-cost/fixed-cost distinctions must use variable costing.' Do you agree? Explain.

7.5 'The main trouble with variable costing is that it ignores the increasing importance of fixed costs in modern manufacturing.' Do you agree? Why?

7.6 Give an example of how, under absorption costing, operating profit could fall even though the unit sales level rises.

7.7 Critics of absorption costing have increasingly emphasised its potential for promoting undesirable incentives for managers. Give an example.

7.8 What are two ways of reducing the negative aspects associated with using absorption costing to evaluate the performance of a plant manager?

7.9 Which denominator-level concepts emphasise what a plant can supply? Which denominator-level concepts emphasise what customers demand for products produced by a plant?

7.10 Name one reason why many companies prefer the master-budget utilisation-level concept rather than the normal utilisation-level concept.

Exercises

Intermediate level

7.11 **Comparison of actual costing methods** (20–30 minutes)

Haselbach GmbH sells its razors at €3 per unit. The company uses a first-in, first-out actual-costing system. A new fixed manufacturing overhead allocation rate is calculated each year by dividing the actual fixed manufacturing overhead cost by the actual production units. The following simplified data are related to its first two years of operation:

	Year 1	Year 2
Unit data		
Sales	1000	1200
Production	1400	1000
Cost		
Variable manufacturing	€700	€500
Fixed manufacturing	700	700
Variable marketing and administration	1000	1200
Fixed marketing and administration	400	400

Required

1 Prepare income statements based on (a) variable costing and (b) absorption costing for each year.

2 Prepare a reconciliation and explanation of the difference in the operating profit for each year resulting from the use of absorption costing and variable costing.

3 Critics have claimed that a widely used accounting system has led to undesirable stockbuilding levels. (a) Is variable costing or absorption costing more likely to lead to such build-ups? Why? (b) What can be done to prevent undesirable stock build-ups?

*7.12 Effects of denominator-level concept choice (20–35 minutes)

Forza San Marino Srl installed standard costs and a flexible budget on 1 January 2015. The president had been pondering how fixed manufacturing overhead should be allocated to products. Machine-hours had been chosen as the allocation base. Her remaining uncertainty was the denominator-level concept for machine-hours. She decided to wait for the first month's results before making a final choice of what denominator-level concept should be used from that day forward.

In January 2015, the actual units of output had a standard of 70 000 machine-hours allowed. If the company used practical capacity as the denominator-level concept, the fixed manufacturing overhead spending variance would be €10 000, unfavourable and the production-volume variance would be €36 000, unfavourable. If the company used normal utilisation as the denominator-level concept, the production-volume variance would be €20 000, favourable. Budgeted fixed manufacturing overhead was €120 000 for the month.

Required

1 Calculate the denominator level, assuming that the normal utilisation concept is chosen.

2 Calculate the denominator level, assuming that the practical capacity concept is chosen.

3 Suppose you are the executive vice-president. You want to maximise your 2015 bonus, which depends on 2015 operating profit. Assume that the production-volume variance is charged or credited to income at year-end. Which denominator-level concept would you favour? Why?

7.13 Income method alternatives (From ACCA Financial Information for Management, Part 1, June 2006) (30 minutes)

Pinafore Ltd manufactures and sells a single product. The budgeted profit statement for this month, which has been prepared using marginal costing principles, is as follows:

	£000	£000
Sales (24 000 units)		864
Less Variable production cost of sales:		
Opening stock (3000 units)	69	
Production (22 000 units)	506	
Closing stock (1000 units)	(23)	
		(552)
		312
Less Variable selling cost		(60)
Contribution		252
Less Fixed overhead costs:		
Production	125	
Selling and administration	40	
		(165)
Net profit		87

The normal monthly level of production is 25 000 units and stocks are valued at standard cost.

Required

1 Prepare in full a budgeted profit statement for this month using absorption-costing principles. Assume that fixed production overhead costs are absorbed using the normal level of activity.

2 Prepare a statement that reconciles the net profit calculated in (1) with the net profit using marginal costing.

3 Which of the two costing principles (absorption or marginal) is more relevant for short-run decision making, and why?

7.14 **Income method alternatives** (From ACCA Financial Information for Management, Part 1, June 2005) (30 minutes)

Archibald Ltd manufactures and sells one product. Its budgeted profit statement for the first month of trading is as follows:

	£	£
Sales (1200 units at £180 per unit)		216 000
Less Cost of sales:		
Production (1800 units at £100 per unit)	180 000	
Less Closing stock (600 units at £100 per unit)	(60 000)	
		(120 000)
Gross profit		96 000
Less Fixed selling and distribution costs		(41 000)
Net profit		55 000

The budget was prepared using absorption costing principles. If budgeted production in the first month had been 2000 units then the total production cost would have been £188 000.

Required

1 Using the high-low method, calculate:

   a the variable production cost per unit; and
   b the total monthly fixed production cost.

2 If the budget for the first month of trading had been prepared using marginal costing principles, calculate:

a the total contribution; and

b the net profit.

3 Explain clearly the circumstances in which the monthly profit or loss would be the same using absorption or marginal costing principles.

7.15 **Absorption vs marginal costing** (From ACCA Financial Information for Management, Part 1, June 2004) (40 minutes)

Langdale Ltd is a small company manufacturing and selling two different products – the Lang and the Dale. Each product passes through two separate production cost centres – a machining department, where all the work is carried out on the same general purpose machinery, and a finishing section. There is a general service cost centre providing facilities for all employees in the factory. The company operates an absorption costing system using budgeted overhead absorption rates. The management accountant has calculated the machine hour absorption rate for the machining department as £3.10 but a direct labour hour absorption rate for the finishing section has yet to be calculated. The following data have been extracted from the budget for the coming year:

	Product	
	Lang	Dale
Sales (units)	6 000	9 000
Production (units)	7 200	10 400
Direct material cost per unit	£52	£44
Direct labour cost per unit:		
– machining department (£8 per hour)	£72	£40
– finishing section (£6 per hour)	£42	£36
Machining department – machine hours per unit	5	3
Fixed production overhead costs:		
– machining department	£183 120	
– finishing section	£241 320	
– general service cost centre	£82 800	
Number of employees:		
– machining department	14	
– finishing section	32	
– general service cost centre	4	

Service cost centre costs are reapportioned to production cost centres.

Required

1 Calculate the direct labour hour absorption rate for the finishing section.

2 Calculate the budgeted total cost for one unit of product Dale only, showing each main cost element separately.

3 The company is considering a changeover to marginal costing. State, with reasons, whether the total profit for the coming year calculated using marginal costing would be higher or lower than the profit calculated using absorption costing. No calculations are required.

7.16   Overhead cost issues (From CIMA Management Accounting Pillar Managerial Level 1 Paper, November 2006) (25 minutes)

X Ltd has two production departments, Assembly and Finishing, and two service departments, Stores and Maintenance. Stores provides the following service to the production departments: 60% to Assembly and 40% to Finishing. Maintenance provides the following service to the production and service departments: 40% to Assembly, 45% to Finishing and 15% to Stores. The budgeted information for the year is as follows:

Budgeted fixed production overheads	
Assembly	£100 000
Finishing	£150 000
Stores	£50 000
Maintenance	£40 000
Budgeted output	100 000 units

At the end of the year after apportioning the service department overheads, the total fixed production overheads debited to the Assembly department's fixed production overhead control account were £180 000. The actual output achieved was 120 000 units.

Required

1 Calculate the under/over absorption of fixed production overheads for the Assembly department.

Advanced level

7.17   Variable and absorption costing, explaining operating profit differences (30 minutes)

Starzmann GmbH assembles and sells motor vehicles. It uses an actual costing system, in which unit costs are calculated on a monthly basis. Data relating to April and May of 2015 are:

	April	May
Unit data		
Opening stock	0	150
Production	500	400
Sales	350	520
Variable-cost data		
Manufacturing costs per unit produced	€10 000	€10 000
Marketing costs per unit sold	3 000	3 000
Fixed-cost data		
Manufacturing costs	€2 000 000	€2 000 000
Marketing **costs**	600 000	600 000

The selling price per motor vehicle is €24 000.

Required

1 Present income statements for Starzmann in April and May of 2015 under (a) variable costing and (b) absorption costing.

2 Explain any differences between (a) and (b) for April and May.

7.18   Variable and absorption costing, explaining operating profit differences (40 minutes)

Svenborg AS manufactures and sells wide-screen television sets. It uses an actual costing system, in which unit costs are calculated on a monthly basis. Data relating to January, February and March of 2015 are:

	January	February	March
Unit data			
Opening stock	0	300	300
Production	1 000	800	1 250
Sales	700	800	1 500
Variable-cost data			
Manufacturing costs per unit produced	DKK 900	DKK 900	DKK 900
Marketing costs per unit sold	600	600	600
Fixed-cost data			
Manufacturing costs	DKK 400 000	DKK 400 000	DKK 400 000
Marketing costs	140 000	140 000	140 000

The selling price per unit is DKr 2500.

Required

1 Present income statements for Svenborg in January, February and March of 2015 under (a) variable costing and (b) absorption costing.

2 Explain any differences between (a) and (b) for January, February and March.

*7.19   Income statements (SMA, adapted) (30–40 minutes)

Ericsson AB manufactures and sells a single product. The following data cover the two latest years of operations:

		2014	2015
Unit data			
Sales		25 000	25 000
Opening stock		1 000	1 000
Closing stock		1 000	5 000
Selling price per unit		SEK 40	SEK 40
Cost data			
Standard fixed costs			
Manufacturing overhead		SEK 120 000	SEK 120 000
Marketing and administrative		SEK 190 000	SEK 190 000
Standard variable costs per unit:			
Direct materials	SEK 10.50		
Direct manufacturing labour	SEK 9.50		
Manufacturing overhead	SEK 4.00		
Marketing and administrative	SEK 1.20		

The denominator level is 30 000 output units per year. Ericsson's accounting records produce variable-costing information and year-end adjustments are made to produce external reports showing absorption-costing information. All variances are charged to cost of goods sold.

Required

1 Prepare two income statements for 2015, one under variable costing and one under absorption costing.

2 Explain briefly why the operating profit figures calculated in requirement 1 agree or do not agree.

3 Give two advantages and two disadvantages of using variable costing for internal reporting.

7.20   Alternative denominator-level concepts (25–30 minutes)

Bières Ronsard SA recently purchased a brewing plant from a bankrupt company. The brewery is in Montpazier, France. It was constructed only two years ago. The plant has budgeted fixed manufacturing overhead of €42 million (€3.5 million each month) in 2015. Alain Cassandre, the accountant of the brewery, must decide on the denominator-level concept to use in its absorption costing system for 2015. The options available to him are

a Theoretical capacity: 600 barrels an hour for 24 hours a day × 365 days
= 5 256 000 barrels.

b Practical capacity: 500 barrels an hour for 20 hours a day × 350 days
= 3 500 000 barrels.

c Normal utilisation for 2015: 400 barrels an hour for 20 hours a day × 350 days
= 2 800 000 barrels.

d Master-budget utilisation for 2015 (separate rates calculated for each half-year):
   • January to June 2015 budget: 320 barrels an hour for 20 hours a day × 175 days
     = 1 120 000 barrels
   • July to December 2015 budget: 480 barrels an hour for 20 hours a day × 175 days
     = 1 680 000 barrels

Variable standard manufacturing costs per barrel are €45 (variable direct materials, €32; variable manufacturing labour, €6; and variable manufacturing overhead, €7). The Montpazier brewery 'sells' its output to the sales division of Bières Ronsard at a budgeted price of €68 per barrel.

Required

1 Calculate the budgeted fixed manufacturing overhead rate using each of the four denominator-level concepts for (a) beer produced in March 2015 and (b) beer produced in September 2015. Explain why any differences arise.

2 Explain why the theoretical capacity and practical capacity concepts are different.

3 Which denominator-level concept would the plant manager of the Montpazier brewery prefer when senior management of Bières Ronsard is judging plant manager performance during 2015? Explain.

7.21   Operating profit effects of alternative denominator-level concepts (continuation of Exercise 7.20) (30 minutes)

In 2015, the Montpazier brewery of Bières Ronsard showed these results:

Unit data in barrels
Opening stock, 1 January 2015	0
Production	2 600 000
Closing stock, 31 December 2015	200 000

The Montpazier brewery had actual costs of:

Cost data
Variable manufacturing	€120 380 000
Fixed manufacturing overhead	€40 632 000

The sales division of Bières Ronsard purchased 2 400 000 barrels in 2015 at the €68 per barrel rate.

All manufacturing variances are written off to cost of goods sold in the period in which they are incurred.

Required

1 Calculate the operating profit of the Montpazier brewery using the following: (a) theoretical capacity, (b) practical capacity and (c) normal utilisation denominator-level concepts. Explain any differences among (a), (b) and (c).

2 What denominator-level concept would Bières Ronsard prefer for income tax reporting? Explain.

3 Explain the ways in which the tax office might restrict the flexibility of a company like Bières Ronsard, which uses absorption costing, to reduce its reported taxable income.

7.22   Ginnungagap in 2015 (40 minutes)

It is the end of 2015. Ginnungagap Oy began operations in January 2014. The company is so named because it has no variable costs. All its costs are fixed; they do not vary with output.

Ginnungagap is located on the bank of a river and has its own hydroelectric plant to supply power, light and heat. The company manufactures a synthetic fertiliser from air and river water and sells its product at a price that is not expected to change. It has a small staff of employees, all hired on a fixed annual salary. The output of the plant can be increased or decreased by adjusting a few dials on a control panel.

The following are data regarding the operations of Ginnungagap Oy:

	2014	2015*
Sales (units)	10 000	10 000
Production (units)	20 000	–
Selling price per tonne	€30	€30
Costs (all fixed):		
Manufacturing	€280 000	€280 000
Marketing and administrative	€40 000	€40 000

* Management adopted the policy, effective from 1 January 2015, of producing only as much product as was needed to fill sales orders. During 2015, sales were the same as for 2014 and were filled entirely from stock at the start of 2015.

Required

1 Prepare income statements with one column for 2014, one column for 2015 and one column for the two years together, using (a) variable costing and (b) absorption costing.

2 What is the breakeven point under (a) variable costing and (b) absorption costing?

3 What stock costs would be carried on the balance sheets at 31 December 2014 and 2015 under each method?

4 Assume that the performance of the top manager of the company is evaluated and rewarded largely on the basis of reported operating profit. Which costing method would the manager prefer? Why?

*7.23   Audumla in 2015 (30 minutes)

Audumla Oy began operations in 2014 and differs from Ginnungagap (described in Exercise 7.22) in only one respect: it has both variable and fixed manufacturing costs. Its variable manufacturing costs are €7 per tonne, and its fixed manufacturing costs are €140 000 per year. The denominator level is 20 000 tonnes per year.

Required

1 Using the same data as in Exercise 7.22 except for the change in manufacturing cost behaviour, prepare income statements with adjacent columns for 2014, 2015 and the two years together, under (a) variable costing and (b) absorption costing.

2 Why did Audumla have operating profit for the two-year period when Ginnungagap in Exercise 7.22 suffered an operating loss?

3 What value for stock would be shown in the balance sheet as at 31 December 2014 and 31 December 2015 under each method?

4 Assume that the performance of the top manager of the company is evaluated and rewarded largely on the basis of reported operating profit. Which costing method would the manager prefer? Why?

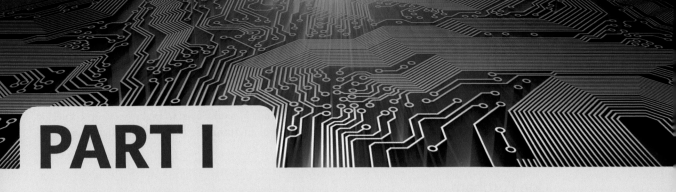

PART I

Case study problems

Case 101

The European Savings Bank

The case considers the ethical issues involved in making illegal copies of a software program by a professional management accountant.

It is a busy day at the office and Joe Fordham is hard at work for the European Savings Bank. Joe is in a quandary. He has a piece of software at work that he believes makes him more efficient and effective at his job. Unfortunately, the bank purchased only one copy. Joe really wants to have access to the software at home and he also wants to share it with his colleagues. The problem is that Joe does not have the necessary funds to purchase an additional copy for himself and he does not want to ask his supervisor for additional copies until he can prove the worth of the software. Joe knows that he can easily copy the software to use at home and to share with his colleagues. He is debating whether he should make the copies.

The following may be affected by Joe's decision.

Nick Stringham

Three years ago Nick graduated from university with a combined major in computer science and accounting. Immediately after graduation, Nick spent two years and €400 000 developing a computer software package, Loan Net, that provides a comprehensive loan analysis system. Loan Net has been proved to predict loan failures six months in advance of the failure date with 87% accuracy, far exceeding older methods that have only a 20% accuracy rate. His software is copyrighted and is being marketed by Data Sources SA. At the current time the software sells for €500 per copy. Sales to date have totalled just over 1000 copies, but the package has been well received and Nick is very excited about the future potential. In fact, he is currently working on an upgrade for the package. A friend recently told Nick that several banks may be using unauthorised copies of the program.

Shelly Norduck

Shelly graduated from university seven years ago with a concentration in marketing and a couple of courses in management information systems. She is currently Director of Sales at Data Sources

Source: Christiansen, A. and Eining, M.M. (1994) 'Software piracy – who does it impact?', *Issues in Accounting Education*, 9(1), Spring 1994. Reproduced with permission from the American Accounting Association.

SA, a medium-sized and rapidly growing software distribution company with current sales of €30 million. All software distributed by Data Sources SA is copyrighted, but because of customer complaints copy protection devices were removed from all software packages this year. Shelly is concerned that, while many customers are pleased that it is now easy to make back-up copies of Data Sources software, it will be difficult to control unauthorised copies. She has also heard rumours about Loan Net being copied.

Joe Fordham

Joe is a young management accountant who was hired last year by European Savings Bank, which has multiple branches throughout Europe. He previously worked for a major accounting firm and specialised in bank audits. He currently works in the loan department of Savings Bank and hopes to advance to Director of Finance within the next five years. Joe has found that competition for promotion to Director is very tight. Joe wants desperately to demonstrate that he is Director material and, therefore, often takes work home. He has a computer at home with a spreadsheet and a word processor, all of which he purchased himself and frequently uses for bank business. Recently, he has been working at the office with the single copy of Loan Net his company purchased and is very impressed with its performance. He believes that he could increase his productivity and, therefore, his chances for promotion if he had a copy of Loan Net for home use. Joe would also like to introduce the program to colleagues at other branches and the four loan officers who he supervises. Joe doesn't want to spend €500 for a copy of Loan Net to use at home. He estimates that he can save the bank a minimum of €2000 by making copies of Loan Net rather than purchasing them.

Judy Wardley

Judy is an internal auditor/accounting information system analyst at European Savings Bank. She is responsible for determining information needs of management, for evaluating the means of providing this information, and for computer education and training. She is in charge of both hardware and software acquisitions. Judy wonders about her responsibility to control software usage and account for copies of software. She knows some people would like additional copies of certain programs, but her budget for software is limited. Judy suspects that some people may be making more than back-up copies of software programs.

Dave Saunders

At 47, Dave is the dynamic and motivated CEO of European Savings Bank. He wants to see the bank rise from being the third most profitable in Europe to the first. He takes an interest in his employees and expects hard work, especially from those who wish to rise in the management ranks. He is interested in identifying those individuals who have insight into making the bank more profitable. Three years ago, he was instrumental in upgrading both the mainframe and personal computer systems at the bank. He is concerned that there is increasing pressure from some individuals to acquire new software and he is unsure how much the software will really be used.

Society

Society in general is affected by the actions of software developers, software vendors and purchasers of the software. The basic objectives of society include an improved standard of living, technological progress, and protection of personal freedom. All behaviours, including software piracy, have potential costs and benefits to society. Society must adopt a stance towards software piracy that will help achieve its goals and objectives.

Question

Discuss the facts relevant to the issue of copying the software program, including the ethical issues involved. Evaluate also the consequences of the different possible courses of action which may be taken.

Case 102

The ethical dilemma at Northlake

The case assumes no technical knowledge of management and cost accounting but deals with ethical issues that often face accounting professionals. It engages in a discussion of how far the notion of 'different costs for different purposes' might extend.

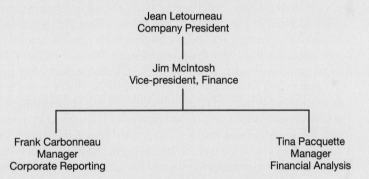

Jean Letourneau
Company President

Jim McIntosh
Vice-president, Finance

Frank Carbonneau
Manager
Corporate Reporting

Tina Pacquette
Manager
Financial Analysis

PART I Case study problems

Our story opens with an irate Jim McIntosh confronting his manager of corporate reporting: 'I thought we had an understanding on this issue, Frank. Tina tells me that you are threatening to go public with your stupid statements about the report. For Pete's sake, Frank, wake up and smell the coffee! You're about to damage all the important things in your life: your career, your friendships, and your company!'

Frank sat quietly in the overstuffed sofa in his VP's expansive office. He thought that the pale green report lying on the desk looked innocent enough, but it certainly had provided the basis for some serious turmoil: Jim stood by his desk trembling with rage. His face was bright red and mottled with anger. Frank had often seen Jim upset, but never in a temper such as this.

'I'm sorry, Jim', Frank replied softly, 'I know how much this means to you, but I don't think that I have a choice in this matter. I can't sit idle while you and that twit from financial analysis allow this report to go forward. You both know that these numbers have no foundation in fact.'

The report, entitled 'Endangered Species: The Pulp and Paper Industry in the Upper Peninsula', laid out the industry's response to the new government proposals to put effluent controls on the discharge of waste water from pulp and paper mills in environmentally sensitive regions of the province. One section of the report detailed the financial consequences of the emission controls as determined by each of the five pulp and paper companies operating in the region. Amalgamated Forest Products had taken the industry lead in developing the report, and the company president,

Source: Grant, R. (1993) 'The ethical dilemma at Northlake', *CMA Magazine*, March. Reproduced with permission from the Centre for Accounting Ethics.

Jean Letourneau, was scheduled to testify before a legislative sub-committee next week, giving the industry perspective on the proposed legislation.

Amalgamated had three major mills, located in some of the more remote locations in the province. The firm had been facing difficult financial times due to the recession, and this had caused substantial hardship in the three small communities where the mills were located. Corporate offices were located in Northlake, a town of approximately 10 000 people.

The section of the report dealing with the dollar impact to Amalgamated Forest Products of installing the emission control equipment had been prepared by Tina Pacquette. Tina, a long-term employee of the firm, had risen through the accounting department to become the manager of financial analysis. While Tina and Frank were at equal levels in the organisational structure, their working relationship had not been particularly cordial. In Frank's opinion, Tina's work was barely adequate, but then, no one asked for his opinion.

'Well, Frank, your pig-headedness has really caused a problem for all of us! Wait here! I'll get Jean Letourneau, and we'll see what he thinks about your efforts.' Jim left the office and slammed the door.

As he waited in the silence of his boss's beautifully decorated office, Frank looked back over his ten years with Amalgamated Forest Products. Just like his father before him, Frank started with the firm after completing high school and his first job was as a yard man sorting out damaged logs before processing. That's when Frank severely damaged his right leg on the job. He had been celebrating the birth of his son the night before and he was unable to manoeuvre his footing with the dexterity required. Surgery saved the leg and he was extremely grateful that the company had brought him inside to the accounting office. An accounting clerk's salary was low compared with being a yard helper, but in a short time his natural talent for analysis brought him to the attention of the Vice President, Finance. Within two years, Jim McIntosh had arranged for him to go to university, complete his CMA designation after graduation, and then return to Amalgamated. The financial support provided by the firm had been adequate but not lavish by any means, and Frank had done well in his studies. He was the gold medallist for his province on the CMA examinations, and he had returned to Northlake in triumph. With three young children and a proud wife, Frank had been appointed to a new position in corporate reporting. After a year of having Jim as his mentor, he rose to the position of manager of corporate reporting.

The office door opened abruptly, and Jim entered with the company president. Jean Letourneau was a distinguished man of approximately 60 years of age. He had a long history with Amalgamated and a solid reputation in the pulp and paper industry.

'What's the problem, Frank?' Jean's voice broke into the silence. 'Jim tells me that you have a few concerns about the report that we're submitting to the legislative committee.'

'Well, Mr Letourneau, I think we – the company – have some major problems here. The report indicates that we'll have severe financial problems if we're forced into building a lagoon for waste water treatment. In fact, the report says we are likely to be pushed into bankruptcy if the legislation is passed. But we all know these estimates of costs are highly inflated. There's no way that our operating costs would be raised by 30%. I could see our operating costs rising by only 8–10%. That's what the internal report Tina wrote a year ago predicts and there's really been no significant change. Moreover, you have to testify before the legislative committee as to the truthfulness of this report – and there's not a shred of truth in it. The other cost estimates are all high, and the prediction of our product demand is based upon a further deepening of the recession. For our internal purposes, we have been using an estimated increase of 10% in demand.'

'Slow down, son', Letourneau's calm voice broke in, 'We have to use different figures for different purposes. When we report to our shareholders, we give them numbers that are substantially altered from the internal documents, right? In this case, we have to make those dunderheads in the government see what all this regulation is doing to us. Besides, they know we're going to use the most effective numbers to justify our position.'

'But this isn't simply a matter of different figures', Frank spluttered. 'These numbers have been totally fabricated. And they don't take into account the damage that we're doing to the Wanawashee River. The same stuff we're dumping was cleaned up by our competition years ago.

The community downstream is still drinking this garbage. We're going to be subject to a huge lawsuit if they ever trace it to us. Then, where will we be? I've got to worry about my professional obligations as well. If this blows up, you could go to jail, and I could get my designation revoked.'

'We'll cross that bridge when we come to it', Jim McIntosh interjected. 'You've got to remember what's at stake here. Northlake's totally dependent on the mill for its economic survival. As the mill goes, so goes the town. It's your buddies you'd be threatening to put out of work, Frank. This legislation may not bankrupt us, but it will certainly put a squeeze on profits. If profits are gone, no more reinvestment by Chicago. Head office is putting lots of pressure on us to improve the bottom line since the takeover last year. They're talking about cutting all of that new production line equipment we requested.'

'The bottom line is this, Frank', Letourneau spoke softly. 'You're an important part of our team – we've invested a lot in you. Jim was talking about working you into a new role: V.P.-controller. We'd hate to let you go because of this small issue. However, we need to have everybody working towards the same goal. Besides, Jim tells me this isn't even your responsibility. If you hadn't picked up the copy of the report on Tina's desk, we wouldn't even have involved you. Now take the rest of the day off, go home to Cheryl and the kids, and take out that new speedboat of yours. Think the problem through, and I'm sure you'll see the long-term benefit of what we're doing. This pollution problem is a "Northern problem" that we can resolve here, not in some fancy legislature in the south. Besides, we've had the problem for as far back as I can remember. So a few extra years certainly won't hurt.'

Question

What would you do if you were Frank?

Case 103

Electronic Boards plc
John Innes and Falconer Mitchell, University of Edinburgh

This is a general case on the design of a management and cost accounting system for a firm operating in a high-tech environment. It provides an opportunity for a broad discussion not only of the appropriateness of particular accounting techniques but also of the need to consider strategic, behavioural and organisational factors.

Introduction

Jack Watson, an electrical engineer, established Electronic Boards plc as a 'one-man' company in the early 1990s. From small beginnings, the company earned a reputation for the quality and reliability of its products, and grew rapidly and consistently until, by 2015, it employed over 200 people and had achieved a turnover of £56 million and a profit after tax of £4.1 million. In addition to Jack Watson, the managing director, the board consists of a production director, a research director and a marketing director.

Source: Innes, J. and Mitchell, F. (1988) 'Electronic Boards plc', in D. Otley, D. Brown and C. Wilkinson (eds) *Case Studies in Management Accounting* (Hemel Hempstead, UK: Philip Allan Publishers). Reproduced with permission.

Market circumstances

The company produces customised batches of electronic circuit boards for approximately 15 major customers in the defence, computer, electrical goods and automotive industries. The market is highly competitive in respect of both price and quality. Market price has fallen steadily in recent years. In addition to several other independent firms from both the UK and the Far East, many of their larger customers have in-house facilities for the production of circuit boards. These latter firms deliberately subcontract a portion of their circuit board requirements for strategic reasons. In a recession they can cease or reduce their subcontracting and bring the work in-house, so stabilising their own employment levels.

Operational circumstances

The production process for circuit boards is complex, multi-stage and highly automated. Production flows continuously through the various processes and any hold-up quickly affects the flow of work at all production stages. Experience has shown that a proportion of the final output contains faults and has to be scrapped. These scrap levels typically vary between 10% and 25% of good output, a considerable learning effect is apparent and the yield on repeat orders is usually significantly improved. At present, faulty products are identified only on completion, although action has been instigated (in the form of an investigative working party) to achieve an earlier identification of faults.

Orders are obtained in three ways:

1 By written tender for large contracts (approximately 40% of business)
2 By telephone quotation for small orders (approximately 20% of business) – a price is normally quoted to the caller during the call
3 By repeat orders (approximately 40% of business).

Prices are calculated by estimating the direct material cost of an order and adding on an allowance for all other costs and profit. This allowance is based on the previous year's direct material cost to sales margin. In recent years the cost structure of the firm's output has been as follows:

Cost structure of current boards	
Direct materials	65%
Direct labour	5
Production overheads	20
Non-production overheads	10
	100%

Direct materials are by far the major cost component and this importance is reflected in the high levels of materials stock which are held by the company.

Financial information

It is generally accepted by the senior members of management that the development of a management accounting system has been neglected. This has been attributed mainly to the dismissive attitude of line management to accountants. Encapsulating this view was the comment of one senior manager, 'they are "bean-counters" who know nothing about the electronics industry, the problems we face and the decisions we have to take'. The consistent success of the company in the absence of any management accounting system has reinforced this type of attitude among managers and directors in the company. No qualified accountants have been appointed to the board, and until 2014 only one qualified accountant was employed by the company. His prime responsibility was the preparation of statutory financial accounting statements for shareholders.

In addition, however, since 2012 a half-yearly company profit and loss account and balance sheet has been prepared for the board.

No product costing system has been in operation. For financial statement preparation, work in progress is simply valued at an estimate of its direct material content cost and finished goods stock is valued at a discounted selling price (using the previous year's gross profit percentage). However, some managers have complained about their lack of knowledge of unit production costs and about their inability to pinpoint which contracts or types of work have been profitable for the company.

Budgets are no longer prepared. Attempts were made to produce annual budgets in 2010 and 2011 but the firm's accountant experienced great difficulty in obtaining reliable estimates from line management. His lack of authority within the firm and the absence of a finance director to provide support rendered his requests for information ineffective. Consequently, acceptance of the budgets which he prepared was not forthcoming. They were quickly viewed as unrealistic by management and after a few months ignored.

Capital budgeting decisions have been based upon the need for the firm to remain at the forefront of production technology. If new equipment became available which would improve the firm's product quality, it was usually purchased and then funds were 'found' to finance it. This had often led to the company having unexpected overdrafts and high bank charges and interest expenses.

Recession

In 2015 the firm experienced its first recession. Market share fell, sales dropped to £21.5 million, a loss of £1.7 million was made and the company's liquidity suffered considerably. The market decline was expected to continue in 2016 and the managing director of Electronic Boards plc sought ways of alleviating the effects of the recession on the company's financial performance. He found, however, that the lack of management accounting information hampered him in pinpointing problem areas and in identifying cost-reduction possibilities. Consequently, he approached a firm of management consultants to provide a blueprint for the development of a management accounting system over the next two years.

Question

Prepare a blueprint for the board of Electronic Boards plc outlining the main factors which it should consider in establishing a useful management accounting function within the company.

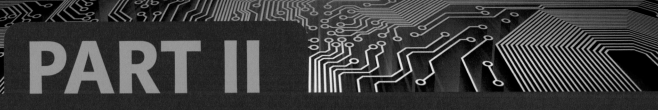

PART II

Accounting information for decision making

Part I introduced fundamental management and cost accounting concepts. Our objective in Part II is to focus on internal accounting concepts which are aimed at assisting managerial decision making. Chapters 8, 9 and 10 discuss long-established perspectives on cost relationships and organisational activity changes. They principally emphasise decision making in the short-term and how a firm's available resources can be influenced and reallocated in the pursuit of immediate goals. The focus in these chapters is largely on scale changes whereas Chapter 11 considers the notion of scope and production complexity *vis-à-vis* cost changes. The cost management approach which allows enterprises to account for volume- and non-volume-based cost drivers is activity-based costing. Chapter 12 introduces pricing considerations and cost-related prioritisation of organisational activities. Chapter 13 provides a perspective on assessing long-term issues in cost change decisions. It considers techniques used to evaluate capital budgeting for investments.

CHAPTER 8

Cost-volume-profit relationships

Cost-volume-profit analysis provides a sweeping financial overview of the planning process. **Cost-volume-profit (CVP) analysis** examines the behaviour of total revenues, total costs and operating profit as changes occur in the output level, selling price, variable costs or fixed costs. CVP analysis is among the most basic tools available to managers. Managers commonly use CVP as a tool to help them answer such questions as: How will revenues and costs be affected if we sell 1000 more units? If we raise or lower our selling prices, how will that affect the output level? If we expand into Far East markets, what will be the impact on costs? These questions have a 'what-if' theme.

Companies need to achieve breakeven before they can produce profits (this is inherent in the definition of breaking even). Consider, for instance, Gaz du Cameroun, which in February 2014 reached breakeven after it managed to average 3.2 million standard cubic feet per day arising from new connections and increased usage by existing customers. Its chairman, Kevin Foo, noted: 'Achieving operational breakeven is an important milestone and we look forward to building on this momentum'. Decisions in most firms, at some stage, inevitably entail an assessment of cost-volume-profit implications. CVP is built on simplifying assumptions about revenue and cost behaviour patterns. This chapter examines CVP analysis and explains how the reasonableness underlying its assumptions affects the reliability of its results.

Learning objectives

After studying this chapter, you should be able to:

- Distinguish between the general case and a special case of CVP

- Explain the relationship between operating profit and net profit

- Describe the assumptions underlying CVP

- Demonstrate three methods for determining the breakeven point and target operating profit

- Explain how sensitivity analysis can help managers cope with uncertainty

- Illustrate how CVP can assist cost planning

- Describe the effect of revenue mix on operating profit

Revenue drivers and cost drivers

Revenues are inflows of assets received in exchange for products or services provided to customers. A **revenue driver** is a factor that affects revenues. Examples of revenue drivers are units of output sold, selling prices and levels of marketing costs. Chapter 2 defined cost as a resource sacrificed or forgone to achieve a specific objective and a *cost driver* as any factor that affects cost – that is, a change in the cost driver will cause a change in the total cost of a related cost object. Examples of cost drivers include units of output manufactured, number of sales visits made and number of packages shipped.

The most detailed way of predicting total revenues and total costs is to consider multiple revenue drivers and multiple cost drivers. We call this the general case. It can require extensive analysis and is likely to be very time-consuming. For now, we focus on a special case where we assume a single revenue driver and a single cost driver. That single driver is units of output (either output units sold or output units manufactured). The term *CVP analysis* is widely used as representing this special case. A single revenue driver and a single cost driver are used in this analysis.

The straightforward relationships provide an excellent base for understanding the more complex relationships that exist with multiple revenues and multiple cost drivers:

General case	Special case
Many revenue drivers	Single revenue driver (output units)
Many cost drivers	Single cost driver (output units)
Various time spans for decisions (short run, long run, product life cycles)	Short-run decisions (time span, typically less than one year, in which fixed costs do not change within the relevant range)

Our restriction to units of output as the sole revenue or cost driver is important to keep in mind. It means that in the CVP model, changes in the level of revenues and costs arise only because the output level changes. This restriction means that we will not consider a revenue driver such as the number of advertisements for a new product. Nor will we consider a cost driver such as the number of calls a customer makes for after-sales service or service repairs. These factors are examples of revenue or cost drivers that are not a function of units of output.

Before we can study CVP, we must understand its terminology. In this chapter, we assume total costs (also termed total expenses) are made up of only two categories: variable costs (variable with respect to units of output) and fixed costs.

$$\text{Total costs} = \text{Variable costs} + \text{Fixed costs}$$

Recall from Chapter 2 (Exhibit 2.6) that variable costs include both direct variable costs and indirect variable costs of a chosen cost object. Similarly, fixed costs include both direct fixed costs and indirect fixed costs of a chosen cost object.

Operating profit is total revenues from operations minus total costs from operations (excluding income taxes):

$$\text{Operating profit} = \text{Total revenues} - \text{Total costs}$$

Net profit is operating profit plus non-operating revenues (such as interest revenue) minus non-operating costs (such as interest cost) minus income taxes. For simplicity, throughout this chapter non-operating revenues and non-operating costs are assumed to be zero. Thus, net profit will be calculated as follows:

$$\text{Net profit} = \text{Operating profit} - \text{Income taxes}$$

In the examples that follow, the measure of output is the number of units manufactured or units sold. Different industries often use different terminology to describe their measure of output. Examples include:

Industry	Measure of output
Airlines	Passenger-kilometres
Cars	Vehicles manufactured
Hospitals	Patient-days
Hotels	Rooms occupied

The following abbreviations are used in this chapter:

USP = Unit selling price
UVC = Unit variable costs
UCM = Unit contribution margin (USP – UVC)
FC   = Fixed costs
Q   = Quantity of output units sold (or manufactured)
OP   = Operating profit
TOP = Target operating profit

CVP assumptions

The CVP analysis that we now discuss is based on the following assumptions:

1 Total costs can be divided into a fixed component and a component that is variable with respect to the level of output.

2 The behaviour of total revenues and total costs is linear (straight-line) in relation to output units within the relevant range.

3 The unit selling price, unit variable costs and fixed costs are known and are constant. (This assumption is discussed later in the chapter and in the appendix to this chapter.)

4 The analysis either covers a single product or assumes that the proportion of different products when multiple products are sold will remain constant as the level of total units sold changes. (This assumption is also discussed later in the chapter.)

5 All revenues and costs can be added and compared without taking into account the time value of money. (Chapter 13 relaxes this assumption.)

6 Changes in the level of revenues and costs arise only because of changes in the number of products (or service) units produced and sold. The number of output units is the only revenue and cost driver.

These CVP assumptions simplify organisational realities. Some managers may prefer a more sophisticated approach. Nevertheless, CVP provides a useful basis for exploring certain business decision situations in which cost–volume–profit relationships are highlighted.

The breakeven point

CVP analysis can be used to examine how various 'what-if' alternatives being considered by a decision maker affect operating profit. The breakeven point is frequently one point of interest in this analysis. Managers wish to avoid the stigma of making a loss. The **breakeven point** is that quantity of output where total revenues and total costs are equal, that is, where the operating profit is zero.

Using the information in the following example, this section examines three methods for determining the breakeven point: the equation method, the contribution margin method and the graph method.

Example 8.1

Mary Frost plans to sell Do-All Software, a software package, at a heavily attended two-day computer convention. Mary can purchase this software from a computer software wholesaler at €120 per package with the privilege of returning all unsold units and receiving a full €120 rebate per package. The units (packages) will be sold at €200 each. Mary has already paid €2000 to Computer Conventions Ltd for the booth rental for the two-day convention. What quantity of units will she need to sell in order to break even? Assume there are no other costs.

Equation method

The first approach for computing the breakeven point is the equation method. Using the terminology in this chapter, the income statement can be expressed in equation form as follows:

$$\text{Revenues} - \text{Variable costs} - \text{Fixed costs} = \text{Operating profit}$$
$$(\text{USP} \times Q) - (\text{UVC} \times Q) - \text{FC} = \text{OP}$$

This equation provides the most general and easy-to-remember approach to any CVP situation. Setting operating profit equal to zero in the preceding equation, we obtain

$$€200Q - €120Q - €2000 = €0$$
$$€80Q = €2000$$
$$Q = €2000 \div €80$$
$$= 25 \text{ units}$$

If Mary sells fewer than 25 units, she will have a loss; if she sells 25 units, she will break even; and if she sells more than 25 units, she will make a profit. This breakeven point is expressed in units. It can also be expressed in sales euros: 25 units × €200 selling price = €5000.

Contribution margin method

A second approach is the contribution margin method, which is simply an algebraic manipulation of the equation method. Contribution margin is equal to revenues minus all costs of the output (a product or service) that vary with respect to the units of output. This method uses the fact that:

$$(\text{USP} \times Q) - (\text{UVC} \times Q) - \text{FC} = \text{OP}$$
$$(\text{USP} - \text{UVC}) \times Q = \text{FC} + \text{OP}$$
$$\text{UCM} \times Q = \text{FC} + \text{OP}$$
$$Q = \frac{\text{FC} + \text{OP}}{\text{UCM}}$$

At the breakeven point, operating profit is, by definition, zero. Setting OP = 0, we obtain:

$$\frac{\text{Breakeven}}{\text{number of units}} = \frac{\text{Fixed costs}}{\text{Unit contribution margin}} = \frac{\text{FC}}{\text{UCM}}$$

The calculations in the equation method and the contribution margin method appear similar because one is merely a restatement of the other. In our example, fixed costs are €2000 and the unit contribution margin is €80 (€200 – €120). Therefore,

Breakeven number of units = €2000 ÷ €80 = 25 units

A **contribution income statement** groups line items by cost behaviour pattern to highlight the contribution margin. The following such statement confirms the preceding breakeven calculations:

Revenues, €200 × 25	€5000
Variable costs, €120 × 25	3000
Contribution margin, €80 × 25	2000
Fixed costs	2000
Operating profit	€0

Graph method

In the graph method, we plot the total costs line and the total revenues line. Their point of intersection is the breakeven point. Exhibit 8.1 illustrates this method for our Do-All example. We need only two points to plot each line if each is assumed to be linear:

1 *Total costs line*. This line is the sum of the fixed costs and the variable costs. Fixed costs are €2000 at all output levels within the relevant range. To plot fixed costs, measure €2000 on the vertical axis (point A) and extend a line horizontally. Variable costs are €120 per unit. To plot

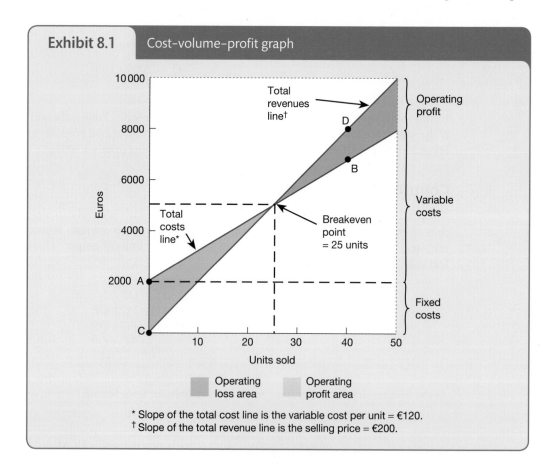

Exhibit 8.1   Cost-volume-profit graph

* Slope of the total cost line is the variable cost per unit = €120.
† Slope of the total revenue line is the selling price = €200.

the total costs line, use as one point the €2000 fixed costs at 0 output units (point A). Select a second point by choosing any other convenient output level (say, 40 units) and determining the corresponding total costs. The total variable costs at this output level are €4800 (40 × €120). Fixed costs are €2000 at all output levels within the relevant range. Hence, total costs at 40 units of output are €6800, which is point B in Exhibit 8.1. The total costs line is the straight line from point A passing through point B.

2 *Total revenues line.* One convenient starting point is zero revenues at the zero output level, which is point C in Exhibit 8.1. Select a second point by choosing any other convenient output level and determining its total revenues. At 40 units of output, total revenues are €8000 (40 × €200), which is point D in Exhibit 8.1. The total revenues line is the straight line from point C passing through point D.

The breakeven point is where the total revenues line and the total costs line intersect. At this point, total revenues equal total costs. But Exhibit 8.1 shows the profit or loss outlook for a wide range of output levels. Many people describe the topics covered in this chapter as breakeven analysis. We prefer to use the phrase cost–volume–profit analysis to avoid overemphasising the single point where total revenues equal total costs. Managers want to know how operating profit differs at many different output levels.

Target operating profit

Let us introduce a profit element by asking the following question: How many units must be sold to earn an operating profit of €1200? The equation method provides a straightforward way to answer this question. Let QT be the number of units sold to earn the target operating profit:

$$\text{Revenues} - \text{Variable costs} - \text{Fixed costs} = \text{Target operating profit}$$
$$€200QT - €120QT - €2000 = €1200$$
$$€80QT = €2000 + €1200$$
$$€80QT = €3200$$
$$QT = €3200 \div €80$$
$$= 40 \text{ units}$$

Alternatively, we could use the contribution margin method. The numerator now consists of fixed costs plus target operating profit:

$$QT = \frac{\text{Fixed costs} + \text{Target operating profit}}{\text{Unit contribution margin}} = \frac{\text{FC} + \text{TOP}}{\text{UCM}}$$

$$QT = \frac{€2000 + €1200}{€80}$$

$$€80QT = €3200$$

$$QT = €3200 \div €80$$

$$= 40 \text{ units}$$

Proof:	Revenues, €200 × 40	€8000
	Variable costs, €120 × 40	4800
	Contribution margin, €80 × 40	3200
	Fixed costs	2000
	Operating profit	€1200

The graph in Exhibit 8.1 indicates that at the 40-unit output level, the difference between total revenues and total costs is the €1200 operating profit.

The PV graph

We can recast Exhibit 8.1 in the form of a profit–volume (PV) graph. A **PV graph** shows the impact on operating profit of changes in the output level. Exhibit 8.2 (Graph A) presents the PV graph for Do-All (fixed costs of €2000, selling price of €200, and variable costs per unit of €120). The PV line can be drawn using two points. One convenient point (X) is the level of fixed costs at zero output – €2000, which is also the operating loss at this output level. A second convenient point (Y) is the breakeven point – 25 units in our example. The PV line is drawn by connecting points X and Y and extending the line beyond Y. Each unit sold beyond the breakeven point will add €80 to operating profit. At the 35-unit output level, for example, operating profit would be €800:

$$(€200 \times 35) - (€120 \times 35) - €2000 = €800$$

A comparison of PV charts representing different what-if possibilities can highlight their effects on operating profit. Graph B in Exhibit 8.2 shows the PV chart for Do-All assuming fixed costs of €3300 (compared with €2000 in Graph A) and variable costs per unit of €90 (compared with €120 in Graph A). The selling price is €200 in both graphs. The unit contribution margin in Graph B is €110. The breakeven point in Graph B is 30 units:

$$€200Q - €90Q - €3300 = 0$$
$$Q = €3300 \div €110$$
$$= 30 \text{ units}$$

Each unit sold beyond the breakeven point will add €110 to operating profit. The PV graph in Graph B has a steeper slope for its operating profit line, which means that the operating profit increases at a faster rate as the level of output increases.

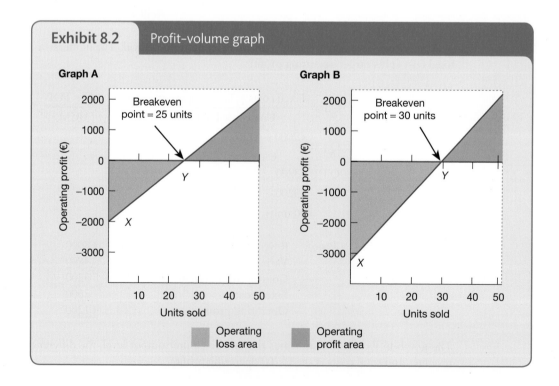

Exhibit 8.2   Profit–volume graph

Impact of income taxes

When we introduced a target operating profit in our earlier Do-All software example, the following income statement was shown:

Revenues, €200 × 40	€8000
Variable costs, €120 × 40	4800
Contribution margin	3200
Fixed costs	2000
Operating profit	€1200

The net profit of Do-All is operating profit minus income taxes. What number of units of Do-All must be sold to earn a net profit of €1200, assuming operating profit is taxed at a rate of 40%? The only change in the equation method of CVP analysis is to modify the target operating profit to allow for income taxes. Recall our previous equation method:

$$\text{Revenues} - \text{Variable costs} - \text{Fixed costs} = \text{Operating profit}$$

We now introduce income tax effects:

$$\text{Target net profit} = (\text{Operating profit}) - [(\text{Operating profit}) \times (\text{Tax rate})]$$
$$\text{Target net profit} = (\text{Operating profit}) \times (1 - \text{Tax rate})$$
$$\text{Operating profit} = \frac{\text{Target net profit}}{1 - \text{Tax rate}}$$

So, taking income taxes into account, the equation method yields:

$$\text{Revenues} - \text{Variable costs} - \text{Fixed costs} = \frac{\text{Target net profit}}{1 - \text{Tax rate}}$$

Substituting numbers from our Do-All example, the equation would now be:

$$\text{€200Q} - \text{€120Q} - \text{€2000} = \frac{\text{Target net profit}}{1 - \text{Tax rate}}$$

$$\text{€200Q} - \text{€120Q} - \text{€2000} = \frac{\text{€1200}}{1 - 0.40}$$

$$\text{€200Q} - \text{€120Q} - \text{€2000} = \text{€2000}$$

$$\text{€80Q} = \text{€4000}$$

$$Q = \text{€4000} \div \text{€80}$$

$$= 50 \text{ units}$$

Proof:

Revenues, €200 × 50	€10 000
Variable costs, €120 × 50	6 000
Contribution margin	4 000
Fixed costs	2 000
Operating profit	2 000
Income taxes, €2000 × 0.40	800
Net profit	€1 200

Suppose the target net profit were set at €1680 instead of €1200. The required number of unit sales would rise from 50 to 60 units:

$$\text{Operating profit} = \frac{\text{Target net profit}}{1 - \text{Tax rate}}$$

$$€200Q - €120Q - €2000 = \frac{€1680}{1 - 0.40}$$

$$€80Q - €2000 = €2800$$

$$€80Q = €4800$$

$$Q = €4800 \div €80$$

$$= 60 \text{ units}$$

The presence of income taxes will not change the breakeven point. Why? Because, by definition, operating profit at the breakeven point is zero, and thus no income taxes will be paid. However, other types of tax may affect the breakeven point. For example, a sales tax paid by the seller that is a fixed percentage of revenues can be treated as a variable cost and hence will increase the breakeven point.

Sensitivity analysis and uncertainty

Sensitivity analysis is a what-if technique that examines how a result will change if the original predicted data are not achieved or if an underlying assumption changes. In the context of CVP, sensitivity analysis answers such questions as: What will operating profit be if the output level decreases by 5% from the original prediction? What will operating profit be if variable costs per unit increase by 10%? The sensitivity to various possible outcomes broadens managers' perspectives as to what might actually occur despite their well-laid plans.

The widespread use of electronic spreadsheets has led to an increase in the use of CVP analysis in many organisations. Using spreadsheets, managers can easily conduct CVP-based sensitivity analyses to examine the effect and interaction of changes in selling prices, unit variable costs, fixed costs and target operating profits. Exhibit 8.3 displays a spreadsheet for our Do-All Software example. Mary Frost can immediately see the revenues that need to be generated to reach particular operating profit levels, given alternative levels of fixed costs and variable costs per unit. For example, revenues of €6000 (30 units at €200 per unit) are required to earn an operating

Exhibit 8.3	Spreadsheet analysis of CVP relationships for Do-All Software				
	Variable costs per unit	Revenue required at €200 selling price to earn operating profit of			
Fixed costs		€0	€1 000	€1 500	€2 000
€2 000	€100	€4 000	6 000	7 000	8 000
	120	5 000	7 500	8 750	10 000
	140	6 667	10 000	11 667	13 333
€2 500	€100	€5 000	7 000	8 000	9 000
	120	6 250	8 750	10 000	11 250
	140	8 333	11 667	13 333	15 000
€3 000	€100	€6 000	8 000	9 000	10 000
	120	7 500	10 000	11 250	12 500
	140	10 000	13 333	15 000	16 667

profit of €1000 if fixed costs are €2000 and variable costs per unit are €100. Mary can also use Exhibit 8.3 to assess whether she wants to sell at the computer convention if, for example, the booth rental is raised to €3000 (thus increasing fixed costs to €3000) or the software supplier raises its price to €140 per unit (thus increasing variable costs to €140 per unit).

One aspect of sensitivity analysis is the **margin of safety**, which is the excess of budgeted revenues over the breakeven revenues. The margin of safety is the answer to the what-if question: If budgeted revenues are above breakeven and drop, how far can they fall below budget before the breakeven point is reached? Such a fall could be due to a competitor having a better product, poorly executed marketing, and so on. Assume that Mary Frost has fixed costs of €3000, a selling price of €200, and variable costs per unit of €140. For 75 units sold, the budgeted revenues are €15 000 and the budgeted operating profit is €1500. The breakeven point for this set of assumptions is 50 units (€3000 ÷ €60) or €10 000 (€200 × 50). Hence, the margin of safety is €5000 (€15 000 − €10 000) or 25 units.

Sensitivity analysis is one approach to recognising **uncertainty**, which is defined here as the possibility that an actual amount will deviate from an expected amount. Another approach is to calculate expected values using probability distributions. The appendix to this chapter illustrates this approach.

Concepts in action   How the 'the biggest rock show ever' turned a big profit

Source: Corbis/David Atlas/Retna Ltd

When U2 embarked on its 2009 world tour, *Rolling Stone* magazine called it 'the biggest rock show ever'. Visiting large stadiums across the United States and Europe, the Irish quartet performed on an imposing 164-foot-high stage that resembled a spaceship, complete with a massive video screen and footbridges leading to ringed catwalks. With an ambitious 48-date trek planned, U2 actually had three separate stages leapfrogging its global itinerary – each one costing nearly $40 million dollars. As a result, the tour's success was dependent not only on each night's concert, but also recouping its tremendous fixed costs – costs that do not change with the number of fans in the audience. To cover its high fixed costs and make a profit, U2 needed to sell a lot of tickets. To maximise revenue, the tour employed a unique in-the-round stage configuration, which boosted stadium capacity by roughly 20%, and sold tickets for as little as $30, far less than most large outdoor concerts. The band's plan worked – despite a broader music industry slump and global recession, U2 shattered attendance records in most of the venues it played. By the end of the tour, the band played to over 3 million fans, racking up almost $300 million in ticket and merchandise sales and turning a profit.

As you read this chapter, you will begin to understand how and why U2 made the decision to lower prices. Many capital intensive companies, such as British Airways and Emirates Airlines in the airlines industry and Telecom Italia, Bharti Airtel and Telenor in the telecommunications industry, have high fixed costs. They must generate sufficient revenues to cover these costs and turn a profit.

Source: Gundersen, E. (2009) 'U2 turns 360 stadium into attendance-shattering sellouts', *USA Today*, 4 October, www.usatoday.com/life/music/news/2009-10-04-u2-stadium-tour_N.htm.

Cost planning and CVP

Alternative fixed-cost/variable-cost structures

Sensitivity analysis highlights the risks that an existing cost structure poses for an organisation. This may lead managers to consider alternative cost structures. CVP helps managers in this task. Consider again Mary Frost and her booth rental agreement with Computer Conventions Ltd. Our original example has Mary paying a €2000 booth rental fee. Suppose, however, Computer Conventions offers her three rental alternatives:

- Option 1: €2000 fixed fee.
- Option 2: €1400 fixed fee plus 5% of the convention revenues from Do-All sales.
- Option 3: 20% of the convention revenues from Do-All sales with no fixed fee.

Mary is interested in how her choice of a rental agreement will affect the risks she faces. Exhibit 8.4 presents these options in the CVP format:

- Option 1 exposes her to fixed costs of €2000 and a breakeven point of 25 units. This option brings €80 additional operating profit for each unit sold above 25 units.
- Option 2 exposes her to lower fixed costs of €1400 and a lower breakeven point of 20 units. There is, however, only €70 in additional operating profit for each unit sold above 20 units.
- Option 3 has no fixed costs. Mary makes €40 in additional operating profit for each unit sold. This €40 addition to operating profit starts from the first unit sold. This option enables Mary to break even if no units are sold.

The breakeven points are calculated as follows:

- The breakeven point of 25 units for option 1 was calculated earlier in this chapter.
- The breakeven point (Q) for option 2 is calculated as follows:

$$\text{Fixed costs} = €1400$$
$$\text{Unit variable costs} = €120 + 0.05(€200) = €130$$
$$\text{Unit contribution margin} = €200 - €130 = €70 \text{ per unit}$$
$$€200Q - €130Q - €1400 = 0$$
$$Q = €1400 \div €70$$
$$= 20 \text{ units}$$

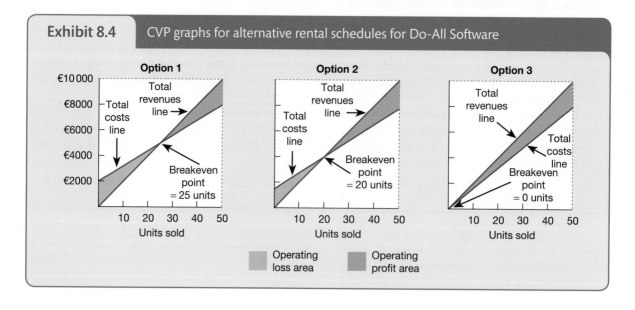

Exhibit 8.4   CVP graphs for alternative rental schedules for Do-All Software

- Option 3 has a breakeven point of zero units because there are no fixed costs. The variable costs per unit are €160 (€120 + 0.20[€200]). The contribution margin per unit is €40 (€200 − €160).

CVP analysis highlights the different risks and different returns associated with each option. For example, while option 1 has the most risk (a €2000 fixed up-front payment), it also has the highest contribution margin per unit. This €80 contribution margin per unit translates to high potential if Mary is able to generate sales above 25 units. By moving from option 1 to option 2, Mary faces less risk (lowers her fixed costs) if demand is low, but she must accept less potential (because of the higher variable costs) if demand is high. The choice among options 1, 2 and 3 will be influenced by her confidence in the level of demand for Do-All software and her willingness to risk money.

The risk–return trade-off across alternative cost structures is usefully summarised in a measure called *operating leverage*. **Operating leverage** describes the effects that fixed costs have on changes in operating profit as changes occur in units sold and hence in contribution margin. Organisations with a high proportion of fixed costs in their cost structures, as is the case under option 1 in our example, have high operating leverage. As a result, small changes in sales lead to large changes in operating profits. Consequently, if sales increase, operating profits increase even more, yielding higher returns. If sales decrease, however, operating profits decline yet more, leading to a greater risk of losses. *At any given level of sales*, the *degree of operating leverage* equals contribution margin divided by operating profit.

The following table shows the degree of operating leverage at sales of 40 units for the three alternative rental options.

	Option 1	Option 2	Option 3
1 Contribution margin per unit (p. 226)	€80	€50	€30
2 Contribution margin (row 1 × 40 units)	€3200	€2000	€1200
3 Operating profit (from Exhibit 8.4)	€1200	€1200	€1200
4 Degree of operating leverage (line 2 ÷ line 3)	$\frac{€3200}{€1200} = 2.67$	$\frac{€2000}{€1200} = 1.67$	$\frac{€1200}{€1200} = 1.00$

These numbers indicate that, when sales are 40 units, a percentage change in sales and contribution margin will result in 2.67 times that percentage change in operating profit for option 1, but the same percentage change in operating profit for option 3. Consider, for example, a sales increase of 50% from 40 units to 60 units. Contribution margin will increase by 50% under each option. Operating profit, however, will increase by 2.67 × 50% = 133% from €1200 to €2800 in option 1 but only by 1.00 × 50% = 50% from €1200 to €1800 in option 3 (see Exhibit 8.5). The degree of operating leverage at a given level of sales helps managers calculate the effect of fluctuations in sales on operating profits.

Exhibit 8.5	Mary Frost's budgets for Do-All and Superword software products

	Do-All	Superword	Total
Units sold	60	30	90
Revenues, €200 and €130 per unit	€12 000	€3 900	€15 900
Variable costs, €120 and €90 per unit	7 200	2 700	9 900
Contribution margin, €80 and €40 per unit	€4 800	€1 200	6 000
Fixed costs			2 000
Operating profit			€4 000

Effect of time horizon

A critical assumption of CVP analysis is that costs can be classified as either variable or fixed. This classification can be affected by the time period being considered. The shorter the time horizon we consider, the higher the percentage of total costs we may view as fixed. Consider Lufthansa. Suppose a Lufthansa plane will depart from its gate in 30 minutes and there are 20 empty seats. A potential passenger arrives bearing a transferable ticket from a competing airline. What are the variable costs to Lufthansa of placing one more passenger in an otherwise empty seat? Variable costs (such as one more meal) would be negligible. Virtually all the costs in that decision situation are fixed. In contrast, suppose Lufthansa must decide whether to include another city in its routes. This decision may have a one-year planning horizon. Many more costs would be regarded as variable and fewer as fixed in this decision.

This example underscores the importance of how the time horizon of a decision affects the analysis of cost behaviour. In brief, whether costs really are fixed depends heavily on the relevant range, the length of the time horizon in question, and the specific decision situation.

Effects of revenue mix on profit

Revenue mix (also called **sales mix**) is the relative combination of quantities of products or services that constitutes total revenues. If the mix changes, overall revenue targets may still be achieved. However, the effects on operating profit depend on how the original proportions of lower or higher contribution margin products have shifted.

Suppose Mary Frost in our computer convention example is now budgeting for the next convention. She plans to sell two software products – Do-All and Superword. Her budgets are set out in Exhibit 8.5.

What is the breakeven point? Unlike the single product (or service) situation, there is not a unique number of units for a multiple-product situation. This number instead depends on the revenue mix. The following approach can be used when it is assumed that the budgeted revenue mix (two units of Do-All sold for each unit of Superword sold) will not change at different levels of total revenue.

Let S be the number of units of Superword that need to be sold in order to break even. Then 2S is the number of units of Do-All that need to be sold in order to break even.

$$\text{Revenues} - \text{Variable costs} - \text{Fixed costs} = \text{Operating profit}$$
$$[\text{€}200(2S) + \text{€}130S] - [\text{€}120(2S) + \text{€}90S] - \text{€}2000 = 0$$
$$\text{€}530S - \text{€}330S = \text{€}2000$$
$$\text{€}200S = \text{€}2000$$
$$S = 10$$
$$2S = 20$$

The breakeven point is 30 units when the revenue mix is 20 units of Do-All and 10 units of Superword. The total contribution margin of €2000 (Do-All €80 × 20 = €1600 plus Superword €40 × 10 = €400) equals the fixed costs of €2000 at this mix.

Alternative revenue mixes (in units) that have a contribution margin of €2000 and thus result in breakeven operations include the following:

Do-All	25	20	15	10	5	0
Superword	0	10	20	30	40	50
Total	25	30	35	40	45	50

Other things being equal, for any given total quantity of units sold, if the mix shifts towards units with higher contribution margins, operating profit will be higher. Thus, if the mix shifts towards

Do-All (say, to 70% Do-All from 60% Do-All) with a contribution margin of twice that of Superword, Mary's operating profit will increase.

Despite their desire to maximise revenues from all products, managers must frequently cope with limited (constrained) resources. For instance, additional production capacity may be unavailable. Which products should be produced? As Chapter 9 explains in more detail, the best decision is not necessarily to make the product having the highest contribution margin per unit. Rather, the best decision recognises the contribution margin per unit of the constraining factor.

Not-for-profit organisations and CVP

CVP can be readily applied to decisions by both not-for-profit and for-profit organisations. Suppose a social welfare department has a government budget appropriation (revenue) for 2015 of €900 000. This not-for-profit agency's major purpose is to assist people with disabilities who are seeking employment. On average, the agency supplements each person's income by €5000 annually. The agency's fixed costs are €270 000. There are no other costs. The agency manager wants to know how many people could be assisted in 2015. We can use CVP analysis here by assuming zero operating profit. Let Q be the number of people to be assisted:

$$\text{Revenue} - \text{Variable costs} - \text{Fixed costs} = €0$$
$$€900\ 000 - €5000Q - €270\ 000 = €0$$
$$€5000Q = €900\ 000 - €270\ 000$$
$$Q = €630\ 000 \div €5000$$
$$= 126 \text{ people}$$

Suppose the manager is concerned that the total budget appropriation for 2015 will be reduced by 15% to a new amount of $(1 - 0.15) \times €900\ 000 = €765\ 000$. The manager wants to know how many people with disabilities will be assisted. Assume the same amount of monetary assistance per person:

$$€765\ 000 - €5000Q - €270\ 000 = €0$$
$$€5000Q = €765\ 000 - €270\ 000$$
$$Q = €495\ 000 \div €5000$$
$$= 99 \text{ people}$$

Note the following two characteristics of the CVP relationships in this not-for-profit situation:

1 The percentage drop in service $(126 - 99) \div 126$, or 21.4%, is more than the 15% reduction in the budget appropriation. Why? Because the existence of €270 000 in fixed costs means that the percentage drop in service exceeds the percentage drop in budget appropriation.

2 If the relationships were graphed, the budget appropriation (revenue) amount would be a straight horizontal line of €765 000. The manager could adjust operations to stay within the reduced appropriation in one or more of three major ways: (a) reduce the number of people assisted; (b) reduce the variable costs (the assistance per person); or (c) reduce the total fixed costs.

Contribution margin and gross margin

Contribution margin is a key concept in this chapter. We now consider how it is related to the gross margin concept discussed in Chapter 2. First some definitions:

Contribution margin = Revenues − All variable costs
Gross margin = Revenues − Cost of goods sold

Cost of goods sold in the merchandising sector is made up of goods purchased for resale. Cost of goods sold in the manufacturing sector consists entirely of manufacturing costs (including fixed manufacturing costs).

Service-sector companies can calculate a contribution margin figure but not a gross margin figure. Service-sector companies do not have a cost of goods sold item in their income statement.

Merchandising sector

The two areas of difference between contribution margin and gross margin for companies in the merchandising sector are fixed cost of goods sold (such as a fixed annual payment to a supplier to guarantee an exclusive option to purchase merchandise) and variable non-cost of goods sold items (such as a salesperson's commission that is a percentage of sales euros). Contribution margin is calculated after all variable costs have been deducted, whereas gross margin is calculated by deducting only cost of goods sold from revenues. The following example for Lia Ltd illustrates this difference. Lia Ltd is a London-based seller of jewellery, lingerie, lounge wear, beachwear and accessories. Figures given are assumed to be in pounds sterling (£).

Contribution margin format

Revenues (£)		200
Variable cost of goods sold	120	
Other variable costs	43	163
Contribution margin		37
Other fixed costs		19
Operating profit (£)		18

Gross margin format

Revenues (£)	200
Cost of goods sold (120)	120
Gross margin	80
Operating costs (43 + 19)	62
Operating profit (£)	18

Manufacturing sector

The two areas of difference between contribution margin and gross margin for companies in the manufacturing sector are fixed manufacturing costs and variable non-manufacturing costs. The following example (figures assumed to be in €million) illustrates this difference:

Revenues (£)		1000	Revenues (£)		1000
Variable manufacturing costs	250		Cost of goods sold (250 + 160)		410
Variable non-manufacturing costs	270	520	Gross margin		590
Contribution margin		480	Non-manufacturing costs (270 + 138)		408
Fixed manufacturing costs	160		Operating profit (£ million)		182
Fixed non-manufacturing costs	138	298			
Operating profit (£)		182			

Fixed manufacturing costs are not deducted from revenues when computing contribution margin but are deducted when computing gross margin. Cost of goods sold in a manufacturing company includes entirely manufacturing costs. Variable non-manufacturing costs are deducted from revenues when computing contribution margins but are not deducted when computing gross margins.

Both the *contribution margin* and the *gross margin* can be expressed as totals, as an amount per unit, or as percentages. The **contribution margin percentage** is the total contribution margin divided by revenues. The **variable-cost percentage** is the total variable costs (with respect to units of output) divided by revenues. The contribution margin percentage in our manufacturing-sector example is 48% (480 ÷ 1000), while the variable-cost percentage is 52% (520 ÷ 1000). The **gross margin percentage** is the gross margin divided by revenues − 59% (590 ÷ 1000) in our manufacturing-sector example.

Summary

The following points are linked to the chapter's learning objectives.

1 General profit planning in its full complexity assumes that there are many revenue drivers and many cost drivers. CVP is a special case that, in a restricted number of settings, can assist managers in understanding the behaviour of total costs, total revenues and operating profit as changes occur in the output level, selling price, variable costs or fixed costs.

2 Operating profit is calculated by subtracting operating costs from operating revenues. Net profit is operating profit plus non-operating revenues minus non-operating costs minus income taxes.

3 Using CVP requires simplifying assumptions, including that costs are either fixed or variable with respect to the number of output units (units produced and sold) and that total sales and total cost relationships are linear.

4 Managers often select the method they find easiest for computing the breakeven point: the equation method, the contribution margin method or the graph method. Income taxes can be incorporated into CVP analysis in a straightforward way by adjusting operating profit by the income tax rate. The breakeven point is unaffected by the presence of income taxes because no income taxes are paid if there is no operating profit.

5 Sensitivity analysis, a 'what-if' technique, can systematically examine the effect on operating profit and net profit of different levels of fixed costs, variable costs per unit, selling prices and output.

6 CVP can highlight to managers the risk and potential reward of alternatives that differ in their fixed costs and variable costs.

7 When CVP is applied to a multiple-product firm, it is assumed that there is a constant sales mix of products as the total quantity of units sold changes.

Appendix

Decision models and uncertainty

Managers make predictions and decisions in a world of uncertainty. This appendix explores the characteristics of uncertainty and describes how managers can cope with it. We also illustrate the additional insights gained when uncertainty is recognised in CVP analysis.

Coping with uncertainty

Role of a decision model

Uncertainty is the possibility that an actual amount will deviate from an expected amount. For example, marketing costs might be forecast at €400 000 but actually turn out to be €430 000. A decision model helps managers deal with uncertainty; it is a formal method for making a choice that often involves quantitative analysis. It usually includes the following elements:

1 A choice criterion, which is an objective that can be quantified. This objective can take many forms. Most often the choice criterion is expressed as a maximisation of income or a minimisation of cost. The choice criterion provides a basis for choosing the best alternative action.

2 A set of the alternative actions being considered.

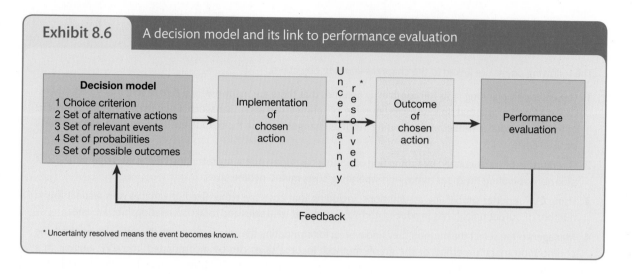

| Exhibit 8.6 | A decision model and its link to performance evaluation |

3   A set of all the relevant events that may occur, where an **event** is a possible occurrence. This set of events should be mutually exclusive and collectively exhaustive. Events are mutually exclusive if they cannot occur at the same time. Events are collectively exhaustive if, taken together, they make up the entire set of possible occurrences (and no other event can occur). Examples are growth or no growth in industry demand, and increase, decrease or no change in interest rates. Only one event in a set of mutually exclusive and collectively exhaustive events will actually occur.

4   A set of probabilities, where a **probability** is the likelihood or chance of occurrence of an event.

5   A set of possible **outcomes** that measures, in terms of the choice criterion, the predicted consequences of the various possible combinations of actions and events.

It is important to distinguish actions from events. Actions are choices made by management – for example, the prices it should charge for the company's products. Events are occurrences that management cannot control – for example, a growing or declining economy. The outcome is the operating profit the company makes, which depends on both the action management selects (pricing strategy) and the event that occurs (how the economy performs). Exhibit 8.6 presents an overview of a decision model, the implementation of the chosen action, its outcome and subsequent performance evaluation.

Probabilities

Assigning probabilities is a key aspect of the decision model approach to coping with uncertainty. A **probability distribution** describes the likelihood (or probability) of each of the mutually exclusive and collectively exhaustive set of events. The probabilities of these events will add to 1.00 because they are collectively exhaustive. In some cases there will be much evidence to guide the assignment of probabilities. For example, the probability of obtaining a head in the toss of a fair coin is $\frac{1}{2}$; that of drawing a particular playing card from a standard, well-shuffled pack is $\frac{1}{52}$. In business, the probability of having a specified percentage of defective units may be assigned with great confidence, on the basis of production experience with thousands of units. In other cases, there will be little evidence supporting estimated probabilities. For example, how many units of a new pharmaceutical product will be sold next year?

Expected value

An **expected value** is a weighted average of the outcomes with the probability of each outcome serving as the weight. Where the outcomes are measured in monetary terms, expected value is often called **expected monetary value**.

Managers often prefer being presented with the entire probability distribution. Information can also be presented in three categories: best-case scenario, most likely and worst-case scenario. All three categories remind the user that uncertainty exists in the decision at hand.

Illustrative problem

Reconsider Mary Frost and the booth rental alternatives offered by Computer Conventions to sell Do-All software:

- Option 1: €2000 fixed fee.
- Option 2: €1400 fixed fee plus 5% of the convention revenues from Do-All sales.
- Option 3: 20% of the convention revenues from Do-All sales (but no fixed fee).

Mary estimates a 0.60 probability that sales will be 40 units and a 0.40 probability that sales will be 70 units. Each Do-All software package will be sold for €200. Mary will purchase the package from a computer software wholesaler at €120 per unit with the privilege of returning all unsold units. Which booth rental alternative should Mary choose?

General approach to uncertainty

The construction of a decision model consists of five steps that are keyed to the five characteristics described at the beginning of this appendix.

Step 1 Identify the choice criterion of the decision maker. Assume that Mary's choice criterion is to maximise expected net cash inflow at the convention.

Step 2 Identify the set of alternative actions under consideration. The notation for an action is a. Mary has three possible actions:

$$a_1 = \text{Pay €2000 fixed fee}$$
$$a_2 = \text{Pay €1400 fixed fee plus 5% of convention revenues}$$
$$a_3 = \text{Pay 20% of convention revenues (but no fixed fee).}$$

Step 3 Identify the set of relevant events that can occur. Mary's only uncertainty is the number of units of Do-All software that she can sell. Using x as the notation for an event,

$$x_1 = 40 \text{ units}$$
$$x_2 = 70 \text{ units}$$

Step 4 Assign the set of probabilities for the events that can occur. Mary assesses a 60% chance that she will sell 40 units and a 40% chance that she will sell 70 units. Using $P(x)$ as the notation for the probability of an event, the probabilities are:

$$P(x_1) = 0.60$$
$$P(x_2) = 0.40$$

Step 5 Identify the set of possible outcomes that are dependent on specific actions and events. The outcomes in this example take the form of six possible net cash flows that are displayed in a decision table in Exhibit 8.7. A **decision table** is a summary of the contemplated actions, events, outcomes and probabilities of events.

Mary can now use the information in Exhibit 8.7 to calculate the expected net cash inflow of each action as follows:

Pay €2000 fixed fee:	$E(a_1) = 0.60 \ (€1200) + 0.40 \ (€3600) = €2160$
Pay €1400 fixed fee plus 5% of revenues:	$E(a_2) = 0.60 \ (€1400) + 0.40 \ (€3500) = €2240$
Pay 20% of revenues (but no fixed fee):	$E(a_3) = 0.60 \ (€1600) + 0.40 \ (€2800) = €2080$

Exhibit 8.7	Decision table for Do-All software	
	Probability of events	
Actions	$x_1 = 40$ **units sold** $P(x_1) = 0.60$	$x_2 = 70$ **units sold** $P(x_2) = 0.40$
a_1: Pay €2000 fixed fee	€1200*	€3600[†]
a_2: Pay €1400 fixed fee plus 5% of convention revenues	€1400[‡]	€3500[§]
a_3: Pay 20% of convention revenues (but no fixed fee)	€1600[#]	€2800**

* Net cash flows = (€200 − €120)(40) − €2000 = €1200.
[†] Net cash flows = (€200 − €120)(70) − €2000 = €3600.
[‡] Net cash flows = (€200 − €120 − €10[‖])(40) − €1400 = €1400.
[§] Net cash flows = (€200 − €120 − €10[‖])(70) − €1400 = €3500.
[‖] €10 = 5% of selling price of €200.
[#] Net cash flows = (€200 − €120 − €40[††])(40) = €1600.
** Net cash flows = (€200 − €120 − €40[††])(70) = €2800.
[††] €40 = 20% of selling price of €200.

To maximise expected net cash inflows, Mary should select action a_2, that is, contracting to pay Computer Conventions a €1400 fixed fee plus 5% of convention revenues.

Consider the effect of uncertainty on the preferred action choice. If Mary was certain that she would sell only 40 units of Do-All software (that is, $P(x_1) = 1$), she would prefer alternative a_3 – pay 20% of revenues and no fixed fee. To follow this reasoning, examine Exhibit 8.7. When 40 units are sold, alternative a_3 yields the maximum net cash inflows of €1600. Because fixed costs are zero, booth rental costs are low when sales are low.

However, if Mary was certain that she would sell 70 units of Do-All software (that is, $P(x_2) = 1$), she would prefer alternative a_1 – pay a €2000 fixed fee. Exhibit 8.7 indicates that when 70 units are sold, alternative a_1 yields the maximum net cash inflows of €3600. Rental payments under a_2 and a_3 increase with units sold but are fixed under a_1.

Good decisions and good outcomes

Always distinguish between a good decision and a good outcome. One can exist without the other. By definition, uncertainty rules out guaranteeing, after the fact, that the best outcome will always be obtained. It is possible that bad luck will produce unfavourable consequences even when good decisions have been made.

Suppose you are offered a one-time-only gamble tossing a fair coin. You will win €20 if the event is heads, but you will lose €1 if the event is tails. As a decision maker, you proceed through the logical phases: gathering information, assessing outcomes and making a choice. You accept the bet. Why? Because the expected value is €9.50 [0.5(€20) + 0.5(−€1)]. The coin is tossed and the event is tails. You lose. From your viewpoint, this was a good decision but a bad outcome.

A decision can be made only on the basis of information available at the time of the decision. Hindsight is flawless, but a bad outcome does not necessarily mean that a bad decision was made. Making a good decision is our best protection against a bad outcome.

Key terms

cost–volume–profit (CVP) analysis (216)
revenues (217)
revenue driver (217)
operating profit (217)
net profit (217)
breakeven point (218)
contribution income statement (220)
PV graph (222)
sensitivity analysis (224)
margin of safety (225)
uncertainty (225)
operating leverage (227)
revenue mix (228)
sales mix (228)

contribution margin (229)
gross margin (229)
contribution margin percentage (230)
variable-cost percentage (230)
gross margin percentage (230)
decision model (231)
choice criterion (231)
event (232)
probability (232)
outcomes (232)
probability distribution (232)
expected value (232)
expected monetary value (232)
decision table (233)

CHAPTER 8

Assessment material

Review questions

Note: To underscore the basic CVP relationships, the assessment material ignores income taxes unless stated otherwise.

8.1 Describe how the special case labelled CVP is different from the general case for predicting total revenues, total costs and operating profit.

8.2 Distinguish between operating profit and net profit.

8.3 Describe the assumptions underlying CVP analysis.

8.4 'CVP is both simple and simplistic. If you want realistic analysis to underpin your decisions, look beyond CVP.' Do you agree? Explain.

8.5 Define contribution margin, gross margin, contribution margin percentage, variable-cost percentage and margin of safety.

8.6 Give an example of how a manager can decrease variable costs while increasing fixed costs.

8.7 Give an example of how a manager can increase variable costs while decreasing fixed costs.

8.8 'There is no such thing as a fixed cost. All costs can be "unfixed" given sufficient time.' Do you agree? What is the implication of your answer for CVP analysis?

8.9 How can a company with multiple products calculate its breakeven point?

8.10 How does an increase in the income tax rate affect the breakeven point?

Exercises

Basic level

*8.11 **CVP computations** (20 minutes)

Fill in the blanks for each of the following independent cases.

Case	Selling price	Variable costs per unit	Total units sold	Total contribution margin	Total fixed costs	Operating profit/loss
a	£30	£20	70 000	£?	£?	−£15 000
b	25	?	180 000	900 000	800 000	?
c	?	10	150 000	300 000	220 000	?
d	20	14	?	120 000	?	12 000

8.12   CVP, changing revenues and costs (15–20 minutes)

Soleil Voyages SA is a travel agency specialising in flights between Paris and London. It books passengers on Air Chanson. Air Chanson charges passengers €1000 per round-trip ticket. Soleil Voyages receives a commission of 8% of the ticket price paid by the passenger. Soleil Voyages's fixed costs are €22 000 per month. Its variable costs are €35 per ticket, including an €18 delivery fee by Lièvre-Express SA. (Assume each ticket purchased is delivered in a separate package; thus the delivery fee applies to every individual ticket.)

Required

1   What is the number of tickets Soleil Voyages must sell each month to (a) break even, and (b) make a target operating profit of €10 000?

2   Assume Tortue-Express SA offers to charge Soleil Voyages only €12 per ticket delivered. How would accepting this offer affect your answers to (a) and (b) in requirement 1?

8.13   CVP, changing revenues and costs (continuation of Exercise 8.12) (20 minutes)

Air Chanson changes its commission structure to travel agents. Up to a ticket price of €600, the 8% commission applies. For tickets costing €600 or more, there is a fixed commission of €48. Assume Soleil Voyages has fixed costs of €22 000 per month and variable costs of €29 per ticket (including a €12 delivery fee by Lièvre-Express).

Required

1   What is the number of Paris-to-London round-trip tickets Soleil Voyages must sell each month to (a) break even, and (b) make a target operating profit of €10 000? Comment on the results.

2   Soleil Voyages decides to charge its customers a delivery fee of €5 per ticket. How would this change affect your answers to (a) and (b) in requirement 1? Comment on the results.

8.14   CVP exercises (20 minutes)

Grünberg Lehrmittelverlag GmbH manufactures and sells pens. Present sales output is 5 million annually at a selling price of €0.50 per unit. Fixed costs are €900 000 per year. Variable costs are €0.30 per unit.

Required

(Consider each case separately.)

1   a   What is the present operating profit for a year?

    b   What is the present breakeven point in revenues?

Calculate the new operating profit for each of the following changes:

2   A €0.04 per unit increase in variable costs.

3   A 10% increase in fixed costs and a 10% increase in units sold.

4   A 20% decrease in fixed costs, a 20% decrease in selling price, a 10% decrease in variable costs per unit, and a 40% increase in units sold.

Calculate the new breakeven point in units for each of the following changes:

5   A 10% increase in fixed costs.

6   A 10% increase in selling price and a €20 000 increase in fixed costs.

8.15   CVP, changing cost inputs (5–10 minutes)

Maria Kabaliki is planning to sell a vegetable slicer-dicer for €15 per unit at a country fair. She purchases units from a local distributor for €6 each. She can return any unsold units for a full refund. Fixed costs for booth rental, set-up and cleaning are €450.

Required

1 Calculate the breakeven point in units sold.

2 Suppose the unit purchase cost is €5 instead of €6, but the selling price is unchanged. Calculate the new breakeven point in units sold.

8.16   **CVP, international cost structure differences** (10 minutes)

Knitwear Ltd is considering three countries for the sole manufacturing site of its new sweater: Cyprus, Turkey and Ireland. All sweaters are to be sold to retail outlets in Ireland at €32 per unit. These retail outlets add their own mark-up when selling to final customers. The three countries differ in their fixed costs and variable costs per sweater.

	Annual fixed costs	Variable manufacturing costs per sweater	Variable marketing and distribution costs per sweater
Cyprus	€6.5 million	€8.00	€11.00
Turkey	4.5 million	5.50	11.50
Ireland	12.0 million	13.00	9.00

Required

1 Calculate the breakeven point of Knitwear Ltd in both (a) units sold, and (b) revenues for each of the three countries considered for manufacturing the sweaters.

2 If Knitwear Ltd sells 800 000 sweaters in 2015, what is the budgeted operating profit for each of the three countries considered for manufacturing the sweaters? Comment on the results.

8.17   **CVP, income taxes** (10–15 minutes)

Koninklijke BolsWessanen NV has fixed costs of €300 000 and a variable-cost percentage of 80%. The company earns net profit of €84 000 in 2015. The income tax rate is 40%.

Required

Calculate (1) operating profit, (2) contribution margin, (3) total revenues and (4) breakeven revenues.

8.18   **CVP, movie production** (10 minutes)

Espasso SA has just finished production of *Tornado*, the latest action film directed by Domingos Vieira and starring Arnaldo Moura and Victoria Rebello. The total production cost to Espasso was €5 million. All the production personnel and actors on *Tornado* received a fixed salary (included in the €5 million) and will have no 'residual' (equity interest) in the revenues or operating income from the movie. Artes e Media Ltda will handle the marketing of *Tornado*. Media agrees to invest a minimum €3 million of its own money in marketing the movie and will be paid 20% of the revenues Espasso itself receives from the box-office receipts. Espasso receives 62.5% of the total box-office receipts (out of which comes the 20% payment to Artes e Media).

Required

1 What is the breakeven point to Espasso for *Tornado* expressed in terms of (a) revenues received by Espasso, and (b) total box-office receipts?

2 Assume in its first year of release, the box-office receipts for *Tornado* total €300 million. What is the operating income to Espasso from the movie in its first year?

8.19   CVP, cost structure differences, movie production (continuation of Exercise 8.18)
(20 minutes)

Espasso is negotiating for *Tornado 2*, a sequel to its mega-blockbuster *Tornado*. This negotiation is proving more difficult than for the original movie. The budgeted production cost (excluding payments to the director Vieira and the stars Moura and Rebello) for *Tornado 2* is €21 million. The agent negotiating for Vieira, Moura and Rebello proposes either of two contracts:

- *Contract A*: Fixed-salary component of €15 million for Vieira, Moura and Rebello (combined) with no residual interest in the revenues from *Tornado 2*.
- *Contract B*: Fixed-salary component of €3 million for Vieira, Moura and Rebello (combined) plus a residual of 15% of the revenues Espasso receives from *Tornado 2*.

Artes e Media will market *Tornado 2*. It agrees to invest a minimum of €10 million of its own money. Because of its major role in the success of *Tornado*, Artes e Media will now be paid 25% of the revenues Espasso receives from the total box-office receipts. Espasso receives 62.5% of the total box-office receipts (out of which comes the 25% payment to Artes e Media).

Required

1 What is the breakeven point for Espasso expressed in terms of:
   a revenues received by that company
   b total box-office receipts for *Tornado 2*

   for contracts A and B? Explain the difference between the breakeven points for contracts A and B.
2 Assume *Tornado 2* achieves the same €300 million in box-office revenues as *Tornado*. What is the operating income to Espasso from *Tornado 2* if it accepts contract B? Comment on the difference in operating income between the two films.

8.20   Not-for-profit institution (15–25 minutes)

The Ville de Genève, Switzerland, makes a SFr 400 000 lump-sum budget appropriation to an agency to conduct a counselling programme for drug addicts for a year. All of the appropriation is to be spent. The variable costs for drug prescriptions average SFr 400 per patient per year. Fixed costs are SFr 150 000.

Required

1 Calculate the number of patients that could be served in a year.
2 Suppose the total budget for the following year is reduced by 10%. Fixed costs are to remain the same. The same level of service to each patient will be maintained. Calculate the number of patients that could be served in a year.
3 As in requirement 2, assume a budget reduction of 10%. Fixed costs are to remain the same. The drug counsellor has discretion over how much in drug prescriptions to give to each patient. She does not want to reduce the number of patients served. On average, what is the cost of drugs that can be given to each patient? Calculate the percentage decline in the annual average cost of drugs per patient.

8.21   Appendix: CVP under uncertainty (15 minutes)

Bomuldstaft AS is considering two new colours for their umbrella products – emerald green and shocking pink. Either can be produced using present facilities. Each product requires an increase in annual fixed costs of €400 000. The products have the same selling price (€10) and the same variable costs per unit (€8).

Management, after studying past experience with similar products, has prepared the following probability distribution:

Event (units demanded)	Probability for	
	Emerald green umbrella	Shocking pink umbrella
50 000	0.0	0.1
100 000	0.1	0.1
200 000	0.2	0.1
300 000	0.4	0.2
400 000	0.2	0.4
500 000	0.1	0.1
	1.0	1.0

Required

1 What is the breakeven point for each product?

2 Which product should be chosen, assuming the objective is to maximise expected operating profit? Why? Show your computations.

3 Suppose management is absolutely certain that 300 000 units of shocking pink will be sold, but it still faces the same uncertainty about the demand for emerald green as outlined in the problem. Which product should be chosen? Why? What benefits are available to management from having the complete probability distribution instead of just an expected value?

Intermediate level

*8.22   CVP, income taxes (20–25 minutes)

La Pilotta has two restaurants in Lausanne that are open 24 hours a day. Fixed costs for the two restaurants together total SFr 450 000 per year. Service varies from a cup of coffee to full meals. The average bill for each customer is SFr 8.00. The average cost of food and other variable costs for each customer is SFr 3.20. The income tax rate is 30%. Target net profit is SFr 105 000.

Required

1 Calculate the revenues needed to obtain the target net profit.

2 How much in sales terms is needed (a) to earn net income of SFr 105 000, and (b) to break even?

3 Calculate net income if the number of bills is 150 000.

8.23   Appendix: uncertainty, CVP (15–20 minutes)

Kristina Larsson is the Stockholm promoter for Gustav Häglund. Larsson is promoting a new world championship fight for Häglund. The key area of uncertainty is the size of the cable pay-per-view TV market. Larsson will pay Häglund a fixed fee of SEK 2 million and 25% of net cable pay-per-view revenue. Every cable TV home receiving the event pays SEK 29.95, of which Larsson receives SEK 16. Larsson pays Häglund 25% of the SEK 16.

Larsson estimates the following probability distribution for homes purchasing the pay-per-view event:

Demand	Probability
100 000	0.05
200 000	0.10
300 000	0.30
400 000	0.35
500 000	0.15
1 000 000	0.05

Required

1 What is the expected value of the payment Larsson will make to Häglund?

2 Assume the only uncertainty is cable TV demand for the fight. Larsson wants to know the breakeven point given her own fixed costs of SEK 1 million and her own variable costs of SEK 2 per home. (Also include Larsson's payments to Häglund in your answer.)

8.24   CVP, shoe stores (20–30 minutes)

Walk-About Ltd operates a chain of shoe stores. The stores sell ten different styles of inexpensive men's shoes with identical unit costs and selling prices. A unit is defined as a pair of shoes. Each store has a store manager who is paid a fixed salary. Individual salespeople receive a fixed salary and a sales commission. Walk-About is trying to determine the desirability of opening another store, which is expected to have the following revenue and cost relationships:

	Per pair
Unit variable data	
Selling price	£30.00
Cost of shoes	£19.50
Sales commissions	1.50
Total variable costs	£21.00
Annual fixed costs	
Rent	£60 000
Salaries	200 000
Advertising	80 000
Other fixed costs	20 000
Total fixed costs	£360 000

Required

(Consider each question independently.)

1 What is the annual breakeven point in (a) units sold, and (b) revenues?

2 If 35 000 units are sold, what will be the store's operating profit (loss)?

3 If sales commissions were discontinued for individual salespeople in favour of an £81 000 increase in fixed salaries, what would be the annual breakeven point in (a) units sold, and (b) revenues?

4 Refer to the original data. If the store manager were paid £0.30 per unit sold in addition to his current fixed salary, what would be the annual breakeven point in (a) units sold, and (b) revenues?

5 Refer to the original data. If the store manager were paid £0.30 per unit commission on each unit sold in excess of the breakeven point, what would be the store's operating profit if 50 000 units were sold? (This £0.30 is in addition to both the commission paid to the sales staff and the store manager's fixed salary.)

8.25   CVP, shoe stores (continuation of Exercise 8.24) (20–25 minutes)

Refer to requirement 3 of Exercise 8.24.

Required

1 Calculate the number of units sold where the operating profit under (a) a fixed-salary plan, and (b) a lower fixed-salary and commission plan (for salespeople only) would be equal. Above that number of units sold, one plan would be more profitable than the other; below that number of units sold, the reverse would occur.

2 Calculate the operating profit or loss under each plan in requirement 1 at sales levels of (a) 50 000 units, and (b) 60 000 units.

3 Suppose the target operating profit is £168 000. How many units must be sold to reach the target under (a) the fixed-salary plan, and (b) the lower fixed-salary and commission plan?

8.26   Sensitivity and inflation (continuation of Exercise 8.24) (10–20 minutes)

As chairman of Walk-About, you are concerned that inflation may squeeze your profitability. Specifically, you feel committed to the £30 selling price, and fear that lowering the quality of the shoes in the face of rising costs would be an unwise marketing move. You expect the cost of shoes to rise by 10% during the coming year. You are tempted to avoid the cost increase by placing a non-cancellable order with a large supplier that would provide 50 000 units of the specified quality for each store at £19.50 per unit. (To simplify this analysis, assume that all stores will face identical demands.) These shoes could be acquired and paid for as delivered throughout the year. However, all shoes must be delivered to the stores by the end of the year.

As a shrewd merchandiser, you foresee some risks. If sales were less than 50 000 units, you feel that markdowns of the unsold merchandise would be necessary to sell the goods. You predict that the average selling price of the leftover units would be £18.00. The regular commission of 5% of revenues would be paid to salespeople.

Required

1 Suppose that actual sales at £30 for the year are 48 000 units and that you contracted for 50 000 units. What is the operating profit for the store?

2 If you had perfect forecasting ability, you would have contracted for 48 000 units rather than 50 000 units. What would the operating profit have been if you had ordered 48 000 units?

3 Given actual sales of 48 000 units, by how much would the average cost per unit have had to rise before you would have been indifferent between having the contract for 50 000 units and not having the contract?

*8.27   Revenue mix, two products (20–25 minutes)

Presencia Equipajes SA retails two products, a standard and a deluxe version of a luggage carrier. The budgeted income statement is as follows:

	Standard carrier	Deluxe carrier	Total
Units sold	150 000	50 000	200 000
Revenues			
@ €20 and €30 per unit	€3 000 000	€1 500 000	€4 500 000
Variable costs			
@ €14 and €18 per unit	2 100 000	900 000	3 000 000
Contribution margins			
@ €6 and €12 per unit	€900 000	€600 000	1 500 000
Fixed costs			1 200 000
Operating profit			€300 000

Required

1 Calculate the breakeven point in units, assuming that the planned revenue mix is maintained.

2 Calculate the breakeven point in units (a) if only standard carriers are sold, and (b) if only deluxe carriers are sold.

3 Suppose 200 000 units are sold, but only 20 000 are deluxe. Calculate the operating profit. Calculate the breakeven point if these relationships persist in the next period. Compare your

answers with the original plans and the answer in requirement 1. What is the major lesson of this problem?

8.28   **Budget issues** (From CIMA Management Accounting Pillar Managerial Level Paper, May 2006) (25 minutes)

S plc produces and sells three products, X, Y and Z. It has contracts to supply products X and Y, which will utilise all of the specific materials that are available to make these two products during the next period. The revenue these contracts will generate and the contribution to sales (c/s) ratios of products X and Y are as follows:

	Product X	Product Y
Revenue	£10 million	£20 million
C/S ratio	15%	10%

Product Z has a c/s ratio of 25%.

The total fixed costs of S plc are £5.5 million during the next period and management have budgeted to earn a profit of £1 million.

Required

Calculate the revenue that needs to be generated by Product Z for S plc to achieve the budgeted profit.

CHAPTER 9

Determining how costs behave

This chapter focuses on how to determine cost behaviour, that is, on understanding how costs change with changes in activity levels, units of products produced, and so on. Knowing how costs vary by identifying the drivers of costs and by distinguishing fixed from variable costs is frequently the key to making considered management decisions. Many managerial functions such as planning and control rely on knowing how costs will behave. For example, consider the following questions: Should a component part be made or purchased? What price should we charge for altering a product's packaging? Should we make the item or buy it? What effect will a 20% increase in units sold have on operating profit? Decisions in the control area, such as the interpretation of some variances, similarly rely heavily on knowledge of cost behaviour. Determining and understanding how costs behave are among the most important functions of the management accountant.

Learning objectives

After studying this chapter, you should be able to:

- Explain the two assumptions frequently used in cost-behaviour estimation

- Describe linear cost functions and three common ways in which they behave

- Recognise various approaches to cost estimation

- Outline six steps in estimating a cost function on the basis of current or past cost relationships

- Describe three criteria to evaluate and choose cost drivers

- Explain and give examples of non-linear cost functions

- Distinguish between the cumulative average-time learning model and the incremental unit-time learning model

General issues in estimating cost functions

Basic assumptions and examples of cost functions

A cost function is a mathematical function describing cost behaviour patterns – how costs change with changes in the cost driver. Cost functions can be plotted on graph paper by measuring the cost driver on the x-axis and the corresponding amount of total costs on the y-axis.

Two assumptions are frequently made when estimating cost functions:

1 Variations in the total costs of a cost object are explained by variations in a single cost driver.

2 Cost behaviour is adequately approximated by a **linear cost function** of the cost driver within the relevant range. A linear cost function is a cost function where, within the relevant range, the graph of total costs versus a single cost driver forms a straight line.

We use these assumptions throughout much of this chapter. Later sections give examples of non-linear cost behaviour patterns in which the plot of the relationship between the cost driver and total costs is not a straight line. The last section in the appendix describes how changes in two or more cost drivers can explain changes in the level of total costs. We illustrate cost functions in the context of negotiations between Verre-Laine and Nord-Sud Communications (NSC) for exclusive use of a telephone line between Paris and Barcelona. NSC offers Verre-Laine three alternative cost structures.

- *Alternative 1*: €5 per minute of phone use. As we saw in Chapter 2, this is a *strictly variable cost* for Verre-Laine. The number of phone-minutes used is the cost driver; that is, the number of phone-minutes used is the factor whose change causes a change in total costs.

  Graph 1 in Exhibit 9.1 presents the *strictly variable or proportionately variable* cost. Total costs (measured along the vertical y-axis) change in proportion to the number of phone-minutes used (measured along the horizontal x-axis) within the relevant range. The *relevant range,* described in Chapter 2, is the range of the cost driver where the relationship between total costs and the driver is valid. There are no fixed costs. Every additional minute adds €5 to total costs. Graph 1 of Exhibit 9.1 illustrates the €5 **slope coefficient**, the amount by which total costs change for a unit change in the cost driver within the relevant range.

  We can write the cost function in Graph 1 of Exhibit 9.1 as:

  $$y = €5X$$

  where X measures the number of phone-minutes used and y measures the total costs of the phone-minutes determined from the cost function.

- *Alternative 2*: €10 000 per month. Under this alternative, Verre-Laine has a fixed cost of €10 000. Graph 2 in Exhibit 9.1 presents the *fixed cost*. The total costs will be €10 000 per month regardless of the number of phone-minutes used. (We use the same cost driver, the number of phone-minutes used, to compare cost-behaviour patterns under various alternatives.)

  Graph 2 in Exhibit 9.1 refers to the fixed cost of €10 000 as a **constant** or **intercept**, the component of total costs that, within the relevant range, does not vary with changes in the level of the cost driver. Under alternative 2, the constant or intercept accounts for all the costs, since there are no variable costs. The slope is zero.

  We can write the cost function in Graph 2 of Exhibit 9.1 as:

  $$y = €10\ 000$$

  showing that total costs will be €10 000, regardless of the number of phone-minutes used by Verre-Laine.

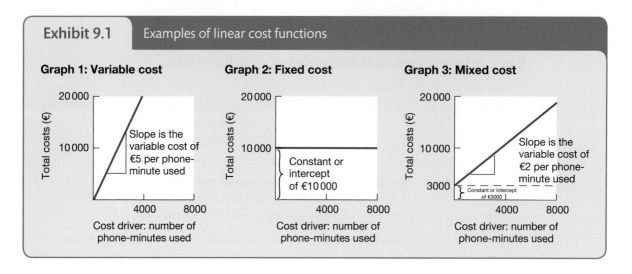

Exhibit 9.1 | Examples of linear cost functions

Graph 1: Variable cost

Slope is the variable cost of €5 per phone-minute used

Graph 2: Fixed cost

Constant or intercept of €10 000

Graph 3: Mixed cost

Slope is the variable cost of €2 per phone-minute used

Constant or intercept of €3000

- *Alternative 3*: €3000 per month plus €2 per minute of phone use. This is an example of a *mixed cost*. A **mixed cost** (or **semivariable cost**) is a cost that has both fixed and variable elements. Graph 3 in Exhibit 9.1 presents the mixed cost. It has one component that is fixed regardless of the number of phone-minutes used (€3000 per month) and another component that is variable with respect to the number of phone-minutes used (€2 per minute of phone use). In this example, the constant or intercept is €3000 and the slope coefficient is €2.

We can write the cost function in Graph 3 of Exhibit 9.1 as:

$$y = €3000 + €2X$$

In the case of mixed costs, the total costs in the relevant range increase as the number of phone-minutes used increases in the relevant range. *However, total costs do not change in proportion to the change in the number of phone-minutes used in the relevant range.* For example, when 4000 phone-minutes are used, the total costs are [€3000 + (€2 × 4000)] = €11 000, but when 8000 phone-minutes are used, the total costs are [€3000 + (€2 × 8000)] = €19 000. Although the number of phone-minutes used has doubled, the total costs have increased to only 1.73 (€19 000 ÷ €11 000) times the original costs.

Understanding cost-behaviour patterns is a crucial input in choosing among the alternatives. Suppose Verre-Laine expects to use at least 4000 phone-minutes per month. Its costs for 4000 phone-minutes under the three alternatives would be: alternative 1, €20 000 (€5 × 4000); alternative 2, €10 000; alternative 3, €11 000 [€3000 + (€2 × 4000)]. Alternative 2 is the least costly. Moreover, if Verre-Laine used more than 4000 phone-minutes, alternatives 1 and 3 would be even more costly than alternative 2. Verre-Laine would prefer alternative 2.

Basic terms

Note two features of the cost functions in the Verre-Laine/NSC example. For specificity, consider Graph 3 in Exhibit 9.1.

1 Variations in a *single* cost driver (number of phone-minutes used) explain variations in total costs.

2 The cost functions are linear; that is, the plot of total costs versus phone-minutes used is a straight line. Because Graph 3 is a straight line, the only information we need to draw is the

constant or intercept term (€3000) and the slope coefficient (€2 per phone-minute used). These two pieces of information describe total costs for the entire relevant range of the number of phone-minutes used. That is, within the relevant range, linear cost functions (in the single cost driver case) can be described by a single constant or intercept (called a) and a single slope coefficient (called b). We write the linear cost function as:

$$y = a + bX$$

Under alternative 1, $a = €0$ and $b = €5$ per phone-minute used; under alternative 2, $a = €10\,000$, $b = €0$ per phone-minute used; and under alternative 3, $a = €3000$, $b = €2$ per phone-minute used.

The Verre-Laine/NSC example illustrates variable, fixed and mixed cost functions using information about future cost structures proposed to Verre-Laine by NSC. Often, however, cost functions are estimated from past cost data. **Cost estimation** is the attempt to measure *past* cost relationships between total costs and the drivers of those costs. For example, managers could use cost estimation to understand what causes marketing costs to change from year to year (the number of cars sold or the number of new models introduced), and its fixed and variable cost components. Managers are interested in estimating past cost-behaviour patterns primarily because these estimates can help them make more accurate **cost predictions**, or forecasts, about future costs. Better cost predictions help managers make more informed planning and control decisions, such as the marketing costs budget for next year.

Chapter 2 outlined three other specifications necessary to classify costs into their variable and fixed cost components. We review them briefly here.

Choice of cost object

A particular cost item could be variable with respect to one cost object and fixed with respect to another. For example, annual van registration and licence costs would be a variable cost with respect to the number of vans owned and operated by Reise-Plus GmbH, an airport transportation company, but registration and licence costs for a particular van are a fixed cost with respect to the number of kilometres that the van covered during the year.

Time span

Whether a cost is variable or fixed with respect to a particular driver depends on the time span considered in the decision situation. The longer the time span, other things being equal, the more likely that the cost will be variable. For example, inspection salaries and costs at Aérospatiale are typically fixed in the short run with respect to hours of inspection activity. But in the long run, Aérospatiale's total inspection costs will vary with the inspection time required: more inspectors will be hired if more inspection is needed, while some inspectors will be reassigned to other tasks if less inspection is needed.

Relevant range

Accountants and managers use linear cost functions to approximate the relation of total costs to cost drivers within a relevant range. Exhibit 9.2 plots the relationship over several years between total direct manufacturing labour costs and the number of valves produced each year by an industrial machinery component producer, AMC Ltd, at its Leeds plant. Costs are non-linear outside the relevant range. In this case, non-linearities occur when the valve output is low because of inefficiencies in using manufacturing labour. Non-linearities occur at very high levels of production because of greater congestion in the plant and the need for more coordination.

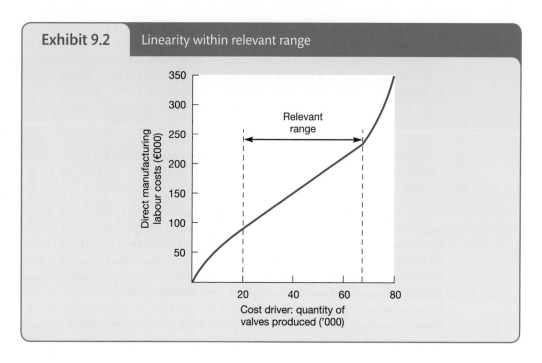

Exhibit 9.2   Linearity within relevant range

The cause-and-effect criterion in choosing cost drivers

The most important issue in estimating a cost function is to determine whether a cause-and-effect relationship exists between the cost driver and the resulting costs. The cause-and-effect relationship might arise in several ways.

1 It may be due to a physical relationship between costs and the cost driver. An example of a physical relationship is when units of production is used as the cost driver of materials costs. To produce more units requires more materials, which results in higher materials costs.

2 Cause and effect can arise from a contractual arrangement, as in the Verre-Laine example described earlier, where the number of phone-minutes used is the cost driver of the telephone line costs.

3 Cause and effect can be implicitly established by logic and knowledge of operations. An example is when the number of component parts is used as a cost driver of design costs. It seems intuitively clear that a complex product design with many component parts that must fit together precisely will incur higher design costs than a simple product with few parts.

Be careful not to interpret a high correlation, or connection, between two variables to mean that either variable causes the other. A high correlation between two variables, u and v, indicates merely that the two variables move together. It is possible that u may cause v; v may cause u; u and v may interact; both may be affected by a third variable z; or the correlation may be due to chance. No conclusions about cause and effect are warranted by high correlations. For example, higher production generally results in higher materials costs and higher labour costs. Materials costs and labour costs are highly correlated, but neither causes the other.

Consider another example. Observation in a Swedish town revealed that 'in years when more storks build their nests on house chimneys, more babies were born in the town and vice versa' (Rees 2000). There is, however, no plausible cause-and-effect explanation for this correlation.

Only a true cause-and-effect relationship, not merely correlation, establishes an economically plausible relationship between costs and their cost drivers. Economic plausibility gives the analyst confidence that the estimated relationship will appear again and again in other similar sets of data. Establishing economic plausibility is a vital aspect of cost estimation.

Cost estimation approaches

There are four approaches to cost estimation:

1 industrial engineering method
2 conference method
3 account analysis method
4 quantitative analysis of current or past cost relationships.

These approaches differ in the costs of conducting the analysis, the assumptions they make, and the evidence they provide about the accuracy of the estimated cost function. They are not mutually exclusive. Many organisations use a combination of these approaches.

Industrial engineering method

The **industrial engineering method**, also called the **work-measurement method**, estimates cost functions by analysing the relationship between inputs and outputs in physical terms. This method has its roots in studies and techniques developed by Frank and Lillian Gilbreth in the early twentieth century. Consider, for example, a carpet manufacturer that uses inputs of cotton, wool, dyes, direct labour, machine time and power. Production output is square metres of carpet. Time-and-motion studies analyse the time and materials required to perform the various operations to produce the carpet. For example, a time-and-motion study may conclude that to produce 20 square metres of carpet requires 2 kilograms of cotton and 3 litres of dye. Standards and budgets transform these physical input and output measures into costs. The result is an estimated cost function relating total manufacturing costs to the cost driver, square metres of carpet.

The industrial engineering method can be very time-consuming. Some government contracts mandate its use. Many organisations, however, find it too costly for analysing their entire cost structure. More frequently, organisations use this approach for direct-cost categories such as materials and labour but not for indirect-cost categories such as manufacturing overhead. Physical relationships between inputs and outputs may be difficult to specify for individual overhead cost items.

Conference method

The **conference method** estimates cost functions on the basis of analysis and opinions about costs and their drivers gathered from various departments of an organisation (purchasing, process engineering, manufacturing, employee relations, and so on). The Metro Bank in the UK has a cost-estimating department that develops cost functions for its retail banking products (current account, Mastercards, mortgages, and so on) on the basis of a consensus of estimates from the relevant departments. The bank uses this information to price products, to adjust its product mix to the products that are most profitable, and to monitor and measure cost improvements over time.

The conference method allows cost functions and cost estimates to be developed quickly. The pooling of expert knowledge from each value-chain area gives the conference method credibility. The accuracy of the cost estimates largely depends on the care and detail taken by the people providing the inputs.

Account analysis method

The **account analysis method** estimates cost functions by classifying cost accounts in the ledger as variable, fixed, or mixed with respect to the identified cost driver. Typically, managers use qualitative rather than quantitative analysis when making these cost-classification decisions. The account analysis approach is widely used.

Consider indirect manufacturing labour costs for a small production area (or cell) at Møre-Teppe AS which weaves carpets for homes and offices and uses state-of-the-art automated weaving machines. These costs include maintenance, quality control and set-up costs for the machines. During the most recent twelve-week period, Møre-Teppe worked the machines in the cell for a total of 862 hours and incurred total indirect manufacturing labour costs of €12 501. Management wants the cost analyst to use the account analysis method to estimate a linear cost function for indirect manufacturing labour costs with machine-hours as the cost driver.

The cost analyst decides to separate total indirect manufacturing labour costs (€12 501) into costs that are fixed (€2157) and costs that are variable (€10 344) with respect to the number of machine-hours worked. Variable costs per machine-hour are €10 344 ÷ 862 = €12. The general cost equation, $y = a + bX$, is indirect manufacturing labour costs = €2157 + (€12 × number of machine-hours). The indirect manufacturing labour cost per machine-hour is €12 501 ÷ 862 = €14.50.

Management at Møre-Teppe can use the cost function to estimate the indirect manufacturing labour costs of using 950 machine-hours to produce carpet in the next twelve-week period. Using the cost function, estimated costs = €2157 + (950 × 12) = €13 557. The indirect manufacturing labour costs per machine-hour decrease to €13 557 ÷ 950 = €14.27, as fixed costs are spread over a greater number of units.

Organisations differ with respect to the care taken in implementing account analysis. In some organisations, individuals thoroughly knowledgeable about the operations make the cost-classification decisions. For example, manufacturing personnel may classify costs such as machine lubricants and materials-handling labour, while marketing personnel may classify costs such as advertising brochures and sales salaries. In other organisations, only cursory analysis is conducted, sometimes by individuals with limited knowledge of operations, before cost-classification decisions are made. Clearly, the former approach would provide more reliable cost classifications, and hence estimates of the fixed and variable components of the cost, than the latter. Supplementing the account analysis method by the conference method improves its credibility.

One survey of 300 UK manufacturing companies reports that 59% of these companies used a subjective approach to classify costs in terms of their behaviour. Twenty-eight per cent viewed all overheads as fixed costs and direct costs as variable costs. Only 2% of these companies used statistical regression techniques (see below) and 11% did not distinguish between fixed and variable costs.

Steps in estimating a cost function

Quantitative analyses of cost relationships are formal methods to fit linear cost functions to past data observations. Columns 1 and 2 of Exhibit 9.3 break down the €12 501 of total indirect manufacturing labour costs and the 862 total machine-hours for the most recent twelve-week period into weekly data. Note that the data are paired. For example, week 12 shows indirect manufacturing labour costs of €963 and 48 machine-hours. In this section, the data in Exhibit 9.3 are used to illustrate how to use quantitive analysis.

There are six steps in estimating a cost function on the basis of an analysis of current or past cost relationships. (1) Choose the dependent variable (the variable to be predicted, which is some type of cost); (2) identify the cost driver(s) (independent variable(s)); (3) collect data on the

Week	Indirect manufacturing labour costs (1)	Cost driver: machine-hours (2)	Alternative cost driver: direct manufacturing labour-hours (3)
1	€1190	68	30
2	1211	88	35
3	1004	62	36
4	917	72	20
5	770	60	47
6	1456	96	45
7	1180	78	44
8	710	46	38
9	1316	82	70
10	1320	94	30
11	752	68	29
12	963	48	38

Exhibit 9.3 Weekly indirect manufacturing labour costs, machine-hours and direct manufacturing labour-hours for Møre-Teppe

dependent variable and the cost driver(s); (4) plot the data; (5) estimate the cost function; and (6) evaluate the estimated cost function. As we discussed earlier in this chapter, choosing a cost driver is not always straightforward. Frequently, the cost analyst will cycle through these steps several times trying alternative economically plausible cost drivers to see which cost driver best fits the data.

Step 1: Choose the dependent variable Choice of the **dependent variable** (the cost variable to be predicted) will depend on the purpose for estimating a cost function. For example, if the purpose is to determine indirect manufacturing costs for a production line, then the dependent variable should incorporate all costs that are classified as indirect with respect to the production line.

Step 2: Identify the independent variable(s) or cost driver(s) The **independent variable** (level of activity or cost driver) is the factor used to predict the dependent variable (costs). Usually we use the term 'cost driver' to describe the independent variable. The chosen cost driver should have an economically plausible relationship with the dependent variable and be accurately measurable. Ideally, all the individual items included in the dependent variable should have the same cost driver(s). Where a single relationship does not exist, the cost analyst should investigate the possibility of estimating more than one cost function.

Consider several types of fringe benefit paid to employees and their cost drivers:

Fringe benefit	Cost driver
Health benefits	Number of employees
Canteen meals	Number of employees
Pension benefits	Salaries of employees
Life insurance	Salaries of employees

The costs of health benefits and cafeteria meals can be combined into one cost pool because they both have the same cost driver, number of employees. Pension benefits and life insurance costs have a different cost driver, salaries of employees, and hence should not be combined with health benefits and canteen meals. Instead, they should be combined into a separate cost pool and estimated using salaries of employees receiving the benefits as the cost driver.

Step 3: Collect data on the dependent variable and the cost driver(s) This step is usually the most difficult one in cost analysis. Cost analysts obtain data from company documents, from interviews with managers, and through special studies. These data may be time-series data or cross-sectional data. *Time-series data* pertain to the same entity (organisation, plant, activity area, and so on) over a sequence of past time periods. Weekly observations of indirect manufacturing labour costs and machine-hours in the Møre-Teppe illustration are an example of time-series data. The ideal time-series database would contain numerous observations for a firm whose operations have not been affected by economic or technological change. Stable technology ensures that data collected in the estimation period represent the same underlying relationship between the dependent variable and the cost driver(s). Moreover, the time periods (for example, daily, weekly or monthly) used to measure the dependent variable and the cost driver(s) should be identical. *Cross-sectional data* pertain to different entities for the same time period. For example, studies of personnel costs and loans processed at 50 individual branches of a bank during March would produce cross-sectional data for March.

Step 4: Plot the data The expression 'a picture is worth a thousand words' conveys the benefits of plotting the data. The general relation between the dependent variable and the cost driver can readily be observed in a plot of the data. Moreover, the plot highlights extreme observations that analysts should check. Was there an error in recording the data or an unusual event, such as a strike, that makes these observations unrepresentative of the normal relationship between the dependent variable and the cost driver? Plotting the data can also provide insight into whether the relation is approximately linear and what the relevant range of the cost function is.

Exhibit 9.4 plots the weekly data from columns 1 and 2 of Exhibit 9.3. There is strong visual evidence of a positive relation between indirect manufacturing labour costs and machine-hours (that is, when machine-hours go up, so do costs). There do not appear to be any extreme observations in Exhibit 9.4. The relevant range is from 46 to 96 machine-hours per week.

Step 5: Estimate the cost function We show how to estimate the cost function for our Møre-Teppe data using the high–low method and regression analysis.

Step 6: Evaluate the estimated cost function We describe criteria for evaluating a cost function after illustrating the high–low method and regression analysis.

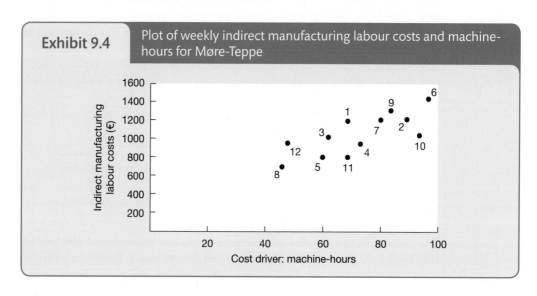

| Exhibit 9.4 | Plot of weekly indirect manufacturing labour costs and machine-hours for Møre-Teppe |

High–low method

Managers, at times, use very simple methods to estimate cost functions. An example is the **high–low method**, which entails using only the highest and lowest observed values of the *cost driver* within the relevant range. The line connecting these two points becomes the estimated cost function.

We illustrate the high–low method using data from Exhibit 9.3.

	Cost driver: machine-hours	Indirect manufacturing labour costs
Highest observation of cost driver (week 6)	96	€1456
Lowest observation of cost driver (week 8)	46	710
Difference	50	€746

$$\text{Slope coefficient } b = \frac{\text{Difference between costs associated with highest and lowest observations of the cost driver}}{\text{Difference between highest and lowest observations of the cost driver}}$$

$$= €746 \div 50$$

$$= €14.92 \text{ per machine-hour}$$

To compute the constant, we can use either the highest or the lowest observation of the cost driver. Both calculations yield the same answer (because the solution technique solves two linear equations with two unknowns, the slope coefficient and the constant).

$$\text{Since } y = a + bX, a = y - bX$$

At the highest observation of the cost driver,

$$\text{Constant } a = €1456 - (€14.92 \times 96)$$
$$= €23.68$$

At the lowest observation of the cost driver,

$$\text{Constant } a = €710 - (€14.92 \times 46)$$
$$= €23.68$$

Therefore, the high–low estimate of the cost function is:

$$y = a + bX$$
$$= €23.68 - (€14.92 \times \text{machine-hours})$$

The blue line in Exhibit 9.5 shows the estimated cost function using the high–low method. The estimated cost function is a straight line joining the observations with the highest and lowest values of the cost driver (machine-hours). The constant, or intercept, term does not serve as an estimate of the fixed costs of Møre-Teppe if no machines were run. Why? Because running no machines and shutting down the plant is outside the relevant range. The intercept term is the constant component of the equation that provides the best (linear) approximation of how a cost behaves within the relevant range.

Suppose indirect manufacturing labour costs in week 6 were €1280 instead of €1456 while 96 machine-hours were worked. In this case, the highest observation of the cost driver (machine-hours

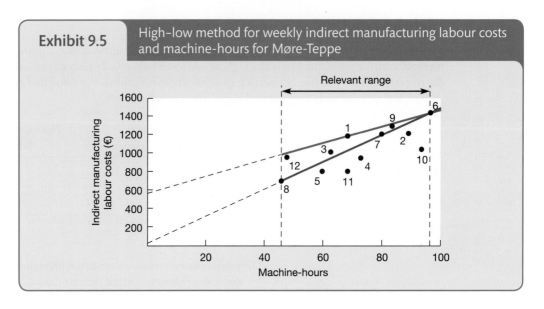

Exhibit 9.5 | High–low method for weekly indirect manufacturing labour costs and machine-hours for Møre-Teppe

of 96 in week 6) will not coincide with newly highest observation of the dependent variable (costs of €1316 in week 9). Given that causality runs from the cost driver to the dependent variable in a cost function, choosing the highest and lowest observation of the cost driver is appropriate. The high–low method would estimate the new cost function still using data from weeks 6 and 8.

There is an obvious danger of relying on only two observations. Suppose that because of certain provisions in the labour contract that guarantee certain minimum payments, indirect manufacturing labour costs in week 8 were €1000 instead of €710 when only 46 machine-hours were worked. The green line in Exhibit 9.5 shows the revised estimated cost function using the high–low method. It lies above the data. In this case, picking the highest and lowest observations for the machine-hours variable can result in an estimated cost function that poorly describes the underlying (linear) cost relationship between indirect manufacturing labour costs and machine-hours.

Sometimes the high–low method is modified so that the two observations chosen are a representative high and a representative low. The reason is that management wants to avoid having extreme observations, which arise from abnormal events, affecting the cost function. Even with such a modification, this method ignores information from all but two observations when estimating the cost function.

Regression analysis method

Unlike the high–low method, regression analysis uses all available data to estimate the cost function. **Regression analysis** is a statistical method that measures the average amount of change in the dependent variable that is associated with a unit change in one or more independent variables. In the Møre-Teppe example, the dependent variable is total indirect manufacturing labour costs. The independent variable, or cost driver, is machine-hours. **Simple regression** analysis estimates the relationship between the dependent variable and one independent variable; **multiple regression** analysis estimates the relationship between the dependent variable and multiple independent variables.

We emphasise the interpretation and use of output from computer software programs for regression analysis and so only present detailed computations for deriving the regression line in the chapter appendix. Commonly available programs calculate almost all the statistics referred to in this chapter.

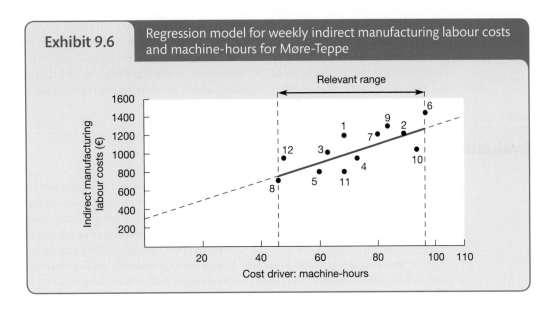

Exhibit 9.6 Regression model for weekly indirect manufacturing labour costs and machine-hours for Møre-Teppe

Exhibit 9.6 shows the line developed using regression analysis that best fits the data in columns 1 and 2 of Exhibit 9.3. The estimated cost function is:

$$y = €300.98 + €10.31X$$

where y is the predicted indirect manufacturing labour costs for any level of machine-hours (X). The constant, or intercept, term of the regression, a, is €300.98, and the slope coefficient b is €10.31 per machine-hour.

How do we derive the regression equation and regression line in Exhibit 9.6? We use the least-squares technique. We draw the regression line to minimise the sum of the squared vertical distances from the data points (the various points on the graph) to the regression line. Vertical differences measure distance between actual cost and the estimated cost for each observation. The difference between actual and predicted cost is called the **residual term**. The smaller the residual term, the better the fit between predicted costs and actual cost observations. Goodness of fit indicates the strength of the relationship between the cost driver and costs. The regression line in Exhibit 9.6 rises reasonably steeply from left to right. The positive slope of this line indicates that, on average, indirect manufacturing labour costs increase as machine-hours increase.

The vertical dashed lines in Exhibit 9.6 indicate the relevant range. As discussed previously, the estimated cost function applies to cost driver levels only *within the relevant range*, not to cost driver levels outside the relevant range.

The estimate of the slope coefficient b indicates that the average indirect manufacturing labour costs vary at the rate of €10.31 for every machine-hour within the relevant range. Management can use this equation when budgeting for future indirect manufacturing labour costs. For instance, if 90 machine-hours are budgeted for the coming week, the predicted indirect manufacturing labour costs would be:

$$y = €300.98 + (€10.31 \times 90)$$
$$= €1228.88$$

Compare the regression equation with the high–low equation in the preceding section, which was €23.68 + €14.92 per machine-hour. For 90 machine-hours, the predicted cost based on the high–low equation is €23.68 + (€14.92 × 90) = €1366.48. Suppose that for three weeks over the next twelve-week period, Møre-Teppe runs its machines for 90 hours each week. Assume average indirect manufacturing labour costs for those three weeks is €1300. Based on the high–low prediction of €1366.48, Møre-Teppe would conclude it has performed well. But comparing the €1300 performance with the €1228.88 prediction of the regression model tells a different story, and would probably prompt Møre-Teppe to search for ways to improve its cost performance.

Evaluating and choosing cost drivers

Correctly identifying the cost driver is aided substantially by a thorough understanding of both operations and cost accounting. Suppose management at Møre-Teppe is thinking of introducing a new style of carpet. Sales of 650 square metres of this carpet are expected each week at a price of €12 per square metre. To make this decision, management needs to estimate costs. The key to doing so is identifying the correct cost drivers and cost functions. This requires some knowledge of the underlying operational processes. Consider, in particular, indirect manufacturing labour costs. Management believes that both machine-hours and direct manufacturing labour-hours are plausible cost drivers of indirect manufacturing labour costs. It estimates 72 machine-hours and 21 direct manufacturing labour-hours would be required to produce the square metres of carpet it needs.

What guidance do the different cost estimation methods provide for choosing among cost drivers? The industrial engineering method relies on analysing physical relationships between costs and cost drivers, which are difficult to specify in this case. The conference method and the account analysis method use subjective assessments to choose a cost driver and to estimate the fixed and variable components of the cost function. In these cases, management must go with its best judgement. Management cannot use these methods to test and try alternative cost drivers. The major advantage of quantitative methods is that managers can use these methods to evaluate different cost drivers. We illustrate how using the regression analysis approach.

Suppose Møre-Teppe wants to evaluate whether direct manufacturing labour-hours is a better cost driver than machine-hours for indirect manufacturing labour costs. The cost analyst at Møre-Teppe inputs the data in columns 1 and 3 of Exhibit 9.3 into a computer program and estimates the cost function:

$$y = €744.67 + €7.72X$$

Exhibit 9.7 shows the plots for indirect manufacturing labour costs and direct manufacturing labour-hours, and the regression line that best fits the data.

Which cost driver should Møre-Teppe choose? We consider three of the most important criteria.

1 *Economic plausibility*. Both cost drivers are economically plausible. However, in the state-of-the-art, highly automated production environment of Møre-Teppe, costs are likely to be more closely related to machine-hours than to direct manufacturing labour-hours.

2 *Goodness of fit*. Compare Exhibits 9.6 and 9.7. The vertical differences between actual and predicted costs are much smaller for machine-hours than for direct manufacturing labour-hours – machine-hours has a stronger relationship with indirect manufacturing labour costs.

3 *Slope of regression line*. Again compare Exhibits 9.6 and 9.7. The machine-hours regression line has a relatively steep slope while the direct manufacturing labour-hours regression line is relatively flat (small slope). A relatively flat regression line indicates a weak or no relationship between indirect manufacturing labour costs and direct manufacturing labour-hours since, on average, changes in direct manufacturing labour-hours appear to have a minimal effect on indirect manufacturing labour costs.

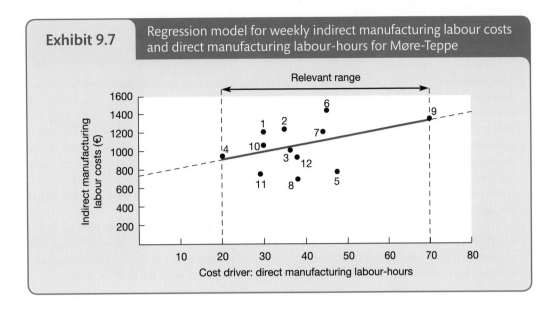

Exhibit 9.7 Regression model for weekly indirect manufacturing labour costs and direct manufacturing labour-hours for Møre-Teppe

Møre-Teppe should prefer machine-hours as the cost driver and use the cost function $y = €300.98 + (€10.31 × \text{machine-hours})$ to predict future indirect manufacturing labour costs. Using this model, Møre-Teppe would predict costs of $y = €300.98 + (€10.31 × 72) = €1043.30$. Had it used direct manufacturing labour-hours as the cost driver, it would have incorrectly predicted costs of $€744.67 + (€7.72 × 21) = €906.79$. If Møre-Teppe systematically underestimates costs and chooses incorrect cost drivers for other indirect costs as well, it would conclude that the costs of manufacturing the new style of carpet are quite low and essentially fixed (the regression line is relatively flat). But the actual costs driven by machine-hours would prove to be much higher. Without identifying the correct cost drivers, management would be misled into believing that the new style of carpets are more profitable than they actually are.

Incorrectly estimating the cost function will also have repercussions for cost management and cost control. Suppose direct manufacturing labour-hours was used as the cost driver, and actual indirect manufacturing labour costs were €970. Actual costs would then be higher than the predicted costs of €906.79. Management would feel compelled to find ways to cut costs. In fact, on the basis of the preferred machine-hour cost driver, the plant has actual costs lower than the predicted amount (€1043.30) – a performance that management should seek to replicate, not change.

Cost drivers and activity-based costing

In activity-based costing (ABC) systems (discussed more fully in Chapter 11), operations managers and cost analysts identify key activities, and the cost drivers and costs of each activity at the output unit-level, batch-level or product-sustaining level. The basic approach to evaluating cost drivers described in the previous section applies to ABC systems as well. An ABC system, however, has a greater number and variety of cost drivers and cost pools.

Generally, ABC systems emphasise long-run relationships between the cost driver (level of activity) and cost. The long-run focus means that more costs are variable, which leads to a stronger cause-and-effect relationship between the cost driver and the corresponding cost. Hence, the ideal database to estimate cost driver rates will contain data over a longer time period. If the time period used to estimate the cost relationship is short, the relationship between changes in the cost driver and changes in cost may be weak. Why? Because many costs are acquired in lump-sum amounts and hence are fixed in the short run while the levels of activity vary.

Concepts in action   Activity-based costing and cost estimation

Cost estimation in activity-based costing and other systems blend the various methods presented in this chapter. To determine the cost of an activity, ABC systems often rely on expert analyses and opinions gathered from operating personnel (the conference method). For example, Loan Department staff at the Co-operative Bank in the UK subject-ively estimates the costs of the loan processing activity and the cost driver of loan processing costs (the number of loans processed, a batch-level cost driver, rather than the value of the loans, an output unit-level cost driver), to derive the cost of processing a loan. ABC systems sometimes use input–output relationships (the industrial engineer-ing method) to identify cost drivers and the cost of an activity. For example, John Deere and Company uses work-measurement methods to identify a batch-level cost driver (the number of standard loads moved) and the cost per load moved within its components plant.

In complex environments, multiple cost drivers are necessary for accurate product costing. Consider how heavy equipment manufacturer Caterpillar identifies the cost driver for receiving costs in its ABC system. Three plausible cost drivers are the weight of parts received, the number of parts received, or the number of shipments received. The weight of parts and number of parts are output unit-level cost drivers, while the number of shipments is a batch-level cost driver. Caterpillar uses the weight of parts as the basis for cost assignment because a regression analysis showed that it is the primary driver of the costs of receiving material. Caterpillar also uses a variety of other cost drivers in assigning costs to its products.

Sources: Kaplan, R.S. and Datar, S.M. (1995) 'The Co-operative Bank', *Harvard Business School Cases*, No. 9-195-196, 23 March (revised 22 April 1997); March, A. and Kaplan, R.S. (1987) 'John Deere Component Works (A)', *Harvard Business School Cases*, No. 9-187-107, 4 May (revised 4 November 1998); and discussions with the company's management.

Consider, for example, salaries and fringe benefits of engineers and line managers responsible for supervising the set-up activity. In the short run, these costs are fixed and will not vary with changes in the quantity of set-up hours. In the long run, however, there is a clear cause-and-effect relationship between set-up hours and indirect set-up costs – increases in set-up hours will cause more engineers and line managers to be hired while decreases will result in engineers and line managers being assigned to other tasks.

As the Concepts in Action feature indicates, managers implementing ABC systems use a variety of methods – conference, industrial engineering and regression – to estimate cost driver rates. In making these choices, managers trade off level of detail, accuracy, feasibility and costs of estimating cost functions.

Non-linearity and cost functions

So far we have assumed linear cost functions. In practice, cost functions are not always linear. A **non-linear cost function** is a cost function where, within the relevant range, the graph of total costs versus the level of a single activity is not a straight line. Exhibit 9.2 graphically illustrated a cost function that is non-linear over the range from 0 to 80 000 valves produced. Consider another example. Economies of scale in advertising may enable an advertising agency to double the number of advertisements for less than double the costs. Even direct materials costs are not always linear variable costs. Consider quantity discounts on direct materials purchases. As shown in Exhibit 9.8, the total direct materials costs rise, but they rise more slowly as the cost driver increases because of quantity discounts. The cost function in Exhibit 9.8 has $b = €25$ for

1–1000 units purchased; b = €15 for 1001–2000 units purchased; and b = €10 for 2001 or more units purchased (a = €0 for all ranges of the units purchased). The cost per unit falls at each price break; that is, the cost per unit decreases with larger orders.

Step cost functions are also examples of non-linear cost functions. A **step cost function** is a cost function in which the cost is constant over various ranges of the cost driver, but the cost increases by discrete amounts (that is, in steps) as the cost driver moves from one range to the next. The graph in Exhibit 9.9 shows a *step variable-cost function*, a step cost function in which cost is constant over narrow ranges of the cost driver in each relevant range. Exhibit 9.9 shows the relationship between set-up costs and units of production. The pattern is a step cost function because set-up costs are incurred only when each production batch is started. This step-pattern behaviour also occurs when inputs such as production scheduling, product design labour and process engineering labour are acquired in discrete quantities but used in fractional quantities. As shown in Exhibit 9.9, management often approximates step variable costs with a variable cost function.

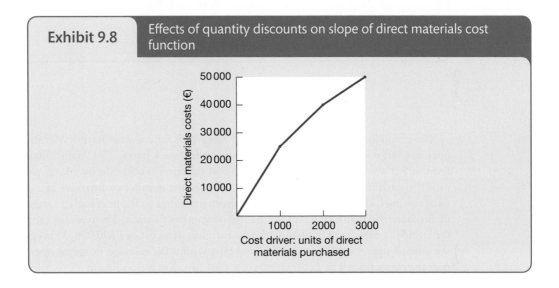

| Exhibit 9.8 | Effects of quantity discounts on slope of direct materials cost function |

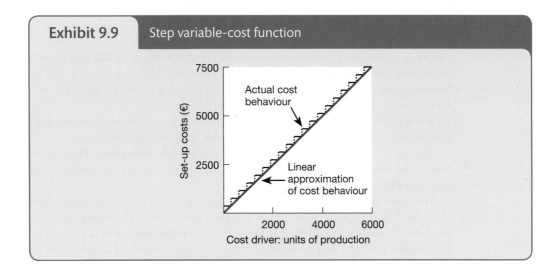

| Exhibit 9.9 | Step variable-cost function |

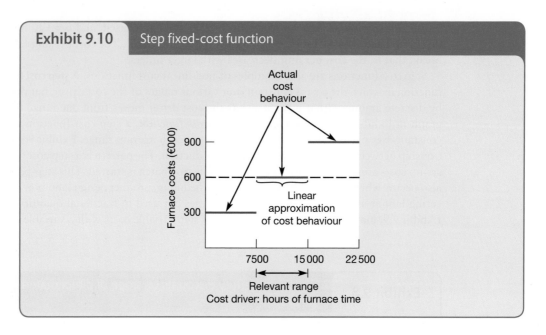

Exhibit 9.10   Step fixed-cost function

The graph in Exhibit 9.10 shows a *step fixed-cost function* for Bayern Metal, a company that operates large heat-treatment furnaces to harden steel parts. The main difference relative to Exhibit 9.9 is that the cost in a step fixed-cost function is constant over large ranges of the cost driver in each relevant range. The ranges indicate the number of furnaces being used (each furnace costing €300 000). The cost changes from one range to the next higher range when the hours of furnace time demanded require the use of another furnace. The relevant range indicates that the company expects to operate with two furnaces at a cost of €600 000. Management considers the cost of operating furnaces as a fixed cost within the relevant range of operation. However, over the range from 0 to 22 500 hours, the cost function is non-linear.

Learning curves and non-linear cost functions

Learning curves also result in cost functions being non-linear. A **learning curve** is a function that shows how labour-hours per unit decline as units of production increase and workers learn and become better at what they do. Managers use learning curves to predict how labour-hours (or labour costs) will change as more units are produced.

The aircraft-assembly industry first documented the effect that learning has on efficiency. As workers become more familiar with their tasks, their efficiency improves.

Managers learn how to improve the scheduling of work shifts. Plant operators learn how best to operate the facility. Unit costs decrease as productivity increases, which means that the unit-cost function behaves non-linearly.

Managers are now extending the learning-curve notion to include other cost areas in the value chain, such as marketing, distribution and customer service. The term *experience curve* describes this broader application of the learning curve. An **experience curve** is a function that shows how full product costs per unit (including manufacturing, marketing, distribution, and so on) decline as units of output increase.

We now describe two learning-curve models: the cumulative average-time learning model and the incremental unit-time learning model.

Cumulative average-time learning model

In the **cumulative average-time learning model**, the cumulative average time per unit declines by a constant percentage each time the cumulative quantity of units produced doubles. Exhibit 9.11 illustrates the cumulative average-time learning model with an 80% learning curve. The 80% means that when the quantity of units produced is doubled from X to 2X, the cumulative average time *per unit* for the 2X units is 80% of the cumulative average time *per unit* for the X units. In other words, average time per unit has dropped by 20%. Graph 1 in Exhibit 9.11 shows the cumulative average time *per unit* as a function of units produced. Graph 2 in Exhibit 9.11 shows the cumulative *total* labour-hours as a function of units produced. The data points underlying Exhibit 9.11 and the details of their calculation are presented in Exhibit 9.12. To obtain the cumulative total time, multiply the cumulative average time per unit by the cumulative number of units produced. For example, to produce 4 cumulative units would require 256.00 labour-hours (4 × 64).

Incremental unit-time learning model

In the **incremental unit-time learning model**, the incremental unit time (the time needed to produce the last unit) declines by a constant percentage each time the cumulative quantity of units produced doubles. Exhibit 9.13 illustrates the incremental unit-time learning model with an 80% learning curve. The 80% here means that when the quantity of units produced is doubled from X to 2X, the time needed to produce the *last unit* at the 2X production level is 80% of the time needed to produce the *last unit* at the X production level. Graph 1 in Exhibit 9.13 shows the cumulative average time *per unit* as a function of cumulative units produced. Graph 2 in Exhibit 9.13 shows the cumulative *total* labour-hours as a function of units produced. The data points underlying Exhibit 9.13 and the details of their calculation are presented in Exhibit 9.14. We obtain the cumulative total time by summing the individual unit times. For example, to produce 4 cumulative units would require 314.21 labour-hours (100.00 + 80.00 + 70.21 + 64.00).

The incremental unit-time model predicts that a higher cumulative total time is required to produce two or more units than the cumulative average-time model predicts, assuming the same learning rate for the two models (compare results in Exhibit 9.12 with results in Exhibit 9.14). For example, to produce 4 cumulative units, the 80% incremental unit-time learning model predicts 314.21 labour-hours whereas the 80% cumulative average-time learning model predicts 256.00 labour-hours.

Which of these two models is preferable? The one that more accurately approximates the behaviour of manufacturing labour-hour usage as production levels increase. The choice can be decided only on a case-by-case basis. Engineers, plant managers and workers are good sources of information on the amount and type of learning actually occurring as production increases. Plotting this information is helpful in selecting the appropriate model.

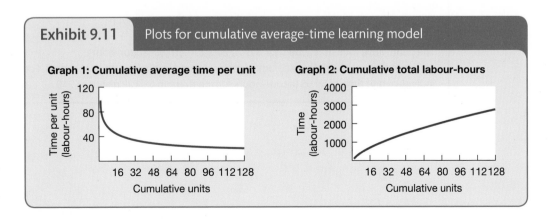

Exhibit 9.11 Plots for cumulative average-time learning model

Exhibit 9.12	Cumulative average-time learning model		

Cumulative number of units (1)	Cumulative average time per unit (y): labour-hours (2)	Cumulative total time: labour-hours (3) = (1) × (2)	Individual unit time for Xth unit: labour-hours (4)
1	100.00	100.00	100.00
2	80.00 (100 × 0.8)	160.00	60.00
3	70.21	210.63	50.63
4	64.00 (80 × 0.8)	256.00	45.37
5	59.57	297.85	41.85
6	56.17	337.02	39.17
7	53.45	374.15	37.13
8	51.20 (64 × 0.8)	409.60	35.45
–	–	–	–
–	–	–	–
–	–	–	–
16	40.96 (51.2 × 0.8)	655.36	28.06

Note: The mathematical relationship underlying the cumulative average-time learning model is:

$$y = p X^q$$

where y = cumulative average time (labour-hours) per unit
   X = cumulative number of units produced
   p = time (labour-hours) required to produce the first unit
   q = rate of learning.

The value of q is calculated as:

$$q = \frac{\ln(\% \text{ learning})}{\ln 2}$$

For an 80% learning curve,

$$q = \frac{-0.2231}{0.6931} = -0.3219$$

As an illustration, when $X = 3$, $p = 100$, and $q = -0.3219$,

$$y = 100 \times 3^{-0.3219} = 70.21 \text{ labour-hours}$$

The cumulative total time when $X = 3$ is 70.21 × 3 = 210.63 labour-hours.

The individual unit times in column 4 are calculated using the data in column 3. For example, the individual unit time of 50.63 labour-hours for the third unit is calculated as 210.63 – 160.00.

Exhibit 9.13   Plots for incremental unit-time learning model

Graph 1: Cumulative average time per unit

Graph 2: Cumulative total labour-hours

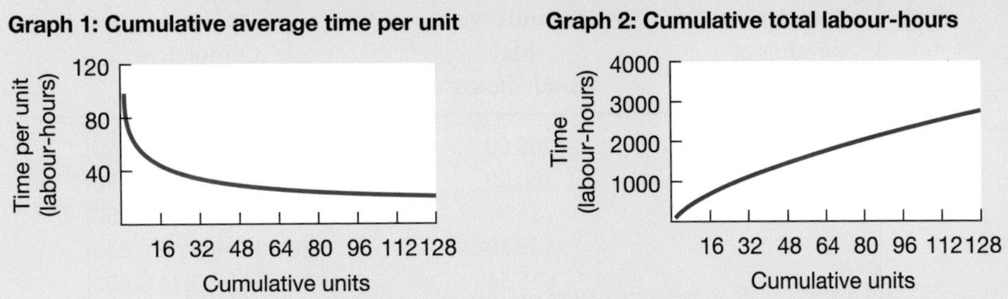

Exhibit 9.14   Incremental unit-time learning model

Cumulative number of units (1)	Individual unit time for Xth unit (m): labour-hours (2)	Cumulative total time: labour-hours (3)	Cumulative average time per unit: labour-hours (4) = (3) ÷ (1)
1	100.00	100.00	100.00
2	80.00 (100 × 0.8)	180.00	90.00
3	70.21	250.21	83.40
4	64.00 (80 × 0.8)	314.21	78.55
5	59.57	373.78	74.76
6	56.17	429.95	71.66
7	53.45	483.40	69.06
8	51.20 (64 × 0.8)	534.60	66.82
–	–	–	–
–	–	–	–
–	–	–	–
16	40.96 (51.2 × 0.8)	892.00	55.75

Note: The mathematical relationship underlying the incremental unit-time learning model is:

$$m = pX^q$$

where m = time (labour-hours) taken to produce the last single unit

X = cumulative number of units produced

p = time (labour-hours) required to produce the first unit

q = rate of learning.

The value of q is calculated as:

$$q = \frac{\ln\ (\%\ \text{learning})}{\ln\ 2}$$

For an 80% learning curve,

$$q = \frac{-0.2231}{0.6931} = -0.3219$$

As an illustration, when $X = 3$, $p = 100$, and $q = -0.3219$,

$$m = 100 \times 3^{-0.3219} = 70.21 \text{ labour-hours}$$

The cumulative total time when $X = 3$ is $100 + 80 + 70.21 = 250.21$ labour-hours.

Exhibit 9.15	Predicting costs using learning curves		
Cumulative number of units	Cumulative total labour-hours*	Cumulative costs	Additions to cumulative costs
1	100.00	€5 000 (100.00 × €50)	€5 000
2	160.00	8 000 (160.00 × €50)	3 000
4	256.00	12 800 (256.00 × €50)	4 800
8	409.60	20 480 (409.60 × €50)	7 680
16	655.36	32 768 (655.36 × €50)	12 288

* Based on the cumulative average-time learning model. See Exhibit 9.12 for the computation of these amounts.

Setting prices, budgets and standards

Predictions of costs should allow for learning. Consider the data in Exhibit 9.12 for the cumulative average-time learning model. Suppose the variable costs subject to learning effects consist of direct manufacturing labour (€20 per hour) and related overhead (€30 per hour). Management should predict the costs shown in Exhibit 9.15.

These data show that the effects of the learning curve could have a major influence on decisions. For example, a company might set an extremely low selling price on its product in order to generate high demand. As the company's production increases to meet this growing demand, costs per unit drop. The company rides the product down the learning curve as it establishes a higher market share. Although the company may have earned little on its first unit sold – it may actually have lost money – the company earns more profit per unit as output increases.

Alternatively, subject to legal and other considerations, the company might set a low price on just the final eight units. After all, the labour and related overhead costs per unit are predicted to be only €12 288 for these final eight units (€32 768 – €20 480). The per unit costs of €1536 on these final eight units (€12 288 ÷ 8) are much lower than the €5000 costs per unit of the first unit produced.

Many companies incorporate learning-curve effects when evaluating performance. For example, the Nissan Motor Company sets assembly-labour efficiency standards for new models of cars after taking into account the learning that will occur as more units are produced.

The learning-curve models examined in Exhibits 9.11 to 9.14 assume that learning is driven by a single variable (production output). Other models of learning have been developed by companies such as Analog Devices and Yokogowa Hewlett-Packard that focus on how quality (rather than manufacturing labour-hours) will change over time (rather than as more units are produced). Some recent studies suggest that factors other than production output – such as job rotation and organising workers into teams – contribute to learning that improves quality.

Summary

The following points are linked to the chapter's learning objectives.

1 Two assumptions frequently made in cost-behaviour estimation are: (a) that changes in total costs can be explained by changes in the level of a single cost driver, and (b) that cost behaviour can adequately be approximated by a linear function of the cost driver within the relevant range.

2 A linear cost function is a cost function where, within the relevant range, the graph of total costs versus a single cost driver forms a straight line. Linear cost functions can be described by a single constant (a), which represents the estimate of the total cost component that does not vary with changes in the level of the cost driver, and a slope coefficient (b), which represents the estimate of the amount by which total costs change for each unit change in the level of the cost driver. Three types of linear cost functions are: variable, fixed and mixed (or semivariable).

3 Four broad approaches to estimating cost functions are: the industrial engineering method, the conference method, the account analysis method, and quantitative analysis of cost relationships (the high–low method and regression analysis method). Regression analysis is a systematic approach to estimating a cost function on the basis of identified cost drivers. Ideally, the cost analyst applies more than one approach; each approach serves as a check on the others.

4 The six steps in estimating a cost function on the basis of an analysis of current or past cost relationships are: (a) choose the dependent variable; (b) identify the cost driver(s); (c) collect data on the dependent variable and the cost driver(s); (d) plot the data; (e) estimate the cost function; and (f) evaluate the estimated cost function. In most situations, the cost analyst will cycle through these steps several times before identifying an acceptable cost function.

5 Three criteria for evaluating and choosing cost drivers are: (a) economic plausibility, (b) goodness of fit, and (c) the slope of the regression line.

6 A non-linear cost function is a cost function where, within the relevant range, the graph of total costs versus a single cost driver does not form a straight line. Non-linear costs can arise due to economies of scale, quantity discounts, step cost functions and learning-curve effects.

7 The learning curve is an example of a non-linear cost function. Labour-hours per unit decline as units of production increase. In the cumulative average-time learning model, the cumulative average-time per unit declines by a constant percentage each time the cumulative quantity of units produced doubles. In the incremental unit-time learning model, the incremental unit time (the time needed to produce the last unit) declines by a constant percentage each time the cumulative quantity of units produced doubles.

Appendix

Regression analysis

This appendix describes formulae for estimating the regression equation and several commonly used statistics. We use the data for Møre-Teppe presented in Exhibit 9.3. The appendix also discusses goodness of fit, significance of independent variables, and specification analysis of estimation assumptions for regression analysis.

Estimating the regression line

The least-squares technique for estimating the regression line minimises the sum of the squares of the vertical deviations (distances) from the data points to the estimated regression line.

The object is to find the values of a and b in the predicting equation $y = a + bX$, where y is the predicted cost value as distinguished from the observed cost value, which we denote by Y. We wish to find the numerical values of a and b that minimise $\Sigma(Y - y)^2$. This calculation is accomplished by using two equations, usually called the normal equations:

$$\Sigma Y = na + b(\Sigma X)$$
$$\Sigma XY = a(\Sigma X) + b(\Sigma X^2)$$

where n is the number of data points; ΣX and ΣY are, respectively, the sums of the given X and Y values; ΣX^2 is the sum of squares of the X values; and ΣXY is the sum of the amounts obtained by multiplying each of the given X values by the associated observed Y value.

Exhibit 9.16 shows the calculations required for obtaining the line that best fits the data of indirect manufacturing labour costs and machine-hours for Møre-Teppe. Substituting into the two normal equations simultaneously, we obtain:

$$12\ 501 = 12a + 862b$$
$$928\ 716 = 862a + 64\ 900b$$

The solution is $a = €300.98$ and $b = €10.31$, which can be obtained by direct substitution if the normal equations are re-expressed symbolically as:

$$a = \frac{(\Sigma Y)(\Sigma X^2) - (\Sigma X)(\Sigma XY)}{n(\Sigma X^2) - (\Sigma X)(\Sigma X)}$$

$$b = \frac{n(\Sigma XY) - (\Sigma X)(\Sigma Y)}{n(\Sigma X^2) - (\Sigma X)(\Sigma X)}$$

Exhibit 9.16	Computation for least-squares regression between indirect manufacturing labour costs and machine-hours for Møre-Teppe							
Week (1)	Machine-hours* X (2)	Indirect manufacturing labour costs* Y (3)	X^2 (4)	XY (5)	y (6)	Variance of Y $(Y - \bar{Y})^2$ (7)	Unexplained variance $(Y - y)^2$ (8)	Variance of X $(X - \bar{X})^2$ (9)
1	68	1 190	4 624	80 920	1 002.06	21 978	35 321	15
2	88	1 211	7 744	106 568	1 208.26	28 646	8	261
3	62	1 004	3 844	62 248	940.20	1 425	4 070	97
4	72	917	5 184	66 024	1 043.30	15 563	15 952	0
5	60	770	3 600	46 200	919.58	73 848	22 374	140
6	96	1 456	9 216	139 776	1 290.74	171 603	27 311	584
7	78	1 180	6 084	92 040	1 105.16	19 113	5 601	38
8	46	710	2 116	32 660	775.24	110 058	4 256	667
9	82	1 316	6 724	107 912	1 146.40	75 213	28 764	103
10	94	1 032	8 836	97 008	1 270.12	95	56 701	491
11	68	752	4 624	51 136	1 002.06	83 955	62 530	15
12	48	963	2 304	46 224	795.86	6 202	27 936	568
Total	862	12 501	64 900	928 716	≈12 501	607 699	290 824	2 979

* Same data as in columns 1 and 2 of Exhibit 9.3.

For our illustration, we now have:

$$a = \frac{(12\,501)(64\,900) - (862)(928\,716)}{12(64\,900) - (862)(862)} = €300.98$$

$$b = \frac{12(928\,716) - (862)(12\,501)}{12(64\,900) - (862)(862)} = €10.31$$

Placing the amounts for a and b in the equation of the least-squares line, we have:

$$y = €300.98 + €10.31X$$

where y is the predicted indirect manufacturing labour costs for any specified number of machine-hours within the relevant range. Generally, these computations are done using software packages such as SPSS, SAS and Statistica.

Goodness of fit

Goodness of fit measures how well the predicted values, y, based on the cost driver, X, match actual cost observations, Y. The regression analysis method computes a formal measure of goodness of fit, called the coefficient of determination. The **coefficient of determination**, r^2, measures the percentage of variation in Y explained by X (the independent variable). The coefficient of determination (r^2) indicates the proportion of the variance of Y, $(Y - \bar{Y})^2 \div n$, that is explained by the independent variable X (where $\bar{Y} = \sum Y \div n$). It is more convenient to express the coefficient of determination as 1 minus the proportion of total variance that is not explained by the independent variable. The unexplained variance arises because of differences between the actual values of Y and the predicted values of y:

$$r^2 = 1 - \frac{\text{Unexplained variation}}{\text{Total variation}} = 1 - \frac{\Sigma(Y - y)^2}{\Sigma(Y - \bar{Y})^2}$$

$$= 1 - \frac{290\,824}{607\,699}$$

$$= 0.52$$

The calculations indicate that r^2 increases as the predicted values y more closely approximate the actual observations Y. The range of r^2 is from 0 (implying no explanatory power) to 1 (implying perfect explanatory power). When $r^2 = 1$, the predicted cost values exactly equal actual cost values; that is, the independent variable X has perfectly explained variations in actual costs Y. Generally, an r^2 of 0.30 or higher passes the goodness-of-fit test. Do not rely exclusively on goodness of fit. It can lead to the indiscriminate inclusion of independent variables that increase r^2 but have no economic plausibility as cost driver(s). Goodness of fit has meaning only if the relationship between costs and the drivers is economically plausible.

Significance of independent variables

A key question that managers ask is: Do changes in the economically plausible independent variable result in significant changes in the dependent variable, or alternatively, is the slope b of the regression line significant? Recall, for example, that in the regression of machine-hours on indirect manufacturing labour costs in the Møre-Teppe illustration, b is estimated from a sample of 12 observations. The estimate b is subject to random factors, as are all sample statistics. That is, a different sample of 12 data points will give a different estimate of b. The **standard error of the estimated coefficient** indicates how much the estimated value b is likely to be affected by random factors. The t-value of the b coefficient measures how large the value of the estimated coefficient is relative to its standard error. A t-value with an absolute value greater than 2.00 suggests that the b coefficient is significantly different from zero. In other words, a relationship exists between the independent variable and the dependent variable that cannot be attributed to chance alone.

The benchmark for inferring that a b coefficient is significantly different from zero is a function of the degrees of freedom in a regression. The benchmark of 2.00 assumes a sample size of 60 observations. The number of degrees of freedom is calculated as the sample size minus the number of a and b parameters estimated in the regression. For a simple regression, the benchmark values for the t-values are:

Sample size	Benchmark*
12	$\|t\| > 2.23$
15	$\|t\| > 2.16$
20	$\|t\| > 2.10$
30	$\|t\| > 2.05$
60	$\|t\| > 2.00$

* $|t|$ denotes the absolute value of the t-value.

For simplicity, we use a cut-off t-value of 2.00 throughout this appendix.

Exhibit 9.17 presents a convenient format for summarising the regression results for indirect manufacturing labour costs and machine-hours. The t-value for the slope coefficient b is €10.31 ÷ €3.12 = 3.30, which exceeds the benchmark of 2.00. Therefore, the coefficient of the machine-hours variable is significantly different from zero. The probability is low (less than 5%) that random factors could have caused the coefficient b to be positive. Alternatively, we can restate our conclusion in terms of a 'confidence interval': there is less than a 5% chance that the true value of the machine-hours coefficient lies outside the range €10.31 ± (2.00 × €3.12) or €10.31 ± €6.24, or from €4.07 and €16.55. Therefore, we can conclude that changes in machine-hours do affect indirect manufacturing labour costs. Similarly, using data from Exhibit 9.17, the t-value for the constant term a is €300.98 ÷ €229.76 = 1.31, which is less than 2.00. This value indicates that, within the relevant range, the constant term is not significantly different from zero.

Specification analysis of estimation assumptions

Specification analysis is the testing of the assumptions of regression analysis. If the assumptions of (1) linearity within the relevant range, (2) constant variance of residuals, (3) independence of residuals, and (4) normality of residuals hold, the simplest regression procedures give reliable estimates of unknown coefficient values. This section provides a brief overview of specification analysis. When these assumptions are not satisfied, more complex regression procedures are necessary to obtain the best estimates. For details see, for example, Watson et al. (1993) and Greene (2000).

Exhibit 9.17	Simple regression results with indirect manufacturing labour costs as dependent variable and machine-hours as independent variable for Møre-Teppe

Variable	Coefficient (1)	Standard error (2)	t-value (3) = (1) ÷ (2)
Constant	€300.98	€229.75	1.31
Independent variable 1:			
Machine-hours	€10.31	€3.12	3.30

$r^2 = 0.52$; Durbin–Watson statistic = 2.05.

1 *Linearity within the relevant range.* A common assumption is that a linear relationship exists between the independent variable X and the dependent variable Y within the relevant range. If a linear regression model is used to estimate a fundamentally non-linear relationship, however, the coefficient estimates obtained will be inaccurate.

Where there is only one independent variable, the easiest way to check for linearity is by studying the data on a scatter diagram, a step that often is unwisely skipped. Exhibit 9.6 presents a scatter diagram for the indirect manufacturing labour costs and machine-hours variables of Møre-Teppe shown in Exhibit 9.3. The scatter diagram reveals that linearity appears to be a reasonable assumption for these data.

The learning-curve models discussed in the chapter are examples of non-linear cost functions; costs increase when the level of production increases, but by lesser amounts than would occur with a linear cost function. In this case, the analyst should estimate a non-linear cost function that explicitly incorporates learning effects.

2 *Constant variance of residuals.* The vertical deviation of the *observed* value Y from the regression line estimate y is called the *residual term*, *disturbance term* or *error term*, $u = Y - y$. The assumption of constant variance implies that the residual terms are unaffected by the level of the independent variable. The assumption also implies that there is a uniform scatter, or dispersion, of the data points about the regression line. The scatter diagram is the easiest way to check for *constant variance*. This assumption holds for Graph A of Exhibit 9.18 but not for Graph B. Constant variance is also known as *homoscedasticity*. Violation of this assumption is called *heteroscedasticity*.

Heteroscedasticity does not affect the accuracy of the regression estimates a and b. It does, however, reduce the reliability of the estimates of the standard errors, and thus affects the precision with which inferences can be drawn.

3 *Independence of residuals.* The assumption of the independence of residuals is that the residual term for any one observation is not related to the residual term for any other observation. The problem of *serial correlation* in the residuals (also called *autocorrelation*) arises when the residuals are not independent. Serial correlation means that there is a systematic pattern in the sequence of residuals such that the residual in observation n conveys information about the residuals in observations $n + 1$, $n + 2$, and so on. In time-series data, inflation is a common cause of autocorrelation because it causes costs (and hence residuals) to be related over time. Autocorrelation can also occur in cross-sectional data as, for example, in Exhibit 9.19. The scatter diagram helps in identifying autocorrelation. Autocorrelation does not exist in Graph A of Exhibit 9.19 but does exist in Graph B. Observe the systematic pattern

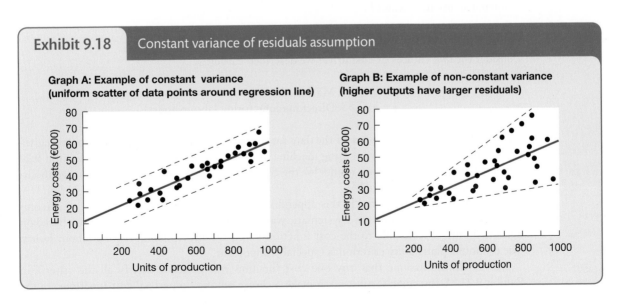

Exhibit 9.18   Constant variance of residuals assumption

Graph A: Example of constant variance
(uniform scatter of data points around regression line)

Graph B: Example of non-constant variance
(higher outputs have larger residuals)

Exhibit 9.19   Independence of residuals assumption

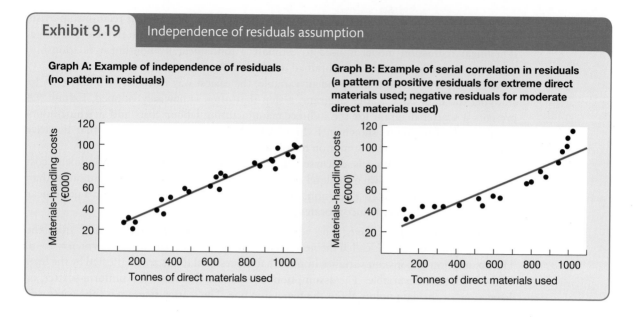

Graph A: Example of independence of residuals (no pattern in residuals)

Graph B: Example of serial correlation in residuals (a pattern of positive residuals for extreme direct materials used; negative residuals for moderate direct materials used)

of the residuals in Graph B: positive residuals for extreme quantities of direct materials used and negative residuals for moderate quantities of direct materials used. No such systematic pattern prevails for Graph A.

Like non-constant variance in residuals, serial correlation does not affect the accuracy of the regression estimates a and b. It does, however, affect the standard errors of the coefficients, which in turn affect the precision with which inferences about the population parameters can be drawn from the regression estimates.

The *Durbin–Watson statistic* is one measure of serial correlation in the estimated residuals. For samples of 10–20 observations, a Durbin–Watson statistic in the 1.10–2.90 range suggests that the residuals are independent. The Durbin–Watson statistic for the regression results of Møre-Teppe in Exhibit 9.17 is 2.05. Therefore, an assumption of independence in the estimated residuals seems reasonable for this regression model.

4 *Normality of residuals.* The normality of residuals assumption means that the residuals are distributed normally around the regression line. This assumption is necessary for making inferences about y, a and b.

Using regression output to choose cost drivers of cost functions

Consider the two choices of cost driver we described earlier:

$$y = a + (b \times \text{Machine-hours})$$
$$y = a + (b \times \text{Direct manufacturing labour-hours})$$

Exhibits 9.6 and 9.7 present plots of the data for the two regressions. Exhibit 9.17 reports regression results for the cost function using machine-hours as the independent variable. Exhibit 9.20 presents comparable regression results for the cost function using direct manufacturing labour-hours as the independent variable.

On the basis of the material in this appendix, which regression is better? Exhibit 9.21 compares these two cost functions in a systematic way. For several criteria, the cost function based on machine-hours is preferable to the cost function based on direct manufacturing labour-hours. The economic plausibility criterion is especially important.

Do not always assume that any one cost function will perfectly satisfy all the criteria in Exhibit 9.21. A cost analyst must often make a choice among 'imperfect' cost functions, in the

Exhibit 9.20	Simple regression results with indirect manufacturing labour costs as dependent variable and direct manufacturing labour-hours as independent variable for Møre-Teppe		
Variable	Coefficient (1)	Standard error (2)	t-value (3) = (1) ÷ (2)
Constant	€744.67	€217.61	3.42
Independent variable 1: Direct manufacturing labour-hours	€7.72	€5.40	1.43

$r^2 = 0.17$; Durbin–Watson statistic = 2.26.

Exhibit 9.21	Comparison of alternative cost functions for indirect manufacturing labour costs estimated with simple regression for Møre-Teppe	
Criterion	Cost function 1: machine-hours as independent variable	Cost function 2: direct manufacturing labour-hours as independent variable
Economic plausibility	A positive relationship between indirect manufacturing labour costs (technical support labour) and machine-hours is economically plausible in a highly automated plant	A positive relationship between indirect manufacturing labour costs and direct manufacturing labour-hours is economically plausible, but less so than machine-hours in a highly automated plant on a week-to-week basis
Goodness of fit	$r^2 = 0.52$ Excellent goodness of fit	$r^2 = 0.17$ Poor goodness of fit
Significance of independent variable(s)	The t-value of 3.30 is significant	The t-value of 1.43 is not significant
Specification analysis of estimation assumptions	Plot of the data indicates that assumptions of linearity, constant variance, independence of residuals and normality of residuals hold, but inferences drawn from only 12 observations are not reliable; Durbin–Watson statistic = 2.05	Plot of the data indicates that assumptions of linearity, constant variance, independence of residuals and normality of residuals hold, but inferences drawn from only 12 observations are not reliable; Durbin–Watson statistic = 2.26

sense that the data of any particular cost function will not perfectly meet one or more of the assumptions underlying regression analysis.

Multiple regression and cost hierarchies

In some cases, a satisfactory estimation of a cost function may be based on only one independent variable, such as machine-hours. In many cases, however, basing the estimation on more than one independent variable is more economically plausible and improves accuracy. The most widely used equations to express relationships between two or more independent variables and a dependent variable are linear in the form

$$Y = a + b_1 X_1 + b_2 X_2 + \ldots + u$$

where

$$Y = \text{cost variable to be predicted}$$
$$X_1, X_2, \ldots = \text{independent variables on which the prediction is to be based}$$
$$a, b_1, b_2, \ldots = \text{estimated coefficients of the regression model}$$
$$u = \text{residual term that includes the net effect of other factors not in the model and measurement errors in the dependent and independent variables.}$$

Example 9A.1

Consider the Møre-Teppe data in Exhibit 9.22. Indirect manufacturing labour costs include sizable costs incurred for set-up and changeover costs when production on one carpet batch is stopped and production on another batch is started. Management believes that in addition to machine-hours (an output unit-level cost driver), indirect manufacturing labour costs are also affected by the number of different batches of carpets produced during each week (a batch-level driver). Møre-Teppe estimates the relation between two independent variables, machine-hours and number of separate carpet jobs worked on during the week, and indirect manufacturing labour costs.

Exhibit 9.23 presents results for the following multiple regression model, using data in columns 1, 2 and 4 of Exhibit 9.22:

$$y = €42.58 + €7.60X_1 + €37.77X_2$$

where X_1 is the number of machine-hours and X_2 is the number of production batches. It is economically plausible that both machine-hours and production batches would help explain variations in indirect manufacturing labour costs at Møre-Teppe. The r^2 of 0.52 for the simple

Exhibit 9.22	Weekly indirect manufacturing labour costs, machine-hours, direct manufacturing labour-hours and number of production batches for Møre-Teppe			
Week	Indirect manufacturing labour costs (1)	Machine-hours (2)	Direct manufacturing labour-hours (3)	Number of production batches (4)
1	€1190	68	30	12
2	1211	88	35	15
3	1004	62	36	13
4	917	72	20	11
5	770	60	47	10
6	1456	96	45	12
7	1180	78	44	17
8	710	46	38	7
9	1316	82	70	14
10	1032	94	30	12
11	752	68	29	7
12	963	48	38	14

Exhibit 9.23	Multiple regression results with indirect manufacturing labour costs and two independent variables (machine-hours and production batches) for Møre-Teppe		
Variable	Coefficient (1)	Standard error (2)	t-value (3) = (1) ÷ (2)
Constant	€42.58	€213.91	0.20
Independent variable 1: Machine-hours	€7.60	€2.77	2.74
Independent variable 2: Production batches	€37.77	€15.25	2.48
$r^2 = 0.72$; Durbin–Watson statistic = 2.49.			

regression using machine-hours (Exhibit 9.17) increases to 0.72 with the multiple regression in Exhibit 9.23. The t-values suggest that the independent variable coefficients of both machine-hours and production batches are significantly different from zero ($t = 2.74$ for the coefficient on machine-hours, and $t = 2.48$ for the coefficient on production batches). The multiple regression model in Exhibit 9.23 satisfies both economic and statistical criteria, and it explains much greater variation in indirect manufacturing labour costs than does the simple regression model using only machine-hours as the independent variable. The information in Exhibit 9.23 indicates that both machine-hours and production batches are important cost drivers of monthly indirect manufacturing labour costs at Møre-Teppe.

In Exhibit 9.23, the slope coefficients – €7.60 for machine-hours and €37.77 for production batches – measure the change in indirect manufacturing labour costs associated with a unit change in an independent variable (assuming that the other independent variable is held constant). For example, indirect manufacturing labour costs increase by €37.77 when one more production batch is added, assuming that the number of machine-hours is held constant.

An alternative approach would create two separate cost pools – one for costs tied to machine-hours and another for costs tied to production batches. Møre-Teppe would then estimate the relationship between the cost driver and overhead costs separately for each cost pool. The difficult task under that approach would be properly dividing overhead costs into the two cost pools.

Multicollinearity

A major concern that arises with multiple regression is multicollinearity. **Multicollinearity** exists when two or more independent variables are highly correlated with each other. Generally, users of regression analysis believe that a coefficient of correlation between independent variables greater than 0.70 indicates multicollinearity. Multicollinearity increases the standard errors of the coefficients of the individual variables. The result is that there is greater uncertainty about the underlying value of the coefficients of the individual independent variables. That is, variables that are economically and statistically significant will appear insignificant.

The coefficients of correlation between the potential independent variables for Møre-Teppe in Exhibit 9.22 are:

Pairwise combinations	Coefficient of correlation
Machine-hours and direct manufacturing labour-hours	0.12
Machine-hours and production batches	0.40
Direct manufacturing labour-hours and production batches	0.31

These results indicate that multiple regressions using any pair of the independent variables in Exhibit 9.23 are not likely to encounter multicollinearity problems.

If severe multicollinearity exists, try to obtain new data that does not suffer from multicollinearity problems. Do not drop an independent variable (cost driver) that should be included in a model because it is correlated with another independent variable. Omitting such a variable will cause the estimated coefficient of the independent variable included in the model to be biased away from its true value.

Key terms

linear cost function (245)	**simple regression** (254)
slope coefficient (245)	**multiple regression** (254)
constant (245)	**residual term** (255)
intercept (245)	**non-linear cost function** (258)
mixed cost (246)	**step cost function** (259)
semivariable cost (246)	**learning curve** (260)
cost estimation (247)	**experience curve** (260)
cost predictions (247)	**cumulative average-time learning model** (261)
industrial engineering method (249)	
work-measurement method (249)	**incremental unit-time learning model** (261)
conference method (249)	**coefficient of determination (r^2)** (267)
account analysis method (250)	**standard error of the estimated coefficient** (267)
dependent variable (251)	
independent variable (251)	**specification analysis** (268)
high–low method (253)	**multicollinearity** (273)
regression analysis (254)	

References and further reading

Rees, D.G. (2000) *Essential Statistics*, 4th edn (London: Chapman and Hall).

Greene, W.H. (2000) *Econometric Analysis*, 4th edn (New York: Macmillan).

Watson, C.J., Billingsley, P., Croft, D.J. and Huntsberger, D.V. (1993) *Statistics for Management and Economics*, 5th edn (Needham Heights: Allyn and Bacon).

CHAPTER 9

Assessment material

Review questions

9.1 Describe three alternative linear cost functions.

9.2 What two assumptions are frequently made when estimating a cost function?

9.3 What is the difference between a linear and a non-linear cost function? Give an example of each type of cost function.

9.4 'High correlation between two variables means that one is the cause and the other is the effect.' Do you agree? Explain.

9.5 Name four approaches to estimating a cost function.

9.6 Describe three criteria for evaluating cost functions and choosing cost drivers.

9.7 Define learning curve. Outline two models that can be used when incorporating learning into the estimation of cost functions.

9.8 What are the four key assumptions examined in specification analysis in the case of simple regression?

9.9 'All the independent variables in a cost function estimated with regression analysis are cost drivers.' Do you agree? Explain.

9.10 'Multicollinearity exists when the dependent variable and the independent variable are highly correlated.' Do you agree? Explain.

Exercises

Basic level

*9.11 Estimating a cost function (10 minutes)

The controller of Iso-Metsä Oy wants you to estimate a cost function from the following two observations in a general-ledger account called Maintenance:

Month	Machine-hours	Maintenance costs incurred
January	4000	€3000
February	7000	3900

Required

1 Estimate the cost function for maintenance.

2 Can the constant in the cost function be used as an estimate of fixed maintenance cost per month? Explain.

9.12   Identifying variable, fixed and mixed cost functions (15 minutes)

Bellingwolde BV operates car rental agencies at over 20 airports. Customers can choose from one of three contracts for car rentals of one day or less:

- Contract 1: €50 for the day.
- Contract 2: €30 for the day plus €0.20 per km travelled.
- Contract 3: €1.00 per km travelled.

Required

1 Present separate plots for each of the three contracts, with costs on the vertical axis and kilometres travelled on the horizontal axis.
2 Describe each contract as a linear cost function of the form $y = a + bX$.
3 Describe each contract as a variable, fixed or mixed cost function.

9.13   Matching graphs with descriptions of cost behaviour (20 minutes)

Given below are a number of charts, each indicating some relationship between cost and a cost driver. No attempt has been made to draw these charts to any particular scale; the absolute numbers on each axis may be closely or widely spaced.

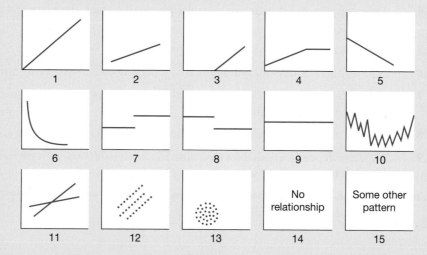

Required

Indicate by number which one of the charts best fits each of the situations or items described. Each situation or item is independent of all the others; all factors not stated are assumed to be irrelevant. Some charts will be used more than once; some may not apply to any of the situations. Note that category 14, 'No relationship', is not the same as 15, 'Some other pattern'.

If the horizontal axis represents the production output over the year and the vertical axis represents total cost or revenue, indicate the one best pattern or relationship for:

1 Direct material costs.
2 Supervisors' salaries.
3 A breakeven chart.
4 Mixed costs – for example, fixed electrical power demand charge plus variable usage rate.
5 Depreciation of plant, calculated on a straight-line basis.
6 Data supporting the use of a variable cost rate, such as manufacturing labour cost of SFr 14 per unit produced.
7 Incentive bonus plan that pays managers SFr 0.10 for every unit produced above some level of production.

8 Interest charges on money borrowed at a fixed rate of interest to finance the acquisition of a plant, before any payments on principal.

Intermediate level

9.14 Account analysis method (20 minutes)

Lorenzo-Netto, Srl, operates a brushless car wash. Incoming cars are put on an automatic, continuously moving conveyor belt. Cars are washed as the conveyor belt carries the car from the start station to the finish station. After the car moves off the conveyor belt, the car is dried manually. Workers then clean and vacuum the inside of the car. Workers are managed by a single supervisor. Lorenzo-Netto serviced 80 000 cars in 2015. Lorenzo-Netto reports the following costs for 2015:

Account description	Costs
Car wash labour	€240 000
Soap, cloth and supplies	32 000
Water	28 000
Power to move conveyor belt	72 000
Depreciation	64 000
Supervision	30 000
Cashier	16 000

Required

1 Classify each account as variable or fixed with respect to cars washed. Explain.

2 Lorenzo-Netto expects to wash 90 000 cars in 2016. Use the cost classification you developed in requirement 1 to estimate Lorenzo-Netto's total costs in 2016.

3 Calculate the average cost of washing a car in 2015 and 2016. (Use the expected 90 000 car wash level for 2016.)

9.15 Linear cost approximation (25 minutes)

Pierre Corneille, managing director of Marre-Quise Consultants SA, is examining how overhead costs behave with variations in monthly professional labour-hours billed to clients. Assume the following historical data:

Total overhead costs	Professional labour-hours billed to clients
€340 000	3000
400 000	4000
435 000	5000
477 000	6000
529 000	7000
587 000	8000

Required

1 Calculate the linear cost function, relating total overhead cost to professional labour-hours, using the representative observations of 4000 and 7000 hours. Plot the linear cost function. Does the constant component of the cost function represent the fixed overhead costs of Marre-Quise Consultants? Why?

2 What would be the predicted total overhead costs for (a) 5000 hours and (b) 8000 hours using the cost function estimated in requirement 1? Plot the predicted costs and actual costs for 5000 and 8000 hours.

3   Corneille had a chance to accept a special job that would have boosted professional labour-hours from 4000 to 5000 hours. Suppose Corneille, guided by the linear cost function, rejected this job because it would have brought a total increase in contribution margin of €38 000, before deducting the predicted increase in total overhead cost, €43 000. What is the total contribution margin actually forgone?

9.16   Regression analysis, service company (CMA, adapted) (25 minutes)

Hans Mehrlich owns a catering company that prepares banquets and parties for both individual and business functions throughout the year. Mehrlich's business is seasonal, with a heavy schedule during the summer months and the year-end holidays and a light schedule at other times. During peak periods there are extra costs.

One of the major events Mehrlich's customers request is a cocktail party. He offers a standard cocktail party and has developed the following cost structure on a per-person basis:

Food and beverages	€15.00
Labour (0.5 hour × €10 per hour)	5.00
Overhead (0.5 hour × €14 per hour)	7.00
Total costs per person	€27.00

Mehrlich is quite certain about his estimates of the food, beverages and labour costs but is not as comfortable with the overhead estimate. This estimate was based on the actual data for the past 12 months presented below. These data indicate that overhead expenses vary with the direct labour-hours expended. The €14 estimate was determined by dividing total overhead expended for the 12 months by total labour-hours.

Month	Labour-hours	Overhead costs
January	2 500	€55 000
February	2 700	59 000
March	3 000	60 000
April	4 200	64 000
May	4 500	67 000
June	5 500	71 000
July	6 500	74 000
August	7 500	77 000
September	7 000	75 000
October	4 500	68 000
November	3 100	62 000
December	6 500	73 000
Total	57 500	€805 000

Mehrlich has recently become aware of regression analysis. He estimated the following regression equation with overhead costs as the dependent variable and labour-hours as the independent variable:

$$y = €48\ 271 + €3.93X$$

Required

1   Plot the relationship between overhead costs and labour-hours. Draw the regression line and evaluate it using the criteria of economic plausibility, goodness of fit and slope of the regression line.

2   Using data from the regression analysis, what is the variable cost per person for a cocktail party?

3 Hans Mehrlich has been asked to prepare a bid for a 200-person cocktail party to be given next month. Determine the minimum bid price that Mehrlich would be willing to submit to earn a positive contribution margin.

9.17 Learning curve, cumulative average-time learning curve (20 minutes)

Genève Défense Systèmes manufactures radar systems. It has just completed the manufacture of its first newly designed system, RS-32. It took 3000 direct manufacturing labour-hours (DMLH) to produce this one unit. Genève Défense Systèmes believes that a 90% cumulative average-time learning model for direct manufacturing labour-hours applies to RS-32. (A 90% learning curve implies $q = -0.1520$.) The variable costs of producing RS-32 are:

Direct materials costs	SFr 80 000 per RS-32
Direct manufacturing labour costs	SFr 25 per DMLH
Variable manufacturing overhead costs	SFr 15 per DMLH

Required

Calculate the total variable costs of producing 2, 4 and 8 units.

9.18 Learning curve, incremental unit-time learning curve (20 minutes)

Assume the same information for Genève Défense Systèmes as in Exercise 9.17 except that Genève Défense Systèmes uses a 90% *incremental unit-time* learning curve as a basis for forecasting direct manufacturing labour-hours. (A 90% learning curve implies $q = -0.1520$.)

Required

1 Calculate the total variable costs of producing 2, 3 and 4 units.

2 If you solved Exercise 9.17, compare your cost predictions in the two exercises for 2 and 4 units. Why are the predictions different?

9.19 Evaluating alternative simple regression models, not for profit (Chapter appendix) (30–40 minutes)

Pauline Raphaël, executive assistant to the principal of Ecole Supérieure des Mines de St Etienne, is concerned about the overhead costs at her university. Cost pressures are severe, so controlling and reducing overheads is very important. Raphaël believes overhead costs incurred are generally a function of the number of different academic programmes (including different specialisations, degrees and research programmes) that the university has and the number of enrolled students. Both have grown significantly over the years. She collects the following data:

Year	Overhead costs ('000)	Number of academic programmes	Number of enrolled students
1	€13 500	29	3400
2	19 200	36	5000
3	16 800	49	2600
4	20 100	53	4700
5	19 500	54	3900
6	23 100	58	4900
7	23 700	88	5700
8	20 100	72	3900
9	22 800	83	3500
10	29 700	73	3700
11	31 200	101	5600
12	38 100	103	7600

She finds the following results for two separate simple regression models:

● *Regression 1.* Overhead costs = $a + (b \times$ Number of academic programmes)

Variable	Coefficient	Standard error	*t*-value
Constant	€7127.75	€3335.34	2.14
Independent variable 1: Number of academic programmes	€240.64	€47.33	5.08

$r^2 = 0.72$; Durbin–Watson statistic = 1.81

● *Regression 2.* Overhead costs = $a + (b \times$ Number of enrolled students)

Variable	Coefficient	Standard error	*t*-value
Constant	€5991.75	€5067.88	1.18
Independent variable 1: Number of enrolled students	€3.78	€1.07	3.53

$r^2 = 0.55$; Durbin–Watson statistic = 0.77

Required

1 Plot the relationship between overhead costs and each of the following variables: (a) number of academic programmes, and (b) number of enrolled students.

2 Compare and evaluate the two simple regression models estimated by Raphaël. Use the comparison format employed in Exhibit 9.20.

3 What insights do the analyses provide about controlling and reducing overhead costs at the Ecole Supérieure?

*9.20   Evaluating multiple regression models, not for profit (continuation of Exercise 9.19) (Chapter appendix) (30 minutes)

Required

1 Given your findings in Exercise 9.19, should Raphaël use multiple regression analysis to better understand the cost drivers of overhead costs? Explain your answer.

2 Raphaël decides that the simple regression analysis in Exercise 9.19 should be extended to a multiple regression analysis. She finds the following result:

● *Regression 3.* Overhead costs = $a + (b_1 \times$ Number of academic programmes) + $(b_2 \times$ Number of enrolled students)

Variable	Coefficient	Standard error	*t*-value
Constant	€2779.62	€3620.05	0.77
Independent variable 1: Number of academic programmes	€178.37	€51.54	3.46
Independent variable 2: Number of enrolled students	€1.87	€0.92	2.03

$r^2 = 0.81$; Durbin–Watson statistic = 1.84

The coefficient of correlation between number of academic programmes and number of students is 0.60. Use the format in Exhibit 9.21 to evaluate the multiple regression model.

(Assume linearity, and constant variance and normality of residuals.) Should Raphaël choose the multiple regression model over the two simple regression models of Exercise 9.19?

3 How might the principal of the Ecole Supérieure use these regression results to manage overhead costs?

Advanced level

*9.21 High–low and regression approaches (Chapter appendix) (30–40 minutes)

Bildt-Östersund AN wishes to set a flexible budget for its power costs, which are primarily a function of machine-hours worked. Data for the first four periods follows:

Period	Power costs (Y)	Machine-hours (X)
1	SKr 350	200
2	450	300
3	300	100
4	500	400

Required

1 Plot the relationship between power costs and machine-hours.

2 Calculate the constant a and slope coefficient b of the function $y = a + bX$ using (i) the high–low approach, and (ii) the regression approach. Comment on the results.

3 For the regression approach, calculate the coefficient of determination, r^2. Comment on the result.

CHAPTER 10

Relevant information for decision making

The provision of decision-relevant information is one important function of the management accountant. In this chapter, we focus on decisions such as accepting or rejecting a one-time-only special order, insourcing or outsourcing products or services, and replacing or keeping equipment. We stress the importance of distinguishing between relevant and irrelevant items in making these decisions.

Learning objectives

After studying this chapter, you should be able to:

- Describe a five-step sequence in the decision process

- Differentiate relevant costs and revenues from irrelevant costs and revenues

- Distinguish between quantitative factors and qualitative factors in decisions

- Identify two potential problems in relevant-cost analysis

- Describe the opportunity cost concept; explain why it is used in decision making

- Describe the key concept in choosing which among multiple products to produce when there are capacity constraints

- Explain why the book value of equipment is irrelevant in equipment-replacement decisions

Information and the decision process

Managers often adopt a personalised approach for deciding among different courses of action. The approach may be highly stylised, informal and subjective. It will also draw differentially on formally structured information. A decision model is here taken to signify a formal method for making a choice, frequently involving quantitative and qualitative analyses. Accountants aim to supply managers with relevant data to guide their decisions. This information is usually structured and acts as an input to decision making which will rely also on other information forms.

Consider a decision that Home Appliances, a manufacturer of vacuum cleaners, faces: Should it rearrange a manufacturing assembly line to reduce manufacturing labour costs? For simplicity, assume that the only alternatives are 'do not rearrange' and 'rearrange'. The rearrangement will eliminate all manual handling of materials. The current manufacturing line uses 20 workers – 15 workers operate machines, and 5 workers handle materials. Each worker puts in 2000 hours annually. The rearrangement is predicted to cost €90 000. The predicted production output of 25 000 units for the next year will be unaffected by the decision. Also unaffected by the decision are the predicted selling price per unit of €250, direct materials costs per unit of €50, other manufacturing overhead of € 750 000, and marketing costs of €2 000 000. The cost driver is units of production.

To make the decision, management may hypothetically proceed in a sequence of steps. The first step is to gather more information about manufacturing labour costs. The historical manufacturing labour rate of €14 per hour is the starting point for predicting total manufacturing labour costs under both alternatives. The manufacturing labour rate is expected to increase to €16 per hour following a recently negotiated increase in employee benefits.

The second step is to predict future costs under the two alternatives. Predicted manufacturing labour costs under the 'do not rearrange' alternative are 20 workers × 2000 hours × €16 per hour = €640 000. Predicted manufacturing labour costs under the 'rearrange' alternative are 15 workers × 2000 hours × €16 per hour = €480 000. Predicted costs of rearrangement are €90 000.

As the third step, Home Appliances' management compares the predicted savings from eliminating materials handling labour costs (5 workers × 2000 hours × €16 per hour) = €160 000 to the costs of rearrangement of €90 000. It also takes into account other qualitative considerations such as the effect that reducing the number of workers will have on employee morale. After weighing the costs and benefits, management chooses the 'rearrange' alternative. Management next implements the decision in the fourth step by rearranging the manufacturing assembly line.

As the fifth and final step, management gathers information about the actual results of the plant rearrangement to evaluate performance and to provide feedback. Actual results show that the new manufacturing labour costs are €550 000 (due to, say, lower than expected manufacturing labour productivity) rather than the predicted €480 000. This feedback may lead to better implementation through, for example, a change in supervisory behaviour, employee training or personnel so that the €480 000 target is achieved in subsequent periods. However, the feedback may convince the decision maker that the prediction method, rather than the implementation, was faulty. Perhaps the prediction method for similar decisions in the future should be modified to allow for worker training or learning time.

Exhibit 10.1 summarises the five-step decision process that we just described: gathering information, making predictions, choosing an alternative, implementing the decision, and evaluating actual performance to provide feedback. The feedback, in turn, might affect future predictions, the prediction method itself, the decision model or the implementation.

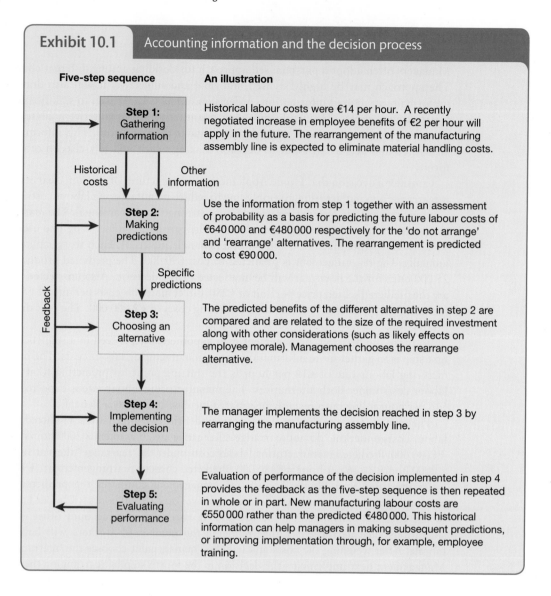

Exhibit 10.1 | Accounting information and the decision process

Five-step sequence   **An illustration**

Step 1: Gathering information

Historical labour costs were €14 per hour. A recently negotiated increase in employee benefits of €2 per hour will apply in the future. The rearrangement of the manufacturing assembly line is expected to eliminate material handling costs.

Historical costs   *Other information*

Step 2: Making predictions

Use the information from step 1 together with an assessment of probability as a basis for predicting the future labour costs of €640 000 and €480 000 respectively for the 'do not arrange' and 'rearrange' alternatives. The rearrangement is predicted to cost €90 000.

Specific predictions

Step 3: Choosing an alternative

The predicted benefits of the different alternatives in step 2 are compared and are related to the size of the required investment along with other considerations (such as likely effects on employee morale). Management chooses the rearrange alternative.

Step 4: Implementing the decision

The manager implements the decision reached in step 3 by rearranging the manufacturing assembly line.

Step 5: Evaluating performance

Evaluation of performance of the decision implemented in step 4 provides the feedback as the five-step sequence is then repeated in whole or in part. New manufacturing labour costs are €550 000 rather than the predicted €480 000. This historical information can help managers in making subsequent predictions, or improving implementation through, for example, employee training.

Feedback

The concept of relevance

Relevant costs and relevant revenues

The most important decision-making concepts in this chapter are relevant costs and relevant revenues. **Relevant costs** are those *expected future costs* that differ among alternative courses of action. The two key aspects to this definition are that the costs must occur in the future and that they must differ among the alternative courses of action. We focus on the future because *every decision deals with the future – nothing can be done to alter the past.* Also, the future costs must differ among the alternatives because if they do not, there will be no difference in costs no matter what decision is made. Likewise, **relevant revenues** are those expected future revenues that differ among alternative courses of action.

In Exhibit 10.2, the €640 000 and €480 000 manufacturing labour costs are relevant costs – they are expected future costs that differ between the two alternatives. The past manufacturing labour rate of €14 per hour and total past manufacturing labour costs of €560 000 (2000 hours × 20 workers × €14 per hour) are not relevant, even though they may play a role in preparing the

€640 000 and €480 000 labour cost predictions. Although they may be a useful basis for making informed judgements for predicting expected future costs, historical costs in themselves are irrelevant to a decision. Why? Because they deal strictly with the past, not the future.

Exhibit 10.2 presents the quantitative data underlying the choice between the 'do not rearrange' and the 'rearrange' alternatives. The first two columns present all data. The last two columns present only relevant costs or revenues. The revenues, direct materials, manufacturing overhead and marketing items can be ignored. Why? Because although they are expected future costs, they do not differ between the alternatives. They are thus irrelevant. The data in Exhibit 10.2 indicate that rearranging the production line will increase next year's predicted operating profit by €70 000. Note that we reach the same conclusion whether we use all data or include only the relevant data in the analysis. By confining the analysis to only the relevant data, managers can clear away related but irrelevant data that might confuse them.

The difference in total cost between two alternatives is a **differential cost**. The differential cost between alternatives 1 and 2 in Exhibit 10.2 is €70 000.

Exhibit 10.2	Determining relevant revenues and relevant costs for Home Appliances			
	All data		**Relevant data**	
	Alternative 1: Do not rearrange	**Alternative 2: Rearrange**	**Alternative 1: Do not rearrange**	**Alternative 2: Rearrange**
Revenues*	€6 250 000	€6 250 000	–	–
			–	–
Costs				
Direct materials[†]	1 250 000	1 250 000	–	–
Manufacturing labour	640 000[‡]	480 000[§]	€640 000[‡]	€480 000[§]
Manufacturing overhead	750 000	750 000	–	–
Marketing	2 000 000	2 000 000	–	–
Rearrangement costs	–	90 000	–	90 000
Total costs	4 640 000	4 570 000	640 000	570 000
Operating profit	€1 610 000	€1 680 000	€(640 000)	€(570 000)
	€70 000 difference		€70 000 difference	

* 25 000 × €250 = €6 250 000.
[†] 25 000 × €50 = €1 250 000.
[‡] 20 × 2000 × €16 = €640 000.
[§] 15 × 2000 × €16 = €480 000.

Qualitative factors can be relevant

We divide the consequences of alternatives into two broad categories: quantitative and qualitative. **Quantitative factors** are outcomes that are measured in numerical terms. Some quantitative factors are financial, that is, they can be easily expressed in financial terms. Examples include the costs of direct materials, direct manufacturing labour and marketing. Other quantitative factors are non-financial, that is, they can be measured numerically, but they are not expressed in financial terms. Reduction in page download time for an Internet company and the percentage of on-time flight arrivals for an airline company are examples of quantitative, non-financial factors. **Qualitative factors** are outcomes that cannot be measured in numerical terms. Employee morale is an example.

Cost analysis generally emphasises quantitative factors that can be expressed in financial terms. But just because qualitative factors and non-financial quantitative factors cannot be easily measured in financial terms does not make them unimportant. Managers must at times give more weight to qualitative or non-financial quantitative factors. For example, Home Appliances may find that it can purchase a part from an outside supplier at a price that is lower than what it costs to manufacture the part in-house. Home Appliances may still choose to make the part in-house because it feels that the supplier is unlikely to meet the demanding delivery schedule – a quantitative non-financial factor – and because purchasing the part from outside may adversely affect employee morale – a qualitative factor. Trading off non-financial and financial considerations, however, is seldom easy.

An illustration of relevance: choosing output levels

Managers often make decisions that affect output levels. For example, managers must choose whether to introduce a new product or sell more units of an existing product. When changes in output levels occur, managers are interested in the effect it has on the organisation and on operating profit. Why? Because maximising organisational objectives (typically operating profit in our illustrations) also increases managers' rewards.

One-off special orders

Management sometimes faces the decision of accepting or rejecting one-off special orders when there is idle production capacity and where the order has no long-run implications. We assume that all costs can be classified as either variable with respect to a single driver (units of output) or fixed. The following example illustrates how focusing on revenues, variable costs and contribution margins can provide key information for decisions about the choice of output level. The example also indicates how reliance on unit-cost numbers calculated after allocating fixed costs can mislead managers about the effect that increasing output has on operating profit.

Exhibit 10.3 presents data in an absorption-costing format: fixed manufacturing costs are included as product costs. The manufacturing cost per unit is €12 (€7.50 of which is variable and €4.50 of which is fixed), which is above the €11 price offered by the hotel chain. Using the €12 absorption cost as a guide in decision making, a manager might reject the offer.

Example 10.1

Huber GmbH manufactures quality bath towels at its highly automated Heidelberg plant. The plant has a production capacity of 48 000 towels each month. Current monthly production is 30 000 towels. Retail department stores account for all existing sales. Expected results for the coming month (August) are shown in Exhibit 10.3. (Note that these amounts are predictions.) The manufacturing costs per unit of €12 consist of direct materials €6 (all variable), direct manufacturing labour €2 (€0.50 of which is variable), and manufacturing overhead €4 (€1 of which is variable). The marketing costs per unit are €7 (€5 of which is variable). Huber GmbH has no R&D costs or product-design costs. Marketing costs include distribution costs and customer-service costs.

A luxury hotel chain offers to buy 5000 towels per month at €11 a towel for each of the next three months. No subsequent sales to this customer are anticipated. No marketing costs will be necessary for the 5000-unit one-off special order. The acceptance of this special order is not expected to affect the selling price or the quantity of towels sold to regular customers. Should Huber GmbH accept the hotel chain's offer?

Exhibit 10.3	Budgeted income statement for August, absorption-costing format for Huber GmbH	

	Total	Per unit
Sales (30 000 towels × €20)	€600 000	€20
Cost of goods sold	360 000	12
Gross margin (gross profit)	240 000	8
Marketing costs	210 000	7
Operating profit	€30 000	€1

Exhibit 10.4 presents data in a contribution income statement format. The relevant costs are the expected future costs that differ between the alternatives – the variable manufacturing costs of €37 500 (€7.50 per unit × 5000 units). The fixed manufacturing costs and all marketing costs (including variable marketing costs) are irrelevant in this case; they will not change in total whether or not the special order is accepted. Therefore, the only relevant items here are sales revenues and variable manufacturing costs. Given the €11 relevant revenue per unit (the special-order price) and the €7.50 relevant costs per unit, Huber would gain an additional €17 500 [(€11.00 − €7.50) × 5000] in operating profit per month by accepting the special order. In this example, comparisons based on either total amounts or relevant amounts (Exhibit 10.4) avoid the misleading implication of the absorption cost per unit (Exhibit 10.3).

Exhibit 10.4	Comparative income statements for August, contribution income statement format for Huber GmbH			

	Without one-off special order, 30 000 units		With one-off special order, 35 000 units	Difference, 5000 units
	Per unit	Total	Total	Total
Sales	€20.00	€600 000	€655 000	€55 000[†]
Variable costs				
Manufacturing	7.50*	225 000	262 500	37 500[§]
Marketing	5.00	150 000	150 000	–[‖]
Total variable costs	12.50	375 000	412 500	37 500
Contribution margin	7.50	225 000	242 500	17 500
Fixed costs				
Manufacturing	4.50[†]	135 000	135 000	–[#]
Marketing	2.00	60 000	60 000	–[#]
Total fixed costs	6.50	195 000	195 000	–
Operating profit	€1.00	€30 000	€47 500	€17 500

* Variable manufacturing costs = direct materials, €6 + direct manufacturing labour, €0.50 + manufacturing overhead, €1 = €7.50.
[†] Fixed manufacturing costs = direct manufacturing labour, €1.50 + manufacturing overhead, €3 = €4.50.
[‡] 5000 × €11.00 = €55 000.
[§] 5000 × €7.50 = €37 500.
[‖] No variable marketing costs would be incurred for the 5000-unit one-off special order.
[#] Fixed manufacturing costs and fixed marketing costs are also unaffected by the special order.

The additional costs of €7.50 per unit that Huber will incur if it accepts the special order for 5000 towels are sometimes called **incremental costs**. Incremental costs are additional costs to obtain an additional quantity, over and above existing or planned quantities, of a cost object. Huber could avoid these costs if it did not accept the special order. Huber incurs no incremental fixed manufacturing costs if it accepts the special order; those costs will not change whether or not the special order is accepted. Fixed manufacturing costs do not change because the analysis in Exhibit 10.4 assumes that the 5000-towel special order will use already acquired capacity that will otherwise remain idle for each of the next three months.

The assumption of no long-run or strategic implications is crucial in the analysis we present for the one-off special order decision. Suppose, for example, that Huber is concerned that the retail department stores (its regular customers) will demand a lower price if it sells towels at €11 each to the luxury hotel chain. In this case, the analysis of the luxury hotel chain order must be modified to consider both the short-term benefits from accepting the order and the long-term consequences on Huber's business and profitability.

Potential problems in relevant-cost analysis

It is important in relevant-cost analysis not to assume that all variable costs are relevant. In the Huber GmbH example, the marketing costs of €5 per unit are variable but not relevant. Why? Because for the special-order decision, Huber incurs no extra marketing costs.

Similarly, it is important not to assume that all fixed costs are irrelevant. Consider fixed manufacturing costs. In our example, we assume that the extra production of 5000 towels per month does not affect fixed manufacturing costs. That is, we assume that the relevant range is at least between 30 000 and 35 000 towels per month. In some cases, however, the extra 5000 towels might increase fixed manufacturing costs. Assume that Huber would have to run three shifts of 16 000 towels per shift to achieve full capacity of 48 000 towels per month. Increasing the monthly production from 30 000 to 35 000 would require a partial third shift because two shifts alone could produce only 32 000 towels. This extra shift would probably increase fixed manufacturing costs, thereby making any partial additional fixed manufacturing costs relevant for this decision.

The best way to avoid these problems is to require each item included in the analysis *both* (1) to be an expected future revenue or cost, and (2) to differ among the alternatives. Note also that unit-cost data mislead decision makers in two major ways: (a) when costs that are irrelevant to a particular decision are included in unit costs, and (b) when unit costs that are calculated at different output levels are used to choose among alternatives. Unitised fixed costs are often erroneously interpreted as if they behave like unit variable costs. Generally, use total costs rather than unit costs in relevant-cost analysis.

Outsourcing and make-or-buy decisions

We now consider the strategic decision of whether a company should make a part or buy it from a supplier. We again assume idle capacity.

Outsourcing and idle facilities

Outsourcing is the process of purchasing goods and services from outside vendors rather than producing the same goods or providing the same services within the organisation, which is called **insourcing**. Outsourcing is an increasingly common practice. Yahoo! uses Hewlett-Packard's E-Services Division for sales, marketing, system integration, and ongoing customer support. Hallmark UK, the greetings card manufacturer, outsourced 80% of its card production to the Far East in 2014. Likewise, BlackBerry, which recorded record losses in 2013, took the decision to outsource its hardware business to Foxcom, the Taiwanese electronics manufacturer which also acts as an outsourcee for Apple Inc. and Amazon.com. Similarly, Sears Canada decided to outsource jobs in call centres to IBM after extensive losses in 2013. Toyota relies on outside suppliers to supply some parts and components but chooses to manufacture other parts internally. The BBC likewise outsources much of its accounting-based activities as does British Airways. Saab, too, prefers an outside firm to undertake part of its finance function. In making decisions about outsourcing and insourcing, cost is a major factor.

Decisions about whether a producer of goods or services will insource or outsource are also called **make-or-buy decisions**. Often qualitative factors dictate management's make-or-buy decision.

In the Brumaire SA example described here, assume that financial factors predominate in the make-or-buy decision. The question we address is: What financial factors are relevant?

Brumaire SA manufactures thermostats for home and industrial use. Thermostats consist of relays, switches and valves. Brumaire makes its own switches. Columns 1 and 2 of Exhibit 10.5 report the current costs for its heavy-duty switch (HDS) based on an analysis of its various manufacturing activities.

Materials handling and set-up activities occur each time a batch of HDS is made. Brumaire produces the 10 000 units of HDS in 25 batches of 400 units each. The cost driver is the number of batches. Total materials handling and set-up consist of fixed costs of €5000 plus variable costs of €500 per batch, amounting to €5000 + 25 × €500 = €17 500. Brumaire only commences production after it receives a firm customer order. Brumaire's customers are pressuring the company to supply thermostats in smaller batch sizes. Brumaire anticipates that next year, the 10 000 units of HDS will be manufactured in 50 batches of 200 units each. Through continuous improvement, Brumaire expects to reduce variable costs per batch for materials handling and set-up costs to €300 per batch. No other changes in fixed costs or unit variable costs are anticipated.

Another manufacturer offers to sell Brumaire 10 000 units of HDS next year for €16 per unit on whatever delivery schedule Brumaire wants. Should Brumaire make or buy the part?

Columns 3 and 4 of Exhibit 10.5 indicate the expected total costs and the expected per unit cost of producing 10 000 units of HDS next year. Direct materials, direct manufacturing labour, and variable manufacturing overhead costs that vary with units produced are not expected to change since Brumaire plans to continue to produce 10 000 units next year at the same variable costs per unit as this year. The costs of materials handling and set-ups are expected to increase

Exhibit 10.5	Financial data for HDS manufacturing at Brumaire SA			
	Total current costs of producing 10 000 units (1)	**Current cost per unit (2) = (1) ÷ 10 000**	**Expected total costs of producing 10 000 units next year (3)**	**Expected cost per unit (4) = (3) ÷ 10 000**
Direct materials	€80 000	€8.00	€80 000	€8
Direct manufacturing labour	10 000	1.00	10 000	1
Variable manufacturing overhead costs for power and utilities	40 000	4.00	40 000	4
Mixed overhead costs of materials handling and set-ups	17 500	1.75	20 000	2
Fixed overhead costs of plant depreciation, insurance and administration	30 000	3.00	30 000	3
Total manufacturing costs	€177 500	€17.75	€180 000	€18

even though there is no expected change in the total production quantity. Why? Because these costs vary with the number of batches started, not the quantity of production. Expected total materials handling and set-up costs = €5000 + 50 batches × the cost per batch of €300 = €5000 + €15 000 = €20 000. Brumaire expects fixed overhead costs to remain the same. The expected manufacturing cost per unit equals €18. At this cost, it seems that the company should buy HDS from the outside supplier because making the part appears to be more costly than the €16 per unit to buy it. A make-or-buy decision, however, is rarely obvious. A key question for management is: What is the difference in relevant costs between the alternatives?

For the moment, suppose the capacity now used to make HDS will become idle if HDS is purchased and that the €30 000 of fixed manufacturing overhead will continue to be incurred next year, regardless of the decision made. Assume that the €5000 in fixed clerical salaries to support set-up, receiving and purchasing will not be incurred if the manufacture of HDS is completely shut down. Further suppose that the €30 000 in plant depreciation, insurance and administration costs represents fixed manufacturing overhead that will not vary regardless of the decision made.

Exhibit 10.6 presents the relevant cost calculations. Brumaire saves €10 000 by making HDS rather than buying it from the outside supplier. Alternatively stated, purchasing HDS costs €160 000 but saves only €150 000 in manufacturing costs. Making HDS is thus the preferred alternative. Exhibit 10.6 excludes the €30 000 of plant depreciation, insurance and administration costs under both the make and the buy alternatives. Why? Because these costs are irrelevant; they do not differ between the two alternatives. Alternatively, the €30 000 could be included under both alternatives since the €30 000 will continue to be incurred whether HDS is bought or made. Exhibit 10.6 includes the €20 000 of materials handling and set-up costs under the make alternative but not under the buy alternative. Why? Because buying HDS and not having to manufacture it saves both the variable costs per batch and the avoidable fixed costs. The €20 000 of costs differ between the alternatives and hence are relevant to the make-or-buy decision.

In Exhibit 10.6, the incremental cost of making HDS is the additional cost of €150 000. Likewise, the incremental cost of buying HDS from an outside supplier is the additional cost of €160 000. The differential cost between making and buying HDS is €10 000. Note that, in practice, incremental and differential costs are often used interchangeably.

Exhibit 10.6	Relevant (incremental) items for make-or-buy decision for HDS at Brumaire SA			
	Total relevant costs		**Per unit relevant costs**	
Relevant items	Make	Buy	Make	Buy
Outside purchase of parts		€160 000		€16
Direct materials	€80 000		€8	
Direct manufacturing labour	10 000		1	
Variable manufacturing overhead	40 000		4	
Mixed materials handling and set-up overhead*	20 000		2	
Total relevant costs	€150 000	€160 000	€15	€16
Difference in favour of making HDS	€10 000		€1	

* Alternatively, the €30 000 of depreciation, plant insurance and plant administration costs could be included under both alternatives. These are, however, irrelevant to the decision.

The figures in Exhibit 10.6 are valid only if the released facilities remain idle. If the component part is bought from the outside supplier, the released facilities can potentially be used for other, more profitable purposes. More generally, then, the choice in our example is not fundamentally whether to make or buy, it is how best to use available facilities.

The use of otherwise idle resources can often increase profitability. For example, consider the machine-repair plant of Beijing Engineering, where the decision was whether to drop or keep a product. The *China Daily* noted that workers were 'busy producing electric plaster-spraying machines' even though the unit cost exceeded the selling price. According to the prevailing method of calculating its cost, each sprayer costs 1230 yuan to make. However, each sprayer sells for only 985 yuan, resulting in a loss of 245 yuan per sprayer. Still, to meet market demand, the plant continues to produce sprayers. Workers and machines would otherwise be idle, and the plant would still have to pay 759 yuan even if no sprayers were made. In the short run, the production of sprayers, even at a loss, actually helps cut the company's operating loss.

Opportunity costs, outsourcing and capacity constraints

Reconsider the Brumaire SA example where we assumed that the capacity currently used to make HDS became idle if the parts were purchased. Suppose instead that Brumaire has alternative uses for the extra capacity. The best available alternative is for Brumaire to use the capacity to produce 5000 units each year of a regular switch (RS) that Ventôse SA wants. Charlotte de Calonne, the accountant at Brumaire, estimates the following future revenues and future costs if RS is manufactured and sold:

Expected additional future revenues		€80 000
Expected additional future costs		
Direct materials	€30 000	
Direct manufacturing labour	5 000	
Variable overhead (power, utilities)	15 000	
Materials handling and set-up overheads	5 000	
Total expected additional future costs		55 000
Expected additional operating profit		€25 000

Since Brumaire cannot make both HDS and RS, the three alternatives available to management are as follows:

1 Make HDS and do not make RS for Ventôse.

2 Buy HDS and do not make RS for Ventôse.

3 Buy HDS and use excess capacity to make and sell RS to Ventôse.

Exhibit 10.7, Panel A, summarises the 'total-alternatives' approach – the incremental expected future costs and expected future revenues for *all* alternatives. Buying HDS and using the excess capacity to make RS and sell it to Ventôse is the preferred alternative. The incremental costs of buying HDS from an outside supplier are more than the incremental costs of making HDS in-house (€160 000 to buy versus €150 000 to make). But the capacity freed up by buying HDS from the outside supplier enables Brumaire to gain €25 000 in operating profit (expected additional future revenues of €80 000 minus expected additional future costs of €55 000) by making RS and selling to Ventôse. The total relevant costs of buying HDS (and making and selling RS) are €160 000 − €25 000 = €135 000.

Deciding to use a resource in a particular way causes a manager to give up the opportunity to use the resource in alternative ways. The lost opportunity is a cost that the manager must take into account when making a decision. **Opportunity cost** is the contribution to income that is forgone (rejected) by not using a limited resource in its next-best alternative use.

Exhibit 10.7	Total-alternatives approach and opportunity-costs approach to make-or-buy decisions for Brumaire

Panel A: Total-alternatives approach to make-or-buy decisions

	Choices for Brumaire		
Relevant items	Make HDS and do not make RS	Buy HDS and do not make RS	Buy HDS and make RS
Total incremental costs of making/buying HDS (from Exhibit 10.6)	€150 000	€160 000	€160 000
Excess of future revenues over future costs from RS	0	0	(25 000)
Total relevant costs	€150 000	€160 000	€135 000

Panel B: Opportunity-costs approach to make-or-buy decisions

	Choices for Brumaire	
Relevant items	Make HDS	Buy HDS
Total incremental costs of making/buying HDS (from Exhibit 10.6)	€150 000	€160 000
Opportunity cost: Profit contribution forgone because capacity cannot be used to make RS, the next-best alternative	25 000	0
Total relevant costs	€175 000	€160 000
Difference in favour of buying HDS	€15 000	

Exhibit 10.7, Panel B, displays the opportunity-costs approach for analysing the alternatives faced by Brumaire. Management focuses on the two alternatives before it: whether to make or buy HDS. It does not explicitly include RS in the analysis. Focus first on the make HDS column and ask what are all the costs of choosing this alternative? Certainly, Brumaire incurs €150 000 of incremental costs to make HDS. But is this the entire cost? No, because by using limited manufacturing resources to make HDS, Brumaire gives up the opportunity to earn €25 000 from not using these resources to make RS. Therefore, the relevant costs of making HDS are the incremental costs of €150 000 plus the opportunity cost of €25 000. Next consider the buy alternative. The incremental costs are €160 000. The opportunity cost is zero because choosing this alternative does not require the use of a limited resource – Brumaire's manufacturing capacity is still available to make and sell RS. Panel B leads management to the same conclusion as Panel A does – buying HDS is the preferred alternative by an amount of €15 000.

Panels A and B of Exhibit 10.7 describe two consistent approaches to decision making with capacity constraints. The total-alternatives approach in Panel A includes only incremental costs and benefits and no opportunity costs. Why? Because the incremental benefit from making RS when HDS is bought is explicitly considered under the alternatives. Panel B does not explicitly consider the incremental benefits from selling RS. Instead, it factors in the forgone benefit as a cost of the make alternative. Panel B highlights the idea that when capacity is constrained, relevant costs equal the incremental costs plus the opportunity cost.

Opportunity costs are seldom incorporated into formal financial accounting reports because these costs do not entail cash receipts or disbursements. Accountants usually confine their systematic recording to costs that require cash disbursements currently or in the near future.

Historical record keeping is limited to alternatives selected rather than those rejected, because once rejected, there are no transactions to record. For example, if Brumaire makes HDS, it would not make RS, and it would not record any accounting entries for RS. Yet the opportunity cost of making HDS, which equals the profit contribution that Brumaire forgoes by not making RS, is a crucial input into the make-versus-buy decision. Consider again Exhibit 10.7, Panel B. On the basis of incremental costs alone, the costs systematically recorded in the accounting system, it is less costly for Brumaire to make rather than buy HDS. Recognising the opportunity cost of €25 000 leads to a different conclusion. It is preferable to buy HDS.

Suppose Brumaire has sufficient excess capacity to make RS (and indeed any other part) even if it makes HDS. Under this assumption, the opportunity cost of making HDS is zero. Why? Because Brumaire gives up nothing even if it chooses to manufacture HDS. It follows from Panel B (substituting opportunity costs equal to zero) that, under these conditions, Brumaire would prefer to make HDS.

Our analysis emphasises purely quantitative considerations. The final decision, however, should consider qualitative factors as well. For example, before deciding to buy HDS from an outside supplier, Brumaire management will consider such qualitative factors as the supplier's reputation for quality and the supplier's dependability for on-time delivery.

Carrying costs of stock

The notion of opportunity cost can also be illustrated for a direct-materials purchase-order decision. Suppose Nøkleby, AS, has enough cash to pay for whatever quantity of direct materials it buys.

Annual estimated direct-materials requirements for the year	120 000 kg
Cost per kg for purchase orders below 120 000 kg	€10.00
Cost per kg for purchase orders equal to or greater than 120 000 kg; €10.00 minus 2% discount	€9.80
Alternatives under consideration:	
A. Buy 120 000 kg at start of year	
B. Buy 10 000 kg per month	
Average investment in stock:	
A. (120 000 kg × €9.80) ÷ 2*	€588 000
B. (10 000 kg × €10.00) ÷ 2*	€50 000
Annual interest rate for investment in government bonds	6%

* The example assumes that the direct materials purchased will be used up uniformly at the rate of 10 000 kg per month. If direct materials are purchased at the start of the year (month), the average investment in stock during the year is the cost of the stock at the beginning of the year (month) plus the cost of stock at the end of the year (month) divided by 2.

The following table presents the two alternatives.

	Alternative A: Purchase 120 000 kg at beginning of year (1)	Alternative B: Purchase 10 000 kg at beginning of each month (2)	Difference (3) = (1) − (2)
Annual purchase (incremental) costs (120 000 × €9.80; 120 000 × €10)	€1 176 000	€1 200 000	€(24 000)
Annual interest income that could be earned if investment in stock were invested in government bonds (opportunity cost) (6% × €588 000; 6% × €50 000)	35 280	3 000	32 280
Relevant costs	€1 211 280	€1 203 000	€8 280

The opportunity cost of holding stock is the income forgone from not investing this money elsewhere. These opportunity costs would not be recorded in the accounting system because they are not incremental or outlay costs. Column 3 indicates that, consistent with the trends towards holding smaller stocks as in just-in-time systems (see Chapter 21), purchasing 10 000 kg per month is preferred to purchasing 120 000 kg at the beginning of the year because the lower opportunity cost of holding smaller stock exceeds the higher purchase cost. If other incremental benefits of holding lower stock such as lower insurance, materials handling, storage, obsolescence and breakage costs were considered, alternative B would be preferred even more.

Concepts in action   VW takes outsourcing to the limit

Volkwagen's bus and truck plant in Resende, Brazil, is a virtual plant: VW has completely outsourced manufacturing to a team of carefully selected supplier-partners in a radical experiment in production operations. At Resende, VW is transformed from manufacturer to general contractor, overseeing assembly operations performed by seven German, US, Brazilian and Japanese components suppliers, with not one VW employee so much as turning a screw. Only 200 of the total 1000 Resende workers are actual VW employees.

When designing the Resende plant, VW asked suppliers to bid for the opportunity to own one of seven major modules required to build a car, such as axles and brakes or engine and transmission. Suppliers have invested US$50 million to build, equip and stock their areas. VW's contract with suppliers is for 10- to 15-year periods, with the conditions that suppliers must achieve specified cost and performance targets and maintain cutting-edge technologies.

The plant is divided into seven zones, demarcated by yellow floor stripes. Within the boundaries of its zone, each supplier assembles its component from subcomponents sourced from 400 minor suppliers. In parallel with subcomponent assembly, final assembly occurs as the chassis (the vehicle platform) passes through the zones, and each company adds its respective component-module until the finished VW rolls off the line. Following each vehicle through the line is a single VW employee – a master craftsman assigned to track the vehicle and solve problems on the spot. Suppliers are paid for each completed vehicle that passes final inspection.

Despite representing seven different companies, the suppliers operate as a tightly integrated team, wearing the same uniforms and receiving the same pay. The assembly line is highly cross-functional, with representatives from each supplier meeting each morning to plan the day's production and each evening to address issues and solve any problems. Each supplier has visibility of the entire production process, which stimulates ideas for simplification, streamlining, and product and process changes.

The specialisation and component knowledge of each supplier, combined with the close interaction among suppliers, improves quality and efficiency. Locating the major component and final assemblies together at the same plant improves production flow and compresses total assembly time. It also simplifies logistics and reduces materials-handling, production control, manufacturing engineering and coordination costs.

Although the plant has made some adjustments that make its operations more conventional, preliminary results look promising. Resende employs 1500 manufacturing workers, instead of 2500 at a comparable older VW plant. The time to assemble a truck has been reduced from 52 to 35 hours. These improvements have enabled VW to quickly earn more than a 20% share in the Brazilian truck and bus markets.

Sources: Schemo, D.J. (1996) 'Is VW's new plant lean, or just mean?', *New York Times*, 19 November; Friedland, J. (1996) 'VW puts suppliers on production lines', *The Wall Street Journal*, 15 February; Goering, L. (1997) 'Revolution at plant X', *Chicago Tribune*, 13 April; Sedgwick, D. (2000) 'Just what does an automaker make?', *Automotive News International*, 1 September; 'Mercedes and VW fight from factory floor up', *Gazeta Mercantil Online*, 4 April 2001; and Arellano, J. (2006) 'Is outsourcing bad for Volkswagen?', www.autoblog.com/tag/outsourcing, 6 March.

Product-mix decisions under capacity constraints

Companies with capacity constraints, such as Brumaire, must also often decide which products to make and in what quantities. When a multiple-product plant operates at full capacity, managers must often make decisions regarding which products to emphasise. These decisions frequently have a short-run focus. For example, BMW must continually adapt the mix of its different models of cars to short-run fluctuations in materials costs, selling prices and demand. Throughout this section, we assume that as short-run changes in product mix occur, the only costs that change are those that are variable with respect to the number of units produced (and sold).

Analysis of individual product contribution margins provides insight into the product mix that maximises operating profit. Consider Tiilikainen, a company that manufactures engines for a broad range of commercial and consumer products. At its Helsinki plant, it assembles two engines: a snowmobile engine and a boat engine. Information on these products is as follows:

	Snowmobile engine	Boat engine
Selling price	€800	€1000
Variable costs per unit	560	625
Contribution margin per unit	€240	€375
Contribution margin ratio	30%	37.5%

At first glance, boat engines appear more profitable than snowmobile engines. The product to be emphasised, however, is not necessarily the product with the higher individual contribution margin per unit or contribution margin percentage. Rather, managers should aim for the *highest contribution margin per unit of the constraining factor* – that is, the scarce, limiting or critical factor. The constraining factor restricts or limits the production or sale of a given product. (See also Chapter 20 on the theory of constraints.)

Assume that only 600 machine-hours are available daily for assembling engines. Additional capacity cannot be obtained in the short run. Tiilikainen can sell as many engines as it produces. The constraining factor, then, is machine-hours. It takes two machine-hours to produce one snowmobile engine and five machine-hours to produce one boat engine.

	Snowmobile engine	Boat engine
Contribution margin per engine	€240	€375
Machine-hours required to produce one engine	2 machine-hours	5 machine-hours
Contribution margin per machine-hour (240 ÷ 2; 375 ÷ 5)	€120	€75
Total contribution margin for 600 machine-hours (€120 × 600; €75 × 600)	€72 000	€45 000

Producing snowmobile engines contributes more margin per machine-hour, which is the constraining factor in this example. Therefore, choosing to emphasise snowmobile engines is the correct decision. Other constraints in manufacturing settings can be the availability of direct materials, components or skilled labour, as well as financial and sales considerations. In a retail department store, the constraining factor may be linear metres of display space. The greatest possible contribution margin per unit of the constraining factor yields the maximum operating profit.

As you can imagine, in many cases a manufacturer or retailer must meet the challenge of trying to maximise total operating profit for a variety of products, each with more than one constraining factor. The problem of formulating the most profitable production schedules and the most profitable product mix is essentially that of maximising the total contribution margin in the face of many constraints. Optimisation techniques, such as the linear-programming technique discussed in the appendix to this chapter, help solve these complicated problems.

Concepts in action   The LEGO Group

For decades, Denmark-based LEGO Group has delighted children of all ages with its sets of construction toys. The fifth-largest toymaker in the world produces billions of its small building bricks annually, but a decision to outsource a major chunk of its production nearly jeopardised the company's global supply chain and operations.

In response to near bankruptcy in 2004, the company outsource 80% of its internal Western European production to three lower-cost countries: the Czech Republic, Hungary, and Mexico. While LEGO Group sought to reduce costs and gain economies of scale, it failed to account for managing the complexity of an outsourced global production network. LEGO Group's challenges include controlling its multi-continent production facilities, transferring production knowledge to its outsourcing partners, and allowing for seasonal fluctuations in demand (60% of LEGO production occurs in the second half of the year to accommodate Christmas holiday demand).

These problems led to unanticipated production delays and costs. As a result, the company cancelled its outsourcing contracts and brought all production back in-house by 2009.

LEGO Group's experience demonstrates the costs of outsourcing and offshoring, the outsourcing of business processes and jobs to other countries. While offshoring often yields significant cost savings, there are significant costs associated with international taxation, global supply chain coordination, and shuttering existing facilities.

Sources: LEGO Group (2012) Annual Report 2011; LEGO Group (2013) Annual Report 2012; Larsen, M.M., Pedersen, T. and Slepniov, D. (2010) *Lego Group: An Offshore Outsourcing Journey towards a New Future* (London, Ontario: Richard Ivey School of Business, No. 910M94).

Customer profitability and relevant costs

In addition to making choices among products, companies must often decide whether they should add some customers and drop others. This section illustrates relevant-revenue and relevant-cost analysis when different cost drivers are identified for different activities. The cost object in our example is customers. The analysis focuses on customer profitability at Imbro-Glio, the Naples sales office of Papa-Geno Srl, a wholesaler of specialised furniture.

Imbro-Glio supplies furniture to three local retailers, Lucrezia, Borgia and Rigo-Letto. Exhibit 10.8 presents representative revenues and costs of Imbro-Glio by customers for the coming year. Additional information on Imbro-Glio's costs for different activities at various levels of the cost hierarchy is as follows:

Exhibit 10.8   Analysis of Imbro-Glio customer profits

	Lucrezia	Borgia	Rigo-Letto	Total
Sales	€500 000	€300 000	€400 000	€1 200 000
Cost of goods sold	370 000	220 000	330 000	920 000
Materials handling labour	41 000	18 000	33 000	92 000
Materials handling equipment cost written off as depreciation	10 000	6 000	8 000	24 000
Rent	14 000	8 000	14 000	36 000
Marketing support	11 000	9 000	10 000	30 000
Purchase orders and delivery processing	13 000	7 000	12 000	32 000
General administration	20 000	12 000	16 000	48 000
Total operating costs	479 000	280 000	423 000	1 182 000
Operating profit	€21 000	€20 000	€(23 000)	€18 000

1 Materials handling labour costs vary with the number of units of furniture shipped to customers.

2 Different areas of the warehouse stock furniture for different customers. Materials handling equipment in an area and depreciation costs on the equipment are identified with individual customer accounts. Any equipment not used remains idle. The equipment has a one-year useful life and zero disposal price.

3 Imbro-Glio allocates rent to each customer account on the basis of the amount of warehouse space occupied by the products to be shipped to that customer.

4 Marketing costs vary with the number of sales visits made to customers.

5 Purchase-order costs vary with the number of purchase orders received; delivery-processing costs vary with the number of shipments made.

6 Imbro-Glio allocates fixed general administration costs to customers on the basis of euro sales made to each customer.

Relevant-cost analysis of dropping a customer

Exhibit 10.8 indicates a loss of €23 000 on sales to Rigo-Letto. Imbro-Glio's manager believes this loss occurred because Rigo-Letto places many low-volume orders with Imbro-Glio, resulting in high purchase-order and delivery processing, and materials handling and marketing activity. Imbro-Glio is considering several possible actions with respect to the Rigo-Letto account – reducing its own costs of supporting Rigo-Letto by becoming more efficient, cutting back on some of the services it offers Rigo-Letto, charging Rigo-Letto higher prices, or dropping the Rigo-Letto account. The following analysis focuses on the operating profit effect of dropping the Rigo-Letto account. Exhibit 10.8 is essentially a customer profitability analysis (this management accounting approach is further discussed in Chapter 12).

The key question is: What are the relevant costs and relevant revenues? The following information about the effect of reducing various activities related to the Rigo-Letto account is available.

1 Dropping the Rigo-Letto account will save cost of goods sold, materials handling labour, marketing support, purchase-order and delivery processing costs incurred on the Rigo-Letto account.

2 Dropping the Rigo-Letto account will mean that the warehouse space currently occupied by products for Rigo-Letto and the materials handling equipment used to move them will become idle.

3 Dropping the Rigo-Letto account will have no effect on fixed general administration costs.

Exhibit 10.9 presents the relevant-revenue and relevant-cost calculations. Imbro-Glio's operating profit will be €15 000 lower if it drops the Rigo-Letto account, so Imbro-Glio decides to keep the Rigo-Letto account. The last column in Exhibit 10.9 shows that the cost savings from dropping the Rigo-Letto account, €385 000, are not enough to offset the loss of €400 000 in revenue. The key reason is that depreciation, rent and general administration costs will not decrease if the Rigo-Letto account is dropped.

Now suppose that if Imbro-Glio drops the Rigo-Letto account, it could lease the extra warehouse space to Nessun-Dorma, which has offered €20 000 per year for it. Then the €20 000 that Imbro-Glio would receive would be the opportunity cost of continuing to use the warehouse to service Rigo-Letto. Imbro-Glio would gain €5000 by dropping the Rigo-Letto account (€20 000 from lease revenue minus lost operating profit of €15 000). Before reaching a final decision, however, Imbro-Glio must examine whether Rigo-Letto can be made more profitable so that supplying products to Rigo-Letto earns more than the €20 000 from leasing to Nessun-Dorma. Imbro-Glio must also consider qualitative factors such as the effect of the decision on Imbro-Glio's reputation for developing stable, long-run business relationships.

Exhibit 10.9	Relevant-cost analysis for Imbro-Glio dropping the Rigo-Letto account

	Amount of total revenues and total costs		Difference: incremental (loss in revenue) and savings in costs from dropping Rigo-Letto account
	Keep Rigo-Letto account	Drop Rigo-Letto account	
Sales	€1 200 000	€800 000	€(400 000)
Cost of goods sold	920 000	590 000	330 000
Materials handling labour	92 000	59 000	33 000
Materials handling equipment cost written off as depreciation	24 000	24 000	0
Rent	36 000	36 000	0
Marketing support	30 000	20 000	10 000
Purchase orders and delivery processing	32 000	20 000	12 000
General administration	48 000	48 000	0
Total operating costs	1 182 000	797 000	385 000
Operating profit (loss)	€18 000	€3 000	€(15 000)

Relevant-cost analysis of adding a customer

Suppose that in addition to Lucrezia, Borgia and Rigo-Letto, Imbro-Glio is evaluating the profitability of adding a fourth customer, Bocca-Negra. Imbro-Glio is already paying rent of €36 000 for the warehouse and is incurring general administration costs of €48 000. These costs will not change if Bocca-Negra is added as a customer. Bocca-Negra is a customer with a profile much like Rigo-Letto's. Suppose Imbro-Glio predicts other revenues and costs of doing business with Bocca-Negra to be the same as those described under the Rigo-Letto column of Exhibit 10.8. Should Imbro-Glio add Bocca-Negra as a customer? Exhibit 10.10 shows incremental revenues

Exhibit 10.10	Relevant-cost analysis for adding the Bocca-Negra account

	Amount of total revenues and total costs		Difference: incremental revenue and (incremental costs) from adding Bocca-Negro account
	Do not add Bocca-Negra account	Add Bocca-Negra account	
Sales	€1 200 000	€1 600 000	€400 000
Cost of goods sold (variable)	920 000	1 250 000	(330 000)
Materials handling labour	92 000	125 000	(33 000)
Materials handling equipment cost written off as depreciation	24 000	32 000	(8 000)
Rent	36 000	36 000	0
Marketing support	30 000	40 000	(10 000)
Purchase orders and delivery processing	32 000	44 000	(12 000)
General administration	48 000	48 000	0
Total operating costs	1 182 000	1 575 000	393 000
Operating profit	€18 000	€25 000	€7 000

exceed incremental costs by €7000. Imbro-Glio would prefer to add Bocca-Negra as a customer. Note that both volume and non-volume factors drive costs. This is the principle underlying activity-based costing which is further discussed in the next chapter. The key point is that the cost of acquiring new equipment to support the Bocca-Negra order (written off as depreciation of €8000 in Exhibit 10.10) is included as a relevant cost. Why? Because this cost can be avoided if Imbro-Glio decides not to do business with Bocca-Negra. Note the critical distinction here. Depreciation cost is irrelevant in deciding whether to drop Rigo-Letto as a customer (because it is a past cost), but the purchase cost of the new equipment that will then be written off as depreciation in the future is relevant in deciding whether to add Bocca-Negra as a new customer.

Irrelevance of past costs and equipment-replacement decisions

The illustrations in this chapter have shown that expected future costs that do not differ among alternatives are irrelevant. Now we return to the idea that all past costs are irrelevant.

Consider an example of equipment replacement. The irrelevant cost illustrated here is the **book value** (original cost minus total depreciation) of the existing equipment. Assume that Bjørnstjerne is considering replacing a metal-cutting machine for kitchen parts with a more technically advanced model. The new machine has an automatic quality-testing capability and is more efficient than the old machine. The new machine, however, has a shorter life. Bjørnstjerne uses the straight-line depreciation method. Sales from kitchen parts (€1.1 million per year) will be unaffected by the replacement decision. Summary data on the existing machine and the replacement machine are as follows:

	Existing machine	Replacement machine
Original cost	€1 000 000	€600 000
Useful life in years	5 years	2 years
Current age in years	3 years	0 years
Useful life remaining in years	2 years	2 years
Total depreciation	€600 000	Not acquired yet
Book value	€400 000	Not acquired yet
Current disposal price (in cash)	€40 000	Not acquired yet
Terminal disposal price (in cash 2 years from now)	€0	€0
Annual operating costs (maintenance, energy, repairs, coolants, and so on)	€800 000	€460 000

To focus on the main concept of relevance, we ignore the time value of money in this illustration. Exhibit 10.11 presents a cost comparison of the two machines.

We can apply our definition of relevance to four important items in the equipment-replacement decision facing Bjørnstjerne:

1 *Book value of old machine.* Irrelevant, because it is a past (historical) cost. All past costs are 'down the drain'. Nothing can change what has already been spent or what has already happened.

2 *Current disposal price of old machine.* Relevant, because it is an expected future cash inflow that differs between alternatives.

3 *Gain or loss on disposal.* This is the algebraic difference between items 1 and 2. It is a meaningless combination blurring the distinction between the irrelevant book value and the relevant disposal price. Each item should be considered separately.

4 *Cost of new machine.* Relevant, because it is an expected future cash outflow that will differ between alternatives.

Exhibit 10.11	Cost comparison: replacement of machinery, including relevant and irrelevant items for Bjørnstjerne

	Two years together		
	Keep	**Replace**	**Difference**
Sales	€2 200 000	€2 200 000	–
Operating costs			
Cash-operating costs	1 600 000	920 000	€680 000
Old machine book value			
Periodic write-off as depreciation or	400 000	–	–
Lump-sum write-off	–	400 000*	
Current disposal price of old machine	–	(40 000)*	40 000
New machine cost, written off periodically as depreciation	–	600 000	(600 000)
Total operating costs	2 000 000	1 880 000	120 000
Operating profit	€200 000	€320 000	€(120 000)

* In a formal income statement, these two items would be combined as 'loss on disposal of machine' of €360 000.

Exhibit 10.11 should clarify these four assertions. The difference column in Exhibit 10.11 shows that the book value of the old machine is not an element of difference between alternatives and could be completely ignored for decision-making purposes. No matter what the timing of the charge against revenue, the amount charged is still €400 000 regardless of the alternative chosen because it is a past (historical) cost (note that the advantage of replacing is €120 000 for the two years together). In contrast, the €600 000 cost of the new machine is relevant because it can be avoided by deciding not to replace.

Past costs that are unavoidable because they cannot be changed, no matter what action is taken, are sometimes described as **sunk costs**. In our example, old equipment has a book value of €400 000 and a current disposal price of €40 000. What are the sunk costs in this case? The entire €400 000 is sunk and down the drain because it represents an outlay made in the past that cannot be changed. Thus, past costs and sunk costs are synonyms.

Exhibit 10.12 concentrates on relevant items only. Note that the same answer (the €120 000 net difference) will be obtained even though the book value is completely omitted from the calculations. The only relevant items are the cash-operating costs, the disposal price of the old machine and the cost of the new machine (represented as depreciation in Exhibit 10.12).

Exhibit 10.12	Cost comparison – replacement of machinery, relevant items only for Bjørnstjerne

	Two years together		
	Keep	**Replace**	**Difference**
Cash-operating costs	€1 600 000	€920 000	€680 000
Current disposal price of old machine	–	(40 000)	40 000
New machine, written off periodically as depreciation	–	600 000	(600 000)
Total relevant costs	€1 600 000	€1 480 000	€120 000

Summary

The following points are linked to the chapter's learning objectives.

1 The five steps which managers might undertake in a decision process are: (a) obtain information, (b) make predictions, (c) choose alternative courses of action, (d) implement decisions, and (e) evaluate performance.

2 To be relevant to a particular decision, a revenue or cost must meet two criteria: (a) it must be an expected future revenue or cost, and (b) it must differ among alternative courses of action.

3 The consequences of alternative actions can be quantitative and qualitative. Quantitative factors are outcomes that are measured in numerical terms. Some quantitative factors can be easily expressed in financial terms, others cannot. Qualitative factors, such as employee morale, cannot be measured in numerical terms. Due consideration must be given to both financial and non-financial factors in making decisions.

4 There are two common problems in relevant-cost analysis: (a) assuming all variable costs are relevant, and (b) assuming all fixed costs are irrelevant.

5 Opportunity cost is the maximum available contribution to income that is forgone (rejected) by not using a limited resource in its next-best alternative use. The idea of an opportunity cost arises when there are multiple uses for resources and some alternatives are not selected. Opportunity cost is often included in decision making because it represents the best alternative way in which an organisation may have used its resources had it not made the decision it did.

6 In choosing among multiple products when resource capacity is constrained, managers should emphasise the product that yields the highest contribution margin per unit of the constraining or limiting factor.

7 Expected future revenues and costs are the only revenues and costs relevant in any decision model. The book value of existing equipment in equipment-replacement decisions represents past (historical) cost and therefore is irrelevant.

Appendix

Linear programming

Linear programming (LP) is an optimisation technique used to maximise total contribution margin (the objective function), given multiple constraints. LP models typically assume that all costs can be classified as either variable or fixed with respect to a single driver (units of output). LP models also require certain other linear assumptions to hold. When these assumptions fail, other decision models should be considered. Such models are described in Nahmias (2008).

Consider the Tiilikainen example described earlier in the chapter. Suppose that both the snowmobile and boat engines must be tested on a very expensive machine before they are shipped to customers. The available testing-machine time is limited. Production data are as follows:

Department	Available daily capacity in hours	Use of capacity in hours per unit of product		Daily maximum production in units	
		Snowmobile engine	Boat engine	Snowmobile engine	Boat engine
Assembly	600 machine-hours	2.0	5.0	300*	120
Testing	120 testing-hours	1.0	0.5	120	240

* For example, 600 machine-hours ÷ 2.0 machine-hours per snowmobile engine = 300, the maximum number of snowmobile engines that the Assembly Department can make if it works exclusively on snowmobile engines.

Exhibit 10.13 summarises these and other relevant data. Note that snowmobile engines have a contribution margin of €240 and that boat engines have a contribution margin of €375. Material shortages for boat engines will limit production to 110 boat engines per day. How many engines of each type should be produced daily to maximise operating profit?

Steps in solving an LP problem

We use the data in Exhibit 10.13 to illustrate the three steps in solving an LP problem. Throughout this discussion, S equals the number of units of snowmobiles produced and B equals the number of units of boat engines produced.

| **Exhibit 10.13** | Operating data for Tiilikainen | | | | |

| | Department capacity (per day) in product units | | Selling price | Variable cost per unit | Contribution margin per unit |
Product	Assembly	Testing			
Only snowmobile engines	300	120	€800	€560	€240
Only boat engines	120	240	€1 000	€625	€375

Step 1: Determine the objective

The **objective function** of a linear program expresses the objective or goal to be maximised (for example, operating profit) or minimised (for example, operating costs). In our example, the objective is to find the combination of products that maximises total contribution margin in the short run. Fixed costs remain the same regardless of the product mix chosen and are therefore irrelevant. The linear function expressing the objective for the total contribution margin (TCM) is

$$TCM = €240S + €375B$$

Step 2: Specify the constraints

A **constraint** is a mathematical inequality or equality that must be satisfied by the variables in a mathematical model. The following linear inequalities depict the relationships in our example:

Assembly Department constraint	$2S + 5B \leq 600$
Testing Department constraint	$1S + 0.5B \leq 120$
Material shortage constraint for boat engines	$B \leq 110$
Negative production is impossible	$S \geq 0$ and $B \geq 0$

The coefficients of the constraints are often called technical coefficients. For example, in the Assembly Department, the technical coefficient is 2 machine-hours for snowmobile engines and 5 machine-hours for boat engines.

The three solid lines on the graph in Exhibit 10.14 show the existing constraints for Assembly and Testing and the material shortage constraint. The feasible alternatives are those combinations of quantities of snowmobile engines and boat engines that satisfy all the constraining factors. The shaded 'area of feasible solutions' in Exhibit 10.14 shows the boundaries of those product combinations that are feasible, or technically possible.

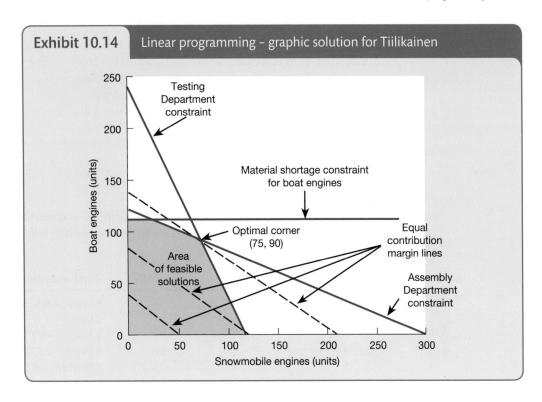

| Exhibit 10.14 | Linear programming – graphic solution for Tiilikainen |

As an example of how the lines are plotted in Exhibit 10.14, use equal signs instead of inequality signs and assume for the Assembly Department that $B = 0$; then $S = 300$ (600 machine-hours ÷ 2 machine-hours per snowmobile engine). Assume that $S = 0$; then $B = 120$ (600 machine-hours ÷ 5 machine-hours per boat engine). Connect those two points with a straight line.

Step 3: Calculate the optimal solution

We present two approaches for finding the optimal solution: the trial-and-error approach and the graphic approach. These approaches are easy to use in our example because there are only two variables in the objective function and a small number of constraints. An understanding of these two approaches provides insight into LP modelling. In most real-world LP applications, however, managers use computer software packages to calculate the optimal solution.

Although the trial-and-error and graphic approaches can be useful for two or possibly three variables, they are impractical when many variables exist. Standard computer software packages rely on the *simplex method*. The simplex method is an iterative step-by-step procedure for determining the optimal solution to an LP problem. It starts with a specific feasible solution and then tests it by substitution to see whether the result can be improved. These substitutions continue until no further improvement is possible and the optimal solution is obtained.

Trial-and-error approach The optimal solution can be found by trial and error, by working with coordinates of the corners of the area of feasible solutions. The approach is simple.

First, select any set of corner points and calculate the total contribution margin. Five corner points appear in Exhibit 10.14. It is helpful to use simultaneous equations to obtain the exact graph coordinates. To illustrate, the point ($S = 75$; $B = 90$) can be derived by solving the two pertinent constraint inequalities as simultaneous equations:

$$2S + 5B = 600 \qquad (1)$$
$$1S + 0.5B = 120 \qquad (2)$$

Multiplying (2) by 2, we get $\qquad 2S + 1B = 240 \qquad (3)$

Subtracting (3) from (1): $\qquad\qquad\qquad 4B = 360$

Therefore, $\qquad\qquad\qquad B = 360 \div 4 = 90$

Substituting for B in (2): $\qquad 1S + 0.5(90) = 120$
$$S = 120 - 45 = 75$$

Given $S = 75$ and $B = 90$,

$$\text{TCM} = \text{€}240(75) + \text{€}375(90) = \text{€}51\ 750$$

Second, move from corner point to corner point, computing the total contribution margin at each corner point. The total contribution margin, at each corner point is as follows:

Trial	Corner point (S, B)	Snowmobile engines (S)	Boat engines (B)	Total contribution margin
1	(0, 0)	0	0	€240(0) + €375(0) = €0
2	(0, 110)	0	110	€240(0) + €375(110) = 41 250
3	(25, 110)	25	110	€240(25) + €375(110) = 47 250
4	(75, 90)	75	90	€240(75) + €375(90) = 51 750*
5	(120, 0)	120	0	€240(120) + €375(0) = 28 800

* Indicates the optimal solution.

The optimal product mix is the mix that yields the highest total contribution: 75 snowmobile engines and 90 boat engines.

Graphic approach   Consider all possible combinations that will produce an equal total contribution margin of, say, €12 000. That is,

$$\text{€}240S + \text{€}375B = \text{€}12\ 000$$

This set of €12 000 contribution margins is a straight dashed line in Exhibit 10.14 through $(S = 50; B = 0)$ and $(S = 0; B = 32)$. Other equal total contribution margins can be represented by lines parallel to this one. In Exhibit 10.14, we show three dashed lines. The equal total contribution margins increase as the lines get farther from the origin because lines drawn farther from the origin represent more sales of both snowmobile and boat engines.

The optimal line is the one farthest from the origin but still passing through a point in the area of feasible solutions. This line represents the highest contribution margin. The optimal solution is the point at the corner $(S = 75; B = 90)$. This solution will become apparent if you put a ruler on the graph and move it outward from the origin and parallel with the €12 000 line. The idea is to move the ruler as far away from the origin as possible (that is, to increase the total contribution margin) without leaving the area of feasible solutions. In general, the optimal solution in a maximisation problem lies at the corner where the dashed line intersects an extreme point of the area of feasible solutions. Moving the ruler out any further puts it outside the feasible region.

Sensitivity analysis

What are the implications of uncertainty about the accounting or technical coefficients used in the LP model? Changes in coefficients affect the slope of the objective function (the equal contribution margin lines) or the area of feasible solutions. Consider how a change in the contribution margin of snowmobile engines from €240 to €300 per unit might affect the optimal solution.

Assume the contribution margin for boat engines remains unchanged at €375 per unit. The revised objective function will be

$$TCM = €300S + €375B$$

Using the trial-and-error approach, calculate the total contribution margin for each of the five corner points described in the table above. The optimal solution is still ($S = 75$; $B = 90$). What if the contribution margin falls to €160? Again, the optimal solution remains the same ($S = 75$; $B = 90$). Big changes in the contribution margin per unit of snowmobile engines have no effect on the optimal solution in this case.

Key terms

relevant costs (284)

relevant revenues (284)

differential cost (285)

quantitative factors (285)

qualitative factors (285)

incremental costs (288)

outsourcing (288)

insourcing (288)

make-or-buy decisions (289)

opportunity cost (291)

book value (299)

sunk costs (300)

objective function (302)

constraint (302)

References and further reading

Bhimani, A. (2015) *Strategic Finance: Achieving High Corporate Performance* (London, Strategy Press).

Bhimani, A. and Bromwich, M. (2010) *Management Accounting: Retrospect and Prospect* (Oxford: CIMA/Elsevier, chapter 4).

Kaplan, R.S. et al. (1990) 'Contribution margin analysis: no longer relevant/strategic cost management: the new paradigm', *Journal of Management Accounting Research*, pp. 1–32.

Nahmias, S. (2008) *Production and Operations Analysis* (New York: McGraw-Hill/Irwin).

Shank, J. and Govindarajan, V. (1992) 'Strategic cost management: the value chain perspective', *Journal of Management Accounting Research*, pp. 179–97.

CHAPTER 10

Assessment material

Review questions

10.1 Outline the five-step sequence in a decision process.

10.2 Define relevant cost. Why are historical costs irrelevant?

10.3 'All future costs are relevant.' Do you agree? Why?

10.4 Distinguish between quantitative and qualitative factors in decision making.

10.5 'Variable costs are always relevant, and fixed costs are always irrelevant.' Do you agree? Why?

10.6 'A component part should be purchased whenever the purchase price is less than its total unit manufacturing cost.' Do you agree? Why?

10.7 Define opportunity cost.

10.8 'Cost written off as depreciation is always irrelevant.' Do you agree? Why?

10.9 'Managers will always choose the alternative that maximises operating profit or minimises costs in the decision model.' Do you agree? Why?

10.10 How might the optimal solution of a linear programming problem be determined?

Exercises

Basic level

10.11 **Relevant costs, contribution margin, product emphasis** (20–25 minutes)

Monteagudo-Playa SA is a take-away food store at a popular beach resort. Consuelo Herreros, owner of Monteagudo-Playa, is deciding how much refrigerator space to devote to four different drinks. Pertinent data on these four drinks are as follows:

	Cola	Lemonade	Punch	Natural orange juice
Selling price per case	€108.00	€115.20	€158.40	€230.40
Variable costs per case	€81.00	€91.20	€120.60	€181.20
Cases sold per metre of shelf-space per day	25	24	4	5

Consuelo has a maximum front shelf-space of 12 metres to devote to the four drinks. She wants a minimum of 1 metre and a maximum of 6 metres of front shelf-space for each drink.

Required

1 What is the contribution margin per case of each type of drink?

2 A co-worker of Consuelo's recommends that she maximise the shelf-space devoted to those drinks with the highest contribution margin per case. Evaluate this recommendation.

3 What shelf-space allocation for the four drinks would you recommend for Monteagudo-Playa?

Intermediate level

10.12 Customer profitability, choosing customers (20–25 minutes)

Jours-Daim SA operates a printing press with a monthly capacity of 2000 machine-hours. Jours-Daim has two main customers, Harpes-à-Gonds, SNC and Fourbe-Riz SA. Data on each customer for January follow:

	Harpes-à-Gonds	Fourbe-Riz	Total
Revenues	€120 000	€80 000	€200 000
Variable costs	42 000	48 000	90 000
Fixed costs (allocated on the basis of revenues)	60 000	40 000	100 000
Total operating costs	102 000	88 000	190 000
Operating profit	€18 000	€(8 000)	€10 000
Machine-hours required	1500 hours	500 hours	2000 hours

Each of the following requirements refers only to the preceding data; there is *no connection* between the requirements.

Required

1 Should Jours-Daim drop the Fourbe-Riz business? If Jours-Daim drops the Fourbe-Riz business, its total fixed costs will decrease by 20%.

2 Fourbe-Riz indicates that it wants Jours-Daim to do an *additional* €80 000 worth of printing jobs during February. These jobs are identical to the existing business Jours-Daim did for Fourbe-Riz in January in terms of variable costs and machine-hours required. Jours-Daim anticipates that the business from Harpes-à-Gonds in February would be the same as that in January. Jours-Daim can choose to accept as much of the Harpes-à-Gonds and Fourbe-Riz business for February as it wants. Assume that total fixed costs for February will be the same as the fixed costs in January. What should Jours-Daim do? What will Jours-Daim's operating profit be in February?

10.13 Relevance of equipment costs (30–40 minutes)

Jääskinen Oy has just today paid for and installed a special machine for polishing cars at one of its several outlets. It is the first day of the company's fiscal year. The machine cost €20 000. Its annual operating costs total €15 000, exclusive of depreciation. The machine will have a four-year useful life and a zero terminal disposal price.

After the machine has been used for a day, a machine salesperson offers a different machine that promises to do the same job at a yearly operating cost of €9000, exclusive of depreciation. The new machine will cost €24 000 cash, installed. The 'old' machine is unique and can be sold outright for only €10 000, minus €2000 removal cost. The new machine, like the old one, will have a four-year useful life and zero terminal disposal price.

Sales, all in cash, will be €150 000 annually, and other cash costs will be €110 000 annually, regardless of this decision.

For simplicity, ignore income taxes, interest and present-value considerations.

Required

1 a Prepare a statement of cash receipts and disbursements for each of the four years under both alternatives. What is the cumulative difference in cash flow for the four years taken together?

b Prepare income statements for each of the four years under both alternatives. Assume straight-line depreciation. What is the cumulative difference in operating profit for the four years taken together?

c What are the irrelevant items in your presentations in requirements (a) and (b)? Why are they irrelevant?

2 Suppose the cost of the 'old' machine was €1 million rather than €20 000. Nevertheless, the old machine can be sold outright for only €10 000, minus €2000 removal cost. Would the net differences in requirements 1 and 2 change? Explain.

3 'To avoid a loss, we should keep the old machine.' What is the role of book value in decisions about replacement of machines?

*10.14 Contribution approach, relevant costs (30 minutes)

Air Calabria owns a single jet aircraft and operates between Cantazaro and Venice. Flights leave Cantazaro on Mondays and Thursdays and depart from Venice on Wednesdays and Saturdays. Air Calabria cannot offer any more flights between Cantazaro and Venice. Only tourist-class seats are available on its planes. An analyst has collected the following information:

Seating capacity per plane	360 passengers
Average number of passengers per flight	200 passengers
Flights per week	4 flights
Flights per year	208 flights
Average one-way fare	€500
Variable fuel costs	€14 000 per flight
Food and beverage service cost (no charge to passenger)	€20 per passenger
Commission to travel agents paid by Air Calabria (all tickets are booked by travel agents)	8% of fare
Fixed annual lease costs allocated to each flight	€53 000 per flight
Fixed ground services (maintenance, check in, baggage handling) cost allocated to each flight	€7000 per flight
Fixed flight crew salaries allocated to each flight	€4000 per flight

For simplicity, assume that fuel costs are unaffected by the actual number of passengers on a flight.

Required

1 What is the operating profit that Air Calabria makes on each one-way flight between Cantazaro and Venice?

2 The Market Research Department of Air Calabria indicates that lowering the average one-way fare to €480 will increase the average number of passengers per flight to 212. Should Air Calabria lower its fare?

3 Cima-Rosa, a tour operator, approaches Air Calabria on the possibility of chartering (renting out) its jet aircraft twice each month, first to take Cima-Rosa's tourists from Cantazaro to Venice and then to bring the tourists back from Venice to Cantazaro. If Air Calabria accepts Cima-Rosa's offer, Air Calabria will be able to offer only 184 (208 – 24) of its own flights each year. The terms of the charter are as follows: (a) For each one-way flight, Cima-Rosa will pay Air Calabria €75 000 to charter the plane and to use its flight crew and ground service staff; (b) Cima-Rosa will pay for fuel costs; and (c) Cima-Rosa will pay for all food costs. On purely financial considerations, should Air Calabria accept Cima-Rosa's offer? What other factors should Air Calabria consider in deciding whether or not to charter its plane to Cima-Rosa?

10.15 Optimal production plan, computer manufacturer (Chapter appendix) (30 minutes)

Fiordi-Ligi Srl assembles and sells two products: printers and desktop computers. Customers can purchase either (a) a computer, or (b) a computer plus a printer. The printers are not sold without the computer. The result is that the quantity of printers sold is equal to or less than the quantity of desktop computers sold. The contribution margins are €200 per printer and €100 per computer.

Each printer requires 6 hours assembly time on production line 1 and 10 hours assembly time on production line 2. Each computer requires 4 hours assembly time on production line 1 only. (Many of the components of each computer are preassembled by external suppliers.) Production line 1 has 24 hours of available time per day. Production line 2 has 20 hours of available time per day.

Let X represent units of printers and Y represent units of desktop computers. The production manager must decide on the optimal mix of printers and computers to manufacture.

Required

1 Express the production manager's problem in an LP format.

2 Which combination of printers and computers will maximise the operating profit of Fiordi-Ligi? Use both the trial-and-error and the graphic approaches.

10.16 Optimal sales mix for a retailer, sensitivity analysis (Chapter appendix) (30–40 minutes)

Vier-und-Zwanzig GmbH operates a chain of food stores open 24 hours a day. Each store has a standard 4000 square metres of floor space available for merchandise. Merchandise is grouped in two categories: grocery products and dairy products. Vier-und-Zwanzig requires each store to devote a minimum of 1000 square metres to grocery products and a minimum of 800 square metres to dairy products. Within these restrictions, each store manager can choose the mix of products to carry.

The manager of the Salzburg store estimates the following weekly contribution margins per square metre: grocery products, €100; dairy products, €30.

Required

1 Formulate the decision facing the store manager as an LP model. Use G to represent square metres of floor space for grocery products and D to represent square metres of floor space for dairy products.

2 Why might Vier-und-Zwanzig set minimum bounds on the floor space devoted to each line of products?

3 Compute the optimal mix of grocery products and dairy products for the Salzburg store.

4 Will the optimal mix determined in requirement 3 change if the contribution margins per square metre change to grocery products, €80, and dairy products, €50?

10.17 Relevant costing (From ACCA Financial Information for Management, Part 1, June 2004) (40 minutes)

Ennerdale Ltd has been asked to quote a price for a one-off contract. The company's management accountant has asked for your advice on the relevant costs for the contract. The following information is available:

Materials

The contract requires 3000 kg of material K, which is a material used regularly by the company in other production. The company has 2000 kg of material K currently in stock which had been purchased last month for a total cost of £19 600. Since then the price per kilogram for material K has increased by 5%. The contract also requires 200 kg of material L. There are 250 kg of material L in stock which are not required for normal production. This material originally cost a total of £3125. If not used on this contract, the stock of material L would be sold for £11 per kg.

Labour

The contract requires 800 hours of skilled labour. Skilled labour is paid £9.50 per hour. There is a shortage of skilled labour and all the available skilled labour is fully employed in the company in the manufacture of product P. The following information relates to product P:

	£ per unit
Selling price	100
Less	
Skilled labour	38
Other variable costs	22
	(60)
	40

Required

1 Prepare calculations showing the total relevant costs for making a decision about the contract in respect of the following cost elements:

  a materials K and L; and

  b skilled labour.

2 Explain how you would decide which overhead costs would be relevant in the financial appraisal of the contract.

Advanced level

*10.18 Special-order decision (35–40 minutes)

Fri-Flask specialises in the manufacture of one-litre plastic bottles. The plastic moulding machines are capable of producing 100 bottles per hour. The firm estimates that the variable cost of producing a plastic bottle is 25 øre. The bottles are sold for 55 øre each.

Management has been approached by a local toy company that would like the firm to produce a moulded plastic toy for them. The toy company is willing to pay DKK 3.00 per unit for the toy. The unit variable cost to manufacture the toy will be DKK 2.40. In addition, Fri-Flask would have to incur a cost of DKK 20 000 to construct the mould required exclusively for this order. Because the toy uses more plastic and is of a more intricate shape than a bottle, a moulding machine can produce only 40 units per hour. The customer wants 100 000 units. Assume that Fri-Flask has a total capacity of 10 000 machine-hours available during the period in which the toy company wants delivery of the toys. The firm's fixed costs, excluding the costs to construct the toy mould, during the same period will be DKK 200 000.

Required

1 Suppose the demand for its bottles is 750 000 units, and the special toy order has to be either taken in full or rejected totally. Should Fri-Flask accept the special toy? Explain your answer.

2 Suppose the demand for its bottles is 850 000 units, and the special toy order has to be either taken in full or rejected totally. Should Fri-Flask accept the special toy order? Explain your answer.

3 Suppose the demand for its bottles is 850 000 units, and Fri-Flask can accept any quantity of the special toy order. How many bottles and toys should it manufacture?

4 Suppose the demand for its bottles is 900 000 units, and the special toy order has to be either taken in full or rejected totally. Should Fri-Flask accept the special toy order? Explain your answer.

5 Suppose the demand for its bottles is 900 000 units, and Fri-Flask can accept any quantity of the special toy order. How many bottles and toys should it manufacture?

6 Suppose the demand for its bottles is 950 000 units and Fri-Flask can accept any quantity of the special toy order. How many bottles and toys should it manufacture?

7 The management has located a firm that has just entered the moulded plastic business. This firm has considerable excess capacity and more efficient moulding machines, and is willing to subcontract the toy job, or any portion of it, for DKK 2.80 per unit. It will construct its own toy mould. Suppose the demand for its bottles is 900 000 units, and Fri-Flask can accept any quantity of the special toy order. How many toys should it subcontract out?

CHAPTER 11

Activity-based costing

Managers find cost information useful in making many types of decisions. What should the selling price of a product/service be relative to the costs incurred? Does the market price allow a profit to be made? How far do existing cost allocation practices reflect the resource consumption of a company's different product lines? Simple costing systems often cannot answer such questions. Changing organisational circumstances at times lead management accounting systems to lose their effectiveness in providing effective costings. Investment in capital-intensive technology, for instance, can alter the material/labour/overhead cost mix of an organisation's products. Operational knowledge of how resources are consumed may not tally with information reported by the costing system. Consequently, a difficult-to-make product may attract very little cost allocation under the prevailing accounting system which may be outdated. Likewise, the life of a product type may be getting shorter because of more intensive competition by technologically driven companies. Under such situations, managers may find themselves with cost information provided by an accounting system relying on product-life assumptions which are rapidly becoming inappropriate. Managers may even reduce the selling price of a loss-making product based on costing information indicating that the product is very profitable. The costing approaches discussed in Chapters 3 and 4 are appropriate starting points for tackling such questions. However, refinement is often seen as necessary when circumstances dictate enhanced cost-information complexity in pursuit of greater cost accuracy. Activity-based costing and activity-based management systems aim to provide such refinement. Activity-based accounting systems have been implemented in many organisations, including Siemens, Hoffman La Roche, Royal Bank of Scotland, Philips, Volvo, Ericsson and the BBC. Activity-based costing/management as a major management accounting approach emerged in the 1990s – it continues to alter managerial views of product costs today in a very significant manner.

Learning objectives

After studying this chapter, you should be able to:

- Explain undercosting and overcosting of products
- Present three guidelines for refining a costing system
- Distinguish between the traditional and the activity-based costing approaches to designing a costing system
- Describe a four-part cost hierarchy
- Cost products or services using activity-based costing
- Use activity-based costing systems for activity-based management
- Compare activity-based costing and department-costing systems
- Appreciate the significance of organisational context issues in activity-based costing/ management system design and implementation

Undercosting and overcosting

We might use the term **cost smoothing** to describe a costing approach that uses broad averages to uniformly assign the cost of resources to cost objects (such as products, services or customers) when the individual products, services or customers in fact use those resources in a non-uniform way.

Cost smoothing can lead to undercosting or overcosting of products or services:

- **Product undercosting.** A product consumes a relatively high level of resources but is reported to have a relatively low total cost.

- **Product overcosting.** A product consumes a relatively low level of resources but is reported to have a relatively high total cost.

Companies that undercost products may actually make sales that result in losses under the erroneous impression that these sales are profitable. That is, these sales bring in less revenue than the cost of the resources they use. Companies that overcost products run the risk of losing market share to existing or new competitors. Because these products actually cost less than what is reported to management, the company could cut selling prices to maintain or enhance market shares and still make a profit on each sale.

Product-cost cross-subsidisation

Product-cost cross-subsidisation means that at least one miscosted product is resulting in the miscosting of other products in the organisation. A classic example arises when a cost is uniformly spread across multiple users without recognition of their different resource demands. Consider the costing of a restaurant bill for four colleagues who meet once a month to discuss business developments. Each diner orders separate entrées, desserts and drinks. The restaurant bill for the most recent meeting is as follows:

	Entrée	Dessert	Drinks	Total
Emmanuelle	€55	€0	€20	€75
Jean-Paul	100	40	70	210
Nathalie	75	20	40	135
Christophe	70	20	30	120
Total	€300	€80	€160	€540
Average	€75	€20	€40	€135

The €540 total restaurant bill produces a €135 average cost per dinner. This broad-average costing approach treats each diner the same. Emmanuelle would probably object to paying €135 because her actual cost is only €75. Indeed, she ordered the lowest-cost entrée, had no dessert, and had the lowest drink bill. When costs are averaged across all four diners, both Emmanuelle and Christophe are overcosted, Jean-Paul is undercosted and Nathalie is accurately costed.

The restaurant example is both simple and intuitive. The amount of cost cross-subsidisation of each diner can be readily calculated given that all cost items can be traced as direct costs to each diner. More complex costing issues arise, however, when there are indirect costs. Then resources are used by two or more individual diners. By definition, indirect costs require allocation – for example, the cost of a bottle of wine shared by two or more diners.

To see the effects of cost smoothing on both direct and indirect costs, we consider the existing costing system at Plastim Limited.

Costing system at Plastim Limited

Plastim Limited manufactures lenses for the tail-lights of cars. The lens, made from black, red, orange or white plastic, is the part of the lamp visible on the car's exterior. Lenses are made using injection moulding. The moulding operation consists of injecting molten plastic into a mould to give the lamp its desired shape. The mould is cooled to allow the molten plastic to solidify, and the part is removed.

Under its contract with Giovanni Motors, a major car manufacturer, Plastim makes two types of lens: a complex lens, CL5, and a simple lens, S3. The complex lens is a large lens with special features such as multicolour moulding (where more than one colour is injected into the mould) and complex shapes that wrap around the corner of the car. Manufacturing these lenses is more complex because various parts in the mould must align and fit precisely. The simple lens is smaller and has few special features.

Design, production and distribution processes

The sequence of steps to design, produce and distribute lenses, whether simple or complex, is as follows:

1 *Design of products and processes.* Each year Giovanni Motors specifies some modifications to the simple and complex lenses. Plastim's Design Department designs the moulds from which the lenses will be made and defines the processes needed (details of the manufacturing operations).

2 *Manufacturing operations.* The lenses are moulded, as described earlier, finished, cleaned and inspected.

3 *Shipping and distribution.* Finished lenses are packed and sent to Giovanni Motors.

Plastim is operating at capacity and incurs very low marketing costs. Because of its high-quality products, Plastim has minimal customer-service costs. Plastim's business environment is very competitive with respect to simple lenses. At a recent meeting, Giovanni's purchasing manager indicated that a new competitor, who makes only simple lenses, was offering to supply the S3 lens to Giovanni at a price of around €53, well below Plastim's price of €63. Unless Plastim lowers its selling price, it will be in jeopardy of losing the Giovanni business for the simple lens, similar to S3, for the upcoming model year. Plastim's management is very concerned about this development. The same competitive pressures do not exist for the complex lens, which Plastim currently sells to Giovanni at a price of €137 per lens.

Plastim's management has various alternatives available to them. Plastim can give up the Giovanni business in simple lenses if it is going to be this unprofitable. It can reduce the price on the simple lens and either accept a lower margin or aggressively seek to reduce costs. But first, management needs to understand what it costs to make and sell the S3 and CL5 lenses. To guide their pricing and cost management decisions, Plastim's managers assign all costs, both manufacturing and non-manufacturing, to the S3 and CL5 lenses. Had the focus been on inventory costing, they would only assign manufacturing costs to the lenses.

Existing single indirect-cost pool system

To cost products, Plastim currently uses a job-costing system with a single indirect-cost rate, similar to the system described in Chapter 3. The steps are as follows.

Step 1: Identify the chosen cost objects   The cost objects are the 60 000 simple S3 lenses, and the 15 000 complex CL5 lenses that Plastim makes. Plastim's goal is to calculate the *total* costs of manufacturing and distributing these lenses. Plastim then determines unit costs of each lens by dividing total costs of each lens by 60 000 for S3 and 15 000 for CL5.

Step 2: Identify the direct costs of the products Plastim identifies the direct costs of the lenses
– direct materials and direct manufacturing labour – as follows:

	60 000 Simple lenses (S3)		15 000 Complex lenses (CL5)		
	Total (1)	Per unit (2) = (1) ÷ 60 000	Total (3)	Per unit (4) = (3) ÷ 15 000	Total (5) = (1) + (3)
Direct materials	€1 125 000	€18.75	€675 000	€45.00	€1 800 000
Direct manufacturing labour	600 000	10.00	195 000	13.00	795 000
Total direct costs	€1 725 000	€28.75	€870 000	€58.00	€2 595 000

Step 3: Select the cost-allocation bases to use for allocating indirect costs to the products Most of the indirect costs consist of salaries paid to supervisors, engineers, manufacturing support and maintenance staff that support direct manufacturing labour. Hence, Plastim uses direct manufacturing labour-hours as the only allocation base to allocate all indirect costs to S3 and CL5. In the current year, Plastim used 39 750 actual direct manufacturing labour-hours.

Step 4: Identify the indirect costs associated with each cost-allocation base Plastim groups all indirect costs totalling €2 385 000 into a single overhead cost pool.

Step 5: Compute the rate per unit of each cost-allocation base used to allocate indirect costs to the products

$$\text{Actual indirect-cost rate} = \frac{\text{Actual total costs in indirect-cost pool}}{\text{Actual total quantity of cost-allocation base}}$$

$$= \frac{€2\,385\,000}{39\,750\text{ hours}} = €60 \text{ per direct manufacturing labour-hour}$$

Exhibit 11.1, Panel A, shows an overview of Plastim's existing costing system.

Step 6: Compute the indirect costs allocated to the products Plastim uses 30 000 total direct manufacturing labour-hours to make the simple S3 lenses and 9750 direct manufacturing labour-hours to make the complex CL5 lenses. Exhibit 11.1, Panel B, shows indirect costs of €1 800 000 (€60 per direct manufacturing labour-hour × 30 000) allocated to the simple lens and €585 000 (€60 per direct manufacturing labour-hour × 9750) allocated to the complex lens.

Step 7: Compute the total cost of the products by adding all direct and indirect costs assigned to them Exhibit 11.1, Panel B, presents the product costs for the simple and complex lenses. The direct costs are calculated in step 2 and the indirect costs in step 6. Note the correspondence between the costing system overview diagram (Exhibit 11.1, Panel A) and the costs calculated in step 7. Panel A shows two direct-cost categories and one indirect-cost pool. Hence the cost of each type of lens in step 7 (Panel B) has three line items: two for direct costs and one for allocated indirect costs.

Plastim's management begins investigating why the S3 lens costs €58.75, well above the €53 price quoted by Plastim's competitor. Are Plastim's technology and processes inefficient in manufacturing and distributing the simple S3 lens? Further analysis indicates that such inefficiency is not the reason. Plastim has years of experience in manufacturing and distributing lenses like S3. Because Plastim often makes process improvements, management is confident that their technology and processes for making simple lenses are not inferior to their competitors. However, management is less certain about Plastim's capabilities in manufacturing and distributing complex lenses. Indeed, Plastim has only recently started making this type of lens. Management is pleasantly surprised to learn that Giovanni Motors considers the prices of CL5 lenses to be very competitive. It is puzzling that, even at these prices, Plastim earns very large margins on the CL5 lenses:

	60 000 Simple lenses (S3)		15 000 Complex lenses (CL5)		
	Total (1)	Per unit (2) = (1) ÷ 60 000	Total (3)	Per unit (4) = (3) ÷ 15 000	Total (5) = (1) + (3)
Revenues	€3 780 000	€63.00	€2 055 000	€137.00	€5 835 000
Costs	3 525 000	58.75	1 455 000	97.00	4 980 000
Operating profit	€255 000	€4.25	€600 000	€40.00	€855 000
Operating profit ÷ Revenues		6.75%		29.20%	

Exhibit 11.1   Product costs at Plastim Ltd using existing single overhead cost pool

Panel A: Overview of Plastim's existing costing system

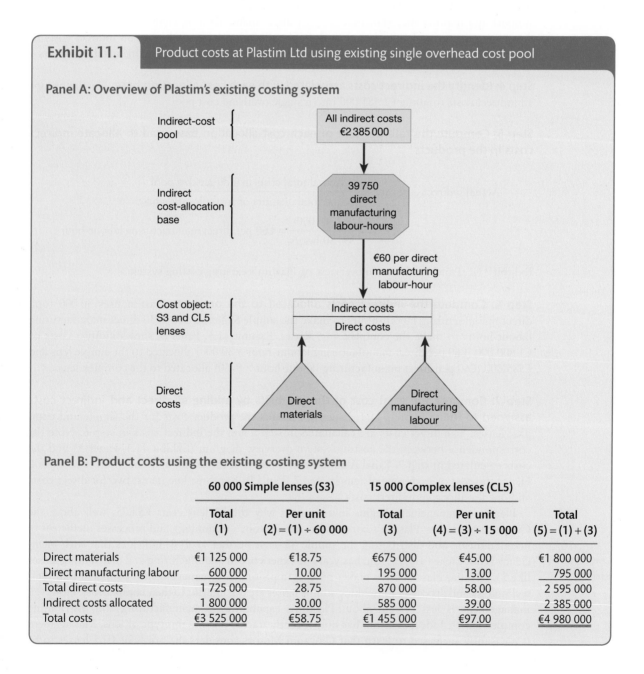

Panel B: Product costs using the existing costing system

	60 000 Simple lenses (S3)		15 000 Complex lenses (CL5)		
	Total (1)	Per unit (2) = (1) ÷ 60 000	Total (3)	Per unit (4) = (3) ÷ 15 000	Total (5) = (1) + (3)
Direct materials	€1 125 000	€18.75	€675 000	€45.00	€1 800 000
Direct manufacturing labour	600 000	10.00	195 000	13.00	795 000
Total direct costs	1 725 000	28.75	870 000	58.00	2 595 000
Indirect costs allocated	1 800 000	30.00	585 000	39.00	2 385 000
Total costs	€3 525 000	€58.75	€1 455 000	€97.00	€4 980 000

Plastim's managers are surprised that the margins are low on the S3 product where the company has strong capabilities, whereas the margins are quite high on the newer, less-established CL5 product. Since they are not deliberately charging a low price for S3, they wonder whether the costing system overcosts the simple S3 lens (assigning excessive costs to it) and undercosts the complex CL5 lens (assigning too little costs to it).

Plastim's management is quite confident about the direct materials and direct manufacturing labour costs of the lenses. Why? Because these costs can be traced to the lenses in an economically feasible way. They are less certain about the accuracy of the costing system in measuring the overhead resources used by each type of lens. The key question then is: How might the system of allocating overhead costs to lenses be refined?

Refining a costing system

A **refined costing system** reduces the use of broad averages for assigning the cost of resources to cost objects (such as jobs, products, and services) and provides better measurement of the costs of indirect resources used by different cost objects – no matter how differently the different cost objects use indirect resources.

Many companies – such as John Deere, the American manufacturer of farm equipment; Kanthal, the Swedish manufacturer of heating elements; Owens and Minor, the American distributor of medical products; and the NatWest bank in the United Kingdom – have refined their costing systems. What has caused companies in such diverse industries, operating in different parts of the world, to do so? There are four principal reasons:

- **Increase in product diversity**. Customers are demanding more customised products and, to differentiate themselves from competitors, companies are producing and selling many more products than in the past. Kanthal, for example, produces more than 10 000 different types of electrical heating wires and thermostats. Banks are offering many different types of account and service: special passbook accounts, ATM and credit cards, electronic payments, and investment and insurance services. These different products make different demands on the resources needed to produce them because of differences in volume, process and complexity. The resources demanded by these different products cannot be measured by a simple costing system that allocates indirect costs on the basis of, say, direct manufacturing labour-hours. Using such a simple costing system will result in inaccurate and misleading product costs.

- **Increase in indirect costs**. Advances in product and process technology have led to increases in indirect costs and decreases in direct costs, particularly direct manufacturing labour costs (see Bhimani 2015). For example, plant automation, such as computer-integrated manufacturing (CIM) and flexible manufacturing systems (FMS), has significantly reduced the direct manufacturing labour costs of products. Computers on the manufacturing floor give instructions to set up and run equipment quickly and automatically. The computers accurately measure hundreds of production parameters and directly control the manufacturing processes to achieve high-quality output. Managing more complex technology and producing very diverse products requires committing an increasing amount of resources for various support functions, such as production scheduling and product and process design and engineering. Because direct manufacturing labour is not a cost driver of these costs, allocating indirect costs on the basis of direct manufacturing labour often does not accurately measure how resources are being used by different products.

- **Advances in information technology**. Costing system refinements require more data gathering and more analysis and make the costing system more detailed. Improvements in information technology and the accompanying decline in the costs of tracking data make it more cost-effective to implement refinements in costing systems. It is more practical now to create systems that have multiple pools of indirect costs for allocating costs to products.

- **Competition in product markets**. As markets have become more competitive managers have felt the need to obtain more-accurate cost information to help them make important strategic decisions, such as how to price products and which products to sell. Making correct pricing and product mix decisions is critical in competitive markets because competitors quickly capitalise on a company's mistakes.

This chapter describes three guidelines for refining a costing system:

- **Direct-cost tracing**. Classify as many of the total costs as direct costs of the cost object as is economically feasible. This guideline aims to reduce the amount of costs classified as indirect.

- **Indirect-cost pools**. Expand the number of indirect-cost pools until each of these pools is more homogeneous. In a *homogeneous cost pool*, all of the costs have the same or a similar cause-and-effect (or benefits-received) relationship with the cost-allocation base. For example, a single indirect cost pool containing both indirect machining costs and indirect distribution costs that are allocated to products using machine-hours is not homogeneous because machining costs and distribution costs do not have the same cause-and-effect relationship with machine-hours. Increases in machine-hours – the cause – have the effect of increasing machining costs but not distribution costs. Now, suppose machining costs and distribution costs are subdivided into two separate indirect cost pools using machine-hours as the cost-allocation base for the machining cost pool and the number of shipments as the cost-allocation base for the distribution cost pool. Each indirect cost pool would now be homogeneous, which means that within each cost pool, all costs have the same cause-and-effect relationship with their respective cost-allocation base.

- **Cost-allocation bases**. Use the cause-and-effect criterion, when possible, to identify the cost-allocation base (the cause) for each indirect cost pool (the effect).

Activity-based costing systems

One often-used approach for refining a costing system is *activity-based costing*. **Activity-based costing (ABC)** systems refine costing systems by focusing on individual activities as the fundamental cost objects. An **activity** is an event, task, or unit of work with a specified purpose, for example designing products, setting up machines, operating machines and distributing products. ABC systems calculate the costs of individual activities and assign costs to cost objects such as products and services on the basis of the activities undertaken to produce each product or service.

We describe key ideas of an ABC system in the context of our Plastim example. ABC systems focus on indirect costs because direct costs can be traced to products and jobs relatively easily. A key step in implementing ABC at Plastim is to identify activities that help explain why Plastim incurs the costs that it currently classifies as indirect. To define these activities, Plastim organises a cross-functional team from design, manufacturing, distribution, and accounting and administration. The team identifies key activities using a flowchart of all the steps and processes needed to design, manufacture and distribute lenses.

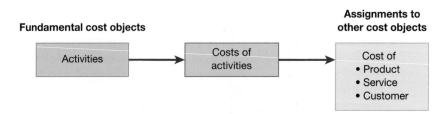

Plastim's team identifies seven major activities:

1   Design products and processes.

2   Set up moulding machine to ensure the mould is properly held in place and parts are properly aligned before manufacturing starts.

3   Operate machines to manufacture lenses.

4   Maintain and clean the mould after lenses are manufactured.

5   Set up batches of finished lenses for shipment.

6   Distribute lenses to customers.

7   Administer and manage all processes at Plastim.

By defining activities and identifying the costs of performing each activity, ABC systems seek a greater level of detail in understanding how an organisation uses its resources. As we describe ABC systems, keep in mind three features:

1   ABC systems create smaller cost pools linked to the different activities. Plastim partitions its original single overhead cost pool into seven activity-related cost pools.

2   For each activity-cost pool, a measure of the activity performed serves as the cost-allocation base. For example, Plastim defines set-up hours as a measure of set-up activity and cubic metres of packages moved as a measure of distribution activity. Because each activity-cost pool pertains to a narrow and focused set of costs (e.g. set-up or distribution), the cost pools are homogeneous – over time, the costs in each cost pool have a cause-and-effect relationship with the cost-allocation base. At Plastim, over the long run, set-up hours is a cost driver of set-up costs, and cubic metres of packages moved is a cost driver of distribution costs.

3   In some cases, costs in a cost pool can be traced directly to products. In the Plastim example, the cleaning and maintenance activity consists of salaries and wages paid to workers responsible for cleaning the mould. Following guideline 1 of refining a costing system, these costs can be traced directly to the specific mould used to produce the lens. Direct tracing of costs improves cost accuracy because it makes no assumptions about the cause-and-effect relationship between the cost pool and the cost-allocation base.

The logic of ABC systems is that more finely structured activity-cost pools with activity-specific cost-allocation bases, which are cost drivers for the cost pool, are considered to lead to more accurate costing of activities (see Cooper and Kaplan 1999). Allocating costs to products by measuring the cost-allocation bases of different activities used by different products may be seen to lead to more accurate product costs. In contrast, consider the case when the cause-and-effect relationship between overhead costs and the cost-allocation base(s) is weak. For example, in its existing costing system, Plastim uses direct manufacturing labour-hours as the cost-allocation base for all overhead costs, whether in set-up or distribution. Direct manufacturing labour-hours do not drive the costs in these activity-cost pools. Consequently, measuring the direct manufacturing labour-hours used by various products does not capture the overhead costs demanded by the different products.

By focusing on the set-up activity, we illustrate the effect of allocating all overhead costs to products using direct manufacturing labour-hours versus an ABC system with its emphasis on individual activities. Set-ups frequently entail trial runs, fine-tuning and adjustments. Improper set-ups cause quality problems such as scratches on the surface of the lens. The resources needed for each set-up depend on the complexity of the manufacturing operation: complex lenses require more set-up resources per set-up than do simple lenses. Furthermore, complex lenses can be produced only in small batches because the mould needs to be cleaned more often. Relative to simple lenses, complex lenses not only use more resources per set-up, they also need more frequent set-ups.

Set-up data for the simple S3 lens and the complex CL5 lens are as follows:

		Simple S3 lens	Complex CL5 lens	Total
1	Quantity of lenses produced	60 000	15 000	
2	Number of lenses produced per batch	240	50	
3 = (1) ÷ (2)	Number of batches	250	300	
4	Set-up time per batch	2 hours	5 hours	
5 = (3) × (4)	Total set-up-hours	500 hours	1500 hours	2000 hours

Plastim identifies the total costs of set-ups (consisting mainly of allocated costs of process engineers, supervisors and set-up equipment) of €300 000. The following table shows how set-up costs are allocated to the simple and complex lenses using direct manufacturing labour-hours and set-up-hours, respectively, as the allocation bases. The set-up cost per direct manufacturing labour-hour equals €7.54717 (€300 000 ÷ 39 750). The set-up cost per set-up-hour equals €150 (€300 000 ÷ 2000 set-up-hours).

	Simple S3 lens	Complex CL5 lens	Total
Cost allocated using direct manufacturing labour-hours			
€7.54717 × 30 000; €7.54717 × 9750	€226 415	€73 585	€300 000
Cost allocated using set-up-hours			
€150 × 500; €150 × 1500	€75 000	€225 000	€300 000

Which allocation base should Plastim use? Plastim should allocate set-up costs on the basis of set-up-hours. Why? Because, following guidelines 2 and 3, there is a strong cause-and-effect relationship between set-up-related overhead costs and set-up-hours, but there is almost no relationship between set-up-related overhead costs and direct manufacturing labour-hours. Set-up costs depend on the number of batches and the complexity of the set-ups and hence set-up-hours drive set-up costs. The simple S3 lens attracts more of the set-up costs when costs are allocated on the basis of direct manufacturing labour-hours. This occurs because more direct manufacturing labour-hours are needed to produce S3 lenses. However, direct manufacturing labour-hours required by the S3 and CL5 lenses bear no relationship to the set-up-hours demanded by the S3 and CL5 lenses.

Note that set-up-hours are related to batches (groups) of lenses made, not individual lenses. An important feature of activity-based costing is how it highlights the different levels of activities – for example, individual units of output versus batches of output – when identifying cause-and-effect relationships. As our discussion of set-ups illustrates, limiting the drivers of costs to only units of output (or cost-allocation bases related to units of output such as direct manufacturing labour-hours) frequently will weaken the cause-and-effect relationship between costs in a cost pool and the cost-allocation base. The *cost hierarchy* distinguishes costs by whether the cost driver is a unit of output (or variables such as machine-hours or direct manufacturing labour-hours that are a function of units of output), or a *group* of units of a product (such as a batch in the case of set-up costs), or the *product itself* (such as the complexity of the mould in the case of design costs).

Cost hierarchies

A **cost hierarchy** categorises costs into different cost pools on the basis of the different types of cost driver (or cost-allocation base) or different degrees of difficulty in determining cause-and-effect (or benefits-received) relationships.

ABC systems commonly use a four-part cost hierarchy – output-unit-level costs, batch-level costs, product-sustaining costs and facility-sustaining costs – to identify cost-allocation bases that are preferably cost drivers of costs in activity cost pools.

Output-unit-level costs are resources sacrificed on activities performed on each individual unit of a product or service. Manufacturing operations costs (such as energy, machine depreciation, and repair) that are related to the activity of running the automated moulding machines are output-unit-level costs. Why? Because the cost of this activity increases with each additional unit of output produced (or machine-hour run).

Suppose that in our Plastim example, each S3 lens requires 0.15 moulding machine-hours. Then S3 lenses require a total of 9000 moulding machine-hours (0.15 hour × 60 000 lenses). Similarly, suppose CL5 lenses require 0.25 moulding machine-hours. Then the CL5 lens requires 3750 moulding machine-hours (0.25 hour × 15 000 lenses). The *total* moulding machine costs allocated to S3 and CL5 depend on the quantity of each type of lens produced, regardless of the number of batches in which the lenses are made. Plastim's ABC system uses machine-hours, an output-unit-level cost-allocation base, to allocate manufacturing operation costs to products.

Batch-level costs are resources sacrificed on activities that are related to a group of units of product(s) or service(s) rather than to each individual unit of product or service. In the Plastim example, set-up costs are batch-level costs. Set-up resources are used each time moulding machines are set up to produce a batch of lenses. The S3 lens requires 500 set-up-hours (2 hours per set-up × 250 batches). The CL5 lens requires 1500 set-up-hours (5 hours per set-up × 300 batches). The *total* set-up costs allocated to S3 and CL5 depend on the total set-up-hours required by each type of lens, not on the number of units of S3 and CL5 produced. Plastim's ABC system uses set-up-hours, a batch-level cost-allocation base to allocate set-up costs to products.

In companies that purchase many different types of direct materials (Plastim purchases mainly plastic pellets), procurement costs can be significant. Procurement costs include the costs of placing purchase orders, receiving materials, and paying suppliers. These costs are batch-level costs because they are related to the number of purchase orders placed rather than to the quantity or value of materials purchased.

Product-sustaining (or **service-sustaining**) **costs** are resources sacrificed on activities undertaken to support individual products or services. In the Plastim example, design costs are product-sustaining costs. Design costs for each type of lens depend largely on the time spent by designers on designing and modifying the product, mould and process. These costs are a function of the complexity of the mould, measured by the number of parts in the mould multiplied by the area (in square metres) over which the molten plastic must flow (12 parts × 2.5 square metres or 30 parts-square metres for the S3 lens, and 14 parts × 5 square metres or 70 parts-square metres for the CL5 lens). The *total* design costs allocated to S3 and CL5 depend on the complexity of the mould, regardless of the number of units or batches in which the units are produced. Design costs cannot be linked in any cause-and-effect way to individual units of products or to individual batches of products. Plastim's ABC system uses parts-square metres, a product-sustaining cost-allocation base, to allocate design costs to products. Another example of product-sustaining costs is engineering costs incurred to change product designs, although such changes are infrequent at Plastim.

Facility-sustaining costs are resources sacrificed on activities that cannot be traced to individual products or services but which support the organisation as a whole. In the Plastim example, the general administration costs (including rent and building security) are facility-sustaining costs. It is usually difficult to find good cause-and-effect relationships between these costs and a cost-allocation base. This lack of a cause-and-effect relationship causes some companies not to allocate these costs to products and instead to deduct them from operating income. Other companies, such as Plastim, allocate facility-sustaining costs to products on some basis – for example, direct manufacturing labour-hours – because management believes all costs should be allocated to products. Allocating all costs to products or services becomes particularly important when management wants to set selling prices on the basis of a cost number that seeks to include all costs.

Implementing ABC at Plastim Limited

Now that we understand the basic concepts of ABC, we use it to refine Plastim's existing costing system. We again follow the seven-step approach to costing presented at the beginning of the chapter and the three guidelines for refining costing systems (increasing direct-cost tracing, creating homogeneous indirect-cost pools, and identifying cost-allocation bases that have a cause-and-effect relationship with costs in the cost pool).

Step 1: Identify the chosen cost objects   The cost objects are the S3 and CL5 lenses. Plastim's goal is to first calculate the *total* costs of manufacturing, and distributing these lenses and then the per-unit costs.

Step 2: Identify the direct costs of the products   Plastim identifies direct materials costs, direct manufacturing labour costs, and mould-cleaning and maintenance costs as direct costs of the lenses. In its existing costing system, Plastim classified mould-cleaning and maintenance costs as indirect costs and allocated them to products using direct manufacturing labour-hours. However, these costs can be traced directly to a lens because each type of lens can only be produced from a specific mould. Note that because mould-cleaning and maintenance costs consist of workers' wages for cleaning moulds after each batch of lenses is produced, cleaning and maintenance costs are direct batch-level costs. Complex lenses incur more cleaning and maintenance costs than simple lenses because Plastim produces more batches of complex lenses than simple lenses and because the moulds of complex lenses are more difficult to clean. Direct manufacturing labour-hours do not capture the demand that complex and simple lenses place on mould-cleaning and maintenance resources.

Plastim's direct costs are as follows:

Description	Cost hierarchy category	60 000 Simple lenses (S3)		15 000 Complex lenses (CL5)		Total
		Total (1)	Per unit (2) = (3) ÷ 60 000	Total (3)	Per unit (4) = (3) ÷ 15 000	Total (5) = (1) + (3)
Direct materials	Output-unit level	€1 125 000	€18.75	€675 000	€45.00	€1 800 000
Direct mfg. labour	Output-unit level	600 000	10.00	195 000	13.00	795 000
Cleaning and maintenance	Batch level	120 000	2.00	150 000	10.00	270 000
Total direct costs		€1 845 000	€30.75	€1 020 000	€68.00	€2 865 000

Step 3: Select the cost-allocation bases to use for allocating indirect costs to the products   Plastim identifies six activities – design, moulding machine set-ups, manufacturing operations, shipment set-up, distribution and administration – for allocating indirect costs to products. Exhibit 11.2, column 4, shows the cost-allocation base and the quantity of the cost-allocation base for each activity.

The cost-allocation base is pivotal in defining the number of activity pools in an ABC system. For example, rather than define the design activities of product design, process design and prototyping as separate activities, Plastim defines these activities as part of a combined design activity. Why? Because the complexity of the mould is an appropriate cost driver for costs incurred in all three design subactivities.

A second consideration in choosing a cost-allocation base is the availability of reliable data and measures. Consider, for example, the problem of choosing a cost-allocation base for the design activity. The driver of design cost, a product-sustaining cost, is the complexity of the mould – more complex moulds take more time to design. In its ABC system, Plastim measures complexity in terms of the number of parts in the mould and the surface area of the mould. If these data are difficult to obtain, or if measurement errors are large, Plastim may be forced to use some other measure of complexity, such as the amount of material flowing through the mould. The problem then is that the quantity of material flow may not adequately represent the complexity of the design activity.

Exhibit 11.2	Activity-cost rates for Plastim's indirect-cost pools				
Activity (1)	**Cost hierarchy category (2)**	**(Step 4) Total costs (3)**	**(Step 3) Quantity of cost-allocation base (4)**	**(Step 5) Overhead allocation rate (5) = (3) ÷ (4)**	**Brief explanation of the cause-and-effect relationship that motivates the choice of the allocation base (6)**
Design	Product-sustaining	€450 000	100 parts-square metres	€4500 per parts-square metres	Complex moulds (more parts and larger surface area) require greater Design Department resources
Set-ups of moulding machines	Batch level	€300 000	2000 set-up-hours	€150 per set-up-hour	Overhead costs of the set-up activity increase as set-up-hours increase
Manufacturing operations	Output-unit level	€637 500	12 750 moulding machine-hours	€50 per moulding machine-hour	Plastim has mostly automated moulding machines. Manufacturing overhead costs support automated moulding machines and hence increase with moulding machine usage
Shipment set-up	Batch level	€81 000	200 shipments	€405 per shipment	Costs incurred to prepare batches for shipment increase with the number of shipments
Distribution	Output-unit level	€391 500	67 500 cubic metres	€5.80 per cubic metre	Overhead costs of the distribution activity increase with cubic metres of packages shipped
Administration	Facility-sustaining	€255 000	39 750 direct manufacturing labour-hours	€6.4151 per direct manufacturing labour-hour	Administration Department resources support direct manufacturing labour-hours because the demand for these resources increases with direct manufacturing labour-hours

Step 4: Identify the indirect costs associated with each cost-allocation base In this step, overhead costs incurred by Plastim are assigned to activities, to the extent possible, on the basis of a cause-and-effect relationship between the costs of an activity and the cost-allocation base for the activity. For example, costs in the distribution-cost pool have a cause-and-effect relationship to cubic metres of packages moved. Of course, the strength of the cause-and-effect relationship between costs of an activity and its respective cost-allocation base varies across cost pools. For example, the cause-and-effect relationship between administration activity costs and direct manufacturing labour-hours is not as strong as the relationship between set-up activity costs and set-up-hours.

Some costs can be directly identified with a particular activity. For example, salaries paid to design engineers are directly identified with the design activity. Other costs need to be allocated across activities. For example, on the basis of interviews or time records, manufacturing engineers and supervisors identify the time spent on design activities, moulding machine set-up activity and manufacturing operations. The time spent on these activities serves as a basis for allocating manufacturing engineers' and supervisors' salary costs to various activities. Similarly, other costs are allocated to activity-cost pools using allocation bases that best describe the costs incurred for the different activities. For example, space costs are allocated on the basis of square metres used for different activities. However, the allocation base chosen may sometimes be constrained by the availability of reliable data.

The key point here is that all costs do not fit neatly into activity categories. Often, costs may first need to be allocated to activities before the costs of the activities can be allocated to products.

Step 5: Compute the rate per unit of each cost-allocation base used to allocate indirect costs to the products Exhibit 11.2 summarises the calculation of the activity-cost rates using the cost-allocation bases selected in step 3 and the indirect costs of each activity calculated in step 4. Exhibit 11.3, Panel A, presents an overview of the ABC system.

Step 6: Compute the indirect costs allocated to the products Exhibit 11.3, Panel B, shows indirect costs of €1 153 953 allocated to the simple lens and €961 047 allocated to the complex lens. To calculate indirect costs of each lens, the total quantity of the cost-allocation base used for each activity by each type of lens (using data provided by Plastim's operations personnel) is multiplied by the cost-allocation rate calculated in step 5 (see Exhibit 11.2, column 5). For example, of the 2000 hours of the set-up activity (Exhibit 11.2, column 4), the S3 lens uses 500 set-up-hours and the CL5 lens uses 1500 set-up-hours. Hence the total costs of the set-up activity allocated to the S3 lens is €75 000 (500 set-up-hours × €150, the set-up rate calculated in Exhibit 11.2, column 5) and to the CL5 lens is €225 000 (1500 set-up-hours × €150). The set-up cost per unit can then be calculated as €1.25 (€75 000 ÷ 60 000 units) for the S3 lens and as €15 (€225 000 ÷ 15 000 units) for the CL5 lens.

Step 7: Compute the total costs of the products by adding all direct and indirect costs assigned to them Exhibit 11.3, Panel B, presents the product costs for the simple and complex lenses. The direct costs are calculated in step 2 and the indirect costs in step 6. The activity-based costing system overview in Exhibit 11.3, Panel A, shows three direct-cost categories and six indirect cost pools. Hence, the cost of each lens type in Exhibit 11.3, Panel B, has nine line items, three for direct costs and six for indirect costs. The differences in the ABC product costs of S3 and CL5 calculated in Exhibit 11.3, Panel B, highlight how these products use different amounts of direct costs and different amounts of resources in each activity area.

We emphasise two key features of ABC systems. First, these systems identify all costs used by products, whether the costs are variable or fixed in the short run. Why? Because the focus of ABC systems is on longer-run decisions when more of the costs can be managed and fewer costs are regarded as fixed and given. Hence, ABC systems identify all resources used by products regardless of how individual costs behave in the short run. Second, as we have already described, recognising the hierarchy of costs is critical when allocating costs to products. It is easiest to use the cost hierarchy to calculate *total* costs. For this reason, we recommend calculating total costs first. The per-unit costs can then be easily calculated by dividing total costs by the number of units produced.

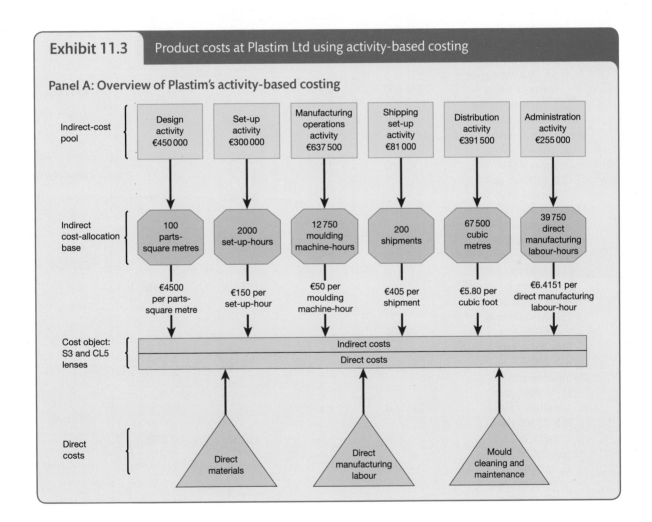

Exhibit 11.3   Product costs at Plastim Ltd using activity-based costing

Panel A: Overview of Plastim's activity-based costing

Exhibit 11.3   continued

Panel B: Product costs using the activity-based costing system

Description of Cost and and the Quantity of Activity Used by Each Type of Lens	60 000 Simple lenses (S3)		15 000 Complex lenses (CL5)		
	Total (1)	Per unit (2) = (1) ÷ 60 000	Total (3)	Per unit (4) = (3) ÷ 15 000	Total (5) = (1) + (3)
Direct costs					
Direct materials	€1 125 000	€18.75	€675 000	€45.00	€1 800 000
Direct manufacturing labour	600 000	10.00	195 000	13.00	795 000
Direct mould-cleaning and maintenance costs	120 000	2.00	150 000	10.00	270 000
Total direct costs	1 845 000	30.75	1 020 000	68.00	2 865 000
Indirect costs					
Design activity costs					
S3, 30 parts-square metres × €4500	135 000	2.25			450 000
CL5, 70 parts-square metres × €4500			315 000	21.00	
Set-up activity costs					
S3, 500 set-up-hours × €150	75 000	1.25			300 000
CL5, 1500 set-up-hours × €150			225 000	15.00	
Manufacturing operations activity costs					
S3, 9000 moulding machine-hours × €50	450 000	7.50			637 500
CL5, 3750 moulding machine-hours × €50			187 500	12.50	
Shipping set-up activity					
S3, 100 shipments × €405	40 500	0.67			81 000
CL5, 100 shipments × €405			40 500	2.70	
Distribution activity					
S3, 45 000 cubic metres × €5.80	261 000	4.35			391 500
CL5, 22 500 cubic metres × €5.80			130 500	8.70	
Administration activity					
S3, 30 000 direct manufacturing labour-hours × €6.4151	192 453	3.21			255 000
CL5, 9750 direct manufacturing labour-hours × €6.4151			62 547	4.17	
Total indirect costs	1 153 953	19.23	961 047	64.07	2 115 000
Total costs	€2 998 953	€49.98	€1 981 047	€132.07	€4 980 000

Comparing alternative costing systems

Exhibit 11.4 compares key features of and differences resulting from Plastim's existing single indirect-cost pool system (Exhibit 11.1) and the ABC system (Exhibit 11.3). We emphasise three points in Exhibit 11.4: (1) ABC systems trace more costs as direct costs; (2) ABC systems create more cost pools linked to different activities; and (3) for each activity-cost pool, ABC systems seek a cost-allocation base that has a cause-and-effect relationship with costs in the cost pool.

The homogeneous cost pools and the choice of cost-allocation bases, tied to the cost hierarchy, gives Plastim's managers greater confidence in the activity and product cost numbers from the ABC system. Allocating costs to lenses using only an output-unit-level allocation base, direct manufacturing labour-hours, as in the existing single indirect-cost pool system, overcosts the simple S3 lens and undercosts the complex CL5 lens. The CL5 (S3) lens uses a disproportionately larger (smaller) amount of output-unit-level, batch-level and product-sustaining costs than is represented by the direct manufacturing labour-hour cost-allocation base.

Exhibit 11.4	Comparing alternative costing systems		
	Existing single indirect-cost pool system **(1)**	**ABC system** **(2)**	**Difference** **(3) = (2) − (1)**
Direct-cost categories	2	3	1
	Direct materials Direct manufacturing labour	Direct materials Direct manufacturing labour Direct cleaning and maintenance labour	
Total direct costs	€2 595 000	€2 865 000	€270 000
Indirect-cost pools	1	6	5
	Single indirect-cost pool allocated using direct manufacturing labour-hours	Design cost pool allocated using parts-square metres Moulding machine set-up-cost pool allocated using set-up-hours Manufacturing operations-cost pool allocated using machine-hours Shipment set-up-cost pool allocated using number of shipments Distribution-cost pool allocated using cubic metres of packages shipped Administration-cost pool allocated using direct manufacturing labour-hours	
Total indirect costs	€2 385 000	€2 115 000	(€270 000)
Total costs assigned to simple (S3) lens	€3 525 000	€2 998 953	(€526 047)
Cost per unit of simple (S3) lens	€58.75	€49.98	(€8.77)
Total costs assigned to complex (CL5) lens	€1 455 000	€1 981 047	€526 047
Cost per unit of complex (CL5) lens	€97.00	€132.07	€35.07

The benefits of ABC systems arise in part from using ABC information in seeking to make decisions that are different from those in the absence of ABC (see Bhimani 2015). But these benefits must be traded off against the measurement and implementation costs and challenges of these systems. We focus on these issues next.

Concepts in action Hospitals use time-driven activity-based costing to reduce costs and improve care

In the United States, health care costs in 2012 exceeded 17% of gross domestic product and are expected to rise to 19.6% by 2021. Several medical centers, such as the M.D. Anderson Cancer Center in Houston and Children's Hospital in Boston, are using time-driven activity-based costing (TDABC) to help bring accurate cost and value measurement practices into the health care delivery system.

TDABC assigns all of the organisation's resource costs to cost objects using a framework that requires two sets of estimates. TDABC first calculates the cost of supplying resource capacity, such as a doctor's time. The total cost of resources – including personnel, supervision, insurance, space occupancy, technology and supplies – is divided by the available capacity – the time available for doctors to do their work – to obtain the capacity cost rate. Next, TDABC uses the capacity cost rate to drive resource costs to cost objects, such as the number of patients seen, by estimating the demand for resource capacity (time) that the cost object requires.

Medical centres implementing TDABC have succeeded in reducing costs. For head and neck procedures at the M.D. Anderson Cancer Center, the TDABC-modified process resulted in a 16% reduction in process time, a 12% decrease in costs for technical staff, and a 36% reduction in total cost per patient. Prior to implementing TDABC, managers did not have the necessary information to make decisions to reduce costs.

More broadly, health care providers implementing TDABC have found that better outcomes for patients often go hand in hand with lower total costs. For example, spending more on early detection and better diagnosis of disease reduces patient suffering and often leads to less-complex and less-expensive care. With the insights from TDABC, health care providers can utilise medical staff, equipment, facilities and administrative resources far more efficiently; streamline the path of patients through the system; and select treatment approaches that improve outcomes while eliminating services that do not.

Sources: Kaplan, R.S. and Anderson, S.R. (2007) 'The innovation of time-driven activity-based costing', *Cost Management*, March–April; Kaplan, R.S. and Anderson, S.R. (2007) *Time-driven Activity-based Costing: A Simpler and More Powerful Path to Higher Profits* (Boston, MA: Harvard Business School Press); Kaplan, R.S. and Porter, M.E. (2011) 'How to solve the cost crisis in health care', *Harvard Business Review*, September; Radnofsky, L. (2012) 'Steep rise in health costs projected', *Wall Street Journal*, 12 June.

Using ABC systems for cost and profit management

The emphasis of this chapter so far has been on the role of ABC systems in obtaining altered activity and product costs. Companies use ABC information for pricing, product mix, and cost management decisions. **Activity-based management (ABM)** describes management decisions that use activity-based costing information to satisfy customers and manage profitability. Although ABM has many definitions, we define it broadly to include pricing and product-mix decisions, cost reduction and process improvement decisions, and product design decisions.

Pricing and product-mix decisions

An ABC system gives management particular insights into the cost structures for making and selling diverse products. As a result, management can make pricing and product-mix decisions. For example, the ABC system indicates that Plastim can reduce the price of S3 to the €53 range and still make a profit, because the ABC cost of S3 is €49.98. Without this ABC information, Plastim management might erroneously conclude that they would incur an operating loss on the

S3 lens at the €53 price. This incorrect conclusion might cause Plastim to reduce its business in simple lenses and focus instead on complex lenses, where its existing single indirect-cost pool system indicates it is very profitable.

Focusing on complex lenses would be a mistake. The ABC system indicates that the cost of making the complex lens is much higher (€132.07 versus €97 under Plastim's existing direct manufacturing labour-based costing system). As Plastim's operations staff had thought all along, Plastim has no comparative advantage in making CL5 lenses. At a price of €137 per lens for CL5, the margins look very small. As Plastim reduces prices on simple lenses, it will probably have to negotiate a higher price for the complex lenses.

Cost reduction and process improvement decisions

Manufacturing and distribution personnel use ABC systems to focus cost reduction efforts. Managers set cost reduction targets in terms of reducing the cost per unit of the cost-allocation base in different activity areas. For example, the supervisor of the distribution activity area at Plastim could have a performance target of decreasing the distribution cost per cubic metre of products shipped from €5.80 to €5.40 by reducing distribution labour and warehouse rental costs.

Doing an analysis of the cost of important activities (activity cost pools) and the factors that cause these costs to be incurred (cost drivers and cost-allocation bases) reveals many opportunities for improving efficiency. Management can evaluate whether particular activities can be reduced or eliminated by improving processes. Each of the indirect cost-allocation bases in the ABC system is a non-financial variable (number of hours of set-up time, cubic metres shipped, and so on). Controlling physical items such as set-up-hours or cubic metres shipped is often the most fundamental way that operating personnel manage costs. For example, Plastim can decrease distribution costs by packing the lenses in a way that reduces the bulkiness of the shipment.

The following table shows the reduction in distribution costs of the S3 and CL5 lenses as a result of process and efficiency improvements that lower the cost per cubic metre (from €5.80 to €5.40) and the total cubic metres of shipments (from 45 000 to 40 000 for S3 and 22 500 to 20 000 for CL5).

	60 000 S3 lenses		15 000 CL5 lenses	
	Total (1)	Per unit (2) = (1) ÷ 60 000	Total (3)	Per unit (4) = (3) ÷ 15 000
Distribution cost per unit (from Exhibit 11.3, Panel B)	€261 000	€4.35	€130 500	€8.70
Distribution costs as a result of process improvements				
S3, 40 000 cubic metres × €5.40	216 000	3.60		
CL5, 20 000 cubic metres × €5.40			108 000	7.20
Savings in distribution cost from process improvements	€45 000	€0.75	€22 500	€1.50

Design decisions

Management can identify and evaluate new designs to improve performance by evaluating how product and process designs affect activities and costs. Companies can then work with their customers to evaluate the costs and prices of alternative design choices. For example, creative design decisions that decrease the complexity of the mould reduce costs of design, materials, labour, set-ups, moulding machine operations, and mould cleaning and maintenance.

If Plastim uses its existing direct manufacturing labour-hour-based system to choose among alternative designs, which design choices will Plastim favour? Those designs that reduce direct manufacturing labour-hours the most. Why? Because the cost system would erroneously signal that reducing direct manufacturing labour-hours reduces overhead costs. However, as our discussion of ABC systems indicates, direct manufacturing labour-hours have little impact on Plastim's overhead costs.

Planning and managing activities

As was the case with Plastim, most companies implementing ABC systems for the first time analyse actual costs to identify activity-cost pools and activity-cost rates. Many companies then use ABC systems for planning and managing activities. They specify budgeted costs for activities and use budgeted cost rates to cost products using normal costing. At year-end, budgeted and actual costs are compared in order to provide feedback on how well activities were managed. Adjustments are also made for under- or overallocated indirect costs for each activity area using the methods described in Chapter 3 (adjusted allocation-rate approach, proration or write-off to cost of goods sold). Kaplan and Cooper (1998) suggest that four stages subsume cost system designs. Stage I systems are inadequate for financial reporting or control purposes. They are 'broken'. Stage II systems are financial-reporting driven. They meet criteria for external financial statements but provide inadequate or even distorted cost information. Stage III systems fulfil financial reporting and many cost management needs. They may comprise several stand-alone ABC and performance measurement systems. Stage IV systems integrate cost management and financial reporting. Here ABM systems are integrated with other operational and strategic performance systems as well as financial reporting systems.

ABC and department-costing systems

Companies often use costing systems that have features of ABC systems – such as multiple cost pools and multiple cost-allocation bases – but that do not emphasise individual activities. Many companies have broadened their costing systems from using a single indirect-cost rate system, to using separate indirect-cost rates for each department (for example, design, manufacturing, distribution, and so on) or sub-department (for example, machining and assembly departments within manufacturing). Why? Because the cost drivers of resources in each department or sub-department differ from the single, company-wide, cost-allocation base. ABC systems are a further refinement of department costing systems. In this section, we compare ABC systems and department costing systems.

Reconsider our Plastim illustration. The indirect-cost rate for the design activity is, in fact, a Design Department indirect-cost rate. Plastim calculates the design activity rate by dividing total Design Department costs by a measure of the complexity of the mould (the driver of Design Department costs). Plastim does not find it worthwhile to calculate separate activity rates within the design department. Why? Because the complexity of the mould is an appropriate cost-allocation base for costs incurred for all design activities – the Design Department costs are homogeneous.

In contrast, in the Manufacturing (also in the Distribution) Department, Plastim identifies two activity-cost pools – a set-up-cost pool and a manufacturing operations-cost pool – instead of using a single Manufacturing Department indirect-cost pool. Why? For two reasons. First, each of these activities within manufacturing incurs significant costs and has a different driver of costs. Second, the S3 and CL5 lenses do not use resources from these two activity areas in the same proportion. For example, CL5 uses 75% (1500 ÷ 2000) of the set-up-hours but only 29.4% (3750 ÷ 12 750) of the machine-hours. Using only machine-hours, say, to allocate all Manufacturing Department costs at Plastim would result in CL5 being undercosted because it would not be charged for the significant set-up resources it actually uses.

The preceding discussion suggests the following. Using department indirect-cost rates to allocate costs to products results in the same product costs as activity-cost rates if (1) a single activity accounts for a sizable fraction of the department's costs, or (2) significant costs are incurred on different activities within a department but each activity has the same cost-allocation base, or (3) significant costs are incurred on different activities with different cost-allocation bases within a department but different products use resources from the different activity areas in the same proportions.

Where any one of these three conditions holds, using department indirect-cost rates rather than activity rates is often adequate. In companies where none of these conditions hold, department costing systems can be refined using ABC. Emphasising activities leads to more focused and homogeneous cost pools, and aids in identifying activity-cost-allocation bases that have a better cause-and-effect relationship with the costs in activity-cost pools. But the benefits of an ABC system must be balanced against its costs and limitations.

Implementing ABC systems

Managers choose the level of detail in their costing systems by evaluating the costs of the system against the benefits that accrue from using these systems while also taking into account the context in which such systems are to operate. There are 'tell-tale' signs that indicate when ABC systems are likely to provide benefits. We list some signals here:

1 Significant amounts of indirect costs are allocated using only one or two cost pools.

2 All or most indirect costs are identified as output-unit-level costs (i.e. few indirect costs are described as batch-level, product-sustaining or facility-sustaining costs).

3 Products make diverse demands on resources because of differences in volume, process steps, batch size or complexity.

4 Products that a company is well suited to make and sell show small profits, whereas products that a company is less suited to produce and sell show large profits.

5 Complex products appear to be very profitable, and simple products appear to be losing money.

6 Operations staff have significant disagreements with the accounting staff about the costs of manufacturing and marketing products and services.

Even when a company decides to implement ABC, it must make important choices about the level of detail. Should it choose many finely specified activities, cost drivers and cost pools, or would a few suffice? For example, Plastim could define a different moulding machine-hour rate for each different type of moulding machine. In making such choices, managers consider the context, costs and limitations of refining costing systems.

ABC systems require management to estimate costs of activity pools and to identify and measure cost drivers for these pools to serve as cost-allocation bases. Even basic ABC systems require many calculations to determine costs of products and services. These measurements are costly. Activity-cost rates also need to be updated regularly. Very detailed ABC systems are costly to operate and difficult to understand.

In very detailed ABC systems, the allocations necessary to calculate activity costs often result in activity-cost pools being measured with error. At times, companies are also forced to use substitute allocation bases for which data are readily available rather than preferred allocation bases. For example, a company might be forced to use the number of loads moved, instead of the complexity and distance of different loads moved as the allocation base for material handling costs because the former is easier to measure. When measurement errors are large, activity-cost information can be misleading. For example, if the cost per load moved decreases, a company may conclude that it has become more efficient in its materials-handling operations. In fact, the lower cost per load moved may have resulted solely from moving lighter loads over shorter distances.

Managers always trade off the expected benefits of designing a more detailed and accurate ABC system against the expected measurement and implementation costs of the system. Improvements in information technology and accompanying declines in technology costs have enabled ABC to be a practical costing system in many organisations. Understanding the organisational context is important for any accounting systems change. This is discussed next.

Concepts in action   Do banks provide 'free' services?

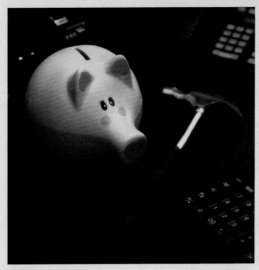

Source: Stockbyte

A major source of profitability in retail banks is the interest rate spread (the difference between the rate at which a bank lends or invests money and the rate it pays its depositors). Banks use this interest rate spread to cover the costs of the many 'free' services provided to customers, such as 'free' cheques and 'free' overdrafts. Many banks use activity-based costing (ABC) to determine the costs of their many individual services. This involves examining how each service (such as a current account) uses the resources of the bank. Some banks believe that they have been losing money on customers who hold small balances and make frequent use of the many 'free' services. In contrast, customers holding large balances and making limited use of the 'free' services are highly profitable to banks. These customers cross-subsidise those with small-balance accounts. This situation has particularly affected banks with a physical high-street retail presence. Likewise, e-banking services require fewer resources than the provision of off-line banking services. Banks offering both may also experience some level of cross-subsidisation. Consider, for instance, how the Lloyds TSB bank in the UK differentiates the net rate it pays savers on the 'e-Savings' versus 'Easy Saver' accounts with £1 or more:

'Easy Saver' account	'e-Savings' account
0.5% AER/Gross Variable	0.55% AER/Gross Variable (0.75% for £10 000+)

Many banks have responded to increased competition by instituting a detailed set of charges for services such as the following:

- non-approved overdraft over a preset limit
- banker's draft preparation
- special statement requests
- cheque stop-payment request
- cheque returned because of insufficient funds in account.

These charges may be derived following an analysis of the activities underlying each service. For example, returning a cheque because of lack of funds uses up more resources than putting a stop-payment on a cheque into effect. ABC information enables the magnitude of costs (and cross-subsidisation) to be known. This is useful to managers in understanding the effects of flat-fee pricing.

Source: From www.lloydstsb.com (July 2014). Please note that Lloyds TSB regularly reviews its accounts and the rates are subject to change.

Concepts in action   Successfully championing ABC

Source: Digital Vision Ltd/Lester Boswell

Successfully implementing ABC systems requires more than an understanding of the technical details. ABC implementation often represents a significant change in the costing sytem and, as the chapter indicates, it requires a manager to make major choices with respect to the definition of activities and the level of detail. What then are some of the behavioural issues that the management accountant must be sensitive to?

1 Gaining support of top management and creating a sense of urgency for the ABC effort

This requires management accountants to lay out the vision for the ABC project and to clearly communicate its strategic benefits (for example, the resulting improvements in product and process design). It also requires selling the idea to end-users and working with members of other departments as business partners of the managers in the various areas affected by the ABC project.

2 Creating a guiding coalition of managers throughout the value chain for the ABC effort

ABC systems measure how the resources of an organisation are used. Managers responsible for these resources have the best knowledge about activities and cost drivers. Getting managers to cooperate and take the initiative for implementing ABC is essential for gaining the required expertise, the proper credibility, and the necessary leadership. Gaining wider participation among managers has other benefits. Managers who feel more involved in the process are likely to commit more time to and be less sceptical of the ABC effort. Engaging managers throughout the value chain also creates greater opportunities for coordination and cooperation across the different functions, for example, design and manufacturing.

3 Educating and training employees in ABC as a basis for employee empowerment

Disseminating information about ABC throughout an organisation allows workers in all areas of a business to use their knowledge of ABC to make improvements. For example, WS Industries, an Indian manufacturer of insulators, not only shared ABC information with its workers but also established an incentive plan that gave employees a percentage of the cost savings. The results were dramatic because employees were empowered and motivated to implement numerous cost-saving projects.

4 Seeking small short-run successes as proof that the ABC implementation is yielding results

Too often, managers and management accountants seek big results and major changes far too quickly. In many situations, achieving a significant change overnight is difficult. However, showing how ABC information has helped improve a process and save costs, even if only in small ways, motivates the team to stay on course and build momentum. The credibility gained from small victories leads to additional and bigger improvements involving larger numbers of people and different parts of the organisation. Eventually, ABC and ABM become rooted in the culture of the organisation. Sharing short-term successes may also help motivate employees to be innovative.

5 Recognising that ABC information is not perfect because it balances the need for better information against the costs of creating a complex system that few managers and employees can understand

The management accountant must help managers recognise both the value and the limitations of ABC and not oversell it. Open and honest communication about ABC ensures that managers use ABC thoughtfully to make good decisions. Critical judgements can then be made without being adversarial, and tough questions can be asked to help drive better decisions about the system.

ABC and the organisational context

Throughout this book we have emphasised the need to consider technical management accounting issues in the light of organisational context. Organisations are subject to a variety of social and behavioural influences. One manager's aspirations will differ from the pursuits of another at the personal level. Different individuals tend to be motivated in different ways by common reward criteria. Moreover, individuals behave differently when working in teams as opposed to operating individually. Organisations have distinct cultures and sub-cultures and, often, political influence at the corporate level is tied to 'belonging' to particular groups or cliques or is simply determined by functional specialism. It is important to recognise that the implementation of a novel cost management approach can, in part, be the outcome of pressure for change as articulated by influential groups within the enterprise who show a preference for more financially oriented approaches to managerial control. One investigation revealed that bureaucracies are more likely to adopt and implement ABC (see Gosselin 1997) than other types of organisation. Indeed, Hopwood (1999, p. 5) notes that ABC 'focuses only on giving the most bureaucratic of insights into why costs are as they are'. He warns that: 'before too long we may come to see ABC as a technique of the past'.

The consequences of implementing an activity-based costing system may lead to novel insights about a company's operations. In one company, the director of activity-based management noted: 'there's a common language of our 150 activities and we now know that we do 150 things in our building a year and everybody understands what they are. It's incorporated into the culture' (Friedman and Lyne 1999, p. 69). Perhaps it is important to have an ABC system 'fit the current culture of the organisation' (see Henning and Undahn 1995) but resistance to change is sometimes dealt with in drastic ways. In one company adopting ABC, the finance director indicated that there had been some resistance to activity-based techniques among finance staff. He stated:

> **Yes, let's be honest about it, if they weren't prepared to work with us, they'd be sacked. We will not spend hours trying to convert people to a different way of thinking, we will change the people.**   (Friedman and Lyne 1995, p. 63)

It is often the case that relations between management accountants and operational managers improve significantly following the implementation of activity-based costing. Perhaps this is due partly to ABC systems' requiring the management accountant to integrate operational information based on first-hand observation and discussions with individuals across different departments, functions and activities within the enterprise. Nevertheless, resistance to accounting systems change is often present. The cure is not always management education. As one extensive study of ABC implementations in Finnish organisations suggests: 'Resistance is an important source of ABC failure and has different origins. These include economic rationale, political concerns and organisational culture' (see Malmi 1997).

Aside from organisational culture and related contextual factors, it is likely that attitudes towards and preferences for cost management practices are influenced by wider factors which can be nationally rooted. For instance, the traditional French full costing method is very similar to ABC. Therefore, many French managers perceive little or no incremental benefit from introducing ABC in their companies. Language also may be an obstacle, especially since there is no precise translation in French for ABC concepts. Activity-based costing has been developed in the USA and is based on a contractual system that clearly sets out the performances expected of each manager in each department. This system is consistent with the traditional 'managing by numbers' style that is prevalent in many American business organisations. The logic of this style of management stipulates that each person responsible for a budget must be assessed according to clearly defined objectives that were negotiated beforehand. As ABC identifies activities and cost drivers, it also defines activities in which managers have complete freedom to manoeuvre and the progress for which managers are individually or jointly responsible. It is possible that French cultural specificities may explain why the implementation of the ABC method has been slower in France than in Anglo-Saxon countries.

Sometimes, the intended objectives of an ABC or ABM system do not fully materialise and, indeed, a variety of unanticipated consequences arise. Changes in accounting systems rarely produce effects which are fully anticipated at the outset. Accounting systems changes tend to become enmeshed with interactions between individuals, processes, technologies, markets and other institutional factors, in often unpredictable ways. A good accounting system implementation is one which recognises the organisational state of flux within which it operates. Successful cost management can be considered an interdisciplinary and multi-functional activity. There are many good examples of ABC implementation, and 'ABC has many satisfied customers' (www.economist.com/node/13933812, 29 June 2009).

Summary

The following points are linked to the chapter's learning objectives.

1 Product undercosting (or overcosting) occurs when a product or service consumes a relatively high (low) level of resources, but is reported to have a relatively low (high) cost. Cost smoothing, a common cause of under- or over-costing, is the result of using broad averages that uniformly assign (spread) the cost of resources to products when the individual products use those resources in a non-uniform way. Product-cost cross-subsidisation exists when one or more undercosted (overcosted) products results in one or more other products being overcosted (undercosted).

2 Refining a costing system means making changes that result in cost numbers that better measure the way cost objects (such as jobs) differentially use the resources of the organisation. These changes can require additional direct-cost tracing, the choice of more indirect-cost pools, or the use of different cost-allocation bases.

3 An ABC approach differs from the traditional approach by its fundamental focus on activities. An ABC approach typically results in (a) more indirect-cost pools than the traditional approach, (b) more cost drivers used as cost-allocation bases, and (c) more frequent use of non-financial variables as cost-allocation bases.

4 A cost hierarchy is a categorisation of costs into different cost pools on the basis of different classes of cost drivers or different degrees of difficulty in determining cause-and-effect (or benefits received) relationships. Four levels of costs are output-unit-level costs, batch-level costs, product-sustaining costs and facility-sustaining costs.

5 In ABC, costs of activities are used to assign costs to other cost objects such as products or services.

6 Activity-based management (ABM) describes management decisions that use ABC information to satisfy customers and improve profits. ABM information can assist in decisions concerning pricing, product mix, costs reductions, process improvement, process or product redesign, and planning or managing activities.

7 Department costing systems approximate ABC systems only when each department has a single activity or a single allocation base for different activities or when different products use departmental activities in the same proportions.

8 Organisational context influences the decision to adopt ABC as well as its consequences. National contextual factors are also likely to have an effect.

Key terms

cost smoothing (313)
product undercosting (313)
product overcosting (313)
product-cost cross-subsidisation (313)
refined costing system (317)
activity-based costing (ABC) (318)
activity (318)

cost hierarchy (320)
output-unit-level costs (321)
batch-level costs (321)
product-sustaining costs (321)
service-sustaining costs (321)
facility-sustaining costs (321)
activity-based management (ABM) (328)

References and further reading

Bhimani, A. (2015) *Strategic Finance: Achieving High Corporate Performance* (London: Strategy Press), Chapter 4.

Cokins, G. (2001) *Activity-based Cost Management* (New York: John Wiley).

Cooper, R. and Kaplan, R.S. (1999) *The Design of Cost Management Systems* (Harlow: Prentice Hall).

Friedman, A. and Lyne, S. (1995) *Activity Based Techniques: The Real Life Consequences* (London: CIMA).

Friedman, A. and Lyne, S. (1999) *Success and Failure of Activity-based Techniques: A Long-term Perspective* (London: CIMA).

Gosselin, M. (1997) 'The effects of strategy and organisational structure on the adoption and implementation of ABC', *Accounting, Organisations and Society*, pp. 105–22.

Henning, K.L. and Undahn, F.W. (1995) 'Implementing ABC: the link between individual motivation and system design', *Advances in Management Accounting*, pp. 42–62.

Hopwood, A.G. (1999) 'Strategy and information: time to look out', http://ft.mastering.com/strategy.

Kaplan, R.S. and Cooper, R. (1998) *Cost and Effect* (Boston: Harvard Business School Press).

Labro, E. (2006) 'Analytics of costing system design', in A. Bhimani (ed.) *Contemporary Issues in Management Accounting* (Oxford: Oxford University Press), pp. 217–42.

Major, M. (2007) 'Activity-based costing and management: a critical review', in T. Hopper, D. Northcott and R. Scapens (eds) *Issues in Management Accounting* (Harlow: FT Prentice Hall).

Malmi, T. (1997) 'Adoption and implementation of activity-based costing: practice, problems and motives', PhD dissertation, Helsinki School of Economics and Business Administration.

CHAPTER 11

Assessment material

Review questions

11.1 Define cost smoothing, and explain how managers can determine whether it occurs with their costing system.

11.2 Why should managers worry about product over- or undercosting?

11.3 What is costing system refinement? Describe three guidelines for such refinement.

11.4 What is an activity-based approach to designing a costing system?

11.5 'Increasing the number of indirect-cost pools is guaranteed to sizably increase the accuracy of product, service or customer costs.' Do you agree? Why?

11.6 The accountant of a retailer has just had a €50 000 request to implement an activity-based costing system quickly turned down. A senior vice-president, in rejecting the request, noted, 'Given a choice, I will always prefer a €50 000 investment in improving things a customer sees or experiences, such as our shelves or our store layout. How does a customer benefit by our spending €50 000 on a supposedly better accounting system?' How should the accountant respond?

11.7 What are the most frequently used allocation bases for manufacturing overhead costs?

11.8 Describe four levels of a manufacturing cost hierarchy.

11.9 'The existence of non-output-unit-level costs means that managers should not calculate unit product costs based on total manufacturing costs in all levels of the cost hierarchy.' Do you agree? Explain.

11.10 How is an activity-based approach different from a traditional approach to designing a job-costing system?

Exercises

Intermediate level

*11.11 ABC, product-cost cross-subsidisation (30 minutes)

McCarthy Potatoes processes potatoes into chips at its highly automated Longford plant. For many years, it processed potatoes for only the retail consumer market where it had a superb reputation for quality. Recently, it started selling chips to the institutional market that includes hospitals, cafeterias and university halls of residence. Its penetration into the institutional market has been slower than predicted. McCarthy's existing costing system has a single direct-cost category (direct materials, which are the raw potatoes) and a single indirect-cost pool (production support). Support costs are allocated on the basis of kilograms of chips processed. Support costs include packaging material. This year's total actual costs for producing 1 000 000 kg of chips (900 000 for the retail market and 100 000 for the institutional market) are:

Direct materials used	€150 000
Production support	€983 000

The existing costing system does not distinguish between chips produced for the retail or the institutional markets.

At the end of the year, McCarthy unsuccessfully bid for a large institutional contract. Its bid was reported to be 30% above the winning bid. This came as a shock as McCarthy included only a minimum profit margin on its bid. Moreover, the Longford plant was widely acknowledged as the most efficient in the industry.

As part of its lost contract bid review process, McCarthy decided to explore several ways of refining its costing system. First, it identified that €188 000 of the €983 000 pertains to packaging materials that could be traced to individual jobs (€180 000 for retail and €8000 for institutional). These will now be classified as a direct material. The €150 000 of direct materials used were classified as €135 000 for retail and €15 000 for institutional. Second, it used activity-based costing (ABC) to examine how the two products (retail chips and institutional chips) used the support area differently. The finding was that three activity areas could be distinguished and that different usage occurred in two of these three areas. The indirect cost per kilogram of finished product at each activity area is as follows:

Activity area	Retail chips	Institutional chips
Cleaning	€0.120	€0.120
Cutting	0.240	0.150
Packaging	0.480	0.120

There was no opening or closing amount of any stock (materials, work in progress or finished goods).

Required

1 Using the current costing system, what is the cost per kilogram of chips produced by McCarthy?

2 Using the refined costing system, what is the cost per kilogram of (a) retail market chips, and (b) institutional market chips?

3 Comment on the cost differences shown between the two costing systems in requirements 1 and 2. How might McCarthy use the information in requirement 2 to make better decisions?

*11.12 ABC, activity area cost driver rates (continuation of Exercise 11.11) (30 minutes)

Exercise 11.11 reports ABC data for the three activity areas (cleaning, cutting and packaging) on a per output unit basis (per kilogram of chips). This format emphasises product costing. An alternative approach that emphasises the costs of individual processes (activities) is to identify (a) the costs at each activity area, and (b) the rate per unit of the cost driver at each activity area. The following information pertains to (a) and (b):

● Cleaning activity area: McCarthy used 1.2 million kilograms of raw potatoes to yield 1 million kilograms of chips. No distinction is made as to the end-product when cleaning potatoes. The cost driver is kilograms of raw potatoes cleaned.

- Cutting activity area: McCarthy processes raw potatoes for the retail market independently of those processed for the institutional market. The production line produces (a) 250 kg of retail chips per cutting-hour, and (b) 400 kg of institutional chips per cutting-hour. The cost driver is cutting-hours on the production line.

- Packaging activity area: McCarthy packages chips for the retail market independently of those packaged for the institutional market. The packaging line packages (a) 25 kg of retail chips per packaging-hour, and (b) 100 kg of institutional chips per packaging-hour. The cost driver is packaging-hours on the production line.

Required

1 What are the total activity costs in the (a) cleaning, (b) cutting and (c) packaging activity areas?

2 What is the cost rate per unit of the cost driver in the (a) cleaning, (b) cutting and (c) packaging activity areas?

3 How might McCarthy Potatoes use information about the cost driver rates calculated in requirement 2 to better manage the Longford plant?

11.13 Activity-based costing, product-cost cross-subsidisation (30–40 minutes)

Starkuchen GmbH has been in the food-processing business for three years. For its first two years (2013 and 2014), its sole product was raisin cake. All cakes were manufactured and packaged in 1 kg units. A normal costing system was used by Starkuchen. The two direct-cost categories were direct materials and direct manufacturing labour. The sole indirect manufacturing cost category – manufacturing overhead – was allocated to products using a units of production allocation base.

In its third year (2015) Starkuchen added a second product – layered carrot cake – that was packaged in 1 kg units. This product differs from raisin cake in several ways:

- more expensive ingredients are used
- more direct manufacturing labour time is required
- more complex manufacturing is required.

In 2015, Starkuchen continued to use its existing costing system where a unit of production of either cake was weighted the same.

Direct materials costs in 2015 were €0.60 per kg of raisin cake and €0.90 per kg of layered carrot cake. Direct manufacturing labour cost in 2015 was €0.14 per kg of raisin cake and €0.20 per kg of layered carrot cake.

During 2015, Starkuchen sales people reported greater-than-expected sales of layered carrot cake and less-than-expected sales of raisin cake. The budgeted and actual sales volumes for 2015 were as follows:

Budgeted	Actual	
Raisin cake	160 000 kg	120 000 kg
Layered carrot cake	40 000 kg	80 000 kg

The budgeted manufacturing overhead for 2015 was €210 800.

At the end of 2015, Wolfgang Iser, the accountant of Starkuchen, decided to investigate how use of an activity-based costing system would affect the product cost numbers. After consultation with operating personnel, the single manufacturing overhead cost pool was subdivided into five activity areas. These activity areas, their driver, their 2015 budgeted rate and the driver units used per kilogram of each cake are as follows:

Activity	Driver	Budgeted 2015 cost per driver unit	Driver units per kg of raisin cake	Driver units per kg of layered carrot cake
1 Mixing	Labour time	€0.04	5	8
2 Cooking	Oven time	€0.14	2	3
3 Cooling	Cool room time	€0.02	3	5
4 Creaming/icing	Machine time	€0.25	0	3
5 Packaging	Machine time	€0.08	3	7

Required

1 Calculate the 2015 unit product cost of raisin cake and layered carrot cake with the normal costing system used in the 2013 to 2014 period.

2 Calculate the 2015 unit product cost per cake under the activity-based normal costing system.

3 Explain the differences in unit product costs calculated in requirements 1 and 2.

4 Describe three uses Starkuchen might make of the activity-based cost numbers.

11.14 Activity-based costing, under- or overallocated indirect costs (continuation of Exercise 11.13) (40 minutes)

Wolfgang Iser, the accountant of Starkuchen, wants to further examine the relative profitability of raisin cake and layered carrot cake. He questions the accuracy of the activity-based normal costing numbers. He notes that the 2015 actual manufacturing indirect cost was €256 256. This differs sizably from the €210 800 budgeted amount. The 2015 actual indirect costs per activity area were as follows:

Activity area	2015 actual costs
Mixing	€62 400
Cooking	83 840
Cooling	12 416
Creaming/icing	36 000
Packaging	61 600
	€256 256

Required

1 Calculate the under- or overallocated manufacturing indirect costs in 2015 for:

   a Each of the five activity area indirect cost pools.
   b The *aggregate* of individual activity area indirect costs.

2 Assume that Starkuchen allocates under- or overallocated indirect costs to individual accounts based on the allocated overhead component in that account. What are the pros and cons of using:

   a Five separate under- or overallocated adjustments (one for each activity area)?
   b One under- or overallocated adjustment for the aggregate of all activity area indirect costs?

3 Calculate the 2015 actual unit product cost for raisin cake and layered carrot cake using the information calculated in requirement 1a.

4 Comment on the implications of the product cost numbers in requirement 3 for Starkuchen's pricing decisions in 2016.

11.15 **ABC and Budgets** (From CIMA Management Accounting Pillar Managerial Level Paper 21 November 2006) (25 minutes)

CJD Ltd manufactures plastic components for the car industry. The following budgeted information is available for three of their key plastic components:

	W £ per unit	X £ per unit	Y £ per unit
Selling price	200	183	175
Direct material	50	40	35
Direct labour	30	35	30
Units produced and sold	10 000	15 000	18 000

The total number of activities for each of the three products for the period is as follows:

	W	X	Y
Number of purchase requisitions	1 200	1 800	2 000
Number of set ups	240	260	300

Overhead costs have been analysed as follows:

Receiving/inspecting quality assurance	£1 400 000
Production scheduling/machine set up	£1 200 000

Required

1 Calculate the budgeted profit per unit for each of the three products using activity-based budgeting.

Advanced level

11.16 **Activity-based job-costing system** (40 minutes)

Henriksen AS manufactures and sells packaging machines. It recently used an activity-based approach to refine the job-costing system at its Vejle plant. The resulting job-costing system has one direct-cost category (direct materials) and four indirect manufacturing cost pools. These four indirect-cost pools and their allocation bases were chosen by a team of product designers, manufacturing personnel and marketing personnel:

Indirect manufacturing cost pool	Cost-allocation base	Budgeted cost-allocation rate
1 Materials handling	Component parts	DKr 8 per part
2 Machining	Machine-hours	DKr 68 per hour
3 Assembly	Assembly-line-hours	DKr 75 per hour
4 Inspection	Inspection-hours	DKr 104 per hour

Langeland recently purchased 50 can-packaging machines from Henriksen AS. Each machine has direct materials costs of DKr 3000, requires 50 component parts, 12 machine-hours, 15 assembly-hours and 4 inspection-hours.

Henriksen's prior costing system had one direct-cost category (direct materials) and one indirect-cost category (manufacturing overhead, allocated using assembly-hours).

Required

1 Present overview diagrams of the prior job-costing system and the refined activity-based job-costing system.

2 Calculate the unit manufacturing costs (using ABC) of each machine and the total manufacturing cost of the Langeland job.

3 The activity-based job-costing system of Henriksen has only one manufacturing direct-cost category: direct materials. A competitor of the Henriksen Company has two direct-cost categories at its manufacturing plant: direct materials and direct manufacturing labour. Why might Henriksen not have a direct manufacturing labour costs category in its job-costing system? Where are the manufacturing labour costs included in the Henriksen costing system?

4 What information might members of the team that refined the prior costing system find useful in the activity-based job-costing system?

11.17 Activity-based job costing (15 minutes)

Baden-Möbel GmbH manufactures a variety of prestige boardroom chairs. Its job-costing system was designed using an activity-based approach. There are two direct-cost categories (direct materials and direct manufacturing labour) and three indirect-cost pools. These three cost pools represent three activity areas at the plant:

Manufacturing activity area	Budgeted costs for 2015	Cost driver used as allocation base	Cost-allocation rate
Materials handling	200 000	Parts	€0.25
Cutting	2 160 000	Parts	2.50
Assembly	2 000 000	Direct manufacturing labour-hours	25.00

Two styles of chairs were produced in March, the executive chair and the chairman chair. Their quantities, direct material costs and other data for March 2015 are as follows:

	Units produced	Direct material costs	Number of parts	Direct manufacturing labour-hours
Executive chair	5 000	€600 000	100 000	7 500
Chairman chair	100	25 000	3 500	500

The direct manufacturing labour rate is €2 per hour. Assume no opening or closing stock.

Required

1 Calculate the March 2015 total manufacturing costs and unit costs of the executive chair and the chairman chair.

2 Suppose that the upstream activities to manufacturing (R&D and design) and the downstream activities (marketing, distribution and customer service) were analysed. The unit costs in 2015 were budgeted to be as follows:

	Upstream activities	Downstream activities
Executive chair	€60	€110
Chairman chair	146	236

Calculate the full product costs per unit of each line of chairs. (Full product costs are the sum of the costs in all business function areas.)

*11.18 Activity-based job costing, unit-cost comparisons (30 minutes)

Aircomposystèmes SA has a machining facility specialising in work for the aircraft components market. The prior job-costing system had two direct-cost categories (direct materials and direct manufacturing labour) and a single indirect-cost pool (manufacturing overhead, allocated using direct labour-hours). The indirect cost-allocation rate of the prior system for the year would have been SFr 115 per direct manufacturing labour-hour. Recently, a team with members from product design, manufacturing and accounting used an activity-based approach to refine its job-costing system. The two direct-cost categories were retained. The team decided to replace the single indirect-cost pool with five indirect-cost pools. These five cost pools represent five activity areas at the facility, each with its own supervisor and budget responsibility. Pertinent data are as follows:

Activity area	Cost driver used as allocation base	Cost-allocation rate
Materials handling	Parts	SFr 0.40
Lathe work	Turns	0.20
Milling	Machine-hours	20.00
Grinding	Parts	0.80
Testing	Units tested	15.00

Information-gathering technology has advanced to the point where all the data necessary for budgeting in these five activity areas are automatically collected. Two representative jobs processed under the new system at the facility in the most recent period had the following characteristics:

	Job 410	Job 411
Direct materials cost per job	SFr 9 700	SFr 59 900
Direct manufacturing labour cost per job	750	11 250
Direct manufacturing labour-hours per job	25	375
Parts per job	500	2 000
Turns per job	20 000	60 000
Machine-hours per job	150	1 050
Units per job	10	200

Required

1 Calculate the per-unit manufacturing costs of each job under the prior job-costing system.

2 Calculate the per-unit manufacturing costs of each job under the activity-based job-costing system.

3 Compare the per-unit cost figures for Jobs 410 and 411 calculated in requirements 1 and 2. Why do the prior and the activity-based costing systems differ in their job cost estimates for each job? Why might these differences be important to Aircomposystèmes?

11.19 **Question from the Association of Chartered Certified Accountants, Pilot Paper 2.4, Financial Management and Control** (45 minutes)

a Discuss the conditions under which the introduction of ABC is likely to be most effective, paying particular attention to:

- product mix;
- the significance of overheads and the ABC method of charging costs;
- the availability of information collection procedures and resources; and
- other appropriate factors. (17 marks)

b Explain why ABC might lead to a more accurate assessment of management performance than absorption costing. (8 marks)

(Total marks = 25)

CHAPTER 12

Pricing, target costing and customer profitability analysis

Pricing decisions are concerned with what to charge for the products and services delivered by organisations. For brevity, we use the term 'pricing decision' in this chapter to include decisions about the profitability of products. These decisions impact upon the revenues a company earns, which must exceed total costs if profits are to be achieved. Consequently, determining product costs is important for pricing decisions. There is, however, no single way of computing a product cost that is universally relevant for all pricing decisions. Why? Because pricing decisions differ greatly in both their time horizons and their contexts. For instance, McDonald's may set a price of £1.99 for a hamburger. This is a 'take it or leave it' price. A house-seller may set an asking price of £495 000 for her property and expect potential buyers to negotiate downwards from this price. Lufthansa.com may auction some of its airline seats whereby the buyer offers a price for a round-trip flight between two cities. Internet technologies have enabled many business models to use variable as opposed to fixed pricing. We emphasise how an understanding of cost-behaviour patterns and cost drivers can lead to more informed pricing decisions and also apply the relevant-revenue and relevant-cost framework described in Chapter 10. Proper pricing can heighten a company's profits. Baker et al. (2010) report that a one-percentage-point improvement in the average price of goods and services leads to an 8.7% increase in operating profits for the typical Global 1200 company. Yet 30% of pricing decisions companies make every year fail to deliver the best prices.

Economic theory indicates that companies acting optimally should produce and sell units until the marginal revenue (the additional revenue from selling an additional unit based on the demand for a product) equals the marginal or variable cost (the additional cost of supplying an additional unit). The market price is the price that creates a demand for these optimal numbers of units. This chapter describes how managers evaluate demand at different prices, manage their costs to influence supply, and earn a profit. We also consider the analysis of customer revenues and customer costs. Customer profitability analysis provides important information on profits generated by different customers rather than generic profits by product types.

Learning objectives

After studying this chapter, you should be able to:

- Discuss the three major influences on pricing decisions

- Distinguish between short-run and long-run pricing decisions

- Describe the target-costing approach to pricing

- Distinguish between cost incurrence and locked-in costs

- Describe the cost-plus approach to pricing

- Explain how life-cycle product budgeting and costing assist in pricing decisions

- Discuss why revenues can differ across customers purchasing the same product

- Apply the concept of cost hierarchy to customer costing

- Show how customer profitability reports can be prepared to highlight differences across customers in their profitability

Major influences on pricing

There are three major influences on pricing decisions: customers, competitors and costs.

Customers

Managers must always examine pricing problems through the eyes of their customers. A price increase may cause customers to reject a company's product and choose a competing or substitute product. Understanding customers' price and product characteristic preferences is a core competitive strength for business today. Indeed, a technology-driven revolution is under way where organisations are embracing 'dynamic pricing'. The idea of continuous variable pricing which prevailed in the pre-industrial world is proving a reality for today's web-enabled businesses. Firms can price dynamically to respond to demand, to create demand, to reduce waste and to turn over stock more rapidly. Many businesses use customer profiling and targeted pricing to refine product offerings to match individual customers' price sensitivities. Although price comparison websites such as Kelkoo or PriceGrabber can help potential customers identify the lowest prices for specific products, 'one-to-one' and private offers to customers cannot be tracked down in this way. Customer knowledge becomes a core technological-driven strength which helps render real prices opaque, invisible to the price crawlers that trawl through websites indiscriminately (see Lawrence 2007). Additionally, companies can harness 'Big Data' arising from the flood of customer interactions to enable more effective pricing. Companies which use Big Data in setting their prices have seen their profit margins lift by between 3% and 8% (Baker et al., 2014).

Competitors

Competitors' reactions influence pricing decisions. At one extreme, a rival's prices and products may force a business to lower its prices to be competitive. At the other extreme, a business without a rival in a given situation can set higher prices. A business with knowledge of its rivals' technology, plant capacity and operating policies is able to estimate its rivals' costs, which is valuable information in setting competitive prices.

Competitor analysis takes different forms. Many companies across the globe have established departments to search out information on their competitors' financial performance, patents, technologies, revenue and cost structures, and strategic alliances. Competitors themselves and their customers, suppliers and former employees are important sources of information. Another form of obtaining information is via reverse engineering – a process of analysing and tearing down competitors' products – to incorporate the best features, materials and technology in a company's own designs.

Competition spans international borders. For example, when companies have excess capacity in their domestic markets, they often take an aggressive pricing policy in their export markets. Today, managers often take a global viewpoint, and it is increasingly common for them to consider both domestic and international rivals in making pricing decisions.

Costs

Companies generally price products to exceed the costs of making them. The study of cost-behaviour patterns gives insight into the income that results from different combinations of price and output quantities sold for a particular product.

Surveys and corporate case studies of how executives make pricing decisions reveal that companies weigh customers, competitors and costs differently. Companies selling commodity-type products in highly competitive markets must accept the price determined by market forces. For example, sellers of wheat, rice and soya beans have many competitors, each offering the identical product at the same price. The market sets the price, but cost data can help these sellers to decide, say, on the output level that best meets a company's particular objective.

In less competitive markets, such as for cameras or mobile phones, products are differentiated and all three factors affect price. The pricing decision depends on how much customers value the product, the pricing strategies of competitors, and the costs of the product. As competition lessens even more, the key factor affecting pricing decisions is the customer's willingness to pay; costs and competitors become less important in the pricing decision.

Product-cost categories and time horizon

When reducing costs, a company must consider costs across all its value-chain business functions, from R&D to customer service. In computing the costs within these functions that are relevant in a pricing decision, the time horizon of the decision is critical. Most pricing decisions are either short run or long run. Short-run decisions include (1) pricing for a one-off special order with no long-term implications, and (2) adjusting product mix and output volume in a competitive market. The time horizon used to calculate those costs that differ among the alternatives for short-run decisions is typically six months or less but sometimes as long as a year. Long-run decisions include pricing a product in a major market where price setting has considerable leeway. A time horizon of a year or longer is used when computing relevant costs for these long-run decisions. Many pricing decisions have both short-run and long-run implications. We next examine short-run pricing decisions.

Costing and pricing for the short run

A one-off special order

Consider a one-off special order from a customer to supply products for the next four months. Acceptance or rejection of the order will not affect the revenues (units sold or the selling price per unit) from existing sales outlets. The customer is unlikely to place any future sales orders.

The English Tea Company (ETC) operates a plant with a monthly capacity of 1 million cases (each case consisting of 200 cans) of iced tea. Current production and sales are 600 000 cases per month. The selling price is €90 per case. Costs of R&D and product and process design at ETC are negligible. Customer-service costs are also small and are included in marketing costs. All variable costs vary with respect to output units (cases), and production is equal to sales. The variable cost per case and the fixed cost per case (based on a production quantity of 600 000 cases per month) are as follows:

	Variable cost per case	Fixed cost per case	Variable and fixed cost per case
Manufacturing costs			
Direct materials costs	€7	–	€7
Packaging costs	18	–	18
Direct manufacturing labour costs	4	–	4
Manufacturing overhead costs	6	€13	19
Manufacturing costs	35	13	48
Marketing costs	5	16	21
Distribution costs	9	8	17
Full product costs	€49	€37	€86

Variable manufacturing overhead of €6 per case is the cost of heating, cooling and lighting. Details of the fixed manufacturing overhead costs and their per case unitised costs (based on a production quantity of 600 000 cases per month) are as follows:

	Total fixed manufacturing overhead costs	Fixed manufacturing overhead cost per case
Depreciation and production support costs	€3 000 000	€5
Materials procurement costs	600 000	1
Salaries paid for process changeover	1 800 000	3
Product and process engineering costs	2 400 000	4
Total fixed manufacturing overhead costs	€7 800 000	€13

Uganda Tea (UT) is constructing a new plant to make iced tea in Kampala. The plant will not open for four months. UT's management, however, wants to start selling 250 000 cases of iced tea each month for the next 4 months in Uganda. UT has asked ETC and two other companies to bid on this special order. From a manufacturing-cost viewpoint, the iced tea to be made for UT is identical to that currently made by ETC.

If ETC makes the extra 250 000 cases, the existing total fixed manufacturing overhead (€7 800 000 per month) would continue to be incurred. In addition, ETC would incur a further €300 000 in fixed manufacturing overhead costs (materials procurement costs of €100 000 and process-changeover costs of €200 000) each month. No additional costs will be required for R&D, design, marketing, distribution or customer service. The 250 000 cases will be marketed by UT in Uganda, where ETC does not sell its iced tea.

A senior manager of UT notifies each potential bidder that a bid above €45 per case will probably be non-competitive. ETC knows that one of its competitors, with a highly efficient plant, has sizable idle capacity and will definitely bid for the contract. What price should ETC bid for the 250 000-case contract?

To calculate the relevant costs for the price-bidding decision, ETC systematically analyses the costs in each business function of the value chain. In this example, only manufacturing costs are relevant. All other costs in the value chain will be unaffected if the special order is accepted, so they are irrelevant.

Exhibit 12.1 presents an analysis of the relevant costs. They include all manufacturing costs that will change in total if the special order is obtained: all direct and indirect variable manufacturing costs plus materials procurement costs and process-changeover salaries related to the special order. *Existing* fixed manufacturing overhead costs are irrelevant. Why? Because these costs will not change if the special order is accepted. But the *additional* materials procurement and process-changeover salaries of €300 000 per month for the special order are relevant because these additional fixed manufacturing costs will only be incurred if the special order is accepted.

Exhibit 12.1 shows the total relevant costs of €9 050 000 per month (or €36.20 per case) for the 250 000-case special order. Any bid above €36.20 per case will improve ETC's profitability. For example, a successful bid of €40 per case, well under UT's ceiling of €45 per case, will add €950 000 to ETC's monthly operating profit: 250 000 × (€40 − €36.20) = €950 000. Note again how unit costs can mislead. The first table in this example reports total manufacturing costs to be €48 per case. The €48 cost might erroneously suggest that a bid of €45 per case for the UT special order will result in ETC sustaining a €3 per case loss on the contract. Why erroneous? Because total manufacturing cost per case includes €13 of fixed manufacturing cost per case that will not be incurred on the 250 000-case special order. These costs are hence irrelevant for the special-order bid.

Cost data, though key information in ETC's decision on the price to bid, are not the only inputs. ETC must also consider business rivals and their likely bids. For example, if ETC knows that its under-capacity rival plans to bid €39 per case, ETC will bid €38 per case instead of €40 per case.

Exhibit 12.1	Monthly relevant costs for ETC: the 250 000-case one-off special order	
Direct materials (250 000 cases × €7)		€1 750 000
Packaging (250 000 cases × €18)		4 500 000
Direct manufacturing labour (250 000 cases × €4)		1 000 000
Variable manufacturing overhead (250 000 × €6)		1 500 000
Fixed manufacturing overhead		
Materials procurement	€100 000	
Salaries paid for process changeover	200 000	
Total fixed manufacturing overhead		300 000
Total relevant costs		€9 050 000
Per case relevant costs: €9 050 000 ÷ 250 000 cases = €36.20		

Costing and pricing for the long run

Many pricing decisions are made for the long run. Buyers – whether a person buying a bar of chocolate, a construction company, such as Tarmac, buying a fleet of tractors, or Lloyd's bank buying audit services – prefer stable prices over an extended time horizon. A stable price reduces the need for continuous monitoring of suppliers' prices. Greater price stability also improves planning and builds long-run buyer–seller relationships.

Calculating product costs

Obtaining appropriate product-cost information is useful to a manager making a pricing decision. In industries such as oil and gas and mining, competitive forces set the price for a product, and knowledge of long-run product costs can guide decisions about entering or remaining in the market. In other industries such as specialised machines, appliances and motor vehicles, managers have some control over the price charged for a product, and long-run product costs can be used as a base for setting that price.

Consider the Astel Computer Company. Astel manufactures two brands of personal computers (PCs): Deskpoint and Provalue. Deskpoint is Astel's top-of-the-range product, a 4th generation Intel® Core™-i7 processor-based PC sold through computer dealers to large organisations and government accounts. Our analysis focuses on pricing Provalue, a less powerful Intel® Core™-based machine sold through catalogues and mass merchandisers to individual consumers and small organisations.

The manufacturing costs of Provalue are calculated using the activity-based costing (ABC) approach described in Chapter 11. Astel has three direct manufacturing cost categories (direct materials, direct manufacturing labour and direct machining costs) and three indirect manufacturing cost pools (materials handling, testing and inspection, and rework) in its accounting system. Astel treats machining costs as a direct cost of Provalue because it is manufactured on machines that are used for no other products. The following table summarises the activity-cost pools, the cost driver for each activity, and the cost per unit of cost driver Astel uses to allocate manufacturing overhead costs to products.

Manufacturing activity	Description of activity	Cost driver	Cost per unit of cost driver
1 Materials handling	Placing orders, receiving and paying for components	Number of orders	€80 per order
2 Testing and inspection	Testing components and final product	Testing-hours	€2 per testing-hour
3 Rework	Correcting and fixing errors and defects	Units reworked	€100 per unit reworked

Astel uses a long-run time horizon to price Provalue. Over this horizon, Astel's management views direct materials costs and direct manufacturing labour costs as variable with respect to the units of Provalue produced, and manufacturing overhead costs as variable with respect to their chosen cost drivers. For example, ordering and receiving costs vary with the number of orders. Staff members responsible for placing orders can be reassigned or laid off in the long run if fewer orders need to be placed. Direct machining costs (rent paid on leased machines) do not vary over this time horizon for the relevant range of production; they are fixed long-run costs.

Astel has no opening or closing stock of Provalue in 2015 and manufactures and sells 150 000 units. How does Astel calculate Provalue's manufacturing costs? It uses the following information, which indicates the resources used to manufacture Provalue in 2015:

1 Direct materials costs per unit of Provalue are €460.

2 Direct manufacturing labour costs per unit of Provalue are €64.

3 Direct fixed costs of machines used exclusively for the manufacture of Provalue are €11 400 000.

4 Number of orders placed to purchase components required for the manufacture of Provalue is 22 500. (We assume for simplicity that Provalue has 450 components supplied by different suppliers, and that 50 orders are placed for each component to match Provalue's production schedule.)

5 Number of testing-hours used for Provalue is 4 500 000 (150 000 Provalue units are tested for 30 hours per unit).

6 Number of units of Provalue reworked during the year is 12 000 (8% of the 150 000 units manufactured).

The detailed calculations underlying each of these numbers are shown in Exhibit 12.2. This exhibit indicates that the total costs of manufacturing Provalue are €102 million, and the manufacturing cost per unit of Provalue is €680. Manufacturing, however, is just one business function in the value chain. For setting long-run prices and for managing costs, Astel determines the full product costs of Provalue.

For brevity, we do not present any detailed analyses or calculations for the other value-chain functions. Astel chooses cost drivers and cost pools in each value-chain function to measure the cause-and-effect relationship between the activities and costs within each activity's cost pool. Costs are allocated to Provalue on the basis of the quantity of cost driver units that Provalue requires. Exhibit 12.3 summarises the product operating profit statement for Provalue for the year 2015 based on an activity analysis of costs in its value-chain functions (supporting calculations for non-manufacturing value-chain functions are not given). Astel earned €15 million from Provalue, or €100 per unit sold. We next consider the role of costs in long-run pricing decisions.

Alternative long-run pricing approaches

The starting point for pricing decisions can be

1 market-based

2 cost-based (also called cost-plus).

The market-based approach to pricing *starts* by asking: Given what our customers want and how our competitors will react to what we do, what price should we charge? The cost-based approach to pricing *starts* by asking: What does it cost us to make this product, and hence what

Exhibit 12.2	Manufacturing costs of Provalue in 2015 using activity-based costing	
	Total manufacturing costs for 150 000 units (1)	**Manufacturing cost per unit (2) = (1) ÷ 150 000**
Direct manufacturing costs		
Direct materials costs (150 000 units × €460)	€69 000 000	€460
Direct manufacturing labour costs		
(150 000 units × €64)	9 600 000	64
Direct machining costs (fixed costs of		
€11 400 000)	11 400 000	76
Direct manufacturing costs	90 000 000	600
Manufacturing overhead costs		
Ordering and receiving costs		
(22 500 orders × €80)	1 800 000	12
Testing and inspection costs		
(4 500 000 hours × €2)	9 000 000	60
Rework costs (12 000 units × €100)	1 200 000	8
Manufacturing overhead costs	12 000 000	80
Total manufacturing costs	€102 000 000	€680

Exhibit 12.3	Product profitability of Provalue in 2015 based on value-chain activity-based costing	
	Total for 150 000 units (1)	**Per unit (2) = (1) ÷ 150 000**
Revenues	€150 000 000	€1000
Cost of goods sold*		
(from Exhibit 12.2)		
Direct materials costs	69 000 000	460
Direct manufacturing labour costs	9 600 000	64
Direct machining costs	11 400 000	76
Manufacturing overhead costs	12 000 000	80
Cost of goods sold	102 000 000	680
Operating costs		
R&D costs	5 400 000	36
Design costs of products and processes	6 000 000	40
Marketing costs	15 000 000	100
Distribution costs	3 600 000	24
Customer-service costs	3 000 000	20
Operating costs	33 000 000	220
Full product costs	135 000 000	900
Operating profit	€15 000 000	€100

* Cost of goods sold = Total manufacturing costs since there is no opening or closing stock of Provalue in 2015.

price should we charge that will recoup our costs and produce a desired profit? Both approaches consider customers, competitors and costs. Only their starting points differ.

In very competitive markets (for example, oil and gas, and airlines) the market-based approach is logical. The items produced or services provided by one company are very similar to those produced or provided by others, so companies have no influence over the prices to charge. In other industries, where there is more product differentiation (for example, motor vehicles, management consulting and legal services) firms have some discretion over prices, products and services. Companies choose prices and product and service features on the basis of anticipated customer and competitor reactions. A final decision on price, product and service is made after evaluating these external influences on pricing along with the costs to produce and sell the product.

Under the cost-plus approach, price is first calculated on the basis of the costs to produce and sell a product. Typically, a mark-up, representing a reasonable return, is added to cost. Often, the price is then modified on the basis of anticipated customer reaction to alternative price levels and the prices charged by competitors for similar products. In short, market forces dictate the eventual size of the mark-up and thus the final price. Recent surveys of pricing practices report widespread use of cost-plus pricing.

Concepts in action — Extreme target pricing and cost management at IKEA

Around the world, IKEA has exploded into a furniture-retailing-industry phenomenon. Known for products named after small Swedish towns, modern design, flat packaging, and do-it-yourself instructions, IKEA has grown from humble beginnings to become the world's largest furniture retailer with 301 stores in 38 countries. How did this happen? Through aggressive target pricing, coupled with relentless cost management. IKEA's prices typically run 30%–50% below its competitors' prices. Moreover, while the prices of other companies' products rise over time, IKEA says it has reduced its retail prices by about 2% to 3% per year since 2000. During the conceptualisation phase, product developers identify gaps in IKEA's current product portfolio. For example, they might identify the need to create a new flat-screen-television stand. 'When we decide about a product, we always start with the consumer need', IKEA Product Developer, June Deboehmler, said. Second, product developers and their teams survey competitors to determine how much they charge for similar items, if offered, and then select a target price that is 30%–50% less than the competitor's price. With a product and price established, product developers then determine what materials will be used and what manufacturer will do the assembly work – all before the new item is fully designed. For example, a brief describing a new couch's target cost and basic specifications like colour and style is submitted for bidding among IKEA's over 1800 suppliers in more than 50 countries. Suppliers vie to offer the most attractive bid based on price, function and materials to be used. This value-engineering process promotes volume-based cost effectiveness throughout the design and production process.

Aggressive cost management does not stop there. All IKEA products are designed to be shipped unassembled in flat packages. The company estimates that shipping costs would be at least six times greater if all products were assembled before shipping. To ensure that shipping costs remain low, packaging and shipping technicians work with product developers throughout the product development process. When IKEA recently designed its Lillberg chair, a packaging technician made a small tweak in the angle of the chair's arm. This change allowed more chairs to fit into a single shipping container, which meant a lower cost to the consumer.

What about products that have already been developed? IKEA applies the same cost management techniques to those products, too. For example, one of IKEA's best selling products is the Lack bedside table, which has retailed for the same low price since 1981. How is this possible, you may ask. Since hitting store shelves, more than 100 technical development projects have been performed on the Lack table. Despite the steady increase in the cost of raw materials and wages, IKEA has aggressively sought to reduce product and distribution costs to maintain the Lack table's initial retail price without jeopardising the company's profit on the product. As founder, Ingvar Kamprad, once summarised, 'Waste of resources is a mortal sin at IKEA. Expensive solutions are a sign of mediocrity, and an idea without a price tag is never acceptable.'

Sources: Baraldi, E. and Strömsten, T. (2009) 'Managing product development the IKEA way. Using target costing in inter-organizational networks', working paper, December; Margonelli, L. (2002) 'How IKEA designs its sexy price tags', *Business 2.0*, October; Terdiman, D. (2008) 'Anatomy of an IKEA product', CNET News.com, 19 April; Ringstrom, A. (2013) 'IKEA founder to leave board', *New York Times*, 6 June.

Target costing for target pricing

An important form of market-based price is the *target price*. A **target price** is the estimated price for a product (or service) that potential customers will be willing to pay. This estimate is based on an understanding of customers' perceived value for a product and competitors' responses. A **target operating profit per unit** is the operating profit that a company wants to earn on each unit of a product (or service) sold. The target price leads to a *target cost*. A **target cost per unit** is the estimated long-run cost per unit of a product (or service) that, when sold at the target price, enables the company to achieve the target operating profit per unit. Target cost per unit is derived by subtracting the target operating profit per unit from the target price.

What relevant costs should we include in the target cost calculations? *All* costs, both variable and fixed. Why? Because in the long run, a company's prices and revenues must recover all its costs. If not, the company's best alternative is to shut down. Relative to the shutting-down alternative, all costs, whether fixed or variable, are relevant.

Target cost per unit is often lower than the existing full product cost per unit. To achieve the target cost per unit and the target operating profit per unit, the organisation must improve its products and processes. Target costing is widely used among different industries around the world. General Motors, Renault, Toyota, Daimler-Chrysler, Fiat and Volvo in the motor vehicle industry, and Siemens, Panasonic, Sharp and HP in the electronics and personal computer industries, are examples of companies that use target pricing and target costing.

Implementing target pricing and target costing

Developing target prices and target costs typically entails the following steps:

- Step 1: Develop a product that satisfies the needs of potential customers.

- Step 2: Choose a *target price* based on customers' perceived value for the product and the prices competitors charge, and a *target operating profit per unit*.

- Step 3: Derive a *target cost per unit* by subtracting the target operating profit per unit from the target price.

- Step 4: Perform *value engineering* to achieve target costs. **Value engineering** is a systematic evaluation of all aspects of the value-chain business functions, with the objective of reducing costs while satisfying customer needs. Value engineering can result in improvements in product designs, changes in materials specifications or modifications in process methods.

We illustrate the above steps for target pricing and target costing using the Astel Computer example introduced earlier in the chapter.

Step 1: Product planning for Provalue   Astel is in the process of planning design modifications for Provalue. Astel is very concerned about severe price competition from several competitors.

Step 2: Target price of Provalue   Astel expects its competitors to lower the prices of PCs that compete against Provalue by 15%. Astel's management believes that it must respond aggressively by reducing Provalue's price by 20%, from €1000 per unit to €800 per unit. At this lower price, Astel's marketing manager forecasts an increase in annual sales from 150 000 to 200 000 units.

Step 3: Target cost per unit of Provalue   Astel's management wants a 10% target operating profit on sales revenues.

Total target sales revenues	= €800 × 200 000 units = €160 000 000
Total target operating profit	= 10% × €160 000 000 = €16 000 000
Target operating profit per unit	= €16 000 000 ÷ 200 000 units = €80 per unit
Target cost per unit	= Target price – Target operating profit per unit
	= €800 – €80 = €720
Total current costs of Provalue	= €135 000 000 (from Exhibit 12.3)
Current cost per unit of Provalue	= €135 000 000 ÷ 150 000 units = €900 per unit

The target cost per unit of €720 is substantially lower than Provalue's existing unit cost of €900. The goal is to find ways to reduce the cost per unit of Provalue by €180, from €900 to €720. The challenge in step 4 is to achieve the target cost through value engineering.

Step 4: Value engineering for Provalue An important element of Astel's value engineering is determining the kind of low-end PC that will meet the needs of potential customers. For example, the existing Provalue design accommodates various upgrades that can make the PC run faster and perform calculations more quickly. It also comes with special audio features. An essential first step in the value-engineering process is to determine whether potential customers are willing to pay the price for these features. Customer feedback indicates that customers do not value Provalue's extra features. They want Astel to redesign Provalue into a no-frills PC and sell it at a much lower price. Value engineering at Astel then proceeds with cross-functional teams consisting of marketing managers, product designers, manufacturing engineers and production supervisors making suggestions for design improvements and process modifications. Cost accountants estimate the savings in costs that would result from the proposed changes.

Managers often find the distinction between value-added and non-value-added activities and costs introduced in Chapter 2 useful in value engineering. A *value-added cost* is a cost that customers perceive as adding value, or utility (usefulness), to a product or service. Determining value-added costs requires identifying attributes that customers perceive to be important. For Provalue, these attributes include the PC's features and its price. Activities undertaken within the company (such as the manufacturing line) influence the attributes that customers value. Astel assesses whether each activity adds value or not. Activities and the costs of these activities do not always fall neatly into value-added or non-value-added categories. Some costs fall in the grey area in between, and include both value-added and non-value-added components. The following classification typifies value-added and non-value-added categories in a manufacturing organisation:

Category	Examples
Value-added costs	Costs of assembly, design, tools and machinery
Non-value-added costs	Costs of rework, expediting, special delivery and obsolete stock
Grey area	Costs of testing, materials movement and ordering

In the Provalue example, direct materials, direct manufacturing labour and machining costs are value-added costs, ordering and testing costs fall in the grey area (customers perceive some portion but not all of these costs as necessary for adding value), while rework costs are non-value-added costs.

Value engineering seeks to reduce or eliminate non-value-added activities and hence non-value-added costs by reducing the cost drivers of the non-value-added activities. For example, to reduce rework costs, Astel must reduce rework-hours. Value engineering also focuses on achieving greater efficiency in value-added activities to reduce value-added costs. For example, to reduce direct manufacturing labour costs, Astel must reduce the time it takes to make Provalue. But how should Astel reduce rework time and direct manufacturing labour time? We focus on these issues next.

Cost incurrence and locked-in costs

Two key concepts in value engineering and in managing value-added and non-value-added costs are cost *incurrence* and *locked-in costs*. **Cost incurrence** occurs when a resource is sacrificed or used up. Costing systems emphasise cost incurrence. They recognise and record costs only when costs are incurred. Astel's costing system, for example, recognises the direct materials costs of Provalue as each unit of Provalue is assembled and sold. But Provalue's direct materials costs per unit are determined much earlier when designers finalise the components that will go into Provalue. Direct materials costs per unit of Provalue are *locked in* (or *designed in*) at the product-design stage. **Locked-in costs (designed-in costs)** are those costs that have not yet been incurred but that will be incurred in the future on the basis of decisions that have already been made.

Why is it important to distinguish between when costs are locked in and when costs are incurred? Because it is difficult to alter or reduce costs that have already been locked in. For example, if Astel experiences quality problems during manufacturing, its ability to improve quality and reduce scrap may be limited by Provalue's design. Scrap costs are incurred during manufacturing, but they may be locked in by a faulty design. Similarly, in the software industry, costs of producing software are often locked in at the design and analysis stage. Costly and difficult-to-fix errors that appear during coding and testing are frequently locked in by bad designs.

Exhibit 12.4 illustrates how the locked-in cost curve and the cost-incurrence curve might appear in the case of Provalue. (The numbers underlying the graph are assumed.) The bottom curve plots the cumulative costs per unit incurred in different business functions. The top curve plots the cumulative costs locked in. Both curves deal with the same total cumulative costs per unit. The graph emphasises the wide divergence between the time when costs are locked in and the time when those costs are incurred. In our example, once the product and processes are designed, more than 86% (say, €780 ÷ €900) of the unit costs of Provalue are locked in when only about 8% (say, €76 ÷ €900) of the unit costs are actually incurred. For example, at the end of the design stage, costs such as direct materials, direct manufacturing labour, direct machining, and

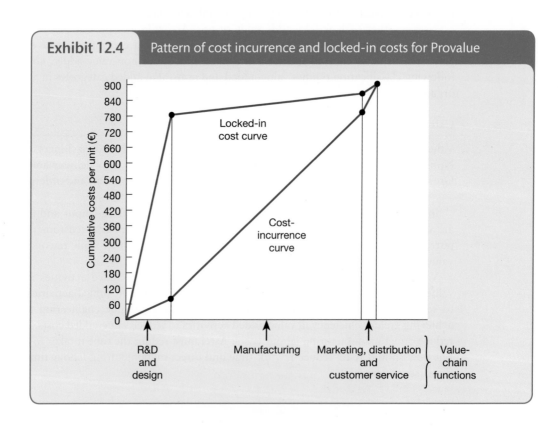

| **Exhibit 12.4** | Pattern of cost incurrence and locked-in costs for Provalue |

many manufacturing, marketing, distribution and customer-service overheads are all locked in. To reduce total costs, Astel must act to modify the design before costs get locked in.

We caution that it is not always the case that costs are locked in early in the design stage as was the case with Provalue. In some industries, such as mining, costs are locked in and incurred at about the same time. When costs are not locked in early, cost-reduction activities can be successful right up to the time that costs are incurred. In these industries, the key to lowering costs is improved operational efficiency and productivity rather than better design.

When a sizable fraction of the costs is locked in at the design stage, as in the Provalue example, the focus of value engineering is on making innovations and modifying designs at the product design stage. The best way to evaluate the effect of alternative design decisions on the target cost per unit is to organise a cross-functional value-engineering team consisting of marketing managers, product designers, manufacturing engineers, production supervisors, purchasing managers, suppliers and cost accountants. Why a cross-functional team? Because only a cross-functional team can evaluate the impact of design decisions on all value-chain functions.

The cross-functional team generates cost reduction ideas and tests them. The management accountant's challenge is to estimate cost savings and explain cost implications of alternative design decisions. To do so, the management accountant must develop a solid understanding of the technical and business aspects of the entire value chain and interact knowledgeably with other team members. A cross-functional team makes it easier to choose and implement new designs. Why? Because all parts of the organisation have 'bought into' the new design.

Achieving the target cost per unit for Provalue

Astel's value-engineering teams focus their cost-reduction efforts on analysing the Provalue design. Their goal? To design a high-quality, highly reliable machine with fewer features that meets customers' price expectations and achieves target cost.

Provalue is discontinued. In its place, Astel introduces Provalue II. Provalue II has fewer components than does Provalue and is easier to manufacture and test. The following tables compare the direct costs and the manufacturing overhead costs and cost drivers of Provalue and Provalue II. In place of the 150 000 Provalue units manufactured and sold in 2015, Astel expects to make and sell 200 000 Provalue II units in 2016.

Direct costs

| | Costs per unit | | |
Cost category	Provalue	Provalue II	Explanation of costs for Provalue II
1 Direct materials	€460	€385	The Provalue II design will use a simplified main printed circuit board, fewer components and no audio features
2 Direct manufacturing labour	€64	€53	Provalue II will require less assembly time
3 Direct machining costs	€76	€57	Machining costs are fixed at €11 400 000. Astel can use the machine capacity to produce 200 000 units of Provalue II. The new design will enable Astel to manufacture each unit of Provalue II in less time than a unit of Provalue. Direct machining costs per unit of Provalue II will equal €57 (€11 400 000 ÷ 200 000)

Manufacturing overhead costs

Cost driver	Quantity of cost driver Provalue*	Quantity of cost driver Provalue II	Explanation for quantity of cost driver used by Provalue II
1 Number of orders	22 500	21 250	Astel will place 50 orders for each of the 425 components in Provalue II. Total orders for Provalue II will equal 21 250 (425 × 50)
2 Testing-hours	4 500 000	3 000 000	Provalue II is easier to test and will require 15 testing-hours per unit. Total number of expected testing-hours will equal 3 000 000 (15 × 200 000)
3 Units reworked	12 000	13 000	Provalue II will have a lower rework rate of 6.5% because it is easier to manufacture. Total units reworked will equal 13 000 (6.5% × 200 000)

* From Exhibit 12.2.

Exhibit 12.5	**Target manufacturing costs of Provalue II**		
	Provalue II		**Provalue**
	Estimated manufacturing costs for 200 000 units (1)	Estimated manufacturing costs per unit (2) = (1) ÷ 200 000	Manufacturing costs per unit (Exhibit 12.2, column 2) (3)
Direct manufacturing costs			
Direct material costs			
(200 000 units × €385)	€77 000 000	€385.00	€460.00
Direct manufacturing labour costs			
(200 000 units × €53)	10 600 000	53.00	64.00
Direct machining costs			
(fixed costs of €11 400 000)	11 400 000	57.00	76.00
Direct manufacturing costs	99 000 000	495.00	600.00
Manufacturing overhead costs			
Ordering and receiving costs			
(21 250 orders × €80)	1 700 000	8.50	12.00
Testing and inspection costs			
(3 000 000 hours ×€2)	6 000 000	30.00	60.00
Rework costs (13 000 units × €100)	1 300 000	6.50	8.00
Manufacturing overhead costs	9 000 000	45.00	80.00
Total manufacturing costs	€108 000 000	€540.00	€680.00

Note that value-engineering activities reduce both value-added and non-value-added costs. For example, direct manufacturing labour cost per unit, a value-added cost, is reduced by designing a product that requires fewer direct manufacturing labour-hours (the cost driver for direct manufacturing labour costs). Rework cost per unit, a non-value-added cost, is reduced by simplifying the design to reduce defects during manufacturing and hence rework-hours (the cost driver for rework costs).

Exhibit 12.5 presents the target manufacturing costs of Provalue II, assuming no change in the cost per unit of the cost drivers. For comparison, Exhibit 12.5 also reproduces the manufacturing costs per unit of Provalue from Exhibit 12.2. Exhibit 12.5 shows that the new design is expected to reduce the manufacturing cost per unit by €140 to €540 from €680. A similar analysis (not presented) estimates the expected effect of the new design on costs in other value-chain business functions. Exhibit 12.6 shows that the estimated full product cost per unit equals €720 – the target cost per unit for Provalue II. Astel's goal is to sell Provalue II at the target price, achieve target cost, and earn the target operating profit.

Unless managed properly, value engineering and target costing can have undesired consequences (see also Cooper and Slagmulder 1997):

- The cross-functional team may add too many features in an attempt to accommodate the different wishes of team members.

- Long development times may result as alternative designs are evaluated endlessly.

- Organisational conflicts may develop as the burden of cutting costs falls unequally on different parts of the organisation.

To avoid these pitfalls, target-costing efforts should always focus on the customer, pay attention to schedules, and build a culture of teamwork and cooperation across business functions.

Exhibit 12.6	Target product profitability of Provalue II in 2016	
	Total for 200 000 units	**Per unit**
	(1)	**(2) = (1) ÷ 200 000**
Revenues	€160 000 000	€800
Cost of goods sold* (from Exhibit 12.5)		
Direct materials costs	77 000 000	385
Direct manufacturing labour costs	10 600 000	53
Direct machining costs	11 400 000	57
Manufacturing overhead costs	9 000 000	45
Cost of goods sold	108 000 000	540
Operating costs		
R&D costs	4 000 000	20
Design of products and processes costs	6 000 000	30
Marketing costs	18 000 000	90
Distribution costs	5 000 000	25
Customer-service costs	3 000 000	15
Operating costs	36 000 000	180
Full product costs	144 000 000	720
Operating profit	€16 000 000	€80

* Cost of goods sold = Total manufacturing costs (since we assume no opening or closing stock for Provalue II in 2016).

Concepts in action	Tata Motors and target pricing

Despite India's rapid economic growth and growing market for consumer goods, transport options in the world's most populous country remain limited. Historically, Indians relied on public transport, bicycles and motorcycles to get around. Less than 1% owned cars, with most foreign models ill-suited to India's unique traffic conditions. Most cars had unnecessary product features and were priced too high for the vast majority of Indians. But Ratan Tata, ex-chairman of India's Tata Motors, saw India's dearth of cars as an opportunity. In 2003, after seeing a family riding dangerously on a two-wheel scooter, Mr Tata set a challenge for his company to build a 'people's car' for the Indian market with three requirements: it should (1) adhere to existing regulatory requirements, (2) achieve certain performance targets for fuel efficiency and acceleration, and (3) cost only 1 lakh rupees (with £1400), about the price of the optional DVD player in a new Lexus sport utility vehicle sold in Europe.

The task was daunting: the target price was about half the price of the cheapest Indian car. One of Tata's suppliers said, 'It's basically throwing out everything the auto industry has thought about cost structures in the past and taking a clean sheet of paper and asking, 'What's possible?' Mr Tata and his managers responded with what some analysts have described as 'Gandhian engineering' principles: deep frugality with a willingness to challenge conventional wisdom. At a fundamental level, Tata Motors' engineers created a new category of car by doing more with less. Extracting costs from traditional car development, Tata eschewed traditional long-term supplier relationships, and instead forced suppliers to compete for its business using Internet-based auctions. Engineering innovations led to a hollowed-out steering-wheel shaft, a smaller diameter drive shaft, a trunk with space for a briefcase, one windshield wiper instead of two, and a rear-mounted engine not much more powerful than a high-end ride-on lawnmower. Moreover, Tata's car has no radio, no power steering, no power windows and no air conditioning – features that are standard on most vehicles. But when Tata Motors introduced the 'Nano' in 2008, the company had successfully built a one-lakh-rupee entry-level car that is fuel efficient; does 50 miles to the gallon; reaches 65 miles per hour; and meets all current Indian emission, pollution and safety standards. Due to rising material costs the price was raised to 1.5 lakh rupees as of 2012. The second-generation Nano is about to be marketed in the West.

While revolutionising the Indian automotive marketplace, the 'Nano' is also changing staid global automakers. Already, the French–Japanese alliance of Renault–Nissan and the Indian–Japanese joint venture of Maruti Suzuki are trying to make ultra-cheap cars for India, while Ford recently made India the manufacturing hub for all of its low-cost cars. Just like Ratan Tata, managers at many innovative companies are taking a fresh look at their strategic pricing decisions. How managers evaluate demand at different prices and manage costs across the value chain and over a product's life cycle to achieve profitability is of the essence.

Sources: Giridharadas, A. (2008) 'Four wheels for the masses: the $2,500 car'. *New York Times*, 9 January http://www.nytimes.com/2008/01/08/business/worldbusiness/08indiacar.html; Kripalani, M. (2008) 'Inside the Tata Nano factory', *Business Week*, 9 May http://www.businessweek.com/print/innovate/content/may2008/id20008059_312111.htm.

Cost-plus pricing

As illustrated in the last section, Astel uses an external market-based approach in its long-run pricing decisions. An alternative approach is to determine a cost-based price. Managers can turn to numerous pricing formulas based on cost. The general formula for setting a price adds a mark-up to the cost base:

Cost base	€X
Mark-up component	Y
Prospective selling price	€X + Y

Cost-plus target rate of return on investment

Consider a cost-based pricing formula that Astel could use for Provalue II. Assume that Astel's engineers have redesigned Provalue into Provalue II as described earlier and that Astel uses a 12% mark-up on the full product cost per unit in developing the prospective selling price.

Cost base (full product cost per unit, from Exhibit 12.6)	€720.00
Mark-up component (12% × €720)	86.40
Prospective selling price	€806.40

How is the mark-up percentage of 12% determined? One approach is to choose a mark-up to earn a *target rate of return on investment*. The **target rate of return on investment** is the target operating profit that an organisation must earn divided by invested capital. Invested capital can be defined in many ways. In this chapter, we define it as total assets (long-term or fixed assets plus current assets). Companies usually specify the target rate of return required on investments. Suppose Astel's (pre-tax) target rate of return on investment is 18%. Assume that the capital investment needed for Provalue II is €96 million. The target operating profit that Astel must earn from Provalue II can then be calculated as follows:

Invested capital	€96 000 000
Target rate of return on investment	18%
Total target operating profit (18% × €96 000 000)	€17 280 000
Target operating profit per unit of Provalue II (€17 280 000 ÷ 200 000 units)	€86.40

The calculation indicates that Astel would like to earn a target operating profit of €86.40 on each unit of Provalue II. What mark-up does this return amount to? Expressed as a percentage of the full product cost per unit of €720, the mark-up is equal to 12% (€86.40 ÷ €720). Do not confuse the 18% target rate of return on investment with the 12% mark-up percentage. The 18% target rate of return on investment expresses Astel's expected operating profit as a percentage of investment. The 12% mark-up expresses operating profit per unit as a percentage of the full product cost per unit. Astel first calculates the target rate of return on investment, and then determines the mark-up percentage.

Companies sometimes find it difficult to determine the capital invested to support a product. Computing invested capital requires allocations of investments in equipment and buildings (used for design, production, marketing, distribution and customer service) to individual products – a difficult and sometimes arbitrary task. Some companies therefore prefer to use alternative cost bases and mark-up percentages that do not require calculations of invested capital to set price. We illustrate these alternatives using the Astel example. Exhibit 12.7 separates the cost per unit for each value-chain business function into its variable and fixed components (without providing details of the calculations). The following table illustrates some alternative cost bases and mark-up percentages.

Exhibit 12.7	Estimated cost structure for Provalue II

Business function	Variable cost per unit	Fixed cost per unit*	Business function cost per unit
R&D	€8.00	€12.00	€20.00
Design of product/process	10.00	20.00	30.00
Manufacturing	483.00	57.00	540.00
Marketing	25.00	65.00	90.00
Distribution	15.00	10.00	25.00
Customer service	6.00	9.00	15.00
Product costs	€547.00	€173.00	€720.00
	Variable product cost per unit	Fixed product cost per unit	Full product cost per unit

* Based on budgeted annual production of 200 000 units.

Cost base	Estimated cost per unit of Provalue II (1)	Mark-up percentage (2)	Mark-up component for Provalue II (3) = (1) × (2)	Prospective selling price for Provalue II (4) = (1) + (3)
Variable manufacturing costs	€483.00	65%	€313.95	€796.95
Variable product costs	547.00	45	246.15	793.15
Manufacturing function costs	540.00	50	270.00	810.00
Full product cost	720.00	12	86.40	806.40

To illustrate the mark-up calculations, we have assumed (but not derived) the mark-up percentages in the table. The different cost bases and mark-up percentages that we use in the table give prospective selling prices that are relatively close to one another. In practice, a company will choose a cost base that it regards as reliable, and a mark-up percentage on the basis of its experience in pricing products to recover its costs and earn a desired return on investment. For example, a company may choose a full product cost base if it is unsure about variable- and fixed-cost distinctions.

The mark-up percentages in the table vary a great deal, from a high of 65% on variable manufacturing costs to a low of 12% on full product costs. Why? Because the mark-up based on variable manufacturing costs takes into account the need to earn a profit, and to recoup fixed manufacturing costs and other business function costs such as R&D, marketing and distribution. The greater these costs relative to variable manufacturing costs, the higher the mark-up percentage. The mark-up percentage on full product costs is much lower. Why? Because full product costs already include all costs incurred to sell the product. The precise mark-up percentage also depends on the competitiveness of the product market. Mark-ups and profit margins tend to be lower the more competitive the market.

The advantages cited by many companies for including fixed costs per unit for pricing decisions include the following:

1 *Full product cost recovery.* For long-run pricing decisions, full product costs inform managers of the bare minimum costs they need to recover to continue in business rather than shut down. Using variable costs as a base does not give managers this information. There is then a temptation to engage in excessive long-run price cutting as long as prices give a positive contribution margin. Long-run price cutting, however, may result in long-run revenues being less than long-run (full product) costs, resulting in the company going out of business.

2 *Price stability.* Managers believe that full-cost formula pricing promotes price stability, because it limits the ability of managers to cut prices. Managers prefer price stability because it facilitates planning.

3 *Simplicity.* A full-cost formula for pricing does not require a detailed analysis of cost-behaviour patterns to separate costs into fixed and variable components for each product. Calculating variable costs for each product is expensive and prone to errors. For these reasons, many managers believe that full-cost formula pricing meets the cost–benefit test.

Including unit fixed costs when pricing is not without its problems. Allocating fixed costs to products can be somewhat arbitrary. Calculating fixed cost per unit requires an estimate of expected future sales quantities. If actual sales fall short of this estimate, the actual full product cost per unit could exceed price. There are instances where non-cost factors are relevant in price setting.

Price discrimination is the practice of charging some customers a higher price than is charged to other customers. Peak-load pricing is the practice of charging a higher price for the same product or service when demand approaches physical capacity limits. Under price discrimination and peak-load pricing, prices differ among market segments even though the outlay costs of providing the product or service are approximately the same. For instance, airlines often charge business travellers higher fares than pleasure travellers. This is possible because business travellers tend to return home within the same week. Likewise, telephone companies can charge higher prices for telephone calls made during business hours. There are illustrations of price discrimination and peak-load pricing.

Life-cycle product budgeting and costing

The **product life cycle** spans the time from initial R&D to the time at which support to customers is withdrawn. For motor vehicles, this time span may range from 5 to 10 years. For some pharmaceutical products, the time span may be 3–5 years. For fashion clothing products, the time span may be less than 1 year.

Using **life-cycle budgeting**, managers estimate the revenues and costs attributable to each product from its initial R&D to its final customer servicing and support in the marketplace. **Life-cycle costing** tracks and accumulates the actual costs attributable to each product from start to finish. The terms 'cradle-to-grave costing' and 'womb-to-tomb costing' convey the sense of fully capturing all costs associated with the product.

There are, according to Baker et al. (2010), two essential points 'to price effectively throughout the life of a product or service. First, companies should actively manage the trade-off between price and volume or profit and market share to maximise returns [...]. Second, companies must make pricing decisions in the context of their broader product portfolios.' We consider here and in later chapters both volume and portfolio-mix issues.

Life-cycle budgeting and pricing decisions

Life-cycle budgeted costs can provide important information for pricing decisions. For some products, the development period is relatively long, and many costs are incurred prior to manufacturing. Consider Fjalar AS, a computer software company developing a new accounting package, 'General Ledger'. Assume the following budgeted amounts for General Ledger over a six-year product life cycle:

Years 1 and 2	
R&D costs	€240 000
Design costs	€60 000

Years 3 to 6		
	One-time set-up costs	Costs per package
Production costs	€100 000	€25
Marketing costs	70 000	24
Distribution costs	50 000	16
Customer-service costs	80 000	30

To be profitable, Fjalar must generate revenues to cover costs in all six business functions. A product life-cycle budget highlights the importance of setting prices and budgeting revenues to recover costs in *all* the value-chain business functions rather than costs in only some of the functions (such as production). The life-cycle budget also indicates the costs to be incurred over the life of the product. Exhibit 12.8 presents the life-cycle budget for General Ledger.

Three combinations of the selling price per package and predicted demand are shown. The high non-production costs at Fjalar are readily apparent in Exhibit 12.8. For example, R&D and product-design costs constitute over 30% of total costs for each of the three combinations of selling price and predicted sales quantity. Fjalar should put a premium on having as accurate a set of revenue and cost predictions for General Ledger as possible, given the high percentage of total life-cycle costs incurred before any production begins and before any revenue is received.

Exhibit 12.8 assumes that the selling price per package is the same over the entire life cycle. For strategic reasons, however, Fjalar may choose to 'skim the market' by charging higher prices to customers eager to try General Ledger when it first comes out, and lower prices to customers who are willing to wait. The life-cycle budget will then express this strategy.

Developing life-cycle reports

Most accounting systems emphasise reporting on a calendar basis – monthly, quarterly and annually. In contrast, product life-cycle reporting does not have this calendar-based focus. Consider the life spans of four Fjalar products:

	Year 1	Year 2	Year 3	Year 4	Year 5	Year 6
General Ledger Package						
Law Package						
Payroll Package						
Engineering Package						

Each product spans more than one calendar year.

Exhibit 12.8	Budgeted life-cycle revenues and costs for 'general ledger' softwarepackage of Fjalar AS*

	Alternative selling price/sales-quantity combinations		
	1	2	3
Selling price per package:	€400	€480	€600
Sales quantity in units:	5000	4000	2500
Life-cycle revenues (€400 × 5000);			
(€480 × 4000; €600 × 2500)	€2 000 000	€1 920 000	€1 500 000
Life-cycle costs			
R&D costs	240 000	240 000	240 000
Design costs of product/process	160 000	160 000	160 000
Production costs			
€100 000 + (€25 × 5000);			
€100 000 + (€25 × 4000);			
€100 000 + (€25 × 2500)	225 000	200 000	162 500
Marketing costs			
€70 000 + (€24 × 5000);			
€70 000 + (€24 × 4000);			
€70 000 + (€24 × 2500)	190 000	166 000	130 000
Distribution costs			
€50 000 + (€16 × 5000);			
€50 000 + (€16 × 4000);			
€50 000 + (€16 × 2500)	130 000	114 000	90 000
Customer-service costs			
€80 000 + (€30 × 5000);			
€80 000 + (€30 × 4000);			
€80 000 + (€30 × 2500)	230 000	200 000	155 000
Total life-cycle costs	1 175 000	1 080 000	937 500
Life-cycle operating profit	€825 000	€840 000	€562 500

* This exhibit does not take into consideration the time value of money when computing life-cycle revenues or life-cycle costs. Chapter 13 outlines how this important factor can be incorporated into such calculations.

Developing life-cycle reports for each product requires tracking costs and revenues on a product-by-product basis over several calendar periods. For example, the R&D costs included in a product life-cycle cost report are often incurred in different calendar years. When R&D costs are tracked over the entire life cycle, the total magnitude of these costs for each individual product can be calculated and analysed.

A product life-cycle reporting format offers at least three important benefits:

1 The full set of revenues and costs associated with each product becomes visible. Manufacturing costs are highly visible in most accounting systems. However, the costs associated with upstream areas (for example, R&D) and downstream areas (for example, customer service) are frequently less visible on a product-by-product basis.

2 Differences among products in the percentage of their total costs incurred at early stages in the life cycle are highlighted. The higher this percentage, the more important it is for managers to develop, as early as possible, accurate predictions of the revenues for that product.

3 Interrelationships among business function cost categories are highlighted. For example, companies that cut back their R&D and product-design costs may experience major increases in customer-service costs in subsequent years. Those costs arise because products fail to meet promised quality-performance levels. A life-cycle revenue and cost report prevents such causally related changes among business function costs from being hidden (buried) as they are in calendar profit statements.

Life-cycle costs further reinforce the importance of locked-in costs, target costing and value engineering in pricing and cost management. For products with long life cycles, a very small fraction of the total life-cycle costs are actually incurred at the time when costs are locked in. But locked-in costs will determine how costs will be incurred over several years. Motor vehicle manufacturers combine target costing with life-cycle budgeting. For example, Ford, General Motors, Nissan and Volvo determine target prices and target costs for their car models on the basis of estimated costs and revenues over a multi-year horizon.

Customer profitability analysis

Customer profitability analysis refers to the reporting and analysis of customer revenues and customer costs. Managers need to ensure that customers contributing sizably to the profitability of an organisation receive a comparable level of attention from the organisation. An accounting system that reports customer profitability helps managers in this task. See Bhimani (2015), Kaplan and Cooper (1998) and Smith (1997) for discussions and further examples of the application of customer-profitability analysis.

The marketing efforts of companies aim to attract and retain profitable customers. This section examines the reporting and analysis of customer revenues and customer costs. We will discuss the Spring Distribution Company, a distributor of water bottled by Spring Products. Spring Distribution buys bottled water from Spring Products at €0.50 a bottle. It sells to wholesale customers at a list price of €0.60 a bottle. Customers range from large supermarkets, hospitals and university canteens to small corner shops. It does not sell to final end-point consumers.

Customer revenues

Customer revenues are inflows of assets from customers received in exchange for products or services being provided to those customers. More accurate customer revenues can likewise be obtained by tracing as many revenue items (such as sales returns and coupons) as possible to individual customers.

The analysis of customer profitability is enhanced by retaining as much detail as possible about revenue. A key concern here is **price discounting**, which is the reduction of selling prices below listed levels in order to encourage an increase in purchases by customers. Accounting systems differ with respect to how details on discounting are recorded. Spring Distribution offers price discounts below its €0.60 list price per bottle to key customers. Individual sales representatives have discretion as to the amount of discounting. Its largest customer is SuperMart, to which it sold 1 million bottles at €0.56 per bottle in November 2015. The two main revenue recording options are:

Option A.   Recognise the list price (€0.60 per bottle) and the discount (€0.04 per bottle) from this list price as separate line items.

Revenues at list prices, €0.60 × 1 000 000	€600 000
Deduct revenue discounting, €0.04 × 1 000 000	40 000
Reported revenues	€560 000

Option B.   Record only the actual price when reporting revenues.

Reported revenues, €0.56 × 1 000 000	€560 000

Option A has the benefit of highlighting the extent of price discounting. It facilitates further analysis that could examine which customers had price discounting and which sales representatives at Spring Distribution most frequently resorted to price discounting. Option B effectively precludes such systematic analysis of price discounting.

Studies on customer profitability in companies have found large price discounting to be an important explanation for a subset of customers being below their expected profitability. Sales representatives may have given these customers large price discounts that are unrelated to their current or potential future value to a company.

Customer costs

Chapters 5 and 11 discussed the *cost hierarchy* concept. Here we apply this concept to customers. A **customer cost hierarchy** categorises costs related to customers into different cost pools on the basis of different types of cost drivers (or cost-allocation bases) or different degrees of difficulty in determining cause-and-effect (or benefits received) relationships. Spring Distribution has an activity-based costing system that focuses on customers rather than products.

Spring's ABC system has one direct cost, the cost of bottles, and multiple indirect-cost pools. The indirect costs belong to different categories of the customer cost hierarchy. Spring identifies five categories in its customer cost hierarchy:

1 *Customer output-unit-level costs* – resources sacrificed on activities performed to sell each unit (bottle) to a customer. An example is product-handling costs of each bottle sold.

2 *Customer batch-level costs* – resources sacrificed on activities that are related to a group of units (bottles) sold to a customer. Examples are costs incurred to process orders or to make deliveries.

3 *Customer-sustaining costs* – resources sacrificed on activities undertaken to support individual customers, regardless of the number of units or each batch of product delivered to customers. Examples are costs of customer visits or costs of displays at customer sites.

4 *Distribution-channel costs* – resources sacrificed on activities that are related to a particular distribution channel rather than to each unit of product, batches of product, or specific customers. An example is the salary of the manager of Spring's retail distribution channel.

5 *Corporate-sustaining costs* – resources sacrificed on activities that cannot be traced to individual customers or distribution channels. Examples are senior management and general administration costs.

Spring has one additional cost hierarchy category, distribution channel costs, for the costs it incurs to support each of its distribution channels. We now consider decisions made at the individual customer level.

Customer-level costs

Customer-level costs include cost of goods sold and costs incurred in the first three categories of the customer cost hierarchy: customer output-unit-level costs, customer batch-level costs and customer-sustaining costs. The following table shows five activities (in addition to cost of goods sold) that Spring identifies as resulting in customer-level costs. The table indicates the cost drivers and cost driver rates for each activity as well as the cost-hierarchy category for each activity.

Activity	Cost driver and rate	Cost-hierarchy category
Order taking	€100 per purchase order	Customer batch-level costs
Customers visits	€80 per customer visit	Customer-sustaining costs
Delivery vehicles	€2 per delivery mile travelled	Customer batch-level costs
Product handling	€0.02 per bottle sold	Customer output-unit-level costs
Expedited deliveries	€300 per expedited delivery	Customer batch-level costs

Exhibit 12.9 shows a customer profitability analysis for four customers. Data underlying this exhibit are as follows:

	Customer			
	A	B	G	J
Bottles sold	1 000 000	800 000	70 000	60 000
List selling price	€0.60	€0.60	€0.60	€0.60
Actual selling price	€0.56	€0.59	€0.55	€0.60
Number of purchase orders	30	25	15	10
Number of sales visits	6	5	4	3
Number of deliveries	60	30	20	15
Kilometres travelled per delivery	5	12	20	6
Number of expedited deliveries	1	0	2	0

Spring Distribution can use the information underlying Exhibit 12.9 to persuade its customers to reduce usage of the cost drivers. For example, consider customer G, which is only 7% the size of customer A (in terms of bottles purchased – G purchased 70 000 while A purchased 1 000 000). Yet, G uses 50% of purchase orders, $66\frac{2}{3}$% of sales visits, $33\frac{1}{3}$% of deliveries, and twice the number of expedited deliveries in comparison to customer A. Spring Distribution could seek to have customer G make fewer purchase orders, require fewer customer visits, have fewer deliveries and reduce expedited deliveries, while preserving opportunities for higher sales to customer G in the future.

The ABC system underlying Exhibit 12.9 provides a road map that facilitates less use of cost drivers by individual customers in order to promote cost reduction. Another advantage of ABC is that it highlights a second way cost reduction can be promoted by Spring Distribution. Spring can take actions to reduce the costs in each of its own activities. For example, order taking currently is estimated to cost €100 per purchase order. By making its own ordering process more efficient (such as having its customers order electronically), Spring can reduce its costs even if its customers place the same number of orders.

Exhibit 12.10 shows the monthly operating income for Spring Distribution. The customer-level operating profit of customers A and B in Exhibit 12.9 are shown in columns 8 and 9 of Exhibit 12.10. The format of Exhibit 12.10 is structured on Spring Distribution's cost hierarchy. This format dovetails with the different levels at which Spring Distribution makes decisions.

Exhibit 12.9	Customer profitability analysis for four retail channel customers of Spring Distribution for June 2015

	Customer			
	A	B	G	J
Revenues at list prices €0.60 × 1 000 000; 800 000; 70 000; 60 000	€600 000	€480 000	€42 000	€36 000
Discount €0.04 × 1 000 000; €0.01 × 800 000; €0.05 × 70 000; €0 × 60 000	40 000	8 000	3 500	0
Revenues (at actual prices)	560 000	472 000	38 500	36 000
Cost of goods sold €0.50 × 1 000 000; 800 000; 70 000; 60 000	500 000	400 000	35 000	30 000
Gross margin	60 000	72 000	3 500	6 000
Customer-level operating costs				
Order taking €100 × 30; 25; 15; 10	3 000	2 500	1 500	1 000
Customer visits €80 × 6; 5; 4; 3	480	400	320	240
Delivery vehicles €2 × (5 × 60); (12 × 30); (20 × 20); (6 × 15)	600	720	800	180
Product handling €0.02 × 1 000 000; 800 000; 70 000; 60 000	20 000	16 000	1 400	1 200
Expedited deliveries €300 × 1; 0; 2; 0	300	0	600	0
Total	24 380	19 620	4 620	2 620
Customer-level operating profit	€35 620	€52 380	€(1 120)	€3 380

Exhibit 12.10	Income statement of Spring Distribution for June 2015

	Customer distribution channels										
	Wholesale customers						Retail customers				
	Total (1)	Total (2)	A1 (3)	A2 (4)	... (5)	... (6)	Total (7)	A* (8)	B* (9)	... (10)	... (11)
Revenues	€12 470 000	€10 470 000	€1 946 000	€1 476 000			€2 000 000	€560 000	€472 000		
Customer-level costs	11 939 000	10 073 000	1 868 000	1 416 000			1 866 000	524 380	419 620		
Customer-level operating profit	531 000	397 000	€78 000	€60 000			134 000	€35 620	€52 380		
Distribution-channel costs	190 000	132 000					58 000				
Distribution-channel-level operating income	341 000	€265 000					€76 000				
Corporate-sustaining costs	263 000										
Operating profit	€78 000										

* Full details are presented in Exhibit 12.9.

Customer profitability profiles

Exhibit 12.11 shows two approaches to presenting customer profitability profiles. For simplicity, we assume Spring Distribution has only 10 customers. Panel A ranks customers on operating profit. Column 4 shows the cumulative operating profit for these customers. This column is calculated by cumulatively adding up the individual customer profits. For example, row three for customer C has a cumulative profit of €108 650 in column 4. This is the sum of €52 380 for customer B, €35 620 for customer A, and €20 650 for customer C. Column 5 shows what percentage this €108 650 amount is of the total operating profit of €134 000. Thus, the three most profitable customers contribute 81% of total operating profit. This high percentage contribution by a small number of customers is a common finding in many studies. It highlights the importance of Spring Distribution maintaining good relations with this pivotal set of customers.

Exhibit 12.11	Customer profitability analysis for Spring Distribution

Panel A: Customers ranked on 2015 operating profit

Customer code (1)	Customer operating profit (2)	Customer revenue* (3)	Cumulative operating profit (4)	Percentage of cumulative operating profit to total operating profit (5)
B	€52 380	€480 000	€52 380	39%
A	35 620	600 000	88 000	66
C	20 650	247 000	108 650	81
D	16 840	227 000	125 490	94
F	6 994	99 000	132 484	99
J	3 380	36 000	135 864	101
E	3 176	193 000	139 040	104
G	−1 120	42 000	137 920	103
H	−1 760	39 000	136 160	102
I	−2 160	37 000	134 000	100
	€134 000	€2 000 000		

Panel B: Customers ranked on 2015 revenues

Customer code (1)	Customer revenue* (2)	Customer operating profit (3)	Operating profit revenues (4)	Cumulative revenues (5)	Percentage of cumulative revenue to total revenues (6)
A	€600 000	€35 620	0.059	€600 000	30%
B	480 000	52 380	0.109	1 080 000	54
C	247 000	20 650	0.084	1 327 000	66
D	227 000	16 840	0.074	1 554 000	78
E	193 000	3 176	0.016	1 747 000	87
F	99 000	6 994	0.071	1 846 000	92
G	42 000	−1 120	(0.027)	1 888 000	94
H	39 000	−1 760	(0.045)	1 927 000	96
I	37 000	−2 160	(0.058)	1 964 000	98
J	36 000	3 380	0.094	2 000 000	100
	€2 000 000	€134 000			

* Customer revenue is gross revenue prior to price offset items such as a price discount.

Exhibit 12.11, Panel B, ranks customers on revenue (before price discounts). Three of the four smallest customers (based on revenue) are unprofitable. Moreover, customer E, with revenues of €193 000, is only marginally profitable. Further analysis revealed that a former sales representative gave customer E an excessively high price discount in an attempt to meet a monthly sales-volume target.

Managers often find the bar chart presentation in Exhibit 12.12 to be the most intuitive way to analyse customer profitability. The highly profitable customers clearly stand out. Moreover, the number of loss-customers and the magnitude of their losses are apparent.

Exhibit 12.12	Bar chart presentation of customer profitability for Spring Distribution

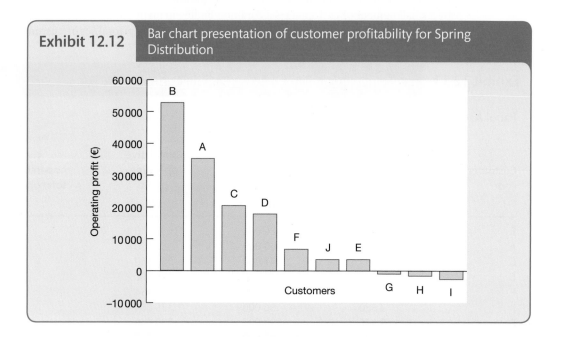

Concepts in action   Managing profits by understanding customers

Technological advances can alter the customer base of a company, creating diverse customer groupings each with differing levels of profitability. Creating customer profitability profiles is important for organisations facing market-based and technological changes, in particular.

In 2009, Pandora Radio was growing rapidly. While the startup company was still unprofitable, widespread adoption gave founder Tim Westergren hope of turning a profit. Some venture capitalists, however, wanted Pandora to get rid of its heaviest users or at least recover the cost of supporting them. Essentially, they wanted Pandora to fire its unprofitable customers!

The venture capitalists found a troubling trend in Pandora's advertising-supported free service. The company's business model was based on selling advertising at a rate of $6 to $7 for every 1000 customer impressions. That is, advertisers paid for reach, not duration. While Pandora streamed music at no charge to listeners, the company was contractually bound to pay a royalty on each song played. Thus, heavy users cost Pandora more. In fact, the 'sweet spot' for Pandora would have been a lot of users who were in the light- to middle-usage range. Some potential investors wanted Pandora to charge the heavy users for the service or deliver more advertising to them if they listened to the radio for a longer period of time.

Westergren worried about whether such changes were really in the company's best interests, as heavy users were Pandora's greatest evangelists. Pandora ultimately decided not to fire its unprofitable customers. The company announced that free listening would be limited to 40 hours per month, but could be extended to unlimited listening for that month for $0.99. By the end of 2009, Pandora turned consistently profitable. The company grew to 43 million members, achieved $50 million in revenues, and became the second-largest volume streamer of bits on the Internet after YouTube. Today, more than 200 million users—including 140 million mobile users—enjoy music through Pandora's profitable service.

Consider also Gjuensidige NOR, or Union Bank of Norway (UBN), which is the country's largest savings bank group with approximately €50 billion in assets and serving over 1 million consumer and commercial customers. Customers traditionally visited branches, interacting with bank officers. As customers began to use ATMs and automated voice response telephone systems, data about customer needs became more difficult to obtain and analyse. Kari Opdal, the bank's head of customer relationship management, noted that 'we began to lose touch with customers'. This limited the bank's ability to understand its customers, to see how specific customers, products and services drove profitability, and to target new services. UBN decided to implement, firstly, a data warehousing system developed by the business service firm Teradata, and, ultimately, a full-scale customer relationship management (CRM) system. The result was customer profitability profiles which could be acted upon. The system helped UBN to market the right product to the right customer at the right time – as soon as the customer showed a need that was unmet. The bank also launched a successful loyalty programme aimed at its most profitable customers. The system communicated to customers how much they were losing by not using the right product. UBN paid for the data warehousing system from returns within a year and expects to recoup the CRM system costs within three years.

Sources: Kay, A. (2004) 'The visionary elite', *Business 2.0*, 9 January (reproduced with permission); Shih, W. and Tesco, H. (2011) 'Pandora Radio: fire unprofitable customers?', HBS No. 9-610-077 (Boston: Harvard Business School Publishing); Pandora Media, Inc. (2013) 'Pandora is now 200 million music fans strong', 9 April (Oakland, CA: Pandora Media, Inc.).

Assessing customer value

The information in Exhibits 12.9 to 12.12 relates to customer profitability in a monthly accounting period. This is one of several factors that managers should consider in deciding how to allocate resources across customers. Other factors include:

1 *Short-run and long-run customer profitability*. This factor will be influenced by factors 2 and 3 below as well as by the level of resources likely to be required to retain the accounts.

2 *Likelihood of customer retention*. The more likely a customer is to continue doing business with a company, the more valuable the customer. Customers can differ in their loyalty and their willingness to 'take their business elsewhere' on a frequent basis.

3 *Potential for customer growth*. This factor will be influenced by the likely growth of the customer's industry and the likely growth of the customer (due to, say, its ability to develop new products). This factor will also be influenced by cross-selling opportunities, that is, when a customer of one of the company's products becomes a customer of one or more of the company's other products.

4 *Increases in overall demand from having well-known customers*. Some customers with established reputations are often worth mentioning during customer visits to drive sales. Other customers are valuable because of their willingness to provide product endorsements.

5 *Ability to learn from customers*. Customers can be an important source of ideas about new products or ways to improve existing products. Customers willing to provide such input can be especially valuable.

Managers should be particularly cautious when deciding to drop customers. Long-run profitability reports may provide misleading signals about their short-run profitability. Not all costs assigned to a customer are variable in the short run. Dropping a currently unprofitable customer will not necessarily eliminate in the short run all the costs assigned to that customer.

Summary

The following points are linked to the chapter's learning objectives.

1 Three major influences on pricing decisions are customers, competitors and costs.

2 Short-run pricing decisions focus on a period of a year or less and have no long-run implications. Long-run pricing decisions focus on a product in a major market with a time horizon of longer than one year. The time horizon appropriate to a decision on pricing dictates which costs are relevant.

3 One approach to pricing is to use a target price. Target price is the estimated price that potential customers are willing to pay for a product (or service). A target operating profit per unit is subtracted from the target price to determine the target cost per unit. The target cost per unit is the estimated long-run cost of a product (or service) that when sold enables the firm to achieve the targeted profit. The challenge for the organisation is to make the cost improvements necessary through value-engineering methods to achieve the target cost.

4 Cost incurrence arises when resources are actually sacrificed or used up. Locked-in costs refer to costs that have not yet been incurred but which, based on decisions that have already been made, will be incurred in the future.

5 The cost-plus approach to pricing chooses prospective prices by using a general formula that adds a mark-up to a cost base. Many different costs (such as full product costs or manufacturing costs) can serve as the cost base in applying the cost-plus formula. Prices are then modified on the basis of customers' reactions and competitors' responses.

6 Life-cycle budgeting and life-cycle costing estimate, track and accumulate the costs (and revenues) attributable to each product from its initial R&D to its final customer service and support in the marketplace. Life-cycle costing offers three important benefits: (a) the full set of costs associated with each product become visible; (b) differences among products in the percentage of their total costs incurred at early stages in the life cycle are highlighted; and (c) interrelationships among value-chain business function costs are emphasised. Companies choose prices to maximise the profits earned over a product's life cycle.

7 The revenues of customers purchasing the same product can differ due to differences in the quantity of units purchased and discounts from list price.

8 Customer-cost hierarchies highlight how some costs can be reliably assigned to individual customers while other costs can be reliably assigned only to distribution channels or to corporate-wide efforts.

9 Customer profitability reports, shown in a cumulative form, often reveal that a small percentage of customers contribute a large percentage of profits. It is important that companies devote sufficient resources to maintaining and expanding relationships with these key contributors to profitability.

Key terms

target price (352)

target operating profit per unit (352)

target cost per unit (352)

value engineering (352)

cost incurrence (354)

locked-in costs (354)

designed-in costs (354)

target rate of return on investment (359)

product life cycle (361)

life-cycle budgeting (361)

life-cycle costing (361)

customer profitability analysis (363)

customer revenues (363)

price discounting (364)

customer cost hierarchy (364)

References and further reading

Ansari, S. and Bell, J. (1997) *Target Costing: The Next Frontier* (Chicago: Irwin).

Baker, W., Marn, M. and Zawada, C. (2010) 'Do you have a long-term pricing strategy?', *McKinsey Quarterly*, pp. 47–52.

Baker, W., Kiewell, D. and Winkler, G. (2014) 'Using big data to make better pricing decisions', *McKinsey Quarterly*, pp. 2–5.

Bellis-Jones, R. (1989) 'Customer profitability analysis', *Management Accounting* (UK), February, pp. 26–8.

Bhimani, A. (2006) 'Management accounting and digitization', in A. Bhimani (ed) *Contemporary Issues in Management Accounting* (Oxford: Oxford University Press) pp. 69–91.

Bhimani, A. (2015) *Strategic Finance: Achieving High Corporate Performance* (London: Strategy Press).

Bhimani, A. and Neike, C. (1999) 'How Siemens designed its target costing system to redesign its products', *Journal of Cost Management*, July/August, pp. 29–34.

Cooper, R. and Slagmulder, R. (1997) *Target Costing and Value Engineering* (Portland, Oregon: Productivity Press).

Kaplan, R.S. and Cooper, R. (1998) *Cost and Effect* (Boston: Harvard Business School Press).

Kato, Y., Böer, G. and Chow, C. (1995) 'Target costing: an integrative management process', *Journal of Cost Management*, Spring, pp. 39–51.

Lawrence, A. (2007) 'Junk strategies', *Information Age*, pp. 16–18.

Monden, Y. and Hamade, K. (1991) 'Target costing and kaizen costing in Japanese automobile companies', *Journal of Management Accounting Research*, pp. 16–35.

Smith, M. (1997) *Strategic Management Accounting* (Oxford: Butterworth-Heinemann).

CHAPTER 12

Assessment material

Review questions

12.1 What are the three major influences on pricing decisions?

12.2 Give two examples of pricing decisions with a short-run focus.

12.3 How is activity-based costing useful for pricing decisions?

12.4 What is a target cost per unit?

12.5 Give two examples each of a value-added cost and a non-value-added cost.

12.6 'It is not important for a firm to distinguish between cost incurrence and locked-in costs.' Do you agree? Explain.

12.7 Describe three alternative cost-plus methods.

12.8 Give two examples where the difference in the costs of two products or services is much smaller than the difference in their prices.

12.9 Why is customer profitability analysis a vitally important topic to managers?

12.10 'A customer profitability profile highlights those customers that should be dropped to improve profitability.' Do you agree?

Exercises

Intermediate level

12.11 **Relevant-cost approach to short-run pricing decisions** (20–30 minutes)

Alexon SL is an electronics business with eight product lines. Profit data for one of the products (XT-107) for the month just ended (June 2016) are as follows:

Sales, 200 000 units at average price of €100		€20 000 000
Variable costs		
Direct materials at €35 per unit	€7 000 000	
Direct manufacturing labour at €10 per unit	2 000 000	
Variable manufacturing overhead at €5 per unit	1 000 000	
Sales commissions at 15% of sales	3 000 000	
Other variable costs at €5 per unit	1 000 000	
Total variable costs		14 000 000
Contribution margin		6 000 000
Fixed costs		5 000 000
Operating profit		€1 000 000

Xuclà Mecàniques Fluvià SA, an instruments company, has a problem with its preferred supplier of XT-107 component products. This supplier has had a three-week strike and will not be able to supply Xuclà 3000 units next month. Xuclà approaches the sales representative of Alexon SL, Angela Zamora, about providing 3000 units of XT-107 at a price of €80 per unit. Zamora informs the XT-107 product manager, Francisco García-Salve, that she would accept a flat commission of €6000 rather than the usual 15% if this special order were accepted. Alexon has the capacity to produce 300 000 units of XT-107 each month, but demand has not exceeded 200 000 units in any month in the last year.

Required

1 If the 3000-unit order from Xuclà is accepted, what will be the effect on monthly operating profit? (Assume the same cost structure as occurred in June 2016.)

2 Francisco ponders whether to accept the 3000-unit special order. He is afraid of the precedent that might be set by cutting the price. He says, 'The price is below our full cost of €95 per unit. I think we should quote a full price, or Xuclà will expect favoured treatment again and again if we continue to do business with them.' Do you agree with Francisco? Explain.

12.12 Target prices, target costs, activity-based costing (25–30 minutes)

Pagnol-Carrelages SNC is a small distributor of marble tiles. Pagnol-Carrelages identifies its three major activities and cost pools as ordering, receiving and storage, and shipping, and reports the following details for 2015:

Activity	Quantity of cost driver	Cost per unit of cost driver	Cost driver
1 Placing and paying for orders of marble tiles	Number of orders	500	€50 per order
2 Receiving and storage	Number of loads moved	4000	€30 per load
3 Shipping of marble tiles to retailers	Number of shipments	1500	€40 per shipment

Pagnol-Carrelages buys 250 000 marble tiles at an average cost of €3 per tile and sells them to retailers at an average price of €4 per tile. Fixed costs are €40 000.

Required

1 Calculate Pagnol-Carrelages' operating profit for 2015.

2 For 2016, retailers are demanding a 5% discount off the 2015 price. Pagnol-Carrelages' suppliers are only willing to give a 4% discount. Pagnol-Carrelages expects to sell the same quantity of marble tiles in 2016 as it did in 2015. If all other costs and cost driver information remain the same, what will Pagnol-Carrelages' operating profit be in 2016?

3 Suppose further that Pagnol-Carrelages decides to make changes in its ordering, and receiving and storing practices. By placing long-term orders with its key suppliers, it expects to reduce the number of orders to 200 and the cost per order to €25. By redesigning the layout of the warehouse and reconfiguring the crates in which the marble tiles are moved, Pagnol-Carrelages expects to reduce the number of loads moved to 3125 and the cost per load moved to €28. Will Pagnol-Carrelages achieve its target operating profit of €0.30 per tile in 2016? Show your calculations.

*12.13 Cost-plus and market-based pricing (25 minutes)

Hospedeiras de Portugal Lda, a large labour contractor, supplies contract labour to building construction companies. For 2015, Hospedeiras has budgeted to supply 80 000 hours of contract labour. Its variable cost is €12 per hour and its fixed costs are €240 000. Manuel Girardi, the general manager, has proposed a cost-plus approach for pricing labour at full cost plus 20%.

Required

1 Calculate the price per hour that Hospedeiras should charge based on Manuel's proposal.

2 Mirella Restrepo, the marketing manager, has supplied the following information on demand levels at different prices:

Price per hour	Demand (hours)
€16	120 000
17	100 000
18	80 000
19	70 000
20	60 000

Hospedeiras can meet any of these demand levels. Fixed costs will remain unchanged for all the preceding demand levels. On the basis of this additional information, what price per hour should Hospedeiras charge?

3 Comment on your answers to requirements 1 and 2. Why are they the same or not the same?

*12.14 Relevant-cost approach to pricing decisions (30 minutes)

Østerbro AS cans peaches for sale to food distributors. All costs are classified as either manufacturing or marketing. Østerbro prepares monthly budgets. The March 2015 budgeted absorption-costing income statement is as follows:

Sales (1000 crates × DKK 100 a crate)	DKK 100 000	100%
Cost of goods sold	60 000	60
Gross profit	40 000	40
Marketing costs	30 000	30
Operating profit	DKK 10 000	10%
Normal mark-up percentage:		
DKK 40 000 ÷ DKK 60 000 = 66.7% of absorption cost		

Monthly costs are classified as fixed or variable (with respect to the cans produced for manufacturing costs and with respect to the cans sold for marketing costs):

	Fixed	Variable
Manufacturing	DKK 20 000	DKK 40 000
Marketing	16 000	14 000

Østerbro has the capacity to can 1500 crates per month. The relevant range in which monthly fixed manufacturing costs will be 'fixed' is from 500 to 1500 crates per month.

Required

1 Calculate the normal mark-up percentage based on total variable costs.

2 Assume that a new customer approaches Østerbro to buy 200 crates at DKK 55 per crate. The customer does not require additional marketing effort except that additional manufacturing costs of DKK 2000 (for special packaging) will be required. Østerbro believes that this is a one-time-only special order because the customer is discontinuing business in six weeks' time. Østerbro is reluctant to accept this 200-crate special order because the DKK 55 per crate price is below the DKK 60 per crate absorption cost. Do you agree with this reasoning? Explain.

3 Assume that the new customer decides to remain in business. How would this longevity affect your willingness to accept the DKK 55 per crate offer? Explain.

12.15 Product costs, activity-based costing systems (20–25 minutes)

Combrai Informatique (CI) manufactures and sells computers and computer peripherals to several nationwide retail chains. Marcel Proust is the manager of the printer division. Its two largest selling printers are P-41 and P-63.

The manufacturing cost of each printer is calculated using CI's activity-based costing system. CI has one direct-manufacturing cost category (direct materials) and the following five indirect-manufacturing cost pools:

Indirect-manufacturing cost pool	Allocation base	Allocation rate
1 Materials handling	Number of parts	€1.20 per part
2 Assembly management	Hours of assembly time	€40 per hour of assembly time
3 Machine insertion of parts	Number of machine-inserted parts	€0.70 per machine-inserted part
4 Manual insertion of parts	Number of manually inserted parts	€2.10 per manually inserted part
5 Quality testing	Hours of quality testing time	€25 per testing-hour

Product characteristics of P-41 and P-63 are as follows:

	P-41	P-63
Direct material costs	€407.50	€292.10
Number of parts	85 parts	46 parts
Hours of assembly time	3.2 hours	1.9 hours
Number of machine-inserted parts	49 parts	31 parts
Number of manually inserted parts	36 parts	15 parts
Hours of quality testing	1.4 hours	1.1 hours

Required

What is the manufacturing cost of P-41? Of P-63?

12.16 Profit calculation (From ACCA Financial Information for Management, Part 1, June 2005) (40 minutes)

Ella Ltd recently started to manufacture and sell product DG. The variable cost of product DG is £4 per unit and the total weekly fixed costs are £18 000. The company has set the initial selling price of product DG by adding a mark up of 40% to its total unit cost. It has assumed that production and sales will be 3000 units per week. The company holds no stocks of product DG.

Required

1 Calculate for product DG:

   a the initial selling price per unit; and
   b the resultant weekly profit.

The management accountant has established that a linear relationship between the unit selling price (P in £) and the weekly demand (Q in units) for product DG is given by:

$$P = 20 - 0.002Q$$

The marginal revenue (MR in £ per unit) is related to weekly demand (Q in units) by the equation:

$$MR = 20 - 0.004Q$$

2 Calculate the selling price per unit for product DG that should be set in order to maximise weekly profit.

3 Distinguish briefly between penetration and skimming pricing policies when launching a new product.

Advanced level

*12.17 Life-cycle product costing, product emphasis (30–40 minutes)

Decision Support Systems (DSS) is examining the profitability and pricing policies of its software division. The DSS software division develops software packages for engineers. DSS has collected data on three of its more recent packages:

- EE-46: package for electrical engineers
- ME-83: package for mechanical engineers
- IE-17: package for industrial engineers.

Summary details on each package over their two-year 'cradle-to-grave' product lives are as follows:

		Number of units sold	
Package	Selling price	Year 1	Year 2
EE-46	€250	2000	8000
ME-83	300	2000	3000
IE-17	200	5000	3000

Assume that no stock remains on hand at the end of year 2.

DSS is deciding which product lines to emphasise in its software division. In the past two years, the profitability of this division has been mediocre. DSS is particularly concerned with the increase in R&D costs in several of its divisions. An analyst at the software division pointed out that for one of its most recent packages (IE-17), major efforts had been made to cut back R&D costs.

Last week Kari Pystynen, the software division manager, attended a seminar on product life-cycle management. The topic of life-cycle reporting was discussed. Kari decides to use this approach in her own division. She collects the following life-cycle revenue and cost information for the EE-46, ME-83 and IE-17 packages:

	EE-46		ME-83		IE-17	
	Year 1	Year 2	Year 1	Year 2	Year 1	Year 2
Revenues	€500 000	€2 000 000	€600 000	€900 000	€1 000 000	€600 000
Costs						
R&D	700 000	0	450 000	0	240 000	0
Design of product	185 000	15 000	110 000	10 000	80 000	16 000
Manufacturing	75 000	225 000	105 000	105 000	143 000	65 000
Marketing	140 000	360 000	120 000	150 000	240 000	208 000
Distribution	15 000	60 000	24 000	36 000	60 000	36 000
Customer service	50 000	325 000	45 000	105 000	220 000	388 000

Required

1 How does a product life-cycle income statement differ from an income statement that is calendar-based? What are the benefits of using a product life-cycle reporting format?

2 Present a product life-cycle income statement for each software package. Which package is the most profitable, and which is the least profitable?

3 How do the three software packages differ in their cost structure (the percentage of total costs in each cost category)?

12.18 Target cost, activity-based costing systems (continuation of Exercise 12.15) (50–60 minutes)

Assume all the information in Exercise 12.15. Marcel has just received some bad news. A foreign competitor has introduced products very similar to P-41 and P-63. Given their announced selling prices, he estimates the P-41 clone to have a manufacturing cost of approximately €680 and the

P-63 clone to have a manufacturing cost of approximately €390. He calls a meeting of product designers and manufacturing personnel at the printer division. They all agree to have the €680 and €390 figures become target costs for redesigned versions of CI's P-41 and P-63, respectively. Product designers examine alternative ways of designing printers with comparable performance but lower cost. They come up with the following revised designs for P-41 and P-63 (termed P-41 REV and P-63 REV, respectively):

	P-41 REV	P-63 REV
Direct material costs	€381.20	€263.10
Number of parts	71 parts	39 parts
Hours of assembly time	2.1 hours	1.6 hours
Number of machine-inserted parts	59 parts	29 parts
Number of manually inserted parts	12 parts	10 parts
Hours of quality testing	1.2 hours	0.9 hours

Required

1 What is a target cost per unit?

2 Using the activity-based costing system outlined in Exercise 12.15, calculate the manufacturing costs of P-41 REV and P-63 REV. How do they compare with the €680 and €390 target costs per unit?

3 Explain the differences between P-41 and P-41 REV and between P-63 and P-63 REV.

4 Assume now that Marcel has achieved major cost reductions in one of the activity areas. As a consequence, the allocation rate in the assembly-management activity area will be reduced from €40 to €28 per assembly-hour. How will this activity-area cost reduction affect the manufacturing costs of P-41 REV and P-63 REV? Comment on the results.

12.19 Life-cycle product costing, activity-based costing (35–40 minutes)

Les Saturniens SA makes digital watches. Les Saturniens is preparing a product life-cycle budget for a new watch, MX3. Development on the new watch with features such as a calculator and a daily diary is to start shortly. Les Saturniens expects the watch to have a product life cycle of three years. Estimates about MX3 are as follows:

	Year 1	Year 2	Year 3
Units manufactured and sold	50 000	200 000	150 000
Price per watch	€45	€40	€35
R&D and design costs	€900 000	€100 000	–
Manufacturing			
Variable cost per watch	€16	€15	€15
Variable cost per batch	€700	€600	€600
Watches per batch	400	500	500
Fixed costs	€600 000	€600 000	€600 000
Marketing			
Variable cost per watch	€3.60	€3.20	€2.80
Fixed costs	€400 000	€300 000	€300 000
Distribution			
Variable cost per watch	€1	€1	€1
Variable cost per batch	€120	€120	€100
Watches per batch	200	160	120
Fixed costs	€240 000	€240 000	€240 000
Customer service costs per watch	€2	€1.50	€1.50

Ignore the time value of money in your answers.

Required

1 Calculate the budgeted life-cycle operating profit for the new watch.

2 What percentage of the budgeted product life-cycle costs will be incurred at the end of the R&D and design stages?

3 An analysis reveals that 80% of the total product life-cycle costs of the new watch will be locked in at the end of the R&D and design stages. What implications would this finding have on managing MX3's costs?

4 Les Saturniens' Market Research Department estimates that reducing MX3's price by €3 each year will increase sales by 10% each year. If sales increase by 10%, Les Saturniens plans to increase manufacturing and distribution batch sizes by 10% as well. Assume that all variable costs per watch, variable costs per batch and fixed costs will remain the same. Should Les Saturniens reduce MX3's price by €3?

12.20 Customer profitability, service company (20–30 minutes)

Overloon BV is a repair-service company specialising in the rapid repair of photocopying machines. Each of its 10 clients pays a fixed monthly service fee (based on the type of photocopying machines owned by that client and the number of employees at that site). Overloon keeps records of the time technicians spend at each client as well as the cost of the equipment used to repair each photocopying machine. Overloon recently decided to calculate the profitability of each customer. The following data (in thousands) pertain to May 2015:

	Customer revenues	Customer costs
Hytop BV	€260	€182
Koninklijk Nederlands Meteorologisch Instituut	180	184
Hoogovens Scrap Processing	163	178
Borgh Pensioen Consultancy	322	225
Edah Supermarkten	235	308
Hogeschool Eindhoven	80	74
Koninklijk Instituut voor de Marine	174	100
Eindhovens Dagblad	76	108
Randmeer College	137	110
NRC Handelsblad	373	231

Required

1 Calculate the operating profit of each customer. Prepare exhibits for Overloon that are similar to Exhibits 12.11 and 12.12. Comment on the results.

2 What options regarding individual customers should Overloon consider in light of your customer profitability analysis in requirement 1?

3 What problems might Overloon encounter in accurately estimating the operating cost of each customer?

12.21 Customer profitability, distribution (40 minutes)

Spring Distribution has decided to analyse the profitability of another five customers (see pages 363–9 of the text). It buys bottled water at €0.50 per bottle and sells to wholesale customers at a list price of €0.60 per bottle. Data pertaining to five customers are:

	Customer				
	P	Q	R	S	T
Bottles sold	50 000	210 000	1 460 000	764 000	94 000
List selling price	€0.60	€0.60	€0.60	€0.60	€0.60
Actual selling price	€0.60	€0.59	€0.55	€0.58	€0.54
Number of purchase orders	15	25	30	25	30
Number of sales visits	2	4	6	2	3
Number of deliveries	10	30	60	40	20
Kilometres travelled per delivery	14	4	3	8	40
Number of expedited deliveries	0	0	0	0	1

Its five activity areas and their cost drivers are:

Activity area	Cost driver and rate
Order taking	€100 per purchase order
Sales visits	€80 per sales visit
Delivery vehicles	€2 per delivery kilometre travelled
Product handling	€0.02 per bottle sold
Expedited deliveries	€300 per expedited delivery

Required

1 Calculate the operating profit of each of the five customers now being examined (P, Q, R, S and T). Comment on the results.

2 What insights are gained by reporting both the list selling price and the actual selling price for each customer?

3 What factors should Spring Distribution consider in deciding whether to drop one or more of customers P, Q, R, S or T?

CHAPTER 13

Capital investment decisions

Organisations are often required to make decisions whose consequences are felt over many future years. Such decisions frequently involve large investments of money and have uncertain actual outcomes that have long-lasting effects on the organisation. For example, Carlos Ghosn, CEO and President of Nissan and Renault, believes that by 2020, electric vehicles (EV) will account for 10% of the global auto market. His belief in EVs rather than hybrids is clear: 'A hybrid is like a mermaid – if you want a fish you get a woman; if you want a woman, you get a fish.' As a consequence, Nissan is investing globally including €430 million in Spain for the production of e-NV200, a zero-emission vehicle (www.nissan-global.com, 5 May 2014). In Brazil, a number of luxury car makers decided to set up domestic car production operations after the country raised taxes on imported vehicles but offered tax breaks for in-country manufacturing. Consequently, Tata Motors invested €420 million to expand Jaguar Land Rover car production from 2015.

Many investment decisions can span many years. The investments and the outcomes from those investments are collectively referred to as investment projects or investment programmes. Poor long-term investment decisions can affect the future stability of an organisation because it is often difficult for organisations to recover money tied up in bad investments. Sometimes, such investments can alter an enterprise's strategy, brand and even culture. Thus there may be qualitative effects from long-term investment decisions which may indirectly influence financial performance and economic viability. Some managers desire a long-range planning tool or process to analyse and control investments with long-term consequences. This is the emphasis of this chapter.

Capital budgeting is the decision process relating to long-term capital investment programmes. Income determination and the planning and control of routine operations focus primarily on the current time period. Capital budgeting is a decision-making and control approach that focuses primarily on projects or programmes whose effects span multiple years.

Learning objectives

After studying this chapter, you should be able to:

- Differentiate between project and period issues

- Identify the six stages of capital budgeting for a project

- Understand the time value of money concept and opportunity costs

- Apply the net present-value (NPV) method and the internal rate-of-return (IRR) method

- Understand the value of sensitivity analysis in capital budgeting

- Identify relevant cash flows used in discounting

- Apply the payback method and the accounting rate-of-return (ARR) method

- Assess capital budgeting project management issues

- Identify the impact of tax and inflation on investment cash flows

- Distinguish between the real rate of return and the nominal rate of return and recognise risk in investment decisions

- Understand the assumptions made by the NPV and the IRR methods

Two focuses of cost analysis

Recall a central theme of this book: different costs for different purposes. Capital-budgeting decisions focus on the project, which spans multiple time periods. There is a great danger in basing capital-budgeting decisions on the current accounting period's profit and loss statement, ignoring the future implications of investing in a project. Investment in a project might depress the current period's reported profit, but it may still be a worthwhile investment because of the high future cash inflows that it is expected to generate.

Exhibit 13.1 illustrates two different dimensions of cost analysis: (1) the project dimension, and (2) the time dimension. Each project is represented in Exhibit 13.1 as a distinct horizontal rectangle. The life of each project is longer than one accounting period. Capital budgeting focuses on the entire life of the project in order to consider all cash inflows or cash savings from the investment. The lighter area in Exhibit 13.1 illustrates the accounting-period focus on profit determination and routine planning and control. This cross-section emphasises the company's performance for the 2015 accounting period. Accounting profit is of particular interest to the manager because bonuses are frequently based on reported profit. Profit reported in an accounting period is also important to a company because of its impact on the company's stock price. Excessive focus on short-run accounting profit, however, can cause a company to forgo long-term profitability. Many managers balance short-term accounting-period considerations and longer-term project considerations in their decision process.

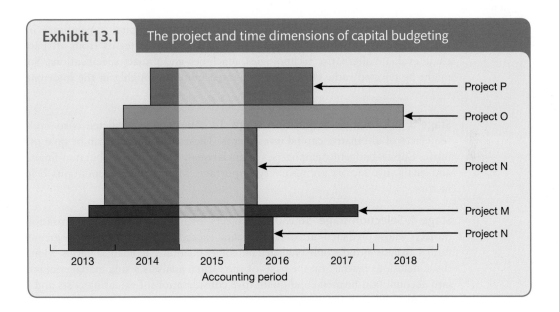

Exhibit 13.1   The project and time dimensions of capital budgeting

Project P
Project O
Project N
Project M
Project N

2013   2014   2015   2016   2017   2018
Accounting period

The accounting system that corresponds to the project dimension in Exhibit 13.1 is termed *life-cycle costing*. This system, described in Chapter 12, accumulates revenues and costs on a project-by-project basis. For example, a life-cycle costing statement for a new car project at Fiat could encompass a seven-year period and would accumulate costs for all business functions in the value chain, from R&D to customer service. This accumulation expands the accounting system, which measures profit on a period-by-period basis, to a system that calculates profit over the entire project covering many accounting periods.

Any system that focuses on the life span of a project ordinarily covers several years and thus might consider the time value of money. The *time value of money* takes into account the fact that a euro (or any other monetary unit) received today is worth more than a euro received tomorrow.

The reason is that €1 received today can be invested to start earning a return of 15% per year (say) so that it grows to €1.15 at the end of the year. The time value of money is the opportunity cost (the return of €0.15 forgone) from not having the money today.

Capital budgeting focuses on projects that can be accounted for using life-cycle costing and that must be evaluated taking into consideration the time value of money.

Stages of capital budgeting

Capital budgeting decisions ought to take into account an organisation's objectives as well as its strategies. Strategy may be regarded as the manner in which an organisation attempts to match its own capabilities with the opportunities in the marketplace to accomplish its overall objectives (see Chapter 22).

We describe six stages in capital budgeting.

Stage 1: Identification stage To distinguish which types of capital expenditure projects are necessary to accomplish organisation objectives. Capital expenditure initiatives are closely tied to the strategies of an organisation or an organisational subunit. For example, an organisation's strategy could be to increase revenues by targeting new products, customers or markets, or to reduce costs by improving productivity and efficiency. Identifying which types of capital investment projects to invest in is largely the responsibility of line management.

Stage 2: Search stage To explore several alternative capital expenditure investments that will achieve organisation strategies and goals. Employee teams from all parts of the value chain evaluate alternative technologies, machines and project specifications. Some alternatives might be rejected early. Others are evaluated more thoroughly in the information-acquisition stage.

Stage 3: Information-acquisition stage To consider the predicted costs and predicted consequences of alternative capital investments. These consequences can be quantitative and qualitative. Capital budgeting emphasises financial quantitative factors, but non-financial quantitative and qualitative factors are also very important. Management accountants help identify these factors.

Stage 4: Selection stage To choose projects for implementation. Organisations choose those projects whose predicted outcomes (benefits) exceed predicted costs by the greatest amount. The formal analysis includes only predicted outcomes quantified in financial terms. Managers re-evaluate the conclusions reached on the basis of the formal analysis, using managerial judgement to take into account non-financial and qualitative considerations. Evaluating costs and benefits is often the responsibility of the management accountant.

Stage 5: Financing stage To obtain project funding. Sources of financing include internally (within the organisation) generated cash and the capital market (equity and debt securities). Financing is often the responsibility of the treasury function of an organisation. This stage may precede stage 4 in contexts where financing must be identified prior to investment choices being made.

Stage 6: Implementation and control stage To put the project in motion and monitor performance. As the project is implemented, the company must evaluate whether capital investments are being made as scheduled and within the budget. As the project generates cash inflows, monitoring and control may include a post-investment audit, in which the predictions made at the time the project was selected are compared with the actual results.

In practice, the capital budgeting process in most organisations entails these formal stages but is also influenced by behavioural, organisational and political factors. Beyond the numbers, the ability of individual managers to 'sell' their own projects to senior management is often pivotal in the acceptance or rejection of projects.

We use information from Hôpital-Nord to illustrate capital budgeting. Hôpital-Nord is a not-for-profit organisation that is not subject to taxes. Tax considerations in capital budgeting are introduced later in the chapter.

One of Hôpital-Nord's goals is to improve the productivity of its X-Ray Department. To achieve this goal, the manager of Hôpital-Nord *identifies* a need to purchase a new state-of-the-art X-ray machine to replace an existing machine. The *search* stage yields several alternative models, but the hospital's technical staff focuses on one machine, XCAM8, as being particularly suitable. They next begin to *acquire information* for a more detailed evaluation. Quantitative financial information for the formal analysis is as follows:

1 Regardless of whether the new X-ray machine is acquired or not, revenue will not change. Hôpital-Nord charges a fixed rate for a particular diagnosis, regardless of the number of X-rays taken. The only relevant financial benefit in evaluating Hôpital-Nord's decision to purchase the X-ray machine is the cash savings in operating costs. The existing X-ray machine can operate for another five years and will have a disposal value of zero at the end of five years. The required net initial investment for the new machine is €379 100. The initial investment consists of the cost of the new machine – €372 890 – plus an additional cash investment in working capital (supplies and spare parts for the new machine) of €10 000 minus cash of €3790 obtained from the disposal of the existing machine (€372 890 + €10 000 − €3790 = €379 100).

2 The manager expects the new machine to have a five-year useful life and a disposal value of zero at the end of five years. The new machine is faster and easier to operate and has the ability to X-ray a larger area. This will decrease labour costs and will reduce the average number of X-rays taken per patient. The manager expects the investment to result in annual cash savings of €100 000. These cash flows will generally occur throughout the year; however, to simplify calculations, we assume that the cash flows occur at the end of each year. The cash inflows are expected to come from cash savings in operating costs of €100 000 for each of the first four years and €90 000 in year 5 plus recovery of working capital investment of €10 000 in year 5.

Managers at Hôpital-Nord also identify the following non-financial quantitative and qualitative benefits of investing in the new X-ray equipment:

1 *The quality of X-rays.* Higher-quality X-rays will lead to improved diagnoses and better patient treatment.

2 *The safety of technicians and patients.* The greater efficiency of the new machine would mean that X-ray technicians and patients are less exposed to the possibly harmful effects of X-rays.

These benefits are not considered in the formal financial analysis.

In the *selection* stage, managers must decide whether Hôpital-Nord should purchase the new X-ray machine. They start with financial information. This chapter discusses the following methods that they can use:

- discounted cash-flow methods:
  - net present-value (NPV) method
  - internal rate-of-return (IRR) method
- payback method
- accounting rate-of-return method.

Concepts in action | International capital budgeting at Disney

Source: Corbis/Pascal Della Zuana/Sygma

The Walt Disney Company, one of the world's leading entertainment producers, had more than $45 billion in 2013 revenue through movies, television networks, branded products, and theme parks and resorts. Within its theme park business, Disney spends around $1 billion annually in capital investments for new theme parks, rides and attractions, and other park construction and improvements. This money is divided between its domestic properties and international parks in Paris, Hong Kong and Tokyo.

Years ago, Disney developed a robust capital-budgeting approval process. Project approval relied heavily on projected returns on capital investment as measured by net present value (NPV) and internal rate of return (IRR) calculations. While this worked well for Disney's investments in its domestic theme park businesses, the company experienced challenges when it considered building the DisneySea theme park near Tokyo, Japan. While capital budgeting in the United States relies on discounted cash flow analysis, Japanese firms frequently use the average accounting return (AAR) method instead. AAR is analogous to an accrual accounting rate of return (AARR) measure based on average investment. However, it focuses on the first few years of a project (five years, in the case of DisneySea) and ignores terminal values. Disney discovered that the difference in capital budgeting techniques between US and Japanese firms reflected the difference in corporate governance in the two countries. The use of NPV and IRR in the United States underlined the perspective of shareholder-value maximisation. On the other hand, the preference for the simple accounting-based measure in Japan reflected the importance of achieving complete consensus among all parties affected by the investment decision.

When the DisneySea project was evaluated, it was found to have a positive NPV, but a negative AAR. To account for the differences in philosophies and capital-budgeting techniques, managers at Disney introduced a third calculation method called average cash flow return (ACFR). This hybrid method measured the average cash flow over the first five years, with the asset assumed to be sold for book value at the end of that period as a fraction of the initial investment in the project. The resulting ratio was found to exceed the return on Japanese government bonds and, hence, to yield a positive return for DisneySea. As a result, the DisneySea theme park was constructed next to Tokyo Disneyland and has since become a profitable addition to Disney's Japanese operations.

Sources: Misawa, M. (2006) 'Tokyo Disneyland and the DisneySea Park: corporate governance and differences in capital budgeting concepts and methods between American and Japanese companies', University of Hong Kong, No. HKU568, Hong Kong: University of Hong Kong Asia Case Research Center; The Walt Disney Company (2013) *Annual Report* (Burbank, CA: The Walt Disney Company).

Discounted cash-flow methods

Discounted cash flow (DCF) measures the cash inflows and outflows of a project as if they occurred at a single point in time so that they can be compared in an appropriate way. The discounted cash-flow methods recognise that the use of money has an opportunity cost – return forgone. Because the DCF methods explicitly and routinely weight cash flows by the time value of money, they are often considered as better methods to use for long-run decisions.

DCF focuses on *cash* inflows and outflows rather than on *operating profit* as used in conventional accounting. Cash is invested now with the expectation of receiving a greater amount of cash in the future. Injecting accrual concepts of accounting into DCF analysis should be avoided, as it can create confusion. For example, depreciation is deducted as an accrual expense when calculating operating profit under accounting. Depreciation is not deducted in DCF analysis because depreciation expense entails no cash outflow.

The compound interest tables and formulae used in DCF analysis are included in Appendix B to this book.

There are two main DCF methods:

- net present value (NPV)
- internal rate of return (IRR).

NPV is calculated using the **required rate of return (RRR)**, which is the minimum acceptable rate of return on an investment. It is the return that the organisation could expect to receive elsewhere for an investment of comparable risk. This rate is also called the **discount rate, hurdle rate** or **opportunity cost of capital** because it typically must exceed the cost of funds as determined by the return expected by those who provide the funds. When working with IRR, the RRR is used as a point of comparison.

Assume that the required rate of return, or discount rate, for the Hôpital-Nord X-ray machine project is 8%.

Net present-value method

The **net present-value (NPV) method** calculates the expected net monetary gain or loss from a project by discounting all expected future cash inflows and outflows to the present point in time, using the required rate of return. Only projects with a positive net present value are acceptable. Why? Because the return from these projects exceeds the cost of capital (the return available by investing the capital elsewhere). Managers prefer projects with higher NPVs to projects with lower NPVs, if all other things are equal. Using the NPV method entails the following steps:

Step 1: Sketch the relevant cash inflows and outflows The right side of Exhibit 13.2 shows how these cash flows are portrayed. Outflows appear in parentheses. The sketch helps the decision maker organise the data in a systematic way. Note that Exhibit 13.2 includes the outflow for the new machine at year 0, the time of the acquisition. The NPV method focuses only on cash flows. NPV analysis is indifferent to where the cash flows come from (operations, purchase or sale of equipment, or investment or recovery of working capital) and to the financial accounting treatments of individual cash-flow items (for example, depreciation costs on equipment purchases).

Step 2: Choose the correct compound interest table from Appendix B In our example, we can discount each year's cash flow separately using Table 2 (Appendix B), or we can calculate the present value of an annuity using Table 4 (Appendix B). If we use Table 2, we find the discount factors for periods 1 to 5 under the 8% column. Approach 1 in Exhibit 13.2 presents the five discount factors. Because the investment produces an annuity, a series of equal cash flows at equal intervals, we may use Table 4. We find the discount factor for five periods under the 8% column. Approach 2 in Exhibit 13.2 shows that this discount factor is 3.993 (3.993 is the sum of the five discount factors used in approach 1). To obtain the present-value figures, multiply the discount factors by the appropriate cash amounts in the sketch in Exhibit 13.2.

Step 3: Sum the present-value figures to determine the net present value If the sum is zero or positive, the NPV model indicates that the project should be accepted. That is, its expected rate of return equals or exceeds the required rate of return. If the total is negative, the project is undesirable. Its expected rate of return is below the required rate of return.

Exhibit 13.2 indicates an NPV of €20 200 at the required rate of return of 8%; the expected return from the project exceeds the 8% required rate of return. Therefore, the project is desirable. The cash flows from the project are adequate to (1) recover the net initial investment in the project, and (2) earn a return greater than 8% on the investment tied up in the project from period to period. Had the NPV been negative, the project would be undesirable on the basis of financial considerations.

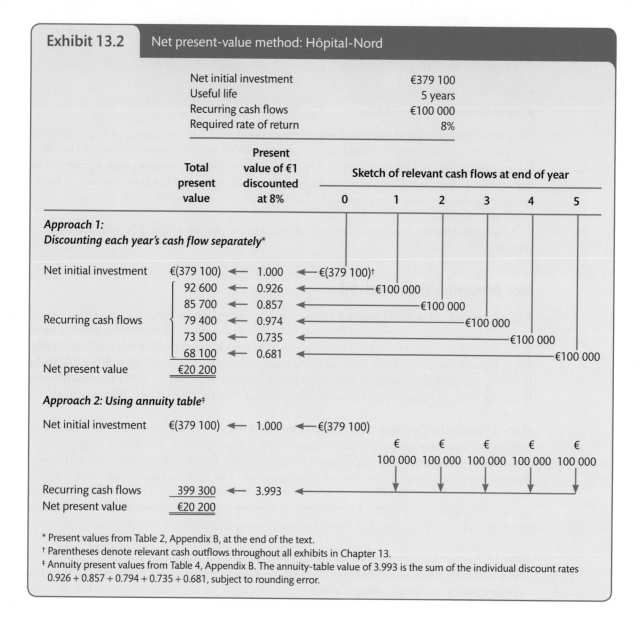

Exhibit 13.2   Net present-value method: Hôpital-Nord

Net initial investment		€379 100	
Useful life		5 years	
Recurring cash flows		€100 000	
Required rate of return		8%	

	Total present value	Present value of €1 discounted at 8%	Sketch of relevant cash flows at end of year

Approach 1:
Discounting each year's cash flow separately*

Net initial investment   €(379 100) ← 1.000 ← €(379 100)†

Recurring cash flows:
- 92 600 ← 0.926 ← €100 000 (year 1)
- 85 700 ← 0.857 ← €100 000 (year 2)
- 79 400 ← 0.974 ← €100 000 (year 3)
- 73 500 ← 0.735 ← €100 000 (year 4)
- 68 100 ← 0.681 ← €100 000 (year 5)

Net present value   €20 200

Approach 2: Using annuity table‡

Net initial investment   €(379 100) ← 1.000 ← €(379 100)

€ 100 000 100 000 100 000 100 000 100 000 (years 1–5)

Recurring cash flows   399 300 ← 3.993
Net present value   €20 200

* Present values from Table 2, Appendix B, at the end of the text.
† Parentheses denote relevant cash outflows throughout all exhibits in Chapter 13.
‡ Annuity present values from Table 4, Appendix B. The annuity-table value of 3.993 is the sum of the individual discount rates 0.926 + 0.857 + 0.794 + 0.735 + 0.681, subject to rounding error.

Of course, the manager of the hospital must also weigh non-financial factors. Consider the reduction in the average number of individual X-rays taken per patient with the new machine. This reduction is a qualitative benefit of the new machine given the health risks to patients and technicians. Other qualitative benefits of the new machine are the better diagnoses and treatments that patients receive. Had the NPV been negative, the manager would need to judge whether the non-financial benefits outweigh the negative NPV.

It is important that you do not proceed until you thoroughly understand Exhibit 13.2. Compare approach 1 with approach 2 in Exhibit 13.2 to see how Table 4 in Appendix B merely aggregates the present-value factors of Table 2. That is, the fundamental table is Table 2; Table 4 reduces calculations when there is an annuity – a series of equal cash flows at equal intervals.

Internal rate-of-return method

The **internal rate of return (IRR)** is the discount rate at which the present value of expected cash inflows from a project equals the present value of expected cash outflows of the project. That is, the IRR is the discount rate that makes NPV = €0. IRR is sometimes called the **time-adjusted rate of return**. As in the NPV method, the sources of cash flows and the accounting treatment of individual cash flows are irrelevant to the IRR calculations. We illustrate the computation of the IRR using the X-ray machine project of Hôpital-Nord. Exhibit 13.3 presents the cash flows and shows the calculation of the NPV using a 10% discount rate. At a 10% discount rate, the NPV of the project is zero. Therefore, the IRR for the project is 10%.

How do we determine the 10% discount rate that yields NPV = €0? In most cases, analysts solving capital-budgeting problems have a calculator or computer programmed to provide the internal rate of return. Without a calculator or computer program, a trial-and-error approach can provide the answer.

Step 1 Try a discount rate and calculate the NPV of the project using that discount rate.

Step 2 If the NPV is less than zero, try a lower discount rate. (A lower discount rate will increase the NPV; remember, we are trying to find a discount rate for which NPV = €0.) If the NPV is greater than zero, try a higher discount rate to lower the NPV. Keep adjusting the discount rate until NPV = €0. In the Hôpital-Nord example, a discount rate of 8% yields NPV of +€20 200 (see Exhibit 13.2). A discount rate of 12% yields NPV of −€18 600 (3.605, the present-value annuity factor from Table 4 × €100 000 − €379 100). Therefore, the discount rate that makes NPV = €0 must lie between 8% and 12%. We happen to try 10% and get NPV = €0. Hence, the IRR is 10%.

The step-by-step computations of an internal rate of return are easier when the cash inflows are equal, as in our example. Information from Exhibit 13.3 can be expressed in the following equation:

€379 100 = Present value of annuity of €100 000 at x% for 5 years

Or, using Table 4 (Appendix B), what factor F will satisfy the following equation?

$$€379\ 100 = €100\ 000F$$
$$F = 3.791$$

On the five-period line of Table 4, find the percentage column that is closest to 3.791. It is exactly 10%. If the factor F falls between the factors in two columns, straight-line interpolation is used to approximate the IRR. The formula for straight-line interpolation is:

$$LR + \frac{LN}{LN - HN}\ (HR - LR)$$

Where LR is the required rate of return of the low estimate, HR is the rate of return of the high estimate, LN is the NPV of cash inflow of the low estimate and HN is the NPV of cash inflow of the high estimate (see Exercises 13.18 and 13.22 for examples). The use of computer spreadsheets can facilitate this exercise.

A project is accepted only if the internal rate of return exceeds the required rate of return (the opportunity cost of capital). In the Hôpital-Nord example, the X-ray machine has an IRR of 10%, which is greater than the required rate of return of 8%. On the basis of financial factors, Hôpital-Nord should invest in the new machine. If the IRR exceeds the RRR, then the project has a positive NPV when project cash flows are discounted at the RRR. If the IRR equals the RRR, NPV = €0. If the IRR is less than the RRR, NPV is negative. Obviously, managers prefer projects with higher IRRs to projects with lower IRRs, if all other things are equal. The IRR of 10% means that the cash inflows from the project are adequate to (1) recover the net initial investment in the project, and (2) earn a return of exactly 10% on investment tied up in the project over its useful life.

Exhibit 13.3	Internal rate-of-return method: Hôpital-Nord

			Net initial investment			€379 100		
			Useful life			5 years		
			Recurring cash flows			€100 000		
			Required rate of return			10%*		

	Total present value	Present value of €1 discounted at 10%	Sketch of relevant cash flows at end of year					
			0	1	2	3	4	5
Approach 1: Discounting each year's cash flow separately†								
Net initial investment	€(379 100) ←	1.000	€(379 100)					
Recurring cash flows	90 900 ←	0.909		€100 000				
	82 600 ←	0.826			€100 000			
	75 100 ←	0.751				€100 000		
	68 300 ←	0.683					€100 000	
	62 100 ←	0.621						€100 000
Net present value‖	€0§							
Approach 2: Using annuity table‖								
Net initial investment	€(379 100) ←	1.000	€(379 100)					
				€ 100 000	€ 100 000	€ 100 000	€ 100 000	€ 100 000
Recurring cash flows	379 100 ←	3.791						
Net present value	€0							

* The internal rate of return is computed by methods explained in the text.
† Present values from Table 2, Appendix B.
‡ The zero difference (subject to rounding error) proves that the internal rate of return is 10%.
§ Sum is €(100) due to rounding errors. We round to €0.
‖ Annuity present values from Table 4, Appendix B. The annuity-table value of 3.791 is the sum of the individual discount rates of 0.909 + 0.826 + 0.751 + 0.683 + 0.621, subject to rounding error.

Comparison of NPV and IRR methods

This text emphasises the NPV method, which has the important advantage that the end result of the computations is euros, not a percentage. We can therefore add the NPVs of individual independent projects to estimate the effect of accepting a combination of projects. In contrast, the IRRs of individual projects cannot be added or averaged to derive the IRR of the combination of projects.

A second advantage of the NPV method is that we can use it in situations where the required rate of return varies over the life of the project. For example, suppose in the X-ray machine example, Hôpital-Nord has a required rate of return of 8% in years 1, 2 and 3 and 12% in years 4 and 5. The total present value of the cash inflows is as follows:

Year	Cash inflows	Required rate of return	Present value of €1 discounted at required rate	Total present value of cash inflows
1	€100 000	8%	0.926	€92 600
2	100 000	8	0.857	85 700
3	100 000	8	0.794	79 400
4	100 000	12	0.636	63 600
5	100 000	12	0.567	56 700
				€378 000

Given the net initial investment of €379 100, NPV calculations indicate that the project is unattractive: it has a negative NPV of −€1100 (€378 000 − €379 100). However, it is not possible to use the IRR method to infer that the project should be rejected. The existence of different required rates of return in different years (8% for years 1, 2 and 3 versus 12% for years 4 and 5) means there is not a single RRR that the IRR (a single figure) must exceed for the project to be acceptable.

Sensitivity analysis

To highlight the basic differences between the NPV and IRR methods, we have assumed that the anticipated values of cash flows will occur for certain. Obviously, managers know that their predictions are imperfect and thus uncertain. To examine how a result will change if the predicted financial outcomes are not achieved or if an underlying assumption changes, managers can use *sensitivity analysis.*

Sensitivity analysis can take various forms. For example, suppose Hôpital-Nord management believes forecast savings are uncertain and difficult to predict. Management could then ask: What is the minimum annual cash savings that will cause us to invest in the new X-ray machine (that is, for NPV = €0)? For the data in Exhibit 13.2, let ACI = annual cash inflows and let NPV = €0. The net initial investment is €379 100, and the present-value factor at the 8% required rate of return for a five-year annuity of €1 is 3.993. Then,

$$NPV = €0$$
$$3.993 \times ACI - €379\ 100 = €0$$
$$3.993 \times ACI = €379\ 100$$
$$ACI = €94\ 941$$

Thus, at the discount rate of 8%, annual cash inflows can decrease to €94 941 (a decline of €100 000 − €94 941 = €5059) before NPV falls below zero. If management believes it can attain annual cash savings of at least €94 941, it could justify investing in the new X-ray machine on financial grounds alone.

Computer spreadsheets enable managers to conduct systematic, efficient sensitivity analysis. Exhibit 13.4 shows how the net present value of the X-ray machine project is affected by variations in (1) the annual cash inflows, and (2) the required rate of return. NPVs can also vary with the useful life of a project. Sensitivity analysis helps a manager focus on those decisions that are most sensitive, and it eases the manager's mind about those decisions that are not so sensitive. For the X-ray machine project, Exhibit 13.4 shows that variations in either the annual cash inflows or the required rate of return have sizable effects on NPV.

Exhibit 13.4	Net present-value calculations for Hôpital-Nord under different assumptions of annual cash inflows and required rates of return				
	Annual cash inflows*				
Required rate of return	**€80 000**	**€90 000**	**€100 000**	**€110 000**	**€120 000**
6%	€(42 140)	€(22)	€42 100	€84 220	€126 340
8%	(59 660)	(19 730)	20 200	60 130	100 060
10%	(75 820)	(37 910)	0	37 910	75 820

* All entries in cells assume a useful project life of five years.

The use of probabilities for different possible cash-flow outcomes can readily be integrated within sensitivity analyses (see Chapter 8 appendix for a discussion of decision analysis under conditions of uncertainty and the calculation of expected values). A real options approach to investment analysis may also be adopted whereby cash flows are discounted after considering such options as waiting before investing, or abandoning the investment temporarily, depending on certain outcomes, or even integrating investment possibilities in the future that are contingent on different present-day investment options (Bhimani et al. 2006; see also Dixit and Pindyck 1994).

Relevant cash flows in discounted cash-flow analysis

The key point of discounted cash-flow (DCF) methods is to focus exclusively on differences in expected future cash flows that result from implementing a project. All cash flows are treated the same, whether they arise from operations, purchase or sale of equipment, or investment in or recovery of working capital. The opportunity cost and the time value of money are tied to the cash flowing in or out of the organisation, not to the source of the cash.

One of the biggest challenges in DCF analysis is determining those cash flows that are relevant to making the decision. Relevant cash flows are expected future cash flows that differ among the alternatives. At Hôpital-Nord, the alternatives are either to continue to use the old X-ray machine or to replace it with the new machine. The relevant cash flows are the *differences* in cash flows between continuing to use the old machine and purchasing the new one. When reading this section, focus on identifying future expected cash flows of each alternative and differences in cash flows between alternatives.

Capital investment projects (for example, purchasing a new machine) typically have five major categories of cash flows: (1) initial investment in machine and working capital, (2) cash flow from current disposal of the old machine, (3) cash flows from operations, (4) cash flow from terminal disposal of machine and recovery of working capital, and (5) income tax impacts on cash flows. We discuss the first four categories here, using Hôpital-Nord's purchase decision of the X-ray machine as an illustration. Income tax impacts are described later in the chapter.

1 **Initial investment.** Two components of investment cash flows are (a) the cash outflow to purchase the machine, and (b) the working-capital cash outflows.

   a *Initial machine investment.* These outflows, made for purchasing plant, equipment and machines, occur in the early periods of the project's life and include cash outflows for transporting and installing the item. In the Hôpital-Nord example, the €372 890 cost (including transportation and installation costs) of the X-ray machine is an outflow in year 0. These cash flows are relevant to the capital-budgeting decision because they will be incurred only if Hôpital-Nord decides to purchase the new machine.

   b *Initial working-capital investment.* Investments in plant, equipment and machines and in the sales promotions for product lines are invariably accompanied by incremental investments in working capital. These investments take the form of current assets, such as receivables and stocks (supplies and spare parts for the new machine in the Hôpital-Nord example), minus current liabilities, such as creditors. Working-capital investments are similar to machine investments. In each case, available cash is tied up.

   The Hôpital-Nord example assumes a €10 000 incremental investment in working capital (supplies and spare parts stock) if the new machine is acquired. The incremental working-capital investment is the difference between the working capital required to operate the new machine (say, €15 000) and the working capital required to operate the old machine (say, €5000). The €10 000 additional investment in working capital is a cash outflow in year 0.

2 **Current disposal price of old machine.** Any cash received from disposal of the old machine is a relevant cash inflow (in year 0) because it is an expected future cash flow that differs between the alternatives of investing and not investing in the new project. In some situations the

terminal disposal value can be critical to projects. If Hôpital-Nord invests in the new X-ray machine, it will be able to dispose of its old machine for €3790. These proceeds are included as cash inflow in year 0.

Recall from Chapter 10 that the book value (original cost minus total depreciation) of the old equipment is irrelevant. It is a past cost. Nothing can change what has already been spent or what has already happened.

The net initial investment for the new X-ray machine, €379 100, is the initial machine investment plus the initial working-capital investment minus current disposal value of the old machine: €372 890 + €10 000 − €3790 = €379 100.

3 **Annual cash flow from operations**. This category includes the difference between each year's cash flow from operations under the alternatives. Organisations make capital investments to generate cash inflows in the future. These inflows may result from producing and selling additional goods or services, or, as in the Hôpital-Nord example, from savings in operating cash costs. Annual cash flow from operations can be net outflows in some periods. For example, oil production may require large expenditures every five years (say) to improve oil extraction rates. Focus on operating cash flows, not on accrued revenues and costs.

To underscore this point, consider the following additional facts about the Hôpital-Nord X-ray machine example:

- Total X-Ray Department overhead costs will not change whether the new machine is purchased or the old machine is kept. The X-Ray Department overhead costs are allocated to individual X-ray machines – Hôpital-Nord has several – on the basis of the labour costs for operating each machine. Because the new X-ray machine will have lower labour costs, overhead allocated to it will be €30 000 less than the amount allocated to the machine it is replacing.
- Depreciation on the new X-ray machine using the straight-line method is €74 578 [(original cost, €372 890 − expected terminal disposal value, €0) ÷ useful life, 5 years].

The savings in operating cash flows (labour and materials) of €100 000 in each of the first four years and €90 000 in the fifth year are clearly relevant because they are expected future cash flows that will differ between the alternatives of investing and not investing in the new machine. But what about the decrease in allocated overhead costs of €30 000? What about depreciation of €74 578?

a *Overhead costs.* The key question is: Do total overhead cash flows decrease as a result of acquiring the new machine? In our example, they do not. Total X-Ray Department overhead costs remain the same whether or not the new machine is acquired. Only the overhead allocated to individual machines changes. The overhead costs allocated to the new machine are €30 000 less. This €30 000 will be allocated to *other* machines in the department. No cash flow savings in total overhead occur. Therefore, the €30 000 should not be included as part of annual cash savings from operations.

b *Depreciation.* Ignoring possible income tax considerations (which differ from country to country), depreciation is irrelevant. It is a non-cash allocation of costs whereas DCF is based on inflows and outflows of *cash*. In DCF methods, the initial cost of equipment is regarded as a *lump-sum* outflow of cash at year 0. Deducting depreciation from operating cash inflows would be counting the *lump-sum* amount twice.

4 **Terminal disposal of investment**. The disposal of the investment at the date of termination of a project generally increases cash inflow in the year of disposal. Errors in forecasting the terminal disposal value are seldom critical on long-duration projects because the present value of amounts to be received in the distant future is usually small. Two components of the terminal disposal value of an investment are (a) the terminal disposal value of the machine, and (b) the recovery of working capital.

a *Terminal disposal value of machine.* At the end of the useful life of the project, the initial machine investment may not be recovered at all, or it may be only partially recovered in the amount of the terminal disposal value.

Exhibit 13.5	Relevant cash inflows and outflows for Hôpital-Nord					

	Sketch of relevant cash flows at end of year					
	0	1	2	3	4	5
1 a Initial machine investment	€(372 890)					
b Initial working-capital investment	(10 000)					
2 Current disposal price of old machine	3790					
Net initial investment	(379 100)					
3 Recurring operating cash flows		€100 000	€100 000	€100 000	€100 000	€100 000
4 a Terminal disposal value of machine						0
b Recovery of working capital						10 000
Total relevant cash inflows and outflows as shown in Exhibits 13.2 and 13.3	€(379 100)	€100 000	€100 000	€100 000	€100 000	€100 000

The relevant cash inflow is the difference in expected terminal disposal values at the end of five years under the two alternatives – the terminal disposal value of the new machine (zero in the case of Hôpital-Nord) minus the terminal disposal value of the old machine (also zero in the Hôpital-Nord example).

b *Recovery of working capital.* The initial investment in working capital is usually fully recouped when the project is terminated. At that time, stocks and receivables necessary to support the project are no longer needed. The relevant cash inflow is the difference in the expected working capital recovered under the two alternatives. If the new X-ray machine is purchased, Hôpital-Nord will recover €15 000 of working capital in year 5. If the new machine is not acquired, Hôpital-Nord will recover €5000 of working capital in year 5, at the end of the useful life of the old machine. The relevant cash inflow in year 5 if Hôpital-Nord invests in the new machine is €10 000 (€15 000 – €5000).

Some capital investments *reduce* working capital. Assume that a computer-integrated manufacturing (CIM) project with a seven-year life will reduce stocks and hence working capital by €20 million from, say, €50 million to €30 million. This reduction will be represented as a €20 million cash inflow for the project at year 0. At the end of seven years, the recovery of working capital will show a relevant cash *outflow* of €20 million. Why? Because the company recovers only €30 million of working capital under CIM rather than the €50 million of working capital it would have recovered had it not implemented CIM.

Exhibit 13.5 presents the relevant cash inflows and outflows for Hôpital-Nord's decision to purchase the new machine as described in items 1 to 4 in the above list. The total relevant cash flows for each year are the same as the relevant cash flows used in Exhibits 13.2 and 13.3 to illustrate the NPV and IRR methods.

Payback method

Uniform cash flows

We now consider a third method for analysing the financial aspects of projects. The **payback method** measures the time it will take to recoup, in the form of net cash inflows, the net initial investment in a project. Like NPV and IRR, the payback method does not distinguish the sources of cash inflows (operations, disposal of equipment or recovery of working capital). In the

Hôpital-Nord example, the X-ray machine costs €379 100, has a five-year expected useful life, and generates a €100 000 uniform cash inflow each year. The payback calculations are as follows:

$$\text{Payback} = \frac{\text{Net initial investment}}{\text{Uniform increase in annual cash flows}}$$

$$= \frac{\text{€379 100}}{\text{€100 000}} = 3.791 \text{ years}$$

Cash savings from the new X-ray machine occur *throughout* the year, but for simplicity in calculating NPV and IRR, we assume they occur at the *end* of each year. A literal interpretation of this assumption would imply a payback of four years because Hôpital-Nord will recover its investment only when cash inflows occur at the end of the fourth year. The calculations shown in this chapter, however, better approximate Hôpital-Nord's payback on the basis of uniform cash flows throughout the year.

Under the payback method, organisations often choose a cutoff period for a project. The greater the risks of a project, the smaller the cutoff period. Why? Because, faced with higher risks, managers would like to recover the investments they have made more quickly. For example, Hualtenbanken Hydro uses a payback period of 3–4 years for investment decisions at its Ormen Lange oil refinery. Projects with a payback period less than the cutoff period are acceptable. Those with a payback period greater than the cutoff period are rejected. If Hôpital-Nord's cutoff period under the payback method is three years, Hôpital-Nord will reject the new machine. If Hôpital-Nord uses a cutoff period of four years, Hôpital-Nord will consider the new machine to be acceptable.

The major strength of the payback method is that it is easy to understand. Like the DCF methods described previously, the payback method is not affected by accounting conventions such as depreciation. Advocates of the payback method argue that it is a handy measure when (1) estimates of profitability are not crucial and preliminary screening of many proposals is necessary, and (2) the predicted cash flows in later years of the project are highly uncertain.

Two major weaknesses of the payback method are (1) it neglects the time value of money, and (2) it neglects to consider project cash flows after the net initial investment is recovered. Consider an alternative to the €379 100 X-ray machine mentioned earlier. Assume that another X-ray machine, with a three-year useful life and zero terminal disposal value, requires only a €300 000 net initial investment and will also result in cash inflows of €100 000 per year. First, compare the two payback periods:

$$\text{Payback period for machine 1} = \frac{\text{€379 100}}{\text{€100 000}} = 3.8 \text{ years}$$

$$\text{Payback period for machine 2} = \frac{\text{€300 000}}{\text{€100 000}} = 3.0 \text{ years}$$

The payback criterion would favour buying the €300 000 machine, because it has a shorter payback. In fact, if the cutoff period is three years, then Hôpital-Nord would not acquire machine 1 because it fails to meet the payback criterion. Consider next the NPV of the two investment options using Hôpital-Nord's 8% required rate of return for the X-ray machine investment. At a discount rate of 8%, the NPV of machine 2 is –€42 300 (2.577, the present-value annuity factor for 3 years at 8% from Table 4 €100 000 = €257 700 – the net initial investment of €300 000). Machine 1, as we know, has a positive NPV of €20 200 (from Exhibit 13.2). The NPV criterion suggests that Hôpital-Nord should acquire machine 1. Machine 2, with a negative NPV, would fail to meet the NPV criterion. The payback method gives a different answer from the NPV method because the payback method (1) does not consider cash flows after the payback period, and (2) does not discount cash flows.

There are situations where payback calculations suggest indifference between two projects. For instance, if Project A yields €10 000 in year 1 and €90 000 in year 6, and Project B yields €90 000 in year 1 and €10 000 in year 6, the two projects would have identical payback periods. The NPV rule would naturally point to Project B as the preferred option. An added problem with the payback method is that choosing too short a cutoff period for project acceptance may promote the selection of only short-lived projects. The organisation will tend to reject long-term, positive-NPV projects.

Non-uniform cash flows

The payback formula presented above is designed for uniform annual cash inflows. When annual cash inflows are not uniform, the payback computation takes a cumulative form. The years' net cash inflows are totalled until the amount of the net initial investment has been recovered. Assume that the solicitors' firm Slaughter and Ogilvy is considering the purchase of a €150 000 video-conferencing facility that will enable its solicitors and clients to interact in a conference format without physically travelling. This facility is expected to produce a total cash saving of €380 000 over the next five years (primarily due to a reduction in travel costs and more effective use of senior staff time). The cash savings occur evenly throughout each year but non-uniformly across five years. Payback occurs during the third year:

Year	Cash savings	Cumulative cash savings	Net initial investment yet to be recovered at end of year
0	–	–	€150 000
1	€50 000	€50 000	100 000
2	60 000	110 000	40 000
3	80 000	190 000	–
4	90 000	280 000	–
5	100 000	380 000	–

Straight-line interpolation within the third year reveals that the final €40 000 needed to recover the €150 000 investment (that is, €150 000 − €110 000 recovered by the end of year 2) will be achieved halfway through year 3 (in which €80 000 of cash savings occur):

$$\text{Payback} = 2 \text{ years} + \left(\frac{€40\,000}{€80\,000} \times 1 \text{ year} \right) = 2.5 \text{ years}$$

The video-conferencing example has a single cash outflow of €150 000 at year 0. Where a project has multiple cash outflows occurring at different points in time, these outflows are added to derive a total cash outflow figure for the project. No adjustment is made for the time value of money when adding these cash outflows in computing the payback period.

Accounting rate-of-return method

We now consider a fourth method for analysing the financial aspects of capital-budgeting projects. The **accounting rate of return (ARR)** is an accounting measure of income divided by an accounting measure of investment. It is also called the *return on investment (ROI)*. We illustrate ARR for the Hôpital-Nord example using the project's net initial investment as the denominator.

$$\text{ARR} = \frac{\text{Increase in expected average annual operating profit}}{\text{Net initial investment}}$$

If Hôpital-Nord purchases the new X-ray machine, the increase in expected average annual savings in operating costs will be €98 000: this amount is the total operating savings of €490 000 (€100 000 for 4 years and €90 000 in year 5) ÷ 5. The new machine has a zero terminal disposal value. Straight-line depreciation on the new machine is €372 890 ÷ 5 = €74 578. The net initial investment is €379 100. The accounting rate of return is equal to:

$$\text{ARR} = \frac{€98\,000 - €74\,578}{€379\,100} = \frac{€23\,422}{€379\,100} = 6.18\%$$

The ARR of 6.18% indicates the rate at which a euro of investment generates operating profit. Projects whose ARR exceeds an accounting return required for the project are considered desirable.

Managers using this method prefer projects with higher, rather than lower, ARR, if all other things are equal.

The ARR method is similar in spirit to the IRR method – both methods calculate a rate-of-return percentage. Whereas the ARR computation calculates return using operating profit numbers after considering accruals, the IRR method calculates return on the basis of cash flows and the time value of money. For capital-budgeting decisions, the IRR method is conceptually superior to the ARR method in terms of financial theory and financial decision making.

The ARR computations are simple and easy to understand, and use routinely maintained accounting numbers. Unlike the payback method, the ARR method considers profitability. Unlike the NPV and IRR methods, however, the ARR focuses on operating profit effects and hence considers accruals. It does not track cash flows and ignores the time value of money. Critics cite these arguments as major drawbacks of the ARR computations.

Concepts in action   International comparison of capital-budgeting methods

What methods of analysing capital investment decisions do companies around the world value? One study of automotive components businesses covering German, US, British and Japanese operations reported considerable diversity associated with differences in national values in respect of strategic investment decisions. The study (Carr and Harris 2004), however, reported points of convergence in relation to processes driven by common industrial globalisation pressures.

The following table indicates the ranking level of usage by companies of particular capital-budgeting methods across six countries. The reported percentages show the overall usage of the four capital-budgeting methods considered significant by the 321 companies responding to the survey (Bhimani et al., 2006; 2007).

	Percentage of usage overall	Canada	France	Germany	Italy	UK	USA
Payback	70%	1	1	3	1	1	1
IRR	69%	4	2	1	2	2	2
NPV	71%	2	3	2	3	4	3
ARR	26%	3	4	4	4	3	4

Sources: Bhimani et al. (2006, 2007); Carr and Harris (2004).

Managing the project

This section discusses stage 6 of capital budgeting, which deals with implementation and control. Two different aspects of management control are discussed: management control of the investment activity itself and management control of the project as a whole.

Management control of the investment activity

Some initial investments such as purchasing an X-ray or a video-conferencing facility are relatively easy to implement. Other initial investments such as building retail centres or new manufacturing plants are more complex and take more time. In the latter case, monitoring and controlling the investment schedules and budgets is critical to the success of the overall project.

Management control of the project: post-investment audit

A post-investment audit compares the predictions of investment costs and outcomes made at the time a project was selected to the actual results. It provides management with feedback about their performance. Suppose, for example, that actual outcomes (operating cash savings from the new X-ray machine in the Hôpital-Nord example) are much lower than predicted outcomes. Management must then investigate whether this occurred because the original estimates were too optimistic or because there were problems in implementing the project. Both types of problem are a concern.

Optimistic estimates are a concern because they may result in the acceptance of a project that would otherwise have been rejected. To discourage optimistic estimates, some companies in the West maintain records comparing actual performance to the estimates made by individual managers when seeking approval for capital investments. These companies believe that post-investment audits discourage managers from making unrealistic forecasts. Problems in implementing a project can be a concern because the returns from the project will not meet expectations. Post-investment audits can point to areas requiring corrective action.

Care should be exercised when performing a post-investment audit. It should be done only after project outcomes have stabilised. Doing the audit early may give a misleading picture. Obtaining actual data to compare against estimates is often not easy. For example, actual labour cost savings from the new X-ray machine may not be comparable to the estimated savings because the actual number and types of X-ray taken may be different from the quantities assumed during the capital-budgeting process. Other benefits, such as the impact on patient treatment, may be difficult to quantify.

We next examine how managers analyse income taxes and changing prices in capital budgeting.

Income tax factors

The importance of income taxes

Income taxes often have a large influence on investment decisions. For example, income taxes can sizably reduce the net cash inflows from individual projects and so change their relative desirability. Decisions to locate plants in certain countries such as Ireland or Jersey are often motivated by tax incentive reasons. The benefits of lower taxes sometimes outweigh lower project operating costs.

Treatment of depreciation for tax purposes

Tax rules regarding income measurement are sometimes the same as the generally accepted accounting principles used for preparing financial statements. But, in most countries, there are tax rules, such as those pertaining to depreciation, which differ from those suitable for preparing financial accounts. Income tax laws frequently allow taxpayers to use shorter useful lives for depreciation.

We emphasise income tax provisions affecting depreciation. A general framework for examining income tax factors in business decisions is presented in Götze et al. (2008). Tax laws for depreciation deductions in many countries typically cover the amount allowable for depreciation, the time period over which the asset is to be depreciated, and the pattern of allowable depreciation.

Under such circumstances, tax can be an important consideration in assessing the financial value of capital investment projects. In computing tax it is necessary first to calculate taxable profit as distinct from the reported profit in external financial accounts. The amount of tax payable is based on this figure at the prevailing statutory level.

Under most tax regimes, the depreciation used by financial accountants in calculating the profit figure is not regarded as an allowable expense. Instead, an alternative schedule of tax allowances is used which provides a depreciation framework valid for tax calculation only. In the UK these tax allowances are referred to as capital allowances. For instance, most plant and equipment in the UK qualifies for 'writing-down allowances'. This means that each year, for example, 25% of the written-down value of an asset can be claimed as tax depreciation. Thus, for an asset costing €5000, we should have the following:

Year	Written-down value (opening)	25% allowance	Written-down value (closing)
0	5000.00	1250.00	3750.00
1	3750.00	937.50	2812.50
2	2812.50	703.13	2109.38
3	2109.38	527.34	1582.03
4	1582.03	395.51	1186.52

The allowance continues indefinitely. Sometimes, when an asset is disposed of, the remaining written-down value may be claimed as an allowance. Other less generous allowances apply to certain assets.

We now consider the tax paid by a company which uses the asset to generate net revenues (before depreciation) of €1500 per year. For simplicity, we assume a corporate tax rate of 40%. In year 0, instead of assessing tax on €1500, the taxable profit is €250 (= €1500 − €1250), i.e. the tax is €100 instead of €600. (Note that if the accountant applies 10% **straight-line depreciation (SL)**, in which an equal amount of depreciation is taken each year, then reported profits will be €1000.) Similar calculations apply in subsequent years. The timing of tax payments can also be a relevant factor. In most countries, tax payments generally take place one year after the end of a company's accounting year.

Capital budgeting and inflation

Inflation can be defined as the decline in the general purchasing power of the monetary unit (for example, the pound in the UK or the Swiss franc). An inflation rate of 10% in 1 year means that what could be bought with €100 (say) at the start of the year will cost €110 [€100 + (10% × €100)] at the end of the year. Some countries – for example, Argentina, Brazil, Israel, Mexico and Russia – have in the past experienced annual inflation rates of 15% to over 400%. Even an annual inflation rate of 5% over, say, a 5-year period can result in sizable declines in the general purchasing power of the monetary unit over that time.

Why is it important to account for inflation in capital budgeting? Because declines in the general purchasing power of the monetary unit (pounds, say) will inflate future cash flows above what they would have been had there been no inflation. We now examine how inflation can be explicitly recognised in capital-budgeting analysis.

Real and nominal rates of return

When analysing inflation, distinguish between the real rate of return and the nominal (money) rate of return:

- **Real rate of return** is the rate of return required to cover return and investment risk.
- **Nominal rate of return** is the rate of return required to cover return, investment risk and the anticipated decline, due to inflation, in the general purchasing power of the cash that the investment generates. The rates of return (or interest) earned on the financial markets are nominal rates, because they compensate investors for both risk and inflation.

We next describe the relationship between real and nominal rates of return. Assume that the real rate of return for investments in high-risk cellular data-transmission equipment at Surrey Communications is 20% and that the expected inflation rate is 10%. The nominal rate of return is:

$$\text{Nominal rate} = (1 + \text{Real rate})(1 + \text{Inflation rate}) - 1$$
$$= (1 + 0.20)(1 + 0.10) - 1$$
$$= [(1.20)(1.10)] - 1 = 1.32 - 1 = 0.32$$

The nominal rate of return is also related to the real rate of return and the inflation rate as follows:

Real rate of return	0.20
Inflation rate	0.10
Combination (0.20×0.10)	0.02
Nominal rate of return	0.32

The real rate of return can be expressed in terms of the nominal rate of return as follows:

$$\text{Real rate} = \frac{(1 + \text{Nominal rate})}{(1 + \text{Inflation rate})} - 1$$
$$= \frac{(1 + 0.32)}{(1 + 0.10)} - 1$$
$$= 0.20$$

Note that the nominal rate is slightly higher than the real rate (0.20) plus the inflation rate (0.10). Why? Because the nominal rate recognises that inflation also decreases the purchasing power of the real rate of return earned during the year.

Net present-value method and inflation

The watchwords when incorporating inflation into the net present-value (NPV) method are internal consistency. There are two internally consistent approaches:

- *Nominal approach.* Predict cash inflows and outflows in nominal monetary units and use a nominal rate as the required rate of return.
- *Real approach.* Predict cash inflows and outflows in real monetary units and use a real rate as the required rate of return.

Consider an investment that is expected to generate sales of 100 units and a net cash inflow of €1000 (€10 per unit) each year for two years *without inflation*. If inflation of 10% is expected each year, net cash inflows from the sale of each unit would be €11 (€10 × 1.10) in year 1 and €12.10 [€11 × 1.10 or €10 × $(1.10)^2$] in year 2, resulting in net cash inflows of €1100 in year 1 and €1210 in year 2. The net cash inflows of €1100 and €1210 are nominal cash inflows because they include the impact of inflation. *These are the cash flows recorded by the accounting system.* The cash inflows of €1000 each year are real cash flows because they exclude inflationary effects. Note that the real cash flows equal the nominal cash flows discounted for inflation, €1000 = €1100 ÷ 1.10 = €1210 ÷ $(1.10)^2$. Many managers find the nominal approach easier to understand and use because they observe nominal cash flows in their accounting systems and the nominal rates of return on financial markets.

Choosing between the net present-value and the internal rate-of-return decision approaches

The NPV method, subject to the assumptions made, always indicates the project (or set of projects) that maximises the NPV of future cash flows. However, surveys of practice report widespread use of the internal rate-of-return (IRR) method. Why? Probably because managers find this method easier to understand and because, in most instances, their decisions would be unaffected by using one method or the other. In some cases, however, the two methods will not indicate the same decision as being optimal.

Where mutually exclusive projects have unequal lives or unequal investments, the IRR method can rank projects differently from the NPV method. Consider Exhibit 13.6. The ranking by the IRR method favours project X, while the ranking by the NPV method favours project Z. The projects ranked in Exhibit 13.6 differ in both life (5, 10 and 15 years) and net initial investment (€286 400, €419 200 and €509 200).

Exhibit 13.6 concentrates on differences in project lives. Similar conflicting results can occur when the terminal dates are the same but the sizes of the net initial investments differ.

Managers using the IRR method implicitly assume that the reinvestment rate is equal to the indicated rate of return for the shortest-lived project. Managers using the NPV method implicitly assume that the funds obtainable from competing projects can be reinvested at the company's required rate of return. The NPV method is generally regarded as conceptually superior. Students should refer to corporate finance texts for more details on these issues, and on the problems of ranking projects with unequal lives or unequal investments.

Exhibit 13.6			Ranking of projects using IRR and NPV						
			IRR method				NPV method		
Project	Life	Net initial investment	Annual cash flow from operations, net of income taxes	IRR	Ranking		PV of annual cash flow from operations, net of income taxes	NPV	Ranking
X	5	€286 400	€100 000	22%	1		€379 100	€92 700	3
Y	10	419 200	100 000	20	2		614 500	195 300	2
Z	15	509 200	100 000	18	3		760 600	251 400	1

Summary

The following points are linked to the chapter's learning objectives.

1 Capital budgeting is long-term planning for proposed capital projects. The life of a project is usually longer than one year, so capital-budgeting decisions consider revenues and costs over relatively long periods. In contrast, accounting measures income on a year-by-year basis.

2 Capital budgeting can be viewed as a six-stage process: (a) identification stage, (b) search stage, (c) information-acquisition stage, (d) selection stage, (e) financing stage, and (f) implementation and control stage.

3 The time value of money takes into account this fact: a euro received today can be invested to start earning a return (for example, interest), so it is worth more than a euro received tomorrow. The time value of money is the opportunity cost (return forgone) from not having the money today.

4 Discounted cash-flow (DCF) methods explicitly include all project cash flows and the time value of money in capital-budgeting decisions. Two DCF methods are the net present-value (NPV) method and the internal rate-of-return (IRR) method. The NPV method calculates the expected net monetary gain or loss from a project by discounting all expected future cash inflows and outflows to the present point in time, using the required rate of return. A project is acceptable if it has a positive NPV. The IRR method calculates the rate of return (discount rate) at which the present value of expected cash inflows from a project equals the present value of expected cash outflows from a project. A project is acceptable if its IRR exceeds the required rate of return.

5 Non-financial and qualitative factors, such as the effects of investment decisions on employee learning and on the company's ability to respond faster to market changes, are often not explicitly considered in capital-budgeting decisions. However, non-financial and qualitative factors can be extremely important. In making decisions, managers must consider different possible scenarios by engaging in sensitivity analysis.

6 Relevant cash inflows and outflows are the expected future cash flows that differ among the alternatives. Only cash inflows and outflows matter. Accounting concepts such as accrued revenues and accrued expenses are irrelevant for the discounted cash-flow methods.

7 The payback method measures the time it will take to recoup, in the form of cash inflows, the total amount invested in a project. The payback method neglects profitability and the time value of money. The accounting rate of return (ARR) is operating profit divided by a measure of investment. The ARR considers profitability but ignores the time value of money.

8 Three factors influence the amount of depreciation claimed as a tax deduction: (a) the amount allowable for depreciation (called 'capital allowances' in the UK), (b) the time period over which the asset is to be depreciated, and (c) the pattern of allowable depreciation. The real rate of return is the rate of return required to cover investment risk and return. The nominal rate of return is the rate of return required to cover return, investment risk and the anticipated decline, due to inflation, in the general purchasing power of the cash that the investment generates. Two internally consistent ways to account for inflation in capital budgeting are (a) to predict cash inflows and outflows in nominal terms and to use a nominal discount rate, and (b) to predict cash inflows and outflows in real terms and to use a real discount rate. The nominal and real approaches are equivalent: both yield the same net present value, but many managers find the nominal approach easier to work with.

9 The net present-value and internal rate-of-return methods make different assumptions about the rate at which project cash inflows are reinvested. Consequently, the two methods may rank projects differently.

Key terms

investment projects (380)

investment programmes (380)

capital budgeting (380)

discounted cash flow (DCF) (384)

required rate of return (RRR) (385)

discount rate (385)

hurdle rate (385)

opportunity cost of capital (385)

net present-value (NPV) method (385)

internal rate of return (IRR) (386)

time-adjusted rate of return (387)

payback method (392)

accounting rate of return (ARR) (394)

straight-line depreciation (SL) (397)

inflation (397)

real rate of return (398)

nominal rate of return (398)

References and further reading

Bhimani, A., Ncube, M. and Soonawalla, K. (2006) 'Intuition and real options-based investment appraisal. A cross-national study of financial executives', *Journal of Applied Management Accounting Research* 4(2), pp. 11–34.

Bhimani, A., Gosselin, M., Soonawalla, K. and Ncube, M. (2007) 'The value of accounting information in assessing investment risk', *Cost Management* 21(1), pp. 29–35.

Carr, C. and Harris, S. (2004) 'The impact of diverse national values on strategic investment decisions in the context of globalization', *International Journal of Cross Cultural Management*, 4(1), pp. 77–99.

Dixit, A. and Pindyck, R. (1994) *Investment under Uncertainty* (Princeton, New Jersey: Princeton University Press).

Gordon, L., Loeb, M. and Tseng, C. (2006) 'Capital budgeting and informational impediments: a management accounting perspective', in A. Bhimani (ed) *Contemporary Issues in Management Accounting* (Oxford: Oxford University Press), pp. 146–65.

Götze, U., Northcott, D. and Schuster, P. (2008) *Investment Appraisal: Methods and Models* (Berlin: Springer-Verlag).

Kaplan, R.S. (1986) 'Must CIM be justified by faith alone?', *Harvard Business Review*, March/April, pp. 87–95.

Northcott, D. and Alkaran, F. (2007) 'Strategic investment appraisal', in T. Hopper, D. Northcott, and R. Scapens (eds) *Issues in Management Accounting* (Harlow: FT Prentice Hall).

CHAPTER 13

Assessment material

Review questions

13.1 What is the essence of the discounted cash-flow method?

13.2 'Only quantitative outcomes are relevant in capital-budgeting analyses.' Do you agree? Explain.

13.3 What is the payback method? What are its main strengths and weaknesses?

13.4 Describe the accounting rate-of-return method. What are its main strengths and weaknesses?

13.5 How is the accounting rate-of-return method different from the payback method?

13.6 'Let's be more practical. DCF is not the gospel. Managers should not become so enchanted with DCF that strategic considerations are overlooked.' Do you agree? Explain.

13.7 What is a post-investment audit? Why is it important?

13.8 'Corporation tax only plays a role in capital budgeting because of capital allowances.' Do you agree? Explain.

13.9 Distinguish between the nominal rate of return and the real rate of return.

13.10 What approaches might be used to recognise risk in capital budgeting?

13.11 'Discounted cash-flow techniques are relevant only to for-profit organisations.' Do you agree? Explain.

Exercises

Basic level

13.12 Comparison of approaches to capital budgeting (22–25 minutes)

Bayern-Bauwerk is thinking of buying, at a cost of €220 000, some new packaging equipment that is expected to save €50 000 in cash-operating costs per year. Its estimated useful life is 10 years, and it will have zero terminal disposal value. The required rate of return is 16%.

Required

1 Calculate the payback period.

2 Calculate the net present value.

3 Calculate the internal rate of return.

4 Calculate the accounting rate of return based on net initial investment. Assume straight-line depreciation.

13.13   **Special order, relevant costs, capital budgeting** (A. Spero, adapted) (30 minutes)

Euro-Jouets SNC sells neon-coated 'Feu-Follet' cars to several local toy stores. It has the capacity to make 250 000 of these units per year, but during the year ending 31 December 2015, it made and sold 130 000 cars to its existing customers. It makes these cars by dipping its highly unsuccessful 'Garou-Garou' model plastic toy cars into a vat of neon paint. It originally purchased 780 000 of the Garou-Garous but has been unable to sell them as Garou-Garous. These plastic cars originally cost €20 per unit, and 650 000 of them remain in stock.

Euro-Jouets' accountant has prepared the following cost sheet per Feu-Follet car:

Selling price per car		**€59**
Manufacturing costs per car		
Direct materials		
Plastic cars	€20	
Neon paint	6	
Boxes	3	29
Direct manufacturing labour		8
Depreciation of vat		10
Allocated plant manager's salary		5
Manufacturing costs per car		52
Gross margin per car		7
Marketing costs per car (€2 of which is variable)		6
Operating margin per car		€1

On 31 December 2015, the Mille-Fontaines chain asked Euro-Jouets to provide 100 000 Feu-Follet cars at a special price of €50 per car. Euro-Jouets will not need to incur any marketing cost for the Mille-Fontaines sale.

Euro-Jouets expected to sell the Feu-Follet cars to its existing customers for the next four years at the current level of demand of 130 000 units per year and none thereafter. At the end of four years, Euro-Jouets will dispose of the VAT and whatever cars remain at zero net disposal value. If Euro-Jouets accepts the Mille-Fontaines order, it is certain that its other customers will refuse to pay the current price of €59 and will demand a discount. Euro-Jouets estimates a required rate of return of 16%.

Required

1 Should Euro-Jouets accept the special order if it must also offer the same price of €50 to its existing customers for the next four years?

2 Suppose Euro-Jouets is uncertain about the discount the existing customers would demand. Determine the price that Euro-Jouets would have to offer its existing customers for the next four years to be indifferent between accepting and rejecting Mille-Fontaines' special order.

*13.14   **Question from the Association of Chartered Certified Accountants, Pilot Paper 2.4, Financial Management and Control** (45 minutes)

Bread Products Ltd is considering the replacement policy for its industrial size ovens which are used as part of a production line that bakes bread. Given its heavy usage, each oven has to be replaced frequently. The choice is between replacing every two years or every three years. Only one type of oven is used, each of which costs £24 500.

Maintenance costs and resale values are as follows:

Year	Maintenance per annum	Resale value
1	£500	
2	£800	£15 600
3	£1 500	£11 200

Original cost, maintenance costs and resale values are expressed in current prices. That is, for example, maintenance for a two-year-old oven would cost £800 for maintenance undertaken now. It is expected that maintenance costs will increase at 10% per annum and oven replacement cost and resale values at 5% per annum. The money discount rate is 15%.

Required

a Calculate the preferred replacement policy for the ovens in a choice between a two-year or three-year replacement cycle.   (12 marks)

b Identify the limitations of net present value techniques when applied generally to investment appraisal.   (13 marks)

(Total marks = 25)

Intermediate level

13.15 **Net present value, internal rate of return, sensitivity analysis** (20–30 minutes)

Carmelo, SA, is planning to buy equipment costing €120 000 to improve its materials handling system. The equipment is expected to save €40 000 in cash-operating costs per year. Its estimated useful life is six years, and it will have zero terminal disposal value. The required rate of return is 14%.

Required

1 Calculate the net present value. Calculate the internal rate of return.

2 What is the minimum annual cash savings that will make the equipment desirable on a net present-value basis?

3 When might a manager calculate the minimum annual cash savings described in requirement 2 rather than use the €40 000 savings in cash-operating costs per year to calculate the net present value or internal rate of return?

13.16 **DCF, accounting rate of return, working capital, evaluation of performance** (20–30 minutes)

Meer has been offered a special-purpose metal-cutting machine for €110 000. The machine is expected to have a useful life of eight years with a terminal disposal value of €30 000. Savings in cash-operating costs are expected to be €25 000 per year. However, additional working capital is needed to keep the machine running efficiently and without stoppages. Working capital includes such items as filters, lubricants, bearings, abrasives, flexible exhaust pipes and belts. These items must continually be replaced so that an investment of €8000 must be maintained in them at all times, but this investment is fully recoverable (will be 'cashed in') at the end of the useful life. Meer's required rate of return is 14%.

Required

1 a Calculate the net present value.
   b Calculate the internal rate of return.

2 Calculate the accounting rate of return based on the net initial investment. Assume straight-line depreciation.

3 You have the authority to make the purchase decision. Why might you be reluctant to base your decision on the DCF model?

13.17 **Sporting contract, net present value, payback** (30 minutes)

Aalesund Fotballklubb is a Norwegian football team with a long tradition of winning. However, the last three years have been traumatic. The team has not won a major championship, and attendance at games has dropped considerably. Norsk Fiskevær AS is Aalesund Fotballklubb's major corporate sponsor. Sverre Aspelund, the president of Norsk Fiskevær, is also the president of Aalesund Fotballklubb. Sverre proposes that the team purchase the services of Brazilian star, Monteiro. Monteiro would create great excitement for Aalesund Fotballklubb's fans and sponsors. Monteiro's agent notifies Aspelund that terms for the superstar's signing with Aalesund Fotballklubb are a bonus of NOK 3 million payable now (start of 2015) plus the following four-year contract (assume all amounts are in millions and are paid at the end of each year):

	2016	2017	2018	2019
Salary	NOK 4.5	NOK 5.0	NOK 6.0	NOK 6.5
Living and other costs	1.0	1.2	1.3	1.4

Aspelund's initial reaction is one of horror. As president of Norsk Fiskevær, he has never earned more than NOK 800 000 a year. However, he swallows his pride and decides to examine the expected additions to Aalesund Fotballklubb's cash inflows if Monteiro is signed for the four-year contract (assume all cash inflows are in millions and are received at the end of each year):

	2016	2017	2018	2019
Net gate receipts	NOK 2.0	NOK 3.0	NOK 3.0	NOK 3.0
Corporate sponsorship	3.0	3.5	4.0	4.0
Television royalties	0.0	1.2	1.4	2.0
Merchandise income (net of costs)	0.6	0.6	0.7	0.7

Aspelund believes that a 12% required rate of return is appropriate for investments by Aalesund Fotballklubb.

Required

1 For Monteiro's proposed four-year contract, calculate (a) the net present value, and (b) the payback period.

2 What other factors should Aspelund consider when deciding whether to sign Monteiro the four-year contract?

13.18 Comparison of projects with unequal lives (20–30 minutes)

The manager of the Robin Hood Company is considering two investment projects that are mutually exclusive. The after-tax required rate of return of this company is 10%, and the anticipated cash flows are as follows:

		Cash inflows			
Project no.	Investment required now	Year 1	Year 2	Year 3	Year 4
1	€10 000	€12 000	€0	€0	€0
2	10 000	0	0	0	17 500

Required

1 Calculate the internal rate of return of both projects. Which project is preferable?

2 Calculate the net present value of both projects. Which project is preferable?

3 Comment briefly on the results in requirements 1 and 2. Be specific in your comparisons.

Advanced level

13.19 **Ranking projects** (adapted from NAA Research Report No. 35, pp. 83–5) (40 minutes)

Assume that six projects, A–F in the table that follows, have been submitted for inclusion in the coming year's budget for capital expenditures:

| | Year | Project cash flows | | | | | |
		A	B	C	D	E	F
Investment	0	€(100 000)	€(100 000)	€(200 000)	€(200 000)	€(200 000)	€(50 000)
	1	0	20 000	70 000	0	5 000	23 000
	2	10 000	20 000	70 000	0	15 000	20 000
	3	20 000	20 000	70 000	0	30 000	10 000
	4	20 000	20 000	70 000	0	50 000	10 000
	5	20 000	20 000	70 000	0	50 000	
Per year	6–9	20 000	20 000		200 000	50 000	
	10	20 000	20 000			50 000	
Per year	11–15	20 000					
Internal rate of return		14%	?	?	?	12.6%	12.0%

Required

1 Calculate the internal rates of return (to the nearest half per cent) for projects B, C and D. Rank all projects in descending order in terms of the internal rate of return. Show your calculations.

2 Based on your answer in requirement 1, state which projects you would select, assuming a 10% required rate of return (a) if €500 000 is the limit to be spent, (b) if €550 000 is the limit, and (c) if €650 000 is the limit.

3 Assuming a 16% required rate of return and using the net present-value method, calculate the net present values and rank all the projects. Which project is more desirable, C or D? Compare your answer with your ranking in requirement 1.

4 What factors other than those considered in requirements 1 to 3 would influence your project rankings? Be specific.

13.20 **Equipment replacement, relevant costs, sensitivity analysis** (30–40 minutes)

A toy manufacturer that specialises in making fad items has just developed a £50 000 moulding machine for producing a special toy. The machine has been used to produce only one unit so far. The company will depreciate the £50 000 initial machine investment evenly over four years, after which production of the toy will be stopped. The company's expected annual costs will be direct materials, £10 000; direct manufacturing labour, £20 000; and variable manufacturing overhead, £15 000. Variable manufacturing overhead varies with direct manufacturing labour costs. Fixed manufacturing overhead, exclusive of depreciation, is £7500 annually, and fixed marketing and administrative costs are £12 000 annually.

Suddenly a machine salesperson appears. He has a new machine that is ideally suited for producing this toy. His automatic machine is distinctly superior. It reduces the cost of direct materials by 10% and produces twice as many units per hour. It will cost £44 000 and will have a zero terminal disposal value at the end of four years.

Production and sales of 25 000 units per year (sales of £100 000) will be the same whether the company uses the old machine or the new machine. The current disposal value of the toy company's moulding machine is £5000. Its terminal disposal value in four years will be £2600.

Required

1 Assume that the required rate of return is 18%. Using the net present-value method, show whether the new machine should be purchased. What is the role of the book value of the old machine in the analysis?

2 What is the payback period for the new machine?

3 As the manager who developed the £50 000 old moulding machine, you are trying to justify not buying the new £44 000 machine. You question the accuracy of the expected cash operating savings. By how much must these cash savings fall before the point of indifference – the point where the net present value of investing in the new machine – reaches zero?

13.21 Capital budgeting, computer-integrated manufacturing, sensitivity (25 minutes)

Dinamica Lda is planning to replace one of its production lines, which has a remaining useful life of 10 years, book value of €9 million, a current disposal value of €5 million, and a neglible terminal disposal value 10 years from now. The average investment in working capital is €6 million.

Dinamica plans to replace the production line with a computer-integrated manufacturing (CIM) system at a cost of €45 million. Manuel Ericeira, the production manager, estimates the following annual cash-flow effects of implementing CIM:

a Cost of maintaining software programs and CIM equipment, €1.5 million.

b Reduction in lease payments due to reduced floor-space requirements, €1 million.

c Fewer product defects and reduced rework, €4.5 million.

In addition, Manuel estimates the average investment in working capital will decrease to €2 million. The estimated disposal value of the CIM equipment is €14 million at the end of 10 years. Dinamica uses a required rate of return of 14%.

Required

1 Calculate the net present value of the CIM proposal. On the basis of this criterion, should Dinamica adopt CIM?

2 Manuel argues that the higher quality and faster production resulting from CIM will also increase Dinamica's revenues. He estimates additional cash revenues net of cash-operating costs from CIM of €3 million per year. Calculate the net present value of the CIM proposal under this assumption.

3 Management is uncertain if the cash flows from additional revenues will occur. Calculate the minimum annual cash flow from additional revenues that will cause Dinamica to invest in CIM on the basis of the net present-value criterion.

4 Discuss the effects of reducing the investment horizon for CIM to five years, Dinamica's usual time period for making investment decisions. Assume disposal values at the end of five years of CIM line, €20 million; and of old production line, €4 million. Also assume additional cash revenues net of cash-operating costs from CIM of €3 million per year.

*13.22 Question from CIMA 2010 Chartered Institute of Management Accountants, Specimen Examination Paper 1 (30 minutes)

The Board of Directors of a company is considering two mutually exclusive projects. Both projects necessitate buying new machinery, and both projects are expected to have a life of five years.

Project One

This project has already been evaluated. Details of the project are:

Initial investment needed £500 000
Net present value £41 000
Accounting rate of return 31%.

Project Two

Details of Project Two are:

Year	1	2	3	4	5
Revenue (£000)	370	500	510	515	475
Operating costs (£000)	300	350	380	390	400
Depreciation (£000)	90	90	90	90	90

The figures for revenue and operating costs in the table above are cash flow estimates, have been stated at current values and are assumed to occur at the year end. However, differential inflation is expected: 8% per annum for revenue and 6% per annum for operating costs. The machinery will cost £500 000 and will be sold for £50 000 cash at the end of year 5.

Additional information

The company pays tax at 30%. Tax is paid and/or received one year in arrears.

The machines qualify for tax depreciation at the rate of 25% per annum on a reducing balance basis.

The company's cost of capital is 12% per annum. The current rate of return on investments in the money market is 7%.

The project chosen will be funded by internal funds.

The target accounting rate of return is 30%. The company defines 'Accounting rate of return' as the average profit before tax divided by the average investment.

Required

a (i) Calculate the Net Present Value and the Accounting Rate of Return of Project Two.

(12 marks)

(ii) Prepare a report for the Board of Directors which:
- recommends which of the projects, if any, they should invest in;
- identifies two non-financial factors that are relevant to the decision;
- explains the strengths and weaknesses of net present value and accounting rate of return. (8 marks)

b A government organisation has a fixed interest ten-year loan. The rate on the loan is 8% per annum. The loan is being repaid in equal annual instalments at the end of each year. The amount borrowed was £250 000. The loan has just over four years to run.

Ignore taxation.

Required

Calculate the present value of the amount outstanding on the loan. (5 marks)

(Total for question = 25 marks)

PART II

Case study problems

Case 201

Permaclean Products plc
David Otley, University of Lancaster

The central issue in this case concerns product pricing. The analysis requires the estimation of appropriate costs and assessing price-demand information using past sales data.

Permaclean Products is an old-established firm, located in Dunstable, manufacturing a comprehensive range of domestic cleaning materials. It has a sound reputation and a well-known brand name which has made it a market leader in a wide range of products designed for home use. Although Permaclean has several competitors, the total sales of each are small in comparison with those of Permaclean, mainly because none offers such a complete product range.

In 2013 the price of one of Permaclean's major products, Permashine, was raised from 75p per bottle to 99p when the product was repackaged in a newly designed bottle; however, the contents were identical to the previous pack, both in formulation and quantity. During the following two years sales fell by 27%. At 75p per bottle Permashine had been competitively priced but when its price was increased manufacturers of similar products had not followed. In the period from 2011 to 2014 the price of competing products had been raised by only 5p.

Prices were fixed once a year, to come into force on 1 February, before the annual peak demand which occurred in the spring. In January 2015, John Williams, the marketing manager, met with Andrew Dutton, the chief accountant, to review the company's pricing policy for the coming year.

Permashine

Permashine is a proprietary cleaning product for bathrooms and in 2012 had accounted for over 10% of the company's sales. Although there are a variety of competing products on the market, Permashine has special properties which make it especially suitable for cleaning baths made of acrylic materials. Such baths are becoming increasingly common, but great care has to be taken to avoid scratching them when they are being cleaned. Permashine contains no abrasive materials yet is able to clean acrylic surfaces with great efficiency, giving a surface shine that is very durable. No competing product appears to have this combination of advantages.

The process used in the manufacture of Permashine involves a hazardous chemical reaction that has to be precisely controlled. Production therefore takes place in a separate building on the

Source: Otley, D. (1988) 'Permaclean Products plc', in D. Otley, D. Brown and C. Wilkinson (eds) *Case Studies in Management Accounting* (Hemel Hempstead, UK: Philip Allan Publishers). Reproduced with permission.

same site as the main factory where the other products are made but some distance from it. This production unit, which was constructed in 2007 for safety reasons, is not capable of being adapted for the manufacture of other Permaclean products without substantial expenditure. Although the manufacture of Permashine is potentially hazardous, no serious accidents have occurred during the 15 years in which it has been produced and the final product is itself completely harmless.

In early 2014, Andrew Dutton had installed an improved cost accounting system which allowed product costs to be determined and product profitability to be reviewed. With regard to Permashine, this took into account the new packaging costs, as well as the overhead costs that were separately attributable to the production unit. His analysis, shown in Exhibit 201.1, indicated that the total cost of Permashine was greater than the current selling price of 75p. As a result, at the annual pricing review in 2013 the selling price was increased to 99p.

Although total industry sales continued to rise during 2013 and 2014, Permashine suffered a reduction in both its market share and its total sales, as shown in Exhibit 201.2.

The 2015 pricing review

Both Mr Williams and Mr Dutton were concerned to improve the profitability of Permashine, as it was one of the company's major products. Mr Williams had joined the company in 2007 and had introduced a number of changes in the firm's marketing methods. One of his major successes had been his decision to replace wholesalers with a team of salaried sales representatives who sold the company's full product range direct to retailers. Mr Dutton had been appointed in 2011, following the retirement of the previous chief accountant, and had been responsible for installing a modern computer-based accounting system.

Exhibit 201.1   Estimated costs of Permashine at various production volumes

	Annual production ('000 bottles)						
Cost (p/bottle)	250	300	400	500	600	700	800
Direct labour	17.5	17.5	17.0	17.0	17.0	17.5	18.0
Materials	8.0	8.0	8.0	8.0	8.0	8.0	8.0
Dept. overhead							
Variable	9.0	9.0	9.0	9.0	9.0	9.0	9.0
Fixed	14.4	12.0	9.0	7.2	6.0	5.1	4.5
Factory overhead (20% of direct labour)	3.5	3.5	3.4	3.4	3.4	3.5	3.6
Factory cost	52.4	50.0	46.4	44.6	43.4	43.1	43.1
Selling and administration cost at 80% of factory cost	41.9	40.0	37.1	35.7	34.7	34.5	34.5
Total cost	94.3	90.0	82.7	80.3	78.1	77.6	77.6

Exhibit 201.2   Permashine: sales and price

	2008	2009	2010	2011	2012	2013	2014
Permashine sales ('000 bottles)	400	429	486	525	536	462	391
Total industry sales ('000 bottles)	2000	2050	2250	2200	2300	2650	2900
Permashine % of market	20	21	22	24	23	17.5	13.5
Permashine price (p)	60	70	70	75	75	99	99
Competitors' price range (p)	56–62	65–70	65–70	69–75	69–75	70–80	75–80

Mr Williams pressed for a return to the previous price of 75p for Permashine; at this price he was confident that the market share of the product could be increased to 20% in 2015. He thought that total industry sales would continue to increase to at least 3 million bottles in 2015, and that Permashine was capable of regaining its previous position, provided that it was competitively priced. Because Permaclean had a modern production facility and a manufacturing output greater than any competitor, he was confident that factory production costs were the lowest in the industry. He therefore supported a policy of reducing the price so that other firms would find it uneconomic to continue to compete.

Mr Williams was convinced that sales would continue to fall if the price were to be maintained at 99p, although he believed that there would always be a premium market for Permashine because of its unique qualities. He thought that annual sales were unlikely to fall below 250 000 bottles even at the current price.

Mr Dutton replied that he was well aware of the problems being experienced in selling the higher-priced product. Nevertheless, his analysis showed that the 99p price covered the costs of the product, even at the lowest volume envisaged. If the price were reduced to 75p costs would fail to be covered, even if sales volume rose to the 800 000 bottles which represented the maximum practical capacity of the plant. He referred to his detailed costings (Exhibit 201.1) to support his argument. These figures, he stated, were based on actual data from past years; where data were not available, he had made what he regarded as realistic assumptions.

Question

What price would you recommend for Permashine? Support your recommendation with detailed calculations, making the underlying assumptions on which your analysis is based as clear as possible.

Case 202

Tankmaster Manufacturing Company
Based on a case written by Ken Bates, Warwick University

This case requires students to consider the merits of activity-based costing in an altered production environment. It also deals with behavioural and organisational culture issues.

The Tankmaster Manufacturing Company, a large manufacturer of domestic oil tanks, is located in Amersham, Buckinghamshire. Since it came into existence in 1975, the company has enjoyed steady growth in both sales and profits.

Davina Tankmaster, the founder's daughter, joined the company in 2009 after graduating with a degree in Accounting and Finance from Manchester University. One of her first tasks was to revise the costing system, as there was a need for more accurate product cost information to support the company's strategy of offering keen prices in a highly competitive market dominated by a few large firms.

Davina had faced considerable opposition to the changes she had suggested, with several managers being willing to accept the shortcomings of the old system because they had 'learned to live

Source: Based on a case written by Ken Bates, Warwick University.

with it'. Davina won the day largely because of her father's support as the latter was convinced that 'learned to live with' was a euphemism for 'learned to manipulate to our own advantage'.

Davina's father has now retired so that Davina is now conscious of the need to prove herself. Accordingly, the last thing she wants at present is the upset of another major change in the costing system. However, profits are below budget and the accountant is critical of the current costing system, saying that it is hopelessly out of line with the company's updated manufacturing methods and also with current theories on product costing. He says, 'We are still absorbing overheads on labour-hours and we have an absurdly high overhead absorption rate of £150 per labour-hour. We are pricing ourselves out of the market on our old established products. Product costs would be more meaningful if we absorbed overheads on machine-hours.'

Davina decides she must investigate. Over the past five years, overhead costs had risen to £599 300 per month, a 46% increase, while direct labour-hours have risen from £168 200 to £170 000, a negligible amount. The product processes are now largely mechanised with a relatively high level of automation. Direct labour-hours are 4000 compared with machine-hours of 6500 (it is possible that some labour is still being classed as direct when in fact changes in technology have altered its nature to indirect).

Davina asks the production manager about the rise in overhead costs, causing him to virtually explode: 'How can I keep costs down when marketing ignore our standard specifications and insist on 23 different versions of every product? I need more specialist engineers to monitor the changes, and they don't come cheap. Also there are completely new parts coming through from design with huge material costs; materials handling is a real headache. And the number of specials going through on small production runs continues to increase. I need many more set-ups per shift and that is skilled work, but you can't pick up that sort of skilled labour easily, so overtime is through the roof.'

Davina talks to the marketing manager next: 'We are facing fierce competition for our bread-and-butter, high-volume lines and we just can't match the low prices in the market. However, we have successfully increased our sales of the more specialised tanks despite an increase in prices forced on us by production. So we are meeting our overall sales targets and as we encourage this trend towards the higher margin specialist products, our profits will rise. I don't see any problem here at present, but there will be if you don't make production get control of the cost increases.'

Davina starts to pull the information together, and gets frustrated at the inconsistencies: 'We are meeting our sales targets but production costs are rising because of the switch to specialist products. However, as these are sold at higher margins, we should be improving profits. I don't understand why profits are falling.'

As Davina designed the costing system, she is reluctant to admit that it is at fault and she remembers clearly the opposition she had when she last recommended changes. She no longer has her father to support her so that she decides to bring in a consultant (you) to help identify the problem and to advise on the necessary changes and on a suitable implementation policy. Davina supplies you with the following information:

Budgeted overhead costs per month:

	£
Machines	279 500
Set-up and engineering support	200 200
Materials handling	119 600
Total overhead	599 300
Direct labour	170 000
Total manufacturing cost excluding direct materials	769 300

Further details:

Budgeted labour rate*	£42.500/labour-hour
Budgeted overhead burden*	£149.825/labour-hour
Total cost per labour-hour	£192.325

* Based on budgeted direct labour-hours of 4000.

	Labour-hours	Machine-hours	No. of set-ups	No. of stores orders
Standard products (high volume)	2500	3500	80	160
Specialised products (low volume)	1500	3000	200	300
Total	4000	6500	280	460

Questions

1 Analyse the problem and give advice as to the advantages of switching to machine-hours as the overhead recovery base.

2 Show how an ABC system would change the analysis of the costs between the standard and specialist products.

3 Advise on the implementation of an ABC system. How can Davina's fears be allayed?

Case 203

Siemens Electric Motor Works

Ten years ago our electric motor business was in real trouble. Low labour rates allowed the Eastern Bloc countries to sell standard motors at prices we were unable to match. We had become the high cost producer in the industry. Consequently, we decided to change our strategy and become a specialty motor producer. Once we adopted our new strategy, we discovered that while our existing cost system was adequate for costing standard motors, it gave us inaccurate information when we used it to cost specialty motors.

Mr Karl-Heinz Lotte, Director of Business Operations, EMW

Siemens Corporation

Headquartered in Munich, Siemens AG, a producer of electrical and electronic products, was one of the world's largest corporations. Revenues totalled 51 billion deutschmarks in 1987, with roughly half this amount representing sales outside the Federal Republic of Germany. The Siemens organisation was split into seven major groups and five corporate divisions. The largest group, Energy and Automation, accounted for 24% of total revenues. Low wattage alternating current (A/C) motors were produced at the Electric Motor Works (EMW), which was part of the Manufacturing Industries Division of the Engery and Automation Group. High wattage motors were produced at another facility.

Professors Robin Cooper and Karen Hopper Wruck prepared this case as the basis for class discussion rather than to illustrate either effective or ineffective handling of an administrative situation.

The Electric Motor Works

Located in the small town of Bad Neustadt, the original Siemens EMW plant was built in 1937 to manufacture refrigerator motors for 'Volkskuhlschraenke' (people's refrigerators). Less than a year later, Mr Siemens halted the production of refrigerator motors and began to produce electric motors for other applications. At the end of World War II, the Bad Neustadt plant was the only Siemans factory in West Germany capable of producing electric motors. All the other Siemens production facilities had been completely destroyed or seized by Eastern Bloc countries. After an aggressive rebuilding programme, Bad Neustadt emerged as the firm's primary producer of electric motors.

Through the 1970s, EMW produced about 200 different types of standard motors, at a total annual volume around 230 000 motors. Standard motors accounted for 80 per cent of sales volumes – the remaining 20 per cent was customised motors. The production process was characterised by relatively long runs of a single type of motor. Because identical motors were used by a wide range of customers, standard motors were inventoried and shipped as orders were received. The market for standard A/C motors was extremely competitive. The firm was under constant pressure to reduce costs so that it could price aggressively and still make a profit. Despite a major expansion and automation programme begun in 1974, by the early 1980s EMW found it could not lower its costs sufficiently to offset the lower labour rates of its Eastern Bloc competitors.

Change in strategy

An extensive study revealed that EMW could become a profitable producer of low volume, customised A/C motors. To help implement this strategy, the Bad Neustadt plant was enlarged and dedicated to the manufacture A/C motors with power ratings ranging from 0.06 to 18.5 kilowatts. These motors supported a number of applications including automation engineering, machine tools, plastic processing and paper and printing machines. Exhibit 203.1 presents a detailed diagram of an A/C motor and shows one standard and one customised version of three motors.

For the new strategy to succeed, EMW needed to be able to manufacture efficiently a large variety of motors in small production runs. Between 1985 and 1988 EMW spent DM50 million a year to replace almost every machine on the shopfloor and thereby create a production environment that could support its new strategy.

By 1987 the production process was highly automated with numerically controlled machines, flexible machining centres and robotically fed production processes used throughout the factory. Large volume common components were manufactured using dedicated automated equipment, while very low volume components might be made in manual production processes. Where possible flexible manufacturing was used to produce small volume specialty components. While a normal annual production volume for common components might be 100 000 units, a single component could have up to 10 000 custom variations that might have to be produced one at a time.

To design a custom motor, modifications were made to a standard motor design. The process involved determining where standard components could not be used. These standard components were replaced by custom components that provided the functionality required by the customer.

By 1987, the EMW strategy seemed to be successful (see Exhibit 203.2). Of a total of 65 625 orders accepted, 90 per cent were for custom motors; 48 per cent for only one motor and 74 per cent for fewer than five motors. But EMW high-volume standard motors still accounted for almost half the total annual output of 630 000 motors.

Exhibit 203.1

A small part of our large supply programme. Photo, top left: Three examples of three-phase standard motors; Diagram, right: Three custom-built variants

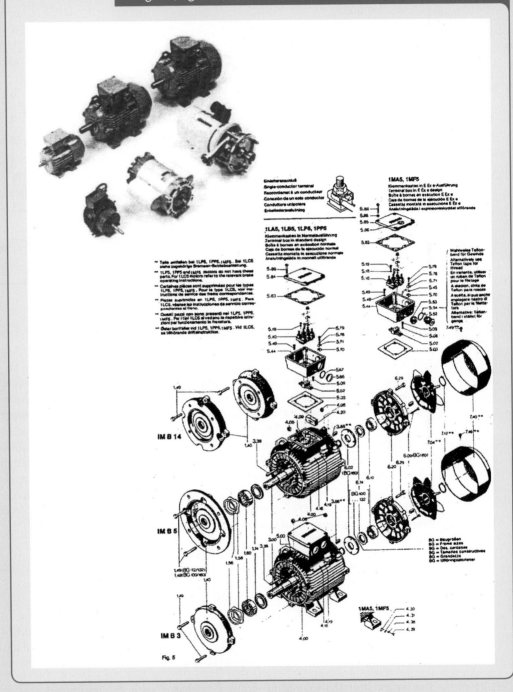

Exhibit 203.2

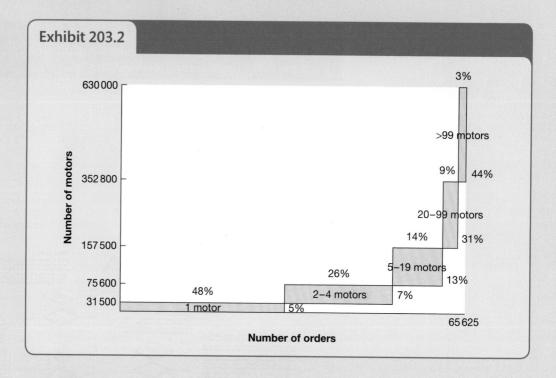

Number of orders

Change in the calculation of product costs

EMW's product cost system assigned materials and labour costs directly to the products. Overhead costs were divided into three categories: materials related, production related and support related. **Materials-related overhead,** containing costs associated with material acquisition, was allocated to products based on their direct materials costs. **Production-related overhead** was directly traced to the 600 production cost centres. A production cost centre had been created for each type of machine. Cost centres with high labour intensity used direct labour hours to allocate costs to products. For centres with automated machines whose operation required few direct labour hours, machine-hours were used as the allocation base. **Support-related overhead** was allocated to products based on manufacturing costs to date: the sum of direct materials and direct labour costs, materials overhead and production overhead. The breakdown of each cost category as a percent of total costs was as follows:

	Percentage of total costs	Burden rate
Direct materials	29%	
Direct labour	10	
Materials overhead	2	6% of materials cost
Production overhead	33	DSM/DLhour or DM/Mhr (600 rates)
Support related overhead	26	35% of other manufacturing costs
Total	100%	

Two years after the change in strategy, problems with the traditional cost system became apparent. The traditional cost system seemed unable to capture the relation between the increased support costs and the change in product mix. Management felt that most support costs related more closely to the number of orders received or the number of customised components in a motor rather than to materials expense or to the quantity of labour and machine hours required to build the motor.

An extensive study was undertaken to identify the support costs that management believed were driven by the processing of orders and the processing of special components. The following departments' costs were most affected by the large increases in number of orders and number of special components.

Costs related to order processing	Costs related to special components
Billing	Inventory handling
Order receiving	Product costing and bidding
Product costing and bidding	Product development
Shipping and handling	Purchasing
	Receiving
	Scheduling and production control
	Technical examination of incoming orders

An analysis of the order processing costs revealed that the same resources were required to process an order of one custom motor as for an order of 200 standard motors. A similar analysis indicated that the number of different types of special components in each motor design determined the work load for the departments affected by special components. The demand for work in these departments was not strongly affected by the total number of special components produced. For example, an order of five custom motors requiring ten special components per unit generated the same amount of work as an order of one custom motor with a design requiring ten special components. In 1987, the factory used 30 000 different special components to customise their motors. The special components were processed 325 000 different times for customised orders.

The costs in each support department associated with these two activities were removed from the support related cost pool and assigned to two new cost pools. Exhibit 203.3 illustrates, for 1987, the formation of the two new cost pools. The first column presents total costs grouped by traditional costing system definitions. The new cost system removes 6.3 million from engineering support costs and 27.0 million from administrative support costs. These expenses are then assigned to the new cost pools. 13.8 million to order processing costs and 19.5 million to special components costs.

Exhibit 203.3	1987 Reconciliation transforming the traditional cost system (000 DM)					
	Traditional		**Transferred**		**New**	
Materials	105 000				105 000	
Materials overhead	6 000				6 000	
Labour	36 000				36 000	
Labour or machine overhead	120 000				120 000	
Manufacturing cost	267 000	(74%)*			267 700	(74%)
Engineering costs	12 000		6 300		5 700	
Tooling costs	22 500		0		22 500	
Administrative costs	60 000		27 000		33 000	
Support related costs	94 500	(26%)	33 300	(9%)	61 200	(17%)
Order processing cost			13 800		13 800	
Special components cost			19 500		19 500	
Total cost	361 500		0		361 500	

* Percentage of total cost

	A	B	C	D	E
Exhibit 203.4 Manufacturing costs for five motor orders					
Cost of base motor (without assignment from new cost pools)	304.0	304.0	304.0	304.0	304.0
Cost of all special components[a] (without assignment from new cost pools)	39.6	79.2	118.8	198.0	396.0
Number of different types of special components per motor	1	2	3	5	10
Number of motors ordered	1	1	1	1	1

	Base motor cost	Special components cost
Materials	90	12.0
Materials overhead	5	0.7
Direct labour	35	4.5
Manufacturing overhead	117	15.0
	247	32.2
Support related overhead[b]	57	7.4
Unit manufacturing costs	304	39.6

[a] For illustrative purposes, all different types of special components are assumed to cost 39.6 a piece.
[b] Support related overhead excludes the expenses associated with processing individual customer orders and handling special components.

Exhibit 203.4 shows the cost buildup for five typical motor orders. The base motor cost includes direct materials and labour costs, materials and production overhead and the portion of support overhead not assigned to the two new cost pools. To this base motor cost must be added the cost of processing the order and the materials, labour, production overhead and support overhead required for the special components.

Effect of the new cost system

In 1987 EMW received close to DM1 billion in orders, accepted only DM450 million and ran the factory at 115 per cent of rated capacity. Mr Karl-Heinz Lottes, Director of Business Operations, EMW commented on the role of redesigned cost system with the new strategy:

> Without the new cost system, our new strategy would have failed. The information it generated helped us to identify those orders we want to accept. While some orders we lose to competitors, most we turn down because they are not profitable. Anyone who wants to understand the importance of the system, can simply compare some typical orders costed with the traditional system with the costs produced by our new system.

Question

How does the new system support EMW's strategy?

Case 204

Colombo Frozen Yogurt
Jane Saly, University of St Thomas, and Jon Guy, General Mills

This case illustrates the strategy adopted by one of the first movers in the frozen yogurt industry in order to stay competitive and maintain market share. The case requires analysis of customer profitability using activity based costing.

In 1997, General Mills Plc, a multi-billion £ consumer goods company, acquired Colombo Frozen Yogurt. General Mills Plc (GMP) believed they could add Colombo frozen yogurt to their existing product line-up to increase net sales with little addition in marketing cost.

Frozen yogurt is sold through two distinct market segments: independent shops and impulse locations such as cafeterias, colleges and buffets. The shop business revolves around frozen yogurt and speciality items made from yogurt. In the impulse segment, yogurt is an add-on to the main business. GMP's large salesforce already served the impulse market with various 'snack' food items.

The financial results in the first couple of years were mixed. Profits increased along with sales volume. However, when sales hit a plateau, earnings dropped. The sales-people were dissatisfied with yogurt sales and said their customers weren't happy either. The GMP salesforce focused on the impulse segments and saw increases in volume there. However, volume in the shop segment declined at alarming rates. While GMP knew sales by segment, they didn't track costs by segment. Instead costs were allocated based on £ sales. Therefore, they needed a new method to track costs: activity-based costing.

Frozen yogurt market structure

Colombo Yogurt Company, an early innovator in the frozen yogurt market, did well during the early craze when customers flocked to frozen yogurt as a healthy alternative to ice cream. As the market continued to develop, Colombo chose to market mainly to independent shop owners. As a result, Colombo lost customers when franchise operations such as TCBY encouraged independent shops to become a franchise and purchase the product from the franchiser. In the early 1990s, the market changed again as food service operators such as cafeterias, colleges and buffets started to add soft-serve yogurt to their business. By the late 1990s, these impulse locations accounted for two-thirds of the soft-serve market.

The economics of shops is similar to that of restaurants. The shops focus on maximising profit per square foot. While they are aware of food cost, shop owners are rooted in a culture dominated by guest counts (new and repeat) and receipt averages. These variables are more linked to the kind of customer referrals where word of mouth brings in new customers and the total experience brings them back again. The key variable is the quality of the product and experience (service and feeling). To compete with other shops, they must innovate by adding distinctive new products such as smoothies, juices, etc. Otherwise they may go out of business as thousands have done in the last decade.

The economics of impulse locations is very different. They make their living from other items, and the soft-serve trade is only performance topspin. These firms are unwilling to take any risk (new equipment or extra labour) to serve highly differentiated products such as smoothies or juices. They generally are interesting in providing a quality service for a reasonable price. They

Source: Adapted from Saly, J. and Guy, T. (2000) 'Colombo Frozen Yogurt: activity-based costing applied to marketing costs', *Cases from Management Accounting Practice*, Volume 15 (Montvale, New Jersey: Institute of Management Accounting Practice).

PART II Case study problems

typically measure performance with cost per serving, and they have a difficult time understanding profit contribution as opposed to food cost. Impulse locations are typically small.

The GMP–Colombo marketing plan

It was the impulse business in the Foodservice operations that made Colombo an attractive acquisition for General Mills. The GMP Foodservice Division was already marketing well-known brands to food management firms, hospitals, and schools. Colombo yogurt was added to this product line-up, and the Foodservice salesforce covered both shop and impulse locations.

Salesforce

Colombo's salesforce was merged into the Foodservice salesforce. Customers were reassigned to salespeople who already serviced that geographical area. The salespeople varied in their reaction to the product. Some found shops easy to sell to, while others avoided the shops despite the possible lost commission. Many spent a lot of time helping their impulse customers understand how to use the machinery.

Merchandising promotions

Colombo traditionally charged the shops for merchandising that was large scale and eye popping (neon signs). The shops used these signs to draw customers inside. Since GMP traditionally provided merchandising at no cost, they stopped charging for it. Salespeople used the merchandising as a reason to visit the customers, and the same merchandising was provided to both shops and impulse locations. While shops expressed interest in the kits, some salespeople noticed that the impulse locations didn't even hang them up.

Pricing promotions

Pricing promotions are a mainstay of GMP's impulse location approach. GMP's salesforce generally used these promotion events as an opportunity to visit their accounts and take advantage of the occasion to meet service needs and sell other products that might not be featured. GMP made price promotions available to both segments of the market. While the deals were typically around £5 per case, they averaged £3 per case against all the volume shipped during the year. GMP marketing knew price was not a major decision factor for shops, and they did not aim pricing promotions to them. However, shops were aware of the promotions and took advantage of them.

The business case pre-ABC

Profit and loss by segment pre-ABC

Category	Impulse segment	Yogurt shops	Total
Sales in cases	1 200 000	300 000	1 500 000
Sales revenue	£23 880 000	£5 970 000	£29 850 000
Less: price promotions	−3 600 000	−900 000	−4 500 000
Net sales	20 280 000	5 070 000	25 350 000
Less: cost of goods sold	−13 800 000	−3 450 000	−17 250 000
Gross margin	6 480 000	1 620 000	8 100 000
Less: merchandising	−1 380 000	−345 000	−1 725 000
Less: SG&A	−948 000	−237 000	−1 185 000
Net income	£4 152 000	£1 038 000	£5 190 000

ABC analysis of cost of goods sold

Cost of goods sold is made up of £14 250 000 for ingredients, packaging and storage, and £3 000 000 for pick/pack and shipping. Since the product is the same across segments, the cost to produce should be the same. However, pick/pack and shipping costs vary according to whether or not the order is for a full pallet. Full pallets cost £75 to pick and ship whereas individual orders cost £2.25 per case. There are 75 cases in a pallet and the segments differ in their utilisation of full pallets, as shown below.

	Impulse segment	Yogurt shops	Total
Cases in full pallets	60 000	240 000	300 000
Individual cases	1 140 000	60 000	1 200 000
Total cases	1 200 000	300 000	1 500 000

ABC analysis of merchandising

Merchandising costs consist mainly of kits costing £500 each. A review of where the kits were sent indicated that a total of 3,450 kits were delivered, 90 of them to shops.

ABC analysis of selling, general, and administrative (SG&A)

Since sales representatives service several products, their costs were allocated to the various products based on gross £ sales. GMP gave diaries to 10% of the salesforce in randomly selected markets of the country and asked them to track their time in activity classifications for 60 days. The diaries indicated that sales representatives spent much more time per pound of sale on yogurt than other products. When SG&A costs were allocated based on time, the total allocation to yogurt jumped from £1 185 000 to £3 900 000. Of their time spent on yogurt, only 1% of the time was spent on the shops.

Questions

1 Briefly summarise Colombo's competitive environment and General Mills' strategy in response to that environment.

2 Using the ABC analysis, determine new segment profitability statements.

3 Based on your analysis in questions 1 and 2, what changes would you suggest to General Mills?

PART II Case study problems

PART III

Planning and budgetary control systems

This part of the book focuses on what managers need to know about expected outcomes once decisions have been made and to build on such information in making further decisions. We look at ways in which management accounting approaches may assist in planning for the future and in learning from past activities. Chapter 14 looks at organisational and behavioural issues which affect the design of internal accounting systems and considers also the consequences of using the information output of such systems. Chapters 15, 16 and 17 stress calculative considerations in the formal planning and control process.

CHAPTER 14

Motivation, budgets and responsibility accounting

Budgets are one of the most widely used tools for planning and controlling organisations. Surveys show an almost universal use of budgets by medium and large companies in many parts of the globe. Budgeting systems turn managers' perspectives forward. A forward-looking perspective enables managers to be in a better position to exploit opportunities. It also enables them to anticipate problems and take steps to eliminate or reduce their severity. As one observer said, 'Few businesses plan to fail, but many of those that flop failed to plan.' Consider Coors Brewers Ltd which achieves high levels of customer service in two very different supply chains. The 'on-trade' channel is seasonal but predictable whereas the 'take-home' channel is very volatile. Accurate demand forecasts enable Coors to lower stock, replenish overnight and optimise customer service.

This chapter examines budgeting as a planning and coordinating device. Topics covered in prior chapters are widely used in this discussion. By understanding cost behaviour (covered in Chapters 2 and 9), managers can better predict how total budgeted costs are affected by different projected output levels. By understanding cost tracing and cost allocation (covered in Chapters 3, 4 and 5), managers can show how different projected revenue and cost amounts will impact upon the budgeted profit and loss statement and balance sheet.

Chapter 1 described some newly evolving management themes that impact upon management accounting. Budgets give financial expression to many of these themes. For example, budgets can quantify the planned financial effects of activities aimed at continuous improvement and cost reduction.

The material covered in this chapter is also integral to subsequent chapters. For example, Chapters 15 and 16 examine how the numbers used in budgets assist in evaluating the performance of managers or the business areas for which they have responsibility.

Learning objectives

After studying this chapter, you should be able to:

- Define what a master budget is and explain its major benefits to an organisation
- Describe major components of the master budget
- Prepare the budgeted profit statement and its supporting budget schedules
- Describe the uses of computer-based financial planning models
- Explain kaizen budgeting and its importance for cost management
- Illustrate an activity-based budgeting approach
- Describe responsibility centres and responsibility accounting
- Explain how controllability relates to responsibility accounting

Major features of budgets

Definition and role of budgets

A *budget* is a quantitative expression of a proposed plan of action by management for a future time period and is an aid to the coordination and implementation of the plan. It can cover both financial and non-financial aspects of these plans and acts as a blue-print for the company to follow in the forthcoming period.

Budgets covering financial aspects quantify management's expectations regarding future income, cash flows and financial position. Just as individual financial statements are prepared covering past periods, so they can be prepared covering future periods – for example, a budgeted income statement, a budgeted cash-flow statement and a budgeted balance sheet. Underlying these financial budgets can be non-financial budgets for, say, units manufactured, number of new products introduced to the market, or head count.

Many organisations adopt the following budgeting cycle:

1 Planning the performance of the organisation as a whole as well as its subunits. The entire management team agrees upon what is expected.

2 Providing a frame of reference, a set of specific expectations against which actual results can be compared.

3 Investigating variations from plans. If necessary, corrective action follows investigation.

4 Planning again, considering feedback and changed conditions.

The **master budget** coordinates all the financial projections in the organisation's individual budgets in a single organisation-wide set of budgets for a given time period. It embraces the impact of both *operating* decisions and *financing* decisions. Operating decisions are about the acquisition and use of scarce resources. Financing decisions centre on how to obtain the funds to acquire resources. This book concentrates on how accounting helps managers make operating decisions, and we emphasise operating budgets in this chapter.

The term *master* in 'master budget' refers to it being a comprehensive, organisation-wide set of budgets. Consider the Credit Suisse Group, which operates the Credit Suisse Bank. It is one of the world's most profitable and important banks upon which international financial stability depends. Fortune Magazine has recently considered it one of the globe's most admired companies. It has three divisions, Investment Banking, Private Banking and Wealth Management, and a Shared Services Group which provides legal, IT, marketing and support to the other divisions. Each division has a separate budgeted income statement, a separate budgeted cash-flow statement, and so on. The master budgeted income statement for the Credit Suisse Group is a single income statement that combines information from all these individual budgeted income statements. Similarly, the master budgeted cash-flow statement is a single cash-flow statement that combines information from all these individual budgeted cash-flow statements.

Roles of budgets

Budgets are a major feature of management control systems in general. Current thinking concerning budgetary control systems suggests two opposite views. On the one hand, there is the view that espouses incremental improvement to budgetary processes in terms of linking such processes more closely to operational requirements and planning systems and increasing the frequency of budget revisions and the deployment of rolling budgets. Conversely, an alternative view advocates the abandonment of budgetary control and its replacement with alternative techniques to enable firms to become more adaptive and agile.

The level of formal budgetary controls perceived as essential by micro (one to nine employees) and small (ten to fifty employees) businesses has been found to be minimal (Pilkington and

Crowther 2007). Micro-businesses believe they can survive 'perfectly well' without any formal budgeting process. Small businesses have more role formality and in these the power of personality is used by management to impose control rather than adopt formal participative elements of budgetary controls. They can (1) compel strategic planning including the implementation of plans, (2) provide performance criteria, (3) promote communication and coordination within the organisation, and (4) affect motivating and wider organisational processes.

Strategy and plans

Budgeting is most useful when done as an integral part of an organisation's strategic analysis. **Strategy** can be viewed as describing how an organisation matches its own capabilities with the opportunities in the marketplace to accomplish its overall objectives. It includes consideration of such questions as:

1 What are the overall objectives of the organisation?

2 Are the markets for its product local, regional, national or global? What trends will affect its markets? How is the organisation affected by the economy, its industry and its competitors?

3 What forms of organisational and financial structures serve the organisation best?

4 What are the risks of alternative strategies, and what are the organisation's contingency plans if its preferred plan fails?

Consider the diagram in Exhibit 14.1. Strategic analysis underlies both long-run and short-run planning. In turn, these plans lead to the formulation of budgets. The arrows in the diagram are pointing in two directions. Why? Because strategy, plans and budgets are interrelated and affect one another. Budgets provide feedback to managers about the likely effects of their strategic plans. Managers then use this feedback to revise their strategic plans. In an increasingly competitive business climate, consumers shop around and demand greater returns for the prices they pay. The communications industry is no exception. BT Retail, for instance, places great reliance on 'top-down' and 'bottom-up' forecasts to ensure all customer requirements are taken into account. For its core telephony revenue, BT takes into account myriad factors, including the incorporation of new products, customer segmentation, external economic and social factors, in its budget forecasts.

A framework for judging performance

Budgeted performance measures can overcome two key limitations of using past performance as a basis for judging actual results. One limitation is that past results incorporate past miscues and substandard performance. Consider a mobile phone company (Mobile Communications)

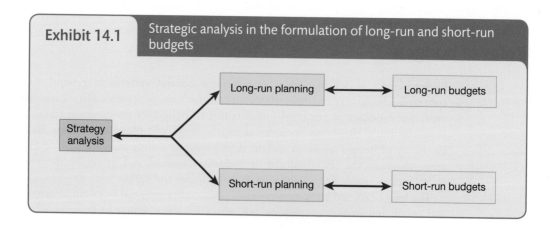

| Exhibit 14.1 | Strategic analysis in the formulation of long-run and short-run budgets |

examining the 2015 performance of its sales-force. Suppose the past performance in 2014 incorporates the efforts of many departed salespeople who left because they did not have an understanding of the marketplace. (As the president of Mobile said, 'They could not sell ice cream in a heatwave.') Using the sales record of those departed employees would set the performance bar for new salespeople too low.

A second limitation of past performance is that the future may be expected to be very different from the past. Consider again our mobile phone company. Suppose that Mobile Communications had a 20% revenue increase in 2015 compared with a 10% increase in 2014. Does this indicate excellent sales performance? Before saying yes, consider two additional facts. Fact one is that in November 2014, an industry trade association forecast that the 2015 growth rate in industry revenues would be 40%. Fact two is that in 2015, the actual growth rate in industry revenues was 50%. The 20% actual revenue gain in 2015 takes on a negative connotation given these facts, even though it exceeds the 2014 actual growth rate of 10%. Use of the 40% figure as the budgeted rate provides a better way to evaluate the 2015 sales performance than does use of the 2014 actual rate of 10%. A cycling analogy is appropriate here. A budgeted industry growth rate of 40% is equivalent to the cyclist going downhill on a steep slope. Top management of Mobile Communications expects that good performance will achieve above-average speed compared with other cyclists in similar conditions.

Coordination and communication

Coordination is the meshing and balancing of all factors of production or service and of all the departments and business functions so that the company can meet its objectives. *Communication* is getting those objectives understood and accepted by all departments and functions.

Coordination forces executives to think of relationships among individual operations, departments, the company as a whole and across companies. Coordination implies, for example, that purchasing officers make material purchase plans based on production requirements. Also, production managers plan personnel and machinery needs to produce the number of products necessary to meet revenue forecasts. How does a budget lead to coordination? Consider budgeting at Pace, a UK-based manufacturer of electronic products. A key product is their decoder boxes for cable television. The Pace production manager for decoder boxes can better budget production schedules by coordinating and communicating with the marketing personnel at Pace. These marketing personnel, in turn, can make better predictions as to future demand for decoder boxes by coordinating and communicating with Pace's customers. Suppose BSkyB, one of Pace's largest customers, is planning to launch a new digital satellite service nine months from now. If Pace's marketing group is able to obtain advance information about the launch date for the digital satellite service, it can share this information with Pace's manufacturing group. This group must then coordinate and communicate with Pace's materials procurement group, and so on. The key point is that Pace is more likely to have a satisfied customer (decoder boxes available for BSkyB in sufficient quantities at the launch date) if Pace coordinates and communicates both within its own business functions and with its suppliers and customers during the budgeting process as well as during the production process.

Motivation and wider organisational issues

Budgets help managers, but budgets need help. Top management has the ultimate responsibility for the budgets of the organisation they manage. Management at all levels, however, should understand and support the budget and all aspects of the management control system. To achieve an ambitious five-year master plan, the Unilever Group stated that 'Our strategic objectives and the imperative for change are clear. To translate strategy into action, we must now align the entire company and all our employees behind our strategic aims.' Top management support is especially critical for obtaining active line participation in the formulation of budgets and for successful administration of the budget. If line managers feel that top management does not 'believe' in the budget, these managers are unlikely to be active participants in the budget process. Similarly, a top management that always mechanically institutes 'across the board' cost reductions (say, a 10% reduction in all areas) in the face of revenue reductions is unlikely to have line managers willing to be 'fully honest' in their budget communications.

The manner in which a budget is administered can adversely impact on the managers' behaviour. Budgets should not be administered rigidly. Managers sometimes use budgeted targets to effect changes in a forceful way. But 'decentralisation and an anti-control ethos seem to characterise a growing number of successful businesses' (Colvin 2006). Consider the Brazilian firm Semco, where there are virtually no job titles: a few executives trade the CEO post every six months, and workers set their own hours and choose their managers by vote. But according to Jack Welch, the ex-CEO of GE, budgets can sometimes just be 'an uncanny way of sucking the energy and fun out of an organization' (Welch and Welch 2007). Jack and Suzy Welch explain that 'The goal of the people in the field is to come up with targets that they absolutely positively think they can hit. So they construct plans with layer upon layer of conservative thinking.' Conversely,

> **headquarters executives are also preparing for the budget review, but with exactly the opposite agenda – they want targets that push the limits. People in the field are paid to hit their targets. They get a stick in the eye (or worse) for missing them. So why in the world should they dream big?**
>
> (Welch and Welch 2007)

These commentators advocate different reward systems where 'bonuses are not based on an internally negotiated number but on real world measures: how the business performed compared with the previous year and how it did compared with the competition'. Hope and Fraser (2003a, p. 5) concur and note that, for some companies, budgets play 'a powerful role in defining and enforcing cultural norms that discourage frontline people from taking responsibility for their performance'. Instances also exist where businesses thrive because of constrained budgets. Consider Elio Sceti, the Chief Executive Officer of Iglo Group, one of Europe's largest frozen food companies:

> **Our business did not grow in 2013 and profitability declined. . . . under a new strategy the potential for our business is much stronger . . . we minimise food waste due to the longer lifecycle of our products. . . . we are all familiar with the current economic crisis increasing pressure on food budgets. Our category plays well in the era of austerity . . .**
>
> (www.iglo.com/business-overview/chief-executive-officers-q-and-a.aspx)

Budgetary control entails more than the simple application of rules and calculative procedures and the quantitative evaluation of performance. Budgeting activities achieve specific significance depending on the organisational processes through which budgetary pressures and demands arise. Having a formal document such as the budget is an effective way to communicate a consistent set of plans to the organisation as a whole. There are instances where budgets serve to send strategic messages. For instance, Hyundai, the Korean car manufacturer, makes it publicly 'understood that impossible targets are part of its way of doing business' (Taylor 2010). In practice, it is rarely possible to disentangle the organisational from the technical aspects of budgeting emphasised in this chapter. An enterprise can set a 'difficult to attain' budget in an attempt to motivate good performance. This is because, in practice, budgets that are set up to a certain degree of tightness often become stronger motivators, although motivation tends to decline after a certain point (see the aspirations budget in Exhibit 14.2). The expectation may be that the budget target set to motivate high performance from employees will not be attained. An alternative budget for financial planning purposes may therefore have to be established based on what is expected to be achieved. Such alternative uses of budgets sometimes require a 'write-down' to be determined. If such 'write-downs' become known in the organisation, relationships between managers and subordinates and across departments will possibly be adversely affected. Consequently, the motivational role of the aspirations budget is certain to suffer.

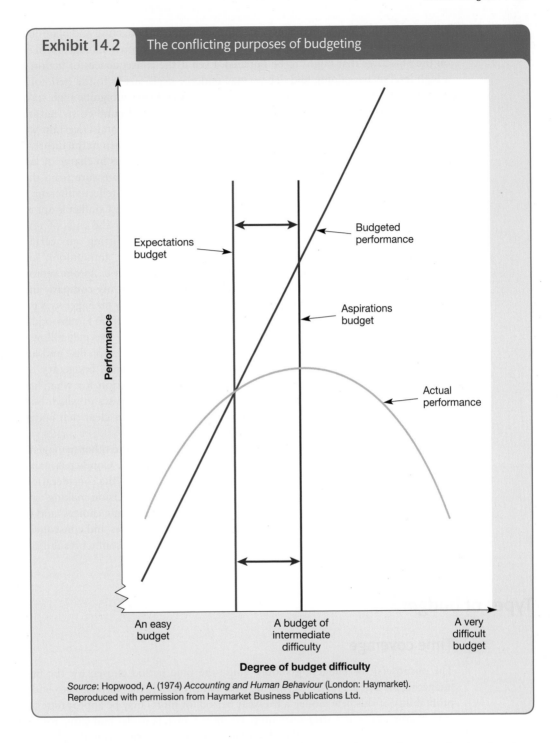

Exhibit 14.2   The conflicting purposes of budgeting

Expectations budget

Budgeted performance

Aspirations budget

Actual performance

Performance

An easy budget

A budget of intermediate difficulty

A very difficult budget

Degree of budget difficulty

Source: Hopwood, A. (1974) *Accounting and Human Behaviour* (London: Haymarket). Reproduced with permission from Haymarket Business Publications Ltd.

Situations where decision makers agree about the aims of particular organisational actions or over the activities of particular organisational units sometimes coincide with certainty about what will ensue if certain actions are taken. In such instances, we can think of budgets as facilitating the coordination and integration of organisational activities through direct computation. For instance, expected budgeted cash-flow changes can readily be assessed and future overdraft requirements can be anticipated in advance. If, however, there exists uncertainty over what might happen as a consequence of taking some action, we can think of the budget as offering the possibility of helping managers to learn rather than to provide computational answers. In other words, managers can simulate different budgeting and planning situations and can ponder over 'what-if' scenarios. It is clear, however, that often managers will not see eye to eye on the objectives that ought to be pursued. Even if the consequences of action are undisputed, a high level of bargaining and debate may underlie decisions as to the best course of action to be pursued. Often, top managers face situations with high ambiguity, high stakes and extreme uncertainty. Discord, contention, debate, disagreement and conflict are natural in such situations. Reasonable people are likely to perceive an ambiguous and uncertain world in different ways and to make differing assessments about what might happen in the future. They will show different preferences for alternatives. Moreover, senior executives in charge of large and important sectors of the organisation will receive information and pressure from their own unique constituencies within the firm and will form objectives that reflect different responsibilities. Executives will act as forceful advocates for 'truth' as they see it. Conflict is apt to ensue. In such circumstances, budgetary controls may be deployed to further the ends of only some groups of managers by, for instance, highlighting, measuring and reporting only certain activities but omitting others. As such, budgets can become synonymous with 'ammunition' in that they determine what is regarded as relevant and worthwhile or problematic. As one senior manager once remarked: 'You will never understand the budgetary system in my company unless you realise that it is like a rosary bead: it quite simply makes sure that every manager says profit, cost, cash, working capital, etc., at least a thousand times a year' (adapted from Hopwood, 1980). There are even times when both what is to be aimed for and what consequences may follow from particular actions are uncertain. Budgets can in such circumstances help rationalise and justify courses of action over which there is already commitment. In other words, budgetary activities do not enhance the quality of decisions but simply provide legitimation for what has been decided beforehand. Although managers often prefer to acknowledge ways in which budgets are useful in providing answers or in helping them to probe and learn, it is clear that budgets also exist in organisations as ammunition and rationalisation means.

The design and functioning of budgetary control systems (and other management accounting practices) will reflect the realities of organisational processes. Conflict is part of managerial affairs and can be valuable. High-conflict situations can lead to 'the consideration of more alternatives, better understanding of choices and more effective decision making' (Eisenhardt et al. 1997, p. 43). Low-conflict management teams make 'poor strategic choices' and their actions are 'easy for competitors to anticipate'. Disagreement over objectives and consequences of action is a fact of organisational life. Accounting reflects and influences conflict resolution.

Types of budget

Time coverage

The purpose(s) for budgeting should guide the time period chosen for the budget. Consider budgeting for a new Harley-Davidson 500cc motorcycle. If the purpose is to budget for the total profitability of this new model, a five-year period (or more) may be appropriate (covering design, manufacture, sales and after-sales support). In contrast, consider budgeting for a Christmas play. If the purpose is to estimate all cash outlays, a 14-month period from the planning to staging of the play may be adequate.

The most frequently used budget period is one year. The annual budget is often subdivided by months for the first quarter and by quarters for the remainder of the year. The budgeted data for a year are frequently revised as the year unfolds. For example, at the end of the first quarter, the budget for the next three quarters is changed in light of new information.

Some businesses use *rolling budgets*. A **rolling budget** is a budget or plan that is always available for a specified future period by adding a month, quarter or year in the future as the month, quarter or year just ended is dropped. Thus, a 12-month rolling budget for the March

2015 to February 2016 period becomes a 12-month rolling budget for the April 2015 to March 2016 period the next month, and so on. There is always a 12-month budget in place. Rolling budgets constantly force management to think concretely about the forthcoming 12 months, regardless of the month at hand. Consider Electrolux, the global appliance company, which has a three- to five-year strategic plan and a one-year rolling budget. A one-year rolling budget for the April 2015 to March 2016 period is superseded by a one-year rolling budget for July 2015 to June 2016 and so on. Rolling budgets force Electrolux's management to constantly think about the forthcoming 12 months.

Sometimes excessive focus on desired outcomes can lead to gross underestimates of budget requirements. In 2007, when Russia was bidding to host the 2014 Winter Olympics, the huge amounts it was willing to spend were a matter of pride and intended to entice officials of the International Olympic Committee. Russia's President Vladimir Putin pledged to spend $12 billion in Sochi, dwarfing other contenders' bids. Still the Sochi Games budget fell well short of the $51 billion actually spent.

Many companies have drastically altered the manner in which budgetary control is exercised. Some companies have abandoned the practice. For instance, when Jan Wallander became the chief executive officer of Svenska Handelsbanken – one of the most profitable international banks in Europe – he abolished the budget process, viewing it as an 'unnecessary evil'. Control is now undertaken using alternative management approaches. Other companies, such as Ikea, Volvo, Ericsson, Boots and Diageo, have moved away from traditional department-focused budgetary control systems.

An illustration of a master budget

A good way to explain the budgeting process is to walk through the development of an actual budget. We shall use a master budget because it provides a comprehensive picture of the entire budgeting process at Wessex Engineering, a manufacturer of aircraft replacement parts. Its job costing system for manufacturing costs has two direct-cost categories (direct materials and direct manufacturing labour) and one indirect cost pool (manufacturing overhead). Manufacturing overhead (both variable and fixed) is allocated to products using direct manufacturing labour-hours as the allocation base.

Exhibit 14.3 shows a simplified diagram of the various parts of the master budget for Wessex Engineering. The master budget summarises the financial projections of all the organisation's individual budgets. The master budget results in a set of related financial statements for a set time period, usually a year. The bulk of Exhibit 14.3 presents a set of budgets that together is often called the **operating budget**, which is the budgeted profit statement and its supporting budget schedules. The supporting budget schedules cut across different categories of the value chain from R&D to customer service. The **financial budget** is that part of the master budget that comprises the capital budget, cash budget, budgeted balance sheet, and budgeted statement of cash flows. It focuses on the impact of operations and planned capital outlays on cash.

The final master budget is often the result of several iterations. Each of its drafts involves interaction across the various business functions of the value chain.

The terminology used to describe budgets varies among organisations. For example, budgeted financial statements are sometimes called **pro forma statements**. The budgeted financial statements of many companies include the budgeted profit statement, the budgeted balance sheet, and the budgeted statement of cash flows. Some organisations, such as Hewlett-Packard, refer to budgeting as *targeting*. Indeed, to give a more positive thrust to budgeting, many organisations – for example, the Nissan Motor Company – describe the budget as a *profit plan*.

Basic data and requirements

Wessex Engineering is a machine shop that uses skilled labour and metal alloys to manufacture two types of aircraft replacement parts: Regular and Heavy-Duty. Wessex managers are ready to

Exhibit 14.3 Overview of the master budget for Wessex Engineering

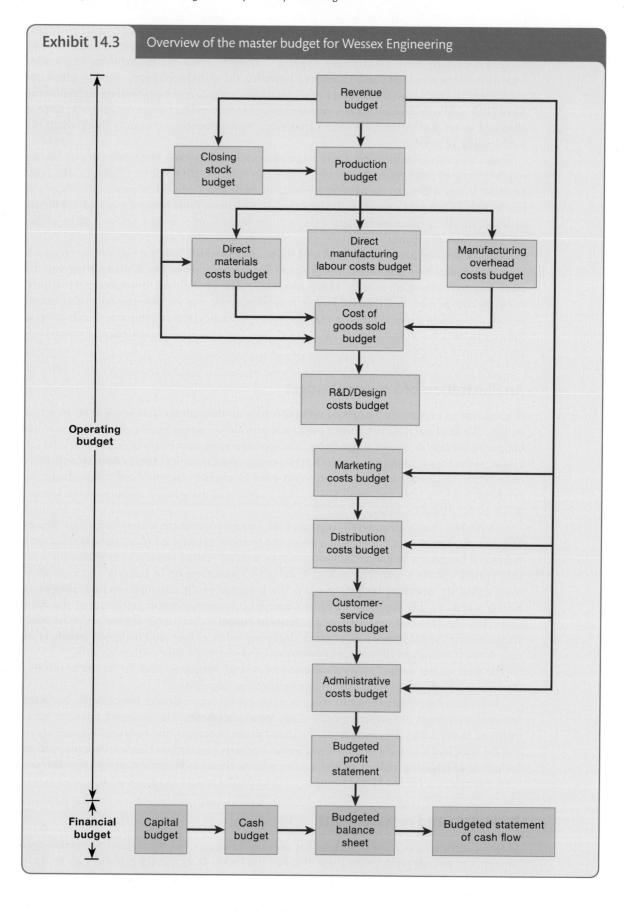

prepare a master budget for the year 2016. To keep our illustration manageable for clarifying basic relationships, we make the following assumptions:

1 The only source of revenues is sales of the two parts. Non-sales-related revenue, such as interest income, is assumed to be zero.

2 Work-in-progress stock is negligible and is ignored.

3 Direct materials stock and finished goods stock are costed using the first-in, first-out (FIFO) method.

4 Unit costs of direct materials purchased and finished goods sold remain unchanged throughout the budget year (2016).

5 Variable production costs are variable with respect to direct manufacturing labour-hours. Variable non-production costs are variable with respect to revenues. Both assumptions are simplifying ones made to keep our example relatively straightforward.

6 For computing inventoriable costs, all manufacturing costs (fixed and variable) are allocated using a single allocation base – direct manufacturing labour-hours.

After carefully examining all relevant factors, the executives of Wessex Engineering forecast the following figures for 2016:

Direct materials	
Material 111 alloy	€7 per kilogram
Material 112 alloy	€10 per kilogram
Direct manufacturing labour	€20 per hour

	Product	
Content of each product unit	Regular aircraft part	Heavy-Duty aircraft part
Direct materials 111 alloy	12 kilograms	12 kilograms
Direct materials 112 alloy	6 kilograms	8 kilograms
Direct manufacturing labour	4 hours	6 hours

All direct manufacturing costs are variable with respect to the units of output produced. Additional information regarding the year 2016 is as follows:

	Product	
	Regular	Heavy-Duty
Expected sales in units	5 000	1 000
Selling price per unit	€600	€800
Target closing stock in units*	1 100	50
Opening stock in units	100	50
Opening stock in euros	€38 400	€26 200

	Direct materials	
	111 Alloy	112 Alloy
Opening stock in kilograms	7000	6000
Target closing stock in kilograms*	8000	2000

* Target stocks depend on expected sales, expected variation in demand for products, and management philosophies such as just-in-time stock management.

At the anticipated output levels for the Regular and Heavy-Duty aircraft parts, management believes the following manufacturing overhead costs will be incurred:

Variable: €26 per direct manufacturing labour-hour
Fixed: €420 000 manufacturing overhead cost for production within relevant range

Other (non-production) costs expected to be incurred:

Variable:	R&D/product design	€76 000	
	Marketing	133 000	
	Distribution	66 500	
	Customer service	47 500	
	Administrative	152 000	€475 000
Fixed:	R&D/product design	60 000	
	Marketing	67 000	
	Distribution	33 500	
	Customer service	12 500	
	Administrative	222 000	395 000
	Total		€870 000

Our task at hand is to prepare a budgeted operating profit statement for the year 2016. As shown in Exhibit 14.3, this is one component of Wessex's master budget. Other components of the master budget – the budgeted balance sheet and the cash budget – are discussed in the appendix to this chapter.

The following supporting budget schedules will be prepared when developing Wessex's budgeted profit statement:

1 Revenue budget

2 Production budget (in units)

3 Direct materials usage budget and direct materials purchases budget

4 Direct manufacturing labour budget

5 Manufacturing overhead budget

6 Closing stock budget

7 Cost of goods sold budget

8 Other (non-production) costs budget.

Most organisations have a budget manual, which contains instructions and relevant information for preparing budgets. Although the details differ among organisations, the following basic steps are common for developing a budgeted profit statement. Beginning with the revenue budget, each budget follows step by step in logical fashion. In most cases, computer software speeds the budget computations.

Steps in preparing an operating budget

Step 1: Revenue budget The revenue budget (schedule 1) is the usual starting point for budgeting. Why? Because production (and hence costs) and stock levels generally depend on the forecast level of revenue.

Schedule 1: Revenue budget for the year ending 31 December 2016

	Units	Selling price	Total revenues
Regular	5 000	€600	€3 000 000
Heavy-Duty	1 000	800	800 000
Total			€3 800 000

The €3.8 million is the amount of revenues in the budgeted income statement. The revenue budget is often the outcome of elaborate information gathering and discussions among sales managers and field sales representatives.

Pressures can exist for budgeted revenues to be either over- or underestimates of the expected amounts. Pressure for employees to underestimate budgeted revenues can occur when a company uses the difference between actual and budget amounts to evaluate marketing managers. These managers may respond by giving highly conservative forecasts. **Padding** the budget or introducing **budgetary slack** refers to the practice of underestimating budgeted revenues (or overestimating budgeted costs) in order to make budgeted targets more easily achievable. Introducing budgetary slack makes it more likely that actual revenues will exceed budgeted amounts. From the marketing manager's standpoint, budgetary slack hedges against unexpected adverse circumstances.

Occasionally, revenues are limited by available production capacity. For example, unusually heavy market demand, shortages of personnel or materials, or strikes may cause a company to exhaust its finished goods stock completely. Additional sales cannot be made because no stock of the product is available. In such cases, the production capacity – the factor that limits revenue – is the starting point for preparing the revenue budget.

Step 2: Production budget (in units) After revenues are budgeted, the production budget (schedule 2) can be prepared. The total finished goods units to be produced depends on planned sales and expected changes in stock levels:

$$\begin{array}{c} \text{Budgeted} \\ \text{production} = \\ \text{(units)} \end{array} \begin{array}{c} \text{Budgeted} \\ \text{sales} \\ \text{(units)} \end{array} + \begin{array}{c} \text{Target closing} \\ \text{finished goods} \\ \text{stock (units)} \end{array} - \begin{array}{c} \text{Opening} \\ \text{finished goods} \\ \text{stock (units)} \end{array}$$

Schedule 2: Production budget (in units) for the year ending 31 December 2016

	Product	
	Regular	Heavy-Duty
Budgeted sales (schedule 1)	5000	1000
Add target closing finished goods stock	1100	50
Total requirements	6100	1050
Deduct opening finished goods stock	100	50
Units to be produced	6000	1000

When unit sales are not stable throughout the year, managers must decide whether (1) to adjust production levels periodically to minimise stock held, or (2) to maintain constant production levels and let stock rise and fall. Increasingly, managers are choosing to adjust production. Chapter 21 discusses just-in-time production systems whose objective is to keep extremely low levels of stock throughout the year.

Step 3: Direct materials usage budget and direct materials purchases budget The decision on the number of units to be produced (schedule 2) is the key to computing the usage of direct materials in quantities and in euros.

Schedule 3A: Direct materials usage budget in kilograms and euros for the year ending 31 December 2016

| | Material | | |
	111 Alloy	112 Alloy	Total
Direct materials to be used in production of Regular parts (6000 units × 12 and 6kg – see schedule 2)	72 000	36 000	
Direct materials to be used in production of Heavy-Duty parts (1000 units × 12 and 8 kg – see schedule 2)	12 000	8 000	
Total direct materials to be used (kg)	84 000	44 000	
Direct materials to be used from opening stock (under a FIFO cost-flow assumption)	7 000	6 000	
Multiply by cost per kilogram of opening stock	€7	€10	
Cost of direct materials to be used from opening stock: (a)	€49 000	€60 000	€109 000
Direct materials to be used from purchases (84 000 – 7000; 44 000 – 6000)	77 000	38 000	
Multiply by cost per kilogram of purchased materials	€7	€10	
Cost of direct materials to be used from purchases: (b)	€539 000	€380 000	€919 000
Total costs of direct materials to be used: (a) + (b)	€588 000	€440 000	€1 028 000

Schedule 3B calculates the budget for direct materials purchases, which depends on the budgeted direct materials to be used, the opening stock of direct materials, and the target closing stock of direct materials:

$$\begin{matrix} \text{Purchases} \\ \text{of direct} \\ \text{materials} \end{matrix} = \begin{matrix} \text{Usage} \\ \text{of direct} \\ \text{materials} \end{matrix} + \begin{matrix} \text{Target closing} \\ \text{stock of direct} \\ \text{materials} \end{matrix} - \begin{matrix} \text{Opening stock} \\ \text{of direct materials} \end{matrix}$$

Schedule 3B: Direct materials purchases budget for the year ending 31 December 2016

| | Material | | |
	111 Alloy	112 Alloy	Total
Direct materials to be used in production from schedule 3A (kg)	84 000	44 000	
Add target closing direct materials stock (kg)	8 000	2 000	
Total requirements (kg)	92 000	46 000	
Deduct opening direct materials stock (kg)	7 000	6 000	
Direct materials to be purchased (kg)	85 000	40 000	
Multiply by cost per kilogram of purchased materials	€7	€10	
Total direct materials purchase costs	€595 000	€400 000	€995 000

Step 4: Direct manufacturing labour budget These costs depend on wage rates, production methods and hiring plans. The computations of budgeted direct manufacturing labour costs appear in schedule 4.

Schedule 4: Direct manufacturing labour budget for the year ending 31 December 2016

	Output units produced (schedule 2)	Direct manufacturing labour-hours per unit	Total hours	Hourly wage rate	Total
Regular	6 000	4	24 000	€20	€480 000
Heavy-Duty	1 000	6	6 000	20	120 000
Total			30 000		€600 000

Step 5: Manufacturing overhead budget The total of these costs depends on how individual overhead costs vary with the assumed cost driver, direct manufacturing labour-hours. The specific variable- and fixed-cost categories may be obtained, following discussions with company personnel in different areas. The calculations of budgeted manufacturing overhead costs appear in schedule 5.

Schedule 5: Manufacturing overhead budget for the year ending 31 December 2016

	At budgeted level of 30 000 direct manufacturing labour-hours	
Variable manufacturing overhead costs		
Supplies	€90 000	
Indirect manufacturing labour	210 000	
Direct and indirect manufacturing labour fringe costs	300 000	
Power	120 000	
Maintenance	60 000	€780 000
Fixed manufacturing overhead costs		
Depreciation	220 000	
Property taxes	50 000	
Property insurance	10 000	
Supervision	100 000	
Power	22 000	
Maintenance	18 000	420 000
Total manufacturing overhead costs		€1 200 000

Wessex treats both variable and fixed manufacturing overhead as inventoriable costs. This stock costing method is termed *absorption costing*; see Chapter 6 for further discussion. It stocks manufacturing overhead at the budgeted rate of €40 per direct manufacturing labour-hour (total manufacturing overhead, €1 200 000 ÷ 30 000 budgeted direct manufacturing labour-hours). It does not use separate variable and fixed manufacturing overhead rates.

Step 6: Closing stock budget Schedule 6A shows the computation of unit costs for the two products. These unit costs are used to calculate the costs of target closing stocks of direct materials and finished goods in schedule 6B.

Schedule 6A: Computation of unit costs of manufacturing finished goods in 2016

		Product			
	Cost per unit of input*	Regular		Heavy-Duty	
		Inputs*	Amount	Inputs*	Amount
Material 111 alloy	€7	12	€84	12	€84
Material 112 alloy	10	6	60	8	80
Direct manufacturing labour	20	4	80	6	120
Manufacturing overhead	40†	4	160	6	240
Total			€384		€524

* In kilograms or hours.
† Direct manufacturing labour-hours are the sole allocation base for manufacturing overhead (both variable and fixed). The budgeted manufacturing overhead rate per direct manufacturing labour-hour of €40 was calculated in step 5.

Schedule 6B: Closing stock budget as at 31 December 2016

	Kilograms	Cost per kilogram		Total
Direct materials				
111 alloy	8 000	€7	€56 000	
112 alloy	2 000	10	20 000	€76 000
	Units	Cost per unit		
Finished goods				
Regular	1 100	€384*	€422 400	
Heavy-duty	50	524*	26 200	448 600
Total closing stock				€524 600

* From schedule 6A, this is based on 2016 costs of manufacturing finished goods because under the FIFO costing method, the units in finished goods closing stock consist of units that are produced during 2016.

Step 7: Cost of goods sold budget The information from schedules 3 to 6 leads to schedule 7:

Schedule 7: Cost of goods sold budget for the year ending 31 December 2016

	From schedule		Total
Opening finished goods stock, 1 January 2016	Given*		€64 600
Direct materials used	3A	€1 028 000	
Direct manufacturing labour	4	600 000	
Manufacturing overhead	5	1 200 000	
Cost of goods manufactured			2 828 000
Cost of goods available for sale			2 892 600
Deduct closing finished goods stock, 31 December 2016	6B		448 600
Cost of goods sold			€2 444 000

* Given in the description of basic data and requirements (Regular €38 400, Heavy-Duty €26 200).

Note that the following holds:

$$\text{Cost of goods sold} = \text{Opening finished goods stock} + \text{Cost of goods manufactured} - \text{Closing finished goods stock}$$

Step 8: Other (non-production) costs budget Schedules 2 to 7 cover budgeting for Wessex's production area of the value chain. For brevity, other areas of the value chain are combined into a single schedule.

Schedule 8: Other (non-production) costs budget for the year ending 31 December 2016

Variable costs		
R&D/product design	€76 000	
Marketing	133 000	
Distribution	66 500	
Customer service	47 500	
Administrative	<u>152 000</u>	475 000*
Fixed costs		
R&D/product design	60 000	
Marketing	67 000	
Distribution	33 500	
Customer service	12 500	
Administrative	<u>222 000</u>	<u>395 000</u>
Total costs		<u><u>€870 000</u></u>

* Total variable cost for schedule 8 is €0.125 per revenue euro (€475 000 ÷ €3 800 000).

Step 9: Budgeted operating profit statement Schedules 1, 7 and 8 provide the necessary information to complete the budgeted operating profit statement, shown in Exhibit 14.4. Of course, more details could be included in the profit statement, and then fewer supporting schedules would be prepared.

Top management's strategies for achieving revenue and operating profit goals influence the costs planned for the different business functions of the value chain. As strategies change, the budget allocations for different elements of the value chain will also change. For example, a shift in strategy towards emphasising product development and customer service will result in increased resources being allocated to these parts of the master budget. The actual data resulting from this strategy will be compared with budgeted results. Management can then evaluate whether the focus on product development and customer service has been successful. This feedback is an important input in subsequent plans.

Exhibit 14.4	Budgeted operating profit for Wessex Engineering for the year ending 31 December 2016		
Revenues	Schedule 1	€3 800 000	
Costs			
Cost of goods sold	Schedule 7	<u>2 444 000</u>	
Gross margin		1 356 000	
Operating costs			
R&D/product design costs	Schedule 8	€136 000	
Marketing costs	Schedule 8	200 000	
Distribution costs	Schedule 8	100 000	
Customer service costs	Schedule 8	60 000	
Administration costs	Schedule 8	<u>374 000</u>	<u>870 000</u>
Operating profit			<u><u>€486 000</u></u>

Computer-based financial planning models

Exhibit 14.1 shows how strategic analysis, planning and budgeting are interrelated. The value of budgets to managers in their strategic analysis and planning is enhanced by conducting sensitivity analysis. Sensitivity analysis is a 'what-if' technique that examines how a result will change if the original predicted data are not achieved or if an underlying assumption changes. In its simplest form, it can be performed in the straightforward way shown in Chapter 8. Here a hand-held calculator would suffice to do the calculations. Commercial software packages are now available for more complex tasks, such as sensitivity analysis for the financial statements found in a master budget. These packages do the calculations for **financial planning models**, which are mathematical representations of the relationships across operating activities, financial activities and financial statements.

Consider Wessex Engineering. Its financial planning model assumes the following:

- Direct materials and direct manufacturing labour costs vary proportionately with the quantities of Regular and Heavy-Duty parts produced.
- Variable manufacturing overhead costs vary with direct manufacturing labour-hours.
- Variable non-manufacturing costs vary with revenues.

Exhibit 14.5 presents the budgeted operating profit for three what-if scenarios for Wessex Engineering:

- *Scenario 1*. A 3% decrease in the selling price of the Regular part and a 3% decrease in the selling price of the Heavy-Duty part.
- *Scenario 2*. A 4% decrease in units sold of the Regular part and a 4% decrease in units sold of the Heavy-Duty part.
- *Scenario 3*. A 5% increase in the price per kilogram of 111 alloy and a 5% increase in the price per kilogram of 112 alloy.

Exhibit 14.5 indicates that, relative to the master budget, budgeted operating profit decreases by 21% under scenario 1, by 10% under scenario 2, and by 9% under scenario 3. Managers can use this information to plan actions that they may need to take if faced with these scenarios.

Exhibit 14.5	Effect of changes in budget assumptions on budgeted operating profit for Wessex Engineering						

	Key assumptions						
	Units sold		**Selling price**		**Direct materials cost***		**Budgeted operating profit**
What-if scenario	Regular	Heavy-Duty	Regular	Heavy-Duty	111 Alloy	112 Alloy	€	Change from master budget
Master budget	5000	1000	€600	€800	€7.00	€10.00	€486 000	–
Scenario 1	5000	1000	582	776	7.00	10.00	386 250	21% decrease
Scenario 2	4800	960	600	800	7.00	10.00	438 273	10% decrease
Scenario 3	5000	1000	600	800	7.35	10.50	448 380	9% decrease

* Per kilogram.

Concepts in action | Web-enabled budgeting and Hendrick Motorsports

Source: Corbis/Brent Smith/Reuters

In recent years, an increasing number of companies have implemented comprehensive software packages that manage budgeting and forecasting functions across the organisation. One such option is Microsoft Forecaster, which was originally designed by FRx Software for businesses looking to gain control over their budgeting and forecasting process within a fully integrated web-based environment. Among the more unique companies implementing web-enabled budgeting is Hendrick Motorsports.

Featuring champion drivers Jeff Gordon and Jimmie Johnson, Hendrick is the premier NASCAR Sprint Cup stock car racing organisation. According to *Forbes* magazine, Hendrick is NASCAR's most valuable team, with an estimated value of $350 million. Headquartered on a 12-building, 600 000-square-foot campus near Charlotte, North Carolina, Hendrick operates four full-time teams in the Sprint Cup series, which runs annually from February through November and features 36 races at 22 speedways across the United States. The Hendrick organisation has annual revenues of close to $195 million and more than 500 employees, with tasks ranging from accounting and marketing to engine building and racecar driving. Such an environment features multiple functional areas and units, varied worksites, and ever-changing circumstances. Patrick Perkins, director of marketing, noted, 'Racing is a fast business. It's just as fast off the track as it is on it. With the work that we put into development of our teams and technologies, and having to respond to change as well as anticipate change, I like to think of us in this business as change experts.'

Microsoft Forecaster, Hendrick's Web-enabled budgeting package, has allowed Hendrick's financial managers to seamlessly manage the planning and budgeting process. Authorised users from each functional area or team sign on to the application through the corporate intranet. Security on the system is tight: access is limited to only the accounts that a manager is authorised to budget. (For example, Jeff Gordon's crew chief is not able to see what Jimmie Johnson's team members are doing.) Forecaster also allows users at the racetrack to access the application remotely, which allows managers to receive or update real-time 'actuals' from the system. This way, team managers know their allotted expenses for each race. Forecaster also provides users with additional features, including seamless links with general ledger accounts and the option to perform what-if (sensitivity) analyses. Scott Lampe, chief financial officer, said, 'Forecaster allows us to change our forecasters to respond to changes, either rule changes [such as pilot testing NASCAR's new, safer "Car of Tomorrow"] throughout the racing season.'

Hendrick's web-enabled budgeting system frees the finance department so it can work on strategy, analysis and decision making. It also allows Hendrick to complete its annual budgeting process in only six weeks, a 50% reduction in the time spent budgeting and planning, which is critical given NASCAR's extremely short season. Patrick Pearson from Hendrick Motorsports believes the system gives the organisation a competitive advantage: 'In racing, the team that wins is not only the team with the fastest car, but the team that is the most disciplined and prepared week in and week out. Forecaster allows us to respond to that changing landscape.'

Sources: Gage, J. (2009) 'Nascar's most valuable teams', Forbes.com, 3 June http://www.forbes.com/2009/06/03/nascar-most-valuable-teams-business-sports-nascar.html; Goff, J. (2004) 'In the fast lane', *CFO Magazine*, 1 December; Hendrick Motorsports (2010) 'About Hendrick Motorsports', Hendrick Motorsports website, 28 May www.hendrickmotorsports.com; Lampe, S. (2003) 'NASCAR racing team stays on track with FRx Software's comprehensive budget planning solution', *DM Review*, 1 July; Microsoft Corporation (200) 'Microsoft Forecaster: Hendrick Motorsports customer video', 8 October http://microsoft.com/BusinessSolutions/frx_hendrick_video.m.sox; Ryan, N. (2006) 'Hendrick empire strikes back with three contenders in chase for the Nextel Cup', *USA Today*, 17 September.

Kaizen budgeting

Chapter 1 noted how continuous improvement is one of the key issues facing management today. The Japanese use the term *kaizen* for continuous improvement. **Kaizen budgeting** is a budgetary approach that explicitly incorporates continuous improvement during the budget period into the resultant budget numbers.

Consider our Wessex Engineering example in schedule 4. The 2016 budget assumes that it will take 4.0 and 6.0 manufacturing labour-hours, respectively, for each Regular and Heavy-Duty aircraft part. A kaizen budgeting approach would incorporate continuous reduction in these manufacturing labour-hour requirements during 2016. Assume Wessex budgets the following labour-hour amounts:

	Budgeted amounts (labour-hours)	
	Regular	Heavy-Duty
January–March 2016	4.00	6.00
April–June 2016	3.90	5.85
July–September 2016	3.80	5.70
October–December 2016	3.70	5.55

Unless Wessex meets these continuous improvement goals, unfavourable variances will be reported. Note that in the Wessex budget, the implications of these direct labour-hour reductions would extend to reductions in variable manufacturing overhead costs, given that direct manufacturing labour-hours is the driver of these costs.

Cost reductions are effected in a similar manner at Citizen Watch which is one of the world's largest manufacturers of watches. The assembly areas at its plants are highly automated. Component part costs for each watch are a sizable percentage of the unit cost of each watch. A central part of Citizen's cost management system is kaizen budgeting. All parts of the entire production area, including component suppliers, are required to continually seek out cost reduction opportunities. For example, at its Tokyo plant, it budgets that all external suppliers will have a steady cost reduction of 3% per annum. Suppliers who exceed this 3% target retain for at least one year any cost reductions above the 3% level. Suppliers who do not attain the 3% target receive the 'assistance' of Citizen engineers in the following year.

Activity-based budgeting

Chapter 11 explained how activity-based costing systems can lead to detailed reportings of past and current costs. Activity-based costing principles can also be extended in the budgeting of future costs. **Activity-based budgeting** focuses on the cost of activities necessary to produce and sell products and services. It separates indirect costs into separate homogeneous activity cost pools. Management uses the cause-and-effect criterion to identify the cost drivers for each of these indirect-cost pools.

Four key steps in activity-based budgeting are:

1 Determine the budgeted costs of performing each unit of activity at each activity area.

2 Determine the demand for each individual activity based on budgeted, production, new product development and so on.

3 Calculate the costs of performing each activity.

4 Describe the budget as costs of performing various activities (rather than budgeted costs of functional or conventional value-chain spending categories).

Many UK managers have reported the following ranking of the benefits from activity-based budgeting: (1) ability to set more realistic budgets, (2) better identification of resource needs,

(3) linking of costs to outputs, (4) clearer linking of costs with staff responsibilities, and (5) identification of budgetary slack.

Consider activity-based budgeting for the R&D/product design parts of the value chain at Ahamed Company. Five activity areas and their cost drivers have been identified. The budgeted 2016 rates for the costs at each activity area are as follows:

Activity	Cost driver/budgeted cost rate
• Computer-aided design (CAD) – using computer software to design aircraft parts	CAD hours, €80 per hour
• Manual design – manually designing aircraft parts	Manual design hours, €50 per hour
• Prototyping development – building actual versions of aircraft parts	Prototyping hours, €60 per hour
• Testing – examining how new aircraft parts 'perform' in different operating conditions	Testing hours, €40 per hour
• Procurement – purchasing supplies and component parts	Purchase orders, €25 per purchase order

Exhibit 14.6 presents the activity-based budget for January to December 2016. Ahamed Company budgets usage of the cost driver in each activity area based on budgeted production and new product development. This budgeted usage of the cost driver for each activity is multiplied by the respective budgeted costs rate per activity to obtain the budgeted activity costs. The budgeted total costs for R&D/product design is the sum of the budgeted costs of the individual activities in that part of the value chain.

The activity-based budget in Exhibit 14.6 is for one part of Ahamed's value chain. In many cases, the same activity will appear in more than one part of the value chain. For example, procurement activities such as purchase ordering and supplier payment are found in most areas of the value chain. Companies using activity-based budgeting may choose to present their budgets at either the individual value-chain level or at some more basic activity level such as procurement by combining budgeted procurement costs from different parts of the value chain.

Exhibit 14.6	Activity-based budget for R&D/product design costs of Ahamed Company: January to December 2016		
Activity area	Budgeted usage of driver	Budgeted rate per cost driver	Budgeted costs
Computer-aided design	200 hours	€80	€16 000
Manual design	70 hours	50	3 500
Prototyping development	80 hours	60	4 800
Testing	280 hours	40	11 200
Procurement	120 purchase orders	25	3 000
Total			€38 500

Budgeting and responsibility accounting

Organisational structure and responsibility

Organisational structure is an arrangement of lines of responsibility within the entity. A company such as British Petroleum may be organised primarily by business function: exploration, refining and marketing. Diageo, a major consumer products company, structures itself by regions: North America, Europe and International. Another company, Norsk Hydro, is organised by product groups such as Agriculture, Oil and Gas, Light Metals and Petrochemicals. The managers of the individual groups each have decision-making authority concerning all the business functions (manufacturing, marketing, and so on) within that group.

To attain the goals described in the master budget, an organisation must coordinate the efforts of all its employees – from the top executive through all levels of management to every supervised worker. Coordinating the organisation's efforts means assigning responsibility to managers who are accountable for their actions in planning and controlling human and physical resources. Management is in essence a human activity. Budgets exist not for their own sake, but to help managers achieve their own pursuits and thereby contribute to meeting those of the organisation.

Each manager, regardless of level, is in charge of a responsibility centre. A **responsibility centre** is a part, segment or subunit of an organisation whose manager is accountable for a specified set of activities. The higher the manager's level, the broader the responsibility centre he or she manages and, generally, the larger the number of subordinates who report to him or her. **Responsibility accounting** is a system that measures the plans (by budgets) and actions (by actual results) of each responsibility centre. Four major types of responsibility centre are:

1 **Cost centre** – manager accountable for costs only.

2 **Revenue centre** – manager accountable for revenues only.

3 **Profit centre** – manager accountable for revenues and costs.

4 **Investment centre** – manager accountable for investments, revenues and costs.

The Maintenance Department of an Hôtel Ibis would be a cost centre because the maintenance manager is responsible only for costs. Hence, the budget would emphasise costs. The Sales Department of the hotel would be a revenue centre because the sales manager is responsible only for revenues. Here the budget would emphasise revenues. The hotel manager would be in charge of a profit centre because the hotel manager is accountable for both revenues and costs. Here the budget would emphasise both revenues and costs. The regional manager responsible for investments in new hotel projects and for revenues and costs would be in charge of an investment centre. Revenue, costs and the investment base would be emphasised in the budget for this manager.

Responsibility accounting affects behaviour. Consider the following incident. The Sales Department requests a rush production run. The plant scheduler argues that it will disrupt his production and will cost a substantial though not clearly determined amount of money. The answer coming from sales is, 'Do you want to take the responsibility of losing the X Company as a customer?' Of course, the production scheduler does not want to take such a responsibility, and he gives up, but not before a heavy exchange of arguments and the accumulation of a substantial backlog of ill feeling. The accountant proposes an innovative solution. He analyses the payroll in the Assembly Department to determine the costs involved in getting out rush orders. This information eliminates the cause for argument. Henceforth, any rush order would be accepted by the production scheduler, 'no questions asked'. The extra costs would be duly recorded and charged to the Sales Department. Within one company which experienced this change, the tension created by rush orders disappeared, and, somehow, the number of rush orders requested by the Sales Department was progressively reduced to an insignificant level.

The responsibility accounting approach traces costs to either (1) the individual who has the best knowledge about why the costs arose, or (2) the activity that caused the costs. In this incident, the cause was the sales activity, and the resulting costs were charged to the Sales Department. If rush orders occur regularly, the Sales Department might have a budget for such costs, and the department's actual performance would then be compared with the budget.

Feedback

Budgets coupled with responsibility accounting provide systematic help for managers, particularly if managers interpret the feedback carefully. Managers, accountants and students of management accounting sometimes use variances (the difference between the actual results and the budgeted results) appearing in the responsibility accounting system to pinpoint fault for operating problems. In looking at variances, managers should focus on whom they should ask and not on whom they should blame. Variances only suggest questions or direct attention to persons who should have the relevant information. Nevertheless, variances, properly used, can be helpful in four ways:

1 *Early warning.* Variances alert managers early to events not easily or immediately evident. Managers can then take corrective actions or exploit available opportunities.

2 *Performance valuation.* Variances inform managers about how well the company has performed in implementing its strategies.

3 *Evaluating strategy.* Variances sometimes signal to managers that their strategies are ineffective.

4 *Communicating the goals of the organisation.* The budget-making exercise and budgeting information are useful in conveying to managers across the organisation the goals of subunits and the wider corporate goals.

Responsibility and controllability

Definition of controllability

Controllability is the degree of influence that a specific manager has over costs, revenues or other items in question. A **controllable cost** is any cost that is primarily subject to the influence of a given manager of a given responsibility centre for a given time span. A responsibility accounting system could either exclude all uncontrollable costs from a manager's performance report or segregate such costs from the controllable costs. For example, a machining supervisor's performance report might be confined to quantities (not costs) of direct materials, direct manufacturing labour, power and supplies.

In practice, controllability is difficult to pinpoint:

1 Few costs are clearly under the sole influence of one manager. For example, costs of direct materials may be influenced by a purchasing manager, but such costs also depend on market conditions beyond the manager's control. Quantities used may be influenced by a production manager, but quantities used also depend on the quality of materials purchased. Moreover, managers often work in teams. How can individual responsibility be evaluated in a team decision?

2 With a long enough time span, all costs will come under somebody's control. However, most performance reports focus on periods of a year or less. A current manager may have inherited problems and inefficiencies from his or her predecessor. For example, present managers may have to work under undesirable contracts with suppliers or trade unions that were negotiated by their predecessors. How can we separate what the current manager actually controls from the results of decisions made by others? Exactly what is the current manager accountable for? Answers to such questions may not be clear cut.

Senior managers differ in how they embrace the controllability notion when evaluating those reporting to them. For example, a newly appointed company president took his management team on a cruise and commented, 'I expect everybody to meet their budget targets no matter what happens, and those who don't should stand a little closer to the railing.' Other presidents and managing directors believe that a more risk-sharing approach with managers is preferable where non-controllable factors are taken into account when making judgements about the performance of managers who miss their budget.

Emphasis on information and behaviour

Managers should avoid overemphasising controllability. Responsibility accounting is more far-reaching. It focuses on *information* and *knowledge*, not control. The key question is: Who is the best informed? Put another way: Who is the person who can tell us the most about the specific item in question, regardless of that person's ability to exert personal control? For instance, purchasing managers may be held accountable for total purchase costs, not because of their ability to affect market prices, but because of their ability to predict uncontrollable prices and explain uncontrollable price changes. Similarly, managers at a Pizza Hut unit may be held responsible for operating income of their units, even though they do not fully control selling prices or the costs for many food items, and have minimal flexibility as to items to sell or their ingredients. Why? Because unit managers are in the best position to explain variances between their actual operating profit and their budgeted operating profit.

Performance reports for responsibility centres may also include uncontrollable items because this approach could change behaviour in the directions top management desires. For example, some companies have changed the accountability of a cost centre to a profit centre. Why? Because the manager will probably behave differently. A cost-centre manager may emphasise production efficiency and de-emphasise the pleas of sales personnel for faster service and rush orders. In a profit centre, the manager is responsible for both costs and revenues. Thus, even though the manager still has no control over sales personnel, the manager will now more likely weigh the impact of his or her decisions on costs and revenues, rather than solely on costs.

Budgeting: a discipline in transition

Many areas of management accounting are subject to ongoing debate and change. Budgeting is no exception. It has been noted that 'budgeting – as most corporations practice it – should be abolished' (Hope and Fraser 2003a). Advocates of new proposals invariably include criticisms of so-called traditional budgeting. These criticisms are often exaggerations of 'current worst practice'. Exhibit 14.7 summarises six proposals relating to improving traditional budgeting systems. Few of the negative features cited in the left-hand column are new; they have long been singled out for criticism. Indeed, prior sections of this chapter have mentioned the importance of avoiding many of these problems. Nonetheless, major changes that address these problems are currently being examined by managers.

Exhibit 14.7	Criticisms of traditional budgeting and proposals for change
Criticism of traditional budgeting	**Proposal for change**
Excessive reliance on extrapolating past trends	Link budgeting explicitly to strategy
Make across-the-board fixed percentage cuts when early iterations of a budget provide 'unacceptable results'	Use activity-based budgeting to guide areas for cost reduction
Budget examines individual functional areas as if they are independent (so-called silos, to use a farming analogy)	Explicitly adopt a cross-functional approach where interdependencies across business function areas of the value chain are recognised
Budget myopically overemphasises a fixed time horizon such as a year. Meeting annual cost targets viewed as key task to be accomplished	Tailor the budget cycle to the purpose of budgeting. Events beyond current period are recognised as important when evaluating current actions. Value creation is given paramount importance
Budget is preoccupied with financial aspects of events in the budget period	Balance financial aspects with both non-financial (such as quality and time) aspects
Budgets are not used until end of budget period to evaluate performance	Signals to all employees the need for continuous improvement of performance (such as revenue enhancement and cost reduction) within the budget period

Source: Adapted from Hope and Fraser (2003a).

Summary

The following points are linked to the chapter's learning objectives.

1 The master budget summarises the financial projections of all the organisation's budgets and plans. It expresses management's comprehensive operating and financial plans – the formalised outline of the organisation's financial objectives and their means of attainment. Budgets are tools that by themselves are neither good nor bad. How managers administer budgets is the key to their value. When administered wisely, budgets compel management planning, provide definite expectations that are an appropriate framework for judging subsequent performance, and promote communication and coordination among the various subunits of the organisation. Budgetary control inevitably affects managerial behaviour and organisational processes.

2 Two major parts of the master budget are the operating budget, which is the budgeted operating profit statement and its supporting budget schedules, and the financial budget, which comprises the capital budget, cash budget, budgeted balance sheet and budgeted statement of cash flows.

3 The foundation for the operating budget is generally the revenue budget. The following supporting budget schedules are geared to the revenue budget: production budget, direct materials usage budget, direct materials purchases budget, direct manufacturing labour budget, manufacturing overhead costs budget, closing stock budget, cost of goods sold budget, R&D/design budget, marketing budget, distribution budget, and customer-service budget. The operating budget ends with the budgeted profit statement.

4 Computer-based financial planning models are mathematical statements of the relationships among operating activities, financial activities and other factors that affect the budget. These models allow management to conduct what-if (sensitivity) analyses of the effects on the master budget of changes in the original predicted data or changes in budget assumptions.

5 Kaizen budgeting captures the continuous improvement notion that is a key management concern. Costs in kaizen budgeting are based on future improvements that are yet to be implemented rather than on current practices or methods.

6 Activity-based budgeting focuses on the costs of activities necessary to produce and sell products and services. It is inherently linked to activity-based costing, but differs in its emphases on future costs and future usage of activity areas.

7 A responsibility centre is a part, segment or subunit of an organisation whose manager is accountable for a specified set of activities. Four major types of responsibility centres are cost centres, revenue centres, profit centres and investment centres. Responsibility accounting systems measure the plans (by budgets) and actions (by actual results) of each responsibility centre.

8 Controllable costs are costs that are primarily subject to the influence of a given manager of a given responsibility centre for a given time span. Performance reports of responsibility-centre managers, however, often include costs, revenues and investments that the managers cannot control. Responsibility accounting associates financial items with managers on the basis of which manager has the most knowledge and information about the specific items, regardless of the manager's ability to exercise full control. The important question is who should be asked, not who should be blamed.

Appendix

The cash budget

The major illustration in the chapter features the operating budget. The other major part of the master budget is the financial budget, which includes the capital budget, cash budget, budgeted balance sheet and budgeted statement of cash flows. This appendix focuses on the cash budget and the budgeted balance sheet. Capital budgeting was covered in Chapter 13; coverage of the budgeted statement of cash flows is beyond the scope of this book.

Suppose Wessex Engineering in our chapter illustration had the balance sheet for the year ended 31 December 2015 shown in Exhibit 14.8. The budgeted cash flows for 2016 are as follows:

	Quarters			
	1	2	3	4
Collections from customers	€913 700	€984 600	€976 500	€918 400
Disbursements				
Direct materials	314 360	283 700	227 880	213 800
Payroll	557 520	432 080	409 680	400 720
Income taxes	50 000	46 986	46 986	46 986
Other costs	184 000	156 000	151 000	149 000
Machinery purchase	–	–	–	35 080

The quarterly data are based on the cash effects of the operations formulated in schedules 1 to 8 in the chapter, but the details of that formulation are not shown here in order to keep the illustration relatively brief and focused.

The company wants to maintain a €35 000 minimum cash balance at the end of each quarter. The company can borrow or repay money in multiples of €1000 at an interest rate of 12% per year. Management does not want to borrow any more cash than is necessary and wants to repay

Exhibit 14.8	Balance sheet for Wessex Engineering for the year ending 31 December 2015

Assets

Current assets		
Cash	€30 000	
Debtors	400 000	
Direct materials	109 000	
Finished goods	64 600	€603 600
Property, plant and equipment		
Land	200 000	
Building and equipment	2 200 000	
Accumulated depreciation	(690 000)	1 710 000
Total		€2 313 600

Liabilities and stockholders' equity

Current liabilities		
Creditors	€150 000	
Income taxes payable	50 000	€200 000
Stockholders' equity		
Common stock, no-par,		
25 000 shares outstanding	350 000	
Retained earnings	1 763 600	2 113 600
Total		€2 313 600

as promptly as possible. By special arrangement, interest is calculated and paid when the principal is repaid. Assume that borrowing takes place at the beginning and repayment at the end of the quarters in question. Interest is calculated to the nearest euro.

Suppose an accountant at Wessex Engineering is given the preceding data and the other data contained in the budgets in the chapter. He is instructed as follows:

1 Prepare a cash budget. That is, prepare a statement of cash receipts and disbursements by quarters, including details of borrowing, repayment and interest expense.

2 Prepare a budgeted balance sheet.

3 Prepare a budgeted profit statement, including the effects of interest expense and income taxes. Assume that income taxes for 2016 (at a tax rate of 40%) are €187 944.

Preparation of budgets

1 The **cash budget** (Exhibit 14.9) is a schedule of expected cash receipts and disbursements. It predicts the effects on the cash position at the given level of operations. Exhibit 14.9 presents the cash budget by quarters to show the impact of cash-flow timing on bank loans and their repayment. In practice, monthly – and sometimes weekly – cash budgets are very helpful for cash planning and control. Cash budgets help avoid unnecessary idle cash and unexpected cash deficiencies. Cash balances are kept in line with needs. Ordinarily, the cash budget has the following main sections:

   a The opening cash balance plus cash receipts equals the total cash available before financing. Cash receipts depend on collections of debtors, cash sales, and miscellaneous recurring sources such as rental or royalty receipts. Information on the prospective collectibility of debtors is needed for accurate predictions. Key factors include bad-debt (uncollectable accounts) experience and average time lag between sales and collections.

   b Cash disbursements include the following items:
      (i) Direct materials purchases – depends on credit terms extended by suppliers and invoice-paying patterns of the buyer.
      (ii) Direct labour and other wage and salary outlays – depends on payroll dates.
      (iii) Other costs – depends on timing and credit terms. *Be sure to note that depreciation does not require a cash outlay.*
      (iv) Other disbursements – outlays for property, plant and equipment, and for long-term investments.

   c Financing requirements depend on how the total cash available for needs, keyed as (a) in Exhibit 14.9, compares with the total cash needed, keyed as (c). Total cash needed includes total disbursements, keyed as (b), plus the minimum closing cash balance desired. The financing plans will depend on the relationship between total cash available for needs and total cash needed. If there is excess cash, loans may be repaid or temporary investments made. The outlays for interest expense are usually shown in this section of the cash budget.

   d The closing cash balance. The total effect of the financing decisions on the cash budget, keyed as (d) in Exhibit 14.9, may be positive (borrowing) or negative (repayment), and the closing cash balance is (a) − (b) + (d).

The cash budget in Exhibit 14.9 shows the pattern of short-term 'self-liquidating cash loans'. Seasonal peaks of production or sales often result in heavy cash disbursements for purchases, payroll and other operating outlays as the products are produced and sold. Cash receipts from customers typically lag behind sales. The loan is *self-liquidating* in the sense that the borrowed money is used to acquire resources that are combined for sale, and the proceeds from sales are used to repay the loan. This **self-liquidating cycle** – sometimes called the **working-capital cycle**, **cash cycle** or **operating cycle** – is the movement from cash to stock to debtors and back to cash.

Exhibit 14.9	Cash budget for Wessex Engineering for the year ending 31 December 2016

| | Quarters | | | | Year as |
	1	2	3	4	a whole
Cash balance, opening	€30 000	€35 820	€35 934	€35 188	€30 000
Add receipts					
Collections from customers	913 700	984 600	976 500	918 400	3 793 200
Total cash available					
for needs (a)	943 700	1 020 420	1 012 434	953 588	3 823 200
Deduct disbursements					
Direct materials	314 360	283 700	227 880	213 800	1 039 740
Payroll	557 520	432 080	409 680	400 720	1 800 000
Income taxes	50 000	46 986	46 986	46 986	190 958
Other costs	184 000	156 000	151 000	149 000	640 000
Machinery purchase	0	0	0	35 080	35 080
Total disbursements (b)	1 105 880	918 766	835 546	845 586	3 705 778
Minimum cash balance					
desired	35 000	35 000	35 000	35 000	35 000
Total cash needed (c)	1 140 880	953 766	870 546	880 586	3 740 778
Cash excess (deficiency)					
(a) – (c)*	€(197 180)	€66 654	€141 888	€73 002	€82 422
Financing					
Borrowing (at beginning)	€198 000	€0	€0	€0	€198 000
Repayment (at end)	–	(62 000)	(130 000)	(6 000)	(198 000)
Interest (at 12% per year)†	–	(3 720)	(11 700)	(720)	(16 140)
Total effects of					
financing (d)	€198 000	€(65 720)	€(141 700)	€(6 720)	€(16 140)
Cash balance, closing					
(a) – (b) + (d)	€35 820	€35 934	€35 188	€101 282	€101 282

* Excess of total cash available over total cash needed before current financing.
† Note that the interest payments pertain only to the amount of principal being repaid at the end of a given quarter. The specific computations regarding interest are €62 000 × 0.12 × $\frac{2}{4}$ = €3720; €130 000 × 0.12 × $\frac{3}{4}$ = €11 700; and €6000 × 0.12 × $\frac{4}{4}$ = €720. Also note that *depreciation does not require a cash outlay*.

2 The budgeted balance sheet is presented in Exhibit 14.10. Each item is projected in light of the details of the business plan as expressed in all the previous budget schedules. For example, the closing balance of debtors of €406 800 is calculated by adding the budgeted revenues of €3 800 000 (from schedule 1) to the opening balance of €400 000 (given) and subtracting cash receipts of €3 793 200 (given in Exhibit 14.10).

3 The budgeted operating profit statement is presented in Exhibit 14.11. It is merely the budgeted operating profit statement in Exhibit 14.4 expanded to include interest expense and income taxes.

Exhibit 14.10	Wessex Engineering: budgeted balance sheet for the year ending 31 December 2016

Assets

Current assets			
Cash (from Exhibit 14.9)		€101 282	
Debtors*		406 800	
Direct materials†		76 000	
Finished goods†		448 600	€1 032 682
Property, plant and equipment			
Land‡		200 000	
Building and equipment§	€2 235 080		
Accumulated depreciation‖	(920 000)	1 315 080	1 515 080
Total			€2 547 762

Liabilities and stockholders' equity

Current liabilities			
Creditors#		€105 260	
Income taxes payable**		46 986	€152 246
Stockholders' equity			
Common stock, no-par, 25 000 shares			
outstanding††		350 000	
Retained earnings‡‡		2 045 516	2 395 516
Total			€2 547 762

Opening balances are used as the starting point for most of the following computations:

* €400 000 + €3 800 000 revenues − €3 793 200 receipts (Exhibit 14.9) = €406 800.

† From schedule 6B.

‡ From opening balance sheet.

§ €2 200 000 + €35 080 purchases = €2 235 080.

‖ €690 000 + €230 000 depreciation from schedule 5.

€150 000 + €995 000 (schedule 3B) − €1 039 740 (Exhibit 14.9) = €105 260.

There are no wages payable. The detailed payroll consists of €600 000 direct manufacturing labour (schedule 4) + €620 000 manufacturing overhead salaries (€200 000 indirect manufacturing labour + €320 000 direct and indirect manufacturing labour fringe cost + €100 000 supervision from schedule 5) + R&D/design salaries €105 000 (schedule 8) + marketing salaries €130 000 (schedule 8) + distribution salaries and wages €60 000 (schedule 8) + customer-service salaries €40 000 (schedule 8) + administration salaries and clerical wages €245 000 (schedule 8) = €1 800 000, all of which was disbursed per Exhibit 14.9.

** €50 000 + €187 944 current year − €190 958 payment = €46 986.

†† From opening balance sheet.

‡‡ €1 763 600 + €281 916 net income per Exhibit 14.11 = €2 045 516.

Exhibit 14.11	Budgeted profit statement for Wessex Engineering for the year ending 31 December 2016			

Revenues	Schedule 1		€3 800 000	
Costs				
Cost of goods sold	Schedule 7		2 444 000	
Gross margin			1 356 000	
Operating costs				
R&D/product design costs	Schedule 8	€136 000		
Marketing costs	Schedule 8	200 000		
Distribution costs	Schedule 8	100 000		
Customer-service costs	Schedule 8	60 000		
Administration costs	Schedule 8	374 000	870 000	
Operating profit			486 000	
Interest expense	Exhibit 14.9		16 140	
Profit before income taxes			469 860	
Income taxes	Given		187 944	
Net profit			€281 916	

For simplicity, the cash receipts and disbursements were given explicitly in this illustration. Frequently, there are lags between the items reported on the accrual basis of accounting in an income statement and their related cash receipts and disbursements. In the Wessex Engineering example, collections from customers are derived under two assumptions: (1) in any month, 10% of sales are cash sales and 90% of sales are on credit, and (2) half the total credit sales are collected in each of the two months subsequent to the sale, as Exhibit 14.12 shows. Of course, such schedules of cash collections depend on credit terms, collection histories and expected bad debts. Similar schedules can be prepared for operating costs and their related cash disbursements.

Exhibit 14.12	Wessex Engineering's collections from customers					

	May	June	July	August	September	Cash collections in Q3 as a whole
Monthly revenue budget for Wessex (given)						
Credit sales, 90%	€307 800	€307 800	€280 800	€280 800	€280 800	
Cash sales, 10%	34 200	34 200	31 200	31 200	31 200	
Total revenues	€342 000	€342 000	€312 000	€312 000	€312 000	
Cash collections from:						
Cash sales this month			€31 200	€31 200	€31 200	
Credit sales last month			153 900*	140 400‡	140 400§	
Credit sales two months ago			153 900†	153 900*	140 400‡	
Total Collections			€339 000	€325 500	€312 000	€976 500

* 0.50 × €307 800 (June sales) = €153 900.
† 0.50 × €307 800 (May sales) = €153 900.
‡ 0.50 × €280 800 (July sales) = €140 400.
§ 0.50 × €280 800 (August sales) = €140 400.

Key terms

master budget (425)	**responsibility accounting** (444)
strategy (426)	**cost centre** (444)
rolling budget (430)	**revenue centre** (444)
operating budget (431)	**profit centre** (444)
financial budget (431)	**investment centre** (444)
pro forma statements (431)	**controllability** (445)
padding (435)	**controllable cost** (445)
budgetary slack (435)	**cash budget** (449)
financial planning models (440)	**self-liquidating cycle** (449)
kaizen budgeting (442)	**working-capital cycle** (449)
activity-based budgeting (442)	**cash cycle** (449)
organisational structure (443)	**operating cycle** (449)
responsibility centre (444)	

References and further reading

Colvin, G. (2006) 'Managing in chaos', *Fortune*, 2 October, p. 32.

Eisenhardt, K., Kahwajy, J. and Bourgeois, L. (1997) 'Conflict and strategic choice: how top management teams disagree', *California Management Review* (Winter).

Hope, J. and Fraser, R. (2003a) *Beyond Budgeting: How Managers Can Break Free from the Annual Performance Trap* (Boston: Harvard Business School Press).

Hope, J. and Fraser, R. (2003b) 'Who needs budgets?' *Harvard Business Review*, February, pp. 42–8.

Hopwood, A.G. (1980) 'Organisational and behavioural aspects of budgeting and control', in J. Arnold, B. Carsberg and R. Scapens (eds) *Topics in Management Accounting* (London: Philip Allan).

Pilkington, M. and Crowther, D. (2007) 'Minimal budgeting: the development of control mechanisms for micro and small businesses', *CIMA Research Update* (May), pp. 6–7.

Taylor, A. (2010) 'Hyundai smokes the competition', *Fortune*, 18 January.

Welch, J. and Welch, S. (2007) 'Stop the BS budgets', *Fortune*, 26 June, p. 114.

CHAPTER 14

Assessment material

Review questions

14.1 Define master budget.

14.2 What are the elements of the budgeting cycle?

14.3 'Strategy, plans and budgets are unrelated to one another.' Do you agree? Explain.

14.4 'Budgeted performance is a better criterion than past performance for judging managers.' Do you agree? Explain.

14.5 'Budgets are wonderful vehicles for communication.' Comment.

14.6 Define kaizen budgeting.

14.7 Cite three benefits companies report from using an activity-based budgeting approach.

14.8 Define responsibility accounting.

14.9 Explain how the choice of the responsibility centre type (cost, revenue, profit or investment) affects budgeting.

14.10 Outline three criticisms of traditional budgeting and a related proposal for change.

Exercises

Basic level

14.11 **Cost of goods sold budget, fill in the missing numbers** (20 minutes)

Embutidos Vallina SA has two direct-cost categories: direct materials and direct manufacturing labour. Its single indirect-cost category (manufacturing overhead) is allocated on the basis of machine-hours. Numbers taken from the monthly budgets for June 2015 and November 2015 are as follows:

	June 2015	November 2015
Direct materials used	€?	€847 000
Opening finished goods stock	87 000	?
Closing finished goods stock	?	94 000
Direct manufacturing labour	481 000	389 000
Manufacturing overhead	772 000	?
Cost of goods manufactured	2 215 000	1 878 000
Cost of goods sold	2 189 000	?
Cost of goods available for sale	?	1 949 000

Required

Fill in the missing numbers.

*14.12 Sales and production budget (5 minutes)

Lux-Ernster expects 2015 sales of 100 000 units of serving trays. Lux-Ernster's opening stock for 2015 is 7000 trays; target closing stock, 11 000 trays.

Required

Calculate the number of trays budgeted for production in 2015.

14.13 Sales and production budget (5 minutes)

Sarandrea Srl had a target closing stock of 70 000 four-litre bottles of burgundy wine. Sarandrea's opening stock was 60 000 bottles, and its budgeted production was 900 000 bottles.

Required

Calculate the budgeted sales in number of bottles.

14.14 Direct materials purchases budget (5 minutes)

Europa-Dyonisos SA produces wine. The company expects to produce 1.5 million two-litre bottles of Chablis in 2015. Europa-Dyonisos purchases empty glass bottles from an outside supplier. Its target closing stock of such bottles is 50 000; its opening stock is 20 000. For simplicity, ignore breakage.

Required

Calculate the number of bottles to be purchased in 2015.

14.15 Budgeting material purchases (10 minutes)

Tiilikainen Oy has prepared a sales budget of 42 000 finished units for a three-month period. The company has a stock of 22 000 units of finished goods on hand at 31 December and has a target finished goods stock of 24 000 units at the end of the succeeding quarter.

It takes 3 litres of direct materials to make 1 unit of finished product. The company has a stock of 90 000 litres of direct materials at 31 December and has a target closing stock of 110 000 litres.

Required

How many litres of direct materials should be purchased during the three months ending 31 March?

14.16 Budgetary slack and ethics (CMA, adapted) (15 minutes)

Jacek Zielinski, the budget manager at Jelenia-Silesia, a manufacturer of child furniture and carriages, is working on the 2015 annual budget. In discussions with Sylwester Czereszewski, the sales manager, Jacek discovers that Sylwester's sales projections are lower than what Sylwester believes are actually achievable. When Jacek asked Sylwester about this, Sylwester said, 'Well, we don't want to fall short of the sales projections, so we generally give ourselves a little breathing room by lowering the sales projections anywhere from 5 to 10%.' Jacek also finds that Andrzej Sazanowicz, the production manager, makes similar adjustments. He pads budgeted costs, adding 10% to estimated costs.

Required

As a management accountant, should Jacek take the position that the behaviour described by Sylwester and Andrzej is unethical?

Intermediate level

14.17 Revenue, production and purchases budget (15–20 minutes)

The Suzuki Company in Japan has a division that manufactures two-wheel motorcycles. Its budgeted sales for Model G in 2016 is 800 000 units. Suzuki's target closing stock is 100 000 units, and its opening stock is 120 000 units. The company's budgeted selling price to its distributors and dealers is 400 000 yen per motorcycle.

Suzuki buys all its wheels from an outside supplier. No defective wheels are accepted. (Suzuki's needs for extra wheels for replacement parts are ordered by a separate division of the company.) The company's target closing stock is 30 000 wheels, and its opening stock is 20 000 wheels. The budgeted purchase price is 16 000 yen per wheel.

Required

1 Calculate the budgeted revenue in yen.

2 Calculate the number of motorcycles to be produced.

3 Calculate the budgeted purchases of wheels in units and in yen.

14.18 Budgeted profit and loss account (CMA, adapted) (30 minutes)

Castelo Branco Lda is a manufacturer of video-conferencing products. Regular units are manufactured to meet marketing projections, and specialised units are made after an order is received. Maintaining the video-conferencing equipment is an important area of customer satisfaction. With the recent downturn in the computer industry, the video-conferencing equipment segment has suffered, leading to a decline in Castelo Branco's financial performance. The following profit and loss account shows results for the year 2015:

Profit and loss account for Castelo Branco for the year ending 31 December 2015 (in thousands)

Sales		
Equipment	€6000	
Maintenance contracts	1800	
Total income		€7800
Cost of goods sold		4600
Gross profit		3200
Operating costs		
Marketing	600	
Distribution	150	
Customer maintenance	1000	
Administration	900	
Total operating costs		2650
Operating profit		€550

Castelo Branco's management team is in the process of preparing the 2016 budget and is studying the following information:

a Selling prices of equipment are expected to increase by 10% as the economic recovery begins. The selling price of each maintenance contract is unchanged from 2015.

b Equipment sales in units are expected to increase by 6%, with a corresponding 6% growth in units of maintenance contracts.

c The cost of each unit sold is expected to increase by 3% to pay for the necessary technology and quality improvements.

d Marketing costs are expected to increase by €250 000, but administration costs are expected to be held at 2015 levels.

e Distribution costs vary in proportion to the number of units of equipment sold.

f Two maintenance technicians are to be added at a total cost of €130 000, which covers wages and related travel costs. The objective is to improve customer service and shorten response time.

g There is no opening or closing stock of equipment.

Required

Prepare a budgeted profit and loss account for 2016.

14.19 Responsibility of purchasing agent (Adapted from a description by R. Villers) (15 minutes)

Ágúst Karlsson is the purchasing agent for the Akureyri Manufacturing Company. Bjarni Jóhannesson is head of the Production Planning and Control Department. Every six months, Bjarni gives Ágúst a general purchasing programme. Ágúst gets specifications from the Engineering Department. He then selects suppliers and negotiates prices. When he took this job, Ágúst was informed very clearly that he bore responsibility for meeting the general purchasing programme once he accepted it from Bjarni. During week 24, Ágúst was advised that Part No. 1234 – a critical part – would be needed for assembly on Tuesday morning of week 32. He found that the regular supplier could not deliver. He called everywhere and finally found a supplier in Selfoss, and accepted the commitment. He followed up by post. Yes, the supplier assured him, the part would be ready. The matter was so important that on Thursday of week 31, Bjarni checked by phone. Yes, the shipment had left in time. Bjarni was reassured and did not check further. But on Tuesday of week 32, the part had not arrived. Enquiry revealed that the shipment had been misdirected and was still in Reykjavik.

Required

What department should bear the costs of time lost in the plant? Why? As purchasing agent, do you think it fair that such costs be charged to your department?

*14.20 Cash budgeting (40–50 minutes)

On 1 December 2014, Tire-Lire, SNC, is attempting to project cash receipts and disbursements to 31 January 2015. On this latter date, a note will be payable in the amount of €100 000. This amount was borrowed in September to carry the company through the seasonal peak in November and December.

The trial balance on 1 December shows in part the following information:

Cash	€10 000	
Debtors	280 000	
Allowance for bad debts		€15 800
Stock	87 500	
Creditors		92 000

Sales terms call for a 2% discount if payment is made within the first 10 days of the month after purchase, with the balance due by the end of the month after purchase. Experience has shown that 70% of the billings will be collected within the discount period, 20% by the end of the month after purchase, 8% in the following month, and that 2% will be uncollectable. There are no cash sales.

The average selling price of the company's products is €100 per unit. Actual and projected sales are

October actual	€180 000
November actual	250 000
December estimated	300 000
January estimated	150 000
February estimated	120 000
Total estimated for year ending 30 June 2015	1 500 000

All purchases are payable within 15 days. Thus approximately 50% of the purchases in a month are due and payable in the next month. The average unit purchase cost is €70. Target closing stocks are 500 units plus 25% of the next month's unit sales.

Total budgeted marketing, distribution and customer-service costs for the year are €400 000. Of this amount, €150 000 is considered fixed (and includes depreciation of €30 000). The remainder varies with sales. Both fixed and variable marketing, distribution and customer-service costs are paid as incurred.

Required

Prepare a cash budget for December and January. Supply supporting schedules for collections of receivables for raw materials, and marketing, distribution and customer-service costs.

14.21   Budgetary control issues (From CIMA Management Accounting Pillar Managerial Level Paper, May 2001) (40 minutes)

M plc designs, manufactures and assembles furniture. The furniture is for home use and therefore varies considerably in size, complexity and value. One of the departments in the company is the Assembly Department. This department is labour intensive; the workers travel to various locations to assemble and fit the furniture using the packs of finished timbers that have been sent to them.

Budgets are set centrally and they are then given to the managers of the various departments who then have the responsibility of achieving their respective targets. Actual costs are compared against the budgets and the managers are then asked to comment on the budgetary control statement. The statement for April for the Assembly Department is shown below.

	Budget	Actual	Variance	
Assembly labour hours	6 400	7 140		
	$	$	$	
Assembly labour	51 970	58 227	6 257	Adverse
Furniture packs	224 000	205 000	19 000	Favourable
Other materials	23 040	24 100	1 060	Adverse
Overheads	62 060	112 340	50 280	Adverse
Total	361 070	399 667	38 597	Adverse

Note: the costs shown are for assembling and fitting the furniture (they do not include time spent travelling to jobs and the related costs). The hours worked by the manager are not included in the figure given for the assembly labour hours.

The Manager of the Assembly Department is new to the job and has very little previous experience of working with budgets but he does have many years' experience as a supervisor in assembly departments. Based on that experience he was sure that the department had performed well. He has asked for your help in replying to a memo he has just received asking him to 'explain the serious overspending in his department'. He has sent you some additional information about the budget:

1 The budgeted and actual assembly labour costs include the fixed salary of $2050 for the Manager of the Assembly Department. All of the other labour is paid for the hours they work.

2 The cost of furniture packs and other materials is assumed by the central finance office of M plc to vary in proportion to the number of assembly labour hours worked.

3 The budgeted overhead costs are made up of three elements: a fixed cost of $9000 for services from central headquarters, a stepped fixed cost which changes when the assembly hours exceed 7000 hours, and some variable overheads. The variable overheads are assumed to vary in proportion to the number of assembly labour hours. Working papers for the budget showed the impact on the overhead costs of differing amounts of assembly labour hours:

Assembly labour hours	5 000	7 500	10 000
Overhead costs	$54 500	$76 500	$90 000

The actual fixed costs for April were as budgeted.

Required

1 Prepare, using the additional information that the manager of the Assembly Department has given you, a budgetary control statement that would be more helpful to him.

2 **a** Discuss the differences between the *format of the statement* that you have produced and that supplied by M plc;

   b Discuss the assumption made by the central office of M plc that costs vary in proportion to assembly labour hours.

3 Discuss whether M plc should change to a system of participative budgeting.

Advanced level

*14.22 Activity-based budgeting (20–30 minutes)

Nyborg Supermarkets AS is preparing its activity-based budget for January 2015 for its operating costs (that is, its non-cost of goods purchased for resale costs). Its current concern is with its four activity areas (which are also indirect-cost categories in its product profitability reporting system):

a *Ordering* – covers purchasing activities. The cost driver is the number of purchase orders

b *Delivery* – covers the physical delivery and receipt of merchandise. The cost driver is the number of deliveries

c *Shelf-stacking* – covers the stacking of merchandise on store shelves and the ongoing restacking before sale

d *Customer support* – covers assistance provided to customers, including check-out and bagging.

Assume Nyborg Supermarkets has only three product areas: soft drinks, fresh produce and packaged food. The budgeted usage of each cost driver in these three areas of the store and the January 2015 budgeted cost driver rates are as follows:

	Cost driver rates		January 2015 budgeted amount of driver used		
Activity area and driver	2014 actual rate	January 2015 budgeted rate	Soft drinks	Fresh produce	Packaged food
Ordering (per purchase order)	DKK 1000	DKK 900	14	24	14
Delivery (per delivery)	DKK 800	DKK 820	12	62	19
Shelf-stacking (per hour)	DKK 200	DKK 210	16	172	94
Customer support (per item sold)	DKK 2.0	DKK 1.8	4 600	34 200	10 750

Required

1 What is the total budgeted cost for each activity area in January 2015?

2 What advantages might Nyborg Supermarkets gain by using an activity-based budgeting approach over (say) an approach for budgeting operating costs based on a budgeted percentage of cost of goods sold times the budgeted cost of goods sold?

14.23 Kaizen approach to activity-based budgeting (continuation of Exercise 14.22) (20–30 minutes)

Nyborg Supermarkets has a kaizen (continuous improvement) approach to budgeting monthly activity area costs for each month of 2015. February's budgeted cost driver rate is 0.998 times the budgeted January 2015 rate. March's budgeted cost driver rate is 0.998 times the budgeted February 2015 rate, and so on. Assume that March 2015 has the same budgeted amount of cost drivers used as did January 2015.

Required

1 What is the total budgeted cost for each activity area in March 2015?

2 What are the benefits of Nyborg Supermarkets adopting a kaizen budgeting approach? What are the limitations?

14.24 **Comprehensive review of budgeting** (50–60 minutes)

British Beverages bottles two soft drinks under licence to Cadbury Schweppes at its Manchester plant. Bottling at this plant is a highly repetitive, automated process. Empty bottles are removed from their carton, placed on a conveyor, and cleaned, rinsed, dried, filled, capped and heated (to reduce condensation). The only stock held is either direct materials or else finished goods. There is no work in progress.

The two soft drinks bottled by British Beverages are lemonade and diet lemonade. The syrup for both soft drinks is purchased from Cadbury Schweppes. Syrup for the regular brand contains a higher sugar content than the syrup for the diet brand.

British Beverages uses a lot size of 1000 cases as the unit of analysis in its budgeting. (Each case contains 24 bottles.) Direct materials are expressed in terms of lots, where one lot of direct materials is the input necessary to yield one lot (1000 cases) of beverage. In 2015, the following purchase prices are forecast for direct materials:

	Lemonade	Diet lemonade
Syrup	£1200 per lot	£1100 per lot
Containers (bottles, caps, etc.)	£1000 per lot	£1000 per lot
Packaging	£800 per lot	£800 per lot

The two soft drinks are bottled using the same equipment. The equipment is cleaned daily, but it is only rinsed when a switch is made during the day between diet lemonade and lemonade. Diet lemonade is always bottled first each day to reduce the risk of sugar contamination. The only difference in the bottling process for the two soft drinks is the syrup.

Summary data used in developing budgets for 2015 are as follows:

a Sales:

- Lemonade, 1080 lots at £9000 selling price per lot.
- Diet lemonade, 540 lots at £8500 selling price per lot.

b Opening (1 January 2015) stock of direct materials:

- Syrup for lemonade, 80 lots at £1100 purchase price per lot.
- Syrup for diet lemonade, 70 lots at £1000 purchase price per lot.
- Containers, 200 lots at £950 purchase price per lot.
- Packaging, 400 lots at £900 purchase price per lot.

c Opening (1 January 2015) stock of finished goods:

- Lemonade, 100 lots at £5300 per lot.
- Diet lemonade, 50 lots at £5200 per lot.

d Target closing (31 December 2015) stock of direct materials:

- Syrup for lemonade, 30 lots.
- Syrup for diet lemonade, 20 lots.
- Containers, 100 lots.
- Packaging, 200 lots.

e Target closing (31 December 2015) stock of finished goods:

- Lemonade, 20 lots.
- Diet lemonade, 10 lots.

f Each lot requires 20 direct manufacturing labour-hours at the 2015 budgeted rate of £25 per hour. Indirect manufacturing labour costs are included in the manufacturing overhead forecast.

g Variable manufacturing overhead is forecast to be £600 per hour of bottling time; bottling time is the time the filling equipment is in operation. It takes two hours to bottle one lot of lemonade and two hours to bottle one lot of diet lemonade. Fixed manufacturing overhead is forecast to be £1 200 000 for 2015.

h Hours of budgeted bottling time is the sole allocation base for all fixed manufacturing overhead.

i Administration costs are forecast to be 10% of the cost of goods manufactured for 2015. Marketing costs are forecast to be 12% of sales for 2015. Distribution costs are forecast to be 8% of sales for 2015.

Required

Assume British Beverages uses the first-in, first-out (FIFO) method for costing all stock. On the basis of the preceding data, prepare the following budgets for 2015:

1 Revenue budget (in £)

2 Production budget (in units)

3 Direct materials usage budget (in units and £)

4 Direct materials purchases budget (in units and £)

5 Direct manufacturing labour budget

6 Manufacturing overhead costs budget

7 Closing finished goods stock budget

8 Cost of goods sold budget

9 Marketing costs budget

10 Distribution costs budget

11 Administration costs budget

12 Budgeted profit and loss account.

CHAPTER 15

Flexible budgets, variances and management control: I

Managers often quantify their plans in the form of budgets. A survey of UK firm finance professionals indicated that 72% believe that the ability to plan ahead is their most important quality. The 2013 Global Budgeting and Planning Survey across 108 countries by Winshuttle and ACCA revealed that over 50% of the companies investigated were happy with their budgeting process and its frequency. The survey revealed that 80% began budgeting three to six months before the end of the financial year. Sales, cash flows and indirect costs were the top three areas of budgeting significance. This chapter focuses on how flexible budgets and variances can play a key role in management planning and control. Flexible budgets and variances help managers gain insights into why the actual results differ from the planned performance. A recent survey by the Chartered Institute of Management Accountants found that variance analysis was the most popular cost tool used by organisations of all sizes.

Each variance we calculate is the difference between an actual result and a budgeted amount. The budgeted amount is a benchmark; that is, it is a point of reference from which comparisons may be made. Benchmarks include:

1 Financial variables reported in a company's own accounting system (such as Nissan's manufacturing cost for a Juke model). This is the focus of this chapter.

2 Financial variables not reported in a company's own accounting system (such as when Nissan uses the estimated cost Mazda incurs to manufacture a CX-9 as the benchmark for evaluating the cost competitiveness of its Juke product line).

3 Non-financial variables (such as Nissan's assembly-line defect rate).

Organisations differ widely in how they calculate and label the budgeted amounts they report in their own accounting system. Some organisations rely heavily on past results; others conduct detailed engineering or time-and-motion studies. The term *standard* is frequently used when such studies underlie the budgeted amounts. A standard is a carefully predetermined amount; it is usually expressed on a per unit basis. In practice, there is not a precise dividing line between a *budgeted amount* and a *standard amount*. We use *budgeted amount* as the more general term because some budgeted amounts may not be carefully predetermined amounts. However, all of the variances we discuss can be calculated using standard amounts or budgeted amounts. Variances assist managers in their planning and control decisions. Management by exception is the practice of concentrating on areas not operating as anticipated and giving less attention to areas operating as expected.

Learning objectives

After studying this chapter, you should be able to:

- Describe the difference between a static budget and a flexible budget

- Illustrate how a flexible budget can be developed and calculate flexible-budget and sales-volume variances

- Interpret the price and efficiency variances for direct-cost input categories

- Explain why purchasing-performance measures should focus on more factors than just price variances for inputs

- Describe how the continuous improvement theme can be integrated into variance analysis

- Perform variance analysis in activity-based costing systems

- Describe benchmarking and how it can be used by managers in variance analysis

Static budgets and flexible budgets

This chapter illustrates both static budgets and flexible budgets. A **static budget** is a budget that is based on one level of output; it is not adjusted or altered after it is set, regardless of ensuing changes in actual output (or actual revenue and cost drivers). A **flexible budget** is adjusted in accordance with ensuing changes in actual output (or actual revenue and cost drivers). A flexible budget is calculated at the end of the period when the actual output is known. A static budget is developed at the start of the budget period based on the planned output level for the period. As we shall see, a flexible budget enables managers to calculate a richer set of variances than does a static budget. A **favourable variance** – denoted F – is a variance that increases operating income relative to the budgeted amount. An **unfavourable variance** – denoted U – is a variance that decreases operating income relative to the budgeted amount.

Budgets, both static and flexible, can differ in their level of detail. Many organisations present budgets with broad summary figures that can be broken down into more detailed figures via computer software programs. In this book, the term *level* followed by a number denotes the amount of detail indicated by the variance(s) isolated. Level 0 reports the least detail, Level 1 offers more information, and so on.

The example of the Sofiya Company illustrates static budgets and flexible budgets. Sofiya manufactures and sells a single product, a distinctive jacket that requires many materials, tailoring and hand operations. Sales are made to independent clothing stores and retail chains. Sofiya sets budgeted revenues (budgeted selling price ¥ budgeted units sold) based on input from its marketing personnel and on an analysis of general and industry economic conditions.

The costing system at Sofiya includes both manufacturing costs and marketing costs. There are direct and indirect costs in each category:

	Direct costs	Indirect costs
Manufacturing	Direct materials	Variable manufacturing overhead
	Direct manufacturing labour	Fixed manufacturing overhead
Marketing	Direct marketing labour	Variable marketing overhead
	Fixed marketing overhead	

Sofiya's manufacturing costs include direct materials (all variable), direct manufacturing labour (all variable) and manufacturing overhead (both variable and fixed). Its marketing costs (which include distribution and customer service costs as well as advertising costs) are made up of direct marketing labour (primarily distribution personnel, which are all variable) and marketing overhead (both variable and fixed). The cost driver for direct materials, direct manufacturing labour and variable manufacturing overhead is the *number of units manufactured*. The cost driver for direct marketing labour and variable marketing overhead is the *number of units sold*. The revenue driver is the *number of units sold*. The relevant range for the €180 selling price per jacket and for the cost drivers in both manufacturing and marketing is from 8000 to 16 000 units. All costs at Sofiya are either driven by output units or are fixed. We make this simplifying assumption to highlight the basic approach to flexible budgeting.

In order to focus on the key concepts, we assume Sofiya has no opening or closing stocks. Chapter 7 discussed some of the complexities that occur when opening or closing stocks exist.

Static-budget variances

The actual results and the static-budget amounts of Sofiya for April 2015 are as follows:

	Actual results	Static-budget amounts
Units sold	10 000	12 000
Revenues	€1 850 000	€2 160 000
Variable costs	1 120 000	1 188 000
Fixed costs	705 000	710 000
Operating profit	25 000	262 000

Exhibit 15.1 presents the Level 0 and Level 1 variance analyses for April 2015. Level 0 gives the least-detailed comparison of the actual and budgeted operating profit. The unfavourable variance of €237 000 is simply the result of subtracting the budgeted operating profit of €262 000 from the actual operating profit of €25 000:

$$\text{Static-budget variance} = \text{Actual results} - \text{Static-budget amount of operating profit}$$
$$= €25\,000 - €262\,000$$
$$= €237\,000 \text{ U}^*$$

* U = unfavourable effort on operating profit.

Exhibit 15.1   Static-budget-based variance analysis for Sofiya for April 2015

Level 0 analysis

Actual operating profit	€25 000
Budgeted operating profit	262 000
Static-budget variance of operating profit	237 000 U*

Level 1 analysis

	Actual results (1)	Static-budget variances (2) = (1) − (3)	Static budget (3)
Units sold	10 000	2 000 U	12 000
Revenues	€1 850 000	€310 000 U	€2 160 000
Variable costs	1 120 000	68 000 F	1 188 000
Contribution margin	730 000	242 000 U	972 000
Fixed costs	705 000	5 000 F	710 000
Operating profit	€25 000	€237 000 U	€262 000
		€237 000 U	

Total static-budget variance

* F = favourable effect on operating profit; U = unfavourable effect on operating profit.

This variance is often called a static-budget variance because the number used for the budgeted amount (€262 000) is taken from a static budget.

Level 1 analysis in Exhibit 15.1 provides managers with more detailed information on the static-budget variance of operating profit of €237 000 U. The additional information added in Level 1 pertains to revenues, variable costs and fixed costs. The budgeted contribution margin percentage of 45.0% (€972 000 ÷ €2 160 000) decreases to 39.5% (€730 000 ÷ €1 850 000) for the actual results.

While Level 1 contains more information than Level 0, additional insights into the causes of variances can be gained by incorporating a flexible budget into the computation of variances.

Steps in developing a flexible budget

Sofiya's five-step approach to developing a flexible budget is relatively straightforward given the assumption that all costs are either variable with respect to output units or fixed. The five steps are as follows.

Step 1: Determine the budgeted selling price per unit, the budgeted variable costs per unit, and the budgeted fixed costs Each output unit (a jacket) has a budgeted selling price of €180. The budgeted variable cost is €99 per jacket. Column 2 of Exhibit 15.2 has a breakdown of this €99 amount. The budgeted fixed costs total €710 000 (€276 000 manufacturing and €434 000 marketing).

Exhibit 15.2	Flexible-budget data for Sofiya for April 2015		
Line item (1)	**Bugeted cost amount per unit** (2)	**Flexible budget amount 10 000** (3)	**Actual results for 10 000 units** (4)
Revenue	€180	€1 800 000	€1 850 000
Variable costs			
Direct materials	60	600 000	688 200
Direct manufacturing labour	16	160 000	198 000
Direct marketing labour	6	60 000	57 600
Variable manufacturing overhead	12	120 000	130 500
Variable marketing overhead	5	50 000	45 700
Total variable costs	99	990 000	1 120 000
Contribution margin	€81	810 000	730 000
Fixed costs			
Manufacturing overhead		276 000	285 000
Marketing overhead	–	434 000	420 000
Total fixed costs	–	710 000	705 000
Total costs	–	1 700 000	1 825 000
Operating profit		€100 000	€25 000

Step 2: Determine the actual quantity of the revenue driver Sofiya's revenue driver is the number of units sold. In April 2015, Sofiya sold 10 000 jackets.

Step 3: Determine the flexible budget for revenue based on the budgeted unit revenue and the actual quantity of the revenue driver

$$\text{Flexible-budget revenues} = €180 \times 10\ 000$$
$$= €1\ 800\ 000$$

Step 4: Determine the actual quantity of the cost driver(s) Sofiya's cost driver for manufacturing costs is units produced. The cost driver for marketing costs is units sold. In April 2015, Sofiya produced and sold 10 000 jackets.

Step 5: Determine the flexible budget for costs based on the budgeted unit variable costs and fixed costs and the actual quantity of the cost driver(s)

Flexible-budget variable costs
Manufacturing   = €88 × 10 000 = €880 000
Marketing   = €11 × 10 000 =   110 000
                                      €990 000

Flexible-budget fixed costs
Manufacturing   =   €276 000
Marketing   =   434 000
                     =   €710 000

These five steps enable Sofiya to move to a Level 2 variance analysis, which helps them better explore reasons for the €237 000 unfavourable static-budget variance of operating profit. Exhibit 15.2 shows the flexible budget for 10 000 units (column 3) as well as the actual results for 10 000 units (column 4).

Flexible-budget variances and sales-volume variances

Exhibit 15.3 presents the Level 2 flexible-budget-based variance analysis for Sofiya. Note that the €237 000 unfavourable static-budget variance of operating profit is now split into two categories: a flexible-budget variance and a sales-volume variance.

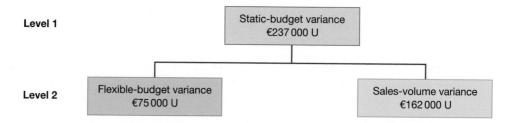

The **flexible-budget variance** is the difference between the actual results and the flexible-budget amount for the actual levels of the revenue and cost drivers. The **sales-volume variance** is the difference between the flexible-budget amount and the static-budget amount; unit selling prices, unit variable costs and fixed costs are held constant. Knowing these variances helps managers better explain the static-budget variance of €237 000 U.

Sales-volume variances

The flexible-budget amounts in column 3 of Exhibit 15.3 and the static-budget amount in column 5 are both calculated using the budgeted selling prices and budgeted costs. This variance is labelled the 'sales-volume variance' because in many contexts the number of units sold is both the revenue driver and the cost driver. For the operating profit line item:

$$\text{Sales-volume variance} = \text{Flexible-budget amount} - \text{Static-budget amount}$$
$$= €100\,000 - €262\,000$$
$$= €162\,000 \text{ U}$$

In our Sofiya example, this sales-volume variance in operating profit arises solely because it sold 10 000 units, which was 2000 less than the budgeted 12 000 units.

Exhibit 15.3	Flexible-budget-based variance analysis for Sofiya for April 2015

Level 2 analysis

	Actual results (1)	Flexible-budget variances (2) = (1) – (3)	Flexible budget (3)	Sales-volume variances (4) = (3) – (5)	Static budget (5)
Units sold	10 000	0	10 000	2 000 U	12 000
Revenues	€1 850 000	€50 000 F*	€1 800 000	€360 000 U	€2 160 000
Variable costs	1 120 000	130 000 U	990 000	198 000 F	1 188 000
Contribution margin	730 000	80 000 U	810 000	162 000 U	972 000
Fixed costs	705 000	5 000 F	710 000	0	710 000
Operating profit	€25 000	€75 000 U	€100 000	€162 000 U	€262 000

€75 000 U   €162 000 U

Total flexible-budget variance   Total sales-volume variance

€237 000 U

Total static-budget variance

* F = favourable effect on operating profit; U = unfavourable effect on operating profit.

Flexible-budget variances

The first three columns of Exhibit 15.3 compare the actual results with the flexible-budget amounts. Flexible-budget variances are reported in column 2 for four line items in the income statement:

$$\text{Flexible-budget variance} = \text{Actual results} - \text{Flexible-budget amount}$$

For the operating profit line item, the flexible-budget variance is €75 000 U (€25 000 – €100 000). This variance arises because the actual selling price, unit variable costs and fixed costs differ from the budgeted amounts. The actual and budgeted unit amounts for the selling price and variable costs are as follows:

	Actual unit amount	Budgeted unit amount
Selling price	€185	€180
Variable cost	112	99

The actual fixed cost of €705 000 is €5000 less than the budgeted €710 000 amount.

The flexible-budget variance pertaining to revenues is often called a **selling-price variance** because it arises solely from differences between the actual selling price and the budgeted selling price:

$$\text{Selling-price variance} = (\text{Actual selling price} - \text{Budgeted selling price}) \times \text{Actual units sold}$$
$$= (€185 - €180) \times 10\ 000$$
$$= €50\ 000\ \text{F}$$

Sofiya has a favourable selling-price variance because the actual selling price exceeds the budgeted amount (by €5). Marketing managers typically are best informed as to why this selling price difference arose.

Price variances and efficiency variances for inputs

The flexible-budget variance (Level 2) captures the difference between the actual results and the flexible budget. The sources of this variance (as regards costs) are the individual differences between actual and budgeted prices or quantities for inputs. The next two variances we discuss – price variances and efficiency variances for inputs – analyse such differences. This information helps managers to better understand past performance and to plan for future performance. We call this a Level 3 analysis as it takes a more detailed analysis of the Level 2 variances.

A **price variance** is the difference between the actual price and the budgeted price multiplied by the actual quantity of input in question (such as direct materials purchased or used). Price variances are sometimes called **input-price variances** or **rate variances** (especially when those variances are for direct labour). An **efficiency variance** is the difference between the actual quantity of input used (such as metres of cloth of direct materials) and the budgeted quantity of input that should have been used, multiplied by the budgeted price. Efficiency variances are sometimes called **input-efficiency variances** or **usage variances**.

The relationship of these two variances to those we have already discussed for Sofiya is as follows:

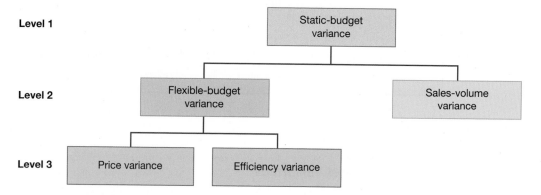

Obtaining budgeted input prices and input quantities

Sofiya's two main sources of information about budgeted input prices and budgeted input quantities are:

1 *Actual input data from past periods*. Most companies have past data on actual input prices and actual input quantities. These past amounts could be used for the budgeted amounts in a flexible budget. Past data are typically available at a relatively low cost. The limitations of using this source are: (a) past data include past inefficiencies, and (b) past data do not incorporate any expected changes planned to occur in the budget period.

2 *Standards developed by Sofiya*. A standard is a carefully predetermined amount; it is usually expressed on a per unit basis. Sofiya uses time-and-motion and engineering studies to determine its standard amounts. For example, it conducts a detailed breakdown of the steps in making a jacket. Each step is then assigned a standard time based on work by a skilled operator using equipment operating in an efficient manner. The advantages of using standard amounts are that: (a) they can exclude past inefficiencies, and (b) they can take into account expected changes in the budget period. An example of (a) is a supplier making dramatic improvements in its ability to consistently meet Sofiya's demanding quality requirements for the cloth material used to make jackets. An example of (b) is the acquisition of new looms that operate at a faster speed and that enable work to be done with lower reject rates.

Sofiya has developed standard inputs and standard costs for each of its variable-cost items. A **standard input** is a carefully predetermined quantity of input (such as kilograms of materials or hours of labour time) required for one unit of output. A **standard cost** is a carefully predetermined cost. Standard costs can relate to units of inputs or units of outputs. Sofiya's budgeted cost for each variable cost item is calculated using the following formula:

Standard inputs allowed for 1 output unit × Standard cost per input unit

The variable-cost items are:

- *Direct materials*: 2.00 square metres of cloth input allowed per output unit (jacket) manufactured, at €30 standard cost per square metre.

  Standard cost = 2.00 × €30 = €60.00 per output unit manufactured

- *Direct manufacturing labour*: 0.80 manufacturing labour-hours of input allowed per output unit manufactured, at €20 standard cost per hour.

  Standard cost = 0.80 × €20 = €16.00 per output unit manufactured

- *Direct marketing labour*: 0.25 marketing labour-hours of input allowed per output unit sold, at €24 standard cost per hour.

  Standard cost = 0.25 × €24 = €6.00 per output unit sold

- *Variable manufacturing overhead*: allocated on the basis of 1.20 machine-hours per output unit manufactured, at €10 standard cost per machine-hour.

  Standard cost = 1.20 × €10 = €12.00 per output unit manufactured

- *Variable marketing overhead*: allocated on the basis of 0.125 direct marketing labour-hours per output unit sold, at €40 standard cost per hour.

  Standard cost = 0.125 × €40 = €5.00 per output unit sold

These standard cost computations explain how Sofiya developed the numbers in column 2 of Exhibit 15.2.

The breakdown of the flexible-budget variance into its price and efficiency components is important when evaluating individual managers. At Sofiya, the production manager is responsible for the efficiency variance, while the purchasing manager is responsible for the price variance. This separate computation of the price variance enables the efficiency variance to be calculated using budgeted input prices. Thus, judgements about efficiency (the quantity of inputs used to produce a given level of output) are not affected by whether actual input prices differ from budgeted input prices. A word of caution, however, is appropriate. As will be discussed in following text, the causes of price and efficiency variances can be interrelated. For this reason, do not interpret these variances in isolation from each other.

An illustration of price and efficiency variances for inputs

Consider Sofiya's three direct-cost categories. The actual cost for each of these three categories is:

Direct materials purchased and used	
Direct materials costs	€688 200
Square metres of cloth input purchased and used	22 200
Actual price per metre	€31
Direct manufacturing labour	
Direct manufacturing labour costs	€198 000
Manufacturing labour-hours of input	9 000
Actual price per hour	€22
Direct marketing labour	
Direct marketing labour costs	€57 600
Marketing labour-hours of input	2 304
Actual price per hour	€25

For simplicity, we assume here that direct materials used is equal to direct materials purchased.

The actual results and the flexible-budget amounts for each category of direct costs for the 10 000 actual output units in April 2015 are:

	Actual results	Flexible budget		Flexible-budget variances
Direct materials	€688 200	€600 000	(10 000 × €60)	€88 200 U
Direct manufacturing labour	198 000	160 000	(10 000 × €16)	38 000 U
Direct marketing labour	57 600	60 000	(10 000 × €6)	2 400 F
Total	€943 800	€820 000		€123 800 U

We now use these Sofiya Company data to illustrate the input-price and input-efficiency variances. Consider first the input-price variances.

Price variances

The formula for calculating a price variance is:

Price variance = (Actual price of input − Budgeted price of input) × Actual quantity of input

Price variances for each of Sofiya's three direct-cost categories are:

Direct-cost category	(Actual price of input − Budgeted price of input)	×	Actual quantity of input	=	Input-price variance
Direct materials	(€31 − €30)	×	22 200	=	€22 200 U
Direct manufacturing labour	(€22 − €20)	×	9 000	=	18 000 U
Direct marketing labour	(€25 − €24)	×	2 304	=	2 304 U

All three price variances are unfavourable (they reduce operating profit) because the actual price of each direct-cost input exceeds the budgeted price; that is, Sofiya incurred more cost per input unit than was budgeted.

Always consider a broad range of possible causes for price variances. For example, Sofiya's unfavourable direct materials price variance could be due to one or more of the following reasons:

- Sofiya's purchasing manager negotiated less skilfully than was assumed in the budget.
- Sofiya's purchasing manager bought in smaller lot sizes than budgeted even though quantity discounts were available for the larger lot sizes.
- Materials prices unexpectedly increased because of disruptive weather conditions.
- Budgeted purchase prices for Sofiya's materials were set without careful analysis of the market.

Sofiya's response to a materials price variance will be vitally affected by the presumed cause of the variance. Assume it decides an unfavourable variance is due to poor negotiating by its purchasing officer. Sofiya may decide to invest more in training this officer in negotiations, or it may decide to employ a more skilful purchasing officer.

When interpreting materials price variances, Sofiya's managers should consider any change in the relationship with the company's suppliers. For example, assume that Sofiya moves to a long-term relationship with a single supplier of material. Sofiya and the supplier agree to a single purchase price per unit for all material purchases in the next six months. It is likely that price variances will be minimal for this material because all purchases will be made from this supplier.

Efficiency variances

Consider now the efficiency variance. Computation of efficiency variances requires measurement of inputs for a given level of output. For any actual level of output, the efficiency variance is the difference between the input that was actually used and the input that should have been used to achieve that actual output, holding input price constant:

$$\text{Efficiency variance} = \left(\begin{array}{c} \text{Actual quantity} \\ \text{of input used} \end{array} - \begin{array}{c} \text{Budgeted quantity} \\ \text{of input allowed} \\ \text{for actual output} \\ \text{units achieved} \end{array} \right) \times \begin{array}{c} \text{Budgeted price} \\ \text{of input} \end{array}$$

The idea here is that an organisation is inefficient if it uses more inputs than budgeted for the actual output units achieved, and it is efficient if it uses less inputs than budgeted for the actual output units achieved.

The efficiency variances for each of Sofiya's direct-cost categories are:

Direct-cost category	$\left(\begin{array}{c}\text{Actual}\\\text{input used}\end{array} - \begin{array}{c}\text{Budgeted input allowed}\\\text{for actual output units}\end{array}\right) \times$	Budgeted price of input	= Efficiency variance
Direct materials	[22 200 metres – (10 000 units × 2.00 metres)] ×	€30	
	(22 200 metres – 20 000 metres) ×	€30	= €66 000 U
Direct manufacturing labour	[9000 hours – (10 000 units × 0.80 hours)] ×	€20	
	(9000 hours – 8000 hours) ×	€20	= €20 000 U
Direct marketing labour	[2304 hours – (10 000 units × 0.25 hours)] ×	€24	
	(2304 hours – 2500 hours) ×	€24	= €4 704 F

The two manufacturing efficiency variances (direct materials and direct manufacturing labour) are both unfavourable because more input was used than was budgeted, resulting in a decrease in operating profit. The marketing efficiency variance is favourable because less input was used than was budgeted, resulting in an increase in operating profit.

As with price variances, Sofiya's managers need to consider a broad range of possible reasons for efficiency variances arising. For example, Sofiya's unfavourable direct manufacturing labour variance could be due to one or more of the following reasons:

- Sofiya's personnel manager took on underskilled workers.
- Sofiya's production scheduler inefficiently scheduled work, resulting in more direct manufacturing labour time per jacket.
- Sofiya's maintenance department did not properly maintain machines, resulting in more direct manufacturing labour time per jacket.
- Budgeted time standards were set without careful analysis of the operating conditions and the employees' skills.

Suppose Sofiya determines that the unfavourable variance is due to poor machine maintenance. It may decide to set up a team consisting of plant machine engineers and machine operators to develop a maintenance schedule so that in the future, jackets can be sewn in shorter times.

Presentation of price and efficiency variances for inputs

Note how the sum of the price variance and the efficiency variance equals the flexible-budget variance:

	Price variance	+	Efficiency variance	=	Flexible-budget variance
Direct materials	€22 200 U		€66 000 U		€88 200 U
Direct manufacturing labour	18 000 U		20 000 U		38 000 U
Direct marketing labour	2 304 U		4 704 F		2 400 F

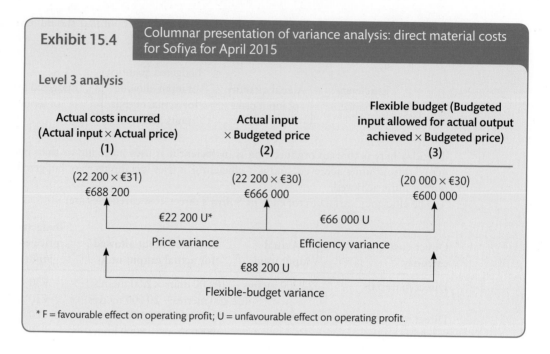

Exhibit 15.4 Columnar presentation of variance analysis: direct material costs for Sofiya for April 2015

Exhibit 15.4 illustrates a convenient way to integrate the actual and budgeted input information used to calculate the price and efficiency variances for direct materials. This exhibit assumes that materials purchased equals materials used.

Overview of variance analysis

Exhibit 15.5 presents a comprehensive road map of where we have been. The Level 0 and Level 1 analyses are reproductions of Exhibit 15.1. Level 2 is a reproduction of Exhibit 15.3. We have just discussed price and efficiency variances, which are Level 3.

Some managers refer to proceeding through successively more detailed data as 'drilling-down' (or 'peeling the onion'). The growing use of online data collection is increasing the number of databases that have this drill-down capability.

Impact of stocks

Our Sofiya Company illustration assumed the following:

1 All units are manufactured and sold in the same accounting period. There are no work-in-progress or finished-goods stocks at either the start or the end of the accounting period.

2 All direct materials are purchased and used in the same accounting period. There are no direct materials stocks at either the start or the end of the period.

Both assumptions can be relaxed without changing the key concepts introduced in this chapter. However, changes in the computation or interpretation of variances would be required when opening or closing stocks exist.

Suppose direct materials are purchased sometime prior to their use and that direct materials stocks exist at the start or end of the accounting period. Managers typically want to pinpoint variances at the earliest possible time so that their decisions can be best informed by the variances.

Exhibit 15.5 Overview of variance analysis for Sofiya for April 2015

Level 0 analysis

Actual operating profit	€25 000
Budgeted operating profit	262 000
Static-budget variance of operating profit	€237 000 U*

Level 1 analysis

	Actual results (1)	Static-budget variances (2) = (1) − (3)	Static budget (3)
Units sold	10 000	2 000 U	12 000
Revenues (sales)	€1 850 000	€310 000 U	€2 160 000
Variable costs	1 120 000	68 000 F	1 188 000
Contribution margin	730 000	242 000 U	972 000
Fixed costs	705 000	5 000 F	710 000
Operating profit	€25 000	€237 000 U	€262 000

€237 000 U

Static-budget variance

Level 2 analysis

	Actual results (1)	Flexible-budget variances (2) = (1) − (3)	Flexible budget (3)	Sales-volume variances (4) = (3) − (5)	Static budget (5)
Units sold	10 000	0	10 000	2 000 U	12 000
Revenues (sales)	€1 850 000	€50 000 F	€1 800 000	€360 000 U	€2 160 000
Variable costs	1 120 000	130 000 U	990 000	198 000 F	1 188 000
Contribution margin	730 000	80 000 U	810 000	162 000 U	972 000
Fixed costs	705 000	5 000 F	710 000	0	710 000
Operating profit	€25 000	€75 000 U	€100 000	€162 000 U	€262 000

€75 000 U   €162 000 U

Total flexible-budget variance   Total sales-volume variance

€237 000 U

Static-budget variance

Level 3 analysis

Revenue variance by customers		Cost variances†			Sales-volume variances‡
Retail chains	€0 F		Price variance	Efficiency variance	Sales-quantity variances
Independent stores	50 000 F				
Sales-price variances	50 000 F	Direct materials	€22 200 U	€66 000 U	Sales-mix variances
		Direct manufacturing labour	18 000 U	20 000 U	
		Direct marketing labour	2 304 U	4 704 F	

* F = favourable effect on operating profit; U = unfavourable effect on operating profit.
† Chapter 16 contains further discussion of Level 3 cost-variance analysis.
‡ These variances are covered in Chapter 17.

For direct materials price variances, the purchase date will almost always be the earliest possible time to isolate them. As a result, many organisations calculate direct materials price variances using the quantities purchased in an accounting period. At the end of this chapter we illustrate how to use two different times (purchase time and use time) to pinpoint direct materials variances.

Concepts in action — Starbucks reduces direct-cost variances to brew a turnaround

Source: Corbis/Wolfgang Kaehler

Starbucks is the largest coffeehouse company in the world, with over 21 000 stores across 64 countries and a workforce exceeding 160 000. Walking around with a coffee drink from Starbucks became prior to 2008 an affordable luxury status symbol. But when consumers tightened their purse strings amid the most recent recession, the company was in serious trouble. With customers cutting back and lower priced competition – from Dunkin' Donuts and McDonald's among others – increasing, Starbucks' profit margins were under attack. For Starbucks, profitability depends on making each high-quality beverage at the lowest possible costs. As a result, an intricate understanding of direct costs is critical.

Variance analysis helps managers assess and maintain profitability at desired levels. In each Starbucks store, the two key direct costs are materials and labour. Materials costs at Starbucks include coffee beans, milk, flavouring syrups, pastries, paper cups and lids. To reduce budgeted costs for materials, Starbucks focused on two key inputs: coffee and milk. For coffee, Starbucks sought to avoid waste and spoilage by no longer brewing decaffeinated and darker coffee blends in the afternoon and evening, when store traffic is slower. Instead, baristas were instructed to brew a pot only when a customer ordered it. With milk prices rising (and making up around 10% of Starbucks' cost of sales), the company switched to 2% milk, which is healthier and costs less, and redoubled efforts to reduce milk-related spoilage.

Labour costs at Starbucks, which cost 24% of company revenue annually, were another area of variance focus. Many stores employed fewer baristas. In other stores, Starbucks adopted many 'lean' production techniques. With 30% of baristas' time involved in walking around behind the counter, reaching for items, and blending drinks, Starbucks sought to make its drink-making processes more efficient. But, while Starbucks closely monitors costs, it is also embarking on other strategies to elevate the brand again. From 2015 the company aims to re-enter the elite coffee business with the opening of 'roastery cafés' which deploy 'coffee masters' who can serve ultra high-end beans such as Colombia Montebonito and Sumatra Peaberry Lake Toba. By 2020, the company aims to open 100 of such Reserve facilities. Continued focus on both direct-cost variances will be critical to the company's future success in any economic climate (http://www.businessweek.com/articles/2014-12-05/starbucks-wants-to-be-fancy-again-opens-new-reserve-cafe by V. Wong).

Sources: Adamy, J. (2009) 'Starbucks brews up new cost cuts by putting lid on afternoon decaf', *Wall Street Journal*, 28 January; Adamy, J. (2008) 'New Starbucks brew attracts customers' flak', *Wall Street Journal*, 1 July; Harris, C. (2007). 'Starbucks slips; lattes rise', *Seattle Post Intelligencer*, 23 July; Jargon, J. (2010) 'Starbucks' growth revives, perked by via', *Wall Street Journal*, 21 January; Jargon, J. (2009) 'Latest Starbucks buzzword: "lean" Japanese techniques', *Wall Street Journal*, 4 August; Kesmodel, D. (2009) 'Starbucks sees demand stirring again', *Wall Street Journal*, 6 November.

Management uses of variances

Performance measurement using variances

A key use of variance analysis is in performance evaluation. Two attributes of performance are commonly measured:

- **Effectiveness** – the degree to which a predetermined objective or target is met.
- **Efficiency** – the relative amount of inputs used to achieve a given level of output.

Be careful to understand the cause(s) of a variance before using it as a performance measure. Assume that a Sofiya purchasing manager has just negotiated a deal that results in a favourable price variance for materials. The deal could have achieved a favourable variance for any or all of three reasons:

1 The purchasing manager bargained effectively with suppliers.

2 The purchasing manager accepted lower-quality materials at a lower price.

3 The purchasing manager secured a discount for buying in bulk. However, she bought higher quantities than necessary for the short run, which resulted in excessive levels of stock.

If the purchasing manager's performance is evaluated solely on materials-price variances, then only reason 1 would be considered acceptable, and the evaluation will be positive. Reasons 2 and 3 would be considered unacceptable, and will probably cause the company to incur additional costs, such as higher materials scrap costs and higher storage costs, respectively.

Performance measures increasingly focus on reducing the total costs of the company as a whole. In the purchasing manager example, the company may ultimately lose more money because of reasons 2 and 3 than it gains from reason 1. Conversely, manufacturing costs may be deliberately increased (for example, because higher costs are paid for better materials or more direct manufacturing labour time) in order to obtain better product quality. In turn, the costs of the better product quality may be more than offset by reductions in customer service costs.

If any single performance measure (for example, a labour efficiency cost variance or a consumer rating report) receives excessive emphasis, managers tend to make decisions that maximise their own reported performance in terms of that single performance measure. Such actions may conflict with the organisation's overall goals. This faulty perspective on performance arises because top management has designed a performance measurement and reward system that does not adequately emphasise total organisational objectives.

Continuous improvement

Variances and flexible budgets can be used to measure specific types of performance goal such as continuous improvement. For example, continuous improvement can be readily incorporated into budgets and thus into variances by the use of a **continuous improvement budgeted cost**. This is a budgeted cost that is successively reduced over succeeding time periods. The budgeted direct materials cost for each jacket that Sofiya Company manufactured in April 2015 is €60 per unit. The budgeted cost used in variance analysis for subsequent periods could be based on a targeted 1% reduction each period:

Month	Prior month's budgeted amount	Reduction in budgeted amount	Revised budgeted amount
April 2015	–	–	€60.00
May 2015	€60.00	€0.600 (0.01 × €60.00)	59.40
June 2015	59.40	0.594 (0.01 × €59.40)	58.81
July 2015	58.81	0.588 (0.01 × €58.81)	58.22

The source of the 1% reduction in budgeted direct materials costs could be efficiency improvements or price reductions. By using continuous improvement budgeted costs, an organisation signals the importance of constantly seeking ways to reduce total costs. For example, managers could avoid unfavourable materials-efficiency variances by continuously reducing materials waste.

Products in the initial months of their production may have higher budgeted improvement rates than those that have been in production for, say, three years. Improvement opportunities may be much easier to identify when products have just started in production. Once the easy opportunities have been identified ('the low-hanging fruit picked'), much more ingenuity may be required to identify successive improvement opportunities.

Variance analysis and organisational learning

Organisations adopting a total value-chain approach to analysing variances are recognising the diversity of the possible sources of variances. Consider an unfavourable materials-efficiency variance in the production area of an organisation. Possible causes of this variance include:

- poor design of products or processes
- poor quality or inadequate availability of materials from suppliers
- poor work in the manufacturing area
- inadequate training of the workforce
- inappropriate assignment of labour or machines to specific jobs
- congestion due to scheduling a large number of rush orders.

This list is far from exhaustive. However, it does indicate that the cause of a variance in one part of the value chain (production in our example) can be actions taken in other parts of the value chain (such as product design or marketing). Note how improvements in early stages of the value chain (such as in product design) can sizably reduce the magnitude of variances in subsequent stages of the value chain.

The most important task in variance analysis is to understand why variances arise and then to use that knowledge to promote learning and improve performance. For instance, in the preceding list of examples, we may seek improvements in product design, in the timeliness of supplier deliveries, in the commitment of the manufacturing workforce to do the job right the first time, and so on. Variance analysis should not be a tool to play the blame game. Rather, it should be an essential ingredient that promotes learning in the organisation.

When to investigate variances

When should the causes of variances be investigated? Frequently, managers base their answer on subjective judgements, or rules of thumb. For critical items, a small variance may prompt a swift follow-up. For other items, a minimum euro variance or a certain percentage of variance from budget may be necessary to prompt an in-depth investigation. Of course, a 4% variance in direct materials costs of €1 million may deserve more attention than a 20% variance in repair costs of €10 000. Therefore, rules such as 'investigate all variances exceeding €5000 or 25% of budgeted cost, whichever is lower' are common. Variance analysis is subject to the same cost–benefit-context test as all other phases of a management control system. For instance, a change in management style can have an impact on reported variances and their repercussions.

Management accounting systems have traditionally implied that a budgeted amount is a single acceptable measure. Practically, managers realise that the budget is a band or range of possible acceptable outcomes and they consequently expect variances to fluctuate randomly within certain normal limits. By definition, a random variance *per se* is within this band or range and thus calls for no corrective action by managers. Random variances are attributable to chance rather than to management's implementation decisions.

Financial and non-financial performance measures

Almost all organisations use a combination of financial and non-financial performance measures rather than relying exclusively on either type. Consider our Sofiya Company illustration. In its cutting room, fabric is laid out and cut into pieces, which are then matched together and assembled. Control is often exercised at the cutting room level by focusing on non-financial measures such as the number of square metres of cloth used to produce 1000 jackets or the percentage of jackets started and completed without requiring any rework. Production managers at Sofiya are also likely to use financial measures to evaluate the overall cost efficiency with which operations are being run and to help guide decisions about, say, changing the mix of inputs used in manufacturing jackets. Financial measures are often critical in an organisation because they summarise the economic impact of diverse physical activities in a way managers readily understand. Moreover, managers are often evaluated on results measured against financial measures.

Concepts in action   Flexible budgets at Corning

Historically, the rule of business budgeting was simple: make a budget and stick to it. In today's fast-changing environment, however, many companies are pairing their annual 'static' budget with a flexible budget that adjusts for changes in the volume of activity. Corning, the 160-year-old maker of speciality glass and ceramics, uses a flexible budget to quickly accommodate the impact of significant changes that affect its business.

Each year, Corning pulls together its annual budget. While managers still work to make sure that budget is achieved, it cannot predict the actions of Corning's customers and competitors with 100% accuracy. For instance, Apple uses the company's scratch-resistant Gorilla Glass on its iPhone screens. If Apple decides to expedite the production of its newest iPhone model, Corning may have to unexpectedly ramp up its Gorilla Glass manufacturing, which has both unexpected costs and revenues. At Corning, management accountants and finance executives produce rolling forecasts each month to address what the company thinks will happen for the rest of the quarter. According to Tony Tripeny, Corning's senior vice president and corporate controller, 'Based on this analysis, we will go to the business units and say, "What are you going to do differently? What actions are you going to take, and how is that different from what we had assumed with the budget?"'

By using a flexible budget, Corning managers can analyse uncertainty, improve performance evaluation, and conduct useful variance analysis that helps the company stay on track. So, why does Corning develop a detailed budget at all? It has specific benefits, explains Tripeny. As an example, he cites the relationship of a budget to Corning's resolve to be the lowest-cost producer in its markets. 'During the budget process, we set up specific objectives, like targets for manufacturing costs,' he says. 'Even though the business might change during the year, it normally doesn't change enough to alter the manufacturing-performance targets. From a control standpoint, a budget still has value, but it shouldn't guide how you manage the business, which is about perceiving what's ahead and acting on it quicker than the competition.'

Sources: Pogue, D. (2010) 'Gorilla Glass, the smartphone's unsung hero', Pogue's Posts (blog), *New York Times*, 9 December, http://pogue.blogs.nytimes.com; Banham, R. (2011) 'Let it roll', *CFO Magazine*, May.

Flexible budgeting and activity-based costing

Activity-based costing (ABC) systems focus on individual activities as the fundamental cost objects. ABC systems classify the costs of various activities into a cost hierarchy: output-unit level, batch level, product sustaining and facility sustaining. The Winshuttle/ACCA survey of over 1800 companies across 108 countries reported that 'incremental', 'activity-based' and 'zero-based' budgeting were the top three budgeting methods used; 32% of companies had adopted activity-based budgeting. The two direct-cost categories in the Sofiya Company example discussed earlier in this chapter are examples of output-unit-level costs. In this section, we show how the basic principles and concepts of flexible budgets and variance analysis presented earlier in the chapter can be applied to other levels of the cost hierarchy. We focus on batch-level costs. Batch-level costs are resources sacrificed on activities that are related to a group of units of product(s) or service(s) rather than to each individual unit of product or service.

Relating batch costs to product output

Consider Lyco Brass Works, a manufacturer of decorative brass taps. Lyco specialises in manufacturing a tap called Jacutap used in jacuzzis. Lyco produces Jacutaps in batches. For each product line, Lyco dedicates materials-handling labour to bring materials to the manufacturing area, transport work in progress from one work centre to the next, and take the finished product to the shipping area. Hence materials-handling labour costs for Jacutaps are direct costs of Jacutaps. Because the materials for a batch are moved together, materials-handling labour costs vary with the number of batches rather than the number of units in a batch. Materials-handling labour costs are direct and variable batch-level costs.

Information regarding Jacutaps for 2015 follows:

	Static-budget amounts	Actual amounts
1 Units of Jacutaps produced and sold	180 000	151 200
2 Batch size (units per batch)	150	140
3 Number of batches (Line 1 ÷ Line 2)	1 200	1 080
4 Materials-handling labour-hours per batch	5	5.25
5 Total materials-handling labour-hours (Line 3 × Line 4)	6 000	5 670
6 Cost per materials-handling labour-hour	€14	€14.50
7 Total materials-handling labour cost (Line 5 × Line 6)	€84 000	€82 215

To prepare the flexible budget for materials-handling labour costs, Lyco starts with the actual units of output produced, 151 200 units, and proceeds in the following steps:

Step 1: Using the budgeted batch size, calculate the number of batches in which the actual output units should have been produced At the budgeted batch size of 150 units per batch, Lyco should have produced the 151 200 units of output in 1008 batches (151 200 ÷ 150).

Step 2: Using the budgeted materials-handling labour-hours per batch, calculate the number of materials-handling labour-hours that should have been used At the budgeted quantity of 5 hours per batch, 1008 batches should have required 5040 materials-handling labour-hours (1008 × 5).

Step 3: Using the budgeted cost per materials-handling labour-hour, calculate the flexible-budget amount for materials-handling labour-hours The flexible-budget amount is 5040 materials-handling labour-hours × €14, the budgeted cost per materials-handling labour-hour = €70 560.

Note how the flexible-budget calculations for materials-handling costs focus on batch-level quantities (materials-handling labour-hours) rather than on output-unit-level amounts (such as materials-handling labour-hours per unit of output). The flexible-budget variance can then be calculated as follows:

$$\text{Flexible-budget variance} = \text{Actual costs} - \text{Flexible-budget costs}$$
$$= 5670 \times €14.50 - 5040 \times €14$$
$$= €82\ 215 - €70\ 560$$
$$= €11\ 655\ \text{U}$$

The unfavourable variance indicates that materials-handling labour costs were €11 655 higher than the flexible-budget target.

Price and efficiency variances

Insight into the possible reasons for this €11 655 unfavourable variance can be gained by examining the price and efficiency components of the flexible-budget variance.

Price variance = (Actual price of input − Budgeted price of input) × Actual quantity of input
= (€14.50 − €14) × 5670 = €0.50 × 5670 = €2835 U

The unfavourable price variance for materials-handling labour indicates that the actual cost per materials-handling labour-hour (€14.50) exceeds the budgeted cost per materials-handling labour-hour (€14). This variance could be due to (1) Lyco's human resources manager negotiating less skilfully than was planned in the budget, or (2) wage rates increasing unexpectedly due to scarcity of labour.

$$\text{Efficiency variance} = \left(\begin{array}{c} \text{Actual} \\ \text{quantity of} \\ \text{input used} \end{array} - \begin{array}{c} \text{Budgeted quantity} \\ \text{of input allowed} \\ \text{for actual output} \end{array} \right) \times \begin{array}{c} \text{Budgeted} \\ \text{price} \\ \text{of input} \end{array}$$

$$= (5670 − 5040) \times €14$$
$$= 630 \times €14$$
$$= €8820 \text{ U}$$

The unfavourable efficiency variance indicates that the actual number of materials-handling labour-hours (5670) exceeded the number of materials-handling labour-hours that Lyco should have used (5040) for the number of units it produced. Two reasons for the unfavourable efficiency variance are (1) smaller actual batch sizes of 140 units instead of the budgeted batch sizes of 150 units; this results in Lyco producing the 151 200 units in 1080 batches instead of in 1008 (151 200 ÷ 150) batches; and (2) higher actual materials-handling labour-hours per batch of 5.25 hours instead of budgeted materials-handling labour-hours per batch of 5 hours.

Reasons for smaller-than-budgeted batch sizes could include (1) quality problems if batch sizes exceed 140 taps, or (2) high costs of carrying inventory.

Reasons for longer actual materials-handling labour-hours per batch could include (1) inefficient layout of the Jacutap product line relative to the plan, (2) materials-handling labour having to wait at work centres before picking up or delivering materials, (3) unmotivated or inexperienced employees, or (4) inappropriate materials-handling time standards.

Identifying the reasons for the efficiency variance helps Lyco's managers to develop a plan for improving materials-handling labour efficiency.

Focus on hierarchy

The key idea is to focus the flexible-budget quantity computations at the appropriate level of the cost hierarchy. Because materials handling is a batch-level cost, the flexible-budget quantity calculations focused at the batch level − the quantity of materials-handling labour-hours that Lyco should have used based on the number of batches it should have taken to produce the actual quantity of 151 200 units. If a cost had been a product-sustaining cost, the flexible-budget quantity computations would focus at the product-sustaining level.

An illustration of journal entries using standard costs

Control feature of standard costs

We now illustrate journal entries when standard costs are used. For illustrative purposes, we focus on direct materials and direct manufacturing labour.

We will continue with the data in the Sofiya Company illustration with one exception. Assume that during April 2015, Sofiya purchases 25 000 square metres of materials. Recall that the actual quantity used is 22 200 metres and that the standard quantity allowed for the actual output achieved is 20 000 metres. The actual purchase price was €31 per square metre, while the standard price was €30.

Note that in each of the following entries, unfavourable variances are always debits and favourable variances are always credits.

Entry 1a Isolate the direct materials price variance at the time of purchase by debiting Materials Control at standard prices. This is the earliest date possible to isolate this variance.

1a Materials control		
(25 000 metres × €30)	€750 000	
Direct materials price variance		
(25 000 metres × €1)	25 000	
Creditors control		
(25 000 metres × €31)		775 000
To record direct materials purchased.		

Entry 1b Isolate the direct materials efficiency variance at the time of usage by debiting Work-in-Progress Control at standard input quantities allowed for actual output units achieved at standard input prices.

1b Work-in-progress control		
(20 000 metres × €30)	€600 000	
Direct materials efficiency variance		
(2200 metres × €30)	66 000	
Materials control		
(22 200 metres × €30)		€666 000
To record direct materials used.		

Entry 2 Isolate the direct manufacturing labour price and efficiency variances at the time this labour is used by debiting Work-in-Progress Control at standard quantities allowed for actual output units achieved at standard input prices. Note that Wages Payable Control measures the payroll liability and hence is always at actual wage rates.

2 Work-in-progress control		
(8000 hours × €20)	€160 000	
Direct manufacturing labour price variance		
(9000 hours × €2)	18 000	
Direct manufacturing labour efficiency		
variance (1000 hours × €20)	20 000	
Wages payable control		
(9000 hours × €22)		€198 000
To record liability for direct manufacturing labour costs.		

A major advantage of this standard costing system is its emphasis on the control feature of standard costs. All variances are isolated at the earliest possible time, when managers can make informed decisions based on those variances.

End-of-period adjustments

Chapter 3 discussed two main approaches to recognising the under- or overallocated manufacturing overhead at the end of a period:

- the adjusted allocation-rate approach, which adjusts every job cost record for the difference between the allocated and actual indirect cost amounts;
- the proration approach, which makes adjustments to one or more of the following end-of-period account balances: materials, work in progress, finished goods and cost of goods sold.

Price and efficiency variances can also be disposed of using these same two approaches.

Benchmarking and variance analysis

The budgeted amounts in the variance formulas discussed in this chapter are *benchmarks* (points of reference from which comparisons may be made). The term **benchmarking** is often used to refer to the continuous process of measuring products, services and activities against the best levels of performance. These best levels of performance may be found in the organisation using internal benchmarking information or by using external benchmarks from competing organisations or from other organisations having similar processes. Consider Gillette, which is well known for its razor-blade products. Gillette sells five times as many blades as its nearest competitor. Given that the profit margin on razor blades is approximately 40% – the most profitable consumer product in the world – this category is clearly an important contributor to Gillette's overall corporate profits. The high profit margins are in part sustained by Gillette learning about the cost structure of its competitors. Gillette operates on a 'zero overhead growth' policy. This requires every Gillette division head to compare their division's costs with a top industry competitor. Each division must decide how to align itself with industry benchmarks. As a result, Human Resource costs have been found to exceed competitors' costs by 20% and its finance division costs are 30–40% higher. This has spurred Gillette divisions to seek ways of bringing down their overhead costs and to further heighten their profit margins as a result. Many consulting firms now also offer benchmarking services. Here we discuss information provided by one such service and then note how the variance computations discussed in this chapter can incorporate this information.

Market Insights (MI), based in Copenhagen, analyses cost information submitted by hospitals to various Danish regulatory bodies. MI develops benchmark reports that show how the cost level at one hospital compares with that at numerous other Danish hospitals. Reports can be prepared at the total hospital level (for example, cost per patient-day) or at a specific diagnostic-group level (for example, cardiology, orthopaedics or gynaecology cost per patient).

Exhibit 15.6 illustrates an MI report for a client hospital. Panel A shows that the client hospital's costs per case is 10% above the average for comparable hospitals. Panel B shows an extract of an MI report at the diagnostic-group level. This report shows that the client hospital has a cost per stroke patient of €33 700 compared with a market average among all hospitals of €31 300. The cost level at this client hospital is well above many hospitals. Cost benchmark reports are attention directing in nature. An individual hospital administrator may well be able to justify an above-average cost level by documenting above-average quality levels or revenue levels. However, in many cases, hospitals with above-average costs have no documentable superiority in their service quality levels, success in surgery operations or revenue per patient-day.

Exhibit 15.6 highlights how hospitals can differ sizably on costs. An administrator of a hospital with above-average costs potentially has much to learn from administrators at hospitals with below-average costs. Be cautious, however, in using benchmark reports such as Exhibit 15.6. The reliability of individual hospital cost data used in benchmark reports varies widely. Many hospitals have not invested heavily in refining their cost accounting systems. In addition, cost figures for individual diagnostic groups require numerous cost allocations, which also vary widely in reliability.

Cost reports like Exhibit 15.6 provide an external benchmark that forces the administrator to ask *why* cost levels differ among hospitals and *how* best practices can be transferred from the more efficient to the less efficient hospitals.

Evaluating the overall performance of a hospital or hospital personnel requires analysing other factors in addition to costs. These factors include the perceived quality of service to patients; the success rate of operations (for example, how many patients who have suffered a stroke survive?); and the morale of the doctors, nurses and other staff. In many cases, however, cost factors have been given too little weighting in the past, in part because of the lack of reliable information on cost relationships in this sector of the economy.

Benchmark reports based on the costs of other companies can be developed for many activities and products. For example, the Sofiya Company could estimate (possibly with the aid of consultants) the materials cost of the jackets manufactured by its competitors. The materials

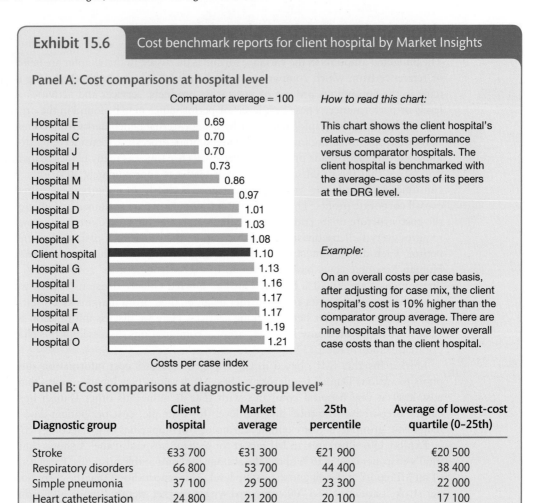

Exhibit 15.6 | Cost benchmark reports for client hospital by Market Insights

Panel A: Cost comparisons at hospital level

Comparator average = 100

Hospital	Costs per case index
Hospital E	0.69
Hospital C	0.70
Hospital J	0.70
Hospital H	0.73
Hospital M	0.86
Hospital N	0.97
Hospital D	1.01
Hospital B	1.03
Hospital K	1.08
Client hospital	1.10
Hospital G	1.13
Hospital I	1.16
Hospital L	1.17
Hospital F	1.17
Hospital A	1.19
Hospital O	1.21

Costs per case index

How to read this chart:

This chart shows the client hospital's relative-case costs performance versus comparator hospitals. The client hospital is benchmarked with the average-case costs of its peers at the DRG level.

Example:

On an overall costs per case basis, after adjusting for case mix, the client hospital's cost is 10% higher than the comparator group average. There are nine hospitals that have lower overall case costs than the client hospital.

Panel B: Cost comparisons at diagnostic-group level*

Diagnostic group	Client hospital	Market average	25th percentile	Average of lowest-cost quartile (0–25th)
Stroke	€33 700	€31 300	€21 900	€20 500
Respiratory disorders	66 800	53 700	44 400	38 400
Simple pneumonia	37 100	29 500	23 300	22 000
Heart catheterisation	24 800	21 200	20 100	17 100

* The cost amounts refer to the insurance premium per month that an insuree would have to pay to the client hospital.

cost estimate of the lowest cost competitor could be used as the budgeted amounts in its variance computations. An unfavourable materials efficiency variance would signal that Sofiya has a higher materials cost than 'best cost practice' in its industry. The magnitude of the cost difference would be of great interest to Sofiya. It could prompt Sofiya to do an extensive search into how to bring its own cost structure in line with that of the lowest in the industry.

Summary

The following points are linked to the chapter's learning objectives.

1   A static budget is a budget that is based on one level of output; when variances are calculated at the end of the accounting period, no adjustments are made to the amounts in the static budget. A flexible budget is a budget that is developed using budgeted revenue or cost amounts; when variances are calculated, the budgeted amounts are adjusted (flexed) to recognise the actual level of output and the actual quantities of the revenue and cost drivers. Flexible budgets help managers gain more insight into the causes of variances than do static budgets.

2 A five-step procedure can be used to develop a flexible budget. Where all costs are either variable with respect to output units or fixed, these five steps require only information about budgeted selling price, budgeted variable cost per output unit, budgeted fixed costs, and the actual quantity of output units achieved. The static-budget variance can be broken into a flexible-budget variance (the difference between the actual result and the flexible-budget amount) and a sales-volume variance. The sales-volume variance arises because the actual output units differ from the budgeted output units.

3 Budgeted input prices and input quantities can be developed from past data (with or without adjustments) or by developing standards based on time and motion studies, engineering studies, and so on. The computation of price variances and efficiency variances helps managers gain insight into two different (but not independent) aspects of performance. Price variances focus on the difference between actual and budgeted input prices. Efficiency variances focus on the difference between actual inputs used and the budgeted inputs allowed for the actual output achieved.

4 Price variances capture only one aspect of a manager's performance. Other aspects include the quality of the inputs the manager purchases and his or her ability to get suppliers to deliver on time.

5 Managers can use continuous improvement budgeted costs in their accounting system to highlight to all employees the importance of continuously seeking ways to reduce total costs and learning from variance investigations to improve organisational performance.

6 The Level 1, 2 and 3 framework can be applied to variance analysis of activity costs (such as set-up costs) to gain insight into why actual activity costs differ from those in the static budget or flexible budget. Interpreting cost variances for different activities requires an understanding of whether the costs are output-unit driven or are of a batch-level, product-sustaining or facility-sustaining kind.

7 Benchmarking is the continuous process of measuring products, services and activities against the best levels of performance. Benchmarking enables companies to use the best levels of performance within their organisation or by competitors or other external companies to gauge the performance of their own managers.

Key terms

benchmark (462)
standard (462)
static budget (463)
flexible budget (463)
favourable variance (463)
unfavourable variance (463)
flexible-budget variance (466)
sales-volume variance (466)
selling-price variance (467)
price variance (468)
input-price variance (468)

rate variance (468)
efficiency variance (468)
input-efficiency variance (468)
usage variance (468)
standard input (468)
standard cost (468)
effectiveness (475)
efficiency (475)
continuous improvement budgeted cost (475)
benchmarking (481)

CHAPTER 15

Assessment material

Review questions

15.1 What is a benchmark? Give an example of three types of benchmark of interest to managers.

15.2 What is the key question in deciding which variances should be calculated and analysed?

15.3 Why might managers find a Level 2 flexible-budget analysis more informative than a Level 1 static-budget analysis?

15.4 'Performance may be both effective and efficient, but either condition can occur without the other.' Do you agree? Give an example of effectiveness. Give an example of efficiency.

15.5 List four reasons for using standard costs.

15.6 Describe why direct materials price and direct materials efficiency variances may be calculated with reference to different points in time.

15.7 'There are many costs associated with acquiring and using materials over and above materials purchase costs.' Give three examples.

15.8 How might the continuous improvement theme be incorporated into the process of setting budgeted costs?

15.9 Why might an analyst examining variances in the production area look beyond that business function for explanations of those variances?

15.10 Comment on the following statement made by a plant supervisor: 'Meetings with my plant accountant are frustrating. All he wants to do is pin the blame for the many variances he reports.'

Exercises

Basic level

15.11 Flexible budget (20–30 minutes)

Abulafia Srl manufactures tyres for the Formula 1 motor racing circuit. For August 2015 Abulafia budgeted to manufacture and sell 3000 tyres at a variable cost of €74 per tyre and a total fixed cost of €54 000. The budgeted selling price was €110 per tyre. Actual results in August 2015 were 2800 tyres manufactured and sold at a selling price of €112 per tyre. The actual total variable costs were €229 600, and the actual total fixed costs were €50 000.

Required

1 Prepare a performance report (akin to Exhibit 15.3) that uses a flexible budget and a static budget.

2 Comment on the results in requirement 1.

*15.12 Materials and manufacturing labour variances (15 minutes)

Consider the following data collected for Helsingør:

	Direct materials	Direct manufacturing labour
Cost incurred: Actual inputs × actual prices	DKK 200 000	DKK 90 000
Actual inputs × standard prices	214 000	86 000
Standard inputs allowed for actual outputs × standard prices	225 000	80 000

Required

Calculate the price, efficiency and flexible-budget variances for direct materials and direct manufacturing labour.

15.13 Professional labour variances, efficiency comparisons (25–30 minutes)

Sharmila Khan is manager of TaxExperts.co.uk, a firm that provides assistance in the preparation of individual tax returns via the Internet. Because of the highly seasonal nature of her business, Sharmila employs staff on a monthly basis from two accounting placement firms – Professional Assist (PA) and Office Support (OS). In July 2015, TaxExperts.co.uk took on 12 staff members from PA and 10 from OS. PA is the prestige firm in its area. OS is a recently formed firm.

Sharmila budgets the following for July 2015:

	PA staff	OS staff
Budgeted hourly rate	£45	£40
Budgeted time per tax return in hours	0.40	0.50

Actual results for July 2015 were as follows:

	PA staff	OS staff
Actual hourly rate	£48	£42
Actual time per tax return in hours	0.42	0.46
Number of tax returns completed	4608	3600

Required

1 Calculate professional labour price and efficiency variances for (a) the 12 PA staff, and (b) the 10 OS staff employed in July 2015.

2 Comment on the efficiency of the PA and OS staff TaxExperts.co.uk employed.

3 What factors other than efficiency might Khan consider in deciding whether to employ staff from PA or OS?

15.14 Comprehensive variance analysis (30–40 minutes)

AKEI is an elite desk manufacturer. At the start of May 2015, the following budgeted unit amounts (based on a standard costing system) related to its manufacture of executive desks (made out of oak):

Direct materials: 16 square metres of oak per desk at €20 per square metre

Direct manufacturing labour: 3 hours per desk at €30 per direct manufacturing labour-hour

Budgeted production for May 2015 was 700 executive desks. There were no opening stocks of direct materials or finished goods on 1 May 2015. Work in progress is minimal.

Actual results for May 2015 are as follows:

Direct materials purchased (12 640 square metres)	€259 120
Direct materials used (11 850 square metres)	?
Direct manufacturing labour (2325 hours at €31 per hour)	?

Actual production in May 2015 is 750 executive desk units. The purchase price for oak wood remained unchanged throughout May 2015.

Required

1 Prepare a detailed flexible-budget variance analysis for May 2015 covering direct materials and direct manufacturing labour.

2 Give two explanations for each of the variances you calculate in requirement 1.

Intermediate level

15.15 **Flexible budget** (15 minutes)

The budgeted prices for direct materials, direct manufacturing labour and direct marketing (distribution) labour per attaché case are €40, €8 and €12, respectively. The chairman is pleased with the following performance report:

	Actual costs	Static budget	Variance
Direct materials	€364 000	€400 000	€36 000 F
Direct manufacturing labour	78 000	80 000	2 000 F
Direct marketing (distribution) labour	110 000	120 000	10 000 F

Required

Actual output was 8800 attaché cases. Is the chairman's pleasure justified? Prepare a revised performance report that uses a flexible budget and a static budget. Assume all three direct costs items are variable costs.

15.16 **Price and efficiency variances** (20–30 minutes)

Ched Ltd manufactures Cheddar cheese pies. For January 2015, it budgeted to purchase and use 15 000 kg of Cheddar cheese at £0.89 per kg; budgeted output was 60 000 pies. Actual purchase and use for January 2015 was 16 000 kg at £0.82 per kg; actual output was 60 800 pies.

Required

1 Calculate the flexible-budget variance.

2 Calculate the price and efficiency variances.

3 Comment on the results in requirements 1 and 2.

15.17 **Flexible budget preparation and analysis** (25–30 minutes)

Norland-Norge AS produces corporate notebooks. Each notebook is designed for an individual customer. The company's operating budget for September 2015 included these data:

Number of notebooks	15 000
Selling price per book	NKR 20
Variable costs per book	NKR 8
Total fixed costs for the month	NKR 145 000

The actual results for September 2015 were:

Number of notebooks produced and sold	12 000
Average selling price per book	NKR 21
Variable costs per book	NKR 7
Total fixed costs for the month	NKR 150 000

The managing director of the company observed that the operating profit for September was much less than anticipated, despite a higher-than-budgeted selling price and a lower-than-budgeted variable cost per unit. You have been asked to provide explanations for the disappointing September results.

Norland-Norge develops its flexible budget on the basis of budgeted revenue per output unit and variable costs per output without a detailed analysis of budgeted inputs.

Required

1 Prepare a Level 1 analysis of the September performance.

2 Prepare a Level 2 analysis of the September performance.

3 Why might Norland-Norge find the Level 2 analysis more informative than the Level 1 analysis? Explain your answer.

15.18 **Price and efficiency variances, journal entries** (30 minutes)

Drogheda Chemical Ltd has set up the following standards per finished output unit for direct materials and direct manufacturing labour.

Direct materials: 10 kg at €3.00 per kg	€30.00
Direct manufacturing labour: 0.5 hour at €20.00 per hour	€10.00

The number of finished output units budgeted for March 2015 was 10 000; 9810 units were actually produced.
Actual results in March 2015 were:

Direct materials: 98 073 kg used	
Direct manufacturing labour: 4900 hours	€102 900

Assume that there were no opening stocks of either direct materials or finished units.

During the month, materials purchases amounted to 100 000 kg, at a total cost of €310 000. Price variances are isolated upon purchase. Efficiency variances are isolated at the time of usage.

Required

1 Calculate the March 2015 price and efficiency variances of direct materials and direct manufacturing labour. Comment on these variances.

2 Prepare journal entries to record the variances in requirement 1.

3 Why might Drogheda Chemical Ltd calculate materials price variances and materials efficiency variances with reference to different points in time?

15.19 **Continuous improvement** (continuation of Exercise 15.18) (20 minutes)

Drogheda Chemical adopts a continuous improvement approach to setting monthly standards' costs. Assume the direct materials standard quantity input of 10 kg per output unit and the direct manufacturing labour quantity input of 0.5 hours per output unit pertain to January 2015. The standard amounts for February 2015 are 0.997 of the January standard amount. The standard amounts for March 2015 are 0.997 of the February standard amount. Assume the same information for March 2015 as in Exercise 15.18 except for these revised standard amounts.

Required

1 Calculate the March 2015 standard quantity input amounts per output unit for direct materials and direct manufacturing labour.

2 Calculate the March 2015 price and efficiency variances of direct materials and direct manufacturing labour.

*15.20 Flexible-budget preparation (20–30 minutes)

The managing partner of Hoofdorp Music Box Fabricators has become aware of the disadvantages of static budgets. She asks you to prepare a flexible budget for October 2015 for the main style of music box. The following partial data are available for the actual operations in August 2015 (a recent typical month):

Boxes produced and sold	4 500
Direct material costs	€90 000
Direct manufacturing labour costs	€67 500
Depreciation and other fixed manufacturing costs	€50 700
Average selling price per box	€70
Fixed marketing costs	€81 350

Assume no opening or closing stocks of music boxes.

A 10% increase in the selling price is expected in October. The only variable marketing cost is a commission of €5.50 per unit paid to the manufacturers' representatives, who bear all their own costs of travelling, entertaining customers, and so on. A patent royalty of €2 per box manufactured is paid to an independent design firm. Salary increases that will become effective in October are €12 000 per year for the production supervisor and €15 000 per year for the sales manager. A 10% increase in direct materials prices is expected to become effective in October. No changes are expected in direct manufacturing labour wage rates or in the productivity of the direct manufacturing labour personnel. Hoofdorp uses a normal costing system and does not have standard costs for any of its inputs.

Required

1 Prepare a flexible budget for October 2015, showing budgeted amounts at each of three output levels of music boxes: 4000, 5000 and 6000 units. (Use the flexible-budget approach of developing budgeted revenue and variable costs on a budgeted per output unit basis.)

2 Why might Hoofdorp Music Box Fabricators find a flexible budget more useful than a static budget? Explain.

15.21 Flexible-budget variances for finance function activities (30 minutes)

Sam Chase is the Finance Director of Flowers.co.ke, an Internet company that enables customers to order home deliveries of flowers by accessing its website. Flowers.co.ke has a network of florists ('strategic partners') who do the physical delivery of flowers. Flowers.co.ke has a group of representatives that continually visit florists and nurseries. This group monitors product and service quality and explores new products or new partners.

Chase is concerned with the efficiency and effectiveness of the finance function at Flowers.co.ke. He collects the following information for three finance activities in 2015:

Finance activity	Activity measure	Budgeted total cost of activity	Budgeted total volume of activity	Actual cost of process	Actual total volume of activity
Creditors	Number of invoices	KSh580 000	200 000	KSh594 020	212 150
Debtors	Number of remittances	639 000	1 000 000	711 000	948 000
Travel and expenses	Number of expense reports	15 200	2 000	13 986	1 890

The budgeted amounts are based on an analysis of costs in past periods at Flowers.co.ke. The output measure is the number of deliveries, which is assumed to be the same as the number of remittances. Debtors is an output-unit-level-driven cost, whereas creditors and travel and expense are batch-driven costs.

Required

1 Prepare a flexible-budget-based report explaining difference between budgeted and actual costs for each of the three finance activities in 2015. Comment on the results.

2 Why might the variances computed in requirement 1 pertain to efficiency but not effectiveness?

3 How might Chase monitor the effectiveness of the three finance processes in this exercise?

15.22 Finance function activities, benchmarking (continuation of Exercise 15.21) (20 minutes)

Sam Chase of Flowers.co.ke receives a brochure from the Hackett Group, a consulting firm specialising in benchmarking. He asks the Hackett Group to provide benchmark data from its recent study of the finance function at over 100 retail companies (both traditional retail and Internet-based retail). Hacketts' 'world-class' cost benchmarks for Flowers.co.ke's three finance activities are:

Finance activity	World-class cost performance
Creditors	KSh0.71 per invoice
Debtors	KSh0.10 per remittance
Travel and expenses	KSh1.58 per expense report

Required

1 What new insights might arise with the Hackett benchmark data using the budgeted amounts in Exercise 15.21?

2 Assume you are in charge of travel and expense report processing. What concerns might you have with Sam Chase using the Hackett benchmark of KSh1.58 per expense report as the key to evaluate your performance next period?

15.23 Price and efficiency variances, problems in standard setting, benchmarking (30–40 minutes)

Poitou-Chemises SARL manufactures shirts for retail chains. Armand Plessis, the accountant, is becoming increasingly disenchanted with Poitou-Chemises' six-month-old standard costing system. The budgeted amounts for both its direct materials and direct manufacturing labour are drawn from its standard costing system. The budgeted and actual amounts for July 2015 were:

	Budgeted	Actual
Shirts manufactured	4 000	4 488
Direct materials cost	€20 000	€20 196
Direct materials units used (rolls of cloth)	400	408
Direct manufacturing labour costs	€18 000	€18 462
Direct manufacturing labour-hours	1 000	1 020

There were no opening or closing stocks of materials.

Armand observes that in the past six months he has rarely seen an unfavourable variance of any magnitude. The standard costing system is based on a study of the operations conducted by an independent consultant. He decides to play detective and makes some unobtrusive observations of the workforce at the plant. He notes that even at their current output levels, the workers seem to have a lot of time to discuss football, sitcoms and cooking recipes.

At a recent industry conference on 'Benchmarking and Competitiveness', Françoise Daubigné, the accountant of Textiles-Georges-Grassens, told Armand that Textiles-Georges-Grassens had employed the same independent consultant to design a standard costing system. However, the company dismissed him after two weeks because Textiles-Georges-Grassens employees quickly became aware of the consultant observing their work.

At the industry conference, Armand participated in seminars on 'benchmarking for the fabric industry'. A consultant for France-Solutions SA showed how she could develop six-month benchmark reports on the estimated costs of Poitou-Chemises' major competitors. She indicated that she was already examining the estimated cost of shirts manufactured by the four largest importers into Europe. These importers had taken much business from Poitou-Chemises in recent years. This information would soon be available by subscribing to the France-Solutions monthly service.

Required

1 Calculate the price and efficiency variances of Poitou-Chemises for direct materials and direct manufacturing labour in July 2015.

2 Describe the types of action the employees at Textiles-Georges-Grassens may have taken to reduce the accuracy of the standards set by the independent consultant. Why would employees take those actions? Is this behaviour ethical?

3 Describe how Poitou-Chemises might use information from France-Solutions when computing the variances in requirement 1.

4 Discuss the pros and cons of Poitou-Chemises using the France-Solutions information to increase its cost competitiveness.

Advanced level

*15.24 Flexible budget preparation, service sector (45 minutes)

Münzel GmbH helps prospective homeowners of substantial means to find low-cost financing and assists existing homeowners in refinancing their current loans at lower interest rates. Münzel works only for customers with excellent borrowing potential. Hence, Münzel is able to obtain a loan for every customer with whom it decides to work.

Münzel charges clients 0.5% of the loan amount it arranges. In 2013, the average loan amount per customer was €199 000. In 2014, the average loan amount was €200 210. In its 2015 flexible budgeting system, Münzel assumes the average loan amount will be €200 000.

Budgeted cost data per loan application for 2015 are:

- Professional labour: 6 budgeted hours at a budgeted rate of €40 per hour
- Loan filing fees: budgeted at €100 per loan application
- Credit checks: budgeted at €120 per loan application
- Courier mailings: budgeted at €50 per loan application.

Office support (the costs of leases, secretarial workers and others) is budgeted to be €31 000 per month. Münzel GmbH views this amount as a fixed cost.

Required

1 Prepare a static budget for November 2015 assuming 90 loan applications.

2 Actual loan applications in November 2015 were 120. Other actual data for November 2015 were:

- Professional labour: 7.2 hours per loan application at €42 per hour
- Loan filing fees: €100 per loan application
- Credit checks: €125 per loan application
- Courier mailings: €54 per loan application.

Office support costs for November 2015 were €33 500. The average loan amount for November 2015 was €224 000. Münzel received its 0.5% fee on all loans. Prepare a Level 2 variance analysis of Münzel GmbH for November 2015. Münzel's output measure in its flexible budgeting system is the number of loan applications.

3 Calculate professional labour price and efficiency variances for November 2015. (Calculate labour price on a per-hour basis.)

4 What factors would you consider in evaluating the effectiveness of professional labour in November 2015?

CHAPTER 16

Flexible budgets, variances and management control: II

Overhead or indirect costs are a major area of concern for many organisations. Chemical, paper, steel and telecommunications companies, for example, incur sizable costs to construct and maintain their physical plant and equipment and other aspects of their infrastructure. Such costs are included in the indirect costs of the individual products or services they produce and sell. Companies like Amazon.co.uk, eBay.com and Facebook.com invest large amounts in software that enable them to provide a broad range of services to their customers. These costs are part of their overhead costs. This chapter covers methods of planning and controlling overhead costs, allocating these costs to products, and analysing overhead variances.

The previous chapter emphasised the direct cost categories of direct materials and direct manufacturing labour. Here, the overhead categories of variable and fixed manufacturing overhead are stressed. Please proceed slowly as you study this chapter. Trace the data to the analysis in a systematic way. In particular, note how fixed manufacturing overhead is accounted for in one way for the planning and control purpose and in a different way for the stock costing purpose.

Learning objectives

After studying this chapter, you should be able to:

- Explain differences in the planning of variable-overhead costs and the planning of fixed-overhead costs

- Explain the computation and meaning of spending and efficiency variances for variable overhead

- Illustrate how to compute the budgeted fixed-overhead rate

- Give two reasons why the production-volume variance may not be a good measure of the opportunity cost of unused capacity

- Explain how a 4-variance analysis can provide an integrated overview of overhead cost variances

- Explain the differing roles of cost allocation bases for fixed manufacturing overhead when (a) planning and controlling, and (b) valuing stock

- Prepare journal entries for variable- and fixed-overhead variances

- Explain how the flexible-budget variance approach can be used in activity-based costing and why managers frequently use both financial and non-financial variables to plan and control overhead costs.

Planning of variable- and fixed-overhead costs

We continue the Chapter 15 analysis of the Sofiya Company. Chapter 15 illustrated how a static-budget variance can be divided into a flexible-budget variance and a sales-volume variance. This chapter focuses on understanding flexible-budget variances for overhead costs and their causes.

Sofiya's cost structure illustrates why it views the planning of overhead costs as important. The following percentages of total static-budget costs (see column 4 of Exhibit 15.2) are based on Sofiya's budget for 12 000 output units for April 2015:

	Variable overhead costs	Fixed overhead costs	Total overhead costs
Manufacturing	7.59%	14.54%	22.13%
Marketing	3.16	22.87	26.03
Total	10.75%	37.41%	48.16%

Total overhead costs amount to almost half (48.16%) of Sofiya's total budgeted costs at 12 000 output units for April 2015. Clearly, Sofiya can greatly improve its profitability by effective planning of its overhead costs, both variable and fixed.

Planning variable-overhead costs

Among Sofiya's variable manufacturing overhead costs are energy, engineering support, indirect materials and indirect manufacturing labour. Effective planning of variable overhead costs involves undertaking only value-added variable-overhead activities and then managing the cost drivers of those activities in the most efficient way. A **value-added cost** is one that, if eliminated, would reduce the value customers obtain from using the product or service. A **non-value-added cost** is one that, if eliminated, would not reduce the value customers obtain from using the product or service. Consider the cost of sewing needles used in the sewing of jackets manufactured by Sofiya. Sewing is an essential element of manufacturing a jacket. Hence, costs associated with sewing (for example, sewing needles) would be classified as adding value. In contrast, consider the cost of a warehouse that stores rolls of cloth to be used in case of an emergency (if, say, a supplier fails to meet the delivery schedule). A jacket sewn from cloth stored in a warehouse is no different from a jacket sewn from cloth delivered by a supplier directly to the production floor. Hence, costs associated with warehousing are likely to be viewed as 'non-value-adding'. There is a continuum between value-added costs and non-value-added costs. Many overhead cost items are in a grey, uncertain area between value-adding and non-value-adding costs.

Planning fixed-overhead costs

Effective planning of fixed-overhead costs includes undertaking only value-added fixed-overhead activities and then determining the appropriate level for those activities. For Sofiya, examples in manufacturing include depreciation or leasing costs on plant and equipment, some administrative costs (for example, the plant manager's salary), and property taxes. Frequently, the most critical issue is how much plant and equipment to acquire. Consider Sofiya's leasing of weaving machines, each of which has a fixed cost per year. Failure to lease sufficient machine capacity will result in an inability to meet demand and thus in lost sales of jackets. In contrast, if Sofiya greatly overestimates demand, it will incur additional fixed leasing costs on machines that are not fully utilised during the year.

At the start of an accounting period, management will probably have made most of the key decisions that determine the level of fixed-overhead costs to be incurred. In contrast, day-to-day, ongoing management decisions play a larger role in determining the level of variable-overhead costs incurred in that period.

Sofiya company data

The Sofiya Company summary information for April 2015 that we use in this chapter is as follows:

Overhead category	Actual results	Flexible-budget amount (for 10 000 output units)	Static-budget amount (for 12 000 output units)
Variable manufacturing overhead	€130 500	€120 000	€144 000
Fixed manufacturing overhead	285 000	276 000	276 000
Variable marketing overhead	45 700	50 000	60 000
Fixed marketing overhead	420 000	434 000	434 000

Developing budgeted variable-overhead rates

Sofiya uses a three-step approach when developing its variable-overhead rate:

Step 1: Identify the costs to include in the variable-overhead cost pool(s) Sofiya groups all of its variable manufacturing overhead costs in a single cost pool. Costs in this pool include energy, engineering support, indirect materials and indirect manufacturing labour.

Step 2: Select the cost allocation base(s) Sofiya's operating managers believe that machine-hours are an important driver of variable manufacturing overhead costs and decided to use this measure as the cost allocation base.

Step 3: Estimate the budgeted variable-overhead rate(s) Several approaches can be used in this step. One approach is to adjust the past actual variable-overhead cost rate per unit of the allocation base – for example, an adjustment to take into account expected inflation. A second approach is to use standard costing.

Sofiya uses the standard costing approach to develop its April 2015 budgeted variable-overhead cost rate of €30 per machine-hour and also its budgeted machine-hour rate of 0.40 hours per actual output unit. These input amounts are used to calculate the budgeted variable manufacturing overhead rate per unit:

$$\begin{array}{l} \text{Budgeted inputs allowed} \\ \text{per output unit} \end{array} \times \begin{array}{l} \text{Budgeted costs per} \\ \text{input unit} \end{array} = 0.40 \times €30$$
$$= €12 \text{ per output unit}$$

Variable-overhead cost variances

We now illustrate how the budgeted variable manufacturing overhead rate is used in computing Sofiya's variable manufacturing overhead cost variances. The following data are for April 2015:

Cost item/allocation base	Actual results	Flexible-budget amount (for 10 000 output units)	Static-budget amount (for 12 000 output units)
1 Variable manufacturing overhead costs	€130 500	€120 000	€144 000
2 Variable manufacturing overhead costs per machine-hour [(1) ÷ (5)]	29	30	30
3 Variable manufacturing overhead costs per output unit [(1) ÷ (4)]	13.05	12	12
4 Output units (jackets)	10 000	10 000	12 000
5 Machine-hours	4 500	4 000	4 800

Static-budget and flexible-budget analyses

The Level 1 static-budget variance for variable manufacturing overhead cost is shown in Exhibit 16.1:

$$\frac{\text{Variable-overhead}}{\text{static-budget variance}} = \frac{\text{Actual}}{\text{results}} - \frac{\text{Static-budget}}{\text{amount}} = €130\ 500 - €144\ 000$$
$$= €13\ 500\ \text{F}$$

Additional insight into the ability of Sofiya's managers to control variable manufacturing overhead can be gained by moving to the Level 2 flexible-budget analysis also shown in Exhibit 16.1. The budgeted amounts in Level 2 recognise that 10 000 output units were produced instead of the budgeted 12 000 output units. The April 2015 flexible budget for variable manufacturing overhead is €120 000 (0.4 × 10 000 × €30).

The variable manufacturing overhead sales-volume variance arises solely because the actual number of output units sold by Sofiya differs from the budgeted number of output units sold:

$$\frac{\text{Variable-overhead}}{\text{sales-volume variance}} = \frac{\text{Flexible-budget}}{\text{amount}} - \frac{\text{Static-budget}}{\text{amount}} = €120\ 000 - €144\ 000$$
$$= €24\ 000\ \text{F}$$

Exhibit 16.1	Static- and flexible-budget analysis of variable manufacturing overhead costs for the Sofiya Company for April 2015

Level 1 analysis

	Actual results (1)	Static-budget variance (2) = (1) – (3)	Static budget (3)
Cost driver: Number of units manufactured	10 000	2000 U*	12 000
Variable manufacturing overhead			(0.40 × 12 000 × €30)
	€130 500		€144 000

€13 500 F

Static-budget variance

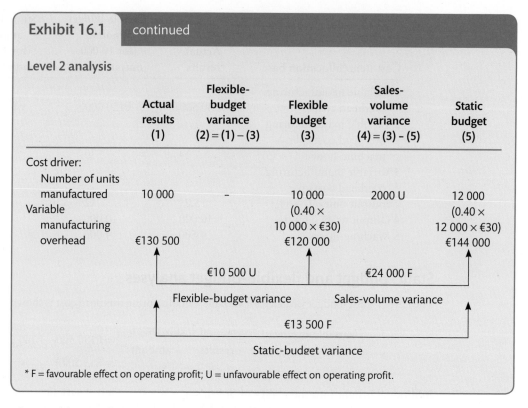

Exhibit 16.1   continued

Level 2 analysis

	Actual results (1)	Flexible-budget variance (2) = (1) − (3)	Flexible budget (3)	Sales-volume variance (4) = (3) − (5)	Static budget (5)
Cost driver: Number of units manufactured	10 000	–	10 000	2000 U	12 000
Variable manufacturing overhead	€130 500		(0.40 × 10 000 × €30) €120 000		(0.40 × 12 000 × €30) €144 000

€10 500 U   €24 000 F

Flexible-budget variance   Sales-volume variance

€13 500 F

Static-budget variance

* F = favourable effect on operating profit; U = unfavourable effect on operating profit.

The variable manufacturing overhead flexible-budget variance arises because Sofiya's actual variable manufacturing overhead cost differs from that budgeted for the actual output units sold:

$$\frac{\text{Variable-overhead}}{\text{flexible-budget variance}} = \frac{\text{Actual}}{\text{results}} - \frac{\text{Flexible-budget}}{\text{amount}} = €130\ 500 - €120\ 000$$
$$= €10\ 500\ \text{U}$$

This €10 500 unfavourable flexible-budget variance shows that Sofiya's actual variable manufacturing overhead exceeded the flexible-budget amount by €10 500 for the 10 000 jackets actually produced in April 2015.

We now discuss how managers can gain additional insight by splitting the Level 2 variable manufacturing overhead flexible-budget variance into its Level 3 efficiency and price (labelled *spending* when dealing with overhead) variances. Exhibit 16.2 is the columnar presentation of these Level 3 efficiency and spending variances.

Variable-overhead efficiency variance

The **variable-overhead efficiency variance** measures the efficiency with which the cost allocation base is used. The formula is:

$$\begin{pmatrix} \text{Variable-} \\ \text{overhead} \\ \text{efficiency} \\ \text{variance} \end{pmatrix} = \begin{pmatrix} \text{Actual units of} \\ \text{variable-overhead} \\ \text{cost allocation base} \\ \text{used for actual} \\ \text{output units} \\ \text{achieved} \end{pmatrix} - \begin{pmatrix} \text{Budgeted units of} \\ \text{variable-overhead} \\ \text{cost allocation base} \\ \text{allowed for actual} \\ \text{output units} \\ \text{achieved} \end{pmatrix} \times \begin{pmatrix} \text{Budgeted} \\ \text{variable-overhead} \\ \text{cost allocation rate} \end{pmatrix}$$

$$= [4500 - (10\,000 \times 0.40)] \times €30$$
$$= (4500 - 4000) \times €30 = 500 \times €30$$
$$= €15\,000\ \text{U}$$

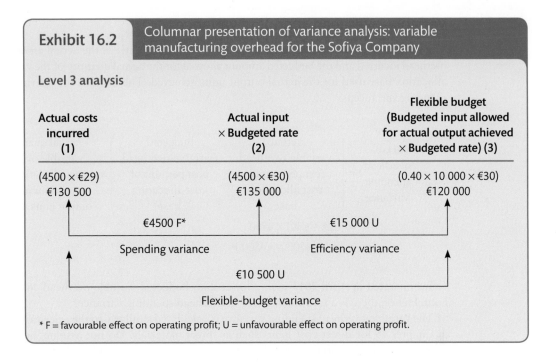

Exhibit 16.2 Columnar presentation of variance analysis: variable manufacturing overhead for the Sofiya Company

Level 3 analysis

Actual costs incurred (1)	Actual input × Budgeted rate (2)	Flexible budget (Budgeted input allowed for actual output achieved × Budgeted rate) (3)
(4500 × €29) €130 500	(4500 × €30) €135 000	(0.40 × 10 000 × €30) €120 000

€4500 F*   Spending variance

€15 000 U   Efficiency variance

€10 500 U

Flexible-budget variance

* F = favourable effect on operating profit; U = unfavourable effect on operating profit.

The variable-overhead efficiency variance is calculated similarly to the efficiency variance described in Chapter 15 for direct-cost items. But the interpretation of the Chapter 15 and 16 efficiency variances differs. In Chapter 15, input-efficiency variances for direct-cost items are based on differences between actual inputs used and the budgeted inputs allowed for actual outputs achieved. In Chapter 16 efficiency variances for variable-overhead costs are based on the efficiency with which the *cost allocation base* is used. Sofiya's unfavourable variable-overhead efficiency variance of €15 000 means that actual machine-hours (the cost allocation base) were higher than the budgeted machine-hours allowed to manufacture 10 000 jackets. Possible causes of this higher-than-budgeted machine-hour usage include the following:

- Sofiya's workers were less skilful in the use of machines than budgeted.
- Sofiya's production scheduler inefficiently scheduled jobs, resulting in higher than budgeted machine usage.
- Sofiya's machines were not maintained in good operating condition.
- Budgeted machine time standards were set without careful analysis of the operating conditions.
- Sofiya promised a distributor a rushed delivery, which resulted in higher machine usage than budgeted.

Management's response to this €15 000 unfavourable variance would be guided by which cause(s) best describes the April 2015 results.

The use of cotton thread for sewing jackets illustrates the difference between the efficiency variance for direct-cost inputs and the efficiency variance for variable-overhead cost categories. If Sofiya classifies cotton thread as a direct-cost item, the direct materials efficiency variance will indicate whether more or less cotton thread per jacket is used than was budgeted for the actual output achieved. In contrast, if Sofiya classifies cotton thread as an indirect-cost item, the variable manufacturing overhead efficiency variance will indicate whether Sofiya used more or fewer machine-hours (the cost allocation base for variable manufacturing overhead) than were budgeted for the actual output achieved. Any variation in cotton thread usage other than that budgeted to vary with respect to machine-hours will be shown in the variable manufacturing overhead spending variance.

Variable-overhead spending variance

The **variable-overhead spending variance** is the difference between the actual amount of variable overhead incurred and the budgeted amount allowed for the actual quantity of the variable-overhead allocation base used for the actual output units achieved. The formula for the variable-overhead spending variance is:

$$\begin{array}{l}\text{Variable-}\\\text{overhead}\\\text{spending}\\\text{variance}\end{array} = \left(\begin{array}{c}\text{Actual}\\\text{variable-overhead}\\\text{cost per unit of}\\\text{cost allocation}\\\text{base}\end{array} - \begin{array}{c}\text{Budgeted}\\\text{variable-overhead}\\\text{cost per unit of}\\\text{cost allocation}\\\text{base}\end{array}\right) \times \begin{array}{c}\text{Actual quanitty of}\\\text{variable-overhead}\\\text{cost allocation base}\\\text{used for actual}\\\text{output units achieved}\end{array}$$

$$= (€29 - €30) \times 4500$$

$$= -€1 \times 4500 = €4500 \text{ F}$$

Sofiya operated in April 2015 with a lower-than-budgeted variable-overhead cost per machine-hour. Hence, there is a favourable variable-overhead spending variance.

The variable-overhead spending variance is calculated similarly to the price variance described in Chapter 15 for direct-cost items such as direct materials. Do not assume, however, that the causes of these two variances are the same. Two main causes could explain a variable-overhead spending variance of €4500 F at Sofiya:

- **Cause A.** The actual prices of individual items included in variable overhead differ from their budgeted prices – for example, the April 2015 purchase price of energy, indirect materials or indirect manufacturing labour was less than budgeted prices.

- **Cause B.** The actual usage of individual items included in variable overhead differs from the budgeted usage – for example, the budgeted usage of energy, indirect materials or indirect manufacturing labour was less than the usage assumed in setting the €30 budgeted variable manufacturing overhead rate per machine-hour.

Cause A has implications for the purchasing area of Sofiya. Cause B has implications for the production area of Sofiya. Distinguishing between these two causes for a variable-overhead spending variance requires detailed information about the budgeted prices and the budgeted quantities of the individual line items in the variable-overhead cost pool.

The following is a summary of the variable manufacturing overhead variances calculated in this section.

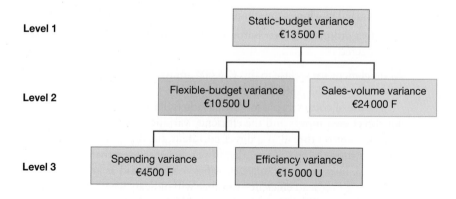

The key cause of Sofiya's unfavourable flexible-budget variance is that the actual use of machine-hours is higher than budgeted.

Developing budgeted fixed-overhead rates

Fixed-overhead costs are, by definition, a lump sum that does not change in total despite changes in a cost driver. While total fixed costs are frequently included in flexible budgets, they remain the same total amount within the relevant range regardless of the output level chosen to 'flex' the variable costs and revenues. The three steps in developing Sofiya Company's budgeted fixed-overhead rate are as follows.

Step 1: Identify the costs in the fixed-overhead cost pool(s)   This is the numerator of the budgeted rate computation. For Sofiya, fixed manufacturing overhead costs include depreciation, plant-leasing costs, property taxes, plant manager's salary and some administrative costs, all of which are included in a single cost pool. Sofiya's budget is €276 000 for April 2015.

Step 2: Estimate the budgeted quantity of the allocation base(s)   This is the denominator of the budgeted rate computation. It is termed the **denominator level**. Sofiya uses machine-hours as its allocation base. It budgets to manufacture 12 000 jackets in April 2011. The budgeted number of machine-hours to manufacture 12 000 jackets is 4800 (12 000 × 0.40 budgeted machine-hours per output unit).

Step 3: Calculate the budgeted fixed-overhead rate(s)

$$\frac{\text{Budgeted fixed-overhead rate per unit of allocation base}}{} = \frac{\text{Budgeted fixed-overhead costs}}{\text{Budgeted quantity of allocation base units}} = \frac{\text{€276 000}}{\text{4800 machine-hours}}$$

$$= \text{€57.50 per machine-hours}$$

In manufacturing settings, the denominator level is commonly termed the **production denominator level** or the **production denominator volume**.

Fixed-overhead cost variances

The Level 1 static-budget variance for Sofiya's fixed manufacturing overhead is €9000 U:

$$\frac{\text{Fixed-overhead static-budget variance}}{} = \frac{\text{Actual results}}{} - \frac{\text{Static-budget amount}}{}$$
$$= \text{€285 000} - \text{€276 000}$$
$$= \text{€9000 U}$$

The actual results for fixed manufacturing overhead are in Exhibit 15.2. The static-budget amount for fixed manufacturing overhead is based on 12 000 output units. Given that it is for a fixed cost, this same €276 000 would be the budgeted amount for all output levels in the relevant range. There is no 'flexing' of fixed costs.

The formula for the fixed manufacturing overhead flexible-budget variance is as follows:

$$\frac{\text{Fixed-overhead flexible-budget variance}}{} = \frac{\text{Actual results}}{} - \frac{\text{Flexible-budget amount}}{}$$
$$= \text{€285 000} - \text{€276 000}$$
$$= \text{€9000 U}$$

The fixed-overhead flexible-budget variance is the same as the fixed-overhead static-budget variance. Why? Because there is no 'flexing' of fixed costs. For Level 3 analysis (decomposing the flexible-budget variance into its efficiency and spending components), all of the flexible-budget variance is attributed to the spending variance because this is precisely why this variance arises for fixed costs.

The €9000 unfavourable variance simply means that Sofiya spent more on fixed manufacturing overhead in April 2015 than it budgeted.

A summary of the Levels 1, 2 and 3 variance analyses for Sofiya's fixed manufacturing overhead in April 2015 is as follows:

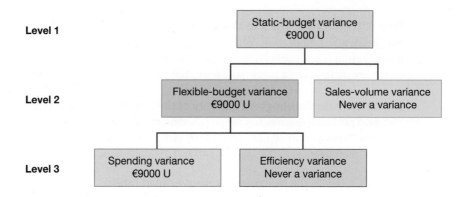

There is never a sales-volume variance in Level 2 for fixed-overhead costs. Why? Because budgeted fixed costs are, by definition, unaffected by sales-volume changes. Similarly, there is never an efficiency variance in Level 3 for fixed-overhead costs. After all, a manager cannot be more or less efficient in dealing with a given amount of fixed costs.

Production-volume variance

The variances discussed so far in this chapter are presented in Exhibit 16.3 – Panel A for variable costs and the first three columns of Panel B for fixed costs. We now discuss a new variance for fixed-overhead costs (shown on the right-hand side of Exhibit 16.3, Panel B). The **production-volume variance** is the difference between budgeted fixed overhead and the fixed overhead allocated. Fixed overhead is allocated based on the budgeted fixed overhead rate times the budgeted quantity of the fixed-overhead allocation base for the actual output units achieved. Other terms for this variance include **denominator-level variance** and **output-level overhead variance**.

The formula for the production-volume variance, expressed in terms of allocation base units (machine-hours for Sofiya), is:

$$\begin{matrix} \text{Production-} \\ \text{volume} \\ \text{variance} \end{matrix} = \begin{matrix} \text{Budgeted} \\ \text{fixed} \\ \text{overhead} \end{matrix} - \left(\begin{matrix} \text{Fixed overhead allocated using} \\ \text{budgeted input allowed for} \\ \text{actual output units achieved} \end{matrix} - \begin{matrix} \text{Budgeted fixed} \\ \text{overhead rate} \end{matrix} \right)$$

$$= €276\,000 - (0.40 \times 10\,000 \times €57.50)$$

$$= €276\,000 - (4000 \times €57.50)$$

$$= €276\,000 - €230\,000$$

$$= €46\,000 \text{ U}$$

The amount used for budgeted fixed overhead will be the same lump sum shown in the static budget and also in any flexible budget within the relevant range. Fixed-overhead costs allocated is the sum of the individual fixed-overhead costs allocated to each of the products manufactured during the accounting period.

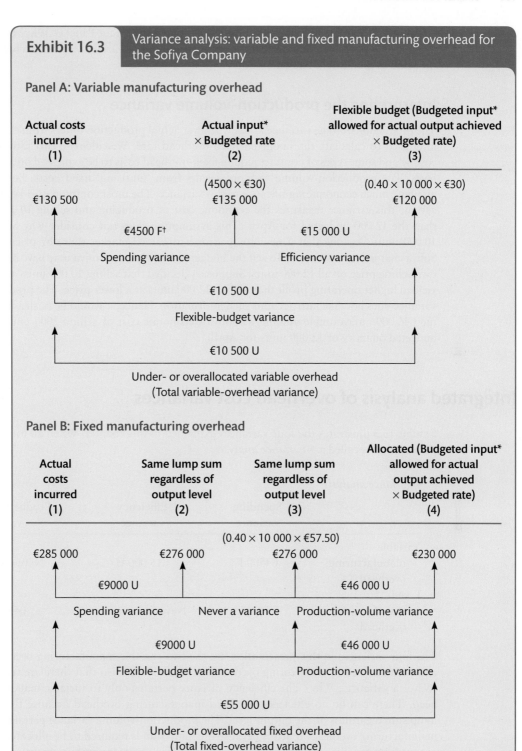

Exhibit 16.3 Variance analysis: variable and fixed manufacturing overhead for the Sofiya Company

Panel A: Variable manufacturing overhead

Actual costs incurred (1)	Actual input* × Budgeted rate (2)	Flexible budget (Budgeted input* allowed for actual output achieved × Budgeted rate) (3)
	(4500 × €30)	(0.40 × 10 000 × €30)
€130 500	€135 000	€120 000

€4500 F† Spending variance   €15 000 U Efficiency variance

€10 500 U Flexible-budget variance

€10 500 U
Under- or overallocated variable overhead
(Total variable-overhead variance)

Panel B: Fixed manufacturing overhead

Actual costs incurred (1)	Same lump sum regardless of output level (2)	Same lump sum regardless of output level (3)	Allocated (Budgeted input* allowed for actual output achieved × Budgeted rate) (4)
		(0.40 × 10 000 × €57.50)	
€285 000	€276 000	€276 000	€230 000

€9000 U Spending variance   Never a variance   €46 000 U Production-volume variance

€9000 U Flexible-budget variance   €46 000 U Production-volume variance

€55 000 U
Under- or overallocated fixed overhead
(Total fixed-overhead variance)

* For overhead costs, input refers to units of cost allocation base.
† F = favourable effect on operating profit; U = unfavourable effect on operating profit.

Panel A of Exhibit 16.3 does not have the column 4 shown for Panel B. Why? Because column 4 does not apply to variable-overhead costs. The amount of variable overhead allocated is always the same as the flexible-budget amount.

Interpreting the production-volume variance

The production-volume variance arises whenever actual production differs from the denominator level used to calculate the budgeted fixed-overhead rate. We calculate this rate because stock costing and some types of contract require fixed-overhead costs to be expressed on a unit-of-output basis. The production-volume variance results from 'unitising' fixed costs. Be careful not to attribute much economic significance to this variance. The most common misinterpretation is to assume this variance measures the economic cost of producing and selling 10 000 units rather than the 12 000 budgeted for April. This assumption does not consider why Sofiya sold only 10 000 units. Assume that a new competitor had gained market share by pricing below what Sofiya charged its customers. To sell the budgeted 12 000 units, Sofiya may have had to reduce its own selling price on all 12 000 units. Suppose it decided that selling 10 000 units at a higher price yielded higher operating profit than selling 12 000 units at a lower price. The production-volume variance does not take into account such information. Hence, it would be misleading to interpret the €46 000 unfavourable amount as Sofiya's economic cost of selling 2000 units less than the budgeted quantity of 12 000 units for April.

Integrated analysis of overhead cost variances

Exhibit 16.3 illustrates the four variances explained in this chapter. When all four variances are presented, it is called a *4-variance analysis*.

4-variance analysis

	Spending variance	Efficiency variance	Production-volume variance
Variable manufacturing overhead	€4500 F	€15 000 U	Never a variance
Fixed manufacturing overhead	€9000 U	Never a variance	€46 000 U

The four variances in this presentation are the two variable manufacturing overhead variances and the two fixed manufacturing overhead variances. Note also that there are two instances of 'Never a variance'. Why? The efficiency variance pertains only to variable manufacturing overhead. There can be no efficiency for fixed manufacturing overhead because this amount is a lump sum regardless of the output level. The production-volume variance pertains only to fixed manufacturing overhead. It arises because the lump sum is required to be allocated to individual output units for stock costing (and, in some cases, for contract reimbursement).

3-variance analysis

	Spending variance	Efficiency variance	Production-volume variance
Total manufacturing overhead	€4500 U	€15 000 U	€46 000 U

The two spending variances from the 4-variance analysis have been combined in the 3-variance analysis. The only loss of information in the 3-variance analysis is the overhead spending variance area – only one spending variance is reported instead of separate variable- and fixed-overhead spending variances. 3-Variance analysis is sometimes called **combined variance analysis**, because it combines variable- and fixed-cost variances when reporting overhead cost variances.

2-variance analysis

	Flexible-budget variance	Production-volume variance
Total manufacturing overhead	€19 500 U	€46 000 U

The spending and efficiency variances from the 3-variance analysis have been combined under the 2-variance analysis.

1-variance analysis

	Total overhead variance
Total manufacturing overhead	€65 500 U

The single variance of €65 500 U in 1-variance analysis is the sum of the flexible-budget variance and the production-volume variance under 2-variance analyses. Using figures from Exhibit 16.3, the total overhead variance is the difference between the total actual manufacturing overhead incurred (€130 500 + €285 000 = €415 500) and the manufacturing overhead allocated (€120 000 + €230 000 = €350 000) to the actual output units produced. The €65 500 unfavourable total manufacturing overhead variance for the Sofiya Company in April 2015 is largely the result of the €46 000 unfavourable production-volume variance. Using the 4-variance analysis presentation, the next largest amount (after the €46 000) is the €15 000 unfavourable variable-overhead efficiency variance. This variance arises from the additional 500 machine-hours used in April 2015 above the 4000 machine-hours allowed to manufacture the 10 000 jackets. The two spending variances (€4500 F and €9000 U) partially offset each other.

The variances in Sofiya's 4-variance analysis are not necessarily independent of each other. For example, Sofiya may purchase lower-quality machine fluids (giving rise to a favourable spending variance); this results in the machines taking longer to operate than budgeted (giving rise to an unfavourable efficiency variance).

Different purposes of manufacturing overhead cost analysis

Different types of cost analysis may be appropriate for different purposes. Consider the planning and control purpose and the stock costing for financial reporting purpose. Panel A of Exhibit 16.4 depicts variable manufacturing overhead for each purpose; Panel B depicts fixed manufacturing overhead for each purpose.

Variable manufacturing overhead costs

Sofiya's variable manufacturing overhead is shown in Panel A of Exhibit 16.4 as being variable with respect to output units (jackets) produced for both the planning and control purpose (graph 1) and the stock costing purpose (graph 2). The greater the number of output units manufactured, the higher the budgeted total variable manufacturing overhead costs and the higher the total variable manufacturing overhead costs allocated to output units.

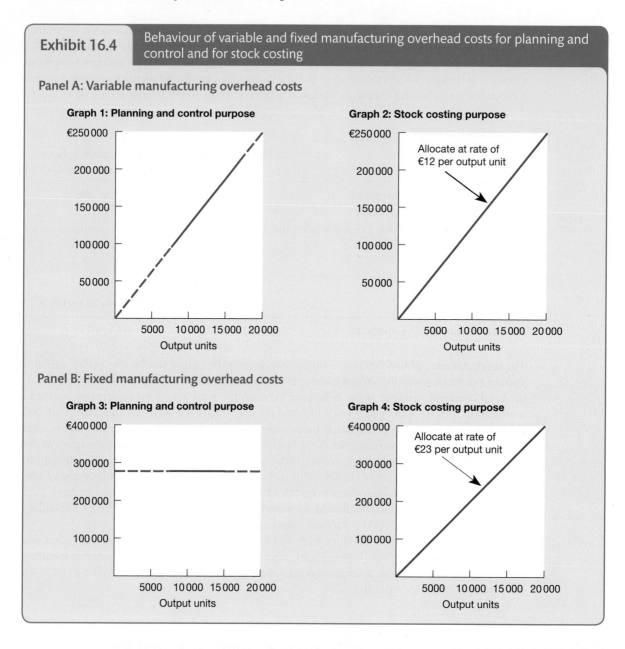

Exhibit 16.4 Behaviour of variable and fixed manufacturing overhead costs for planning and control and for stock costing

Panel A: Variable manufacturing overhead costs

Graph 1: Planning and control purpose

Graph 2: Stock costing purpose
Allocate at rate of €12 per output unit

Panel B: Fixed manufacturing overhead costs

Graph 3: Planning and control purpose

Graph 4: Stock costing purpose
Allocate at rate of €23 per output unit

Graph 1 of Exhibit 16.4 presents an overall picture of how total variable overhead might behave. Of course, variable overhead consists of many items, including energy costs, repairs, indirect labour, and so on. Managers help control variable overhead costs by budgeting each line item and then investigating possible causes for any significant variances.

Fixed manufacturing overhead costs

Panel B of Exhibit 16.4 (graph 3) shows that for the planning and control purpose, fixed overhead costs do not change in the 8000-unit to 16 000-unit output range. Consider a monthly leasing cost of €20 000 for a building under a three-year leasing agreement. Managers control this fixed leasing cost at the time the lease is signed. During any month in the leasing period, management can do little to change this €20 000 lump-sum payment. Contrast this description of fixed overhead with how these costs are depicted for the stock costing purpose, graph 4 of Panel B. Under generally accepted accounting principles, fixed manufacturing costs are capitalised as part of stock on a unit-of-output basis. Every output unit that Sofiya manufactures will increase the fixed overhead allocated to products by €23 (€57.50 per machine-hour × 0.40 machine-hours per output unit). Managers should not use this unitisation of fixed manufacturing overhead costs for their planning and control.

The denominator level in each graph in Exhibit 16.4 is expressed in output units produced. Alternatively, we could also have expressed this denominator in terms of input units. For Sofiya, machine-hours would be the chosen denominator, as this is the allocation base for both variable and fixed manufacturing overhead costs.

Journal entries for overhead costs and variances

Recording overhead costs

The Wallace Company job-costing example (Chapter 3) used a single manufacturing overhead control account. This chapter illustrates separate variable and fixed manufacturing overhead control accounts. Each overhead control account requires its own overhead allocated account.

Consider the following journal entries for the Sofiya Company. Recall that for April 2015:

	Actual results	Flexible-budget amount (10 000 units)	Allocated amount
Variable manufacturing overhead	€130 500	€120 000*	€120 000*
Fixed manufacturing overhead	285 000	276 000†	230 000‡

* 0.40 × 10 000 × €30 = €120 000.
† €276 000 is the budgeted fixed manufacturing overhead.
‡ 0.40 × 10 000 × €57.50 = €230 000.

The budgeted variable-overhead rate is €30 per machine-hour. The denominator level for fixed manufacturing overhead is 4800 machine-hours of input with a budgeted rate of €57.50 per machine-hour. Sofiya uses 4-variance analysis.

During the accounting period, actual variable-overhead and actual fixed-overhead costs are accumulated in separate control accounts. As each unit is manufactured, the budgeted variable- and fixed-overhead rates are used to record the amounts in the respective overhead allocated accounts.

Entries for variable manufacturing overhead for April 2015 are:

1	Variable Manufacturing Overhead Control	130 500	
	Creditors Control and other accounts		130 500
	To record actual variable manufacturing overhead costs incurred.		
2	Work-in-Progress Control	120 000	
	Variable Manufacturing Overhead Allocated		120 000
	To record variable manufacturing overhead cost allocated (0.40 × 10 000 × €30).		
3	Variable Manufacturing Overhead Allocated	120 000	
	Variable Manufacturing Overhead Efficiency Variance	15 000	
	Variable Manufacturing Overhead Control		130 500
	Variable Manufacturing Overhead Spending Variance		4 500
	To isolate variances for the accounting period.		

Entries for fixed manufacturing overhead are:

1 Fixed Manufacturing Overhead Control	285 000	
Wages Payable, Accumulated Depreciation, etc.		285 000
To record actual fixed-overhead costs incurred.		
2 Work-in-Progress Control	230 000	
Fixed Manufacturing Overhead Allocated		230 000
To record fixed manufacturing overhead costs allocated		
$(0.40 \times 10\,000 \times €57.50)$.		
3 Fixed Manufacturing Overhead Allocated	230 000	
Fixed Manufacturing Overhead Spending Variance	9 000	
Fixed Manufacturing Production-Volume Variance	46 000	
Fixed Manufacturing Overhead Control		285 000
To isolate variances for the accounting period.		

The end-of-period adjustments for these variances are now discussed.

Overhead variances and end-of-period adjustments

Chapter 5 outlined the adjusted allocation rate approach and the proration approach to handling the end-of-period difference between manufacturing overhead incurred and manufacturing overhead allocated. Consider Sofiya's variable manufacturing overhead. The budgeted rate was €30 per machine-hour. The actual rate is €29 per machine-hour.

Under the adjusted allocation rate approach, Sofiya would adjust the job record of every job worked on during the year. This adjustment, in effect, would entail using the actual rate per machine-hour of €29 instead of the budgeted rate of €30. Then, Sofiya would accordingly re-calculate the closing stock and cost of goods sold for the accounting period. This approach has several benefits. Individual job records are restated to show actual costs accurately. Also, closing stock and cost of goods sold would accurately show actual variable overhead incurred. A similar approach could be used to restate the fixed manufacturing overhead in job records. Provided all accounting records are on compatible computer systems, the adjusted allocation rate approach can often be done in a low-cost and timely manner.

The proration approach is used where managers view the adjusted allocation rate approach as not being cost-effective. The three main options for disposing of variances under this approach are:

- proration based on the allocated overhead amount (before proration) in the closing balances of Stock and Cost of Goods Sold;

- proration based on total closing balances (before proration) in Stock and Cost of Goods Sold;

- immediate write-off to Cost of Goods Sold.

Sofiya could use any one of these options when prorating the €10 500 of underallocated variable manufacturing overhead (and the €55 000 of underallocated fixed manufacturing overhead).

Concepts in action	Variance analysis and standard costing: helping Sandoz manage overhead costs

Sandoz US is a subsidiary of Swiss-based Novartis AG – one of the largest developers of generic pharmaceutical substitutes for market-leading therapeutic drugs. Competition forces it to operate on razor-thin margins on its sales.

How does a major manufacturing company, such as Sandoz US, maintain its competitive advantage? In addition to its intricate analysis of direct cost variances, Sandoz must also tackle the challenge of accounting for overhead cost variances. Let's examine how Sandoz uses variance analysis and standard costing to manage its overhead costs.

Sandoz is the generic pharmaceutical division of Novartis and a world leader in the generics industry. It employs over 26 000 people who work at its 10 major global development centres and its worldwide network of more than 30 manufacturing sites producing medicines available in more than 160 countries.

Each year, Sandoz prepares an overhead budget based on a detailed production plan, planned overhead spending and other factors, including inflation, efficiency activity-based costing techniques to assign budgeted overhead costs to different work centres (e.g. mixing, blending, tableting, testing and packaging). Finally, overhead costs are assigned to products based on the activity levels required by each product at each work centre. The resulting standard product cost is used in product profitability analysis and as a basis for making pricing decisions. The two main focal points in Sandoz's performance analyses are overhead absorption analysis and manufacturing overhead variance analysis.

Each month, absorption analysis compares actual production and actual costs to the standard costs of processed inventory. The monthly analysis evaluates two key trends: 1. Are costs in line with the budget? If not, the reasons are examined and the accountable managers notified. 2. Are production volume and product mix conforming to plan? If not, machine capacities are reviewed and adjusted if the absorption trend is deemed to be permanent. Absorption analysis acts as a compass for plant management to determine if they are on budget and have an appropriate capacity level to efficiently satisfy the needs of their customers.

Manufacturing overhead variances are examined at the work centre level. These variances help determine when equipment is not running as expected, which leads to repair or replacement. Variances also help in identifying inefficiencies in processing and set-up and cleaning times, which leads to the review and improvement of the standards themselves – a critical element in planning the level of plant capacity. Management reviews current and future capacity utilisation on a monthly basis, using standard hours entered into the plant's Enterprise Resource Planning system. The standards are a useful tool in identifying capacity constraints, enabling performance assessments and determining future capital needs.

Sandoz notes that:

'Our annual performance management process here at Sandoz reflects our dedication to the achievement of outstanding results. This process is implemented in all countries in which we operate, and applies to most positions in our company. At the beginning of each financial year, employees agree on objectives that they will be expected to achieve that year with their manager. These objectives support overall business priorities and are typically both individual and team-based.'

Sources: Novartis Annual Report 2013 and conversations with and documents prepared by Eric Evans and Erich Erchr on 20 March 2004 and 28 May 2004 http://www.sandoz.com/careers/working_at_sandoz/performance_culture.shtml (December 2014).

Engineered, discretionary and infrastructure costs

From a planning and control standpoint, managers often find it useful to classify costs in general, and overhead costs in particular, into three main categories: engineered, discretionary and infrastructure.

- **Engineered costs** result specifically from a clear cause-and-effect relationship between costs and output. In the Sofiya Company example, direct materials and direct manufacturing labour are examples of engineered direct costs, while energy, indirect materials and indirect support labour are examples of engineered overhead costs. Each of these costs increases in a specific way as the units manufactured (jackets) increase. Consider, in particular, the costs of leasing machines (p. 493). This is a fixed cost in the short run, but it is also an example of an engineered cost. Why? Because, over time, there is a clear cause-and-effect relationship between output, machine-hours of capacity required, and machine leasing costs. Thus, engineered costs can be variable or fixed costs.

- **Discretionary costs** have two important features: (1) they arise from periodic (usually yearly) decisions regarding the maximum outlay to be incurred, and (2) they have no clearly measurable cause-and-effect relationship between costs and outputs. There is often a delay between the acquisition of a resource and its eventual use. Examples of discretionary costs include advertising, executive training, R&D, health care and management consulting, and corporate staff department costs such as legal, human resources and public relations. The most noteworthy aspect of discretionary costs is that managers are seldom confident that the 'correct' amounts are being spent. The founder of Lever Brothers, an international consumer-products company, once noted, 'Half the money I spend on advertising is wasted; the trouble is, I don't know which half.' Exhibit 16.5 sets out the differences between engineered and discretionary costs.

- **Infrastructure costs** arise from having property, plant and equipment, and a functioning organisation. Examples are depreciation, long-run lease rental and the acquisition of long-run technical capabilities. The period between when infrastructure costs are committed to and acquired and when they are eventually used is very long. Careful long-range planning, rather than day-to-day monitoring, is the key to managing infrastructure costs. Frequently, there is also a high level of uncertainty about the outputs (cash inflows) resulting from the capital-expenditure decisions.

Exhibit 16.5	Differences between engineered and discretionary costs	
	Engineered costs	**Discretionary costs**
1 Process or activity	a Detailed and physically observable	a Black box (knowledge of process is sketchy or unavailable)
	b Repetitive	b Non-repetitive or non-routine
2 Level of uncertainty	Moderate or small (shipping or manufacturing settings)	Great (R&D or advertising settings)

Source: This exhibit is a modification of one suggested by H. Itami.

Financial and non-financial performance measures

The overhead variances discussed in this chapter are examples of financial performance measures. Managers also find that non-financial measures provide useful information. Examples of such measures that Sofiya would likely find useful in planning and controlling its overhead costs are:

1 Actual indirect materials usage in metres per machine-hour, compared with budgeted indirect materials usage in metres per machine-hour
2 Actual energy usage per machine-hour, compared with budgeted energy usage per machine-hour
3 Actual machining time per job, compared with budgeted machining time per job.

These performance measures, like the variances discussed in this chapter, are best viewed as attention directors, not problem solvers. These performance measures would probably be reported on the manufacturing floor on a daily, or even hourly, basis. The manufacturing overhead variances we discussed in this chapter capture the financial effects of items such as 1, 2 and 3 above, which in many cases first appear as non-financial performance measures.

Both financial and non-financial performance measures are key inputs when evaluating the performance of managers. Exclusive reliance on either is nearly always simplistic.

Actual, normal and standard costing

Chapter 3 presented two possible combinations of actual and budgeted direct-cost rates and actual and budgeted indirect-cost rates. Exhibit 16.6 presents these two costing systems along with a third system – **standard costing** – discussed in Chapters 15 and 16. Standard costing is a costing method that traces direct costs to a cost object by multiplying the standard price(s) or rate(s) times the standard inputs allowed for actual outputs achieved, and allocates indirect costs on the basis of the standard indirect rate(s) times the standard inputs allowed for the actual outputs achieved.

Exhibit 16.6	Actual, normal and standard costing methods		
	Actual costing	**Normal costing**	**Standard costing**
Direct costs	Actual direct price/rate × Actual quantity of direct-cost input	Actual direct price/rate × Actual quantity of direct-cost input	Standard direct price/rate × Standard inputs allowed for actual outputs achieved
Overhead (indirect) costs	Actual indirect rate × Actual quantity of cost-allocation base	Budgeted indirect rate × Actual quantity of cost-allocation base	Standard indirect rate × Standard inputs allowed for actual outputs achieved

With a standard costing system, the costs of every product or service planned to be worked on during that period can be calculated at the start of that period. This feature enables a simplified recording system to be used. No record need be kept of the actual costs of items used or of the actual quantity of the cost allocation base used on individual products or services worked on during the period. Once standards have been set, the costs of operating a standard costing system can be low relative to an actual or normal costing system.

Suppose the Sofiya Company is analysing its marketing overhead costs. It uses a 4-variance analysis of its marketing overhead costs. The following information was collected for April 2015.

1 Variable marketing overhead is allocated to products using budgeted direct marketing labour-hours per jacket. Fixed marketing overhead is allocated to products on a per-jacket basis.

2 Budgeted amounts for April 2015 are:

   a Direct marketing labour-hours: 0.25 hours per jacket
   b Variable marketing overhead rate: €20 per direct marketing labour-hour
   c Fixed marketing overhead: €434 000
   d Output, which is used as the denominator level of output: 12 000 jackets.

3 Actual results for April 2015 are:

   a Variable marketing overhead: €45 700
   b Fixed marketing overhead: €420 000
   c Direct marketing labour-hours: 2304
   d Actual output: 10 000 jackets.

Suppose we wish to present an analysis of the April 2015 marketing overhead costs using the format shown in both panels of Exhibit 16.3. Exhibit 16.7 is the columnar presentation of variances.

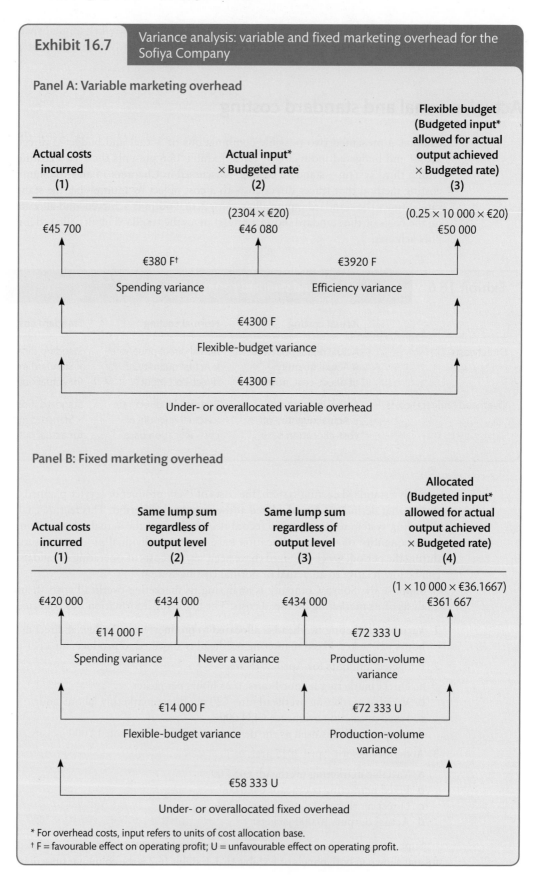

Exhibit 16.7   Variance analysis: variable and fixed marketing overhead for the Sofiya Company

Panel A: Variable marketing overhead

	Actual costs incurred (1)	Actual input* × Budgeted rate (2)	Flexible budget (Budgeted input* allowed for actual output achieved × Budgeted rate) (3)

(2304 × €20)   (0.25 × 10 000 × €20)

€45 700   €46 080   €50 000

←——— €380 F† ———→   ←——— €3920 F ———→

Spending variance   Efficiency variance

←——————————— €4300 F ———————————→

Flexible-budget variance

←——————————— €4300 F ———————————→

Under- or overallocated variable overhead

Panel B: Fixed marketing overhead

	Actual costs incurred (1)	Same lump sum regardless of output level (2)	Same lump sum regardless of output level (3)	Allocated (Budgeted input* allowed for actual output achieved × Budgeted rate) (4)

(1 × 10 000 × €36.1667)

€420 000   €434 000   €434 000   €361 667

←——— €14 000 F ———→   ←——— €72 333 U ———→

Spending variance   Never a variance   Production-volume variance

←——————— €14 000 F ———————→   ←——————— €72 333 U ———————→

Flexible-budget variance   Production-volume variance

←——————————————— €58 333 U ———————————————→

Under- or overallocated fixed overhead

* For overhead costs, input refers to units of cost allocation base.
† F = favourable effect on operating profit; U = unfavourable effect on operating profit.

The budgeted fixed marketing overhead rate is €36.1667 (rounded) per jacket. These variances can be summarised as follows:

	Spending variance	Efficiency variance	Production-volume variance
Variable marketing overhead	€380 F	€3920 F	Never a variance
Fixed marketing overhead	€14 000 F	Never a variance	€58 333 U

We would also like to determine why variances occurred in marketing overhead costs.

- *Variable marketing overhead spending variance* (€380 F). The reasons for this variance include:
  - Lower-than-expected prices for line items in the variable marketing overhead budget, such as lower wage rates for marketing support staff, lower prices for long-distance telephone calls and lower prices for petrol used by salespeople.
  - Lower-than-expected usage of line items in the variable marketing overhead budget, such as fewer marketing support staff, fewer long-distance telephone calls and fewer litres of petrol per direct marketing labour-hour.
- *Variable marketing overhead efficiency variance* (€3920 F). The reason for this variance is more productive use of the cost-allocation base (direct marketing labour-hours); 2304 direct marketing labour-hours were used, compared with a budgeted 2500 hours. Perhaps marketing personnel classified as direct labour were more efficient, maybe because of a new incentive plan, a better training programme, or greater-than-expected continuous improvement.
- *Fixed marketing overhead spending variance* (€14 000 F). The possible reasons for this variance include:
  - Lower-than-expected prices for line items in the fixed marketing overhead budget. Perhaps a marketing department supervisor resigned and was replaced by a lower-paid supervisor, or maybe a building lease was renegotiated at a lower than budgeted amount.
  - Lower-than-expected usage of line items in the fixed marketing overhead budget, such as the marketing salesforce renting five rather than six cars and thus reducing the fixed monthly car rental payment.
- *Production-volume variance* (€72 333 U). This variance arises because the output level (sales) was 10 000 jackets rather than 12 000 jackets. One explanation is that marketing sales personnel were much less effective than budgeted. Other explanations include a downturn in the economy, poor-quality work at Sofiya's manufacturing plant, a new competitor entering the market, and a reduction in tariffs, resulting in the import of lower-cost jackets.

How might Sofiya plan and control its marketing overhead costs? The main approaches to planning and controlling are: variable and fixed.

- Working creatively at the design stage to avoid non-value-added activities (for example, double-checking marketing mailings).
- Working on reducing the rate per cost driver or the number of cost driver units per output. For example, marketing managers could exert tighter control over the price of department purchases.
- Monitoring variances on an ongoing basis.
- Assigning responsibilities for the marketing variance to managers who will promote the productivity of the marketing staff.

The main approaches to planning and controlling fixed marketing overhead costs are:

- Planning capacity needs in detail, including providing incentives for managers to estimate their budgeted usage in an unbiased way.
- Having marketing managers make careful, cost-conscious planning decisions on individual line items.

Day-to-day monitoring of variances is likely to play only a minor role in the control of fixed marketing overhead costs.

Activity-based costing and variance analysis

ABC systems classify costs of various activities into a cost hierarchy – output-unit level, batch level, product sustaining, and facility sustaining. The basic principles and concepts for variable and fixed manufacturing overhead costs presented earlier in the chapter can be extended to ABC systems. In this section, we illustrate variance analysis for variable and fixed batch-level set-up overhead costs. Batch-level costs are resources sacrificed on activities that are related to a group of units of product(s) or service(s) rather than to each individual unit of product or service.

We continue the Chapter 15 example of Lyco Brass Works, which manufactures Jacutaps, a line of decorative brass taps for jacuzzis. Lyco manufactures Jacutaps in batches. To manufacture a batch of Jacutaps, Lyco must set up the machines and moulds. Set-up costs are batch-level costs because they are associated with batches rather than individual units of products. Doing set-ups is a skilled activity. Hence, a separate Set-up Department is responsible for setting up machines and moulds for different types of Jacutap. Lyco regards set-up costs as overhead costs of products.

Set-up costs consist of some costs that are variable and some costs that are fixed with respect to the number of set-up-hours. Variable costs of set-ups consist of wages paid to hourly set-up labour and indirect support labour, costs of maintenance of set-up equipment, and costs of indirect materials and energy used during set-ups. Fixed set-up costs consist of costs of engineers, supervisors and set-up equipment leases.

Information regarding Jacutaps for 2015 follows:

		Static-budget amounts	Actual amounts
1	Units of Jacutaps produced and sold	180 000	151 200
2	Batch size (units/batch)	150	140
3	Number of batches (Line 1 ÷ Line 2)	1 200	1 080
4	Set-up-hours per batch	6	6.25
5	Total set-up-hours (Line 3 × Line 4)	7 200	6 750
6	Variable overhead cost per set-up-hour	€20	€21
7	Variable set-up overhead costs (Line 5 × Line 6)	€144 000	€141 750
8	Total fixed set-up overhead costs	€216 000	€220 000

Flexible budget and variance analysis for variable set-up overhead costs

To prepare the flexible budget for variable set-up overhead costs, Lyco starts with the actual units of output produced, 151 200 units, and proceeds in the following steps.

Step 1: Using the budgeted batch size, calculate the number of batches that should have been used to produce the actual output Lyco should have manufactured the 151 200 units of output in 1008 batches (151 200 ÷ 150).

Step 2: Using budgeted set-up-hours per batch, calculate the number of set-up-hours that should have been used At the budgeted quantity of 6 set-up-hours per batch, 1008 batches should have required 6048 set-up-hours (1008 × 6).

Step 3: Using the budgeted variable cost per set-up-hour, calculate the flexible budget for variable set-up overhead costs The flexible-budget amount is 6048 set-up-hours × €20 per set-up-hour = €120 960.

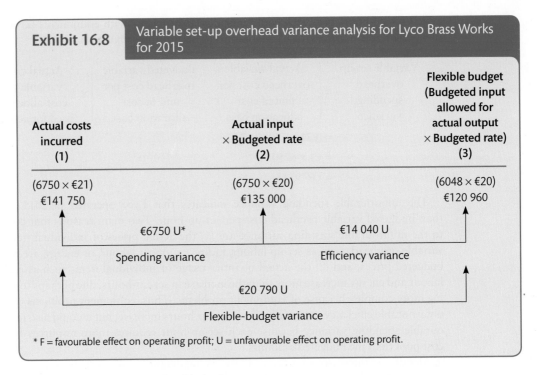

Exhibit 16.8	Variable set-up overhead variance analysis for Lyco Brass Works for 2015

Actual costs incurred (1)	Actual input × Budgeted rate (2)	Flexible budget (Budgeted input allowed for actual output × Budgeted rate) (3)
(6750 × €21) €141 750	(6750 × €20) €135 000	(6048 × €20) €120 960

€6750 U*   €14 040 U

Spending variance   Efficiency variance

€20 790 U

Flexible-budget variance

* F = favourable effect on operating profit; U = unfavourable effect on operating profit.

$$\begin{array}{l}\text{Flexible-budget}\\ \text{variance for}\\ \text{variable set-up}\\ \text{overhead costs}\end{array} = \begin{array}{l}\text{Actual}\\ \text{costs}\end{array} - \begin{array}{l}\text{Flexible-budget}\\ \text{costs}\end{array}$$

$$= 6750 \times €21 - 6048 \times €20$$
$$= €141\,750 - €120\,960$$
$$= €20\,790\ U$$

Exhibit 16.8 presents the variances for variable set-up overhead costs in columnar form.

The flexible-budget variance for variable set-up overhead costs can be subdivided into efficiency and spending variances.

$$\begin{array}{l}\text{Variable set-up}\\ \text{overhead}\\ \text{efficiency}\\ \text{variance}\end{array} = \left(\begin{array}{l}\text{Actual units of}\\ \text{variable overhead}\\ \text{cost-allocation base}\\ \text{used for}\\ \text{actual output}\end{array} - \begin{array}{l}\text{Budgeted units of}\\ \text{variable overhead}\\ \text{cost-allocation base}\\ \text{allowed for}\\ \text{actual output}\end{array}\right) \times \begin{array}{l}\text{Budgeted}\\ \text{variable}\\ \text{overhead}\\ \text{rate}\end{array}$$

$$= (6750 - 6048) \times €20$$
$$= 702 \times €20$$
$$= €14\,040\ U$$

The unfavourable variable set-up overhead efficiency variance of €14 040 arises because the actual number of set-up-hours (6750) exceeds the number of set-up-hours that Lyco should have used (6048) for the number of units it produced. Two reasons for the unfavourable efficiency variance are (1) smaller actual batch sizes of 140 units instead of budgeted batch sizes of 150 units, which results in Lyco producing the 151 200 units in 1080 batches instead of 1008 batches, and (2) higher actual set-up-hours per batch of 6.25 hours instead of the budgeted set-up-hours per batch of 6 hours.

Explanations for smaller-than-budgeted batch sizes could include (1) quality problems if batch sizes exceed 140 taps, or (2) high costs of carrying inventory. Explanations for longer actual set-up-hours per batch could include: (1) problems with equipment, (2) demotivated or inexperienced employees, or (3) inappropriate set-up-time standards.

$$\begin{array}{c} \text{Variable set-up} \\ \text{overhead} \\ \text{spending} \\ \text{variance} \end{array} = \left(\begin{array}{c} \text{Actual variable} \\ \text{overhead cost per} \\ \text{unit of cost-} \\ \text{allocation base} \end{array} - \begin{array}{c} \text{Budgeted variable} \\ \text{overhead cost per} \\ \text{unit of cost-} \\ \text{allocation base} \end{array} \right) \times \begin{array}{c} \text{Actual quantity of} \\ \text{variable overhead} \\ \text{cost-allocation base} \\ \text{used for actual output} \end{array}$$

$$= (€21 - €20) \times 6750$$
$$= €1 \times 6750$$
$$= €6750 \text{ U}$$

The unfavourable spending variance indicates that Lyco operated in 2015 with a higher-than-budgeted variable overhead cost per set-up-hour. Two main reasons that could contribute to the unfavourable spending variance are (1) the actual prices of individual items included in variable overhead, such as set-up labour, indirect support labour, or energy, are higher than the budgeted prices, and (2) the actual quantity usage of individual items such as indirect support labour and energy increase more than the increase in set-up-hours, due perhaps to set-ups becoming more complex because of equipment problems. Thus, equipment problems could lead to an unfavourable efficiency variance because set-up-hours increase, but it could also lead to an unfavourable spending variance because each set-up-hour requires more resources from the set-up cost pool than the budgeted amounts.

Identifying the reasons for the variances is important because it helps managers plan for corrective action. We now consider fixed set-up overhead costs.

Flexible budget and variance analysis for fixed set-up overhead costs

For fixed set-up overhead costs, the flexible-budget amount equals the static-budget amount of €216 000. Why? Because there is no 'flexing' of fixed costs.

$$\begin{array}{c} \text{Fixed set-up} \\ \text{overhead} \\ \text{flexible-budget} \\ \text{variance} \end{array} = \begin{array}{c} \text{Actual} \\ \text{costs} \end{array} - \begin{array}{c} \text{Flexible-budget} \\ \text{costs} \end{array}$$

$$= €220\ 000 - €216\ 000$$
$$= €4000 \text{ U}$$

The fixed set-up overhead spending variance is the same amount as the fixed over-head flexible-budget variance (because fixed overhead costs have no efficiency variance).

$$\begin{array}{c} \text{Fixed set-up} \\ \text{overhead} \\ \text{spending} \\ \text{variance} \end{array} = \begin{array}{c} \text{Actual} \\ \text{costs} \end{array} - \begin{array}{c} \text{Flexible-budget} \\ \text{costs} \end{array}$$

$$= €220\ 000 - €216\ 000$$
$$= €4000 \text{ U}$$

The unfavourable fixed set-up overhead spending variance could be due to lease costs of new set-up equipment, or higher salaries paid to engineers and supervisors. Lyco may have incurred these costs to alleviate some of the difficulties it was having in setting up machines.

To calculate the production-volume variance, Lyco first computes the budgeted cost-allocation rate for fixed set-up overhead costs using the four-step approach described below.

Step 1: Choose the time period used to calculate the budget Lyco uses a period of 12 months (the year 2015).

Step 2: Select the cost-allocation base to use in allocating fixed overhead costs to the cost object(s) Lyco uses budgeted set-up-hours as the cost-allocation base for fixed set-up overhead costs. Budgeted set-up-hours for 2015 per the static budget are 7200 hours.

Step 3: Identify the fixed overhead costs associated with the cost-allocation base Lyco's fixed set-up overhead cost budget for 2015 is €216 000.

Step 4: Calculate the rate per unit of the cost-allocation base used to allocate fixed overhead costs to the cost object(s) Dividing the €216 000 from step 3 by the 7200 set-up-hours from step 2, Lyco estimates a fixed set-up overhead cost rate of €30 per set-up-hour:

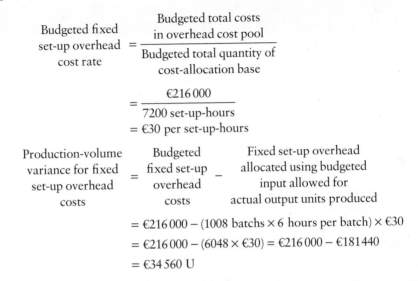

$$\begin{array}{c}\text{Budgeted fixed}\\\text{set-up overhead}\\\text{cost rate}\end{array} = \dfrac{\begin{array}{c}\text{Budgeted total costs}\\\text{in overhead cost pool}\end{array}}{\begin{array}{c}\text{Budgeted total quantity of}\\\text{cost-allocation base}\end{array}}$$

$$= \dfrac{€216\,000}{7200\ \text{set-up-hours}}$$

$$= €30\ \text{per set-up-hours}$$

$$\begin{array}{c}\text{Production-volume}\\\text{variance for fixed}\\\text{set-up overhead}\\\text{costs}\end{array} = \begin{array}{c}\text{Budgeted}\\\text{fixed set-up}\\\text{overhead}\\\text{costs}\end{array} - \begin{array}{c}\text{Fixed set-up overhead}\\\text{allocated using budgeted}\\\text{input allowed for}\\\text{actual output units produced}\end{array}$$

$$= €216\,000 - (1008\ \text{batchs} \times 6\ \text{hours per batch}) \times €30$$

$$= €216\,000 - (6048 \times €30) = €216\,000 - €181\,440$$

$$= €34\,560\ \text{U}$$

Exhibit 16.9 presents the variances for fixed set-up overhead costs in columnar form.

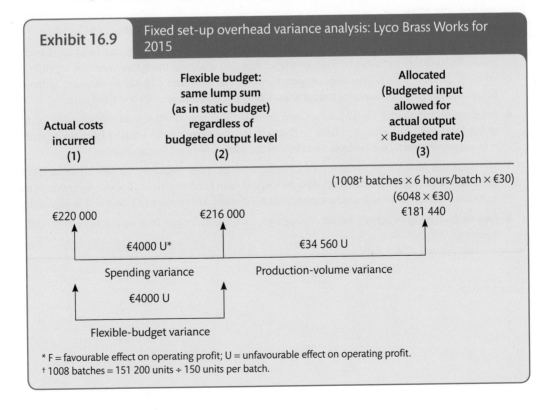

Exhibit 16.9 Fixed set-up overhead variance analysis: Lyco Brass Works for 2015

Actual costs incurred (1)	Flexible budget: same lump sum (as in static budget) regardless of budgeted output level (2)	Allocated (Budgeted input allowed for actual output × Budgeted rate) (3)
		(1008† batches × 6 hours/batch × €30) (6048 × €30)
€220 000	€216 000	€181 440
	€4000 U*	€34 560 U
	Spending variance	Production-volume variance
	€4000 U	
	Flexible-budget variance	

* F = favourable effect on operating profit; U = unfavourable effect on operating profit.
† 1008 batches = 151 200 units ÷ 150 units per batch.

During 2015 Lyco planned to produce 180 000 units of Jacutaps but actually produced only 151 200 units. The unfavourable production-volume variance measures the amount of extra fixed set-up costs that Lyco incurred for set-up capacity it planned to use but did not. One interpretation is that the unfavourable €34 560 production-volume variance represents inefficient utilisation of set-up capacity. However, Lyco may have earned higher operating income by selling 151 200 units at a higher price than what it would have earned by selling 180 000 units at a lower price. The production-volume variance should be interpreted cautiously because it does not consider such information.

Summary

The following points are linked to the chapter's learning objectives.

1 Planning of variable-overhead costs involves undertaking only value-added variable-cost activities and then efficiently managing the cost drivers of those activities. Planning of fixed-overhead costs includes undertaking only value-added fixed-cost activities and then determining the appropriate level of those activities, given the expected demand and the level of uncertainty pertaining to that demand.

2 When the flexible budget for variable overhead is developed, a spending overhead variance and an efficiency variance can be calculated. The variable-overhead spending variance is the difference between the actual amount of variable overhead incurred and the budgeted amount that is allowed for the actual quantity of the variable-overhead allocation base used for the actual output units achieved. The variable-overhead efficiency variance measures the efficiency with which the cost-allocation base is used; this is a different type of efficiency variance from that calculated in Chapter 15 for direct-cost items, such as direct materials.

3 The budgeted fixed-overhead rate is calculated by dividing the budgeted fixed-overhead costs by the budgeted quantity of allocation base units.

4 Production-volume variances are rarely a good measure of the opportunity cost of unused capacity. For example, the plant capacity level may exceed the budgeted level, hence some unused capacity may not be included in the denominator. Moreover, the production-volume variance focuses only on costs. It does not take into account any price changes necessary to spur extra demand that would in turn make use of any idle capacity.

5 A 4-variance analysis presents spending and efficiency variances for variable-overhead costs and spending and production-volume variances for fixed-overhead costs. By analysing these four variances together, managers can consider possible interrelationships among them. These variances collectively measure differences between actual and budgeted amounts for output level, selling prices, variable costs and fixed costs.

6 For planning and control, fixed manufacturing overhead is a lump sum that is unaffected by the budgeted quantity of the fixed-overhead allocation base. In contrast, for stock costing the unitised fixed manufacturing overhead rate will be affected by the budgeted quantity of the fixed-overhead allocation base.

7 The separate analysis of variable- and fixed-overhead costs requires the use of separate variable- and fixed-overhead control accounts and separate variable- and fixed-overhead allocated accounts. At the end of each accounting period, any variances for variable- or fixed-overhead costs can be disposed as illustrated in Chapter 5.

8 Flexible budgeting in activity-based costing systems enables insight into why activity costs differ from those budgeted.

Key terms

value-added cost (493)
non-value-added cost (493)
variable-overhead efficiency variance (496)
variable-overhead spending variance (498)
denominator level (499)
production denominator level (499)
production denominator volume (499)
production-volume variance (500)

denominator-level variance (500)
output-level overhead variance (500)
combined variance analysis (503)
engineered costs (507)
discretionary costs (508)
infrastructure costs (508)
standard costing (509)

CHAPTER 16

Assessment material

Review questions

16.1   What are the steps in planning variable-overhead costs?

16.2   How does the planning of fixed-overhead costs differ from the planning of variable-overhead costs?

16.3   What are the steps in developing a budgeted variable-overhead cost rate?

16.4   Budgeting for variable manufacturing overhead requires a knowledge of cost drivers. Name three possible cost drivers.

16.5   Both financial and non-financial measures are used to control variable manufacturing overhead. Give two examples of each type of measure.

16.6   Assume variable manufacturing overhead is allocated using machine-hours. Give three possible reasons for a €25 000 favourable variable-overhead efficiency variance.

16.7   Describe the difference between a direct materials efficiency variance and a variable manufacturing overhead efficiency variance.

16.8   Why is the flexible-budget variance the same amount as the spending variance for fixed manufacturing overhead?

16.9   Explain how 4-variance analysis differs from 1-, 2- and 3-variance analyses.

16.10   The 4-variance analysis format shows 'never a variance' for two areas. Which two areas? Why?

Exercises

Basic level

*16.11   Variable manufacturing overhead, variance analysis (20 minutes)

Lavertezzo Srl is a manufacturer of designer suits. The cost of each suit is the sum of three variable costs (direct material costs, direct manufacturing labour costs and manufacturing overhead costs) and one fixed-cost category (manufacturing overhead costs). Variable manufacturing overhead cost is allocated to each suit on the basis of budgeted direct manufacturing labour-hours per suit. For June 2015, each suit is budgeted to take 4 labour-hours. Budgeted variable manufacturing overhead cost per labour-hour is SFr 12. The budgeted number of suits to be manufactured in June 2015 is 1040.

Actual variable manufacturing overhead costs in June 2015 were SFr 52 164 for 1080 suits started and completed. There was no opening or closing stock of suits. Actual direct manufacturing labour-hours for June were 4536.

Required

1 Calculate the static-budget variance, the flexible-budget variance and the sales-volume variance for variable manufacturing overhead.

2 Comment on the results.

Intermediate level

16.12 Fixed manufacturing overhead, variance analysis (continuation of Exercise 16.11) (20 minutes)

Lavertezzo allocates fixed manufacturing overhead to each suit using budgeted direct manufacturing labour-hours per suit. Data pertaining to fixed manufacturing overhead costs for June 2015 are budgeted, SFr 62 400, and actual, SFr 63 916.

Required

1 Calculate the spending variance and the flexible-budget variance for fixed manufacturing overhead. Comment on these results.

2 Calculate the production-volume variance for June 2015. What inferences can Lavertezzo draw from this variance?

16.13 Comprehensive review of Chapters 15 and 16, static budget (15 minutes)

L'Evénement du Dimanche budgets to produce 300 000 copies of its monthly newspaper for August 2015. It is budgeted to run 15 000 000 print pages in August with 50 print pages per newspaper. Actual production in August 2015 was 320 000 copies with 17 280 000 print pages run. Each paper was only 50 print pages, but quality problems with paper led to many pages being unusable.

Variable costs comprise direct materials, direct labour, and variable indirect costs. Variable and fixed indirect costs are allocated to each copy on the basis of print pages. The driver for all variable costs is the number of print pages. Data pertaining to August 2015 are:

	Budgeted	Actual
Direct materials	SFr 180 000	SFr 224 640
Direct labour costs	45 000	50 112
Variable indirect costs	60 000	63 936
Fixed indirect costs	90 000	97 000

Data pertaining to revenues for *L'Evénement du Dimanche* in August 2015 are:

	Budgeted	Actual
Circulation revenue	SFr 140 000	SFr 154 000
Advertising revenue	360 000	394 600

L'Evénement du Dimanche sells for SFr 0.50 per copy in 2015. No change from this budgeted price of SFr 0.50 per copy occurred in August 2015. The actual direct labour rate in August 2015 was SFr 29.00 per hour. Actual and budgeted pages produced per direct labour-hour in August 2015 were 10 000 print pages. Copies produced but not sold have no value. Advertising revenue covers payments from all advertising sources.

Required

1 Present a static-budget variance (Level 1) report for *L'Evénement du Dimanche*.

2 Comment on the results in requirement 1.

16.14 Engineered and discretionary overhead costs (20 minutes)

Willem Nijmegen manages the warehouse of Stientje NV, a mail-order firm. Nijmegen is concerned about controlling the fixed costs of the 20 workers who collect merchandise in the warehouse and bring it to the area where orders are assembled for shipment. Each employee works 180 hours per month at a budgeted cost of €15 per hour. Studies show that it takes an average of 12 minutes for a worker to locate an article of merchandise and move it to the order assembly area, and that the average order is for two different articles. In August, Stientje processed 8500 orders. Actual costs were €56 000.

Required

1 Calculate the spending and production-volume variances for Stientje using an engineered overhead cost approach.

2 Calculate the spending and production-volume variances for Stientje using a discretionary overhead cost approach.

3 Comment on the differences in the approaches to controlling costs under requirements 1 and 2.

16.15 Standard Costing (From ACCA Financial Information for Management, Part 1, June 2005) (40 minutes)

Murgatroyd Ltd, which manufactures a single product, uses standard absorption costing. A summary of the standard product cost is as follows:

	£ per unit
Direct materials	15
Direct labour	20
Fixed overheads	12

Budgeted and actual production for last month were 10 000 units and 9000 units respectively. The actual costs incurred were:

	£
Direct materials	138 000
Direct labour	178 000
Fixed overheads	103 000

Required

1 Prepare a statement that reconciles the standard cost of actual production with its actual cost for last month and highlights the total variance for each of the three elements of cost.

2 Last month 24 000 litres of direct material were purchased and used by the company. The standard allows for 2.5 litres of the material, at £6 per litre, to be used in each unit of product.

Provide an appropriate breakdown of the total direct materials cost variance included in your statement in 1.

3 Explain who in the company should be involved in setting:
a the standard price; and
b the standard quantity for direct materials.

16.16 Variance calculations (From ACCA Financial Information for Management, Part 1, June 2004) (25 minutes)

Coledale Ltd manufactures and sells product CC. The company operates a standard marginal costing system. The standard cost card for CC includes the following:

	£ per unit
Direct material	20
Direct labour (6 hours at £7.50 per hour)	45
Variable production overheads	27
	92

The budgeted and actual activity levels for the last quarter were as follows:

	Budget units	Actual units
Sales	20 000	19 000
Production	20 000	21 000

The actual costs incurred last quarter were:

	£
Direct material	417 900
Direct labour (124 950 hours)	949 620
Variable production overheads	565 740

Required

1 Calculate the *total* variances for direct material, direct labour and variable production overheads.

2 Provide an appropriate breakdown of the total variance for direct labour calculated in 1.

3 Suggest TWO possible causes for EACH variance calculated in 2.

16.17 **Cost behaviour issues** (From ACCA Financial Information for Management, Part 1, June 2004) (25 minutes)

Braithwaite Ltd manufactures and sells a single product. The following data have been extracted from the current year's budget:

Contribution per unit	£8
Total weekly fixed costs	£10 000
Weekly profit	£22 000
Contribution to sales ratio	40%

The company's production capacity is not being fully utilised in the current year and three possible strategies are under consideration. Each strategy involves reducing the unit selling price on all units sold with a consequential effect on the budgeted volume of sales. Details of each strategy are as follows:

Strategy	Reduction in unit weekly selling price %	Expected increase in sales volume over budget %
A	2	10
B	5	18
C	7	25

The company does not hold stocks of finished goods.

Required

1 Calculate for the current year:
   a the selling price per unit for the product; and
   b the weekly sales (in units).

2 Determine, with supporting calculations, which one of the three strategies should be adopted by the company in order to maximise weekly profits.

3 Briefly explain the practical problems that a management accountant might encounter in separating costs into their fixed and variable components.

16.18 **Variance calculation** (From CIMA Management Accounting Pillar Managerial Level Paper, November 2006) (20 minutes)

PP Ltd operates a standard absorption costing system. The following information has been extracted from the standard cost card for one of its products:

Budgeted production	1500 units	
Direct material cost:	7 kg × £4.10	£28.70 per unit

Actual results for the period were as follows:

Production	1600 units
Direct material (purchased and used):	12 000 kg £52 200

It has subsequently been noted that due to a change in economic conditions the best price that the material could have been purchased for was £4.50 per kg during the period.

Required

1 Calculate the material price planning variance.

2 Calculate the operational material usage variance.

Advanced level

16.19 **Manufacturing overhead, variance analysis** (30–40 minutes)

Mondragon SA assembles its CardioX product at its Toledo plant. Manufacturing overhead (both variable and fixed) is allocated to each CardioX unit using budgeted assembly-time hours. Budgeted assembly time per CardioX product is 2 hours. The budgeted variable manufacturing overhead cost per assembly time hour is €40. The budgeted number of CardioX units to be assembled in March 2015 is 8000. Budgeted fixed manufacturing overhead costs are €480 000.

Actual variable manufacturing overhead costs for March 2015 were €610 500 for 7400 units actually assembled. Actual assembly-time hours were 16 280. Actual fixed manufacturing overhead costs were €503 420.

Required

1 Conduct a 4-variance analysis (Exhibit 16.3) for Mondragon's Toledo plant.

2 Comment on the results in requirement 1.

3 How does the planning and control of variable manufacturing overhead costs differ from that of fixed manufacturing overhead costs?

16.20 **Spending and efficiency overhead variances, service sector** (20–25 minutes)

Danskmat AS operates a home meal delivery service. It has agreements with 20 restaurants to pick up and deliver meals to customers who phone or fax in orders. Danskmat is currently examining its overhead costs for May 2015.

Variable-overhead costs for May 2015 were budgeted at DKK 20 per hour of home delivery time. Fixed-overhead costs were budgeted at DKK 240 000. The budgeted number of home deliveries in May 2015 was 8000. Delivery time, the allocation base for variable- and fixed-overhead costs, is budgeted to be 0.80 hour per delivery.

Actual results for May 2015 were:

Variable overhead	DKK 141 740
Fixed overhead	DKK 276 000
Number of home deliveries	7 460
Hours of delivery time	5 595

Customers are charged DKK 120 per delivery. The delivery driver is paid DKK 70 per delivery. Danskmat receives a 10% commission on the meal costs that the restaurants charge the customers who use Danskmat.

Required

1 Calculate spending and efficiency variances for Danskmat's variable and fixed overhead in May 2015. Comment on the results.

2 How might Danskmat manage its variable-overhead costs differently from the way it manages its fixed-overhead costs?

16.21 Total overhead, 3-variance analysis (35–50 minutes)

The Olsson-Langkilde Air Force Base has an extensive repair facility for jet engines. It developed standard costing and flexible budgets to account for this activity. Budgeted variable overhead at a level of 8000 standard monthly direct labour-hours was SEK 64 000; budgeted total overhead at 10 000 standard direct labour-hours was SEK 197 600. The standard cost allocated to repair output included a total overhead rate of 120% of standard direct labour cost.

Total overhead incurred for October was SEK 249 000. Direct labour costs incurred were SEK 202 440. The direct labour price variance was SEK 9640 U. The direct labour flexible-budget variance was SEK 14 440 U. The standard labour price was SEK 16 per hour. The production-volume variance was SEK 14 000 F.

Required

1 Calculate the direct labour efficiency variance and the spending, efficiency and production-volume variances for overhead. Also, calculate the denominator level.

2 Describe how individual variable manufacturing overhead items are controlled from day to day. Also, describe how individual fixed manufacturing overhead items are controlled.

16.22 Comprehensive review of Chapters 15 and 16, flexible budget (continuation of Exercise 16.13) (40 minutes)

Required

1 Prepare a comprehensive set of variances for each of the four categories of cost of *L'Evénement du Dimanche*.

2 Comment on the results in requirement 1. What extra insights are available with a flexible-budget analysis over that of a static-budget analysis?

16.23 Flexible budgets, 4-variance analysis (CMA, adapted) (15–25 minutes)

Nolton-Ragnvald AS uses a standard costing system. It allocates manufacturing overhead (both variable and fixed) to products on the basis of standard direct manufacturing labour-hours (DLH). Nolton develops its manufacturing overhead rate from the current annual budget. The manufacturing overhead budget for 2015 is based on budgeted output of 720 000 units requiring 3 600 000 direct manufacturing labour-hours. The company is able to schedule production uniformly throughout the year.

A total of 66 000 output units requiring 315 000 direct labour-hours was produced during May 2015. Manufacturing overhead (MOH) costs incurred for May amounted to NOK 375 000. The actual costs as compared with the annual budget and 1/12 of the annual budget are shown below.

Annual manufacturing overhead budget 2015

	Total amount	Per output unit	Per DLH input unit	Monthly MOH budget, May 2015	Actual MOH costs for May 2015
Variable MOH					
Indirect mfg labour	NOK 900 000	NOK 1.25	NOK 0.25	NOK 75 000	NOK 75 000
Supplies	1 224 000	1.70	0.34	102 000	111 000
Fixed MOH					
Supervision	648 000	0.90	0.18	54 000	51 000
Utilities	540 000	0.75	0.15	45 000	54 000
Depreciation	1 008 000	1.40	0.28	84 000	84 000
Total	NOK 4 320 000	NOK 6.00	NOK 1.20	NOK 360 000	NOK 375 000

Required

Calculate the following amounts for Nolton-Ragnvald for May 2015:

1 Total manufacturing overhead costs allocated.

2 Variable manufacturing overhead spending variance.

3 Fixed manufacturing overhead spending variance.

4 Variable manufacturing overhead efficiency variance.

5 Production-volume variance.

Be sure to identify each variance as favourable (F) or unfavourable (U).

16.24 Review of Chapters 15 and 16, 3-variance analysis (CPA, adapted) (30–50 minutes)

Madetoja Oy's job-costing system has two direct-cost categories: direct materials and direct manufacturing labour. Manufacturing overhead (both variable and fixed) is allocated to products on the basis of standard direct manufacturing labour-hours (DLH). At the beginning of 2015, Madetoja adopted the following standards for its manufacturing costs:

	Input	Cost per output unit
Direct materials	3 kg at €5.00 per kg	€15.00
Direct manufacturing labour	5 hours at €15.00 per hour	75.00
Manufacturing overhead		
Variable	€6.00 per DLH	30.00
Fixed	€8.00 per DLH	40.00
Standard manufacturing cost per output unit		€160.00

The denominator level for total manufacturing overhead per month in 2015 is 40 000 direct manufacturing labour-hours. Madetoja's flexible budget for January 2015 was based on this denominator level. The records for January indicate the following:

Direct materials purchased	25 000 kg at €5.20 per kg
Direct materials used	23 100 kg
Direct manufacturing labour	40 100 hours at €14.60 per hour
Total actual manufacturing overhead (variable and fixed)	€600 000
Actual production	7800 output units

Required

1 Prepare a schedule of total standard manufacturing costs for the 7800 output units in January 2015.

2 For the month of January 2015, calculate the following variances, indicating whether each is favourable (F) or unfavourable (U):

a Direct materials price variance, based on purchases
b Direct materials efficiency variance
c Direct manufacturing labour price variance
d Direct manufacturing labour efficiency variance
e Total manufacturing overhead spending variance
f Variable manufacturing overhead efficiency variance
g Production-volume variance.

CHAPTER 17

Measuring yield, mix and quantity effects

Comparing actual results with budgets can help managers evaluate operations and focus on areas that deserve more attention. Chapters 15 and 16 illustrated various uses of variance information relating to direct materials, direct manufacturing labour, direct marketing labour, manufacturing overhead and marketing overhead. While Chapters 15 and 16 focused on a single input in each cost category (for example, only one direct material), this chapter considers multiple inputs in each cost category (for example, many types of direct materials). Also, we discuss revenue and sales mix and quantity analysis for companies with multiple products.

Learning objectives

After studying this chapter, you should be able to:

- Distinguish between variance analysis procedures where inputs cannot be substituted for one another and those where inputs can be so substituted

- Understand how direct materials yield and mix variances highlight trade-offs among material inputs

- Explain direct manufacturing labour yield and mix variances

- Describe the insight gained from dividing the sales-volume variance into the sales-mix and sales-quantity variances

- Explain how market-size and market-share variances provide different explanations for a sales-quantity variance

Input variances

Here we focus on variance analysis for inputs in manufacturing organisations. Manufacturing processes often require that a number of different direct materials and different direct manufacturing labour skills be combined to obtain a unit of finished product. In the case of some materials and labour skills, this combination must be exact. For example, the manager of an HP plant that assembles laptop computers prespecifies the make of chip to be used in each computer. Substituting an Intel chip for an AMD chip will alter the final product. We refer to these materials as *non-substitutable* materials. In the case of other materials, a manufacturer has some leeway in combining the materials. For example, to manufacture fertilisers, Cargill Fertilisers can combine materials (for example, elemental phosphorus and acids) in varying proportions. Elemental phosphorus and acids are *substitutable* materials.

When inputs are substitutable, *mix* refers to the relative proportion or combination of the different inputs used within an input category such as direct materials or direct manufacturing labour to produce a quantity of finished output. *Yield* refers to the quantity of finished output units produced from a budgeted or standard mix of inputs within an input category. Yield and mix variances are useful when examining direct materials and direct-labour inputs. Consider, for example, the production of ice-cream. Ice-creams contain multiple material ingredients. Nut 'n Crunch ice-cream, for example, has milk, cream, cocoa, chocolate, caramel and different kinds of nuts. Managing the total quantity and mix of ingredients is essential to making high-quality ice-cream at a competitive cost. Direct materials yield and mix variances help managers to achieve these goals. Recall from Chapter 15 that a *variance* is the difference between an actual result and a budgeted amount, when that budgeted amount is a financial variable reported by the accounting system. Budgeted figures discussed in this chapter can be obtained from:

- internally generated actual costs from the most recent accounting period, sometimes adjusted for expected improvement;
- internally generated *standard* costs based on best performance standards or *currently attainable standards*;
- externally generated *target* cost numbers based on an analysis of the cost structures of the leading competitors in an industry.

Direct materials yield and mix variances

When we initially examined materials and labour variances in Chapter 15, we saw that managers sometimes make trade-offs between price and efficiency variances. For example, an orange-juice bottler may use oranges whose juice content is lower than budgeted if their price is significantly lower than the price of oranges with the budgeted juice content. The yield and mix variances calculated in this section provide additional insight into the effect that yield and mix factors have on operating income. Yield and mix variances divide the efficiency variance calculated in Chapter 15; hence, we start by reviewing efficiency and price variances.

Direct materials efficiency and price variances

Consider a specific example of multiple direct materials inputs and a single product output. Aliya Ltd makes cider. To produce cider of the desired consistency, colour and taste, Aliya mixes three types of apples grown in three different regions: Golden Delicious from Brittany, British Coxes from Kent, and Jonagold from Italy. Aliya's production standards require 1.6 tonnes of apples to produce 1 tonne of cider, with 50% of the apples being Golden Delicious, 30% British Coxes, and 20% Jonagold. The direct materials input standards to produce 1 tonne of cider are:

0.80 (50% of 1.6) tonne of Golden Delicious at €70 per tonne	€56.00	
0.48 (30% of 1.6) tonne of British Coxes at €80 per tonne	38.40	
0.32 (20% of 1.6) tonne of Jonagold at €90 per tonne	28.80	
Total standard cost of 1.6 tonnes of apples	€123.20	

Budgeted cost per tonne of apples is €123.20 ÷ 1.6 tonnes = €77.

Because Aliya uses fresh apples to make cider, no stocks of apples are kept. Purchases are made as needed, so all price variances relate to apples purchased and used. Actual results for June 2015 show that a total of 6500 tonnes of apples were used to produce 4000 tonnes of cider:

3250 tonnes of Golden Delicious at actual cost of €70 per tonne	€227 500
2275 tonnes of British Coxes at actual cost of €82 per tonne	186 550
975 tonnes of Jonagold at actual cost of €96 per tonne	93 600
6500 tonnes of apples	507 650
Standard cost of 4000 tonnes of cider at €123.20 per tonne	492 800
Total variance to be explained	€14 850 U

Given the standard ratio of 1.6 tonnes of apples to 1 tonne of cider, 6400 tonnes of apples should be used to produce 4000 tonnes of cider. At the standard mix, the quantities of each type of apple required are:

Golden Delicious	0.50 × 6400 = 3200 tonnes
British Coxes	0.30 × 6400 = 1920 tonnes
Jonagold	0.20 × 6400 = 1280 tonnes

Exhibit 17.1 presents the familiar approach to analysing the flexible-budget direct materials variance discussed in Chapter 15. The direct materials price and efficiency variances are calculated separately for each input material and then added together. The variance analysis prompts Aliya to investigate the unfavourable price and efficiency variances – why did they pay more for the apples and use greater quantities than they should have? Were the market prices of apples

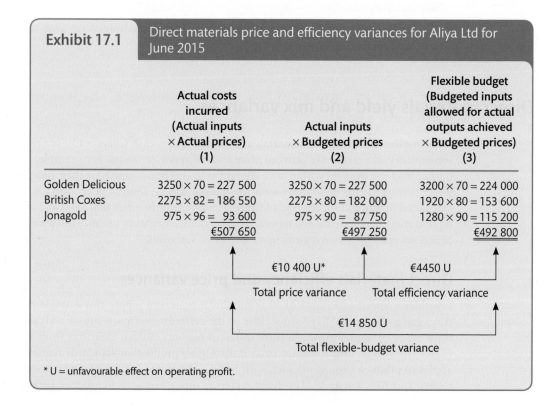

Exhibit 17.1	Direct materials price and efficiency variances for Aliya Ltd for June 2015

	Actual costs incurred (Actual inputs × Actual prices) (1)	Actual inputs × Budgeted prices (2)	Flexible budget (Budgeted inputs allowed for actual outputs achieved × Budgeted prices) (3)
Golden Delicious	3250 × 70 = 227 500	3250 × 70 = 227 500	3200 × 70 = 224 000
British Coxes	2275 × 82 = 186 550	2275 × 80 = 182 000	1920 × 80 = 153 600
Jonagold	975 × 96 = 93 600	975 × 90 = 87 750	1280 × 90 = 115 200
	€507 650	€497 250	€492 800

€10 400 U*   €4450 U

Total price variance   Total efficiency variance

€14 850 U

Total flexible-budget variance

* U = unfavourable effect on operating profit.

higher, in general, or could the Purchasing Department have negotiated lower prices? Did the inefficiencies result from inferior apples or from problems in processing?

The analysis in Exhibit 17.1 may suffice when the three direct materials used are not substitutes. Managers control each individual input, and no discretion is permitted regarding the substitution of materials inputs. For example, there is often a specified mix of parts needed for the assembly of cars, radios and washing machines. A car needs both an engine and a gear box – one cannot be substituted for the other. In these cases, all deviations from the input–output relationships are due to efficient or inefficient usage of individual direct materials. Thus, the price and efficiency variances individually calculated for each material typically provide the information necessary for decisions.

The role of direct materials yield and direct materials mix variances

Managers sometimes do have discretion to substitute one material for another. For example, the manager of Aliya's cider plant has some leeway in combining Golden Delicious, British Coxes and Jonagold without affecting quality. We will assume that to maintain quality, the mix percentages of each type of apple can vary only up to 5% in the standard mix. For example, the percentage of British Coxes in the mix can vary between 25% and 35% (30% ± 5%). When inputs are substitutable, direct materials efficiency improvement relative to budgeted costs can come from two sources: (1) using less input to achieve a given output, and (2) using a cheaper mix to produce a given output. The direct materials yield and mix variances divide the efficiency variance into two variances: the yield variance focusing on total inputs used and the mix variance focusing on how the inputs are combined.

Given that the budgeted input mix is unchanged, the **total direct materials yield variance** is the difference between two amounts: (1) the budgeted cost of direct materials based on the actual total quantity of all direct materials inputs used, and (2) the flexible-budget cost of direct materials based on the budgeted total quantity of direct materials inputs for the actual output achieved. Given that the actual total quantity of all direct materials inputs used is unchanged, the **total direct materials mix variance** is the difference between two amounts: (1) the budgeted cost for the actual direct materials input mix, and (2) the budgeted cost if the budgeted direct materials input mix had been unchanged.

Exhibit 17.2 presents the total direct materials yield and mix variances for Aliya Ltd. We start with column 3 and work our way to column 1.

Total direct materials yield variance

Compare columns 3 and 2 of Exhibit 17.2. Column 3 calculates the flexible-budget cost based on the budgeted cost of the budgeted total quantity of all inputs used (6400 tonnes of apples) for the actual output achieved (4000 tonnes of cider) times the budgeted input mix (Golden Delicious, 50%; British Coxes, 30%; Jonagold, 20%). Column 2 also calculates costs using the budgeted input mix and the budgeted prices. The *only* difference in the two columns is that column 3 uses the *budgeted total quantity of all inputs used* (6400 tonnes), while column 2 uses the *actual total quantity of all inputs used* (6500 tonnes). Hence, the difference in costs between the two columns is the total direct materials yield variance, due solely to differences in actual and budgeted total input quantity used. The total direct materials yield variance is the sum of the direct materials yield variances for each input.

$$
\begin{array}{l}
\text{Direct materials} \\
\text{yield variance for} \\
\text{each input}
\end{array}
=
\left(
\begin{array}{l}
\text{Actual total} \\
\text{quantity of all} \\
\text{direct materials} \\
\text{inputs used}
\end{array}
-
\begin{array}{l}
\text{Budgeted total} \\
\text{quantity of all} \\
\text{direct materials} \\
\text{inputs allowed} \\
\text{for actual} \\
\text{output achieved}
\end{array}
\right)
\times
\begin{array}{l}
\text{Budgeted} \\
\text{direct materials} \\
\text{input mix} \\
\text{percentage}
\end{array}
\times
\begin{array}{l}
\text{Budgeted} \\
\text{price of} \\
\text{direct materials} \\
\text{input}
\end{array}
$$

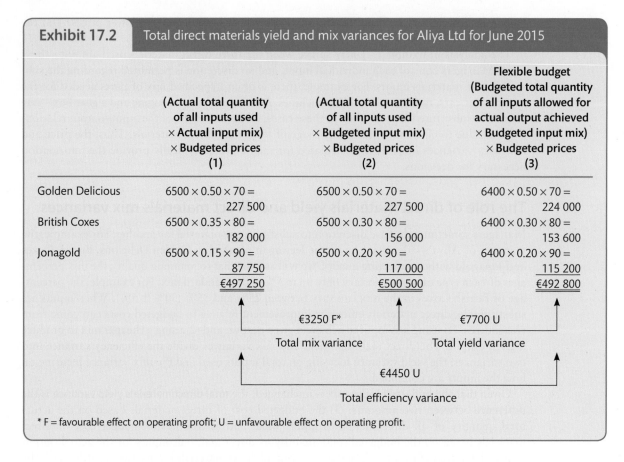

	Exhibit 17.2 Total direct materials yield and mix variances for Aliya Ltd for June 2015		

	(Actual total quantity of all inputs used × Actual input mix) × Budgeted prices (1)	(Actual total quantity of all inputs used × Budgeted input mix) × Budgeted prices (2)	Flexible budget (Budgeted total quantity of all inputs allowed for actual output achieved × Budgeted input mix) × Budgeted prices (3)
Golden Delicious	6500 × 0.50 × 70 = 227 500	6500 × 0.50 × 70 = 227 500	6400 × 0.50 × 70 = 224 000
British Coxes	6500 × 0.35 × 80 = 182 000	6500 × 0.30 × 80 = 156 000	6400 × 0.30 × 80 = 153 600
Jonagold	6500 × 0.15 × 90 = 87 750	6500 × 0.20 × 90 = 117 000	6400 × 0.20 × 90 = 115 200
	€497 250	€500 500	€492 800

€3250 F*   €7700 U

Total mix variance   Total yield variance

€4450 U

Total efficiency variance

* F = favourable effect on operating profit; U = unfavourable effect on operating profit.

The direct materials yield variances are:

Golden Delicious	$(6500 - 6400) \times 0.50 \times €70 = 100 \times 0.50 \times €70 =$	€3500 U
British Coxes	$(6500 - 6400) \times 0.30 \times €80 = 100 \times 0.30 \times €80 =$	2400 U
Jonagold	$(6500 - 6400) \times 0.20 \times €90 = 100 \times 0.20 \times €90 =$	1800 U
Total direct materials yield variance		€7700 U

The total direct materials yield variance is unfavourable because Aliya uses 6500 tonnes of apples rather than the 6400 tonnes that it should have used to produce 4000 tonnes of cider. Holding constant the budgeted mix and budgeted prices of apples, the budgeted cost per tonne of apples in the budgeted mix is €77 per tonne. The unfavourable yield variance represents the budgeted cost of using 100 more tonnes of apples $(6500 - 6400) \times €77 = €7700$ U.

Total direct materials mix variance

Compare columns 2 and 1 in Exhibit 17.2. Both columns calculate cost using the actual total quantity of all inputs used (6500 tonnes) and budgeted input prices (Golden Delicious, €70; British Coxes, €80; and Jonagold, €90). The only difference is that column 2 uses *budgeted input mix* (Golden Delicious, 50%; British Coxes, 30%; and Jonagold, 20%), and column 1 uses *actual input mix* (Golden Delicious, 50%; British Coxes, 35%; Jonagold, 15%). The difference in costs between the two columns is the total direct materials mix variance, attributable solely to differences in the mix of inputs used. The total direct materials mix variance is the sum of the direct materials mix variances for each input.

$$\begin{array}{c} \text{Direct materials mix} \\ \text{variance for each input} \end{array} = \left(\begin{array}{c} \text{Actual} \\ \text{direct materials} \\ \text{input mix} \\ \text{percentage} \end{array} - \begin{array}{c} \text{Budgeted} \\ \text{direct materials} \\ \text{input mix} \\ \text{percentage} \end{array} \right) \times \begin{array}{c} \text{Actual total} \\ \text{quantity of all} \\ \text{direct materials} \\ \text{inputs used} \end{array} \times \begin{array}{c} \text{Budgeted} \\ \text{price of} \\ \text{direct materials} \\ \text{input} \end{array}$$

The direct materials mix variances are:

Golden Delicious	$(0.50 - 0.50) \times 6500 \times €70 = 0 \times 6500 \times €70$	=	€0
British Coxes	$(0.35 - 0.30) \times 6500 \times €80 = 0.05 \times 6500 \times €80$	=	26 000 U
Jonagold	$(0.15 - 0.20) \times 6500 \times €90 = (-0.05) \times 6500 \times €90$	=	29 250 F
Total direct materials mix variance			€3 250 F

The favourable total direct materials mix variance (3250 F) occurs because the average budgeted cost per tonne of apples in the actual mix [€497 250 (Exhibit 17.2, column 1) ÷ 6500 = €76.50] is less than the average budgeted cost per tonne of apples in the budgeted mix [€500 500 (Exhibit 17.2, column 2) ÷ 6500 = €77]. The favourable mix variance represents the difference in cost of the budgeted mix and the actual mix for the 6500 tonnes of apples used (€76.50 – €77) × 6500 = €3250 F. The total direct materials mix variance helps managers understand how total budgeted costs change as the actual direct materials mix varies from the budgeted mix. The mix variance of an individual input is favourable (unfavourable) if Aliya uses a smaller (greater) percentage of that input in its actual mix relative to the budgeted mix. The individual variances help managers identify the reasons why the total mix variance is favourable – substituting some lower (budgeted) priced British Coxes (€80 per tonne) in place of the more costly Jonagold (€90 per tonne) while using the budgeted mix of Golden Delicious reduces costs.

How should we interpret the analysis in Exhibit 17.2? The total direct materials yield variance is €7700 U, and the total direct materials mix variance is €3250 F. There was a trade-off among ingredients (perhaps because of the high cost or lack of availability of Jonagold) that reduced the (budgeted) cost of the mix of inputs used but hurt yield. That is, the benefit of the cheaper mix was more than offset by the lower yield. This analysis helps Aliya's managers to understand that using the cheaper mix of inputs in the future will only be worthwhile if they can improve yield. Managers would need to understand the reasons for the poor yield – for example, did the poor yield result from inadequate testing of the apples received, from lax quality control during processing, or simply from using a cheaper mix? Identifying these reasons enables managers to find ways to overcome these problems and improve performance.

The direct materials variances calculated in Exhibits 17.1 and 17.2 can be summarised as follows:

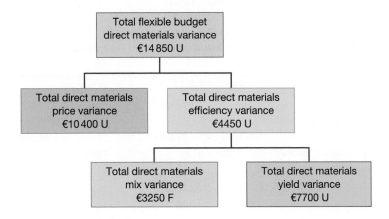

Direct manufacturing labour yield and mix variances

Direct manufacturing labour variances are calculated in much the same way as direct materials variances. We again use the Aliya Ltd example to illustrate direct manufacturing labour price, efficiency, yield and mix variances. Aliya has three grades of direct manufacturing labour: Grade 1, Grade 2 and Grade 3. Budgeted costs for June 2015 follow:

3000	hours of Grade 3 labour at €24 per hour	€72 000
2100	hours of Grade 2 labour at €16 per hour	33 600
900	hours of Grade 1 labour at €12 per hour	10 800
6000	total hours	€116 400

Actual results for June 2015 show that the work was completed in 5900 hours:

3245	hours of Grade 3 labour at €23 per hour	€74 635
1770	hours of Grade 2 labour at €18 per hour	31 860
885	hours of Grade 1 labour at €13 per hour	11 505
5900	total hours	118 000
	Budgeted costs	116 400
	Total direct manufacturing labour variance to be explained	€1600 U

Exhibit 17.3 presents the direct manufacturing labour price and efficiency variances for each employee category and in total. The total price variance is unfavourable (€1180 U) because of the higher wage rates paid to Grade 1 and Grade 2 labour. Managers would want to understand why the wage rates were higher – for example, did the higher rate result from a general shortage of Grade 2 labour or from factors specific to Aliya? The total efficiency variance is unfavourable (€420 U), primarily because of the greater number of hours worked by Grade 3 labour. The budgeted costs of these hours were only partially offset by the fewer hours worked by Grade 1 and Grade 2 labour and the fewer total hours worked. Aliya's managers would want to explore the reasons for the unfavourable efficiency variance – for example, was it caused by absenteeism, labour turnover, processing problems or the change in the mix of workers? To further understand this last issue, the unfavourable total direct manufacturing labour efficiency variance of €420 may be divided into yield and mix variances in the same way that we divided the direct materials efficiency variance in the preceding section.

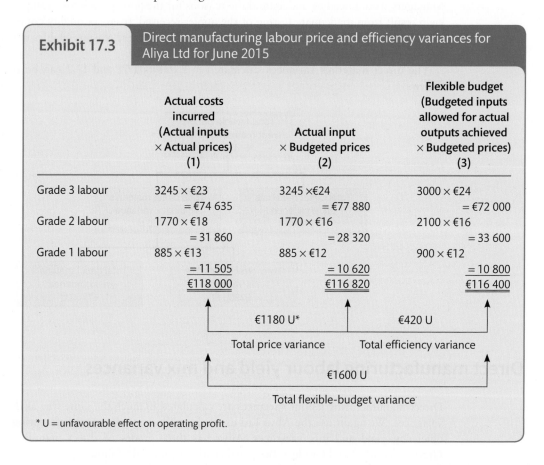

Exhibit 17.3   Direct manufacturing labour price and efficiency variances for Aliya Ltd for June 2015

	Actual costs incurred (Actual inputs × Actual prices) (1)	Actual input × Budgeted prices (2)	Flexible budget (Budgeted inputs allowed for actual outputs achieved × Budgeted prices) (3)
Grade 3 labour	3245 × €23 = €74 635	3245 × €24 = €77 880	3000 × €24 = €72 000
Grade 2 labour	1770 × €18 = 31 860	1770 × €16 = 28 320	2100 × €16 = 33 600
Grade 1 labour	885 × €13 = 11 505	885 × €12 = 10 620	900 × €12 = 10 800
	€118 000	€116 820	€116 400

€1180 U*   €420 U

Total price variance   Total efficiency variance

€1600 U

Total flexible-budget variance

* U = unfavourable effect on operating profit.

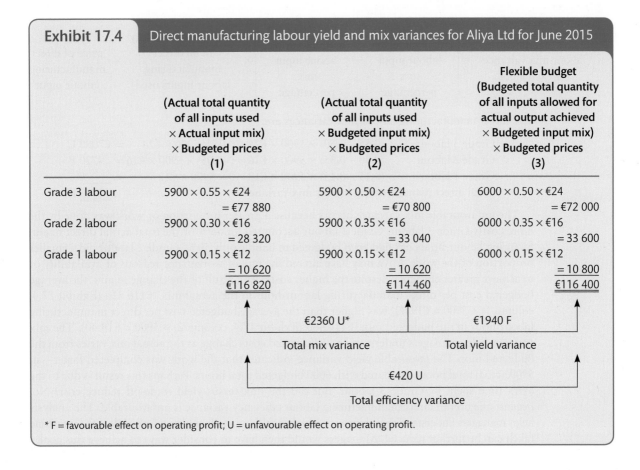

Exhibit 17.4   Direct manufacturing labour yield and mix variances for Aliya Ltd for June 2015

	(Actual total quantity of all inputs used × Actual input mix) × Budgeted prices (1)	(Actual total quantity of all inputs used × Budgeted input mix) × Budgeted prices (2)	Flexible budget (Budgeted total quantity of all inputs allowed for actual output achieved × Budgeted input mix) × Budgeted prices (3)
Grade 3 labour	5900 × 0.55 × €24 = €77 880	5900 × 0.50 × €24 = €70 800	6000 × 0.50 × €24 = €72 000
Grade 2 labour	5900 × 0.30 × €16 = 28 320	5900 × 0.35 × €16 = 33 040	6000 × 0.35 × €16 = 33 600
Grade 1 labour	5900 × 0.15 × €12 = 10 620 €116 820	5900 × 0.15 × €12 = 10 620 €114 460	6000 × 0.15 × €12 = 10 800 €116 400

€2360 U*
Total mix variance

€1940 F
Total yield variance

€420 U
Total efficiency variance

* F = favourable effect on operating profit; U = unfavourable effect on operating profit.

Keeping the budgeted input mix unchanged, the **total direct manufacturing labour yield variance** is the difference between two amounts: (1) the budgeted cost of direct manufacturing labour based on the actual total quantity of all direct manufacturing labour used, and (2) the flexible-budget cost of direct manufacturing labour based on the budgeted total quantity of direct manufacturing labour for the actual output achieved. Taking the actual total quantity of all direct manufacturing labour used as given, the **total direct manufacturing labour mix variance** is the difference between two amounts: (1) the budgeted cost of inputs in the actual mix of direct manufacturing labour, and (2) the budgeted cost of inputs in the budgeted mix of direct manufacturing labour.

Exhibit 17.4 presents the computations for the *total direct manufacturing labour yield* and *mix variances* for Aliya Ltd in columnar format. These variances can also be calculated as follows:

$$\begin{array}{c}\text{Direct manufacturing} \\ \text{labour yield vairance} \\ \text{for each input}\end{array} = \left(\begin{array}{c}\text{Actual} \\ \text{total quantity} \\ \text{of all direct} \\ \text{manufacturing} \\ \text{labour inputs} \\ \text{used}\end{array} - \begin{array}{c}\text{Budgeted} \\ \text{quantity of all} \\ \text{direct manufacturing} \\ \text{labour inputs} \\ \text{allowed for actual} \\ \text{output achieved}\end{array}\right) \times \begin{array}{c}\text{Budgeted direct} \\ \text{manufacturing} \\ \text{labour input} \\ \text{mix percentage}\end{array} \times \begin{array}{c}\text{Budgeted} \\ \text{price of direct} \\ \text{manufacturing} \\ \text{labour input}\end{array}$$

The direct manufacturing labour yield variances are:

Grade 3 labour	$(5900 - 6000) \times 0.50 \times €24 = (-100) \times 0.50 \times €24 =$	€1200 F
Grade 2 labour	$(5900 - 6000) \times 0.35 \times €16 = (-100) \times 0.35 \times €16 =$	560 F
Grade 1 labour	$(5900 - 6000) \times 0.15 \times €12 = (-100) \times 0.15 \times €12 =$	180 F
Total direct manufacturing labour yield variance		€1940 F

$$\begin{array}{l} \text{Direct manufacturing} \\ \text{labour mix vairance} \\ \text{for each input} \end{array} = \left(\begin{array}{c} \text{Actual} \\ \text{manufacturing} \\ \text{labour input} \\ \text{mix} \\ \text{percentage} \end{array} - \begin{array}{c} \text{Budgeted direct} \\ \text{manufacturing} \\ \text{labour input} \\ \text{mix} \\ \text{percentage} \end{array} \right) \times \begin{array}{c} \text{Actual total quantity} \\ \text{of all direct} \\ \text{manufacturing} \\ \text{labour inputs used} \end{array} \times \begin{array}{c} \text{Budgeted} \\ \text{price of direct} \\ \text{manufacturing} \\ \text{labour input} \end{array}$$

The direct manufacturing labour mix variances are:

Grade 3 labour	$(0.55 - 0.50) \times 5900 \times €24 = 0.05 \times 5900 \times €24$	$= €7080$ U
Grade 2 labour	$(0.30 - 0.35) \times 5900 \times €16 = (-0.05) \times 5900 \times €16 =$	4720 F
Grade 1 labour	$(0.15 - 0.15) \times 5900 \times €12 = 0 \times 5900 \times €12$	$= \quad 0$
Total direct manufacturing labour mix variance		$\underline{€2360}$ U

The unfavourable mix variance occurs because a greater proportion of work was done by the more costly Grade 3 labour. Grade 3 labour accounted for 55% of the total actual direct manufacturing labour-hours but had been budgeted to handle only 50%. Grade 2 labour did a smaller proportion of the work. Aliya may have altered the mix of workers for reasons of availability or to achieve greater efficiency despite the higher costs. As a result of the change in mix, the average budgeted cost per direct manufacturing labour-hour in the actual mix [€116 820 (Exhibit 17.4, column 1) ÷ 5900 = €19.80] was higher than the average budgeted cost per direct manufacturing labour-hour in the budgeted mix [€114 460 (Exhibit 17.4, column 2) ÷ 5900 = €19.40]. The mix variance helps managers understand how budgeted costs change as the actual mix varies from the budgeted mix. The favourable yield variance indicates that the work was completed faster – in 5900 actual total hours compared with 6000 budgeted total hours. Perhaps this result is due to the extra time spent by Grade 3 labour. But did the mix-versus-yield trade-off reduce cost? No, because the overall direct manufacturing labour efficiency variance is unfavourable. The analysis helps managers understand that shifting to a higher skills mix will only be worthwhile if the total time taken can be further reduced. Managers would then have to consider ways to achieve this goal.

Revenue and sales variances

We now examine how variances that use revenue information as a key output can be calculated. Special attention is paid to companies with multiple products or services.

The revenue variances we discuss are most frequently called sales variances, in large part because sales are the single largest component of revenue for many companies. For example, sales of new or used vehicles in a motorcar dealership are typically a larger source of revenues than are after-sales revenue items such as servicing and repairs.

The levels approach introduced in Chapter 15 shows how the variances we now discuss are linked to each other:

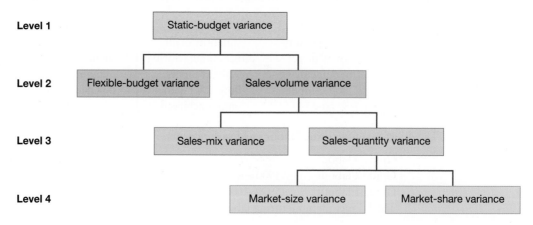

We discuss how each variance can be calculated for the revenues of Global Air, which has multiple classes of air service on its flights. The variances in this section could be calculated for any line item in the income statement. For exposition purposes, we calculate variances for the revenue line item of Global Air. Airlines face many challenges in increasing their revenues, such as the level of price discounting and the special airline club promotions to use. The variances discussed in the next section help managers to evaluate how well budgeted revenue targets are met. A second reason for Global Air's emphasis on revenues (as opposed to, say, contribution margin per passenger) is that variable costs per passenger are minimal. A third reason is that many marketing or sales divisions are run as revenue centres.

Variance analysis for multiple products

Global Air operates flights between New York and London. It has three classes of service: first class, business class and economy class. It is currently examining results for August 2015. Unit volume is measured in terms of a round-trip ticket (one-way tickets are converted into equivalent round-trip tickets). Budgeted and actual results for August 2015 are as follows:

	Budget for August 2015				Actual for August 2015			
	Selling price per unit	Unit volume	Sales mix	Revenue	Selling price per unit	Unit volume	Sales mix	Revenue
First class	€3200	1 000	5%	€3 200 000	€2600	2 400	10%	€6 240 000
Business class	2400	3 000	15%	7 200 000	1600	6 000	25%	9 600 000
Economy class	900	16 000	80%	14 400 000	700	15 600	65%	10 920 000
Total		20 000	100%	€24 800 000		24 000	100%	€26 760 000

In July 2015, Pan Air, a major competitor of Global, went bankrupt. It was acquired by Easy Travel, a low-cost economy travel operator. Pan Air had a sizable presence in the first- and business-class markets. Easy Travel immediately offered deep price discounts for all classes of travel. Its reputation among first-class and business-class travellers, however, was poor. Global Air dropped all its fares in late July (after its budget was prepared) to meet the new competition.

Static-budget variance

The *static-budget variance* for revenues is the difference between the actual revenues and the budgeted revenues from the static budget.

$$\text{Static-budget variance of revenues} = \text{Actual results} - \text{Static-budget amount}$$

First class	=	€6 240 000	–	€3 200 000	= €3 040 000	F
Business class	=	€9 600 000	–	€7 200 000	= €2 400 000	F
Economy class	=	€10 920 000	–	€14 400 000	= €3 480 000	U
Total					€1 960 000	F

Global Air has favourable variances for first class and business class and an unfavourable variance for economy class. More information about the €1 960 000 favourable total variance can be gained by examining the flexible-budget variance and the sales-volume variance.

Flexible-budget and sales-volume variances

The *flexible-budget variance* for revenues is the difference between the actual revenues and the flexible-budget amount for the actual unit volume of sales.

$$\begin{array}{ccc} \text{Fiexible-budget variance} \\ \text{of revenues} \end{array} = \begin{array}{c} \text{Actual} \\ \text{results} \end{array} - \begin{array}{c} \text{Flexible-budget} \\ \text{amount} \end{array}$$

First class	=	€6 240 000	–	(€3200 × 2400)		
	=	€6 240 000	–	€7 680 000	=	€1 440 000 U
Business class	=	€9 600 000	–	(€2400 × 6000)		
	=	€9 600 000	–	€14 400 000	=	€4 800 000 U
Economy class	=	€10 920 000	–	(€900 × 15 600)		
	=	€10 920 000	–	€14 040 000	=	€3 120 000 U
Total						€9 360 000 U

The €9 360 000 unfavourable total variance arises because Global Air sizably reduced the price for each class of travel relative to the budgeted price.

The *sales-volume variance* shows the effect of the difference between the actual and budgeted quantity of the variable used to 'flex' the flexible budget. For the revenues of Global Air, this variable is units sold. This variance can be calculated for each class of service of Global Air:

$$\begin{array}{c} \text{Sales-volume} \\ \text{variance of} \\ \text{revenues} \end{array} = \left(\begin{array}{c} \text{Actual sales} \\ \text{quantity} \\ \text{in units} \end{array} - \begin{array}{c} \text{Budgeted sales} \\ \text{quantity} \\ \text{in units} \end{array} \right) \times \begin{array}{c} \text{Budgeted} \\ \text{selling price} \\ \text{per unit} \end{array}$$

First class	=	(2400 – 1000)	×	€3200	=	€4 480 000 F
Business class	=	(6000 – 3000)	×	€2400	=	€7 200 000 F
Economy class	=	(15 600 – 16 000)	×	€900	=	€360 000 U
Total						€11 320 000 F

While the total sales-volume variance for revenues is €11 320 000 favourable, there is a combination of favourable variances for first class and business class and an unfavourable variance for economy class. Managers can gain additional insight into sales-volume changes by separating the sales-volume variance into a sales-quantity variance and a sales-mix variance.

Sales-quantity variance

The **sales-quantity variance** is the difference between two amounts: (1) the budgeted amount based on actual quantities sold of all products and the budgeted mix, and (2) the amount in the static budget (which is based on the budgeted quantities to be sold of all products and the budgeted mix). The formula for computing the sales-quantity variance in terms of revenues and the amounts for Global Air is:

$$\begin{array}{c} \text{Sales-quantity} \\ \text{variance of} \\ \text{revenues} \end{array} = \left(\begin{array}{c} \text{Actual units} \\ \text{of all products} \\ \text{sold} \end{array} - \begin{array}{c} \text{Budgeted units} \\ \text{of all products} \\ \text{sold} \end{array} \right) \times \begin{array}{c} \text{Budgeted} \\ \text{sales-mix} \\ \text{percentage} \end{array} \times \begin{array}{c} \text{Budgeted} \\ \text{selling price} \\ \text{per unit} \end{array}$$

First class	=	(24 000 – 20 000)	×	0.05 × €3200	=	€640 000 F
Business class	=	(24 000 – 20 000)	×	0.15 × €2400	=	€1 440 000 F
Economy class	=	(24 000 – 20 000)	×	0.80 × €900	=	€2 880 000 F
Total						€4 960 000 F

This variance is favourable when the actual units of product sold exceed the budgeted units of product sold. Global sold 4000 more round-trip tickets than was budgeted. Hence, its sales-quantity variance for revenues is favourable.

Sales-mix variance

The **sales-mix variance** is the difference between two amounts: (1) the budgeted amount for the actual sales mix, and (2) the budgeted amount if the budgeted sales mix had been unchanged.

The formula for computing the sales-mix variance in terms of revenue and the amounts for Global Air is:

$$\begin{array}{c} \text{Sales-mix} \\ \text{variance of} \\ \text{revenues} \end{array} = \begin{array}{c} \text{Actual units} \\ \text{of all} \\ \text{products sold} \end{array} \times \left(\begin{array}{c} \text{Actual} \\ \text{sales-mix} \\ \text{percentage} \end{array} - \begin{array}{c} \text{Budgeted} \\ \text{sales-mix} \\ \text{percentage} \end{array} \right) \times \begin{array}{c} \text{Budgeted} \\ \text{selling price} \\ \text{per unit} \end{array}$$

First class	=	24 000 × (0.10 − 0.05) × €3200 =	€3 840 000 F
Business class	=	24 000 × (0.25 − 0.15) × €2400 =	€5 760 000 F
Economy class	=	24 000 × (0.65 − 0.80) × €900 =	€3 240 000 U
Total			€6 360 000 F

A favourable sales-mix variance arises at the individual product level when the actual sales-mix percentage exceeds the budgeted sales-mix percentage. This situation applies to both first class (10% actual versus 5% budgeted) and business class (25% actual versus 15% budgeted). In contrast, economy class has an unfavourable variance because the actual sales mix percentage (65%) is less than the budgeted sales-mix percentage (80%).

The concept behind the sales-mix variance for revenues of €6 360 000 F is best explained in terms of the budgeted selling prices per composite unit of the sales mix. A **composite product unit** is a hypothetical unit with weights related to the individual products of the company. The weights for the revenue-based variances are calculated as follows in column 3 for the actual mix and column 5 for the budgeted mix:

	Budgeted selling price per unit (1)	Actual sales-mix percentage (2)	Budgeted selling price per composite unit for actual mix (3) = (1) × (2)	Budgeted sales-mix percentage (4)	Budgeted selling price per composite unit for budgeted mix (5) = (1) × (4)
First class	€3200	0.10	€320	0.05	€160
Business class	2400	0.25	600	0.15	360
Economy class	900	0.65	585	0.80	720
Total			€1505		€1240

The actual sales mix has a budgeted selling price per composite unit of €1505 (where the composite unit comprises 0.10 of first class, 0.25 of business class and 0.65 of economy class). The budgeted sales mix had a budgeted selling price per composite unit of €1240 (where the composite unit comprises 0.05 of first, 0.15 of business and 0.80 of economy). Thus, the effect of the 2015 sales-mix shift for Global Air is to increase the budgeted selling price per composite unit by €265 (€1505 − €1240). For the 24 000 units actually sold, this increase translates to a favourable sales-mix variance of €6 million.

Exhibit 17.5 shows how both the sales-mix and sales-quantity variances can be calculated using the columnar approach introduced in Chapter 15. Exhibit 17.5 highlights the revenue effect of the shift towards a mix with higher revenue generating units (first class and business class) and the revenue effect of the 20% increase in total units sold (actual of 24 000 round-trips versus 20 000 budgeted).

Market-size and market-share variances

Sales depend on overall market demand as well as the company's ability to maintain its share of the market. Assume that the budgeted unit sales of 20 000 units (round-trip tickets) came from a management estimate of a 50% market share on the New York to London route in August 2015 and an industry sales forecast by the Travel Information Group (TIG) of 40 000 round-trip tickets for the route. In September, TIG reported the following:

Exhibit 17.5	Sales-mix and sales-quantity variance analysis for revenues of Global Air on New York to London route for August 2015

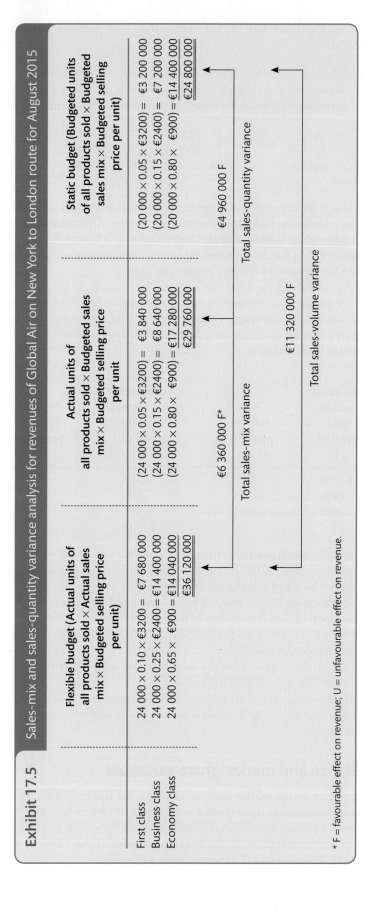

Flexible budget (Actual units of all products sold × Actual sales mix × Budgeted selling price per unit)

Actual units of all products sold × Budgeted sales mix × Budgeted selling price per unit

Static budget (Budgeted units of all products sold × Budgeted sales mix × Budgeted selling price per unit)

First class
Business class
Economy class

24 000 × 0.10 × €3200 = €7 680 000
24 000 × 0.25 × €2400 = €14 400 000
24 000 × 0.65 × €900 = €14 040 000
€36 120 000

(24 000 × 0.05 × €3200) = €3 840 000
(24 000 × 0.15 × €2400) = €8 640 000
(24 000 × 0.80 × €900) = €17 280 000
€29 760 000

(20 000 × 0.05 × €3200) = €3 200 000
(20 000 × 0.15 × €2400) = €7 200 000
(20 000 × 0.80 × €900) = €14 400 000
€24 800 000

€6 360 000 F*

Total sales-mix variance

€4 960 000 F

Total sales-quantity variance

€11 320 000 F

Total sales-volume variance

* F = favourable effect on revenue; U = unfavourable effect on revenue.

	Budgeted industry volume for August 2015	Actual industry volume for August 2015
First class	1 500	3 000
Business class	6 000	9 000
Economy class	32 500	38 000
Total	40 000	50 000

Global Air's actual market share was 48% of unit volume (24 000 ÷ 50 000) in contrast to its budgeted share of 50%. TIG noted that Easy Travel was highly successful in generating economy travel but had been unsuccessful in attracting first- and business-class travellers. In contrast, it noted Global Air's great success in expanding its first- and business-class presence.

Global Air can use this industry information from TIG to get further insight into the sales-quantity variance by dividing it into a market-size variance and a market-share variance. The **market-size variance** is the difference between two amounts: (1) the budgeted amount based on the *actual market size in units* and the budgeted market share, and (2) the static-budget amount based on the *budgeted market size in units* and the budgeted market share. The formula and the 2015 amount for Global Air for revenues are:

$$
\begin{aligned}
\text{Market-size variance of revenues} &= \left(\begin{array}{c} \text{Actual} \\ \text{market size} \\ \text{in units} \end{array} - \begin{array}{c} \text{Budgeted} \\ \text{market size} \\ \text{in units} \end{array} \right) \times \begin{array}{c} \text{Budgeted} \\ \text{market} \\ \text{share} \end{array} \times \begin{array}{c} \text{Budgeted average} \\ \text{selling price} \\ \text{per unit} \end{array} \\
&= (50\,000 - 40\,000) \times 0.50 \times €1\,240 \\
&= €6\,200\,000 \text{ F}
\end{aligned}
$$

The budgeted average selling price per (composite) unit is calculated by dividing the total budgeted revenues of €24 800 000 by the total budgeted units of 20 000. The €6 200 000 market-size variance for revenues is favourable because it is the additional revenue expected as a result of the 25% increase in market size (50 000 ÷ 40 000 = 125%), provided Global Air maintains both its budgeted market share of 50% and its budgeted average selling price of €1240.

The **market-share variance** is the difference between two amounts: (1) the budgeted amount at budgeted mix based on the actual market size in units and the actual market share, and (2) the budgeted amount at budgeted mix based on actual market size in units and the *budgeted market share*. The formula and the 2015 amounts for Global Air for revenues are:

$$
\begin{aligned}
\text{Market-share variance for revenues} &= \begin{array}{c} \text{Actual} \\ \text{market size} \\ \text{in units} \end{array} \times \left(\begin{array}{c} \text{Actual} \\ \text{market} \\ \text{share} \end{array} - \begin{array}{c} \text{Budgeted} \\ \text{market} \\ \text{share} \end{array} \right) \times \begin{array}{c} \text{Budgeted average} \\ \text{selling price} \\ \text{per unit} \end{array} \\
&= 50\,000 \times (0.48 - 0.50) \times €1\,240 \\
&= €1\,240\,000 \text{ U}
\end{aligned}
$$

Global Air lost total market share from that budgeted – from the 50% budgeted to the actual of 48%. The €1 240 000 unfavourable variance highlights the revenue impact of this 2 percentage-point decline in market share.

Exhibit 17.6 shows both the market-share and market-size variances using the columnar approach introduced in Chapter 15. Exhibit 17.7 presents an overview of the Level 1 to Level 4 variances calculated for Global Air. Note how offsetting variances occur in both Levels 2 and 4. In some cases, these offsetting variances may be causally related. The €9 360 000 unfavourable flexible-budget variance arises because of the decline in actual ticket prices from that budgeted. The €11 320 000 favourable sales-volume variance reflects the unit-volume increase stimulated by this decrease in selling prices.

The phrase 'drilling down' or 'peeling the onion' is sometimes used to describe starting at the most aggregate level (Level 1) and then progressively seeking more detail on the factors underlying

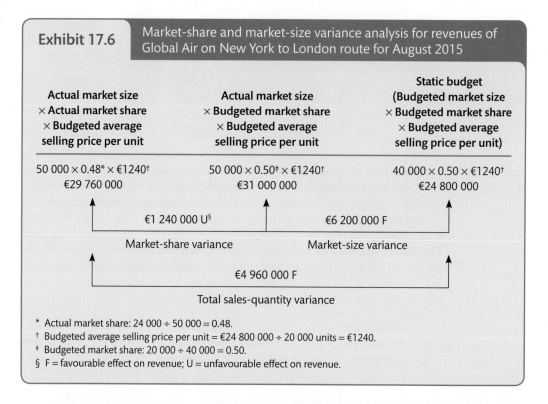

Exhibit 17.6   Market-share and market-size variance analysis for revenues of Global Air on New York to London route for August 2015

		Static budget
Actual market size × Actual market share × Budgeted average selling price per unit	Actual market size × Budgeted market share × Budgeted average selling price per unit	(Budgeted market size × Budgeted market share × Budgeted average selling price per unit)
50 000 × 0.48* × €1240† €29 760 000	50 000 × 0.50‡ × €1240† €31 000 000	40 000 × 0.50 × €1240† €24 800 000

€1 240 000 U§   €6 200 000 F

Market-share variance   Market-size variance

€4 960 000 F

Total sales-quantity variance

* Actual market share: 24 000 ÷ 50 000 = 0.48.
† Budgeted average selling price per unit = €24 800 000 ÷ 20 000 units = €1240.
‡ Budgeted market share: 20 000 ÷ 40 000 = 0.50.
§ F = favourable effect on revenue; U = unfavourable effect on revenue.

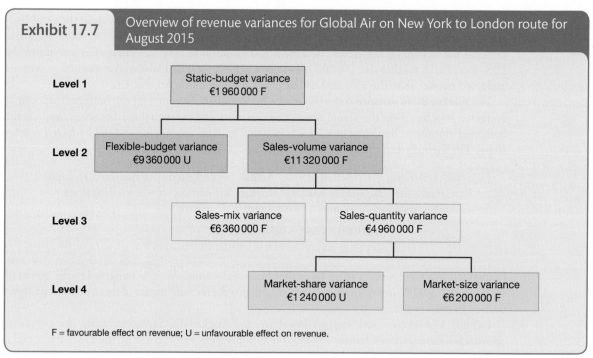

Exhibit 17.7   Overview of revenue variances for Global Air on New York to London route for August 2015

Level 1
Static-budget variance
€1 960 000 F

Level 2
Flexible-budget variance
€9 360 000 U
Sales-volume variance
€11 320 000 F

Level 3
Sales-mix variance
€6 360 000 F
Sales-quantity variance
€4 960 000 F

Level 4
Market-share variance
€1 240 000 U
Market-size variance
€6 200 000 F

F = favourable effect on revenue; U = unfavourable effect on revenue.

specific variance amounts. Managers are increasingly able to access software programs that start at Level 1 and then proceed to Levels 2, 3 and 4.

Is dividing the sales-quantity variance into the market-size and market-share variances useful for evaluating the marketing manager's performance? Suppose market size and the demand for an industry's products are largely influenced by factors such as growth and interest rates in the economy. Then the market-size variance does not tell us much about the marketing manager's performance because it is largely determined by factors outside the manager's control. Senior management may therefore put greater weight on the market-share variance in their evaluation of the marketing manager.

A caution when computing market-size and market-share variances is appropriate. Reliable information on market size and market share is available for some, but not all, industries. For example, the soft-drinks and television industries are ones where market size and share statistics are widely available. In other industries such as management consulting, information about market size and market share is far less reliable and is usually not published on a regular basis.

Summary

The following points are linked to the chapter's learning objectives.

1. When inputs, such as three direct materials, are not substitutes, price and efficiency variances individually calculated for each material typically provide the information necessary for decisions. In the case of substitutable inputs, however, various combinations of inputs can be used to produce the same output. Further splitting the efficiency variance into yield and mix variances provides additional information.

2. Many products use multiple direct materials that can be substituted for one another. In these cases, direct materials efficiency can come from two sources: (1) using fewer inputs of one or more of the materials, and (2) using a cheaper mix of materials to produce output. The total direct materials yield and mix variances divide the total direct materials efficiency variance into two components, with the yield variance focusing on the total inputs used and the mix variance evaluating how the inputs are combined.

3. Multiple direct-labour inputs that are substitutes for one another are often used to manufacture a product or provide a service. The total direct manufacturing labour yield and mix variances indicate the sources of direct manufacturing labour efficiency. A favourable total direct manufacturing labour yield variance results when fewer total direct manufacturing labour-hours are used to produce a given quantity of product. A favourable total direct manufacturing labour mix variance results when a cheaper mix of direct manufacturing labour inputs is used to produce the actual quantity of product.

4. A sales-volume variance can occur because of (a) a change in the actual unit sales from the budgeted unit sales (a sales-quantity variance), and (b) a change in the actual sales mix from the budgeted sales mix (a sales-mix variance). Sales-quantity and sales-mix variances can be calculated for companies selling multiple products or services or the same product or service in multiple markets.

5. The sales-quantity variance can occur because of (a) a change in the actual market size in units from that budgeted (the market-size variance), and (b) a change in the actual share of the market compared to its budgeted share (the market-share variance).

Key terms

total direct materials yield variance (529)
total direct materials mix variance (529)
total direct manufacturing labour yield variance (533)
total direct manufacturing labour mix variance (533)

sales-quantity variance (536)
sales-mix variance (536)
composite product unit (537)
market-size variance (539)
market-share variance (539)

CHAPTER 17

Assessment material

Review questions

17.1 Distinguish between total direct materials yield and mix variances.

17.2 'Direct materials yield and mix variances are particularly useful when materials are substitutable.' Do you agree? Explain.

17.3 Name three sources of the standards used in the total direct materials yield and mix variances.

17.4 'Changes in the mix of direct materials used from the budgeted mix always hurt yield.' Do you agree? Explain.

17.5 How might managers use information about direct-labour yield and mix variances in improving the performance of a business?

17.6 Give an example of an input other than direct materials and direct labour where calculating yield and mix variances might be useful. Explain your reasoning briefly.

17.7 The manager of a highly automated plant that assembles desktop computers commented, 'Yield and mix variance information is irrelevant to my cost management decisions.' Give two possible reasons for the manager's statement.

17.8 Explain why a favourable sales-quantity variance occurs.

17.9 Distinguish between a market-size variance and a market-share variance.

17.10 Why might some companies not calculate market-size and market-share variances?

Exercises

Intermediate level

*17.11 Direct materials efficiency, yield and mix variances (CMA, adapted) (20–25 minutes)

Paix-Trolls SARL produces a petrol additive, Elysium, that increases engine efficiency and reduces petrol consumption. The actual and budgeted quantities (in litres) of materials required to produce Elysium and the budgeted prices of materials in August 2015 are as follows:

Chemical	Actual quantity	Budgeted quantity	Budgeted price
Echol	24 080	25 200	€0.20
Protex	15 480	16 800	0.45
Benz	36 120	33 600	0.15
CT-40	10 320	8 400	0.30

Required

1 Calculate the total direct materials efficiency variance for August 2015.

2 Calculate the total direct materials yield and mix variances for August 2015.

3 What conclusions would you draw from the variance analysis?

17.12 Direct nursing labour efficiency, yield and mix variances (25 minutes)

Les Cliniques du Parc reports the following information for July 2015 regarding its nursing staff consisting of nurses, nursing assistants and orderlies.

	Actual hours	Budgeted hours	Budgeted rate per hour
Nurses	8750	8100	SFr 25
Nursing assistants	4900	5400	17
Orderlies	3850	4500	12

Required

1 Calculate the total direct nursing labour efficiency variance for July 2015.

2 Calculate the total direct nursing labour yield and mix variances for July 2015.

3 Briefly describe the conclusions you would draw from the variance analysis.

17.13 Variance analysis of revenues, multiple products (30–40 minutes)

The Antwerp Lions play in the Flemish Football League. The Lions play in the Antwerp Stadium (owned and managed by the City of Antwerp), which has a capacity of 30 000 seats (10 000 lower-tier seats and 20 000 upper-tier seats). The Antwerp Stadium charges the Lions a per-ticket charge for use of their facility. All tickets are sold by the Reservation Network, which charges the Lions a reservation fee per ticket. The Lions budgeted net revenue for each type of ticket in 2015 is calculated as follows:

	Lower-tier tickets	Upper-tier tickets
Selling price	€35	€14
Antwerp Stadium fee	10	6
Reservation Network fee	5	3
Net revenue per ticket	20	5

The budgeted and actual average attendance figures per game in the 2015 season are:

	Budgeted seats sold	Actual seats sold
Lower tier	8 000	6 600
Upper tier	12 000	15 400
Total	20 000	22 000

There was no difference between the budgeted and actual net revenue for lower-tier or upper-tier seats.

The manager of the Lions was delighted that actual attendance was 10% above budgeted attendance per game, especially given the depressed state of the local economy in the past six months.

Required

1 Calculate the sales-volume variance for individual 'product' net revenues and total net revenues for the Antwerp Lions in 2015.

2 Calculate the sales-quantity and sales-mix variances for individual 'product' net revenues and total net revenues in 2015.

3 Present a summary of the variances in requirements 1 and 2. Comment on the results.

17.14 Standard Costing (From ACCA Financial Information for Management, Part 1, June 2006) (40 minutes)

Deadeye Ltd operates a standard costing system in which all stocks are valued at standard cost. The standard direct material cost of one unit of product MS is £36, made up of 4.8 kg of material H at £7.50 per kg. Material H is used only in the manufacture of product MS. The following information relates to last month:

Material H:	
Purchased 40 000 kg for	£294 000
Issued into production	36 500 kg
Finished output of MS	7200 units

Required

1 Calculate the direct material price and usage variances for last month.

2 Prepare a statement that reconciles the actual cost of material H purchased with the standard material cost of actual production of MS for last month. The statement should incorporate the variances calculated in 1.

3 a Suggest ONE possible cause for EACH of the variances calculated in 1.
  b Who should the direct material price variance be reported to, and why?

17.15 Variance calculations (From CIMA Management Accounting Pillar Managerial Level Paper, November 2006) (40 minutes)

X Ltd uses an automated manufacturing process to produce an industrial chemical, Product P. X Ltd operates a standard marginal costing system. The standard cost data for Product P is as follows:

Standard cost per unit of Product P	
Materials	
A 10 kg @ £15 per kilo	£150
B 8 kg @ £8 per kilo	£64
C 5 kg @ £4 per kilo	£20
23 kg	
Total standard marginal cost	£234
Budgeted fixed production overheads	£350 000

In order to arrive at the budgeted selling price for Product P the company adds 80% mark-up to the standard marginal cost. The company budgeted to produce and sell 5000 units of Product P in the period. There were no budgeted inventories of Product P. The actual results for the period were as follows:

Actual production and sales	5450 units
Actual sales price	£445 per unit
Material usage and cost	
A 43 000 kg	£688 000
B 37 000 kg	£277 500
C 23 500 kg	£99 875
103 500 kg	
Fixed production overheads	£385 000

Required

1 Prepare an operating statement which reconciles the budgeted profit to the actual profit for the period. The statement should include the material mix and material yield variances.

2 The Production Manager of X Ltd is new to the job and has very little experience of management information. Write a brief report to the Production Manager of X Ltd that:

a interprets the material price, mix and yield variances;

b discusses the merits, or otherwise, of calculating the materials mix and yield variances for X Ltd.

Advanced level

*17.16 Direct materials price, efficiency, yield and mix variances (35 minutes)

Granoline SA manufactures cereal products such as multi-grain porridge and breakfastcereals. It makes multi-grain porridge by blending barley, wheat and rye. Budgeted costs to produce 100 000 kg of multi-grain porridge in November 2015 are as follows:

45 000 kg of barley at €0.30 per kg	€13 500
180 000 kg of wheat at €0.26 per kg	46 800
75 000 kg of rye at €0.22 per kg	16 500

Actual costs in November 2015 are

62 000 kg of barley at €0.28 per kg	€17 360
155 000 kg of wheat at €0.26 per kg	40 300
93 000 kg of rye at €0.20 per kg	18 600

Required

1 Calculate the total direct materials price and efficiency variances for November 2015.

2 Calculate the total direct materials mix and yield variances for November 2015.

3 Comment on your results in requirements 1 and 2.

17.17 Direct materials price and efficiency variances, direct materials yield and mix variances, perfume manufacturing (SMA, adapted) (40 minutes)

Markku Antero Oy produces perfume. To make this perfume, Markku Antero uses three different types of fluid. Tartarus, Erebus and Uranus are used in standard proportions of $\frac{4}{10}$, $\frac{3}{10}$ and $\frac{3}{10}$, and their standard costs are €6.00, €3.50 and €2.50 per litre, respectively. The chief engineer reported that in the past few months the standard yield has been at 80% on 100 litres of mix. The company maintains a policy of not carrying any direct materials, as stock storage space is costly.

Last week, the company produced 75 000 litres of perfume at a total direct materials cost of €449 500. The actual number of litres used and costs per litre for the three fluids are as follows:

Direct materials	Actual litres	Costs per litre
Tartarus	45 000	€5.50
Erebus	35 000	4.20
Uranus	20 000	2.75

Required

1 Calculate the total direct materials price and efficiency variances for perfume made in the last week.

2 Calculate the total direct materials yield and mix variances for the last week.

3 Explain the significance of the price, yield and mix variances from management's perspective.

17.18 Direct materials price and efficiency variances, direct materials yield and mix variances, food processing (50 minutes)

Tropica AB processes tropical fruit into fruit salad mix, which it sells to a food-service company. Tropica has in its budget the following standards for the direct materials inputs to produce 80 kg of tropical fruit salad:

50 kg of pineapple at SFr 1.00 per kg	SFr 50
30 kg of watermelon at SFr 0.50 per kg	15
20 kg of mango at SFr 0.75 per kg	15
100	SFr 80

Note that 100 kg of input quantities are required to produce 80 kg of fruit salad. No stocks of direct materials are kept. Purchases are made as needed, so all price variances are related to direct materials used. The actual direct materials inputs used to produce 54 000 kg of tropical fruit salad for the month of October were

36 400 kg of pineapple at SFr 0.90 per kg	SFr 32 760
18 200 kg of watermelon at SFr 0.60 per kg	10 920
15 400 kg of mango at SFr 0.70 per kg	10 780
70 000	SFr 54 460

Required

1 Calculate the total direct materials price and efficiency variances in October.

2 Calculate the total direct materials yield and mix variances for October.

3 Comment on your results in requirements 1 and 2.

4 How might the management of Tropica use information about the direct materials yield and mix variances?

17.19 Direct materials efficiency variance, mix and yield variances; working backward (30–40 minutes)

Calypso SA manufactures and sells fertilisers. Calypso uses the following standard direct materials costs to produce 1 tonne of fertiliser:

75% of the input materials is Alpha at €400 per tonne	€360
25% of the input materials is Gamma at €200 per tonne	60
Total standard cost of 1.2 tonnes of inputs	€420

Note that 1.2 tonnes of input quantities are required to produce 1 tonne of fertiliser. No stocks of direct materials are kept. Purchases are made as needed, so all price variances are related to direct materials used. Calypso produced 2000 tonnes of fertiliser in a particular period. The total direct materials yield variance for the period was €35 000 U. The actual input mix for the period was 50% of Alpha and 50% of Gamma.

Required

1 Calculate the individual direct materials yield variances for the period.

2 Calculate the individual and total direct materials mix variances for the period.

3 Calculate the individual and total direct materials efficiency variances for the period.

4 Briefly describe the conclusions you would draw from the variance analyses.

17.20 Direct service labour price, efficiency, yield and mix variances (40 minutes)

O'Connell & Associates, a firm of architects, has three levels of professional staff: principals (managers), who manage all aspects of the architectural job; senior architects, who are responsible for the main designs; and junior architects, who provide technical support. Budgeted costs for five architectural jobs done over a recent period are as follows:

600 principal-hours at €105 per hour	€63 000
1800 senior-hours at €75 per hour	135 000
3600 junior-hours at €25 per hour	90 000

Actual hours worked and the actual rates per hour to complete the five jobs are

295 principal-hours at €108 per hour	€31 860
2360 senior-hours at €70 per hour	165 200
3245 junior-hours at €30 per hour	97 350

Required

1 Calculate the total direct labour price and efficiency variances for the five jobs.

2 Calculate the total direct labour mix and yield variances for the five jobs.

3 Comment on your results in requirements 1 and 2.

4 How might managers use information about the direct labour yield and mix variances?

*17.21 Variance analysis of contribution margin, multiple products; working backwards (30 minutes)

Rusti-Verres SNC sells two brands of wine glasses – Choc and Chic. Rusti-Verres provides the following information for sales in the month of June 2015:

Static-budget total contribution margin	SFr 5600
Budgeted units to be sold of all glasses in June 2015	2000 units
Budgeted contribution margin per unit of Choc	SFr 2 per unit
Budgeted contribution margin per unit of Chic	SFr 6 per unit
Total sales-quantity variance	SFr 1400 U
Actual sales-mix percentage of Choc	60%

All variances are to be calculated in contribution-margin terms.

Required

1 Calculate the sales-quantity variances for each product for June 2015.

2 Calculate the individual product and total sales-mix variances for June 2015. Calculate. the individual product and total sales-volume variances for June 2015.

3 Briefly describe the conclusions you would draw from the variances.

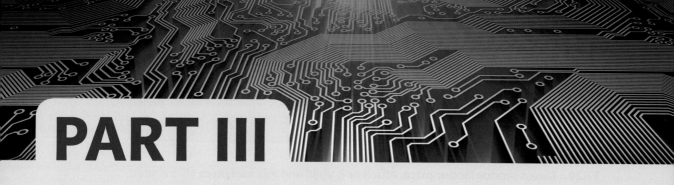

PART III

Case study problems

Case 301

Zeros plc
Falconer Mitchell, University of Edinburgh

This case is concerned with the use of ROI to measure divisional performance. It also addresses the use of an integrated standard costing system to produce meaningful profit statements where standard setting is problematic.

The board of Zeros plc assesses divisional performance within the company primarily on the basis of a return on investment ratio. This is computed as follows:

$$\frac{\text{Operating profit}}{\text{Book value of total assets}} \times 100 = \text{ROI}$$

The figure of operating profit is obtained from a standard-costing-based profit statement (see Exhibit 301.1 for the two most recent such statements).

The Blank Division

In terms of turnover the Blank Division is the second largest division within the company. The divisional manager is Joe Cool who has worked in the division for over 30 years, initially as a management accountant and then as manager from 2005. He is 63 years old and will retire in 18 months' time. In accordance with a board policy introduced to improve motivation at divisional level, his current remuneration contains a substantial bonus element based on divisional operating profit. In addition, his retirement pension will be based upon his average total earnings in his last three working years.

Source: Mitchell, F. (1988) 'Zeros plc', in D. Otley, D. Brown and C. Wilkinson (eds) *Case Studies in Management Accounting* (Hemel Hempstead, UK: Philip Allan Publishers). Reproduced with permission.

Exhibit 301.1   Annual profit statement

	2014 (£000)	2015 (£000)
Budgeted sale	8000	10 940
Selling price variance	–	–
Sales volume variance	(1600) U	(2 735) U
Actual sales	6400	8 205
Standard cost of sales	4800	6 150
Standard operating profit	1600	2 055
Cost variances		
Direct material price	(100) U	(80) U
Direct material usage	(220) U	(280) U
Labour rate	(150) U	(130) U
Labour efficiency	(200) U	(300) U
Variable overhead spending	(180) U	(300) U
Variable overhead efficiency	(250) U	(275) U
Fixed overhead spending	(120) U	(150) U
Fixed overhead volume	–	–
Operating profit	380	540

Exhibit 301.2   Unit standard costs and selling price

	2014	2015
Unit standard cost		
Direct material	0.50	0.60
Direct labour	0.75	0.90
Variable overheads	0.50	0.60
Fixed overheads	1.25	2.00
	3.00	4.10
Actual unit selling prices	4.00	5.47

The Blank Division was resituated in a town-centre freehold site which was purchased in 1999. A custom-built factory was erected on the site with considerable financial aid from the government, and was equipped with what were, at the time, the most modern machines available. It is a matter of considerable pride to Joe that much of this equipment has been conscientiously maintained and is still in use today. In the accounting records the freehold site and factory building are still valued at historic cost.

The Blank Division produces a wide range of sizes of surgical needles, although all are sold at a standard price (see Exhibit 301.2). Although the market is growing the competition is intense, being based on both price and, particularly, product quality.

Standard costs are revised at the start of each financial year (see Exhibit 301.2) and are based on the middle-range size of surgical needle produced in the division.

Exhibit 301.3	Records of production and sales	
	2014 ('000 units)	2015 ('000 units)
Opening stock	200	600
Production	2000	2000
Sales	(1600)	(1500)
Closing stock	600	1100

It is frequently pointed out at board meetings by Joe Cool that the Blank Division can still achieve a 33% mark-up on its standard unit cost, and that no competing firm can approach this level of margin.

In recent years the Blank Division has produced highly satisfactory return-on-investment figures and a reasonable profit growth. The board has, however, been concerned by the large unfavourable variances which have been consistently reported. The normal retort of the Blank Division manager to queries on the size of variances has been to state unequivocally that 'it is the bottom line that matters; if that's OK you can forget the rest'. He has also consistently promoted the performance of his division during 2014 and 2015 to the board as 'excellent' and rebuffed any judgements to the contrary. Results for the last two years are given in Exhibits 301.1 and 301.3.

Questions

1 What criticism would you make of the approach to divisional-performance assessment employed by the board of Zeros plc?

2 Would you agree with Joe Cool's assessment that his division's performance was 'excellent' during 2014 and 2015?

3 What suggestions would you make for improving the divisional-performance measurement in Zeros plc?

Case 302

Instrumental Ltd

Vijay Govindarajan and John Shank

This case requires the analysis of budgeted versus actual performance for different organisational functions and considers strategic versus operational issues.

David Jones, president and principal shareholder of Instrumental Ltd, sat at his desk reflecting on the 2015 results (Exhibit 302.1). For the second year in succession the company had exceeded its profit target. David was obviously happy with the 2015 results. All the same, he wanted to get a better feel for the relative contributions of the R&D, manufacturing and marketing departments in this overall success. With this in mind, he called his assistant, Jennifer, a recent MBA graduate of the London Business School, into his office.

Exhibit 302.1	Profit and loss account for year ending 2015			
		Budget (£000)		Actual (£000)
Sales		16 872		17 061
Cost of goods sold		9 668		9 865
Gross margin		7 204		7 196
Less:				
Operating expenses				
Marketing	1856		1440	
R&D	1480		932	
Administration	1340	4 676	1674	4 046
Profit before taxes		2 528		3 150

Source: Adapted from a case written by Govindarajan, V. and Shank, J. (1989) 'Profit variance analysis: a strategic focus', *Issues in Accounting Education*, Fall, pp. 396–410. Reproduced with permission from the American Accounting Association.

'Jennifer,' he started, 'as you can see from our recent financial results, we have exceeded our profit target by £622 000. Could you please prepare an analysis showing how much R&D, manufacturing and marketing contributed to this?'

Jennifer, flushed with all the fervour and enthusiasm of a total convert to professional management, got down to work immediately. She collected all the data in Exhibit 302.2 and then wondered somewhat disconsolately what her next step should be.

Exhibit 302.2	Instrumental Ltd: additional information

	Electric motors (EM)	Electronic instruments (EI)
Selling prices per unit		
Average standard price	£40.00	£180.00
Average actual prices, 2015	30.00	206.00
Variable product costs per unit		
Average standard manufacturing cost	20.00	50.00
Average actual manufacturing cost	21.00	54.00
Volume information		
Units produced and sold – actual	141 770	62 172
Units produced and sold – planned	124 800	66 000
Total industry sales, 2015 – actual	£44 million	£76 million
Total industry variable product costs,		
2015 – actual	£16 million	£32 million
Instrumental's share of the market		
(% of physical units)		
Planned	10%	15%
Actual	16%	9%

	Planned	Actual
Firm-wide fixed expenses (£000)		
Fixed manufacturing expenses	£3872	3530
Fixed marketing expenses	1856	1440
Fixed administrative expenses	1340	1674
Fixed R&D expenses		
(exclusively for EI)	1480	932

Instrumental's products can be grouped into two main lines of business: electric motors (EM) and electronic instruments (EI). Both EM and EI are industrial measuring instruments and perform almost identical functions. However, EM is based on mechanical and electrical technology, whereas EI is based on the microchip.

Instrumental Ltd uses a variable costing system for internal reporting purposes.

Question

You are required to put yourself in Jennifer's position and state what you would do in your analysis of Instrumental's performance across its different departments and what you would recommend to the president.

Case 303

Hereford Steak Houses
Thomas Ahrens, United Arab Emirates University and Christopher Chapman, Imperial College London and Copenhagen Business School

I'd love to know where I am as an area manager. I don't know what to do with food margin. Shall I say to my restaurant managers, well done? Thank you? You're fired?

Hereford Steak Houses operated a chain of more than 200 wholly owned, full-service restaurants across the UK. Over the past 10 years the division had achieved substantial growth in revenues and earnings through the addition of new restaurants. More recently, however, with increasing numbers of new entrants to the UK eating-out market and the growing saturation of Hereford Steak Houses' own outlets, senior managers were increasingly turning their attention to internal financial controls as a means to sustain earnings growth.

National branding and marketing for the chain was managed centrally by Hereford Steak Houses' head office. Most significant to this was the nationwide menu that defined the food specifications, cost and price of all dishes for sale in all outlets. Menus were designed to deliver a target food gross profit margin that was agreed between the boards of Hereford Steak Houses and the corporate leisure group of which it was part, and applied to all of Hereford Steak Houses' outlets. While food cost was a primary element of restaurant controllable costs, as the above quotation from an area manager indicates, there was a lack of agreement on how the food margin reports should be used to evaluate a restaurant manager. Restaurant managers emphasised that they wanted leeway to meet the demand of their local clientele.

Source: Thomas Ahrens, United Arab Emirates University and Christopher Chapman, Imperial College London.

Exhibit 303.1	Menu design ingredients database report			

	Standard wastage percentage:			**1%**
Ingredient no.	**Description**	**Input cost**	**Wastage**	**Standard cost**
100	1 pat butter	0.05	0.001	0.05
101	1 standard garnish	0.20	0.002	0.20
102	1 sachet ketchup	0.05	0.001	0.05
151	1 bread roll	0.15	0.002	0.15
297	1 portion of fries	0.60	0.006	0.61
314	1 carton vegetable soup	2.40	0.024	2.42
601	9 oz rump steak	6.00	0.060	6.06
907	6 oz frozen cod fillet	3.60	0.036	3.64
915	1 fish finger	0.25	0.003	0.25

The gross profit margin was defined as sales minus cost of food used, and was generally referred to as the 'food margin'. For each new menu a selection of dishes was iteratively developed in order to achieve the target food margin (in terms of percentage and cash). This was a complicated process since the menu needed to contain dishes at a range of price points to appeal to different customers. Depending on the selling price, different levels of margin were realistic. For example, a very high margin on high-cost dishes resulted in unrealistic sales prices, but could be sustainable on low-cost dishes. High-volume dishes offered scope for the centralised purchasing department on negotiate substantial price discounts. Hereford Steak Houses' position as a buyer of large quantities of food also allowed them to enforce strict quality standards for raw materials.

The process of developing individual restaurant budgets started with an estimation of the achievable level of sales growth based on expected number of dishes and prices from the central menu. Budgets were painstakingly built up. They drew on the database of standard ingredient costs, which included a standard allowance for wastage (Exhibit 303.1). Then dish specifications, prices and expected sales mix were decided (Exhibit 303.2). For weekly management reporting this data was used to generate a target food margin based on each restaurant's actual dish-mix that could be compared with the actual cost of food used (Exhibit 303.3). The actual cost of food was calculated by adding the opening inventory to deliveries received minus closing inventory (see Exhibit 303.4).

Exhibit 303.2	Dish specification and costing report @ standard cost

Dish no.	Description	% sales	Ingredients	Cost (£)	Sales price (£)	Gross profit margin (%)	Gross profit margin (£)
1	Soup	10.0%					
			1 pat butter	0.05			
			1 bread roll	0.15			
			1 carton vegetable soup	2.42			
			Total	£2.62	£5.50	52.3%	£2.87
11	Steak and chips	45.0%					
			1 standard garnish	0.20			
			1 portion of fries	0.61			
			9 oz rump steak	6.06			
			Total	£6.87	£11.95	42.5%	£5.08
12	Fish and chips	25.0%					
			1 standard garnish	0.20			
			1 portion of fries	0.61			
			6 oz frozen cod fillet	3.64			
			Total	£4.45	£8.50	47.7%	£4.06
21	Fish fingers	20.0%					
			1 sachet ketchup	0.05			
			1 portion of fries	0.61			
			3 fish fingers	0.75			
			Total	£1.41	£4.95	71.4%	£3.54

Exhibit 303.3	Restaurant no. 219 budget report – week 48

	Budget	Actual
Dishes	1 500	1 600
Revenue	13 563.75	13 116.00
Cost	7120.50	6 805.50
Gross profit margin (£)	6433.25	6 310.50
Gross profit margin (%)	47.5%	48.1%

	Actual dishes sold
Soup	240
Steak and chips	480
Fish and chips	480
Fish fingers	400

PART III Case study problems

Exhibit 303.4	Restaurant no. 219 stock-keeping report – week 48			
Ingredient no.	Description	Opening stock count	Purchases during week	Closing stock count
100	1 pat butter	200	120	30
101	1 standard garnish	200	1300	300
102	1 sachet ketchup	300	400	300
151	1 bread roll	300	100	60
297	1 portion of fries	2000	900	1840
314	1 carton vegetable soup	100	180	40
601	9 oz rump steak	300	400	160
907	6 oz frozen cod fillet	250	300	70
915	1 fish finger	200	1200	200

In order to take advantage of centralised purchasing and also to ensure tight control over quality standards, restaurants sourced all their food purchases through the centralised supply chain. Especially for seasonal produce it was normal for Hereford Steak Houses to agree price bands with their food suppliers. Fluctuations in the price of food purchased were accounted for by the central purchasing department. The weekly budget reports for the restaurants were based on the standard costs that had been defined during the design of the menu.

Questions

1 Calculate the following variances for restaurant no. 219: Static budget variance, sales volume variance, sales mix variance, sales quantity variance and the flexible budget variance.

2 Calculate usage variances for all ingredients for restaurant no. 219.

3 If you were the manager of restaurant no. 219, what would you do?

4 Recently the central purchasing department managed to secure a 5% reduction on the input cost for steaks and a 15% reduction in the input costs of portions of fries compared with those shown in Exhibit 304.1. Calculate the resulting price variances for restaurant no. 219 for week 48.

PART IV

Management control systems and performance issues

Part III emphasised planning and control considerations in management and cost accounting. The aim in Part IV is to build on costing system design and implementation issues by considering further ways in which managerial action is guided and affected by internal accounting information. In particular, notions of how the structuring of the organisation influences accounting practices and performance assessment approaches are considered in Chapters 18 and 19.

CHAPTER 18

Control systems and transfer pricing

Aside from studying the technical aspects of management control systems, it is essential to consider how the system will influence the behaviour of the people who use it. What role can accounting information play in management control systems? For example, how does cost and budget information help in planning and coordinating the actions of multiple divisions within companies such as Philips and Ericsson? This chapter explores some links between strategy, organisation structure, management control systems and accounting information. It examines the benefits and costs of centralised and decentralised organisational structures and looks at the pricing of products or services transferred between subunits of the same organisation. A large proportion of global trade consists of internal transactions within transnational companies. Over half of international transactions are inter-company transactions (European Parliament Briefing 2013, http://www.europarl.europa.eu/RegData/bibliotheque/briefing/2013/130574/LDM_BRI(2013)130574_REV1_EN.pdf). The mechanisms used to establish the pricing of these transactions (transfer prices) can be complex. Relevant transfer pricing issues are considered in this chapter.

Learning objectives

After studying this chapter, you should be able to:

- Describe a management control system

- Recognise important elements of effective management control systems

- Describe the benefits and costs of decentralisation

- Identify three general methods for determining transfer prices and understand how a transfer-pricing method can affect the operating profit of individual subunits

- Illustrate how market-based transfer prices generally promote goal congruence in perfectly competitive markets

- Recognise when a transfer price may lead to suboptimal decisions

- Understand the range over which two divisions generally negotiate the transfer price when there is unused capacity

- Present a general guideline for determining a minimum transfer price in transfer-pricing situations

- Recognise income tax considerations in multinational transfer pricing

Management control systems

A **management control system** is a means of gathering and using information to aid and coordinate the process of making planning and control decisions throughout the organisation and to guide employee behaviour. The goal of the system is to improve the collective decisions within an organisation.

Consider part of the management control system at Siemens, the German electrical and electronics company. Information for management control is gathered and reported at various levels:

1 *Total-organisation level* – for example, stock price, net income, return on investment, cash flow from operations, total employment, pollution control, and contributions to the community.

2 *Customer/market level* – for example, customer satisfaction, time taken to respond to customer requests for products, and cost of competitors' products.

3 *Individual-facility level* – for example, materials costs, labour costs, absenteeism and accidents in various divisions or business functions (such as R&D, manufacturing and distribution).

4 *Individual-activity level* – for example, the time taken and costs incurred for receiving, storing, assembling and dispatching goods in a warehouse; scrap rates, defects and units reworked on a manufacturing line; the number of sales transactions and sales euros per salesperson; and the number of shipments per employee at distribution centres.

As the preceding examples indicate, formal elements of management control systems collect both financial data (for example, net income, materials costs and storage costs) and non-financial data (for example, the time taken to respond to customer requests for products, absenteeism and accidents). Some of the information is obtained from within the company (such as net profit and number of shipments per employee); other information is obtained from outside the company (such as stock price and cost of competitors' products). Some companies present financial and non-financial information in a single report called the balanced scorecard (see Chapter 22).

The levels indicate the different kinds of information that are needed by managers performing different tasks. For example, stock price information is important at the total-organisation level but not at the individual-activity level in the warehouse, where information about the time taken for receiving and storing is more relevant. At the individual-activity level, management control reports focus on internal financial and non-financial data. At higher levels, management control reports also emphasise external financial and non-financial data.

Management control systems have both formal and informal components. The formal management control system of an organisation includes those explicit rules, procedures, performance measures and incentive plans that guide the behaviour of its managers and employees. The formal control system itself consists of several systems. The management accounting system is a formal accounting system that provides information on costs, revenues and income. Examples of other formal control systems are human resource systems (providing information on recruiting, training, absenteeism and accidents) and quality systems (providing information on scrap, defects, rework and late deliveries to customers).

The informal part of the management control system includes such aspects as shared values, loyalties and mutual commitments among members of the organisation and the unwritten norms about acceptable behaviour for promotion that also influence employee behaviour.

Evaluating management control systems

To be effective, management control systems should be closely aligned to an organisation's strategies and goals. Examples of strategies are doubling net profit in four years, increasing market share by 50% in two years, or maximising short-run profit. Suppose management decides, wisely or unwisely, to emphasise maximising short-run profit as a strategy. Then the management control system must attempt to reinforce this strategy. It should aim to provide managers with information that will help them make short-run decisions – for example, contribution margins on individual products. It should tie managers' incentives to short-run net profit figures in contexts where such remuneration is desirable.

A second important feature of formal management control systems is that they should be designed to fit the organisation's structure and the decision-making responsibility of individual managers. For example, management control should align with leadership approach. A professor at Kyung Kee School of Management in Seoul commented that 'Samsung became a world leader only because chairman Lee could keep his management control distant from external influence' (www.businessweek.com/news/2014.07.22). The company will likely see a changed approach to its management controls. This may follow after chairman Lee's hospitalisation in mid-2014. Until that time, Lee had deployed an 'autocratic management style based on the principle of always rewarding good job performances and punishing poor ones' which included removing very senior managers whose performance were sub-standard. Lee Jae-Yong, the ailing chairman's heir apparent, shows a style more focused on avoiding risks (http://asia.nikkei.com/Business/Companies/Embracing-the-Internet-of-Things-for-a-turnaround (29 December 2014)). Asda's CEO, Andy Clarke, communicated to his staff in March 2014 why he was making significant management control changes: 'In order to deliver our strategy we need to have an organisation structure where accountabilities are clear, duplication is removed, and decision making is swift and decisive' (www.thegrocer.co.uk/channels/supermarkets/asda/asda-brand-director-mckeon-departs-in-restructuring/355885.article). The supermarket chain moved to cut costs by laying off 1360 jobs and retraining 700 managers by November 2014 (http://www.standard.co.uk/business/business-news/asda-boss-vows-to-win-supermarket-war-against-discounters-despite-sales-slump-9858432.html (29 December 2014)).

Finally, effective management control systems motivate managers and employees. **Motivation** is the desire to attain a selected goal (the goal-congruence aspect) combined with the resulting drive towards that goal (the effort aspect).

Goal congruence exists when individuals and groups work towards the organisational goals that top management desires – that is, managers working in their own best interest take actions that further the overall goals of top management. Goal-congruence issues have arisen in earlier chapters. For example, in capital-budgeting decisions, making decisions by discounting long-run cash flows at the required rate of return best achieves organisational goals. But if the management control system evaluates managers on the basis of short-run accrual accounting income, managers will be tempted to make decisions to maximise accrual accounting income that may not be in the best interests of the organisation.

Effort is defined as exertion towards a goal. Effort goes beyond physical exertion, such as a worker producing at a faster rate, to include all conscientious actions (physical and mental).

Management control systems can aim to motivate employees to exert effort towards attaining organisational goals through a variety of incentives tied to the achievement of those goals. These incentives can be monetary (cash, stock, use of a company car and membership of a club) or non-monetary (power, self-esteem, and pride in working for a successful company).

One criterion for evaluating formal elements of a management control system is how far the attainment of top management's goals are promoted in a cost-effective manner.

Organisational stucture and decentralisation

Given that organisations are in a constant state of flux in terms of their markets, customers, workers, technology, and so on, it is in practice difficult ever to attain a 'fit' which might be deemed desirable between, for instance, strategy, structure and motivation of individuals. What is clear is that any such attempts need to be continuous since organisational processes are never static.

Top management makes decisions about decentralisation that affect day-to-day operations at all levels of the organisation. The essence of **decentralisation** is the freedom for managers at lower levels of the organisation to make decisions.

As we discuss the issues of decentralisation, we use the term *subunit* to refer to any part of an organisation. In practice, a subunit may be a large division (the Premier Banking subunit of Barclays plc – a UK-based financial services group) or a small group (the two-person advertising department of a local clothing boutique).

Total decentralisation means *minimum constraints and maximum freedom* for managers at the lowest levels of an organisation to make decisions. Total centralisation means *maximum constraints and minimum freedom* for managers at the lowest levels. Most companies' structures fall somewhere between these two extremes.

Benefits of decentralisation

How should top managers decide how far to decentralise? Conceptually, they might try to choose the degree of decentralisation that maximises the excess of benefits over costs bearing in mind organisational context factors. From a practical standpoint, top managers can seldom quantify either the benefits or the costs. But thought can be given to the advantages and drawbacks of decentralisation.

Advocates of decentralising decision making and granting responsibilities to managers of subunits claim the following benefits:

1 *Creates greater responsiveness to local needs.* Information is the key to intelligent decisions. Compared with top managers, subunit managers are better informed about their customers, competitors, suppliers and employees, as well as about factors that affect the performance of their jobs such as ways to decrease costs and improve quality.

2 *Leads to quicker decision making.* An organisation that gives lower-level managers the responsibility for making decisions can make decisions quickly, creating a competitive advantage over organisations that are slower because they send the decision-making responsibility upwards through layer after layer of management.

3 *Increases motivation.* Subunit managers are usually more highly motivated when they can exercise greater individual initiative.

4 *Aids management development and learning.* Giving managers more responsibility promotes the development of an experienced pool of management talent – a pool that the organisation can draw from to fill higher-level management positions. The organisation also learns which people are not management material.

5 *Sharpens the focus of managers.* In a decentralised setting, the manager of a small subunit has a concentrated focus. A small subunit is more flexible and nimble than a larger subunit and better able to adapt itself quickly to a fast-developing market opportunity. Also, top management, relieved of the burden of day-to-day operating decisions, can spend more time and energy on strategic planning for the entire organisation.

Costs of decentralisation

Advocates of more centralised decision making point out the following costs of decentralising decision making:

1 *Leads* to **suboptimal** (*also called* **incongruent) decision making,** which arises when a decision's benefit to one subunit is more than offset by the costs or loss of benefits to the organisation as a whole. This cost arises because top management has given up some control over decision making. Suboptimal decision making may occur (1) when there is a lack of harmony or congruence among the overall organisational goals, the subunit goals and the individual goals of decision makers, or (2) when no guidance is given to subunit managers concerning the effects of their decisions on other parts of the organisation. Suboptimal decision making is most likely to occur when the subunits in the organisation are highly interdependent, such as when the end-product of one subunit is the direct material of another subunit.

2 *Results in duplication of activities.* Several individual subunits of the organisation may undertake the same activity separately. For example, there may be a duplication of staff functions (accounting, employee relations and legal) if an organisation is highly decentralised. Centralising these functions helps to consolidate, streamline and downsize these activities. Consider, for instance, Microsoft CEO Satya Nadella's decision in July 2014 to fire 18 000 employees over the following year. His intent was 'to have fewer layers of management, both top down and sideways, to accelerate the flow of information and decision making. This includes flattening organizations and increasing the span of control of people managers' (www.businessweek.com/articles/2014-07-17/microsoft).

3 *Focuses managers' attention on the subunit rather than the organisation as a whole.* Individual subunit managers may regard the managers of other subunits in the same organisation as external parties. Consequently, managers may be unwilling to share significant information or to assist when another subunit faces an emergency. They may also use information they have about local conditions to further their own self-interest rather than the organisation's goals. For instance, they may ask for more resources than they need from the organisation in order to reduce the effort they need to exert.

4 *Increases costs of gathering information.* Managers may spend too much time negotiating the prices for internal products or services transferred among subunits.

To choose an appropriate organisation structure, top managers need to consider the benefits and costs of decentralisation, often on a function-by-function basis. For example, the controller's function may be highly decentralised for many attention-directing and problem-solving purposes (such as preparing operating budgets and performance reports) but highly centralised for other purposes (such as processing creditors and developing income tax strategies). Decentralising budgeting and cost reporting enables the marketing manager of a subunit, for example, to influence the design of product-line profitability reports for the subunit. Tailoring the report to the specific information that the manager may need helps the manager make more informed decisions. Centralising income tax strategies, on the other hand, allows the organisation to trade off profits in some subunit with losses in others to evaluate the impact on the organisation as a whole.

Multinational corporations are often decentralised. Language, customs, cultures, business practices, rules, laws and regulations vary significantly across countries. Decentralisation enables country managers to make decisions that exploit their knowledge of local business and political conditions and to deal with uncertainties in their individual environments. Philips, the Dutch electronics conglomerate, delegates marketing and pricing decisions for its television business in the Indian and Singaporean markets to its respective country managers. Multinational corporations often rotate managers between foreign locations and the home office. Job rotation combined with decentralisation helps develop managers' abilities to operate in global environments.

Choices about responsibility centres

To measure the performance of subunits in centralised or decentralised organisations, the management control system uses one or a mix of the four types of responsibility centre presented in Chapter 14:

- *Cost centre* – manager accountable for costs only.
- *Revenue centre* – manager accountable for revenues only.
- *Profit centre* – manager accountable for revenues and costs.
- *Investment centre* – manager accountable for investments, revenues and costs.

Centralisation or decentralisation is not mentioned in these descriptions. This is because each of these responsibility units can be found in either of the extremes of centralised and decentralised organisations.

A common misconception is that the term *profit centre* (and, in some cases, *investment centre*) is a synonym for a decentralised subunit, and that *cost centre* is a synonym for a centralised subunit. But profit centres can also be coupled with a highly centralised organisation, and cost centres can exist within a highly decentralised organisation. For example, managers in a division organised as a profit centre may have little leeway in making decisions. They may need to obtain approval from corporate headquarters for every expenditure over, say, €10 000 and may be forced to accept central-staff 'advice'. In another company, divisions may be organised as cost centres, but their managers may have great latitude on capital expenditures and on where to purchase materials and services. In short, the labels 'profit centre' and 'cost centre' are independent of the degree of decentralisation in an organisation.

Transfer pricing

In decentralised organisations, individual subunits of an organisation act as separate units. In these settings, the management control system often uses transfer prices to coordinate actions and to evaluate performance of the subunits.

An **intermediate product** is a product transferred from one subunit to another subunit of the same organisation. This product may be processed further and sold to an external customer. A **transfer price** is the price one subunit (segment, department, division, and so on) of an organisation charges for a product or service supplied to another subunit of the same organisation. The transfer price creates revenue for the selling subunit and a purchase cost for the buying subunit, affecting operating profit for both subunits. The operating profits can be used to evaluate the performance of each subunit and to motivate managers.

Alternative transfer-pricing methods

There are three general methods for determining transfer prices:

1 *Market-based transfer prices.* Upper management may choose to use the price of a similar product or service publicly listed in, say, a trade association website. Also, upper management may select, for the internal price, the external price that a subunit charges to outside customers.

2 *Cost-based transfer prices.* Upper management may choose a transfer price based on the costs of producing the product in question. Examples include variable manufacturing costs, manufacturing (absorption) costs and full product costs. 'Full product costs' include all production costs as well as costs from other business functions (R&D, design, marketing, distribution and customer service). The costs used in cost-based transfer prices can be actual costs or budgeted costs.

3 *Negotiated transfer prices.* In some cases, the subunits of a company are free to negotiate the transfer price between themselves and then to decide whether to buy and sell internally or deal with outside parties. Subunits may use information about costs and market prices in these negotiations, but there is no requirement that the chosen transfer price bear any specific relationship to either cost or market-price data. Negotiated transfer prices are often employed when market prices are volatile and change occurs constantly. The negotiated transfer price is the outcome of a bargaining process between the selling and the buying subunits.

Ideally, the chosen transfer-pricing method should lead each subunit manager to make optimal decisions for the organisation as a whole. As in all management control systems, transfer pricing should help achieve an organisation's strategies and goals, and fit its structure. In particular, it should promote *goal congruence* and a sustained high level of *management effort*. Sellers should be motivated to hold down costs of supplying a product or service, and buyers should be motivated to acquire and use inputs efficiently. If top management favours a high degree of decentralisation, transfer pricing should also promote a high level of *subunit autonomy* in decision making. **Autonomy** is the degree of freedom to make decisions.

An illustration of transfer pricing

Stavanger-Oil AS has three divisions. Each operates as a profit centre. The Production Division manages the production of crude oil from a petroleum field near Heimberg. The Transportation Division manages the operation of a pipeline that transports crude oil from the Heimberg area to Nordstad. The Refining Division manages a refinery at Nordstad that processes crude oil into petrol. (For simplicity, assume that petrol is the only saleable product the refinery makes and that it takes two barrels of crude oil to yield one barrel of petrol.)

Variable costs in each division are assumed to be variable with respect to a single cost driver in each division: barrels of crude oil produced by the Production Division, barrels of crude oil transported by the Transportation Division, and barrels of petrol produced by the Refining Division. The fixed costs per unit are based on the budgeted annual output of crude oil to be produced and transported and the amount of petrol to be produced. Stavanger-Oil reports all costs and revenues of its non-European operations in euros using the prevailing exchange rate.

- The Production Division can sell crude oil to outside parties in the Heimberg area at €13 per barrel.

- The Transportation Division 'buys' crude oil from the Production Division, transports it to Nordstad, and then 'sells' it to the Refining Division. The pipeline from Heimberg to Nordstad has the capacity to carry 40 000 barrels of crude oil per day.

- The Refining Division has been operating at capacity, 30 000 barrels of crude oil a day, using oil from Stavanger-Oil's Production Division (an average of 10 000 barrels per day) and oil bought from other producers and delivered to the Nordstad Refinery (an average of 20 000 barrels per day, at €18 per barrel).

- The Refining Division sells the petrol it produces at €52 per barrel.

Exhibit 18.1 summarises Stavanger-Oil's variable and fixed costs per unit of the cost driver in each division, the external market prices of buying and selling crude oil, and the external market prices of selling petrol. Consider the divisional operating profits resulting from three transfer-pricing methods applied to a series of transactions involving 100 barrels of crude oil produced by Stavanger-Oil's Production Division.

- Method A: Market-based transfer prices.

- Method B: Cost-based transfer prices at 110% of full costs, where full costs are the cost of the transferred-in product plus the division's own variable and fixed costs.

- Method C: Negotiated transfer prices.

The transfer prices per barrel of crude oil under each method are as follows. The transferred-in cost component in method B is denoted by an asterisk (*).

- *Method A: Market-based transfer prices:*

  From Production Division to Transportation Division = €13
  From Transportation Division to Refining Division = €18

- *Method B: Cost-based transfer prices at 110% of full costs:*

  From Production Division to Transportation Division =
  $1.10 \times (€2 + €6) = €8.80$
  From Transportation Division to Refining Division =
  $1.10 \times (€8.80^* + €1 + €3) = €14.08$

- *Method C: Transfer prices negotiated by divisions to be between market-based and cost-based transfer prices:*

  From Production Division to Transportation Division = €10
  From Transportation Division to Refining Division = €16.75

| Exhibit 18.1 | Operating data for Stavanger-Oil |

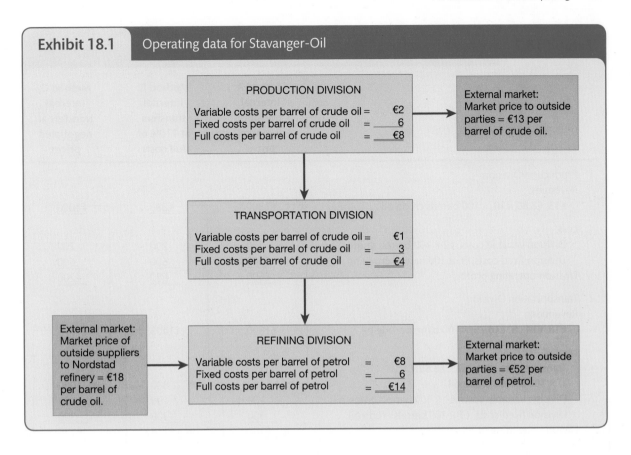

Exhibit 18.2 presents divisional operating profits per 100 barrels of crude oil reported under each transfer-pricing method. Transfer prices create income for the 'selling' division and corresponding costs for the 'buying' division that cancel out when divisional results are consolidated. The exhibit assumes that the different transfer-pricing methods have no effect on the decisions and actions taken by the Production, Transportation and Refining Division managers. Stavanger-Oil's total operating profit from producing, transporting and refining the 100 barrels of crude oil is therefore the same, €700 (revenues of €2600 minus costs of €800 in production, €400 in transportation and €700 in refining), regardless of internal transfer prices used. Keeping total operating profit the same focuses attention on the effects of different transfer-pricing methods on divisional operating profits. These profits differ under the three methods. The operating profit amounts span a €420 range (€80 to €500) in the Production Division, a €175 range (€100 to €275) in the Transportation Division, and a €392 range (€100 to €492) in the Refining Division. Note that each division would choose a different transfer-pricing method if its sole criterion were to maximise its own divisional operating profit: the Production Division would choose market prices, the Transportation Division would favour negotiated prices, and the Refining Division would choose 110% of full costs. Little wonder that divisional managers take considerable interest in the setting of transfer prices, especially those managers whose compensation or promotion directly depends on their division's operating profit.

Exhibit 18.2 maintains company-wide operating profit at €700 and illustrates how the choice of a transfer-pricing method divides the company-wide operating profit pie among individual divisions. Subsequent sections of this chapter illustrate that the choice of a transfer-pricing method can also affect the decisions that individual division managers make and hence the size of the operating profit pie itself. We consider this effect as we expand our discussion of market-based, cost-based and negotiated transfer prices.

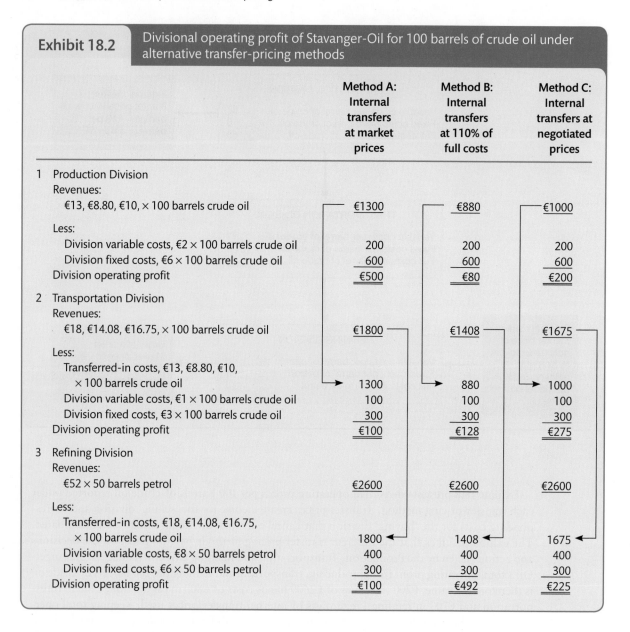

Exhibit 18.2 Divisional operating profit of Stavanger-Oil for 100 barrels of crude oil under alternative transfer-pricing methods

	Method A: Internal transfers at market prices	Method B: Internal transfers at 110% of full costs	Method C: Internal transfers at negotiated prices
1 Production Division			
Revenues:			
€13, €8.80, €10, × 100 barrels crude oil	€1300	€880	€1000
Less:			
Division variable costs, €2 × 100 barrels crude oil	200	200	200
Division fixed costs, €6 × 100 barrels crude oil	600	600	600
Division operating profit	€500	€80	€200
2 Transportation Division			
Revenues:			
€18, €14.08, €16.75, × 100 barrels crude oil	€1800	€1408	€1675
Less:			
Transferred-in costs, €13, €8.80, €10, × 100 barrels crude oil	1300	880	1000
Division variable costs, €1 × 100 barrels crude oil	100	100	100
Division fixed costs, €3 × 100 barrels crude oil	300	300	300
Division operating profit	€100	€128	€275
3 Refining Division			
Revenues:			
€52 × 50 barrels petrol	€2600	€2600	€2600
Less:			
Transferred-in costs, €18, €14.08, €16.75, × 100 barrels crude oil	1800	1408	1675
Division variable costs, €8 × 50 barrels petrol	400	400	400
Division fixed costs, €6 × 50 barrels petrol	300	300	300
Division operating profit	€100	€492	€225

Market-based transfer prices

Perfectly competitive market case

Transferring products or services at market prices generally leads to optimal decisions when three conditions are satisfied: (1) the intermediate market is perfectly competitive, (2) interdependencies of subunits are minimal, and (3) there are no additional costs or benefits to the corporation as a whole in using the market instead of transacting internally. A **perfectly competitive market** exists when there is a homogeneous product with equivalent buying and selling prices and no individual buyers or sellers can affect those prices by their own actions. By using market-based transfer prices in perfectly competitive markets, a company can meet the criteria of goal congruence, management effort and (if desired) subunit autonomy.

Reconsider the Stavanger-Oil example, assuming that there is a perfectly competitive market for crude oil in the Heimberg area. As a result, the Production Division can sell and the Transportation Division can buy as much crude oil as each wants at €13 per barrel. Stavanger-Oil would like its managers to buy or sell crude oil internally. Think about the decisions that Stavanger-Oil's division managers would make if each had the option to sell or buy crude oil externally. If the transfer price between Stavanger-Oil's Production Division and Transportation Division is set below €13, the manager of the Production Division will be motivated to sell all production to outside buyers at €13 per barrel. If the transfer price is set above €13, the manager of the Transportation Division will be motivated to purchase all its crude oil requirements from outside suppliers. A transfer price of €13 will motivate the Production Division and the Transportation Division to buy and sell internally.

Suppose each division manager is motivated to maximise his or her own divisional operating profit. The Production Division will sell (either internally or externally) as much crude oil as it can profitably sell, and the Transportation Division will buy (either internally or externally) as much crude oil as it can profitably transport. At a transfer price of €13, the actions that maximise divisional operating profit are also the actions that maximise operating profit of Stavanger-Oil as a whole. Market prices also serve to evaluate the economic performance and profitability of each division individually.

Distress prices

When supply outstrips demand, market prices may drop well below their historical average. If the drop in prices is expected to be temporary, these low market prices are sometimes called 'distress prices'. Deciding whether a current market price is a distress price is often difficult. The market prices of several agricultural commodities, such as wheat and oats, have stayed for many years at what observers initially believed were temporary distress levels.

Which transfer-pricing method should be used for judging performance if distress prices prevail? Some companies use the distress prices themselves, but others use long-run average prices, or 'normal' market prices. In the short run, the manager of the supplier division should meet the distress price as long as it exceeds the incremental costs of supplying the product or service; if not, the supplying division should stop producing and the buying division should buy the product or service from an outside supplier. These actions would increase overall company-wide operating income. If the long-run average market price is used, forcing the manager to buy internally at a price above the current market price will hurt the buying division's short-run performance and understate its profitability. If, however, prices remain low in the long run, the manager of the supplying division must decide whether to dispose of some manufacturing facilities or shut down and get the buying division to purchase the product from outside.

Cost-based transfer prices

Cost-based transfer prices are helpful when market prices are unavailable, inappropriate, or too costly to obtain. For example, the product may be specialised or unique, price lists may not be widely available, or the internal product may be different from the products available externally in terms of quality and service.

Full-cost bases

In practice, many companies use transfer prices based on full costs. These prices, however, can lead to suboptimal decisions. Assume that Stavanger-Oil makes internal transfers at 110% of full cost. The Nordstad Refining Division purchases, on average, 20 000 barrels of crude oil per day from a local Nordstad supplier, who delivers the crude oil to the refinery. Purchase and delivery cost €18 per barrel. To reduce crude oil costs, the Refining Division has located an independent producer in Heimberg who is willing to sell 20 000 barrels of crude oil per day at €13 per barrel, delivered to Stavanger-Oil's pipeline in Heimberg. Given Stavanger-Oil's organisation structure, the Transportation Division would purchase the 20 000 barrels of crude oil in Heimberg, transport it to Nordstad and then sell it to the Refining Division. The pipeline has excess capacity and can ship the 20 000 barrels at its variable costs of €1 per barrel without affecting the shipment of crude oil from Stavanger-Oil's own Production Division. Will Stavanger-Oil incur lower costs by purchasing crude oil from the independent producer in Heimberg or by purchasing crude oil from the Nordstad supplier? Will the Refining Division show lower crude oil purchasing costs by using oil from the Heimberg producer or by using its current Nordstad supplier?

The following analysis shows that operating profit of Stavanger-Oil as a whole would be maximised by purchasing oil from the independent Heimberg producer. The analysis compares the incremental costs in all divisions under the two alternatives.

- *Alternative 1.* Buy 20 000 barrels from Nordstad supplier at €18 per barrel.

  Total costs to Stavanger-Oil = 20 000 × €18 = €360 000

- *Alternative 2.* Buy 20 000 barrels in Heimberg at €13 per barrel and transport it to Nordstad at €1 per barrel variable costs.

  Total costs to Stavanger-Oil = 20 000 × (€13 + €1) = €280 000

There is a reduction in total costs to Stavanger-Oil of €80 000 by using the independent producer in Heimberg.

In turn, suppose the Transportation Division's transfer price to the Refining Division is 110% of full cost. The Refining Division will see its reported division costs increase if the crude oil is purchased from the independent producer in Heimberg:

$$\text{Transfer price} = 1.10 \times \left(\begin{matrix} \text{Purchase price} \\ \text{from Heimberg} \\ \text{producer} \end{matrix} = \begin{matrix} \text{Unit variable cost} \\ \text{of Transportation} \\ \text{Division} \end{matrix} + \begin{matrix} \text{Unit fixed cost} \\ \text{of Transportation} \\ \text{Division} \end{matrix} \right)$$

$$= 1.10 \times (€13 + €1 + €3) = 1.10 \times €17 = €18.70$$

- *Alternative 1.* Buy 20 000 barrels from Nordstad supplier at €18 per barrel.

  Total costs to Refining Division = 20 000 × €18 = €360 000

- *Alternative 2.* Buy 20 000 barrels from the Transportation Division of Stavanger-Oil that are purchased from the independent producer in Heimberg.

  Total costs to Refining Division = 20 000 × €18.70 = €374 000

As a profit centre, the Refining Division can maximise its short-run divisional operating profit by purchasing from the Nordstad supplier (€360 000 versus €374 000).

The transfer-pricing method has led the Refining Division to regard the fixed cost (and the 10% mark-up) of the Transportation Division as a variable cost. Why? Because the Refining Division looks at each barrel that it obtains from the Transportation Division as a variable cost of €18.70 – if 10 barrels are transferred, it costs the Refining Division €187; if 100 barrels are transferred, it costs €1870. From the point of view of Stavanger-Oil as a whole, its variable costs per barrel are €14 (€13 to purchase the oil from the independent producer and €1 to transport it to Nordstad). The remaining €4.70 (€18.70 − €14) per barrel are fixed costs and mark-ups of the Transportation Division. Buying crude oil in Nordstad costs Stavanger-Oil an additional €18 per barrel. For the company, it is cheaper to buy from Heimberg. But the Refining Division sees the problem differently. From its standpoint, it prefers buying from the Nordstad supplier at a cost of €360 000 (20 000 barrels × €18 per barrel) because buying from Heimberg costs the division €374 000 (20 000 barrels × €18.70). Goal incongruence is induced by the transfer price based on full cost plus a mark-up.

What transfer price will promote goal congruence for both the Transportation Division and the Refining Division? The minimum transfer price is €14 per barrel; a transfer price below €14 does not provide the Transportation Division with an incentive to purchase crude oil from the independent producer in Heimberg, while a transfer price above €14 generates contribution margin to cover fixed costs. The maximum transfer price is €18 per barrel; a transfer price above €18 will cause the Refining Division to purchase crude oil from the external market rather than from the Transportation Division. A transfer price between the minimum and maximum transfer prices of €14 and €18, respectively, will promote goal congruence – both divisions will increase their own reported divisional operating profit by purchasing crude oil from the independent producer in Heimberg. In particular, a transfer price based on the full costs of €17 without a mark-up will achieve goal congruence. The Transportation Division will show no operating profit and will be evaluated as a cost centre. Surveys indicate that managers prefer to use full-cost transfer pricing because it yields relevant costs for long-run decisions and because it facilitates pricing on the basis of full product costs.

Using full-cost transfer prices that include an allocation of fixed overhead costs raises other issues. How are indirect costs allocated to products? Have the correct activities, cost pools and cost drivers been identified? Are the chosen overhead rates actual or budgeted rates? The issues here are similar to the issues that arise in allocating fixed costs (Chapter 5). Full-cost-based transfer prices calculated using activity-based cost drivers can provide more refined allocation bases for allocating costs to products. Using budgeted costs and budgeted rates lets both divisions know the transfer price in advance. Also variations in the quantity of units produced by the selling division do not affect the transfer price.

Prorating the difference between minimum and maximum transfer prices

An alternative cost-based approach is for Stavanger-Oil to choose a transfer price that splits the €4 difference between the maximum transfer price the Refining Division is willing to pay and the minimum transfer price the Transportation Division wants on some equitable basis. Suppose Stavanger-Oil allocates the €4 difference on the basis of the budgeted variable costs incurred by the Transportation Division and the Refining Division for a given quantity of crude oil. Using the data in Exhibit 18.2, the variable costs are as follows:

Transportation Division to transport 100 barrels of crude oil	€100
Refining Division to refine 100 barrels of crude oil	400
	€500

The Transportation Division gets to keep (€100/€500) × €4.00 = €0.80, and the Refining Division gets to keep (€400/€500) × €4.00 = €3.20 of the €4 difference. That is, the transfer price between the Transportation Division and the Refining Division would be €14.80 per barrel of crude oil (€13 purchase cost + €1 variable costs + €0.80 that the Transportation Division gets to keep). In essence, this approach is a budgeted variable cost plus transfer price; the 'plus' indicates the setting of a transfer price above variable costs.

To decide on the €0.80 and €3.20 allocation of the €4.00 contribution to total corporate operating profit per barrel, the divisions must share information about their variable costs. In effect, each division does not operate (at least for this transaction) in a totally decentralised manner. Because most organisations are hybrids of centralisation and decentralisation anyway, this approach deserves serious consideration when transfers are significant. Note, however, that each division has an incentive to overstate its variable costs in order to receive a more favourable transfer price.

Dual pricing

There is seldom a *single* transfer price that simultaneously meets the criteria of goal congruence, management effort and subunit autonomy. Some companies turn to **dual pricing**, using two separate transfer-pricing methods to price each interdivisional transaction. An example of dual pricing arises when the selling division receives a full cost plus mark-up-based price and the buying division pays the market price for the internally transferred products. Assume that Stavanger-Oil purchases crude oil from the independent producer in Heimberg at €13 per barrel. One way of recording the journal entry for the transfer between the Transportation Division and the Refining Division is as follows:

1 Credit the Transportation Division (the selling division) with the 110%-of-full-cost transfer price of €18.70 per barrel of crude oil.

2 Debit the Refining Division (the buying division) with the market-based transfer price of €18 per barrel of crude oil.

3 Debit a corporate cost account for the €0.70 (€18.70 − €18.00) difference between the two transfer prices for the cost of crude oil borne by corporate rather than the Refining Division.

The dual-price method promotes goal congruence because it makes the Refining Division no worse off if it purchases the crude oil from the Transportation Division rather than from the outside supplier. In either case, the Refining Division's cost is €18 per barrel of crude oil. This dual-price system in essence gives the Transportation Division a corporate subsidy. The results of dual pricing? The operating profit for Stavanger-Oil as a whole is less than the sum of the operating profit of the divisions.

Dual pricing is not widely used in practice even though it reduces the goal-congruence problems associated with a pure cost-plus-based transfer-pricing method. One concern of top management is that the manager of the supplying division does not have sufficient incentive to control costs with a dual-price system. A second concern is that the dual-price system confuses division managers about the level of decentralisation top management seeks. Above all, dual pricing tends to insulate managers from the frictions of the marketplace. Managers should know as much as possible about their subunit's buying and selling markets, and dual pricing reduces the incentive to gain this knowledge.

Negotiated transfer prices

Negotiated transfer prices arise as the outcome of a bargaining process between selling and buying divisions. Consider again the choice of a transfer price between the Transportation and Refining Divisions of Stavanger-Oil. The Transportation Division has excess capacity that it can use to transport oil from Heimberg to Nordstad. The Transportation Division will only be willing to 'sell' oil to the Refining Division if the transfer price equals or exceeds €14 per barrel of crude oil (its variable costs). The Refining Division will only be willing to 'buy' crude oil from the Transportation Division if the cost equals or is below €18 per barrel (the price at which the Refining Division can buy crude oil in Nordstad).

From the viewpoint of Stavanger-Oil as a whole, operating profit would be maximised if the Refining Division purchased from the Transportation Division rather than from the Nordstad market (incremental costs of €14 per barrel versus incremental costs of €18 per barrel). Both divisions would be interested in transacting with each other if the transfer price is set between €14 and €18. For example, a transfer price of €16.75 per barrel will increase the Transportation Division's operating profit by €16.75 − €14 = €2.75 per barrel. It will increase the Refining Division's operating profit by €18 − €16.75 = €1.25 per barrel because Refining can now 'buy' the oil for €16.75 inside rather than for €18 outside.

The key question is where between the €14 and €18 will the transfer price be? The answer depends on the bargaining strengths of the two divisions. Negotiations become particularly sensitive if Stavanger-Oil evaluates each division's performance on the basis of divisional operating profit. The price negotiated by the two divisions will, in general, have no specific relationship to either costs or market price. But cost and price information are often useful starting points in the negotiation process.

A general guideline for transfer-pricing situations

Is there an all-pervasive rule for transfer pricing that leads towards optimal decisions for the organisation as a whole? No. Why? Because the three criteria of goal congruence, management effort and subunit autonomy must all be considered simultaneously. The following general guideline, however, has proved to be a helpful first step in setting a minimum transfer price in many specific situations:

$$\begin{array}{c}\text{Minimum} \\ \text{transfer price}\end{array} = \begin{array}{c}\text{Additional } \textit{incremental} \text{ or } \textit{outlay costs} \text{ per} \\ \text{unit incurred up to the point of transfer}\end{array} + \begin{array}{c}\textit{Opportunity costs} \text{ per unit} \\ \text{to the supplying division}\end{array}$$

The term *incremental* or *outlay costs* in this context represents the additional costs that are directly associated with the production and transfer of the products or services. *Opportunity costs* are defined here as the maximum contribution forgone by the supplying division if the products or services are transferred internally. For example, if the supplying division is operating at capacity, the opportunity cost of transferring a unit internally rather than selling it externally is equal to the market price minus variable costs. We distinguish incremental costs from opportunity costs because the accounting system typically records incremental costs but not opportunity costs. We illustrate the general guideline in some specific situations using data from the Production and Transportation Divisions of Stavanger-Oil.

1 A perfectly competitive market for the intermediate product exists, and the supplying division has no idle capacity. If the market for crude oil is perfectly competitive, the Production Division can sell all the crude oil it produces to the external market at €13 per barrel, and it will have no idle capacity. The Production Division's incremental costs (see Exhibit 18.1) are €2 per barrel of crude oil. The Production Division's opportunity cost per barrel of transferring the oil internally is the contribution margin per barrel of €11 (market price, €13 − variable cost, €2) forgone by not selling the crude oil in the external market. In this case,

$$\begin{array}{c}\text{Minimum transfer} \\ \text{price per barrel}\end{array} = \begin{array}{c}\text{Incremental} \\ \text{costs per barrel}\end{array} + \begin{array}{c}\text{Opportunity} \\ \text{costs per barrel}\end{array}$$
$$= €2 + €11$$
$$= €13 = \text{Market price per barrel}$$

Market-based transfer prices are ideal in perfectly competitive markets when there is no idle capacity.

2 An intermediate market exists that is not perfectly competitive, and the supplying division has idle capacity. In markets that are not perfectly competitive, capacity utilisation can be increased only by cutting prices. Idle capacity exists because cutting prices is often not worthwhile − it decreases operating profit.

   If the Production Division has idle capacity, its opportunity cost of transferring the oil internally is zero because the division does not forgo any external sales and hence does not forgo any contribution margin from internal transfers. In this case,

$$\text{Minimum transfer price per barrel} = \text{Incremental costs per barrel} = €2 \text{ per barrel}$$

Note that any transfer price between €2 and €13 (the price at which the Transportation Division can buy crude oil in Heimberg) motivates the Production Division to produce and sell crude oil to the Transportation Division and the Transportation Division to buy crude oil from the Production Division. In this situation, the company could either use a cost-based transfer price or allow the two divisions to negotiate a transfer price between themselves.

   In general, though, in markets that are not perfectly competitive, the potential to influence demand and operating profit through prices makes measuring opportunity costs more complicated. The transfer price depends on constantly changing levels of supply and demand. There is not just one transfer price; rather, a transfer-pricing schedule yields the transfer price for various quantities supplied and demanded, depending on the incremental costs and opportunity costs of the units transferred.

3 No market exists for the intermediate product. This would occur, for example, in the Stavanger-Oil case if oil from the production well flows directly into the pipeline and cannot be sold to outside parties. Here, the opportunity cost of supplying crude oil internally is zero because the inability to sell crude oil externally means no contribution margin is forgone. At the Production Division of Stavanger-Oil, the minimum transfer price under the general guideline would be the incremental costs per barrel of €2. As in the previous case, any transfer price between €2 and €13 will achieve goal congruence. If the transfer price is set at €2, of course, the Production Division would never record positive operating profit and would show poor performance. One approach to overcoming this problem is to oblige the Transportation Division to make a lump-sum payment to cover fixed costs and generate some operating profit for the Production Division while the Production Division continues to make transfers at incremental costs of €2 per barrel.

Transfer pricing and tax considerations

Transfer prices often have tax implications. Tax factors include not only income taxes, but also payroll taxes, customs duties, tariffs, sales taxes, value added taxes, environment-related taxes and other government levies on organisations. Full consideration of tax aspects of transfer-pricing decisions is beyond the scope of this book. Our aim here is to highlight tax factors and, in particular, income taxes as an important consideration in transfer-pricing decisions.

Consider the Stavanger-Oil data in Exhibit 18.2. Assume that the Production Division based in the Heimberg area pays income taxes at 30% of operating profit and that both the Transportation and Refining Divisions based in Nordstad pay profit taxes at 20% of operating profit. Stavanger-Oil would minimise its total profit tax payments with the 110%-of-full-costs transfer-pricing method, as shown in the following table:

	Operating profit for 100 barrels of crude oil			Income tax on 100 barrels of crude oil		
Transfer-pricing method	Production Division (1)	Transportation and Refining Divisions (2)	Total (3) = (1) + (2)	Production Division (4) = 0.30 × (1)	Transportation and Refining Divisions (5) = 0.20 × (2)	Total (6) = (4) + (5)
A Market price	€500	€200	€700	€150	€40	€190
B 110% of full costs	80	620	700	24	124	148
C Negotiated price	200	500	700	60	100	160

Tax considerations raise additional issues that may conflict with other objectives of transfer pricing. Suppose that the market for crude oil in Heimberg is perfectly competitive. In this case, the market-based transfer price achieves goal congruence and provides effort incentives. It also helps Stavanger-Oil to evaluate the economic profitability of the Production Division. But it is costly from an income tax standpoint.

Stavanger-Oil would favour using 110% of full costs for tax reporting. Tax laws in the Nordstad area and the Heimberg area constrain this option. In particular, the Heimberg tax authorities are fully aware of Stavanger-Oil's incentives to minimise income taxes by reducing the profits reported in Heimberg. They would challenge any attempts to shift profits to the Transportation and Refining Divisions through a low transfer price.

The perfectly competitive market for crude oil in Heimberg would probably force Stavanger-Oil to use the market price for transfers from the Production Division to the Transportation Division. Stavanger-Oil might successfully argue that the transfer price should be set below the market price because the Production Division incurs no marketing and distribution costs when 'selling' crude oil to the Transportation Division.

Concepts in action   Transfer pricing dispute temporarily stops the flow of Fiji Water

Source: Alamy Images/Lenscap

Tax authorities and government officials across the globe pay close attention to taxes paid by multinational companies operating within their boundaries. At the heart of the issue are the transfer prices that companies use to transfer products from one country to another. Since 2008, Fiji Water, LLC, a US-based company that markets its famous brand of bottled water in more than a dozen countries, has been engaged in a fierce transfer-pricing dispute with the government of the Fiji Islands, where its water bottling plant is located. While Fiji Water is produced in the Fiji Islands, all other activities in the company's value chain – importing, distributing, and retailing – occur in the countries where Fiji Water is sold. Over time, the Fiji Islands government became concerned that Fiji Water was engaging in transfer price manipulations, selling the water shipments produced in the Fiji Islands at a very low price to the company headquarters in Los Angeles. It was feared that very little of the wealth generated by Fiji Water, the country's second largest exporter, was coming into the Fiji Islands as foreign reserves from export earnings, which Fiji badly needed to fund its imports. To the Fiji Islands government, Fiji Water was funnelling most of its cash to the United States. As a result of these concerns, the Fiji Islands Revenue and Customs Authority (FIRCA) decided to take action against Fiji Water. The FIRCA halted exports in January 2008 at ports in the Fiji Islands by putting 200 containers loaded with Fiji Water bottled under armed guard, and issuing a statement accusing Fiji Water of transfer price manipulations. FIRCA's chief executive, Jitoko Tikolevu, said, 'The wholly US-owned Fijian subsidiary sold its water exclusively to its US parent at the declared rate, in Fiji, of $4 a carton. In the US, though, the same company then sold it for up to $50 a carton.' Fiji Water immediately filed a lawsuit against the FIRCA in the High Court of Fiji. The court issued an interim order, allowing the company to resume shipment of the embargoed containers upon payment of a bond to the court. In the media and subsequent court filings, the company stated that on a global basis it sold each carton of water for $20–28, and it did not make a profit due to 'heavy investments in assets, employees, and marketing necessary to aggressively grow a successful branded product'.

The dispute between the FIRCA and Fiji Water ultimately resolved with the $4 transfer price for water produced at its bottling plant in the Fiji Islands being maintained. But a 15-cents-per-litre excise tax on water produced in the country was imposed.

Sources: Bloxham, A. (2011) 'Fiji Water accused of environmentally misleading claims', The Telegraph, 20 June; Matau, R. (2008) 'Fiji Water explains saga', Fiji Times, 9 February; McMaster, J. and Novak, J. (2009) 'Fiji Water and corporate social responsibility – Green makeover or "green-washing"?', University of Western Ontario Richard Ivey School of Business, No. 909A08, London, ON: Ivey Publishing.

To meet multiple transfer-pricing objectives, a company may choose to keep one set of accounting records for tax reporting and a second set for internal management reporting. The difficulty here is that tax authorities may interpret two sets of books as suggestive of the company manipulating its reported taxable profits to avoid tax payments.

Additional factors that arise in multinational transfer pricing include tariffs and customs duties levied on imports of products into a country. The issues here are similar to the income tax considerations discussed earlier – companies will have incentives to lower transfer prices for products imported into a country to reduce the tariffs and customs duties that those products will attract.

In addition to the various motivations for choosing transfer prices described so far, multinational transfer prices are sometimes influenced by restrictions that some countries place on the payment of income or dividends to parties outside their national borders. By increasing the prices of goods or services transferred into divisions in these countries, companies can increase the funds paid out of these countries without appearing to violate income or dividend restrictions.

Summary

The following points are linked to the chapter's learning objectives.

1 A management control system is a means of gathering and using information to aid and coordinate the process of making planning and control decisions throughout the organisation, and to guide employee behaviour.

2 Effective management control systems are closely aligned to the organisation's strategy, fit the organisation's structure, and motivate managers and employees to give effort to achieve the organisation's goals.

3 The benefits of decentralisation include (a) greater responsiveness to local needs, (b) gains from quicker decision making, (c) increased motivation of subunit managers, (d) greater management development and learning, and (e) sharper management focus. The costs of decentralisation include (a) dysfunctional decision making (control loss), (b) duplication of activities, (c) decreased loyalty towards the organisation, and (d) increased costs of information gathering.

4 Transfer prices can be (a) market-based, (b) cost-based, or (c) negotiated. Different transfer-pricing methods produce different revenues and costs for individual subunits, and hence different operating profits for them.

5 In perfectly competitive markets, there is no idle capacity, and division managers can buy and sell as much as they want at the market price. Setting the transfer price at the market price motivates division managers to deal internally and to take exactly the same actions as they would if they were dealing in the external market.

6 A transfer price based on full cost plus a mark-up may lead to suboptimal decisions because it leads the 'buying' division to regard the fixed costs and the mark-up of the selling division as variable costs.

7 When there is excess capacity, the transfer price range for negotiations generally lies between the minimum price at which the selling division is willing to sell (its variable costs) and the maximum price the buying division is willing to pay (the price at which the product is available from outside suppliers).

8 The general guideline for transfer pricing states that the minimum transfer price equals the incremental costs per unit incurred up to the point of transfer plus the opportunity costs per unit to the supplying division resulting from transferring products or services internally.

9 Transfer prices can reduce income tax payments by recognising higher profits in low-tax-rate countries and lower profits in high-tax-rate countries.

Key terms

management control system (561)
motivation (562)
goal congruence (562)
effort (562)
decentralisation (562)
suboptimal decision making (563)

incongruent decision making (563)
intermediate product (565)
transfer price (565)
autonomy (565)
perfectly competitive market (568)
dual pricing (571)

CHAPTER 18

Assessment material

18.1 What is a management control system?

18.2 Describe three criteria you would use to evaluate whether a management control system is effective.

18.3 What is the relationship among motivation, goal congruence and effort?

18.4 Name three benefits and two costs of decentralisation.

18.5 'Organisations typically adopt a consistent decentralisation or centralisation philosophy across all their business functions.' Do you agree? Explain.

18.6 'Transfer pricing is confined to profit centres.' Do you agree? Why?

18.7 Under what conditions is a market-based transfer price optimal?

18.8 Give two reasons why a dual-price approach to transfer pricing is not widely used.

18.9 'Under the general transfer-pricing guideline, the minimum transfer price will vary depending on whether the supplying division has idle capacity or not.' Do you agree? Explain.

18.10 Why should managers consider income tax issues when choosing a transfer-pricing method?

Exercises

Basic level

18.11 Goals of public accounting firms (10 minutes)

All personnel, including partners, of public accounting firms must usually turn in biweekly time reports, showing how many hours were devoted to their various duties. These firms have traditionally looked unfavourably on idle or unassigned staff time. They have looked favourably on heavy percentages of chargeable time because this maximises revenue.

Required

What effect is such a policy likely to have on the behaviour of the firm's personnel? Can you relate this practice to the problem of goal congruence that was discussed in this chapter? How?

18.12 Decentralisation, goal congruence, responsibility centres (15 minutes)

Montaigne-Chimie SA consists of seven operating divisions each of which operates independently. The operating divisions are supported by a number of support divisions such as R&D, labour relations and environmental management. The environmental management group consists of 20 environmental engineers. These engineers must seek out business from the operating divisions – that is, the projects they work on must be mutually agreed to and paid for by one of the operating divisions. Under Montaigne-Chimie's rules, the environmental group is required to charge the operating divisions for environmental services at cost.

Required

1 Is the environmental management organisation centralised or decentralised?

2 What type of responsibility centre is the environmental management group?

3 What benefits and problems do you see in structuring the environmental management group the way Montaigne-Chimie has? Does it lead to goal congruence and motivation?

18.13 Transfer-pricing dispute (20 minutes)

Gustavsson AB, manufacturer of tractors and other heavy farm equipment, is organised along decentralised lines, with each manufacturing division operating as a separate profit centre. Each divisional manager has been delegated full authority on all decisions involving the sale of that division's output both to outsiders and to other divisions of Gustavsson. Division C has in the past always purchased its requirement of a particular tractor-engine component from Division A. However, when informed that Division A is increasing its selling price to €150, Division C's manager decides to purchase the engine component from outside suppliers.

Division C can purchase the component for €135 on the open market. Division A insists that, because of the recent installation of some highly specialised equipment and the resulting high depreciation charges, it will not be able to earn an adequate return on its investment unless it raises its price. Division A's manager appeals to top management of Gustavsson for support in the dispute with Division C and supplies the following operating data:

C's annual purchases of tractor-engine component	1000 units
A's variable costs per unit of tractor-engine component	€120
A's fixed costs per unit of tractor-engine component	€20

Required

1 Assume that there are no alternative uses for internal facilities. Determine whether the company as a whole will benefit if Division C purchases the component from outside suppliers for €135 per unit.

2 Assume that internal facilities of Division A would not otherwise be idle. By not producing the 1000 units for Division C, Division A's equipment and other facilities would be used for other production operations that would result in annual cash-operating savings of €18 000. Should Division C purchase from outside suppliers?

3 Assume that there are no alternative uses for Division A's internal facilities and that the price from outsiders drops €20. Should Division C purchase from outside suppliers?

18.14 Transfer-pricing problem (continuation of Exercise 18.13) (5 minutes)

Refer to Exercise 18.13. Assume that Division A can sell the 1000 units to other customers at €155 per unit with variable marketing costs of €5 per unit.

Required

Determine whether Gustavsson will benefit if Division C purchases the 1000 components from outside suppliers at €135 per unit.

*18.15 Ethics, transfer pricing (20 minutes)

The Leipzig Division of Bohemia Industries makes two component parts, X23 and Y99. It supplies X23 to the Hanover Division to be used in the manufacture of car engines and supplies Y99 to the Bremen Division to be used in the manufacture of car gearboxes. The Leipzig Division is the only supplier of these specialised components. When transfers are made in-house, Bohemia Industries transfers products at full cost (calculated using an activity-based cost system) plus 10%. The unit cost information for X23 and Y99 is as follows:

	X23	Y99
Variable costs per unit	€11	€8
Allocated fixed costs per unit	€14	€7

The Hanover Division feels that the price for X23 is too high and has told Leipzig that it is trying to locate an outside vendor to supply the part at a lower price. Wilhelm von Kalkstein, Leipzig Division's management accountant, calls Eberhard Dunkelmann, his assistant, into his office. 'We can't afford to lose the Hanover Division business. Our fixed costs won't go away even if we stop supplying Hanover, and this means that the costs of supplying Y99 to Bremen will increase. Then they'll start wanting to buy from outside. We're seriously looking at possibly shutting down the entire division if we lose the Hanover business. See if you can find a different method of allocating fixed costs that will decrease X23's transfer price to €23.65. I think Bremen will be willing to pay a somewhat higher price for Y99.'

Eberhard is uncomfortable making any changes because he knows that any other allocation method would violate corporate guidelines on overhead cost allocation. Still, he believes that changing the fixed-cost allocations is in the best interest of Bohemia Industries. Eberhard is confused about what he should do.

Required

1 Calculate the transfer prices for X23 and Y99.

2 Calculate the fixed cost per unit that Eberhard would have to allocate to X23 to enable Leipzig to transfer X23 at €23.65 per unit.

3 Evaluate whether Wilhelm von Kalkstein's suggestion to Eberhard to change the fixed-cost allocations is ethical. Would it be ethical for Eberhard to revise the fixed-cost allocations at his boss's urging? What steps should he take to resolve this situation?

Intermediate level

18.16   **Transfer-pricing methods, goal congruence** (30 minutes)

Ilmajoki-Lumber Oy has a Raw Lumber Division and Finished Lumber Division. The variable costs are:

- Raw Lumber Division: €100 per 100 board-metres of raw lumber.
- Finished Lumber Division: €125 per 100 board-metres of finished lumber.

Assume that there is no waste incurred in processing raw lumber into finished lumber. Raw lumber can be sold at €200 per 100 board-metres. Finished lumber can be sold at €275 per 100 board-metres.

Required

1 Should Ilmajoki-Lumber process raw lumber into its finished form?

2 Assume that internal transfers are made at 110% of variable costs. Will each division maximise its contribution to divisional operating profit by adopting the action that is in the best interests of Ilmajoki-Lumber?

3 Assume that internal transfers are made at market prices. Will each division maximise its contribution to divisional operating profit by adopting the action that is in the best interests of Ilmajoki-Lumber?

18.17 Effect of alternative transfer-pricing methods on divisional operating profit
(CMA, adapted) (30 minutes)

Escuelas SA has two divisions. The Mining Division makes toldine, which is then transferred to the Metals Division. The toldine is further processed by the Metals Division and is sold to customers at a price of €150 per unit. The Mining Division is currently required by Escuelas to transfer its total yearly output of 400 000 units of toldine to the Metals Division at 110% of full manufacturing cost. Unlimited quantities of toldine can be purchased and sold on the outside market at €90 per unit. To sell the toldine it produces at €90 per unit on the outside market, the Mining Division would have to incur variable marketing and distribution costs of €5 per unit. Similarly, if the Metals Division purchased toldine from the outside market, it would have to incur variable purchasing costs of €3 per unit.

The following table gives the manufacturing costs per unit in the Mining and Metals Divisions for the year 2015:

	Mining Division	Metals Division
Direct materials	€12	€6
Direct manufacturing labour costs	16	20
Manufacturing overhead costs	32*	25†
Manufacturing costs per unit	€60	€51

* Manufacturing overhead costs in the Mining Division are 25% fixed and 75% variable.
† Manufacturing overhead costs in the Metals Division are 60% fixed and 40% variable.

Required

1 Calculate the operating profits for the Mining and Metals Divisions for the 400 000 units of toldine transferred under each of the following transfer-pricing methods: (a) market price, and (b) 110% of full manufacturing costs.

2 Suppose Escuelas rewards each division manager with a bonus, calculated as 1% of divisional operating profit (if positive). What is the amount of bonus that will be paid to each division manager under each of the transfer-pricing methods in requirement 1? Which transfer-pricing method will each division manager prefer to use?

3 What arguments would Arturo Tuzón, manager of the Mining Division, make to support the transfer-pricing method that he prefers?

18.18 Goal congruence, negotiated transfer prices (continuation of Exercise 18.17) (20 minutes)

Refer to the information in Exercise 18.17. Suppose that the Mining Division is not required to transfer its yearly output of 400 000 units of toldine to the Metals Division.

Required

1 From the standpoint of Escuelas, SA, as a whole, what quantity of toldine should the Mining Division transfer to the Metals Division?

2 Now suppose each division manager acts autonomously to maximise the division's operating profit. What range of transfer prices will result in managers of the Metals and Mining Divisions achieving the actions determined to be optimal in requirement 1? Explain your answer.

3 Would you recommend that Escuelas allow the divisions to buy and sell toldine in the open market, and to negotiate the transfer price between themselves? Explain your answer.

*18.19 Pertinent transfer price (20–30 minutes)

Liberaki SA has two divisions, A and B, which manufacture bicycles. Division A produces the bicycle frame, and Division B assembles the bicycle components onto the frame. There is a market for both the subassembly and the final product. Each division has been designated as a profit centre. The transfer price for the subassembly has been set at the long-run average market price. The following data are available to each division:

Estimated selling price for final product	€300
Long-run average selling price for intermediate product	200
Incremental costs for completion in Division B	150
Incremental costs in Division A	120

The manager of Division B has made the following calculation:

Selling price for final product		€300
Transferred-in costs (market)	€200	
Incremental costs for completion	150	
		350
Contribution (loss) on product		€(50)

Required

1 Should transfers be made to Division B if there is no excess capacity in Division A? Is the market price the correct transfer price?

2 Assume that Division A's maximum capacity for this product is 1000 units per month and sales to the intermediate market are now 800 units. Should 200 units be transferred to Division B? At what transfer price? Assume that for a variety of reasons, A will maintain the €200 selling price indefinitely; that is, A is not considering lowering the price to outsiders even if idle capacity exists.

3 Suppose Division A quoted a transfer price of €150 for up to 200 units. What would be the contribution to the company as a whole if the transfer were made? As manager of Division B, would you be inclined to buy at €150?

18.20 **Transfer pricing issues** (From CIMA Management Accounting Pillar Managerial Level Paper, November 2006) (25 minutes)

ZP Plc operates two subsidiaries, X and Y. X is a component manufacturing subsidiary and Y is an assembly and final product subsidiary. Both subsidiaries produce one type of output only. Subsidiary Y needs one component from subsidiary X for every unit of Product W produced. Subsidiary X transfers to Subsidiary Y all of the components needed to produce Product W. Subsidiary X also sells components on the external market. The following budgeted information is available for each subsidiary:

	X	Y
Market price per component	$800	
Market price per unit of W	$1 200	
Production costs per component	$600	
Assembly costs per unit of W	$400	
Non production fixed costs	$1.5m	$1.3m
External demand	10 000 units	12 000 units
Capacity	22 000 units	
Taxation rates	25%	30%

The production cost per component is 60% variable. The fixed production costs are absorbed based on budgeted output. X sets a transfer price at marginal cost plus 70%.

Required

Calculate the post tax profit generated by each subsidiary.

18.21 **Transfer pricing issues** (From CIMA Management Accounting Pillar Managerial Level Paper)
(40 minutes)

The ZZ Group has two divisions, X and Y. Each division produces only one type of product: X produces a component, C and Y produces a finished product, FP. Each FP needs one C. It is the current policy of the group for C to be transferred to Division Y at the marginal cost of £10 per component and that Y must buy all the components it needs from X. The markets for the component and the finished product are competitive and price sensitive. Component C is produced by many other companies but it is thought that the external demand for the next year could increase to 1000 units more than the sales volume shown in the current budget for Division X. Budgeted data, taken from the ZZ Group internal information system, for the divisions for the next year is as follows:

Division X
Income statement

Sales	£70 000
Cost of sales	
Variable costs	£50 000
Contribution	£20 000
Fixed costs (controllable)	£15 000
Profit	£5 000
Production/Sales (units)	5000 (3000 of which are transferred to Division Y)
External demand (units)	3000 (Only 2000 of which can be currently satisfied)
Capacity (units)	5000
External market price per unit	£20

Balance sheet extract

Capital employed	£60 000

Other information

Cost of capital charge	10%

Division Y
Income statement

Sales	£270 000
Cost of sales	
Variable costs	£114 000
Contribution	£156 000
Fixed costs (controllable)	£100 000
Profit	£56 000
Production/Sales (units)	3000
Capacity (units)	7000
Market price per unit	£90

Balance sheet extract

Capital employed	£110 000

Other information

Cost of capital charge	10%

Four measures are used to evaluate the performance of the divisional managers. Based on the data above, the budgeted performance measures for the two divisions are as follows:

	Division X	Division Y
Residual income	(£1 000)	£45 000
Return on capital employed	8.33%	50.91%
Operating profit margin	7.14%	20.74%
Asset turnover	1.17	2.46

Proposed policy

ZZ Group is thinking of giving the divisional managers the freedom to set their own transfer price and to buy the components from external suppliers but there are concerns about problems that could arise by granting such autonomy.

Required

1 If the transfer price of the component is set by the manager of Division X at the current market price (£20 per component), recalculate the budgeted performance measures for each division.

2 Discuss the changes to the performance measures of the divisions that would arise as a result of altering the transfer price to £20 per component.

3 a Explain the problems that could arise for each of the divisional managers and for ZZ Group as a whole as a result of giving full autonomy to the divisional managers.

   b Discuss how the problems you have explained could be resolved without resorting to a policy of imposed transfer prices.

Advanced level

*18.22 **Pricing in imperfect markets** (continuation of Exercise 18.19) (30–40 minutes)

Refer to Exercise 18.19.

Required

1 Suppose the manager of Division A has the option of (a) cutting the external price to €195 with the certainty that sales will rise to 1000 units, or (b) maintaining the outside price of €200 for the 800 units and transferring the 200 units to Division B at some price that would produce the same operating profit for Division A. What transfer price would produce the same operating profit for Division A? Does that price coincide with that produced by the general guideline in the chapter so that the desirable decision for the company as a whole would result?

2 Suppose that if the selling price for the intermediate product is dropped to €195, outside sales can be increased to 900 units. Division B wants to acquire as many as 200 units if the transfer price is acceptable. For simplicity, assume that there is no outside market for the final 100 units of Division A's capacity.

   a Using the general guideline, what is (are) the minimum transfer price(s) that should lead to the correct economic decision? Ignore performance-evaluation considerations.

   b Compare the total contributions under the alternatives to show why the transfer price(s) recommended lead(s) to the optimal economic decision.

18.23 **Question from the Chartered Institute of Management Accountants, Intermediate Level, Management Accounting – Decision Making, November 2003** (45 minutes)

P Ltd has two divisions, Q and R, that operate as profit centres. Division Q has recently been set up to provide a component (Comp1) which division R uses to produce its product (ProdX). Prior to division Q being established, division R purchased the component on the external market at a price of £160 per unit. Division Q has an external market for Comp1 and also transfers to division R. Division R uses one unit of Comp1 to produce ProdX which is sold externally. There are no other products produced and sold by the divisions.

Costs associated with the production of Comp1 and ProdX are as follows:

	Comp1	ProdX
Fixed costs	£50 000 per annum	£100 000 per annum
Variable costs		£250 per unit*
Direct labour	£15 per hour	
Materials	£25 per unit	
Variable overheads	£3 per labour-hour	

* The variable cost for ProdX excludes the cost of the component.

The first unit of Comp1 will take 20 labour-hours to produce. However, it is known that the work of direct labour is subject to a 90% learning curve.

The forecast external annual sales and capacity levels for the divisions are as follows:

External sales

Division Q	Comp1	5000 units at a price of £150 per unit
Division R	ProdX	10 000 units at a price of £500 per unit

Production capacity

Division Q	Comp1	13 000 units
Division R	ProdX	15 000 units

Required

a State, with reasons, the volume of Comp1 which division Q would choose to produce in the first year and calculate the marginal cost per unit of Comp1 at this volume. (6 marks)

b (i) Explain the criteria an effective system of transfer pricing should satisfy. (6 marks)

(ii) Discuss one context in which a transfer price based on marginal cost would be appropriate and describe any issues that may arise from such a transfer pricing policy. (5 marks)

(iii) Identify the minimum transfer price that division Q would wish to charge and the maximum transfer price which division R would want to pay for the Comp1. Discuss the implications for the divisions and for the group as a whole of the transfer prices that you have identified. (8 marks)

(Total marks = 25)

CHAPTER 19

Control systems and performance measurement

We have discussed performance measurement in many of the earlier chapters, each time within a specific accounting context. We have, for example, described situations where the correct decision based on a relevant-cost analysis (buying new equipment, say) may not be implemented because the performance measurement system induced the manager to act differently. This chapter discusses the design, implementation and uses of performance measures more generally.

Performance measures are a central component of a management control system. Planning and control decisions requires information about how different subunits of the organisation have performed. To be effective, management control systems must also motivate managers and employees to strive to achieve organisation goals. Performance evaluation and rewards are key elements for motivating employees.

Performance measurement of an organisation's subunits should be a prerequisite for allocating resources within that organisation. When a subunit undertakes new activities, it forecasts revenues, costs and investments. Periodic comparisons of the actual revenues, costs and investments with the budgeted amounts can help guide top management's decisions about future allocations.

Performance measurement of managers is used in decisions about their salaries, bonuses, future assignments and career advancement. Moreover, the very act of measuring their performance can motivate managers to strive for the goals used in their evaluation.

This chapter examines issues in designing performance measures for different levels of an organisation and for managers at these different levels. We discuss both financial and non-financial performance measures.

Learning objectives

After studying this chapter, you should be able to:

- Provide examples of financial and non-financial measures of performance

- Design an accounting-based performance measure

- Understand the return on investment (ROI) method of profitability analysis

- Describe the residual-income (RI) measure

- Describe the economic value added (EVA®) method

- Distinguish between current-cost and historical-cost asset measurement methods

- Recognise the role of salaries and incentives in compensation arrangements

- Describe the management accountant's role in designing incentive systems

- Describe the incentive problems arising when employees perform multiple tasks

- Describe the four levers of control and understand their effects

Financial and non-financial performance measures

Chapter 18 noted how the information used in a management control system can be financial or non-financial. Many common performance measures such as operating profit rely on internal financial and accounting information. Increasingly, companies are supplementing internal financial measures with measures based on external financial information (for example, stock prices), internal non-financial information (such as manufacturing lead time) and external non-financial information (such as customer satisfaction). In addition, companies are benchmarking their financial and non-financial measures against other companies that are regarded as the 'best performers'. To compete effectively in the global market, companies need to perform at or near the 'best of the breed'.

Some companies present financial and non-financial performance measures for various organisation subunits in a single report called the *balanced scorecard* (see Chapter 22). Different companies stress various elements in their scorecards, but most scorecards include (1) profitability measures; (2) customer-satisfaction measures; (3) internal measures of efficiency, quality and time; and (4) innovation measures (see Kaplan and Norton 1996, 2001, 2004).

The balanced scorecard highlights trade-offs that the manager may have made. For example, it indicates whether improvements in financial performance resulted from sacrificing investments in new products or from on-time delivery. The specific non-financial measures chosen signal to employees the areas that top management views as critical to the company's success.

Some performance measures, such as the number of new patents developed, have a long-run time horizon. Other measures, such as direct materials efficiency variances, overhead spending variances and yield, have a short-run time horizon. We focus on the most widely used performance measures covering an intermediate to long-run time horizon. These are internal financial measures based on accounting numbers routinely maintained by organisations.

Non-financial performance measures offer some distinct benefits. Ittner and Larcker (2000) suggest that they:

- provide a closer link to long-term organisational stategies;
- provide indirect quantitative information on a company's intangible assets;
- can be good indicators of future financial performance;
- can improve managers' performance by providing more transparent evaluation of their actions.

However, these researchers also note that non-financial performance measures:

- can be time consuming and costly to implement;
- do not have a common denominator and entail different denominators such as time, percentages, quantities, etc;
- sometimes lack verifying links to accounting profits or stock prices and may have weak statistical reliability;
- may be too numerous to translate into main drivers of success.

Designing an accounting-based performance measure

The design of an accounting-based performance measure might entail the following general steps:

- *Step 1: Choosing the variable(s) that represents top management's financial goal(s).* Does operating profit, net profit, return on assets or revenues, for example, best measure a division's financial performance?

- *Step 2: Choosing definitions of the items included in the variables in step 1.* For example, should assets be defined as total assets or net assets (total assets minus total liabilities)?
- *Step 3: Choosing measures for the items included in the variables in step 1.* For example, should assets be measured at historical cost, current cost or present value?
- *Step 4: Choosing a target against which to gauge performance.* For example, should all divisions have as a target the same required rate of return on assets?
- *Step 5: Choosing the timing of feedback.* For example, should manufacturing performance reports be sent to top management daily, weekly or monthly?

These five steps need not be done sequentially. The issues considered in each step are interdependent and a decision maker will often proceed through these steps several times before deciding on an accounting-based performance measure. The answers to the questions raised at each step depend on top management's beliefs about how cost-effectively and how well each alternative fulfils the behavioural criteria of goal congruence, employee effort and subunit autonomy discussed in Chapter 18.

Different performance measures

Heads of enterprises tend to align reporting structures to performance-measurement systems to obtain the best information for monitoring activities. Consider Alan Mulally, who, when he was CEO of the Ford Motor Company, held weekly meetings for the Business Plan Review. He noted that 'everybody in this place has to be involved and has to know everything'. At the meeting, presentations were made by Ford's four profit centres: Americas, Europe, East Pacific and Ford Credit. Then came the presentations from 12 functional areas, such as product development, manufacturing, human resources, etc. To monitor operations, Mulally set up two rooms that he and others can visit at any time with 280 performance charts arranged by areas of responsibility with pictures of executives in charge of each of these. This enabled Mulally to 'keep his finger on every piece of this large and complex company' (Taylor 2009, p. 42).

This section presents step 1 by describing four measures commonly used to evaluate the economic performance of organisation subunits. Good performance measures promote goal congruence with the organisation's objectives and facilitate comparisons across different subunits. We illustrate these measures using the example of Hôtels Desfleurs.

Hôtels Desfleurs owns and operates three hotels, located in Vaison-la-Romaine, Perpignan and La Rochelle. Exhibit 19.1 summarises data for each of the three hotels for the most recent year (2015). At present, Hôtels Desfleurs does not allocate to the three separate hotels the total long-term debt of the company. Exhibit 19.1 indicates that the La Rochelle hotel generates the highest operating profit, €510 000. The Perpignan hotel generates €300 000; the Vaison hotel, €240 000. But is this comparison appropriate? Is the La Rochelle hotel the most 'successful'? Actually, the comparison of operating profit ignores potential differences in the *size* of the investments in the different hotels. **Investment** refers to the resources or assets used to generate profits. The question then is not how large operating profit is *per se*, but how large it is given the resources that were used to earn it.

Three approaches include investment in performance measures: return on investment (ROI), residual income (RI) and economic value added (EVA®). A fourth approach measures return on sales (ROS).

Exhibit 19.1	Annual financial data for Hôtels Desfleurs for 2015			
	Vaison hotel (1)	Perpignan hotel (2)	La Rochelle hotel (3)	Total (4) = (1) + (2) + (3)
Hotel revenues (sales)	€1 200 000	€1 400 000	€3 185 000	€5 785 000
Hotel variable costs	310 000	375 000	995 000	1 680 000
Hotel fixed costs	650 000	725 000	1 680 000	3 055 000
Hotel operating profit	€240 000	€300 000	€510 000	1 050 000
Interest costs on long-term debt at 10%	–	–	–	450 000
Profit before income taxes	–	–	–	600 000
Income taxes at 30%	–	–	–	180 000
Net profit	–	–	–	€420 000
Average book values for 2015				
Current assets	€400 000	€500 000	€600 000	€1 500 000
Long-term assets	600 000	1 500 000	2 400 000	4 500 000
Total assets	€1 000 000	€2 000 000	€3 000 000	€6 000 000
Current liabilities	€50 000	€150 000	€300 000	€500 000
Long-term debt	–	–	–	4 500 000
Stockholders' equity	–	–	–	1 000 000
Total liabilities and shareholders' equity				€6 000 000

Return on investment

Return on investment (ROI) is an accounting measure of income divided by an accounting measure of investment.

$$\text{Return on investment (ROI)} = \frac{\text{Income}}{\text{Investment}}$$

ROI is the most popular approach to incorporating the investment base into a performance measure. ROI appeals conceptually because it blends all the major ingredients of profitability (revenues, costs and investment) into a single number. ROI can be compared with the rate of return on opportunities elsewhere, inside or outside the company. Like any single performance measure, however, ROI should be used cautiously and in conjunction with other performance measures.

ROI is also called the accounting rate of return. Managers usually use the term ROI in the context of evaluating the performance of a division or subunit and accrual accounting rate of return when evaluating a project. Companies vary in the way they define both the numerator and the denominator of the ROI. For example, some firms use operating profit for the numerator. Other firms use net profit. Some firms use total assets in the denominator. Others use total assets minus current liabilities.

Hôtels Desfleurs can increase ROI by increasing revenues or decreasing costs (both these actions increase the numerator), or by decreasing investments (decreases the denominator). ROI can often provide more insight into performance when it is divided into the following components:

$$\frac{\text{Revenues}}{\text{Investment}} \times \frac{\text{Income}}{\text{Revenues}} = \frac{\text{Income}}{\text{Investment}}$$

This approach is widely known as the *DuPont method of profitability analysis*. The DuPont approach recognises that there are two basic ingredients in profit making: using assets to generate more revenue, and increasing income per euro of revenue. An improvement in either ingredient without changing the other increases return on investment.

Consider the ROI of each of the three Hôtels Desfleurs in Exhibit 19.1. For our calculations, we are using the operating profit of each hotel for the numerator and total assets of each hotel for the denominator.

Hotel	Operating profit	÷	Total assets	=	ROI
Vaison	€240 000	÷	€1 000 000	=	24%
Perpignan	€300 000	÷	€2 000 000	=	15%
La Rochelle	€510 000	÷	€3 000 000	=	17%

Using these ROI figures, the Vaison hotel appears to make the best use of its total assets.

Assume that the top management at Hôtels Desfleurs adopts a 30% target ROI for the Vaison hotel. How can this return be attained? The DuPont method (Exhibit 19.2) illustrates the present situation and three alternatives. Other alternatives such as increasing the selling price per room could increase both the revenue per euro of total assets and the operating profit per euro of revenue.

Exhibit 19.2	The DuPont method applied to the present situation and three alternatives for Hôtels Desfleurs

	$\dfrac{\text{Revenues}}{\text{Revenues}}$ × $\dfrac{\text{Operating profit}}{\text{Total asses}}$		$\dfrac{\text{Operating profit}}{\text{Total asses}}$
Present situation	$\dfrac{€1200000}{€1000000}$ × $\dfrac{€240000}{€1200000}$	= 1.20 × 0.20 =	0.24 or 24%
Alternatives			
A. Decrease assets (for example, debtors) keeping revenues and operating profit per euro of revenue constant	$\dfrac{€1200000}{€800000}$ × $\dfrac{€240000}{€1200000}$	= 1.50 × 0.20 =	0.30 or 30%
B. Increase revenues (by selling more rooms) keeping assets and operating profit per euro of revenue constant	$\dfrac{€1500000}{€1000000}$ × $\dfrac{€300000}{€1500000}$	= 1.50 × 0.20 =	0.30 or 30%
C. Decrease costs (for example, via efficient maintenance) to increase operating profit per euro of revenue, keeping revenues and assets constant	$\dfrac{€1200000}{€1000000}$ × $\dfrac{€300000}{€1200000}$	= 1.50 × 0.25 =	0.30 or 30%

ROI highlights the benefits that managers can obtain by reducing their investments in current or fixed assets. Some managers are conscious of the need to boost revenues or to control costs but pay less attention to reducing their investment base. Reducing investments means decreasing idle cash, managing credit judiciously, determining proper stock levels and spending carefully on fixed assets.

Residual income

Residual income is income minus a required euro return on the investment:

$$\text{Residual income} = \text{Income} - (\text{Required rate of return} \times \text{Investment})$$

The required rate of return multiplied by investment is also called the **imputed cost** of the investment. **Imputed costs** are costs recognised in particular situations that are not regularly recognised by accrual accounting procedures. An imputed cost is not recognised in accounting records because it is not an incremental cost but instead represents the return forgone by Hôtels Desfleurs as a result of tying up cash in various investments of similar risk. Assume that each hotel faces similar risks. Hôtels Desfleurs defines residual income for each hotel as hotel operating profit minus a required rate of return of 12% of the total assets of the hotel:

Hotel	Operating profit	–	Required rate of return × Investment	=	Income
Vaison	€240 000	–	€120 000 (12% × €1 000 000)	=	€120 000
Perpignan	€300 000	–	€240 000 (12% × €2 000 000)	=	€60 000
La Rochelle	€510 000	–	€360 000 (12% × €3 000 000)	=	€150 000

Given the 12% required rate of return, the La Rochelle hotel is performing best in terms of residual income.

Some firms favour the residual-income approach because managers will concentrate on maximising an absolute amount (euros of residual income) rather than a percentage (return on investment). The objective of maximising residual income assumes that as long as a division earns a rate in excess of the required return for investments, that division should expand.

The objective of maximising ROI may induce managers of highly profitable divisions to reject projects that, from the viewpoint of the organisation as a whole, should be accepted. To illustrate, assume that Hôtels Desfleurs' required rate of return on investment is 12%. Assume also that an expansion of the Vaison hotel will increase its operating profit by €160 000 and increase its total assets by €800 000. The ROI for the expansion is 20% (€160 000 ÷ €800 000), which makes it attractive to Hôtels Desfleurs as a whole. By making this expansion, however, the Vaison manager will see the hotel's ROI decrease:

$$\text{Pre-expansion ROI} = \frac{€240\,000}{1\,000\,000} = 24\%$$

$$\text{Pre-expansion ROI} = \frac{€240\,000 + €160\,000}{€1\,000\,000 + €800\,000} = \frac{€400\,000}{1\,800\,000} = 22.2\%$$

The annual bonus paid to the Vaison manager may decrease if ROI is a key component in the bonus calculation and the expansion option is selected. In contrast, if the annual bonus is a function of residual income, the Vaison manager will view the expansion favourably:

Pre-expansion residual income = €240 000 − (12% × €1 000 000) = €120 000
Post-expansion residual income = €400 000 − (12% × €1 800 000) = €184 000

Goal congruence is more likely to be promoted by using residual income rather than ROI as a measure of the division manager's performance.

Both ROI and residual income represent the results for a single time period (such as a year). Managers could take actions that cause short-run increases in ROI or residual income but are in conflict with the long-run interests of the organisation. For example, managers may curtail R&D and plant maintenance in the last three months of a fiscal year to achieve a target level of annual operating profit. For this reason, some companies evaluate subunits on the basis of ROI and residual income over multiple years.

Economic value added (EVA®)

Economic value added (EVA®) is a specific type of residual income calculation that has attracted considerable attention for the past two decades (Bouwens and Speklé 2007; Stewart 1994; Young and O'Byrne, 2001). Joel Stern, a partner at consultants Stern Stewart which developed and markets EVA®, argues that EVA® is a superior measure for certain management decisions and performance tracking. Many companies have adopted this measure, including Boots, Burton Group, Coca-Cola, Siemens, Pirelli, Lucas, Lloyds TSB and Telecom Italia Group. Economic value added equals after-tax operating profit *minus* the (after-tax) weighted-average cost of capital *multiplied by* total assets minus current liabilities.

$$\begin{array}{c} \text{Economic value} \\ \text{added (EVA}^{\circledR}) \end{array} = \begin{array}{c} \text{After-tax} \\ \text{operating profit} \end{array} - \left[\begin{array}{c} \text{Weighted-average} \\ \text{cost of capital} \end{array} \times \left(\begin{array}{c} \text{Total} \\ \text{assets} \end{array} - \begin{array}{c} \text{Current} \\ \text{liabilities} \end{array} \right) \right]$$

EVA® substitutes the following numbers in the residual-income calculations: (1) income equal to after-tax operating profit, (2) a required rate of return equal to the weighted-average cost of capital and (3) investment equal to total assets minus current liabilities. We use the Hôtels Desfleurs data in Exhibit 19.1 to illustrate EVA®.

The key calculation is the weighted-average cost of capital (WACC), which equals after-tax average cost of all the long-term funds used by Hôtels Desfleurs. The company has two sources of long-term funds: long-term debt with a market and book value of €4.5 million issued at an interest rate of 10% and equity capital that has a market value of €3 million (and a book value of €1 million). (The market value of Hôtels Desfleurs' equity exceeds book value because book values, based on historical costs, do not reflect the current values of the company's assets and because various intangible assets, such as the company's brand name, are not shown at current value on the balance sheet.) Since interest costs are tax deductible, the after-tax cost of debt financing equals $0.10 \times (1 - \text{tax rate}) = 0.10 \times (1 - 0.30) = 0.10 \times 0.70 = 0.07$, or 7%. The cost of equity capital is the opportunity cost to investors of not investing their capital in another investment that is similar in risk to Hôtels Desfleurs. Suppose that Hôtels Desfleurs' cost of equity capital is 15%. The WACC computation, which uses market values of debt and equity, is as follows:

$$\text{WACC} = \frac{(0.07 \times €4\,500\,000) + (0.15 \times €3\,000\,000)}{€4\,500\,000 + €3\,000\,000}$$

$$= \frac{€315\,000 + €450\,000}{€7\,500\,000} = \frac{€765\,000}{€7\,500\,000}$$

$$= 0.102 \text{ or } 10.2\%$$

The company applies the same WACC to all its hotels since each hotel faces similar risks.

Long-term assets minus current liabilities (see Exhibit 19.1) can also be calculated as:

$$\text{Total assets} - \text{Current liabilities} = \text{Long-term assets} + \text{Current Assets} - \text{Current liabilities}$$
$$= \text{Long-term assets} + \text{Working capital}$$

where working capital = current assets − current liabilities. After-tax hotel operating profit is:

$$\text{Hotel operating profit} \times (1 - \text{Tax rate}) = \text{Hotel operating profit} \times (1 - 0.30)$$
$$= \text{Hotel operating profit} \times 0.70$$

EVA® calculations for Hôtels Desfleurs are as follows:

Hotel	After-tax operating profit	−	Weighted-average cost of capital	×	Total assets − Current liabilities	= Economic value added (EVA®)
Vaison	€240 000 × 0.7	−	[10.2%	×	(€1 000 000 − €50 000)] = €168 000 − €96 900 =	€71 100
Perpignan	€300 000 × 0.7	−	[10.2%	×	(€2 000 000 − €150 000)] = €210 000 − €188 700 =	€21 300
La Rochelle	€510 000 × 0.7	−	[10.2%	×	(€3 000 000 − €300 000)] = €357 000 − €275 400 =	€81 600

The La Rochelle hotel has the highest EVA®. EVA®, like residual income, charges managers for the cost of their investments in long-term assets and working capital. Value is created only if after-tax operating profit exceeds the cost of investing the capital. To improve EVA®, managers must earn more operating profit with the same capital, use less capital, or invest capital in high-return projects.

Return on sales

The income-to-revenue (sales) ratio, often called *return on sales* (ROS), is a frequently used financial performance measure. ROS is one component of ROI in the DuPont method of profit-ability analysis. To calculate the ROS of each of the Desfleurs hotels, we use operating profit divided by revenues. The ROS for each hotel is:

Hotel	Operating profit	÷	Revenues (sales)	=	ROS
Vaison	€240 000	÷	€1 200 000	=	20.0%
Perpignan	€300 000	÷	€1 400 000	=	21.4%
La Rochelle	€510 000	÷	€3 185 000	=	16.0%

The following table summarises the performance and ranking of each hotel under each of the four performance measures:

Hotel	ROI (rank)	Residual income (rank)	EVA® (rank)	ROS (rank)
Vaison	24% (1)	€120 000 (2)	€71 100 (2)	20.0% (2)
Perpignan	15% (3)	€60 000 (3)	€21 300 (3)	21.4% (1)
La Rochelle	17% (2)	€150 000 (1)	€81 600 (1)	16.0% (3)

The residual-income and EVA® rankings differ from the ROI and ROS rankings. Consider the ROI and residual-income rankings for the Vaison and Perpignan hotels. The La Rochelle hotel has a smaller ROI. Although its operating profit is only slightly more than twice that of the Vaison hotel (€510 000 versus €240 000), its total assets are three times as large (€3 million versus €1 million). The return on assets invested in the La Rochelle hotel is not as high as the return on assets invested in the Vaison hotel. The La Rochelle hotel has a higher residual income because it earns a higher operating income after covering the 12% required return on investment. The Perpignan hotel has the highest ROS but the lowest ROI. Why? Because although it earns very high profit per euro of revenue, it generates very low revenues per euro of assets invested. Is any one method superior to the others? No, because each evaluates a slightly different aspect of per-formance. For example, in markets where revenue growth is limited, return on sales is the most meaningful indicator of a subunit's performance. To evaluate overall aggregate performance, ROI or residual-income-based measures are more appropriate since they consider both income earned and investments made. Residual-income and EVA® measures overcome some of the goal-congruence problems that ROI measures might introduce. Some managers favour EVA® because it explicitly considers tax effects while pre-tax residual-income measures do not. Other managers favour pre-tax residual-income because it is easier to calculate and because it often leads to the same conclusions as EVA®.

Exhibit 19.3 presents the key financial performance measures used by seven companies. Note the diversity in the use of income-based measures, ROS, ROI and EVA®.

Exhibit 19.3	Company examples of key financial performance measures		
Company name	Country headquarters	Product/ business	Key financial performance measures
Quaker Oats	USA	Food products	EVA®
Guinness	Ireland	Consumer products	Profit and ROS
Krones	Germany	Machinery/equipment	Sales and income
Mayne Nickless	Australia	Security/transportation	ROI and ROS
Mitsui	Japan	Trading	Sales and income
Pirelli	Italy	Tyres/manufacturing	Income and cash flow
Swedish Match	Sweden	Consumer products	ROI

Source: Business International (1989, 1992b); Stewart (1994).

Concepts in action   Misalignment between CEO compensation and performance at Lloyds

Source: Getty images/AFP

After the September 2008 collapse of HBOS, the UK based banking and insurance company was taken over by the Lloyds Banking Group. The following year, through a UK bank rescue package, the British government took a large stake in Lloyds Banking Group. Currently, the group is 25% owned by the UK government. The compensation package of its CEO is thus a significant concern given the part public ownership. Lloyds had net income before tax of £576m (a loss) in 2012 but reported pre-tax 2013 profits of £415m – the first since its £20.5bn bailout. Lloyds Bank chief executive Antonio Horta-Osorio believes that his bonus, worth £1.7m, given this value creation in terms of profits aligns his 'interests with the interests of the taxpayer'. However, the union's national officer Rob Macgregor states that: 'The chief executive's £1.7m bonus, on top of shares worth millions . . . is a kick in the teeth to the taxpayer, and to hard-working staff who don't know if they will be next in line for the chop.'

In 2014, there were a number of publicised revolts in the UK against high executive pay at FTSE 100 companies. Investors in luxury group Burberry voted down a £20m pay deal for its chief executive. Likewise, Barclays, AstraZeneca, HSBC, Standard Chartered and WPP, among others, witnessed challenges from shareholders in relation to pay

Alternative definitions of investment

We use the different definitions of investment that companies use to illustrate step 2 when designing accounting-based performance measures. Definitions include the following:

1 *Total assets available* – includes all business assets, regardless of their particular purpose.

2 *Total assets employed* – defined as total assets available minus idle assets and minus assets purchased for future expansion. For example, if the La Rochelle hotel in Exhibit 19.1 has unused land set aside for potential expansion, the total assets employed by the hotel would exclude the cost of that land.

3 *Working capital (current assets minus current liabilities) plus long-term assets* – this definition excludes that portion of current assets financed by short-term creditors.

4 *Shareholders' equity* – use of this definition for each individual hotel in Exhibit 19.1 requires allocation of the long-term liabilities of Hôtels Desfleurs to the three hotels, which would then be deducted from the total assets of each hotel.

Most companies that employ ROI, residual income or EVA® for performance measurement use either total assets available or working capital plus long-term assets as the definition of investment. However, when top management directs a division manager to carry extra assets, total assets employed can be more informative than total assets available. The most common rationale for using working capital plus long-term assets is that the division manager often influences decisions on the short-term debt of the division.

Alternative performance measures

To illustrate step 3 in the design of accounting-based performance measures, consider different ways to measure assets included in the investment calculations. Should they be measured at historical cost or at current cost? Should gross book value or net book value be used for depreciable assets? We now examine these issues.

Current cost

Current cost is the cost of purchasing an asset today identical to the one currently held. It is the cost of purchasing the services provided by that asset if an identical asset cannot currently be purchased. Of course, measuring assets at current costs will result in different ROIs compared with the ROIs calculated based on historical costs.

We illustrate the current-cost ROI calculations using the Hôtels Desfleurs example (see Exhibit 19.1) and then compare ROIs based on current and historical costs. Assume the following information about the long-term assets of each hotel:

	Vaison	Perpignan	La Rochelle
Age of facility (at end of 2016)	8 years	4 years	2 years
Gross book value	€1 400 000	€2 100 000	€2 800 000
Total depreciation	€800 000	€600 000	€400 000
Net book value (at end of 2016)	€600 000	€1 500 000	€2 400 000
Depreciation for 2016	€100 000	€150 000	€200 000

Hôtels Desfleurs assumes a 14-year estimated useful life, assumes no terminal disposal price for the physical facilities and calculates depreciation on a straight-line basis.

An index of construction costs for the eight-year period that Hôtels Desfleurs has been operating is as follows:

Year	2009	2010	2011	2012	2013	2014	2015	2016
Construction cost index	110	122	136	144	152	160	174	180

Earlier in this chapter, we calculated an ROI of 24% for Vaison, 15% for Perpignan and 17% for La Rochelle. One possible explanation of the high ROI for Vaison is that this hotel's long-term assets are expressed in terms of 2008 construction price levels, and that the long-term assets for the Perpignan and La Rochelle hotels are expressed in terms of the higher, more recent construction price levels, which depress ROIs for these hotels.

Exhibit 19.4 illustrates a step-by-step approach for incorporating current-cost estimates for long-term assets and depreciation into the ROI calculation. The aim is to approximate what it would cost today to obtain assets that would produce the same expected operating profit that the subunits currently earn. (Similar adjustments to represent current costs of capital employed and depreciation can also be made in the residual income and EVA® calculations.) The current-cost adjustment dramatically reduces the ROI of the Vaison hotel.

	Historical-cost ROI	Current-cost ROI
Vaison	24%	10.81%
Perpignan	15%	11.05%
La Rochelle	17%	14.70%

Adjusting for current costs negates differences in the investment base caused solely by differences in construction price levels. Consequently, compared to historical-cost ROI, current-cost ROI is a better measure of the current economic returns from the investment. For example, current-cost ROI indicates that taking into account current construction price levels, investing in a new hotel in Vaison will result in an ROI closer to 10.81% than to 24%. If Hôtels Desfleurs were to invest in a new hotel today, investing in one like the La Rochelle hotel offers the best ROI.

A drawback of the current-cost method is that obtaining current-cost estimates for some assets can be difficult. Why? Because the estimate requires a company to consider technological advances when determining the current cost of assets needed to earn today's operating profit. (When a specific cost index, such as the construction cost index, is not available, companies use a general index, such as the consumer price index, to approximate current costs.)

Long-term assets: gross or net book value?

Because historical-cost investment measures are used often in practice, there has been much discussion about the relative merits of using gross book value (original cost) or net book value (original cost minus depreciation). Using the data in Exhibit 19.1 and the accompanying text, the ROI calculations using net book values and gross book values of plant and equipment are as follows:

	Vaison		Perpignan		La Rochelle	
ROI for 2016 using net book value of total assets given in Exhibit 19.1 and calculated earlier	$\dfrac{€240\,000}{€1\,000\,000}$	$= 24\%$	$\dfrac{€300\,000}{€2\,000\,000}$	$= 15\%$	$\dfrac{€510\,000}{€3\,000\,000}$	$= 17\%$
ROI for 2016 using gross book value of total assets obtained by adding depreciation under 'Current cost' above to net book value of total assets in Exhibit 19.1	$\dfrac{€240\,000}{€1\,800\,000}$	$= 13.33\%$	$\dfrac{€300\,000}{€2\,600\,000}$	$= 11.54\%$	$\dfrac{€510\,000}{€3\,400\,000}$	$= 15\%$

Exhibit 19.4	ROI for Hôtels Desfleurs computed using current-cost estimates as of the end of 2016 for depreciation and long-term assets

Step 1: Restate long-term assets from gross book value at historical cost to gross book value at current cost as of the end of 2016.

$$\begin{array}{c}\text{Gross book value of long-term assets}\\\text{at current cost at the end of 2016}\end{array} = \begin{array}{c}\text{Gross book value of long-term}\\\text{assets at historical cost}\end{array} \times \dfrac{\begin{array}{c}\text{Construction cost}\\\text{index in 2016}\end{array}}{\begin{array}{c}\text{Construction cost index}\\\text{in year of construction}\end{array}}$$

Vaison	€1 400 000 × (180 ÷ 100) = €2 520 000
Perpignan	€2 100 000 × (180 ÷ 144) = €2 625 000
La Rochelle	€2 800 000 × (180 ÷ 160) = €3 150 000

Step 2: Derive the net book value of long-term assets at current cost as of the end of 2016. (The estimated useful life of each hotel is 14 years.)

$$\begin{array}{c}\text{Net book value of long-term assets at}\\\text{current cost at the end of 2016}\end{array} = \begin{array}{c}\text{Gross book value of}\\\text{long-term assets at current}\\\text{cost at the end of 2016}\end{array} \times \dfrac{\text{Estimated useful life remaining}}{\text{Estimated total useful life}}$$

Vaison	€2 520 000 × (6 ÷ 14) = €1 080 000
Perpignan	€2 625 000 × (10 ÷ 14) = €1 875 000
La Rochelle	€3 150 000 × (12 ÷ 14) = €2 700 000

Step 3: Compute the current cost of total assets at the end of 2016. (Assume that the current assets of each hotel are expressed in 2016 euros.)

$$\begin{array}{c}\text{Current cost of total assets}\\\text{at the end of 2016}\end{array} = \begin{array}{c}\text{Current assets at the end of}\\\text{2016 (from Exhibit 19.1)}\end{array} + \begin{array}{c}\text{Net book value of long-term}\\\text{assets at current cost at the}\\\text{end of 2016 (from step 2)}\end{array}$$

Vaison	€400 000 + €1 080 000 = €1 480 000
Perpignan	€500 000 + €1 875 000 = €2 375 000
La Rochelle	€600 000 + €2 700 000 = €3 300 000

Exhibit 19.4   continued

Step 4: Compute the current-cost depreciation expense in 2016 euros.

$$\text{Current-cost depreciation expense in 2016 euros} = \frac{\text{Gross book value of long-term assets at current cost at the end of 2016 (from step 1)}}{} \times \frac{1}{\text{Estimated total useful life}}$$

Vaison	€2 520 000 × (1 ÷ 14) = €180 000
Perpignan	€2 625 000 × (1 ÷ 14) = €187 500
La Rochelle	€3 150 000 × (1 ÷ 14) = €225 000

Step 5: Compute 2016 operating profit using 2016 current-cost depreciation.

$$\text{Operating profit for 2016 using 2016 current-cost depreciation} = \text{Historical-cost operating profit} \times \left(\text{Current-cost depreciation expense in 2016 euros (from step 4)} - \text{Historical-cost depreciation} \right)$$

Vaison	€240 000 − (€180 000 − €100 000) = €160 000
Perpignan	€300 000 − (€187 500 − €150 000) = €262 500
La Rochelle	€510 000 − (€225 000 − €200 000) = €485 000

Step 6: Compute the ROI using current-cost estimates for long-term assets and depreciation.

$$\text{ROI using current-cost estimates} = \frac{\text{Operating profit for 2016 using 2016 current cost depreciation (from step 5)}}{\text{Current cost of total assets at the end of 2016 (from step 3)}}$$

Vaison	€160 000 ÷ €1 480 000 = 10.81%
Perpignan	€262 500 ÷ €2 375 000 = 11.05%
La Rochelle	€485 000 ÷ €3 300 000 = 14.70%

Using the gross book value, the ROI of the older Vaison hotel (13.33%) is lower than that of the newer La Rochelle hotel (15%). Those who favour using gross book value claim that it enables more accurate comparisons across subunits. For example, using gross book value calculations, the return on the original plant and equipment investment is higher for the newer La Rochelle hotel than for the older Vaison hotel. This probably reflects the decline in earning power of the Vaison hotel. In contrast, using the net book value masks this decline in earning power because the constantly decreasing base results in a higher ROI (24%); this higher rate may mislead decision makers into thinking that the earning power of the Vaison hotel has not decreased.

The proponents of using net book value as a base maintain that it is less confusing because (1) it is consistent with the total assets shown on the conventional balance sheet, and (2) it is consistent with net profit computations that include deductions for depreciation. Surveys of company practice report net book value to be the dominant asset measure used by companies in their internal performance evaluations.

Choosing targeted levels of performance and timing of feedback

Choosing targets to compare performance

We next consider step 4 and the setting of targets to compare actual performance against. Recall that historical-cost-based accounting measures are often inadequate for evaluating economic returns on new investments and sometimes create disincentives for new expansion. Despite these problems, historical-cost ROIs can be used to evaluate current performance by adjusting target ROIs. Consider our Hôtels Desfleurs example. The key is to recognise that the hotels were built at different times, which in turn means they were built at different levels of the construction-cost index. Top management could adjust the target historical cost ROIs accordingly, perhaps setting Vaison's ROI at 26%, Perpignan's at 18% and La Rochelle's at 19%.

Nevertheless, the alternative of comparing actual with target performance is frequently overlooked in the literature. Critics of historical cost have indicated how high rates of return on old assets may erroneously induce a manager not to replace assets. Regardless, the manager's mandate is often 'Go forth and attain the budgeted results'. The budget, then, should be carefully negotiated with full knowledge of historical-cost accounting pitfalls. *The desirability of tailoring a budget to a particular subunit and a particular accounting system cannot be overemphasised.* For example, many problems of asset valuation and profit measurement (whether based on historical cost or current cost) can be satisfactorily solved if top management gets everybody to focus on what is attainable in the forthcoming budget period – regardless of whether the financial measures are based on historical costs or some other measure, such as current costs.

Top management often sets continuous improvement targets. Consider companies implementing EVA®. These companies have generally found it cost-effective to use historical-cost net assets rather than estimates of market or replacement values. Why? Because top management evaluates operations on year-to-year changes in EVA®, not on absolute measures of EVA®. Evaluating performance on the basis of *improvements* in EVA® makes the initial method of calculating EVA® less important.

Timing of feedback

The fifth and final step in designing accounting-based performance measures is the timing of feedback. Timing of feedback depends largely on how critical the information is for the success of the organisation, the specific level of management that is receiving the feedback, and the sophistication of the organisation's information technology. For example, hotel managers responsible for room sales will want information on the number of rooms sold each day on a daily or, at most, weekly basis. Why? Because a large percentage of hotel costs are fixed costs, so that achieving high room sales and taking quick action to reverse any declining sales trends are critical to the financial success of each hotel. Supplying managers with daily information about room sales would be much easier if Hôtels Desfleurs had a computerised room reservation and check-in system. Senior management, on the other hand, in their overseeing role may look at information about daily room sales only on a monthly basis. In some instances, for example, because of concern about the low sales to total assets ratio of the Perpignan hotel, they may want the information weekly.

Distinction between managers and organisational units[1]

As noted before in this and several earlier chapters, the performance evaluation of a manager should be distinguished from the performance evaluation of an organisation subunit, such as a division of a company. For example, historical-cost-based ROIs for a particular division can be used to evaluate a manager's performance relative to a budget or over time, even though historical-cost ROIs may be unsatisfactory for evaluating economic returns earned by the subunit. But using historical-cost ROIs to compare the performance of managers of different subunits can be misleading. Why? Because among other factors, one subunit's ROI may have been adversely affected relative to another's because of legal, political and government regulations as well as economic conditions over which certain subunit managers have no control.

---

[1] The presentations here draw (in part) from teaching notes prepared by S. Huddart, N. Melumad and S. Reichelstein.

Likewise, companies often put the most skilful division manager in charge of the weakest division in an attempt to change its fortunes. Such an effort may take years to bear fruit. Furthermore, the manager's efforts may result merely in bringing the division up to a minimum acceptable ROI. The division may continue to be a poor profit performer in comparison with other divisions, but it would be a mistake to conclude from the poor performance of the division that the manager is necessarily performing poorly.

This section focuses on developing basic principles for evaluating the performance of a division manager of an individual subunit. The concepts we discuss apply, however, to all organisation levels. Later sections consider specific examples at the individual-activity level and the total-organisation level. For specificity, we use the residual-income (RI) performance measure throughout.

The basic trade-off: creating incentives versus imposing risk

The performance evaluation of managers and employees often affects their compensation. Compensation arrangements run the range from a flat salary with no direct performance-based bonus (as in the case of some government officials) to rewards based only on performance (as in the case of door-to-door salespeople). Most often, however, a manager's total compensation includes some combination of salary and a performance-based bonus. An important consideration in designing compensation arrangements is the trade-off between creating incentives and imposing risk. We illustrate this trade-off in the context of our Hôtels Desfleurs example.

Antoinette Kessel owns the Hôtels Desfleurs chain of hotels. Joseph Saint-Exupéry manages the Hôtels Desfleurs Vaison (HDV) hotel. Assume that Antoinette uses RI to measure performance. To achieve good results as measured by RI, Antoinette would like Joseph to control costs, provide prompt and courteous service and reduce receivables. But even if he did all those things, good results are by no means guaranteed. HDV's RI is affected by many factors outside their control, such as a recession in the Vaison economy, or recent floods that might negatively affect HDV. Alternatively, non-controllable factors might have a positive influence on HDV's RI. Non-controllable factors make HDV's profitability uncertain and risky.

Antoinette is an entrepreneur and does not mind bearing risk, but Joseph does not like being subject to risk. One way of insuring Joseph against risk is to pay him a flat salary, regardless of the actual amount of residual income attained. All the risk would then be borne by Antoinette. There is a problem here, however, because the effort that Joseph puts in is difficult to monitor and the absence of performance-based compensation will provide him with no incentive to work harder or undertake extra physical and mental effort beyond what is necessary to retain his job or to uphold his own personal values.

Moral hazard describes contexts in which an employee prefers to exert less effort (or report distorted information) than the effort (or information) desired by the owner because the employee's effort (or information) cannot be accurately monitored and enforced. In some repetitive jobs – for example, in electronic assembly – a supervisor can monitor the workers' actions and the moral hazard problem may not arise. However, the manager's job is often to gather information and exercise judgement on the basis of the information obtained and monitoring a manager's effort is thus considerably more difficult.

The term *moral hazard* originated in insurance contracts to represent situations where insurance coverage caused insured parties to take less care of their properties than they might otherwise. One response to moral hazard in insurance contracts is the system of deductibles (that is, the insured pays for damages below a specified amount). For a fuller discussion of principal–agent contract issues, see Baiman (2006).

Paying no salary and rewarding Joseph *only* on the basis of some performance measure – RI, in our example – raises different concerns. He would now be motivated to strive to increase RI because his rewards would increase with increases in RI. But compensating Joseph on RI also subjects him to risk. Why? Because HDV's RI depends not only on Joseph's effort, but also on random factors such as the local economy over which he has no control.

To compensate Joseph (who does not like being subject to risk) for taking on uncontrollable risk, Antoinette must pay him some extra compensation within the structure of the RI-based arrangement. Thus, using performance-based incentives will cost Antoinette more money, *on average*, than paying Joseph a flat salary. Why 'on average'? Because her compensation payment to Joseph will vary with RI outcomes. When averaged over these outcomes, the RI-based compensation will cost Antoinette more than would paying Joseph a flat salary. The motivation for having some salary and some performance-based bonus in compensation arrangements is to balance the benefits of incentives against the extra costs of imposing uncontrollable risk on the manager.

Intensity of incentives and financial and non-financial measurements

What dictates the intensity of the incentives? That is, how large should the incentive component be relative to salary? A key question is, How well does the performance measure capture the manager's ability to influence the desired results?

Measures of performance that are preferred change significantly with the manager's performance and not very much with changes in factors that are beyond the manager's control. Consequently, superior performance measures motivate the manager but limit the manager's exposure to uncontrollable risk and hence reduce the cost of providing incentives to get the manager to accept the incentive programme. On the other hand, measures of performance are inferior if they fail to capture the manager's performance and fail to induce managers to improve. When owners have superior performance measures available to them, they place greater reliance on incentive compensation.

Suppose Joseph has no authority to determine investments. Further suppose revenue is determined largely by external factors such as the local economy. His actions influence only costs. Using RI as a performance measure in these circumstances subjects Joseph's bonus to excessive risk because two components of the performance measure (investments and revenues) are unrelated to his actions. The management accountant might suggest that, to create stronger incentives, Antoinette should consider using a different performance measure for Joseph – perhaps HDV's costs – that more closely captures his effort. Note that, in this case, RI may be a perfectly good measure of the economic viability of HDV, but it is not a good measure of Joseph's performance.

The benefits of tying performance measures more closely to a manager's efforts encourage the use of non-financial measures. Consider two possible measures for evaluating the manager of the Housekeeping Department at one of Desfleurs' hotels – the costs of the Housekeeping Department and the average time taken by the housekeeping staff to clean a room. Suppose housekeeping costs are affected by factors such as wage rates, which the housekeeping manager does not determine. In this case, the average time taken to clean a room may more precisely capture the manager's performance.

The salary component of compensation dominates in the absence of good measures of performance (as in the case of some corporate staff and government officials). This is not to say, however, that incentives are completely absent; promotions and salary increases do depend on some overall measure of performance, but the incentives are less direct. Employers give stronger incentives when superior measures of performance are available to them and when monitoring the employee's effort is very difficult (estate agencies, for example, reward employees mainly on commissions on houses sold).

Benchmarks and relative performance evaluation

Owners can use *benchmarks* to evaluate performance. Benchmarks representing best practice may be available inside or outside the overall organisation. In our Hôtels Desfleurs example, benchmarks could be other similar hotels, either within or outside the Hôtels Desfleurs chain. Suppose Joseph has authority over revenues, costs and investments. In evaluating his performance, Antoinette would want to use, as a benchmark, a hotel of a similar size that is influenced by the same uncontrollable factors – for example, location, demographic trends and economic conditions – that affect HDV. *Differences* in performances of the two hotels occur only because of differences in the two managers' performances, not because of random factors. Thus, benchmarking, also called *relative performance evaluation,* 'filters out' the effects of the common non-controllable factors.

Benchmarking is important in this light, but the element of surprise has recently been found to motivate people at work. Consider the experiment run by Professor Hayagreeva Rao at Stanford University. In one study he provides three groups of people with puzzles to solve. The first group received $1 immediately after solving a puzzle. The second knew they would get $1 for solving each puzzle but did not know when. The third group knew only that its members would be randomly rewarded – they completed most of the puzzles. Rao reports: 'It's the element of surprise, not the size of the award that really moves people.'

Globoforce, a $90 million Boston firm, has similarly reported what may not be intuitive in relation to motivation and rewards. Its CEO, Eric Mosley, considers that small awards, all the time to almost everyone 'really works'. Moreover, 'even high earners can appreciate a small award if it is unexpected' (Rao and Mosley cited in Demos 2010).

Can the performance of two managers responsible for running similar operations within a company be benchmarked against one another? Yes, but one problem is that the use of these benchmarks may reduce incentives for these managers to help one another. That is, a manager's performance evaluation measure improves either by doing a better job or by making the other manager look bad. Not working together as a team is not in the best interests of the organisation as a whole. In this case, using benchmarks for performance evaluation can lead to *goal incongruence*.

Performance measures at the individual activity level

This section focuses on incentive issues that arise in the context of individual activities. The principles described here, however, can be applied at all levels of the organisation.

Performing multiple tasks

Most employees perform more than one task as part of their job. Marketing representatives sell products, provide customer support and gather market information. Other jobs have multiple aspects to them. Manufacturing workers, for example, are responsible for both the quantity and quality of their products. Employers want employees to allocate their time and effort intelligently among various tasks or aspects of their jobs.

Consider, for example, garage mechanics. Their jobs have at least two distinct and important aspects. The first aspect is the repair work. Performing more repair work would generate more revenues for the workshop. The second aspect is customer satisfaction. The higher the quality of the job, the more likely the customer will be pleased. If the employer wants an employee to focus on both these aspects, then the employer must measure and compensate performance on both.

Suppose the employer can easily measure the quantity of repairs but not their quality. If the employer rewards workers on a piece-rate system – which pays workers only on the basis of the number of repairs performed – mechanics will probably increase the number of repairs they make at the expense of quality. Some companies experience this problem when they introduce by-the-job rates for their mechanics. The following steps might be taken to motivate workers to balance both quantity and quality:

1 Management can drop the piece-rate system and pay mechanics an hourly wage, a step that de-emphasises the quantity of repair. Mechanics' promotions and pay increases can be determined on the basis of management's assessment of each mechanic's overall performance regarding quantity and quality of repairs.

2 Management can evaluate employees, in part, using data such as customer-satisfaction surveys, the number of dissatisfied customers or the number of customer complaints.

3 Management can also employ independent staff to randomly monitor whether the repairs performed are of high quality.

Note that non-financial measures (such as customer-satisfaction measures) can play a central role in motivating the mechanics to emphasise both quantity and quality. The goal is to measure both aspects of the mechanics' jobs and to balance incentives so that both aspects are properly emphasised.

Environmental and ethical responsibilities

Managers in all organisations shoulder environmental and ethical responsibilities. Environmental violations (such as water and air pollution) and unethical and illegal practices (such as bribery and corruption) carry heavy fines and are prison offences under the laws of many European countries. But environmental responsibilities and ethical conduct extend beyond legal requirements.

Socially responsible companies set stringent environmental targets and measure and report their performance against them. German, Swiss, Dutch and Scandinavian companies report on environmental performance as part of a larger set of social responsibility disclosures (which include employee welfare and community development information). Some companies make environmental performance a line item on every employee's salary appraisal sheet.

Ethical behaviour on the part of managers is paramount. In particular, the numbers that sub-unit managers report should not be tainted by 'cooking the books' – they should be uncontaminated by, for example, padded assets, understated liabilities, fictitious sales and understated costs.

Many of the world's largest organisations have had to pay large fines for engaging in corrupt business practices. Such companies include Daimler and BHP Hilton. Siemens recently had to pay fines of $1.6 billion to the American and German governments. A study by Transparency International of 500 prominent firms reported that the average company only scored 17 out of a possible 50 points on 'anti-corruption practices', but many companies have an excellent anti-corruption reputation, including Reebok, Google, Novo Nordisk, Ikea and Chevron. Companies adopting explicit codes of conduct on corruption recognise that 'grease' is not very efficient. Schumpeter (2010) reports that 'the hidden costs of corruption are almost always much higher than companies imagine'.

Codes of business conduct are circulated in some organisations to signal appropriate and inappropriate individual behaviour. Division managers often cite enormous top-management pressures 'to make the budget' as excuses or rationalisations for not adhering to ethical accounting policies and procedures. A healthy amount of motivational pressure is not bad – as long as the 'tone from the top' simultaneously communicates the absolute need for all managers to behave ethically at all times. Management should promptly and severely reprimand unethical conduct irrespective of the benefits that accrue to the company from such actions. Some companies emphasise ethical behaviour by routinely evaluating employees against a business code of ethics.

Strategy and levers of control[1]

Given the management accounting focus of this book, this chapter has emphasised the role of quantitative financial and non-financial performance–evaluation measures that companies use to implement their strategies. These measures – such as ROI, RI, EVA, customer satisfaction and

[1] For a more detailed discussion see R. Simons (1995) 'Control in an age of empowerment', *Harvard Business Review*.

employee satisfaction – monitor critical performance variables that help managers track progress towards achieving a company's strategic goals. Because these measures help diagnose whether a company is performing to expectations, they are collectively called **diagnostic control systems**. Companies motivate managers to achieve these goals by holding managers accountable for, and by rewarding them for, meeting these goals. The concern, however, is that the pressure to perform may cause managers to cut corners and misreport numbers to make their performance look better than it is, as happened at companies such as Enron, Polly Peck, Parmalat and Lernout and Hauspie. WorldCom, Tycol and Health South. To avoid unethical behaviour, companies need to balance the push for performance resulting from diagnostic control systems, the first of four levers of control, with three other levers: *boundary systems, belief systems* and *interactive control systems*.

Boundary systems describe standards of behaviour and codes of conduct expected of all employees, especially action that are off-limits. Ethical behaviour on the part of managers is paramount. In particular, numbers that subunit managers report should not be tainted by 'cooking the books'. They should be free of, for example overstated assets, understated liabilities, fictitious revenues and understated costs.

Codes of practice conduct signal appropriate and inappropriate individual behaviours. The following is from Caterpillar Tractor's 'Code of Worldwide Business Conduct and Operating Principles':

The law is a floor. Ethical business conduct should normally exist at a level well above the minimum required by law. Caterpillar employees shall not accept costly entertainment or gifts (excepting mentors and novelties of nominal value) from dealers, suppliers and others with whom we do business. And we won't tolerate circumstances that produce, or reasonably appear to produce, conflict between personal interests and interests of the company.

Division managers often cite enormous pressure from top management 'to make the budget' as excuses or rationalisations for not adhering to ethical accounting policies and procedures. A healthy amount of motivational pressure is desirable, as long as the 'tone from the top' and the code of conduct simultaneously communicate the absolute need for all managers to behave ethically at all times. Managers should train employees to behave ethically. They should promptly and severely reprimand unethical conduct, regardless of the benefits that might accrue to the company from unethical actions. Some companies, such as Lockheed-Martin, emphasise ethical behaviour by routinely evaluating employees against a business code of ethics.

Many organisations also set explicit boundaries precluding actions that harm the environment. Environmental violations (such as water and air pollution) carry heavy fines and are prison offences under the laws of the United States and other countries. But, in many companies, environmental responsibilities extend beyond legal requirements.

Socially responsible companies, such as BP, set aggressive environmental goals and measure and report their performance against them. German, Swiss, Dutch and Scandanavian companies report on environmental performance as part of a larger set of social responsibility disclosures (such as employee welfare and community development activities). Some companies, such as DuPont, make environmental performance a line item on every employee's salary appraisal report. Duke Power Company appraises employees on their performance in reducing solid waste, cutting emissions and discharges, and implementating environmental plans. The result? Duke Power has met all its environmental goals.

Belief systems articulate the mission, purpose and core values of a company. They describe the accepted norms and patterns of behaviour expected of all managers and employees with respect to each other, shareholders, customers and communities. Johnson & Johnson described its values and norms in its credo statement:

We believe our first responsibility is to the doctors, nurses and patients, to mothers and fathers and all others who use our products and services . . . Everything we do must be of high quality.

> We are responsible to our employees . . . We must respect their dignity and recognise their merit. They must have a sense of security in their jobs . . . We must be mindful of ways to help our employees fulfil their family responsibilities and provide opportunity for development and advancement . . . Our actions must be just and ethical.
>
> We are responsible to the communities in which we live . . . We must support good works and charities and bear our fair share of taxes . . . We must encourage better health and education.
>
> Our final responsibility is to our stockholders. Business must make a sound profit . . . We must experiment with new ideas . . . develop innovative programs and pay for mistakes.

Johnson & Johnson's credo is intended to inspire all managers and other employees to do their best. Belief systems play to employees' intrinsic motivations.

Intrinsic motivation is the desire to achieve self-satisfaction from good performance regardless of external rewards such as bonuses or promotion. Intrinsic motivation comes from being given greater responsibility, doing interesting and creative work, having pride in doing that work, establishing commitment to the organisation, and developing personal bonds with co-workers. High intrinsic motivation enhances performance because managers and worker have a sense of achievement in doing something important, feel satisfied with their jobs, and see opportunities for personal growth.

Interactive control systems are formal information systems that managers use to focus organisation attention and learning on key strategic issues. An excessive focus on diagnostic control systems and critical performance variables can cause an organisation to ignore emerging threats and opportunities – changes in technology, customer preferences, regulations and industry competition that can undercut a business.

Interactive control systems track strategic uncertainties that businesses face, such as the emergence of digital imaging in the case of Kodak and Fujifilm, airline deregulation in the case of American Airlines and Southwest Airlines, and the shift in customer preferences for mini- and microcomputers in the case of IBM. The result is ongoing discussion and debate about assumptions and action plans. New strategies emerge from the dialogue and debate surrounding the interactive process. Interactive control systems force busy managers to step back from the actions needed to manage the business today and to shift their focus forward to positioning the organisation for the opportunities and threats of tomorrow.

Measuring and rewarding managers for achieving critical performance variables is an important driver of corporate performance. But these diagnostic control systems must be counterbalanced by the other levers of control – boundary systems, belief systems and interactive control systems – to ensure that proper business ethics, inspirational values and attention to future threats and opportunities are not sacrificed while achieving business results.

Summary

The following points are linked to the chapter's learning objectives.

1 Financial measures such as return on investment and residual income can capture important aspects of both manager performance and organisation-subunit performance. In many cases, however, financial measures are supplemented with non-financial measures of performance, such as those relating to customer service time, number of defects and productivity.

2 The steps in designing an accounting-based performance measure are (a) choosing variables to include in the performance measure, (b) defining the terms, (c) measuring the items included in the variables, (d) choosing a target for performance and (e) choosing the timing of feedback.

3 The DuPont method describes return on investment (ROI) as the product of two components: revenues divided by investment and income divided by revenues. ROI can be increased in three ways: increase revenues, decrease costs and decrease investment.

4 Residual income is income minus a required monetary return on the investment. Residual income was designed to overcome some of the limitations of ROI. For example, residual income is more likely than ROI to promote goal congruence. That is, actions that are in the best interests of the organisation maximise residual income. The objective of maximising ROI, conversely, may induce managers of highly profitable divisions to reject projects that, from the viewpoint of the organisation as a whole, should be accepted.

5 Economic value added (EVA®) is a specific type of residual income calculation. It equals the after-tax operating profit minus the after-tax weighted-average cost of capital multiplied by total assets minus current liabilities.

6 The current cost of an asset is the cost now of purchasing an identical asset to the one currently held. Historical-cost asset measurement methods consider the original cost of the asset net of total depreciation.

7 Organisations create incentives by rewarding managers on the basis of performance. But managers may face risks because random factors beyond their control may also affect performance. Owners choose a mix of salary and incentive compensation to trade off the incentive benefit against the cost of imposing risk.

8 Obtaining measures of employee performance that are superior is critical for implementing strong incentives. Many management accounting practices, such as the design of responsibility centres and the establishment of financial and non-financial measures, have as their goal better performance evaluation.

9 Most employees perform multiple tasks as part of their jobs. In some situations, one aspect of a job is easily measured (for example, the quantity of work done), while another aspect is not (for example, the quality of work done). Creating incentives to promote the aspect of the job that is easily measured (quantity) may cause workers to ignore an aspect of their job that is more difficult to measure (quality).

10 Implementing the four levers of control can assist a company to achieve its pursued performance, engage in ethical behaviour, inspire its employees and to act proactively in the fact of strategic threats and opportunities.

Key terms

investment (588)
return on investment (ROI) (589)
residual income (590)
imputed costs (591)
economic value added (EVA®) (592)
current cost (595)

moral hazard (600)
diagnostic control systems (604)
boundary systems (604)
belief systems (604)
interactive control systems (605)

References and further reading

Baiman, S. (2006) 'Contract theory analysis of managerial accounting issues', in A. Bhimani (ed) *Contemporary Issues in Management Accounting* (Oxford: Oxford University Press), chapter 2.

Bouwens, J. and Speklé, R. (2007) 'Does EVA add value?', in T. Hopper, D. Northcott and R. Scapens (eds) *Issues in Management Accounting* (Harlow: FT Prentice Hall).

Demos, T. (2010) 'Motivate without spending millions', *Fortune*, 12 April.

Ittner, C. and Larcker, D. (2000) 'A bigger yardstick for company performance', *FT Mastering Management*, 20 November, pp. 8–11.

Kaplan, R.S. and Norton, D.P. (1996) *The Balanced Scorecard* (Boston: Harvard Business School Press).

Kaplan, R.S. and Norton, D. (2001) *The Strategy Focused Organization: How Balanced Scorecard Companies Thrive in the New Business Environment* (Boston: Harvard Business School Press).

Kaplan, R.S. and Norton, D. (2004) *Strategy Maps: Converting Intangible Assets into Tangible Outcomes* (Boston: Harvard Business School Press).

Schumpeter, J.A. (2010) 'The corruption eruption', *Economist*, 1 May, p. 68.

Stewart, G.B., III (1994) 'EVA®: fact and fantasy', *Journal of Applied Corporate Finance* (Summer).

Taylor, A. (2009) 'Fixing up Ford', *Fortune*, 25 May, p. 42.

Young, S.D. and O'Byrne, S.F. (2001) *EVA® and Value-based management: A Practical Guide to Implementation* (New York: McGraw-Hill).

CHAPTER 19

Assessment material

Review questions

19.1 What factors affecting ROI does the DuPont method highlight?

19.2 'Residual income is not identical to ROI although both measures incorporate profit and investment into their computations.' Do you agree? Explain.

19.3 Describe economic value added (EVA®).

19.4 Give three definitions of investment used in practice when computing ROI.

19.5 Distinguish between measuring assets based on current cost and historical cost.

19.6 Why is it important to distinguish between the performance of a manager and the performance of the organisation subunit for which the manager is responsible? Give examples.

19.7 Describe moral hazard.

19.8 'Managers should be rewarded only on the basis of their performance measures. They should be paid no salary.' Do you agree? Explain.

19.9 Explain the management accountant's role in helping organisations design stronger incentive systems for their employees.

19.10 Explain the role of benchmarking in evaluating managers.

Exercises

Basic level

19.11 **ROI and residual profit** (10–15 minutes)

Récré-Gaules SARL produces and distributes a wide variety of recreational products. One of its divisions, the Idefix Division, manufactures and sells 'menhirs', which are very popular with cross-country skiers. The demand for these menhirs is relatively insensitive to price changes. The Idefix Division is considered to be an investment centre and in recent years has averaged a return on investment of 20%. The following data are available for the Idefix Division and its product:

Total annual fixed costs	€1 000 000
Variable costs per menhir	€300
Average number of menhirs sold each year	10 000
Average operating assets invested in the division	€1 600 000

Required

1 What is the minimum selling price per unit that the Idefix Division could charge in order for Marie-Aimée Obelix, the division manager, to get a favourable performance rating? Management considers an ROI below 20% to be unfavourable.

2 Assume that Récré-Gaules judges the performance of its investment centre managers on the basis of residual income rather than ROI, as was assumed in requirement 1. The company's required rate of return is considered to be 15%. What is the minimum selling price per unit that the Idefix Division should charge for Obelix to receive a favourable performance rating?

19.12 Pricing and return on investment (30 minutes)

Salvador SA assembles motorcycles and uses long-run (defined as 3–5 years) average demand to set the budgeted production level and costs for pricing. Prices are then adjusted only for large changes in assembly wage rates or direct materials prices. You are given the following data:

Direct materials, assembly wages and other variable costs	€1320 per unit
Fixed costs	€300 000 000 per year
Target return on investment	20%
Normal utilisation of capacity (average output)	1 000 000 units
Investment (total assets)	€900 000 000

Required

1 What operating profit percentage on revenues is needed to attain the target return on investment of 20%? What is the selling price per unit?

2 Using the selling price per unit calculated in requirement 1, what rate of return on investment will be earned if Salvador assembles and sells 1 500 000 units? 500 000 units?

3 The company has a management bonus plan based on yearly division performance. Assume that Salvador assembled and sold 1 000 000 units, 1 500 000 units and 500 000 units in three successive years. Each of three people served as divisional manager for one year before being killed in a car accident. As the principal heir of the third manager, comment on the bonus plan.

*19.13 Residual income, economic value added (EVA®) (25 minutes)

Intervilles SA operates two divisions, a Lorry Rental Division that rents to individuals and a Transportation Division that transports goods from one city to another. Results reported for the last year are as follows:

	Lorry Rental Division	Transportation Division
Total assets	€650 000	€950 000
Current liabilities	120 000	200 000
Operating profit before tax	75 000	160 000

Required

1 Calculate the residual income for each division using operating profit before tax and investment equal to total assets minus current liabilities. The required rate of return on investments is 12%.

2 The company has two sources of funds: long-term debt with a market value of €900 000 at an interest rate of 10% and equity capital with a market value of €600 000 at a cost of equity of 15%. Intervilles' income tax rate is 40%. Intervilles applies the same weighted-average cost of capital to both divisions, since each division faces similar risks. Calculate the economic value added (EVA®) for each division.

3 Using your answers to requirements 1 and 2, what would you conclude about the performance of each division? Explain briefly.

19.14   **Ethics, manager's performance evaluation** (25 minutes)

Serra-Mica Srl is a maker of ceramic coffee cups. It imprints company logos and other sayings on the cups for both commercial and wholesale markets. The firm has the capacity to produce 3 000 000 cups per year, but the recession has cut production and sales last year to 1 500 000 cups. The summary operating statement for 2015 was as follows:

Sales (1 500 000 × €2)	€3 000 000
Cost of goods sold	2 700 000
Gross profit	300 000
Marketing, distribution and administration costs (fixed)	400 000
Operating profit	€(100 000)

Cost of goods sold consists of variable costs of €750 000 (or €0.50 per cup) and fixed costs of €1 950 000 (or €1.30 per cup). There was no opening and no closing stock of finished goods in 2015.

Concerned about the loss, the board of directors hired a new CEO, Antonio Pirelli, and offered him an incentive-based compensation contract rather than the fixed-salary contract of the previous CEO. Pirelli's contract paid €50 000 per year in salary plus a 15% bonus on the firm's operating profits (if any) before deducting the bonus. Operating profits are calculated using full absorption costing – that is, fixed manufacturing costs per unit manufactured are inventoried and expensed only when the goods are sold.

Pirelli took the following actions for 2016:

a Increased production to 2 500 000 cups.

b Increased sales to 1 800 000 cups.

c Increased marketing, distribution and administration costs to €650 000. (Pirelli's salary of €50 000 is included in these costs.)

The selling price per cup in 2016 of €2, the variable manufacturing costs per cup of €0.50 and total fixed manufacturing costs of €1 950 000 were all unchanged from 2015.

At the end of 2016, Pirelli met with the board of directors and announced that he had accepted another job. He noted that he had put Serra-Mica successfully on track and thanked the board for the opportunity. His new job was to turn around another struggling company.

Required

1 Calculate Pirelli's bonus for 2016.

2 Evaluate Pirelli's performance. Did he do as good a job as the numbers in requirement 1 suggest? Explain.

3 Did Pirelli behave ethically? Explain your answer.

Intermediate level

*19.15   **Return on investment; comparisons of three companies** (CMA, adapted) (30 minutes)

Return on investment is often expressed as follows:

$$\frac{\text{Income}}{\text{Investment}} = \frac{\text{Revenues}}{\text{Investment}} \times \frac{\text{Income}}{\text{Revenues}}$$

Required

1 What advantages are there in the breakdown of the computation into two separate components?

2   Fill in the following blanks:

	Companies in same industry		
	A	B	C
Revenue	€1 000 000	€500 000	?
Profit	€100 000	€50 000	?
Investment	€500 000	?	€5 000 000
Profit as % of revenue	?	?	0.5%
Investment turnover	?	?	2
Return on investment	?	1%	?

After filling in the blanks, comment on the relative performance of these companies as thoroughly as the data permit.

19.16   Financial and non-financial performance measures, goal congruence (CMA, adapted) (25 minutes)

Thor-Equip AS specialises in the manufacture of medical equipment, a field that has become increasingly competitive. Approximately two years ago, Knut Solbær, president of Thor-Equip, decided to revise the bonus plan (based, at the time, entirely on operating profit) to encourage divisional managers to focus on areas that were important to customers and that added value without increasing cost. In addition to a profitability incentive, the revised plan also includes incentives for reduced rework costs, reduced sales returns and on-time deliveries. Bonuses are calculated and awarded semi-annually on the following basis. A base bonus is calculated at 2% of operating profit. The bonus amount is then adjusted by the following amounts:

a (i)   Reduced by excess of rework costs over 2% of operating profit.

   (ii) No adjustment if rework costs are less than or equal to 2% of operating profit.

b Increased by €5000 if over 98% of deliveries are on time, by €2000 if 96–98% of deliveries are on time and by €0 if on-time deliveries are below 96%.

c (i)   Increased by €3000 if sales returns are less than or equal to 1.5% of sales.

   (ii) Decreased by 50% of excess of sales returns over 1.5% of sales.

Note: If the calculation of the bonus results in a negative amount for a particular period, the manager simply receives no bonus and the negative amount is *not* carried forward to the next period.

Results for Thor-Equip's Kari and Siri Divisions for the year 2015, the first year under the new bonus plan, follow. In the previous year, 2014, under the old bonus plan, the Kari Division manager earned a bonus of €27 060 and the Siri Division manager a bonus of €22 440.

	Kari Division		Siri Division	
	1 January 2015 to 30 June 2015	1 July 2015 to 31 December 2015	1 January 2015 to 30 June 2015	1 July 2015 to 31 December 2015
Sales	€4 200 000	€4 400 000	€2 850 000	€2 900 000
Operating profit	€462 000	€440 000	€342 000	€406 000
On-time delivery	95.4%	97.3%	98.2%	94.6%
Rework costs	€11 500	€11 000	€6000	€8000
Sales returns	€84 000	€70 000	€44 750	€42 500

Required

1   Why did Knut need to introduce these new performance measures? That is, why does he need to use these performance measures over and above the operating profit numbers for the period?

2   Calculate the bonus earned by each manager for each six-month period and for the year 2015.

3 What effect did the change in the bonus plan have on each manager's behaviour? Did the new bonus plan achieve what he desired? What changes, if any, would you make to the new bonus plan?

Advanced level

19.17 **Risk sharing, incentives, benchmarking, multiple tasks** (20–30 minutes)

The Portimão Division of Amica Lda sells car batteries. Amica's corporate management gives Portimão management considerable operating and investment autonomy in running the division. Amica is considering how it should compensate Manuel Belem, the general manager of the Portimão Division. Proposal 1 calls for paying him a fixed salary. Proposal 2 calls for paying him no salary and compensating him only on the basis of the division's ROI (calculated based on operating profit before any bonus payments). Proposal 3 calls for paying him some salary and some bonus based on ROI. Assume that Manuel does not like bearing risk.

Required

1 a Evaluate each of the three proposals, specifying the advantages and disadvantages of each.

   b Suppose that Amica competes against Tiara-Iberica SA in the car battery business. Tiara is roughly the same size and operates in a business environment that is very similar to Portimão's. The senior management of Amica is considering evaluating Manuel on the basis of Portimão's ROI minus Tiara's ROI. He complains that this approach is unfair because the performance of another firm, over which he has no control, is included in his performance evaluation measure. Is his complaint valid? Why or why not?

2 Now suppose that Manuel has no authority for making capital investment decisions. Corporate management makes these decisions. Is return on investment a good performance measure to use to evaluate him? Is return on investment a good measure to evaluate the economic viability of the Portimão Division? Explain.

3 Portimão's salespersons are responsible for selling and providing customer service and support. Sales are easy to measure. Although customer service is very important to Portimão in the long run, it has not yet implemented customer-service measures. Manuel wants to compensate his salesforce only on the basis of sales commissions paid for each unit of product sold. He cites two advantages to this plan: (a) it creates very strong incentives for the salesforce to work hard, and (b) the company pays salespersons only when the company itself is earning revenues and has cash. Do you like his plan? Why or why not?

19.18 **Relevant costs, performance evaluation, goal congruence** (30 minutes)

Mikkeli Oy has three operating divisions. The managers of these divisions are evaluated on their divisional operating profit, a figure that includes an allocation of corporate overhead *proportional to the revenues of each division*. The operating profit statement (in thousands) for the first quarter of 2016 is as follows:

	Tampere Division	Oulu Division	Kotka Division	Total
Revenues	€2000	€1200	€1600	€4800
Cost of goods sold	1050	540	640	2230
Gross profit	950	660	960	2570
Division overhead	250	125	160	535
Corporate overhead	400	240	320	960
Divisional operating profit	€300	€295	€480	€1075

The manager of the Tampere Division is unhappy that his profitability is about the same as the Oulu Division's and is much less than the Kotka Division's, even though his revenues are much higher than either of these other two divisions'. The manager knows that he is carrying one line of products with very low profitability. He was going to replace this line of business as soon as more profitable product opportunities became available, but he has kept it because the line is marginally profitable and uses facilities that would otherwise be idle. That manager now realises, however, that the sales from this product line are attracting a fair amount of corporate overhead because of the allocation procedure and maybe the line is already unprofitable for him. This low-margin line of products had the following characteristics for the most recent quarter (in thousands):

Revenues	€800
Cost of goods sold	600
Avoidable division overhead	100

Required

1 Prepare the operating profit statement for Mikkeli Oy for the second quarter of 2016. Assume that revenues and operating results are identical to the first quarter except that the manager of the Tampere Division has dropped the low-margin product line from his product group.

2 Is Mikkeli Oy better off from this action?

3 Is the Tampere Division manager better off from this action?

4 Suggest changes for Mikkeli's system of division reporting and evaluation that will motivate division managers to make decisions that are in the best interest of Mikkeli Oy as a whole. Discuss any potential disadvantages of your proposal.

*19.19 Evaluating managers, ROI, value-chain analysis of cost structure (40–50 minutes)

User Friendly Computer is one of the largest personal computer companies in the world. The board of directors was recently (March 2015) informed that User Friendly's president, Felix Lechat, was resigning to 'pursue other interests'. An executive search firm recommends that the board consider appointing Peter Diamond (current CEO of Computer Power) or Rachida Kamel (current CEO of Plum Computer). You collect the following financial information on Computer Power and Plum Computer for 2013 and 2014 (in millions):

	Computer Power		Plum Computer	
	2013	2014	2013	2014
Total assets	€360.0	€340.0	€160.0	€240.0
Revenues	€400.0	€320.0	€200.0	€350.0
Costs				
R&D	36.0	16.8	18.0	43.5
Design	15.0	8.4	3.6	11.6
Production	102.0	112.0	82.8	98.6
Marketing	75.0	92.4	36.0	66.7
Distribution	27.0	22.4	18.0	23.2
Customer service	45.0	28.0	21.6	46.4
Total costs	300.0	280.0	180.0	290.0
Operating profit	€100.0	€40.0	€20.0	€60.0

In early 2015, a computer magazine gave Plum Computer's main product five stars (its highest rating on a five-point scale). Computer Power's main product was given three stars, down from five stars a year ago because of customer-service problems. The computer magazine also ran an article on new-product introductions in the personal computer industry. Plum Computer received high marks for new products in 2014. Computer Power's performance was called 'mediocre'. One 'unnamed insider' of Computer Power commented: 'Our new-product cupboard is empty.'

Required

1 Use the DuPont method to analyse the ROI of Computer Power and Plum Computer in 2013 and 2014. Comment on the results.

2 Calculate the percentage of costs in each of the six business-function cost categories for Computer Power and Plum Computer in 2013 and 2014. Comment on the results.

3 Rank Diamond and Kamel as potential candidates for CEO of User Friendly Computer.

19.20 **ROI, residual income, investment decisions, division manager's compensation** (CMA, adapted) (50 minutes)

Faulkenheim GmbH is a manufacturer of tool and die machinery. Faulkenheim is a vertically integrated company that is organised into two divisions. The Frankfurt Steel Division manufactures alloy steel plates. The Tool and Die Machinery Division uses the alloy steel plates to make machines. Faulkenheim operates each of its divisions as an investment centre.

Faulkenheim monitors its divisions on the basis of return on investment (ROI) with investment defined as average operating assets employed. Faulkenheim uses ROI to determine management bonuses. All investments in operating assets are expected to earn a minimum return of 11% before income taxes. For many years, Frankfurt's ROI has ranged from 11.8% to 14.7%. During the fiscal year ending 31 December 2014, Frankfurt contemplated a capital acquisition with an estimated ROI of 11.5%; division management, however, decided against the investment because it believed that the investment would decrease Frankfurt's overall ROI.

Frankfurt's 2014 operating income statement follows. The division's operating assets employed were €15 750 000 at 31 December 2014, a 5% increase over the previous year-end balance.

**Frankfurt Steel Division operating profit statement
for the year ending 31 December 2014**

Revenue		€25 000 000
Cost of goods sold		16 500 000
Gross profit		8 500 000
Operating costs		
Administrative	€3 955 000	
Marketing	2 700 000	
Total operating costs		6 655 000
Operating profit		€1 845 000

Required

1 Calculate the return on investment in average operating assets employed (ROI) for 2014 for the Frankfurt Steel Division.

2 Calculate Frankfurt Steel Division's residual income on the basis of average operating assets employed.

3 Would the management of Frankfurt Steel Division have been more likely to accept the investment opportunity it had in 2014 if residual income were used as a performance measure instead of ROI? Explain.

4 Frank Weissmann, the chairman of Faulkenheim GmbH is considering one of four alternative ways to compensate division managers.

  a Pay each division manager only a flat salary and no bonus.

  b Make all of each division manager's compensation depend on division residual income.

  c Make all of each division manager's compensation depend on company-wide (Faulkenheim GmbH) residual income rather than divisional residual income.

  d Use benchmarking and compensate each division manager on the basis of his or her own division's residual income minus the residual profit of the other division. Assume the two divisions have comparable levels of investment and required rates of return.

Assume that division managers do not like bearing risk. Evaluate each of the four alternatives Weissmann is considering, in the context of the structure and businesses of Faulkenheim GmbH. Indicate the positive and negative features of each proposal.

5 What compensation arrangement would you recommend? Explain your answer briefly.

PART IV

Case study problems

Case 401

BBR plc
Clive Emmanuel, University of Glasgow

This case highlights a transfer-pricing problem where divisional interests are pitted against total corporate profitability. The case requires some analysis of the potential costs and benefits of a transfer pricing procedure based on divisional management negotiation.

'BBR prides itself on being a growing, prosperous company, its success being partly due to a good management team which fully participates in its development via a decentralised control system.' This statement was questioned at the meeting which took place between John North, group finance director of BBR and Paul Giddings, divisional general manager of the Shrewsbury plant. The surprise came when Paul revealed that he did not believe he was responsible for his division's profitability. This, he claimed, was due to the company's transfer-pricing policy.

Historically, Paul's division bought over 50% of its total input of rubber hose from a sister division located in Preston. This trade annually accounted for about 25–35% of the Preston division's total output. Paul felt that the transfer price was unfair, and hence his division's reported profit was not a true reflection of his operational effectiveness. In the ensuing conversation both men agreed in principle that divisional general managers are delegated discretionary control over short-term strategy development, day-to-day operating decisions and capital expenditure decisions up to a prescribed limit. However, Paul claimed that in practice other factors intervened to reduce the divisional manager's degree of control and took, as an example, the inter-divisional trade in rubber hose.

The rubber hose trade

Fundamentally, the Preston division produces rubber hose which is then sold to, among others, Paul's Shrewsbury division where it is 'tailored' for hydraulic uses in pit props, aircraft undercarriages and heavy plant and equipment.

Before the annual budgets are compiled, the divisional general managers enter into negotiations about fixing the transfer price. Three months' notice is required before any mutually agreed price can be revised. The managers themselves spend one or two days negotiating the transfer price for the forthcoming months. At this meeting, information provided by their respective

Source: Emmanuel, C.R. (1988) 'BBR plc', in D. Otley, D. Brown and C. Wilkinson (eds) *Case Studies in Management Accounting* (Hemel Hempstead, UK: Philip Allan Publishers). Reproduced with permission.

management accountants and annual cost variances provided by the central purchasing officer of BBR are available. The Preston division provides cost data relating to standard variable and fixed costs traceable to the division, plus an apportionment for selling, administrative and distribution costs. Normally, these data provide a platform price for the negotiations. The forecasts given by the central purchasing officer are included in these cost estimates. The Preston subsidiary is unaware of the assumptions on which the purchasing forecasts are based, but nevertheless accepts them as relevant to the fixing of the transfer price.

The Shrewsbury division also compiles standard cost data, and in addition presents price list information with the likely allowable discounts it can hope to receive from alternative suppliers. On some occasions these latter estimates form the ceiling price for the negotiations on the transfer price. One of the difficulties that has been experienced is that the range between the cost estimates at Preston and the competitor list prices at Shrewsbury can be vast. So much so that the platform price exceeds the ceiling price. This may occur when excess supply is expected to characterise the external market. Hard-nosed negotiations can result in the ultimate transfer price being less than satisfactory to both parties and there is always the possibility for unrelated disputes to interfere with the unstructured negotiations on the transfer price.

When a transfer price has been negotiated, this is incorporated in the annual budgets of the divisions resulting in separate profit targets. The Preston division requires large volume production in order to obtain economies of scale and to maintain its competitive position in the external market. Manufacturing set-up costs are high, and hence there are real cost savings in having long production runs. The Shrewsbury division, on the other hand, is committed to increasing its share of the final product market which is price-sensitive. The end-users are mainly multinational companies and have access to world-wide suppliers. The differing orientations are perhaps best illustrated by the responses to a question put to the respective divisional managers about the degree of autonomy which they exercise.

Does the authority to use external markets freely, to develop and innovate products, and to plan the division's future:

		Preston division	Shrewsbury division
(a)	reduce the interdependence between the companies of the group?	Agree	Disagree
(b)	make compliance with corporate plans more difficult?	Agree	Disagree
(c)	allow your division's performance to be a more realistic reflection of your worth or effort?	Agree	Agree
(d)	motivate you to use more your ingenuity, imagination, and creativity?	Agree	Agree
(e)	cause corporate/group objectives to give ground to division's goals?	Agree	Disagree
(f)	enhance the competitive effectiveness of the group as a whole?	Disagree	Agree

Paul Giddings feels that at the transfer-price negotiating stage, he is always in a weak position. There are only two other domestic suppliers and three overseas who could supply the rubber hose in the volume he requires. Even then it is unlikely that any one of these five external suppliers would be willing to handle more than 20% of his division's total needs. His input to the negotiations is based on volume discounts likely to be available from the external suppliers and he argues that the Preston division should give a substantially better discount when he is buying internally because Preston avoids the problems of the settlement and payments, advertising and some transportation costs. In fact, he argues that the economies of scale Preston enjoys from the internal trade are being passed on in disproportionately lower prices to potential competitors of the Shrewsbury division. The Preston division counters that the savings obtained by the large volume of internal sales enables it to be cost-efficient and innovative in developing new production techniques.

Exhibit 401.1 provides cost data which the managers are using in their current negotiations. The transfer price proposed by the Preston division is £12.50 per metre of rubber hose.

Exhibit 401.1	Cost data available for the transfer pricing negotiations

Preston Division

Output ('000 metres of rubber hose)	Average material cost (£ per metre)	Average direct labour cost (£ per metre)
100	8.00	5.00
200	7.70	4.80
300	7.50	4.70
400	7.20	4.50
500	7.00	4.10
600	6.50	4.00
700	6.00	3.80
800	5.50	3.60
900	5.00	3.40
1000	4.50	3.20

Annual budgeted divisional fixed costs	£160 000
Annual budgeted allocation of selling, administration and transportation costs	£40 000
Proposed transfer price	£12.50 per metre

Shrewsbury Division

Buy-in order size ('000 metres of rubber hose)	Average external suppliers list price (£ per metre)	Average discount (% per metre)
100	14	nil
200	14	3.57
300	14	7.15
400	14	11.6
500	14	15.0

Overlaying all of this is the difficulty both parties have in trying to forecast whether the future market will exhibit excess demand or excess supply. It is this problem which had led to the regular revision of the transfer price during the budget year in which it has been set.

Questions

1 Using the data provided, explain Paul Giddings' misgivings about a transfer price of £12.50. Indicate the actions he may take to source his rubber hose requirements and identify those which are in BBR's best interests.

2 Analyse the transfer pricing procedure of BBR within the management-control system (Exhibit 401.2 below). Outline clearly all the hidden costs associated with the existing procedure.

3 Suggest and examine alternative transfer pricing procedures and transfer prices which may lead to an improvement.

Exhibit 401.2   Procedures governing transfer-price setting

A Policy

1 The transfer price between operating units of the *same* operating company is purely a matter for the Chief Executive of the operating company concerned, for he is responsible for the total profitability of the organisation under his management. However, where supply/demand is between operating units of the *same* operating company it is important that a check is maintained on the market, or 'going' price for the products/services in question to enable the efficiency of the supplier to be reviewed.

2 Transfer prices, where applicable, will be between operating companies/units who are organisationally separate, i.e. those who are an independent operating unit not within an operating company or who are within a different operating company to the unit with whom they are dealing.

3 Operating companies/units will *normally* draw their requirements from within Group resources except where:

   a fiscal/political constraints make this impossible;

   b added cost (e.g. freight, transport, duty, etc.) make the price wholly uncompetitive;

   c the supplying operating unit requires a transfer price in excess of that *actually paid* by the purchasing operating unit to third parties for 25% of their annual consumption for comparable quality, delivery and quantities of the product in question.

B Guidelines

4 Transfer prices agreed between supplying operating units and purchasing operating units will have reference to the market price on the willing buyer/willing seller basis for the comparable qualities and deliveries.

5 The agreed quantities and prices of products to be transferred between operating companies to be clearly and separately shown in the documentation submitted by each operating company.

6 It is not in the interests of the Group for the purchasing operating units to play off a Group supplier against a third party; such action serves to debase the whole market price where significant quantities are involved.

C Reference

7 If the purchasing operating unit is unable to arrive at an agreed transfer price with the supplying operating unit and where the quantities of products involved are in excess of £10 000 p.a., the matter will be referred to the Headquarters Office, in which event the Chief Executive (or the executive concerned) of the purchasing operating unit will be expected to show that:

   a he can buy on a regular basis (NOT spot lots) at significantly lower prices than his colleague is offering

   b he is unable to maintain the gross margins that he has heretofore achieved, or, if selling retail, his standard mark-up inclusive of quantity or special discounts

   c his operations are seriously prejudiced by his having to accept an inflated transfer price from Group resources.

8 It will be important that (a) a firm supply/demand plan is established and (b) the buying operating unit can rely on the same quality and service which is available to them from third parties. Thus the provision contained in para. 5 (i.e. that the *planned* Inter-Group Transfer Price is shown in the documentation, working programme section and represents the basis on which *both* parties are operating) will establish a quasi-contractual situation between the parties concerned.

9 If operating unit A erects a plant for the purpose of supplying operating unit B then clearly B is committed to accepting the planned transfer price over the planned time scale, while A is responsible for ensuring that its output costs are in accordance with the original plan submitted in the sanction documents.

D Conclusion

10 Nothing in the foregoing will be interpreted as an intention that one operating unit should subsidise inefficient (in quality) or uneconomic (in cost) production of another; it is intended that the policy set out in paras 2 and 3 above shall be complied with in order that maximum throughput at transfer prices which will optimise the total Group profitability can be achieved.

Case 402

Cresta Plating Company Ltd

This case focuses on the design of a management control system in a company where 'control by observation' is no longer deemed appropriate and where management by objectives is being implemented. It engages in a discussion of decentralisation and responsibility accounting issues.

Company background

Cresta Plating Company Ltd was purchased in 1995 by a group of companies to carry out the plating works of its many subsidiary companies. Cresta is one company within a division of the main group, the division being concerned predominantly with metal finishing in the widest sense. The company is located in the London area, and this was a significant factor in the decision to purchase, since the majority of the companies in the group were also situated in the south east of England.

Apart from plating work for companies within the division and within the group generally, the company carries out a substantial amount of plating for companies outside the group. The proportions of work for group companies and non-group companies have recently been equal.

The company had its origins in the early 1980s, and from tin-shed beginnings it expanded by the time of the purchase in 1995 to a reasonable size and had gained a sound technical

Source: Adapted from 'Cresta Plating Company Ltd', *Management Accounting*, 1988.

reputation. All the remnants of private family business management have now disappeared. However, despite the efforts of the parent company, and a number of recent executive appointments which have been group-inspired, the 'group image' is not well established.

Production and progress

The company is in the electro-plating jobbing industry, and this presents problems not met in a plating shop in a factory handling work that is produced in that factory alone. This is an important factor, for it results in the company having limited knowledge of the orders that are coming into the factory premises. Production planning and control is extremely difficult, especially when linked to the quick delivery so vital to secure orders. The company aims at a 48-hour turnaround from the receipt of an order to its despatch.

Since 1995 the company has grown rapidly and now employs about 350 people at two factories in London, one in Newcastle and another in Sheffield, the last two fac-tories being recent acquisitions of family businesses which, although technically sound, have not been satis-factory in the financial sense.

At Cresta, both barrel plating and vat plating are used. Most of the vats are hand-operated in order to achieve a flexibility necessary to cope with the different mixes of products. On the barrel-plating side, there are two large automatic plants to cope with the steady flow of work from group companies. There are also a few hand-operated barrels. The company handles a wide variety of work, ranging from small orders of a few kilograms weight, to huge orders where the total weight of the products involved could be as much as one tonne. A wide variety of finishes is catered for, such as zinc, cadmium, tin, chromium, nickel, copper, precious metals such as gold and silver, and also plastics.

The company has been profitable for a number of years and the continuation of this trend can be seen in recent results. This success has been partly due to the fact that the company has an assured market within the group. Intra-group pricing is a touchy matter within the company, and Cresta is under constant pressure to reduce transfer prices which, by the strength of its top management, it seems to withstand successfully.

Accounting methods

The accounting department has a staff of 12 who cover the duties of financial accounting, cost accounting and wages for all the factories. There are, however, two clerical workers on routine accounting and wages matters, both at Newcastle and Sheffield. Until a few months ago, the only costing work being done was the recalculation of cost rates for the purpose of estimating for price fixing. This recalculation was undertaken annually and was on an absorption costing basis. Overhead costs are cat-egorised as fixed or variable on a basis specified by head office, and this analysis is a requirement of the trading statement prepared and submitted to head office.

In 2014 a new man was appointed to the post of company secretary/chief accountant. He has proved to be quite an innovator, and one of the first tasks he undertook was to review the financial and cost accounting procedures. At one of the early board meetings he attended it was stressed that better financial controls were needed. This attitude was supported by the argument that, as the company was continuing to expand, control by observation became increasingly difficult. The new man formed the impression that a certain amount of lip-service was being paid to the idea of management accounting and information services. He found that monthly and quarterly interim trading statements were being prepared, but he was disappointed that these were only total trading statements for the company. He proceeded to give immediate thought to the departmentalisation of the figures. One of the factors which weighed heavily with him was the fact that during his four weeks 'acclimatisation' at head office, he had been introduced to a management by objectives programme which was in the process of being launched throughout the group. Two points that particularly impressed him about this programme were:

1 The overall financial objective which was to be built into the programme, namely a return on capital employed of 20% before tax.

2 The desire to set objectives and key tasks for individual managers and executives.

This second point matched comments which had been made at the Cresta board meeting that production managers needed measures which they did not have at the moment.

Budgets

The accountant also had work to do on accounting returns for head office. The statements in Exhibit 402.1 include a budget and actual trading statement return, prepared to the group uniform pattern. The budget is an annual affair and worries the accountant somewhat, since he believes that it should have its roots in departmental budgets. This is not so at the moment, because it is produced as an overall business budget.

Exhibit 402.1   Budget and actual trading statements, September 2015

	September 2015		January to September 2015	
	Budget	Actual	Budget	Actual
Sales: to group companies	£22 000	£29 161	£220 000	£287 103
Sales: outside group	38 000	27 277	380 000	285 046
Total sales	60 000	56 438	600 000	572 149
Variable costs of sales	35 000	32 231	350 000	335 203
Gross margin	25 000	24 207	250 000	236 946
Other costs				
Depreciation	2 600	2 416	26 000	24 720
Fixed works expenses	5 200	6 637	52 000	58 634
Admin. expenses	2 800	3 029	28 000	29 327
Fixed sales expenses	2 400	1 448	24 000	20 772
	£13 000	£13 530	£130 000	£133 012
	£12 000	£10 677	£120 000	£103 934

Accounting developments

As far as Cresta was concerned, it seemed to the accountant that departmentalisation could logically be carried to profit centres. There was vat plating and barrel plating, and there were some less significant sections; further, there were natural subsections in each of which were definite factory locations with directly identifiable sales. There was already in being a simple sales analysis to these profit centres. To develop the existing records into a departmental system of accounting was only a matter of arranging the necessary cost analysis procedures. These were partly in existence in a rough-and-ready fashion and were used to facilitate the task of recalculating cost rates annually. The extra work created by a full-scale cost allocation and apportionment exercise carried out each monthly accounting period was performed by two additional cost office staff especially appointed for the purpose.

There were, inevitably, some joint costs and much thought had to be given to them, particularly on the matter of how these should be apportioned between the profit centres. In addition, there were service department costs, administration expenses and some general fixed costs, and for all of these bases of apportionment had to be determined. It was a hard slog, but it was finally done and it was possible to produce interim profit centre trading statements.

Profit centre trading statements

The first man to see the new statements was the managing director, who took some time to warm to them, but he eventually did. The other executives were brought into a meeting to study them, and there was general agreement that they were very informative. This was the first information which top management had ever received on the profitability of different units, so that inevitably some surprise was registered about some of the figures. On this first set of departmental trading statements, the new accountant had gone no further than to analyse sales, costs and profits or losses. There was, however, a feeling at the meeting that the next statement should show an analysis of capital employed in profit centres in order that 'profitability' could be computed on a departmental basis. Interest was running high, and the accountant was pleased.

The next step was the analysis of capital employed, and the accountant and his staff found this analysis to profit centres was just as difficult as cost analysis. Some of the fixed capital could be identified directly with departments, but some was of a more general type. He was not at all sure about the working capital, which he felt was very much more a function of the product itself and of the customer than it was of any production department. There was also the problem of capital employed in the service departments of the company. But again, the interest in department profitability was something to be cultivated, and he felt that the management accounting service had an opportunity here to justify itself. The net result of all these efforts is the type of trading statement which appears in Exhibit 402.2.

Exhibit 402.2   Profit centre analysis

Panel A

	Totals	Barrel	Vat	HD	Spec. fin.	Misc.
September 2015						
Sales: group companies	£29 161	£21 625	£2 604	£1 445	£1 877	£1 610
Others	27 277	3 630	7 564	3 457	11 426	1 200
Total	56 438	25 255	10 168	4 902	13 303	2 810
Process materials	8 271	3 599	1 885	502	1 857	428
Direct labour	7 140	1 374	2 003	818	2 702	243
Indirect labour	1 501	497	474	28	455	47
Labour overheads	1 296	282	366	112	497	39
Consumables	2 308	127	470	195	857	659
Power	4 653	1 851	452	603	1 278	469
Maintenance	1 947	974	238	100	575	60
Jigs	576	–	133	203	240	–
Services	4 539	1 950	726	633	1 205	25
Variable costs	32 231	10 654	6 747	3 194	9 666	1 970
Gross margin	24 207	14 601	3 421	1 708	3 637	840
Fixed works expenses	9 053	3 589	1 487	1 352	2 303	322
Admin. and sales expenses	4 477	2 037	729	395	93	1 223
	13 530	5 626	2 216	1 747	2 396	1 545
Profit (loss)	£10 677	£8 975	£1 205	(£39)	£1 241	(£705)
January–September 2015						
Sales	572 149	260 093	105 623	61 078	120 467	24 888
Profit (loss)	103 934	77 909	8 101	4 568	9 356	4 000
% of sales	18.2	29.9	7.6	7.5	7.8	16.0
Annual rate of profit	138 578	103 879	10 801	6 091	12 475	5 333
Assets employed	350 000	130 000	58 000	43 000	109 000	10 000
ROI%	39.5	79.8	18.6	14.2	11.4	53.3

Panel B

	Total Barrel	A Automatic	B Automatic	Horizontal	Chrome	Small orders	Anodising	Spec. fin.
September 2015								
Sales								
Group companies	£21 625	£5 791	£3 191	£7 985	£3 923	£427	£150	£158
Others	3 630	247	1 926	1 177	63	217	–	–
Total	25 255	6 038	5 117	9 162	3 986	644	150	158
Process materials	5 599	516	533	2 105	137	213	18	77
Direct labour	1 374	282	226	474	165	112	40	75
Indirect labour	497	65	190	150	45	39	8	–
Labour overheads	282	50	67	94	30	25	6	10
Consumables	127	26	47	44	–	10	–	–
Power	1 851	520	568	570	118	40	15	20
Maintenance	974	65	261	375	209	64	–	–
Services	1 930	378	379	666	370	100	32	25
Variable costs	10 654	1 902	2 271	4 478	1 074	603	119	207
Gross margin	14 601	4 136	2 846	4 684	2 912	41	31	(49)
Fixed works expenses	3 589	754	1 095	1 065	465	170	20	20
Admin. and Sales								
expenses	2 037	486	412	738	324	52	12	13
	5 626	1 240	1 507	1 803	789	222	32	33
Profit (loss)	£8 975	£2 896	£1 339	£2 881	£2 123	(£181)	(£1)	(£82)
January–September 2015								
Sales	260 093	73 424	57 916	82 491	35 228	7 326	1 802	1 906
Profit (loss)	77 909	24 969	10 734	24 003	19 026	(700)	180	(303)
% of sales	29.9	34.0	14.6	23.1	54.0	(9.7)	10.0	(16.0)
Annual rate of profit	103 879	33 292	14 312	32 004	25 368	(933)	240	(404)
Assets employed	130 000	27 000	44 000	37 000	14 000	6 000	1 000	1 000
ROI%	79.8	123.3	32.5	86.5	181.2	(15.5)	24.0	(40.4)

'Can these assessments be right?'

The next phase in relationships between accounting and management generally at Cresta can best be described as a 'Can these assessments be right?' phase. Arguments raged about the allocation and apportionment of costs to profit centres. Time and again the accountant made the point that any allocation is arbitrary, no matter how detailed the process by which the allocation rule is determined. On the other hand, he never failed to add that each profit centre must bear its fair share of all expenses. There is no doubt that many of the management team at Cresta had been shattered by the figures. Some profit centres were shown to be less profitable than they had been thought to be. Perhaps it was natural that there were recriminations. There were comments like 'We always felt that Bert was efficient, but look how much money he's losing us.' All this worried the accountant. Surely it was logical to have profit centre reporting? But where were the ties between profitability and efficiency, if any?

Transfer pricing

Discussions between the accountant, managers and parties aggrieved by his efforts brought out many points which he felt deserved attention. The overriding one seemed to be the subject of transfer pricing. The point was made that there were inconsistencies in pricing which stemmed from two main causes: firstly, insufficient work measurement had been done to enable the establishment of reasonable standards or estimating; and secondly, the managing director had involved himself extensively in pricing decisions. On the first point, everyone agreed that proper work measurement was difficult in this type of manufacture. Then, since it had never been seen in this company's history as providing much more than a basis for wages payment, no very clear need had been established. On the second point, the managing director had been very successful in price negotiations with group companies. Using the argument of quick turnround and quality, coupled with his prestige in the trade and his forcefulness of character, he had been able to extract advantageous prices from group companies. Clearly, this was a factor in the profitability of the various profit centres.

Question

Matters were brought to a head when the group management accountant called a meeting of executives at head office to consider a wide variety of matters, which included the profit centre reporting at Cresta. The managing director and the accountant were invited to this meeting.

As the accountant, you have been asked to prepare a short review of the management accounting system in use at Cresta. This should review the main problems with the present system, as you see them, and any possibilities which you see for improvement.

Case 403

Clayton Industries

In late September 2009, Peter Arnell, country manager of Clayton SpA, the Italian subsidiary of U.S.-based Clayton Industries, faced some daunting challenges as the global recession took its toll. Sales were down 19%, and after decades of solid returns, Clayton SpA was in its third year of losses, now accumulating at more than $1 million a month.

Arnell's attention was sharpened by the imminent visit of Dan Briggs, Clayton's recently appointed CEO, and Simonne Buis, Arnell's direct boss and President of Clayton Europe. Both expected him to turn around Clayton SpA and position it for future growth. And although he had only been in Italy for just over two months, Arnell knew that Briggs and Buis would want to know exactly what action he intended to take.

The Parent Company: Clayton Industries

Founded in Milwaukee in 1938, Clayton Industries Inc. had built a successful business around window-mounted room air conditioners which it sold for residential and light-commercial applications. In the early 1980s, management perceived two important growth opportunities –

HBS Professor Christopher A. Bartlett and writer Benjamin H. Barlow prepared this case solely as a basis for class discussion and not as an endorsement, a source of primary data, or an illustration of effective or ineffective management. The authors thank Sisto Merolla (HBS MBA 2002) of Merloni Termosanitari Spa of Fabriano, Italy, for his helpful contributions to the development of this case.

This case, though based on real events, is fictionalised, and any resemblance to actual persons or entities is coincidental. There are occasional references to actual companies in the narration. From Clayton Industries, reproduced with permission.

one in the North American commercial sector, and the other in residential and commercial markets in Europe – and took steps to exploit both.

As it expanded abroad, Clayton established its position in Europe by acquiring four companies:

- Corliss, a U.K.-based manufacturer of home heating, ventilation, and air conditioning (HVAC) systems.
- Fontaire, a Brussels-based manufacturer of fans and ventilating equipment.
- Control del Clima, a Barcelona-based manufacturer of climate control products for industrial and commercial applications.
- AeroPuro, a Brescia, Italy-based manufacturer of compression chillers for large commercial, public, and institutional installations. (Chillers are the units at the core of most industrial air conditioners.)

To manage international expansion, Clayton restructured its organization in 1988. All operations in the United States and Canada were placed under Clayton North America, while the European acquisitions reported to a newly created Clayton Europe. Each of these entities was headed by a regional company president. (See Exhibit 403.1 for the organizational chart.)

Clayton Europe

In 1989, Clayton Europe adopted the Brussels offices formerly occupied by Fontaire as its head-quarters. Recognizing the need for strong management in each country where it had a presence, the new president of Clayton Europe appointed four country managers. They were given respon-sibility for sales of the full line of Clayton products in their home country and their allocated export markets in Europe.

Early progress was slow. While the European market for air conditioning began to grow in the 1990s, it was from a low base. Even in 1998, air-conditioning was in only 7% of homes in Italy, and 11% in Spain, compared with US penetration of 71%. Many Europeans saw air condition-ing as an expensive American luxury that harmed the environment.

Clayton's slow market penetration also reflected Europeans' different needs and national brand preferences. For example, Clayton's window units (assembled in Belgium from components shipped from the United States) did not sell as well as familiar local brands that Europeans seemed to prefer. And its central AC units also struggled in Europe where few buildings had duct work required for such systems. But a couple of Asian producers had been able to gain penetra-tion in Europe, largely on the basis of price.

As a result of Europeans' strong national brand preferences, the Corliss-sourced HVAC systems and the Fontaire line of fans both sold much better in their home markets than elsewhere in Europe. But no product represented this geographic concentration more strongly than the chiller line built in Italy. A decade after it had been offered to all Clayton's European companies, sales outside Italy accounted for only 12% of the total.

In 2001, Simonne Buis, previously the hard-driving head of the Belgian company, was named president of Clayton Europe. Determined to create a more integrated European organization, her first priority was to increase the operational efficiency of Clayton's diverse portfolio of inherited plants. She set tough targets that required them to slash costs, build scale, or both. Then, to encourage Europe-wide penetration of the entire product line, she informed country managers that in addition to their national sales responsibility, they would now be held respon-sible for Europe-wide profitability of products produced in their plants. She encouraged them to emerge from their country subsidiary silos and collaborate. The simple geographic-based structure was evolving toward a product-overlaid matrix.

Over the next seven years, Europe became a major growth engine for Clayton, increasing its share of the company's global revenue from 33% in 2000 to 45% by 2009. During this period, Belgium/France overtook Italy as Clayton Europe's lead market, its 38% of 2009 revenues ahead of Italy's 30%. Spain accounted for 20%, and the UK for 12%.

Exhibit 403.1   Clayton Industries: Organization of Operations, August 2009

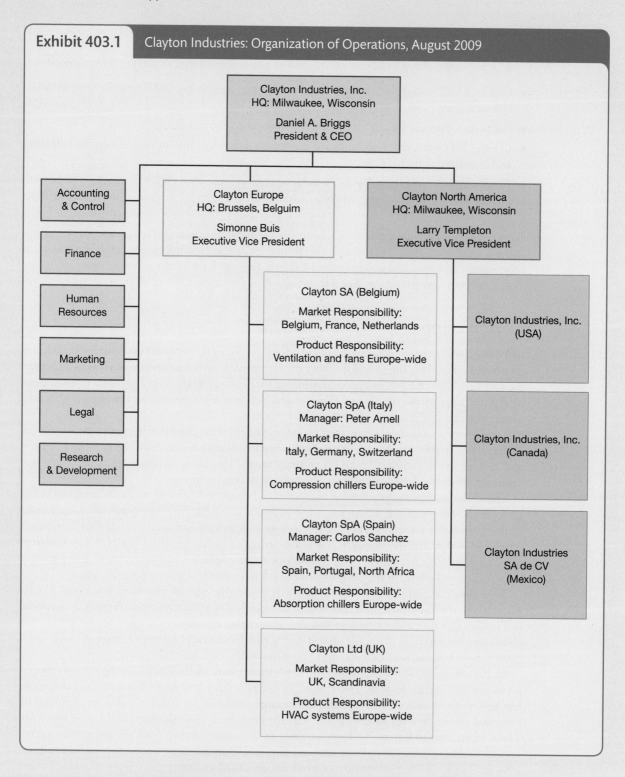

But the European growth engine stalled when the global recession of 2008–09 hit. (**Exhibit 403.2** summarizes Clayton's financial statements.) It was a crisis that triggered strategic adjustments and management changes in both the U.S. and European operations.

Crisis response in the United States and Europe

As the economic crisis deepened in 2009, the Clayton Industries board convinced its 63-year-old, long-time CEO to step aside in favor of Dan Briggs, a 16-year company veteran who, along with Buis, had been groomed as a potential CEO successor. Briggs was a no-nonsense manager who was previously EVP of Clayton North America.

On assuming his new role in March 2009, Briggs quickly established two priorities. Facing a cash crisis, he underlined the urgency of reducing capital use and bringing costs under control. But he also emphasized that 'great opportunities always reside inside crisis', and urged managers to use the downturn to rationalize the company's portfolio and focus on products that could position it for post-recession profitable growth.

As he discussed these priorities with Buis, Briggs told her that he saw Europe as a continued source of growth. But he questioned whether the company should continue its attempts to penetrate the commercial air conditioning sector. In Briggs's view, it was a business in which only the top three or four competitors in any market could make money, and he was skeptical that Clayton could get there from its current situation.

Buis argued that several record-breaking hot European summers were changing consumer attitudes and that the market was on the cusp of embracing air-conditioning. She felt that the company should be positioning for a post-recession expansion. Recognizing Buis's successes in Europe, Briggs asked her to prepare a growth plan to review with him.

To translate Briggs's corporate priorities into European actions, Buis met with her country managers and told them she wanted all country operations to achieve a 10/10/10 plan to cut both receivables and inventories by 10 days, and reduce headcount by 10%. She also announced the 'Top Four in Four' initiative, and asked each manager to prepare plans showing how the product for which he had Europe-wide responsibility would be in the top four in European market share within four years.

Problems at Clayton SpA

While these new targets would be difficult for all of Clayton's European companies, in Italy they would be a real challenge. Lagging other countries in revenue growth since 2004, Clayton SpA actually recorded a 5.3% sales decline in 2008, followed by a 19.4% drop in the first half of 2009. As a result, receivables and inventories were both above 120 days sales. In addition, headcount reduction faced tough local laws and a tense union relationship. In short, achieving the 10/10/10 plan would be very difficult.

The 'Top Four in Four' requirement would also be a challenge for the Italian unit's Europe-wide responsibility for chillers. While this line accounted for 55% of 2009 Italian revenues, it generated only 12% of sales for the rest of Europe. (See Exhibits 403.3 and 403.4 for industry sales and projections). Of the seven companies in the European chiller market, Clayton was in a distant fifth place with a 7% overall market share.

As performance declined, Paolo Lazzaro, president of Clayton SpA since 1998, claimed that the problems were due to the commodity cycle, and suggested that Clayton should 'weather the storm.' Frustrated by this attitude, Buis terminated Lazzaro in June 2009. As she began thinking about who could take over, her mind turned to Peter Arnell.

Exhibit 403.2	Clayton Industries: Income Statement – Summary, 2004–2009					

Millions of USD (except where indicated)	2004	2005	2006	2007	2008	1H09
Revenues						
Clayton N. America (USA/Canada/Mexico)	565.7	577.1	590.0	598.1	557.7	216.6
% Change		2.0%	2.2%	1.4%	(6.8%)	(22.3%)
% Contribution	63.2%	61.8%	60.7%	59.6%	58.0%	54.7%
Clayton SA (Belgium/France/Netherlands)	107.5	118.6	129.7	142.3	148.7	68.0
% Change		10.3%	9.3%	9.8%	4.4%	(8.5%)
% Contribution	12.0%	12.7%	13.3%	14.2%	15.5%	17.2%
Clayton SpA (Italy/Germany/Switzerland)	125.0	132.5	138.0	141.8	134.3	54.1
% Change		6.0%	4.2%	2.7%	(5.3%)	(19.4%)
% Contribution	14.0%	14.2%	14.2%	14.1%	14.0%	13.7%
Clayton SA (Spain/Portugal/N. Africa)	58.1	62.9	68.1	72.3	72.2	36.0
% Change		8.1%	8.4%	6.2%	(0.1%)	(0.3%)
% Contribution	6.5%	6.7%	7.0%	7.2%	7.5%	9.1%
Clayton Ltd (UK/Scandinavia)	39.3	42.8	45.9	48.3	48.6%	21.6
% Change		8.9%	7.2%	5.2%	0.6%	(11.1%)
% Contribution	4.4%	4.6%	4.7%	4.8%	5.1%	5.5%
Total	895.7	933.8	971.7	1,002.8	961.4	396.3
% Change		4.3%	4.1%	3.2%	(4.1%)	(17.6%)
EBITDA						
Clayton N. America (USA/Canada/Mexico)	70.7	69.2	53.1	47.8	27.9	6.5
% Margin	12.5%	12.0%	9.0%	8.0%	5.0%	3.0%
Clayton SA (Belgium/France/Netherlands)	20.2	21.3	17.5	17.1	11.1	3.1
% Margin	18.8%	18.0%	13.5%	12.0%	7.5%	4.5%
Clayton SpA (Italy/Germany/Switzerland)	25.1	24.5	18.1	5.2	(12.8)	(7.6)
% Margin	20.1%	18.5%	13.1%	3.7%	(9.5%)	(14.1%)
Clayton SA (Spain/Portugal/N. Africa)	10.0	10.4	8.4	6.9	6.6	3.2
% Margin	17.2%	16.5%	12.4%	9.5%	9.1%	8.9%
Clayton Ltd (UK/Scandinavia)	7.0	7.3	5.9	4.8	2.9	0.7
% Margin	17.9%	17.2%	12.9%	9.9%	6.0%	3.4%
Total	133.0	132.8	103.0	81.8	35.8	5.9
% Margin	14.8%	14.2%	10.6%	8.2%	3.7%	1.5%
Net income (loss)						
Clayton N. America (USA/Canada/Mexico)	31.1	28.9	11.8	(6.0)	(22.3)	(17.3)
% Margin	5.5%	5.0%	2.0%	(1.0%)	(4.0%)	(8.0%)
Clayton SA (Belgium/France/Netherlands)	8.9	9.5	10.1	10.2	5.9	0.7
% Margin	8.3%	8.0%	7.8%	7.2%	4.0%	1.0%
Clayton SpA (Italy/Germany/Switzerland)	10.8	10.5	6.0	(1.1)	(11.9)	(6.7)
% Margin	8.7%	7.9%	4.4%	(0.8%)	(8.8%)	(12.3%)
Clayton SA (Spain/Portugal/N. Africa)	4.1	4.1	3.7	1.9	0.2	0.0
% Margin	7.1%	6.5%	5.4%	2.6%	0.3%	0.1%
Clayton Ltd (UK/Scandinavia)	2.9	2.9	2.6	1.3	(0.3)	(0.9)
% Margin	7.4%	6.8%	5.6%	2.7%	(0.5%)	(4.2%)
Total	57.9	55.8	34.2	6.4	(28.3)	(24.2)
% Margin	6.5%	6.0%	3.5%	0.6%	(2.9)%	(6.1)%

| Exhibit 403.3 | Clayton Industries: Balance Sheet – Summary, 2004–2009 | | | | | |

Millions of USD	2004	2005	2006	2007	2008	1H09
Current assets	**$277.0**	**$291.6**	**$303.8**	**$308.8**	**$284.2**	**$254.4**
Clayton SpA	$ 9.0	$ 54.1	$ 58.7	$ 62.6	$ 61.6	$ 59.6
Other Europe	$ 60.6	$ 66.5	$ 71.7	$ 75.2	$ 72.5	$ 71.5
North America	$167.4	$171.0	$173.5	$171.0	$150.1	$123.3
Facilities	**$417.6**	**$400.4**	**$385.5**	**$371.1**	**$354.4**	**$336.6**
Clayton SpA	$ 50.4	$ 54.6	$ 48.9	$ 44.7	$ 40.7	$ 38.0
Other Europe	$139.4	$129.4	$124.9	$118.7	$112.6	$109.6
North America	$227.9	$216.4	$211.6	$207.8	$201.1	$189.1
Other assets	**$ 88.0**	**$118.7**	**$124.1**	**$141.3**	**$125.2**	**$140.2**
Clayton SpA	$ 12.3	$ 16.8	$ 17.6	$ 20.0	$ 17.5	$ 19.1
Other Europe	$ 20.1	$ 28.5	$ 31.1	$ 37.0	$ 35.1	$ 44.4
North America	$ 55.6	$ 73.4	$ 75.4	$ 84.3	$ 72.6	$ 76.6
Total assets	**$782.7**	**$810.7**	**$813.4**	**$821.2**	**$763.8**	**$731.2**
Clayton SpA	$111.6	$125.5	$125.2	$127.2	$119.7	$116.7
Other Europe	$220.2	$224.4	$227.7	$230.9	$220.2	$225.5
North America	$450.9	$460.8	$460.5	$463.1	$423.8	$389.0
Current liabilities	**$204.3**	**$224.3**	**$238.6**	**$255.3**	**$251.7**	**$255.4**
Clayton SpA	$ 28.5	$ 32.9	$ 36.7	$ 41.2	$ 42.7	$ 45.5
Other Europe	$ 46.7	$ 51.3	$ 54.6	$ 58.4	$ 57.6	$ 58.4
North America	$129.0	$140.1	$147.3	$155.6	$151.4	$151.5
Long-term debt	**$310.5**	**$340.9**	**$362.6**	**$388.0**	**$382.5**	**$388.2**
Clayton SpA	$ 43.3	$ 50.0	$ 55.8	$ 62.7	$ 64.9	$ 69.1
Other Europe	$ 71.1	$ 81.9	$ 91.5	$102.8	$106.4	$113.4
North America	$196.1	$209.0	$215.3	$222.5	$211.3	$205.7
Stockholders' equity	**$267.9**	**$245.5**	**$212.3**	**$177.9**	**$129.6**	**$ 87.6**
Clayton SpA	$ 37.4	$ 32.2	$ 23.1	$ 12.2	$ (0.9)	$(14.8)
Other Europe	$ 61.3	$ 61.5	$ 57.9	$ 54.1	$ 50.1	$ 59.9
North America	$169.2	$151.8	$131.3	$111.6	$ 80.4	$ 42.5
Total liabilites and equity	**$782.7**	**$810.7**	**$813.4**	**$821.2**	**$763.8**	**$731.2**
Clayton SpA	$109.2	$115.0	$115.6	$116.1	$106.7	$ 99.8
Other Europe	$179.1	$194.7	$204.0	$215.3	$214.1	$231.7
North America	$494.4	$501.0	$493.9	$489.8	$443.0	$399.6

Peter Arnell

Peter Arnell was the 42-year-old head of the British subsidiary, Clayton Ltd. Raised in a working-class family on the outskirts of London, Arnell served seven years in the Royal Marines where he rose to the rank of Captain before attending business school in London. A brief stint in management consulting left him missing the sense of impact he had experienced in the Royal Marines. So in 1998 he joined Clayton's Birmingham office in a sales and marketing job that he thought would let him test himself again on the front lines.

An avid weekend footballer, Arnell was a born competitor, quick with both a handshake and a smile. He drove himself hard and expected the same from others. While very outgoing, he expressed opinions bluntly and had alienated a few colleagues during his time at Clayton.

Exhibit 403.4	Industry Sales of Air Treatment Products (including Chillers) 2003–2008

Millions of USD (except where indicated)	2003	2004	2005	2006	2007	2008
Units ('000)						
United States	61,263.4	64,104.4	67,137.1	70,380.4	71,142.0	71,410.2
% Change		4.6%	4.7%	4.8%	1.1%	0.4%
Europe	15,315.9	16,667.1	18,127.0	19,706.5	20,986.9	22,137.2
% Change		8.8%	8.8%	8.7%	6.5%	5.5%
Italy	2,718.9	2,832.2	2,940.5	3,074.6	3,273.6	3,482.5
% Change		4.2%	3.8%	4.6%	6.5%	6.4%
Millions of USD – current prices						
United States	5,794.7	6,012.4	6,386.9	6,862.9	6,886.9	6,921.7
% Change		3.8%	6.2%	7.5%	0.3%	0.5%
Europe[a]	1,997.4	2,386.8	2,519.8	2,683.3	3,502.2	4,274.1
% Change		19.5%	5.6%	6.5%	30.5%	22.0%
Italy[a]	775.7	861.0	887.8	934.5	1,149.3	1,336.4
% Change		13.9%	3.1%	5.3%	23.0%	16.3%
Millions of USD – constant prices						
United States	5,794.7	5,855.6	6,016.2	6,262.6	6,107.3	5,959.4
% Change		1.1%	2.7%	4.1%	(2.5%)	(2.4%)
Europe[a]	1,945.4	2,335.5	2,499.8	2,691.4	3,540.2	NA
% Change		20.0%	7.0%	7.7%	31.5%	
Italy[a]	736.1	820.5	829.7	855.3	1,030.2	NA
% Change		11.5%	1.1%	3.1%	20.5%	

[a] Converted annually at following exchange rates:

	2003	2004	2005	2006	2007	2008
EUR / US$	0.8854	0.8051	0.8045	0.7970	0.7308	0.6834

Source: Euromonitor International and casewriter estimates.

Quickly promoted to marketing manager, Arnell had expanded Clayton's distribution network from four distributors in central England to 14 throughout the U.K. and Ireland, positioning Clayton's product line to capitalize on the U.K. real estate boom. In 2002, when the head of Clayton Ltd. retired, Buis promoted Arnell to fill the role.

Within weeks, Arnell took the tough decision of closing the old Corliss boiler plant – a move that was in line with the cost cutting program that Buis had initiated a few months earlier. After enduring months of labor pressure and personal threats over the closure, he set about revitalizing the UK business by replacing the lost revenue. He solicited support from product managers of other Clayton lines to help them understand the UK market.

Buis was impressed by Arnell's military discipline and propensity for bold action and felt he could be the change agent Italy needed. She was also aware that years of summers spent in Italy with his maternal grandparents had given him a good command of Italian. When she asked him to consider taking on Clayton SpA, Arnell saw it as a career advancing opportunity to turn around a larger operation that was key to Clayton's European strategy.

A new subsidiary manager arrives

Arnell arrived in Brescia alone on July 20, 2009, having asked his wife and two children to follow in October so he could focus his energies on work. Buis met him and took him around the offices, personally introducing him to Brescia's 10 senior managers. At a group lunch, she told them that

Exhibit 403.5   Forecast Sales of Air Treatment Products (including Chillers), 2009–2013

Millions of USD (except where indicated)	2009	2010	2011	2012	2013
Units ('000)					
United States	72,391.6	73,911.5	75,532.5	77,253.8	79,130.0
% Change	*1.4%*	*2.1%*	*2.2%*	*2.3%*	*2.4%*
Europe	22,441.4	23,651.7	24,925.7	26,266.3	27,295.5
% Change		*5.4%*	*5.4%*	*5.4%*	*5.4%*
Italy	3,692.2	3,910.4	4,128.6	4,347.9	NA
% Change	*6.0%*	*5.9%*	*5.6%*	*5.3%*	
Millions of USD – current prices					
United States	7,013.6	7,139.2	7,287.8	7,462.0	7,632.0
% Change	*1.3%*	*1.8%*	*2.1%*	*2.4%*	*2.3%*
Europe	4,249.4	4,687.6	5,106.9	5,486.5	NA
% Change		*10.3%*	*8.9%*	*7.4%*	
Italy[a]	1,328.1	1,414.9	1,493.2	1,558.7	NA
% Change	*(0.6%)*	*6.5%*	*5.5%*	*4.4%*	

[a] Converted annually at following exchange rates:

	2009	2010	2011	2012	2013
EUR / US$	0.7389	0.7389	0.7389	0.7389	0.7389

Source: Euromonitor International and casewriter estimates.

Exhibit 403.6   Brescia Plant Economics

Millions of USD (except where indicated)	2004	2005	2006	2007	2008	1H09
Units	348.0	372.0	382.0	386.0	375.0	155.0
Revenue Italy	67.1	73.2	76.7	79.0	76.0	29.9
Contribution to Clayton SpA	*53.7%*	*55.3%*	*55.6%*	*55.7%*	*56.6%*	*55.2%*
Other	10.9	11.3	11.1	11.3	11.5	4.1
Total	75.2	82.4	86.7	89.6	86.7	34.0
Operating Expense						
Direct materials	19.7	23.7	29.2	37.5	50.1	18.5
Labor	16.1	16.6	16.9	15.3	15.7	7.2
Overhead – Fixed	29.0	31.3	32.2	34.9	33.6	15.7
Total	64.8	71.5	78.3	87.6	99.4	41.3
EBITDA	10.4	10.9	8.4	2.0	(12.8)	(7.3)
EBITDA Margin	*13.8%*	*13.2%*	*9.7%*	*2.3%*	*(14.7%)*	*(21.5%)*
Capital Expenditures	10.8	11.2	2.3	2.8	3.0	0.8
Capex Margin	*14.4%*	*13.6%*	*2.7%*	*3.1%*	*3.5%*	*2.3%*
Headcount	190	196	204	208	204	203

[a] Converted annually at following exchange rates:

	2004	2005	2006	2007	2008	1H09
EUR / US$	0.851	0.8045	0.7970	0.7308	0.6834	0.7389

PART IV Case study problems

the future of Clayton SpA was in their hands. Reflecting her commitment to empowering country managers and encouraging them to take initiative, she said she would 'get out of their way,' and returned to Brussels.

That afternoon, Arnell called a management meeting to share his early assessment of Brescia's grave situation and to ask for their support. Emphasizing that this was a time for immediate action, he requested all of them to postpone vacation plans until further notice. August being the Italian vacation month, three managers expressed misgivings – the plant manager, the QC manager, and the company controller. Arnell asked them to meet with him individually before the end of the day. In those meetings, after each manager reiterated an unwillingness to change plans, Arnell dismissed them on the spot.

The following day, after a meeting with his HR director to identify strong successors, he announced internal replacements for all three positions. He then met individually with his top team, asking each to help him use his first 60 days to understand the situation and develop a strategy for the company. He then scheduled follow-up meetings with each of them to share their perspectives on the operations, and also to review their individual work plans for the next 60 days.

But events at Clayton SpA did not wait for Arnell to complete his 60-day analysis. On his second day, he arrived at work to find four union officials from Federazione dei Lavoratori della Manifatture (FILM) outside his office with a local TV news crew. These officials suggested he was a hatchet man sent to close the Brescia plant and implement a mass layoff. Arnell assured them he had no such directive, that his mind was open, and that all options were on the table. He told them he would keep them informed, and promised to meet with union representatives the following week.

On August 4, Arnell met seven FILM representatives to show them how much money the operations were losing. He explained that in the current economic environment, Clayton's U.S. parent could not subsidize these losses. (It was a presentation he had made earlier that day to Brescia's Mayor who expressed concern about a plant closure and had arrived for his appointment with press photographers in tow.) After hours of acrimonious discussion, FILM agreed to recommend shortened shifts to its Brescia members. But Arnell knew that the concessions were far less than the company needed to break even.

The following week, Arnell made an appointment to meet with Clayton's bank to renegotiate terms on the company's credit line. As a gesture of goodwill, and because he thought it would help his case, he invited a politically connected union representative to accompany him and his finance manager. The three men secured the bank's agreement to postpone large payments due over the coming quarter. Arnell knew that while these few changes would not return the plant to profitability, they might buy the company some time as he completed his assessment of the situation.

Assessing Clayton SpA's situation

Over the next few weeks, in meetings with his management team, Arnell learned a great deal about the company's current situation as well as the history that brought it there. He learned that despite being given Europe-wide responsibility for compression chiller sales, Lazzaro had continued to focus on building political relationships to support large projects in Italy. As a result, chillers accounted for 55% of Italy's revenues, and its strong position in the public and institutional segments ensured its 'top three' competitive position at home. However, it lagged among commercial customers who increasingly favored Asian products that promised lower lifecycle costs through more efficient design.

He also learned that Clayton's other product lines were struggling in Italy. Its central air-conditioning system fit poorly with Italian buildings, many of which lacked the duct work an integrated system required. In room air conditioners and ventilators, the market was split between low-priced foreign imports and familiar Italian brands. Offering neither low-price nor name familiarity, the Clayton and Fontaire brands struggled in Italy's residential climate-control market. And by focusing resources on the chiller line, the company had failed to develop a broader marketing capability needed to sell these other products.

On the production side, Arnell discovered that the unionized work force (which had tried to block Clayton's 1985 acquisition of AeroPuro) still enjoyed very generous benefits. For many years, the plant's high cost position was masked by political relationships that gave it an inside track on government contracts. It was because of these relationships that Lazzaro refused to consider permanent layoffs which were permitted in Italy only for 'good cause' in firms with more than 15 employees. He even rejected using the Cassa Ingrazione Guardagni (CIG), a temporary layoff provision that exempted workers coming to work in exchange for a significant pay cut, with costs shared between the companies and the state.

This vulnerable cost position had put Brescia under threat in 2004 when Buis announced the second phase of her plant efficiency drive. Focusing on efficient sourcing, she had insisted that all plants become cost-effective European-scale operations. An early focus of the program was to decide whether Brescia or Barcelona should become Clayton's European source of commercial air conditioning chillers.

In conversations with Carlos Sanchez who headed the Spanish company, Arnell learned that after much political maneuvering, Lazzaro had convinced Buis to make Brescia the European source. Barcelona was smaller and older than the Italian plant, and was able to build only 300 to 1000 kW units compared to the 500 to 2000 kW units Brescia could make. So despite Barcelona's 20% lower labor costs and its more flexible work force, Buis felt that only the Italian operation had the capacity to meet European demand. She committed $18 million to upgrade and expand its operation, which eventually employed 203 people. But Sanchez told Arnell that he felt Brescia's staffing levels were still 20% to 30% too high.

Nonetheless, as Sanchez explained, with the support of labor, he had kept the Barcelona plant open by licensing technology to manufacture specialized absorption chillers suitable for Spain's growing thermal industry.[1] Sanchez was proud that with growing exports, this line contributed $35 million to his company's revenues in 2008, and with a 10% EBITDA, was already far more profitable than compression chillers had ever been.

Arnell also wanted to understand why Brescia's chiller penetration outside Italy was poor. Its 7% European market share (well below the 21% Italy boasted) made Clayton a distant number five behind competitors with shares of 36%, 23%, 16%, and 12% respectively. He spoke with country manager colleagues in other major European markets as well as several major customers who told him that the product was too expensive and also behind competitors in innovative features such as variable speed technology. Furthermore, the Clayton chillers lagged the operating efficiencies of market-leading units by 15%.

Customers in some markets – particularly Scandinavia and Germany – told Arnell of a trend toward 'district energy systems' which produced steam, hot water, or chilled water at a central plant and then piped it to buildings in the district for space heating, hot water, and air conditioning. Such systems favored absorption technology over the compression chillers Brescia produced. While compression chillers still had 85% of the market, environmentalists emphasized that absorption chillers were less carbon-intensive and used water instead of the ozone-depleting refrigerants that compression systems required.

Finally, Arnell's financial director reviewed current results showing that the company was currently losing more than $1 million a month. He felt the losses were primarily due to a 27% increase in steel prices in the past two years – a cost that could not be recouped due to foreign competitors' aggressive pricing. And rather than recognizing the problem, FILM, wielding great influence during a time of high unemployment, had increased its demands.

---

[1] While compression chillers such as those made in Brescia rely on electricity, absorption chillers are driven by heat, often from waste hot water, and are increasingly solar-powered.

Decision options

In early September, to help his senior team develop their plans, Arnell organized two internal conferences to expose them to outside input. At a manufacturing conference, production, engineering, and QC managers from Brescia described their situation and tested their emerging ideas with respected counterparts from the Spanish, Belgian, and UK plants. And in the marketing conference, the sales, marketing, and product development managers exchanged views with colleagues invited from other Clayton country organizations.

Not surprisingly, the Italian managers' presentations focused on restoring Brescia's profitability and ensuring its long-term viability. Their emerging plan involved programs to boost plant efficiency, product development initiatives to revitalize the compression chiller line, and a sales and marketing plan to expand market share outside Italy. Early cost estimates were about $5 million, with most of that investment in the first 12 months.

Meanwhile, Arnell had been in ongoing discussions with Sanchez who had raised an alternative option. He explained to Arnell that he had approached Buis several times to fund a major new plant in Spain, but she had told him she was not convinced that absorption chillers would ever be more than a niche market. She had also told them that she had placed her investment bet on Brescia, and wanted to give Italy a chance to prove itself.

'But the absorption chiller is the market of the future, and we have the license for a first-class technology,' Sanchez said. 'We still can't produce large-scale chillers in Barcelona, and we're site-constrained to grow the plant. Why don't you phase out your compression chiller line and convert capacity to absorption chillers to meet the growing market? Together, we could make Clayton a dominant force in this segment.'

It was an intriguing idea, but one that would involve significant costs in layoffs and restructuring, even with the gradual phased changeover process. Arnell estimated the investment would be about $15 million over five years, with most costs starting in the phase-out and re-structuring stages two to three years out.

A third option was proposed by Arnell's finance director who felt that it was too early to make major strategic commitments in an economy that was still unstable. He was skeptical of the government's July draft budget which projected a 2009 contraction of 4.8% in the Italian economy, before a rebound to 0.7% growth in 2010. He argued for a tight focus on efficiency measures to restore profitability while studying the various strategic options for at least another six months or until things became clearer.

In considering these alternatives, Arnell knew that while he did not have all the answers, what he did know was that Briggs and Buis were booked at the Hotel Ambasciatori for two nights the following week. They would expect to hear his analysis, his vision for a healthy Clayton SpA, his plans for a turnaround, and the results he expected to achieve.

Questions

1 What are Peter Arnell's main challenges?

2 Which plan should he recommend?

PART V

Quality, time and the strategic management of costs

The first four parts of the book provided an overview of management and cost accounting concepts and practices. As suggested in previous chapters, not only are many organisations concerned with the management of costs within a narrow focus, but they also take into account cost-based relationships with quality, flexibility, time, strategy and other organisational issues. This last part aims to discuss how such concerns are more directly being addressed by management accountants. In particular, Chapters 20, 21 and 22 discuss quality, time, strategy and emerging issues which are of growing significance in management accounting.

CHAPTER 20

Quality and throughput concerns in managing costs

As we stated in Chapter 1, global competition and demanding customers have forced managers to improve the quality of their products and to deliver them to customers faster. But achieving higher quality and faster delivery requires managers to identify and overcome a variety of organisational constraints. This chapter examines how management accounting can assist managers in taking initiatives in relation to quality and time priorities and in making decisions under different resource constraints.

Learning objectives

After studying this chapter, you should be able to:

- Explain four cost categories in a cost of quality programme

- Describe three methods that companies use to identify quality problems

- Identify the relevant costs and benefits of quality improvements

- Provide examples of non-financial quality measures of customer satisfaction and internal performance

- Understand why companies use both financial and non-financial measures of quality

- Define the three main measurements in the theory of constraints

- Explain how to manage bottlenecks

Quality as a competitive weapon

Many companies throughout the world – for example, Hewlett-Packard in the USA, BT in the UK, Renault in France, Fujitsu in Japan, Crysel in Mexico, and Samsung in Korea – view total quality management as providing an important competitive edge. This is because a quality focus reduces costs and increases customer satisfaction. Several prestigious, high-profile awards – for example, the European Quality Award, the UK Quality Award, the Malcolm Baldrige Quality Award (USA) and the Deming Prize (Japan) – have been instituted to recognise exceptional quality (see Goetsch and Davis 2009; Hoyle 2007).

International quality standards have emerged. For example, ISO 9000, developed by the International Organisation for Standardisation, is a set of five international standards for quality management adopted by more than 85 countries. ISO 9000 was created to enable companies to document and certify their quality system elements effectively. Some companies, such as BT and General Electric, require their suppliers to obtain ISO 9000 certification. Why? To reduce their own costs by evaluating, assessing and working to improve the quality of their suppliers' products. Thus, certification and an emphasis on quality are rapidly becoming conditions for competing in the global market.

Why this emphasis on quality? Because quality costs can be as much as 20% of sales revenue for many organisations. Quality-improvement programmes can result in substantial savings and higher revenues. Consider a general effect that quality has on revenues. If competitors are improving quality, then a company that does not invest in quality improvement will probably suffer a decline in its market share and revenues. In this case, the benefit of better quality is in preventing lower revenues, not in generating higher revenues.

Quality improvement also has non-financial and qualitative effects that improve a company's long-term performance. For example, managers and workers focusing on quality gain expertise about product and process. This knowledge may lead to lower costs in the future. Manufacturing a product of high quality can enhance a company's reputation and increase customer goodwill, which may lead to higher future revenues.

As corporations' responsibilities towards the environment grow, many managers are paying increasing attention to environmental quality and the problems of air pollution, waste water, oil and chemical spills, hazardous waste and waste management. The costs of environmental damage (failure costs) can be extremely high. For example, BP, the sixth largest global company in 2013 with revenues of $396 billion and profits in excess of $23 billion, was responsible for a mega oil spill in the Gulf of Mexico, which was caused by an explosion on an oil rig in April 2010. BP pleaded guilty to multiple counts of manslaughter and misdemeanour and of lying to Congress. The company has agreed to pay $4.5 billion in fines and penalties. Further fines following civil trials which are ongoing could amount to additional damage payments of £25 billion.

An environmental management standard, ISO 14000, encourages organisations to pursue environmental goals vigorously by developing (1) environmental management systems to improve the environmental impact of an organisation's activities, products and services, and (2) environmental auditing and performance evaluation systems to review and provide feedback on how well an organisation has achieved its environmental goals.

Quality has been defined in many different ways as it can mean different things to different people. Generally, the term *quality* refers to a wide variety of factors: fitness for use, the degree to which a product satisfies the needs of a customer and the degree to which a product conforms to design specification and engineering requirements. We discuss two basic aspects of quality: *quality of design* and *conformance quality* (see Feigenbaum 2015; Hoyle 2007).

Quality of design measures how closely the characteristics of products or services match the needs and wants of customers. Suppose customers of photocopying machines want copiers that combine copying, faxing, scanning and electronic printing. Photocopying machines that fail to meet these customer needs fail in the quality of their design. Similarly, if customers of a bank want an online banking system, then not providing this facility would be a quality of design failure.

Conformance quality is the performance of a product or service according to design and production specifications. For example, if a photocopying machine mishandles paper or breaks down, it will have failed to satisfy conformance quality. Products not conforming to specifications must be repaired, reworked or scrapped at an additional cost to the organisation. If non-conformance errors are not corrected within the plant and the product breaks down at the customer site, even greater repair costs as well as the loss of customer goodwill – often the highest quality cost of all – may result. In the banking industry, depositing a customer's cheque into the wrong bank account is an example of conformance quality failure.

The following diagram illustrates our framework:

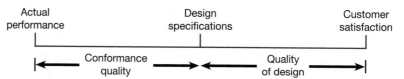

To travel the road from actual performance to customer satisfaction, companies must meet design specifications through conformance quality, but they must also design products to satisfy customers through quality of design.

Costs of quality

The **costs of quality (COQ)** are costs incurred to prevent, or costs arising as a result of, the production of a low-quality product. These costs focus on conformance quality and are incurred in all business functions of the value chain. Costs of quality are classified into four categories:

1 **Prevention costs** – costs incurred in precluding the production of products that do not conform to specifications.

2 **Appraisal costs** – costs incurred in detecting which of the individual units of products do not conform to specifications.

3 **Internal failure costs** – costs incurred when a non-conforming product is detected before it is shipped to customers.

4 **External failure costs** – costs incurred when a non-conforming product is detected after it is shipped to customers.

Exhibit 20.1 presents examples of individual cost of quality items in each of these four categories reported on COQ reports. Note that the items included in Exhibit 20.1 come from all value-chain business functions and are broader than the internal failure costs of spoilage, rework and scrap in manufacturing.

We illustrate the various issues in managing quality – from computing the costs of quality, to identifying quality problems, to taking actions to improve quality – using Braganza Lda as our example. Braganza makes many products. Our presentation focuses on Braganza's photocopying machines, which earned an operating profit of €24 million on sales of €300 million (20 000 copiers) in 2015. Braganza determines its costs of quality using an activity-based approach with five steps.

- **Step 1.** Identify all quality-related activities and activity cost pools. Column 1 of Exhibit 20.2, Panel A, classifies costs into prevention, appraisal, internal failure and external failure categories and indicates the value-chain functions in which the costs occur. One such activity is inspecting (including testing) the photocopying machines.

- **Step 2.** Determine the quantity of the cost-allocation base for each quality-related activity (see Exhibit 20.2, Panel A, column 2). For example, Braganza identifies inspection hours, the primary cost driver, as the cost-allocation base of the inspection activity. Assume that

Exhibit 20.1	Items pertaining to costs of quality reports		
Prevention costs	**Appraisal costs**	**Internal failure costs**	**External failure costs**
Design engineering	Inspection	Spoilage	Customer support
Process engineering	Online product manufacturing and process inspection	Rework	Transportation costs
Quality engineering		Scrap	Manufacturing/ process engineering
Supplier evaluations	Product testing	Breakdown maintenance	
Preventive equipment maintenance		Manufacturing/ process engineering on internal failure	Warranty repair costs
Quality training			Liability claims
New materials used to manufacture products			

photocopying machines use 240 000 hours (12 hours per copier × 20 000 copiers) of the cost-allocation base.

- **Step 3.** Calculate the rate per unit of each cost-allocation base (see Exhibit 20.2, Panel A, column 3). Owing to space considerations, we do not provide details of the calculations. Allocation rates are calculated using methods described in Chapters 3 and 11. In the Braganza example, the total (fixed and variable) costs of inspection are €40 per hour.

- **Step 4.** Calculate the costs of each quality-related activity for photocopying machines by multiplying the quantity of the cost-allocation base determined in step 2 by the rate per unit of the cost-allocation base calculated in step 3 (see Exhibit 20.2, Panel A, column 4). In our example, quality-related inspection costs are €9 600 000 (240 000 hours × €40 per hour).

- **Step 5.** Obtain the total costs of quality by adding the costs of all quality-related activities for photocopying machines in all value-chain business functions. Exhibit 20.2, Panel A, shows Braganza's total costs of quality reported on the COQ report for photocopying machines at €40.02 million, of which the largest categories are €14.52 million in total external failure costs and €10 million in total internal failure costs – a sum of €24.52 million. Total reported costs of quality are 13.34% of current sales.

Do not assume, however, that costs reported on COQ reports represent the total costs of quality for a company. COQ reports typically exclude opportunity costs, such as forgone contribution margins and profit from lost sales, lost production or lower prices that result from poor quality. Why? Because opportunity costs are difficult to estimate and generally not recorded in accounting systems. Nevertheless, opportunity costs can be substantial and important driving forces in quality-improvement programmes. Exhibit 20.2, Panel B, presents the analysis of the opportunity costs of poor quality at Braganza. Braganza Corporation's Market Research Department estimates lost sales of 2000 photocopying machines because of external failures. The forgone contribution and operating profit of €12 million measures the financial costs from dissatisfied customers who have returned machines to Braganza and from sales lost because of quality problems. Total costs of quality (including opportunity costs) equal €52.02 million (Panel A, €40.02 million + Panel B, €12 million), or 17.34% of current sales. Opportunity costs account for 23% (€12 million ÷ €52.02 million) of Braganza's total costs of quality.

The COQ report and the opportunity cost analysis highlight Braganza's high internal and external failure costs. To reduce costs of quality, Braganza must identify and reduce failures caused by quality problems.

Exhibit 20.2   Activity-based cost of quality analysis for Braganza

Panel A: Cost of quality report

	Allocation base or cost driver			
Costs of quality and value-chain category (1)	Quantity (2)	Rate (number assumed) (3)	Total costs (4) = (2) × (3)	Percentage of sales (5) = (4) ÷ €300 000 000
Prevention costs				
Design engineering (R&D/Design)	40 000* hours	€80 per hour	€3 200 000	1.07%
Process engineering (R&D/Design)	45 000* hours	€60 per hour	2 700 000	0.90
Total prevention costs			5 900 000	1.97
Appraisal costs				
Inspection (Manufacturing)	240 000† hours	€40 per hour	9 600 000	3.20
Total appraisal costs			9 600 000	3.20
Internal failure costs				
Rework (Manufacturing)	2500‡ copiers reworked	€4000 per copier reworked	10 000 000	3.33
Total internal failure costs			10 000 000	3.33
External failure costs				
Customer support (Marketing)	3000§ copiers repaired	€200 per copier repaired	600 000	0.20
Transportation costs (Distribution)	3000 copiers repaired	€240 per copier repaired	720 000	0.24
Warranty repair (Customer service)	3000 copiers repaired	€4400 per copier repaired	13 200 000	4.40
Total external failure costs			14 520 000	4.84
Total costs of quality			€40 020 000	13.34%

Panel B: Opportunity cost analysis

Costs of quality category (1)	Quantity of lost sales (2)	Contribution margin per copier (number assumed) (3)	Total estimated contribution margin lost (4) = (2) × (3)	Percentage of sales (5) = (4) ÷ €300 000 000
External failure costs				
Estimated forgone contribution margin and income on lost sales	2000# copiers	€6000	€12 000 000	4.00%
Total costs of quality			€12 000 000	4.00%

* Based on special studies.
† 12 hours per copier × 20 000 copiers.
‡ 12.5% of 20 000 copiers manufactured required rework.
§ 15% of 20 000 copiers manufactured required warranty repair service.
# Estimated by Braganza's Market Research Department.

Techniques used to identify quality problems

Control charts

Statistical quality control (SQC) or statistical process control (SPC) is a formal means of distinguishing between random variation and non-random variation in an operating process. A key tool in SQC is a control chart. A **control chart** is a graph of a series of successive observations of a particular step, procedure or operation taken at regular intervals of time. Each observation is plotted relative to specified ranges that represent the expected distribution. Only those observations outside the specified limits are ordinarily regarded as non-random and worth investigating.

Exhibit 20.3 presents control charts for the daily defect rates observed at Braganza's three production lines. Defect rates in the prior 60 days for each plant were assumed to provide a good basis from which to calculate the distribution of daily defect rates. The arithmetic mean (μ, read mu) and standard deviation (σ, read sigma) are the two parameters of the distribution that are used in the control charts in Exhibit 20.3. On the basis of experience, the company decides that any observation outside the $\mu \pm 2\sigma$ range should be investigated.

Exhibit 20.3	Statistical quality-control charts: Daily defect rate at Braganza

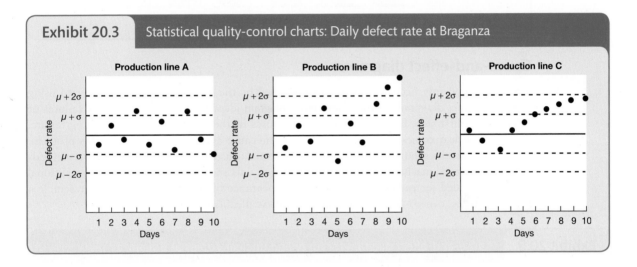

For production line A in Exhibit 20.3, all observations are within the range of $\mu \pm 2\sigma$ from the mean. Management, then, believes no investigation is necessary. For production line B, the last two observations signal that an out-of-control occurrence is highly likely. Given the $\mu \pm 2\sigma$ rule, both observations would lead to an investigation. Production line C illustrates a process that would not prompt an investigation under the $\mu \pm 2\sigma$ rule but may well be out of control. Note that the last eight observations show a clear direction and that the direction by day 5 (the third point in the last eight) is away from the mean. Statistical procedures have been developed using the trend as well as the level of the variable in question to evaluate whether a process is out of control.

Pareto diagrams

Observations outside control limits serve as inputs to *Pareto diagrams*. A **Pareto diagram** indicates how frequently each type of failure (defect) occurs. Exhibit 20.4 presents a Pareto diagram for Braganza's quality problems. Fuzzy and unclear copies are the most frequently recurring problem.

The fuzzy copy problem results in high rework costs because, in many cases, Braganza discovers the fuzzy image problem only after the copier has been built. Sometimes fuzzy images occur at customer sites, resulting in high warranty and repair costs.

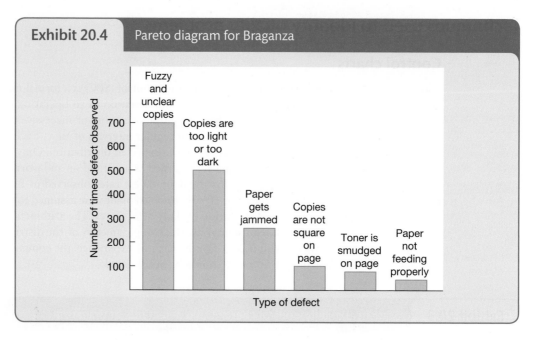

Exhibit 20.4 | Pareto diagram for Braganza

Cause-and-effect diagrams

The most frequently occurring problems identified by the Pareto diagram are analysed using *cause-and-effect diagrams*. A **cause-and-effect diagram** identifies potential causes of failures or defects. As a first step, Braganza analyses the causes of the most frequently occurring failure, fuzzy and unclear copies. Exhibit 20.5 presents the cause-and-effect diagram for this problem. The exhibit identifies four major categories of potential causes of failure: human factors, methods and design factors, machine-related factors, and materials and components factors. As additional arrows are added for each cause, the general appearance of the diagram begins to resemble a fishbone (hence, cause-and-effect diagrams are also called *fishbone diagrams*).

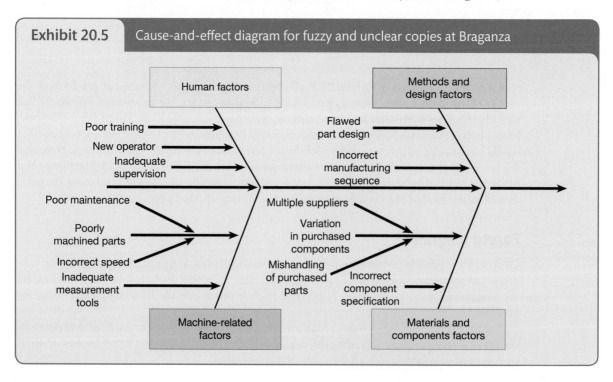

Exhibit 20.5 | Cause-and-effect diagram for fuzzy and unclear copies at Braganza

Relevant costs and benefits of quality improvement

Careful analysis of the cause-and-effect diagram reveals that the steel frame (or chassis) of the copier is often mishandled as it travels from the suppliers' warehouses to Braganza's plant. The frame must satisfy very precise specifications and tolerances; otherwise, various copier components (such as drums, mirrors and lenses) attached to the frame will be improperly aligned. Mishandling causes the dimensions of the frame to vary from specifications, resulting in fuzzy images.

| Exhibit 20.6 | Estimated effect of quality-improvement actions on costs of quality |

	Incremental costs and benefits of:	
Description	Further inspecting incoming frame (1)	Redesigning frame (2)
Costs of quality items		
Additional design engineering costs		
€80 × 2 000 hours	–	€160 000
Additional process engineering costs		
€60 × 5 000 hours	–	300 000
Additional inspection and testing costs		
€40 × 10 000 hours	€400 000	–
Savings in rework costs		
€1 600 × 600 fewer copiers reworked	(960 000)	
€1 600 × 800 fewer copiers reworked		(1 280 000)
Savings in customer-support costs		
€80 × 500 fewer copiers repaired	(40 000)	
€80 × 700 fewer copiers repaired		(56 000)
Savings in transportation costs for repair parts		
€180 × 500 fewer copiers repaired	(90 000)	
€180 × 700 fewer copiers repaired		(126 000)
Savings in warranty repair costs		
€1 800 × 500 fewer copiers repaired	(900 000)	
€1 800 × 700 fewer copiers repaired		(1 260 000)
Opportunity costs		
Contribution margin from increased sales		
€6 000 × 250 additional copiers sold	(1 500 000)	
€6 000 × 300 additional copiers sold	–	(1 800 000)
Net cost savings and additional contribution margin	€(3 090 000)	€(4 062 000)
Difference in favour of redesigning frame	€972 000	

Suppose the team of engineers working to solve the fuzzy image problem offers two alternative solutions: (1) to improve the inspection of the frame immediately upon delivery, or (2) to redesign and strengthen the frame and the containers used to transport them to better withstand mishandling during transportation.

Should Braganza inspect incoming frames more carefully or redesign them and their containers? Exhibit 20.6 shows the costs and benefits of each choice. Management estimates that additional inspection will cost €400 000 (€40 per hour × 10 000 hours). Redesign will cost an additional €460 000 (design engineering, €80 per hour × 2000 hours; process engineering, €60 per hour × 5000 hours). The potential benefits of incurring these costs are lower internal and external failure costs. The key question here is: What are the relevant cost savings and other relevant benefits? Braganza considers only a one-year time horizon for analysing this decision because Braganza plans to introduce a completely new line of copiers at the end of the year. Braganza believes that even as it improves quality, it will not be able to save any of the fixed costs of internal and external failure. To identify the relevant cost savings, Braganza divides each category of failure costs into its fixed and variable components.

Consider first the internal failure costs of rework. Fixed and variable costs for each reworked copier are:

Variable costs (including direct materials, direct rework labour and supplies)	€1600
Allocated fixed costs (equipment, space and allocated overhead)	2400
Total costs (Exhibit 20.2, Panel A, column 3)	€4000

If Braganza chooses to inspect the frame more carefully, it expects to eliminate rework on 600 copiers and save variable costs of €960 000 (€1600 × 600) in rework: see Exhibit 20.6, column 1. Braganza believes that fixed rework costs will be unaffected. If Braganza chooses the redesign alternative, it expects to eliminate rework on 800 copiers, saving €1 280 000 (€1600 × 800): see Exhibit 20.6, column 2.

Next consider external failure costs. Braganza currently repairs 3000 copiers at customer sites. If incoming frames are inspected more carefully, Braganza estimates that 500 fewer copiers will require warranty repair and that it will be able to sell 250 additional copiers. If the frame is redesigned, Braganza estimates that 700 fewer copiers will require warranty repair and that it will be able to sell 300 additional copiers.

Variable and fixed costs per copier repaired of individual external failure COQ items described in Exhibit 20.2 (Panel A, column 4) are as follows:

	Variable costs	Fixed costs	Total costs
Customer-support costs	€80	€120	€200
Transportation costs	180	60	240
Warranty repair costs	1800	2600	4400

As Braganza eliminates repair work on copiers, it expects to save only the variable costs of customer support, transportation and warranty repair.

Note that the savings per copier in cost of rework, customer-support, transportation and warranty repair in Exhibit 20.6 differ from the costs per copier for each of these items in Exhibit 20.2. Why? Because Exhibit 20.6 shows only the variable costs that Braganza expects to save. Exhibit 20.2 shows the total (fixed and variable) costs of each of these items. Also note that Exhibit 20.6 includes the incremental contribution margin from the estimated increases in sales due to the improved quality and performance of Braganza's copiers.

Braganza's management chooses to redesign the frame since Exhibit 20.6 indicates that the net estimated cost savings are €972 000 greater under this alternative. The costs of a poorly designed frame appear in the form of higher manufacturing, marketing, distribution and customer-service costs as internal and external failures begin to mount. But these costs are locked in when the frame is designed. Thus, it is not surprising that redesign will yield significant savings.

In the Braganza example, lost contribution margin occurs because Braganza's repeated external failures damage its reputation for quality, resulting in lost sales. Lost contribution margin can also occur as a result of internal failures. Suppose Braganza's manufacturing capacity is fully

Concepts in action   Does Mercedes stand for quality? What about Toyota?

Mercedes buyers in the UK voiced their concerns over quality problems during the early years of this century. Complaints included faulty key fobs, leaky sunroofs, baulky electronics, airbags that failed to inflate in accidents and malfunctioning navigation systems, among others. One customer who faced more than 60 mechanical problems with his C-class car, parked it in front of his dealership with a sign that read: 'Mercedes is unfair to consumers'. In 2003, J.D. Power and Associates ranked Mercedes, quality in the USA in 26th place. Web forums such as lemonmb.com, mercedesproblems.com and troublebenz.com became vocal, with customers complaining about Mercedes quality.

Following a focused drive to improve its quality, Mercedes-Benz was ranked second by J.D. Power and Associates in 2014 with 104 problems per 100 vehicles versus an industry average of 133.

Another car maker with a long established reputation for building high-quality cars found its reputation severely damaged from mid 2009. Toyota issued a dozen recalls covering defects from faulty accelerator pedals to rusted spare-tyre carriers. The company appointed a Chief Quality Officer and restructured its reporting system to communicate defect issues in a more timely manner. Again in April 2014 Toyota recalled 6.5 million cars worldwide to fix a variety of problems including faulty steering wheels and seats. Over the prior two years the company recalled 20 million vehicles and sold 18.7 million.

Source: Dave Caulkin/Pool/Reuters/Corbis

Regaining lost reputation for quality can prove expensive for an auto company in paying fines, dealing with payouts in class-action lawsuits and spending on marketing incentives. The reputational costs are difficult to quantify but always prove to be high. Peter Shervington, a legal expert on product liability, noted: 'Each announcement puts another dent in Toyota's efforts to recover its reputation and resurrects questions about the impact of its strategy of rapid expansion on previously enviable standards of design and production quality' (www.theguardian.com, 9 April 2014). In the J.D. Power and Associates rankings, Toyota ranked eighth in 2014. The car in front may not be a Toyota for quite some time. For 2014, it is Lexus – the luxury vehicle division of Toyota.

Source: Taylor, A. (2010) 'How Toyota lost its way', *Fortune*, 26 July, pp. 84–90; www.jdpower.com.

used. In this case, rework uses up valuable manufacturing capacity and causes the company to forgo contribution margin from producing and selling additional copiers. Suppose Braganza could produce (and subsequently) sell an additional 600 copiers by improving quality and reducing rework. The costs of internal failure would then include lost contribution margin of €3 600 000 (€6000 contribution margin per copier × 600 copiers). This €3 600 000 is the opportunity cost of poor quality.

Braganza can use its COQ report to examine interdependencies across the four categories of quality-related costs. In our example, redesigning the frame increases costs of prevention activities (design and process engineering), decreases costs of internal failure (rework) and decreases costs of external failure (warranty repairs). Costs of quality give more insight when managers compare trends over time. In successful quality programmes, the costs of quality as a percentage of sales and the costs of internal and external failure as a percentage of total costs of quality should decrease over time. Many companies believe they should eliminate all failure costs and have zero defects.

Non-financial measures of quality and customer satisfaction

To evaluate how well their actual performance satisfies customer needs, companies supplement the available financial measures with non-financial measures of quality of design and conformance quality. Non-financial measures are helpful in revealing the future needs and preferences of customers and in indicating the specific areas that need improvement. Hence, non-financial quality measures are useful indicators of future long-run performance, unlike financial measures of quality that have a short-run quality focus. Management accountants are often responsible for maintaining and presenting these non-financial measures. We focus first on non-financial measures of customer satisfaction (that include non-financial measures of quality of design and external failure) and then on internal performances measures (that include non-financial measures of prevention, appraisal and internal failure).

Non-financial measures of customer satisfaction

To evaluate how well they are doing, many companies track customer-satisfaction measures over time. Some of these measures are:

- market research information on customer preferences and customer satisfaction with specific product features;
- the number of defective units shipped to customers as a percentage of total units shipped;
- the number of customer complaints. (Companies estimate that for every customer who complains, there are 10–20 others who have had bad experiences with the product but did not complain);
- percentage of products that experience early or excessive failure;
- delivery delays (the difference between scheduled delivery date and date requested by the customer);
- on-time delivery rate (percentage of shipments made on or before the scheduled delivery date).

Management investigates if these numbers deteriorate over time. If these numbers improve over time, management can be more confident about operating profit being strong in future years.

In addition to these routine non-financial measures, many companies such as Xerox conduct surveys to measure customer satisfaction. Surveys serve two objectives. First, they provide a deeper perspective into customer experiences and preferences. Second, they provide a glimpse of features that customers would like future products to have.

Non-financial measures of internal performance

To satisfy their customers, companies need constantly to improve the quality of work done inside the company. Companies can use prevention costs, appraisal costs, and internal failure costs to measure quality performance inside the company in financial terms. But most companies supplement these financial measures with non-financial measures of internal quality. For example, Analog Devices, a semiconductor manufacturer, follows trends in these gauges of quality:

- the number of defects for each product line
- process yield (ratio of good output to total output)
- employee turnover (ratio of the number of employees who leave the company to the total number of employees).

Many companies go further and try to understand the factors that lead to better internal quality (see also Chapter 22 on the balanced scorecard). For example, some companies measure employee empowerment and employee satisfaction because managers at these companies believe that these measures are important determinants of quality.

- A measure of employee empowerment is the ratio of the number of processes where employees have the right to make decisions without consulting supervisors to the total number of processes.

- A measure of employee satisfaction is the ratio of employees indicating high satisfaction ratings on employee surveys to the total number of employees surveyed.

For a single reporting period, non-financial measures of quality have limited meaning. They are more informative when managers examine trends over time. To provide this information clearly, the management accountant must review the non-financial measures for accuracy and consistency. Thus, management accountants help companies improve quality in multiple ways: they calculate the costs of quality, assist in developing cost-effective solutions to quality problems, and provide feedback about quality improvement.

Evaluating quality performance

Measuring the financial costs of quality and the non-financial aspects of quality have distinctly different advantages. Those of costs of quality (COQ) measures are as follows:

1 COQ focuses attention on how costly poor quality can be.

2 Financial COQ measures are a useful way of comparing different quality-improvement programmes and setting priorities for achieving maximum cost reduction.

3 Financial COQ measures serve as a common denominator for evaluating trade-offs among prevention and failure costs. COQ provides a single, summary measure of quality performance.

The advantages of non-financial measures of quality are:

1 Non-financial measures of quality are often easy to quantify and easy to understand.

2 Non-financial measures direct attention to physical processes and hence focus attention on the precise problem areas that need improvement.

3 Non-financial measures provide immediate short-run feedback on whether quality improvement efforts have, in fact, succeeded in improving quality.

The advantages cited for COQ are disadvantages of non-financial measures and vice versa. Most organisations use both financial and non-financial quality measures to measure quality performance.

Theory of constraints

We consider problems which arise when products are made from multiple parts and processed on different machines. With multiple parts and multiple machines, dependencies arise among operations; some operations cannot be started until parts from a previous operation are available. Some operations are bottlenecks; others are not.

The **theory of constraints (TOC)** describes methods to maximise operating profit when faced with some bottleneck and some non-bottleneck operations. It defines three measurements:

1 **Throughput contribution**, equal to sales revenue minus direct materials costs.

2 Investments (stock), equal to the sum of materials costs of direct materials stock, work-in-progress stock and finished goods stock; R&D costs; and costs of equipment and buildings.

3 Operating costs, equal to all operating costs (other than direct materials) incurred to earn throughput contribution. Operating costs include salaries and wages, rent, utilities and depreciation.

The objective of TOC is to increase throughput contribution while decreasing investments and operating costs. *The theory of constraints considers short-run time horizons and assumes other current operating costs to be fixed costs.* The key steps in managing bottleneck resources are as follows:

- **Step 1**. Recognise that the bottleneck resource determines throughput contribution of the plant as a whole.

- **Step 2**. Search and find the bottleneck resource by identifying resources with large quantities of stock waiting to be worked on.

- **Step 3**. Keep the bottleneck operation busy and subordinate all non-bottleneck resources to the bottleneck resource. That is, the needs of the bottleneck resource determine the production schedule of non-bottleneck resources.

Step 3 represents a key notion: to maximise overall contribution margin, the plant must maximise contribution margin (in this case, throughput contribution) of the constrained or bottleneck resource. For this reason, step 3 suggests that the bottleneck machine always be kept running, not waiting for jobs. To achieve this, companies often maintain a small buffer stock of jobs waiting for the bottleneck machine. The bottleneck machine sets the pace for all non-bottleneck machines. That is, the output at the non-bottleneck operations are tied or linked to the needs of the bottleneck machine. For example, workers at non-bottleneck machines are not motivated to improve their productivity if the additional output cannot be processed by the bottleneck machine. Producing more non-bottleneck output only creates excess stock; it does not increase throughput contribution.

Concepts in action	Overcoming wireless data bottlenecks: the wired world is quickly going wireless

In 2014, sales of smartphones – such as the Apple iPhone 6 and iPhone 6 Plus and Samsung's Galaxy Alpha – were predicted to be 1.3 million units. In addition to the smartphone boom, emerging devices including smartwatches and machine-to-machine appliances (the so-called 'Internet of things') will add to rapidly growing data traffic. With every new device that lets users browse the Internet, and every new business that taps into the convenience and speed of the wireless world, the invisible information superhighway gets a little more crowded.

Source: Alamy Images

Cisco recently forecast that data traffic will grow at a compound rate of 66% to produce 11.2 exabytes per month by 2017 (an exabyte is one billion gigabytes, or about 50 000 years' worth of DVD-quality video). This astronomical growth already causes many users to suffer from mobile bottlenecks caused by too many users trying to transfer mobile data at the same time in a given area. These bottlenecks are most harmful to companies buying and selling products and services over the mobile Internet. Without access, Amazon.com Kindle owners cannot download new e-books and mobile brokerage users cannot buy and sell stocks 'on the go'. To relieve mobile bottlenecks, wireless providers and other high-tech companies are working on more efficient mobile broadband networks, such as 4G LTE, that make use of complementary technologies to automatically choose the best available wireless network to increase capacity. Technology providers are also deploying Wi-Fi Direct, which allows mobile users to freely transfer video, digital music and photos between mobile devices without choking up valuable bandwidth.

Companies and government agencies around the world are also trying to increase the wireless broadband spectrum. In some countries, for example, current holders of spectrum – such as radio stations – are being encouraged to sell their excess capacity to wireless providers in exchange for a share of the profits.

Source: Based on data from Cisco Systems Inc. (2013) 'Global Mobile Data Traffic Forecast, 2012–2017', 6 February; http://www.idc.com/prodserv/smartphone-market-share.jsp (29 December 2014).

- **Step 4.** Take actions to increase bottleneck efficiency and capacity – the objective is to increase throughput contribution minus the incremental costs of taking such actions. The management accountant plays a key role in step 4 by calculating throughput contribution, identifying relevant and irrelevant costs and doing a cost–benefit analysis of alternative actions to increase bottleneck efficiency and capacity.

We illustrate step 4 using the example of Häussermann-Plattenvertriebs AG. Häussermann-Plattenvertriebs manufactures car doors in two operations: stamping and pressing. Additional information is as follows:

	Stamping	Pressing
Capacity per hour	20 units	15 units
Annual capacity (6000 hours of capacity available in each of stamping and pressing)	120 000 units	90 000 units
Annual production	90 000 units	90 000 units
Fixed operating costs (excluding direct materials)	€720 000	€1 080 000
Fixed operating costs per unit produced (€720 000 ÷ 90 000; €1 080 000 ÷ 90 000)	€8 per unit	€12 per unit

Each door sells for €100 and has direct materials costs of €40. Variable costs in other functions of the value chain – R&D, design of products and processes, marketing, distribution and customer service – are negligible. Häussermann-Plattenvertriebs' output is constrained by the capacity of 90 000 units at the pressing operation. What can Häussermann-Plattenvertriebs do to relieve the bottleneck constraint at the pressing operation?

1 *Eliminate idle time* (time when the pressing machine is neither being set up to process products nor actually processing products) at the bottleneck operation. Häussermann-Plattenvertriebs is considering permanently positioning two workers at the pressing operation. Their sole responsibility would be to unload finished units as soon as one batch of units is processed and to set up the machine to process the next batch. Suppose the annual cost of this action is €48 000 and the effect of this action is to increase bottleneck output by 1000 units per year. Should Häussermann-Plattenvertriebs incur the additional costs? Yes, because Häussermann-Plattenvertriebs' relevant throughput contribution increases by €60 000 [1000 units × (selling price, €100 – direct materials costs, €40)], which exceeds the additional cost of €48 000. All other costs are irrelevant.

2 *Process only those parts or products that increase sales and throughput contribution*, not parts or products that remain in finished goods or spare parts stock. Manufacturing products that sit in stock does not increase throughput contribution.

3 *Shift products that do not have to be made on the bottleneck machine to non-bottleneck machines or to outside facilities.* Suppose Kontrol, AG, an outside contractor, offers to press 1500 doors at €15 per door from direct materials that Häussermann-Plattenvertriebs supplies. Kontrol's quoted price is greater than Häussermann-Plattenvertriebs' own operating costs in the Pressing Department of €12 per door. Should Häussermann-Plattenvertriebs accept the offer? Yes, because pressing is the bottleneck operation. Getting additional doors pressed from outside increases throughput contribution by €90 000 [(€100 – €40) × 1500 doors], while relevant costs increase by €22 500 (€15 × 1500). The fact that Häussermann-Plattenvertriebs' unit cost is less than Kontrol's quoted price is irrelevant.

Suppose Ahrens AG, another outside contractor, offers to stamp 2000 doors from direct materials that Häussermann-Plattenvertriebs supplies at €6 per door. Ahrens' price is lower than Häussermann-Plattenvertriebs' operating cost of €8 per door in the Stamping Department. Should Häussermann-Plattenvertriebs accept the offer? Since other operating costs are fixed costs, Häussermann-Plattenvertriebs will not save any costs by subcontracting the stamping operations. Total costs will be greater by €12 000 (€6 × 2000) under the subcontracting alternative. Stamping more doors will not increase throughput contribution, which is constrained by pressing capacity. Häussermann-Plattenvertriebs should not accept Ahrens' offer.

4   *Reduce set-up time and processing time at bottleneck operations* (for example, by simplifying the design or reducing the number of parts in the product). Suppose Häussermann-Plattenvertriebs can reduce set-up time at the pressing operation by incurring additional costs of €55 000 a year. Suppose further that reducing set-up time enables Häussermann-Plattenvertriebs to press 2500 more doors a year. Should Häussermann-Plattenvertriebs incur the costs to reduce set-up time? Yes, because throughput contribution increases by €150 000 [(€100 − €40) × 2500], which exceeds the additional costs incurred of €55 000. Will Häussermann-Plattenvertriebs find it worthwhile to incur costs to reduce machining time at the stamping operation? No. Other operating costs will increase, but throughput contribution will remain unaffected. Throughput contribution increases only by increasing bottleneck output; increasing non-bottleneck output has no effect.

5   *Improve the quality of parts or products manufactured at the bottleneck operation.* Poor quality is often more costly at a bottleneck operation than it is at a non-bottleneck operation. The cost of poor quality at a non-bottleneck operation is the cost of materials wasted. If Häussermann-Plattenvertriebs produces 1000 defective doors at the stamping operation, the cost of poor quality is €40 000 (direct materials cost per unit, €40 × 1000 doors). No throughput contribution is forgone because stamping has excess capacity. Despite the defective production, stamping can produce and transfer 90 000 doors to the pressing operation. At a bottleneck operation, the cost of poor quality is the cost of materials wasted plus the opportunity cost of lost throughput contribution. Bottleneck capacity not wasted in producing defective units could be used to generate additional sales and throughput contribution. If Häussermann-Plattenvertriebs produces 1000 defective units at the pressing operation, the cost of poor quality is €100 000: direct materials cost of €40 000 (direct materials cost per unit, €40 × 1000 units) plus forgone throughput contribution of €60 000 [(€100 − €40) × 1000 doors].

The high costs of poor quality at the bottleneck operation mean that bottleneck time should not be wasted processing units that are defective. That is, inspection should be done before processing parts at the bottleneck to ensure that only good-quality units are transferred to the bottleneck operation. Also, quality-improvement programmes should focus on ensuring that bottlenecks produce minimal defects.

The theory of constraints emphasises the management of bottlenecks as the key to improving the performance of the system as a whole. It focuses on the short-run maximisation of throughput contribution − revenues minus materials costs. It is less useful for the long-run management of costs because it does not model the behaviour of costs or identify individual activities and cost drivers. By contrast, activity-based costing (ABC) systems take a longer-term perspective by attempting to eliminate non-value-added activities and to reduce the costs of performing value-added activities. The theory of constraints is in this respect complementary to ABC systems (Holmes 1995).

Summary

The following points are linked to the chapter's learning objectives:

1   Four cost categories in a costs of quality programme are *prevention costs* (costs incurred in precluding the manufacture of products that do not conform to specifications), *appraisal costs* (costs incurred in detecting which of the individual products produced do not conform to specifications), *internal failure costs* (costs incurred when a non-conforming product is detected before its shipment to customers) and *external failure costs* (costs incurred when a non-conforming product is detected after its shipment to customers).

2   Three methods that companies use to improve quality are *control charts*, to distinguish random variations from other sources of variation in an operating process; Pareto diagrams, which indicate how frequently each type of failure occurs; and *cause-and-effect diagrams*, which identify potential factors or causes of failure.

3 The relevant costs of quality improvement are the incremental costs incurred to implement the quality programme. The relevant benefits are the savings in total costs and the estimated increase in contribution margin from the higher sales that will result from the quality improvements.

4 Non-financial measures of customer satisfaction include the number of customer complaints, the on-time delivery rate and the customer-response time. Non-financial measures of internal performance include product defect levels, process yields and manufacturing lead times.

5 Financial measures are helpful to evaluate trade-offs among prevention and failure costs. They focus attention on how costly poor quality can be. Non-financial measures help focus attention on the precise problem areas that need attention.

6 The three main measurements in the theory of constraints are *throughput contribution* (equal to sales minus direct materials costs); *investments or stock* (equal to the sum of materials costs of direct materials stock, work-in-progress stock and finished goods stock, R&D costs and costs of equipment and buildings); and *operating costs* (equal to all operating costs other than direct materials costs incurred to earn throughput contribution).

7 The four steps in managing bottlenecks are (a) to recognise that the bottleneck operation determines throughput contribution, (b) to search for and find the bottleneck, (c) to keep the bottleneck busy and subordinate all non-bottleneck operations to the bottleneck operation and (d) to increase bottleneck efficiency and capacity.

Key terms

costs of quality (COQ) (638)
prevention costs (638)
appraisal costs (638)
internal failure costs (638)
external failure costs (638)

control chart (641)
Pareto diagram (641)
cause-and-effect diagram (642)
theory of constraints (TOC) (647)
throughput contribution (647)

References and further reading

Bhimani, A. (2015) *Strategic Finance: Achieving High Corporate Performance* (London: Strategy Press), Chapter 3.

Cooper, R. and Slagmulder, R. (2007) 'Integrated cost management', in A. Bhimani (ed.) *Contemporary Issues in Management Accounting* (Oxford: Oxford University Press) pp. 117–45.

Feigenbaum, A. (2015) *Total Quality Control* (New York: McGraw-Hill).

Goetsch, D. and Davis, S. (2009) *Quality Management for Organisational Excellence* (NY: Prentice Hall).

Goldman, S. (2000) 'The next generation enterprise', Emerging Issues Paper, Strategic Cost Management (Mississauga, Ontario: CMA Canada).

Holmes, J.S. (1995) 'ABC vs TOC: it's a matter of time', *Management Accounting*, January, pp. 37–40.

Hoyle, D. (2007) *Quality Management Essentials* (Oxford: Butterworth-Heinemann).

Taylor, A. (2010) 'How Toyota lost its way', *Fortune*, 26 July, pp. 84–90.

CHAPTER 20

Assessment material

Review quesions

20.1 Describe some of the benefits of improving quality.

20.2 How does conformance quality differ from quality of design? Explain.

20.3 Name two items classified as prevention costs.

20.4 Distinguish between internal failure costs and external failure costs.

20.5 'Companies should focus on financial measures of quality because these are the only measures of quality that can be linked to bottom-line performance.' Do you agree? Explain.

20.6 Give examples of non-financial measures of customer satisfaction.

20.7 Give examples of non-financial measures of internal performance.

20.8 Give two reasons why waiting lines and delays occur.

20.9 'Companies should always make and sell all products whose selling prices exceed variable costs.' Do you agree? Explain.

20.10 Describe the three main measures used in the theory of constraints.

Exercises

Basic level

20.11 **Cost of quality programme, non-financial quality measures** (15 minutes)

Zaccaria Srl manufactures automotive parts. A major customer has just given Zaccaria an edict: 'Improve quality or no more business.' Lorenzo Da Ponte, the controller of Zaccaria, is given the task of developing a COQ programme. He seeks your advice on classifying each of items (a) to (g) as (i) a prevention cost, (ii) an appraisal cost, (iii) an internal failure cost, or (iv) an external failure cost.

a Cost of inspecting products on the production line by Zaccaria quality inspectors.

b Payment of travel costs for a Zaccaria customer representative to meet a customer who detected defective products.

c Costs of reworking defective parts detected by Zaccaria's quality-assurance group.

d Labour cost of the product designer at Zaccaria whose task is to design components that will not break under extreme temperature variations.

e Cost of automotive parts returned by customers.

f Seminar costs for 'Supplier Day', a programme aimed at communicating to suppliers the new quality requirements for purchased components.

g Costs of spoiled parts.

Required

1 Classify the seven individual cost items into one of the four categories of prevention, appraisal, internal failure or external failure.

2 Give two examples of non-financial performance measures Zaccaria could monitor as part of a total-quality-control effort.

20.12 Quality improvement, relevant costs and revenues, service (25 minutes)

Colombe-Déménagements SA is a removals company that transports household goods from one Belgian city to another. It measures service quality in terms of (a) time required to transport goods, (b) on-time delivery (within two days of agreed-upon delivery date) and (c) lost or damaged shipments. Colombe-Déménagements is considering investing in a new scheduling and tracking system costing €160 000 per year that should help it improve performance with respect to items (b) and (c). The following information describes Colombe-Déménagements' current performance and the expected performance if the new system is implemented:

	Current performance	Future expected performance
On-time delivery performance	85%	95%
Variable costs per carton lost or damaged	€60	€60
Number of cartons lost or damaged per year	3000 cartons	1000 cartons

Colombe-Déménagements expects that each percentage point increase in on-time performance will result in sales increases of €20 000 per year. Colombe-Déménagements' contribution margin percentage is 45%.

Required

1 What are the annual additional costs to Colombe-Déménagements of choosing the new scheduling and tracking system?

2 What are the annual additional benefits of the new system?

3 Should Colombe-Déménagements acquire the new system?

20.13 Theory of constraints, throughput contribution, relevant costs (15 minutes)

Salamanca SA manufactures filing cabinets in two operations: machining and finishing. Additional information is as follows.

	Machining	Finishing
Annual capacity	100 000 units	80 000 units
Annual production	80 000 units	80 000 units
Fixed operating costs (excluding direct materials)	€640 000	€400 000
Fixed operating costs per unit produced (€640 000 ÷ 80 000; €400 000 ÷ 80 000)	€8 per unit	€5 per unit

Each cabinet sells for €72 and has direct materials costs of €32 incurred at the start of the machining operation. Salamanca has no other variable costs. Salamanca can sell whatever output it produces. The following requirements refer only to the preceding data; there is no connection between the situations.

Required

1 Salamanca is considering using some modern jigs and tools in the finishing operation that would increase annual finishing output by 1000 units. The annual cost of these jigs and tools is €30 000. Should Salamanca acquire these tools?

2 The production manager of the Machining Department has submitted a proposal to do faster set-ups that would increase the annual capacity of the Machining Department by 10 000 units and cost €5000 per year. Should Salamanca implement the change?

20.14 **Theory of constraints, throughput contribution, relevant costs** (15 minutes)

Refer to the information in Exercise 20.13 in answering the following requirements; there is no connection between the situations.

Required

1 An outside contractor offers to do the finishing operation for 12 000 units at €10 per unit, double the €5 per unit that it costs Salamanca to do the finishing in-house. Should Salamanca accept the subcontractor's offer?

2 The Hunt Corporation offers to machine 4000 units at €4 per unit, half the €8 per unit that it costs Salamanca to do the machining in-house. Should Salamanca accept the subcontractor's offer?

*20.15 **Theory of constraints, throughput contribution, quality** (15 minutes)

Refer to the information in Exercise 20.13 in answering the following requirements; there is no connection between the situations.

Required

1 Salamanca produces 2000 defective units at the machining operation. What is the cost to Salamanca of the defective items produced? Explain your answer briefly.

2 Salamanca produces 2000 defective units at the finishing operation. What is the cost to Salamanca of the defective items produced? Explain your answer briefly.

Intermediate level

20.16 **Costs of quality analysis, non-financial quality measures** (20 minutes)

Alcazarquivir Lda manufactures and sells industrial grinders. The following table presents financial information pertaining to quality in 2014 and 2015 (in €000):

	2015	2014
Sales	€12 500	€10 000
Line inspection	85	110
Scrap	200	250
Design engineering	240	100
Cost of returned goods	145	60
Product-testing equipment	50	50
Customer support	30	40
Rework costs	135	160
Preventive equipment maintenance	90	35
Product liability claims	100	200
Incoming materials inspection	40	20
Breakdown maintenance	40	90
Product-testing labour	75	220
Training	120	45
Warranty repair	200	300
Supplier evaluation	50	20

Required

1 Classify the cost items in the table into prevention, appraisal, internal failure or external failure categories.

2 Calculate the ratio of each COQ category to sales in 2014 and 2015. Comment on the trends in costs of quality between 2014 and 2015.

3 Give two examples of non-financial quality measures that Alcazarquivir could monitor as part of a total-quality-control effort.

20.17 Quality improvement, relevant costs and relevant revenues (25 minutes)

Braganza manufactures and sells 20 000 copiers each year. The variable and fixed costs of reworking and repairing copiers are as follows:

	Variable costs	Fixed costs	Total costs
Rework costs per copier	€1600	€2400	€4000
Repair costs per copier			
Customer-support costs	80	120	200
Transportation costs for			
repair parts	180	60	240
Warranty repair costs	1800	2600	4400

Braganza's engineers are currently working to solve the problem of copies being too light or too dark. They propose changing the lens of the copier. The new lens will cost €50 more than the old lens. Each copier uses one lens. Braganza uses a one-year time horizon for this decision, since it plans to introduce a new copier at the end of the year. Braganza believes that even as it improves quality, it will not be able to save any of the fixed costs of rework or repair.

By changing the lens, Braganza expects that it will (1) rework 300 fewer copiers, (2) repair 200 fewer copiers and (3) sell 100 additional copiers. Braganza's unit contribution margin on its existing copier is €6000.

Required

1 What are the additional costs of choosing the new lens?

2 What are the additional benefits of choosing the new lens?

3 Should Braganza use the new lens?

20.18 Quality improvement, relevant costs and relevant revenues (30 minutes)

Carmody Ltd sells 300 000 V262 valves to the car and truck industry. Carmody has a capacity of 110 000 machine-hours and can produce three valves per machine-hour. V262's contribution margin per unit is €8. Carmody sells only 300 000 valves because 30 000 valves (10% of the good valves) need to be reworked. It takes one machine-hour to rework three valves so that 10 000 hours of capacity are lost in the rework process. Carmody's rework costs are €210 000. Rework costs consist of:

Direct materials and direct rework labour (variable costs)	€3 per unit
Fixed costs of equipment, rent and overhead allocation	€4 per unit

Carmody's process designers have come up with a modification that would maintain the speed of the process and would ensure 100% quality and no rework. The new process would cost €315 000 per year. The following additional information is available:

- The demand for Carmody's V262 valves is 370 000 per year.

- Clohisey has asked Carmody to supply 22 000 T971 valves if Carmody implements the new design. The contribution margin per T971 valve is €10. Carmody can make two T971 valves per machine-hour on the existing machine with 100% quality and no rework.

Required

1 Suppose Carmody's designers implemented the new design. Should Carmody accept Clohisey's order for 22 000 T971 valves? Explain.

2 Should Carmody implement the new design?

3 What non-financial and qualitative factors should Carmody consider in deciding whether to implement the new design?

*20.19 Theory of constraints, throughput contribution, relevant costs (20 minutes)

Autronic AG manufactures electronic testing equipment. Autronic also installs the equipment at the customer's site and ensures that it functions smoothly. Additional information on the Manufacturing and Installation Departments is as follows (capacities are expressed in terms of the number of units of equipment):

	Equipment manufactured	Equipment installed
Annual capacity	400 units per year	300 units per year
Equipment manufactured and installed	300 units per year	300 units per year

Autronic manufactures only 300 units per year because the Installation Department has only enough capacity to install 300 units. The equipment sells for €40 000 per unit (installed) and has direct materials costs of €15 000. All costs other than direct materials costs are fixed. The following requirements refer only to the preceding data; there is no connection between the situations.

Required

1 Autronic's engineers have found a way to reduce equipment manufacturing time. The new method would cost an additional €50 per unit and would allow Autronic to manufacture 20 additional units a year. Should Autronic implement the new method?

2 Autronic's designers have proposed a change in the direct materials that would increase direct materials costs by €2000 per unit. This change would enable Autronic to install 320 units of equipment each year. If Autronic makes the change, it will implement the new design on all equipment sold. Should Autronic use the new design?

3 A new installation technique has been developed that will enable Autronic's engineers to install 10 additional units of equipment a year. The new method will increase installation costs by €50 000 each year. Should Autronic implement the new technique?

4 Autronic is considering how to motivate workers to improve their productivity (output per hour). One proposal is to evaluate and compensate workers in the Manufacturing and Installation Departments on the basis of their productivities. Do you think the new proposal is a good idea? Explain briefly.

20.20 Theory of constraints, throughput contribution, quality, relevant costs (30–40 minutes)

Lappalainen Oy manufactures pharmaceutical products in two departments: Mixing and Tablet Making. Additional information on the two departments follows. Each tablet contains 0.5 gram of direct materials.

	Mixing	Tablet Making
Capacity per hour	150 grams	200 tablets
Monthly capacity (2000 hours available in each of mixing and tablet making)	300 000 grams	400 000 tablets
Monthly production	200 000 grams	390 000 tablets
Fixed operating costs (excluding direct materials)	€16 000	€39 000
Fixed operating costs per tablet (€16 000 ÷ 200 000; €39 000 ÷ 390 000)	€0.08 per gram	€0.10 per tablet

The Mixing Department makes 200 000 grams of direct materials mixture (enough to make 400 000 tablets) because the Tablet-Making Department has only enough capacity to process 400 000 tablets. All direct materials costs are incurred in the Mixing Department. Lappalainen incurs €156 000 in direct materials costs. The Tablet-Making Department manufactures only 390 000 tablets from the 200 000 grams of mixture processed; 2.5% of the direct materials mixture is lost in the tablet-making process. Each tablet sells for €1. All costs other than direct materials costs are fixed costs. The following requirements refer only to the preceding data; there is no connection between the situations.

Required

1 An outside contractor makes the following offer: if Lappalainen will supply the contractor with 10 000 grams of mixture, the contractor will manufacture 19 500 tablets for Lappalainen (allowing for the normal 2.5% loss during the tablet-making process) at €0.12 per tablet. Should Lappalainen accept the contractor's offer?

2 Another firm offers to prepare 20 000 grams of mixture per month from direct materials Lappalainen supplies. The company will charge €0.07 per gram of mixture. Should Lappalainen accept the company's offer?

3 Lappalainen's engineers have devised a method that would improve quality in the tablet-making operation. They estimate that the 10 000 tablets currently being lost would be saved. The modification would cost €7000 a month. Should Lappalainen implement the new method?

4 Suppose that Lappalainen also loses 10 000 grams of mixture in its mixing operation. These losses can be reduced to zero if the company is willing to spend €9000 per month on quality-improvement methods. Should Lappalainen adopt the quality-improvement method?

5 What are the benefits of improving quality at the mixing operation compared with the benefits of improving quality at the tablet-making operation?

20.21 **Ethics and quality** (30–35 minutes)

Anna-Greta Lantto, the assistant controller of Kiruna AB had recently prepared the following quality report comparing 2015 and 2014 quality performances.

	2015	2014
Sales	€90 000 000	€80 000 000
On-line inspection	€700 000	€600 000
Warranty liability	€2 250 000	€3 600 000
Product testing	€2 000 000	€1 000 000
Scrap	€2 700 000	€2 000 000
Design engineering	€1 800 000	€800 000
Percentage of customers complaining about quality	3%	4%

Just two days after preparing the report, Lars Törnman, the controller, had called Lantto into his office. 'Our plant manager, Sven Töyrä, is quite upset with the recent costs of quality and non-financial measures of quality reports that you prepared. He feels his workers have made significant progress in improving quality at the plant but that our reports are just not showing this. He wants to apply for various quality awards that would bring a lot of prestige to Kiruna, but he obviously cannot do so on the basis of the numbers we are reporting. Can you look over these quality numbers and see what you can do? I think Sven has a point. Nobody wants Kiruna to miss out on all the wonderful press we'd get if we won one of these quality awards.' Lantto is quite certain that her numbers are correct. Yet she would very much like Kiruna to win these prestigious quality awards. She is confused about how to handle Törnman's request.

Required

1　Calculate the ratio of each costs of quality category (prevention, appraisal, internal failure and external failure) to sales in 2014 and 2015.

2　What do the reports indicate about the plant's quality performance?

3　Is Lars Törnman's suggestion to Lantto to recalculate her quality numbers unethical? Would it be unethical for Lantto to modify her analysis? What steps should Lantto take to resolve this situation?

Advanced level

*20.22　Statistical quality control, airline operations (30–40 minutes)

Air Gascogne operates daily round-trip flights on the Toulouse–Stockholm route using a fleet of three 747s, the Eclair des Cévennes, the Eclair des Vosges and the Eclair des Alpilles. The budgeted quantity of fuel for each round-trip flight is the mean (average) fuel usage. Over the last 12 months, the average fuel usage per round-trip is 1000 litre-units with a standard deviation of 100 litre-units. A litre-unit is 1000 litres.

Gervaise Plassans, the operations manager of Air Gascogne, uses a statistical quality control (SQC) approach in deciding whether to investigate fuel usage per round-trip flight. She investigates those flights with fuel usage greater than two standard deviations from the mean.

In October, Plassans receives the following report for round-trip fuel usage by the three planes operating on the Toulouse–Stockholm route:

Flight	Eclair des Cévennes (litre-units)	Eclair des Vosges (litre-units)	Eclair des Alpilles (litre-units)
1	1040	1030	970
2	940	940	1040
3	970	960	1110
4	1010	1070	1040
5	1050	920	1220
6	1070	1130	1180
7	1110	990	1260
8	1120	1060	1140
9	1150	1010	1170
10	1190	930	1230

Required

1　Using the $\pm 2\sigma$ rule, what variance investigation decisions would be made?

2　Present SQC charts for round-trip fuel usage for each of the three 747s in October. What inferences can you draw from them?

3　Some managers propose that Air Gascogne present its SQC charts in monetary terms rather than in physical quantity terms (litre-units). What are the advantages and disadvantages of using euro fuel costs rather than litre-units in the SQC charts?

CHAPTER 21

Accounting for just-in-time systems

Modern organisations manage costs in the context of a variety of constraints. Increasingly, time is becoming a key issue. When is the best time for materials or merchandise to be purchased? How should purchasing arrangements with suppliers be structured? What is the best way to handle materials or merchandise once received? Are there essential trade-offs between ordering and carrying and storage costs? In this chapter, we look at just-in-time production and purchasing issues. Ultimately, the concern of this chapter is stock management. Stock management is a major part of profit planning for manufacturing and merchandising companies. Material costs often account for more than 40% of total costs of manufacturing companies and over 70% of total costs in merchandising companies. Management accounting information can play a key role in stock management.

Learning objectives

After studying this chapter, you should be able to:

- Describe a just-in-time (JIT) production system

- Identify the major features of a JIT production system

- Describe journal entries for backflush-costing systems

- Explain the economic order quantity (EOQ) decision model and how it balances ordering costs and carrying costs

- Explain the reorder point and safety stocks

- Compare EOQ and JIT purchasing models

- Determine the relevant benefits and relevant costs in JIT purchasing and JIT production

- Describe measures for evaluating JIT production performance

Just-in-time systems

Just-in-time (JIT) refers to a system in which materials arrive exactly as they are needed. Demand drives the procurement or production of any needed materials and immediate delivery eliminates waiting times and the need for stock. Managers in such companies as Renault in France, AT&T in the USA, Honda Motors in Japan, Siemens in Germany, Cummins Engines in the UK and DAF Trucks in Holland, which have implemented just-in-time systems, believe stock is waste that can be minimised and even eliminated through careful planning. A key element of just-in-time is *just-in-time production*.

Just-in-time production is a system in which each component on a production line is produced immediately as needed by the next step in the production line. In a JIT production line, manufacturing activity at any particular workstation is prompted by the need for that station's output at the following station. Demand triggers each step of the production process, starting with customer demand for a finished product at one end of the process and working all the way back to the demand for direct materials at the other end of the process. In this way, demand pulls a product through the production line. The demand-pull feature of JIT production systems achieves close coordination among workcentres. It smoothes the flow of goods, despite low quantities of stock.

There are many ways to implement the demand-pull feature of JIT production, but perhaps the most common is a kanban system. *Kanban* is the Japanese term for a visual record or card. In the simplest kanban system, workers at one operation use a kanban card to signal those at another operation to produce a specified quantity of a particular part. For example, suppose the assembly department of a silencer manufacturer receives an order for ten silencers. The assembly department triggers production of the ten metal pipes it needs to make the ten silencers by sending a kanban card to the machining department. Only after receiving the kanban card does the machining department begin production of the pipes. When production is complete, the machining department attaches the kanban card to the box containing the metal pipes and ships the package downstream to the assembly department. The assembly department starts the cycle over again when it receives the next customer order.

Major features of JIT production systems

There are five main features in a JIT production system:

1 Production is organised in **manufacturing cells**, a grouping of all the different types of equipment used to manufacture a given product.

2 Workers are trained to be multiskilled so that they are capable of performing a variety of operations and tasks.

3 Total quality management is aggressively pursued to eliminate defects.

4 Emphasis is placed on reducing *set-up time*, which is the time required to get equipment, tools and materials ready to start the production of a component or product, and *manufacturing lead time*, which is the time from when an order is ready to start on the production line to when it becomes a finished good.

5 Suppliers are carefully selected to obtain delivery of quality-tested parts in a timely manner.

Organising manufacturing cells

Conventional manufacturing plants generally have a *functional layout*, in which machines that perform the same function are located in the same area or department. JIT plants, however, organise machines in cells designed around products. Different types of machines that perform different functions needed to manufacture a product, or a family of products, are placed close to each other. Materials move from one machine to another where various operations are performed in sequence. Incoming and outgoing material stock points for individual cells are located near the cell rather than at a central location. Cells reduce materials handling costs. Forklifts and forklift operators are no longer needed to transport materials between central storerooms and between departments as in conventional manufacturing. Instead, workers or small conveyor belts carry materials from one cell station to the next.

Consider the manufacture of metal pipes for silencer assembly described earlier. Exhibit 21.1 contrasts the functional layout in conventional manufacturing with the cell layout in JIT plants in this case. Note the U-shaped layout of the cell. This layout ensures that all machines and workers are located near each other. Multiskilled workers may then be able to operate more than one machine.

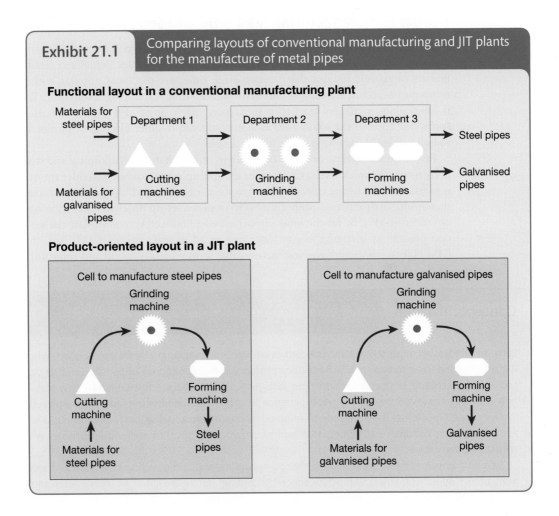

Exhibit 21.1 Comparing layouts of conventional manufacturing and JIT plants for the manufacture of metal pipes

Multiskilled workers

Workers in a cell are trained to perform all operations within the cell. Workers can then be assigned to different machines as needed to achieve smooth production flow. Workers are also trained and expected to perform minor repairs and do routine maintenance. Quality testing and inspection are also the responsibility of the workers in a cell rather than of a quality assurance department.

Total quality management

If a worker at any cell discovers a defect, he or she must set off an alarm to alert others of the problem and that operation is shut down. Because of the dynamics of the demand-pull system, when one operation shuts down, all production shuts down until the problem is solved. JIT creates an urgency for solving problems immediately and eliminating the root causes of defects as quickly as possible. Therefore, total quality management is an essential component of any JIT production system.

In contrast, in many traditional production systems, extra parts and subassemblies are held at workstations in anticipation of shortages or production breakdowns. These stocks can service a downstream operation even if a defect occurs. Consequently, there is less need for and emphasis on preventing rework and spoilage relative to JIT systems.

Reducing manufacturing lead time and set-up time

Reducing manufacturing lead time enables a company to respond better to changes in customer demand. For example, a short manufacturing lead time enables Siemens to rapidly restock those models of mobile phones that, at any given time, are the most popular with consumers. An important aspect of reducing manufacturing lead time is reducing set-up time. When set-up time is long, plant managers tend to manufacture many units of a product because they want to spread the costs of the set-up over as many units as possible. The higher production causes stock to build up until such time as the units are sold.

Reducing set-up time makes production in smaller batches economical and worthwhile, which in turn reduces stock levels. Companies use multiple approaches to reduce set-up time. One way is to use manufacturing cells dedicated to the manufacture of a product or product family rather than multiple products. Another way is to improve set-up processes and train workers to do set-ups more quickly. By far the most important way, however, is to automate the set-up and production process by investing in *computer-integrated manufacturing* (CIM) (see Bhimani 2015). In CIM plants, computers give instructions that automatically set up and run equipment.

Concepts in action   After the encore: just-in-time live concert recordings

Each year, millions of music fans flock to concerts to see artists ranging from Metallica to Bon Jovi. When fans stop by the merchandise stand to pick up a T-shirt or poster after the show ends, they often have another option: buying a professional recording of the concert they just saw! Just-in-time production, enabled by advances in technology, now allows fans to re-live the live concert experience just a few minutes after the final chord is played.

Live concert recordings have long been hampered by production and distribution difficulties. Live albums typically sold few copies, and retail outlets that profit from volume-driven merchandise turnover were somewhat reluctant to carry them.

Several companies now employ microphones, recording and audio mixing hardware and software, and an army of high-speed computers to produce concert recordings during the show. As soon as each song is complete, MP3 or FLAC based downloads are available. Recordings thus become available instantly. Live Nation's online store for instance provides fast and high quality playbacks. Though some critics say this is often done at prices 'far out of line with the industry standard as to be baffling' in Bruce Springsteen's case.

Sources: Chartrand, S. (2004) 'How to take the concert home', *New York Times*, 3 May; Humphries, S. (2003) 'Get your official "bootleg" here', *Christian Science Monitor*, 21 November; Van Buskirk, E. (2009) 'Apple unveils "live music" in iTunes', Wired Business (blog), 24 November, http://www.wired.com/business/; Smith, C. (2011) 'Nugs.net appetizer puts direct-to-fan download sales in Facebook newsfeed', Hypebot.com (blog), 12 August, http://www.hypebot.com. http://stayhardstayhungry.wordpress.com/2014/01/18/total-disaster-as-springsteen-tries-to-sell-recordings-of-live-shows/.

Strong supplier relationships

Many companies implementing JIT production also implement *JIT purchasing*. **Just-in-time purchasing** is the purchase of goods or materials such that delivery immediately precedes demand or use. JIT plants expect JIT suppliers to provide high-quality goods and make frequent deliveries of the exact quantities specified on a timely basis. Suppliers often deliver materials directly to the plant floor to be immediately placed into production. Consequently, JIT plants require suppliers to inspect their own goods and guarantee their quality. These procedures completely eliminate the non-value-adding costs of incoming inspection, storage, stock and materials handling and this saves the JIT purchaser money.

Strong relationships with suppliers are a critical component of JIT purchasing because production stops if a supplier fails to deliver materials on time. Building partnerships with suppliers is time consuming and costly. It entails the negotiation of long-run contracts so that minimal paperwork is involved in each individual transaction. A single telephone call or computer entry via an electronic link triggers the delivery of material. Hence, JIT companies choose to work with only a few reliable and dependable suppliers. Since JIT purchasing demands a lot from supplier companies, many suppliers are unable to provide the needed service levels.

Financial benefits of JIT

JIT tends to focus broadly on the control of *total manufacturing costs* instead of individual costs such as direct manufacturing labour. For example, idle time may rise because production lines are starved of materials more frequently than before. Nevertheless, many manufacturing costs will decline. JIT can provide many financial benefits, including:

- lower investment in stocks
- reductions in carrying and handling costs of stocks
- reductions in risk of obsolescence of stocks
- lower investment in plant space for stocks and production
- reductions in set-up costs and total manufacturing costs
- reduction in costs of waste and spoilage as a result of improved quality
- higher revenues as a result of responding faster to customers
- reductions in paperwork.

Exhibit 21.2 summarises the effects Hewlett-Packard reported after adopting JIT at several of its production plants.

Product-costing benefits of JIT

In reducing the need for materials handling, warehousing, inspection of supplies and other activities, JIT systems reduce overhead costs. JIT systems also facilitate the direct tracing of some costs that were formerly classified as overhead. For example, the use of manufacturing cells makes it easy to trace materials handling and machine operating costs to specific products or product families made in specific cells. These costs then become direct costs of those products. Also, the use of multiskilled workers in these cells allows the costs of set-up, minor maintenance and quality inspection to become easily traced, direct costs.

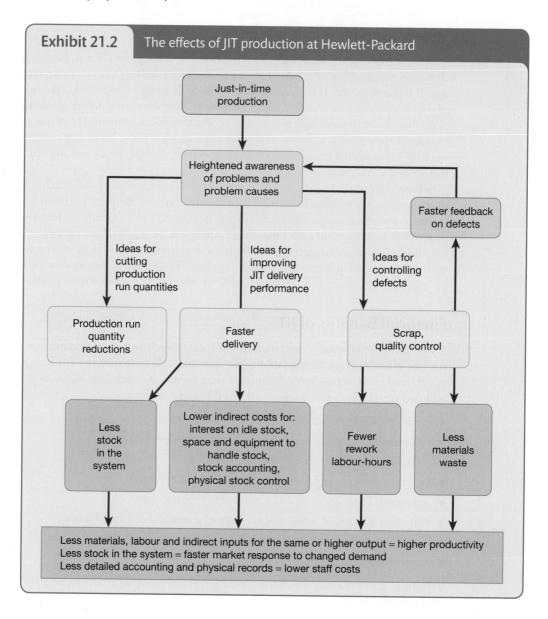

Exhibit 21.2   The effects of JIT production at Hewlett-Packard

Enterprise resource planning (ERP) systems

The success of a JIT system hinges on the speed of information flows from customers to manufacturers to suppliers. Information flows is a problem for large companies that have fragmented information systems (for sales, manufacturing and purchasing) spread over dozens of unlinked computer systems. The enterprise resources planning (ERP) system comprises a single database that collects data and feeds it into applications supporting all of a company's business activities. For example, using an ERP system, a salesperson can generate a contract for a customer in Germany, verify the customer's credit limits and place a production order. The system schedules manufacturing in, say, Brazil; requisitions materials from inventory, orders components from suppliers; and schedules shipment. Its also credits sales commissions to the salesperson and records all the costing and financial accounting information.

ERP systems give low-level managers, workers, customers and suppliers access to operating information. This benefit, coupled with tight coordination across business function, enables ERP systems to rapidly shift manufacturing and distribution plans in response to changes in supply and demand. Companies believe that an ERP system is essential to support JIT initiatives because of the effect it has on lead times. Using an ERP system, Autodesk, a maker of computer-aided design software, reduced order lead times from 2 weeks to 1 day; Fujitsu reduced lead times from 18 to 1.5 days. ERP systems also help in demand forecasting and materials requirements planning as part of their operations and logistics modules.

Although the tight coupling of systems throughout a business streamlines administrative and financial processes and saves costs, it can also make the system large and unwieldly. Because of its complexity, suppliers of ERP systems such as SAP, Sage, Microsoft dynamics and Oracle provide software packages that are standard, but that can be customised, although at considerable cost. Without some customisation, unique and distinctive features that confer strategic advantage will not be available. The challenge when implementing ERP systems is to strike the right balance between systems that are common across all of a company's business and geographical locations and systems that for strategic reasons are designed to be unique.

Concepts in action   RFID at Selexys

Stock tracking systems can combine with other resource management systems within ERPs. Tracking merchandise in bulk can be achieved by putting radio frequency ID (RFID) tags on boxes and pallets. A survey by IDTechEx Research suggests that by 2018 the RFID market will exceed $20 billion globally. At present the market is growing at 22% per year, with the total market for RFID goods and services reaching $9.2 billion in 2014.

Consider Selexys, the Netherlands' largest book chain, which has been testing an RFID stock management system at an outlet in the town of Altmere. The system enabled the store to increase sales by 25% in less than nine months relative to the average store in the chain. Selexys will install RFID systems across all its 42 Selexys stores. The implementation cost is approximately €100 000 per store. According to Jan Vink, Selexys's Chief Information Officer, the chain's overall sales will grow and its overall profits will increase by up to 40%.

How does Selexys's RFID system work? The company's distributor places an RFID tag – usually the size of a strip of tape – on every book being shipped to the store. The tag also contains a barcode and can be used as an anti-theft device. Each tag costs 20 cents. When boxes of books are delivered to the store, they go through an RFID scanning tunnel which compares receipts with what was ordered and enters every book into the stock system. Vink notes that, 'in 5 seconds, we check each box'. Prior to the RFID system, only spot checks of boxes were undertaken and required hand-scanning of the barcodes. Now, three times a week, employees roll an RFID scanning cart through the store to check the stock. A wand is waved over each shelf and the books and their locations are identified within the system. Two employees can scan through 38 000 books in 2.5 hours. This contrasts with what happens in other Selexys stores where a complete stocktake is done once a year requiring the store to be shut down for a whole day at a cost of about €650 000 in labour expenses and lost sales.

The RFID system allows customers to search for books, identify their exact shelf location and order books online for next day home or store delivery. The system, in addition, suggests other books customers might want. Vink notes that half the customers using the system end up making a purchase. The system's costs are quickly covered by reduced stock management expenses, lower pilferage, higher sales, increased profits and greater customer life values, with returning loyal customers satisfied with the Selexys buying experience.

Source: Schonfeld, E. (2006) 'Tagged for growth', *Business 2.0*, December, pp. 58–9; www.idtechex.com/research, 31 July 2014; http://www.rfid24-7.com/2014/03/13/rfid-market-exceeds-9b-in-2014-retail-drives-strong-growth/.

Backflush costing

A unique production system such as JIT leads to its own unique costing system. Organising manufacturing in cells, reducing defects and manufacturing lead time and ensuring timely delivery of materials enables purchasing, production and sales to occur in quick succession with minimal stocks. The absence of stocks makes choices about cost-flow assumptions (such as weighted-average or first-in, first-out) or stock costing methods (such as absorption or variable costing) unimportant – all manufacturing costs of a period flow directly into cost of goods sold. The rapid conversion of direct materials to finished goods that are immediately sold simplifies job costing.

Simplified normal or standard job costing

Traditional normal and standard costing systems (discussed in Chapters 3, 15 and 16) use **sequential tracking** (also called **synchronous tracking**), which is any product-costing method in which the accounting system entries occur in the same order as actual purchases and production. These traditional systems track costs sequentially as products pass from direct materials, to work in progress, to finished goods and finally to sales. Sequential tracking is often expensive, especially if management tries to track direct materials requisitions and labour time tickets to individual operations and products.

An alternative to the sequential tracking approach in many costing systems is to delay the recording of journal entries until after the physical sequences have occurred. The term **backflush costing** (also called **delayed costing**, **endpoint costing** or **post-deduct costing**) describes a costing system that delays recording changes in the status of a product being produced until good finished units appear; it then uses budgeted or standard costs to work backwards to flush out manufacturing costs for the units produced. An extreme form of such delay is to wait until sale of finished units has occurred. Typically, no record of work in progress appears in backflush costing.

In companies that adopt backflush costing, the following occurs:

1 Management wants a simple accounting system. Detailed tracking of direct costs through each step of the production system to the point of completion is deemed unnecessary.

2 Each product has a set of budgeted or standard costs.

3 Backflush costing reports approximately the same financial results as sequential tracking would generate.

If stocks are low, managers may not believe it worthwhile to spend resources tracking costs through Work in Progress, Finished Goods and Cost of Goods Sold. Backflush costing, therefore, is especially attractive in companies that have low stocks resulting from JIT. Backflush costing and sequential tracking will also produce approximately the same results, however, when stock is present, provided stocks maintain stable values. Constant amounts of costs will be deferred in stock each period.

The following examples illustrate backflush costing. To underscore basic concepts, we assume no direct materials variances in any of the examples. (We do, however, discuss variances in a separate section following Example 21.1.) These examples differ in the number and placement of points at which journal entries are made in the accounting system to accumulate production costs of units (also called trigger points):

	Number of journal entry trigger points	Location of journal entry trigger points
Example 21.1	2	1 Purchase of direct materials (also called raw materials) 2 Completion of good finished units of product
Example 21.2	2	1 Purchase of raw materials 2 Sale of good finished units of product
Example 21.3	1	1 Completion of good finished units of product

Example 21.1

Trigger points are materials purchases and finished goods completion

This example uses two trigger points to illustrate how backflushing can eliminate the need for a separate Work in Progress account. A hypothetical company, Henley-on-Thames Computer (HTC), produces keyboards for personal computers. For April, there were no opening stocks of raw materials. Moreover, there is zero opening and closing work in progress.

HTC has only one direct manufacturing cost category (direct or raw materials) and one indirect manufacturing cost category (conversion costs). All labour costs at the manufacturing facility are included in conversion costs. From its bill of materials (description of the types and quantities of materials) and an operations list (description of operations to be undergone), HTC determines the April standard direct materials costs per keyboard unit of €19 and the standard conversion costs of €12. HTC has two stock accounts:

Type	Account title
Combined direct materials and any direct materials in work in progress	Stock: Raw and In-Progress Control
Finished goods	Finished Goods Control

Trigger point 1 occurs when materials are purchased. These costs are charged to Stock: Raw and In-Progress Control.

Actual conversion costs are recorded as incurred under backflush costing, just as in other costing systems and charged to Conversion Costs Control. Conversion costs are allocated to products at trigger point 2 – the transfer of units to Finished Goods. This example assumes that under- or overallocated conversion costs are written off to cost of goods sold monthly.

HTC takes the following steps when assigning costs to units sold and to stocks.

Step 1: Record the direct materials purchased during the accounting period
Assume April purchases of €1 950 000:

| Entry (a) Stock: Raw and In-Progress Control | 1 950 000 | |
| Creditors Control | | 1 950 000 |

Step 2: Record the incurrence of conversion costs during the accounting period
Assume that conversion costs are €1 260 000:

| Entry (b) Conversion Costs Control | 1 260 000 | |
| Various accounts (such as, Creditors Control and Wages Payable) | | 1 260 000 |

Step 3: Determine the number of finished units manufactured during the accounting period
Assume that 100 000 keyboard units were manufactured in April.

Step 4: Calculate the budgeted or standard costs of each finished unit
The standard cost is €31 (€19 direct materials + 12 conversion costs) per unit.

Step 5: Record the cost of finished goods completed during the accounting period
In this case, 100 000 units × €31 = €3 100 000. This step gives backflush costing its name. Up to this point in the operations, the costs have not been recorded sequentially with the flow of product along its production route. Instead, the output trigger reaches back and pulls the standard costs of direct materials from Stock: Raw and In-Progress Control and the standard conversion costs for manufacturing the finished goods.

Entry (c) Finished Goods Control	3 100 000	
Stock: Raw and In-Progress Control		1 900 000
Conversion Costs Allocated		1 200 000

Example 21.1 continued

Step 6: Record the cost of goods sold during the accounting period

Assume that 99 000 units were sold in April (99 000 units × €31 = €3 069 000).

Entry (d) Cost of Goods Sold	3 069 000	
Finished Goods Control		3 069 000

Step 7: Record under- or overallocated conversion costs

Actual conversion costs may be under- or overallocated in any given accounting period. Chapter 11 discussed various ways to account for under- or overallocated manufacturing overhead costs. Many companies write off underallocations or overallocations to cost of goods sold only at year-end; other companies, like HTC, do so monthly. Companies that use backflush costing typically have low stocks, so proration of under- or overallocated costs between finished goods and cost of goods sold is less often necessary. The journal entry for the €60 000 difference between actual conversion costs incurred and standard conversion costs allocated would be:

Entry (e) Conversion Costs Allocated	1 200 000	
Cost of Goods Sold	60 000	
Conversion Costs Control		1 260 000

The April closing stock balances are:

Stock: Raw and In-Progress Control	€50 000
Finished Goods, 1000 units × €31	31 000
Total stocks	€81 000

Exhibit 21.3, Panel A, summarises the journal entries for this example. Exhibit 21.4 provides an overview of this version of backflush costing. The elimination of the typical Work in Progress account reduces the amount of detail in the accounting system. Units on the production line may still be tracked in physical terms, but there is 'no attaching of costs' to specific work orders as they flow along the production cycle. In fact, there are no work orders or labour time tickets in the accounting system (see Bhimani 2015).

Exhibit 21.3   Journal entries in backflush costing (€)

Panel A: Example 21.1. Two trigger points – purchases of raw materials and finished units produced

Transactions

a	Purchases of raw materials	Stock: Raw and In-Progress Control	1 950 000	
		Creditors Control		1 950 000
b	Incur conversion costs	Conversion Costs Control	1 260 000	
		Various Accounts		1 260 000
c	Finished units produced	Finished Goods Control	3 100 000	
		Stock: Raw and In-Progress Control		1 900 000
		Conversion Costs Allocated		1 200 000
d	Finished units sold	Cost of Goods Sold	3 069 000	
		Finished Goods Control		3 069 000
e	Under- or overallocated conversion costs	Conversion Costs Allocated	1 200 000	
		Cost of Goods Sold	60 000	
		Conversion Costs Control		1 260 000

Panel B: Example 21.2. Two trigger points – in purchases of raw materials and finished units sold

Transactions

a	Purchases of raw materials	Stock Control	1 950 000	
		Creditors Control		1 950 000
b	Incur conversion costs	Conversion Costs Control	1 260 000	
		Various Accounts		1 260 000
c	Finished units produced		No entry	
d	Finished units sold	Cost of Goods Sold	3 069 000	
		Stock Control		1 881 000
		Conversion Costs Allocated		1 188 000
e	Under- or overallocated conversion costs	Conversion Costs Allocated	1 188 000	
		Cost of Goods Sold	72 000	
		Conversion Costs Control		1 260 000

Panel C: Example 21.3. One trigger point – finished units produced

Transactions

a	Purchases of raw materials		No entry	
b	Incur conversion costs	Conversion Costs Control	1 260 000	
		Various Accounts		1 260 000
c	Finished units produced	Finished Goods Control	3 100 000	
		Creditors Control		1 900 000
		Conversion Costs Allocated		1 200 000
d	Finished units sold	Cost of Goods Sold	3 069 000	
		Finished Goods Control		3 069 000
e	Under- or overallocated conversion costs	Conversion Costs Allocated	1 200 000	
		Cost of Goods Sold	60 000	
		Conversion Costs Control		1 260 000

Exhibit 21.4   Overview of backflush costing, Example 21.1

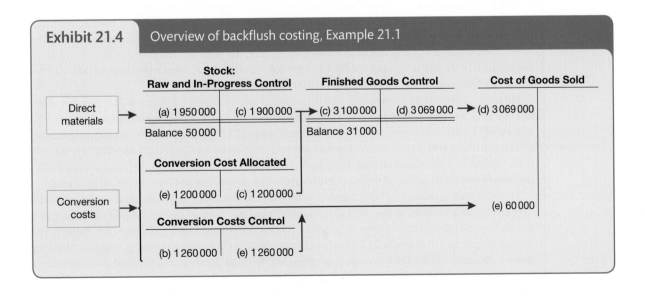

Accounting for variances

The accounting for variances between actual costs incurred and standard costs allowed and the disposition of variances is basically the same under all standard costing systems. The procedures are described in Chapters 15 and 16. In Example 21.1, suppose the direct materials purchased had an unfavourable price variance of €42 000. Entry (a) would then be:

Stock: Raw and In-Progress Control	1 950 000	
Raw Materials Price Variance	42 000	
Creditors Control		1 992 000

Example 21.2

Trigger points are materials purchases and finished goods sales

This example, also based on HTC and using the same data, presents a backflush costing system that, relative to Example 21.1, is a more dramatic departure from a sequential tracking stock costing system. The first trigger point in this example is the same as the first trigger point in Example 21.1 (the purchase of direct materials), but the second trigger point is the sale – not the completed manufacture – of finished units. Toyota's cost accounting at its Burnaston (UK) plant is similar to this type of costing system. There are two justifications for this accounting system:

1 To remove the incentive for managers to produce for stock. If the value of finished goods stock includes conversion costs, managers can bolster operating profit by producing more units than are sold. Having trigger point 2 as the sale instead of the completion of production, however, reduces the attractiveness of producing for stock by recording conversion costs as period costs instead of capitalising them as inventoriable costs.

2 To increase managers' focus on selling units.

The stock account in this example is confined solely to direct materials (whether they are in storerooms, in process or in finished goods). There is only one stock account:

Type	Account title
Combined direct materials stock and any direct materials in work in progress and finished goods	Stock Control

Exhibit 21.3, Panel B, presents the journal entries in this case. Entry (a) is prompted by the same trigger point 1 as in Example 21.1, the purchase of direct materials. Entry (b) for the conversion costs incurred is recorded in an identical manner as in Example 21.1. Trigger point 2 is the sale of good finished units (not their production, as in Example 21.1), so there is no entry corresponding to entry (c) of Example 21.1. The cost of finished units is calculated only when finished units are sold (which corresponds to entry (d) of Example 21.1): 99 000 units sold × €31 = €3 069 000, consisting of direct materials (99 000 × €19 = €1 881 000) and conversion costs allocated (99 000 × €12 = €1 188 000).

No conversion costs are inventoried. That is, compared with Example 21.1, Example 21.2 does not attach €12 000 (€12 per unit × 1000 units) of conversion costs to finished goods stock. Hence, Example 21.2 allocates €12 000 less in conversion costs relative to Example 21.1. Of the €1 260 000 in conversion costs, €1 188 000 is allocated at standard cost to the units sold. The remaining €72 000 (€1 260 000 – €1 188 000) of conversion costs is underallocated. Entry (e) in Exhibit 21.3, Panel B, presents the journal entry if HTC, like many companies, writes off these underallocated costs monthly as additions to cost of goods sold.

The April ending balance of Stock Control is €69 000 (€50 000 direct materials still on hand + €19 000 direct materials embodied in the 1000 units manufactured but not sold during the period). Exhibit 21.5 provides an overview of this version of backflush costing. Entries are keyed to Exhibit 21.3, Panel B. The approach described in Example 21.2 closely approximates the costs calculated using sequential tracking when a company holds minimal work in progress and finished goods stocks because the approach in Example 21.2 does not maintain these stock accounts.

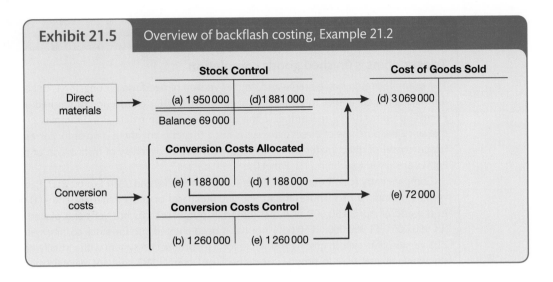

| Exhibit 21.5 | Overview of backflash costing, Example 21.2 |

Stock Control

Direct materials → (a) 1 950 000 | (d) 1 881 000 → (d) 3 069 000   **Cost of Goods Sold**

Balance 69 000

Conversion Costs Allocated

Conversion costs → (e) 1 188 000 | (d) 1 188 000

Conversion Costs Control

(b) 1 260 000 | (e) 1 260 000 → (e) 72 000

Direct materials are often a large proportion of total manufacturing costs, sometimes over 60%. Consequently, many companies will at least measure the direct materials efficiency variance in total by physically comparing what remains in direct materials stock against what should be remaining, given the output of finished goods for the accounting period. In our example, suppose that such a comparison showed an unfavourable materials efficiency variance of €90 000. The journal entry would be:

Raw Materials Efficiency Variance	90 000	
Stock: Raw and In-Progress Control		90 000

The under- or overallocated manufacturing overhead costs may be split into various overhead variances (spending variance, efficiency variance and production-volume variance) as explained in Chapters 15 and 16.

Extending Example 21.3, backflush costing systems could also use the sale of finished goods (instead of the production of finished goods) as the only trigger point. This version of backflush costing would be most suitable for a JIT production system with minimal direct materials, work-in-progress and finished goods stocks. Why? Because this backflush costing system would maintain no stock accounts.

Special considerations in backflush costing

The accounting illustrated in Examples 21.1, 21.2 and 21.3 does not strictly adhere to generally accepted accounting principles of external reporting. For example, work in progress (an asset) exists but is not recognised in the accounting system. Advocates of backflush costing, however, cite the materiality concept in support of these versions of backflushing. They claim that if stocks are low or their total costs are not subject to significant change from one accounting period to the next, operating profit and stock costs developed in a backflush costing system will not differ materially from the results generated by a system that adheres to generally accepted accounting principles.

Suppose material differences in operating profit and stocks do exist between the results of a backflush costing system and those of a conventional standard costing system. An adjustment can be recorded to make the backflush numbers satisfy external reporting requirements. For example, the backflush entries in Example 21.2 would result in regarding all conversion costs as a part of Cost of Goods Sold (€1 188 000 at standard costs + €72 000 write-off of underallocated conversion costs = €1 260 000). But suppose conversion costs were regarded as sufficiently material in amount to be included in Stock Control. Then entry (d), closing the Conversion Costs accounts, would change as shown below.

Example 21.3

Trigger point is finished goods completion

This example presents an extreme and simpler version of backflush costing. It has only one trigger point for making journal entries to stock. The trigger point is HTC's completion of finished units. Exhibit 21.3, Panel C, presents the journal entries in this case, using the same data as in Examples 21.1 and 21.2. Note that since the purchase of direct materials is not a trigger point, there is no entry corresponding to entry (a), purchases of direct materials. Exhibit 21.6 provides an overview of this version of backflush costing. Entries are keyed to Exhibit 21.3, Panel C.

Compare entry (c) in Exhibit 21.3, Panel C, with entries (a) and (c) in Exhibit 21.3, Panel A. The simpler version in Example 21.3 ignores the €1 950 000 purchases of direct materials (entry (a) of Example 21.1). At the end of April, €50 000 of direct materials purchased has not yet been placed into production (€1 950 000 – €1 900 000 = €50 000), nor has it been entered into the stock costing system. The Example 21.3 version of backflush costing is suitable for a JIT production system with virtually no direct materials stock and minimal work-in-progress stocks because Example 21.3 does not maintain these stock accounts. It is less feasible otherwise.

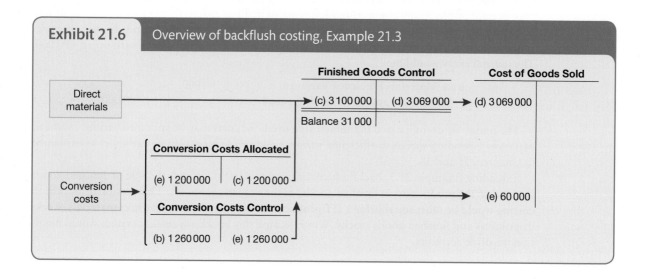

Exhibit 21.6   Overview of backflush costing, Example 21.3

Original entry (d) Conversion Costs Allocated	1 188 000	
Cost of Goods Sold	72 000	
Conversion Costs Control		1 260 000
Revised entry (d) Conversion Costs Allocated	1 188 000	
Stock Control (1000 units × €12)	12 000	
Cost of Goods Sold	60 000	
Conversion Costs Control		1 260 000

Criticisms of backflush costing focus mainly on the absence of audit trails – the ability of the accounting system to pinpoint the uses of resources at each step of the production process. The absence of large amounts of materials and work-in-progress stock means that managers can keep track of operations by personal observations, computer monitoring and non-financial measures.

What are the implications of JIT and backflush costing systems for activity-based costing (ABC) systems? Simplifying the production process, as in a JIT system, makes more of the costs direct and so reduces the extent of overhead cost allocations. Simplified ABC systems are often adequate for companies implementing JIT. But even these simpler ABC systems can enhance backflush costing. Costs from ABC systems give more accurate budgeted conversion costs per unit for different products, which are then used in the backflush costing system. The activity-based cost data are also useful for product costing, decision making and cost management.

Managing goods for sale in retail organisations

Accounting information can play a key role in **stock management**. This section illustrates the importance of accounting information in two areas:

1 the management of goods for sale in retail organisations;

2 the management of materials, work in progress and finished goods in organisations with manufacturing operations.

Stock management is of little concern in service companies since these companies hold minimal materials and stock.

Cost of goods sold measures the costs of stock sold, including the costs of purchasing and managing stock. Cost of goods sold constitutes the largest single cost item for most retailers.

Sales		100.0%
Less costs:		
Cost of goods sold	75.8%	
Selling, general and administration costs	19.7	
Other costs, interest and taxes	3.3	
Total costs		98.8
Net profit		1.2%

This means that better decisions regarding the purchasing and managing of goods for sale can cause dramatic percentage increases in net income.

Costs associated with goods for sale

The following cost categories are important when managing stocks and goods for sale.

1 **Purchasing costs** consist of the costs of goods acquired from suppliers including incoming freight or transportation costs. These costs usually make up the largest single cost category of goods for sale. Discounts for different purchase-order sizes and supplier credit terms affect purchasing costs.

2 **Ordering costs** consist of the costs of preparing and issuing a purchase order. Related to the number of purchase orders processed are special processing, receiving, inspection and payment costs.

3 **Carrying costs** arise when a business holds stocks of goods for sale. These costs include the opportunity cost of the investment tied up in stock (see Chapter 10) and the costs associated with storage, such as storage-space rental and insurance, obsolescence and spoilage.

4 **Stockout costs.** A stockout occurs when a company runs out of a particular item for which there is customer demand. A company may respond to the shortfall or stockout by expediting an order from a supplier. Expediting costs of a stockout include the additional ordering costs plus any associated transportation costs. Alternatively, the company may lose a sale owing to

the stockout. In this case, stockout costs include the lost contribution margin on the sale plus any contribution margin lost on future sales hurt by customer ill-will caused by the stockout.

5 **Quality costs.** The quality of a product or service is its conformance with a preannounced or prespecified standard. As described in Chapter 20, four categories of costs of quality are often distinguished: (a) prevention costs, (b) appraisal costs, (c) internal failure costs and (d) external failure costs.

The descriptions of the cost categories indicate that some of the relevant costs for making stock decisions and managing goods for sale are not available in existing accounting systems. Opportunity costs, which are not typically recorded in accounting systems, are an important component in several of these cost categories.

The inclusion of costs from all five categories makes cost of goods sold substantial. (In some cases, stock 'shrinkage' from shoplifting and employee theft can also add to cost of goods sold.) Advances in information-gathering technology, however, are attempting to increase the reliability and timeliness of stock data and reduce costs in these five categories. For example, electronic data interchange (EDI) links a company to its suppliers via computers. An order is often initiated by a single keystroke, increasing timeliness and reducing costs of ordering. Similarly, barcoding technology allows a scanner to capture purchases and sales of individual units. This creates an instantaneous record of stock movements and helps in the management of purchasing, carrying and stockout costs.

Economic order quantity decision model

The first major decision in managing goods for sale is deciding how much of a given product to order. The **economic order quantity** (EOQ) decision model calculates the optimal quantity of stock to order. The simplest version of this model incorporates only ordering costs and carrying costs into the calculation. It assumes the following:

1 The same fixed quantity is ordered at each reorder point.

2 Demand, ordering costs and carrying costs are certain. The **purchase-order lead time** – the time between the placement of an order and its delivery – is also certain.

3 Purchasing costs per unit are unaffected by the quantity ordered. This assumption makes purchasing costs irrelevant to determining EOQ, because purchasing costs of all units acquired will be the same, whatever the order size in which the units are ordered.

4 No stockouts occur. One justification for this assumption is that the costs of a stockout are prohibitively high. We assume that to avoid these potential costs, management always maintains adequate stock so that no stockout can occur.

5 In deciding the size of the purchase order, management considers the costs of quality only to the extent that these costs affect ordering costs or carrying costs.

Given these assumptions, EOQ analysis ignores purchasing costs, stockout costs and quality costs. To determine EOQ, we minimise the relevant ordering and carrying costs (those ordering and carrying costs that are affected by the quantity of stock ordered):

$$\text{Total relevant costs} = \text{Total relevant ordering costs} + \text{Total relevant carrying costs}$$

Exhibit 21.7 shows a graph analysis of the total annual relevant costs of ordering (DP/Q) and carrying stock ($QC/2$) under various order sizes (Q) and illustrates the trade-off between the two types of costs. The larger the order quantity, the higher the annual relevant carrying costs, but the lower the annual relevant ordering costs. *The total annual relevant costs are at a minimum where total relevant ordering costs and total relevant carrying costs are equal* (in the Video Galore example, each equals €2600).

Example 21.4

Video Galore sells packages of blank video tapes to its customers; it also rents out tapes of movies and sporting events. It purchases packages of video tapes from Sontek at €14 a package. Sontek pays all incoming freight. No incoming inspection is necessary, as Sontek has a superb reputation for delivering quality merchandise. Annual demand is 13 000 packages, at a rate of 250 packages per week. Video Galore requires a 15% annual return on investment. The purchase-order lead time is two weeks. The following cost data are available:

Relevant ordering costs per purchase order		€200.00
Relevant carrying costs per package per year:		
Required annual return on investment, 15% × €14	€2.10	
Relevant insurance, materials handling, breakage, etc., per year	3.10	
		5.20

What is the economic order quantity of packages of video tapes?

The formula underlying the EOQ model is:

$$EOQ = \sqrt{\frac{2DP}{C}}$$

where:

EOQ = Economic order quantity
   D = Demand in units for a specified time period (1 year in this example)
   P = Relevant ordering costs per purchase order
   C = Relevant carrying costs of 1 unit in stock for the time period used for D (1 year in this example).

The formula indicates that EOQ increases with demand and ordering costs and decreases with carrying costs.

We can use this formula to determine the EOQ for Video Galore as follows:

$$EOQ = \sqrt{\frac{2 \times 13\,000 \times €200}{€5.20}} = \sqrt{1\,000\,000} = 1000 \text{ packages}$$

Therefore, Video Galore should order 1000 tape packages each time to minimise total ordering and carrying costs.

The total annual relevant costs (TRC) for any order quantity Q can be calculated using the following formula:

TRC = Total annual relevant ordering costs + Total annual relevant carrying costs

$$= \begin{matrix}\text{Number of} \\ \text{purchase orders} \\ \text{per year}\end{matrix} \times \begin{matrix}\text{Relevant} \\ \text{ordering costs per} \\ \text{purchase order}\end{matrix} + \begin{matrix}\text{Average} \\ \text{stock} \\ \text{in units}\end{matrix} \times \begin{matrix}\text{Annual relevant} \\ \text{carrying costs of} \\ \text{1 unit for a year}\end{matrix}$$

$$= \frac{D}{Q} \times P + \frac{Q}{2} \times C$$

$$= \frac{DP}{Q} + \frac{QC}{2}$$

(Note that in this formula, Q can be any order quantity, not just the EOQ.)

When Q 1000 units,

$$TRC = \frac{13\,000 \times €200}{1000} + \frac{1000 \times €5.20}{2} = €2600 + €2600 = €5200$$

The number of deliveries each time period (in our example, 1 year) is:

$$\frac{D}{EOQ} = \frac{13\,000}{1000} = 13 \text{ deliveries}$$

Exhibit 21.7	Ordering costs and carrying costs for Video Galore

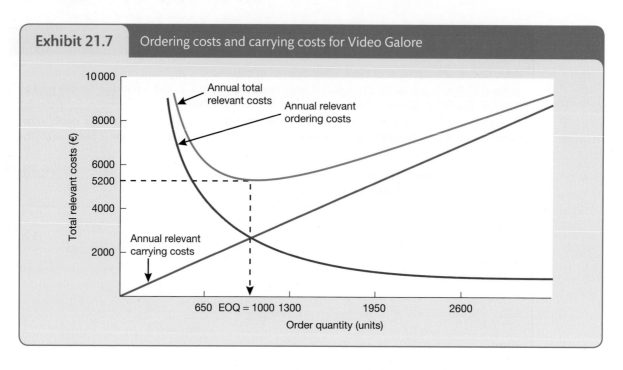

When to order, assuming certainty

The second major decision in dealing with cost of goods for sale is when to order. The **reorder point** is the quantity level of the stock on hand that triggers a new order. The reorder point is simplest to calculate when both demand and lead time are certain:

$$\text{Reorder point} = \text{Number of units sold per unit of time} \times \text{Purchase-order lead time}$$

Consider our Video Galore example. We choose a week as the unit of time:

Economic order quantity	1000 packages
Number of units sold per week	250 packages
Purchase-order lead time	2 weeks

Thus,

$$\begin{aligned}\text{Reorder point} &= \text{Number of units sold per unit of time} \times \text{Purchase-order lead time}\\ &= 250 \times 2\\ &= 500 \text{ packages}\end{aligned}$$

So, Video Galore will order 1000 packages of tapes each time its stock falls to 500 packages.

The graph in Exhibit 21.8 presents the behaviour of the stock level of tape packages, assuming demand occurs uniformly throughout each week. If the purchase-order lead time is two weeks, a new order will be placed when the stock level reaches 500 tape packages so that the 1000 packages ordered are received at the time stock reaches zero.

This handy formula does not apply when the receipt of the order fails to increase stock to the reorder-point quantity (for example, when the lead time is three weeks and the order is a one-week supply). In these cases, orders will overlap.

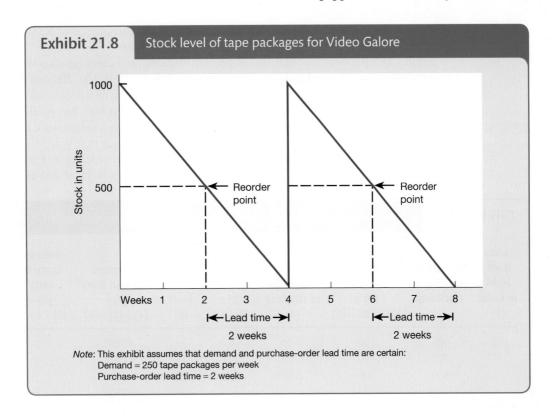

Exhibit 21.8   Stock level of tape packages for Video Galore

Note: This exhibit assumes that demand and purchase-order lead time are certain:
Demand = 250 tape packages per week
Purchase-order lead time = 2 weeks

Safety stock

So far, we have assumed that demand and purchase-order lead time are certain. When retailers are uncertain about the demand, the lead time or the quantity that suppliers can provide, they often hold safety stock. **Safety stock** is stock held at all times regardless of stock ordered using EOQ. It is used as a buffer against unexpected increases in demand or lead time and unavailability of stock from suppliers. In our Video Galore example, expected demand is 250 packages per week, but the company's managers feel that a maximum demand of 400 packages per week may occur. If Video Galore's managers decide that the costs of stockout are prohibitive, they may decide to hold safety stock of 300 packages. This amount is the maximum excess demand of 150 packages per week for the two weeks of purchase-order lead time. The computation of safety stock hinges on demand forecasts. Managers will have some notion – usually based on experience – of the range of weekly demand.

A frequency distribution based on prior daily or weekly levels of demand provides data for computing the associated costs of maintaining safety stock. Assume that one of seven different levels of demand will occur over the two-week purchase-order lead time at Video Galore:

	Units						
Total demand for 2 weeks	200	300	400	500	600	700	800
Probability (sums to 1.00)	0.06	0.09	0.20	0.30	0.20	0.09	0.06

We see that 500 is the most likely level of demand for two weeks because it is assigned the highest probability of occurrence. We also see that there is a 0.35 probability that demand will be either 600, 700 or 800 packages (0.20 + 0.09 + 0.06 = 0.35).

If a customer calls Video Galore to buy video tapes and the store has none in stock, it can 'rush' them to the customer at a cost to Video Galore of €4 per package. The relevant stockout costs in this case are €4 per package. The optimal safety stock level is the quantity of safety stock that minimises the sum of the relevant annual stockout and carrying costs. Recall that the relevant carrying costs for Video Galore are €5.20 per unit per year.

Exhibit 21.9 presents the total annual relevant stockout and carrying costs when the reorder point is 500 units. We need only consider safety stock levels of 0, 100, 200 and 300 units, since demand will exceed the 500 units of stock available at reordering by 0 if demand is 500, by 100 if demand is 600, by 200 if demand is 700 and by 300 if demand is 800. The total annual relevant stockout and carrying costs would be minimised at €1352, when a safety stock of 200 packages is maintained. Think of the 200 units of safety stock as extra stock that Video Galore maintains. For example, Video Galore's total stock of tapes at the time of reordering its EOQ of 1000 units would be 700 units (the reorder point of 500 units plus the safety stock of 200 units).

Exhibit 21.9	Computation of safety stock for Video Galore when reorder point is 500 units

Safety stock level in units (1)	Demand realisations resulting in stockouts (2)	Stockout in units* (3) = (2) − 500 − (1)	Probability of stockout (4)	Relevant stockout costs† (5) = (3) × €4	No. of orders per year‡ (6)	Expected stockout costs§ (7) = (4) × (5) × (6)	Relevant carrying costs# (8) = (1) × €5.20	Total relevant costs (9) = (7) + (8)
0	600	100	0.20	€400	13	€1040		
	700	200	0.09	800	13	936		
	800	300	0.06	1200	13	936		
						€2912	€0	€2912
100	700	100	0.09	400	13	€468		
	800	200	0.06	800	13	624		
						€1092	€520	€1612
200	800	100	0.06	400	13	€312	€1040	€1352
300	–	–	–	–	–	€0‖	€1560	€1560

* Realised demand − stock available during lead time (excluding safety stock), 500 units − safety stock.
† Stockout units × relevant stockout costs of €4.00 per unit.
‡ Annual demand 13 000 ÷ 1000 EOQ = 13 orders per year.
§ Probability of stockout × relevant stockout costs × number of orders per year.
# Safety stock × annual relevant carrying costs of €5.20 per unit (assumes that safety stock is on hand at all times and that there is no overstocking caused by decreases in expected usage).
‖ At a safety stock level of 300 units, no stockouts will occur and hence expected stockout costs = €0.

Challenges in estimating stock-related costs and their effects

Considerations in obtaining estimates of relevant costs

Obtaining accurate estimates of the cost parameters used in the EOQ decision model is a challenging task. For example, the relevant annual carrying costs of stock consist of *incremental or outlay costs* plus the *opportunity cost of capital*.

What are the relevant incremental costs of carrying stock? Only those costs that vary with the quantity of stock held – for example, insurance, property taxes, costs of obsolescence and costs of breakage. Consider the salaries paid to clerks, storekeepers and materials handlers. These costs are irrelevant if they are unaffected by changes in stock levels. Suppose, however, that as stocks decrease, these salary costs also decrease as the clerks, storekeepers and materials handlers are transferred to other activities or laid off. In this case, the salaries paid to these persons are relevant incremental costs of carrying stock. Similarly, the costs of storage space owned that cannot be used for other profitable purposes as stocks decrease are irrelevant. But if the space has other profitable uses, or if rental cost is tied to the amount of space occupied, storage costs are relevant incremental costs of carrying stock.

What is the relevant opportunity cost of capital? It is the return forgone by investing capital in stock rather than elsewhere. It is calculated as the required rate of return multiplied by those costs per unit that vary with the number of units purchased and that are incurred at the time the units are received. (Examples of these costs per unit are purchase price, incoming freight and incoming inspection.) Opportunity costs are not calculated on investments, say, in buildings, if these investments are unaffected by changes in stock levels. In the case of stockouts, calculating the relevant opportunity costs requires an estimate of the lost contribution margin on that sale as well as on future sales hurt by customer ill-will resulting from the stockout.

Our discussion suggests that predicting relevant costs requires care and is difficult. Managers understand that their projections will seldom be flawless. This leads to the question: What is the cost of an incorrect prediction when actual relevant costs are different from the relevant predicted costs used for decision making?

Cost of a prediction error

Continuing our example, suppose Video Galore's relevant ordering costs per purchase order are €242 instead of the predicted €200. We can calculate the cost of this prediction error with a three-step approach.

Step 1: Calculate the monetary outcome from the best action that could have been taken, given the actual amount of the cost input The appropriate inputs are $D = 13\,000$ units, $P = €242$ and $C = €5.20$. The economic order quantity size is:

$$EOQ = \sqrt{\frac{2DP}{C}}$$

$$EOQ = \sqrt{\frac{2 \times 13\,000 \times €242}{€5.20}} = \sqrt{1\,210\,000}$$

$$= 1\,100 \text{ packages}$$

The total annual relevant costs when EOQ = 1100 is:

$$TRC = \frac{DP}{Q} + \frac{QC}{2}$$

$$= \frac{13\,000 \times €242}{1000} + \frac{1\,100 \times €5.20}{2}$$

$$= €286 + €2860$$

$$= €3146$$

Step 2: Calculate the monetary outcome from the best action based on the incorrect amount of the predicted cost input The planned action when the relevant ordering costs per purchase order are predicted to be €200 is to purchase 1000 packages in each order. The total annual relevant costs using this order quantity when $D = 13\,000$ units, $P = €242$ and $C = €5.20$ are:

$$TRC = \frac{13\,000 \times €242}{1000} + \frac{1000 \times €5.20}{2}$$

$$= €314.60 + €2600$$

$$= €2914.60$$

Step 3: Calculate the difference between the monetary outcomes from steps 1 and 2

	Monetary outcome
Step 1	€3146
Step 2	2914.60
Difference	(€231.40)

The cost of the prediction error is €231.40. Note that the total annual relevant costs curve in Exhibit 21.8 is relatively flat over the range of order quantities from 650 to 1300. An important feature of the EOQ model is that the *total relevant costs are rarely sensitive to minor variations in cost predictions*. The square root in the EOQ model reduces the sensitivity of the decision to errors in predicting its inputs.

Just-in-time purchasing

As described earlier in the chapter, organisations are giving increased attention to *just-in-time (JIT) purchasing* – the purchase of goods or materials such that a delivery immediately precedes demand or use. JIT purchasing requires organisations to restructure their relationship with suppliers and place smaller and more frequent purchase orders. We next explore the relationship between EOQ decision models and JIT purchasing.

Companies moving towards JIT purchasing argue that the full costs of carrying stocks (including stock storage space, spoilage and opportunity costs not recorded in the accounting system) have been dramatically underestimated in the past. At the same time, building close partnerships with suppliers and using electronic commerce systems for order-related activities significantly reduce ordering costs.

EOQ implications of JIT purchasing

Exhibit 21.10 analyses the sensitivity of Video Galore's EOQ to illustrate the economics of smaller and more frequent purchase orders. The analysis presented in Exhibit 21.10 supports JIT purchasing – that is, having a smaller EOQ and placing orders more frequently – as relevant carrying costs increase and relevant ordering costs per purchase order decrease. One factor driving down ordering costs is the use of electronic links, such as the Internet, to place purchase orders. The cost of placing some orders on the Internet is estimated to be less than one-tenth – sometimes less than one-hundredth – of the cost of placing those orders by telephone, facsimile or post.

Exhibit 21.10	Sensitivity of EOQ to variations in relevant ordering and carrying costs for Video Galore*			
Relevant carrying costs per package per year	**Relevant ordering costs per purchase order**			
	€200	**€150**	**€100**	**€30**
€5.20	EOQ = 1000	EOQ = 866	EOQ = 707	EOQ = 387
€7.00	862	746	609	334
€10.00	721	624	510	279
€15.00	589	510	416	228
* Assuming annual demand is always 13 000 packages.				

Relevant benefits and relevant costs of JIT purchasing

The JIT purchasing model is not guided solely by the EOQ model. As discussed earlier, the EOQ model is designed to emphasise only the trade-off between carrying and ordering costs. Stock management extends beyond ordering and carrying costs to include purchasing costs, stockout costs and quality costs. The quality of materials and goods and timely deliveries are important motivations for using JIT purchasing and stockout costs are an important concern. We add these features as we move from the EOQ decision model to the JIT purchasing model.

Let us revisit the Video Galore example and consider the following information. Video Galore has recently established an Internet business-to-business purchase-order link with Sontek. Video Galore triggers a purchase order for tapes by a single computer entry. Payments are made electronically for batches of deliveries rather than for each individual delivery. These changes make ordering costs negligible. Video Galore is negotiating for Sontek to deliver 100 packages of video tapes 130 times each year (five times every two weeks) instead of delivering 1000 packages 13 times each year as calculated in Exhibit 21.7. Sontek is willing to make these frequent deliveries, but it will tack on a small additional amount of €0.02 to the price per package. Video Galore's required return on investment remains 15%. Assume that relevant annual carrying costs of insurance, materials handling, breakage and so on remain at €3.10 per package per year.

Suppose that Video Galore incurs no stockout costs under its current purchasing policy because demand and purchase-order lead times over each four-week period are certain. Video Galore's major concern is that lower stock levels from implementing JIT purchasing will lead to more stockouts because demand variations and delays in supplying tapes are more likely to occur in the short intervals between supplies under JIT purchasing. Sontek assures Video Galore that its new manufacturing processes enable it to respond rapidly to changing demand patterns. Consequently, stockouts may not be a serious problem. Video Galore expects to incur stockout costs on 50 tape packages each year under a JIT purchasing policy. In the event of a stockout, Video Galore will have to rush-order tape packages at a cost of €4 per package. Should Video Galore implement JIT purchasing?

Exhibit 21.11 compares (1) the incremental costs Video Galore incurs when it purchases video tapes from Sontek under its current purchasing policy, with (2) the incremental costs Video Galore would incur if Sontek supplied video tapes under a JIT policy. The difference in the two incremental costs is the relevant savings of JIT purchasing. In other methods of comparing the two purchasing policies, the analysis would include only the relevant costs – those costs that differ between the two alternatives. Exhibit 21.11 shows a net cost savings of €1879.85 per year from shifting to a JIT purchasing policy.

Supplier evaluation and relevant costs of quality and timely deliveries

As we saw earlier, costs of quality and timely deliveries are particularly crucial in JIT purchasing environments. Defective materials and late deliveries often bring the whole plant to a halt, resulting in forgone contribution margin on lost sales. Companies that implement JIT purchasing choose their suppliers carefully and pay special attention to developing long-run supplier partnerships. Some suppliers are very cooperative with a business's attempts to adopt JIT purchasing. For example, Convent, which is one of the market leaders in Germany for savoury snack products, makes more frequent deliveries to retail outlets than does many of its competitors. The company's corporate strategy emphasises service to retailers and consistency, freshness and quality of the delivered product. Through a highly customised service, Convent offers its customers the possibility to maximise return on shelf-space – a major service strength.

When evaluating suppliers, companies have to pay special attention to quality costs of goods or materials (for example, incoming materials inspection costs, returns, scrap costs and rework costs); costs of late deliveries (expediting costs, idle time on machines and forgone contribution margin on lost sales); and costs of early deliveries (carrying costs).

Exhibit 21.11	Annual relevant costs of current purchasing policy and JIT purchasing policy for Video Galore		
Relevant item		**Incremental costs under current purchasing relevant item**	**Incremental costs under JIT purchasing policy**
Purchasing costs			
€14 per unit × 13 000 units per year		€182 000.00	
€14.02 per unit × 13 000 units per year		€182 260.00	
Required return on investment			
15% per year × €14 cost per unit × 500* units of average stock per year		1 050.00	
15% per year × €14.02 cost per unit × 50† units of average stock per year			105.15
Outlay carrying costs (insurance, materials handling, breakage, and so on)			
€3.10 per unit per year × 500* units of average stock per year		1 550.00	
€3.10 per unit per year × 50† units of average stock per year			155.00
Stockout costs			
No stockouts		0	
€4 per unit × 50 units per year			200.00
Total annual relevant costs		€184 600.00	€182 720.15
Annual difference in favour of JIT purchasing		€1 879.85	

* Order quantity ÷ 2 = 1000 ÷ 2 = 500.
† Order quantity ÷ 2 = 100 ÷ 2 = 50.

What are the relevant costs when choosing suppliers? Consider again our Video Galore example. The Denton Corporation also supplies video tapes. It offers to supply all of Video Galore's video tape needs at a price of €13.60 per package (less than Sontek's price of €14.02) under the same JIT delivery terms that Sontek offers. Denton proposes an Internet purchase-order link identical to Sontek's that would make Video Galore's ordering costs negligible. Video Galore's relevant outlay carrying costs of insurance, materials handling, breakage and so on, per package per year, is €3.10 if it purchases video tapes from Sontek and €3.00 if it purchases from Denton. Should Video Galore buy from Denton? Not before considering the relevant costs of quality and also the relevant costs of failing to deliver on time.

Video Galore has used Sontek in the past and knows that Sontek fully deserves its reputation for delivering quality merchandise on time. Video Galore does not, for example, find it necessary to inspect the tape packages that Sontek supplies. Denton, however, does not enjoy so sterling a reputation for quality. Video Galore anticipates the following negative aspects of using Denton:

- Video Galore would incur additional inspection costs of €0.05 per package.

- Average stockouts of 360 tape packages each year would occur, largely resulting from late deliveries. Denton cannot rush-order tape packages to Video Galore on short notice. Video Galore anticipates lost contribution margin per unit of €8 from stockouts.

- Customers would probably return 2% of all packages sold owing to poor quality of the tapes. Video Galore estimates its additional costs to handle each returned package are €25.

Exhibit 21.12 presents the relevant costs of purchasing from Sontek and from Denton. Even though Denton is offering a lower price per package, the total relevant costs of purchasing goods from Sontek are lower by €4361.85 per year. Selling high-quality merchandise also has non-financial and qualitative benefits. For example, offering Sontek's high-quality tapes enhances Video Galore's reputation and increases customer goodwill, which may lead to higher future profitability.

Exhibit 21.12	Annual relevant costs of purchasing from Sontek and Denton	
Relevant item	**Incremental costs of purchasing from Sontek**	**Incremental costs of purchasing from Denton**
Purchasing costs		
€14.02 per unit × 13 000 units per year	€182 260.00	
€13.60 per unit × 13 000 units per year		€176 800.00
Inspection costs		
No inspection necessary	0	
€0.05 per unit × 13 000 units		650.00
Required return on investment		
15% per year × €14.02 × 50* units of average stock per year	105.15	
15% per year × €13.60 × 50* units of average stock per year		102.00
Outlay carrying costs (insurance, materials handling, breakage, and so on)		
€3.10 per unit per year × 50* units of average stock per year	155.00	
€3.00 per unit per year × 50* units of average stock per year		150.00
Stockout costs		
€4 per unit × 50 units per year	200.00	
€8 per unit × 360 units per year		2 880.00
Customer returns costs		
No customer returns	0	
€25 per unit returned × 2% × 13 000 units returned		6 500.00
Total annual relevant costs	€182 720.15	€187 082.00
Annual difference in favour of Sontek	€4 361.85	

* Order quantity ÷ 2 = 100 ÷ 2 = 50.

Stock costs and their management in manufacturing organisations

Managers in companies with manufacturing facilities face the challenging task of producing high-quality products at competitive cost levels. Numerous systems have been developed to help managers plan and implement production and stock activities. Earlier, we described the two most basic types of system:

- A *just-in-time (JIT) production system*, a 'demand-pull' system under which products are manufactured only to satisfy a specific customer order.
- A *materials requirements planning (MRP) system*, a 'push-through' system that manufactures finished goods for stock on the basis of demand forecasts.

Companies implementing JIT production systems manage stocks by eliminating them. When stocks are present, as in MRP systems, the management accountant plays several important roles. First, the management accountant must maintain accurate and timely information pertaining to materials, work-in-progress and finished goods stocks. A major cause of unsuccessful attempts to implement MRP systems has been the problem of collecting and updating stock records. Calculating the full cost of carrying finished goods stock motivates other actions.

A second role of the management accountant consists of providing estimates of the costs of setting up each production run at a plant, the costs of downtime and the costs of holding stock. Costs of setting up the machine are analogous to ordering costs in the EOQ model. When the costs of setting up machines or sections of the production line are high (for example, as with a blast furnace in an integrated steel mill), processing larger batches of materials and incurring larger stock-carrying costs is the optimal approach because it reduces the number of times the machine must be set up. When set-up costs are small, processing smaller batches is optimal because it reduces carrying costs. Similarly, when the costs of downtime are high, there can be sizable benefits from maintaining continuous production.

JIT production, quality and relevant costs

Early advocates of JIT production emphasised the benefits of lower carrying costs of stock. *An important benefit of lower stocks, however, is the heightened emphasis on eliminating the root causes of rework, scrap and waste and on reducing the manufacturing lead time of their products.* In computing the relevant benefits and relevant costs of reducing stocks in JIT production systems, the cost analyst must consider all benefits.

Consider the Hudson Corporation, a manufacturer of brass fittings. Hudson is considering implementing a JIT production system. Suppose that to implement JIT production, Hudson must incur €100 000 in annual tooling costs to reduce set-up times. Suppose further that JIT will reduce average stock by €500 000. Also, relevant costs of insurance, space, materials handling and set-up will decline by €30 000 per year. The company's required rate of return on stock investments is 10% per year. Should Hudson implement JIT? On the basis of the numbers provided, we would be tempted to say no. Why? Because annual relevant cost savings in carrying costs amount to €80 000 [(10% of €500 000) + €30 000], which is less than the additional annual tooling costs of €100 000.

Our analysis, however, has not considered other benefits of lower stocks in JIT production. For example, Hudson estimates that implementing JIT will reduce rework on 500 units each year, resulting in savings of €50 per unit. Also, better quality and faster delivery will allow Hudson to charge €2 more per unit on the 20 000 units that it sells each year. The annual relevant quality and delivery benefits from JIT and lower stock levels equal €65 000 (rework savings, €50 × 500 + additional contribution margin, €2 × 20 000). Total annual relevant benefits and cost savings equal €145 000 (€80 000 + €65 000), which exceeds annual JIT implementation costs of €100 000. Therefore, Hudson should implement a JIT production system.

Performance measures and control in JIT production

To manage and reduce stocks, the management accountant must also design performance measures to evaluate and control JIT production. Examples of information the management accountant may use include (see Dodd 1998):

- personal observation by production line workers and team leaders;
- financial performance measures (such as stock turnover ratios) and variances based on standard materials costs and conversion costs;
- non-financial performance measures of time, stock and quality, such as manufacturing lead time, units produced per hour and days stock on hand;
- $$\frac{\text{Total set-up time for machines}}{\text{Total manufacturing time}}$$
- $$\frac{\text{Number of units requiring rework or scrap}}{\text{Total number of units started and completed}}$$

Personal observation and non-financial performance measures are the dominant methods of control. Why? Because they are the most timely, intuitive and easy-to-comprehend measures of plant performance. Rapid, meaningful feedback is critical because the lack of buffer stocks in a demand-pull system creates added urgency to detect and solve problems quickly.

Summary

The following points are linked to the chapter's learning objectives:

1 Just-in-time production systems take a 'demand-pull' approach in which each component on a production line is produced immediately as needed by the next step in the production line to directly satisfy customer orders.

2 The five major features of a JIT production system are (a) organising production in manufacturing cells, (b) employing and training multiskilled workers, (c) emphasising total quality management, (d) reducing manufacturing lead time and set-up time, and (e) building strong supplier relationships.

3 Journal entries in a backflush costing system are not made sequentially to match the flow of a product in a plant. Rather, some or all journal entries relating to the cycle from purchase of direct materials to the sale of finished goods are delayed.

4 The economic order quantity (EOQ) decision model calculates the optimal quantity of stock to order. The larger the order quantity, the higher the annual carrying costs and the lower the annual ordering costs. The EOQ model includes those transactions routinely recorded in the accounting system and opportunity costs not routinely recorded.

5 The reorder point is the quantity level of stock that triggers a new order. It equals the sales per unit of time multiplied by the purchase-order lead time. Safety stock is the buffer stock held as a cushion against unexpected unavailability of stock from suppliers.

6 Just-in-time (JIT) purchasing is the purchase of goods or materials such that delivery immediately precedes demand or use. EOQ models support smaller and more frequent purchase orders (as in JIT purchasing) as relevant carrying costs increase and relevant ordering costs per order decrease.

7 A relevant cost–benefit analysis of JIT purchasing includes relevant costs of purchasing, carrying stock, ordering and stockout, quality-related costs of inspection and customer returns and lost contribution margins due to late deliveries. The relevant benefits and relevant costs of JIT production include relevant costs of set-up and carrying stock, better quality and faster delivery.

8 Performance measurements and control in JIT production systems emphasise personal observation and non-financial rather than financial performance measures.

Key terms

just-in-time production (660)	**purchasing costs** (673)
manufacturing cells (660)	**ordering costs** (673)
just-in-time purchasing (663)	**carrying costs** (673)
sequential tracking (666)	**stockout costs** (673)
synchronous tracking (666)	**quality costs** (674)
backflush costing (666)	**economic order quantity** (674)
delayed costing (666)	**purchase-order lead time** (674)
endpoint costing (666)	**reorder point** (676)
post-deduct costing (666)	**safety stock** (677)
stock management (673)	

References and further reading

Bhimani, A. (2015) *Strategic Finance: Achieving High Corporate Performance* (London: Strategy Press), chapter 3.

Dodd, A.J. (1998) 'The just-in-time environment', in A. Oldman and R. Mills (eds) *Handbook of Cost Management* (London: CIMA/Gee).

Hansen, A. and Mouritsen, J. (2007) 'Management accounting and changing operations management', in T. Hopper, D. Northcott and R. Scapens, *Issues in Management Accounting* (Harlow: FT Prentice Hall), pp. 3–26.

Johnson, H.T. and Kaplan, R.S. (1987) *Relevance Lost: The Rise and Fall of Management Accounting* (Boston, MA: Harvard Business School Press).

CHAPTER 21

Assessment material

Review questions

21.1 Distinguish a demand-pull from a push-through system.

21.2 List five major features of JIT production systems.

21.3 Describe how JIT systems affect product costing.

21.4 Companies adopting backflush costing often meet three conditions. Describe these three conditions.

21.5 Outline how three different versions of backflush costing can differ.

21.6 What assumptions are made when using the simplest version of the economic order quantity (EOQ) decision model?

21.7 Give examples of costs included in annual carrying costs of stock when using the EOQ decision model.

21.8 'Holding safety stocks needlessly ties up capital in stock.' Comment on this statement.

21.9 Name two cost factors that can explain why an organisation finds it cost-effective to make smaller and more frequent purchase orders.

21.10 'Accountants have placed stocks on the wrong side of the balance sheet. They are a liability, not an asset.' Comment on this statement by a plant manager.

Exercises

Basic level

*21.11 Backflush costing and JIT production (20 minutes)

Papadopoulou SA manufactures electrical meters. For August, there were no opening stocks of direct (raw) materials and no opening and closing work in progress. Papadopoulou uses a JIT production system and backflush costing with two trigger points for making entries in the accounting system:

a Purchase of direct materials debited to Stock: Raw and In-Progress Control

b Completion of good finished units of product debited to Finished Goods Control at standard costs.

Papadopoulou's August standard costs per unit are direct materials, €25; conversion costs, €20. The following data apply to August manufacturing:

Direct (raw) materials purchased	€550 000
Conversion costs incurred	€440 000
Number of finished units manufactured	21 000
Number of finished units sold	20 000

Required

1 Prepare summary journal entries for August (without disposing of under- or overallocated conversion costs). Assume no direct materials variances.

2 Post the entries in requirement 1 to the following T-accounts if applicable: Stock Control, Conversion Costs Control, Conversion Costs Allocated and Cost of Goods Sold.

21.12   Backflush, second trigger is sale (20 minutes)

Assume the same facts as in Exercise 21.11. Assume that the second trigger point for Papadopoulou is the sale – rather than the production – of finished units. Also, the Stock Control account is confined solely to direct materials, whether these materials are in a storeroom, in work in progress or in finished goods. No conversion costs are 'inventoried'. They are allocated at standard cost to the units sold. Any under- or overallocated conversion costs are written off monthly to Cost of Goods Sold.

Required

1 Prepare summary journal entries for August, including the disposition of under- or overallocated conversion costs. Assume no direct materials variances.

2 Post the entries in requirement 1 to the following T-accounts if applicable: Stock Control, Conversion Costs Control, Conversion Costs Allocated and Cost of Goods Sold.

21.13   Backflush, one trigger point (20 minutes)

Assume the same facts as in Exercise 21.11. Now assume that there is only one trigger point, the completion of good finished units of product, which are debited to Finished Goods Control at standard costs. Any under- or overallocated conversion costs are written off monthly to cost of goods sold.

Required

1 Prepare summary journal entries for August, including the disposition of under- or overallocated conversion costs. Assume no direct materials variances.

2 Post the entries in requirement 1 to the following T-accounts if applicable: Stock Control, Conversion Costs Control, Conversion Costs Allocated and Cost of Goods Sold.

21.14   EOQ for a retailer (15 minutes)

Kari-Klær AS buys and sells fabrics to a wide range of industrial and consumer users. One of the products it carries is denim cloth, used in the manufacture of jeans and carrying bags. The supplier for the denim cloth pays all incoming freight. No incoming inspection of the denim is necessary because the supplier has a track record of delivering high-quality merchandise. The purchasing officer of Kari-Klær has collected the following information:

Annual demand for denim cloth	20 000 metres
Ordering costs per purchase order	€160
Carrying costs per year	20% of purchase cost
Safety stock requirements	None
Cost of denim cloth	€8 per metre

The purchasing lead time is two weeks. Kari-Klær is open 250 days a year (50 weeks for 5 days a week).

Required

1 Calculate the EOQ for denim cloth.

2 Calculate the number of orders that will be placed each year.

3 Calculate the reorder point for denim cloth.

21.15 EOQ for manufacturer (20 minutes)

Keep-Kool makes air conditioners. It purchases 12 000 units of a particular type of compressor part, CU29, each year at a cost of £50 per unit. Keep-Kool requires a 12% annual return on investment. In addition, relevant carrying costs (for insurance, materials handling, breakage and so on) are £2 per unit per year. Relevant costs per purchase order are £120.

Required

1 Calculate Keep-Kool's EOQ for CU29.

2 Calculate Keep-Kool's total ordering and carrying costs using EOQ.

3 Assume that demand is uniform throughout the year and is known with certainty. The purchasing lead time is half a month. Calculate Keep-Kool's reorder point for CU29.

21.16 Choosing suppliers for JIT purchasing (30 minutes)

Arjun Manraj runs a print shop. Manraj requires 100 000 boxes of printing paper each year. He wants his suppliers to deliver the boxes on a JIT basis in order quantities of 400 boxes. Papyrus Ltd currently supplies the paper to Manraj. Papyrus charges £100 per box and has a superb reputation for quality and timely delivery. Manraj reports the following revenue and cost information for a typical print job:

Sales	£100 000
Costs of printing paper (£100 per box × 400 boxes)	40 000
Other direct materials (ink, etc.)	2 000
Variable printing costs (other than materials)	3 000
Fixed printing costs	25 000
Variable marketing and distribution overhead	1 000
Fixed marketing and distribution overhead	12 000

Suffolk Leaves Ltd has approached Manraj with a proposal to supply all 100 000 boxes to Manraj at a price of £95 a box. The savings in purchase costs are substantial and Manraj is tempted to accept Suffolk Leaves's offer, but before doing so, Manraj decides to check on Suffolk Leaves's reputation for quality and timely delivery. The information Manraj gathers is not all positive. Manraj estimates that late deliveries from Suffolk Leaves would lead to his incurring overtime and subcontracting costs of £30 000 per job on ten jobs during the coming year. Manraj also recognises that Suffolk Leaves's paper quality is not uniformly high and ink sometimes smudges after printing. Manraj expects that smudging would occur on five jobs during the year. Manraj would then have to buy paper in the open market at £110 per box and rerun the job. Manraj does not expect both delivery problems and quality problems to occur on the same jobs. Manraj requires a rate of return of 15% per year on investments in stock.

Required

1 Calculate changes costs if he purchases paper from (a) Papyrus and (b) Suffolk Leaves. Which supplier should Manraj choose only on the basis of the financial numbers given in the problem?

2 What other factors should Manraj consider before choosing a supplier?

21.17 Stock management, ethics (CMA, adapted) (20 minutes)

Range-Tout SARL builds and distributes industrial storage racks using a just-in-time system and maintaining minimal stocks. Range-Tout's earnings increased sharply in 2014 and earnings-based bonuses were paid to the management staff for the first time in several years. Nathalie Carotte, Range-Tout's president, wants earnings to continue growing, even to the point that the 2015 bonuses would be double those of 2014.

Albert Capus, Range-Tout's vice-president of finance, met with Boris Carême of Génie du Bois SA, a primary vendor of Range-Tout's manufacturing supplies and equipment. Capus asked Carême to invoice all of Range-Tout's 2015 purchases (€2 million in equipment and €3 million in supplies) as equipment. The reason Capus gave for his request was that Range-Tout's president had imposed stringent budget constraints on operating costs but not on capital expenditures. Carême agreed to do as Capus asked. Range-Tout expenses all supplies purchases immediately. It depreciates equipment on a straight-line basis over 10 years, assuming a zero disposal price.

While analysing the second-quarter financial statements, Jules Ballès, Range-Tout's financial controller, noticed that only equipment and no supplies had been purchased from Génie du Bois. Ballès, who reported to Capus, immediately brought this matter to Capus's attention. Capus told Ballès of President Carotte's high expectations and of the arrangement made with Boris Carême of Génie du Bois. Ballès requested that he be allowed to correct the accounts and urged that the arrangement with Génie du Bois be discontinued. Capus refused and told Ballès not to become involved in the Génie du Bois arrangement.

After thinking about the matter for a while, Ballès arranged to meet with Nathalie Carotte and he disclosed the arrangement Capus had made with Génie du Bois.

Required

1 Calculate the effect on Range-Tout's 2015 operating profit of showing supplies purchased in 2015 as equipment purchases. Do you agree with Jules Ballès, Range-Tout's financial controller, that the supplies purchased from Génie du Bois SA were accounted for improperly? Explain your answer.

2 Refer to the discussion of professional ethics in the appendix to Chapter 1. Explain why the use of the alternative accounting method to manipulate reported earnings is unethical.

3 Without prejudice to your answers to requirements 1 and 2, assume that Albert Capus's arrangement with Génie du Bois SA is not ethical in a professional sense. Discuss whether Ballès's actions were appropriate.

Intermediate level

21.18 Backflush journal entries and JIT production (15–20 minutes)

Krügsmann AG has a plant that manufactures transistor radios. The production time is only a few minutes per unit. The company uses a just-in-time production system and a backflush costing system with two trigger points for journal entries:

- Purchase of direct (raw) materials
- Completion of good finished units of product.

There are no opening stocks. The following data pertain to April manufacturing:

Direct (raw) materials purchased	€8 800 000
Direct (raw) materials used	8 500 000
Conversion costs incurred	4 220 000
Allocation of conversion costs	4 000 000
Costs transferred to finished goods	12 500 000
Cost of goods sold	11 900 000

Required

1 Prepare summary journal entries for April (without disposing of under- or overallocated conversion costs). Assume no direct materials variances.

2 Post the entries in requirement 1 to the following T-accounts if applicable: Stock Control, Conversion Costs Control, Conversion Costs Allocated and Cost of Goods Sold.

3 Under an ideal JIT production system, how would the amounts in your journal entries differ from those in requirement 1?

21.19 JIT purchasing, choosing suppliers (20–25 minutes)

Grano BV and Henco BV manufacture fairly similar remote-controlled toy cars. Sido BV, a retailer of children's toys, expects to buy and sell 4000 of these cars each year. Both Grano and Henco can supply all of Sido's needs and Sido prefers to use only one supplier for these cars. An electronic link will make ordering costs negligible for either supplier. Sido wants 80 cars delivered 50 times each year. Sido obtains the following additional information.

	Grano	Henco
Purchase price of the car	€50	€49
Relevant incremental carrying costs of insurance, materials handling, breakage, etc., per car per year	€11	€10
Expected number of stockouts per year resulting from late deliveries	20 cars	150 cars
Stockout costs per car	€25	€26
Expected number of cars sold that will be returned owing to quality and other problems	40 cars	140 cars
Additional costs to Sido of handling each returned car	€21	€21
Inspection costs per delivery	€20	€28

Sido requires a rate of return of 15% per year on investments in stock.

Required

1 Which supplier should Sido choose? Show all calculations.

2 What other factors should Sido consider before choosing a supplier?

21.20 JIT production, relevant benefits, relevant costs (20 minutes)

Turun Telelaitos Oy manufactures cordless telephones. Turun Telelaitos is planning to implement a JIT production system, which requires annual tooling costs of €150 000. Turun Telelaitos estimates that the following annual benefits would arise from JIT production.

a Average stock will decline by €700 000, from €900 000 to €200 000.

b Insurance, space, materials handling and set-up costs, which currently total €200 000, would decline by 30%.

c The emphasis on quality inherent in JIT systems would reduce rework costs by 20%. Turun Telelaitos currently incurs €350 000 on rework.

d Better quality would enable Turun Telelaitos to raise the prices of its products by €3 per unit. Turun Telelaitos sells 30 000 units each year.

Turun Telelaitos's required rate of return on stock investment is 12% per year.

Required

1 Calculate the net benefit or cost to Turun Telelaitos from implementing a JIT production system.

2 What other non-financial and qualitative factors should Turun Telelaitos consider before deciding on whether it should implement a JIT system?

21.21 Just-in-time systems, ethics (30 minutes)

Anna de Noailles, the plant manager at Electro-Sons, calls Pauline Eluard, the plant controller, into her office. She had just finished reviewing Eluard's report on the financial benefits from implementing JIT. The report described the following annual benefits and costs.

	First year after implementation	Subsequent years
Annual expected benefits from:		
Lower investment in stocks	€290 000	€350 000
Reductions in set-up costs	110 000	150 000
Reduction in costs of waste, spoilage and rework	200 000	250 000
Operating profit from higher sales as a result of responding faster to customers	180 000	300 000
Annual expected costs of implementing JIT	950 000	750 000

'We have been working on getting organised for JIT for almost a year now. Some of the financial benefits you have calculated seem optimistic to me. I don't think we are quite there yet, but if you continue to use the financial numbers you have, we would be forced to implement JIT sooner than we should. Please look over the numbers and see what you can do. I think some of the numbers are rather soft anyway. I also understand that plant profitability might take a hit in the year JIT is first implemented. I retire next year and I don't want to go out with a losing record.' Eluard is quite certain that her numbers are correct. She is also aware that Noailles would lose most of her performance bonuses if plant earnings decrease next year. It does not seem fair to her that Noailles should be penalised in the short term for what is in the long-run interest of the company.

Required

1 On the basis of Eluard's report, calculate the effect of JIT implementation on plant profitability in the first year after implementation and in subsequent years. On the basis of Eluard's report, should Electro-Sons implement JIT?

2 Is Noailles correct in characterising some of the financial benefits as 'soft'? Which items do you think she is referring to? If the benefits you identify as 'soft' are not realised, should Electro-Sons implement JIT?

3 Is Noailles being unfairly penalised if she implements JIT? What should Noailles do? What should Eluard do?

21.22 Effect of different order quantities on ordering costs and carrying costs, EOQ (30 minutes)

Rêve Andalou retails a broad line of Spanish merchandise at its Mont-St-Michel store. It sells 26 000 Juanita linen bedroom packages (two sheets and two pillow cases) each year. Rêve Andalou pays Juanita, SA, €104 per package. Its ordering costs per purchase order are €72. The carrying costs per package are €10.40 per year.

Simone Voirbeau, manager of the Mont-St-Michel store, seeks your advice on how ordering costs and carrying costs vary with different order quantities. Juanita, SA, guarantees the €104 purchase cost per package for the 26 000 units budgeted to be purchased in the coming year.

Required

1 Calculate the annual ordering costs, the annual carrying costs and their sum for purchase-order quantities of 300, 500, 600, 700 and 900, using the formulae described in this chapter. What is the economic order quantity? Comment on your results.

2 Assume that Juanita SA introduces a computerised ordering network for its customers. Simone Voirbeau estimates that Rêve Andalou's ordering costs will be reduced to €40 per purchase order. How will this reduction in ordering costs affect the EOQ for Rêve Andalou on their linen bedroom packages?

21.23 JIT production, operating efficiency (30 minutes)

Mannklein AG is a major manufacturer of metal-cutting machines. It has plants in Frankfurt and Stuttgart. The managers of these two plants have different manufacturing philosophies.

Liisa Kurunmäki, the recently appointed manager of the Frankfurt plant, is a convert to JIT production and has fully implemented JIT by January 2014.

Thomas Ahrens, manager of the Stuttgart plant, has adopted a wait-and-see approach to JIT. He commented to Kurunmäki: 'In my time, I have forgotten more manufacturing acronyms than you have read about in your five-year career. In two years' time, JIT will join the manufacturing buzzword scrapheap.' Ahrens continues with his 'well-honed' traditional approach to manufacturing at the Stuttgart plant.

Summary operating data for the two plants in 2014 are as follows:

	January–March	April–June	July–September	October–December
Manufacturing lead time (days)				
Frankfurt	9.2	8.7	7.4	6.2
Stuttgart	8.3	8.2	8.4	8.1
$\dfrac{\text{Total set-up time for machines}}{\text{Total production time}}$				
Frankfurt	52.1%	49.6%	43.8%	39.2%
Stuttgart	47.6	48.1	46.7	47.5
$\dfrac{\text{Number of units requiring rework}}{\text{Total number of units started and completed}}$				
Frankfurt	64.7%	59.6%	52.1%	35.6%
Stuttgart	53.8	56.2	51.6	52.7

Required

1 What are the key features of JIT production?

2 Compare the operating performance of the Frankfurt and Stuttgart plants in 2014. Comment on any differences you observe.

3 Kurunmäki is concerned about the level of detail on the job-cost records for the cutting machines manufactured at the Frankfurt plant during 2014. What reasons might lead Kurunmäki to simplify the job-cost records?

*21.24 Backflushing (35–40 minutes)

The following conversation occurred between Nicos Stavrou, plant manager at Sarantis Engineering, and Thanasis Bakogiorgos, plant controller. Sarantis manufactures automotive component parts such as gears and crankshafts for automobile manufacturers. Stavrou has been very enthusiastic about implementing JIT and about simplifying and streamlining the production and other business processes.

Stavrou: Thanasis, I would like to substantially simplify our accounting in the new JIT environment. Can't we just record one accounting entry at the time we ship products to our customers? I don't want our staff to be spending time tracking stock from one stage to the next, when we have as little stock as we do.

Bakogiorgos: Nicos, I think you are right about simplifying the accounting, but we still have a fair amount of raw material and finished goods stock that varies from period to period depending on the demand for specific products. Doing away with all stock accounting may be a problem.

Stavrou: Well, you know my desire to simplify, simplify, simplify. I know that there are some costs of oversimplifying, but I believe that, in the long run, simplification pays big dividends. Why don't you and your staff study the issues involved and I will put it on the agenda for our next senior plant management meeting?

Required

1 What backflush costing method would you recommend that Bakogiorgos adopt? Remember Stavrou's desire to simplify the accounting as much as possible. Develop support for your recommendation.

2 Think about the three examples of backflush costing described in this chapter. These examples differ with respect to the number and types of trigger point used. Suppose your goal of implementing backflush costing is to simplify the accounting, but only if it closely matches the sequential tracking approach. Which backflush costing method would you propose if:

a Sarantis had no raw materials or work-in-progress stocks but did have finished goods stock?
b Sarantis had no work-in-progress or finished goods stocks but did have raw material stock?
c Sarantis had no raw material, work-in-progress or finished goods stocks?

3 Backflush costing has its critics. In an article in the magazine *Management Accounting*, entitled 'Beware the new accounting myths', R. Calvasina, E. Calvasina and G. Calvasina state:

> **The periodic (backflush) system has never been reflective of the reporting needs of a manufacturing system. In the highly standardized operating environments of the present JIT era, the appropriate system to be used is a perpetual accounting system based on an up-to-date, realistic set of standard costs. For management accountants to backflush on an actual cost basis is to return to the days of the outdoor privy.**

Comment on this statement.

21.25   Stock issues (From ACCA Financial Information for Management, Part 1, June 2005)
(25 minutes)

Jane plc purchases its requirements for component RB at a price of £80 per unit. Its annual usage of component RB is 8760 units. The annual holding cost of one unit of component RB is 5% of its purchase price and the cost of placing an order is £12.50.

Required

1 Calculate the economic order quantity (to the nearest unit) for component RB.

2 Assuming that usage of component RB is constant throughout the year (365 days) and that the lead time from placing an order to its receipt is 21 days, calculate the stock level (in units) at which an order should be placed.

3 a Explain the terms 'stockout' and 'buffer stock'.
  b Briefly describe the circumstances in which Jane plc should consider having a buffer stock of component RB.

Advanced level

*21.26   EOQ, cost of prediction error (30–45 minutes)

Ronald van Hooijdonk is the owner of a truck repair shop. He uses an EOQ model for each of his truck parts. He initially predicts the annual demand for heavy-duty tyres to be 2000. Each tyre has a purchase price of €50. The incremental ordering costs per purchase order are €40. The incremental carrying costs per year are €4 per unit plus 10% of the supplier's purchase price.

Required

1 Calculate the EOQ for heavy-duty tyres, along with the sum of annual relevant ordering costs and carrying costs.

2 Suppose van Hooijdonk is correct in all his predictions except the purchase price. (He ignored a new law that abolished tariff duties on imported heavy-duty tyres, which led to lower prices from foreign competitors.) If he had predicted events correctly, he would have foreseen that the purchase price would drop to €30 at the beginning of the year and then remain unchanged throughout the year. What is the cost of the prediction error?

CHAPTER 22

Strategic management accounting and emerging issues

A pervasive theme of this book is that accounting usage within organisations is affected by many interacting factors including managers' behaviour, technological changes, competitive forces and nation-specific features. Just as there are different costs for different purposes, different organisations design and use management accounting systems in different ways. Many scholars, consultants and practitioners have called for changes in management accounting systems to more closely align them with the operations and strategies of organisations. This requires management accountants to develop an understanding of strategy and to devise ways in which a more strategic management accounting (SMA) orientation can be adopted in practice. We have already discussed in previous chapters the cost management implications of customer profitability analysis, life-cycle issues, quality concerns, activity-based management and target costing practices which may be viewed as SMA approaches. Our discussion here includes an assessment of the balanced scorecard as an approach to performance measurement and management control as well as other emerging issues.

Many managers consider that emerging issues of relevance to management accounting including governance, risk management, ethics, green business and digitisation and globalisation should, alongside strategy, inform the operations of a company and guide managers' short-run and long-run decisions. We start by discussing what strategy is and then consider ways in which organisations attempt to operationalise strategic concepts into management accounting practices. We then consider the implications of modern day emerging organisational concerns on management accounting.

Learning objectives

After studying this chapter, you should be able to:

- Recognise that different conceptions of strategy exist

- Consider how some organisations adopt identifiable generic strategies such as product differentiation and cost leadership

- Identify key aspects of SMA practices

- Understand the objectives of balanced scorecards as systems of performance measurement

- Design and illustrate a tableau de bord

- Describe how a strategic scorecard can contribute to enterprise governance

- Consider the scope of SMA in practice

- Understand how the potential of SMA systems relies on understanding the organisational context

- Consider some emerging issues affecting management accounting including the rise of social media, 'Big Data', environmental management accounting and knowledge management and intellectual capital creation

Conceptions of strategy

There is no single, universally accepted definition of strategy. The origins of the term strategy go back to ancient Greece whereby *strategos* signified the role of a general in command of an army. By 450 BC, the term was associated with skills in administration, leadership and oration (see Hoskin, Macve and Stone 2006). Today, different management writers and practitioners use the term differently. In analysing over 400 research articles on strategy, Mintzberg et al. (1998) identify ten key schools of thought. Mintzberg (1985) distinguishes between the notion that strategy can be *deliberate* and formally espoused and strategy as being *emergent*, sometimes by accident, and often arising from some level of bottom-up input from the lower reaches of the enterprise. For our purposes, it is sufficient to recognise that some management theorists view strategy in terms of how it is supposed to be according to them (the prescriptive or normative approach) while others prefer to explore how strategies arise in organisations (the descriptive approach). While the prescriptive approach has tended to dominate writings on the design of strategic management accounting systems and techniques, the descriptive perspective has been useful in explaining the process by which such techniques emerge and are operationalised.

The term 'strategic management accounting' is not used extensively in organisations but many firms engage in collecting and using information about competitors, matching accounting metrics and qualitative data with the strategic intents of the firm, pursuing cost-reduction opportunities manifested by the value chain, undertaking cost driver and competitive advantage analyses and using customer/marketing information. All these can be regarded as dimensions of SMA (see Lord 2007 and Langfield-Smith 2006). The term is increasingly used by professional management accounting associations. For instance, the leading association in Canada, CMA Canada, states that its mission is to lead the 'advancement of accounting, management and strategy' (www.cma-canada.org). Likewise, the UK's CIMA has 'strategic' level examination papers which require the application of strategic management accounting techniques to business contexts.

Some modern management writers have maintained the emphasis on militaristic notions of the term to identify essential dimensions of strategy (Porter 1980, 1985; Quinn 1980). This perspective has been particularly influential in a number of strategic management accounting writings (Shank 2006; Simmonds 1981; Simmonds et al. 1997). Adopting this view, we might describe strategy in terms of how an organisation matches its own capabilities with the opportunities in the marketplace in order to accomplish its overall objectives. In formulating its strategy, an organisation would seek to understand the industry in which it operates. Industry analysis might focus on five forces: (a) competitors, (b) potential entrants into the market, (c) equivalent products, (d) bargaining power of customers, and (e) bargaining power of input suppliers. These five dimensions have been posited by Porter (1980, 1985, 1996). The collective effect of these forces shapes an organisation's profit potential. In general, profit potential decreases with greater competition, stronger potential entrants, products that are similar, and tougher customers and suppliers.

We illustrate these five forces using the example of Chipset Ltd, a manufacturer of linear integrated circuit devices (LICDs) used in modems and communication networks. Chipset produces a single specialised product, CX1. This standard, high-performance microchip can be used in numerous applications that require instant processing of real-time data. CX1 was designed with extensive inputs from key customers.

- *Competitors*. Chipset has many growth opportunities, but it also faces significant competition from many small competitors. Companies in the industry have high fixed costs. There is steady pressure to utilise capacity fully; in turn, there is ceaseless pressure on selling prices. Reducing prices of products is critical for industry growth because it allows LICDs to be incorporated into mass-market modems. CX1 enjoys a reputation of having slightly superior product features relative to competitive products, but competition is severe along the dimensions of price, timely delivery and quality. Quality is important because LICD failure disrupts the communication network.

- *Potential entrants into the market.* This is not an attractive industry for new entrants. Competition keeps profit margins small, and significant capital is needed to set up a new manufacturing facility. Companies that have been making LICDs are further down the learning curve and hence are likely to have lower costs. Existing companies also have the advantage of close relationships with customers.

- *Equivalent products.* Chipset uses a technology that allows its customers to use CX1 flexibly to best meet their needs. The flexible design of CX1, and the fact that it is closely integrated into end-products made by Chipset's customers, reduces the potential for equivalent products or new technologies to replace CX1 during the next few years. This risk is reduced even further if Chipset continuously improves CX1's design and processes to decrease costs.

- *Bargaining power of customers.* Customers have bargaining power because each buys large quantities of product. Customers can also obtain microchips from other potential suppliers. Signing a contract to deliver microchips is very important to Chipset. Recognising this fact, customers negotiate hard to keep prices down.

- *Bargaining power of input suppliers.* Chipset purchases high-quality materials such as silicon wafers, pins for connectivity, and plastic or ceramic packaging from its suppliers. Chipset also requires skilled engineers, technicians and manufacturing labour. Materials suppliers and employees have some bargaining power to demand higher prices and higher wages.

In summary, strong competition and the bargaining powers of customers and suppliers put significant pressure on prices. Chipset is considering responding to these challenges by adopting one of two basic strategies: *differentiating its product* or *achieving cost leadership*.

Product differentiation is an organisation's ability to offer products or services that are perceived by its customers to be superior and unique relative to those of its competitors. For example, Samsung has successfully differentiated its products in the mobile telephony industry, as have Cross with pens, Rolex with watches and Coca-Cola with soft drinks. Through innovative product R&D, and by developing processes that bring products to market rapidly, each of these companies has been able to provide enhanced and differentiated products. This differentiation increases brand loyalty and the prices that customers are willing to pay.

Cost leadership is an organisation's ability to achieve lower costs relative to competitors through productivity and efficiency improvements, elimination of waste, and tight cost control. Some cost leaders in their respective industries are Hyundai (cars), BIC (pens), Dell (PCs) and Asda (consumer retailing). These companies all provide products and services that are similar to, not differentiated from, those of their competitors, but generally at a lower cost to the customer. Lower selling prices – rather than unique products or services – provide a competitive advantage for these cost leaders.

What strategy should Chipset follow? CX1 is already somewhat differentiated from competing products. Differentiating CX1 further will be costly but it may allow Chipset to charge a higher price. Conversely, reducing the cost of manufacturing and selling CX1 will allow Chipset to reduce the price of CX1 and spur growth. The CX1 technology allows Chipset's customers to achieve different performance levels by simply altering the number of CX1 units in their products. This solution is more cost effective than designing new, customised microchips for different applications. Customers want Chipset to keep the current design of CX1 but to lower its price. Chipset's current engineering staff is also more oriented towards making product and process improvements than towards creatively designing brand new products and technologies. Chipset concludes that it should pursue a cost leadership strategy. Of course, successful cost leadership would generally increase Chipset's market share and help the company to grow.

Porter (2001) believes that many companies which have invested heavily in Internet-based business processes have ignored strategy at their peril. He suggests that many such companies have undermined the structure of their industries, hastened competitive convergence and reduced the likelihood that they or anyone else will gain a competitive advantage. Porter states that 'the Internet actually makes strategy more essential than ever'. Indeed he claims that 'Only by

Concepts in action   Changing strategic gears

Source: Alexandra Winkler/Reuters/Corbis

In 1948, Rudolf Dassler had an argument with his brother, Adi, in the German town of Herzogenaurauch where they had founded a sports-shoe company. Adi set up the company Adidas and, across the road, Rudolf founded Puma. Like Adidas, Puma grew swiftly until 1986, when Rudolf's son Armin took the company public and retired. The company faced numerous problems, not least the lack of a focused strategy given the rapid succession of chief executives appointed to the helm. In 1993, Puma asked Jochen Zeitz, the company's marketing director, to become chief executive of what was, in his own words, 'probably the most undesirable sports name around'. Zeitz tackled three related problems head-on: Puma's centralised corporate structure, the high-cost German production base and the company's inability to keep pace with global trends. Strategic management accounting recognises that organisational structure, market intelligence and cost management are intimately intertwined. Zeitz's strategy, based on such information, worked. In 2013, Bjørn Gulden, Puma's new CEO, introduced a new strategy for the company: 'To be the fastest sports brand in the world'. The objective for Puma is 'to be fast in reacting to new trends, fast in bringing new innovations, fast in decision making and fast in problem solving for our partners'. The company ensures that employees are paid a fixed wage as well as participating in bonus schemes that are part of a performance-based remuneration system and profit-sharing programmes which allow employees to participate in the company's success. As Gulden says: 'It's about the instinct which will make you faster.' In 2013, Puma earned €191.4 million on sales of €3.2 billion. The new campaign for its brand 'Forever Faster' is designed to put the company back on track.

Another company stands at a strategic crossroads which will reflect on what it stands for. In 1994, a 'very seriously financially distressed' Finnish conglomerate, according to its ex-CEO, bet all it had on an unproven digital technology for mobile phones. The company divested itself of its consumer electronics, nappy and rubber boots operations and allowed Jorma Ollila to reinvent Nokia. Nokia went on to become the world's biggest manufacturer and seller of mobile phones, dominating the industry share of the market. In 2009, the world bought 1.14 billion mobile devices, of which 432 million were Nokia products and 20 million were Apple.

But Nokia's competition has been tough. In 2010 it was being squeezed by low-cost producers of handsets as well as by Apple's iPhone and Samsung smartphones which Nokia had developed over a decade before but failed to commercialise. By 2013, Nokia's global market share halved to 16%. The company sold its handset and services business to Microsoft for $7.2 billion on 25 April 2014 and appointed Rajeev Suri as its President and CEO six days later. Nokia's intention is to focus on three areas: the Networks-based products and services needed by telecoms operators to manage the increasing wireless data traffic; the HERE business based on further development of its location cloud to provide location intelligence across different operating systems and platforms; and finally, its Technologies business, which will see expansion of Nokia's intellectual property licensing programmes and technologies-based breakthrough innovations. Suri believes that 'With our three strong businesses – Networks, HERE and Technologies – and position as one of the world's largest software companies, we are well placed to meet our goal to be a leader in the technologies for a world where everybody and everything is connected.'

Sources: Halper, M. (2006) 'Nokia vs. Qualcomm: the handset maker wants to cut its royalty payments for using technology', *Fortune* (European edition), 25 December, pp. 23–5; Guyon, J. (2004) 'Nokia tries to reinvent itself – again', *Fortune* (European edition), 8 March; and Tomlinson, R. (2004) 'The cat that came back', *Fortune* (European edition), 2 March, pp. 60–4; puma.com and nokia.com; Smith, K. (2014) 'In the money: Forever Faster strategy to drive Puma turnaround', www.just-style.com, 21 February; Puma Group Management Report 2013; Nokia Corporation Stock Exchange Release, 29 April 2014; Steinbock, D. (2013) 'Nokia's failure: no flexibility in US, emerging markets', www.cnbc.com/id/101040631, 17 September.

integrating the Internet into overall strategy will this powerful new technology become an equally powerful force for competitive advantage' (p. 78).

The Internet thus seems to have brought new challenges for linking a company's strategy to management controls. Some commentators believe that 'what killed most first generation internet ventures – those of traditional business as well as startups – was not a failure of strategy, it was a failure of execution' (Downes 2001, p. 75). Digitisation of business activities and the deployment of Internet technologies by enterprises has had a significant impact on pricing issues, cost-volume-profit parameters, quality and throughput factors, cost management concerns and strategic considerations (Bhimani and Bromwich 2010).

Strategy development and implementation affects different firms' needs in different ways (Bhimani and Langfield-Smith 2007). The advent of digitisation and the Internet will no doubt continue to give rise to new ways of dealing with the interplay between strategic action and cost and financial management information. These concerns will further refine and redefine what is understood by strategic management accounting. We consider next the implications of this term. Clearly, just as there are many views on strategy and its implications for managing an enterprise, so there are different notions of how an organisation should deal with strategic concerns. How strategic intent arises and with what potential for affecting organisational affairs is still part of an evolving knowledge base.

What is strategic management accounting?

The Chartered Institute of Management Accountants in the UK defines **strategic management accounting (SMA)** in its *Official Terminology* (CIMA 2000, p. 50) as:

> **A form of management accounting in which emphasis is placed on information which relates to factors external to the firm, as well as non-financial information and internally generated information.**

SMA may be viewed as an attempt to integrate insights from *marketing management* and *management accounting* within a *strategic management* framework (Roslender and Hart 2003). But it has also been noted that many views on the relationships between strategy and management accounting are in evidence. These entail dimensions of firms' strategic positioning, competitor action, value chain concerns, time and innovation issues and market defined valuation of product characteristics (see Bhimani 2015 and Lord 2007). Such a view enables this emerging area to be understood in the context of more established disciplines.

The concern with the implications of external changes for the ways in which organisations reconstruct themselves has been prevalent in the applied management literature for a number of decades. Business process reengineering, benchmarking, total quality management, just-in-time methodologies, SWOT (strengths, weaknesses, opportunities and threats) analysis as well as the Boston Consulting Group's growth–share matrix have all called for a more extensive assessment of factors external to the enterprise. Although an all-emcompassing and comprehensive conceptual framework for strategic management accounting does not exist, the literature suggests that strategic management accounting (SMA) should incorporate strategic product costing and performance measurement, analyses of the firm's product markets and competitive market forces, and the assessment of organisational strategies over extended periods of time.

Certain key differences between conventional management accounting and SMA have been identified. While conventional management accounting adopts a historical orientation coupled with a focus on single decisions, single periods and single entities, SMA is oriented towards the future. Moreover, it seeks to emphasise the cohesiveness and consistency of macro- and micro-level activities and of short- and long-term decisions. Emphasis in SMA is also placed on an enterprise's position relative to that of its competitors in the context of sequences of decisions over multiple time periods. For instance, Shank (2006) places considerable weight on Porter's notion of strategic positioning. Here a value-chain perspective on strategic cost management requires that firms recognise their product in the total value-creating chain of activities, and that they endeavour to develop accounting information that enables improvement of internal cost management performance. The emphasis is not simply on competition, but also on the interaction that firms have with their suppliers.

The strategic evaluation of organisational issues entails the analysis of a range of diverse factors. A variety of contextual elements of organisational practices and their contingencies influence enterprise action and accounting practices including performance management (Ahrens and Chapman 2004, 2006). Many factors may be relevant in the provision of strategically oriented management accounting information. These include financial and non-financial information, competitor activities, product characteristics, market share data and other value-chain-related information.

What specific management accounting techniques might be considered as addressing strategic concerns? We have discussed in earlier chapters how external factors relating to the consumer, the market and technological advances have given rise to management accounting innovations such as activity-based management (Chapter 11), target costing (Chapter 12), product life-cycle costing (Chapter 12), customer profitability analysis (Chapter 12) and backflush accounting (Chapter 21). These have all been categorised by many management accounting commentators as dimensions of SMA. To these we might add the balanced scorecard, which has been adopted by many enterprises around the world in an attempt to explicitly link an organisation's operational activities to its strategic objectives. We consider the balanced scorecard and a French precursor – the tableau de bord – in more detail below.

The balanced scorecard

Consistent with the scorekeeping function, the management accountant has an important role to play in the implementation of strategy. This role takes the form of designing reports to help managers track progress in implementing strategy. Many organisations have introduced a balanced scorecard and a French precursor – the tableau de bord – approach to manage the implementation of their strategies.

The **balanced scorecard** translates an organisation's mission and strategy into a comprehensive set of performance measures that provides the framework for implementing its strategy (Kaplan and Norton 1996a, b). The balanced scorecard does not focus solely on achieving financial objectives. It also highlights the non-financial objectives that an organisation must achieve in order to meet its financial objectives. The balanced scorecard measures an organisation's performance from four key perspectives: (1) financial, (2) customer, (3) internal business process, and (4) learning and growth. A company's strategy influences the measures used in each of these perspectives.

The balanced scorecard gets its name from the attempt to balance financial and non-financial performance measures to evaluate both short-run and long-run performance in a single report. Consequently, the balanced scorecard reduces managers' emphasis on short-run financial performance, such as quarterly earnings. Why? Because the non-financial and operational indicators measure fundamental changes that a company is making. The financial benefits of these changes may not be captured in short-run earnings, but strong improvements in non-financial measures signal the prospect of creating economic value in the future. For example, an increase in customer satisfaction signals higher sales and income in the future. By balancing the mix of financial and non-financial measures, the balanced scorecard focuses management's attention on both short-run and long-run performance (Albertsen and Lueg 2014, Hoque 2014, Norreklit and Mitchell 2007).

We illustrate the four perspectives of the balanced scorecard using the Chipset example. To understand the measures Chipset uses to monitor progress under each perspective, it is important to recognise key elements of Chipset's cost leadership strategy: improve quality and reengineer processes. As a result of these initiatives, Chipset plans to reduce costs and downsize and eliminate capacity in excess of that needed to support future growth. However, it does not want to make deep cuts in personnel that would adversely affect employee morale and hinder future growth.

Quality improvement and reengineering at Chipset

One key element of Chipset's strategy to reduce costs is improving quality – that is, reducing defects and improving yields in its manufacturing process. To improve quality, Chipset needs to obtain real-time data about manufacturing process parameters and to implement advanced process control methods. The goal is to ensure that process parameters such as temperature and pressure are maintained within tight ranges. Chipset must also train its frontline workers in quality management techniques to help them identify and resolve defects and problems. Following this training, Chipset desires to give its workforce greater ability both to make timely decisions and continuously improve the process.

Another key element of Chipset's strategy to reduce costs is reengineering its order delivery process. **Reengineering** is the fundamental rethinking and redesign of business processes in seeking to achieve improvements in critical measures of performance such as cost, quality, service, speed and customer satisfaction (see Hammer and Champy 1993). To illustrate the concept of reengineering, we examine the order delivery system at Chipset in 2015. Chipset's salespeople work with customers to identify and plan customer needs. A copy of each purchase order received from a customer is sent to Manufacturing where a production scheduler begins the planning for manufacturing the order. Frequently, there is a long waiting time before production begins. After manufacturing is complete, the CX1 chips are sent to the Shipping Department, which matches the quantities of CX1 to be shipped against customer purchase orders. Often, the completed CX1 chips are held in inventory until a vehicle is available for shipment to the customer. If the quantity shipped does not match the number of chips requested by the customer, a special shipment is scheduled. The shipping documents are sent to the Invoicing Department for issuing of invoices. Credit controllers in the Accounting Department follow up customer payments.

Chipset discovered that the many transfers across departments (Sales, Manufacturing, Shipping, Invoicing and Accounting) to satisfy a customer order slowed down the process and created delays. A multifunction team from the various departments has reengineered the order delivery process for 2016. Its goal is to make the entire organisation more customer-focused and reduce delays by eliminating the number of interdepartmental transfers. Under the new system, a customer relationship manager will be responsible for the entire customer relationship. Chipset will enter into long-term contracts with customers that specify quantities and prices. The customer relationship manager will work closely with the customer and with manufacturing to specify delivery schedules for CX1 one month in advance. The schedule of customer orders will be sent electronically to Manufacturing. Completed chips will be shipped directly from Manufacturing to customer sites. Each shipment will automatically trigger an invoice that will be sent electronically to the customer.

The experiences of many companies, such as B T, British American Tobacco, Banca di America e di Italia, Hewlett-Packard and Siemens, indicate that the benefits from reengineering are most significant when reengineering cuts across functional lines to focus on an entire business process (as in the Chipset example). Reengineering only the shipping or invoicing activity at Chipset rather than the entire order delivery process would not be particularly beneficial. Successful reengineering efforts involve changing roles and responsibilities, eliminating unnecessary activities and tasks, using information technology, and developing employee skills. Chipset's balanced scorecard for 2016 must track Chipset's progress in reengineering the order delivery process from both a non-financial and a financial perspective.

The four perspectives of the balanced scorecard

Exhibit 22.1 presents Chipset's balanced scorecard. It highlights the four key perspectives of performance: financial, customer, internal business process, and learning and growth. At the beginning of the year 2016, Chipset specifies the objectives, measures, initiatives to achieve the objectives, and target performance (the first four columns of Exhibit 22.1). The target performance levels for non-financial measures are based on competitor benchmarks. They indicate the performance levels necessary to meet customer needs, compete effectively and achieve financial goals. The fifth column, which describes actual performance, is completed at the end of the year 2016. This column shows how well Chipset has performed relative to its target performance.

1 *Financial perspective.* This perspective evaluates the profitability of the strategy. Because cost reduction relative to competitors and growth are Chipset's key strategic initiatives, the financial perspective focuses on how much of operating income and return on capital employed results from reducing costs and selling more units of CX1.

2 *Customer perspective.* This perspective identifies the targeted market segments and measures the company's success in these segments. To monitor its growth objectives, Chipset uses measures such as market share in the communication networks segment, number of new customers and customer satisfaction.

3 *Internal business process perspective.* This perspective focuses on internal operations that further both the customer perspective by creating value for customers and the financial perspective by increasing shareholder wealth. Chipset determines internal business process improvement targets after benchmarking against key competitors. There are different sources of competitor cost analysis: published financial statements, prevailing prices, customers, suppliers, former employees, industry experts and financial analysts. Chipset also physically takes apart competitors' products to compare them with its own designs. This activity also helps Chipset to estimate competitors' costs. The internal business process perspective comprises three principal subprocesses:

   a *The innovation process* – creating products, services and processes that will meet the needs of customers. At Chipset, the key to lowering costs and promoting growth is improving the technology of manufacturing.
   b *The operations process* – producing and delivering existing products and services to customers. Chipset's key strategic initiatives are (a) improving manufacturing quality, (b) reducing delivery time to customers, and (c) meeting specified delivery dates.
   c *After-sales service* – providing service and support to the customer after the sale or delivery of a product or service. Chipset's sales staff work closely with customers to monitor and understand how well product features of CX1 match customer needs.

4 *Learning and growth perspective.* This perspective identifies the capabilities in which the organisation must excel in order to achieve superior internal processes that create value for customers and shareholders. Chipset's learning and growth perspective emphasises three capabilities: (1) employee capabilities measured using employee education and skill levels, surveys of employee satisfaction, employee turnover (proportion of employees who have left the company annually) and employee productivity; (2) information system capabilities measured by percentage of frontline employees that have online access to customer information, and percentage of business processes with real-time feedback; and (3) motivation and empowerment measured by number of suggestions per employee, percentage of suggestions implemented, and percentage of compensation based on individual and team incentives.

The arrows in Exhibit 22.1 indicate how gains in the learning and growth perspective lead to improvements in internal business processes, which in turn lead to higher customer satisfaction and market share, and finally to superior financial performance. Note how key elements of Chipset's strategy implementation – empowering workers, training, information systems, quality and process improvements, reengineering and customer focus – filter through the scorecard. These initiatives have been successful from a financial perspective in 2016. Chipset has earned significant operating income from its cost leadership strategy that has also translated into growth.

Aligning the balanced scorecard to strategy

Different strategies call for different scorecards. Suppose that Visilog, another company in the microchip industry, follows a product differentiation strategy by designing custom chips for the communication networks business. Visilog designs its balanced scorecard to fit its strategy. For example, in the financial perspective, Visilog evaluates how much of its operating income comes from charging premium prices for its products. In the customer perspective, Visilog measures the percentage of its revenues from new products (and new customers). In the internal business process perspective, Visilog measures the development of advanced manufacturing capabilities to produce custom chips. In the learning and growth perspective, Visilog measures new product development time. Of course, Visilog uses some of the measures described in the balanced scorecard in Exhibit 22.1. For example, revenue growth, customer satisfaction ratings, order delivery time, on-time delivery, percentage of frontline workers empowered to manage processes, and employee satisfaction ratings, are important measures under the new strategy. The key point, though, is to align the balanced scorecard to company strategy. For simplicity, we have presented the balanced scorecard in the context of companies that have followed either a cost leadership or a product differentiation strategy. Of course, a company may have some products for which cost leadership is critical and other products for which product differentiation is important. The company will then develop separate scorecards to implement the different product strategies. In still other contexts, product differentiation may be of primary importance, but some cost leadership must also be achieved. The balanced scorecard measures would then link to this strategy.

Exhibit 22.2 presents some common balanced scorecard measures that companies have used.

Features of a good balanced scorecard

A good balanced scorecard design has several features:

1 It tells the story of a company's strategy by articulating a sequence of cause-and-effect relationships. For example, because Chipset's goal is to be a low-cost producer and to emphasise growth, the balanced scorecard describes the specific objectives and measures in the learning and growth perspective that lead to improvements in internal business processes. These, in turn, lead to increased customer satisfaction and market share, as well as higher operating profit and shareholder wealth. Each measure in the scorecard is part of a cause-and-effect chain, a linkage from strategy formulation to financial outcomes.

2 It helps to communicate the strategy to all members of the organisation by translating the strategy into a coherent and linked set of understandable and measurable operational targets. Guided by the scorecard, managers and employees take actions and make decisions that aim to achieve the company's strategy. To focus these actions, some companies, such as Halifax and Barclays, have pushed down and developed scorecards at the division and department levels.

3 In for-profit companies, the balanced scorecard places strong emphasis on financial objectives and measures. Managers sometimes tend to focus too much on innovation, quality and customer satisfaction as ends in themselves even if they do not lead to tangible pay-offs. A balanced scorecard emphasises non-financial measures as a part of a programme to achieve future financial performance. When financial and non-financial performance measures are properly linked, many of the non-financial measures serve as leading indicators of future financial performance. In the Chipset example, the improvements in non-financial factors have, in fact, led to improvements in financial factors.

4 The balanced scorecard limits the number of measures used by identifying only the most critical ones. Avoiding a proliferation of measures focuses management's attention on those that are key to the implementation of strategy.

Exhibit 22.1	The balanced scorecard for Chipset Ltd for the year 2016			

Objectives	Measures	Initiatives	Target performance	Actual performance
Financial perspective				
Increase shareholder value	Operating profit from productivity gain	Manage costs and unused capacity	£2 000 000	£2 100 000
	Operating profit from growth	Build strong customer relationships	£3 000 000	£3 420 000
	Revenue growth	Build strong customer relationships	6%	6.48%*
Customer perspective				
Increase market share	Market share in communication networks segment	Identify future needs of customers	6%	7%
	New customers	Identify new target customer segments	5	66†
Increase customer satisfaction	Customer satisfaction survey	Increase customer focus of sales organisation	90% of customers give top two ratings	87% of customers give top two ratings
Internal business process perspective				
Improve manufacturing capability	Percentage of processes with advanced controls	Organise R&D/ manufacturing teams to implement advanced controls	75%	75%
Improve manufacturing quality and productivity	Yield	Identify root causes of problems and improve quality	78%	79.3%‡
Reduce delivery time to customers	Order delivery time	Reengineer order delivery process	30 days	30 days
Meet specified delivery dates	On-time delivery	Reengineer order delivery process	92%	90%
Learning and growth perspective				
Develop process skill	Percentage of employees trained in process and quality management	Employee training programmes	90%	92%
Empower workforce	Percentage of front-line workers empowered to manage processes	Have supervisors act as coaches rather than decision makers	85%	90%
Align employee and organisation goals	Employee satisfaction survey	Employee participation and suggestions programme to build teamwork	80% of employees give top two ratings	88% of employees give top two ratings
Enhance information system capabilities	Percentage of manufacturing processes with real-time feedback	Improve offline data gathering	80%	80%
Improve manufacturing processes	Number of major improvements in process controls	Organise R&D/ manufacturing teams to modify processes	5	5

* Revenues in 2016 – Revenues in 2015) ÷ Revenues in 2015 = (£28 750 000 – £27 000 000) ÷ £27 000 000 = 6.48%.
† Customers increased from 40 to 46 in the year 2016.
‡ Yield = Units of CX1 produced ÷ Units of CX1 started × 100 = 1 150 000 ÷ 1 450 000 × 100 = 79.3%.

Exhibit 22.2	Frequently cited balanced scorecard measures

Financial perspective

- Operating profit, revenue growth, revenues from new products, gross margin percentage, cost reductions in key areas, economic value added (EVA®)*, return on investment*.

Customer perspective

- Market share, customer satisfaction, customer retention percentage, time taken to fulfil customer's requests.

Internal business process perspective

- *Innovation process* – manufacturing capabilities, number of new products or services, new product development times, number of new patents.

- *Operations process* – yield, defect rates, time taken to deliver product to customers, percentage of on-time deliveries, average time taken to manufacture orders, set-up time, manufacturing downtime.

- *After-sales service* – time taken to replace or repair defective products, hours of customer training for using the product.

Learning and growth perspective

- Employee education and skill levels, employee satisfaction scores, employee turnover rates, information system availability, percentage of processes with advanced controls, percentage of employee suggestions implemented, percentage of compensation based on individual and team incentives.

* These measures are described in Chapter 19.

5 The scorecard highlights suboptimal trade-offs that managers may make when they fail to consider operational and financial measures together. For example, a company for which innovation is key could achieve superior short-run financial performance by reducing spending on R&D. A good balanced scorecard would signal that the short-run financial performance may have been achieved by taking actions that hurt future financial performance because a leading indicator of that performance, R&D spending and R&D output, has declined.

Correct implementation is key to the successful deployment of a balanced scorecard. It is particularly important that some common objectives drive the desire to use a balanced scorecard within an organisation. Many unintended forces can shape the way in which a balanced scorecard is ultimately implemented (Kasurinen 2000). If it is incorrectly implemented, 'the organisation may actually go faster in the wrong direction' (Rousseau and Rousseau 2000, p. 25). This appears to be true across for-profit as well as not-for-profit and governmental organisations (Kloot and Martin 2000). One study of 17 Finnish companies with balanced scorecard applications suggests that specific emphasis was being placed on management by objectives in some organisations but on more directly deploying the balanced scorecard as an information system in others (Malmi 2001). More recent research suggests that successful balanced scorecard implementation depends on managers' understanding of the linkages between performance measures, business units' strategy and firm decisions (Ding and Beaulieu 2011). In a significant review of balanced scorecard research over two decades, Hoque (2014) notes that, for some organisations, integrating the balanced scorecard with other managerial control tools such as budgeting is difficult. Also, some organisations have a tendency to use too many measures in a scorecard and may end up measuring the wrong things.

Pitfalls to avoid when implementing a balanced scorecard

Points to note when implementing a balanced scorecard include the following:

1 Do not assume the cause-and-effect linkages to be precise. They are merely hypotheses. A critical challenge is to identify the strength and speed of the causal linkages among the non-financial and financial measures. Hence, an organisation must gather evidence of these linkages over time. With experience, organisations should alter their scorecards to include those non-financial objectives and measures that are the best leading indicators of subsequent financial performance (a lagging indicator). Committing to evolve the scorecard over time avoids the paralysis associated with trying to design the perfect scorecard at the outset.

2 Do not seek improvements across all of the measures all of the time. This approach may be inappropriate because trade-offs may need to be made across various strategic goals. For example, emphasising quality and on-time performance beyond a point may not be worthwhile – further improvement in these objectives may be inconsistent with profit maximisation.

3 Do not use only objective measures in the scorecard. Chipset's scorecard includes both objective measures (such as operating income from cost leadership, market share and manu-facturing yield), as well as subjective measures (such as customer and employee satisfaction ratings). When using subjective measures, though, management must be careful to trade off the benefits of the richer information these measures provide against the imprecision and potential for manipulation.

4 Do not fail to consider both costs and benefits of initiatives such as spending on information technology and R&D before including these objectives in the scorecard. Otherwise, management may focus the organisation on measures that will not result in overall long-run financial benefits.

5 Do not ignore non-financial measures when evaluating managers and employees. Managers tend to focus on what their performance is measured by. Excluding non-financial measures when evaluating performance will reduce the significance and importance that managers give to non-financial scorecard measures. Extensive research by Larker (2004) suggests that it is crucial for an organisation to think carefully about linking balanced scorecard categories to performance measures. He notes that companies often experience problems of 'disbalance' when incorporating non-financial measures stemming from the balanced scorecard into remuneration plans. In one investigation of the use of balanced scorecards at Citibank, Larker noted that 45% of branch managers were not satisfied with the scorecard process whereas only 32% were. A major problem was managers not knowing 'who gets what and why' when it came to scorecard-based bonuses.

In reviewing the evidence available on the balanced scorecard, Mitchell and Norreklit (2014, p. 426) noted that 'BSC (balanced scorecards) implementation can vary among organisations due to different interpretations of the BSC' and 'few organisations seem to follow the instructions of linking compensation to all areas of measurements'. Hoque (2014, p. 56) notes that 'Until another improved innovation appears, the balanced scorecard will continue to provide organisations with a valuable option as a strategy map, an enabler of policy implementation, and an organisational control and accountability tool'.

Concepts in action | The growth versus profitability choice at Facebook

Source: Getty images

Competitive advantage comes from product differentiation or cost leadership. Successful implementation of these strategies helps a company to be profitable and to grow. Many Internet start-ups pursue a strategy of short-run growth to build a customer base, with the goal of later benefiting from such growth by either charging user fees or sustaining a free service for users supported by advertisers. However, during the 1990s dot-com boom (and subsequent bust), the most spectacular failures occurred in dot-com companies that followed the 'get big fast' model but then failed to differentiate their products or reduce their costs. Today, many social networking companies face this same challenge.

At Facebook, the most notable of the social networking sites, users can create personal profiles that allow them to interact with friends through messaging, chat, sharing website links and video clips, and more. In 2003, Mark Zuckerberg launched Facemash at Harvard to allow university students to exchange information about themselves. The online facility attracted 450 visitors and 22 000 photoviews within hours. Three months later Zuckerberg launched 'thefacebook', later to become facebook.com. Within ten years, one out of six people on the planet were Facebook members. The company's market value by end of 2014 exceeded $225 billion with a net income of $1.5 billion on revenues exceeding $7.8 billion the previous year. Facebook remains intent on maintaining leadership in social networking. In 2012 it bought the photo-sharing mobile application Instagram, which was only 18 months old, for $1 billion. In early 2014, Facebook purchased the five-year-old WhatsApp cross-platform instant messaging service for $19 billion. A question that faces Facebook is that its business model presumes ever extending friendships. For this reason, many online users prefer less 'noisy' social networks. Smaller networks such as Snapchat, Kik and WhatsApp may have surfaced to avoid extreme size. Yet it is clear that Facebook's offerings continue to lure new members for the time being.

Sources: Arrington, M. (2010) 'Facebook may be growing too fast and hitting the capital markets again', 'Tech Crunch', blog, 31 October, http://tech-crunch.com/2010/10/31/facebooks-growing-problem/; Mourdoukoutas, P. (2014) 'What's wrong with Facebook's business model and innovation strategy?', www.forbes.com/panosmourdoukoutas/2014/02/23.

Evaluating the success of a strategy

To evaluate how successful it has been in implementing its strategy, Chipset compares the target and actual performance columns of its balanced scorecard in Exhibit 22.1. This comparison indicates that Chipset met most of the targets it had set on the basis of competitor benchmarks. Meeting the targets suggests that the strategic initiatives that Chipset had identified and measured for learning and growth resulted in improvements in internal business processes, customer measures and financial performance. The financial measures show that Chipset achieved targeted cost savings and growth. The key question is: How does Chipset isolate operating profit from specific sources such as cost savings and growth instead of emphasising only the aggregate change in operating profit?

Some companies might be tempted to gauge the success of their strategies by measuring the change in their operating profits from one year to the next, but this approach is inadequate. For example, operating profit can increase simply because entire markets are expanding, not because a specific strategy has been successful. Also, changes in operating profit might be caused by factors outside the strategy. For example, a company such as Chipset that has chosen a cost leadership strategy may find that operating profit increases have instead been caused incidentally by some degree of product differentiation. Managers and accountants need to evaluate the success of a strategy on the basis of whether the sources of operating profit increases are the result of implementing the chosen strategy.

To use operating profit numbers for evaluating the success of a strategy, a company needs to isolate the operating profit due to cost leadership from the operating profit due to product differentiation. Of course, successful cost leadership or product differentiation generally increases market share and helps a company to grow. To evaluate the success of a company's strategy, one can subdivide changes in operating profit into components that can be identified with growth, product differentiation and cost leadership. Subdividing the change in operating profit to evaluate the success of a company's strategy is similar to variance analysis, discussed in Chapters 15 and 16. The focus is on comparing actual operating performance over two different time periods and explicitly linking it to strategic choices. A company is considered to be successful in implementing its strategy when the amounts of the product differentiation, cost leadership and growth components align closely with its strategy.

The balanced scorecard seems useful to some organisations if it is adopted in a flexible manner. Some management accounting commentators believe that developing a balanced scorecard without the input and participation of those who implement the enterprise's strategies and plans will 'doom the balanced scorecard to being a source of controversy rather than an integrating and focusing force in the organisation' (Atkinson and Epstein 2000, p. 26). Subscribing to this view is the global telecommunications company British Telecom (BT) which has implemented the balanced scorecard in a manner that recognises certain core value elements of the organisation. Creelman (2000, p. 11) cited BT's director of organisational excellence as considering that getting the 'culture fit' right is critical, saying 'I would make "culture" the fifth balanced scorecard perspective' and noting that 'the scorecard enables us to measure, on one piece of paper, whether we are practising our values'. Other researchers have similarly highlighted the need for the balanced scorecard to fit the adopting organisation's culture (Bontis et al. 1999; Chesley and Wenger 1999; Ding and Beaulieu 2011; England 2001). Larker (2004) and Albertsen and Lueg (2014) report that managers subjected to performance evaluation systems based on balanced scorecards need to understand explicit ties between performance outcomes and rewards. Qu and Cooper (2011) have produced evidence of how organisational employees and consultants engaged in implementing a balanced scorecard play a significant role in affecting the system's outcomes.

Although organisations differ in the way that they use the balanced scorecard, there is some evidence that there are country-specific ways in which it is implemented and deployed. Thus, the notion of a specifically 'Scandinavian balanced scorecard' has been reported (Ax and Bjornenak 2007). In some countries, organisations have shown reticence in the use of balanced scorecards. Similarly, in the UK, the balanced scorecard does not seem to be operationalised in the classic form. Rather the process of developing an appropriate scorecard reflects an organisation's specific strategy and culture (Keasey et al. 2000). One study of 54 publicly listed companies in the Netherlands has cast doubt on the effectiveness of the balanced scorecard for controlling business unit performance in larger Dutch corporations (Groot 2001). In France, the **tableau de bord** (effectively a 'dashboard') has been used as a performance measurement and control approach by many enterprises for over five decades (see discussion of the tableau de bord below). A comparative survey of the use of the balanced scorecard by European enterprises showed revealed that familiarity with the approach among German, British, Italian and French firms extended to 98%, 83%, 72% and 41% respectively (Gehrke cited in Norreklit et al. 2001). Possibly there may be socio-economic reasons for this (Mendoza and Zrihen, 1999). The French reaction to the balanced scorecard may be rooted in the nature of the 'French ideology' (Norreklit et al. 2001). These authors have identified important differences between the tableau de bord and the balanced scorecard in terms of underlying strategic concept, focus, deployment and main emphasis as well as distinctive features which identify French and US society (see Exhibit 22.3). Broadly, there is growing evidence that managers place different values on different aspects of management accounting systems including balanced scorecards. While organisational values are an important element in the implementation of balanced scorecards, broader-level factors, including nation-specificity can also influence their nature and use.

Name	France	USA
Performance measurement system	**Tableau de bord**	**Balanced scorecard**
Underlying strategic concept	Managers' subjective perception	External (objective)
Focus	Process of construction (conceptual)	Ready-to-use indicators
Deployment	Open to local initiative	Strictly top-down
Main emphasis	Learning	Rewards
Basic elements of society		
Individualism	Lower	Higher
Hierarchy in society	Omnipresent	No hierarchy
Centralisation	Higher	Lower
Basic social demand	Respect of honour	Respect of contract and fairness
Demand for objectivity	Lower	Higher
Social ascension	Perceived as limited	Perceived as unlimited
Perception of performance-based rewards	Threat	Opportunity
Social control	Self-control	External control
Attitude towards external control	Negative	Positive
Employee dismissal	Almost taboo	Legitimate
Dominating professional culture	Engineer	Manager
Top management	Practically no management education	Extensive management education
Perception regarding manager's qualities	Given by birth	Given by education
Social status of management	Lower	Higher
Belief in management tools	Lower	Higher
Future orientation	Lower	Higher
Political past	Absolutist monarchy and revolution	Contractual agreement
Philosophical tradition	Intellectualism and idealism	Pragmatism
Grammatical structure of language	Clear, with many exceptions	Less clear

Exhibit 22.3 title: The distinctive features of French and American societies and related differences in performance management systems

Source: Adapted from Norreklit et al. (2001).

The tableau de bord

The tableau de bord (TdB) is a management tool bearing similarities to the balanced scorecard which is used by many French enterprises, including Air France, Lafarge, Pechiney, Saint-Gobain and IBM (France) (see Chiapello and Delmond 1994; Epstein and Manzoni 1997; Lebas 1996; Pezet 2009). TdBs are founded on multicriteria models of control that use financial as well as non-financial means to identify and measure objectives, key variables and indicators. French companies use a series of TdBs carved to overlay their organisational structure. Localised responsibilities are assigned and hierarchical lines of authority are respected.

At the apex of the pyramid, the managing director has a TdB detailing overall company objectives and attainments. The managing director's TdB aggregates data from subordinate TdBs such as those of divisional heads, functional heads, geographical heads or product group heads as the case may be. For instance, there might be TdBs for manufacturing, finance and marketing. The manufacturing TdB itself would aggregate those of its departments: production, purchases, receiving and storage. Production in turn would have TdBs for line A, line B and so on down to the nadir of the pyramid. Exhibit 22.4 provides an illustration of a network of tableaux de bord

Exhibit 22.4	Illustration of a network of tableaux de bord nesting one inside the other

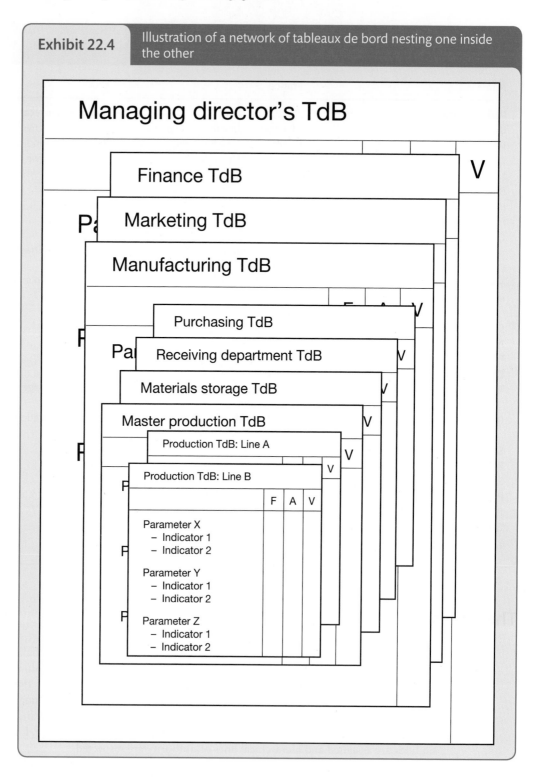

nesting one inside the other. The TdB is 'an ad-hoc tool, completely custom designed for a firm and for every one of its managers' (Chiapello and Lebas 1996). TdBs consist of a range of diverse information. TdBs report forecasts, actual results and variances in the conventional manner, but this information relates to non-financial data as well as financial data. Thus, a TdB might report number of units produced, consumption of different materials, production hours, reject rates, returns and unsold products, in addition to financial information such as contribution margins. Beyond financial and non-financial informational differences, TdBs include externally sourced information and general information on the business environment.

Control systems are based on a vision of activities that they portray. Management accounting control systems are based on a vision that digests various facts, reinterpreting them in a financial perspective. TdBs go beyond measuring values; they attempt to understand processes that create value. The use of TdBs can lead to rapid action. Managers can respond more readily to physical indicators than financial indicators of performance. Sales figures, for instance, are a measure of results of action but not determinant of performance, and physical events occur ahead of financial results. Physical indicators enable future financial results to be anticipated and indicate where action is needed. TdBs provide real-time information to guide an organisation towards the attainment of its objectives.

Enterprise governance and strategy

Well-run companies sometimes fall prey to the demands of financial-performance-driven short-termism. Many recent corporate failures have been the result of laxity in corporate governance whereby problems exist with the structure of boards, their stipulated roles and remuneration issues. The types of mechanisms enterprises have at hand to achieve acceptable corporate governance tend to focus on conformance whereby assurance activities and audits attempt to ensure compliance with what is desirable in terms of corporate and stakeholder welfare.

Some **corporate governance** characteristics which can affect effectiveness in compliance include executive compensation package design, workings and structure of the board of directors, internal control mechanisms and top management style of control and thinking. Bad corporate governance practices can result in the aggressive management of earnings by senior enterprise officers. Many cases of outright fraudulent accounting, such as at Polly Peck, Enron, AIG, Lehman Brothers and Satyam, can result when corporate governance practices are so inadequate as to lead to extremes of distorted behaviour in managing earnings.

But whilst corporate governance practices are important for organisations to put into place, they may simply ensure conformance with stipulated responsibilities rather than enabling the assessment of effective strategic corporate action. At issue is that sound governance within an enterprise does not arise solely from adhering to required corporate governance practices. One perspective taken by CIMA (2007) is that **enterprise governance** constitutes the entire accountability framework of the organisation. Two dimensions of enterprise governance exist: corporate governance and **business governance**. To complement the activities of organisational audit committees which seek to ensure corporate governance, companies also need some means of monitoring corporate performance. Boards of directors should be able to focus on key criteria for success and need some basis for asking appropriate questions to ensure strategic oversight.

To bring together all the important issues relating to an organisation's strategic process, the CIMA/IFAC (2004) report proposes the CIMA-developed **strategic scorecard**. The strategic scorecard 'forces boards to consider where the company is now, what its options are, how it will implement the options it chooses and how it will manage risk' according to the chairman of IFAC's PAIB Committee and chairman of CIMA's Technical Committee (Connell 2004, p. 19).

The strategic scorecard has to be adapted to fit the needs of individual organisations but its four generic dimensions provide pointers to areas of relevance. These are as follows:

- *Strategic position.* An organisation needs to continuously review its strategic position. This should include the micro environment (market, competition, customers); the macro environment (economic, political, regulatory); threats from significant/abrupt changes; business position (pricing, quality, service differentiation, share of market); capabilities (capabilities – strengths/weaknesses/opportunities/threats – issues); and stakeholders (investors, suppliers, employees).

- *Strategic options.* The board needs to understand decision points on change. It must be aware of change of scope (geography, product, industrial sector) and change of direction (high/low growth, price/quality offerings, high/low diversity of products). For each business there may only be three or four strategic options. The board needs to ensure that proper evaluation of these options is (or has been) undertaken and that the perceived resource constraints were sufficiently analysed, and to determine the soundness of process by which decisions of strategic import are/were assessed.

- *Strategic implementation.* Once a project is embarked upon, its progress needs to be tracked. Milestones and timelines have to be developed and monitored. Much as with the traditional planning and control framework, reasons for the achievement of, or failure to meet, targets need to be established and an analysis of implications and consequent actions carried out. Decisions to accelerate, alter, switch or abort strategies should also be assessed.

- *Strategic risk.* The board needs to understand what can go wrong and what must go right. The strategic scorecard might seek to provide assurance on risk encompassing; a review of risks on strategy; probability analyses of key risks; strategic risks embedded in company/ divisional plans and structures; and risk management embedded in major projects and acquisitions.

CIMA itself uses its own strategic scorecard to assist its governing council in the oversight of strategy which it claims 'has been very successful in ensuring greater focus on the major issues' (CIMA 2007).

The strategic management accounting potential

Many organisations formally or informally combine their strategic concerns and priorities with management accounting information in controlling their operational activities and engaging in longer-term decision making. While the term *strategic management accounting* is specific to the extent that it connotes the integration of external with internal financial and non-financial information, it is also used as an umbrella term to include cost management approaches such as life-cycle costing, value-chain analysis, target costing, activity-based management, quality costing and the balanced scorecard among others. Given that these approaches to managing costs have very particular roots where they are found to be present, it should not come as a surprise that SMA is deployed in organisations in ways that are unique.

Diverse notions of SMA exist. Although management accounting techniques such as standard costing, cost–volume–profit analysis, responsibility accounting and activity-based accounting can be accorded quite precise definitions, their deployment and the roles they play within organisations tend to be contextually determined. SMA should likewise not be expected to evidence a level of operational rigour that is standard across systems or organisations since it represents a variety of different management possibilities.

While strategic objectives entail the effective use of cost management systems, likewise, cost changes imply a potential re-addressing of strategic priorities. Cost management cannot be purely cost focused. It must entail an assessment of operational functions, marketing concerns, design constraints, human resource issues and other aspects of organisational activities. This makes cost management an interdisciplinary and multifunctional activity. What is essential is the enablement of organisational insight, learning and adaptation. Organisations implementing innovative costing solutions need to be cognisant that the origins of these approaches may relate to very different local contexts and challenges rather than being generic.

If an organisation seeks to find ways of transforming costs, it must make cost knowledge accessible to different managers who are able to share the language of costs irrespective of their functional training. Effective cost management should stem from an understanding that resource management and utilisation is a complex endeavour. Accounting metrics as well as formal non-financial measures rarely fully grasp the complexities of organisational resource flows. It is therefore inappropriate to indiscriminately seek cost reductions without knowledge of how these resources relate to value creation. Lord (2007, p. 151) thus notes that 'if accountants want to be involved with strategic management accounting they will need to work with other functions, such as marketing and production'.

What is evident from reports of management accounting systems in action and the manner in which they have been designed and implemented, is that they exhibit a high degree of specificity. The transplanting of a seemingly effective and successful management accounting approach from one particular context to another is likely to produce different consequences and effects. This applies both to traditional management accounting techniques and to the newer approaches described in this book. Ultimately, it is the responsibility of the management accounting system's designers and users to ponder over the organisation-wide circumstances and effects influencing the system's potential.

Emerging issues impacting management accounting

The past few years have witnessed significant changes in the environment within which organisations operate. External events can affect enterprises in important ways. The global financial crisis which began in 2008, the rise of social networking and the pursuit of sustainability as a corporate strategy shape the functioning and actions of companies. No organisation today can ignore the impact of external events. Indeed, the labelling of external/internal factors and the notion of organisational boundaries is being questioned in many contexts. The impact of changes has to be made visible to managers to allow them to act on what is perceived. The 'making visible' of transactions and the development of formal systems to allow managerial action has been central to the role of management accountants in organisations for many years. Moreover, management accounting systems have increasingly sought to assist managers to assess trends and to evaluate potential organisational action. It is likely that, in a world of continuous and integrated change, this role will continue to grow. Consider, for instance, a survey of executives from 18 countries which reported that over two-thirds of respondents were seeking to reduce selling, general and administrative overhead expenses over the following 12 to 24 months by 10% (www.Alixpartners.com/pressrelease/821, 16 April 2014). The respondents noted the need to focus on integrated cost reductions entailing organisational design, supplier sourcing and other indirect cost categories. Problematically, many executives feel that their companies are not totally committed to pursuing focused strategies. One study of 501 executives from companies from every continent reported that 42% felt their companies are not aligned behind their strategy and that parts of the organisation do not understand it or support it. These factors are of direct concern to management accounting work. But techniques and strategies in management accounting must also keep pace with changing perceptions by managers of the type of information they require. We highlight below three emerging issues of significance: social media and 'Big Data' implications, environmental management accounting, and how knowledge management practices and intellectual capital factors shape enterprise actions and value creation.

Social media and 'Big Data'

Many organisations have extensively invested in internet technology and resources which promote automation and online networking. But the rising popularity of user-driven online services has led to a group of technological developments referred to as 'Web 2.0' which are affecting organisational activities and corporate pursuits. Services such as Twitter, Wikipedia and YouTube are recent, though extensively deployed developments. Blogs, collective intelligence, P2P networks, Podcasts, RSS feeds, wikis, social networks and mashups continue to change the face of consumerism and business practices.

Consequently, management accounting thinkers and practitioners continue to develop ways of adapting to the pace of enterprise environment changes. For instance, there is recognition that strategic, technological and cost management issues are co-mingled and cannot be assessed as independent considerations in a highly structured and linear manner by managers. Likewise, while activity-based costing arguments have altered how we think of organisational processes drive costs, so internet technologies are enabling many enterprises to establish variable pricing alongside variable costing mechanisms. Quality costing is also being rethought in some organisations where the relationships between voluntary and non-voluntary quality costs are very complex and where quality and service input costs exhibit dynamic interlinkages.

Advances in web-based technologies and telephony combined with the plummeting costs of information production and retrieval and the falling cost of hardware are making easier the input of consumer desires into organisational-design and product-fabrication functions. E-business technologies are enabling customers to be turned into 'product makers'. Whereas firms over the past three decades have become more prone to allowing the customer to dictate prices only recently, has there been a fundamental shift towards allowing them also to design products. Social websites (e.g. facebook.com, linkedin.com, secondlife.com, flickr.com) allow consumers to create the products they consume, but increasingly firms encourage the co-innovation of physical products, where consumers and producers come together as 'prosumers' (Tapscott 2009). In these contexts, management accountants must very carefully engage with other organisational employees to seek new ways of adding value and insight (see Bhimani and Bromwich 2010; Bhimani 2006, 2015).

Digitised communication technologies are beginning to very extensively impact the world of management accounting (Bhimani and Willcocks 2014). Globally produced data doubles about every 18 months, with data volume processed by organisations expanding by 35–50% per year. The proliferation of mobile devices, applications and operating systems is altering how we work, what we work on, where we work and what we work with. Additionally, the physical world itself is becoming a type of information system via the 'Internet of Things' (Chui et al. 2010) where every thing is becoming connected to everyone. New possibilities arise for organisations to alter the speed of their operations, the flexibility of their decision making, their strategic positioning and how they use accounting information to achieve their objectives. Major technologies affecting business firms include mobile technologies, social media, cloud computing and 'Big Data'. The cloud has enabled enterprises to store, access and share resources at lower costs and with much greater ease, economy and flexibility. Most of the data that organisations collect, store, create and manage today is unstructured, and the deployment of this data, which was impossible in the past, now enables companies windows affording new business intelligence, more informed strategies and greater speed of service. The rise of 'Big Data' is thus altering the premise on which accounting information provision is based.

What consumers do which results in economic transactions has always affected what executives want from accounting information systems. But a shift in information design structures is leading enterprises to realise that the information which information systems have traditionally discarded because of the lack of a direct link to economic transactions can be of significant relevance and usefulness as a source of business intelligence for companies (Bhimani 2015). A customer making online searches and collecting product information will leave a trail of information disclosure about choice and information assessment prior to making the purchase. This 'data exhaust', if effectively captured and analysed, can help organisations determine how customers search and arrive at the purchase point and the specific path dependencies of buying decisions. Google.com, for instance, learns from every search process carried out by users and generates greater search value as the magnitude of prior searches grows. Amazon.co.uk gathers information from online customer behaviour irrespective of whether a purchase is made. EBay monitors buyer and seller activities even if no bidding transactions are carried out. Such information at a mass level can allow predictive customised marketing ploys to be mobilised. Data that are non-economic-transaction-related and derived via the analysis of data exhaust offer the potential of developing management accounting intelligence and shaping cost management strategies. The potential for this is extreme and is likely to affect the work of management accountants in the very near future at an increasing pace. Some enterprises are beginning to derive new insights from existing and newly available sources of information in this way (Davenport 2014). Technology, the growing sophistication of analytical methods and the lowered costs of such information processing allow potentially new roles for cost management. More widely sourced information content points to the capacity for using information to alter corporate strategy rather than simply to support it and for effecting restructuring rather than only just promoting alignment with ready existing organisational arrangements. The significance of harnessing such business intelligence is growing apace. Recognising the value of 'Big Data' and developing the ability to apply data analysis techniques is for many companies becoming essential to allow their executives access to empirical information, both structured and unstructured, relating to market trends and customer behaviour and to alter corporate strategy (Bhimani (in press)).

Environmental management accounting

In recent years many organisations have made more public a 'social conscience' even though environmental accounting and management concerns have been the subject of corporate action and extra-organisational stakeholder attention for over three decades. Many techniques and approaches have been advanced over this period to quantify, measure and communicate environmental factors relevant to enterprises in accounting terms. The International Federation of Accountants has issued an International Guidance Document on Environmental Management Accounting to 'be a guidance document that falls into the middle ground between regulatory requirements, standards and pure information . . . its goal is to reduce some of the international confusion on this important topic' (http://www.ifac.org/store). The confusion stems from striking a balance between how much to report, how to report it and how to alter what is reported so that it remains pertinent and informative. Environmental management accounting (EMA) is a complex area with objectives aimed at meeting the specific information needs of a very diverse information base of stakeholders.

Exhibit 22.5 presents the broad social, economic and political forces that interact to create EMA as a strategic, decision-making and accounting approach, which goes beyond the scope achieved by more traditional accounting approaches to considering environmental issues. It shows how non-governmental organisations, the public and governments, spurred by industrial accidents and incidents, interact to force corporate reaction and awareness. Developments in management accounting provide industry with sophisticated tools to respond appropriately. Coupled with these is the rising demand for better financial reporting and disclosure of environmental liabilities and costs, and for information on how these are linked with internal decision processes (see Soonawalla 2006). Also influencing both management accounts and financial reporting, and the corporate world in general, are enhanced corporate governance mechanisms and ethical guidelines. In addition, the emergence of voluntary corporate social responsibility reporting guidelines and management systems, such as the ISO series, permits management to go beyond compliance with government regulations and accounting rules. Finally, advances in the sciences have driven the evolution of eco-efficient production processes, better measurement mechanisms and the use of renewable energy sources. All these together create a setting for EMA to evolve a distinct identity and to function as a compliance, performance and enhancement frame of operation. A key input into EMA is strategic management accounting knowledge, as illustrated in Exhibit 22.5. The concern with the environment more recently has been extended to sustainability. For instance, 'accounting for sustainability' has been the subject of important developments encompassing management accounting systems' metrics-based approaches (see Hopwood et al. 2010).

Knowledge management and intellectual capital

Economies which have shifted from agricultural-based to industrial-based are also seeing an ongoing transformation toward becoming digital economies. Land, labour and capital have been

Exhibit 22.5   A framework for understanding the social, economic, political and scientific forces influencing EMA

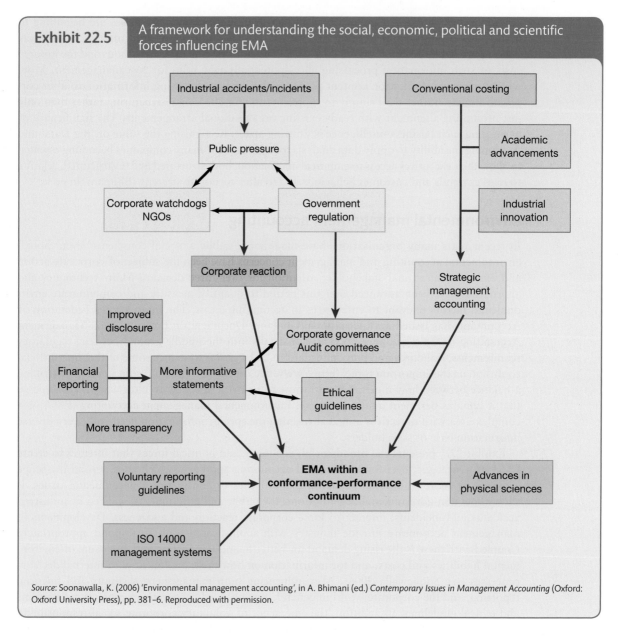

Source: Soonawalla, K. (2006) 'Environmental management accounting', in A. Bhimani (ed.) *Contemporary Issues in Management Accounting* (Oxford: Oxford University Press), pp. 381–6. Reproduced with permission.

regarded as finite and as necessitating capital rationing for organisations in all types of economies. However, management commentators argue that, recently, knowledge and intellectual resources are becoming increasingly important for many organisations. What differentiates these from the traditional factors of production is that, rather than diminishing with usage, these resources grow and can be key drivers of economic value and organisational capability (Bhimani 2015). One approach to theorising about the resources of a firm is to think of it as a locus of technological and organisational knowledge and as integrating informal and tacit, as well as formal and explicit, learning processes (Roberts 2006). The role of management is to create, maintain and change coordination procedures which facilitate the accumulation of knowledge from different localised learning processes. It is argued that management accounting processes can play a key role in the coordination and integration of knowledge (Roberts 2007). To understand how, an intellectual capital model is presented in Exhibit 22.6 which shows how management accounting concepts and procedures can help build collective learning within an enterprise (Roberts 2006).

| Exhibit 22.6 | Categories of intellectual capital and their dynamic relationships |

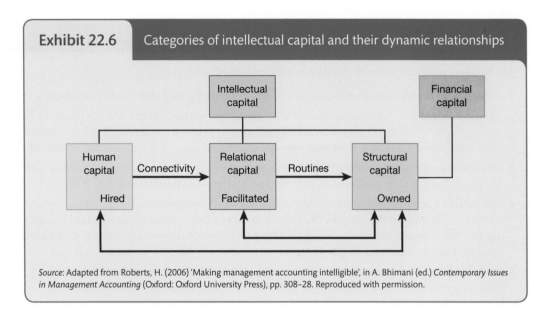

Source: Adapted from Roberts, H. (2006) 'Making management accounting intelligible', in A. Bhimani (ed.) *Contemporary Issues in Management Accounting* (Oxford: Oxford University Press), pp. 308–28. Reproduced with permission.

Intellectual capital is commonly defined as complementary to financial capital, and comprises the accumulated knowledge of a firm, both in dynamic and in static terms (i.e. knowledge flows and knowledge stocks). A common way of analysing intellectual capital is to separate it into the three subcategories of human, relational and structural capital.

Human capital provides the basis of intellectual capital and contains the accumulated knowledge, experience and competences of the firm's employees. Human capital is not limited to the formal education and training of people; it also includes the accumulated work experience of people that is not formally certified by diplomas or degrees. For example, a firm that has a majority of senior employees without formal education can have a higher experience-based human capital than a firm staffed by people with postgraduate degrees. Human capital is not 'owned' by the firm. It is hired or leased and can be accessed by the firm. Typically, human capital is a dominant feature of so-called 'people businesses', and requires appropriate managerial and accounting treatment (Roberts 2006, 2007).

Relational capital encompasses the relational networks between people and groups of people inside and outside the firm. Organisational boundaries matter less than the linkage or connectivity between communities of people. Where human capital addresses the individual human being, relational capital provides the arena for exchange of the knowledge and experience held by human capital while simultaneously providing the arena for sense-making and interpretation. It is in relational capital that the divergent opinions, experiences, formal knowledge and professional insights are combined into new knowledge, either in terms of commercial innovations or in terms of ways of working, organising or administering. It is the 'engine' of intellectual capital and provides the basic source of new revenue streams and innovations. Relational capital cannot be owned or hired by the firm, but only enabled by the appropriate organisational arrangements and systems. The design of management accounting systems can assist in extracting the most value from relational capital.

Structural capital is the only element which an enterprise actually owns as proprietary knowledge, e.g. its management accounting system. It includes elements of proprietary knowledge that are also represented by statutory accounting as its intangible assets, such as intellectual property rights and goodwill. Structural capital remains if capital and labour are stripped away or have gone home after work. Management accounting systems can help interrelationships between the three forms of capital – human, relational and structural. Often, the connectivity between the former two help stage the routines in the latter. It is the interaction between the three which enhances knowledge exchange and value creation.

Summary

The following points are linked to this chapter's learning objectives:

1 Strategy is an elusive concept. Many definitions and notions of strategy exist in the management literature.

2 Two popularised notional strategies that some organisations may be considered to use are product differentiation and cost leadership. Product differentiation refers to offering products and services that are perceived by customers as being superior and unique. Cost leadership refers to the pursuit of low costs relative to those of competitors.

3 Strategic management accounting (SMA) places particular emphasis on blending external with internal organisational information. SMA encompasses both financial and non-financial information.

4 The balanced scorecard seeks to translate an organisation's mission and strategy into a comprehensive set of performance measures that provides the framework for a strategic performance management and measurement system. The scorecard measures performance from four key perspectives: (1) financial, (2) customer, (3) internal business process, and (4) learning and growth.

5 A tableau de bord is a customised multidimensional control system encompassing both financial and non-financial information to identify and measure organisational objectives, key variables and indicators.

6 Enterprise governance is about both corporate governance (conformance) and business governance (performance). The strategic scorecard aims to assist boards of directors achieve effective business governance.

7 Strategic management accounting practices exist in different forms within organisations seeking to use both financial and non-financial information as well as integrating internal with external market-based information. It is also subject to wider contextual influences including nation-specific effects.

8 Strategic management accounting systems may include a wide array of techniques or may be narrowly focused in terms of their cost management priorities. Their implementation and effects within organisations are best considered in visionary and creative rather than in reactive and technical terms. Understanding organisational context is key to the development of an effective SMA potential.

9 A variety of emerging issues has recently made a growing impact on management accounting systems. Social media, 'Big Data', environmental management accounting and knowledge management and intellectual capital value creation practices are discussed.

Key terms

product differentiation (697)
cost leadership (697)
strategic management accounting (SMA) (699)
balanced scorecard (700)
reengineering (701)

tableau de bord (708)
corporate governance (711)
enterprise governance (711)
business governance (711)
strategic scorecard (711)

References and further reading

Ahrens, T. and Chapman, C. (2004) 'Management controls systems and the crafting of strategy: a practice based view', in C.S. Chapman, *Controlling Strategy: Management Accounting and Performance Measurement* (Oxford: Oxford University Press).

Ahrens, T. and Chapman, C. (2006) 'New measures in performance measurement', in A. Bhimani (ed.) *Contemporary Issues in Management Accounting* (Oxford: Oxford University Press (pp. 1–19).

Albertsen, O. and Lueg, R. (2014) 'The balanced scorecard's missing link to compensation: A literature review and an agenda for future research', *Journal of Accounting and Organizational Change*, 10(4), pp. 431–55.

Atkinson, A. and Epstein, M. (2000) 'Measure for measure: realising the power of the balanced scorecard', *CMA Magazine*, September, pp. 23–8.

Ax, C. and Bjornenak, T. (2007) 'Management accounting innovations: origins and diffusion', in T. Hopper, D. Northcott and R. Scapens (eds) *Issues in Management Accounting* (Harlow: FT Prentice Hall).

Bhimani, A. (2006) 'Management accounting and digitisation', in A. Bhimani (ed.) *Contemporary Issues in Management Accounting* (Oxford: Oxford University Press), pp. 69–91.

Bhimani, A. (2015) *Strategic Finance: Achieving High Corporate Performance* (London: Strategy Press).

Bhimani, A. (in press) 'Exploring big data's strategic consequences', *Journal of Information Technology*.

Bhimani, A and Bromwich, M. (2010) *Management Accounting: Retrospect and Prospect* (London: CIMA/Elsevier).

Bhimani, A. and Langfield-Smith, K. (2007) 'The use of financial and non-financial information in strategy development and implementation', *Management Accounting Research*, 18(1), pp. 3–31.

Bhimani, A. and Willcocks, L. (2014) 'Digitisation, "Big Data", and the transformation of accounting', *Accounting and Business Research*, 44(4), pp. 469–90.

Bontis, N., Dragonetti, N.C., Jacobsen, K. and Roos, G. (1999) 'The knowledge toolbox: a review of the tools available to measure and manage intangible resources', *European Management Journal*, 17(4), pp. 391–402.

Chesley, J.A. and Wenger, M.S. (1999) 'Transforming an organisation: using models to foster a strategic conversation', *California Management Review*, 41(3), pp. 54–73.

Chiapello, E. and Delmond, M. (1994) 'Les tableaux de bord de gestion, outil d'introduction du changement', *Revue Française de Gestion*, January/February, pp. 49–58.

Chiapello, E. and Lebas, M. (1996) 'The tableau de bord, a French approach to management information', paper presented at the 19th Annual Congress of the European Accounting Association, Bergen, Norway, 2–4 May.

Chui, M., Loffler, M. and Roberts, R. (2010) 'The Internet of Things', *McKinsey Quarterly*, 20(2), pp. 70–9.

CIMA (2000) *Management Accounting Official Terminology* (London: CIMA).

CIMA (2007) *CIMA Strategy Scorecard: Boards Engaging in Strategy* (London: CIMA).

CIMA/IFAC (2004) *Enterprise Governance: Getting the Balance Right* (New York: IFAC).

Connell, B. (2004) 'Get the balance right', *Accountancy Age*, 19 February, p. 19.

Creelman, J. (2000) 'Culture and the balanced scorecard: is your company practising what it preaches?', *The Balanced Scorecard Report*, July–August, pp. 11–14.

Davenport, T.H. (2014) *Big Data at Work: Dispelling the Myths, Uncovering the Opportunities* (Boston, MA: HBS Press).

Ding, S. and Beaulieu, P. (2011) 'The role of financial incentives in balanced scorecard-based performance evaluations: correcting mood congruency biases', *Journal of Accounting Research*, 49(5), pp. 1223–47.

Downes, L. (2001) 'Strategy can be deadly', *The Industry Standard*, 14 May, pp. 74–5.

England, H. (2001) 'Leaders' activities and their impact on implantation processes: the case of balanced scorecard in the municipality of Nora, Sweden', paper presented at the EAA Conference, Athens, 18–20 April 2001.

Epstein, M. and Manzoni, J. (1997) 'The balanced score card and tableau de bord: translating strategy to action', *Management Accounting* (US), August, pp. 28–36.

Groot, T.L.C.M. (2001) 'Environmental uncertainty, corporate strategy, performance measurement and the creation of economic value', paper presented at the EAA Conference, Athens, 18–20 April.

Guilding, C., Cravens, K.S. and Tayles, M. (2000) 'An international comparison of strategic management accounting practices', *Management Accounting Research*, pp. 113–35.

Hammer, M. and Champy, J. (1993) *Reengineering the Corporation: A Manifesto for Business Revolution* (New York: Harper).

Hopwood, A., Unerman, J. and Fries, J. (2010) *Accounting for Sustainability: Practical Insights* (London: Earthscan).

Hoque, Z. (2014) '20 years of studies on the balanced scorecard: trends, accomplishments, gaps and opportunities for future research', *British Accounting Review*, 46(1), pp. 33–59.

Hoskin, K., Macve, R. and Stone, J. (2006) 'Accounting and strategy: towards understanding the historical genesis of modern business and military strategy', in A. Bhimani (ed.) *Contemporary Issues in Management Accounting* (Oxford: Oxford University Press), pp. 166–97.

Ittner, C.D. and Larker, D.F. (2003) 'Coming up short on non-financial performance measurement', *Harvard Business Review*, November, pp. 46–54.

Kaplan, R.S. and Norton, D.P. (1996a) *The Balanced Scorecard* (Boston: Harvard Business School Press).

Kaplan, R. and Norton, D. (1996b) 'Using the balanced scorecard as a strategic management system', *Harvard Business Review* (January–February).

Kasurinen, T. (2000) 'Exploring management accounting change: the case of balanced scorecard implementation', paper presented at the 23rd Annual Congress of the European Accounting Association, Munich, 29–31 March.

Keasey, K., Aisthorpe, P., Hudson, R., Littler, K. and Vazquez, J. (2000) 'Shareholder and stakeholder approaches to strategic performance measurement using the balanced scorecard', Draft CIMA Research Report.

Kloot, L. and Martin, J. (2000) 'Strategic performance measurement: a balanced approach to performance management issues in local government', *Management Accounting Research*, pp. 169–279.

Langfield-Smith, K. (2006) 'Understanding management control systems and strategy', in A. Bhimani (ed.) *Contemporary Issues in Management Accounting* (Oxford: Oxford University Press) pp. 243–65.

Larker, D.F. (2004) 'Performance measures: insights and challenges', plenary speech made at the LSE Management Accounting Research Group Conference, 25 March.

Lebas, M. (1996) 'Management accounting practice in France', in A. Bhimani (ed.), *Management Accounting: European Perspectives* (Oxford: Oxford University Press), pp. 74–99.

Lord, B.R. (2007) 'Strategic management accounting', in T. Hopper, D. Northcott and R. Scapens (eds) *Issues in Management Accounting* (Harlow: FT Prentice Hall), pp. 135–54.

Malmi, T. (2001) 'Balanced scorecard in Finnish companies: a research note', *Management Accounting Research*, 12, 207–20.

Mendoza, C. and Zrihen, R. (1999) 'Le tableau de bord, une version Américaine?' *Revue Française de Comptabilité*, pp. 60–6.

Mintzberg, H. (1985) 'Of strategies, deliberate and emergent', *Strategic Management Journal*, pp. 257–72.

Mintzberg, H., Ahlstrand, B. and Lampel, J. (1998) *Strategy Safari* (New York: Free Press).

Mitchell, F. and Norreklit, H. (2014) 'Guest Editorial: Contemporary issues on the balanced scorecard', *Journal of Accounting and Organizational Change*, 10(4), pp. 426–9.

Norreklit, H. and Mitchell, F. (2007) 'The balanced scorecard', in T. Hopper, D. Northcott and R. Scapens (eds) *Issues in Management Accounting* (Harlow: FT Prentice Hall) pp. 175–98.

Norreklit, H., Malleret, V. and Bourguignon, A. (2001) 'Tableau de bord and French reaction on the balanced scorecard', paper presented at the EAA Conference, Athens, 18–20 April.

Nyamori, R.O., Perera, M.H.B. and Lawrence, S.R. (2001) 'The concept of strategic change and implications for management accounting research', *Journal of Accounting Literature*, pp. 62–83.

Pezet, A. (2009) 'The history of the French *tableau de bord* (1885–1975): evidence from the archives', *Accounting, Business and Financial History*, 19(2), pp. 103–25.

Porter, M. (1980) *Competitive Strategy* (New York: Free Press).

Porter, M. (1985) *Competitive Advantage* (New York: Free Press).

Porter, M. (1996) 'What is strategy?' *Harvard Business Review*, November–December.

Porter, M. (2001) 'Strategy and the Internet', *Harvard Business Review*, March, pp. 63–98.

Qu, S. and Cooper, D. (2011) 'The role of inscription in producing a balanced scorecard', *Accounting, Organizations and Society*, 36(2), pp. 344–62.

Quinn, B. (1980) *Strategies for Change: Logical Incrementalism* (New York: Irwin).

Roberts, H. (2006) 'Making management accounting intelligible', in A. Bhimani (ed.) *Contemporary Issues in Management Accounting* (Oxford: Oxford University Press), pp. 308–28.

Roberts, H. (2007) 'Knowledge resources and management accounting', in T. Hopper, D. Northcott and R. Scapens (eds) *Issues in Management Accounting* (London: FT/Prentice Hall, 2007), pp. 317–34.

Roberts, R. and Sikes, J. (2010) 'How IT is managing new demands', www.McKinseyQuarterly.com (November).

Roslender, R. and Hart, S.J. (2003) 'In search of strategic management accounting: theoretical and field study perspectives', *Management Accounting Research*, pp. 255–81.

Rousseau, Y. and Rousseau, P. (2000) 'Turning strategy into action in financial services', *CMA Management*, December–January, pp. 25–9.

Shank, J.K. (2006) 'Strategic cost management: upsizing, downsizing and rightsizing', in A. Bhimani (ed.) *Contemporary Issues in Management Accounting* (Oxford: Oxford University Press), pp. 355–79.

Simmonds, K. (1981) 'Strategic management accounting', *Management Accounting* (UK), pp. 26–9.

Simmonds, K., Bonshor, R. and Fisher, L. (1997) *Strategic Management Accounting in Practice* (London: CIMA).

Soonawalla, K. (2006) 'Environmental management accounting', in A. Bhimani (ed.) *Contemporary Issues in Management Accounting* (Oxford: Oxford University Press), pp. 381–406.

Tapscott, D. (2009) *Grown Up Digital* (New York: McGraw-Hill).

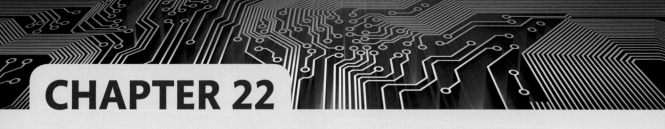

CHAPTER 22

Assessment material

Review questions

22.1 Define strategy.

22.2 Describe two generic strategies.

22.3 What are the four key perspectives in the balanced scorecard?

22.4 What is reengineering?

22.5 Describe three features of a good balanced scorecard.

22.6 What are three important pitfalls to avoid when implementing a balanced scorecard?

22.7 How does an engineered cost differ from a discretionary cost? Are these strategic costs?

22.8 Define SMA.

22.9 Why is SMA practice organisation-specific?

22.10 What affects SMA's potential?

Exercises

Basic level

*22.11 Balanced scorecard (20 minutes)

La Quinta Ltd manufactures corrugated cardboard boxes. It competes and plans to grow by producing high-quality boxes at a low cost that are delivered to customers in a timely manner. There are many other manufacturers who produce similar boxes. La Quinta believes that continuously improving its manufacturing processes and having satisfied employees are critical to implementing its strategy in 2016.

Required

1 Is La Quinta's 2016 strategy one of product differentiation or cost leadership? Explain briefly.

2 Indicate two measures you would expect to see under each perspective in La Quinta's balanced scorecard for 2016. Explain your answer briefly.

22.12 Strategy, balanced scorecard (30 minutes)

Meredith Ltd makes a special-purpose machine D4H used in the textile industry. Meredith has designed the D4H machine for 2015 to be distinct from its competitors. It has been generally regarded as a superior machine. Meredith presents the following data for the years 2014 and 2015.

	2014	2015
1 Units of D4H produced and sold	200	210
2 Selling price	£40 000	£42 000
3 Direct materials (kilograms)	300 000	310 000
4 Direct materials cost per kilogram	£8	£8.50
5 Manufacturing capacity in units of D4H	250	250
6 Total conversion costs	£2 000 000	£2 025 000
7 Conversion costs per unit of capacity	£8 000	£8 100
8 Selling and customer-service capacity	100 customers	95 customers
9 Total selling and customer-service costs	£1 000 000	£940 500
10 Selling and customer-service capacity cost per customer	£10 000	£9 900
11 Design staff	12	12
12 Total design costs	£1 200 000	£1 212 000
13 Design costs per employee	£100 000	£101 000

Meredith produces no defective machines, but it wants to reduce direct materials usage per D4H machine in 2015. Conversion costs in each year depend on production capacity defined in terms of D4H units that can be produced, not the actual units of D4H produced. Selling and customer-service costs depend on the number of customers that Meredith can support, not the actual number of customers Meredith serves. Meredith has 75 customers in 2014 and 80 customers in 2015. At the start of each year, management uses its discretion to determine the number of design staff for the year. The design staff and costs have no direct relationship with the quantity of D4H produced or the number of customers to whom D4H is sold.

Required

1 Is Meredith's strategy one of product differentiation or cost leadership? Explain briefly.

2 Describe briefly key elements that you would include in Meredith's balanced scorecard and the reasons for doing so.

*22.13 **Strategy, balanced scorecard, service company** (30 minutes)

Snyder & Partners is a small information systems consulting firm that specialises in helping companies implement sales management software. The market for Snyder's products is very competitive. To compete, Snyder must deliver quality service at a low cost. Snyder invoices clients in terms of units of work performed, which depends on the size and complexity of the sales management system. Snyder presents the following data for the years 2014 and 2015.

	2014	2015
1 Units of work performed	60	70
2 Selling price	£50 000	£48 000
3 Software implementation labour-hours	30 000	32 000
4 Cost per software implementation labour-hour	£60	£63
5 Software implementation support capacity (in units of work)	90	90
6 Total cost of software implementation support	£360 000	£369 000
7 Software implementation support capacity cost per unit of work	£4 000	£4 100
8 Number of employees doing software development	3	3
9 Total software development costs	£375 000	£390 000
10 Software development costs per employee	£125 000	£130 000

Software implementation labour-hour costs are variable costs. Software implementation support costs for each year depend on the software implementation support capacity (defined in terms of units of work) that Snyder chooses to maintain each year. It does not vary with the actual units of work performed that year. At the start of each year, management uses its discretion to determine the number of software development employees. The software development staff and costs have no direct relationship with the number of units of work performed.

Required

1 Is Snyder's strategy one of product differentiation or cost leadership? Explain briefly.

2 Describe briefly key elements that you would include in Snyder's balanced scorecard and your reasons for doing so.

*22.14 Balanced scorecard (R. Kaplan, adapted) (40 minutes)

Caltex GmbH refines petrol and sells it through its own Caltex petrol stations. On the basis of market research, Caltex determines that 60% of the overall petrol market consists of 'service-oriented customers', medium- to high-income individuals who are willing to pay a higher price for petrol if the petrol stations can provide excellent customer service such as a clean facility, a convenience store, friendly employees, a quick turnround, the ability to pay by credit card, and high-octane premium fuel. The remaining 40% of the overall market are 'price shoppers' who look to buy the cheapest petrol available. Caltex's strategy is to focus on the 60% of service-oriented customers. Caltex's balanced scorecard for the year 2015 is given below. For brevity, the initiatives taken under each objective are omitted.

Objectives	Measures	Target performance	Actual performance
Financial perspective			
Increase shareholder value	Operating profit changes from price recovery	€90 000 000	€95 000 000
	Operating profit changes from growth	€65 000 000	€67 000 000
Customer perspective			
Increase market share	Market share of overall petrol market	10%	9.8%
Internal business process perspective			
Improve petrol quality	Quality index	94 points	95 points
Improve refinery performance	Refinery reliability index (%)	91%	91%
Ensure petrol availability	Product availability index (%)	99%	100%
Learning and growth perspective			
Increase refinery process capability	Percentage of refinery processes with advanced controls	88%	90%

Required

1 Was Caltex successful in implementing its strategy in 2015? Explain your answer.

2 Would you have included some measure of employee satisfaction and employee training in the learning and growth perspective? Are these objectives critical to Caltex for implementing its strategy? Why or why not? Explain briefly.

3 Explain how Caltex did not achieve its target market share in the total petrol market but still exceeded its financial targets. Is 'market share of overall petrol market' the correct measure of market share? Explain briefly.

4 Is there a cause-and-effect linkage between improvements in the measures in the internal business process perspective and the measures in the customer perspective? That is, would you add other measures to the internal business process perspective or the customer perspective? Why or why not? Explain briefly.

5 Do you agree with Caltex's decision not to include measures of changes in operating profit from productivity improvements under the financial perspective of the balanced scorecard? Explain briefly.

Intermediate level

22.15 Balanced scorecard (40 minutes)

Lee SA manufactures various types of colour laser printer in a highly automated facility with high fixed costs. The market for laser printers is competitive. The various colour laser printers on the market are comparable in terms of features and price. Lee believes that satisfying customers with products of high quality at low costs is key to achieving its target profitability. For 2016, Lee plans to achieve higher quality and lower costs by improving yields and reducing defects in its manufacturing operations. Lee will train workers and encourage and empower them to take the necessary actions. Currently, a significant amount of Lee's capacity is used to produce products that are defective and cannot be sold. Lee expects that higher yields will reduce the capacity that Lee needs to use to manufacture products. Lee does not anticipate that improving manufacturing will automatically lead to lower costs because Lee has high fixed costs. To reduce fixed costs per unit, Lee could lay off employees and sell equipment or use the capacity to produce and sell more of its current products or improved models of its current products.

Lee's balanced scorecard for the just-completed financial year 2015 is shown below. For brevity, the initiatives taken under each objective are omitted.

Objectives	Measures	Target performance	Actual performance
Financial perspective			
Increase shareholder value	Operating profit changes from productivity	€1 000 000	€400 000
	Operating profit changes from growth	€1 500 000	€600 000
Customer perspective			
Increase market share	Market share in colour laser printers	5%	4.6%
Internal business process perspective			
Improve manufacturing quality	Yield	82%	85%
Reduce delivery time to customers	Order delivery time	25 days	22 days
Learning and growth perspective			
Develop process skills	Percentage of employees trained in process and quality management	90%	92%
Enhance information system capabilities	Percentage of manufacturing processes with real-time feedback	85%	87%

Required

1 Was Lee successful in implementing its strategy in 2015? Explain.

2 Is Lee's balanced scorecard useful in helping Lee understand why it did not reach its target market share in 2015? If it is, explain why. If it is not, explain what other measures you might want to add under the customer perspective and why.

3 Would you have included some measure of employee satisfaction in the learning and growth perspective and new product development in the internal business process perspective? That is, do you think employee satisfaction and development of new products are critical to Lee for implementing its strategy? Why or why not? Explain briefly.

4 What problems, if any, do you see in Lee's improving quality and significantly downsizing to eliminate unused capacity?

22.16 **Balanced scorecard, ethics** (40 minutes)

John Emburey, division manager of the Household Products Division, a maker of kitchen dishwashers, has just seen the balanced scorecard for his division for 2015. He immediately calls Patricia Conley, the management accountant for the division into his office for a meeting. 'I think the employee satisfaction and customer satisfaction numbers are way too low. These numbers are based on a random sample of subjective assessments made by individual managers and customer representatives. My own experience indicates that we are doing well on both these dimensions. Until we do a formal survey of employees and customers sometime next year, I think we are doing a disservice to ourselves and this company by reporting such low scores for employee and customer satisfaction. These scores will be an embarrassment for us at the division managers' meeting next month. We need to get these numbers up.'

Patricia knows that the employee and customer satisfaction scores are subjective, but the procedure she used is identical to the procedures she has used in the past. She knows from the comments she had asked for that the scores represent the unhappiness of employees with the latest work rules and the unhappiness of customers with missed delivery dates. She also knows that these problems will be corrected in time.

Required

1 Do you think that the Household Products Division should include subjective measures of employee satisfaction and customer satisfaction in its balanced scorecard? Explain.

2 What should Patricia do?

Advanced level

22.17 **Downsizing** (CMA, adapted) (60 minutes)

Mayfair Limited currently subsidises cafeteria services for its 200 employees. Mayfair is in the process of reviewing the cafeteria services as cost-cutting measures are needed throughout the organisation to keep the prices of its products competitive. Two alternatives are being evaluated: downsize the cafeteria staff and offer a reduced menu or contract with an outside supplier.

The current cafeteria operation has four employees with a combined base annual salary of €110 000 plus additional employee benefits at 25% of salary. The cafeteria operates 250 days each year, and the costs for utilities and equipment maintenance average €30 000 annually. The daily sales include 100 starters at €4.00 each, 80 sandwiches or salads at an average price of €3.00 each, plus an additional €200 for beverages and desserts. The cost of all cafeteria supplies is 60% of revenues.

The plan for downsizing the current operation envisions retaining two of the current employees whose combined base annual salaries total €65 000. A starter menu would no longer be offered, and prices of the remaining items would be increased slightly. Under this arrangement, Mayfair expects daily sales of 150 sandwiches or salads at a higher average price of €3.60. The additional revenue for beverages and desserts is expected to increase to €230 each day. Because of the elimination of the starter, the cost of all cafeteria supplies is expected to decline to 50% of revenues. All other conditions of operation would remain the same. Mayfair is willing to continue to subsidise this reduced operation but will not spend more than 20% of the current subsidy.

A proposal has been received from Wilco Foods, an outside supplier who is willing to supply cafeteria services. Wilco has proposed to pay Mayfair €1000 per month for use of the cafeteria and utilities. Mayfair would be expected to cover equipment repair costs. In addition, Wilco would pay Mayfair 4% of all revenues received above the breakeven point. This payment would be made at the end of the year. All other costs incurred by Wilco to supply the cafeteria services are variable and equal 75% of revenues. Wilco plans to charge €5.00 for a starter course, and the average price for the sandwich or salad would be €4.00. All other daily sales are expected to average €300. Wilco expects daily sales of 66 starters and 94 sandwiches or salads.

Required

1 Determine whether the plan for downsizing the current cafeteria operation would be acceptable to Mayfair Limited. Show your calculations.

2 Is the Wilco Foods proposal more advantageous to Mayfair Limited than the downsizing plan? Show your calculations.

22.18 **Question from the Chartered Institute of Management Accountants, Intermediate Level, Management Accounting – Performance Management, November 2003** (45 minutes)

E plc provides a computer upgrading, servicing and repair facility to a variety of business and personal computer users.

The management team has managed the business to date by using a standard costing and budgetary control system. However, the team has recently been discussing the possible use of alternative performance measurement systems, such as the 'balanced scorecard'.

Another issue which concerns the management of E plc is the quality of the service provided for clients. The operations manager has suggested that the company should introduce total quality management (TQM) but the management team is unsure how to do this and of the likely costs and benefits of its introduction.

Required

1 Explain the concept of the balanced scorecard and how it may be used by E plc to improve performance measurement.   (10 marks)

2 **a** Briefly explain total quality management in the context of E plc.   (3 marks)
  b Discuss the likely costs and benefits that would arise if E plc introduced a TQM policy.

(12 marks)
(Total marks = 25)

PART V
Case study problems

High-Tech Limited
Jenice Prather-Kinsey, University of Missouri-Columbia

This case demonstrates the importance of strategy and cost allocation in the IT manufacturing environment. The case requires the development of a relevant balanced scorecard for the business together with the construction of an appropriate ABC model.

Background

High-Tech (H-T) is a computer manufacturer founded in Yorkshire, England, in 1901. H-T originated as a commercial scale, cheese and meat slicing, punch card, tabulating and time recording conglomerate. The company began with 1300 employees and with sales in England, Scotland and Wales. The company had a difficult time managing its diversified products in numerous locations. H-T undertook several strategies to overcome its faltering operations. First, H-T increased sales by implementing healthy sales incentives, grooming its salesmen in dark suits, promoting company pride and loyalty in its employees and beefing up customer services. Second, H-T focused on selling tabulating machines, and expanded sales to the USA, Asia, Australia and South America.

These strategies helped H-T overcome its sinking operations. While other companies were folding during the Great Depression, H-T continued to grow and began providing employee benefits such as life insurance and paid vacations. Just-in-time inventory control would not have been useful to H-T during the Depression. Because H-T had large inventories on hand, it was able to undertake large government contracts during the 1930s. H-T had become so large in the computer industry that it was constantly being sued, but unsuccessfully, for monopoly violations. During World War II, H-T continued to grow through government contracts. H-T used some of its profits to finance orphans and widows of war casualties. This goodwill act helped to foster employee loyalty and demonstrated good community citizenship.

Technological development escalated beginning in the 1950s. H-T first developed a 5-ton 50-foot by 8-foot calculator. This calculator was replaced with vacuum tubes and later with a mainframe transistor that was faster and smaller than the vacuum tube. By 1957, H-T had a spinning disk storage system that could assess and process accounting data on as many as 50 disks and introduced the FORTRAN computer language. H-T was so large that it supplied 90% of Europe's computers, had £80 billion in sales and 270 000 employees. Between 1970 and 1980, H-T became the leading manufacturer of mainframe computers, hardware, software and

Source: Adapted from Prather-Kinsey, J. (2001) 'High-Tech Limited', *Cases from Management Accounting Practice*, Volume 16 (Montvale, New Jersey: Institute of Management Accounting Practice).

services. By the 1980s, H-T was manufacturing floppy disks, bank automatic teller machines, and PCs for small businesses, schools and home use.

H-T now has manufacturing plants located in Yorkshire, England, and Essonnes, France. In Yorkshire, H-T manufactures low-end servers and personal computer systems while in Essonnes it manufactures logic and memory chips. H-T is now vertically integrated and produces, services and sells products exclusively in the computer industry. More recently, H-T has experienced a downturn in earnings resulting from a very competitive computer industry.

Systems information

H-T's corporate strategy is to get **multi-year cooperative agreements with SAP adopters to increase H-T's share of the computer hardware market.** H-T uses a normal costing system where manufacturing overhead is applied and estimated annually and quarterly and all other costs are recorded at actual using a stand-alone weighted-average accounting information and inventory system. Stand-alone implies that the cost accounting system is not integrated with financial accounting, finance or logistics ledgers. They hope to install SAP, an electronic resource planning system, but that has not happened yet. Because cost accounting is stand-alone, at the end of each quarter considerable accounting effort is spent integrating cost data with financial accounting and logistics data. Each production location (Yorkshire and Essonnes) is managed separately and within each location there is decentralisation of functions. The cost accountants focus solely on budgeting, recording and analysing costs (Exhibits 501.1 and 501.2).

Exhibit 501.1	High-Tech Corporation: Income statement at 31 December (£ millions except per-share amounts)	
	2011	**2010**
Revenues:		
Hardware sales	36 500	35 700
Services revenues	15 000	12 000
Software sales	13 000	13 000
Maintenance revenues	7 000	7 000
Rentals and financing income	1 600	1 500
Total revenues	73 100	69 200
Cost of sales:		
Hardware sales	24 000	22 000
Services expenses	12 000	10 000
Software expenses	4 000	4 400
Maintenance expenses	3 600	3 600
Rentals and financing expenses	1 600	1 500
Total cost of sales	45 200	41 500
Gross profit	27 900	27 700
Selling expense	15 000	15 200
R & D expense	4 000	4 000
Operating Income	8 900	8 500
Other income	9 000	8 000
Other expenses	710	720
Earnings before income taxes	17 190	15 780
Income tax expense	3 100	3 600
Net income	14 090	12 180
Dividends paid	22	60
Net income to common stockholders	14 068	12 120

| Exhibit 501.2 | High-Tech Corporation: Balance sheet at 31 December (£ millions except per-share amounts) |

	2011	2010		2011	2010
Assets			*Liabilities*		
Current assets:			**Current liabilities:**		
Cash and cash equivalents	7 680	7 260	Taxes payable	3 000	2 600
Marketable securities	500	450	Short-term payables	13 000	11 500
Notes and accounts receivable	16 500	16 400	Accounts payable	5 000	4 500
Sales lease receivables	5 700	6 000	Compensation and benefits	3 000	3 000
Other receivables	900	1 000	Deferred income	3 700	3 500
Inventories	6 000	6 000	Other liabilities	6 600	6 500
Prepaid expenses	3 500	3 200	Total current liabilities	34 300	31 600
Total current assets	40 780	40 310			
			Long-term liabilities	10 000	10 000
Property, plant and equipment	41 200	44 000	Other debt	14 000	14 300
Less: Accumulated depreciation	-25 000	-27 000	Deferred income taxes payable	1 600	1 800
Net property, plant and equipment	16 200	17 000	Total liabilities	59 900	57 700
Software – net	2 000	2 500	Stockholders' equity		
Investments and miscellaneous acct	22 500	20 600	Preferred stock	353	353
			Common stock	8 500	8 400
Total assets	81 480	80 410	Retained earnings	10 327	10 657
			Translation adjustment	2 400	3 300
			Total stockholders' equity	21 580	22 710
			Total liabilities and stockholders' equity	81 480	80 410

Yorkshire, England

The product development cycle for low-end servers and personal computer systems is three months. This means that faster and cheaper computers are developed at least three to four times a year. The computer industry experiences a 2–3% decline in raw material costs and selling prices each quarter. Therefore, product costs are changing constantly. While head count is high at Yorkshire, this cost is stable and represents only about 5% of product cost. Seventy per cent of product cost is materials and 25% is manufacturing overhead. Traditionally, for manufacturing overhead in production, direct labour £s have been the allocation base.

Yorkshire tries to trace most of its costs directly to the product. Labour and materials are traced directly to the product through bar codes. Each material input component is bar-coded and traced directly to the unit to which it is attached. As materials move through assembly, assemblers indicate which unit of output they are assembling through bar codes. For each product produced, a diskette includes the serial number assigned to the finished server, the assembler ID number and the identification number of parts used to make the server.

Since the market fixes the price of labour and materials, H-T hopes to increase profit margins by reducing manufacturing overhead costs. H-T believes that it can reduce costs by reducing throughput time. Throughput is defined as follows:

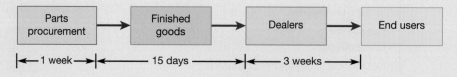

H-T's strongest competitors reduce throughput time by eliminating the dealer. Their competitors sell directly to the final or end customer. However, the dealers provide a level of immediate service to end customers at the end customer's location that is not provided by its competitors. Competitors' customers have to call an 0800 (freephone) number and sometimes wait 30 minutes on the phone before a technician can answer their question. Many customers who have software installation problems must see a computer specialist at their own cost, or for other problems they may have to return their equipment to the vendor and wait 2–3 weeks before the computer is replaced or repaired. Therefore, H-T must weigh the benefits of selling through dealers to its end customers against reducing throughput time by eliminating dealers.

Lead time from dealer order to receipt of goods by the dealer is usually 3–4 weeks. Dealers generally hold five-week inventory levels to avoid stockout costs and to compensate for goods that may be damaged during shipment. If not sold immediately, dealers have unsold obsolete inventory on hand. In the past, H-T has provided rebates to dealers for obsolete inventory. This way, dealers can offer obsolete inventory at discounted prices to their customers. H-T is concerned that this policy sends the wrong message to dealers. That is, if dealers do not move their inventory fast, the dealer does not lose because H-T will discount the merchandise. Therefore, dealers are not motivated to buy from H-T in small quantities or to sell their inventories quickly. H-T wants dealers to more accurately estimate their sales so that they do not end up with large quantities of obsolete inventory on hand. H-T's competitors not only reduce dealer costs by not having dealers, but also reduce costs related to storing outdated inventory at the dealer's location.

H-T records procurement parts costs when invoiced. So if it invoices a purchase in March, it uses February costs because March costs are not known at the time of invoicing. At the end of March, when H-T knows the actual cost of March purchases, it records the under- or overapplied materials/parts cost as the difference between actual and recorded parts cost.

Variances are investigated at the top end of the organisation, outside of the cost accounting department. Some variance is tolerated/expected due to the rapidly decreasing parts cost in the computer industry. Similarly, when dealers are billed for computers purchased, they are billed at the previous month's price and the invoice price is adjusted the following month to reflect the actual selling price. That is, H-T does not know the cost of producing the computers and therefore the selling price of the computers until a month later when their vendors invoice raw materials. This is when H-T knows the actual cost of parts procurement. Sizing or the comparison of ledger to physical inventory is done annually.

Shipment of almost all of H-T's products (servers, PCs and mainframes) is out of Yorkshire. In addition to the production area, Yorkshire has 450 000 square feet of warehousing space. Inventory is in the warehouse for an average of 10–15 days before shipping. H-T uses activity-based costing (ABC) to allocate annual warehousing and shipping costs to each product as follows (in £ millions):

Cost driver

Activities	Indirect head count (£)	Square foot floor space (£)	Hours scanning outbound freight (£)	Hours information systems (£)
Receiving (from mfg)	50			15.5
Shipping parts to shipping lane	120			12.0
Storage		700.5		10.5
Transportation out	185		30	10.0

Annual allocation of expenses to products is then conducted as follows:

	Desktop	Server	Monitor	Laptops	Options
Receiving					
Head count	1000	500	600	1200	400
Info. systems (hours)	600	120	100	800	60
Shipping parts to lane					
Head count	800	100	100	800	20
Info. systems (hours)	80	10	60	80	15
Storage					
Floor space	1000	2000	600	800	400
Info. systems (hours)	100	100	100	100	100
Trans-out					
Head count	70	120	50	80	20
Info. systems (hours)	20	15	10	20	5
Scanning hours	10	5	5	10	2

For some parts, transportation-out is the highest cost (servers). For example, servers have high transportation-out costs because they are heavy. For other products, order filling is the highest cost (desktops). For example, desktops absorb high order-filling costs because desktops are composed of multiple individual parts. The desktops may have 10–15 pieces to a box so it takes more time to fill a desktop order than a server order, which is composed of one or two parts.

Essonnes, France

In Essonnes, France, H-T manufactures logic and memory chips from a silicon wafer. The silicon wafers are sliced from a silicon cylinder. The silicon cylinders are £400 each. Each working day H-T manufactures approximately 1200 wafers.

In Essonnes, production takes place 24 hours a day, 7 days a week and 52 weeks a year. The only days off are 1 May because the French law of 1936 requires it and 25 December. However, accounting executives' working hours are generally 8.30 a.m. to 6.00 p.m., five days a week.

H-T purchases silicon cylinders for £400 each. Approximately 125 wafers can be sliced from each cylinder. During slicing, there is a loss of 20% of the silicon cylinder. It has quality assurance contracts with its vendors to assure the quality and on-time delivery of its production parts (silicon cylinders). After an order is received, H-T slices the silicon cylinders into wafers.

From each wafer H-T can usually get a total of 100 logic chips and 400 memory chips of which 5% of the good output is loss. The loss is detected at the end of production. To minimise costs, H-T is currently focusing on increasing the yield from each cylinder and wafer.

After end-of-line, the chips go to production control where they are distributed to their internal customers at a transfer price of 10% above total production cost. H-T spends considerable effort in developing and implementing its budget. H-T prepares five-year strategic plans from which flow yearly budgets and quarterly budgets. The annual budgets begin with actual data that is negotiated with production managers to produce annual and quarterly budgets. Budgeting involves a cross-functional team to ensure optimal corporate goal congruence (as opposed to unit-focused goals that may be suboptimal to the corporation as a whole). Senior management has weekly technical meetings with production regarding yield, lead time, and quality of shipped output. Each quarter (three months), H-T compares actual with monthly budgets. Usage of the service department centres during 2011 follows.

2011 JOINT PROCESSING COST CENTRE
H-T's actual usage for the year

Suppliers	Information systems (computer-hours)	Utilities (square km)	Maintenance (labour-hours)	Quality assurance (no. people on prod. line)
Users of joint processing service departments				
Utilities	500		70 000	100
Maintenance	1200	1000	60 000	100
Memory chip	500	2000	12 000	500
Logic chip	500	1000	60 000	800

The budgeted charge-out rate for information systems is £10 000 per hour, for utilities is £20 000 per square kilometre, for maintenance is £80 per labour-hour and for quality assurance is £52 000 per person. Information systems include the salaries of personnel, accounting and budgeting costs and costs associated with the mainframe central processing unit. Utilities include building repairs, electricity, water, fuel, property taxes and building depreciation. Maintenance involves servicing the machinery used in production and computers and mainframe systems used throughout H-T.

Quality assurance represents those personnel who measure quality and who conduct surveys on supplier, employee and customer satisfaction. Full absorption costing is used to determine product costs. (For the French definition of full absorption costing, see Bescos and Mendoza (1995).)

H-T wants to assign costs so that managers maximise the quality of output and reduce the percentage of spoiled chips from each cylinder and wafer (yield). Currently H-T uses a traditional normal costing system and allocates all processing costs to the good chips only. H-T also wants a cost system that accurately allocates overhead costs to chips.

To monitor quality, H-T continuously queries its suppliers, employees and customers. Employee satisfaction is important because it believes the more satisfied the employee, the more likely the employee will seek to achieve quality output efficiently. In France, the employees are very concerned about job stability as a result of the downsizing that has taken place. H-T has reduced the number of buildings occupied by 60%, the number of employees by 40% and has increased production 100% over the past five years as a result of increased technology in its production facilities. Thus, employees are working harder to achieve corporate goals in a competitive environment. Customer surveys include questions about on-time delivery. H-T strives to have a 98–99% on-time delivery rate.

Questions

Implementing and monitoring strategy

H-T is in the process of designing a balanced scorecard for the company overall and a tableau de bord for its plant in Yorkshire. Management's overall corporate goal is to get **multi-year cooperative agreements with SAP adopters to increase H-T's share of the computer hardware market**.

1 Develop a value chain for H-T Corporation and for its operations in Yorkshire. Your value-chain models should be illustrated similar to your textbook. Explain functions in the value chain with examples. For instance, define in your own words, research and development costs (R&D) and indicate what projects might be undertaken in R&D. Just because you have the R&D element in the corporate value chain does not imply that you have an R&D element in the Yorkshire value

chain. Therefore, the corporate value chain may look different from or similar to Yorkshire's value chain. You must explain why the chains are similar or dissimilar between the corporate office and the Yorkshire plant site.

2   A balanced scorecard is usually used to depict corporate strategy. A tableau de bord is a reflection of the balanced scorecard but represents a division's responsibility in achieving corporate strategy. For example, a balanced scorecard includes a 5% increase in operating profits as one of its goals. However, a cost centre will usually focus on the cost element of operating profit. Therefore the cost centre's tableau de bord will have cost goals rather than revenue or profit goals. Develop a balanced scorecard for H-T Corporation similar to that of Kaplan and Norton, but be creative in developing your illustration. You must provide objective measures for each of the four perspectives of the balanced scorecard. Explain how your balanced scorecard monitors how well the corporation is meeting its objective(s).

3   Develop a tableau de bord for H-T's operations in Yorkshire. The tableau de bord should be consistent with the corporate balanced scorecard goals. You should contrast the difference of Kaplan's balanced scorecard as you illustrated in question 2 above with the tableau de bord for Yorkshire.

4   Prior to the summary of your paper, you should recommend whether H-T should use the balanced scorecard only or the tableau de bord for Yorkshire as well as the balanced scorecard for corporate headquarters.

Are standard and activity-based costing appropriate for H-T?

H-T is contemplating using activity-based costing (ABC). Answer the following questions about the Yorkshire location.

5   Would you recommend that H-T consider using activity-based-costing throughout the Yorkshire plant site? (H-T is currently using ABC in the warehousing area only.)

6   What costing system is H-T using in the production area: actual, normal or standard? What costing system would you recommend that H-T use and why?

7   Develop a model for H-T to use if it considers adopting ABC at the Yorkshire plant's production department. Your model should include identification of activities and cost drivers for which standards should be developed. To defend the cost drivers used, relate them to the tableau de bord and corporate strategy targets that you developed in the assignment 'Implementing and Monitoring Strategy'.

Allocating costs in a multicultural company

Answer the following questions about the Essonnes plant site.

8   Recommend a method that H-T should use in allocating its joint production costs. Explain how this method would be useful in monitoring company strategy.

9   Use your recommended joint cost allocation method to allocate joint production costs. Provide an illustration of the computations used to allocate joint production costs.

10 What method did you use to allocate service department costs to the production departments? Explain why you recommend your selected service department cost allocation method.

11 How much will H-T charge its internal customers (transfer price) for

a   Memory chips

b   Logic chips?

12 H-T is hesitant about implementing standard costing because the manufacturing system is very complicated and because many products share the same manufacturing machines and/or assembly production lines. Assuming that H-T uses normal costing and is considering ABC and standard costing, explain personnel issues.

Case 502

Empire Glass Company (A)

Peter Small of the Harvard Business School undertook to write case material on the budgetary control system of the Empire Glass Company, a manufacturing company with a number of plants located throughout Canada. In particular, Peter Small was interested in how James Walker, the corporate controller, saw the company's budgetary control system. Therefore, Small focused his research on the budgetary control system in relationship to the company's Glass Products Division. This division was responsible for manufacturing and selling glass food–and–beverage bottles.

Organisation

Empire Glass Company was a diversified company organised into several major product divisions, one of which was the Glass Products Division. Each division was headed by a vice president who reported directly to the company's executive vice president, Landon McGregor. (Exhibit 502.1 shows an organisation chart of the company's top management group.) All of the corporate and divisional management groups were located in British City, Canada.

McGregor's corporate staff included three people in the financial area – the controller, the chief accountant, and the treasurer. The controller's department consisted of only two people – Walker and the assistant controller, Allen Newell. The market research and labour relations departments also reported in a staff capacity to McGregor.

All of the product divisions were organised along similar lines. Reporting to each product division vice president were several staff members in the customer service and product research areas. Reporting in a line capacity to each divisional vice president were also a general manager of manufacturing (responsible for all of the division's manufacturing activities) and a general manager of marketing (responsible for all of the division's marketing activities). Both of these executives were assisted by a small staff of specialists. Exhibit 502.2 presents an organisation chart of the Glass Products Division's top management group. Exhibit 502.3 shows the typical organisation structure of a plant within the Glass Products Division.

Products and technology

The Glass Products Division operated a number of plants in Canada, producing glass food-and-beverage bottles. Of these products, food jars constituted the largest group. Milk bottles, as well as beer and soft drink bottles, were also produced in large quantities. A great variety of shapes and sizes of containers for wines, liquors, drugs, cosmetics, and chemicals were produced in smaller quantities.

Most of the thousands of different products, varying in size, shape, colour, and decoration were produced to order. According to British City executives, the typical lead time between the customer's order and shipment from the plant was between two and three weeks.

Source: Professor David F. Hawkins prepared this case. HBS cases are developed solely as the basis for class discussion. Cases are not intended to serve as endorsements, sources of primary data, or illustrations of effective or ineffective management.

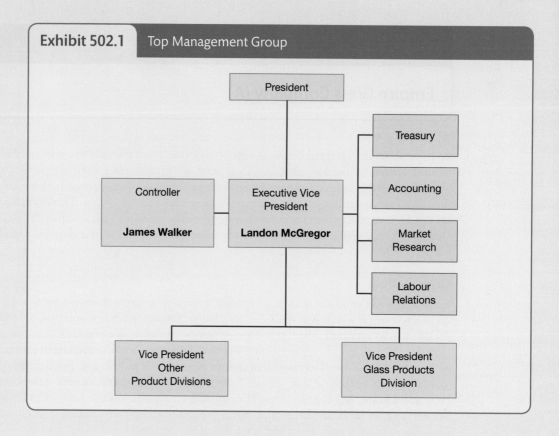

Exhibit 502.1 Top Management Group

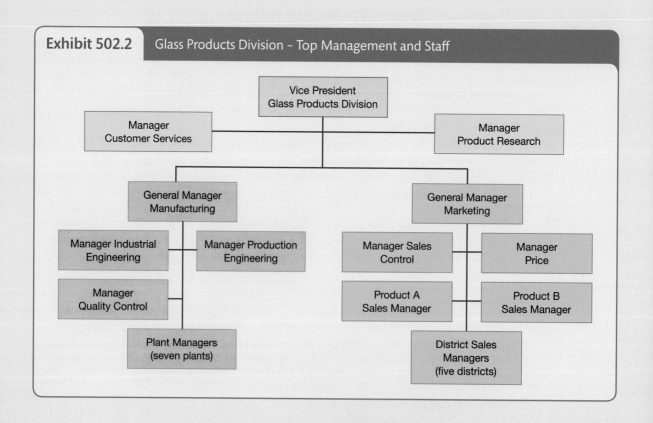

Exhibit 502.2 Glass Products Division – Top Management and Staff

Exhibit 502.3 Glass Product Division – Typical Plant Organisation

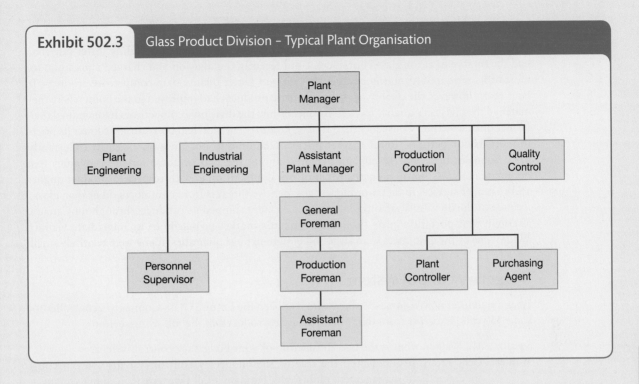

The principal raw materials for container glass were sand, soda ash, and lime. The first step in the manufacturing process was to melt batches of these materials in furnaces or tanks. The molten mass was then passed into automatic or semiautomatic machines which filled moulds with the molten glass and blew the glass into the desired shape. The 'ware' then went through an automatic annealing oven or lehr where it was cooled slowly under carefully controlled conditions. If the glass was to be coated on the exterior to increase its resistance to abrasion and scratches, this coating – often a silicone film – was applied in the lehr. Any decorating (such as a trademark or other design) was then added, the product inspected again, and the finished goods packed in corrugated containers (or wooden cases for some bottles).

Quality inspection was critical in the manufacturing process. If the melt in the furnace was not completely free from bubbles and stones (unmelted ingredients or pieces of refractory material), or if the fabricating machinery was slightly out of adjustment, or moulds were worn, the rejection rate was very high. Although a number of machines were used in the inspection process, including electric eyes, much of the inspection was still done visually.

While glass making was one of the oldest arts, and bottles and jars had been machine-moulded at relatively high speeds for over half a century, the Glass Products Division had spent substantial sums each year modernizing its equipment. These improvements had greatly increased the speed of operations and had reduced substantially the visual inspection and manual handling of glassware.

No hand blowing was done in the division's plants; contrary to the early days of the industry, most of the jobs were relatively unskilled, highly repetitive, and gave the worker little control over work methods or pace. The mould makers who made and repaired the moulds, the machine repairers, and those who made the equipment-setup changes between different products were considered to be the highest-skilled classes of workers.

Wages were relatively high in the glass industry. The rumble of the machinery and the hiss of compressed air in the moulding operation, however, plus the roar of fuel in the furnaces, made the plants extremely noisy. The great amount of heat given off by the furnaces and molten glass also made working conditions difficult. Production employees belonged to two national unions, and for many years bargaining had been conducted on a national basis. Output standards were established for all jobs, but no bonus was paid to hourly plant workers for exceeding standard.

Marketing

Over the years, the sales of the Glass Products Division had grown at a slightly faster rate than had the total market for glass containers. Until recently, the division had charged a premium for most of its products, primarily because they were of better quality than competitive products. In later years, however, the quality of the competitive products had improved to the point where they matched the division's quality level. In the meantime, the division's competitors had retained their former price structure. Consequently, the Glass Products Division had been forced to lower its prices to meet its competitors' lower market prices. According to one division executive: 'Currently, price competition is not severe, particularly among the two or three larger companies that dominate the glass bottle industry. Most of our competition is with respect to product quality and customer service. In fact, our biggest competitive threat is from containers other than glass.'

Each of the division's various plants to some extent shipped its products throughout Canada, although transportation costs limited each plant's market primarily to its immediate vicinity. While some of the customers were large and bought in huge quantities, many were relatively small.

Budgetary control system

Peter Small interviewed James Walker, who had been the Empire Glass Company's controller for some 15 years. Excerpts from that interview are reproduced in the following sections.

Small: Mr. Walker, what is the overall function of your budgetary control system?

Walker: Well, Peter, to understand the role of the budgetary control systems you must first understand our management philosophy. Fundamentally, we have a divisional organisation based on broad product categories. These divisional activities are coordinated by the company's executive vice president, with the head office group providing a policy and review function for the company's executive vice president.

Within the broad policy limits, we operate on a decentralized basis, with each of the decentralised divisions performing the full management job which normally would be inherent in any independent company. The only exceptions to this philosophy is that the head office group is solely responsible for the sources of funds and the labour relations with those bargaining units which cross division lines.

Given this form of organisation, the budget is the principal management tool used by head office to coordinate the efforts of the various segments of the company toward a common goal. Certainly, in our case, the budget is much more than a narrow statistical accounting device.

Sales budget

Walker and Small discussed the preparation of the sales budget. This was the first step in the budget preparation procedure.

Walker: As early as May 15 of the year preceding the budget year, the top management of the company asks the various product division vice presidents to submit preliminary reports stating what they think their division's capital requirements and outlook in terms of sales and income will be during the next budget year. In addition, corporate top management also wants an expression of the division vice president's general feelings toward the trends in the particular items over the two years following the upcoming budget year. At this stage, head office is not interested in too much detail.

Small: Does the market research group get involved in these forecasts?

Walker: No. What we want is an interpretive statement about sales and income based on the operating executives' practical feel for the market. Since all divisions plan their capital requirements five years in advance and have made predictions of the forthcoming budget year's market when the budget estimates were prepared last year, these rough estimates of next year's conditions and requirements are far from wild guesses.

After the opinions of the divisional vice presidents are in, the market research staff go to work. They develop a formal statement of the marketing climate in detail for the forthcoming budget year and in general terms for the subsequent two years.

Small: Putting together the sales forecast, then, is the first step in developing the budget?

Walker: Yes. This is an important first step since practically all of the forecasts or estimates used in planning either start with or depend in some way on a sales forecast.

The market research group begins by projecting such factors as the general economic condition; growth of our various markets; weather conditions related to the end uses of our products; competitive effort; and labour disturbances.

Once these general factors have been assessed, a sales forecast for the company and each division is developed. Consideration is given to the relationship of the general economic climate to our customers' needs and Empire's share of each market. Also, basic assumptions as to price, weather conditions, and so forth, are developed and stated explicitly.

In sales forecasting, consideration is given also to the introduction of new products, gains or losses in particular accounts, forward buying, new manufacturing plants, and any changes in our definition of, say, gross sales.

The probable impact of such information as the following is also taken into account: industry growth trends, packaging trends, inventory carry-overs, and the development of alternative packages to or from glass.

This review of all the relevant factors is followed for each of our product lines, regardless of its size and importance. The completed forecasts of the market research group are then forwarded to the appropriate divisions for review, criticism, and adjustments.

Small: How would you summarise the role of the head office group in developing these sales forecasts?

Walker: Well, I suppose our primary goal is to assure uniformity between the divisions with respect to the basic assumptions on business conditions, pricing, and the treatment of possible emergencies. Also, we provide a yardstick so as to assure us that the company's overall sales forecast will be reasonable and obtainable.

Next, the product division top management goes back to its district sales managers. Each district sales manager is asked to tell his top management what he expects to do in the way of sales during the budget year. Head office and the divisional staffs will give the district sales managers as much guidance as they request, but it is the sole responsibility of each district sales manager to come up with his particular forecast.

After the district sales manager's forecasts are received by the divisional top management, the forecasts are consolidated and reviewed by the division's general manager of marketing. At this time the general manager of marketing may go back to the district sales managers and suggest they revise their budgets. For instance, a situation such as this might arise: We enjoy a very large share of the liquor market. In one year, however, it may be predicted on the basis of the consolidated district sales manager's estimates that we can look forward to a 20%–25% increase in sales.

Obviously, this is unreasonable. What has happened is this: Each district sales manager has been told by each of his liquor customers that they expect an increase in sales. When all these anticipated individual sales increases are summed, it looks like the market is going to grow considerably. However, this is not going to happen. What is going to occur is that company A will take sales from company B and company C will take sales from company D, and so forth.

Individually, the district sales managers know little of what's happening outside their territory. However, from the headquarters' point of view, we can ascertain the size of the whole market and the customer's probable relative market share. That's where the market research group's studies come in handy.

Let me emphasise, however, even in this case nothing is changed in the district sales manager's budget, unless the district manager agrees. Then, once the budget is approved, nobody is relieved of his responsibility without top management approval. Also, no arbitrary changes are made in the approved budgets without the concurrence of all the people responsible for the budget.

Small: At this point, have the plant managers – or the divisional general managers of manufacturing – been involved in the preparation of the sales budget?

Walker: Not in a formal way. Informally, of course, the plant managers know what's going on. For example, when a plant manager prepares his capital equipment investment programme he is sure to talk to the district sales manager closest to his plant about the district's sales plans.

Next, we go through the same process at the division and headquarters levels. We keep on repeating the process until everybody agrees the sales budgets are sound. Then, each level of management takes responsibility for its particular portion of the budget. These sales budgets then become fixed objectives.

Small: Besides coming up with a realistic sales budget, what other objectives do the divisions have in mind when they review the sales forecasts?

Walker: I would say they have four general objectives in mind: First, a review of the division's competitive position, including plans for improving that position. Second, an evaluation of its efforts to gain either a larger share of the market or offset competitors' activities. Third, a consideration of the need to expand facilities to improve the division's products or introduce new products. Finally, a review and development of plans to improve product quality, delivery methods, and service.

Manufacturing budgets

Walker and Small then turned their conversation to the preparation of the manufacturing budgets. According to Walker, each plant had a profit responsibility.

Small: When are the plant budgets prepared?

Walker: Once the vice presidents, executive vice president, and company president have given final approval to the sales budgets, we make a sales budget for each plant by breaking the division sales budget down according to the plants from which the finished goods will be shipped. These plant sales budgets are then further broken down on a monthly basis by price, volume, and end use. With this information available, the plants then budget their gross profit, fixed expenses, and income before taxes.

Small: How do you define gross profit and income?

Walker: Gross profit is the difference between gross sales, less discounts and variable manufacturing costs – such as direct labour, direct material, and variable manufacturing overheads. Income is the difference between the gross profit and the fixed costs.

Small: Is the principal constraint within which the plants work the sales budget?

Walker: That's right. Given his sales budget, it is up to the plant manager to determine the fixed overhead and variable costs – at standard – that he will need to incur so as to meet the demands of the sales budget.

In some companies I know of, the head office gives each plant manager sales and income figures that the plant has to meet. We don't operate that way, however. We believe that type of directive misses the benefit of all the field experience of those at the district sales and plant levels. If we gave a profit figure to our plant managers to meet, how could we say it was their responsibility to meet it?

What we say to the plant managers is this: Assuming that you have to produce this much sales volume, how much do you expect to spend producing this volume? And what do you expect to spend for your programmes allied to obtaining these current and future sales?

Small: Then the plant managers make their own plans?

Walker: Yes. In my opinion requiring the plant managers to make their own plans is one of the most valuable things associated with the budget system. Each plant manager divides the preparation of the overall plant budget among his plant's various departments. First, the departments spell out the programmes in terms of the physical requirements – such as tons of raw material – and then the plans are priced at standard cost.

Small: What items might some of these departmental budgets include?

Walker: Let me tell you about the phase of the budget preparation our industrial engineering people are responsible for. The plant industrial engineering department is assigned the responsibility for developing engineered cost standards and reduced costs. Consequently, the phase of budget preparation covered by the industrial engineers includes budget standards of performance for each operation, cost center, and department within the plant. This phase of the budget also includes budget cost reductions, budgeted unfavorable variances from standards, and certain budgeted programmed fixed costs in the manufacturing area such as service labour. The industrial engineer prepares this phase of the budget in conjunction with departmental line supervision.

Small: Once the plant budgets are completed, are they sent directly to the divisional top management?

Walker: No. Before each plant sends its budget into British City, a group of us from head office goes out and visits each plant. For example, in the case of the Glass Products Division, Allen [Newell, assistant controller] and I, along with representatives of the Glass Products division manufacturing staffs visit each of the division's plants.

Let me stress this point: We do not go on these trips to pass judgment on the plant's proposed budget. Rather, we go with three purposes in mind. First, we wish to acquaint ourselves with the thinking behind the figures that each plant manager will send in to British City. This is helpful because when we come to review these budgets with the top management – that is, the management above our level – we will have to answer questions about the budget, and we will know the answers. Second, the review is a way of giving guidance to the plant managers as to whether or not they are in line with what the company needs to make in the way of profits.

Of course, when we make our field reviews we do not know what each of the other plants is doing. Therefore, we explain to the plant managers that, while their budget may look good now, when we put all the plants together in a consolidated budget, the plant managers may have to make some changes because the projected profit is not high enough. When this happens we have to tell the plant managers that it is not their programmes that are unsound. The problem is that the company cannot afford the programmes.

I think it is very important that each plant manager has a chance to tell his story. Also, it gives them the feeling that we at headquarters are not living in an ivory tower.

Small: How long do these plant visits take?

Walker: They are spread over a three-week period and we spend an average of half a day at each plant.

Small: I gather the role of the head office and divisional staff is to recommend, not decide. That's the plant manager's right.

Walker: Correct.

Small: Who on the plant staff attends these meetings?

Walker: The plant manager is free to bring in any of his supervisors he wishes. We asked him not to bring in anybody below the supervisory level. Then, of course, you get into organised labour.

Small: What do you do on these plant visits?

Walker: During the half-day we spend at each plant we discuss the budget primarily. However, if I have time, I like to wander through the plant and see how things are going. Also, I go over in great detail the property replacement and maintenance budget with the plant engineer.

Small: After you have completed the plant tours, do the plant budgets go to the respective division top management?

Walker: That's right. About September 1, the plant budgets come into British City and the accounting department consolidates them. Then the product division vice presidents review their respective divisional budgets to see if the division budget is reasonable in terms of what the vice president thinks the corporate top management wants. If he is not satisfied with the consolidated plant budgets, he will ask the various plants within the division to trim their budget figures.

When the division vice presidents and the executive vice president are happy, they will send their budgets to the company president. He may accept the division budgets at this point. If he doesn't, he will specify the areas to be reexamined by division and, if necessary, plant management. The final budget is approved at our December board of directors' meeting.

Small: As I understand it, the district sales managers have a responsibility for sales.

Walker: Specifically volume, price, and sales mix.

Small: And the plant manager is responsible for manufacturing costs?

Walker: His primary responsibility extends to profits. The budgeted plant profit is the difference between the fixed sales dollar budget and the budgeted variable costs at standard and the fixed overhead budget. It is the plant manager's responsibility to meet this budgeted profit figure.

Small: Even if actual dollar sales drop below the budgeted level?

Walker: Yes.

Comparison of actual and standard performance

The discussion turned to the procedures and management philosophy related to the periodic comparison by the head office group of the actual and standard performance of the field organisation. In particular, the two men discussed the manufacturing area.

Small: What do you do with the actual results that come in the head office?

Walker: We go over them on the basis of exception: that is, we only look at those figures that are in excess of the budgeted amounts. We believe this has a good effect on morale. The plant managers don't have to explain everything they do. They only have to explain where they go off base.

Small: What cost and revenue items are of greatest interest to you?

Walker: In particular, we pay close attention to the net sales, gross margin, and the plant's ability to meet its standard manufacturing cost. Incidentally, when analyzing the gross sales, we look closely at the price and mix changes. All this information is summarised on a form known as the Profit Planning and Control Report #1 (see Exhibit 502.4). This document is backed up by a number of supporting documents (see Exhibit 502.5).

Small: When you look at the fixed costs, what are you interested in?

Walker: We want to know whether or not the plants carried out the programmes that they said they would carry out. If they have not, we want to know why they have not. Here we are looking for sound reasons. Also, we want to know if they have carried out their projected programmes at the cost they said they would.

Small: Do you have to wait until you receive the monthly PPCR #1 [Profit Planning and Control Report #1] before you know how well the various plants performed during the month?

Walker: No. At the end of the sixth business day after the close of the month, each plant transmits to the head office certain operating variances which we put together on what we call the variance analysis sheet (see Exhibit 502.6). Within a half-hour after the last plant report comes through, variance analysis sheets for the divisions and plants are compiled. On the morning of the seventh business day after the end of the month, these reports are usually on the desks of the interested top management.

The variance analysis sheet highlights the variances in what we consider to be critical areas. Receiving this report as soon as we do helps us at head office to take timely action. Let me emphasise, however, we do not accept the excuse that the plant manager has to go to the end of the month to know what happened during the month. He has to be on top of these particular items daily.

Exhibit 502.4 Profit Planning and Control Report (PPCR) #1

MONTH			REF.		YEAR TO DATE		
GAIN (+) OR LOSS (−) FROM		ACTUAL			ACTUAL	INCOME GAIN (+) OR LOSS (−) FROM	
PREV. YEAR	BUDGET					BUDGET	PREV. YEAR
			1	GROSS SALES TO CUSTOMERS			
			2	DISCOUNTS & ALLOWANCES			
			3	NET SALES TO CUSTOMERS			
%	%	/////	4	% GAIN (+)/LOSS (−)	/////	%	%
				DOLLAR VOLUME GAIN (+)/LOSS (−) DUE TO:			
		/////	5	SALES PRICE	/////		
			6	SALES VOLUME			
			6(a)	TRADE MIX	/////		
			7	VARIABLE COST OF SALES			
			8	PROFIT MARGIN			
				PROFIT MARGIN GAIN (+)/LOSS (−) DUE TO:			
		/////	9	PROFIT VOLUME RATIO (P/V)	/////		
			10	DOLLAR VOLUME			
%	%	%	11	PROFIT VOLUME RATIO (P/V)		%	%	%
	INCOME ADDITION (+)				INCOME ADDITION (+)		
			12	TOTAL FIXED MANUFACTURING COST			
			13	FIXED MANUFACTURING COST - TRANSFERS			
			14	PLANT INCOME (STANDARD)			
%	%	%	15	% OF NET SALES		%	%	%
	INCOME ADDITION (+) INCOME REDUCTION (−)				INCOME ADDITION (+) INCOME REDUCTION (−)		
%	%	%	16	% PERFORMANCE		%	%	%
			17	MANUFACTURING EFFICIENCY			
	INCOME ADDITION (+)				INCOME ADDITION (+)		
			18	METHODS IMPROVEMENTS			
			19	OTHER REVISIONS OF STANDARDS			
			20	MATERIAL PRICE CHANGES			
			21	DIVISION SPECIAL PROJECTS			
			22	COMPANY SPECIAL PROJECTS			
			23	NEW PLANT EXPENSE			
			24	OTHER PLANT EXPENSES			
			25	INCOME ON SECONDS			
			26				
			27				
			28	PLANT INCOME (ACTUAL)			
%	%	/////	29	% GAIN (+)/LOSS (−)	/////	%	%
%	%	%	30	% OF NET SALES		%	%	%
			36A				

EMPLOYED CAPITAL

INCREASE (+) OR DECREASE (−)						INCREASE (+) OR DECREASE (−)	
			37	TOTAL EMPLOYED CAPITAL			
%	%	%	38	% RETURN		%	%	%
			39	TURNOVER RATE			

PLANT _____ DIVISION _____ MONTH _____ 19___

Exhibit 502.4	continued

Notes

During his conversation with James Walker, Small asked him to describe the various items listed on PPCR #I.

Walker: Let's start with reference 3, *net sales to customers*. This is the difference between the gross sales to customers [ref. 1] and any discounts or allowances [ref. 2].

The next line, % gain (+)/*loss* (–) [ref. 4], is the increase or decrease in net sales dollars expressed as a percentage of the budget and previous year's actual figures.

Next, we break the cause of the dollar volume gain or loss into its component parts: namely, changes due to sales price, volume, and mix.

Variable cost of sales [ref. 7] includes such items as direct materials, operating labour, and that part of indirect labour that varies in monthly dollar amounts directly with changes in unit production volume. These costs are constant per unit of production. The amount listed in the budget column is the standard cost of the actual production.

Reference 8, *profit margin*, is the difference between the total net dollar sales and the total variable manufacturing costs of products sold.

Next, we identify further the causes of the change in profit margin.

The item reference 9, *profit margin gain* (+)/*loss* (–) *due to profit volume ratio* (PIV), is that portion of the profit margin gain or loss resulting from changes in the relationship between the net selling price and the standard variable manufacturing costs of the products sold to customers. This relationship, expressed as a percentage, is known as the PIV ratio [see ref. 11].

The *profit margin gain* (+)/*loss* (–) *due to dollar volume* [ref. 10] is that portion of the profit margin or loss resulting from the changes in dollar volume of net sales to customers, exclusive of changes in PN. It is the algebraic difference between the total profit margin variance and reference 9.

We keep a close check on the P/V ratio because it shows us how much we are making over our variable costs. Of course, volume changes alone never affect the P/V ratio.

Total fixed manufacturing costs [ref. 12] are the costs that should remain unchanged irrespective of fluctuation in volume during the year. Included in this category are depreciation, rent, general insurance, general taxes, and most supervision costs. Fixed costs are calculated on an annual basis, and each monthly figure is shown as one-twelfth of the annual total.

The next item, *fixed manufacturing cost-transfers* [ref. 13], doesn't apply to the Glass Products Division as they have very little intra or interdivision transfers.

Therefore, in the case of the Glass Products Division [ref. 14] *plant income (standard) is* the difference between profit margin dollars [ref. 8] and total fixed manufacturing costs [ref. 12].

In the *actual* column of reference 16, % performance, we enter the ratio of the standard to the actual manufacturing cost expressed as a percentage.

In the *gain/loss* columns for this same item, we enter the difference in percentage points between current performance and budget, and between the current performance and previous year.

In the *actual* column of reference 17, *manufacturing efficiency*, we put the difference between standard and actual manufacturing efficiency dollar costs.

In the *gain/loss* columns of reference 17, we enter the increase or decrease in income resulting from changes in manufacturing dollar savings or excesses.

References 18 through 25 are self-explanatory. In addition to cost savings or excesses resulting from efficiency, special conditions may arise to cause other departures from standard cost. These additional differences are classified according to cause and the more significant ones are shown individually on separate lines in this portion of PPCR #1.

Reference 28, *plant income (actual)*, is the income remaining after adjusting reference 14 for all the departures from standard manufacturing listed on references 18 through 25, inclusive.

Total employed capital (ref. 37) is the value of employed capital at the end of the month, and average for the year to date. At the plant level employed capital consists of inventories [mostly work-in-process and finished goods] valued at their standard direct costs plus the replacement value of fixed assets. At the division level, accounts receivable are included in employed capital.

Small: How do you calculate the replacement value of fixed assets?

Walker: We have formulas that give us the current cost of equipment capable of doing the same job as the installed equipment.

Small: Why do you use replacement costs?

Walker: We have two basic reasons. First, within a single division it places all plants on an equal footing from the standpoint of measuring return, since it eliminates distortions arising from the use of widely disparate acquisition costs for similar equipment. Second, it eliminates distortions arising from the use of unrecovered costs which, even though based on comparable replacement values, are heavily influenced by cumulative depreciation charges that vary widely depending upon the length of time a given facility has been in use.

Small: What about the rest of the items on PPCR #1?

Walker: Reference 38 is plant income (actual) dollars expressed as a percentage of *employed capital*. Reference 39 is the net sales dollars divided by employed capital and expressed as a multiple of employed capital.

Small: What are the three most important items on PPCR #1?

Walker: The P/V ratio, *plant income (actual)*, and % return *(employed capital)*.

Small: Are the budgets prepared on forms similar to the PPCR series?

Walker: Yes. The only major difference is that the budget forms include columns for recording the current year's budget figures, and previous year's actual figures. In addition, variances are shown between the proposed budget figures and the current year's estimated actuals' and the previous year's actual figures.

Source: Company document.

Exhibit 502.5   Brief Descriptions of PPCR #2 Through PPCR #11

Report	Description
	Individual Plant Reports
PPCR #2	*Manufacturing Expense*: Plant materials, labour and variable overhead consumed. Detail of actual figures compared with budget and previous years' figures for year-to-date and current month.
PPCR #3	*Plant Expense*: Plant fixed expenses incurred. Details of actual figures compared with budget and previous years' figures for year-to-date and current month.
PPCR #4	*Analysis of Sales and Income*: Plant operating gains and losses due to changes in sales revenue, profit margins, and other sources of income. Details of actual figures compared with budget and previous years' figures for year-to-date and current month.
PPCR #5	*Plant Control Statement*: Analysis of plant raw material gains and losses, spoilage costs, and cost reductions programmes. Actual figures compared with budget figures for current month and year-to-date.
PPCR #6	*Comparison of Sales by Principal and Product Groups*: Plant sales dollars, profit margin and *PN* ratios broken down by end-product use (i.e., soft drinks, beer, etc.). Compares actual figures with budgeted figures for year-to-date and current month.
	Division Summary Reports
PPCR #7	*Comparative Plant Performance, Sales and Income*: Gross sales and income figures by plants. Actual figures compared with budget figures for year-to-date and current month.
PPCR #8	*Comparative Plant Performance, Total Plant Expenses*: Profit margin, total fixed costs, manufacturing efficiency, other plant expenses and *PN* ratios by plants. Actual figures compared with budgeted and previous years' figures for current month and year-to-date.
PPCR #9	*Manufacturing Efficiency*: Analysis of gains and losses by plant in areas of material, spoilage, supplies, and labour. Current month and year-to-date actuals reported in total dollars and as a percentage of budget.
PPCR #10	*Inventory*: Comparison of actual and budget intentory figures by major inventory accounts and plants.
PPCR #11	*Status of Capital Expenditures*: Analysis of the status of capital expenditures by plants, months and relative to budget.

Exhibit 502.6   Variance Analysis Sheet for Various Divisions and Plants

Line No.	Division or Plant	Budget Income	Gross Sales	Sales Price	Manufacturing Cost	Labor	Overtime	Employee Benefits	Outside Warehouse	Utilities	Overhaul and Repair	Depreciation, Plant, Insurance and Taxes	Controllable Plant Fixed Cost	Other Fixed Cost	Manufacturing Efficiency	Cost Reduction	Other Operating Gains and Losses	Income From Seconds	Wage Changes	Price Changes	Division Expenses	Actual Income	Income Adjusted by Volume
1																							
2																							
3																							
4																							
5																							
6																							
7																							
8																							
9																							
10																							
11																							
12																							
13																							
14																							
15																							
16																							
17																							
18																							
19																							
20																							
21																							
22																							
23																							
24																							
25																							
26																							
27																							
28																							
29																							
30																							
31																							
32																							
33																							
34																							
35																							

Source: Company document.

Small: Is there any way head office can detect an adverse trend in operations before you receive the monthly variance analysis sheet?

Walker: Yes. At the beginning of each month, the plant managers prepare current estimates for the upcoming month and quarter on forms similar to the variance analysis sheets.

Since our budget is based on known programmes, the value of this current estimate is that it gets the plant people to look at their programmes. Hopefully, they will realise that they cannot run their plants just on a day-to-day basis.

If we see a sore spot coming up, or if the plant manager draws our attention to a potential trouble area, we may ask for daily reports concerning this item to be sent to the particular division top management involved. In addition, the division top management may send a division staff specialist – say, a quality control expert if it is a quality problem – to the plant concerned. The division staff members can make recommendations, but it is up to the plant manager to accept or reject these recommendations. Of course, it is well known throughout the company that we expect the plant managers to accept gracefully the help of the head office and division staffs.

Small: When is the monthly PPCR #1 received at British City?

Walker: The plant PPCR #1 and the month-end trial balance showing both actual and budget figures are received in British City at the close of the eighth business day after the end of the month. These two very important reports, along with the supporting reports (PPCR #2 through PPCR #11, described in Exhibit 502.5) are then consolidated by the accounting department on PPCR-type forms to show the results of operations by division and company. The consolidated reports are distributed the next day.

Sales-manufacturing relations

Small was curious about the relationship between the sales and manufacturing groups, particularly at the plant level.

Small: If during the year, the actual sales volume is less than the budgeted sales volume, what changes do you make in the plant budget?

Walker: This is one of the biggest risks we run with our budget system. If the sales decline occurs during the early part of the year, and if the plant managers can convince us that the change is permanent, we may revise the plant budgets to reflect these new circumstances.

However, if toward the end of the year the actual sales volume suddenly drops below the predicted sales volume, we don't have much time to change the budget plans. What we do is ask the plant managers to go back over their budget with their staffs and see where reduction of expense programmes will do the least harm. Specifically, we ask them to consider what they may be able to eliminate this year or delay until next year.

I believe it was Confucius who said: 'We make plans so we have plans to discard.' Nevertheless, I believe it is wise to make plans, even if you have to discard them. Having plans makes it a lot easier to figure out what to do when sales fall off from the budgeted level. The understanding of operations that comes from preparing the budget removes a lot of the potential chaos and confusion that might arise if we were under pressure to meet a stated profit-goal and sales-decline quickly and unexpectedly at year-end – just as they did this year.

Under these circumstances, we don't try to ram anything down the plant managers' throats. We ask them to tell us where they can reasonably expect to cut costs below the budgeted level.

Small: What happens when a plant manager's costs are adversely affected by the sales group insisting that a production schedule be changed so as to get out an unexpected rush order?

Walker: As far as we are concerned, the customer's wants are primary – our company is a case where sales wags the rest of the dog.

Whenever a problem arises at a plant between sales and production, the local people are supposed to solve the problem themselves. Let's take your example: a customer's

Exhibit 502.7 — Plant Display Reporting Winners of Housekeeping Contest

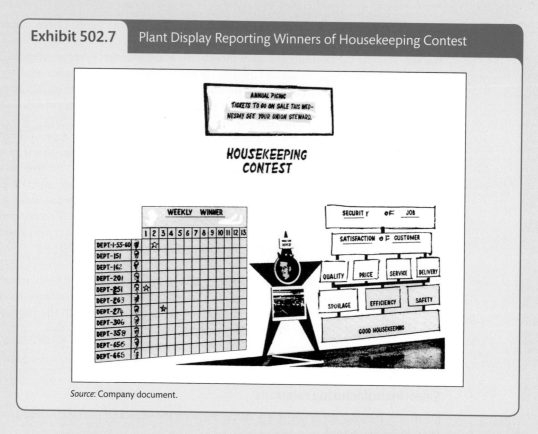

Source: Company document.

purchasing agent insists he wants an immediate delivery and this delivery will disrupt the production department's plans. The production group can make recommendations as to alternative ways to take care of the problem, but it's the sales manager's responsibility to get the product to the customer. The salesmen are supposed to know their customers well enough to judge whether or not the customer really needs the product. If the sales manager says the customer needs the product, that ends the matter.

Of course, if the change in the sales programme involves a major expense at the plant which is out of line with the budget, then the matter is passed up to division for decision.

As I said earlier, the sales department has the sole responsibility for the product price, sales mix, and delivery schedules. They do not have direct responsibility for plant operations or profit. That's the plant management's responsibility. However, it is understood that the sales group will cooperate with the plant people wherever possible.

Small: I guess cooperation is very important to the success of your system.

Walker: Definitely. We believe the whole budgetary control system works best if we can get cooperation. But, within the framework of cooperation the sales and production groups have very clear responsibilities.

Motivation

Small: How do you motivate the plant managers to meet their profit goals?

Walker: Well, first of all, we only promote capable people. Also, a monetary incentive programme has been established that stimulates their efforts to achieve their profit goal.

Small: What other incentive devices do you use?

Walker: Each month we put together a bar chart which shows, by division and plant, the ranking of the various manufacturing units with respect to manufacturing efficiency. We feel the plant managers are one hundred percent responsible for variable manufacturing costs. I believe this is true since all manufacturing standards have to be approved by plant managers. Most of the plant managers give wide publicity to these bar charts. The efficiency bar chart and efficiency measure itself is perhaps a little unfair in some respects when you are comparing one plant with another. Different kinds of products are run through different plants. These require different setups, etc., which have an important impact on a position of the plant. However, in general the efficiency rating is a good indication of the quality of the plant manager and his supervisory staff.

Also, a number of plants run competitions within the plants which reward department heads, or foremen, based on their relative standing with respect to a certain cost item.

Small: While I waited to see you this morning, I read some of the company publications for employees. They all seemed to stress profits and product quality (see Exhibit 502.8).

Walker: That's true. In my opinion, the number one item now stressed at the plant level is quality. The market situation is such that in order to make sales you have to meet the market price and exceed the market quality. By quality I mean not only the physical characteristics of the product but also such things as delivery schedules.

As I read the company employee publications, their message is that if the company is to be profitable it must produce high quality items at a reasonable cost. This is necessary so that the plants can meet their obligation to produce the maximum profits for the company under the circumstances prevailing.

Small: Do you analyze the sales reports?

Exhibit 502.8	Excerpt from Employee Magazine

Source: Company document.

Walker: No. It is the sales group's responsibility to comment on the sales activity. They prepare their own reports. They also control their selling costs against budgets prepared by the sales managers.

Initial sales statistics are developed from plant billings summarised by end use and are available on the third business day after month-end. Detailed sales statistics by end use and customer indicating actual and variance to both budget and prior year are prepared by data processing at British City and available on the eighth business day after month-end. Sales and price and mix variances by plant and end use can be obtained from PPCR #1, PPCR #4, and PPCR #6.

The future

Small: Mr. Walker, do you intend to make any changes in your budgetary control system?

Walker: An essential part of the budgetary control system is planning. We have developed a philosophy that we must begin our plans where the work is done – in the line organisation and out in the field. Perhaps, in the future, we can avoid or cut back some of the budget preparation steps and start putting our sales budget together later on in the year than May 15. However, I doubt if we will change the basic philosophy. Frankly, I doubt if the line operators would want any major change in the system – they are very jealous of the management prerogatives the system gives to them.

It is very important that we manage the budget. We have to be continually on guard against it managing us. Sometimes, the plants lose sight of this fact. They have to be made conscious daily of the necessity of having the sales volume to make a profit. And, when sales fall off and their plant programmes are reduced they do not always appear to see the justification for budget cuts. Although, I do suspect that they see more of the justification for these cuts than they will admit. It is this human side of the budget to which we will have to pay more attention in the future.

Case 503

Osram
John Shank and Lawrence Carr

This case highlights the trade-off faced by organisations between traditionally used consumables, and newer, more efficient ones that have a higher initial cost. The case requires the analysis of the potential savings made by more efficient consumables.

Larry Carter was feeling very optimistic about the new product he wanted to introduce in the European market, the 'Dulux' Compact Fluorescent Lamp. He had lined up two potential test market sites, pending a final pricing decision. Larry's problem now was to determine how to price the Dulux bulbs to provide good value to both end-use customers and Osram's distributors while also earning as good a profit as possible. His compensation as president of Osram Europe (OEU) was largely based on the profitability of the business.

Osram EU's parent company, Osram GmbH, is a German-based lighting firm with €1.5 billion in annual sales. It is part of the German electrical giant Siemens AG (€70 billion in sales). Osram

Source: Adapted from Shank, J. and Carr, L. (2002) 'Osram', *IMA Cases from Management Accounting Practice*, Volume 17 (Montvale, New Jersey: Institute of Management Accounting Practice).

competes in a €12 billion worldwide lightbulb market with a very strong position in North and South America. In 1989, Osram started a new subsidiary, Osram Europe (OEU), to try to compete in the very attractive European market. The European represents 50% of world lighting demand, but it is dominated by three major competitors: GE, Sylvania and Philips. OEU grew very rapidly (25% per year) during its first 10 years, pursuing a niche strategy. OEU, however, was only participating on the fringe of the market. The three dominant players focused primarily on large segments in both the consumer and commercial lightbulb markets. Sales for OEU peaked in 1994 and seemed stuck at €60 million in 2001. This was only 4% of the total European commercial market for 2001, but it was 50% of the speciality segments in which OEU concentrated. Carter felt it was unlikely he could do better than a 50% market share, so his only realistic hope for further high growth, which Siemens expected of him, was to tackle new segments.

A new product opportunity

In 2001, during a factory visit in Germany, the OEU management team was introduced to a patented, innovative light source called Compact Fluorescent Lamps (CFL). Similar in size to an incandescent bulb, CFL bulbs emit the same 'colour' of light (colour temperature 2800 Kelvin). The big differences with CFL are that they last about ten times as long and consume only about one-fifth the energy. For example, an 18 W CFL bulb provides the light of a 100 W incandescent bulb while consuming only 18% of the energy and lasting 10 000 hours, versus about 1000 hours. Of course, this kind of performance comes at a price. The normal incandescent 100 W bulb costs about 18 cents to manufacture and sells retail for about €1.20. The CFL 18 W bulb costs well over €2.00 to manufacture. The retail selling price is yet to be determined. Typically, bulb prices did not vary with wattage. The ten-times life and 80% energy savings factors were thought to more than justify a substantially higher price that would more than compensate for the significantly higher manufacturing cost. 'Customer value' for an 18 W CFL bulb, replacing 10 000 hours of use with a 100 W incandescent bulb (at €0.14 per kWh) is €78.00, as shown below:

$$\text{Annual cost for the incandescent bulb} = €1.20 + \text{Power cost } (1000 \text{ hr} \times 100 \text{ W})$$
$$= 100 \text{ kWh} \times €.14 = €14.00)$$
$$= €15.20$$

10-year present value (10%) of €15.20 per year = €93.40

For the 18 W CFL bulb, 10 years of energy cost has a present value (PV) of €15.40 as shown below:

$$1000 \text{ hours per year} \times 18 \text{ W} = 18 \text{ kWh} \times €.14$$
$$= €2.50 \text{ per year}$$

10-year PV (10%) of €2.50 per year = €15.40

Customer value of the CFL bulb = €93.40 − €15.40 = €78.00

In theory, a consumer should be willing to pay up to €78.00 for the alternative CFL bulb. OEU management was confident that the CFL product had high potential in the European market. They were pleased to have a proprietary technology to compete against the big three in larger segments. The technological superiority would give them immediate credibility with end-users and distributors. Philips Europe owned the European distribution rights to CFL bulbs manufactured in the USA through joint venture agreements with Siemens. OEU could pay Philips a royalty on imported CFL bulbs, or manufacture bulbs in the EU to avoid the royalty. Siemens would license the manufacturing patent to OEU for a nominal fee. Carter was reluctant to commit to EU manufacturing until he was sure of the demand. He wanted to do some test marketing, using bulbs imported from the USA, to introduce the new product.

Market segmentation

The European lighting market can be divided into two basic segments: commercial and consumer. The latter is the channel for retail sales for home use. The product is ultimately purchased from supermarkets, drugstores, hardware stores, lighting stores or mass merchandisers. Mass merchandisers buy bulbs direct from manufacturers. Other outlets use wholesale distributors.

The commercial segment provides lighting for hotels, factories, hospitals, offices, schools, theatres, scientific laboratories, street and sign lighting, and retail lighting fixture salesrooms. Eighty per cent of commercial bulbs are bought through wholesale distributors. Because GE, Sylvania and Philips are so well established with the major distribution companies, Carter thought his best bet for introducing CFL was to target segments that do not use distributors. Because OEU is far too small to deal with the mass merchandisers or the government, Carter decided to explore two particular niches within the commercial segment: (1) energy-saving converters, which are not currently large buyers of lightbulbs; and (2) lighting maintenance companies which supply and maintain bulbs for businesses such as hotels, offices or casinos.

The energy savings converters (ESCO) market

Babson Energy Savers (BES) is a successful ESCO located in London. Its business is energy-saving remodelling projects, such as heating and air-conditioning systems, low-voltage versus high-voltage power conversions, and automatic switching controls. A small part of its current business involves saving building owners energy costs through conversion to fluorescent fixtures. For example, a fluorescent lamp, which consumes about 32 W of power, provides the equivalent of 150 W of incandescent light.

The major drawbacks to fluorescent light are the high cost of the bulb, the harsh light and glare, and the bulky fixtures which are awkward to install and service, and are very unattractive. CFL bulbs could create a new business opportunity for firms such as BES. CFL's small size and simple ballasting allow a much wider range of fixture design options than with fluorescent, as well as the huge energy savings and long-life advantages.

Once the idea was explained to them, the BES engineers shared OEU management's enthusiasm for the compact fluorescent lamp. BES felt that, with proper pricing of the CFL lamp, the cost savings would be very attractive for many of its customers.

In order to test the new product in this segment, OEU convinced BES to propose using CFL lighting as part of an overall energy savings project for one of London's old classic hotels, the Opaque Gardens. OEU would provide financing to the hotel for the cost of retrofitting existing fixtures (12% annual rate and payments over 15 years) through Siemens' captive finance subsidiary. OEU would guarantee the hotel annual savings in power cost at least double the annual payment on the retrofitting loan.

The hotel lighting configuration is as follows:

- *Rooms*: 10 floors with 25 rooms per floor. Each room averages 200 occupied days per year. There are 9 lights in each room (4 table or vanity, 3 overhead and 2 wall) at 100 W each (cost €1.20 each). Average usage per room rental is a total of 7 hours.

- *Halls*: 10 floors with 24 overhead lights per floor (one 50 W bulb each). Average usage of 24 hours per day.

- Bulb life for the hotel, using incandescent bulbs was 800 hours for room lamps and 1400 hours for hall lights. Turning bulbs on and off shortens the useful life.

The cost of electricity in London is high, averaging €.14 per kilowatt-hour (kWh). In other parts of Europe, power costs can be half that rate.

The hotel was currently buying about 1900 bulbs per year:

2250 room bulbs (250 × 9) at 5-year life per bulb (200 × 7 = 1400 ÷ 9 = 155 vs 800)
= 450 bulbs per year

240 hall bulbs at 6 changes per year (8760 hours ÷ 1400) = 1440 bulbs per year
450 + 1440 = 1890 ≈ 1900 bulbs

Bulbs are changed by the hotel maintenance staff as they burn out. BES cost to retrofit the hotel light fixtures is as follows:

A typical incandescent or fluorescent overhead fixture costs €7 for material (reflector, ballast, igniters and housing modifications) and one half-hour of electrical technician labour at €18 per hour to retrofit for CFL use. To retrofit a table or vanity fixture costs €2.50 for material and one quarter-hour of labour. Wall fixtures cost €3 for material and 40 minutes to retrofit.

BES electrical technicians would do the conversion job. Lighting fixtures typically have a life of 15 years.

The lighting maintenance contractors (LMC) market

The second niche market that looked attractive to OEU for CFL bulbs was lighting maintenance contractors (LMCs). This segment bought €144 million in incandescent and fluorescent bulbs in 2001 and was supplied directly by the big three. The ESCO segment was buying only about €36 million in fluorescent bulbs in 2001. Even if OEU could double the ESCO market by switching it to CFL bulbs, the potential was only half that of LMCs.

Farnham Lighting Service (FLS) is based in Farnham, Surrey. FLS contracts with building managers to change the many thousands of lightbulbs that illuminate casino interiors, exterior signs and car parks. A typical job could have 12 000 to 18 000 bulbs. For the Mayfair casino in London, the marquee billboard alone has 33 000 bulbs.

FLS charges the casino a set monthly fee based on the number of light sources. The fee includes labour, equipment usage and the cost of the lightbulbs themselves. Access to the lightbulb can be very difficult, requiring lifts and other power equipment for changes. This is a key factor in determining the monthly fee. Normally, longer-life light sources (fluorescent) are chosen for the least accessible locations. Research showed that burned-out lighting is very unattractive, keeping customers away from the casinos. The standard practice for lighting service companies is to totally relamp a section, known as 'group relamping', at 80% of the bulbs' expected life. This virtually eliminates burned-out lights.

In order to test the new product in this segment, OEU convinced FLS to propose a conversion to CFL bulbs for one large customer, the Victoria Casino. The casino has 15 000 incandescent fixtures (50 W and 100 W) with an expected life of 800 or 1400 hours, similar to a hotel, and 2000 25 W fluorescent fixtures with a rated life of 8000 hours. The casino stays open 24 hours a day. FLS does not relamp the hotel room bulbs, which are changed as they burn out by the regular maintenance staff. It relamps the hall and casino incandescent bulbs 8 times per year (8760 hours ÷ 1400 × 0.8) and the fluorescent fixtures approximately 1.4 times per year (8760 ÷ 8000 × 0.8). With an average labour rate of €20 per hour, an average of 5 minutes to change each bulb, and equipment rental at about €300 per day, the CFL story is very appealing to Farnham.

The CFL bulb offers lower power cost to the casino (18 W bulbs vs 100 W, and 9 W vs 25 or 50 W). CFL bulbs offer lower changeover cost to the service company due to longer bulb lives. The casino would also enjoy less downtime for its 24-hour gambling operation. Sometimes bulbs could be changed without closing down the gambling, but not always. Downtime means lost revenue from the gamblers who move to a different casino.

Once they move, players usually do not return immediately the bulb change is complete. The Victoria Casino, which grosses €250 million a year, once estimated that lost time from lightbulb changes costs about €100 000 each year in lost revenue at, probably, 75% gross margin.

The changeover requires the purchase of more expensive bulbs and a one-time retrofitting of all fixtures to accommodate CFL-compatible sockets. The lighting configuration for the Victoria Casino is as follows:

- A 1000-room hotel, with 9 bulbs (100 W) per room and 1000 hall lights (50 W). This is a total of 10 000 incandescent bulbs.

- The casino, with 5000 100 W incandescent bulbs and 2000 25 W fluorescent bulbs.
- The casino and the hotel halls were lighted 24 hours a day. The hotel rooms average 200 occupied nights per year with 7 hours of bulb usage, combined, per stay.

The one-time retrofitting cost for light fixtures would be:

> 3000 wall fixtures @ €30 each
> 5000 overhead fixtures @ €35 each

> Power cost is €.12 per kWh in Victoria

FLS uses an eight-person crew at the Victoria Casino. The crew averages 7 working hours on each 8-hour shift. The crew is scheduled to spend about 76 days a year on site. The monthly fee is €20 500 (€246 000 per year), which breaks down as follows:

Bulbs: 48 000 incandescent bulbs at €1.00 each	=	€48 000
2800 fluorescent bulbs at €6.00	=	€16 800
Labour: 50 800 bulb changes at 5 minutes (average) per bulb	=	4234 hours
Paid hours = 76 days × 8 hr × 8 persons = 4864 hours × €20 per hour	=	€97 280
Equipment rental (at €300 per crew-day) = €300 × 76	=	€22 800
Subtotal	=	€184 880
Mark-up to cover overhead and profit	=	€61 120
Total	=	€246 000

The CFL bulbs exhibit much smaller variation in bulb life compared with incandescent, whether bulbs are frequently turned on and off or left burning. FLS could go to 'group relamping' at 90% of the 10 000-hour-rated CFL life with very little chance of burned out bulbs.

Questions

1 a For the ESCO test market job, what is the present value of CFL bulbs to the hotel over the 15 years life of the fixtures? (This figure will be equivalent to energy savings and labour saving on bulb replacements, less the cost to retrofit all the fixtures, plus current expenditures for bulb replacement.) This is the maximum price the hotel should be willing to pay BES for the conversion job.

  b What price should OEU charge BES for the CFL bulbs for the Opaque Gardens Hotel job?

  c What price should OEU charge the hotel for replacement bulbs?

2 a For the LMC test market, what is the value to FLS in the first year from the Victoria Casino contract if FLS switched to CFL bulbs? (This figure will be equivalent to the labour and equipment rental savings from longer bulb life.) This is the maximum amount, which FLS might pay to OEU for the 8000 new CFL bulbs (5000 18 W bulbs and 3000 9 W bulbs). Of course, FLS would also know that the casino was achieving large savings which might be shared with FLS and OEU.

  b What is the average annual saving to the Victoria Casino, over the 15-year life of the retrofitted fixtures, of switching to CFL bulbs? (This figure will be equivalent to energy savings, less the retrofit charge, plus the value of reduced casino downtime.) Assume the retrofit contractor earns a 40% gross margin and Siemens' captive finance subsidiary will finance the retrofit with a 15-year instalment loan at 12% interest. This is the maximum amount, which the casino might be willing to pay to FLS for using CFL bulbs. Of course, the casino would also know that FLS was saving on changeover costs.

  c What price should OEU charge FLS for the 8000 replacement bulbs each year?

3 Which of these two markets should OEU pursue? Both?

Case 504

Coors: balanced scorecard

Hugh Grove and Tom Cook, University of Denver, and Ken Richter, Coors Brewing Company

This case demonstrates the importance of supply chain management, and the comparison of various strategies through the use of EVA®. The case also requires the creation of a balanced scorecard to highlight the impact of any changes in strategy.

By the end of 2010, Coors had finished the implementation of a three-year computer-integrated logistics (CIL) project to improve its supply chain management. Coors defined its supply chain as every activity involved in moving production from the supplier's supplier to the customer's customer. (Since, by federal law, Coors cannot sell directly to consumers, Coors customers are its distributors whose customers are retailers whose customers are consumers.) Coors' supply chain included the following processes: purchasing, research and development, engineering, brewing, conditioning, fermenting, packaging, warehouse, logistics and transportation.

This CIL project was a cross-functional initiative to reengineer the business processes by which Coors' logistics or supply chain was managed. The project objective was to increase company profitability by reducing cycle times and operating costs and increasing customer (distributor) satisfaction.

The software vendor used for this project was the German company Systems Applications and Products (SAP), which provided the financial and materials planning software modules. The following major supply chain problems were corrected by this CIL project:

- meeting seasonal demand
- meeting demand surges from sales promotions
- supporting the introduction of more than three new brands each year
- filling routine customer (distributor) orders
- filling rush orders
- moving beer from production through warehouse to distributors before the beer spoiled.

The shelf-lives for Coors products were 60 days for beer kegs and 112 days for all other beer packages.

Matt Vail, head of Coors' Customer Service Department, had been the CIL project leader since the inception of the project. He had developed such expertise with supply chain management that he had just been hired by a supply chain consulting firm. In early 2011, on his last day of work for Coors, he was talking with Ken Rider, head of Coors' Quality Assurance Department.

Ken had just been placed in charge of the new balanced scorecard (BSC) project at Coors. The initial motivation for this project was to assess whether the supply chain improvements were being maintained. However, the project was broadened to become a company-wide BSC. Accordingly, the project strategy was to implement a performance measurement process that: (1) focused on continuous improvement, (2) rewarded reasonable risk taking and learning to improve performance, and (3) enabled employees to understand the opportunity and reward for working productively.

Matt: The supply chain management project was really challenging and rewarding. I hate to leave Coors, but the consulting firm made me such an attractive offer that I could not refuse it. I hope you have such positive experiences with this follow-up balanced scorecard project.

Source: Adapted from Grove, H., Cook, T. and Richter, K. (2000) 'Coors: balanced scorecard', *IMA Cases from Management Accounting Practice*, Volume 15 (Montvale, New Jersey: Institute of Marketing Accounting Practice).

Ken: This new project will be a real challenge. We need to build on all the improvements made by your supply chain project.

Matt: My project team was excited to see that our CEO discussed the supply chain project in his 2010 shareholder letter. He said that significant productivity gains in 2006 were due to our project, which streamlined purchasing, brewing, packaging, transportation and administration of the supply chain.

Ken: Perhaps an economic value added (EVA®) analysis could be done to assess these supply chain productivity gains.

Matt: That's an interesting idea, to analyse performance in the financial quadrant of the balanced scorecard with EVA®.

Ken: Another challenge for my project is how to translate the Coors vision statement and related business strategies into operational performance measures.

Matt: You also need to identify any gaps between the vision statement, business strategies and current performance.

Ken: Do you have any experiences from your project that I could use?

Matt: Well, we did obtain some benchmarking data to develop targets for some performance measures for our supply chain project. I can give you these measures, but they are limited due to confidentiality problems in obtaining such data. Maybe Coors should join one of the commercial benchmarking databases.

Ken: Thanks. I am also aware of certain employee resistance to developing a new set of performance measures for this balanced scorecard approach.

Matt: We had similar employee resistance to changes in the business processes of the supply chain. We were able to use the following crisis motivation. At that time, Coors could not support all the new beer brand introductions proposed by our marketing people, due to the antiquated 1970s software that was then being used for our supply chain management. The marketing people wanted to introduce three new brands each quarter, and we could support only three new brands each year! We also learned that we needed to get more employee involvement in the project.

Ken: That's a good idea. In fact, I've already developed a list of the most frequently asked questions about the balanced scorecard from initial meetings with employees involved in the supply chain.

Matt: You have lots of challenges awaiting you. Good luck in your new project. Make sure that today's improvements in supply chain performance don't become tomorrow's problems!

Company background

Coors had been a family-owned and operated business from its inception in 1873 until 1993 when the first non-family member became president and chief operating officer. However, Coors family members still held the positions of chairman of the board of directors and chief executive officer and also held all voting stock. Only non-voting, Class B common stock was publicly traded. Coors has been financed primarily by equity and has borrowed capital only twice in its corporate history. The first long-term debt, $220 million, 8.5% notes, was issued in 1991, and the final $40 million of principal repaid at the end of 1999. The second long-term debt, $100 million, 7% unsecured notes, was issued in a 1995 private placement. Of this principal, $80 million was due in 2009 and the last $20 million is due in 2012.

Coors had 16 beer brands, including a speciality line, Blue Moon, that competed with the domestic micro brewing industry. However, Coors continued to focus on its four key premium brands: Coors Light, Original Coors, Killian's Irish Red and Zima. Coors Light was the fourth largest selling beer in the United States. In packaging, Coors had to compete with the major competitors' value packaging, such as 12-packs and 30-packs.

Competition in the beer industry was strong, especially in the United States. Anheuser-Busch (A/B) was the market leader with approximately 44% of the US market, 80 million barrels sold,

$8 billion beer sales and $1 billion net profit. Due to its size, A/B was the acknowledged price leader in the industry. A/B also had 13 domestic production plants, including one in Fort Collins, Colorado, to achieve its customer service goal of having no major domestic distributor more than 500 miles away from one of its beer production plants.

Number two in this market was Miller, owned by Philip Morris, with approximately 22% market share, 40 million barrels sold, $4 billion beer sales and $460 million net profit. Miller had seven domestic production plants. Coors was number three with an 11% market share 20 million barrels sold, $2 billion beer sales and $80 million net profit. Coors had three production plants in the United States. Its Colorado plant was the largest brewery in the world and served 70% of the US market with its 10 can lines, 6 bottle lines, and 2 keg lines.

No other domestic brewers had market share in excess of 5%. In the late 1990s, there had been consolidation of the larger companies in the domestic beer industry. The most recent example was Stroh Brewing Company (SBC) with about 5% market share. SBC had signed agreements to sell its major brands to Miller and the remaining brands to Pabst Brewing Company. SBC would then exit the beer industry by 2003.

Benchmarking and performance gaps

Only limited benchmarking information was available since Coors had not yet decided to join any of the commercial benchmarking databases. (The largest one in the United States, the Hackett Group Study, sponsored by the American Institute of CPAs, has about 700 participating companies.) Benchmarking analyses using company annual reports revealed performance gaps with Coors' two major competitors (Exhibit 504.1).

There were insignificant differences in price per barrel as A/B was the industry price leader and the other competitors closely followed A/B's pricing decisions. A/B had this pricing power because its domestic market share of 44% was twice that of Miller and four times that of Coors.

The major motivation for the CIL supply chain project came from the deficiencies in the supply chain performance. The CIL project had become fully operational by the end of 2010, but more time was needed to realise the full benefits of such a project. There was still a significant amount of volatility in the production process that contributed to the Colorado redistribution centre's being the largest bottleneck in the supply chain. For example, Coors often could not meet its goal to load beer product directly off the production line into waiting railroad cars.

Thus, Ken's project team had already added three new non-monetary performance measures and created challenging performance targets for these measures to track anticipated additional efficiencies from the CIL project. Also, top management had created financial goals for key monetary performance measures in an attempt to become more competitive. These key performance measures are shown in Exhibit 504.2.

The gaps in current performance at the end of 2010 indicated problems with Coors' traditional, cost-based performance measures. For example, direct labour variances were becoming less important due to the highly automated nature of the beer production lines. Also, current performance measures were fragmented and inconsistent between plants, unclear, not linking the separate business processes to the organisation goals, not balanced to prevent overemphasis in

Exhibit 504.1	Benchmarking analysis		
Beer industry competitor	Manufacturing cost per barrel ($)	S,G & A cost per barrel ($)	Net profit ($)
Anheuser-Busch	48.00	27.50	12.50
Miller	50.00	27.00	11.00
Coors	55.00	29.00	4.00

| Exhibit 504.2 | Key performance measures | | | |

| | CIL project | | Performance | |
Performance measure	Pre	Post	Target	Gap
Non-monetary:				
Load schedule (1)	30%	60%	100%	40%
Load item accuracy (2)	90%	95%	100%	5%
Production stability (3)	25%	50%	100%	50%
Monetary (per barrel):				
Manufacturing cost	$56	$55	$53	$2
S, G & A cost	$30	$29	$27	$2
Net profit	$3	$4	$6	$2

one area at the expense of another, not able to be acted on at all levels, and used to punish rather than reward continuous improvement.

Balanced scorecard and change management issues

Ken was thinking that he could develop a crisis motivation for his balanced scorecard project, similar to the strategy used by Matt for his CIL project. Ken knew that Coors' traditional, cost-based performance measures were not driving desired results, as indicated by the various performance gaps. He thought that continuous improvement required clearly defined, aligned business process and activity measures that support a balanced scorecard.

Ken had already had preliminary meetings about this BSC project with employees who were involved in supply chain management. He had developed a list of frequently asked questions (FAQs), as follows:

1 Will the balanced scorecard be linked to any incentive plans?

2 What if a measure does not drive the correct behaviour after implementation? What process will be used to evolve the scorecard? How will my input be heard?

3 Won't the measures reduce our ability to be flexible with our distributors and make last-minute changes for them?

4 Why is the window on the load schedule performance measure so tight? What difference does it make if we get a load out within plus/minus two hours? If we get it out the day it is scheduled, won't the load arrive at the distributor as planned?

5 We already have plant measures that are working. Why would we want to change them?

6 The production stability measure does not give the production lines incentive to run ahead. Doesn't it make sense to allow us to run ahead on major brands as a cushion for those times when we have problems? So what should we do when we are more than an hour ahead, shut the line down?

7 Why would you base production stability, load schedule performance and load item accuracy on the initial weekly schedule? The schedule changes constantly. Why measure me against a weekly schedule that has changed as a result of something I had no control over?

8 Will the balanced scorecard be used to compare the performance of the three US plants? Since each plant is different, how can we be expected to use the same scorecard?

9 Product mix can adversely affect the cost per barrel. Will this be taken into consideration in this measure?

10 Some important measures may be excluded from the scorecard. If so, will they eventually be added to the scorecard?

11 Will there be a throughput measure on the scorecard? I cannot affect the number of barrels coming through my plant. That is determined by sales and scheduling that shifts production between plants.

12 How can you hold me responsible for a measure when I am not the only one who can affect it?

Balanced scorecard project: additional thoughts

Ken was wondering whether he should do an EVA® analysis to demonstrate its potential for a BSC financial performance measure. Coors' net operating profit before income taxes had increased from $75 million in 2003 to $105 million in 2010. According to both the CEO's shareholder letter and a value line analysis, the major reason for this increase was the productivity improvement from the supply chain management project, which cost $20 million. This $30 million improvement in net operating profit before income taxes was also predicted to become a permanent improvement for both 2011 and 2012 operations. Ken's project team had compiled five annual adjustments (all increases) and other financial information just in case Ken decided to do an EVA® analysis (Exhibit 504.3).

At the end of 2010, Coors had total stockholder equity of $730 million and total liabilities of $670 million. Total liabilities included $170 million of interest-bearing debt as well as current liabilities, deferred income taxes and pension liabilities. Coors' weighted average cost of capital was 10%. Ken was curious about what gaps might exist between vision statements and current business strategies for both Coors and the O&T department. However, he did not want this gap analysis to wind up overloading the BSC with too many performance measures. He was also concerned about what performance targets and reporting frequencies to establish for various BSC performance measures. Other challenges were how to link BSC performance measures and how to gain employee acceptance of the BSC.

Ken realised that he had some serious challenges ahead of him in order to create and implement a balanced scorecard for Coors. It was now January 2011 and top management was pressing for a quick installation of the balanced scorecard in order to use it for evaluating performance in 2011.

Exhibit 504.3	EVA adjustments (in $ millions)		
Adjustment		**Capital**	**Income**
1 Advertising costs (three-year life)		900	300
2 LIFO reserve		45	3
3 Deferred income tax liability		65	10
4 Capitalisation of operating leases		30	5
5 Net interest expense		0	12

Questions

1 Provide possible explanations for the performance gaps identified by Coors benchmarking analysis.

2 Answer the FAQs already raised by employees about the Coors BSC project.

3 Considering the prior gap and benchmarking analyses, design specific performance measures with benchmarked targets (where feasible) and reporting frequency to create an operational and acceptable BSC for Coors.

4 Perform an economic value added (EVA®) analysis to assess its potential as a BSC financial performance measure for Coors.

APPENDIX A
Solutions to selected exercises

CHAPTER 1

Exercise 1.11

This problem can form the basis of an introductory discussion of the entire field of management accounting.

1 The focus of management accounting is on assisting internal users in their pursuit of better decisions, whereas the focus of financial accounting is on helping external users seeking to make better decisions. Management accounting attempts to assist in making most decisions, including pricing, product choices, investments in equipment, making or buying goods and services, and manager rewards.

2 Generally accepted accounting principles affect both management accounting and financial accounting. However, an organisation's management accounting system is not governed by generally accepted accounting principles. For example, if an organisation wants to account for assets on the basis of replacement costs for internal purposes, no outside agency can prohibit such accounting.

Exercise 1.12

Report statement	Purpose
a	Formulating overall strategies . . .
b	Meeting external regulatory . . .
c	Performance measurement of . . . people
d	Cost planning and cost control
e	Product/customer emphasis decisions

Exercise 1.22

1 Companies with 'codes of conduct' frequently have a 'supplier clause' that prohibits their employees from accepting 'material' (in some cases, any) gifts from suppliers. The motivations include:

- *Integrity/conflict of interest*. Suppose von Stolzing recommends that a Pogner 1-2-3 product subsequently be purchased by Beckmesser. This recommendation could be because he felt he owed them an obligation as his trip to the Marbella conference was fully paid for by Pogner.
- *The appearance of a conflict of interest*. Even if the Pogner 1-2-3 product is the superior one at that time, other suppliers will probably have a different opinion. They may believe that the way to sell products to Beckmesser is via 'fully-paid junkets to resorts'. Those not wanting to do business this way may downplay future business activities with Beckmesser even though Beckmesser may gain much from such activities.

Some executives view the meeting as 'suspect' from the start given the Costa del Sol location and its 'rest and recreation' tone.

2 The pros of attending the user meeting are as follows:

- Able to learn more about the software products of Pogner.
- Able to interact with other possible purchasers and get their opinions.

- Able to influence the future product development plans of Pogner in a way that will benefit Beckmesser. An example is Pogner subsequently developing software modules tailored to food product companies.
- Saves Beckmesser money. Visiting suppliers and their customers typically costs money whereas Pogner is paying for the Marbella conference.

The cons of attending are:

- The ethical issues raised in requirement 1.
- Negative morale effects on other Beckmesser employees who do not get to attend the Marbella conference. These employees may reduce their trust and respect for von Stolzing's judgement, arguing he has been on a 'supplier-paid vacation'.

The conditions on attending that Beckmesser might impose are:

- A sizable part of time in Marbella has to be devoted to business rather than recreation.
- The decision on which Beckmesser executive attends is *not* made by the person who attends (this reduces the appearance of a conflict of interest).
- The person attending (von Stolzing) does not have the final say on a purchase decision (this reduces the appearance of a conflict of interest).
- Beckmesser executives go only when a new major purchase is being contemplated (to avoid the conference becoming a regular 'vacation').

A Conference Board publication *Corporate Ethics* asked executives about a comparable situation:

- 76% said Beckmesser and von Stolzing face an ethical consideration in deciding whether to attend.
- 71% said von Stolzing should not attend as the payment of expenses is a 'gift' within the meaning of a credible corporate ethics policy.

3 Concerning the pros of having a written code, the Conference Board outlines the following reasons why companies adopt codes of ethics:

- Signals commitment of senior management to ethics.
- Promotes public trust in the credibility of the company and its employees.
- Signals the managerial professionalism of its employees.
- Provides guidance to employees as to how difficult problems are to be handled. If adhered to, employees will avoid many actions that are, or appear to be, unethical.
- Drafting of the policy (and its redrafting in the light of ambiguities) can assist management in anticipating and preparing for ethical issues not yet encountered.

The cons of having a written code are:

- Can give the appearance that all issues have been covered. Issues not covered may appear to be 'acceptable' even when they are not.
- Can constrain the entrepreneurial activities of employees. Forces people always to 'behave by the book'.
- The cost of developing such a code can be 'high' if it consumes a lot of employee time.

CHAPTER 2

Exercise 2.12

1

	Fixed costs	Variable costs
Schedule 1	€8000	–
Schedule 2	€2000	€20 per person
Schedule 3	–	€50 per person

2	50 people	200 people	500 people
Schedule 1			
Total costs	€8 000	€8 000	€8 000
Unit costs	160	40	16
Schedule 2			
Total costs	€3 000*	€6 000†	€12 000‡
Unit costs	60	30	24
Schedule 3			
Total costs	€2 500	€10 000	€25 000
Unit costs	50	50	50

* (€20 × 50) + €2000.
† (€20 × 200) + €2000.
‡ (€20 × 500) + €2000.

Schedule 1 has €8000 fixed costs; as the attendance increases, the unit cost decreases. Schedule 2 has both a fixed cost component (€2000) and a variable cost component (€20); the spreading of the €2000 amount over more units as attendance increases causes the unit cost to decrease. Schedule 3 has only a variable cost component; there is no change in unit cost as attendance increases.

Exercise 2.23

1 Target closing stock of finished goods, 31 Dec. 2016 .... 12 000 units
Forecasted sales for 2016 .... 122 000 units
Total finished goods required in 2016 .... 134 000 units
Opening finished goods, 1 Jan. 2016 .... 9 000 units
Finished goods production required in 2016 .... 125 000 units

2 Revenues (122 000 units sold × €4.80) €585 600
Cost of units sold:
  Opening stock of finished goods, 1 Jan. 2016 .... €20 970
  Cost of goods manufactured 281 250
  Cost of goods available for sale 302 220
  Closing stock of finished goods, 31 Dec. 2016 .... 27 000 .... 275 220
  Gross margin 310 380
Operating costs:
  Marketing, distribution and customer-service costs 204 700
  Administrative costs .... 50 000 .... 254 700
Operating profit €55 680

Supporting computations

	Manufacturing costs for 125 000 units		
	Variable	Fixed	Total
Direct materials costs	€175 000	–	€175 000
Direct manufacturing labour costs	37 500	–	37 500
Plant energy costs	6 250	–	6 250
Indirect manufacturing labour costs	12 500	16 000	28 500
Other indirect manufacturing costs	10 000	24 000	34 000
Cost of goods manufactured	€241 250	€40 000	€281 250

- Direct materials costs = 250 000 kg × €0.70 per kg = €175 000.
- The average unit manufacturing costs in 2015 are €281 250 ÷ 125 000 units = €2.25.
- Finished goods, 31 Dec. 2015 = 12 000 × €2.25 = €27 000.
- Variable marketing, distrib. and customer-service costs, 122 000 × €1.35 .... €164 700
  Fixed marketing, distrib. and customer-service costs 40 000
  Fixed administrative costs 50 000
  .... €254 700

Exercise 2.24

1 Variable cost per tonne of beach sand mined:

Subcontractor	€80
Government tax	50
Total	€130

Fixed costs per month:

$$0–100 \text{ tonnes of capacity per day} = €150\,000$$
$$101–200 \text{ tonnes of capacity per day} = €300\,000$$
$$201–300 \text{ tonnes of capacity per day} = €450\,000$$

2

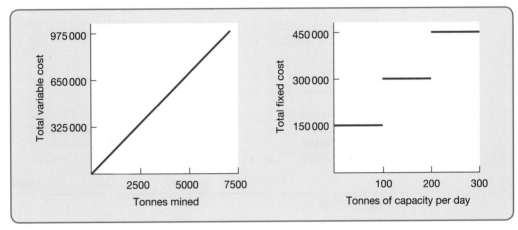

The concept of relevant range is potentially relevant for both graphs. However, the question does not place restrictions on the unit variable costs. The relevant ranges for the total fixed costs are from 0 to 100 tonnes; from 101 to 200 tonnes; from 201 to 300 tonnes, and so on. Within these ranges, the fixed costs do not change in total.

3 Tonnes mined per day (1)	Tonnes mined per month (2) = (1) × 25	Fixed unit cost per tonne (3) = FC ÷ (2)	Variable unit cost per tonne (4)	Total unit cost per tonne (5) = (3) + (4)
a 180	4500	€300 000 ÷ 4500 = €66.67	€130	€196.67
b 220	5500	€450 000 ÷ 5500 =€81.82	€130	€211.82

The unit cost for 220 tonnes mined per day is €211.82, while for 180 tonnes it is only €196.67. This difference is caused by the fixed cost increment from 101 to 200 tonnes being spread over an increment of 80 tonnes, while the fixed cost increment from 201 to 300 tonnes is spread only over an increment of 20 tonnes.

CHAPTER 3

Exercise 3.11

1

		Budgeted fixed indirect costs	Budgeted hours	Budgeted fixed indirect costs rate per hour	Budgeted variable indirect cost rate per hour	Budgeted total indirect cost rate per hour
a	Jan.–March	€50 000	20 000	2.50	10	12.50
	April–June	50 000	10 000	5.00	10	15.00
	July–Sept.	50 000	4 000	12.50	10	22.50
	Oct.–Dec.	50 000	6 000	8.33	10	18.33
b	Jan.–Dec.	€200 000	40 000	5.00	10	15.00

2 **a** All four jobs use 10 hours of professional labour time. The only difference in job costing is the indirect cost rate. The quarterly-based indirect job cost rates are:

Roquelin:	$(10 \times €12.50) = €125.00$
Leduc:	$(6 \times €12.50) + (4 \times €15.00) = €135.00$
Dudet:	$(4 \times €15.00) + (6 \times €22.50) = €195.00$
Leclerc:	$(5 \times €12.50) + (2 \times €22.50) + (3 \times €18.33) = €162.50$

	Roquelin	Leduc	Dudet	Leclerc
Revenues, €65 × 10	€650	650	650	650.00
Direct costs, €30 × 10	300	300	300	300.00
Indirect costs	125	135	195	162.50
Total costs	425	435	495	462.50
Operating profit	€225	215	155	187.50

b Using annual-based indirect job cost rates, all four customers will have the same operating profit:

Revenues, €65 × 10	€650
Direct costs, €30 × 10	300
Indirect costs, €15 × 10	150
Total costs	450
Operating profit	€200

3 All four jobs use 10 hours of professional labour time. Using the quarterly-based indirect cost rates, there are four different operating profit as the work done on them is completed in different quarters. In contrast, using the annual indirect cost rate all four customers have the same operating profit. All these different operating profit figures for jobs with the same number of professional labour-hours are due to the allocation of fixed indirect costs.

An overview of the Tax-Assistance job costing system is:

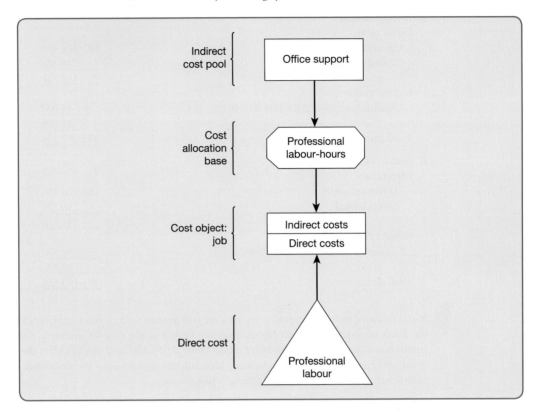

Exercise 3.17

1 a Budgeted indirect-cost rate $= \dfrac{\text{Budgeted indirect costs}}{\text{Budgeted direct labour-hours}} = \dfrac{\text{SKr }8\,000\,000}{160\,000 \text{ hours}}$

$= \text{SKr }50 \text{ per direct labour-hour}$

b Actual indirect-cost rate $= \dfrac{\text{Actual indirect costs}}{\text{Actual direct labour-hour}} = \dfrac{\text{SKr }6\,888\,000}{164\,000 \text{ hours}}$

$= \text{SKr }42 \text{ per direct labour-hour}$

2	Mora model	Solna model
a Normal costing		
Direct costs		
Direct materials	SKr 106 450	SKr 127 604
Direct labour	36 276	41 410
	142 726	169 014
Indirect costs		
Assembly support (SKr 50 × 900; 1010)	45 000	50 500
	45 000	50 500
Total costs	SKr 187 726	SKr 219 514
b Actual costing		
Direct costs		
Direct materials	SKr 106 450	SKr 127 604
Direct labour	36 276	41 410
	142 726	169 014
Indirect costs		
Assembly support (SKr 42 × 900; 1010)	37 800	42 420
	37 800	42 420
Total costs	SKr 180 526	SKr 211 434

3 Normal costing enables Idergard to report a job cost as soon as the job is completed, assuming that both the direct materials and direct labour costs are known at the time of use/work. Once the 900 direct labour-hours are known for the Mora model (June 2015), Idergard can calculate the SKr 187 726 cost figure using normal costing. In contrast, Idergard has to wait until the December 2015 year-end to calculate the SKr 180 526 cost figure using actual costing.

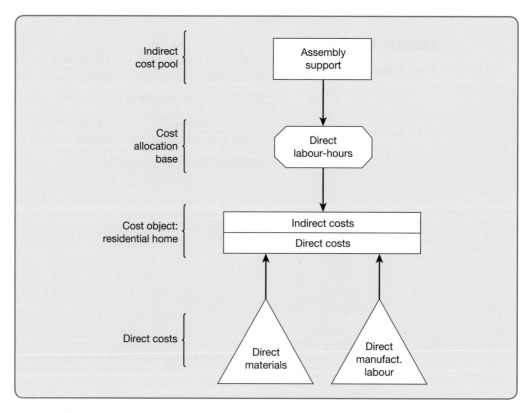

Exercise 3.20

1 Actual indirect cost rate = 190% of professional labour-euros.

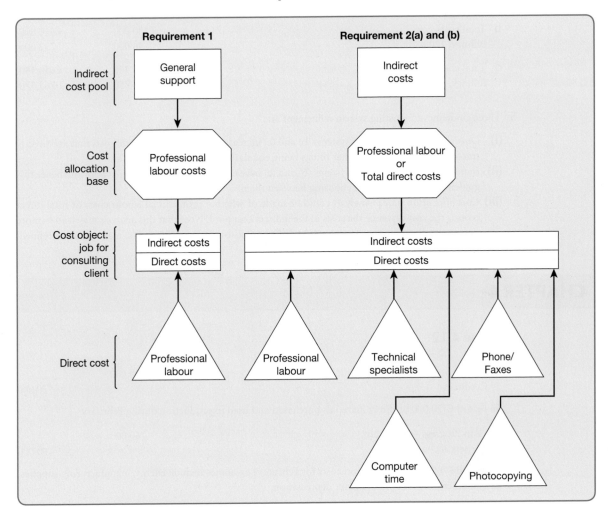

2 a Actual indirect cost rate = 135% of professional labour-euros
  b Actual indirect cost rate = 87.1% of total direct costs

3		Client 304	Client 308
a	Direct costs	€200 000	€200 000
	Indirect costs, 190% × €200 000	380 000	380 000
	Total costs	€580 000	€580 000
b	Direct costs	€260 000	€340 000
	Indirect costs, 135% × €200 000	270 000	270 000
	Total costs	€530 000	€610 000
c	Direct costs	€260 000	€340 000
	Indirect costs, 87.1% × direct costs	226 460	296 140
	Total costs	€486 460	€636 140

4

		Client 304	Client 308
a	Total costs	€580 000	€580 000
	Billings, 120% × total costs	696 000	696 000
b	Total costs	€530 000	€610 000
	Billings, 120% × total costs	636 000	732 000
c	Total costs	€486 460	€636 140
	Billings, 120% × total costs	583 750	763 370

5 Three guidelines for costing system refinement are:

(i) *Direct cost tracing.* Costing systems (b) and (c) increase the percentage of total costs that are directly traced to the cost object. Other things being equal, (b) or (c) is preferred to (a).

(ii) *Indirect cost pools.* Costing systems (b) and (c) have the same single indirect cost pool and hence this guideline does not assist in choosing between them.

(iii) *Cost allocation bases.* Analysis could be made of whether professional labour costs or total direct costs is the cost driver of the costs in the indirect cost pool. Note that this analysis may lead to more than one indirect cost pool being selected. That is, costing systems (b) and (c) may be further refined.

CHAPTER 4

Exercise 4.12

1 Work in Progress – Assembly   720 000
    Creditors   720 000

To record €720 000 of direct materials purchased and used in production during February

2 Work in Progress – Assembly   760 000
    Various accounts   760 000

To record €760 000 of conversion costs for February; examples include energy, manufacturing supplies, all manufacturing labour, and plant depreciation

3 Work in Progress – Testing   1 368 000
    Work in Progress – Assembly   1 368 000

To record 9000 units completed and transferred from Assembly to Testing during February at

$$€152 \times 9000 \text{ units} = €1 \ 368 \ 000$$

Postings to the Work in Progress – Assembly account follows.

Work in Progress – Assembly Department

Opening stock, 1 February	0	3 Transferred out to	
1 Direct materials	720 000	Work in Progress – Testing	1 368 000
2 Conversion costs	760 000		
Closing stock, 28 February	112 000		

Exercise 4.14

1 The reported monthly cost per equivalent unit of either direct materials or conversion costs is lower when the plant manager overestimates the percentage of completion of closing work in progress; the overestimate increases the denominator and thus decreases the cost per equivalent whole unit. By reporting a lower cost per equivalent unit, the plant manager increases the likelihood of being in the top three ranked plants for the benchmarking comparisons.

A plant manager can manipulate the monthly estimate of percentage of completion by understating the number of steps yet to be undertaken before a suit becomes a finished good.

2 There are several options available:

   a Khrishna shows the letters to the line executive to whom the plant managers report directly (say, the corporate manager of manufacturing). This approach is appropriate if the letters allege it is the plant managers who are manipulating the percentage of completion estimates.

   b Khrishna herself shows the letters to the plant managers. This approach runs the danger of the plant managers ignoring or reacting negatively to someone to whom they do not report in a line mode questioning their behaviour. Much will depend here on how Khrishna raises the issue. Unsigned letters need not have much credibility unless they contain specific details.

   c Khrishna discusses the letters with the appropriate plant accountants without including the plant manager in the discussion. While the plant accountant has responsibility for preparing the accounting reports from the plant, the plant accountant in most cases reports directly to the plant manager. If this reporting relationship exists, Khrishna may create a conflict of interest situation for the plant accountant. Only if the plant accountant reports directly to the corporate accountant and has a 'dotted-line' reporting responsibility to the plant manager should Khrishna show the letters to the plant accountant without simultaneously showing them to the plant manager.

3 The plant accountant's ethical responsibilities to Khrishna and to Manchester Suits should be the same. These include:

   - *Competence.* The plant accountant is expected to have the competence to make equivalent unit computations. This competence does not always extend to making estimates of the percentage of completion of a product. In Manchester Suits' case, however, the products are probably easy to understand and observe. Hence, a plant accountant could obtain reasonably reliable evidence on percentage of completion at a specific plant.

   - *Objectivity.* The plant accountant should not allow the possibility of the division being written up favourably in the company newsletter to influence the way equivalent unit costs are calculated.

4 Khrishna could seek evidence on possible manipulations as follows:

   - Instruct plant accountants to report detailed breakdowns on the stages of production and then conduct end-of-month audits to verify the actual stages completed for closing work in progress.

   - Examine trends over time in closing work in progress. Divisions that report low amounts of closing work in progress relative to total production are not likely to be able to affect greatly equivalent cost amounts by manipulating percentage of completion estimates. Divisions that show sizable quantities of total production in closing work in progress are more likely to be able to manipulate equivalent cost computations by manipulating percentage of completion estimates.

Exercise 4.16

1 Solution Exhibit 4.16A calculates equivalent units of (a) opening work in progress and (b) work done in the current period for each cost element. To calculate equivalent units of opening work in progress, divide the value of opening work in progress by the cost per equivalent unit of opening work in progress. Similarly, to calculate equivalent units of work done in the current period divide total costs added in the current period by the cost per equivalent unit of work done in the current period.

Solution Exhibit 4.16A

Step 3: Compute equivalent units under the weighted-average method, thermo-assembly process of Le Roi du Plastique for June.

	Transferred-in costs	Direct materials	Conversion costs
a *Equivalent unit costs of opening work in progress*			
Opening work in progress (given)	€90 000	–	€45 000
Divide by cost per equivalent unit of opening work in progress	÷ €6	–	÷ €5
Equivalent units of opening work in progress	15 000	–	9 000
b *Equivalent unit costs of work done in current period only*			
Costs added in current period (given)	€58 500	€57 000	€57 200
Divide by cost per equivalent unit of work done in current period	÷ €6.50	÷ €3	÷ €5.20
Equivalent units of work done in current period only	9 000	19 000	11 000

Solution Exhibit 4.16B

Steps 1 and 2: Summarise output in physical units and compute equivalent units, thermo-assembly process of Le Roi du Plastique for June.

	(Step 1) Physical units	(Step 2) Equivalent units		
Flow of production		Transferred-in costs	Direct materials	Conversion costs
Completed and transferred out during current period	19 000	19 000	19 000	19 000
Add closing work in progress, (5000 × 100%; 5000 × 0%; 5000 × 20%)	5 000	5 000	0	1 000
Total accounted for	24 000	24 000	19 000	20 000
Deduct opening work in progress (15 000 × 100%; 15 000 × 0%; 15 000 × 60%)	15 000	15 000	0	9 000
Transferred in during current period	9 000			
Work done in current period only		9 000	19 000	11 000

2 and 3 See Solution Exhibit 4.16B.

Using information about physical units given in the exercise:

Physical units completed and transferred out	=	Physical units in opening work in progress	+	Physical units transferred-in during period	–	Physical units in closing work in progress
	=	15 000	+	9000	–	5000
	=	19 000				

Equivalent units of opening work in progress and equivalent units of work done in current period (rows 4 and 5 of Solution Exhibit 4.16B) have been calculated in Solution Exhibit 4.16A. Equivalent units of units completed and transferred out for each cost element equal the 19 000 physical units completed and transferred out. Equivalent units of closing work in progress for each cost element are then given by:

Equivalent units in closing work in progress	=	Equivalent units in opening work in progress	+	Equivalent units of work done in current period	−	Equivalent units completed and transferred out during current period
Equivalent units of transferred-in cost in closing work in progress	=			15 000 + 9000 − 19 000	=	5000 units
Equivalent units of direct materials in closing work in progress	=			0 + 19 000 − 19 000	=	0 units
Equivalent units of conversion costs in closing work in progress	=			9000 + 11 000 − 19 000	=	1000 units

3a Percentage of completion of opening work-in-progress stock:

Transferred-in costs:	15 000 equivalent units ÷ 15 000 physical units	=	100%
Direct materials:	0 equivalent units ÷ 15 000 physical units	=	0%
Conversion costs:	9000 equivalent units ÷ 15 000 physical units	=	60%

3b Percentage of completion of closing work-in-progress stock:

Transferred-in costs:	5000 equivalent units ÷ 5000 physical units	=	100%
Direct materials:	0 equivalent units ÷ 5000 physical units	=	0%
Conversion costs:	1000 equivalent units ÷ 5000 physical units	=	20%

CHAPTER 5

Exercise 5.11

1 Total manufacturing overhead cost pool = €3 600 000 + €2 800 000 = €6 400 000.

Total direct manufacturing labour-hours:

500 cc:	10 000 × 2	=	20 000
1000 cc:	20 000 × 4	=	80 000
			100 000 hours

Manufacturing overhead cost per direct manufacturing labour-hour	=	€64

Manufacturing overhead costs allocated per unit to each brand:

500 cc:	2 × €64	=	€128
1000 cc:	4 × €64	=	€256

2 Machining cost pool = €3 600 000.

Machining hours:

500 cc:	10 000 × 8	=	80 000
1000 cc:	20 000 × 8	=	160 000
			240 000 hours

Machining cost per machining hour	=	€15

Each unit would be charged:

500 cc:	8 × €15	=	€120
1000 cc:	8 × €15	=	€120

General plant overhead cost pool	=	€2 800 000
Direct manufacturing labour-hours (from requirement 1)	=	100 000 hours
General plant overhead costs per direct manufacturing labour-hour	=	€28

Each unit would be charged:

500 cc:	2 × €28	=	€56
1000 cc:	4 × €28	=	€112

The total manufacturing overhead costs allocated per unit of each brand is:

500 cc:	Machining cost pool	8 × €15 =	€120
	General plant overhead cost pool	2 × €28 =	56
			€176
1000 cc:	Machining cost pool	8 × €15 =	€120
	General plant overhead cost pool	4 × €28 =	112
			€232

3 Use of two separate cost pools can provide more refined estimates of unit costs. Different cause-and-effect relationships may exist for the machining costs and the general plant overhead costs, which can be captured by the use of two different allocation bases.

The use of separate cost pools can also aid cost management at Azu-Cena as different cost improvement targets may be appropriate for each manufacturing overhead cost area.

Exercise 5.14

1 The total costs in the single-cost pool are fixed (€1 000 000) and variable (€2 000 000) = €3 000 000. Alxenor could use one of two allocation bases (budgeted usage or actual usage) given the information provided.

- Allocation to Iraklion based on budgeted usage: (60/200) × €3 000 000 = €900 000.
- Allocation to Iraklion based on actual usage: (120/240) × €3 000 000 = €1 500 000.

2 Using the dual-rate method (with separate fixed and variable cost pools), several combinations of the budgeted and actual usage allocation bases are possible:

Fixed cost pool. Total costs of €1 000 000:

- Allocation to Iraklion based on budgeted usage: (60/200) × €1 000 000 = €300 000.
- Allocation to Iraklion based on actual usage: (120/240) × €1 000 000 = €500 000.

Variable cost pool. Total costs of €2 000 000:

- Allocation to Iraklion based on budgeted usage: (60/200) × €2 000 000 = €600 000.
- Allocation to Iraklion based on actual usage: (120/240) × €2 000 000 = €1 000 000.

The combinations possible are:

Combination	Fixed-cost pool	Variable cost pool	Allocation function
I	Budgeted usage	Budgeted usage	= €300 000 + €600 000 = €900 000
II	Budgeted usage	Actual usage	= €300 000 + €1 000 000 = €1 300 000
III	Actual usage	Budgeted usage	= €500 000 + €600 000 = €1 100 000
IV	Actual usage	Actual usage	= €500 000 + €1 000 000 = €1 500 000

Combinations I and IV give the same cost allocations as in requirement 1. Combination II is a frequently used dual-rate method. The fixed costs are allocated using budgeted usage on the rationale that it better captures the cost of providing capacity. The variable costs are allocated using actual usage on a cause-and-effect rationale. Combination III is rarely encountered in practice.

Exercise 5.22

1 The average full cost per unit of the 2000 units of Product Line B produced in 2015 is €27 850 per unit. Details of the €55.7 million full cost for Product Line B, compared with those for Product Line A, are (in €millions):

	Product Line A	Product Line B
Direct costs		
Research and development	€10.0	€5.0
Design	2.0	3.0
Manufacturing/production	15.0	13.0
Marketing	6.0	5.0
Distribution	2.0	3.0
Customer service	5.0	3.0
Total direct costs	40.0	32.0
Indirect costs		
Research and development, 6000/8000; 2000/8000 × €20.0	€15.0	€5.0
Design, 8/12; 4/12 × €6.0	4.0	2.0
Manufacturing/production, 70 000/120 000; 50 000/120 000 × €24.0	14.0	10.0
Marketing, 25/70; 45/70 × €7.0	2.5	4.5
Distribution, 600/2000; 1400/2000 × €2.0	0.6	1.4
Customer service, 1000/5000; 4000/5000 × €1.0	0.2	0.8
Total indirect costs	36.3	23.7
Full product costs	€76.3	€55.7

2 The summary data are (in €millions):

	Product Line A	Product Line B
Upstream	€31.0	€15.0
Manufacturing	29.0	23.0
Downstream	16.3	17.7
	€76.3	€55.7
Upstream		
Direct		
Research and development	€10.0	€5.0
Design	2.0	3.0
	12.0	8.0
Indirect		
Research and development	15.0	5.0
Design	4.0	2.0
	19.0	7.0
Total upstream costs	€31.0	€15.0
Manufacturing		
Direct	€15.0	€13.0
Indirect	14.0	10.0
Total manufacturing cost	€29.0	€23.0
Downstream		
Direct		
Marketing	€6.0	€5.0
Distribution	2.0	3.0
Customer service	5.0	3.0
	13.0	11.0
Indirect		
Marketing	2.5	4.5
Distribution	0.6	1.4
Customer service	0.2	0.8
	3.3	6.7
Total downstream costs	€16.3	€17.7

3 The inventoriable costs are (in €millions):

	Product Line B
Direct costs	
Design	€3.0
Manufacturing	13.0
Total	16.0
Indirect costs	
Design	2.0
Manufacturing	10.0
Total	12.0
Total inventoriable costs	€28.0

The average inventoriable cost per unit of Product Line B is €14 000 per unit.

4 The reimbursable costs for Product Line A are (in €millions):

	Product Line A
Direct costs	
Research and development	€10.0
Design	2.0
Manufacturing/production	15.0
Distribution	2.0
Customer service	5.0
Total direct costs	34.0
Indirect costs	
Research and development	15.0
Design	4.0
Manufacturing/production	14.0
Distribution	0.6
Customer service	0.2
Total indirect costs	33.8
Full reimbursable cost	€67.8

5 No. The answers to requirements 1 to 4 illustrate how a single accounting system (database) can provide relevant data for a diverse set of decisions. The data in this single system can be 'sliced and diced' in many ways without requiring multiple systems to be independently set up.

CHAPTER 6

Exercise 6.13

1 a Sales value at split-off point method

	Kilograms of product	Wholesale selling price per kg	Sales value at split-off	Weighting: sales value at split-off	Joint costs allocated	Allocation costs per kg
Breasts	100	€1.10	€110	0.675	€67.50	€0.6750
Wings	20	0.40	8	0.049	4.90	0.2450
Thighs	40	0.70	28	0.172	17.20	0.4300
Bones	80	0.20	16	0.098	9.80	0.1225
Feathers	10	0.10	1	0.006	0.60	0.0600
	250		€163	1.000	€100.00	

Costs of destroyed product

Breasts:	€0.6750 × 20 = €13.50
Wings:	€0.2450 × 10 = 2.45
	€15.95

b Physical measures method

	Kilograms of product	Weighting: physical measures	Joint costs allocated	Allocation costs per kg
Breasts	100	0.400	€40.00	€0.400
Wings	20	0.080	8.00	0.400
Thighs	40	0.160	16.00	0.400
Bones	80	0.320	32.00	0.400
Feathers	10	0.040	4.00	0.400
	250	1.000	€100.00	

Costs of destroyed product

Breasts:	€0.40 × 20 =	€8
Wings:	€0.40 × 10 =	4
		€12

Note: Although not required, it is useful to highlight the individual product profitability figures:

		Sales value at split-off method		Physical measures method	
Product	Sales value	Joint costs allocated	Gross income	Joint costs allocated	Gross income
Breasts	€110	€67.50	€42.50	€40.00	€70.00
Wings	8	4.90	3.10	8.00	0.00
Thighs	28	17.20	10.80	16.00	12.00
Bones	16	9.80	6.20	32.00	(16.00)
Feathers	1	0.60	0.40	4.00	(3.00)

2 The sales value at split-off method captures the benefits-received criterion of cost allocation. The costs of processing a chicken are allocated to products in proportion to the ability to contribute revenue. Galinha-Esquina's decision to process chicken is heavily influenced by the revenues from breasts and thighs. The bones provide relatively few benefits to Galinha-Esquina despite their high physical volume.

The physical measures method shows profits on breasts and thighs and losses on bones and feathers. Given that Galinha-Esquina has to process jointly all the chicken products, it does not make sense intuitively to single out individual products that are being processed simultaneously as making losses while the overall operations make a profit.

Exercise 6.14

1

	By-product accounting method			
	A	**B**	**C**	**D**
When by-products are recognised in the general ledger	At production	At production	At sale	At sale
Where by-product revenues appear in the profit statement	Reduction of cost	Revenue item	Reduction of cost	Revenue item
Revenues:				
Main product: Pelléas, 8000 × €20.00	€160 000	€160 000	€160 000	€160 000
By-product: Mélisande, 1400 × €2.00	–	2 800	–	2 800
	160 000	162 800	160 000	162 800

	By-product accounting method			
	A	B	C	D
Cost of goods sold:				
Total manufacturing costs	120 000	120 000	120 000	120 000
Deduct by-product revenue, 1400 × €2.00	2 800	–	2 800	–
Net manufacturing costs	117 200	120 000	117 200	120 000
Deduct main product stock, 2000/10 000 × net manufacturing costs	23 440	24 000	23 440	24 000
Deduct by-product stock, 600 × €2.00	1 200	1 200	–	–
Cost of goods sold	92 560	94 800	93 760	96 000
Gross margin	€67 440	€68 000	€66 240	€66 800
Gross margin percentage	42.15%	41.77%	41.40%	41.03%

2	A	B	C	D
Inventoriable costs (30 September):				
Main product – Pelléas	€23 440	€24 000	€23 440	€24 000
By-product – Mélisande	1 200	1 200	0	0

Under methods C and D there is no inventoriable cost shown for the by-product (Mélisande), as by-products are not recognised in the general ledger until sales are made.

3   Method A or B results in a better matching of costs with revenues than does either Method C or D. Method B results in more disclosure about individual product revenues than does Method A. Method A 'buries' information about by-product revenues as a reduction of cost.

Exercise 6.19

A diagram of the situation is shown in Solution Exhibit 6.19.

1	Quantity (kg)	Sales price per kg	Final sales value	Separable processing costs	Estimated net realisable value at split-off	Weighting
Vadstena	20 000	SKr 20	SKr 400 000	SKr 100 000	SKr 300 000	30/56
Vättervik	60 000	6	360 000	200 000	160 000	16/56
Birgitta	100 000	1	100 000	0	100 000	10/56
Totals			SKr 860 000	SKr 300 000	SKr 560 000	

Allocation of Skr 420 000 joint costs:

Vadstena	30/56 × SKr 420 000 =	SKr 225 000
Vättervik	16/56 × SKr 420 000 =	120 000
Birgitta	10/56 × SKr 420 000 =	75 000
		SKr 420 000

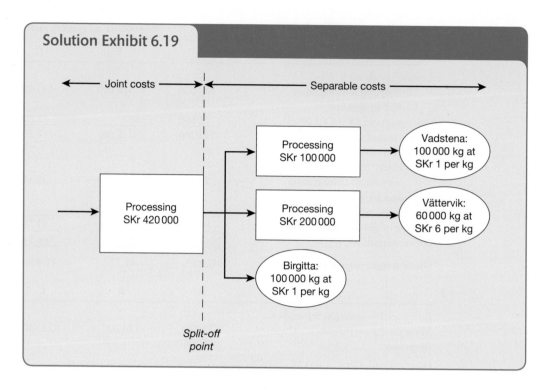

Solution Exhibit 6.19

	Joint costs allocated	Separable processing costs	Total costs	Units	Unit cost
Vadstena	SKr 225 000	SKr 100 000	SKr 325 000	20 000	SKr 16.25
Vättervik	120 000	200 000	320 000	60 000	5.33
Birgitta	75 000	0	75 000	100 000	0.75
Totals	SKr 420 000	SKr 300 000	SKr 720 000	180 000	

The closing stock is:

Vadstena	1000 × SKr 16.25 =	SKr 16 250
Vättervik	1000 × SKr 5.33 =	5 330
Birgitta	1000 × SKr 0.75 =	750
		SKr 22 330

2

	Unit sales price	Unit cost	Gross margin	Gross-margin percentage
Vadstena	SKr 20	SKr 16.25	SKr 3.75	18.75%
Vättervik	6	5.33	0.67	11.17
Birgitta	1	0.75	0.25	25.00

3 Further processing of Vättervik yields incremental profit of SKr 40 000:

Incremental revenue of further processing Vättervik, (SKr 6 − SKr 2) × 60 000	SKr 240 000
Incremental processing costs	200 000
Incremental operating profit from further processing	SKr 40 000

Langholmen-Sverige should process Vättervik further. Note that joint costs are irrelevant to this decision; they remain the same, whichever alternative (sell at split-off or process further) is selected.

CHAPTER 7

Exercise 7.12

1 Normal utilisation (givens denoted by §):

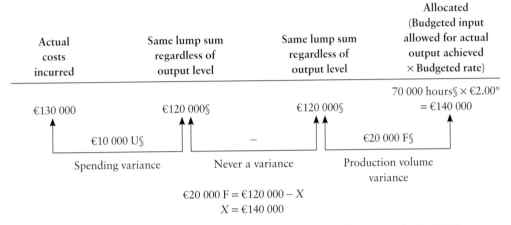

$$€20\ 000\ F = €120\ 000 - X$$
$$X = €140\ 000$$

* Budgeted fixed manufacturing overhead rate per unit = €2 per machine-hour, denominator level = 60 000 machine-hours.

2 Practical capacity (givens denoted by §):

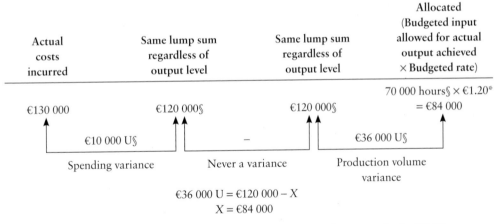

$$€36\ 000\ U = €120\ 000 - X$$
$$X = €84\ 000$$

* Budgeted manufacturing overhead rate per unit = €1.20 per machine-hour, denominator level = 100 000 machine-hours.

3 To maximise operating profit, the executive vice-president would favour using normal utilisation rather than practical capacity. Why? Because normal utilisation is a smaller base than practical capacity, resulting in any year-end stock having a higher unit cost. Thus, less fixed manufacturing overhead would become an expense if normal utilisation were used as the denominator level.

Exercise 7.19

1 Ericsson AB: Income statements for the year (in SEK 000).

Variable costing

Revenues (25 000 × SEK 40)		SEK 1000
Variable costs		
Opening stock (1000 × SEK 24)	SEK 24	
Variable cost of goods manufactured (29 000 × SEK 24)	696	
Cost of goods available for sale	720	
Closing stock (5000 × SEK 24)	120	
Variable manufacturing cost of goods sold	600	
Variable marketing and administrative costs		
(25 000 × SEK 1.20)	30	
Variable costs		630
Contribution margin		370
Fixed costs		
Fixed manufacturing overhead costs	120	
Fixed marketing and administrative costs	190	
Fixed costs		310
Operating profit		SEK 60

Absorption costing

Revenues (25 000 × SEK 40)		SEK 1000
Cost of goods sold		
Opening stock (1000 × SEK 28)	SEK 28	
Variable manufacturing costs (29 000 × SEK 24)	696	
Fixed manufacturing costs (given)	120	
Cost of goods available for sale	844	
Closing stock (5000 × SEK 28)	140	
Cost of goods sold		704
Gross margin		296
Marketing and administrative costs		
Variable marketing and administrative costs		
(25 000 × SEK 1.20)	30	
Fixed marketing and administrative costs	190	
Marketing and administrative costs		220
Operating profit		SEK 76

2 SEK 76 000 − SEK 60 000 = (5000 × SEK 4) − (1000 × SEK 4)
$$= \text{SEK } 20\,000 - \text{SEK } 4000$$
$$= \text{SEK } 16\,000$$

The operating profit figures differ because the amount of fixed manufacturing costs in the closing stock differs from that in the opening stock.

3 *Advantages*

- The fixed costs are reported as period costs (and not allocated to stock), thus increasing the likelihood of better control of these costs.
- Operating profit is directly influenced by changes in unit sales (and not influenced by build-up of stock).
- The impact of fixed costs on operating profit is emphasised.
- The income statements are in the same form as is used for cost–volume–profit analysis.
- Product line, territory, etc., contribution margins are emphasised and more readily ascertainable.

Disadvantages

- Total costs may be overlooked when considering operating problems.
- Distinction between fixed and variable costs is arbitrary for many costs.
- Emphasis on variable costs may cause some managers to ignore fixed costs.
- A new variable-costing system may be too costly to install unless top managers think that operating decisions will be improved collectively.

Exercise 7.23

1 a Variable costing income statements (in €000):

	2014	2015	Together
Revenues		€300	€300	€600
Variable cost of sales		70	70	140
Contribution margin		230	230	460
Fixed manufacturing costs	€140			
Fixed marketing and administrative costs	40	180	180	360
Operating profit		€50	€50	€100

b Absorption statements (in €000):

	Alternative 1			Alternative 2		
	2014	2015	Together	2014	2015	Together
Revenues	€300	€300	€600	€300	€300	€600
Opening stock	–	140	–	–	210	–
Manufacturing costs	280	–	280	420	–	420
Available for sales	280	140	280	420	210	420
Closing stock	140	–	–	210	–	–
Cost of goods sold	140	140	280	210	210	420
Underallocated overhead	–	140	140	–	140	–
Overallocated overhead	–	–	–	(140)	–	–
Marketing and administrative costs	40	40	80	40	40	80
Total costs	180	320	500	110	390	500
Operating profit (loss)	€120	€(20)	€100	€190	€(90)	€100

Alternative 1. Rate for fixed manufacturing overhead allocation based on 20 000 units:

$$\frac{€140\,000}{20\,000} = €7.00 \text{ per tonne}$$

Alternative 2. Rate for fixed manufacturing overhead allocation based on 10 000 units:

$$\frac{€140\,000}{10\,000} = €14.00 \text{ per tonne}$$

2 Audumla Oy has a positive operating profit because some of its costs were variable. They could be avoided when the plant shut down for the second year. Variable costs can be 'stored' as measures of assets, while fixed costs cannot. When Audumla paid €70 000 for direct materials, direct manufacturing labour and variable manufacturing overhead to produce 10 000 additional tonnes of fertiliser during the first year for sale in the second year, it saved that amount of cost in the second year.

3

	Variable costing	Absorption costing 20 000 unit base*	Absorption costing 10 000 unit base
Stock, end of 2014	€70 000	€140 000	€210 000
Stock, end of 2015	0	0	0

* Fixed manufacturing overhead rate is €7.00 when denominator level is 20 000 units and is €14.00 when denominator level is 10 000 units.

4 Reported operating profit is affected by both production *and* sales under absorption costing. Hence, most managers would prefer absorption costing because their performance in any given reporting period, at least in the short run, is influenced by how much production is scheduled near the end of a reporting period.

CHAPTER 8

Exercise 8.11

a   TCM = Q (USP − UVC)
        = 70 000 (£30 − £20)
        = £700 000
    TFC = TCM − OP/L
        = £700 000 − £15 000 = £685 000

b   TCM = Q (USP − UVC)
    £900 000 = 180 000 (£25 − UVC)
        UVC = £20
    OP/L = TCM − TFC
        = £900 000 − £800 000 = £100 000

c   TCM = Q (USP − UVC)
    £300 000 = 150 000 (USP − £10)
        USP = £12
    OP/L = TCM − TFC
        = £300 000 − £220 000 = £80 000

d   Q = TCM ÷ (USP − UVC)
        = £120 000 ÷ (£20 − £14)
        = 20 000
    TFC = TCM − OP/L
        = £120 000 − £12 000 = £108 000

Exercise 8.22

1 Variable cost percentage is SFr 3.20/SFr 8.00 = 40%. Let R = Revenues needed to obtain target net profit, then:

$$R - 0.40R - SFr\ 450\ 000 = SFr\ 150\ 000$$
$$0.60R = SFr\ 450\ 000 + SFr\ 150\ 000$$
$$R = SFr\ 600\ 000 \div 0.60$$
$$= SFr\ 1\ 000\ 000$$

Proof:	Revenues	SFr 1 000 000
	Variable costs (at 40%)	400 000
	Contribution margin	600 000
	Fixed costs	450 000
	Operating profit	150 000
	Income taxes (at 30%)	45 000
	Net profit	SFr 105 000

2 a Sales necessary to earn net profit of SFr 105 000:

$$\frac{\text{SFr } 1\,000\,000}{\text{SFr } 8} = 125\,000 \text{ sales necessary}$$

b Sales necessary to break even:

Contribution margin = SFr 8.00 − SFr 3.20 = SFr 4.80

$$\frac{\text{SFr } 450\,000}{\text{SFr } 4.80} = 93\,750 \text{ sales necessary}$$

3 Using the short-cut approach described in the chapter:

$$\text{Change in net profit} = (150\,000 - 125\,000) \times \text{SFr } 4.80 \times (1 - 0.30)$$
$$= \text{SFr } 120\,000 \times 0.7 = \text{SFr } 84\,000$$
$$\text{New net profit} = \text{SFr } 84\,000 + \text{SFr } 105\,000 = \text{SFr } 189\,000$$

Proof:	Revenues, 150 000 × SFr 8.00	SFr 1 200 000
	Variable costs at 40%	480 000
	Contribution margin	720 000
	Fixed costs	450 000
	Operating profit	270 000
	Income tax at 30%	81 000
	Net profit	SFr 189 000

Exercise 8.27

1 Let Q = Number of units of deluxe product to break even.

$3Q$ = Number of units of standard product to break even.

Revenues − Variable costs − Fixed costs = Zero operating profit.

$$€20(3Q) + €30Q − €14(3Q) − €18Q − €1\,200\,000 = 0$$
$$€60Q + €30Q − €42Q − €18Q = €1\,200\,000$$
$$€30Q = €1\,200\,000$$
$$Q = 40\,000 \text{ units of deluxe}$$
$$3Q = 120\,000 \text{ units of standard}$$

The breakeven point is 120 000 standard units plus 40 000 deluxe carriers, a total of 160 000 units.

2 Unit contribution margins are: standard: €20 − €14 = €6; deluxe: €30 − €18 = €12.

a If only standard carriers were sold, the breakeven point would be:

$$€1\,200\,000/€6 = 200\,000 \text{ units}$$

b If only deluxe carriers were sold, the breakeven point would be:

$$€1\,200\,000/€12 = 100\,000 \text{ units}$$

3 Operating profit = 180 000(€6) + 20 000(€12) − €1 200 000
= €1 080 000 + €240 000 − €1 200 000
= €120 000

Let Q = Number of units of deluxe product to break even.
$9Q$ = Number of units of standard product to break even.

€20(9Q) + €30Q − €14(9Q) − €18Q − €1 200 000 = 0
€180Q + €30Q − €126Q − €18Q = €1 200 000
€66Q = €1 200 000
Q = 18 182 units of deluxe (rounded)
9Q = 163 638 units of standard

The breakeven point is 163 638 standard + 18 182 deluxe, a total of 181 820 units.

The lesson of this problem is that changes in sales mix change breakeven points and operating profits. In this example, the budgeted and actual total sales in number of units were identical, but the proportion of the product having the higher contribution margin declined. Operating profit suffered, falling from €300 000 to €120 000. Moreover, the breakeven point rose from 160 000 to 181 820 units.

CHAPTER 9

Exercise 9.11

1 Slope coefficient = €0.30 per machine-hour.

Constant = Total cost − (Slope coefficient × Quantity of cost driver)
= €3900 − (€0.30 × €7000) = €1800
= €3000 − (€0.30 × 4000) = €1800

The cost function based on the two observations is:

Maintenance costs = €1800 + €0.30 × machine-hours

2 The cost function in requirement 1 is an estimate of how costs behave within the relevant range, not at cost levels outside the relevant range. If there are no months with zero machine-hours represented in the maintenance account, data in that account cannot be used to estimate the fixed costs at the zero machine-hours level. Rather, the constant component of the cost function provides the best available starting point for a straight line that approximates how a cost behaves within the relevant range.

Exercise 9.20

1 It is economically plausible that the correct form of the model of overhead costs includes both number of academic programmes and number of enrolled students as cost drivers. The findings indicate that each of the independent variables affects overhead costs. (Each regression has a significant r^2 and t-value on the independent variable.) Raphäel could choose to divide overhead costs into two cost pools, (i) those overhead costs that are more closely related to the number of academic programmes and (ii) those overhead costs more closely related to the number of enrolled students, and rerun the simple regression analysis on each overhead cost pool. Alternatively, she could run a multiple regression analysis with total overhead costs as the dependent variable and the number of academic programmes and number of enrolled students as the two independent variables.

2 Raphäel should use the multiple regression model over the two simple regression models. The multiple regression model appears economically plausible and the regression model performs very well when estimating overhead costs. It has an excellent goodness-of-fit and significant t-values on both independent variables, and it meets all the specification assumptions for ordinary least-squares regression (see Solution Exhibit 9.20).

Solution Exhibit 9.20	Evaluation of cost function for overhead costs estimated with multiple regression for ESMSE
Criterion	Number of academic programmes and number of enrolled students as independent variables
1 Economic plausibility	A positive relationship between overhead costs and number of academic programmes and number of enrolled students is economically plausible at ESMSE
2 Goodness-of-fit	$r^2 = 0.81$ Excellent goodness-of-fit
3 Significance of independent variable(s)	t-values of 3.46 on number of academic programmes and 2.03 on number of enrolled students are both significant
4 Specification analysis of estimation assumptions	The assumptions of linearity, constant variance, and normality of residuals hold, but inferences drawn from only 12 observations are not reliable; the Durbin–Watson statistic = 1.84 indicates that independence of residuals holds

There is some correlation between the two independent variables, but multicollinearity does not appear to be a problem here. The significance of both independent variables (despite some correlation between them) suggests that each variable is a driver of overhead cost. Of course, as the chapter describes, even if the independent variables exhibited multicollinearity, Raphäel should still prefer to use the multiple regression model over the simple regression models. Omitting any one of the variables will cause the estimated coefficient of the independent variable included in the model to be biased away from its true value.

3 Possible uses for the multiple regression results include:

- *Planning and budgeting at ESMSE.* The regression analysis indicates the variables (number of academic programmes and number of enrolled students) that help predict changes in overhead costs.
- *Cost control and performance evaluation.* Raphäel could compare actual performance with budgeted or expected numbers and seek ways to improve the efficiency of the ESMSE operations, and evaluate the performance of managers responsible for controlling overhead costs.
- *Cost management.* If cost pressures increase, the ESMSE could save costs by closing down academic programmes that have few students enrolled.

Exercise 9.21

1 Solution Exhibit 9.21 plots the relationship between machine-hours and power costs.

2 (i)

	Machine-hours (X)	Power costs (Y)
Highest observation of independent variable	400	SEK 500
Lowest observation of independent variable	100	300
	300	SEK 200

Slope coefficient = SEK 0.667 per machine-hour

Constant = SEK 500 – (SEK 0.667 × 400) = SEK 233.20

= SEK 300 – (SEK 0.667 × 100) = SEK 233.30

(difference in values is due to rounding errors)

Cost function estimated with high–low approach is:

$$y = \text{SEK } 233.20 + \text{SEK } 0.667X$$

Solution Exhibit 9.21   Plot of machine-hours versus power cost

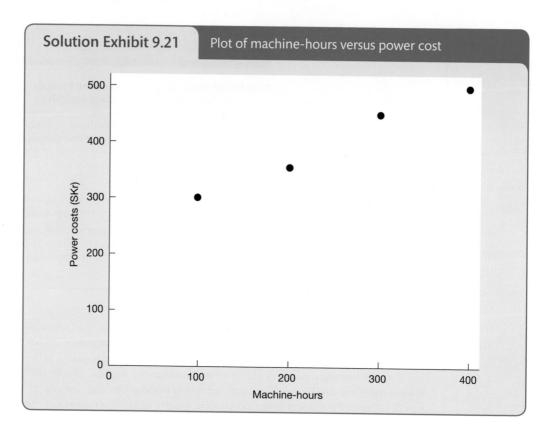

(ii) One way of calculating a and b under the regression approach is to use the equations given in the chapter appendix.

Period (1)	Machine-hours (X) (2)	Power costs (Y) (3)	X^2 (4)	XY (5)
1	200	350	40 000	70 000
2	300	450	90 000	135 000
3	100	300	10 000	30 000
4	400	500	160 000	200 000
Total	1 000	1 600	300 000	435 000

$$\Sigma Y = na + b(\Sigma X)$$
$$\Sigma XY = a(\Sigma X) + b(\Sigma X)^2$$

That is,

$$1600 = 4a + 1000b \qquad R_1$$
$$435\ 000 = 1000a + 300\ 000b \qquad R_2$$
$$400\ 000 = 1000a + 250\ 000b \qquad R_3 = 250(R_1)$$
$$35\ 000 = 50\ 000b \qquad R_4 = R_2 - R_3$$
$$b = \text{SEK } 0.70$$
$$1600 = 4a + 1000\ (0.70)$$
$$900 = 4a$$
$$a = \text{SEK } 225$$

Cost function estimated with the regression approach is:

$$y = \text{SEK } 225 + \text{SEK } 0.70 \times \text{machine-hours}$$

Substituting we get:

$$a = \text{SEK } 225$$

Another approach is to use a computer software package. Results are:

Variable	Coefficient	Standard error	t-value
Constant	SEK 225	SEK 19.36	11.62
Independent variable: machine-hours	SEK 0.70	SEK 0.07	10.00

$r^2 = 0.98$; Durbin–Watson statistic $= 2.20$

In this simple illustration, the high–low estimate using only two observations closely approximates the least-squares regression approach that minimises the sum of squares of the vertical deviations from the observations to the estimated regression line. The regression equation indicates that variable power costs are SEK 0.70 per machine-hour against the high–low estimate of SEK 0.667. The fixed component of power costs within the relevant range equals SEK 225, while the high–low method estimates this component as SEK 233.20. The high–low method gives good results in this case because all the data points fall very close to the regression line.

$A =$ SEK 0.70.

3 $\bar{Y} = \Sigma Y \div 4 =$ SEK $1600 \div 4 =$ SEK 400
$\quad \Sigma(Y - \bar{Y})^2 = (350 - 400)^2 + (450 - 400)^2 + (300 - 400)^2 + (500 - 400)^2$
$\quad\quad\quad\quad\quad = 2500 + 2500 + 10\,000 + 10\,000 = 25\,000$

Period	Y	$y =$ SEK 225 + SEK 0.70X	$Y - y$	$(Y - y)^2$
1	350	365	−15	225
2	450	435	+15	225
3	300	295	+5	25
4	500	505	−5	25
Total	1600			500

$r^2 = 0.98$.

An r^2 of 0.98 indicates excellent goodness-of-fit. Only 2% of the variation in power costs is not explained by machine-hours. Since the relation between machine-hours and power costs is also economically plausible, Bildt-Östersund can be very confident of using the regression results to set its flexible budget for power costs. Machine-hours is a cost driver of power costs.

CHAPTER 10

Exercise 10.14

1

Average one-way fare per passenger		€500
Commission at 8% of €500		40
Net cash to Air Calabria per ticket		€460
Average number of passengers per flight		200
Revenues per flight (€460 × 200)		€92 000
Food & beverage cost per flight (€20 × 200)		4 000
Total contribution from passengers		88 000
Fuel costs per flight		14 000
Contribution per flight		74 000
Fixed costs allocated to each flight:		
Lease costs	€53 000	
Baggage handling	7 000	
Flight crew	4 000	64 000
Operating profit per flight		€10 000

2 If fare is €480.00
Commission at 8% of €480 38.40
Net cash per ticket 441.60
Food and beverage cost per ticket 20.00
Contribution per passenger €421.60
Total contribution margin from passengers
(€421.60 × 212) €89 379.20

All other costs are irrelevant

On the basis of quantitative factors alone, Air Calabria should decrease its fare to €480 because reducing the fare gives Air Calabria a higher contribution margin from passengers (€89 379.20 versus €88 000).

3 In evaluating whether Air Calabria should charter its plane to Cima-Rosa, we compare the charter alternative to the solution in requirement (2) because requirement (2) is preferred to requirement (1).

Under requirement (2), Air Calabria gets €89 379.20
Deduct fuel costs 14 000.00
Total contribution per flight €75 379.20

Air Calabria gets €75 000 per flight from chartering the plane to Cima-Rosa. On the basis of quantitative financial factors Air Calabria is better off not chartering the plane and instead lowering its own fares.

Students who compare the €75 000 that Air Calabria earns from chartering its plane to the contribution from passengers in requirement (1) (€74 000) will conclude that Air Calabria should charter the plane to Cima-Rosa. Strictly speaking, though, the correct answer must compare the charter fee of €75 000 to the €75 379.20 passenger contribution in requirement (2) since lowering the fare is certainly an alternative available to Air Calabria.

Other qualitative factors that Air Calabria should consider in coming to a decision are:

a The lower risk from chartering its plane relative to the uncertainties regarding the number of passengers it might get on its scheduled flights.
b Chartering to Cima-Rosa means that Air Calabria would not have a regular schedule of flights each week. This arrangement could cause inconvenience to some of its passengers.
c The stability of the relationship between Air Calabria and Cima-Rosa. If this is not a long-term arrangement, Air Calabria may lose current market share and not benefit from sustained charter revenues.

Exercise 10.18

1 Time spent on manufacturing bottles $= \dfrac{750\,000 \text{ bottles}}{100 \text{ bottles per hour}} = 7500$ hours

So $10\,000 - 7500 = 2500$ hours available for toys.

The moulded plastic toy requires $\dfrac{100\,000 \text{ units}}{40} = 2500$ hours, so Fri-Flask has enough capacity to accept the toys order. Additional income from accepting the order is:

Revenue DKK 3.00 × 100 000 DKK300 000
Variable costs 2.40 × 100 000 240 000
Contribution margin 60 000
Fixed costs 20 000
Additional income DKK 40 000

So Fri-Flask should accept the order since it has enough excess capacity to make the 100 000 toys.

2 Time spent on manufacturing bottles $= \dfrac{850\,000}{100} = 8500$ hours

So $10\,000 - 8500 = 1500$ hours available for toys.

From requirement (1) moulded plastic toy requires 2500 hours and generates DKK40 000 in operating income.

So if the toy order is accepted, 1000 hours (2500 hours required – 1500 hours available) of bottle making will be forgone, equal to 100 000 bottles (100 bottles/hr × 1000 hrs).

Operating income from accepting	DKK40 000
Forgone contribution margin (100 000 bottles × DKK0.30)	30 000
Increase in operating income	DKK10 000

So Fri-Flask should accept the special order.

3 Without considering the fixed costs of the toy mould, the contribution per machine-hour of the constrained resource for bottles and the special toy are as follows:

	Bottles	Toys
Contribution margin per unit	DKK0.30	DKK0.60
Multiplied by units made in 1 machine-hour	100	40
Contribution margin per machine-hour	DKK30	DKK24

This suggests that Fri-Flask should make as many bottles as it can rather than the special toys because bottles generate a higher contribution margin per machine-hour.

So if Fri-Flask used the 1500 hours available to it for making toys after using the 8500 hours to make bottles, it would be able to make $1500 \times 40 = 60\,000$ toys and earn operating income of:

Contribution margin 60 000 × DKK0.60	DKK36 000
Fixed mould costs	20 000
Increase in operating income	DKK16 000

The contribution margin earned covers the fixed costs of the mould, so Fri-Flask should make 850 000 bottles and 60 000 toys.

4 Time spent on manufacturing bottles $= \dfrac{900\,000}{100} = 9000$ hours

So $10\,000 - 9000 = 1000$ hours available for toys.

So if the toy order is accepted, then 1500 hours (2500 hours required – 1000 hours available) of bottle capacity will be forgone = 150 000 bottles

Contribution from accepting toy offer	DKK40 000
Forgone profits on bottles 150 000 × DKK0.30	(45 000)
Increase (decrease) in operating income	DKK(5 000)

So *reject* the special order.

5 As in requirement (3), Fri-Flask should first use the 9000 hours to make bottles and then consider using the 1000 hours available to it for making toys. It would be able to make 1000 hours × 40 = 40 000 toys and earn operating income of:

Contribution margin 40 000 × DKK0.60	DKK24 000
Fixed mould costs	20 000
Increase in operating income	DKK 4 000

Fri-Flask should make 900 000 bottles and 40 000 toys.

6 As in requirements (3) and (5), Fri-Flask should first use 9500 hours to make bottles and then consider using the 500 hours available to it for making toys. It would be able to make 500 hours × 40 = 20 000 toys and earn operating income of

Contribution margin 20 000 × DKK0.60	DKK12 000
Fixed mould costs	20 000
Increase (decrease) in operating income	DKK (8 000)

So Fri-Flask should refuse to make any of the plastic toys. If it tried to make the toy product more profitable by making more toys, it would have to give up the plastic bottles. This trade-off is not worthwhile because Fri-Flask makes DKK24 per hour from the toys and would lose DKK30 per hour from the plastic bottles.

7 The subcontracting option is a good option because it nets Fri-Flask DKK0.20 per toy (DKK3.00 – DKK2.80) without using up any of its limited capacity.

So long as Fri-Flask is manufacturing in-house, it would prefer to first make bottles (contribution of DKK30 per hour) and then make toys (contribution of DKK24 per hour).

As in requirement (5), Fri-Flask would make 900 000 bottles and be left with 1000 hours available for toy making. It has two options at this stage (1) use 1000 hours of available in-house capacity to make 40 000 toys and subcontract 60 000 toys outside or (2) subcontract all 100 000 toys from outside.

	40 000 toys in-house 60 000 toys subcontracted	100 000 toys subcontracted
Revenues (irrelevant)	DKK300 000	DKK300 000
Costs		
Variable manufacturing costs		
(40,000 × DKK2.40)	96 000	
Incremental fixed costs of mould	20 000	
Subcontract costs (DKK2.80 × 60 000;	168 000	
DKK2.80 × 100 000)		280 000
Total costs	284 000	280 000
Operating income	DKK 16 000	DKK 20 000

So Fri-Flask should use 9000 hours of its capacity to make 900 000 bottles, leave 1000 hours capacity idle and subcontract out all the 100 000 toys.

A short-cut to solving this problem is to calculate when it is worthwhile for Fri-Flask to manufacture toys in-house rather than subcontracting them. Suppose number of toys manufactured is X, the cut-off point is obtained by solving:

$$X = \frac{DKK20\,000}{DKK0.40} = 50\,000 \text{ toys}$$

This means that if the internal manufacturing capacity is for less than 50 000 toys, it is cheaper to subcontract, whereas if the internal manufacturing capacity is for more than 50 000 toys, it is better to manufacture in-house.

In our example, the internal manufacturing capacity is for 40 000 toys, so it is better to subcontract out entirely.

CHAPTER 11

Exercise 11.11

1

Direct costs		
Direct materials	€150 000	€150 000
Indirect costs		
Product support	983 000	983 000
Total costs		€1 133 000

Cost per kilogram of chips = €1.133

2

	(a) Retail chips	(b) Institutional chips
Direct costs		
Direct materials	€135 000	€15 000
Packaging	180 000	8 000
Indirect costs	315 000	23 000
Cleaning		
€0.120 × 900 000	108 000	
€0.120 × 100 000		12 000
Cutting		
€0.24 × 900 000	216 000	
€0.15 × 100 000		15 000
Packaging		
€0.48 × 900 000	432 000	
€0.12 × 100 000		12 000
	756 000	39 000
Total costs	€1 071 000	€62 000
Kilograms produced	900 000	100 000
Cost per kilogram	€1.19	€0.62

Note: The total costs of €1 133 000 (€1 071 000 + €62 000) are the same as those in requirement 1.

3 There is much evidence of product-cost cross-subsidisation.

	Retail	Institutional
Current system	€1.133	€1.133
ABC system	€1.190	€0.620

Assuming the ABC numbers are more accurate, retail is undercosted by approximately 5% (€1.133 ÷ €1.19 = 0.95) while institutional is overcosted by 83% (€1.133 ÷ €0.620 = 1.83).

The current system assumes that each product uses all the activity areas in a homogeneous way. This is not the case. Institutional sales use far fewer resources in the cutting area and the packaging area. The percentage of total costs for each cost category is:

	Retail	Institutional	Total
Direct costs			
Direct materials	90.0%	10.0%	100.0%
Packaging	95.7	4.3	100.0
Indirect costs			
Cleaning	90.0	10.0	100.0
Cutting	93.5	6.5	100.0
Packaging	97.3	2.7	100.0
Units produced	90.0%	10.0%	100.0%

McCarthy Potatoes can use the revised cost information for a variety of purposes:

- *Pricing/product emphasis decisions.* The sizable drop in the reported cost of institutional potatoes makes it possible that McCarthy Potatoes was overpricing potato products in this market. It lost the bid for a large institutional contract with a bid 30% above the winning bid. With its revised product cost dropping from €1.133 to €0.620, McCarthy Potatoes could have bid much lower and still made a profit. An increased emphasis on the institutional market appears warranted.
- *Product design decisions.* ABC provides a roadmap as to how to reduce the costs of individual products. The relative components of costs are:

	Retail	Institutional
Direct costs		
Direct materials	12.6%	24.2%
Packaging	16.8	12.9
Indirect costs		
Cleaning	10.1	19.3
Cutting	20.2	24.2
Packaging	40.3	19.3
Total costs	100.0%	100.0%

Packaging-related costs constitute 57.1% (16.8% + 40.3%) of total costs of the retail product line. Design efforts that reduce packaging costs can have a big impact on reducing total unit costs for retail.

- *Process improvements.* Each activity area is now highlighted as a separate cost. The three indirect cost areas are over 60% of total costs for each product, indicating the upside from improvements in the efficiency of processes in these activity areas.

Exercise 11.12

1   (a) Cleaning activity area

                1 000 000 kg × €0.120   €120 000

          (b) Cutting

                900 000 × €0.24   €216 000

                100 000 × €0.15   15 000

                                    €231 000

          (c) Packaging

                900 000 × €0.480   €432 000

                100 000 × €0.120   12 000

                                    €444 000

2

Cost pool	Costs in pool	Number of driver units	Costs per driver unit
(a) Cleaning	€120 000	1 200 000 raw kilograms	€0.10
(b) Cutting	€231 000	3 850 hours*	€60.00
(c) Packaging	€444 000	37 000 hours†	€12.00

* (900 000 ÷ 250) + (100 000 ÷ 400) = 3600 + 250 = 3850.
† (900 000 ÷ 25) + (100 000 ÷ 100) = 36 000 + 1000 = 37 000.

3 McCarthy Potatoes can use information about cost driver rates in several ways:

- Target the high cost rate areas for process improvement. For example, cutting has a €60 per hour rate. McCarthy Potatoes could seek ways to reduce this by either redesigning processes or employing lower-cost equipment.
- Benchmarking to signal areas capable of improvement. If McCarthy Potatoes has other potato processing plants around the globe, it could compare cost driver rates for the same activity at different plants. It could then seek to transfer knowledge from the most efficient plants to the less efficient plants.

- Use cost driver rates as performance targets when evaluating operating managers. For example, the manager in charge of potato cleaning could be given a target rate of €0.09 per raw kilogram of potatoes cleaned.
- Developing a flexible budget for McCarthy Potatoes. The effect of different product mixes and different output levels can be estimated using the cost driver rates.

Exercise 11.18

1

	Job order 410		Job order 411	
Direct manufacturing costs				
Direct materials	SFr 9 700		SFr 59 900	
Direct manufacturing labour, SFr 30 × 25; 375	750	SFr 10 450	11 250	SFr 71 150
Indirect manufacturing costs, SFr 115 × 25; 375		2 875		43 125
Total manufacturing costs		SFr 13 325		SFr 114 275
Number of units		÷ 10		÷ 200
Unit manufacturing cost per job		SFr 1 332.50		SFr 571.375

2

	Job order 410		Job order 411	
Direct manufacturing costs:				
Direct materials	SFr 9 700		SFr 59 900	
Direct manufacturing labour, SFr 30 × 25; 375	750	SFr 10 450	11 250	SFr 71 150
Indirect manufacturing costs:				
Materials handling, SFr 0.40 × 500; 2000	200		800	
Lathe work, SFr 0.20 × 20 000; 60 000	4 000		12 000	
Milling, SFr 20.00 × 150; 1050	3 000		21 000	
Grinding, SFr 0.80 × 500; 2000	400		1 600	
Testing, SFr 15.00 × 10; 200	150	7 750	3 000	38 400
Total manufacturing costs		SFr 18 200		SFr 109 550
Number of units per job		÷ 10		÷ 200
Unit manufacturing cost per job		SFr 1 820		SFr 547.75

3

	Job order 410	Job order 411
Number of units in job	10	200
Unit cost per job with prior costing system	SFr 1332.50	SFr 571.375
Unit cost per job with activity-based costing	SFr 1820.00	SFr 547.75

Job order 410 has an increase in reported cost of 36.6% [(SFr 1820 − SFr 1332.50) ÷ SFr 1332.50] while Job order 411 has a decrease in reported cost of 4.1% [(SFr 547.75 − SFr 571.375) ÷ SFr 571.375].

A common finding when activity-based costing is implemented is that low-volume products have increases in their reported costs while high-volume products have decreases in their reported cost. This result is also found in requirements 1 and 2 of this problem.

The product cost figures calculated in requirements 1 and 2 differ because:

- the job orders differ in the way they use each of the five activity areas; and
- the activity areas differ in their indirect cost allocation bases (specifically, each area does not use the direct labour-hours indirect cost allocation base).

The following table documents how the two job orders differ in the way they use each of the five activity areas included in indirect manufacturing costs:

Activity area	Usage based on analysis of activity area cost drivers		Usage assumed with direct labour-hours as application base	
	Job order 410	Job order 411	Job order 410	Job order 411
Materials handling	20.0%	80.0%	6.25%	93.75%
Lathe work	25.0	75.0	6.25	93.75
Milling	12.5	87.5	6.25	93.75
Grinding	20.0	80.0	6.25	93.75
Testing	4.8	95.2	6.25	93.75

Areas where the differences in product cost figures might be important to Aircomposystèmes include:

- *Product pricing and product emphasis.* The activity-based accounting approach indicates that Job 410 is being undercosted while Job 411 is being overcosted. Aircomposystèmes may erroneously push Job 410 and de-emphasise Job 411. Moreover, by its actions, Aircomposystèmes may encourage a competitor to enter the market for Job order 411 and take market share away from itself.
- *Product design.* Product designers at Aircomposystèmes will probably find the numbers in the activity-based costing approach more believable and credible than those in the existing system. In a machine-paced manufacturing environment, it is unlikely that direct labour-hours would be the major cost driver. Activity-based costing provides more credible signals to product designers about the ways the costs of a product can be reduced – for example, use fewer parts, require fewer turns on the lathe, and reduce the number of machine-hours in the milling area.

An overview of the product costing system is given by Solution Exhibit 11.18.

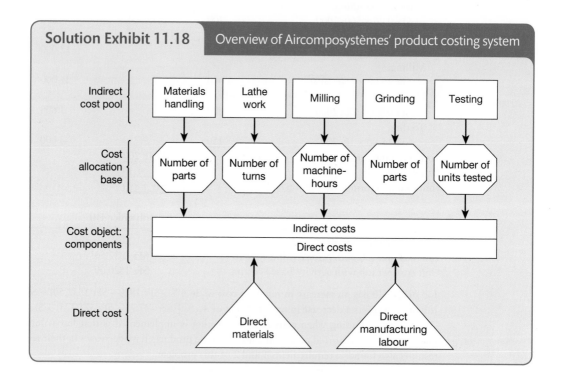

Solution Exhibit 11.18   Overview of Aircomposystèmes' product costing system

CHAPTER 12

Exercise 12.13

1 Hospedeiras de Portugal Lda's full cost per hour of supplying contract labour is:

Variable costs	€12
Fixed costs (€240 000 ÷ 80 000 hours)	3
Full cost per hour	€15

Price per hour at full cost plus 20% = €15 × 1.20 = €18 per hour.

2 Contribution margins for different prices and demand realisations are as follows:

Price per hour (1)	Variable cost per hour (2)	Contribution margin per hour (3) = (1) − (2)	Demand in hours (4)	Total contribution (5) = (3) × (4)
€16	€12	€4	120 000	€480 000
17	12	5	100 000	500 000
18	12	6	80 000	480 000
19	12	7	70 000	490 000
20	12	8	60 000	480 000

Fixed costs will remain the same regardless of the demand realisations. Fixed costs are therefore irrelevant since they do not differ among the alternatives. The table above indicates that Hospedeiras de Portugal can maximise contribution margin and hence operating profit by charging a price of €17 per hour.

3 The cost-plus approach to pricing in requirement 1 does not explicitly consider the effect of prices on demand. The approach in requirement 2 models the interaction between price and demand and determines the optimal level of profitability using concepts of relevant costs. The two different approaches lead to two different prices in requirements 1 and 2. As the chapter describes, pricing decisions should consider both demand or market considerations and supply or cost factors. The approach in requirement 2 is the more balanced approach. In most cases, of course, managers use the cost-plus method of requirement 1 as only a starting point. They then modify the cost-plus price on the basis of market considerations – anticipated customer reaction to alternative price levels and the prices charged by competitors for similar products.

Exercise 12.14

1
Sales (1000 crates at DKK 100 per crate)		DKK 100 000
Variable costs:		
Manufacturing	DKK 40 000	
Marketing	14 000	
Total variable costs		54 000
Contribution margin		46 000
Fixed costs		
Manufacturing	DKK 20 000	
Marketing	16 000	
Total fixed costs		36 000
Operating profit		DKK 10 000

Normal mark-up percentage: DKK 46 000 ÷ DKK 54 000 = 85.19% of total variable costs.

2 Only the manufacturing-cost category is relevant to considering this special order; no additional marketing costs will be incurred. The relevant manufacturing costs for the 200-crate special order are:

Variable manufacturing cost per unit

DKK 40 × 200 crates	DKK 8 000
Special packaging	2 000
	DKK 10 000

Any price above DKK 50 per crate (DKK 10 000 ÷ 200) will make a positive contribution to operating profit.

The reasoning based on a comparison of DKK 55 per crate-price with the DKK 60 per-crate absorption cost ignores monthly cost–volume–profit relationships. The DKK 60 per-crate absorption cost includes a DKK 20 per-crate cost component that is irrelevant to the special order. The relevant range for the fixed manufacturing costs is from 500 to 1500 crates per month; the special order will increase production from 1000 to 1200 crates per month. Furthermore, the special order requires no incremental marketing costs.

3 If the new customer is likely to remain in business, Østerbro should consider whether a strictly short-run focus is appropriate. For example, what is the likelihood of demand from other customers increasing over time? If Østerbro accepts the 200-crate special offer for more than one month, it may preclude accepting other customers at prices exceeding DKK 55 per crate. Moreover, the existing customers may learn about Østerbro's willingness to set a price based on variable cost plus a small contribution margin. The longer the timeframe over which Østerbro keeps selling 200 crates of canned peaches at DKK 55 a crate, the more likely that the existing customers will approach Østerbro for their own special price reductions.

Exercise 12.17

1 A life-cycle profit statement traces revenue and costs of each individual software package from its initial research and development to its final customer servicing and support in the marketplace. The two main differences from a calendar-based profit statement are:

- Costs incurred in different calendar periods are included in the same statement.
- Costs and revenue of each package are reported separately rather than aggregated into company-wide categories.

The benefits of using a product life-cycle report are:

- The full set of revenues and costs associated with each product becomes visible.
- Differences among products in the percentage of total costs committed at early stages in the life cycle are highlighted.
- Interrelationships among business function cost categories are highlighted. What is the effect, for example, of cutting back on R&D and product-design cost categories on customer-service costs in subsequent years?

2

	EE-46		ME-83		IE-17	
Revenue (€000)		€2500		€1500		€1600
Costs (€000)						
R&D	€700		€450		€240	
Design	200		120		96	
Production	300		210		208	
Marketing	500		270		448	
Distribution	75		60		96	
Customer service	375	2150	150	1260	608	1696
Operating profit (€000)		€350		€240		€(96)

As emphasised in this chapter, the time value of money is not taken into account when summing life-cycle revenue or life-cycle costs.

Rankings of the three packages on profitability (and relative profitability) are:

Operating profit

1 EE-46:	€350 000	1 ME-83:	16.0%
2 ME-83:	€240 000	2 EE-46:	14.0%
3 IE-17:	(€96 000)	3 IE-17:	(6.0%)

The EE-46 and ME-83 packages should be emphasised, and the IE-17 package should be de-emphasised. It is interesting that IE-17 had the lowest R&D costs but was the least profitable.

3 The cost structures of the three software packages are:

	EE-46	ME-83	IE-17
R&D	32.5%	35.7%	14.1%
Design	9.3	9.5	5.7
Production	14.0	16.7	12.3
Marketing	23.3	21.4	26.4
Distribution	3.5	4.8	5.7
Customer service	17.4	11.9	35.8
	100.0%	100.0%	100.0%

The major differences are:

- EE-46 and ME-83 have over 40% of their costs in the R&D/product-design categories compared with less than 20% (19.8%) for IE-17.
- IE-17 has 35.8% of its costs in the customer-service category compared with 17.4% for EE-46 and 11.9% for ME-83.

There are several explanations for these differences:

- EE-46 and ME-83 differ sizably from IE-17 in their R&D/product-design intensity. For example, EE-46 and ME-83 may require considerably more interaction with users, and more experimentation with software algorithms than does IE-17.
- The software division should have invested more in the R&D/product-design categories for IE-17. The high percentage for customer service could reflect the correcting of problems that should have been corrected prior to manufacture. Life-cycle reports highlight possible causal relationships among cost categories.

CHAPTER 13

Exercise 13.14

a The optimum approach for this question is to inflate cash flows at their different inflation rates and to discount at the money discount rate. The lowest common multiple is $2 \times 3 = 6$ years. Hence the cash will be presented in these terms.

Two-year cycle: (cash flows are inflated according to their individual inflation rates):

	0	1	2	3	4	5	6
Original cost	24 500		27 011		29 780		
Maintenance		550	968	666	1171	805	1417
Resale values			−17 199		−18 962		−20 905
Total	24 500	550	10 780	666	11 989	805	−19 488
Present values	24 500	478	8151	438	6856	400	−8425
Net present value of costs	32 398						

Three-year cycle: (cash flows are inflated according to their individual inflation rates):

	0	1	2	3	4	5	6
Original cost	24 500			28 362			
Maintenance		550	968	1996	732	1288	2657
Resale values				−12 968			−15 012
Total	24 500	550	968	17 390	732	1288	−12 355
Present values	24 500	478	732	11 434	418	640	−5341
Net present value of costs	32 861						

The two-year cycle is ideal.

b Some of the difficulties with NPV are listed below:

- NPV assumes that firms pursue an objective of maximising the wealth of their shareholders. This is questionable given the wider range of stakeholders whose interests might conflict with those of the shareholders.
- NPV is potentially a difficult method to apply in the context of having to estimate what is the correct discount rate to use. This is particularly so when questions arise as to the incorporation of risk premiums in the discount rate since an evaluation of the riskiness of the business, or of the project in particular, will have to be made and which may be difficult to discern.
- NPV assumes that cash surpluses can be reinvested at the discount rate. This is subject to other projects being available which produce at least a zero NPV at the chosen discount rate.
- NPV can most easily cope with cash flows arising at period ends and is not a technique that is used easily when complicated, mid-period cash flows are present.
- The conclusion from NPV analysis is the present value of the surplus cash generated from a project. If reported profits are important to businesses then it is possible that there may be a conflict between undertaking a positive NPV project and potentially adverse consequences on reported profits. This will particularly be the case for projects with long horizons, large initial investment and very delayed cash inflows.
- Managerial incentive schemes may not be consistent with NPV, particularly when long time horizons are involved. Thus managers may be rewarded on the basis of accounting profits in the short term and may be incentivised to act in accordance with these objectives and thus ignore positive NPV projects.

Exercise 13.22

a (i) Workings £000

Year 0	1	2	3	4	5	6
Money sales		399.600	583.200	642.453	700.652	697.931
Money costs		318.000	393.260	452.586	492.366	535.290
Tax profit		81.600	189.940	189.867	208.286	162.641
Tax		24.480	56.982	56.960	62.486	48.792
Tax offset		24.480	56.982	56.960	62.486	48.792
Capital value		500	375	281.25	210.9375	158.2031
Allowance		125	93.75	70.3125	52.73438	108.2031
C/f		375	281.25	210.9375	158.2031	
Tax		37.5	28.125	21.09375	15.82031	32.46094
Offset		37.5	28.125	21.09375	15.82031	32.46094

Cash flows

Investment	−500	50					
Sales-costs	81.600	189.940	189.867	208.286	162.641		
Tax	−24.480	−56.982	−56.960	−62.486	−48.792		
Tax allow	37.5	28.125	21.09375	15.82031	32.46094		
Net cash flow	−500	81.6	202.96	161.01	172.4194	165.9752	−16.3312
Discount factor	1.00	0.893	0.797	0.712	0.636	0.567	0.507
Present Value	−500	72.87	161.76	114.64	109.66	94.11	−8.28

Net present value = £44,760

Sales revenue	399.600	583.200	642.453	700.652	697.931
Operating costs	318.000	393.260	452.586	492.366	535.290
Depreciation	90.00	90.00	90.00	90.00	90.00
Profit	(8.40)	99.94	99.867	118.286	72.641

Total profit   = £382,334.
Average profit   = £382,334/5 = £76,467
Average investment   = (500,000 + 50,000)/2 = £275,000
Accounting Rate of Return = £76,467/£275,000 = 0.278
Accounting Rate of Return = 28%

(ii) **To: Board of Directors**
From: Management Accountant
Date: July 2009
Subject: Investment projects

From a financial perspective based on the information given and that the projects are mutually exclusive the company should invest in project 2. Investment decisions should be based on net present values as this methodology is consistent with maximising company wealth. However, the company will also need to consider non-financial factors that could affect the decision.

Example include:

- consistency with the company's strategy
- impact on other areas of the business
- technical compatibility and obsolescence.

Accounting rate of return is a simple method of investment appraisal but has many disadvantages. In particular, it is based on accounting profit rather than cash flow. Accounting profit is subjective and dependent on the choice of accounting methods used. Accounting rate of return also ignores the time value of money.

The net present value method is preferable as it ensures that shareholders' wealth is maximised and recognises that cash received in the future is less valuable than cash received today. Net present value does suffer from a number of disadvantages as follows:

- the speed of the repayment of the original investment is not highlighted;
- non-financial managers may have difficulty in understanding the concept;
- determination of the correct discount rate can be difficult.

b   Annual repayment = £250,000/(10 year 8% annuity factor)
                          = £250,000/6.71
                          = £37,258

There are just five years remaining therefore the company will be about to make a payment and then will have four more annual payments to make. The value of these five payments is:

$$£37,258 + (37,258 * 3.312) = £160,656$$

Source: CIMA 2010 Chartered Management Accounting Qualification – Answers for Specimen Examination Paper P1. Published November 2009.

CHAPTER 14

Exercise 14.12

Budgeted sales in units	100 000
Add target closing finished goods stock	11 000
Total requirements	111 000
Deduct opening finished goods stock	7 000
Units to be produced	104 000

Exercise 14.20

Tire-Lire, SNC

Statement of budgeted cash receipts and disbursements for the months of December 2014 and January 2015

	December 2014	January 2015
Cash balance, opening	€10 000	€2 025
Add receipts:		
Collections of receivables (schedule 1)	235 900	285 800
(a) Total cash available for needs	245 900	287 825
Deduct disbursements:		
For merchandise purchases (schedule 2)	183 875	141 750
For variable costs (schedule 3)	50 000	25 000
For fixed costs (schedule 3)	10 000	10 000
(b) Total disbursements	243 875	176 750
Cash balance, end of month (a − b)	€2 025	€111 075

Enough cash should be available for repayment of the note on 31 January 2015.

Schedule 1: Collections of receivables

December: 14 400[a] + 50 000[b] + 171 500[c] = €235 900
January: 20 000[d] + 60 000[e] + 205 800[f] = €285 800

[a] 0.08 ×€180 000   [b] 0.20 × €250 000   [c] 0.70 × €250 000 × 0.98
[d] 0.08 × €250 000   [e] 0.20 × €300 000   [f] 0.70 × €300 000 × 0.98

Schedule 2: Payments for merchandise

	December		January	
Target closing stock (in units)	875	[a]	800	[c]
Add units sold (Sales ÷ €100)	3 000		1 500	
Total requirements	3 875		2 300	
Deduct opening stock (in units)	1 250	[b]	875	
Purchases (in units)	2 625		1 425	
Purchases in euros (units × €70)	€183 750		€99 750	

[a] 500 units + 0.25(150 000 ÷ 100)   [b] 87 500 ÷ 70
[c] 500 units + 0.25(120 000 ÷ 100)

	December	January
Cash disbursements:		
For previous month's purchases at 50%	€92 000	€91 875
For current month's purchases at 50%	91 875	49 875
	€183 875	€141 750

Schedule 3: Marketing, distribution and customer service costs

Total annual fixed costs, €150 000, minus €30 000 depreciation	=	€120 000
Monthly fixed cost requiring cash outlay	=	€10 000
Variable cost ratio to sales $=\frac{1}{6}$		
December variable costs: $\frac{1}{6} \times$ €300 000 sales	=	€50 000
January variable costs: $\frac{1}{6} \times$ €150 000 sales	=	€25 000

Exercise 14.22

1

Activity area	Soft drinks	Fresh produce	Packaged food	Total
Ordering				
DKK 90 × 14; 24; 14	DKK 1 260	DKK 2 160	DKK 1 260	DKK 4 680
Delivery				
DKK 82 × 12; 62; 19	984	5 084	1 558	7 626
Shelf-stacking				
DKK 21 × 16; 172; 94	336	3 612	1 974	5 922
Customer support				
DKK 0.18 × 4600; 34 200;				
10 750	828	6 156	1 935	8 919
	DKK 3 408	DKK 17 012	DKK 6 727	DKK 27 147

2 An ABB approach recognises how different products require different mixes of support activities. The relative percentage of how each product area uses the cost driver at each activity area is:

Activity area	Soft drinks	Fresh produce	Packaged food	Total
Ordering	26.9	46.2	26.9	100.0%
Delivery	12.9	66.7	20.4	100.0
Shelf-stacking	5.7	61.0	33.3	100.0
Customer support	9.3	69.0	21.7	100.0

By recognising these differences, Nyborg Supermarkets managers are better able to budget for different unit sales levels and different mixes of individual product line items sold. Using a single cost driver (such as cost of goods sold, COGS) assumes homogeneity across product lines which does not occur at Nyborg Supermarkets.

Other benefits cited by managers include: (1) better identification of resource needs, (2) clearer linking of costs with staff responsibilities, and (3) identification of budgetary slack.

CHAPTER 15

Exercise 15.12

Direct materials

DKK 200 000		DKK 214 000		DKK 225 000
	DKK 14 000 F		DKK 11 000 F	
	Price variance		Efficiency variance	
		DKK 25 000 F		
		Flexible-budget variance		

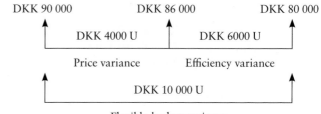

Direct manufacturing labour

| DKK 90 000 | | DKK 86 000 | | DKK 80 000 |

DKK 4000 U　　　　　DKK 6000 U

Price variance　　　　Efficiency variance

DKK 10 000 U

Flexible-budget variance

Exercise 15.20

1　Flexible budget data for Hoofdorp Music Box Fabricators for October.

	Budgeted amount per unit	Alternative levels of output		
		4000 units	5000 units	6000 units
Revenues	€77.00*	€308 000	€385 000	€462 000
Variable costs				
Direct materials	22.00†	88 000	110 000	132 000
Direct manufacturing labour	15.00‡	60 000	75 000	90 000
Variable manufacturing overhead	2.00§	8 000	10 000	12 000
Variable marketing cost	5.50§	22 000	27 500	33 000
Total variable costs	44.50	178 000	222 500	267 000
Contribution margin	€32.50	130 000	162 500	195 000
Fixed costs				
Manufacturing		51 700#	51 700	51 700
Marketing and administrative		82 600‖	82 600	82 600
Total fixed costs		134 300	134 300	134 300
Total costs		312 300	356 800	401 300
Operating profit (loss)		€(4 300)	€28 200	€60 700

*　€70 + 10%(€70) = €77.
†　€90 000 ÷ 4500 = €20; €20 + 10%(€20) = €22.
‡　€67 500 ÷ 4500 = €15.
§　Given.
#　€50 700 + (€12 000 ÷ 12) = €50 700 + €1000 = €51 700.
‖　€81 350 + (€15 000 ÷ 12) = €81 350 + €1250 = €82 600.

2　A flexible budget enables Hoofdorp to calculate a richer set of variances than does a static budget. Hoofdorp will be able to calculate a flexible-budget variance and a sales-volume variance. These additional variances provide more insight into *why* actual results differ from budgeted amounts.

Exercise 15.24

1　Budgeted selling price (revenue per loan application):

$$\tfrac{1}{2}\% \times \text{budgeted average loan amount} = \tfrac{1}{2}\% \times €200\,000 = €1000$$

Budgeted variable costs per output unit are:

Professional labour (6 × €40)	€240
Loan filing fees	100
Credit checks	120
Courier mailings	50
Total budgeted variable costs	€510

Budgeted fixed costs = €31 000 per month.

The static budget for the 90 loan applicant level (and the flexible budget for the 120 loan application level in requirement 2) are:

	Requirement 1: 90 loan applications	Requirement 2: 120 loan applications
Budgeted revenue (90, 120 × €1000)	€90 000	€120 000
Budgeted variable costs (90, 120 × €510)	45 900	61 200
Contribution margin	44 100	58 800
Fixed costs	31 000	31 000
Operating profit	€13 100	€27 800

2 The actual results are:

Revenue (120 × 0.5% × €224 000)		€134 400
Variable costs:		
Professional labour (120 × 7.2 ×€42)	€36 288	
Loan filing fees (120 × €100)	12 000	
Credit checks (120 × €125)	15 000	
Courier mailings (120 × €54)	6 480	69 768
Contribution margin		64 632
Fixed costs		33 500
Operating profit		€31 132

These actual results can be analysed in a Level 2 variance analysis.

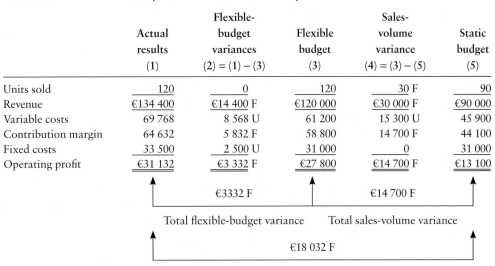

	Actual results (1)	Flexible- budget variances (2) = (1) − (3)	Flexible budget (3)	Sales- volume variance (4) = (3) − (5)	Static budget (5)
Units sold	120	0	120	30 F	90
Revenue	€134 400	€14 400 F	€120 000	€30 000 F	€90 000
Variable costs	69 768	8 568 U	61 200	15 300 U	45 900
Contribution margin	64 632	5 832 F	58 800	14 700 F	44 100
Fixed costs	33 500	2 500 U	31 000	0	31 000
Operating profit	€31 132	€3 332 F	€27 800	€14 700 F	€13 100

€3332 F

€14 700 F

Total flexible-budget variance   Total sales-volume variance

€18 032 F

Total static-budget variance

Note that the €18 032 favourable static-budget variance is largely the result of an increase in loan applications from a budgeted 90 to an actual 120. In addition, the average size of a loan increased from a budgeted €200 000 to €224 000 which explains the flexible-budget variance of €14 400 F for revenues (0.5% × €24 000 × 120 = €14 400). One possible explanation is a rapid decrease in interest rates leading to an increase in demand for loan refinancing.

CHAPTER 16

Exercise 16.11

1

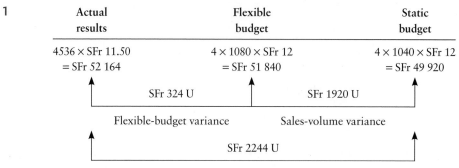

2 Lavertezzo manufactured an extra 40 suits than the 1040 budgeted. This accounts for the unfavourable sales-volume variance of SFr 1920 for variable manufacturing overhead.

The actual variable manufacturing overhead of SFr 52 164 exceeds the flexible budget amount of SFr 51 840 for 1080 suits by SFr 324 – hence the flexible budget variance is SFr 324 U.

Although not required by the exercise, the spending and efficiency variances provide further insight into the flexible-budget variance of SFr 324 U for variable manufacturing overhead:

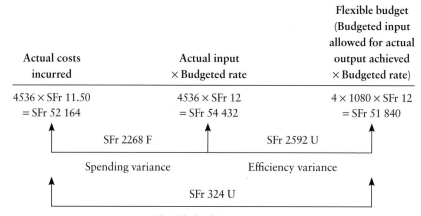

Lavertezzo had a favourable spending variance of SFr 2268 (the actual variable overhead rate was SFr 11.50 per direct manufacturing labour-hour versus SFr 12 budgeted). It had an unfavourable efficiency variance of SFr 2592 U (each suit average 4.2 labour-hours versus 4.00 budgeted).

CHAPTER 17

Exercise 17.11

1 and 2 Actual total quantity of all inputs used and actual input mix percentages for each input are as follows:

Chemical	Actual quantity	Actual mix percentage
Echol	24 080	24 080 ÷ 86 000 = 0.28
Protex	15 480	15 480 ÷ 86 000 = 0.18
Benz	36 120	36 120 ÷ 86 000 = 0.42
CT-40	10 320	10 320 ÷ 86 000 = 0.12
Total	86 000	1.00

Budgeted total quantity of all inputs allowed and budgeted input mix percentages for each input are as follows:

Chemical	Budgeted quantity	Budgeted mix percentage
Echol	25 200	25 200 ÷ 84 000 = 0.30
Protex	16 800	16 800 ÷ 84 000 = 0.20
Benz	33 600	33 600 ÷ 84 000 = 0.40
CT-40	8 400	8 400 ÷ 84 000 = 0.10
Total	84 000	1.00

Solution Exhibit 17.11 presents the total direct materials efficiency, yield and mix variances for August.

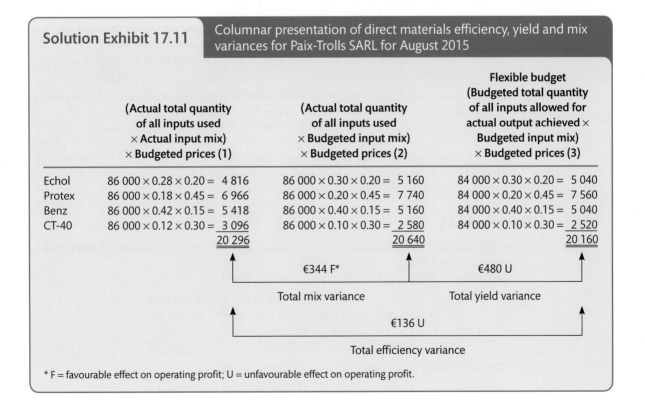

Solution Exhibit 17.11 Columnar presentation of direct materials efficiency, yield and mix variances for Paix-Trolls SARL for August 2015

	(Actual total quantity of all inputs used × Actual input mix) × Budgeted prices (1)	(Actual total quantity of all inputs used × Budgeted input mix) × Budgeted prices (2)	Flexible budget (Budgeted total quantity of all inputs allowed for actual output achieved × Budgeted input mix) × Budgeted prices (3)
Echol	86 000 × 0.28 × 0.20 = 4 816	86 000 × 0.30 × 0.20 = 5 160	84 000 × 0.30 × 0.20 = 5 040
Protex	86 000 × 0.18 × 0.45 = 6 966	86 000 × 0.20 × 0.45 = 7 740	84 000 × 0.20 × 0.45 = 7 560
Benz	86 000 × 0.42 × 0.15 = 5 418	86 000 × 0.40 × 0.15 = 5 160	84 000 × 0.40 × 0.15 = 5 040
CT-40	86 000 × 0.12 × 0.30 = 3 096	86 000 × 0.10 × 0.30 = 2 580	84 000 × 0.10 × 0.30 = 2 520
	20 296	20 640	20 160

€344 F*

Total mix variance

€480 U

Total yield variance

€136 U

Total efficiency variance

* F = favourable effect on operating profit; U = unfavourable effect on operating profit.

Total direct materials efficiency variance can also be calculated as:

$$\begin{array}{c} \text{Direct materials} \\ \text{efficiency variance} \\ \text{for each input} \end{array} = \left(\text{Actual input} - \begin{array}{c} \text{Budgeted inputs} \\ \text{allowed for actual} \\ \text{output achieved} \end{array} \right) \times \begin{array}{c} \text{Budgeted} \\ \text{prices} \end{array}$$

Echol	$= (24\,080 - 25\,200) \times €0.20$	$=$	€224 F
Protex	$= (15\,480 - 16\,800) \times €0.45$	$=$	594 F
Benz	$= (36\,120 - 33\,600) \times €0.15$	$=$	378 U
CT-40	$= (10\,320 - 8400) \times €0.30$	$=$	576 U
Total direct materials efficiency variance		$=$	€136 U

The total direct materials yield variance can also be calculated as the sum of the direct materials yield variances for each input:

Echol	$= (86\,000 - 84\,000) \times 0.30 \times €0.20 = 2000 \times 0.30 \times €0.20 = €120$ U
Protex	$= (86\,000 - 84\,000) \times 0.20 \times €0.45 = 2000 \times 0.20 \times €0.45 = 180$ U
Benz	$= (86\,000 - 84\,000) \times 0.40 \times €0.15 = 2000 \times 0.40 \times €0.15 = 120$ U
CT-40	$= (86\,000 - 84\,000) \times 0.10 \times €0.30 = 2000 \times 0.10 \times €0.30 = 60$ U
Total direct materials yield variance	€480 U

The total direct materials mix variance can also be calculated as the sum of the direct materials mix variances for each input:

$$\begin{array}{c} \text{Direct materials} \\ \text{mix variance} \\ \text{for each input} \end{array} = \left(\begin{array}{c} \text{Actual direct materials} \\ \text{input mix percentage} - \\ \text{Budgeted direct materials} \\ \text{input mix percentage} \end{array} \right) \times \begin{array}{c} \text{Actual total} \\ \text{quantity of all} \\ \text{direct materials} \\ \text{inputs used} \end{array} \times \begin{array}{c} \text{Budgeted} \\ \text{prices of direct} \\ \text{materials} \\ \text{inputs} \end{array}$$

Echol	$= (0.28 - 0.30) \times 86\,000 \times €0.20 = -0.02 \times 86\,000 \times €0.20 = €344$ F
Protex	$= (0.18 - 0.20) \times 86\,000 \times €0.45 = -0.02 \times 86\,000 \times €0.45 = 774$ F
Benz	$= (0.42 - 0.40) \times 86\,000 \times €0.15 = 0.02 \times 86\,000 \times €0.15 = 258$ U
CT-40	$= (0.12 - 0.10) \times 86\,000 \times €0.30 = 0.02 \times 86\,000 \times €0.30 = 516$ U
Total direct materials mix variance	€344 F

3 Paix-Trolls used a larger total quantity of direct materials inputs than budgeted, and so showed an unfavourable yield variance. The mix variance was favourable because the actual mix contained more of the cheapest input, Benz, and less of the costliest input, Protex, than the budgeted mix. The favourable mix variance offset some, but not all, of the unfavourable yield variance – the overall efficiency variance was unfavourable. Paix-Trolls will only find it profitable to shift to the cheaper mix if the yield from this cheaper mix can be improved. Paix-Trolls must also consider the effect on output quality of using the cheaper mix, and the potential consequences for future revenues.

Exercise 17.16

1 Solution Exhibit 17.16A presents the total price variance (€3100 F), the total efficiency variance (€2560 U) and the total flexible-budget variance (€540 F).

Total direct materials price variance can also be calculated as:

Barley	$= (€0.28 - €0.30) \times 62\,000$	$=$	€1240 F
Wheat	$= (€0.26 - €0.26) \times 155\,000$	$=$	0
Rye	$= (€0.20 - €0.22) \times 93\,000$	$=$	1860 F
Total direct materials price variance			€3100 F

Total direct materials efficiency variance can also be calculated as:

Barley	$= (62\,000 - 45\,000) \times €0.30$	$=$	€5100 U
Wheat	$= (155\,000 - 180\,000) \times €0.26$	$=$	6500 F
Rye	$= (93\,000 - 75\,000) \times €0.22$	$=$	3960 U
Total direct materials efficiency variance			€2560 U

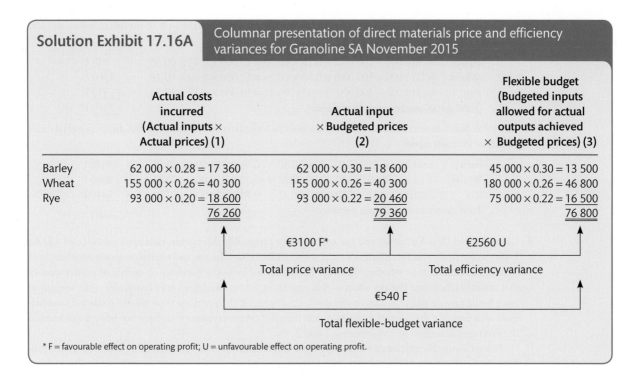

Solution Exhibit 17.16A — Columnar presentation of direct materials price and efficiency variances for Granoline SA November 2015

	Actual costs incurred (Actual inputs × Actual prices) (1)	Actual input × Budgeted prices (2)	Flexible budget (Budgeted inputs allowed for actual outputs achieved × Budgeted prices) (3)
Barley	62 000 × 0.28 = 17 360	62 000 × 0.30 = 18 600	45 000 × 0.30 = 13 500
Wheat	155 000 × 0.26 = 40 300	155 000 × 0.26 = 40 300	180 000 × 0.26 = 46 800
Rye	93 000 × 0.20 = 18 600	93 000 × 0.22 = 20 460	75 000 × 0.22 = 16 500
	76 260	79 360	76 800

€3100 F*
Total price variance

€2560 U
Total efficiency variance

€540 F
Total flexible-budget variance

* F = favourable effect on operating profit; U = unfavourable effect on operating profit.

2 Solution Exhibit 17.16B presents the total direct materials yield and mix variances for Granoline SA for November 2015.

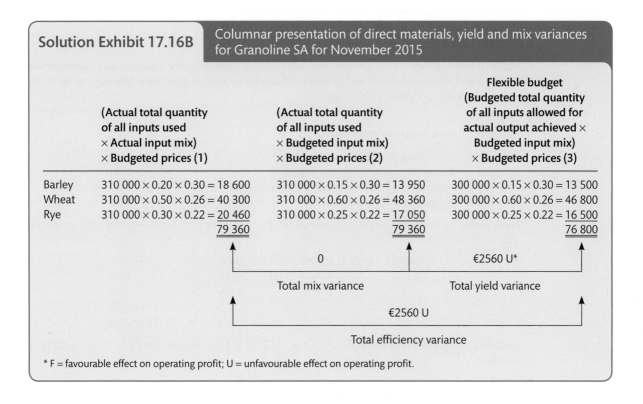

Solution Exhibit 17.16B — Columnar presentation of direct materials, yield and mix variances for Granoline SA for November 2015

	(Actual total quantity of all inputs used × Actual input mix) × Budgeted prices (1)	(Actual total quantity of all inputs used × Budgeted input mix) × Budgeted prices (2)	Flexible budget (Budgeted total quantity of all inputs allowed for actual output achieved × Budgeted input mix) × Budgeted prices (3)
Barley	310 000 × 0.20 × 0.30 = 18 600	310 000 × 0.15 × 0.30 = 13 950	300 000 × 0.15 × 0.30 = 13 500
Wheat	310 000 × 0.50 × 0.26 = 40 300	310 000 × 0.60 × 0.26 = 48 360	300 000 × 0.60 × 0.26 = 46 800
Rye	310 000 × 0.30 × 0.22 = 20 460	310 000 × 0.25 × 0.22 = 17 050	300 000 × 0.25 × 0.22 = 16 500
	79 360	79 360	76 800

0
Total mix variance

€2560 U*
Total yield variance

€2560 U
Total efficiency variance

* F = favourable effect on operating profit; U = unfavourable effect on operating profit.

The total direct materials yield variance can also be calculated as the sum of the direct materials yield variances for each input:

Barley	$= (310\,000 - 300\,000) \times 0.15 \times €0.30 = 10\,000 \times 0.15 \times €0.30$	$=$ 450 U
Wheat	$= (310\,000 - 300\,000) \times 0.60 \times €0.26 = 10\,000 \times 0.60 \times €0.26$	$=$ 1560 U
Rye	$= (310\,000 - 300\,000) \times 0.25 \times €0.22 = 10\,000 \times 0.25 \times €0.22$	$=$ 550 U
Total direct materials yield variance		€2560 U

The total direct materials mix variance can also be calculated as the sum of the direct materials mix variances for each input:

Barley	$= (0.20 - 0.15) \times 310\,000 \times €0.30 = \ \ 0.05 \times 310\,000 \times €0.30$	$=$ €4650 U
Wheat	$= (0.50 - 0.60) \times 310\,000 \times €0.26 = -0.10 \times 310\,000 \times €0.26$	$=$ 8060 F
Rye	$= (0.30 - 0.25) \times 310\,000 \times €0.22 = \ \ 0.05 \times 310\,000 \times €0.22$	$=$ 3410 U
Total direct materials mix variance		€0 U

3 Granoline paid less for barley and rye and so had a favourable direct materials price variance of €3100. It also had an unfavourable efficiency variance of €2560. Granoline would need to evaluate whether these were unrelated events or whether the lower price resulted from the purchase of cereals of poorer quality that affected efficiency. The net effect in this case from a cost standpoint was favourable – the savings in price being greater than the loss in efficiency. Of course, if the porridge is of poorer quality, Granoline must also evaluate the potential effects on current and future revenues that have not been considered in the variances described in requirements 1 and 2.

The unfavourable efficiency variance is attributable entirely to an unfavourable yield. The actual mix does deviate from the budgeted mix, but at the budgeted prices, the greater quantity of barley and rye cereals used in the actual mix exactly offsets the fewer wheat cereals used. Again, management should evaluate the reasons for the unfavourable yield variance. Is it due to poor quality barley and rye cereals (recall from requirement 1 that these cereals were acquired at a price lower than the standard price)? Is it due to the change in mix (recall that the mix used is different from the budgeted mix, even though the mix variance is €0)? Isolating the reasons can lead management to take the necessary corrective actions.

Exercise 17.21

1 and 2 Solution Exhibit 17.21 presents the sales-volume, sales-quantity and sales-mix variances for the Choc and Chic wine glasses and in total for Rusti-Verres SNC in June 2011. The steps to fill in the numbers in Solution Exhibit 17.21 follow:

- *Step 1*
  Consider the static budget column (column 3):

Static budget total contribution margin	SFr 5600
Budgeted units of all glasses to be sold	2000
Budgeted contribution margin per unit of Choc	SFr 2
Budgeted contribution margin per unit of Chic	SFr 6

Suppose that the budgeted sales mix percentage of Choc is y. Then the budgeted sales mix percentage of Chic is $(1 - y)$. Hence,

$(2000 \times y \times \text{SFr } 2) + (2000 \times (1 - y) \times \text{SFr } 6)$	$=$	SFr 5600
$4000y + 12\,000 - 12\,000y$	$=$	5600
$8000y$	$=$	6400
y	$=$	0.8 or 80%
$1 - y = 1 - 0.8$	$=$	0.2 or 20%

Rusti-Verres' budgeted sales mix is 80% of Choc and 20% of Chic. We can then fill in all the numbers in column 3.

- *Step 2*
  Consider next column 2 of Solution Exhibit 17.21.

  The total of column 2 in Panel C is SFr 4200 (the static budget total contribution margin of SFr 5600 – the total sales-quantity variance of SFr 1400 U which was given in the problem).

We need to find the actual units sold of all glasses, which we denote by q. From column 2, we know that:

$$
\begin{aligned}
(q \times 0.8 \times \text{SFr } 2) + (q \times 0.2 \times \text{SFr } 6) &= \text{SFr } 4200 \\
\text{SFr } 1.6q + \text{SFr } 1.2q &= \text{SFr } 4200 \\
\text{SFr } 2.8q &= \text{SFr } 4200 \\
q &= 1500 \text{ units}
\end{aligned}
$$

Hence, the total quantity of all glasses sold is 1500 units. This calculation allows us to fill in all the numbers in column 2.

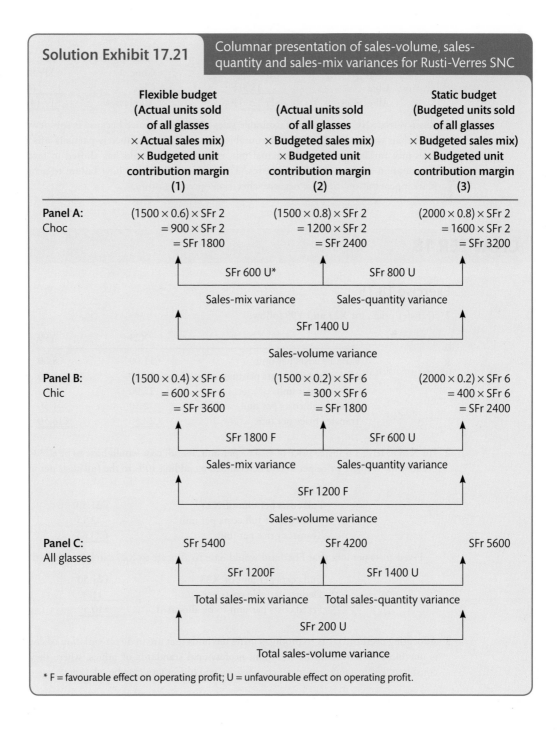

Solution Exhibit 17.21	Columnar presentation of sales-volume, sales-quantity and sales-mix variances for Rusti-Verres SNC

	Flexible budget (Actual units sold of all glasses × Actual sales mix) × Budgeted unit contribution margin (1)	(Actual units sold of all glasses × Budgeted sales mix) × Budgeted unit contribution margin (2)	Static budget (Budgeted units sold of all glasses × Budgeted sales mix) × Budgeted unit contribution margin (3)
Panel A: Choc	(1500 × 0.6) × SFr 2 = 900 × SFr 2 = SFr 1800	(1500 × 0.8) × SFr 2 = 1200 × SFr 2 = SFr 2400	(2000 × 0.8) × SFr 2 = 1600 × SFr 2 = SFr 3200

Panel A:
SFr 600 U*   SFr 800 U
Sales-mix variance   Sales-quantity variance
SFr 1400 U
Sales-volume variance

Panel B: Chic	(1500 × 0.4) × SFr 6 = 600 × SFr 6 = SFr 3600	(1500 × 0.2) × SFr 6 = 300 × SFr 6 = SFr 1800	(2000 × 0.2) × SFr 6 = 400 × SFr 6 = SFr 2400

SFr 1800 F   SFr 600 U
Sales-mix variance   Sales-quantity variance
SFr 1200 F
Sales-volume variance

Panel C: All glasses	SFr 5400	SFr 4200	SFr 5600

SFr 1200F   SFr 1400 U
Total sales-mix variance   Total sales-quantity variance
SFr 200 U
Total sales-volume variance

* F = favourable effect on operating profit; U = unfavourable effect on operating profit.

- *Step 3*

  Consider next column 1 of Solution Exhibit 17.21. We know the actual units sold of all glasses (1500 units), the actual sales-mix percentage (given in the problem information as Choc 60% and Chic 40%), and the budgeted unit contribution margin of each product (Choc SFr 2, Chic SFr 6). We can therefore determine all the numbers in column 1.

  Solution Exhibit 17.21 displays the following sales-quantity, sales-mix and sales-volume variances:

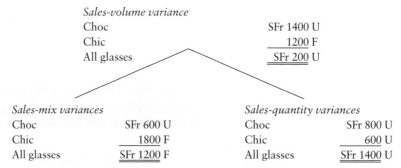

Sales-volume variance

Choc	SFr 1400 U
Chic	1200 F
All glasses	SFr 200 U

Sales-mix variances		*Sales-quantity variances*	
Choc	SFr 600 U	Choc	SFr 800 U
Chic	1800 F	Chic	600 U
All glasses	SFr 1200 F	All glasses	SFr 1400 U

3 Rusti-Verres SNC shows an unfavourable sales-quantity variance because it sold fewer wine glasses in total than was budgeted. This unfavourable sales-quantity variance is partially offset by a favourable sales-mix variance because the actual mix of wine glasses sold has shifted in favour of the higher contribution margin Chic wine glasses. The problem illustrates how failure to achieve the budgeted market penetration can have negative effects on operating profit.

CHAPTER 18

Exercise 18.15

1 Transfer prices for X23 and Y99 follow:

	X23	Y99
Variable costs per unit	€11.00	€8.00
Allocated fixed costs per unit	14.00	7.00
Full costs per unit	25.00	15.00
10% of full costs per unit	2.50	1.50
Transfer price per unit	€27.50	€16.50

2 For X23 to have a transfer price of €23.65 per unit, its full cost would have to be €23.65 ÷ 1.10 = €21.50, because the transfer price per unit is determined by adding 10% to the full costs per unit.

Check

Full costs per unit of X23	€21.50
Add 10% of full costs per unit	2.15
Transfer price per unit	€23.65

Fixed costs per unit that Eberhard would have to allocate to X23 can be calculated as follows:

Full costs per unit of X23	€21.50
Deduct variable costs per unit	11.00
Fixed costs per unit to be allocated	€10.50

3 Allocating overhead costs to products using methods that are in direct violation of corporate guidelines is unethical. In assessing the situation, professional standards of ethics, where they exist, should be consulted. For instance, competence, integrity and objectivity may be relevant.

Competence

Clear reports using relevant and reliable information should be prepared. Reports prepared on the basis of incorrectly allocating fixed costs would violate the management accountant's responsibility to competence. It is unethical for Wilhelm to suggest that Eberhard should change the cost numbers that were prepared for costing product X23 and for Wilhelm to change the numbers in order to reduce the cost and hence the transfer price for X23.

Integrity

The management accountant has a responsibility to avoid actual or apparent conflicts of interest and to advise all appropriate parties of any potential conflict. Lowering the fixed costs allocated to X23 will increase the costs allocated to Y99. If they changed the method of fixed-cost allocation, Wilhelm and Eberhard would appear to favour the Hanover Division (that uses X23) over the Bremen Division (that uses Y99). This action could be viewed as violating the responsibility for integrity. It is desirable for the management accountant to communicate favourable as well as unfavourable information. In this regard both Wilhelm's and Eberhard's behaviour (if Eberhard agrees to reduce the overhead costs allocated to X23) could be viewed as unethical.

Objectivity

Information should be fairly and objectively communicated and all relevant information should be disclosed. From a management accountant's standpoint, allocating fewer costs to a product in violation of company policy clearly violates both these precepts. For the various reasons cited above, we should take the position that the behaviour described by Wilhelm and Eberhard (if he goes along with Wilhelm's wishes) is unethical.

Eberhard should indicate to Wilhelm that the overhead costs allocated to X23 are indeed appropriate, given the long-term nature of the relationship between Leipzig and Hanover, and also as required by company policy. If Wilhelm still insists on making the changes and reducing the costs of making X23, Eberhard should raise the matter with Wilhelm's superior. If, after taking all these steps, there is continued pressure to misallocate costs, Eberhard should consider resigning from the company, and not engage in unethical behaviour.

Some students may raise the issue of whether full-cost transfer pricing is appropriate in this context. The problem does not provide enough details for a complete discussion of this issue. Management may well conclude that full-cost-based transfer prices should not be used. But that is a management decision. The management accountant should not unilaterally use methods of allocating fixed costs that are in direct violation of company policy.

Exercise 18.19

This problem explores the 'general transfer-pricing guideline' discussed in the chapter.

1 No, transfers should not be made to Division B if there is no excess capacity in Division A.

An incremental (outlay) cost approach shows a positive contribution for the company as a whole.

Selling price of final product		€300
Incremental costs in Division A	€120	
Incremental costs in Division B	150	270
Contribution (loss)		€30

However, if there is no excess capacity in Division A, any transfer will result in diverting product from the market for the intermediate product. Sales in this market result in a greater contribution for the company as a whole. Division B should not assemble the bicycle since the incremental revenue Liberaki can earn, €100 per unit (€300 from selling the final product − €200 from selling the intermediate product) is less than the incremental costs of €150 to assemble the bicycle in Division B.

Selling price of intermediate product	€200
Incremental (outlay) costs in Division A	120
Contribution (loss)	€80

The general guideline described in the chapter is:

Minimum transfer price = Additional incremental costs per unit incurred up to the point of transfer
+ Opportunity costs per unit to the supplying division

= €120 + (€200 − €120)
= €200, which is the market price

Market price is the transfer price that leads to the correct decision; that is, do not transfer to Division B unless there are extenuating circumstances for continuing to market the final product. Therefore, B must either drop the product or reduce the incremental costs of assembly from €150 per bicycle to less than €100.

2 If (i) A has excess capacity, (ii) there is intermediate external demand for only 800 units at €200, and (iii) the €200 price is to be maintained, then the opportunity costs per unit to the supplying division are €0. The general guideline indicates a minimum transfer price of: €120 + €0 = €120, which is the incremental or outlay costs for the first 200 units. B would buy 200 units from A at a transfer price of €120 because B can earn a contribution of €30 per unit [€300 − (€120 + €150)]. In fact, B would be willing to buy units from A at any price up to €150 per unit because any transfers at a price of up to €150 will still yield B a positive contribution margin.

Note, however, that if B wants more than 200 units, the minimum transfer price will be €200 as calculated in requirement 1 because A will incur an opportunity cost in the form of lost contribution of €80 (market price, €200 − outlay costs of €120) for every unit above 200 units that are transferred to B.

The following schedule summarises the transfer prices for units transferred from A to B.

Units	Transfer price
0–200	€120–€150
200–1000	€200

For an exploration of this situation when imperfect markets exist, see Exercise 18.22.

3 Division B would show zero contribution, but the company as a whole would generate a contribution of €30 per unit on the 200 units transferred. Any price between €120 and €150 would induce the transfer that would be desirable for the company as a whole. A motivational problem may arise regarding how to split the €30 contribution between Divisions A and B. Unless the price is below €150, B would have little incentive to buy.

Note: The transfer price that may appear optimal in an economic analysis may, in fact, be totally unacceptable from the viewpoints of (1) preserving autonomy of the managers and (2) evaluating the performance of the divisions as economic units. For instance, consider the simplest case discussed above, where there is idle capacity and the €200 intermediate price is to be maintained. To direct that A should sell to B at A's variable cost of €120 may be desirable from the viewpoint of B and the company as a whole. However, the autonomy (independence) of the manager of A is eroded. Division A will earn nothing, although it could argue that it is contributing to the earning of profit on the final product.

If the manager of A wants a portion of the total company contribution of €30 per unit, the question is: How is an appropriate amount determined? This is a difficult question in practice. The price can be negotiated upwards to somewhere between €120 and €150 so that some 'equitable' split is achieved. A dual transfer pricing scheme has also been suggested whereby the supplier gets credit for the full intermediate market price and the buyer is charged only with variable or incremental costs. In any event, when there is heavy interdependence between divisions, such as in this case, some system of subsidies may be needed to deal with the three problems of goal congruence, management effort and subunit autonomy. Of course, where heavy subsidies are needed, a question can be raised as to whether the existing degree of decentralisation is optimal.

Exercise 18.22

An alternative presentation, which contains the same numerical answers, can be found at the end of this solution.

1 Potential contribution from external intermediate sale:

$1000 \times (€195 - €120)$	€75 000
Contribution through keeping price at €200:	
$800 \times €80$.	64 000
Forgone contribution by transferring 200 units	€11 000

Opportunity cost per unit to the supplying division:

By transferring internally = 11 000/200 = €55
Transfer price   = €120 + €55 = €175

An alternative approach to obtaining the same answer is to recognise that the incremental or outlay cost is the same for all 1000 units in question. Therefore, the total revenue desired by A would be the same for selling outside or inside.

Let X equal the transfer price at which Division A is indifferent between selling all units outside versus transferring 200 units inside:

$$1000 \ (€195) = 800 \ (€200) + 200X$$
$$X = €175$$

The €175 price will lead to the correct decision. Division B will not buy from Division A because its total costs of €175 + €150 will exceed its prospective selling price of €300. Division A will then sell 1000 units at €195 to the outside; Division A and the company will have a contribution margin of €75 000. Otherwise, if 800 units were sold at €200 and 200 units were transferred to Division B, the company would have a contribution of €64 000 plus €6000 (200 units of final product × €30), or €70 000.

A comparison might be drawn regarding the calculation of the appropriate transfer prices between the preceding exercise and this:

$$\text{Minimum transfer price} = \frac{\text{Additional incremental costs per unit incurred up to the point of transfer}}{} + \frac{\text{Opportunity costs per unit to Division A}}{}$$

Perfect markets

$$\text{Minimum transfer price} = €120 + (\text{Selling price} - \text{Outlay costs per unit})$$
$$= €120 + (€200 - €120) = €200$$

Imperfect markets

$$\text{Minimum transfer price} = €120 + \frac{\text{Marginal revenues} - \text{Outlay costs}}{\text{Number of units transferred}}$$

The marginal revenues of Division A from selling 200 units outside rather than transferring to Division B are = $(€195 \times 1000) - (€200 \times 800) = €195 000 - €160 000 = €35 000$. The incremental (outlay) costs incurred by Division A to produce 200 units = $€120 \times 200 = €24 000$. Therefore

$$\text{Minimum transfer price} = €120 + [(35 000 - 24 000)/200] = €175$$

Therefore, selling price (€195) and marginal revenues per unit (€175 = €35 000 ÷ 200) are not the same.

Some students will erroneously say that the 'new' market price of €195 is the appropriate transfer price. They will claim that the general guideline says that the transfer price should be €120 + (€195 − €120) = €195, the market price. This conclusion assumes a perfect market. But here there are imperfections in the intermediate market. That is, the market price is *not* a good approximation of alternative revenue. If a division's sales are heavy enough to reduce market prices, marginal revenue will be less than market price.

It is true that *either* €195 *or* €175 will lead to the correct decision by B in this case. But suppose that B's variable costs were €120 instead of €150. Then B would buy at a transfer price of €175, but not at a price of €195, because then B would earn a negative contribution of €15 per unit [€300 − (€195 + €120)]. Note that if B's variable costs were €120, transfers would be desirable:

Division A contribution,	
800 × (200 − 120) + 200 (175 − 120) =	€75 000
Division B contribution,	
200 × [€300 − (€175 + €120)] =	1 000
Total contribution	€76 000

Or the same facts can be analysed for the company as a whole:

Sales of intermediate product, 800 × (€200 − €120) =	€64 000
Sales of final products, 200 × [300 − (€120 + €120)] =	12 000
Total contribution	€76 000

If the transfer price were €195, B would not accept the transfer and would not earn any contribution. As shown above, Division A and the company as a whole will earn a total contribution of €75 000 instead of €76 000.

2 **a** Division A can sell 900 units at €195 to the outside market and 100 units to Division B, or 800 at €200 to the outside market and 200 units to Division B. Note that, under both alternatives, 100 units can be transferred to Division B at no opportunity cost to A.

Using the general guideline, the minimum transfer price of *the first 100 units* [901 to 1000] is TP1 = €120 + 0 = €120. If Division B needs 100 additional units, the opportunity cost to A is not zero, because Division A will then have to sell only 800 units to the outside market for a contribution of 800 × (€200 − €120) = €64 000 instead of 900 units for a contribution of 900 (€195 − €120) = €67 500. Each unit sold to B in addition to the first 100 units has an opportunity cost to A of (€67 500 − €64 000) ÷ 100 = €35.

Using the general guideline, the minimum transfer price of *the next 100 units* [801 to 900] is TP2 = €120 + €35 = €155.

Alternatively, the calculation could be as follows:

Increase in contribution from 100 more units, 100 × €75	€7500
Loss in contribution on 800 units, 800 × (€80 − €75)	4000
Net 'marginal revenue'	€3500
Net 'marginal revenue' per unit, €3500 ÷ 100	€35
(Minimum) transfer price applicable to first 100 units	
offered by A, €120 + €0	€120 per unit
(Minimum) transfer price applicable to next 100 units	
offered by A, €120 + (€3500 ÷ 100)	€155 per unit
(Minimum) transfer price applicable to next 800 units	€195 per unit

b The manager of Division B will not want to purchase more than 100 units because the units at €155 would decrease his contribution (€155 + €150 > €300). Because the manager of B does not buy more than 100 units, the manager of A will have 900 units available for sale to the outside market. The manager of A will strive to maximise the contribution by selling them all at €195.

This solution maximises the company's contribution:

900 × (€195 − €120)	€67 500
100 × (€300 − €270)	3 000
	€70 500

This compares favourably with:

800 × (€200 − €120)	€64 000
200 × (€300 − €270)	6 000
	€70 000

Alternative presentation from company viewpoint (by James Patell)

1   *Sell 1000 outside at €195*

Price	€195
Variable costs	120
Contribution	€75 × 1000 = €75 000

Sell 800 outside at €200, transfer 200

Transfer price	€200
Variable costs	120
Contribution	€80 × 800 = €64 000

Total contribution given up if transfer occurs = €75 000 − €64 000 = €11 000. (The contribution of €30 per unit by B is not given up if transfer occurs, so it is not relevant here.)

On a per-unit basis, the relevant costs are the incremental costs to point of transfer + opportunity costs to Division A of transfer = transfer price, i.e. 120 + 11 000/200 = €175.

By formula, the costs are the incremental costs to point of transfer + lost opportunity to sell 200 at €195 for contribution of €75 − gain when first 800 sell at €200 instead of €195, i.e. €120 + €75 − €20 = €175.

2 **a** At most, Division A can sell only 900 units and can produce 1000. Therefore, at least 100 units should be transferred, at a transfer price no less than €120. The question is whether or not a second 100 units should be transferred.

   Sell 900 outside at €195

Transfer price	€195
Variable cost	120
Contribution	€75 × 900 = €67 500

   Sell 800 outside at €200, transfer 100

Transfer price	€200
Variable cost	120
Contribution	€80 × 800 = €64 000

Total contribution forgone if transfer of 100 units occurs = €67 500 − €64 000 = €3500 (or €35 per unit).

On a per-unit basis, the relevant costs are the incremental costs to point of transfer + opportunity costs to Division A of transfer = transfer price, i.e. €120 + €35 = €155.

   b By formula, the costs are the incremental costs to point of transfer + lost opportunity to sell 100 at €195, for contribution of €75 − gain when first 800 sell at €200 instead of €195, i.e. €120 + €75 − €40 = €155.

Transfer price schedule (minimum acceptable transfer price)

Units	Transfer price
0–100	€120
101–200	€155
201–1000	€195

CHAPTER 19

Exercise 19.13

1

	Lorry Rental Division	Transportation Division
Total assets	€650 000	€950 000
Less: current liabilities	120 000	200 000
Investment	€530 000	€750 000
Required return (12% × investment)	63 600	90 000
Operating profit before tax	75 000	160 000
Residual income (profit − return)	€11 400	€70 000

2   After-tax cost of debt financing $= (1 − 0.4) \times 10\% = 6\%$
   After-tax cost of equity financing $= 15\%$
   Weighted average cost of capital $= 9.6\%$
   Required return for EVA®:

	Lorry Rental Division	Transportation Division
Investment	€530 000	€750 000
9.6% × investment	50 880	72 000
Operating profit after tax = 0.6 × operating profit before tax	45 000	96 000
EVA® (profit after tax − required return)	(€5 880)	€24 000

3   Both the residual profit and the EVA® calculations indicate that the Transportation Division is performing better than the Lorry Rental Division. The Transportation Division has a higher residual profit (€70 000 versus €11 400) and a higher EVA® (€24 000 versus negative €5880). The negative EVA® for the Lorry Rental Division indicates that on an after-tax basis the division is *destroying* value – the after-tax economic return from the Lorry Rental Division's assets is less than the required return. If EVA® continues to be negative, Intervilles may have to consider shutting down the Lorry Rental Division.

Exercise 19.15

1   The separate components highlight several features of return on investment not revealed by a single calculation:

- The importance of investment turnover as a key to profit is stressed.
- The importance of revenues is explicitly recognised.
- The important components are expressed as ratios or percentages instead of monetary figures. This form of expression often enhances comparability of different divisions, businesses and time periods.
- The breakdown stresses the possibility of trading-off investment turnover for income as a percentage of revenues so as to increase the average ROI at a given level of output.

2   (Filled-in blanks are in bold face.)

	Companies in same industry		
	A	B	C
Revenue	€1 000 000	€500 000	€10 000 000
Profit	€100 000	€50 000	€50 000
Investment	€500 000	€5 000 000	€5 000 000
Profit as % of revenue	10%	10%	0.5%
Investment turnover	2.0	0.1	2.0
Return on investment	20%	1%	1%

Income and investment alone shed little light on comparative performances because of disparities in size between Company A and the other two companies. Thus, it is impossible to say whether B's low return on investment in comparison with A's is attributable to its larger investment or to its lower profit. Furthermore the fact that Companies B and C have identical profit and investment may suggest that the same conditions underlie the low ROI, but this conclusion is erroneous. B has higher margins but a lower investment turnover. C has very small margins (1/20 of B's) but turns over investment 20 times faster.

The following analysis of the situation could be made:

> Introducing revenues to measure level of operations helps to disclose specific areas for more intensive investigation. Company B does as well as Company A in terms of profit margin, for both companies earn 10% on revenues. But Company B has a much lower turnover of investment than does Company A. Whereas a euro of investment in Company A supports 2 euros in revenues each period, a euro investment in Company B supports only 10 cents in revenues each period. This suggests that the analyst should look carefully at Company B's investment. Is the company keeping a level of stocks larger than necessary for its revenue level? Are debts being collected promptly? Or did Company A acquire its fixed assets at a price level that was much lower than that at which Company B purchased its plant?
>
> On the other hand, C's investment turnover is as high as A's, but C's profit as a percentage of revenue is much lower. Why? Are its operations inefficient, are its material costs too high, or does its location entail high transportation costs?
>
> Analysis of ROI raises questions such as the foregoing. When answers are obtained, basic reasons for differences between rates of return may be discovered. For example, in Company B's case, it is apparent that the emphasis will have to be on increasing turnover by reducing investment or increasing revenues. Clearly, B cannot appreciably increase its ROI simply by increasing its profit as a percentage of revenue. In contrast, Company C's management should concentrate on increasing the percentage of profit on revenue.

Exercise 19.19

1 *Computer Power*

2013	1.111	0.250	0.278
2014	0.941	0.125	0.118

Plum Computer

2013	1.250	0.100	0.125
2014	1.458	0.171	0.250

Computer Power's ROI has declined sizably from 2013 to 2014, largely because of a decline in operating profit to revenues. Plum Computer's ROI has doubled from 2013 to 2014, in large part due to an increase in operating profit to revenues.

2

	Computer Power		Plum Computer	
Business function	2013	2014	2013	2014
R&D	12.0%	6.0%	10.0%	15.0%
Design	5.0	3.0	2.0	4.0
Production	34.0	40.0	46.0	34.0
Marketing	25.0	33.0	20.0	23.0
Distribution	9.0	8.0	10.0	8.0
Customer service	15.0	10.0	12.0	16.0
Total costs	100.0%	100.0%	100.0%	100.0%

Business functions with increases/decreases in the percentage of total costs from 2013 to 2014 are:

	Computer Power	Plum Computer
Increases	Production	R&D
	Marketing	Design
		Marketing
		Customer service
Decreases	R&D	Production
	Design	Distribution
	Distribution	
	Customer service	

Computer Power has decreased expenditures in several key business functions that are critical to its long-term survival, notably research and development and design. These costs are discretionary and can be reduced in the short run without any short-run effect on customers, but such action is likely to create serious problems in the long run.

3 Based on the information provided, Kamel is the better candidate for president of User Friendly Computer. Both Computer Power and Plum Computer are in the same industry. Kamel has headed Plum Computer at a time when it has considerably outperformed Computer Power:

- The ROI of Plum Computer has increased from 2013 to 2014 while that of Computer Power has decreased.
- The computer magazine has increased the ranking of Plum Computer's main product, while it has decreased the ranking of Computer Power's main product.
- Plum Computer has received high marks for new products (the lifeblood of a computer company), while Computer Power new-product introductions have been described as 'mediocre'.

CHAPTER 20

Exercise 20.15

1 Cost of defective unit at machining operation which is not a bottleneck operation is the loss in direct materials (variable costs) of €32 per unit. Producing 2000 units of defectives does not result in loss of throughput contribution. Despite the defective production, machining can produce and transfer 80 000 units to finishing. Therefore cost of 2000 defective units at the machining operation is €32 × 2000 = €64 000.

2 A defective unit produced at the bottleneck finishing operation costs Salamanca materials costs plus the opportunity cost of lost throughput contribution. Bottleneck capacity not wasted in producing defective units could be used to generate additional sales and throughput contribution. Cost of 2000 defective units at the finishing operation is as follows:

Loss of direct materials: €32 × 2000	€64 000
Forgone throughput contribution: (€72 − €32) × 2000	80 000
Total cost of 2000 defective units	€144 000

Alternatively, the cost of 2000 defective units at the finishing operation can be calculated as the lost revenue of €72 × 2000 = €144 000. That is, the direct materials costs of €32 × 2000 = €64 000 and all fixed operating costs in the machining and finishing operations are irrelevant since these costs would be incurred anyway whether a defective or good unit is produced. The cost of producing a defective unit is the revenue lost of €144 000.

Exercise 20.19

1 It will cost Autronic €50 per unit to reduce manufacturing time. But manufacturing is not a bottleneck operation, installation is. Therefore manufacturing more equipment will not increase sales and throughput contribution. Autronic AG should not implement the new manufacturing method.

2 Additional relevant costs of new direct materials = €2000 × 320 units = €640 000. Increase in throughput contribution = €25 000 × 20 units = €500 000. The additional incremental costs exceed the benefits from higher throughput contribution by €140 000, so Autronic AG should not implement the new design.

   Alternatively, compare throughput contribution under each alternative. Current throughput contribution is €25 000 × 300 = €7 500 000. With the modification, throughput contribution is €23 000 × 320 = €7 360 000. The current throughput contribution is greater than the throughput contribution resulting from the proposed change in direct materials. Hence, Autronic should not implement the new design.

3 Increase in throughput contribution, €25 000 × 10 units = €250 000. Increase in relevant costs = €50 000. The additional throughput contribution exceeds incremental costs by €200 000 so Autronic should implement the new installation technique.

4 Motivating installation workers to increase productivity is worthwhile because installation is a bottleneck operation and any increase in productivity at the bottleneck will increase throughput contribution. On the other hand, motivating workers in the Manufacturing Department to increase productivity is not worthwhile. Manufacturing is not a bottleneck operation, so any increase in output will only result in extra stock of equipment. Autronic AG should only encourage manufacturing to produce as much equipment as the Installation Department needs, not to produce as much as it can. In these circumstances, it would not be a good idea to evaluate and compensate manufacturing workers on the basis of their productivity.

Exercise 20.22

1 The $\pm 2\sigma$ rule will trigger a decision to investigate when the round-trip fuel usage is outside the control limit:

$$\text{Mean} \pm 2\sigma = 1000 \pm 2\sigma = 1000 \pm (2 \times 100)$$
$$= 800 \text{ to } 1200 \text{ litre-units}$$

   Any fuel usage less than 80 litre-units or greater than 1200 litre-units will trigger a decision to investigate.

   The only plane to be outside the specified $\mu \pm 2\sigma$ fuel usage control limit is the Eclair des Alpilles on flights 5 (1220 litre-units), 7 (1260 litre-units) and 10 (1230 litre-units).

2 The Eclair des Cévennes has no observation outside the $\mu \pm 2\sigma$ control limits. However, there was an increase in fuel use in each of the last eight round-trip flights. The probability of eight consecutive increases from an in-control process is very low.

   The Eclair des Vosges appears in control regarding fuel usage.

   The Eclair des Alpilles has three observations outside the $\mu \pm 2\sigma$ control limits. Moreover, the mean on the last six flights is 1200 compared with a mean of 1040 for the first four flights.

3 The advantage of using euro fuel costs as the unit of analysis in an SQC chart is that it focuses on a variable of overriding concern to top managers: operating costs.

   However, the disadvantages of using euro fuel costs are:

   ● Split responsibilities. Operations managers may not control the purchase of fuel, and may want to exclude from their performance measures any variation stemming from factors outside their control.
   ● Offsetting factors may mask important underlying trends when the quantity used and the price paid are combined in a single observation. For example, decreasing litre usage may be offset by increasing fuel costs. Both of these individual patterns are important in budgeting for an airline.

- The distribution of fuel usage in litres may be different from the distribution of fuel prices per litre. More reliable estimates of the μ and σ parameters might be obtained by focusing separately on the individual usage and price distributions.

Note: The above disadvantages are most marked if actual fuel prices are used. The use of standard fuel prices can reduce many of these disadvantages.

CHAPTER 21

Exercise 21.11

1 Journal entries for August are as follows:

Entry (a)	Stock: Raw and In-Progress Control	550 000	
	Creditors' Control		550 000
	(raw materials and components purchased)		
Entry (b)	Conversion Costs Control	440 000	
	Various accounts (such as Creditors Control and Wages Payable)		440 000
	(conversion costs incurred)		
Entry (c)	Finished Goods Control	945 000	
	Stock: Raw and In-Progress Control		525 000
	Conversion Costs Allocated		420 000
	(standard costs of 21 000 units of finished goods produced at €45 per unit; direct materials, €25 per unit; conversion costs, €20 per unit)		
Entry (d)	Cost of Goods Sold	900 000	
	Finished Goods Control		900 000
	(standard costs of 20 000 units of finished goods sold at €45 per unit)		

2

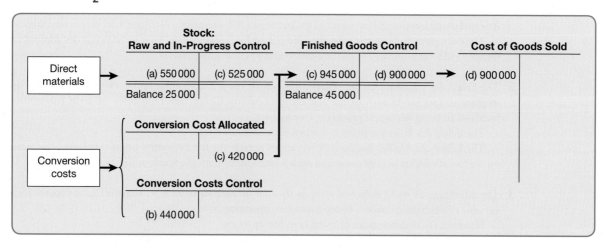

Exercise 21.24

1 Sarantis has successfully implemented JIT in its production operations and hence minimised work-in-progress stock. It still has a fair amount of raw material and finished goods stock. It is therefore recommended that Sarantis adopt a backflush costing system with two trigger points as follows:

- direct materials purchases charged to stock: Raw and In-Progress Control
- finished goods recorded as Finished Goods Control.

The backflush approach described closely approximates the costs calculated using sequential tracking. There is no work in progress so there is no need for a Work-in-Progress stock account.

Further, by maintaining a Raw and In-Progress Stock Control and Finished Goods Control account, Sarantis can keep track of and control the stocks of direct materials and finished goods in its plant.

2 **a** A backflush costing system with a single trigger point: Finished Goods Control. This would approximate the sequential tracking approach since the question assumes Sarantis has no raw materials or work-in-progress stocks. There is therefore no need for these stock accounts.

b A backflush costing system with two trigger points: (1) when purchases are made (debited to Stock Control) and (2) when finished goods are sold, would approximate sequential tracking, since the question assumes Sarantis has no work-in-progress or finished goods stocks.

c A backflush costing system with a single trigger point when finished goods are sold would approximate sequential tracking since the question assumes Sarantis has no raw material, work-in-progress or finished goods stock.

The principle here is that backflushing of costs should be triggered at the finished goods stock stage if Sarantis plans to hold finished goods inventory. If Sarantis plans to hold no finished goods stock, backflushing can be postponed until the finished goods are sold. In other words, the trigger points for backflushing relate to the points where stock is being accumulated. As a result, backflushing matches the sequential tracking approach and also maintains a record for the monitoring and control of the stock.

3 Some comments on the quotation follow:

- The backflush system is a standard costing system, not an actual costing system.
- If standard costing is used, an up-to-date realistic set of standard costs is always desirable – as long as the set meets the cost–benefit test as related to the task of updating.
- The operating environments of 'the present JIT era' have induced many companies towards more simplicity (backflush) and abandoning the typical standard costing system (sequential tracking).
- Backflush is probably closer to being a periodic system than a perpetual system. However, a periodic system may be cost-effective, particularly where physical stocks are relatively low or stable.
- The textbook points out that, to be attractive, backflush costing should generate the same financial measurements as sequential tracking – and at a lower accounting cost.
- The choice of a product costing system is highly contextual. Its characteristics should be heavily affected by its costs, the preferences of operating managers and the underlying operating processes. Sweeping generalisations about any cost accounting system or technique are unjustified.

Exercise 21.26

1    $EOQ = \sqrt{(2DP/C)}$
$D = 2000; P = €40; C = €4 + (10\% \times €50) = €9$
    $EOQ = \sqrt{(2 \times 2000 \times 40/9)} = 133.333$ tyres $\simeq 133$ tyres
    $TRC = DP/Q + QC/2$ where Q can be any quantity, including the EOQ
        $= (2000 \times 40/133.3) + (133.3 \times 9/2) = €600 + €600 = €1200$

If students used an EOQ of 133 tyres (order quantities rounded to the nearest whole number),

$$TRC = €601.5 + €598.5 = €1200$$

The sum of annual relevant ordering and carrying costs equals €1200.

2 The prediction error affects C, which is now:

$$C = €4 + (10\% \times €30) = €7$$
$$D = 2000 \quad P = €40 \quad C = €7$$
$$EOQ = \sqrt{(2 \times 2000 \times 40/7)} = 151.186 \text{ tyres} \simeq 151 \text{ tyres}$$

The cost of the prediction error can be calculated using a three-step procedure.

- *Step 1.* Calculate the monetary outcome from the best action that could have been taken, given the actual amount of the cost input:

$$TRC = DP/Q + QC/2 = €529.15 + €529.15 = €1058.30$$

- *Step 2.* Calculate the monetary outcome from the best action based on the incorrect amount of the predicted cost input:

$$TRC = DP/Q + QC/2 = €600 + €466.67 = €1066.67$$

- *Step 3.* Calculate the difference between the monetary outcomes from steps 1 and 2:

	Monetary outcome
Step 1	€1058.30
Step 2	1066.67
Difference	€(8.37)

The cost of the prediction error is   €8.37

Note: The €20 prediction error for the purchase price of the heavy-duty tyres is irrelevant in computing purchase costs under the two alternatives because the same purchase costs will be incurred whatever the order size.

Some students may prefer to round off the EOQs to 133 tyres and 151 tyres, respectively. The calculations under each step in this case are:

- *Step 1.* TRC = €529.80 + €528.50 = €1058.30
- *Step 2.* TRC = €601.50 + €465.50 = €1067.00
- *Step 3.* Difference = €1058.30 – €1067.00 = €8.70

CHAPTER 22

Exercise 22.11

1 La Quinta's 2016 strategy is a cost leadership strategy. La Quinta plans to grow by producing high-quality boxes at a low cost delivered to customers in a timely manner. La Quinta's boxes are not differentiated and there are many other manufacturers who produce similar boxes. To succeed, La Quinta must achieve lower costs relative to competitors through productivity and efficiency improvements.

2 Measures that we would expect to see on a La Quinta's balanced scorecard for 2015 are:

Financial perspective

- operating income from productivity gain
- operating income from growth
- cost reductions in key areas.

These measures evaluate whether La Quinta has successfully reduced costs and generated growth through cost leadership:

Customer perspective

- market share
- new customers
- customer satisfaction index
- customer retention
- time taken to fulfil customer orders.

The logic is that improvements in these customer measures are leading indicators of superior financial performance:

Internal business process perspective

- yield
- productivity
- order delivery time
- on-time delivery.

Improvements in these measures are expected to lead to more satisfied customers and in turn to superior financial performance:

Learning and growth perspective

- percentage of employees trained in process and quality management
- employee satisfaction
- number of major process improvements.

Improvements in these measures have a cause-and-effect relationship with improvements in internal business processes, which in turn lead to improved customer satisfaction and financial performance.

Exercise 22.13

1 Snyder's strategy in 2015 is cost leadership. Snyder's consulting services for implementing sales management software are not distinct from those of its competitors. The market for these services is very competitive. To succeed, Snyder must deliver quality service at low cost. Improving productivity while maintaining quality is key.

2 Balanced scorecard measures for 2015 follow:

Financial perspective

- increase operating income from productivity gains and growth
- revenues per employee
- cost reductions in key areas, for example, software implementation and overhead costs.

These measures indicate whether Snyder has been able to reduce costs and achieve operating income increases through cost leadership:

Customer perspective

- market share
- new customers
- customer responsiveness
- customer satisfaction.

Improvements in these customer measures are regarded as leading indicators of superior financial performance:

Internal business process perspective

- time to complete customer jobs
- time lost due to errors
- quality of job. (Is system running smoothly after job is completed?)

Improvements in these measures are expected to lead to more satisfied customers, lower costs and superior financial performance:

Learning and growth perspective

- time required to analyse and design implementation steps
- time taken to perform key steps implementing the software
- skill levels of employees
- hours of employee training
- employee satisfaction and motivation.

Improvements in these measures have a cause-and-effect relationship with improvements in internal business processes, leading to improved customer satisfaction and financial performance.

Exercise 22.14

1 Caltex's strategy is to focus on 'service-oriented customers' who are willing to pay a higher price for services. Even though its product is largely a commodity product, petrol, Caltex wants to differentiate itself through the service it provides at its retailing stations.

Does the scorecard represent Caltex's strategy? By and large it does. The focus of the scorecard is on measures of process improvement, quality, market share, and financial success from product differentiation. There are some deficiencies that the subsequent assignment exercises raise but, abstracting from these concerns for the moment, the scorecard does focus on implementing a product differentiation strategy.

Having concluded that the scorecard has been reasonably well designed, how has Caltex performed relative to its strategy in 2015? It appears from the scorecard that Caltex was successful in implementing its strategy in 2015. It achieved all targets in the financial, internal business, and learning and growth perspectives. The only target it missed was the market share target in the customer perspective. At this stage, students may raise some questions about whether this is a good scorecard measure. Requirement 3 gets at this issue in more detail. The bottom line is that measuring 'market share in the overall petrol market' rather than in the 'service-oriented customer' market segment is not a good scorecard measure, so not achieving this target may not be as big an issue as it may at first seem.

2 Yes, Caltex should include some measure of employee satisfaction and employee training in the learning and growth perspective. Caltex's differentiation strategy and ability to charge a premium price is based on customer service. The key to good, fast and friendly customer service is well-trained and satisfied employees. Untrained and dissatisfied employees will have poor interactions with customers and cause the strategy to fail. Hence, training and employee satisfaction are important to Caltex for implementing its strategy. These measures are leading indicators of whether Caltex will be able to successfully implement its strategy and, hence, should be measured on the balanced scorecard.

3 Caltex's strategy is to focus on the 60% of petrol consumers who are service-oriented, not on the 40% price-shopper segment. To evaluate if it has been successful in implementing its strategy, Caltex needs to measure its market share in its targeted market segment, 'service-oriented customers', not its market share in the overall market. Given Caltex's strategy, it should not be concerned if its market share in the price-shopper segment declines. In fact, charging premium prices will probably cause its market share in this segment to decline. Caltex should replace 'market share in overall petrol market' with 'market share in the service-oriented customer segment' in its balanced scorecard customer measure. Caltex may also want to consider putting a customer satisfaction measure on the scorecard. This measure should capture an overall evaluation of customer reactions to the facility, the convenience store, employee interactions and quick turnround. The customer satisfaction measure would serve as a leading indicator of market share in the service-oriented customer segment.

4 Although there is a cause-and-effect link between internal business process measures and customer measures on the current scorecard, Caltex should add more measures to tighten this linkage. In particular, the current scorecard measures focus exclusively on refinery operations and not on petrol station operations. Caltex should add measures of petrol station performance such as cleanliness of the facility, turnround time at the pumps, the shopping experience at the convenience store, and the service provided by employees. Many companies do random audits of their facilities to evaluate how well their branches and retail outlets are performing. These measures would serve as leading indicators of customer satisfaction and market share in Caltex's targeted segments.

5 Caltex is correct in not measuring changes in operating profit from productivity improvements on its scorecard under the financial perspective. Caltex's strategy is to grow by charging premium prices for customer service. The scorecard measures focus on Caltex's success in implementing this strategy. Productivity gains *per se* are not critical to Caltex's strategy and, hence, should not be measured on the scorecard.

Interest is the cost of using money. It is the rental charge for funds, just as renting a building and equipment entails a rental charge. When the funds are used for a period of time, it is necessary to recognise interest as a cost of using the borrowed ('rented') funds. This requirement applies even if the funds represent ownership capital and if interest does not entail an outlay of cash. Why must interest be considered? Because the selection of one alternative automatically commits a given amount of funds that could otherwise be invested in some other alternative.

Interest is generally important, even when short-term projects are under consideration. Interest looms correspondingly larger when long-run plans are studied. The rate of interest has significant enough impact to influence decisions regarding borrowing and investing funds. For example, €100 000 invested now and compounded annually for 10 years at 8% will accumulate to €215 900; at 20%, the €100 000 will accumulate to €619 200.

INTEREST TABLES

Many computer programs and pocket calculators are available that handle computations involving the time value of money. You may also turn to the following four basic tables to calculate interest.

Table 1 Future amount of €1

Table 1 shows how much €1 invested now will accumulate in a given number of periods at a given compounded interest rate per period. Consider investing €1000 now for 3 years at 8% compound interest. A tabular presentation of how this €1000 would accumulate to €1259.70 follows:

Year	Interest per year	Cumulative interest called compound interest	Total at end of year
0	–	–	€1000.00
1	€80.00	€80.00	1080.00
2	86.40	166.40	1166.40
3	93.30	259.70	1259.70

This tabular presentation is a series of computations that could appear as follows:

$$S_1 = €1000(1.08)^1$$
$$S_2 = €1000(1.08)^2$$
$$S_3 = €1000(1.08)^3$$

The formula for the 'amount of 1', often called the 'future value of €1' or 'future amount of €1', can be written:

$$S = P(1 + r)^n$$
$$S = €1000(1 + 0.08)^3$$
$$= €1259.70$$

where S is the future value amount, P is the present value (€1000 in this case), r is the rate of interest, and n is the number of time periods.

Fortunately, tables make key computations readily available. A facility in selecting the *proper* table will minimise computations. Check the accuracy of the preceding answer using Table 1.

Table 2 Present value of €1

In the previous example, if €1000 compounded at 8% per year will accumulate to €1259.70 in 3 years, then €1000 must be the present value of €1259.70 due at the end of 3 years. The formula for the present value can be derived by reversing the process of *accumulation* (finding the future amount) that we just finished.

$$S = P(1 + r)^n$$

If

$$P = \frac{S}{(1 + r)^n}$$

then

$$P = \frac{€1259.70}{(1.08)^3}$$
$$= €1000$$

Use Table 2, to check this calculation.

When accumulating, we advance or roll forward in time. The difference between our original amount and our accumulated amount is called *compound interest*. When discounting, we retreat or roll back in time. The difference between the future amount and the present value is called *compound discount*. Note the following formulae (where $P = €1000$):

$$\text{Compound interest} = P[(1 + r)^n - 1] = €259.70$$

$$\text{Compound discount} = S\left[1 - \frac{1}{(1 + r)^n}\right] = €259.70$$

Table 3 Amount of annuity of €1

An (ordinary) *annuity* is a series of equal payments (receipts) to be paid (or received) at the *end* of successive periods of equal length. Assume that €1000 is invested at the end of each of 3 years at 8%:

End of year			Amount
1st payment $\longrightarrow$ €1000.00 $\longrightarrow$		€1080.00	€1166.40, which is €1000$(1.08)^2$
2nd payment		€1000.00	1080.00, which is €1000$(1.08)^1$
3rd payment			1000.00
Accumulation (future amount)			€3246.40

The preceding arithmetic may be expressed algebraically as the amount of an ordinary annuity of €1000 for 3 years = €1000$(1 + r)^2$ + €1000$(1 + r)^1$ + €1000.

We can develop the general formula for S_n, the amount of an ordinary annuity of €1, by using the example above as a basis:

1            $S_n = 1 + (1 + r)^1 + (1 + r)^2$

2 Substitute: $S_n = 1 + (1.08)^1 + (1.08)^2$

3 Multiply (2) by $(1 + r)$: $(1.08)S_n = (1.08)^1 + (1.08)^2 + (1.08)^3$

4 Subtract (2) from (3): $1.08S_n - S_n = (1.08)^3 - 1$
   Note that all terms on the
   right-hand side are removed
   except $(1.08)^3$ in equation (3)
   and 1 in equation (2).

5 Factor (4): $S_n(1.08 - 1) = (1.08)^3 - 1$

6 Divide (5) by $(1.08 - 1)$: $S_n = \dfrac{(1.08)^3 - 1}{1.08 - 1} = \dfrac{(1.08)^3 - 1}{0.08}$

7 The general formula for
   the amount of an ordinary $S_n = \dfrac{(1 + r)^n - 1}{r}$ or $\dfrac{\text{Compound interest}}{\text{Rate}}$
   annuity of €1 becomes:

This formula is the basis for Table 3. Look at Table 3 or use the formula itself to check the calculations.

Table 4 Present value of an ordinary annuity of €1

Using the same example as for Table 3, we can show how the formula of P_n, *the present value of an ordinary annuity*, is developed.

End of year

1st payment	$\dfrac{1000}{(1.08)^1}$	= €926.14	€1000		
2nd payment	$\dfrac{1000}{(1.08)^2}$	= €857.52		€1000	
3rd payment	$\dfrac{1000}{(1.08)^3}$	= €794.00			€1000
Total present value		€2577.66			

For the general case, the present value of an ordinary annuity of €1 may be expressed as:

1            $P_n = \dfrac{1}{1 + r} + \dfrac{1}{(1 + r)^2} + \dfrac{1}{(1 + r)^3}$

2 Substitute $P_n = \dfrac{1}{1.08} + \dfrac{1}{(1.08)^2} + \dfrac{1}{(1.08)^3}$

3 Multiply by $\dfrac{1}{1.08}$: $P_n \dfrac{1}{1.08} = \dfrac{1}{(1.08)^2} + \dfrac{1}{(1.08)^3} + \dfrac{1}{(1.08)^4}$

4 Subtract (3) from (2): $P_n - P_n \dfrac{1}{1.08} = \dfrac{1}{1.08} - \dfrac{1}{(1.08)^4}$

5 Factor: $P_n \left(1 - \dfrac{1}{(1.08)}\right) = \dfrac{1}{1.08}\left[1 - \dfrac{1}{(1.08)^3}\right]$

6 or $P_n \left(\dfrac{0.08}{1.08}\right) = \dfrac{1}{1.08}\left[1 - \dfrac{1}{(1.08)^3}\right]$

7 Multiply by $\dfrac{1.08}{0.08}$: $P_n = \dfrac{1}{0.08}\left[1 - \dfrac{1}{(1.08)^3}\right]$

The general formula for the present value of an annuity of €1.00 is:

$$P_n = \frac{1}{r}\left[1 - \frac{1}{(1 + r)^n}\right] = \frac{\text{Compound discount}}{\text{Rate}}$$

Solving,

$$P_n = \frac{0.2062}{0.08} = 2.577$$

The formula is the basis for Table 4. Check the answer in the table. The present value tables, Tables 2 and 4, are used most frequently in capital budgeting.

The tables for annuities are not essential. With Tables 1 and 2, compound interest and compound discount can readily be calculated. It is simply a matter of dividing either of these by the rate to get values equivalent to those shown in Tables 3 and 4.

Table 1 Compound amount of €1.00 (the future value of €1.00). $S = P(1 + r)^n$. In this table $P = €1.00$.

Periods	2%	4%	6%	8%	10%	12%	14%	16%	18%	20%	22%	24%	26%	28%	30%	32%	40%	Periods
1	1.020	1.040	1.060	1.080	1.100	1.120	1.140	1.160	1.180	1.200	1.220	1.240	1.260	1.280	1.300	1.320	1.400	1
2	1.040	1.082	1.124	1.166	1.210	1.254	1.300	1.346	1.392	1.440	1.488	1.538	1.588	1.638	1.690	1.742	1.960	2
3	1.061	1.125	1.191	1.260	1.331	1.405	1.482	1.561	1.643	1.728	1.816	1.907	2.000	2.097	2.197	2.300	2.744	3
4	1.082	1.170	1.262	1.360	1.464	1.574	1.689	1.811	1.939	2.074	2.215	2.364	2.520	2.684	2.856	3.036	3.842	4
5	1.104	1.217	1.338	1.469	1.611	1.762	1.925	2.100	2.288	2.488	2.703	2.932	3.176	3.436	3.713	4.007	5.378	5
6	1.126	1.265	1.419	1.587	1.772	1.974	2.195	2.436	2.700	2.986	3.297	3.635	4.002	4.398	4.827	5.290	7.530	6
7	1.149	1.316	1.504	1.714	1.949	2.211	2.502	2.826	3.185	3.583	4.023	4.508	5.042	5.629	6.275	6.983	10.541	7
8	1.172	1.369	1.594	1.851	2.144	2.476	2.853	3.278	3.759	4.300	4.908	5.590	6.353	7.206	8.157	9.217	14.758	8
9	1.195	1.423	1.689	1.999	2.358	2.773	3.252	3.803	4.435	5.160	5.987	6.931	8.005	9.223	10.604	12.166	20.661	9
10	1.219	1.480	1.791	2.159	2.594	3.106	3.707	4.411	5.234	6.192	7.305	8.594	10.086	11.806	13.786	16.060	28.925	10
11	1.243	1.539	1.898	2.332	2.853	3.479	4.226	5.117	6.176	7.430	8.912	10.657	12.708	15.112	17.922	21.199	40.496	11
12	1.268	1.601	2.012	2.518	3.138	3.896	4.818	5.936	7.288	8.916	10.872	13.215	16.012	19.343	23.298	27.983	56.694	12
13	1.294	1.665	2.133	2.720	3.452	4.363	5.492	6.886	8.599	10.699	13.264	16.386	20.175	24.759	30.288	36.937	79.371	13
14	1.319	1.732	2.261	2.937	3.797	4.887	6.261	7.988	10.147	12.839	16.182	20.319	25.421	31.691	39.374	48.757	111.120	14
15	1.346	1.801	2.397	3.172	4.177	5.474	7.138	9.266	11.974	15.407	19.742	25.196	32.030	40.565	51.186	64.359	155.568	15
16	1.373	1.873	2.540	3.426	4.595	6.130	8.137	10.748	14.129	18.488	24.086	31.243	40.358	51.923	66.542	84.954	217.795	16
17	1.400	1.948	2.693	3.700	5.054	6.866	9.276	12.468	16.672	22.186	29.384	38.741	50.851	66.461	86.504	112.139	304.913	17
18	1.428	2.026	2.854	3.996	5.560	7.690	10.575	14.463	19.673	26.623	35.849	48.039	64.072	85.071	112.455	148.024	426.879	18
19	1.457	2.107	3.026	4.316	6.116	8.613	12.056	16.777	23.214	31.948	43.736	59.568	80.731	108.890	146.192	195.391	597.630	19
20	1.486	2.191	3.207	4.661	6.727	9.646	13.743	19.461	27.393	38.338	53.358	73.864	101.721	139.380	190.050	257.916	836.683	20
21	1.516	2.279	3.400	5.034	7.400	10.804	15.668	22.574	32.324	46.005	65.096	91.592	128.169	178.406	247.065	340.449	1171.356	21
22	1.546	2.370	3.604	5.437	8.140	12.100	17.861	26.186	38.142	55.206	79.418	113.574	161.492	228.360	321.184	449.393	1639.898	22
23	1.577	2.465	3.820	5.871	8.954	13.552	20.362	30.376	45.008	66.247	96.889	140.831	203.480	292.300	417.539	593.199	2295.857	23
24	1.608	2.563	4.049	6.341	9.850	15.179	23.212	35.236	53.109	79.497	118.205	174.631	256.385	374.144	542.801	783.023	3214.200	24
25	1.641	2.666	4.292	6.848	10.835	17.000	26.462	40.874	62.669	95.396	144.210	216.542	323.045	478.905	705.641	1033.590	4499.880	25
26	1.673	2.772	4.549	7.396	11.918	19.040	30.167	47.414	73.949	114.475	175.936	268.512	407.037	612.998	917.333	1364.339	6299.831	26
27	1.707	2.883	4.822	7.988	13.110	21.325	34.390	55.000	87.260	137.371	214.642	332.955	512.867	784.638	1192.533	1800.927	8819.764	27
28	1.741	2.999	5.112	8.627	14.421	23.884	39.204	63.800	102.967	164.845	261.864	412.864	646.212	1004.336	1550.293	2377.224	12 347.670	28
29	1.776	3.119	5.418	9.317	15.863	26.750	44.693	74.009	121.501	197.814	319.474	511.952	814.228	1285.550	2015.381	3137.935	17 286.737	29
30	1.811	3.243	5.743	10.063	17.449	29.960	50.950	85.850	143.371	237.376	389.758	634.820	1025.927	1645.505	2619.996	4142.075	24 201.432	30
35	2.000	3.946	7.686	14.785	28.102	52.800	98.100	180.314	327.997	590.668	1053.402	1861.054	3258.135	5653.911	9727.860	16 599.217	130 161.112	35
40	2.208	4.801	10.286	21.725	45.259	93.051	188.884	378.721	750.378	1469.772	2847.038	5455.913	10 347.175	19 426.689	36 118.865	66 520.767	700 037.697	40

Table 2 Present value of €1.00 $P = \dfrac{S}{(1+r)^n}$. In this table $S = €1.00$

Periods	2%	4%	6%	8%	10%	12%	14%	16%	18%	20%	22%	24%	26%	28%	30%	32%	40%	Periods
1	0.980	0.962	0.943	0.926	0.909	0.893	0.877	0.862	0.847	0.833	0.820	0.806	0.794	0.781	0.769	0.758	0.714	1
2	0.961	0.925	0.890	0.857	0.826	0.797	0.769	0.743	0.718	0.694	0.672	0.650	0.630	0.610	0.592	0.574	0.510	2
3	0.942	0.889	0.840	0.794	0.751	0.712	0.675	0.641	0.609	0.579	0.551	0.524	0.500	0.477	0.455	0.435	0.364	3
4	0.924	0.855	0.792	0.735	0.683	0.636	0.592	0.552	0.516	0.482	0.451	0.423	0.397	0.373	0.350	0.329	0.260	4
5	0.906	0.822	0.747	0.681	0.621	0.567	0.519	0.476	0.437	0.402	0.370	0.341	0.315	0.291	0.269	0.250	0.186	5
6	0.888	0.790	0.705	0.630	0.564	0.507	0.456	0.410	0.370	0.335	0.303	0.275	0.250	0.227	0.207	0.189	0.133	6
7	0.871	0.760	0.665	0.583	0.513	0.452	0.400	0.354	0.314	0.279	0.249	0.222	0.198	0.178	0.159	0.143	0.095	7
8	0.853	0.731	0.627	0.540	0.467	0.404	0.351	0.305	0.266	0.233	0.204	0.179	0.157	0.139	0.123	0.108	0.068	8
9	0.837	0.703	0.592	0.500	0.424	0.361	0.308	0.263	0.225	0.194	0.167	0.144	0.125	0.108	0.094	0.082	0.048	9
10	0.820	0.676	0.558	0.463	0.386	0.322	0.270	0.227	0.191	0.162	0.137	0.116	0.099	0.085	0.073	0.062	0.035	10
11	0.804	0.650	0.527	0.429	0.350	0.287	0.237	0.195	0.162	0.135	0.112	0.094	0.079	0.066	0.056	0.047	0.025	11
12	0.788	0.625	0.497	0.397	0.319	0.257	0.208	0.168	0.137	0.112	0.092	0.076	0.062	0.052	0.043	0.036	0.018	12
13	0.773	0.601	0.469	0.368	0.290	0.229	0.182	0.145	0.116	0.093	0.075	0.061	0.050	0.040	0.033	0.027	0.013	13
14	0.758	0.577	0.442	0.340	0.263	0.205	0.160	0.125	0.099	0.078	0.062	0.049	0.039	0.032	0.025	0.021	0.009	14
15	0.743	0.555	0.417	0.315	0.239	0.183	0.140	0.108	0.084	0.065	0.051	0.040	0.031	0.025	0.020	0.016	0.006	15
18	0.728	0.534	0.394	0.292	0.218	0.163	0.123	0.093	0.071	0.054	0.042	0.032	0.025	0.019	0.015	0.012	0.005	16
17	0.714	0.513	0.371	0.270	0.198	0.146	0.108	0.080	0.060	0.045	0.034	0.026	0.020	0.015	0.012	0.009	0.003	17
18	0.700	0.494	0.350	0.250	0.180	0.130	0.095	0.069	0.051	0.038	0.028	0.021	0.016	0.012	0.009	0.007	0.002	18
19	0.686	0.475	0.331	0.232	0.164	0.116	0.083	0.060	0.043	0.031	0.023	0.017	0.012	0.009	0.007	0.005	0.002	19
20	0.673	0.456	0.312	0.215	0.149	0.104	0.073	0.051	0.037	0.026	0.019	0.014	0.010	0.007	0.005	0.004	0.001	20
21	0.660	0.439	0.294	0.199	0.135	0.093	0.064	0.044	0.031	0.022	0.015	0.011	0.008	0.006	0.004	0.003	0.001	21
22	0.647	0.422	0.278	0.184	0.123	0.083	0.056	0.038	0.026	0.018	0.013	0.009	0.006	0.004	0.003	0.002	0.001	22
23	0.634	0.406	0.262	0.170	0.112	0.074	0.049	0.033	0.022	0.015	0.010	0.007	0.005	0.003	0.002	0.002	0.000	23
24	0.622	0.390	0.247	0.158	0.102	0.066	0.043	0.028	0.019	0.013	0.008	0.006	0.004	0.003	0.002	0.001	0.000	24
25	0.610	0.375	0.233	0.146	0.092	0.059	0.038	0.024	0.016	0.010	0.007	0.005	0.003	0.002	0.002	0.001	0.000	25
26	0.598	0.361	0.220	0.135	0.084	0.053	0.033	0.021	0.014	0.009	0.006	0.004	0.002	0.002	0.001	0.001	0.000	26
27	0.586	0.347	0.207	0.125	0.076	0.047	0.029	0.018	0.011	0.007	0.005	0.003	0.002	0.002	0.001	0.001	0.000	27
28	0.574	0.333	0.196	0.116	0.069	0.042	0.026	0.016	0.010	0.006	0.004	0.002	0.002	0.001	0.001	0.000	0.000	28
29	0.563	0.321	0.185	0.107	0.063	0.037	0.022	0.014	0.008	0.005	0.003	0.002	0.001	0.001	0.001	0.000	0.000	29
30	0.552	0.308	0.174	0.099	0.057	0.033	0.020	0.012	0.007	0.004	0.003	0.002	0.001	0.001	0.000	0.000	0.000	30
35	0.500	0.253	0.130	0.068	0.036	0.019	0.010	0.006	0.003	0.002	0.001	0.001	0.000	0.000	0.000	0.000	0.000	35
40	0.453	0.208	0.097	0.046	0.022	0.011	0.005	0.003	0.001	0.001	0.000	0.000	0.000	0.000	0.000	0.000	0.000	40

Table 3 Compound amount of annuity of €1.00 in arrears* (future value of annuity) $S_n = \dfrac{(1+r)^n - 1}{r}$

Periods	2%	4%	6%	8%	10%	12%	14%	16%	18%	20%	22%	24%	26%	28%	30%	32%	40%	Periods
1	1.000	1.000	1.000	1.000	1.000	1.000	1.000	1.000	1.000	1.000	1.000	1.000	1.000	1.000	1.000	1.000	1.000	1
2	2.020	2.040	2.060	2.080	2.100	2.120	2.140	2.160	2.180	2.200	2.220	2.240	2.260	2.280	2.300	2.320	2.400	2
3	3.060	3.122	3.184	3.246	3.310	3.374	3.440	3.506	3.572	3.640	3.708	3.778	3.848	3.918	3.990	4.062	4.360	3
4	4.122	4.246	4.375	4.506	4.641	4.779	4.921	5.066	5.215	5.368	5.524	5.684	5.848	6.016	6.187	6.362	7.104	4
5	5.204	5.416	5.637	5.867	6.105	6.353	6.610	6.877	7.154	7.442	7.740	8.048	8.368	8.700	9.043	9.398	10.946	5
6	6.308	6.633	6.975	7.336	7.716	8.115	8.536	8.977	9.442	9.930	10.442	10.980	11.544	12.136	12.756	13.406	16.324	6
7	7.434	7.898	8.394	8.923	9.487	10.089	10.730	11.414	12.142	12.916	13.740	14.615	15.546	16.534	17.583	18.696	23.853	7
8	8.583	9.214	9.897	10.637	11.436	12.300	13.233	14.240	15.327	16.499	17.762	19.123	20.588	22.163	23.858	25.678	34.395	8
9	9.755	10.583	11.491	12.488	13.579	14.776	16.085	17.519	19.086	20.799	22.670	24.712	26.940	29.369	32.015	34.895	49.153	9
10	10.950	12.006	13.181	14.487	15.937	17.549	19.337	21.321	23.521	25.959	28.657	31.643	34.945	38.593	42.619	47.062	69.814	10
11	12.169	13.486	14.972	16.645	18.531	20.655	23.045	25.733	28.755	32.150	35.962	40.238	45.031	50.398	56.405	63.122	98.739	11
12	13.412	15.026	16.870	18.977	21.384	24.133	27.271	30.850	34.931	39.581	44.874	50.895	57.739	65.510	74.327	84.320	139.235	12
13	14.680	16.627	18.882	21.495	24.523	28.029	32.089	36.786	42.219	48.497	55.746	64.110	73.751	84.853	97.625	112.303	195.929	13
14	15.974	18.292	21.015	24.215	27.975	32.393	37.581	43.672	50.818	59.196	69.010	80.496	93.926	109.612	127.913	149.240	275.300	14
15	17.293	20.024	23.276	27.152	31.772	37.280	43.842	51.660	60.965	72.035	85.192	100.815	119.347	141.303	167.286	197.997	386.420	15
16	18.639	21.825	25.673	30.324	35.950	42.753	50.980	60.925	72.939	87.442	104.935	126.011	151.377	181.868	218.472	262.356	541.988	16
17	20.012	23.698	28.213	33.750	40.545	48.884	59.118	71.673	87.068	105.931	129.020	157.253	191.735	233.791	285.014	347.309	759.784	17
18	21.412	25.645	30.906	37.450	45.599	55.750	68.394	84.141	103.740	128.117	158.405	195.994	242.585	300.252	371.518	459.449	1064.697	18
19	22.841	27.671	33.760	41.446	51.159	63.440	78.969	98.603	123.414	154.740	194.254	244.033	306.658	385.323	483.973	607.472	1491.576	19
20	24.297	29.778	36.786	45.762	57.275	72.052	91.025	115.380	146.628	186.688	237.989	303.601	387.389	494.213	630.165	802.863	2089.206	20
21	25.783	31.969	39.993	50.423	64.002	81.699	104.768	134.841	174.021	225.026	291.347	377.465	489.110	633.593	820.215	1060.779	2925.889	21
22	27.299	34.248	43.392	55.457	71.403	92.503	120.436	157.415	206.345	271.031	356.443	469.056	617.278	811.999	1067.280	1401.229	4097.245	22
23	28.845	36.618	46.996	60.893	79.543	104.603	138.297	183.601	244.487	326.237	435.861	582.630	778.771	1040.358	1388.464	1850.622	5737.142	23
24	30.422	39.083	50.816	66.765	88.497	118.155	158.659	213.978	289.494	392.484	532.750	723.461	982.251	1332.659	1806.003	2443.821	8032.999	24
25	32.030	41.646	54.865	73.106	98.347	133.334	181.871	249.214	342.603	471.981	650.955	898.092	1238.636	1706.803	2348.803	3226.844	11 247.199	25
26	33.671	44.312	59.156	79.954	109.182	150.334	208.333	290.088	405.272	567.377	795.165	1114.634	1561.682	2185.708	3054.444	4260.434	15 747.079	26
27	35.344	47.084	63.706	87.351	121.100	169.374	238.499	337.502	479.221	681.853	971.102	1383.146	1968.719	2798.706	3971.778	5624.772	22 046.910	27
28	37.051	49.968	68.528	95.339	134.210	190.699	272.889	392.503	566.481	819.223	1185.744	1716.101	2481.586	3583.344	5164.311	7425.699	30 866.674	28
29	38.792	52.966	73.640	103.966	148.631	214.583	312.094	456.303	669.447	984.068	1447.608	2128.965	3127.798	4587.680	6714.604	9802.923	43 214.343	29
30	40.568	56.085	79.058	113.263	164.494	241.333	356.787	530.312	790.948	1181.882	1767.081	2640.916	3942.026	5873.231	8729.985	12 940.859	60 501.081	30
35	49.994	73.652	111.435	172.317	271.024	431.663	693.573	1120.713	1816.652	2948.341	4783.645	7750.225	12 527.442	20 188.966	32 422.868	51 869.427	325 400.279	35
40	60.402	95.026	154.762	259.057	442.593	767.091	1342.025	2360.757	4163.213	7343.858	12 936.535	22 728.803	39 792.982	69 377.460	120 392.883	207 874.272	1 750 091.741	40

* Payments (or receipts) at the end of each period.

Table 4 Present value of annuity €1.00 in arrears.* $P_n = \dfrac{1}{r}\left[1 - \dfrac{S}{(1+r)^n} \right]$

Periods	2%	4%	6%	8%	10%	12%	14%	16%	18%	20%	22%	24%	26%	28%	30%	32%	40%	Periods
1	0.980	0.962	0.943	0.926	0.909	0.893	0.877	0.862	0.847	0.833	0.820	0.806	0.794	0.781	0.769	0.758	0.714	1
2	1.942	1.886	1.833	1.783	1.736	1.690	1.647	1.605	1.566	1.528	1.492	1.457	1.424	1.392	1.361	1.331	1.224	2
3	2.884	2.775	2.673	2.577	2.487	2.402	2.322	2.246	2.174	2.106	2.042	1.981	1.923	1.868	1.816	1.766	1.589	3
4	3.808	3.630	3.465	3.312	3.170	3.037	2.914	2.798	2.690	2.589	2.494	2.404	2.320	2.241	2.166	2.096	1.849	4
5	4.713	4.452	4.212	3.993	3.791	3.605	3.433	3.274	3.127	2.991	2.864	2.745	2.635	2.532	2.436	2.345	2.035	5
6	5.601	5.242	4.917	4.623	4.355	4.111	3.889	3.685	3.498	3.326	3.167	3.020	2.885	2.759	2.643	2.534	2.168	6
7	6.472	6.002	5.582	5.206	4.868	4.564	4.288	4.039	3.812	3.605	3.416	3.242	3.083	2.937	2.802	2.677	2.263	7
8	7.325	6.733	6.210	5.747	5.335	4.968	4.639	4.344	4.078	3.837	3.619	3.421	3.241	3.076	2.925	2.786	2.331	8
9	8.162	7.435	6.802	6.247	5.759	5.328	4.946	4.607	4.303	4.031	3.786	3.566	3.366	3.184	3.019	2.868	2.379	9
10	8.983	8.111	7.360	6.710	6.145	5.650	5.216	4.833	4.494	4.192	3.923	3.682	3.465	3.269	3.092	2.930	2.414	10
11	9.787	8.760	7.887	7.139	6.495	5.938	5.453	5.029	4.656	4.327	4.035	3.776	3.543	3.335	3.147	2.978	2.438	11
12	10.575	9.385	8.384	7.536	6.814	6.194	5.660	5.197	4.793	4.439	4.127	3.851	3.606	3.387	3.190	3.013	2.456	12
13	11.348	9.986	8.853	7.904	7.103	6.424	5.842	5.342	4.910	4.533	4.203	3.912	3.656	3.427	3.223	3.040	2.469	13
14	12.106	10.563	9.295	8.244	7.367	6.628	6.002	5.468	5.008	4.611	4.265	3.962	3.695	3.459	3.249	3.061	2.478	14
15	12.849	11.118	9.712	8.559	7.606	6.811	6.142	5.575	5.092	4.675	4.315	4.001	3.726	3.483	3.268	3.076	2.484	15
16	13.578	11.652	10.106	8.851	7.824	6.974	6.265	5.668	5.162	4.730	4.357	4.033	3.751	3.503	3.283	3.088	2.489	16
17	14.292	12.166	10.477	9.122	8.022	7.120	6.373	5.749	5.222	4.775	4.391	4.059	3.771	3.518	3.295	3.097	2.492	17
18	14.992	12.659	10.828	9.372	8.201	7.250	6.467	5.818	5.273	4.812	4.419	4.080	3.786	3.529	3.304	3.104	2.494	18
19	15.678	13.134	11.158	9.604	8.365	7.366	6.550	5.877	5.316	4.843	4.442	4.097	3.799	3.539	3.311	3.109	2.496	19
20	16.351	13.590	11.470	9.818	8.514	7.469	6.623	5.929	5.353	4.870	4.460	4.110	3.808	3.546	3.316	3.113	2.497	20
21	17.011	14.029	11.764	10.017	8.649	7.562	6.687	5.973	5.384	4.891	4.476	4.121	3.816	3.551	3.320	3.116	2.498	21
22	17.658	14.451	12.042	10.201	8.772	7.645	6.743	6.011	5.410	4.909	4.488	4.130	3.822	3.556	3.323	3.118	2.498	22
23	18.292	14.857	12.303	10.371	8.883	7.718	6.792	6.044	5.432	4.925	4.499	4.137	3.827	3.559	3.325	3.120	2.499	23
24	18.914	15.247	12.550	10.529	8.985	7.784	6.835	6.073	5.451	4.937	4.507	4.143	3.831	3.562	3.327	3.121	2.499	24
25	19.523	15.622	12.783	10.675	9.077	7.843	6.873	6.097	5.467	4.948	4.514	4.147	3.834	3.564	3.329	3.122	2.499	25
26	20.121	15.983	13.003	10.810	9.161	7.896	6.906	6.118	5.480	4.956	4.520	4.151	3.837	3.566	3.330	3.123	2.500	26
27	20.707	16.330	13.211	10.935	9.237	7.943	6.935	6.136	5.492	4.964	4.524	4.154	3.839	3.567	3.331	3.123	2.500	27
28	21.281	16.663	13.406	11.051	9.307	7.984	6.961	6.152	5.502	4.970	4.528	4.157	3.840	3.568	3.331	3.124	2.500	28
29	21.844	16.984	13.591	11.158	9.370	8.022	6.983	6.166	5.510	4.975	4.531	4.159	3.841	3.569	3.332	3.124	2.500	29
30	22.396	17.292	13.765	11.258	9.427	8.055	7.003	6.177	5.517	4.979	4.534	4.160	3.842	3.569	3.332	3.124	2.500	30
35	24.999	18.665	14.498	11.655	9.644	8.176	7.070	6.215	5.539	4.992	4.541	4.164	3.845	3.571	3.333	3.125	2.500	35
40	27.355	19.793	15.046	11.925	9.779	8.244	7.105	6.233	5.548	4.997	4.544	4.166	3.846	3.571	3.333	3.125	2.500	40

* Payments (or receipts) at the end of each period.

GLOSSARY

absorption costing Stock costing method in which all variable manufacturing costs and all fixed manufacturing costs are included as inventoriable costs.

account analysis method Approach to cost estimation that classifies cost accounts in the ledger as variable, fixed or mixed with respect to the cost driver. Typically, qualitative rather than quantitative analysis is used in making these classification decisions.

accounting rate of return (ARR) Accounting measure of income divided by an accounting measure of investment. Also called *return on investment (ROI)*.

activity An event, task or unit of work with a specified purpose.

activity-based accounting Examination of activities across the entire chain of value-adding organisational processes underlying causes (drivers) of cost and profit.

activity-based budgeting Approach to budgeting that focuses on the costs of activities necessary to produce and sell products and services.

activity-based costing (ABC) Approach to costing that focuses on activities as the fundamental cost objects. It uses the cost of these activities as the basis for assigning costs to other cost objects such as products, services or customers.

activity-based management (ABM) Management system which uses activity-based costing information to improve profits and enhance value to customers.

actual costing A costing method that traces direct costs to a cost object by using the actual direct cost rate(s) times the actual quantity of the direct cost input(s) and allocates indirect costs based on the actual indirect cost rate(s) times the actual quantity of the cost allocation base.

actual costs Costs incurred (historical costs), as distinguished from budgeted or forecast costs.

appraisal costs Costs incurred in detecting which of the individual units of products do not conform to specifications.

artificial costs See *complete reciprocated cost*.

attention directing Management accountant's function that involves making visible both opportunities and problems on which managers need to focus.

autonomy The degree of freedom to make decisions.

average cost See *unit cost*.

backflush accounting A cost accounting system which focuses on the output of the organisation and then works

backwards to allocate costs between cost of goods sold and stock.

backflush costing Costing system that delays recording changes in the status of a product being produced until good finished units appear; it then uses budgeted or standard costs to work backwards to flush out manufacturing costs for the units produced. Also called *delayed costing, endpoint costing* or *post-deduct costing*.

balanced scorecard A measurement and management system that views a business unit's performance from four perspectives: financial, customer, internal business process, and learning and growth.

batch-level costs The costs of resources sacrificed on activities that are related to a group of units of products or services rather than to each individual unit of product or service.

belief systems Levers of control that articulate the mission, purpose, norms of behaviours and core values of a company; intended to inspire managers and other employees to do their best.

benchmark Point of reference from which comparisons may be made.

benchmarking The continuous process of measuring products, services or activities against the best levels of performance.

book value The original cost minus accumulated depreciation of an asset.

bottleneck An operation where the work required approaches or exceeds the available capacity.

boundary systems Levers of control that describe standards of behaviour and codes of conduct expected of all employees, especially actions that are off-limits.

breakeven point Quantity of output where total revenues and total costs are equal; that is where the operating profit is zero.

budget The quantitative expression of a plan of action and an aid to the coordination and implementation of the plan.

budgetary slack See *padding*.

budgeted costing See *extended normal costing*.

bundled product A package of two or more products or services, sold for a single price, where the individual components of the bundle may be sold as separate items, each with its stand-alone price.

business function costs   The sum of all the costs in a particular business function.

business governance   The performance dimension of an enterprise.

by-product   Product from a joint process that has a low sales value compared with the sales value of the main or joint product(s).

capital budgeting   The process of making long-term planning decisions for investments.

capitalised costs   Costs that are first recorded as an asset (capitalised) when they are incurred.

carrying costs   Costs that arise when a business holds stocks of goods for sale.

cash budget   Schedule of expected cash receipts and disbursements.

cash cycle   See *self-liquidating cycle*.

cause-and-effect diagram   Diagram that identifies the potential causes of failures or defects. Four major categories of potential causes of failure are identified human factors, methods and design factors, machine-related factors and materials and components factors. Also called a *fishbone diagram*.

Chartered Institute of Management Accountants (CIMA)   The principal professional management accounting body in the UK, founded in 1919 as the Institute of Cost and Works Accountants. Today, in terms of membership, it is the third largest professional accounting body in the UK.

chief accounting officer   The financial executive primarily responsible for both management accounting and financial accounting.

choice criterion   Objective that can be quantified in a decision model.

coefficient of determination (r^2)   Measures the percentage of variation in a dependent variable explained by one or more independent variables.

collusive pricing   Companies in an industry conspire in their pricing and output decisions to achieve a price above the competitive price.

combined variance analysis   Approach to overhead variance analysis that combines variable-cost and fixed-cost variances.

common cost   The cost of operating a facility, operation, activity area or like cost object that is shared by two or more users.

complete reciprocated cost   The actual cost incurred by the service department plus a part of the costs of the other support departments that provide services to it; it is always larger than the actual cost. Also called *artificial cost* of the service department.

composite product unit   A hypothetical unit of product with weights related to the individual products of the company.

computer-aided design (CAD)   Computer-based technology allowing interactive design and testing of a manufacturing component on a visual display terminal.

computer-aided manufacturing (CAM)   Computer-based technology to permit the programming and control of production equipment in the manufacturing task.

computer-integrated manufacturing (CIM)   The use of computers and other advanced manufacturing techniques to monitor and perform manufacturing tasks.

conference method   Approach to cost estimation that develops cost estimates on the basis of analysis and opinions gathered from various departments of an organisation (purchasing, process engineering, manufacturing, employee relations, and so on).

constant   The component of total costs that, within the relevant range, does not vary with changes in the level of the cost driver. Also called *intercept*.

constant gross-margin percentage NRV method   Joint cost allocation method that allocates joint costs in such a way that the overall gross-margin percentage is identical for all the individual products.

constraint   A mathematical inequality or equality that must be satisfied by the variables in a mathematical model.

continuous improvement budgeted cost   Budgeted cost that is successively reduced over succeeding time periods.

contribution income statement   Income statement that groups line items by cost behaviour pattern to highlight the contribution margin.

contribution margin   Revenues minus all costs of the output (a product or service) that vary with respect to the number of output units.

contribution margin percentage   Total contribution margin divided by revenues.

control   Covers both the action that implements the planning decision and the performance evaluation of the personnel and operations.

control chart   Graph of a series of successive observations of a particular step, procedure or operation taken at regular intervals of time. Each observation is plotted relative to specified ranges that represent the expected distribution.

controllability   The degree of influence that a specific manager has over costs, revenues or other items in question.

controllable cost   Any cost that is primarily subject to the influence of a given manager of a given responsibility centre for a given time span.

conversion costs   All manufacturing costs other than direct materials costs.

corporate governance The conformance dimension of an enterprise.

cost Resource sacrificed or forgone to achieve a specific objective.

cost accounting Measures and reports financial and other information related to the organisation's acquisition or consumption of resources. It provides information for both management accounting and financial accounting.

cost accumulation The collection of cost data in some organised way through an accounting system.

cost allocation The assigning of indirect costs to the chosen cost object.

cost-allocation base A factor that is the common denominator for systematically linking an indirect cost or group of indirect costs to a cost object.

cost assignment General term that encompasses both tracing accumulated costs to a cost object and allocating accumulated costs to a cost object.

cost-benefit approach Primary criterion for choosing among alternative accounting systems, which is how each system achieves organisational goals in relation to the cost of those systems.

cost centre A responsibility centre in which a manager is accountable for costs only.

cost driver Any factor that affects total costs. That is, a change in the cost driver will cause a change in the level of the total cost of a related cost object.

cost estimation The measurement of past cost relationships.

cost hierarchy Categorisation of costs into different cost pools on the basis of different classes of cost drivers or different degrees of difficulty in determining cause-and-effect (or benefits received) relationships.

cost incurrence Occurs when a resource is sacrificed or used up.

cost leadership An organisation's ability to achieve lower costs relative to competitors through productivity and efficiency improvements, elimination of waste and tight cost control.

cost management Actions by managers undertaken to satisfy customers while continuously reducing and controlling costs.

cost object Anything for which a separate measurement of costs is desired.

cost-plus contract Contract in which reimbursement is based on actual allowable cost plus a fixed fee.

cost pool A grouping of individual cost items.

cost predictions Forecasts of future costs.

cost smoothing A costing approach that uses broad averages to uniformly assign (spread or smooth out) the cost of resources to cost objects (such as products, services or customers) when the individual products, services or customers in fact use those resources in a non-uniform way.

cost tables Databases of all costs involved in production incorporating cost-based knowledge of sub-components.

cost tracing The assigning of direct costs to the chosen cost object.

cost–volume–profit (CVP) analysis Examines the behaviour of total revenues, total costs and operating profit as changes occur in the output level, selling price, variable costs or fixed costs; a single revenue driver and a single cost driver are used in this analysis.

costs of quality (COQ) Costs incurred to prevent or rectify the production of a low-quality product.

cumulative average-time learning model Learning curve model in which the cumulative average time per unit declines by a constant percentage each time the cumulative quantity of units produced is doubled.

current cost Asset measure based on the cost of purchasing an asset today identical to the one currently held. It is the cost of purchasing the services provided by that asset if an identical asset cannot currently be purchased.

customer cost hierarchy Categorisation of costs related to customers into different cost pools on the basis of different classes of cost drivers or different degrees of difficulty in determining cause-and-effect (or benefits received) relationships.

customer life-cycle costs Focuses on the total costs to a customer of acquiring and using a product or service until it is replaced.

customer profitability analysis Examines how individual customers, or groupings of customers, differ in their profitability.

customer-response time Amount of time from when a customer places an order for a product or requests a service to when the product or service is delivered to the customer.

customer revenues Inflows of assets from customers received in exchange for products or services being provided to those customers.

customer service The support activities provided to customers.

decentralisation The freedom for managers at lower levels (subunits) of the organisation to make decisions.

decision model Formal model for making a choice under uncertainty, frequently involving quantitative analysis.

decision table Summary of the contemplated actions, events, outcomes and probabilities of events in a decision.

delayed costing See *backflush costing*.

denominator level Quantity of the allocation base used to allocate fixed overhead costs to a cost object. Also called a *production denominator level* or a *production denominator volume*.

denominator-level variance   See *production-volume variance*.

dependent variable   The cost variable to be predicted in a cost estimation or prediction model.

design of products, services or processes   The detailed planning and engineering of products, services or processes.

designed-in costs   See *locked-in costs*.

diagnostic control systems.   Levers of control that monitor critical performance variables that help managers track progress toward achieving a company's strategic goals. Managers are held accountable for meeting these goals.

differential approach   Approach to decision making and capital budgeting that analyses only those future cash outflows and inflows that differ among alternatives.

differential cost   Difference in total cost between two alternatives. Also called *net relevant cost*.

direct allocation method.   Method of support cost allocation that ignores any service rendered by one support department to another; it allocates each support department's total costs directly to the operating departments. Also called *direct method*.

direct costing   See *variable costing*.

direct costs of a cost object   Costs that are related to the particular cost object and that can be traced to it in an economically feasible way.

direct manufacturing labour costs   Compensation of all manufacturing labour that is considered to be specifically identified with the cost object (say, units finished or in process) and that can be traced to the cost object in an economically feasible way.

direct material costs   The acquisition costs of all materials that eventually become part of the cost object (say, units finished or in progress) and that can be traced to that cost object in an economically feasible way.

direct materials stock   Direct materials in stock and awaiting use in the manufacturing process.

direct method   See *direct allocation method*.

discount rate   See *required rate of return*.

discounted cash flow (DCF)   Capital budgeting method that measures the cash inflows and outflows of a project as if they occurred at a single point in time so that they can be compared in an appropriate way.

discretionary costs   Arise from periodic (usually yearly) decisions regarding the maximum outlay to be incurred. They are not tied to a clear cause-and-effect relationship between inputs and outputs.

distribution   The mechanism by which products or services are delivered to the customer.

downsizing   An integrated approach to configuring processes, products and people in order to match costs to the activities that need to be performed for operating effectively and efficiently.

dual pricing   Approach to transfer pricing using two separate transfer-pricing methods to price each interdivision transaction.

dual-rate cost-allocation method   Allocation method that first classifies costs in one cost pool into two sub-pools (typically into a variable-cost sub-pool and a fixed-cost sub-pool). Each sub-pool has a different allocation rate or a different allocation base.

e-business   The use of digital and Internet technologies incorporating e-commerce in the full range of business functions across the entire value chain.

e-commerce   The exchange and tracking of information, goods and services using digital media.

economic order quantity (EOQ)   Decision model that calculates the optimal quantity of stock to order. Simplest model incorporates only ordering costs and carrying costs.

economic value added (EVA®)   After-tax operating profit minus the (after-tax) weighted average cost of capital multiplied by total assets minus current liabilities.

effectiveness   The degree to which a predetermined objective or target is met.

efficiency   The relative amount of inputs used to achieve a given level of output.

efficiency variance   The difference between the actual quantity of input used (such as metres of materials) and the budgeted quantity of input that should have been used, multiplied by the budgeted price. Also called *input-efficiency variance* or *usage variance*.

effort   Exertion towards a goal.

endpoint costing   See *backflush costing*.

engineered costs   Costs that result specifically from a clear cause-and-effect relationship between costs and outputs.

enterprise governance   The entire accountability framework of an organisation.

equivalent units   Measure of the output in terms of the physical quantities of each of the inputs (factors of production) that have been consumed when producing the units. It is the physical quantities of inputs necessary to produce output of one fully complete unit.

estimated net realisable value (NRV) method   Joint cost allocation method that allocates joint costs on the basis of the relative estimated net realisable value (expected final sales value in the ordinary course of business minus the expected separable costs of production and marketing of the total production of the period).

event   A possible occurrence in a decision model.

excess capacity   See *unused capacity*.

expected monetary value   See *expected value*.

expected value   Weighted average of the outcomes of a decision with the probability of each outcome serving as the weight. Also called *expected monetary value*.

experience curve   Function that shows how full product costs per unit (including manufacturing, distribution, marketing and so on) decline as units of output increase.

extended normal costing   A costing method that traces direct costs to a cost object by using the budgeted direct-cost rate(s) times the actual quantity of the direct-cost input and allocates indirect costs based on the budgeted indirect-cost rate(s) times the actual quantity of the cost-allocation base. Also called *budgeted costing*.

external failure costs   Costs incurred when a non-conforming product is detected after it is shipped to customers.

facility-sustaining costs   The costs of resources sacrificed on activities that cannot be traced to specific products or services but support the organisation as a whole.

factory overhead costs   See *indirect manufacturing costs*.

favourable variance   Variance that increases operating profit relative to the budgeted amount. Denoted F.

finance director   The senior officer empowered with overseeing the financial operations of an organisation. Also called *chief financial officer (CFO)*.

financial accounting   Focuses on external reporting that is guided by generally accepted accounting principles.

financial budget   That part of the master budget that comprises the capital budget, cash budget, budgeted balance sheet and budgeted statement of cash flows.

financial planning models   Mathematical representations of the relationships among all operating activities, financial activities and financial statements.

finished goods stock   Goods fully completed but not yet sold.

first-in, first-out (FIFO) process-costing method   Method of process costing that assigns the cost of the earliest equivalent units available (starting with the equivalent units in opening work-in-progress stock) to units completed and transferred out, and the cost of the most recent equivalent units worked on during the period to closing work-in-progress stock.

fishbone diagram   See *cause-and-effect diagram*.

fixed cost   Cost that does not change in total despite changes in a cost driver.

flexible budget   A budget that is developed using budgeted revenues or cost amounts; when variances are computed, the budgeted amounts are adjusted (flexed) to recognise the actual level of output and the actual quantities of the revenue and cost drivers.

flexible-budget variance   Difference between the actual result and the flexible budget amount for the actual output achieved.

flexible manufacturing system (FMS)   An integrated production system that is computer controlled to produce a family of parts in a flexible manner.

full product costs   The sum of all the costs in all the business functions – R&D, design, production, marketing, distribution and customer service.

functional analysis   An activity aimed at linking product functions and perceived value to customers with the cost of designing functions.

goal congruence   Exists when individuals and groups work towards the organisational goals that top management desires.

gross margin   Revenues minus cost of goods sold.

gross margin percentage   Gross margin divided by revenues.

high–low method   Method used to estimate a cost function that entails using only the highest and lowest observed values of the cost driver within the relevant range.

homogeneous cost pool   Cost pool in which all the activities whose costs are included in the pool have the same or a similar cause-and-effect relationship or benefits-received relationship between the cost allocator and the costs of the activity.

hurdle rate   See *required rate of return*.

hybrid-costing system   Blends of characteristics from both job-costing systems and process-costing systems.

imputed costs   Costs recognised in particular situations that are not regularly recognised by accrual accounting procedures.

incongruent decision making   See *suboptimal decision making*.

incremental cost-allocation method   Cost-allocation method requiring that one user be viewed as the primary party and the second user be viewed as the incremental party.

incremental costs   Additional costs to obtain an additional quantity over and above existing or planned quantities of a cost object. Also called *outlay costs* or *out-of-pocket costs*.

incremental unit-time learning model   Learning curve model in which the incremental unit time (the time needed to produce the last unit) declines by a constant percentage each time the cumulative quantity of units produced is doubled.

independent variable   The level of activity to predict the dependent variable in a cost estimation model.

indirect costs of a cost object   Costs that are related to the particular cost object but cannot be traced to it in an economically feasible way.

indirect manufacturing costs   All manufacturing costs considered to be part of the cost object (say, units finished or in progress) but that cannot be individually traced to that cost object in an economically feasible way. Also called *manufacturing overhead costs* and *factory overhead costs*.

industrial engineering method   Approach to cost estimation that first analyses the relationship between inputs and outputs in physical terms. Also called *work measurement method*.

inflation   The decline in the general purchasing power of the monetary unit.

infrastructure costs   Costs that arise from having property, plant, equipment and a functioning organisation.

input-efficiency variance   See *efficiency variance*.

input-price variance   See *price variance*.

insourcing   Process of producing goods or providing services within the firm rather than purchasing those same goods or services from outside vendors.

institute of Management Accountants (IMA)   The largest association of management accountants in the USA.

interactive control systems   Formal information systems that managers use to focus an organisation's attention and learning on key strategic issues.

intercept   See *constant*.

intermediate product   Product transferred from one subunit to another subunit of the organisation. This product may be processed further and sold to an external customer.

internal failure costs   Costs incurred when a non-conforming product is detected before it is shipped to customers.

internal rate of return (IRR)   Discount rate at which the present value of expected cash inflows from a project equals the present value of expected cash outflows of the project. The IRR is the discount rate that makes net present value (NPV) equal to zero. Also called the *time-adjusted rate of return*.

Internet   The physical network that links computers across the globe. It consists of the infrastructure of network servers and communication links between them, which are used to uphold and transport information. The Internet enables the transfer of messages and transactions between connected computers world-wide.

inventoriable costs   See *stock-related costs*.

investment   Resources or assets used to generate income.

investment centre   A responsibility centre in which a manager is accountable for investments, revenues and costs.

investment programmes   See *investment projects*.

investment projects   Investments and outcomes from those investments (which generally cover a number of years). Also called *investment programmes*.

job cost record   Source document that records and accumulates all the costs assigned to a specific job. Also called *job cost sheet*.

job cost sheet   See *job cost record*.

job-costing system   Costing system in which the cost of a product or service is obtained by assigning costs to a distinct unit, batch or lot of a product or service.

joint cost   Cost of a single process that yields multiple products simultaneously.

joint products   Products from a joint process that have relatively high sales value and are not separately identifiable as individual products until the split-off point.

just-in-time (JIT) production   Production system in which each component on a production line is produced immediately as needed by the next step in the production line.

just-in-time (JIT) purchasing   The purchase of goods or materials such that delivery immediately precedes demand or use.

kaizen budgeting   Budgetary approach that explicitly incorporates continuous improvement during the budget period into the resultant budget numbers.

key success factors   Factors that directly affect customer satisfaction such as cost, quality, time and innovative products and services.

labour-paced operations   Worker dexterity and productivity determine the speed of production.

labour time record   Record used to charge departments and job cost records for labour time used on a specific job.

learning curve   Function that shows how labour-hours per unit decline as units of production increase.

life-cycle budgeting   Budget that incorporates the revenues and costs attributable to each product from its initial R&D to its final customer servicing and support in the marketplace.

life-cycle costing   System that tracks and accumulates the actual costs attributable to each product from start to finish.

line management   Managers directly responsible for attaining the objectives of the organisation.

linear cost function   Cost function in which the graph of total costs versus a single cost driver forms a straight line within the relevant range.

locked-in costs Costs that have not yet been incurred but that will be incurred in the future on the basis of decisions that have already been made. Also called *designed-in costs*.

machine-paced operations Machines conduct most (or all) phases of production, such as movement of materials to the production line, assembly and other activities on the production line and shipment of finished goods to the delivery dock areas.

main product When a single process yielding two or more products yields only one product with a relatively high sales value, that product is termed a main product.

make-or-buy decisions Decisions about whether a producer of goods or services will produce goods or services within the firm or purchase them from outside vendors.

management accounting The application of accounting and financial management principles to create, protect, preserve and increase value so as to deliver that value to stakeholders of for-profit and not-for-profit enterprises, both public and private (see Chapter 1 for an expanded definition).

management by exception The practice of concentrating on areas that are not operating as expected and placing less attention on areas operating as expected.

management control system Means of gathering and using information to aid and coordinate the process of making planning and control decisions throughout the organisation and to guide employee behaviour.

manufacturing cells Grouping of all the different types of equipment used to manufacture a given product.

manufacturing lead time Time from when an order is ready to start on the production line (ready to be set up) to when it becomes a finished good.

manufacturing overhead allocated All manufacturing costs that are assigned to a product (or service) using a cost allocation base because they cannot be traced to a product (or service) in an economically feasible way.

manufacturing overhead costs See *indirect manufacturing costs*.

manufacturing-sector companies Companies that provide to their customers tangible products that have been converted to a different form from that of the products purchased from suppliers.

margin of safety Excess of budgeted revenues over the breakeven revenues.

market-share variance The difference between (a) the budgeted amount at budgeted mix based on the actual market size in units and the actual market share and (b) the budgeted amount at budgeted mix based on actual market size in units and the budgeted market share.

market-size variance The difference between (a) the budgeted amount based on the actual market size in units and the budgeted market share and (b) the static-budget amount based on the budgeted market size in units and the budgeted market share.

marketing The manner by which individuals or groups (a) learn about and value the attributes of products or services and (b) purchase those products or services.

master budget Budget that summarises the financial projections of all the organisation's individual budgets. It describes the financial plans for all value-chain functions.

master-budget utilisation The denominator-level concept based on the anticipated level of capacity utilisation for the coming budget period.

materials requirement planning (MRP) A system that maximises the efficiency of the timing of raw material orders through to the manufacture and assembly of the final product.

materials requisition record Record used to charge departments and job cost records for the cost of the materials used on a specific job.

merchandising-sector companies Companies that provide to their customers tangible products they have previously purchased in the same basic form from suppliers.

mixed cost A cost that has both fixed and variable elements. Also called a *semivariable cost*.

moral hazard Describes contexts in which an employee prefers to exert less effort (or report distorted information) than the effort (or information) desired by the owner because the employee's effort (or information) cannot be accurately monitored and enforced.

motivation The desire to attain a selected goal (the goal-congruence aspect) combined with the resulting drive or pursuit towards that goal (the effort aspect).

multicollinearity Exists when two or more independent variables in a regression model are highly correlated with each other.

multiple regression Regression model that uses more than one independent variable to estimate the dependent variable.

net present-value (NPV) method Discounted cash-flow method that calculates the expected net monetary gain or loss from a project by discounting all expected future cash inflows and outflows to the present point in time, using the required rate of return.

net profit Operating profit plus non-operating revenues (such as interest revenues) minus non-operating costs (such as interest costs) minus income taxes.

net relevant cost See *differential cost*.

new economy A period in which there is discontinuity in the normal progression of economic events resulting from a fundamental change in the structure of the economy.

Currently, this change stems from the convergence of telecommunications and digital technologies.

nominal rate of return   Rate of return required to cover investment risk and the anticipated decline due to inflation, in the general purchasing power of the cash that the investment generates.

non-linear cost function   Cost function in which the graph of total costs versus a single cost driver does not form a straight line within the relevant range.

non-value-added cost   A cost that, if eliminated, would not reduce the value customers obtain from using the product or service.

normal costing   A costing method that traces direct costs to a cost object by using the actual direct cost rate(s) times the actual quantity of the direct cost input and allocates indirect costs based on the budgeted indirect cost rate(s) times the actual quantity of the cost-allocation base.

normal spoilage   Spoilage that arises under efficient operating conditions; it is an inherent result of the particular production process.

normal utilisation   The denominator-level concept based on the level of capacity utilisation that satisfies average customer demand over a period (say, two or three years) that includes seasonal, cyclical or other trend factors.

numerical control machine (NC machine)   A manufacturing tool that can be programmed within predefined performance criteria to perform required production activities. It can be computer controlled (Computer NC, CNC) or centrally controlled (Direct NC, DNC).

objective function   Expresses the objective to be maximised (for example, operating profit) or minimised (for example, operating costs) in a decision model, for example a linear programming model.

operating budget   The budgeted income statement and its supporting schedules.

operating costs   All costs associated with generating revenues, other than cost of goods sold.

operating cycle   See *self-liquidating cycle*.

operating department   A department that adds value to a product or service that is observable by a customer. Also called a *production department* in manufacturing organisations.

operating leverage   The effects that fixed costs have on changes in operating income as changes occur in units sold and hence in contribution margin.

operating profit   Total revenues from operations minus total costs from operations (excluding income taxes).

operation   A standardised method or technique that is performed repetitively regardless of the distinguishing features of the finished good.

operation costing   Hybrid costing system applied to batches of similar products. Each batch of products is often a variation of a single design and proceeds through a sequence of selected (though not necessarily the same) activities or operations. Within each operation all product units use identical amounts of the operation's resources.

opportunity cost   The contribution to income that is forgone (rejected) by not using a limited resource in its best alternative use.

opportunity cost of capital   See *required rate of return*.

ordering costs   Costs of preparing and issuing a purchase order.

organisational structure   The arrangement of activities and possibly lines of responsibility within the entity.

out-of-pocket costs   See *incremental costs*.

outcomes   Predicted consequences of the various possible combinations of actions and events in a decision model.

outlay costs   See *incremental costs*.

output-level overhead variance   See *production-volume variance*.

output-unit-level costs   The costs of resources sacrificed on activities performed on each individual unit of product or service.

outsourcing   Process of purchasing goods and services from outside vendors rather than producing the same goods or providing the same services within the firm.

overabsorbed indirect costs   See *overallocated indirect costs*.

overallocated indirect costs   Allocated amount of indirect costs in an accounting period is greater than the actual (incurred) amount in that period. Also called *overapplied indirect costs* and *overabsorbed indirect costs*.

overapplied indirect costs   See *overallocated indirect costs*.

padding   The practice of underestimating budgeted revenues (or overestimating budgeted costs) in order to make budgeted targets more easily achievable. Also called *budgetary slack*.

Pareto diagram   Diagram that indicates how frequently each type of failure (defect) occurs.

payback method   Capital budgeting method that measures the time it will take to recoup, in the form of net cash inflows, the net initial investment in a project.

perfectly competitive market   Exists when there is a homogeneous product with equivalent buying and selling prices and no individual buyers or sellers can affect those prices by their own actions.

physical measure method   Joint cost allocation method that allocates joint costs on the basis of their relative proportions at the split-off point, using a common physical measure such as weight or volume of the total production of each product.

planning   Choosing goals, predicting results under various ways of achieving those goals and then deciding how to attain the desired goals.

post-deduct costing   See *backflush costing*.

practical capacity   The denominator-level concept that reduces theoretical capacity for unavoidable operating interruptions such as scheduled maintenance time, shutdowns for holidays and other days, and so on.

predatory pricing   Company deliberately prices below its costs in an effort to drive out competitors and restrict supply and then raises prices rather than enlarge demand or meet competition.

present value   An asset measure based on discounted cash-flow estimates.

prevention costs   Costs incurred in precluding the production of products that do not conform to specifications.

previous department costs   See *transferred-in costs*.

price discounting   The reduction of selling prices below listed levels in order to encourage an increase in purchases by customers.

price variance   The difference between actual price and budgeted price multiplied by the actual quantity of input in question. Also called *input-price variance* or *rate variance* (especially when those variances are for direct-labour categories).

prime costs   All direct manufacturing costs.

pro forma statements   Budgeted financial statements of an organisation.

probability   Likelihood or chance of occurrence of an event.

probability distribution   Describes the likelihood (or probability) of each of the mutually exclusive and collectively exhaustive sets of events.

problem solving   Management accountant's function that involves comparative analysis to identify the best alternatives in relation to the organisation's goals.

process-costing system   Costing system in which the cost of a product or service is obtained by using broad averages to assign costs to masses of similar units.

product   Any output sold to a customer that has a positive sales value (or an output used internally that enables an organisation to avoid incurring costs).

product cost   Sum of the costs assigned to a product for a specific purpose.

product-cost cross-subsidisation   Costing outcome where at least one miscosted product is resulting in the miscosting of other products in the organisation.

product differentiation   An organisation's ability to offer products or services that are perceived by its customers to be superior and unique relative to those of its competitors.

product life cycle   Spans the time from initial R&D to the time at which support to customers is withdrawn.

product line   A grouping of similar products.

product overcosting   A product consumes a relatively low level of resources but is reported to have a relatively high total cost.

product-sustaining costs   The costs of resources sacrificed on activities undertaken to support specific products or services.

product undercosting   A product consumes a relatively high level of resources but is reported to have a relatively low total cost.

production   The coordination and assembly of resources to produce a product or deliver a service.

production denominator level   See *denominator level*.

production denominator volume   See *denominator level*.

production department   See *operating department*.

production-volume variance   Difference between budgeted fixed overhead and the fixed overhead allocated. Fixed overhead is allocated based on the budgeted fixed overhead rate times the budgeted quantity of the fixed-overhead allocation base for the actual output units achieved. Also called *denominator-level variance* and *output-level overhead variance*.

productivity   Measures the relationship between actual inputs used (both physical inputs and costs) and actual outputs achieved; the lower the inputs for a given set of outputs or the higher the outputs for a given set of inputs, the higher the level of productivity.

profit centre   A responsibility centre in which a manager is accountable for revenues and costs.

proration   The spreading of underallocated or overallocated overhead among closing stocks and cost of goods sold.

purchase-order lead time   Amount of time between the placement of an order and its delivery.

purchasing costs   Cost of goods acquired from suppliers, including freight and transportation costs.

PV graph   Shows the impact on operating profit of changes in the output level.

qualitative factors   Outcomes that cannot be measured in numerical terms.

quality costs   See *costs of quality (COQ)*.

quantitative factors   Outcomes that are measured in numerical terms.

rate variance   See *price variance*.

real rate of return   The rate of return required to cover only investment risk.

reciprocal allocation method   Method of support-cost allocation that explicitly includes the mutual services rendered among all support departments.

reengineering   The fundamental rethinking and redesign of business processes to achieve improvements in critical measures of performance such as cost, quality, service, speed and customer satisfaction.

refined costing system   Costing system that results in a better measure of the non-uniformity in the use of resources by jobs, products and customers.

regression analysis   Statistical model that measures the average amount of change in the dependent variable that is associated with a unit change in one or more independent variables.

relevant costs   Expected future costs that differ among alternative courses of action.

relevant range   Range of the cost driver in which a specific relationship between cost and driver is valid.

relevant revenues   Expected future revenues that differ among alternative courses of action.

reorder point   The quantity level of the stock on hand that triggers a new order.

required rate of return (RRR)   The minimum acceptable rate of return on an investment; the return that the organisation could expect to receive elsewhere for an investment of comparable risk. Also called *discount rate, hurdle rate* and *opportunity cost of capital.*

research and development (R&D)   The generation of and experimentation with, ideas related to new products, services or processes.

residual income   Income minus a required monetary return on the investment.

residual term   The difference between the actual and predicted amount of a dependent variable (such as a cost) in a regression model. Also called the *disturbance term* or *error term.*

responsibility accounting   System that measures the plans (by budgets) and actions (by actual results) of each responsibility centre.

responsibility centre   A part, segment or subunit of an organisation whose manager is accountable for a specified set of activities.

return on investment (ROI)   See *accounting rate of return.*

revenue centre   A responsibility centre in which a manager is accountable for revenues only.

revenue costs   Costs that are recorded as expenses of the accounting period when they are incurred.

revenue driver   Any factor that affects revenues.

revenue mix   The relative contribution of quantities of products or services that constitutes total revenues. See *sales mix.*

revenues   Inflows of assets received in exchange for products or services provided to customers.

reworked units   Unacceptable units of production that are subsequently reworked and sold as acceptable finished goods.

rolling budget   Budget or plan that is always available for a specified future period by adding a month, quarter or year in the future as the month, quarter or year just ended is dropped.

safety stock   Stock held at all times regardless of stock ordered using EOQ. It is a buffer against unexpected increases in demand or lead time and unexpected unavailability of stock from suppliers.

sales mix   See *revenue mix.*

sales-mix variance   The difference between the budgeted amount for the actual sales mix and the budgeted amount if the budgeted sales mix had been unchanged.

sales-quantity variance   The difference between the budgeted amount based on actual quantities sold of all products and the budgeted-mix and the amount in the static budget (which is based on the budgeted quantities to be sold of all products and the budgeted mix).

sales value at split-off method   Joint cost allocation method that allocates joint costs on the basis of the relative sales value at the split-off point of the total production in the accounting period of each product.

sales-volume variance   Difference between the flexible-budget amount and the static-budget amount; unit selling prices, unit variable costs and fixed costs are held constant.

scorekeeping   Management accountant's function that involves accumulating data and reporting reliable results to all levels of management.

scrap   Product that has a minimal (frequently zero) sales value.

segment   Identifiable part or subunit of an organisation.

self-liquidating cycle   The movement of cash to stocks to receivables and back to cash. Also called *cash cycle* or *operating cycle.*

selling-price variance   Flexible-budget variance that pertains to revenues; arises solely from differences between the actual selling price and the budgeted selling price.

semivariable cost   See *mixed cost.*

sensitivity analysis   A what-if technique that examines how a result will change if the original predicted data are not achieved or if an underlying assumption changes.

separable costs   Costs incurred beyond the split-off point that are assignable to one or more individual products.

sequential allocation method   See *step-down allocation method*.

sequential tracking   Product-costing method in which the accounting system entries occur in the same order as actual purchases and production. Also called *synchronous tracking*.

service department   See *support department*.

service-sector companies   Companies that provide services or intangible products to their customers – for example legal advice or an audit.

service-sustaining costs   The costs of resources sacrificed on activities undertaken to support specific services.

set-up   Process of preparing a machine or manufacturing cell for production.

simple regression   Regression model that uses only one independent variable to estimate the dependent variable.

single-rate cost-allocation method   Allocation method that pools all costs in one cost pool and allocates them to cost objects using the same rate per unit of the single allocation base.

slope coefficient   Coefficient term in a cost estimation model indicates how much total costs change for each unit change in the cost driver within the relevant range.

source documents   The original records that support journal entries in an accounting system.

specification analysis   Testing of the assumptions of regression analysis.

split-off point   Juncture in the process when one or more products in a joint-cost setting become separately identifiable.

spoilage   Unacceptable units of production that are discarded or sold for net disposal proceeds.

staff management   Managers who provide advice and assistance to line management.

stand-alone cost-allocation method   Cost allocation method that allocates the common cost on the basis of each user's percentage of the total of the individual stand-alone costs.

standard   Carefully predetermined amount; it is usually expressed on a per-unit basis.

standard cost   Carefully predetermined cost. Standard costs can relate to units of inputs or units of outputs.

standard costing   Costing method that traces direct costs to a cost object by multiplying the standard price(s) or rate(s) times the standard inputs allowed for actual outputs achieved and allocates indirect costs on the basis of the standard indirect rate(s) times the standard inputs allowed for the actual outputs achieved.

standard error of the estimated coefficient   Regression statistic that indicates how much the estimated value is likely to be affected by random factors.

standard input   Carefully predetermined quantity of inputs (such as kilograms of materials or hours of labour time) required for one unit of output.

static budget   Budget that is based on one level of output; when variances are computed at the end of the period, no adjustment is made to the budgeted amounts.

step allocation method   See *step-down allocation method*.

step cost function   A cost function in which the cost is constant over various ranges of the cost driver, but the cost increases by discrete amounts (that is, in steps) as the cost driver moves from one range to the next.

step-down allocation method   Method of support cost allocation that allows for partial recognition of services rendered by support departments to other support departments. Also called *step* or *sequential allocation method*.

stock management   The planning, organising and control activities focused on the flow of materials into, through and from the organisation.

stock-related costs   Specific type of capitalised costs. Those capitalised costs associated with the purchase of goods for resale (in the costs of merchandise stock) or costs associated with the acquisition and conversion of materials and all other manufacturing inputs into goods for sale (in the case of manufacturing stocks). Also called *inventoriable costs*.

stockout   A stockout arises when a supplier runs out of a particular item for which there is customer demand.

stockout costs   Costs that result when a company runs out of a particular item for which there is customer demand. The company must act to meet that demand or suffer the costs of not meeting it.

straight-line depreciation (SL)   Depreciation method in which an equal amount of depreciation is taken each year.

strategic analysis   Considers how an organisation attempts to best combine its own capabilities with the opportunities in the marketplace in seeking to accomplish its overall objectives.

strategic investment appraisal (SIA)   Linking corporate strategy to costs and benefits associated with AMT adoption by combining both formal and informal evaluation procedures.

strategic management accounting   A form of management accounting in which emphasis is placed on information which relates to factors external to the firm, as well as non-financial information and internally generated information.

strategic scorecard   A method of assisting company boards in the oversight of the strategic process, dealing with strategic choice and change, and giving a view of strategic progress.

strategy   A course of action, including the specification of resources required to achieve a specific objective (see Chapter 22 for an expanded definition).

suboptimal decision making   Decisions in which the benefit to one subunit is more than offset by the costs or loss of benefits to the organisation as a whole. Also called *incongruent decision making*.

sunk costs   Past costs that are unavoidable because they cannot be changed no matter what action is taken.

supply chain   Describes the flow of goods, services and information 'from cradle to grave', irrespective of whether those activities occur in the same organisation or other organisations.

support department   A department that provides the services that maintain other internal departments (operating departments and other support departments) in the organisation. Also called a *service department*.

synchronous tracking   See *sequential tracking*.

tableau de bord   Multicriterial model of control that uses financial as well as non-financial means to identify and measure objectives, key variables and indicators.

target cost per unit   Estimated long-run cost per unit of a product (or service) that when sold at the target price enables the company to achieve the targeted income per unit. Target cost per unit is derived by subtracting the target operating profit per unit from the target price.

target operating profit per unit   Operating profit that a company wants to earn on each unit of a product (or service) sold.

target price   Estimated price for a product (or service) that potential customers will be willing to pay.

target rate of return on investment   The target operating profit that an organisation must earn divided by invested capital.

theoretical capacity   The denominator-level concept that is based on the constant production of output at maximum efficiency.

theory of constraints (TOC)   Describes methods to maximise operating profit when faced with some bottleneck and some non-bottleneck operations.

throughput contribution   Revenues minus all variable direct materials costs.

throughput costing   Stock costing method that treats all costs except those related to variable direct materials as costs of the accounting period in which they are incurred; only variable direct materials costs are inventoriable.

time-adjusted rate of return   See *internal rate of return (IRR)*.

time driver   Any factor where a change in the factor causes a change in the speed with which an activity is undertaken.

total direct manufacturing labour mix variance   The difference between (a) the budgeted cost for the actual direct manufacturing labour input mix and (b) the budgeted cost if the budgeted direct labour input mix had been unchanged, for the actual total quantity of all direct manufacturing labour used.

total direct manufacturing labour yield variance   The difference between (a) the budgeted cost of direct manufacturing labour based on actual total quantity of all direct manufacturing labour used and (b) the flexible budget cost of direct manufacturing labour based on the budgeted total quantity of direct manufacturing labour inputs for the actual output achieved, given that the budgeted labour input mix is unchanged.

total direct materials mix variance   The difference between (a) the budgeted cost for the actual direct materials input mix and (b) the budgeted cost if the budgeted direct materials input mix had been unchanged, for the actual total quantity of all direct material inputs used.

total direct materials yield variance   The difference between (a) the budgeted cost of direct materials based on actual total quantity of all direct materials inputs used and (b) the flexible-budget cost of direct materials based on the budgeted total quantity of direct materials inputs for the actual output achieved, given that the budgeted materials input mix is unchanged.

transactions   Physical and electronic documentation of any production activity.

transfer price   Price that one subunit (segment, department, division, etc.) of an organisation charges for a product or service supplied to another subunit of the same organisation.

transferred-in costs   Costs incurred in a previous department that are carried forward as part of the product's cost as it moves to a subsequent department for processing. Also called *previous department costs*.

uncertainty   The possibility that an actual amount will deviate from an expected amount.

underabsorbed indirect costs   See *underallocated indirect costs*.

underallocated indirect costs   Allocated amount of indirect costs in an accounting period is less than the actual (incurred) amount in that period. Also called *underapplied indirect (overhead) costs* or *underabsorbed indirect costs*.

underapplied indirect costs   See *underallocated indirect costs*.

unfavourable variance   Variance that decreases operating profit relative to the budgeted amount. Denoted U.

unit cost   Computed by dividing some total cost (the numerator) by some number of units (the denominator). Also called *average cost*.

unused capacity   The difference between the productive capacity available and the productive capacity required to meet consumer demand in the current period. Also called *excess capacity*.

usage variance   See *efficiency variance*.

value-added activities   Activities that customers perceive as adding value to the products or services they purchase.

value-added cost   A cost that, if eliminated, would reduce the value customers obtain from using the product or service.

value chain   The sequence of business functions in which utility (usefulness) is added to the products or services of an organisation.

value engineering   Systematic evaluation of all aspects of the value-chain business functions, with the objective of reducing costs while satisfying customer needs.

variable cost   Cost that changes in total in proportion to changes in a cost driver.

variable-cost percentage   Total variable costs (with respect to units of output) divided by revenues.

variable costing   Stock costing method in which all variable manufacturing costs are included as inventoriable costs. All fixed manufacturing costs are excluded from inventoriable costs; they are costs of the period in which they are incurred. Also called *direct costing*.

variable-overhead efficiency variance   The difference between the actual and budgeted quantity of the variable-overhead cost-allocation base allowed, for the actual output units achieved, times the budgeted variable overhead cost allocation rate.

variable-overhead spending variance   The difference between the actual amount of variable overhead incurred and the budgeted amount allowed for the actual quantity of the variable-overhead allocation base used, for the actual output units achieved.

variance   Difference between an actual result and a budgeted amount when that budgeted amount is a financial variable reported by the accounting system.

weighted-average process-costing method   Method of process costing that assigns the average equivalent unit cost of all work done to date (regardless of when it was done) to equivalent units completed and transferred out and to equivalent units in closing stock.

work cell   Grouping of individuals or machines to perform a manufacturing task.

work in process   See *work-in-progress stock*.

work in progress   See *work-in-progress stock*.

work-in-progress stock   Goods partially worked on but not yet fully completed. Also called *work in process*.

working-capital cycle   The movement from cash to stocks to receivables and back to cash.

work-measurement method   See *industrial engineering method*.

World Wide Web   A medium for publishing information on the Internet. It is accessed through web browsers, which display web pages and can be used to run business applications. Company (or other) information is stored on web servers, which are usually referred to as websites.

NAMES INDEX

SUBJECT INDEX